1987

WHO'S WHO

in Canadian Film and Television

QUI EST QUI

au cinéma et à la télévisio
au Canada

Edited by Chapelle Jaffe

Assistant Editor Marie-Claude Poulin

Academy of Canadian Académie canadienne du
Cinema & Television   cinéma et de la télévision

First published in 1986 by the Academy of Canadian Cinema & Television
653 Yonge Street, 2nd Floor
Toronto, Ontario M4Y 1Z9

This book was published with the financial assistance of Telefilm Canada.

Canadian Cataloguing in Publication Data

Main entry under title:
Who's who in Canadian film and television = Qui est qui au cinéma et à la télévision au Canada

Text in English and French.
Includes filmographies and bibliographies.
ISBN 0-919083-08-0

1. Moving-picture writers, producers, directors, production managers, cinematographers, art directors, editors, composers — Canada — Biography — Dictionaries. 2. Television writers, producers, directors, production managers, cinematographers, art directors, editors, composers — Canada — Biography — Dictionaries. I. Jaffe, Chapelle. II. Academy of Canadian Cinema & Television. III. Title: Who's who in Canadian film and television.

C86-030678-XE

Données de catalogage avant publication (Canada)

Vedette principale au titre:
Who's who in Canadian film and television = Qui est qui au cinéma et à la télévision au Canada

Textes en français et an anglais.
Comprend des filmographies et des bibliographies.
ISBN 0-919083-08-0

1. Scénaristes, producteurs, réalisateurs, régisseurs, directeurs-photo, directeurs artistiques, monteurs, compositeurs de cinéma — Canada — Biographies — Dictionnaires. 2. Scénaristes, producteurs, réalisateurs, régisseurs, directeurs-photo, directeurs artistiques, monteurs, compositeurs de télévision — Canada — Biographies — Dictionnaires. I. Jaffe, Chapelle. II. Académie canadienne du cinéma et de la télévision. III. Titre: Qui est qui au cinéma et à la télévision au Canada.

C86-030678-XF

Reasonable effort has been made in the accurate compilation of information contained in this publication; the publisher, however, assumes no liability for errors or omissions, but would appreciate being notified of any that are found.

Cover design by Mort Walsh

Typeset by RBW Graphics

Printed in Canada by WEBCOM Limited

CONTENTS/TABLE DES MATIERES

FOREWORD by John Hunter

Until this prodigious directory shattered the illusion, I thought I was a know-it-all about what Canadians have done in cinema and television. But one read-through of 'Who's Who' showed me I had no real grasp of the amazing scope of our contributions to productions here and everywhere else on the planet. I'm awed by the enormity of the data that's been compacted into a single volume and oh-so-grateful to have it at my fingertips.

Just about everybody I've ever heard of, along with many I should have heard of and a few I hoped I'd never hear of again are rostered on these pages — some 1,400 of us, representing about 15,000 productions of all kinds, spanning 45 years of creative effort. What a treat to have all our credits and discredits enshrined in one reference source. I intend to use it often.

Thank you, 'Who's Who' for giving us such a useful, entertaining book.

AVANT-PROPOS

La parution du prodigieux répertoire que voici m'a fait perdre une grande illusion — celle de m'y connaître comme pas un en production cinématographique et télévisuelle canadienne. Il m'a suffi de feuilleter le présent ouvrage pour constater que je n'avais vraiment aucune idée de l'omniprésence des Canadiens sur les écrans de la planète. J'ai été surpris de constater la masse de renseignements qu'on peut insérer dans un volume aussi pratique que celui que je me propose de garder indéfiniment sous la main.

Ce guide de l'industrie tient compte non seulement de tas de gens que je connais, mais encore d'une foule de gens que je devrais connaître et même de quelques-uns dont j'aurais préféré ne plus entendre parler — quelque 1 400 artistes et artisans responsables de quelque 15 000 productions dans tous les genres réalisées en l'espace de 45 ans. Quelle chance que de trouver tous nos honneurs et déshonneurs en un seul et unique volume! Je me propose de m'en servir abondamment.

Merci, 'Qui est Qui', de nous avoir offert un répertoire aussi utile et aussi rempli de péripéties.

ACKNOWLEDGEMENTS/REMERCIEMENTS

Thank-you, all 1,400 of you who are in this book. Now I can look you up. Remerciements à toute la gang qui ont répondu. I wish the 2,100 others whom we beseeched were here too but they're not so c'est la vie.

Special thanks to Margaret Collier, John Hunter, Penelope Hynam, Debbie Janson, Andra Sheffer, Jennifer Stark, Mort Walsh et Suzanne Blais, Raynald Desmeules, Louise Ferland qui ont tant aidé.

My appreciation to Telefilm Canada, Marcia Hackborn and all the advertisers.

Most of all, my love and thanks to Marie-Claude Poulin, who will no longer be assistant to anyone.

EXPLANATORY NOTES/NOTES EXPLICATIVES

All information has been gathered from the individuals listed in this directory. We have endeavored to verify all the data in order to ensure accuracy. Each listing is printed in the language in which it was submitted. The first line of information about each person contains union/guild memberships; addresses and phone numbers. Under the heading 'Genres' (e.g. Drama, Documentary etc.); we have allowed a maximum of four main genres in which a person has worked. This does not necessarily cover all the genres in which that person has experience.

In 'Selective Filmography', there are various national and international film and television awards noted by the initials or names they are known by, including: ACTRA; EMMY; GENIE; OSCAR. Whenever two or more people share a credit on the same film or television program, each person's credit is preceded by 'Co' (e.g. Co-Prod, Co-Wr).

Following is the key to abbreviations used in the listings.

Les renseignements contenus dans le présent ouvrage ont été fournis par les cinéastes eux-mêmes et vérifiés par la rédaction dans la mesure du possible. Ils sont publiés dans la langue dans laquelle ils ont été remis à l'Académie à commencer par les informations suivantes: syndicats et associations professionnelles; adresses; numéros de téléphone. Dans la catégorie 'Types d'oeuvres', quatre types seulement (ex.: drame, documentaire, etc.), ont été retenus bien que certains cinéastes aient travaillé dans plus que quatre genres.

Les prix nationaux et internationaux mentionnés dans les filmographies sélectives sont représentés par leurs initiales ou abréviation (ex.: ACTRA; EMMY; GENIE; OSCAR). Lorsque deux personnes ou davantage se partagent une mention au générique d'un film ou d'une émission de télévision, leur titre est précédé du préfixe Co (ex.: Co prod, Co sc).

On trouvera le glossaire des abréviations utilisées dans le présent ouvrage dans les pages qui suivent.

The Data Bank/La banque de données

All information found in this publication is also stored in the Academy's "WHO'S WHO/QUI EST QUI" data bank. The computer program has extensive cross-indexing possibilities, which enables the Academy to respond to requests for various kinds of lists concerning people in film and television.

Les renseignements donnés dans la présente publication font partie de la banque de données "QUI EST QUI/WHO'S WHO" de l'Académie. Il existe de nombreuses possibilités de contre-indexation en vue de la compilation de listes specialisée en cinéma et en télévision.

Design/programme conçu par: Arie Litman

ABBREVIATIONS/ABREVIATIONS

Types of Production/Types de production

C	Cinéma (longs et courts métrages)
Cm	Commercial/Annonce
ED	Educational/Education
In	Industrial/Industriel
MV	Music Video/Vidéo-clips
Th	Theatrical (features and shorts)
TV	Television/Télévision

Credits

	1st AD	1st Assistant Director
	1st Assist Cam	1st Assistant Cameraman
	1st Assist Ed	1st Assistant Editor
	1st Assist Snd Ed	1st Assistant Sound Editor
	2nd AD	2nd Assistant Director
	2nd Assist Art Dir	2nd Assistant Art Director
	2nd Assist Cam	2nd Assistant Cameraman
	2nd Assist Ed	2nd Assistant Editor
	2nd Cam	2nd Cameraman
	2nd Cam Op	2nd Camera Operator
	2nd Op	2nd Operator
	2nd U Cam	2nd Unit Cameraman
	2nd U Co-Dir	2nd Unit Co-Director
	2nd U Dir	2nd Unit Director
	2nd U DOP	2nd Unit Director of Photography
	2nd Unit AD	2nd Unit Assistant Director
	2nd Unit Op	2nd Unit Operator
	2nd Unit PM	2nd Unit Production Manager
	3rd AD	3rd Assistant Director
A	Act	Actor
	Adapt	Adaptation
	Add'l Dial	Additional Dialogue
	Add'l Ed	Additional Editing
	Add'l Phot	Additional Photography
	An	Animator
	An Co-Des	Animation Co-Design
	An Des	Animation Design
	An Dir	Animation Director
	An Spv	Animation Supervisor
	Arr	Arranger
	Art Dept Coord	Art Department Coordinator
	Art Dir	Art Director
	Assemb Ed	Assembly Editor
	Assist Art Dir	Assistant Art Director
	Assist Cam	Assistant Cameraman
	Assist Des	Assistant Designer
	Assist Dir	Assistant Director
	Assist Ed	Assistant Editor
	Assist Mus Dir	Assistant Music Director
	Assist PM	Assistant Production Manager
	Assist Pro Acc't	Assistant Production Accountant
	Assist Prod	Assistant Producer
	Assist Set Des	Assistant Set Designer
	Assist SFX	Assistant Special Effects
	Assist Snd Ed	Assistant Sound Editor
	Assist Story Ed	Assistant Story Editor
	Assist Unit M	Assistant Unit Manager
	Assoc Dir	Associate Director
	Assoc Ed	Associate Editor
	Assoc PM	Associate Production Manager
	Assoc Prod	Associate Producer
B	Boom	Boom Operator

C

Cam	Cameraman
Cast	Casting
Ch	Choreographer
Cin	Cinematographer
Co-An	Co-Animator
Co-Art Dir	Co-Art Director
Co-Cam	Co-Cameraman
Co-Cin	Co-Cinematographer
Co-Comp	Co-Composer
Co-Creator	Co-Creator
Co-Dir	Co-Director
Co-DOP	Co-Director of Photography
Co-Ed	Co-Editor
Co-Exec Prod	Co-Executive Producer
Co-Exec Story Ed	Co-Executive Story Editor
Co-Field Prod	Co-Field Producer
Co-Host	Co-Host
Co-Loc M	Co-Location Manager
Comp	Composer
Co-Narr	Co-Narrator
Co-Narr Wr	Co-Narration Writer
Cond	Conductor
Cont	Continuity
Cont Wr	Continuity Writer
Contr Dir	Contributing Director
Contr Wr	Contributing Writer
Co-Op	Co-Operator
Coord Prod	Coordinating Producer
Co-Prod	Co-Producer
Co-Prod Des	Production Co-Designer
Cos	Costumes
Co-Scr	Co-Screenplay
Co-Snd Ed	Co-Sound Editor
Co-Spv Prod	Co-Supervising Producer
Co-Story	Co-Story
Co-Story Ed	Co-Story Editor
Co-T'play	Co-Teleplay
Co-Wr	Co-Writer
Creator	Creator

D

Des	Designer
Dial Dir	Dialogue Director
Dial Ed	Dialogue Editor
Dir	Director
Dir SFX	Director of Special Effects
DOP	Director of Photography

E

Ed	Editor
Exec Prod	Executive Producer
Exec Story Ed	Executive Story Editor

F

Field Dir	Field Director
Field Prod	Field Producer
Fl Dir	Floor Director
Focus Pull	Focus Puller
Foley	Foley

	FX An	Effects Animator
	FX Des	Effects Design
	FX Ed	Effects Editor
G	Gaf	Gaffer
	Grip	Grip
H	Head Wr	Head Writer
	Host	Host
I	Illustr	Illustrator
	Interv	Interviewer
K	Key Grip	Key Grip
L	Lay Art	Layout Artist
	Light Cam	Lighting Cameraman
	Light Dir	Lighting Director
	Line Prod	Line Producer
	Loc Dir	Location Director
	Loc M	Location Manager
	Lyrics	Lyrics
M	Mus Dir	Music Director
	Mus Ed	Music Editor
	Mus Prod	Music Producer
	Mus Spv	Music Supervisor
N	Narr	Narrator
	Narr Wr	Narration Writer
	News Ed	News Editor
O	Op	Operator
	Orch	Orchestrator
P	P Audio	Post Audio
	P Pro Spv	Post Production Supervisor
	P Prod	Post Producer
	PA	Production Assistant
	PM	Production Manager
	Post PM	Post Production Manager
	Pro Acc't	Production Accountant
	Pro Assoc	Production Associate
	Pro Coord	Production Coordinator
	Pro Des	Production Designer
	Pro Exec	Executive in Charge of Production
	Pro Spv	Production Supervisor
	Prod	Producer
	Props	Property Master
R	Report	Reporter
	Res	Researcher
S	Sc Dir	Scene Director
	Scr	Screenplay
	Scr Adapt	Screenplay Adaptation
	Seg An Dir	Segment Animation Director
	Serv Prod	Service Producer
	Set Dec	Set Decorator
	Set Des	Set Designer
	Set Dr	Set Dresser

	SFX	Special Effects
	SFX Des	Special Effects Design
	SFX Makeup	Special Effects Makeup
	SFX Spv	Special Effects Supervisor
	Sing	Singer
	Snd Des	Sound Design
	Snd Ed	Sound Editor
	Snd Mix	Sound Mixer
	Snd Rec	Sound Recordist
	Spv Art Dir	Supervising Art Director
	Spv Assist Ed	Supervising Assistant Editor
	Spv Ed	Supervising Editor
	Spv Lay	Supervisor of Layout
	Spv Pro Acc't	Supervising Production Accountant
	Spv Prod	Supervising Producer
	Spv Snd Ed	Supervising Sound Editor
	Spv St'board	Supervisor of Storyboards
	Sr Ed	Senior Editor
	Sr Prod	Senior Producer
	Sr Spv Lay	Senior Supervisor of Layout
	Sr Spv St'board	Senior Supervisor of Storyboards
	Staff Ed	Staff Editor
	Staff Wr	Staff Writer
	St'board	Storyboards
	St'cam	Steadicam Operator
	Stills	Stills Photographer
	Story	Story
	Story Ed	Story Editor
	Studio Dir	Studio Director
	Sw	Switcher
T	Tech Dir	Technical Director
	Theme Co-Comp	Theme Co-Composer
	Theme Comp	Theme Composer
	Titles Des	Titles Design
	T'play	Teleplay
	Trans	Translation
U	U Loc M	Unit Location Manager
	Uncr Rewr	Uncredited Rewrite
	Unit M	Unit Manager
	Unit PM	Unit Production Manager
V	VFX Des	Visual Effects Design
	Vid Paint Art	Video Paintbox Artist
	VO	Voice Over
	Voice	Voice
W	Wr	Writer
	Wran	Wrangler

Mentions au générique

	1er ass cam	1er assistant caméraman
	1er ass mont	1er assistant monteur
	1er ass réal	1er assistant réalisateur
	2e ass cam	2e assistant caméraman
	2e ass mont	2e assistant monteur
	2e ass réal	2e assistant réalisateur
	3e ass réal	3e assistant réalisateur
A	Acces	Accessoiriste
	Adapt	Adaptation
	An	Animation
	Anim	Animateur
	Arr	Arrangeur
	Ass cam	Assistant caméraman
	Ass comp	Assistant compositeur
	Ass décor	Assistant décorateur
	Ass dir art	Assistant directeur artistique
	Ass dir mus	Assistant directeur musical
	Ass eff sp	Assistant effets spéciaux
	Ass mont	Assistant monteur
	Ass mont son	Assistant monteur son
	Ass pro	Assistant à la production
	Ass prod	Assistant producteur
	Ass réal	Assistant réalisateur
	Ass rég	Assistant régisseur
	Aut	Auteur
	Aut comp	Auteur-compositeur
	Aut cons	Auteur conseil
B	Bruit	Bruitage
C	Cadr	Cadreur
	Cadr 2e ép	Cadreur deuxième équipe
	Cam	Caméraman
	Cam 2e éq	Caméraman deuxième équipe
	Cast	Casting
	Ch	Chorégraphe
	Chant	Chanteur
	Chef décor	Chef décorateur
	Chef d'orch	Chef d'orchestre
	Chef mont	Chef monteur
	Co an	Coanimation
	Co anim	Coanimateur
	Co aut	Coauteur
	Co cam	Cocaméraman
	Co comp	Cocompositeur
	Co comp thème	Cocompositeur thème
	Co conc	Coconcepteur
	Co D phot	Codirecteur-photo
	Co mont	Comonteur
	Co mont son	Comonteur son
	Co op	Co-opérateur
	Co prod	Coproducteur
	Co prod exéc	Coproducteur exécutif

	Co réal	Coréalisateur
	Co sc	Coscénariste
	Com	Comédien
	Comp	Compositeur
	Comp thème	Compositeur thème
	Conc	Concepteur
	Conc gén	Conception du générique
	Conc son	Concepteur son
	Conc vis	Concepteur visuel
	Coord pro	Coordonnateur de production
	Cos	Costumes
D	Décor	Décorateur
	Des	Dessins
	Dial	Dialogue
	Dir art	Directeur artistique
	Dir eff sp	Directeur effets spéciaux
	Dir mus	Directeur musical
	Dir pro	Directeur de production
	Dir tech	Directeur technique
	D phot	Directeur-photo
	D phot 2e éq	Directeur-photo deuxième équipe
E	Eff sp	Effets spéciaux
G	Gén an	Générique animé
I	Ing son	Ingénieur du son
	Interv	Intervieweur
J	Journ	Journaliste
M	Mach	Machiniste
	Mont	Monteur
	Mont 2e eq	Monteur deuxième équipe
	Mont mus	Monteur musique
	Mont son	Monteur son
N	Narr	Narrateur
O	Op	Opérateur
P	Parol	Parolier
	Partic sc	Participation au scénario
	Phot	Photographie
	Phot plat	Photographe de plateau
	Prod	Producteur
	Prod assoc	Producteur associé
	Prod coord	Producteur coordonnateur
	Prod dél	Producteur délégué
	Prod exéc	Producteur exécutif
R	Réal	Réalisateur
	Réal an	Réalisateur d'animation
	Réal dél	Réalisateur délégué
	Rég	Régisseur
	Rég gén	Régisseur général

S	Scripte	Scripte
	Script ed	Script éditeur
	Sup mont	Superviseur montage
	Sup mont son	Superviseur montage son
	Sup p pro	Superviseur de postproduction
	Sup pro	Superviseur de production
T	Textes	Textes
	Trad	Traduction

Countries / Pays

A	Austria/Autriche
AUS	Australia/Australie
B	Belgium/Belgique
CDN	Canada
CH	Switzerland/Suisse
CS	Czechoslovakia/Tchécoslovaquie
D	Germany (Fed. Rep.)/Allemagne (Rép. féd.)
DK	Denmark/Danemark
E	Spain/Espagne
F	France
GB	Great Britain/Grande-Bretagne
H	Hungary/Hongrie
I	Italy/Italie
IND	India/Inde
IL	Israel/Israël
IRL	Ireland/Irlande
J	Japan/Japon
L	Luxembourg
LAO	Laos
MEX	Mexico/Mexique
NL	Netherlands/Pays-Bas
NZ	New Zealand/Nouvelle-Zélande
PE	Peru/Pérou
PL	Poland/Pologne
R	Roumania/Roumanie
RA	Argentina/Argentine
RC	China/Chine
RFC	Cameroon/Cameroun
S	Sweden/Suède
SF	Finland/Finlande
SKO	South Korea/Corée du Sud
SN	Senegal/Sénégal
T	Thailand/Thaïlande
TT	Trinidad-Tobago/Ile de la Trinité-Tobago
UAE	United Arab Emirates/Emirats arabes unis
USA	United States/Etats-Unis
YU	Yugoslavia/Yougoslavie
ZA	South Africa/Afrique du Sud

Unions-Guilds/Syndicats-Associations

ABS	Association of Broadcasting Staff (Britain)
ACFC	Association of Canadian Film Craftspeople
ACFTP	Association of Canadian Film and Television Producers
ACTRA	Alliance of Canadian Cinema, Television and Radio Artists
ACTT	Association of Cinematograph, Television and Allied Technicians (Britain)
AFM	American Federation of Musicians
AFTRA	American Federation of Television and Radio Artists
AGVA	American Guild of Variety Artists
AMPAC	American Motion Picture Association of Composers
APFVQ	Association des producteurs de film et de vidéo du Québec
AR	Association des réalisateurs (Radio-Canada)
ARRFQ	Association des réalisateurs et réalisatrices de films du Québec
ARRQ	Association des réalisateurs de Radio-Québec
ASC	American Society of Cinematographers
ASIFA-CANADA	Association internationale du film d'animation
ATPD	Association of Television Producers and Directors (CBC)
BAE	British Actors Equity
CAMERA	Canadian Association of Motion Picture and Electronic Recording Artists
CAPAC	Composers, Authors and Publishers Association of Canada Limited
CFTA	Canadian Film and Television Association
CLC	Canadian League of Composers
CSC	Canadian Society of Cinematographers
CTPDA	Canadian Television Producers and Directors Association (CBC)
CUPE	Canadian Union of Public Employees
CST	Commission supérieure technique (France)
DGA	Directors Guild of America
DGC	Directors Guild of Canada
GCFC	Guild of Canadian Film Composers
IATSE	International Alliance of Theatrical Stage Employees and Moving Picture Machine Operators
MPEG	Motion Picture Editors Guild (U.S.A.)
NABET	National Association of Broadcast Employees and Technicians
PGA	Producers Guild of America
SACD	Société des auteurs et compositeurs dramatiques (France)
SAG	Screen Actors Guild (U.S.A.)
SARDEC	Société des auteurs, recherchistes, documentalistes et compositeurs
SGCT	Syndicat général du cinéma et de la télévision (ONF)
SMPTE	Society of Motion Picture and Television Engineers
STCQ	Syndicat des techniciennes et techniciens du cinéma du Québec
UDA	Union des Artistes
WGA	Writers Guild of America
WGGB	Writers Guild of Great Britain

WRITERS
★
SCENARISTES

SCENARISTES/WRITERS

ABBOTT, Roger

ACTRA, WGAw. Abbott/Ferguson Prods. Ltd., 66 Gerrard St.E., Toronto, Ont, CAN, M5B 1G3. (416)977-6222.
Types of Production & Categories: TV Film-Wr; TV Video-Wr.
Genres: Comedy-TV; Variety-TV.
Biography: Born 1946, England; emigrated to Canada, 53. Worked for private radio stations as writer, manager, programmer, 55-70; writing, performing, producing, directing comedy (TV, radio, stage) since 70. Has won 4 Actra Awards for radio writing, 3 for radio performing; Juno Award for 'Air Farce Comedy Album'.
Selective Filmography: *ACTRA AWARDS,* TV, 86, CDN, Co-Wr; *'AIR FARCE'* (Co-Prod-1 eps), (14 eps), TV, 85-80, CDN, Co-Wr **(3 ACTRA);** *'MARY AND MICHAEL'* (26 eps), TV, 77, CDN, Head Wr/Pro Spv; *'MIXED DOUBLES'* (26 eps), TV, 76, CDN, Contr Wr; *'CAUGHT IN THE ACT'* (26 eps), TV, 76, CDN, Contr Wr.

A'COURT, Susan

167 Boulton Ave., Toronto, Ont, CAN, M4M 2J8. (416)465-4874.
Types of Production & Categories: TV Film-Wr/Prod.
Genres: Drama-TV; Documentary-TV; Educational-TV; Children's-TV.
Biography: Born 1952, Toronto, Ontario. B.Sc.N., University of Toronto.
Selective Filmography: *HELL & HIGH WATER/HOBIE CATS,* 'ASSIGNMENT ADVENTURE', TV, 86-85, CDN/GB, Wr; *RED SHOES/HOTWALKER/GOING TO WAR/ESSO,* 'BELL CANADA PLAYHOUSE', TV, 86-85, CDN, Co-Prod; *TAPESTRY,* ED, 85, CDN, Wr/Dir; *AIR CANADA: SUN DESTINATIONS,* Cm, 85-84, CDN, Wr/Field Prod; *'KIDS OF DEGRASSI STREET'* (4 eps), TV, 84, CDN, Wr; *TWIN DRAGON ENCOUNTER,* Th, 84, CDN, PM/Line Prod; *'HEALTHWISE'* (4 eps), ED, 80, CDN, Wr.

ALLAN, Ted

ACTRA, WGAw. Linda Butler, Butler, Tilden, Bell Assoc., 501 Yonge St., Ste. 301, Toronto, Ont, CAN, M4Y 1Y4. (416)964-6660. Mike Zimring, William Morris Agency, 151 El Camino Dr., Beverly Hills, CA, USA, 90212. (213)859-4246.
Types of Production & Categories: Th Film-Wr; TV Film-Wr.
Genres: Drama-Th&TV; Documentary-TV.
Biography: Born Montreal, Quebec. Writer, 100's of dramas and comedies for TV (CBC, BBC, ITV); also wrote 100's of radio plays (CBC, BBC). Stageplays include: 'The Money Makers', 'Legend of Paradiso', 'Double Image', 'Gog and Magog', 'Chou Chem', 'Love Streams', 'The Third Day Comes', 'Lies My Father Told Me'. Author: 'The Scalpel, The Sword, The Story of Dr. Bethune' (written with S. Gordon). Oscar nomination for writing *LIES MY FATHER TOLD ME* which also won the Golden Globe Award and a Virgin Island Film Festival Award for Best Screenplay.
Selective Filmography: *LOVE STREAMS,* Th, 84, USA, Co-Scr; *LIES MY FATHER TOLD ME,* Th, 75, CDN, Scr **(CFA).**

ALMOND, Paul - see DIRECTORS

ARCAND, Denys - voir REALISATEURS

ARSENEAU, Joanne

SARDEC. 5766 Hutchison, Outremont, Qué, CAN, H2V 4B6. (514)274-2906.
Types de production et Catégories: TV vidéo-Sc.
Types d'oeuvres: Drame-TV; Comédie-TV; Comédie musicale-TV; Enfants-TV.
Curriculum vitae: Née en 1953, Montréal, Québec; bilingue. Education: Maitrise en Psychologie, Scolarité de Doctorat.
Filmographie sélective: *'A PLEIN TEMPS'* (30 eps), TV, 86-84, CDN, Aut; *'SAMEDI DE RIRE'* (5 eps), TV, 86-84, CDN, Co aut; *'COURT-CIRCUIT'* (6
(cont/suite)

eps), TV, 85, CDN, Aut; *'POP CITROUILLE'* (20 eps), TV, 83-80, CDN, Co aut; *'BOF ET CIE'* (5 eps), TV, 83, CDN, Aut.

BAILEY, Don

ACTRA. 139 Roslyn Rd., Winnipeg, Man, CAN, R3L 0G7. (204)453-2940.
Types of Production & Categories: TV Film-Wr/Prod; TV Video-Wr/Prod.
Genres: Drama-TV; Documentary-TV; Educational-TV; Industrial-TV.
Biography: Born 1942, Toronto, Ontario. Completed grade 8, but read a lot while serving 15 years in prison for bank robbery. Ordained as a United Church Minister and has worked in the church for 15 years as an implementer of social programs; particular interest in youth and the elderly.
Selective Filmography: *ALL SALES FINAL,* TV, 86, CDN, Wr/Prod; *REACHING OUT,* In, 86, CDN, Wr/Prod/Dir; *MOB STORY,* TV, 86, CDN, Wr; *ARE YOU HAPPY,* TV, 86, CDN, Wr/Prod; *CANADA IS YOU,* TV, 85, CDN, Wr; *ROSIE: THE UNWED TEENAGE MOTHER,* TV, 81, CDN, Wr; *HOW TO INVEST IN CANADA,* In, 80, CDN, Wr; *SEER WAS HERE,* 'FOR THE RECORD', TV, 77, CDN, Co-Wr; *HANK,* 'FOR THE RECORD', TV, 76, CDN, Wr; *THE MONEY-GO-ROUND,* TV, 75, CDN, Wr; *PLAYING THE GAME,* TV, 75, CDN, Wr.

BARBEAU, Manon

760 Champagneur, Outremont, Qué, CAN, H2V 3P8. (514)276-5728.
Radio-Québec, 1000 rue Fullum, Montréal, Qué, CAN. (514)521-2424.
Types de production et Catégories: c métrage-Sc; TV film-Sc; TV vidéo-Sc.
Types d'oeuvres: Drame-C&TV; Comédie-C&TV; Comédie musicale-C&TV; Documentaire-C&TV.
Curriculum vitae: Née en 1949, Montréal, Québec; bilingue. Education: Bac. spécialisé en communications.
Filmographie sélective: *'ADELE COMEAU MENE L'ENQUETE'* (6 eps), TV, 86, CDN, Sc/Dial; *AGORA: STEPHANE TREMBLAY, PAROLES ET MUSIQUE,* TV, 85, CDN, Sc; *LES CHERUBINS,* TV, 85, CDN, Sc; *TILT,* TV, 84, CDN, Sc; *T'AS BIEN CHANGE MARIE,* TV, 83, CDN, Sc; *PAYSAGES SONORES,* TV, 82, CDN, Sc; *'BOZEJEUNNES'* (5 eps), TV, 81, CDN, Sc; *NOUS SOMMES PLUSIEURS BEAUCOUP DE MONDE,* TV, 80, CDN, Réal; *L'ATTENTE,* 'CONTREJOUR', TV, 79, CDN, Sc; *'VISAGES'* (2 eps), TV, 78, CDN, Sc; *LES ARPENTEURS DE KARNAK,* C, 77, F, Sc; *'MOI MES CHANSONS'* (22 eps), TV, 76, CDN, Sc; *COMPTINES,* C, 76, CDN, Réal; *'LES PRODUITS DE SOIN'* (5 eps), TV, 74, CDN, Sc.

BARLOW, David - see PRODUCERS

BARNEY, Bryan

ACTRA. 19 Portneuf Court, Toronto, Ont, CAN, M5A 4E4. (416)368-3578. Cdn. Communications Reports, 777 Bay St., Toronto, Ont, CAN. (416)596-5938.
Types of Production & Categories: Th Film-Wr; TV Film-Wr; TV Video-Wr.
Genres: Drama-Th&TV; Comedy-TV; Action-TV.
Biography: Born 1930, Reading, England; Canadian citizen. Worked as magazine editor, journalist; since 80, has edited Maclean Hunter Newsletter, 'Canadian Communications Reports'.
Selective Filmography: *'THE PHOENIX TEAM'* (2 eps), TV, 80, CDN, Wr; *'THE GREAT DETECTIVE'* (1 eps), TV, 78, CDN, Wr; *'FLAPPERS'* (1 eps), TV, 78, CDN, Wr; *'HIGH HOPES'* (32 eps), TV, 78, CDN/USA, Dial; *THE FAR SHORE,* Th, 76, CDN, Scr; *DELILAH,* 'TO SEE OURSELVES', TV, 76, CDN, Wr; *'POLICE SURGEON'* (1 eps), TV, 74, CDN/USA, Story; *CLOSE CALL,* TV, 74, CDN, Wr; *SOME ARE SO LUCKY/RIGMAROLE,* 'CANADIAN SHORT STORIES', TV, 70, CDN, T'play; *THE FUR COAT/FRINGE BENEFITS,* 'ANTHOLOGY', TV, 70/69, CDN, Wr; *'McQUEEN'* (3 eps), TV, 69, CDN, Wr; *TROPHY ROOM,* TV, 67, CDN, Wr.

BARRIE, Scott - see DIRECTORS

BARRIS, Alex

ACTRA, WGAw. 6 Malamute Cr., Agincourt, Ont, CAN, M1T 2C7. (416)292-7488.
Types of Production & Categories: TV Film-Wr; TV Video-Wr.
Genres: Drama-TV; Comedy-TV; Variety-TV; Documentary-TV.
Biography: Born 1922, USA; Canadian citizen since 65. Has written many TV shows in Canada, 56-68; Los Angeles, 69-76; returned to Canada, 77. *A FUNNY THING HAPPENED ON THE WAY TO THE SYMPHONY,* won Best Musical Variety, AMPIA, 86; Emmy nomination for *DORIS DAY SPECIAL.*
Selective Filmography: *'REAR VIEW MIRROR'* (30 eps), TV, 85-81, CDN, Wr; *A FUNNY THING HAPPENED ON THE WAY TO THE SYMPHONY,* TV, 84, CDN, Wr; *JAZZ ALIVE,* TV, 83, CDN/USA, Wr; *'THE PALACE'* (26 eps), TV, 80/79, CDN/USA, Head Wr; *ACTRA AWARDS* (2 shows), TV, 79/78, CDN, Wr; *IRISH ROVERS CELEBRATION,* TV, 78, CDN, Wr; *'KING OF KENSINGTON'* (7 eps), TV, 78, CDN, Wr; *A LITTLE PART OF CANADA,* TV, 78, CDN, Head Wr; *'SO THE STORY GOES'* (16 eps), TV, 77, CDN, Story Ed; *JULIETTE SPECIAL,* TV, 77, CDN, Wr; *'CELEBRITY REVUE'* (120 eps), TV, 76, CDN/USA, Head Wr; *'ENTERTAINMENT HALL OF FAME'* (2 eps), TV, 76/75, USA, Co-Wr; *'WIZARD OF ODDS'* (65 eps), TV, 74, USA, Co-Wr; *DAVID FROST SHOW,* TV, 74, USA, Co-Wr; *CELEBRITY TREASURE HUNT,* TV, 72, USA, Head Wr; *'ROLLIN' WITH KENNY ROGERS AND FIRST EDITION'* (26 eps), TV, 72/71, CDN/USA, Co-Prod/Co-Wr; *'ROLLIN' ON THE RIVER'* (26 eps), TV, 71, CDN/USA, Co-Wr; *FIFTH DIMENSION SPECIAL,* TV, 71, CDN/USA, Head Wr; *BOBBY DARIN SPECIAL,* TV, 71, CDN/USA, Wr; *SONNY & CHER SPECIAL,* TV, 71, CDN/USA, Assoc Prod; *DORIS DAY SPECIAL,* TV, 70, USA, Co-Wr; *'BARBARA McNAIR SHOW'* (52 eps), TV, 70/69, CDN/USA, Co-Wr.

BASEN, Leila

ACTRA. 3777 Hampton Ave., Montreal, Que, CAN, H4A 2K7. (514)485-1886. Stan Colbert, The Colbert Agency, 303 Davenport Rd., Toronto, Ont, CAN, M5R 1K5. (416)964-3302.
Types of Production & Categories: Th Film-Wr; Th Short-Wr; TV Film-Wr.
Genres: Drama-Th&TV; Comedy-Th&TV; Variety-TV; Educational-Th&TV.
Biography: Born 1955, Toronto, Ontario. Education: York University, specialized honours, Film.
Selective Filmography: *'ROCKIT RECORDS'* (pilot), TV, 85, CDN, Wr; *IF YOU WANT A GIRL LIKE ME,* 'BIO ETHICS', ED, 85, CDN, Wr; *MY OWN WAY TO ROCK* (BURTON CUMMINGS VARIETY SPECIAL), TV, 83, CDN, Wr; *MAN IN 5A* (THE MAN NEXT DOOR), Th, 83, CDN, Co-Scr; *'HANGIN' IN'* (4 eps), TV, 82, CDN, Wr; *'FLAPPERS'* (2 eps), TV, 81, CDN, Wr; *YOUR TICKET IS NO LONGER VALID,* Th, 81, CDN, Co-Scr.

BEARDE, Chris - see PRODUCERS

BEAUCHEMIN, Yves

SARDEC. 247 St-Jacques, Longueuil, Qué, CAN, J4H 3B8. (514)670-7430. Jacques Fortin, Editions Québec/Amérique, 450 Sherbrooke E., Ste. 301, Montréal, Qué, CAN, H2L 1J8. (514)288-2371.
Types de production et Catégories: c métrage-Sc.
Types d'oeuvres: Comédie-C.
Curriculum vitae: Né en 1941, Noranda, Québec, Licence ès Lettres (Français, Littérature, Histoire de l'Art), Université de Montréal, 65. Expérience: éditeur, professeur, recherchiste; écrivain: 'L'Enfirouapé' (74), 'Matou'(81). Récipiendaire

(cont/suite)

du Prix France-Québec décerné par l'Association des écrivains de langue française pour 'L'Enfirouapé', 75.
Filmographie sélective: *BURLEX,* C, 70, CDN, Réal/Sc/Com.

BEAUDIN, Jean - voir REALISATEURS
BEAUDRY, Jean - voir REALISATEURS
BENNER, Richard

ACTRA, DGA, DGC, WGAe. 184 Seaton St., Toronto, Ont, CAN, M5A 2T4. (416)967-5371. 150 W. 80th St., #9B, New York, NY, USA, 10014. (212)724-5007. Stan Colbert, The Colbert Agency, 303 Davenport Rd., Toronto, Ont, CAN, M5R 1K5. (416)964-3302.
Types of Production & Categories: Th Film-Wr/Dir; TV Film-Wr/Dir.
Genres: Drama-Th; Comedy-Th; Horror-TV.
Biography: Born 1946, Sterling, Illinois; US citizen; landed immigrant, Canada. M.A., Drama, University of Manchester, England, 68; M.A., Drama, U. of California in Santa Barbara, 69. Professor, U. of Calgary, 69-72; story editor, CBC, 74-76. Writer/director, several off-off-Broadway productions. *OUTRAGEOUS!* was named Best Film, 'Soho News' (NY) and Most Popular Film, Berlin Film Festival, 78.
Selective Filmography: *THE SWAP/PAYMENT OVERDUE,* 'TALES FROM THE DARKSIDE', TV, 86/85, USA, Wr/Dir; *HAPPY BIRTHDAY GEMINI,* Th, 79, CDN/USA, Scr/Dir; *OUTRAGEOUS!,* Th, 77, CDN, Scr/Dir; *FRIDAY NIGHT ADVENTURES,* 'INSIGHT', TV, 76, CDN, Wr; *LONDON DRAG,* Th, 70, USA, Wr/Dir.

BENOIT, Denyse - voir REALISATEURS
BENOIT, Jacques

SARDEC. 4139 ave. Old Orchard, Montréal, Qué, CAN, H4A 3B3. (514)484-3952. La Presse, 7 rue St-Jacques O., Montréal, Qué, CAN. (514)285-7070.
Types de production et Catégories: l métrage-Sc; TV vidéo-Sc.
Types d'oeuvres: Drame-C&TV; Action-C.
Curriculum vitae: Né en 1941. Remporte le Prix du Québec pour son roman 'Jos Carbone', 69; Prix Judith Jasmin (journalisme), 76. Chroniqueur viticole pour La Presse depuis 82.
Filmographie sélective: *'EMPIRE INC.'* (1 eps), TV, 81, CDN, Co sc; *L'AFFAIRE COFFIN* (THE COFFIN AFFAIR), C, 79, CDN, Sc; *REJEANNE PADOVANI,* C, 72, CDN, Co sc (CFA); *LA MAUDITE GALETTE,* C, 72, CDN, Sc.

BERTON, Pierre

R.R. #1, Kleinburg, Ont, CAN, L0J 1C0. (416)893-1103. My Country Productions, 21 Sackville St., Toronto, Ont, CAN, M5A 3E1. (416)864-9753.
Types of Production & Categories: Th Short-Wr; TV Film-Wr; TV Video-Wr.
Genres: Documentary-Th&TV; Educational-TV.
Biography: Born 1920; raised in the Yukon; has 11 honorary degrees. Became Managing Editor of 'Maclean's', 47; assoc. editor, columnist, 'Toronto Star', 58-62; *THE PIERRE BERTON SHOW,* 62-73. Has written revue sketches, a musical comedy (stage), plays, documentaries for radio, film and TV, a daily newspaper column and 31 books; is seen weekly on CBC's *FRONT PAGE CHALLENGE.* Has won 3 Governor General's Awards for Creative non-fiction: 'The Mysterious North', 'Klondike', 'The Last Spike'; 2 National Newspaper Awards, 2 Actra Awards for broadcasting; Officer of the Order of Canada; member, Canadian News Hall of Fame; Director of McClelland and Stewart.
Selective Filmography: *'HERITAGE THEATRE'* (26 eps), TV, 85/84, CDN, Story Ed/Host; *SPIRIT OF BATOCHE,* TV, 85, CDN, Wr/Narr; *THE DIONNE QUINTUPLETS,* TV, 79, CDN, Wr/Narr; *GRENFELL,* TV, 76, CDN, Wr/Narr; *'THE NATIONAL DREAM'* (8 eps), TV, 74, CDN, Narr; *CITY OF GOLD,* Th, 58, CDN, Wr/Narr.

BLUM, Jack
ACTRA. 10 Sackville Pl., Toronto, Ont, CAN, M4X 1A4. (416)923-3357.
Types of Production & Categories: TV Film-Wr; TV Video-Wr.
Genres: Drama-TV; Comedy-TV; Children's-TV.
Biography: Born 1956, Canada; dual citizenship (Can/US). Graduate of National Theatre School of Canada (acting, directing). Has written, directed for the stage, Canada, USA; associate artistic director, LaJolla Playhouse, California, 83; Won the Dora Mavor Moore Award, 83, for 'Getting Out'. Extensive acting experience, film. *HOCKEY NIGHT* won a CFTA.
Selective Filmography: *'STREET LEGAL'* (6 eps), TV, 86, CDN, Story Ed; *JACK OF HEARTS,* 'BELL CANADA PLAYHOUSE', TV, 85, CDN, T'play; *THE HOSPITAL,* 'HOME MOVIES', TV, 85, CDN, Wr; *HOCKEY NIGHT,* TV, 84, CDN, Co-Wr; *THE UMPIRE,* 'HOME MOVIES', TV, 84, CDN, Co-Wr; *THE EDISON TWINS'* (2 eps), TV, 83, CDN, Co-Wr; *R.W.,* 'SONS AND DAUGHTERS', TV, 82, CDN, Co-Wr.

BOMPHRAY, Clinton
ACTRA. 11 Howie Ave., Toronto, Ont, CAN, M4M 2H9. (416)463-6717.
Types of Production & Categories: Th Short-Wr; TV Film-Wr/Dir; TV Video-DOP/Dir/Prod.
Genres: Drama-TV; Action-TV; Documentary-TV.
Biography: Born 1943, Regina, Saskatchewan. Studied English Literature, History, Psychology, University of Saskatchewan. Has worked as writer, director, grip, props, DOP. Received 3 Ontario Arts Council screenwriting grants. *OCTOBER STRANGER* won Best Short Film, Native American Film Festival, 85.
Selective Filmography: *YAD,* TV, 86, CDN, Prod/Dir/DOP; *OCTOBER STRANGER,* Th, 84, CDN, Co-Wr; *'THE GREAT DETECTIVE'* (2 eps), TV, 83/82, CDN, Wr; *TALKIN' UNION,* TV, 78, CDN, Dir.

BOND, Timothy - see DIRECTORS

BORRIS, Clay - see DIRECTORS

BOUCHARD, Michel - voir REALISATEURS

BOWIE, Douglas
ACTRA. 414 Albert St., Kingston, Ont, CAN, K7L 3W3. (613)544-9596. Nancy Colbert, The Colbert Agency, 303 Davenport Rd., Toronto, Ont, CAN, M5R 1K5. (416)964-3302.
Types of Production & Categories: Th Film-Wr; TV Film-Wr.
Genres: Drama-Th&TV; Comedy-Th&TV.
Biography: Canadian citizen; Bachelor of Science. Films he has written have won CFTA, American Film Festival Awards; he received the CBC Centennial Playwrighting Prize, 67.
Selective Filmography: *'CHASING RAINBOWS'* (13 eps), TV, 86, CDN, Wr; *THE BOY IN BLUE,* Th, 84, CDN, Wr; *LOVE AND LARCENY,* TV, 84, CDN, Wr; *'EMPIRE INC.'* (6 eps), TV, 82/81, CDN, Wr; *'THE NEWCOMERS'* (1 eps), TV, 78, CDN, Wr; *THE WAR IS OVER,* TV, 77, CDN, Wr; *SHANTYMEN OF CACHE LAKE/NO WAY OF TELLING,* 'THE MAGIC LIE', TV, 77/76, CDN, T'play; *SCOOP,* 'FOR THE RECORD', TV, 77, CDN, Wr; *A GUN, A GRAND, A GIRL/THE MAN WHO WANTED TO BE HAPPY,* 'PERFORMANCE', TV, 75, CDN, T'play; *BREAKDOWN,* TV, 75, CDN, Wr; *BARGAIN BASEMENT,* TV, 74, CDN, Wr; *U-TURN,* Th, 72, CDN, Wr; *GUNPLAY,* TV, 71, CDN, Wr; *YOU AND ME,* TV, 71, CDN, Wr; *'THE KROKONOL HUSTLERS'* (4 eps), TV, 70, CDN, Wr; *THE CONTEST EATERS,* TV, 69, CDN, Wr; *AMNESTY,* TV, 68, CDN, Wr; *WHO WAS THE LONE RANGER?,* TV, 67, CDN, Wr.

BOYDEN, Barbara - see PRODUCERS

BRANDES, David

ACTRA, WGAw. 717 Copeland Ct., Santa Monica, CA, USA, 90405. (213)399-8901. Stu Robinson, Robinson Weintraub, 8428 Melrose Pl., Ste. C, Los Angeles, CA, USA, 90069. (213)653-5802.
Types of Production & Categories: Th Film-Wr; TV Video-Wr.
Genres: Drama-Th; Horror-Th; Documentary-TV; Children's-TV.
Biography: Born 1944, Kemptville, Ontario. M.F.A., Film Production, UCLA. Has received a Canada Council Award, 2 Ontario Arts Council Awards. Worked for CBC TV and CJOH TV as news reporter, interviewer.
Selective Filmography: *THE DIRT BIKE KID,* Th, 85, USA, Wr; *'FRAGGLE ROCK'* (1 eps), TV, 83, CDN, Wr; *BLOOD ROOT,* Th, 83, CDN, Wr; *MY MOTHER'S HOUSE,* Th, 78, USA, Wr/Dir.

BRESLIN, Mark

ACTRA. 26 Bellair St., Toronto, Ont, CAN, M5R 2C7. (416)923-9124. Yuk-Yuk's Inc., 1280 Bay St., Toronto, Ont, CAN, M5R 3L1. (416)967-6431. Larry Goldhar, Characters, 150 Carlton St., Toronto, Ont, CAN, M5A 2K1. (416)964-8522.
Types of Production & Categories: Th Film-Wr; TV Video-Wr.
Genres: Comedy-Th&TV; Variety-TV.
Biography: Born 1952; Canadian citizen. Founder of Yuk-Yuk's Komedy Kabaret and Funny Business Inc..
Selective Filmography: *'THE JOURNAL'* (4 seg), TV, 86-84, CDN, Wr/Act; *TAKE MY HUSBAND AND LEAVE,* TV, 85, CDN, Wr; *MR. NICE GUY,* Th, 85, CDN, Wr; *YUK-YUK'S GLOBAL PILOT,* TV, 82, CDN, Prod.

BRITTAIN, Donald - see DIRECTORS

BROADFOOT, Dave

ACTRA, AGVA. Broadfoot Productions II Inc., 33 Hawthorn Ave., Toronto, Ont, CAN, M4W 2Z1. (416)960-0012. First Artists Mgmt., 1255 Yonge St., Toronto, Ont, CAN, M4T 1W6. (416)961-7766.
Types of Production & Categories: TV Film-Wr/Act.
Genres: Drama-TV; Comedy-TV; Variety-TV; Documentary-TV.
Biography: Born 1925, North Vancouver, British Columbia. Has appeared in over 30, produced 8 stage reviews; appeared in 4 feature films. Has been with *ROYAL CANADIAN AIR FARCE* for 14 years. Won 10 Actra Awards for writing and performing comedy, TV and radio; Juno Award for comedy recording; C.S.P. (US) Award; Queen's Silver Jubilee Medal; Officer, Order of Canada.

BROWN, Barbara

ACTRA. 14864-17 Ave., White Rock, BC, CAN, V4A 6V4. (604)536-0526.
Types of Production & Categories: TV Film-Wr; TV Video-Wr.
Genres: Drama-TV; Documentary-TV; Educational-TV; Children's-TV.
Biography: Born Edmonton, Alberta. B.A., Journalism, University of Western Ontario. Journalist, radio commentator, TV documentaries (O.E.C.A.), researcher; TV series and movie writing; series developer, story editor.
Selective Filmography: *'THE CAMPBELLS'* (1 eps), TV, 86, CDN/USA/GB, Co-Wr; *'THE BEACHCOMBERS'* (11 eps), TV, 86-81, CDN, Co-Wr; *CHUNG CHUCK,* TV, 85, CDN, Co-Wr; *SILVER RAVEN,* TV, 84, CDN, Co-Wr; *'RITTER'S COVE'* (19 eps), TV, 80/79, CDN, Co-Wr; *WHAT'S IT ALL ABOUT/ RESEARCH,* TV, 70, CDN, Wr; *'EARLY ADOLESCENCE'* (6 eps), TV, 70/69, CDN, Wr; *THE NETHERLANDS,* TV, 70, CDN, Wr; *WHAT'S THE MATTER WITH DONNY?,* TV, 69, CDN, Wr.

BROWN, Jamie

ACTRA, WGAw. 174 Beacon Hill Rd., Beaconsfield, Que, CAN, H9W 1T6. (514)

(cont/suite)

694-6928. Telescene Inc., 360 Place Royale, Montreal, Que, CAN, H2Y 2V1. (514) 288-1638.
Types of Production & Categories: Th Film-Wr/Prod; Th Short-Wr; TV Film-Wr.
Genres: Drama-Th&TV; Comedy-Th&TV; Action-Th; Documentary-Th.
Biography: Born 1945, Brantford, Ontario. Published 5 novels including 'Superbike', the Young Adult Canadian Book of the Year, 83. Head of Feature Film Development for Telescene Productions.
Selective Filmography: *KEEPING TRACK*, Th, 85, CDN, Co-Prod/Co-Wr; *TOBY McTEAGUE*, Th, 85, CDN, Co-Wr; *YOU'VE COME A LONG WAY LADIES* (WOMEN IN SPORTS IN CANADA), TV, 84, CDN, Wr; *'THE WINNERS'* (1 eps), TV, 81, CDN, Wr; *THE WAR IS OVER*, Th, 77, CDN, Co-Wr.

BROWN, Lyal D.

ACTRA, CTPDA. 14864 - 17th Ave., White Rock, BC, CAN, V4A 6V4. (604)536-0526.
Types of Production & Categories: TV Film-Wr/Dir/Prod; TV Video-Wr.
Genres: Drama-TV; Action-TV; Documentary-TV; Children's-TV.
Biography: Born 1929, Medicine Hat, Alberta. Studied journalism, Montana State University; Political Science, History, U. of British Columbia. Worked in radio as continuity writer, announcer; writer for 'CBC Times', 52; after 8 years at CBC as Director of Information Services, Executive Assistant for General Manager, English Network, began freelancing as writer, broadcaster; has written 67 teleplays; won 3 Chris Awards for tourist films.
Selective Filmography: *'THE BEACHCOMBERS'* (20 eps), TV, 86, CDN, Story Ed; *'THE CAMPBELLS'* (1 eps), TV, 86, CDN/USA/GB, Co-Wr; *'THE BEACHCOMBERS'* (13 eps), TV, 85-74, CDN, Co-Wr; *CHUNG CHUCK*, TV, 85, CDN, Co-Wr; *OVER THE EDGE*, 'CONSTABLE, CONSTABLE', TV, 85, CDN, Wr; *'HOME FIRES'* (3 eps), TV, 83, CDN, Wr; *LEGEND OF THE SILVER RAVEN*, TV, 82, CDN, Co-Wr; *'RITTER'S COVE'* (19 eps), TV, 80/79, CDN/D, Co-Wr/Co-Creator; *'THE ALBERTANS'* (3 eps), TV, 79, CDN, Wr; *'SIDESTREET'* (3 eps), TV, 77/76, CDN, Wr; *'COLLABORATORS'* (4 eps), TV, 74/73, CDN, Wr; *THE ROBBER*, TV, 73, CDN, Wr; *A PEACE OF GREEN*, 'THIS LAND', TV, 73, CDN, Dir/Wr; *THE MAN WHO RAN AWAY*, TV, 73, CDN, Wr; *AN ANGEL AGAINST THE NIGHT*, 'PERFORMANCE', TV, 69, CDN, Wr; *THE WAITING ROOM*, 'TELEPLAY', TV, 69, CDN, Wr; *JUNIOR SERGEANT BEATS PAN*, TV, 68, CDN, Wr; *TONGUES OF STONE*, TV, 68, CDN, Wr; *THE FLYING LAMBS*, 'TELESCOPE', TV, 66, CDN, Prod/Dir/Wr; *ASSIGNMENT MANITOBA/LAKE TO MARKET/ENJOY OR DESTROY*, In, 66/65, CDN, Wr; *THE PRAIRIES*, TV, 66, CDN, Wr; *DIARY OF A MOUNTAIN MAN*, 'DIARY OF...', TV, 65, CDN, Wr; *TRAPPER'S FESTIVAL*, 'TAKE 30', TV, 64, CDN, Prod/Dir/Wr; *CITY OF RIVERS*, In, 63, CDN, Wr; *BALLET TO JAMAICA*, '20/20', TV, 63, CDN, Wr; *THE BREWSTERS OF BANFF*. 'TELESCOPE', TV, 63, CDN, Wr; *NO ROOM TO RUN*, TV, 63, CDN, Wr/Narr; *LONG JOURNEY THROUGH CHILDHOOD*, 'EYE TO EYE', TV, 62, CDN, Wr/Narr; *GIVEN HALF A CHANCE*, 'COUNTRY CALENDAR', TV, 61, CDN, Wr.

BRULOTTE, Gaétan

SARDEC. 82 rue des Casernes, Trois-Rivières, Qué, CAN, G9A 1X2. (819)379-6347. University of South Florida, Division of Languages, Tampa, Fl, USA, 33620. (813)974-2547. Louise Myette, 3507 Aylmer, Montréal, Qué, CAN. (514)844-9009.
Types de production et Catégories: 1 métrage-Sc; TV film-Sc.
Types d'oeuvres: Drame-C&TV.
Curriculum vitae: Né en 1945, Lauzon, Québec. Etudes à l'Université Laval et à Paris; détient un Doctorat en Sémiologie. A publié plusieurs livres et des centaines d'articles; a reçu 8 prix littéraires dont le Prix Robert Cliche pour 'L'Emprise'; Prix Adrienne Choquette et Prix France-Québec pour 'Le Surveillant'. Fellow of the

(cont/suite)

World Literary Academy, Cambridge, Angleterre. A réalisé 31 émissions de radio; professeur invité aux Etats-Unis depuis 81.
Filmographie sélective: *L'EMPRISE* (THE ASCENDANCY), C, 81, CDN, Co sc; *L'EMPRISE,* 'LES CHEMINS DE L'IMAGINAIRE', TV, 80, CDN, Aut.

BRUYERE, Christian

ACTRA, WGAw. 3105 West 5th Avenue, Vancouver, BC, CAN, V6K 1V1. (604) 732-9983. Jericho Films Ltd., 3090 Waterloo St., Vancouver, BC, CAN. (604)732-7506.
Types of Production & Categories: Th Film-Wr/Dir/Prod; TV Film-Wr/Dir/Prod; TV Video-Ed/Prod/Wr/Dir.
Genres: Drama-Th&TV; Variety-TV; Documentary-TV; Educational-TV.
Biography: Born 1944, Paris, France; raised in Chicago and Los Angeles. Education: U.S.C., Graduate Film School, specialized in scriptwriting, which he teaches at University of British Columbia. *DADS AND KIDS* won the Golden Sheaf Award, Yorkton, 85; *RAPE: FACE TO FACE* won the Dupont-Columbia Award, 83, the Corporation for Public Broadcasting Award and a Blue Ribbon, American Film Festival.
Selective Filmography: *DADS AND KIDS,* ED, 85, CDN, Wr/Dir/Prod; *'WHO AM I?'* (2 eps), ED, 85, CDN, Dir/Ed; *'DANGER BAY'* (1 eps), TV, 85, CDN, Wr; *'THE BEACHCOMBERS'* (2 eps), TV, 84, CDN, Wr; *'SEX OFFENDER TREATMENT'* (7 eps), ED, 84, CDN, Wr/Prod; *WALLS,* Th, 84, CDN, Co-Prod/ Wr; *UNICEF HALLOWEEN SPECIAL,* TV, 83, CDN, Wr; *RAPE: FACE TO FACE,* TV, 83, CDN/USA, Co-Wr/Co-Dir/Co-Prod.

BRYANT, Peter

2560 Larch St., Vancouver, BC, CAN, V6J 3R1. (604)733-7032. Eighty-Seven Bear Images Inc., 1876 W. First Ave., #4, Vancouver, BC, CAN, V6S 1G4. Cynthia Wilkerson, Triad Artists Inc., 10100 Santa Monica Blvd., 16th Fl., Los Angeles, CA, USA, 90067. (213)556-2727.
Types of Production & Categories: Th Film-Wr/Dir/Prod; TV Film-Wr/Dir/Prod; TV Video-Wr/Dir/Prod.
Genres: Drama-Th&TV; Documentary-Th&TV; Educational-Th&TV; Animation-Th.
Biography: Born 1946, London, England; Canadian citizen. Graduate of Simon Fraser University, 70; attended American Film Institute for advanced film studies, 71. Has taught film production , U. of British Columbia, Southern Alberta Institute of Technology. Owns film development company, Eighty-Seven Bear Images Inc..
Selective Filmography: *THE GREAT ESCAPE,* ED, 86, CDN, Wr/Dir; *VISITATION,* Th, 83, CDN, Prod; *BAD TEDDY,* Th, 83, CDN, Prod; *HELLO GOODBYE,* TV, 82, CDN, Line Prod; *BURN OUT,* TV, 79, CDN, Wr/Dir; *OCTOBER ALMS,* TV, 78, CDN, Prod; *THE SUPREME KID,* Th, 75, CDN, Wr/ Dir/Prod; *ROCCO BROTHERS,* TV, 73, CDN, Wr/Dir/Prod; *MORNING LINE,* Th, 73, CDN, Wr/Dir/Prod.

BUGAJSKI, Richard - see DIRECTORS

BURKE, Martyn - see DIRECTORS

BURT, Jim

ACTRA. 169 Harbord St., Toronto, Ont, CAN, M5S 1H3. (416)537-6216. CBC, Box 500, Stn. A, Toronto, Ont, CAN, M5W 1E6. (416)975-7156. Ralph Zimmerman, Great North Artists Mgmt., 345 Adelaide St.W., #500, Toronto, Ont, CAN, M5V 1R5. (416)593-2587.
Types of Production & Categories: TV Video-Wr.
Genres: Drama-TV.
Biography: Born 1947, Providence, Rhode Island; landed immigrant in Canada, U.S. citizen. B.A., Harvard University, 69; M.F.A., Yale School of Drama, program in

(cont/suite)

directing, 69-70. Background in stage directing, acting, teaching; Director, New School of Theatre, Toronto. Supervisor of Script Development, CBC Independent TV Drama, 86.
Selective Filmography: *AND MILES TO GO,* TV, 85, CDN, Story Ed; *SAM HUGHES'S WAR* (2 parts), 'SOME HONOURABLE GENTLEMEN', TV, 84, CDN, Wr; *ARTICHOKE,* TV, 77, CDN, Story Ed.

BURTON, Robert H. - see PRODUCERS

CAHILL, T.J.

ACTRA, CTPDA. 39 Quidi Vidi Village Rd., St. John's, Nfld, CAN, A1A 1E9. (709)722-2547. CBC, P.O. Box 12010, St. John's, Nfld, CAN, A1B 3T8. (709)737-4140.
Types of Production & Categories: TV Film-Dir/Prod/Wr; TV Video-Dir/Prod/Wr.
Genres: Drama-TV; Comedy-TV; Variety-TV; Documentary-TV.
Biography: Born 1929, St. John's, Newfoundland; B.A., Memorial University, Newfoundland, 53. Journalist; joined CBC, 58. Won Canadian Centennial Award for 'Tomorrow Will Be Sunday'; CBC President's Award, 85.
Selective Filmography: *YARNS FROM PIGEON INLET* (14 eps), TV, 86-80, CDN, Wr/Prod; *CORNERSTONE OF EMPIRE* (SIR HUMPHREY GILBERT), 'THE UNDAUNTED', TV, 83, CDN, Wr/Prod **(ACTRA)**; *YESTERDAYS' HEROES'* (12 eps), TV, 79/78, CDN, Dir/Prod/Wr; *WHERE ONCE THEY STOOD'* (18 eps), TV, 77-75, CDN, Dir/Prod/Wr; *AS LOVED OUR FATHERS,* TV, 76, CDN, T'play/Prod **(ANIK)**.

CAILLOUX, Michel

CAPAC, SARDEC, UDA. 3562 Abbé-Desrosiers, Laval, Qué, CAN, H7E 2K5. (514)661-7624.
Types de production et Catégories: TV vidéo-Sc.
Types d'oeuvres: Comédie-TV; Variété-TV; Education-TV; Enfants-TV.
Curriculum vitae: Né en 1931, Issoudun, France; au Canada depuis 55; naturalisé canadien. Auteur d'émissions de TV pour enfants depuis 30 ans. Récipiendaire du Grand Prix du Children's Broadcast Institute (77) pour *NIC ET PIC.*
Filmographie sélective: *'BOBINO'* (5150 ém), TV, 85-59, CDN, Aut; *'NIC ET PIC'* (72 eps), TV, 77-70, CDN, Sc/Dial; *MICHEL-LE-MAGICIEN* 'LA BOITE A SURPRISES', (480 eps), TV, 68-56, CDN, Aut/Com; *PICOLO* 'LA BOITE A SURPRISES', (40 eps), TV, 68-66, CDN, Co aut; *IL FAUT MARIER COLOMBE,* TV, 58, CDN, Aut; *LES HUTTO PERE ET FILS,* TV, 57, CDN, Aut.

CALLAGHAN, Barry

ACTRA. 69 Sullivan St., Toronto, Ont, CAN, M5T 1C2. (416)977-7937.
Types of Production & Categories: TV Film-Wr/Prod; TV Video-Wr/Prod.
Genres: Drama-TV; Variety-TV; Documentary-TV; Educational-TV.
Biography: Born 1937, Toronto, Ontario. Professor, York University for 21 years; literary critic and editor, 'Toronto Telegram', 66-71; host and documentary filmmaker for CBC TV, 68-71; co-writer, producer, documentaries, Vilions Films, 74-77; weekly commentator, *CANADA A. M.* (CTV), 76-82; host, *ENTERPRISE* (City-TV), 84; 30 appearances, *FIGHTING WORDS* (CHCH-TV), 82-83; founder, editor of 'Exile: A Literary Quarterly', 72; Exile Editions, 76. Magazine journalist; poet; translator; fiction writer. Winner of 6 National Magazine Awards; Canadian Periodical Publication Award for Fiction, 85.
Selective Filmography: *LOVE,* 'ENTERPRISE', TV, 85, CDN, Host; *GAMBLING,* 'ENTERPRISE', TV, 84, CDN, Host **(ACTRA)**; *THE WHITE LAGER,* TV, 77, CDN/USA/J/S, Host/Wr/Interv; *COUNTERPOINT,* TV, 75, CDN/USA/J/S, Host; *CANADA: QUEBEC,* TV, 74, CDN, Wr; *THE TIN CANOE,* TV, 73, CDN, Wr; *MARY QUEEN OF SCOTS/LOUIS RIEL,* 'MAN ALIVE', TV, 72, CDN,

(cont/suite)

Wr; *GOLDA MEIR/DRUGS/ANGELA DAVIS IN PRISON*, 'WEEKEND', TV, 71/70, CDN, Wr/Prod/Interv; *MY LAI/VIETNAM VETERANS/KNAPP COMMISSION (NEW YORK CRIME)*, 'WEEKEND', TV, 71, CDN, Wr/Prod; *ARABS-ISRAELI / SPEED CITY (DRUGS) / BLACK PANTHER JURISPRUDENCE*, 'WEEKEND', TV, 70/69, CDN, Wr/Prod/Interv; *SIX DAYS IN AMWAN(BLACK SEPT.WAR)/EGYPT/MIDDLE EAST(PALESTINIANS)*, 'WEEKEND', TV, 70, CDN, Wr/Prod/Interv; *LEBANON-ISRAEL/QUEBEC ECONOMICS/MICHEL CHARTRAND/QUEBEC CULTURE*, 'WEEKEND', TV, 69, CDN, Wr/Prod/Interv; *CALLAGHAN'S NEW YORK/ISRAEL*, 'THE PUBLIC EYE', TV, 68, CDN, Prod/Wr; *THE BLUES*, 'BELL TELEPHONE HOUR', TV, 66, CDN, Wr/Host; *MARGARET LAURENCE/PATRICK KAVANAGH*, 'UMBRELLA', TV, 66, CDN, Wr/Interv; *MARIE-CLAIRE BLAIS*, 'SHOW OF SHOWS', TV, 64, CDN, Wr/Interv.

CAMERON, B.A.

Southview Rd., R.R. 2, Powell River, BC, CAN, V8A 4Z3. (604)483-9849. The Colbert Agency, 303 Davenport Rd., Toronto, Ont, CAN, M5R 1K5. (416)964-3302.
Types of Production & Categories: Th Film-Wr; TV Film-Wr.
Genres: Drama-Th&TV; Comedy-TV; Action-Th.
Biography: Born 1938, Nanaimo, British Columbia. Several poems and short stories published in anthologies; novels in Canada, USA. Has won poetry, film and literary awards. Writer in residence, Simon Fraser University; teaches creative writing and screenwriting.
Selective Filmography: *MADELEINE*, 'DAUGHTERS OF THE COUNTRY', TV, 86, CDN, Co-Wr; *CALIFORNIA AUNTS*, 'POV', TV, 86, CDN, Wr; *THE TIN FLUTE* (BONHEUR D'OCCASION), (5 eps), TV, 82, CDN, Co-T'Play; *TICKET TO HEAVEN*, Th, 80, CDN, Co-Scr; *HOMECOMING/THEY'RE DRYING UP THE STREETS/A MATTER OF CHOICE*, 'FOR THE RECORD', TV, 79-77, CDN, Wr; *COAL TYEE*, TV, 77, CDN, Wr; *BOMB SQUAD*, TV, 77, CDN, Wr; *DREAMSPEAKER*, 'FOR THE RECORD', TV, 76, CDN, Wr **(CFA)**.

CAMERON, Silver Donald

ACTRA. D'Escousse, NS, CAN, B0E 1K0. (902)226-3165. Nancy Colbert, The Colbert Agency, 303 Davenport Rd., Toronto, Ont, CAN, M5R 1K5. (416)964-3302.
Types of Production & Categories: TV Film-Wr; TV Video-Wr.
Genres: Drama-TV; Documentary-TV.
Biography: Born 1937. B.A., University of British Columbia; M.A., U. of California; Ph.D., U. of London, England. Has taught english language and literature at Dalhousie U., U.B.C., and U. of New Brunswick. Since 71, has been a full-time writer, film, TV, radio; has written for many magazines including: 'Saturday Night', 'Maclean's', 'The Financial Post'; Contributing Editor of 'Weekend', 74-76; has received National Magazine Awards. Television credits include: *THE BUCCANEERING SPIRIT, THE ATLANTIC PROVINCES*. Writer-in-residence, U. of Prince Edward Island, 85-86. Published 7 books including: 'Conversations with Canadian Novelists', 'Dragon Lady'.

CANDY, John

ACTRA, AFTRA, SAG, WGAw. Frostbacks Production Ltd., 12328 Montana Ave., Los Angeles, CA, USA, 90049. John Gaines, Agency for the Perf. Arts, 9000 Sunset Blvd., Los Angeles, CA, USA, 90069. (213)273-0744.
Types of Production & Categories: Th Film-Wr/Prod/Act; TV Video-Wr/Act.
Genres: Comedy-Th&TV; Variety-Th&TV; Children's-Th&TV.
Biography: Born Toronto, Ontario; numerous acting credits in feature films and television.

(cont/suite)

Selective Filmography: *ARMED AND DANGEROUS*, Th, 86, USA, Act/Co-Wr/ Co-Prod; *LITTLE SHOP OF HORRORS*, Th, 86, USA, Act; *VACATION*, Th, 85, USA, Act; *BREWSTER'S MILLIONS*, Th, 85, USA, Act; *VOLUNTEERS*, Th, 85, USA, Act; *SUMMER RENTAL*, Th, 85, USA, Act; *TEARS ARE NOT ENOUGH*, Th, 85, CDN, Act; *SPLASH*, Th, 84, USA, Act; *'SCTV'* (195 eps), TV, 84-76, CDN, Act/Co-Wr (ACTRA/2 EMMY); *GOING BERSERK*, Th, 83, CDN/ USA, Act; *IT CAME FROM HOLLYWOOD*, Th, 82, USA, Act; *STRIPES*, Th, 81, USA, Act; *THE BLUES BROTHERS*, Th, 80, USA, Act; *DOUBLE NEGATIVE*, Th, 79, CDN, Act; *1941*, Th, 79, USA, Act; *THE SILENT PARTNER*, Th, 77, CDN, Act; *TUNNELVISION*, Th, 76, USA, Act.

CAPISTRAN, Michel

SARDEC, UDA. 1680 chemin Athlone, Mont-Royal, Qué, CAN, H3R 3G8. (514) 340-1770. BHMCL inc., 1600 blvd. Dorchester O., Montréal, Qué, CAN. (514)937-7771.
Types de production et Catégories: 1 métrage-Sc; TV film-Sc.
Types d'ocuvres: Drame-C; Documentaire-TV.
Curriculum vitae: Né en 1946, Montréal, Québec. Etudes universitaires en sociologie et psycho-pédagogie. Huit ans à Radio-Canada comme scénariste; cinéma: courts et longs métrages. Consultant en communications et stratégie politique à BHMCL inc. depuis 1980.
Filmographie sélective: *BINGO*, C, 73, CDN, Co sc/Ass réal; *'SI TOUS LES GENS DU MONDE'* (13 eps), TV, 71, CDN, Sc.

CARLE, Gilles - voir REALISATEURS

CARNEY, Robert

ACTRA. The Colbert Agency, 303 Davenport Rd., Toronto, Ont, CAN, M5R 1K5. (416)964-3302.
Types of Production & Categories: TV Film-Wr; TV Video-Wr.
Genres: Drama-TV.
Selective Filmography: *'HOT SHOTS'* (Wr-1 eps), (13 eps), TV, 86, CDN, Story Ed; *'NIGHT HEAT'* (Wr-6 eps), (26 eps), TV, 86-84, CDN, Story Ed; *'BACKSTRETCII'* (2 eps), TV, 83, CDN, Wr; *'THE GREAT DETECTIVE'* (8 eps), TV, 81-79, CDN, Wr; *'TALES OF THE KLONDIKE'* (3 eps), TV, 80, CDN, T'play.

CARON, Louis

SACD, SARDEC. 220 St-Alexandre, Longueuil, Qué, CAN, J4H 3E8. (514)463-1183.
Types de production et Catégories: TV film-Sc.
Types d'oeuvres: Drame-TV; Education-TV.
Curriculum vitae: Né en 1942.
Filmographie sélective: *'LES RACONTAGES DE LOUIS CARON'* (12 eps), TV, 82, CDN, Sc; *'LES FILS DE LA LIBERTE'* (6 eps), TV, 81, CDN/F, Sc; *REGARDE PAPA!*, TV, 79, CDN, Sc.

CARRIERE, Bruno - voir REALISATEURS

CHAD, Sheldon

ACTRA, WGAw. 40 Homewood Ave., #504, Toronto, Ont, CAN, M4Y 2K2. (416)967-6266. Ralph Zimmerman, Great North Artists Mgmt., 345 Adelaide St. W., Ste. 500, Toronto, Ont, CAN, M5V 1R5. (416)593-2587.
Types of Production & Categories: Th Film-Wr; TV Film-Wr; TV Video-Wr.
Genres: Drama-Th&TV; Comedy-Th&TV; Action-Th&TV.
Biography: Education : B.A, McGill University; Lionel Shapiro Award for Literary Merit in English, 76.

(cont/suite)

WRITERS/SCENARISTES

Selective Filmography: *LES FOUS DE BASSAN* (IN THE SHADOW OF THE WIND), Th, 86, CDN, Scr; *ON ANY GIVEN SUNDAY* (PITTSBURGH vs CLEAVELAND), Th, 85, USA, Wr; *'SEEING THINGS'* (8 eps), TV, 84-81, CDN, Wr **(ACTRA)**.

CHAREST, Gaétan - voir REALISATEURS

CHATO, Paul

ACTRA. 77 Carlton St., #703, Toronto, Ont, CAN, M5B 2J7. Barbara Fogler, 3 Charles St.W., #204, Toronto, Ont, CAN. (416)923-9844.
Types of Production & Categories: TV Video-Wr/Act.
Genres: Comedy-TV.
Biography: Born 1954, Canada; Hungarian parents; speaks English and Hungarian. Graduated from Ryerson Polytechnical Institute (Radio/TV Arts). Received the Don Hudson Award. Has been a graphic designer and advertising manager.
Selective Filmography: *'4 ON THE FLOOR'* (13 eps), TV, 85, CDN, Co-Wr/Act.

CHETWYND, Lionel

ACTRA, WGGB, WGAw. Cannon Television, 640 San Vincente Blvd., Los Angeles, CA, USA, 90048. (213)658-2004. Lee Rosenberg, Triad Artists, 10100 Santa Monica Blvd.,#1600, Los Angeles, CA, USA, 90067. (213)556-2727.
Types of Production & Categories: Th Film-Wr/Dir/Prod; TV Film-Wr/Dir/Prod; TV Video-Wr/Dir.
Genres: Drama-Th&TV; Comedy-Th&TV; Variety-TV; Documentary-TV.
Biography: Born 1940, London, England; naturalized Canadian, 64. B.A., Honours, Philosophy, Economics, Sir George Williams University, 63; Bachelor Civil Laws, McGill U., 67. Assistant managing director, Columbia Pictures (U.K.) Ltd., 68-72; freelance writer, film, TV, essays, articles for 'Punch', 'Encounter', 'L'Express'. *MIRACLE ON ICE* won a Chris Award, Columbus; *THE APPRENTICESHIP OF DUDDY KRAVITZ* won the Silver Bear (Berlin), an Oscar nomination (Best Screenplay Adaptation); *TWO SOLITUDES* won the Silver Laurel, Salonika.
Selective Filmography: *CHILDREN IN THE CROSSFIRE*, TV, 84, USA/IRL, Wr; *SADAT*, TV, 82, USA, Wr; *HOT TOUCH* (FRENCH KISS), Th, 82, CDN, Scr; *MIRACLE ON ICE*, TV, 81, USA, Wr; *ESCAPE FROM IRAN: THE CANADIAN CAPER*, TV, 80, CDN, Wr; *A WHALE FOR THE KILLING*, TV, 80, CDN/USA, T'play; *TWO SOLITUDES*, Th, 77, USA, Scr/Dir; *IT HAPPENED ONE CHRISTMAS*, TV, 77, USA, T'play; *QUINTET*, Th, 77, USA, Story; *'THE ADAMS CHRONICLES'* (ep 12 & 13), 'BICENTENNIAL SERIES', TV, 76, USA, Wr; *THE AMERICAN 1776*, Th, 76, USA, Wr; *GOLDENROD*, Th, 76, CDN, Scr/Co-Prod; *JOHNNY WE HARDLY KNEW YE*, TV, 75, USA, Scr/Prod; *THE APPRENTICESHIP OF DUDDY KRAVITZ*, Th, 74, CDN, Scr Adapt (WGA); *THE GUEST ROOM*, 'PLAYHOUSE 90', TV, 73, USA, Wr; *DAY BEGINS*, TV, 73, USA, Wr/Dir; *JOHNNY VELVET*, Th, 71, GB/I, Co-Wr.

CHILCO, Joe

ACTRA. 227 Cassandra Blvd., T.H.#905, Don Mills, Ont, CAN, M3A 1V3. (416) 444-2187. Bookings, 304 Richmond St.W., Toronto, Ont, CAN. (416)599-5816.
Types of Production & Categories: TV Film-Wr/Act; TV Video-Wr/Act.
Genres: Drama-TV; Comedy-TV; Industrial-Th.
Biography: Born 1953, Toronto, Ontario. B.A., York University. Winner of a Graham Award for cable TV Production.
Selective Filmography: *'LIFESTYLE WORKOUT'* (pilot), TV, 85, CDN, Act/Co-Wr; *'HANGIN' IN'* (1 eps), TV, 85, CDN, Act; *'LAUGHING MATTERS'* (13 eps), TV, 85, CDN, Contr Wr; *SOCIETY CENTRAN/BREWER'S RETAIL*, In, 85, CDN, Act; *'SNOWJOB'* (1 eps), TV, 84, CDN, Act; *'HANGIN' IN'* (1 eps), TV, 84, CDN, Wr.

CLARK, Barry

ACTRA, WGAw. Telford-Clark Productions, 316 Spalding Drive, Beverly Hills, CA, USA, 90212. (213)556-3963.
Types of Production & Categories: Th Film-Wr/Dir; Th Short-Wr/Dir; TV Film-Wr/Dir; TV Video-Wr/Dir.
Genres: Drama-Th; Action-Th&TV; Documentary-TV; Educational-TV.
Biography: Born 1937, Lethbridge, Alberta. B.Sc. (Chemistry), McGill University, 57; M.A. (Physics), Harvard University, 59. Officer of Los Angeles Audubon Society. *THE BIG SIX* won 8 awards, Hollywood TV Festival, 78; *AMERICAN DIARY* won a Cine Golden Eagle, Golden Babe, Chicago, 84.
Selective Filmography: *THE SLENDER TRAP*, Th, 86, USA, Wr/Dir; *'THE AMERICAN CHRONICLES'* (10 eps), TV, 86/85, USA, Wr/Dir; *'DANGER BAY'* (5 eps), TV, 85, CDN/USA, Wr; *BIMINI CODE*, Th, 83, USA, Wr/Dir; *'AMERICAN DIARY'* (Wr-2 eps), (6 eps), TV, 83, USA, Story Ed/Dir; *'MYSTERIES, MYTHS AND LEGENDS'* (5 eps), TV, 81, USA, Wr/Dir; *ELEANOR ROOSEVELT: AN UNCOMMON WOMAN*, 'LEGENDS', TV, 80, USA, Wr/Dir; *'NEPTUNE CHRONICLES'* (8 eps), TV, 80, USA, Wr; *'THE BIG SIX'* (5 eps), TV, 78-76, USA, Wr/Dir; *KRAG, KING OF THE KLONDIKE*, 'WONDERFUL WORLD OF DISNEY', TV, 78, USA, Wr; *ESCAPE FROM ANGOLA*, Th, 76, USA/ZA, Wr; *THE WILD AND THE FREE/SHOKEE, THE EVERGLADES PANTHER*, 'WONDERFUL WORLD OF DISNEY', TV, 74/73, USA, Wr; *GO WEST YOUNG DOG*, 'WONDERFUL WORLD OF DISNEY', TV, 74, USA, Wr; *COOMBA, DINGO OF THE OUTBACK/GRINGO*, 'WONDERFUL WORLD OF DISNEY', (5 eps), TV, 73/72, USA, Wr; *'SALTY'* (Co-Wr-1 eps), (2 eps), TV, 71, CDN, Wr; *CINDY AND DONNA*, Th, 71, USA, Wr; *'THE CHALLENGING SEA'* (9 eps), TV, 70/69, CDN/USA, Wr/Dir; *A LA MOD*, Th, 68, USA, Wr/Dir.

COHEN, Annette - see PRODUCERS

COHEN, M. Charles

ACTRA, WGAw. 2045 Grey Ave., Montreal, Que, CAN, H4A 3N3. (514)488-5476. Triad Artists Inc., 10100 Santa Monica Blvd., 16th Fl., Los Angeles, CA, USA, 90067. (213)556-2727.
Types of Production & Categories: Th Film-Wr; Th Short-Wr; TV Film-Wr; TV Video-Wr.
Genres: Drama-Th&TV; Comedy-Th&TV.
Biography: Born 1926, Warner, Alberta. B.A., B.S.W., University of Manitoba; M.S.W., U. of Toronto. Thirty years experience as freelance writer in Canada for CBC and NFB, in USA for the 3 major networks. Awards: Western Heritage Award for *AGE OF THE BUFFALO*, NFB; Humanitas Award, 75, for *SUNSHINE* series; Emmy nomination for *ROOTS* mini-series.

COLLEY, Peter

ACTRA, WGAw. 238 Davenport Rd., Ste. 100, Toronto, Ont, CAN, M5R 1J6. 3960 Laurel Canyon Blvd.,#259, Studio City, CA, USA, 91604. (818)509-8915. John Downey, Noble Talent Mgmt., 2411 Yonge St., Ste. 302, Toronto, Ont, CAN, M4P 2E7. (416)482-6556.
Types of Production & Categories: Th Film-Wr.
Genres: Horror-Th.
Biography: Born 1949, Great Britain. B.A., Honours, Sheffield University. Resident playwright, Grand Theatre, London, Ontario; author of 7 stage plays with over 200 productions in Canada, USA and G.B. including 'I'll Be Back Before Midnight'.
Selective Filmography: *THE MARK OF CAIN*, Th, 85, CDN, Co-Scr.

CORNISH, Christine
ACTRA. Rainy River Pictures Inc., 387 Kingswood Rd., Toronto, Ont, CAN, M4E 3P2. (416)690-4991.
Types of Production & Categories: TV Film-Wr; TV Video-Wr.
Genres: Drama-TV.
Biography: Born London, England; Canadian citizen. Television writer for 7 years.
Selective Filmography: *THE BEACHCOMBERS'* (Co-Wr-2 eps), (5 eps), TV, 86-84, CDN, Wr; *FLOWERS IN THE SAND,* TV, 80, CDN, Wr/Co-Prod; *CLARE'S WISH,* TV, 79, CDN, Wr/Co-Prod.

COUTURE, Jacques
SARDEC. 4372 ave.Laval, Montréal, Qué, CAN, H2W 2J8. (514)288-5940.
Types de production et Catégories: TV film-Sc; TV vidéo-Sc.
Types d'oeuvres: Documentaire-TV; Education-TV.
Curriculum vitae: Né en 1950, Sherbrooke, Québec. Maitrise en études littéraires, Université de Sherbrooke; 12 années de théâtre avant de se consacrer à la production audio-visuelle. Scénariste ayant travaillé pour des compagnies privées autant que pour le gouvernement.
Filmographie sélective: *'COMMENT VA LA SANTE?'* (5 eps), TV, 84, CDN, Textes/Rech/Anim; *'VISITE DE JEAN-PAUL II AU CANADA'* (12 eps), TV, 84, CDN, Textes; *'CHRONIQUE D'UNE VILLE'* (2 eps), TV, 82, CDN, Textes/Rech; *'GALT ET CIE'* (2 eps), TV, 82, CDN, Textes/Rech.

COUTURE, Suzette
ACTRA, UDA. 9 Olive Ave., Toronto, Ont, CAN, M6G 1T7. (416)530-4437.
Types of Production & Categories: TV Film-Wr; TV Video-Wr.
Genres: Drama-TV; Comedy-TV; Variety-TV; Documentary-TV.
Biography: Born 1947, Ottawa, Ontario; bilingual. B.A., Carleton University. Worked as a journalist; actress, Yale School of Drama, Toronto alternate theatres (70's); wrote and starred in 'Joined at the Hip' with partner Chas Lawther; though she has not given up performing, she is writing full time.
Selective Filmography: *'DANGER BAY'* (2 eps), TV, 86, CDN/USA, Wr; *MICHAEL AND KITTY,* TV, 85, CDN, Wr; *'THE CAMPBELLS'* (4 eps), TV, 85, CDN/USA/GB, Wr; *WHERE THE HEART IS,* 'FOR THE RECORD', TV, 84, CDN, Wr; *JOINED AT THE HIP,* TV, 84, CDN, Co-Wr/Act.

CRONENBERG, David - see DIRECTORS

CULLEN, Donald
ACTRA. 86 Gloucester St., #302, Toronto, Ont, CAN, M4Y 2S2. (416)964-2546.
Types of Production & Categories: Th Film-Wr; TV Film-Wr.
Genres: Comedy-Th&TV; Variety-TV.
Biography: Born 1933, London, Ontario. Education: Philosophy, University of Toronto. Has written 200 TV shows, 1100 shows for CBC radio from satire to public affairs; actor, feature films, TV, radio; performed on Broadway, 'Beyond the Fringe'. Won the Gabriel Award for *THE FLYING AGNOSTICS.*
Selective Filmography: *ALL IN GOOD TASTE,* Th, 80, CDN, Co-Wr; *'EVERYTHING GOES'* (100 eps), TV, 74/73, CDN, Head Wr; *THE FLYING AGNOSTICS,* TV, 68, CDN, Wr.

D'ANDREA, Anthony
ACTRA, DGC. 71 Hatherley Rd., Toronto, Ont, CAN, M6E 1V8. (416)653-9287.
Types of Production & Categories: Th Film-Wr/Dir.
Genres: Drama-Th; Action-Th.
Biography: Born 1955, Canada. B.A., Fine Arts Film Program, York University.
Selective Filmography: *THE HAUNTING OF HAMILTON HIGH,* Th, 86, CDN, 1st Assist Ed; *BULLIES,* Th, 85, CDN, Assist Ed; *HIGH STAKES,* Th, 85, CDN,
(cont/suite)

Assist Ed; *FLYING*, Th, 84, CDN, Assist Ed; *THRILLKILL*, Th, 83, CDN, Wr/ Co-Dir.

DANFORTH, Logan N.
ACTRA. c/o ACTRA, 2239 Yonge St., Toronto, Ont, CAN, M4S 2B5. (416)489-1311.
Types of Production & Categories: Th Film-Wr.
Genres: Drama-Th.
Selective Filmography: *CROSS-COUNTRY*, Th, 82, CDN, Co-Scr; *MISDEAL* (BEST REVENGE), Th, 80, CDN, Co-Scr.

DANSEREAU, Mireille - voir REALISATEURS

DARCUS, Jack - see DIRECTORS

DAVIDSON, William - see DIRECTORS

DAVIS, Gerry
ACTRA, WGAw, WGGB. 980 Elkland Pl., #4, Venice, CA, USA, 90291. (213) 396-4620.
Types of Production & Categories: Th Film-Wr; TV Film-Wr; TV Video-Wr/Prod.
Genres: Drama-Th&TV; Action-Th&TV; Science Fiction-Th&TV; Documentary-Th&TV.
Biography: Born 1937, London, England; Canadian citizen; residing in USA. Started in theatre as actor, director in England, Canada; merchant seaman, 4 years; actor, editor, NFB, CBC; writer, editor, producer for ITV, BBC; writer, story editor, Hollywood, 80's. Published 7 novels world-wide.
Selective Filmography: *'JESSIE'* (7 eps), TV, 84, USA, Staff Wr; *'VEGAS'* (3 eps), TV, 80, USA, Wr; *THE FINAL COUNTDOWN*, Th, 80, USA, Co-Scr; *DOOMWATCH*, Th, 75, GB, Scr; *'THE GREAT DETECTIVE'* (13 eps), TV, 75/ 74, CDN, Story Ed; *'SIDESTREET'* (26 eps), TV, 75/74, CDN, Head Wr; *'SOFTLY-SOFTLY'* (80 eps), TV, 74-72, GB, Story Ed/Wr; *'DOOMWATCH'* (39 eps), TV, 73-68, GB, Creator/Wr/Prod/Story Ed; *'THE FIRST LADY'* (40 eps), TV, 68/67, GB, Wr/Story Ed/Prod; *'DR WHO'* (90 eps), TV, 68-66, GB, Wr/Prod/ Story Ed; *'UNITED'* (115 eps), TV, 66/65, GB, Story Ed; *'199 PARKLANE'* (60 eps), TV, 65, GB, Wr/Story Ed

DEFELICE, James
ACTRA. 5611 - 109th St., Edmonton, Alta, CAN, T6H 3A7. (403)434-9702.
Types of Production & Categories: Th Film-Wr; Th Short-Wr; TV Film-Wr; TV Video-Wr.
Genres: Drama-Th&TV; Comedy-Th&TV; Action-Th&TV; Children's-TV.
Biography: Born 1943. Has lived and worked in Edmonton since 69; married with 2 daughters. Studied Journalism, Drama, Northeastern University, Boston; advanced study in drama, Tufts U. and Indiana U. Worked 4 years, sports dept., 'Boston Globe'; has written 20 plays and directed for the stage; acted in professional theatre, film, TV, radio in Canada and USA. Received an Outstanding Alumni Award, Northeastern U., 78; Alberta Achievement Award in Theatre Arts, 78.
Selective Filmography: *HOTWALKER*, 'BELL CANADA PLAYHOUSE', TV, 85, CDN, T'play; *LETTING GO*, TV, 85, CDN, Wr; *THIS MORTAL COIL*, 'STONEY PLAIN', TV, 83, CDN, Wr; *DRAW!*, TV, 83, CDN/USA, Act; *'NUGGETS'* (1 eps), TV, 82, CDN, Wr; *HARRY TRACY*, Th, 80, CDN, Act; *PRISONERS IN THE SNOW*, 'THE MAGIC LIE', TV, 79, CDN, Wr; *WHY SHOOT THE TEACHER*, Th, 76, CDN, Scr (**CFA**); *WINGS OF TIME*, Th, 76, CDN, Wr.

DELMA, Christian
ARRQ. 510 rue Cherrier, Montréal, Qué, CAN, H2L 1H3. (514)845-7917.
Radio-Québec, 1000 rue Fullum, Montréal, Qué, CAN, H2K 3L7. (514)521-2424.
(cont/suite)

Types de production et Catégories: TV film-Sc; TV vidéo/Sc/Réal.
Types d'oeuvres: Drame-TV; Variété-TV; Documentaire-TV; Education-TV.
Curriculum vitae: Né en 1927 à Paris, France; citoyen canadien depuis 67.
Formation originale: acteur; scénariste à l'emploi de Radio-Québec depuis 68;
réalisateur depuis 84. Formation TV: Banff Centre of Performing Arts. Chargé de
cours en scénarisation à l'UQAM.
Filmographie sélective: *LE JARDIN EXTRAORDINAIRE* (DANIEL GUERARD
CHANTE CHARLES TRENET), TV, 85, CDN, Réal; *LA MANIERE NOIRE*
(MARC-AURELE FORTIN), TV, 82, CDN, Sc; *LE GRAND PRIX,* TV, 82,
CDN, Sc; *LA COMMISSION D'ENQUETE/LE CLERGE CANADIEN,* 'AUX
YEUX DU PRESENT', TV, 78/77, CDN, Sc; *MUSSOLINI/LE TRAITE DE
PARIS,* 'AUX YEUX DU PRESENT', TV, 77/76, CDN, Sc; *UN ENFANT BIEN
TRANQUILLE* (LES MALENTENDANTS), TV, 75, CDN, Sc.

DENNIS, Charles - see DIRECTORS

DENSHAM, Pen - see PRODUCERS

DESJARDINS, Normand

SARDEC. 4179 Coloniale, Montréal, Qué, CAN, H2W 2L2. (514)285-1993.
Types de production et Catégories: c métrage-Sc.
Types d'oeuvres: Drame-C; Enfants-C.
Curriculum vitae: Né en 1950, St-Antoine des Laurentides, Québec; bilingue.
Expérience professionnelle: rédacteur, critique littéraire (revue 'Nos Livres',
Montréal); auteur, rédaction de romans, contes et pièces de théâtre; journaliste
pigiste auprès de divers magazines.
Filmographie sélective: *CHER MONSIEUR L'AVIATEUR,* C, 84, CDN, Conc/Sc.

DESROSIERS, Sylvie

SARDEC. 4872 Hutchison, Montréal, Qué, CAN, H2V 4A3. (514)274-7992.
Ludom Inc., 5800 Monkland, Montréal, Qué, CAN. (514)483-6320.
Types de production et Catégories: TV vidéo-Sc.
Types d'oeuvres: Drame-TV; Variété-TV.
Curriculum vitae: Née en 1954, Montréal, Québec; bilingue. Baccalauréat spécialisé
en Histoire de l'Art, Université de Montréal. Auteur au magazine 'Croc' depuis 80;
journaliste; romancière, 'T'as rien compris Jacynthe'.
Filmographie sélective: *SEULE AVEC L'AUTRE,* 'BEAUX DIMANCHES', TV,
86, CDN, Aut; *'SAMEDI DE RIRE'* (5 eps), TV, 86/85, CDN, Aut.

DEVERELL, Rex

ACTRA. 2775 Broder St., Regina, Sask, CAN, S4N 3T8. (306)352-9763. The
Globe Theatre, 1801 Scarth St., Regina, Sask, CAN. (306)525-9553.
Types of Production & Categories: TV Film-Wr; TV Video-Wr.
Genres: Drama-TV; Documentary-Th&TV; Educational-TV; Children's-TV.
Biography: Born 1941, Toronto, Ontario. B.A., B.D., McMaster University; S.T.M.,
Theatre and Theology, Union Theological Seminary, New York, 67. Resident
playwright, Globe Theatre since 75. Winner, Canadian Authors Award, 78; author
of a number of stage and radio plays.
Selective Filmography: *VOYAGE-VOYAGEUR,* TV, 84, CDN, Wr;
BATTLEFORD, TV, 79, CDN, Wr; *WHAT'S A MOOSE JAW?,* TV, 78, CDN,
Wr; *WELCOMED WITH JOY,* ED, 74, CDN, Wr; *VERSE AND WORSE,* 'HI
DIDDLE DAY', TV, 74, CDN, Wr.

DEVERELL, William H.

ACTRA. Razor Point Rd., North Pender Island, BC, CAN, V0N 2M0. (604)629-
6622. Lucinda Vardey Agency, 228 Gerrard St.E., Toronto, Ont, CAN, M5A 2E8.

(cont/suite)

(416)922-0250. Turnham, Green, Higginbottom, Woodland, 844 Courtney, Victoria, BC, CAN, V8N 1C4. (604)385-1122.
Types of Production & Categories: TV Film-Wr.
Genres: Drama-TV.
Biography: Born 1937, Regina, Saskatchewan. Education: B.A. and LL.B.. Has written several radio plays and 4 novels: 'Needles' (also wrote screenplay), 'High Crimes', 'Mecca', 'The Dance of Shiva'.
Selective Filmography: *'STREET LEGAL'* (2 eps), TV, 86, CDN, Wr; *SHELL GAME* (pilot), TV, 85, CDN, Wr.

DEWAR, Stephen W. - see PRODUCERS

DONOVAN, Paul - see DIRECTORS

DORE, Isabelle
CAPAC, SARDEC, UDA. 5578 de l'Esplanade, Montréal, Qué, CAN, H2T 3A1. (514)276-7048.
Types de production et Catégories: TV vidéo-Sc.
Types d'oeuvres: Comédie-TV; Comédie musicale-TV; Education-TV; Enfants-TV.
Curriculum vitae: Née à Montréal, Québec. Expérience à la télévision et au théâtre. Ecrit des paroles de musique.
Filmographie sélective: *'COURT-CIRCUIT'* (40 eps), TV, 85/84, CDN, Aut; *'POP-CITROUILLE'*, TV, 84-78, CDN, Aut; *'LUNDIS DES HA! HA!'* (1 monologue), TV, 84, CDN, Aut; *'ECOUTE MOI DONC QUAND JE TE PARLE'* (13 eps), TV, 81, CDN, Aut; *MEURTRE AU MANOIR,* TV, 80, CDN, Aut; *UNE CLASSE SANS ECOLE,* C, 79, CDN, Aut; *'LA TELEVISION DU BONHEUR'* (4 eps), TV, 76, CDN, Aut; *'LA FRICASSEE'* (22 eps), TV, 72, CDN, Aut.

DRAKE, T.Y.
ACTRA, WGAw. R.R. #1, Winlaw, BC, CAN, V0G 2J0. Project Hill Productions, 434 E. 20th Ave., Vancouver, BC, CAN, V5V 1M5. (604)874-8005. Michael Hamilburg, The Hamilburg Agency, 292 S. La Cienega Blvd., #212, Los Angeles, CA, USA. (213)657-1501.
Types of Production & Categories: Th Film-Wr; TV Film-Wr; TV Video-Wr.
Genres: Drama-Th&TV; Comedy-Th; Science Fiction-TV; Horror-Th.
Biography: Born 1936, Vancouver, British Columbia; Canadian-US citizenship. Executive story consultant: series TV, MGM, Penta One Productions, Calgary.
Selective Filmography: *'HAMILTON'S QUEST'* (7 eps), TV, 86, CDN, Co-Creator/Co-Wr/Story Ed; *TERROR TRAIN,* Th, 80, CDN, Wr; *'MAN FROM ATLANTIS'* (1 eps), TV, 77, USA, Wr; *'WHATEVER HAPPENED TO THE CLASS OF '65'* (3 eps), TV, 76, USA, Staff Wr; *THE KEEPER,* Th, 75, CDN, Wr/Dir; *'PLANET EARTH'* (2 eps), TV, 74, USA, Staff Wr; *PAR FOR THE COURSE,* 'THE PSYCHIATRIST', TV, 71, USA, Wr (WGA); *'THEN CAME BRONSON'* (Wr-2 eps/Co-Wr-3 eps), (5 eps), TV, 71/70, USA, Exec Story Ed; *'THE BILL COSBY SHOW'* (1 eps), TV, 68, USA, Wr.

DROUIN, Dominique
SARDEC. 5881 Hutchison, Montréal, Qué, CAN, H2V 4B7. (514)273-9342.
Types de production et Catégories: TV vidéo-Sc.
Types d'oeuvres: Drame-TV; Documentaire-TV.
Curriculum vitae: Née en 1958; citoyenneté canadienne. Maitrise en Communications, Université de Montréal; participation à titre de conférencière sur le métier d'auteur à la télévision.
Filmographie sélective: *'LE GRAND REMOUS'* (39 eps), TV, 86, CDN, Aut; *'TERRE HUMAINE'* (156 eps), TV, 84-81, CDN, Aut; *L'ENSEIGNEMENT A LA MATERNELLE/LA MUSIQUE AU SECONDAIRE,* ED, 82, CDN, Sc; *'LA DEFICIENCE AUDITIVE'* (13 eps), TV, 81, CDN, Sc/Anim.

DUBE, Marcel

SARDEC. 57 Terrasse Les Hautvilliers, Outremont, Qué, CAN, H2V 4P1. (514) 273-8398.
Types de production et Catégories: l métrage-Sc; TV film-Sc.
Types d'oeuvres: Drame-C&TV.
Curriculum vitae: Né en 1930, Montréal, Québec; bilingue. Education: Faculté des Lettres, Université de Montréal; Ecole de Théâtre, Paris. Ecrit surtout pour le théâtre et la TV, mais aussi pour la radio, un livre, de la poésie, des contes, articles et adaptations de pièces de théâtre en anglais. Environ 30 de ses pièces ont été produites dont 'Zone', 'De l'autre coté du mur', 'Un simple soldat', 'Le temps des lilas', 'Florence, 'Au retour des oies blanches', 'Hold-up!', 'Dites-le avec des fleurs', 'Le testament' et 'L'honneur des hommes'. Ecrit 2 séries pour la TV: *LA COTE DE SABLE* et *DE 9 A 5*; au cinéma, il coscénarise entre autres *LES BEAUX DIMANCHES, ENTRE LA MER ET L'EAU DOUCE.*

DUCHESNE, Christiane

SARDEC. 4426 Boyer, Montréal, Qué, CAN, H2J 3E7. (514)522-4854.
Types de production et Catégories: c métrage-Sc; TV film-Sc.
Types d'oeuvres: Education-TV; Enfants-C&TV.
Curriculum vitae: Née en 1949, Montréal, Québec. Ecrit pour les enfants depuis 72 (scénarios pour TV et livres); 7 livres qu'elle a elle-même illustrés. *MATILDE OU LES BALLOTS DE FOIN* remporte le 1er Prix du Concours des Dramatiques de Radio-Canada et le 1er Prix Court-métrage à Bruxelles.
Filmographie sélective: *'MICHOU ET PILO'* (7 eps), TV, 85/84, CDN, Sc; *VICTOR, LA TERRE EST PLATE?*, C, 83, CDN, Sc; *'SALUT SANTE'* (26 eps), TV, 82/81, CDN, Sc/Rech; *'BONJOUR COMMENT MANGEZ-VOUS?'* (13 eps), TV, 77, CDN, Sc/Rech; *'SURVILLE'* (3 eps), TV, 77, CDN, Sc.

DUFRESNE, Guy

SARDEC, SACD. l ch. Abbott's Corner, Frelighsburg, Qué, CAN, J0J 1C0. (514) 298-5174.
Types de production et Catégories: TV film-Sc; TV vidéo-Sc.
Types d'oeuvres: Drame-TV; Comédie-TV; Documentaire-TV; Enfants-TV.
Curriculum vitae: Né en 1915, Montréal, Québec. Cours classique. Scénariste à la radio, 45-55; télévision, 55-75; théâtre, 59-67. *CAP-AUX-SORCIERS* fut proclamée émission de l'année, 56-57; *DES SOURIS ET DES HOMMES*, meilleur télé-théâtre de l'année, 73.
Filmographie sélective: *L'ENIGME LOUIS RIEL,* TV, 85, CDN, Sc; *NORMAN BETHUNE,* TV, 84, CDN, Sc; *'PROPOS D'ECOLOGIE'* (12 eps), TV, 81-78, CDN, Co sc; *C'EST POUR MATHIEU,* TV, 81, CDN, Sc; *CES DAMES DE L'ESTUAIRE,* TV, 79, CDN, Sc; *DECEMBRE,* TV, 78, CDN, Sc **(ANIK)**; *JOHANNE ET SES VIEUX,* TV, 76, CDN, Sc; *DES SOURIS ET DES HOMMES,* TV, 73, CDN, Aut; *LES TROIS SOEURS,* TV, 69, CDN, Aut; *'SEPTIEME-NORD'* (169 eps), TV, 67-63, CDN, Aut; *COMME TU ME VEUX,* TV, 63, CDN, Aut; *'KANAWRO'* (39 eps), TV, 61/60, CDN, Aut; *CHEMIN PRIVE,* TV, 61, CDN, Aut; *MESURE DE GUERRE,* TV, 60, CDN, Aut; *'CAP-AUX-SORCIERS'* (123 eps), TV, 58-55, CDN, Aut; *KEBEC,* TV, 58, CDN, Aut; *'EAUX VIVES'* (50 eps), TV, 55-53, CDN, Aut; *NICOLAS DUMETS,* TV, 55, CDN, Aut; *MARIE HORDOUIL,* TV, 55, CDN, Aut.

DUMOULIN-TESSIER, Françoise

SARDEC. 1075 Jean-Dumetz, Ste-Foy, Qué, CAN, G1W 4K6. (418)653-8862.
Types de production et Catégories: TV film-Sc.
Types d'oeuvres: Drame-TV; Comédie-TV.
Curriculum vitae: Néc en 1939, Québec; bilingue. Doctorat en Littérature; recherche post-doctorale en dialogue cinéma et TV. Expériences: documentaliste, critique

(cont/suite)

littéraire , enseignement (spécialiste en français); remplaçante en Afrique du Sud, école de métis.
Filmographie sélective: *ANTOINE ET SEBASTIEN,* 'LES BEAUX DIMANCHES', TV, 80, CDN, Aut; *ANTOINE ET SEBASTIEN/ELISE OU LE TEMPS D'AIMER,* 'PREMIER PLAN', TV, 77/76, CDN, Aut.

DUNPHY, Timothy
ACTRA, DGC. 100 Gloucester St., #1003, Toronto, Ont, CAN, M4Y 1M1. (416) 968-2225.
Types of Production & Categories: Th Film-Wr; TV Film-Wr; TV Video-Wr.
Genres: Drama-TV; Comedy-Th&TV; Action-TV.
Biography: Born 1954, New York City; US-Canadian citizen.
Selective Filmography: *'NIGHT HEAT'* (6 eps), TV, 86/85, CDN, Co-Wr; *'HOT SHOTS'* (2 eps), TV, 86, CDN, Wr; *BIG DEAL,* TV, 85, CDN, Co-Wr.

DUSSAULT, Louis - voir REALISATEURS

EAMES, David
ACTRA. 524-133 Wilton St., Toronto, Ont, CAN, M5A 4A4. (416)368-8787.
Types of Production & Categories: Th Film-Wr; TV Film-Wr; TV Video-Wr.
Genres: Drama-Th&TV; Comedy-Th&TV; Children's-Th&TV.
Biography: Born 1950, Toronto, Ontario.
Selective Filmography: *WILDER POINT,* TV, 86, CDN, Story Ed; *CAFE ROMEO,* Th, 86, CDN, Story Ed; *'DANGER BAY'* (1 eps), TV, 85, CDN, Wr; *'THE EDISON TWINS'* (1 eps), TV, 85, CDN, Wr; *MUSCLEBOUND/BEING DEAD/ THE CUPID GAME,* 'WINDOWS', TV, 85, CDN, Wr; *ANIMAL FEVER,* 'PARENTS AND READING', TV, 85, CDN, Wr; *'THE EDISON TWINS'* (12 eps), TV, 85, CDN, Story Ed; *BY DESIGN,* Th, 82, CDN, Co-Wr.

EDWARDS, Cash
WGAw. 1430 Maple St., Vancouver, BC, CAN, V6J 3T9. (604)731-0175. CKVU TV, 180 W. Second Ave., Vancouver, BC, CAN, V5Y 3T9. (604)876-1344.
Types of Production & Categories: Th Film-Wr; Th Short-Wr; TV Video-Prod/Wr.
Genres: Drama-Th&TV; Comedy-TV; Variety-TV; Action-Th&TV.
Biography: Born 1949, Santa Monica, California; U.S. citizen; landed immigrant, Canada. Educated at UCLA.
Selective Filmography: *'VANCOUVER LIVE'* (100 eps), TV, 85, CDN, Sr Prod/Head Wr; *THE LEGEND OF KAHUILIN,* Th, 82, USA/IRL, Wr; *THE HEALER* (pilot), 'JACK OF DIAMONDS', TV, 80, USA, Wr/Creator; *'HART TO HART'* (1 eps), TV, 79, USA, Wr; *SUPERTANKER,* Th, 78, USA, Wr/Assoc Prod.

EGOYAN, Atom - see DIRECTORS

ENDERSBY, Clive
ACTRA. 7224 Hillside Ave., #38, Los Angeles, CA, USA, 90046. (213)874-1641.
Doug Brodax, Stone Masser Manners, 1052 Carol Dr., Los Angeles, CA, USA, 90046. (213)275-9599.
Types of Production & Categories: TV Film-Wr; TV Video-Wr.
Genres: Drama-TV; Documentary-TV; Educational-TV; Children's-TV.
Biography: Born Edinburgh, Scotland; Canadian citizen. Child actor, 150 productions; won scholarship to acting school, England and appeared in numerous stage, TV and film productions. During 70's, returned to Canada as a writer; 200 TV scripts produced, TV Ontario; 5 children's plays; 2 published novels, 'Read All About It' and 'Journey Through the Stars'; has written lyrics to 150 songs. His educational series have won both Silver and Bronze, N.Y. Film Fest.; 2 ACT Awards and the Int'l Reading Assoc. Award of Merit.
Selective Filmography: *'TODAY'S SPECIAL'* (41 eps), TV, 86-81, CDN, Wr; *'DEAR AUNT AGNES'* (11 eps), TV, 86-84, CDN, Wr; *'POLKA DOT DOOR'* (30
(cont/suite)

eps), TV, 85-75, CDN, Wr; *'ARTSCAPE'* (8 eps), TV, 82/81, CDN, Wr; *'IT'S MAINLY MUSIC'* (6 eps), TV, 82, CDN, Wr; *'CANADA - THE GREAT EXPERIMENT'* (14 eps), TV, 81-79, CDN, Wr; *'READ ALL ABOUT IT'* (40 eps), TV, 80-76, CDN, Wr; *'MUSIC BOX'* (2 eps), TV, 79, CDN, Wr; *'LIKE NO OTHER PLACE'* (2 eps), TV, 78, CDN, Wr; *'ONE WORLD'* (13 eps), TV, 78/77, CDN, Wr; *'PERSON TO PERSON'* (7 eps), TV, 77, CDN, Wr; *KNOWLEDGE IS UNDERSTANDING*, TV, 76, CDN, Wr; *'OUR HERITAGE'* (3 eps), TV, 75, CDN, Wr; *'TWO PLUS YOU'* (16 eps), TV, 74, CDN, Wr.

ENGEL, Howard

ACTRA. 281 Major St., Toronto, Ont, CAN, M5S 2L5. (416)960-3829. Beverley Slopen, 131 Bloor St.W., #711, Toronto, Ont, CAN, M5S 1S3. (416)964-9598.
Types of Production & Categories: TV Film-Wr; TV Video-Wr.
Genres: Drama-TV; Comedy-TV; Action-TV.
Biography: Born 1931, Toronto, Ontario. B.A., McMaster University, 54. Freelance writer/producer, CBC radio (wrote thousands of radio programs, 55-85); freelanced in U.K., France, Cyprus, 60-64. Did literary and political interviews for documentaires (Alice B. Toklas, Sylvia Beach, Archbishop Makarios); CBC staff producer, 68-85. Published 5 books beginning with 'The Suicide Murders', 80. Became full-time writer, 85.
Selective Filmography: *MURDER SEES THE LIGHT,* TV, 86, CDN, T'play; *THE SUICIDE MURDERS,* TV, 85, CDN, T'play/Act; *'THE OBSERVER',* TV, 65/64, CDN, Story Ed/Wr.

FAVREAU, Robert - voir REALISATEURS

FERGUSON, Don

ACTRA, WGAw. Air Farce Productions, 66 Gerrard St. E., Toronto, Ont, CAN, M5B 1G3. (416)977-6222.
Types of Production & Categories: Th Film-Wr; TV Video-Wr.
Genres: Drama-Th&TV; Comedy-Th&TV.
Biography: Born 1948, Montreal, Quebec. Languages: English, Italian. B.A., Honours, Loyola University, Montreal. Won Juno Award, Best Comedy Album, 79; 8 Actra Awards for 'Air Farce', radio.
Selective Filmography: *AIR FARCE LIVE AT THE BAYVIEW,* TV, 84, CDN, Co-Wr/Act; *AIR FARCE ENQUIRER,* TV, 82, CDN, Co-Wr/Act; *AIR FARCE FACTORY COMEDY OUTLET,* TV, 81, CDN, Co-Wr/Act (**ACTRA**); *'AIR FARCE'* (10 eps), TV, 81, CDN, Co-Wr/Act (**ACTRA**); *AIR FARCE,* TV, 80, CDN, Co-Wr/Act; *HIGH POINT,* Th, 79, CDN, Uncr Rewr; *IMPROPER CHANNELS,* Th, 79, CDN, Uncr Rewr; *'MARY AND MICHAEL'* (Wr-8 eps)/ Dir-1 eps), (26 eps), TV, 78, CDN, Pro Coord; *'MONEY MAKERS'* (4 eps), TV, 76/75, CDN, Dir; *OUR COSTLY CLEAN-UP,* TV, 75, CDN, Dir; *'THE PLANE GAME'* (4 eps), TV, 74/73, CDN, Wr.

FIELDING, Joy

ACTRA. Owen Laster, William Morris Agency, 1350 Ave. of the Americas, New York, NY, USA, 10019. (212)586-5100.
Types of Production & Categories: Th Film-Wr; TV Film-Wr.
Genres: Drama-Th&TV; Comedy-Th&TV.
Biography: Born 1945, Canada. B.A., University of Toronto. Known primarily as an author; has 7 books published: 'The Best of Friends', 'The Transformation', 'Trance', 'The Other Woman', 'Life Penalty', 'The Deep End' and 'Kiss Mommy Goodbye' which won the Book-of-the-Year Award, Canadian Periodical Society. Has also written for TV, *PROGRAM X*; several film scripts; writes book reviews for the 'Globe & Mail' and CBC radio.

OPEN THE DOOR
To Filming Opportunities

- Script and Project Development
- Interim Financing
- Production, Distribution and Marketing Assistance
- Versioning Assistance
- Co-Productions.

Telefilm Canada

Head Office
Montreal
Tour de la Banque Nationale
600, rue de la Gauchetière Ouest
25e étage
H3B 4L2
Telephone: (514) 283-6363
Telex: 055-60998

Celebrating fifty years of flight.

Across the country and around the world…we're always there serving you.

Nous célébrons notre 50ᵉ anniversaire.

Et un demi-siècle de service aux passagers, tant du Canada que du monde entier!

AIR CANADA

FINNIGAN, Joan

Hartington, Ont, CAN, K0H 1W0. (613)374-3145. Bella Pomer, 22 Shallmar Blvd., Toronto, Ont, CAN, M5N 2Z8. (416)781-8597.
Types of Production & Categories: TV Film-Wr.
Genres: Drama-TV.
Biography: Born 1925, Ottawa, Ontario. B.A, English, History, Economics, Queen's University. Has written many radio scripts; published 17 books including: 'Entrance to the Greenhouse', 68 (Centennial Award for Poetry); 'I Come From the Valley', 'Some of the Stories I Told you Were True', 81, 'Legacies, Legends and Lies', 85.
Selective Filmography: *CELEBRATE THIS CITY*, TV, 73, CDN, Wr; *HOME*, 'THIS LAND', TV, 72, CDN, Wr; *THEY'RE PUTTING US OFF THE MAP*, TV, 70, CDN, Wr; *THE BEST DAMN FIDDLER FROM CALABOGIE TO KALADAR*, TV, 69, CDN, Wr (**CFA**).

FISCHER, Max - see DIRECTORS

FLAHERTY, David

ACTRA, WGA. 30 Beech Ave., Toronto, Ont, CAN, M4E 3H2. (416)691-8576. Deb Miller, William Morris Agency, 151 El Camino Dr., Los Angeles, CA, USA. (213)274-7451.
Types of Production & Categories: TV Film-Wr; TV Video-Wr.
Genres: Comedy-Th&TV; Variety-TV.
Biography: Born 1948, Pittsburg, Pennsylvania; US citizen; Canadian landed immigrant since 73. Attended University of Pittsburgh; married, 3 children. Has writing, directing, editing experience in film; copy writer for J. Walter Thompson, Cockfield Brown, Raymond Lee & Associates.
Selective Filmography: *'REALLY WEIRD TALES'* (2 eps), TV, 86, CDN/USA, Co-Creator/Wr; *'SCTV'* (18 eps), TV, 84, CDN, Co-Wr.

FORCIER, André - voir REALISATEURS

FORSYTH, Rob

ACTRA. The Colbert Agency, 303 Davenport Rd., Toronto, Ont, CAN, M5R 1K5. (416)964-3302.
Types of Production & Categories: TV Film-Wr.
Genres: Drama-TV; Action-TV.
Biography: Born 1949, Saskatoon, Saskatchewan. Also experienced in writing radio drama.
Selective Filmography: *RACE FOR THE BOMB* (mini-series), TV, 86/85, CDN/F, Co-Wr; *'AIRWAVES'* (2 eps), TV, 85, CDN, Wr; *'VANDERBERG'* (Wr-3 eps), (6 eps), TV, 83, CDN, Head Wr; *TAKEOVER* (pilot), 'VANDERBERG', TV, 81, CDN, Wr; *PASSENGERS*, TV, 81, CDN, Wr, *HARVEST*, TV, 80, CDN, Wr; *THE WINNINGS OF FRANKIE WALLS*, 'FOR THE RECORD', TV, 79, CDN, Wr; *'SIDESTREET'* (5 eps), TV, 78-76, CDN, Wr.

FOURNIER, Claude - voir REALISATEURS

FOURNIER, Guy

SARDEC. 335 chemin de la Montagne, St-Paul d'Abbotsford, Qué, CAN. (514) 935-1814. TV Quatre Saisons, 405 rue Ogilvy, Montréal, Qué, CAN, H3N 1M4. (514)271-3535.
Types de production et Catégories: l métrage-Sc/Prod; c métrage-Sc; TV film-Sc; TV vidéo-Sc.
Types d'oeuvres: Drame-C&TV; Comédie-C&TV; Variété-C&TV; Documentaire-C&TV.
Curriculum vitae: Né en 1931. A été journaliste pour divers quotidiens au Québec; a écrit pour la scène; a publié plusieurs livres; tient une chronique dans le 'Journal de Montréal'. Membre fondateur de l'Institut Québécois du Cinéma, 77; président,

(cont/suite)

78-81. *FANTASTICA* fut selectionné au Festival de Film de Cannes. Depuis 85, membre du Conseil d'administration et Vice-président (programmes) du réseau de télévision Quatre Saisons.
Filmographie sélective: *'MANON'* (22 eps), TV, 85, CDN, Sc/Dial; *'PEAU DE BANANE'* (90 eps), TV, 83/82, CDN, Aut; *'ENERGIE, LE TEMPS DES CHOIX'* (11 eps), TV, 82, CDN, Narr; *'L'AGE DE L'ENERGIE'* (13 eps), TV, 80, CDN, Narr; *FANTASTICA*, C, 80, CDN, Co prod; *'PATRICK, JULIE, FELIX ET TOUS LES AUTRES'* (9 eps), TV, 80/79, CDN, Sc/Narr; *'JAMAIS DEUX SANS TOI'* (68 eps), TV, 79-77, CDN, Aut; *UNE AMIE D'ENFANCE*, C, 78, CDN, Prod; *MESDAMES & MESSIEURS, LA FETE*, C, 76, CDN, Sc/Narr; *'LES REGIONS DU QUEBEC'* (6 eps), TV, 76, CDN, Sc/Narr; *'JO GAILLARD'* (2 eps), TV, 75-73, F, Dial; *JOIE DE VIVRE*, C, 75, CDN, Sc/Narr; *LA MER MI-SEL*, C, 75, CDN, Sc/Narr; *SOURIS TU M'INQUIETES*, *'EN TANT QUE FEMMES'*, TV, 73, CDN, Sc/Dial; *GASPESIE, OUI J'ECOUTE*, C, 72, CDN, Narr; *'LA FEUILLE D'ERABLE'* (3 eps), TV, 70, CDN, Sc; *KW*, C, 70, CDN, Sc/Narr; *'BIDULE DE TARMACADAM'* (60 eps), TV, 69-67, CDN, Aut; *LA SAIGNEE*, TV, 67, CDN, Aut; *DU GENERAL AU PARTICULIER*, C, 67, CDN, Narr; *SEBRING LA 5e HEURE*, C, 66, CDN, Narr; *COLUMBIUM*, C, 66, CDN, Sc; *QUEBEC AN 2000*, C, 66, CDN, Narr; *'LE GRAND DUC'* (39 eps), TV, 66-64, CDN, Sc; *'PIERRE D'IBERVILLE'* (39 eps), TV, 65-63, CDN, Aut; *CYBORG*, TV, 65, CDN, Aut; *'RUE DE L'ANSE'* (110 eps), TV, 63-60, CDN, Aut; *MALIOTHENAM*, C, 63, CDN, Narr; *'LA BOITE A SURPRISE'* (250 eps), TV, 59, CDN, Aut.

FOURNIER, Roger

AR, SARDEC. 1202 rue Seymour, Montréal, Qué, CAN, H3H 2A5. (514)937-1900. Radio-Canada, 1400 bd. Dorchester est, Montréal, Qué, CAN, H2L 2N2. (514)285-2887.
Types de production et Catégories: l métrage-Sc/Réal; TV vidéo-Réal.
Types d'oeuvres: Drame-C&TV; Comédie-C&TV.
Curriculum vitae: Né en 1929, St-Anaclet, Québec. Licencié en Lettres, Université Laval. Réalisateur TV depuis 30 ans, Radio-Canada (Montréal); auteur de 13 livres, romans pour la plupart. Récipiendaire du Prix du Gouverneur Général du Canada en 82 et France-Canada, 76; Prix Louis Barthou de l'Académie Française.
Filmographie sélective: *UNE JOURNEE EN TAXI*, C, 81, CDN, Sc; *AU REVOIR.. .A LUNDI (SEE YOU MONDAY)*, C, 78, CDN/F, Co sc; *LES AVENTURES D'UNE JEUNE VEUVE*, C, 75, CDN, Réal/Co sc.

FOX, Beryl - see PRODUCERS

FREEMAN, David E.

ACTRA. John C. Goodwin, 4235 ave. de l'Esplanade, Montreal, Que, CAN, H2W 1T1. (514)844-2139.
Types of Production & Categories: TV Video-Wr.
Genres: Drama-TV.
Biography: Born 1945, Toronto, Ontario. B.A., Political Science, McMaster University, 71. Playwright: 'Creeps' won the Chalmers Award (Best New Play), the New York Drama Desk Award (Outstanding New Playwright) and the L.A. Critics Circle Award. Also writes radio drama.
Selective Filmography: *YOU'RE GONNA BE ALL RIGHT, JAMIE-BOY*, 'OPENING NIGHT', TV, 75, CDN, T'play.

FRIZZELL, John

ACTRA. 30 Wellington St.E., #1805, Toronto, Ont, CAN, M5E 1S3. Stan Colbert, The Colbert Agency, 303 Davenport Rd., Toronto, Ont, CAN, M5R 1K5. (416) 964-3302.
Types of Production & Categories: Th Film-Wr/Dir; TV Film-Wr/Dir.

(cont/suite)

Genres: Drama-Th&TV; Comedy-TV; Documentary-TV; Educational-TV.
Biography: Born Kingston, Ontario. B.A., Queen's University, 1980. Member, Ontario Film and Video Appreciation Society; Advisory Board of Funnel Experimental Film Theatre.
Selective Filmography: *'AIRWAVES'* (Wr-8 eps), (26 eps), TV, 86/85, CDN, Head Wr; *NEON: AN ELECTRIC MEMOIR,* TV, 85, CDN, Wr; *I LOVE A MAN IN A UNIFORM,* 'FOR THE RECORD', TV, 83, CDN, Wr; *AN OUNCE OF CURE,* 'SONS AND DAUGHTERS', TV, 82, CDN, T'play; *WHITE LIES,* 'SONS AND DAUGHTERS', TV, 82, CDN, Wr; *RICKY GOES TO CAMP,* TV, 82, CDN, Dir; *UPROOTED,* TV, 82, CDN, Dir.

FRUET, William - see DIRECTORS

FURIE, Sidney J. - see DIRECTORS

GAGLIARDI, Laurent - voir REALISATEURS

GAGNON, Claude - voir REALISATEURS

GAGNON, Jacques

SARDEC. 2760 Banff, Brossard, Qué, CAN. (514)656-0403.
Types de production et Catégories: TV vidéo-Sc.
Types d'oeuvres: Drame-TV.
Curriculum vitae: Né en 1936. Auteur de pièces de théâtre et pour la radio depuis une vingtaine d'années.
Filmographie sélective: *'A CAUSE DE MON ONCLE'* (78 eps), TV, 79-77, CDN, Aut.

GELINAS, Gratien

ACTRA, UDA. 316 rue Girouard, Oka, Qué, CAN, J0N 1E0. (514)4⁻9-8796. 4207 rue Ste-Catherine ouest, Montréal, Qué, CAN. (514)931-9641.
Types de production et Catégories: l métrage-Sc/Prod/Com; TV film-Sc/Com.
Types d'oeuvres: Drame-C&TV; Comédie-C&TV.
Curriculum vitae: Né en 1909. A reçu des Doctorats honorifiques des universités de Toronto, Nouveau-Brunswick, McGill, Trent, Saskatchewan, Mount Allison. Devient membre de la Société Royale du Canada, 58; reçoit la médaille de l'ordre du Canada, 67. Comédien et auteur à la radio et au théâtre; fonde la Comédie-Canadienne, 57; membre fondateur de l'Ecole Nationale de Théâtre du Canada, 60; Président, Société de développement de l'insdustrie cinématographique canadienne, 69-78. Chef de la délégation du Canada, Festival du Film de Cannes, 72-75; vice-président, Union des Artistes, 84-85.
Filmographie sélective: *IIT-COQ,* TV, 84, CDN, Sc/Prod/Com; *AGNES OF GOD,* C, 84, USA, Com; *BONHEUR D'OCCASION* (THE TIN FLUTE), (aussi TV), C, 82, CDN, Com; *YESTERDAY THE CHILDREN WERE DANCING,* TV, 67, CDN, Sc/Com; *BOUSILLE ET LES JUSTES* (BOUSILLE AND THE JUST), TV, 62, CDN, Sc/Com; *TIT-COQ,* C, 52, CDN, Sc/Com/Prod (CFA); *LA DAME AUX CAMELIAS, LA VRAIE,* C, 43, CDN, Sc/Prod/Com/Réal.

GELINAS, José P.

SARDEC, UDA. 495 de la Colline, C.P.1757, Ste-Adèle, Qué, CAN, J0R 1L0. (514)229-6707.
Types de production et Catégories: TV vidéo-Sc.
Types d'oeuvres: Variété-TV; Enfants-TV.
Curriculum vitae: Née en 1949, Montréal, Québec.
Filmographie sélective: *'TRABOULIDON'* (5 eps), TV, 85/84, CDN, Co aut; *'BRAVO'* (65 eps), TV, 81, CDN, Co conc/Co aut.

GELINAS, Marc - voir COMPOSITEURS

WRITERS/SCENARISTES

GELINAS, Marc F.
SARDEC. 5355 Durocher, Outremont, Qué, CAN, H2V 3X9. (514)279-9485.
Types de production et Catégories: c métrage-Sc; TV film-Sc; TV vidéo-Sc.
Types d'oeuvres: Drame-TV; Comédie-TV; Documentaire-C&TV; Enfants-TV.
Curriculum vitae: Né en 1937. Membre de l'Ordre des Ingénieurs du Québec.
Enseigne à temps partiel à l'Université de Montréal; auteur pigiste.
Filmographie sélective: *MOI AUSSI J'ECRASE* (3 eps), TV, 83, CDN, Conc/Co sc;
CAP AU NORD/NORTHWARD BOUND, TV, 83, CDN, Conc/Sc; *L'ETE DE
MARIE LAPOINTE,* ED, 81, CDN, Sc; *LA QUALITE, LA CLE DU SUCCES/
QUALITY STARTS AT THE TOP,* In, 81, CDN, Sc; *'CHERE ISABELLE'* (39
eps), TV, 76, CDN, Partic sc; *MARGO,* TV, 74, CDN, Aut; *UNE CAUSE CIVILE,*
ED, 73, CDN, Sc; *UN PROCES CRIMINEL,* ED, 73, CDN, Sc; *'PICOLO'* (26
eps), TV, 72/71, CDN, Co aut.

GEOFFRION, Robert
ACTRA. 369 Edouard Charles, Montréal, Qué, CAN, H2V 2N1. (514)276-5262.
John Goodwin, 4235 Esplanade, Montréal, Qué, CAN, H2W 1T1. (514)844-2139.
Types de production et Catégories: l métrage-Sc; c métrage-Sc/Réal.
Types d'oeuvres: Drame-C; Comédie-C; Action-C; Horreur-C.
Curriculum vitae: Né en 1949.
Filmographie sélective: *THE BLUE MAN,* C, 85, CDN, Sc; *THE PURACON
FACTOR,* C, 85, CDN, Co sc; *A FIGHTING CHANCE,* ED, 84, CDN, Sc/Réal;
BLIPSS, ED, 84, CDN, Sc/Réal; *L'ENTREVUE FORMELLE,* ED, 84, CDN,
Réal; *L'OFFICIER D'INFORMATION,* ED, 84, CDN, Réal; *THE SURROGATE,*
C, 83, CDN, Co sc; *SCANDALE,* C, 81, CDN, Sc; *CIVVY STREET,* ED, 81,
CDN, Sc.

GILLARD, Stuart
ACTRA, AFTRA, SAG, WGAw. By The Way Films, Inc., 16400 Ventura
Blvd.,#324, Encino, CA, USA, 91634. (818)789-4066. Elliot Wax & Associates,
9255 Sunset Blvd., Los Angeles, CA, USA, 90069. (213)273-8217.
Types of Production & Categories: Th Film-Wr/Dir/Prod/Act; Th Short-Wr/Dir/
Prod/Act; TV Video-Wr/Dir/Prod/Act.
Genres: Drama-Th&TV; Comedy-Th&TV; Variety-TV; Action-Th.
Biography: Born 1946, Coronation, Alberta. Education: B.A., University of Alberta;
National Theatre School of Canada, Acting; University of Washington, Seattle,
Special Acting Program. Received an Emmy nomination, writing, for *SONNY &
CHER.*
Selective Filmography: *'CHECK IT OUT!'* (44 eps), TV, 86/85, CDN/USA, Prod/
Co-Wr; *HONEYMOON HAVEN,* TV, 83, CDN, Prod/Wr; *IF YOU COULD SEE
WHAT I HEAR,* Th, 82, CDN, Co-Prod/Scr; *PARADISE,* Th, 81, CDN/IL, Dir/
Wr; *'MORK AND MINDY'* (25 eps), TV, 80/79, USA, Dir/Wr; *'DONNY
AND MARIE'* (25 eps), TV, 79/78, USA, Co-Dir/Head Wr; *'SONNY AND
CHER'* (36 eps), TV, 77/76, USA, Co-Wr; *'EXCUSE MY FRENCH'* (50 eps), TV,
76-74, CDN, Act; *WHY ROCK THE BOAT?,* Th, 74, CDN, Act (**CFA/ACTRA**).

GOLDMAN, Alvin
ACTRA, WGAe. 208 Dufferin Rd., Hampstead, Que, CAN, H3X 2Y1. (514)483-
3371.
Types of Production & Categories: Th Film-Wr; Th Short-Wr; TV Film-Wr; TV
Video-Wr.
Genres: Drama-Th&TV; Action-Th&TV; Documentary-Th&TV; Educational-TV.
Biography: Born 1927, Winnipeg, Manitoba. Chancellor's Prize in Literature,
University of Manitoba, 48; French government bursary in arts, U. of Montreal, 50;
post-graduate work in French Literature, Sorbonne, Paris, 50-51. Writer and
filmmaker, NFB, 51-58; freelance writer, 58 onward.

(cont/suite)

Selective Filmography: *THE MAKING OF MARIA CHAPDELAINE* (English Version), TV, 85, CDN, Co-Wr; *NIGHT FLIGHT*, TV, 79, CDN/USA, T'play; *THE HEAT WAVE LASTED FOUR DAYS*, TV, 74, CDN, Add'l Dial; *DUTY FREE*, TV, 74, CDN, Wr; *'SALTY'* (2 eps), TV, 74, CDN/USA, Co-Wr; *THE SLOANE AFFAIR*, TV, 73, CDN, Co-Wr **(CFA)**; *PAMPA GALOPE*, In, 71, CDN/RA, Adapt; *BELUGA DAYS*, TV, 70, CDN, Adapt; *NORTH WEST PASSAGE*, TV, 70, CDN, Adapt; *FREEDOM AFRICA*, TV, 68, CDN, Adapt; *THE PAINTED DOOR/YERMA*, 'FESTIVAL', TV, 68/67, CDN, T'play; *THE BETRAYAL*, 'SHOW OF THE WEEK', TV, 66, CDN, T'play; *MARIA*, 'SEAWAY', TV, 66, CDN, Story; *THE CHEAP BUNCH OF NICE FLOWERS/ THE MAGICIAN OF LUBLIN*, 'FESTIVAL', TV, 65/64, CDN, T'play; *THE PRIVATE MEMOIRS AND CONFESSIONS OF A JUSTIFIED SINNER*, 'FESTIVAL', TV, 64, CDN, T'play; *THE WILD DUCK/THE GAMBLER/THE QUEEN AND THE REBELS*, 'FESTIVAL', TV, 63/62, CDN, T'play; *THE ENDLESS ECHO*, 'FESTIVAL', TV, 63, CDN, T'play/Trans; *'WORLD OF WONDER'* (26 eps), TV, 62, CDN, Cont Wr; *'WOMAN'S WORLD'* (26 eps), TV, 62, CDN, Cont Wr; *'DOCUMENTARY SHOWCASE'* (26 eps), TV, 62, CDN, Cont Wr; *QUEBEC SEPARATISM* (2 parts), 'INQUIRY', TV, 61, CDN, Wr/Dir; *THE MAGIC BARREL/TAKE PITY*, 'SHOESTRING THEATRE', TV, 59, CDN, T'play; *BAR MITZVAH*, Th, 57, CDN, Wr/Dir; *MUSICIAN IN THE FAMILY*, Th, 54, CDN, Wr.

GORDON, Benjamin

ACTRA, SAG, WGAw. 24 Dewbourne Ave., Toronto, Ont, CAN, M5P 1Z4. (416) 489-7799. Ben Gordon Inc., 43 Lesmill Rd., Don Mills, Ont, CAN, M3B 2T8. (416) 444-3512. Prendergast Agency, 260 Richmond St. W., #405, Toronto, Ont, CAN, M5V 1W5. (416)922-5308.
Types of Production & Categories: Th Film-Wr/Act; TV Film-Wr/Act; TV Video-Wr/Prod/Act.
Genres: Drama-Th&TV; Comedy-Th&TV; Variety-TV.
Biography: Born 1951, Toronto, Ontario. Experience in Canada and US; numerous Clio awards for commercial writing and performing. Television host and script editor; motion picture script consultant and ghost writer.
Selective Filmography: *'CHECK IT OUT!'* (23 eps), TV, 86/85, CDN/USA, Exec Story Ed; *'LAUGHING MATTERS'* (13 eps), TV, 86/85, CDN, Co-Wr/Act; *CLUB SANDWICH*, Th, 86, USA, Wr; *'CBC LATE NIGHT'* (157 eps), TV, 85/84, CDN, Host/Wr; *GENIE AWARDS*, TV, 85, CDN, Co-Wr; *LOST SATELLITE NETWORK* (2 shows), TV, 83, CDN/USA, Prod/Wr/Act.

GOTTLIEB, Paul

ACTRA, WGAe. 149 Lytton Blvd., Toronto, Ont, CAN, M4R 1L6, (416)486-7970. Baker Lovick Co., 60 Bloor St. West, Toronto, Ont, CAN, M4W 3B8. (416)924-6861.
Types of Production & Categories: Th Film-Wr; TV Film-Wr.
Genres: Drama-Th&TV; Comedy-Th&TV; Documentary-Th&TV; Commercials-TV.
Biography: Born 1936, Hungary; in Canada since 57; Canadian citizen; speaks English, Hungarian, French, German. M.A., Concordia University, Montreal. Lecturer, screenwriting, Ryerson Polytechnical Institute. Novelist, 'Agency'; screenwriter; reviewer; contributor: 'Maclean's', 'Toronto Life', 'Marketing'. Senior Vice President, Director of Creative Services, Baker-Lovick Advertising Agency, Toronto. Winner of over 30 awards for commercials.
Selective Filmography: *THE GOOD NEWS IN PRINTING*, In, 85, CDN, Wr; *SMART MONEY/VELVET/GOOD NEWS/HARVEY LAZYBONES/MONEY IN ACTION*, Cm, 84-81, CDN, Wr; *MOUNT CARAMEL/FIT-FAT/CHAIRS CONVENTION*, Cm, 81-70, CDN, Wr; *IN PRAISE OF OLDER WOMEN*, Th, 77, CDN, Scr.

GOUGH, Bill

ACTRA, CAPAC. 162 Banff Rd., Toronto, Ont, CAN, M4P 2P7. (416)481-0880.
Types of Production & Categories: TV Film-Prod/Dir/Wr; TV Film-Prod/Dir/Wr.
Genres: Drama-TV; Comedy-TV; Documentary-TV.
Biography: Born 1945, Halifax, Nova Scotia. Education: Graham Jr. College and The Film School, Boston, Mass.; Memorial University of Newfoundland. Publications include: 'Maud's House', 'Finger Prints', 'The Proper Lover'. Lyricist for songs on 'Ryan's Fancy', 'Here and Now', 'Sunday Morning Magazine'; radio plays on 'Terra Nova Theatre', 'CBC Stage'. *ANNE'S STORY* and *CHARLIE GRANT'S WAR* won Chris Bronze Plaques, Columbus; *THE WINNINGS OF FRANKIE WALLS*, a Blue Ribbon, American Film Festival.
Selective Filmography: *'SEEING THINGS'* (9 eps), TV, 86-83, CDN, Co-Wr; *THE MARRIAGE BED*, TV, 86/85, CDN, Prod; *THE SUICIDE MURDERS*, TV, 85, CDN, Prod/Lyrics; *CHARLIE GRANT'S WAR*, TV, 84, CDN, Prod **(ACTRA)**; *ANNE'S STORY*, TV, 84, CDN, Prod/Lyrics; *THE ACCIDENT*, TV, 83, CDN, Prod/Wr/Lyrics; *HIGH CARD*, 'FOR THE RECORD', TV, 82, CDN, Co-Prod/ Dir; *AN HONORABLE MEMBER/COP/RUNNING MAN/A QUESTION OF THE SIXTH*, 'FOR THE RECORD', TV, 82-80, CDN, Prod; *A FAR CRY FROM HOME*, 'FOR THE RECORD', TV, 81, CDN, Wr; *WAR BRIDES*, TV, 81, CDN, Prod **(ANIK/BIJOU)**; *CERTAIN PRACTICES*, 'FOR THE RECORD', TV, 79, CDN, Prod **(GENIE)**; *ONE OF OUR OWN/THE WINNINGS OF FRANKIE WALLS*, 'FOR THE RECORD', TV, 79, CDN, Prod; *DYING HARD*, 'FOR THE RECORD', TV, 78, CDN, Wr; *A FIGGY DUFF CHRISTMAS*, TV, 78, CDN, Dir; *THE BROTHERS BYRNE*, TV, 74, CDN, Dir; *MEDIA OUTPORT*, TV, 74, CDN, Dir; *'TAKE 30'/'ACCESS'/'HERE AND NOW'*, TV, 73-69, CDN, Dir.

GOULET, Stella - voir REALISATEURS

GRAY, Jack

ACTRA, WGGB. 65 Pine St., Brockville, Ont, CAN, K6V 1G6. (613)345-1981. Eastern Productions, 155 Hopewell Ave., Ottawa, Ont, CAN, K1S 2Z4. (613)235-1151. Nancy Colbert, The Colbert Agency, 303 Davenport Rd., Toronto, Ont, CAN, M5R 1K5. (416)964-3302.
Types of Production & Categories: Th Film-Wr; TV Film-Wr; TV Video-Wr.
Genres: Drama-Th&TV; Comedy-Th&TV; Action-Th&TV; Documentary-TV.
Biography: Born 1927.
Selective Filmography: *A QUIET DAY IN BELFAST*, Th, 74/73, CDN/GB, Wr; *'GAMEPLAYERS'*, TV, 73, GB, Wr; *PEACEMAKERS*, TV, 72, GB, Wr; *THE MAN*, TV, 68, CDN, Wr; *VANITY, VANITY*, TV, 68, CDN, Wr; *ONE IS ONE*, TV, 67, GB, Wr; *'QUICK BEFORE THEY CATCH US'* (6 eps), TV, 67, GB, Wr; *'WOJECK'* (1 eps), TV, 67, CDN, Wr; *'FRONT PAGE STORY'* (4 eps), TV, 65, GB, Wr; *UNDERMIND*, TV, 65, USA, Wr; *THE BENEFACTOR*, TV, 65, GB, Wr; *I SPY*, TV, 65, GB, Wr; *DANGER MAN*, TV, 64, GB, Wr; *JEAN DUPUIS*, TV, 64, GB, Wr; *BORDERLINE*, TV, 64, GB, Wr; *THE GUARD*, TV, 64, CDN, Wr; *PLANE MAKERS*, TV, 64, GB, Wr; *MISS HANAGO*, TV, 63, GB, Wr; *THE GLOVE*, TV, 61, GB, Wr; *THE ENEMY*, TV, 61, GB, Wr.

GRAY, John H.

ACTRA. 3392 West 37th Ave., Vancouver, BC, CAN, V6N 2V6. (604)266-7031.
Types of Production & Categories: TV Video-Comp/Wr.
Genres: Drama-TV; Comedy-TV; Musical-TV.
Biography: Born 1946, Ottawa, Ontario. M.A., Theatre (Directing), University of British Columbia. Playwright, composer for theatre: 'Billy Bishop Goes to War', '18 Wheels', 'Rock and Roll'. Many awards including Governor General's Medal, Los Angeles Drama Critics', Golden Globe Awards (Boston); *BILLY BISHOP GOES*

(cont/suite)

TO WAR won an Actra Award; *KING OF FRIDAY NIGHT* won a Gold Medal (N.Y.), 2 CFTA, Silver Hugo (Chicago) and a Rockie at Banff.
Selective Filmography: *KING OF FRIDAY NIGHT*, TV, 84, CDN, Wr/Comp/Co-Dir; *BILLY BISHOP GOES TO WAR*, TV, 82, CDN/GB, Wr/Comp.

GRAY, William

ACTRA, WGAw. Gersh Agency, 222 Canon Dr., Beverly Hills, CA, USA, 90210. (213)274-6611.
Types of Production & Categories: Th Film-Wr.
Genres: Drama-Th; Action-Th; Science Fiction-Th; Horror-Th.
Biography: Born Toronto, Ontario; Canadian citizen.
Selective Filmography: *BLACK MOON RISING*, Th, 86, USA, Co-Scr; *THE PHILADELPHIA EXPERIMENT*, Th, 84, USA, Co-Scr; *CROSS-COUNTRY*, Th, 82, CDN, Co-Scr; *AN EYE FOR AN EYE*, Th, 81, USA, Co-Scr; *PROM NIGHT*, Th, 80, CDN, Co-Scr; *THE CHANGELING*, Th, 79, CDN, Co-Scr (GENIE); *BLOOD & GUTS*, Th, 77, CDN, Co-Scr/Ed.

GREEN, Rick

ACTRA, CAPAC. 69 Wroxeter Ave., Toronto, Ont, CAN. (416)462-0941. Barb Fogler, 3 Charles St.W., Ste. 204, Toronto, Ont, CAN, M4V 1R4. (416)923-9844.
Types of Production & Categories: TV Film-Wr/Act; TV Video-Wr/Act.
Genres: Comedy-TV; Variety-TV; Musical-TV; Educational-TV.
Biography: Born 1953, Canada. B.Sc. in Physics; teacher at Ontario Science Centre, 74-76. Wrote and starred in numerous stage productions with The Frantics; CBC radio show 'Frantic Times', Armstrong Award winner; published numerous humorous articles in 'Globe & Mail'.
Selective Filmography: *WE BARGE IN* (pilot), TV, 86, CDN, Contr Wr; *'4 ON THE FLOOR'* (13 eps), TV, 85, CDN, Co-Wr/Act; *'LAUGHING MATTERS'* (13 eps), TV, 85, CDN, Contr Wr; *THE NO NAME SHOW* (pilot), TV, 84, CDN, Contr Wr/Act; *'SMITH AND SMITH'* (26 eps), TV, 84, CDN, Contr Wr.

GREENE, Charles J. - see PRODUCERS

GUENETTE, Pierre

CAPAC, SARDEC. 4062 rue St-Hubert, Montréal, Qué, CAN, H2L 4A8. (514) 527-8149.
Types de production et Catégories: TV vidéo-Sc.
Types d'oeuvres: Documentaire-TV; Enfants-TV.
Curriculum vitae: Né en 1947, Mont Rolland, Québec. Etudes en pédagogie; auteur de 4 pièces de théâtre; auteur conseil pour une maison d'édition; auteur d'un roman pour enfants publié aux éditions Québec-Amérique.
Filmographie sélective: *ELIZABETH BEGON/PAMPHILE LEMAY/ALBERT LOZEAU/LAURE CONAN*, 'MANUSCRITS', TV, 84-81, CDN, Aut; *'PLACE DU FONDATEUR'* (35 eps), TV, 81-79, CDN, Aut; *'LE GRENIER'* (89 eps), TV, 79-75, CDN, Aut; *'TELE-RESSOURCES'* (25 eps), TV, 78, CDN, Aut.

HACKETT, Bob

ACTRA, WGAw. 330 Dixon Rd., #1505, Weston, Ont, CAN, M9R 1S9. (416) 247-9519.
Types of Production & Categories: TV Film-Wr; TV Video-Wr.
Genres: Comedy-TV; Variety-TV; Educational-TV; Children's-TV.
Biography: Born 1945, Toronto, Ontario. Graduated from Ryerson Polytechnical Institute, Radio & TV Arts (Film major), 70.
Selective Filmography: *'SEEING THINGS'* (1 eps), TV, 85, CDN, Co-Story; *STEVEN AND FRIENDS*, ED, 85, CDN, Wr; *'THE MONEY MAZE'* (5 eps), In, 85, CDN, Contr Wr/Act; *VIDEO GUIDE TO THE TORONTO INTERNATIONAL FESTIVAL*, TV, 84, CDN, Cont Wr; *'FLAPPERS'* (1 eps),

(cont/suite)

TV, 80, CDN, Co-Story; *'THE TOMMY HUNTER SHOW'* (6 eps), TV, 78, CDN, Staff Wr; *KOMEDY TONITE,* TV, 77, USA, Staff Wr; *'MIXED DOUBLES'* (5 eps), TV, 76, CDN, Contr Wr; *'OUTDOOR EDUCATION'* (5 eps), ED, 72, CDN, Narr Wr; *'PARTY GAME'* (100 eps), TV, 72/71, CDN, Contr Wr; *'HART & LORNE TERRIFIC HOUR'* (1 eps), TV, 71, CDN, Contr Wr; *'HILARIOUS HOUSE OF FRIGHTENSTEIN'* (IGOR & COUNT sketches-130-Staff Wr), (ZANY ZOO-130/LIBRARIAN-130), TV, 71, CDN, Wr; *'MISSING LINK'* (26 eps), TV, 71, CDN, Co-Wr; *'SUMMER HOLIDAY'* (30 eps), TV, 70, CDN, Prod/Wr/Host.

HALLER, Ty

2250 Trimble St., Vancouver, BC, CAN, V6R 3Z6. (604)224-2666. Act Four, 640 W.Broadway, Vancouver, BC, CAN. (604)873-3661.
Types of Production & Categories: TV Film-Wr; TV Video-Wr.
Genres: Drama-TV; Comedy-TV; Action-TV.
Biography: Born 1942.
Selective Filmography: *LOST!,* Th, 85, CDN, 1st AD; *OVERNIGHT,* Th, 85, CDN, 2nd AD; *FOR THE WHALES,* 'CENTRE PLAY THEATRE', TV, 78, GB, Wr; *BOY ON DEFENCE,* 'MAGIC LIE', TV, 76, CDN, Wr; *'SIDESTREET'* (1 eps), TV, 75, CDN, Wr; *THE VICTIM,* 'PEEP SHOW', TV, 75, CDN, Wr; *THE WOLFPEN PRINCIPLE,* Th, 73, CDN, 1st AD.

HARRON, Don

ACTRA, AFTRA, SAG, WGAe. 23 Lowther Ave., Toronto, Ont, CAN, M5R 1C5. (416)920-1500.
Types of Production & Categories: Th Short-Wr; TV Film-Wr.
Genres: Comedy-TV; Variety-TV; Musical-TV; Documentary-Th.
Biography: Born 1924, Toronto, Ontario. Television writer since 53; worked for BBC (London), 50-51; Los Angeles and New York, 54-66. Writes for radio; stage, 3 musicals including 'Anne of Green Gables', 2 plays and several reviews; stand up comic; author of 6 books, half-a-million copies sold. Officer, Order of Canada, 80; won an Actra Award, Best Radio Host for 'Morningside', 82.
Selective Filmography: *'REALLY WEIRD TALES'* (1 eps), TV, 86, CDN/USA, Act; *'THE DON HARRON SHOW'* (daily), TV, 84/83, CDN, Host; *'SHH...IT'S THE NEWS'* (52 eps), TV, 75/74, CDN, Prod/Head Wr; *SNOW JOB,* Th, 74, CDN, Wr; *HOSPITAL,* Th, 71, USA, Act; *THE WONDER OF IT ALL,* TV, 70, CDN, Wr; *THE BEST OF EVERYTHING,* Th, 59, USA, Act.

HEALEY, Barry

ACTRA. Ralph Zimmerman, Great North Artists Mgmt, 345 Adelaide St.W., #500, Toronto, Ont, CAN, M5V 1R5. (416)593-2587.
Types of Production & Categories: Th Film-Prod/Wr; Th Short-Prod/Dir/Wr; TV Film-Dir.
Genres: Drama-Th&TV; Comedy-TV.
Biography: Born 1945, Toronto, Ontario. *OUTTAKES* won Best Short Story Award, Athens Int'l Film Festival and Best Director/Best Dramatic Short, Yorkton.
Selective Filmography: *BIG DEAL,* TV, 85, CDN, Dir; *ONE MAGIC CHRISTMAS,* Th, 85, CDN/USA, Co-Story; *MAGGIE,* TV, 81, CDN, Dir; *THE GREY FOX,* Th, 80, CDN, Co-Prod; *THE NIGHT BEFORE THE MORNING AFTER,* Th, 79, CDN, Wr/Dir; *OUTTAKES,* Th, 77, CDN, Wr/Dir/Prod.

HEDLEY, Tom

WGAw. Jim Wiatt, ICM, 8899 Beverly Blvd., Los Angeles, CA, USA, 90048. (213) 550-4000. Bill Essensten, Nanas, Stern, Biers & Co., 9454 Wilshire Blvd., Beverly Hills, CA, USA, 90212. (213)273-2501.
Types of Production & Categories: Th Film-Wr.
Genres: Drama-Th; Musical-Th.

(cont/suite)

Biography: Born 1943 England; Canadian citizen. From 67-74: Entertainment Editor of 'Showcase' for 'Toronto Telegram'; Editor, 'Esquire'; Editor in Chief, 'Toronto Life'.
Selective Filmography: FLASHDANCE, Th, 83, USA, Co-Scr/Story; FIGHTING BACK, Th, 83, USA, Co-Scr/Assoc Prod; DOUBLE NEGATIVE, Th, 80, CDN, Co-Wr; CIRCLE OF TWO, Th, 80, CDN, Scr; MR. PATMAN, Th, 79, CDN, Wr; 'WEEKEND' (4 seg), TV, 78/77, CDN, Prod/Dir.

HELLIKER, John

ACTRA. 8 Shanly St., Toronto, Ont, CAN, M6H 1S1. (416)533-3629.
Types of Production & Categories: TV Film-Wr; TV Video-Wr.
Genres: Drama-TV; Documentary-TV; Educational-TV; Animation-TV.
Biography: Born 1951, Toronto, Ontario. Languages: English, Chinese (Mandarin); education: Ph.D.(Political Thought); M.A., Economics; 2 years study in People's Republic of China (Philosophy and Chinese Language Diploma). DON'T CALL ME STUPID, winner at Columbus Int'l, American Film Festivals.
Selective Filmography: 'INDONESIA: A GENERATION OF CHANGE' (4 eps), TV, 86, CDN, Wr; A FAMILY AFFAIR, ED, 86, CDN, Wr; THE OTHER HALF, ED, 86, CDN, Wr; GETTING THE JOB DONE, ED, 86, CDN, Wr; 'PATHS OF DEVELOPMENT' (6 eps), TV, 85, CDN, Wr; 'AUTOMATING THE OFFICE' (9 eps), TV, 84, CDN, Wr; PATIENCE PLEASE, ED, 83, CDN, Wr/Dir; DON'T CALL ME STUPID, TV, 83, CDN, Wr/Co-Prod.

HELWIG, David

ACTRA. 106 Montreal St., Kingston, Ont, CAN, K7K 3E8. (613)542-8667.
Types of Production & Categories: TV Film-Wr; TV Video-Wr.
Genres: Drama-TV.
Biography: Born 1938, Toronto, Ontario. B.A., Toronto; M.A., Liverpool. Author of 16 books; editor of many others; literary manager, CBC TV drama, 74-76. Extensive magazine journalism and radio drama.
Selective Filmography: 'BACKSTRETCH' (Wr-2 eps/Co-Wr-2 eps), TV, 83/82, CDN, Creator; 'THE GREAT DETECTIVE' (1 eps), TV, 78, CDN, Wr; 'SIDESTREET' (1 eps), TV, 77, CDN, Wr.

HENSHAW, Jim

ACTRA. 75 Walmer Rd., Toronto, Ont, CAN, M5R 2X6. (416)925-0428. Ralph Zimmerman, Great North Artists Mgmt., 345 Adalaide St.W., #500, Toronto, Ont, CAN, M5V 1R5. (416)593-2587.
Types of Production & Categories: Th Film-Wr/Act; Th Short-Wr/Act; TV Film-Wr/Act; TV Video-Wr/Act.
Genres: Drama-Th&TV; Comedy-Th&TV; Action-Th&TV; Children's-TV.
Biography: Born 1949, Bassano, Alberta. B.F.A., University of Saskatchewan, 70. Professional actor, theatre, film and TV; several foreign tours of Canadian theatre; first feature screenplay produced, 75. Writer resident in L.A., 75-79; returned to Canada during film boom. Winner, Crystal Cube (Actra Writers Guild), 80; founding member, Academy of Canadian Cinema; member, Nat'l Writers Council (Actra), 83-86.
Selective Filmography: 'ADDERLY' (Wr-1 eps), (11 eps), TV, 86, CDN, Story Ed; THE SPIRIT OF CHRISTMAS, TV, 85, CDN, Wr; TODD'S BIRTHDAY PRESENT/SPIES AND DETECTIVES/KNIGHTS AND CASTLES, 'PARENTS AND READING', TV, 85, CDN, Wr; 'FITNESS AFTER 40' (6 eps), TV, 85, CDN, Wr; INVISIBLE BURDEN/TIGERS IN A CAGE, 'EDUCATING THE SPECIAL CHILD', TV, 84, CDN, Wr; THE CHRISTINE JESSOP STORY, TV, 84, CDN, Wr; 'PIZZAZZ' (130 eps), TV, 84, CDN, Co-Wr/Host; A SWEETER SONG (SNAPSHOTS), Th, 75, CDN, Co-Wr/Act.

HOLE, Jeremy

ACTRA. R.R. #1, Locust Hill, Ont, CAN, L0H 1J0. (416)683-8838. The Colbert Agency, 303 Davenport Rd., Toronto, Ont, CAN, M5R 1K5. (416)966-3302.
Types of Production & Categories: TV Film-Wr.
Genres: Drama-TV; Action-TV.
Biography: Canadian-British citizenship. Experienced in international co-production.
Selective Filmography: *THE CASK OF AMONTILLADO*, TV, 86, USA, T'play; *'PHILIP MARLOWE PRIVATE EYE'* (Wr-2eps/Co-Wr-3 eps), TV, 85, CDN, Wr.

HUMPHREY, Jack - see PRODUCERS

HUNTER, John

ACTRA, WGAw. Centaur Productions Ltd., 25 St. Mary St., #2410, Toronto, Ont, CAN, M4Y 1R2. (416)967-9180. Paul Schwartzman, ICM, 8899 Beverly Blvd., Los Angeles, CA, USA, 90048. (213)550-4000.
Types of Production & Categories: Th Film-Wr/Prod; TV Film-Wr/Dir; TV Video-Wr.
Genres: Drama-Th&TV; Action-Th&TV; Horror-Th.
Biography: Born 1941, Winnipeg, Manitoba. Bachelor of Commerce, University of British Columbia.
Selective Filmography: *JOHN AND THE MISSUS*, Th, 86, CDN, Co-Prod; *THE BOY NEXT DOOR*, 'FOR THE RECORD', TV, 84, CDN, Dir/Wr; *'VANDERBERG'* (eps 4&5), TV, 83, CDN, Wr; *CLASS OF '84*, Th, 81, CDN/ USA, Uncr Rewr; *THE GREY FOX*, Th, 80, CDN, Wr **(GENIE)**; *PROM NIGHT* (LE BAL DE L'HORREUR), Th, 79, CDN, Uncr Rewr; *BLOOD & GUTS*, Th, 77, CDN, Co-Wr/Co-Prod; *'SIDESTREET'* (4 eps), TV, 77-75, CDN, Wr; *A SWEETER SONG* (SNAPSHOTS), Th, 75, CDN, Prod; *THE KILL*, 'PEEPSHOW', TV, 75, CDN, Wr; *THE HARD PART BEGINS*, Th, 73, CDN, Wr/Prod; *BANANA PEEL*, 'PROGRAM X', TV, 71, CDN, Wr; *BLACK PHOENIX*, 'SUNDAY AT NINE', TV, 69, CDN, Co-Wr.

ISRAEL, Charles

ACTRA, WGAw. 113 Howland Ave., Toronto, Ont, CAN, M5R 3B4. (416)964-6738.
Types of Production & Categories: Th Film-Wr; TV Film-Wr; TV Video-Wr.
Genres: Drama-Th&TV; Action-Th&TV; Documentary-Th&TV.
Biography: Born 1920, Indiana, USA; naturalized Canadian citizen. Holds B.A. and B.H.L. degrees. Has published 7 novels and 2 biographies, including 'Rizpah' (Literary Guild Main Selection) and 'The Mark'(made into movie). *THE VETERAN AND THE LADY* won Best Screenplay, Yorkton Festival; *THE OPEN GRAVE* won the Prix Italia and Best Scenario, Prague Festival.
Selective Filmography: *ARCH OF TRIUMPH*, TV, 84, USA/GB, T'play; *LOUISIANA* (also 6 eps, TV), Th, 83, CDN/F, Co-T'play; *'HARVEST HOME'* (3 eps), TV, 77, USA, T'play; *'THE NEWCOMERS'* (Wr-1 ep/Co-Wr-1 ep), TV, 77/ 76, CDN, Wr; *THE VETERAN AND THE LADY*, TV, 72, CDN, Wr; *'MARCUS WELBY'* (1 eps), TV, 69, USA, Wr; *LET ME COUNT THE WAYS*, TV, 66, CDN, Wr; *THE LABYRINTH*, TV, 65, CDN, Wr; *THE OPEN GRAVE*, TV, 64, CDN, Wr.

JACKSON, Doug - see DIRECTORS

JASMIN, Claude

B.P.24, route #1, Ste-Adèle-en-Haut, Qué, CAN, J0R 1L0.
Types de production et Catégories: l métrage-Sc; c métrage-Sc; TV film-Sc; TV vidéo-Sc.
Types d'oeuvres: Drame-C&TV; Comédie-TV; Variété-TV; Documentaire-C.

(cont/suite)

Curriculum vitae: Né en 1930, Montréal, Québec. A publié une quinzaine de romans, essais, un livre de contes pour enfants; a eu 3 de ses romans adaptés au cinéma dont 'Délivrez-nous du mal' 'La Sablière' (Mario). *CHEMIN DE CROIX DANS LE METRO* remporte le Prix Anik, 71.
Filmographie sélective: *'METRO-BOULOT-DODO'*, TV, 84, CDN, Dial; *'BOOGIE-WOOGIE'* (75 eps), TV, 83-81, CDN, Aut; *PROCES DEVANT JUGE SEUL*, TV, 80, CDN, Textes; *'LA PETITE PATRIE'* (75 eps), TV, 78-76, CDN, Aut; *C'EST TOUJOURS LA MEME HISTOIRE*, TV, 70, CDN, Aut; *UN CERTAIN CHEMIN DE CROIX*, TV, 69, CDN, Sc/Dial/Dir art; *TUEZ LE VEAU GRAS*, TV, 66, CDN, Aut; *BLUES POUR UN HOMME AVERTI*, TV, 65, CDN, Aut; *L'OREILLE DE VAN GOGH*, C, 65, CDN, An; *LA MORT DANS L'AME*, TV, 64, CDN, Aut; *LES MAINS VIDES*, TV, 63, CDN, Aut; *LA CORDE AU COU*, C, 63, CDN/F, Sc; *LA RUE DE LA LIBERTE*, TV, 60, CDN, Aut.

JEAN, André

SARDEC. 330 des Franciscains, #4, Québec, Qué, CAN, G1S 2P8. (418)683-6927.
Types de production et Catégories: c métrage-Sc; TV vidéo-Sc.
Types d'oeuvres: Documentaire-TV; Enfants-TV; Expérimental-C.
Curriculum vitae: Né en 1960, Lévis, Québec. Baccalauréat en Littérature, Université Laval; diplômé en mise en scène, Conservatoire d'Art dramatique de Québec. Auteur d'une dizaine de pièces de théâtre dont: 'A propos de la demoiselle qui pleurait'. Premier Prix au Concours d'écriture du Grand Théâtre de Québec pour 'Altius, Citius, Fortius'. Professeur de littérature et de théatre, 83-86.
Filmographie sélective: *'FELIX ET CIBOULETTE'* (130 eps), TV, 86/85, CDN, Aut; *MONSIEUR LEON*, C, 86, CDN, Dial; *LA QUINZAINE INTERNATIONALE DE THEATRE*, TV, 84, CDN, Aut.

JOBIN, Peter

ACTRA, WGAe. 172 Crawford St., Toronto, Ont, CAN, M6J 2V4. (416)532-6981.
A.C.E., 9 Sultan St., Toronto, Ont, CAN, M5S 1L6. (416)923-5228.
Types of Production & Categories: Th Film-Wr/Prod/Act; TV Film-Wr/Act; TV Video-Wr/Act.
Genres: Drama-Th&TV; Comedy-Th&TV; Action-Th&TV; Horror-Th&TV.
Biography: Born 1944, Montreal, Quebec; bilingual.
Selective Filmography: *YOU GOTTA COME BACK A STAR*, Th, 86, CDN, Wr/Co-Prod; *OAKMOUNT HIGH*, TV, 85, CDN, Co-Wr; *TILL DEATH DO US PART*, TV, 81, CDN, Co-Wr; *HAPPY BIRTHDAY TO ME*, Th, 80, CDN, Co-Scr; *SHE CRIED MURDER*, TV, 74, CDN/USA, Co-Story.

JONES, Cliff

ACTRA, AFM. Cleve Productions Inc., 51 Forest Heights Blvd., Willowdale, Ont, CAN, M2L 2K7. (416)444-1438.
Types of Production & Categories: TV Video-Wr/Prod/Comp; TV Film-Wr/Prod/Comp.
Genres: Drama-TV; Comedy-TV; Variety-TV; Musical-TV.
Biography: Born 1943, Toronto, Ontario. Education: M.A. in Psychology. Active in musical theatre: 'Kronburg', 'Hey Marilyn'; 'Something's Rockin' in Denmark' won Best Writer, Best Composer, L.A. Dramalogue Awards. Recently started independent TV production company, Cleve Productions Inc.. *MAGIC* won Best Variety program at the New York TV Film Festival.
Selective Filmography: *'LIFETIME'* (daily), TV, 86/85, CDN, Comp/Mus Dir; *'HANGIN' IN'* (120 eps), TV, 86-80, CDN, Mus Dir; *'THRILL OF A LIFETIME'* (60 eps), TV, 86-83, CDN/USA, Comp/Mus Dir; *'DEFINITION'* (daily), TV, 86-83, CDN, Comp/Mus Dir; *THE TRUE GIFT OF CHRISTMAS*, TV, 85, CDN, Co-Wr; *'JUST KIDDING'* (40 eps), TV, 85/84, CDN, Comp/Mus Dir; *'SUNDAY'S CHILD'* (14 eps), TV, 83, CDN/USA, Comp/Mus Dir; *PYGMALION*, TV, 83, CDN, Comp/Mus Dir; *FRANK MILLS CHRISTMAS SPECIAL*, TV, 82, CDN,

(cont/suite)

Wr/Mus Dir; *ROBIN HOOD STARRING RICH LITTLE,* TV, 82, CDN/USA, Co-Wr; *'ROMANCE'* (10 eps), TV, 82, CDN, Comp/Mus Dir; *A CHRISTMAS FANTASY,* TV, 82, CDN/D, Mus Dir; *RIVALS,* TV, 82, CDN, Wr; *ANNE MURRAY SPECIALS* (4), TV, 82-78, CDN, Co-Wr; *'FLAPPERS'* (52 eps), TV, 82-78, CDN, Mus Dir; *MAGIC,* TV, 81, CDN, Prod/Co-Wr/Mus Dir; *'THE JULIE SHOW'* (24 eps), TV, 79/78, CDN, Prod/Co-Wr/Mus Dir; *'KIDSTUFF'* (32 eps), TV, 78-76, CDN, Prod/Co-Wr/Mus Dir; *'FLIM FLAM'* (24 eps), TV, 77, CDN, Prod/Co-Wr/Mus Dir; *'THE TOMMY HUNTER SHOW'* (42 eps), TV, 74-72, CDN, Co-Wr; *'MR DRESSUP'* (18 eps), TV, 74-71, CDN, Wr.

JUTRA, Claude - voir REALISATEURS

KANDALAFT, Cécile Gédéon

Les Films Pierka Inc., 1455 rue de Val Brillant, Ste-Dorothée, Laval, Qué, CAN, H7Y 1T7. (514)689-2071.
Types de production et Catégories: c métrage-Sc/Prod; TV film-Sc/Prod; TV vidéo-Sc/Prod.
Types d'oeuvres: Drame-C&TV; Documentaire-C&TV; Enfants-C&TV.
Curriculum vitae: Née en 1937; citoyenneté canadienne. Etudes universitaires en Lettres françaises, Beyrouth, Liban; Art dramatique, Académie Libanaise des Beaux Arts. A travaillé dans le domaine du théâtre au Liban; radio, O.R.T.F., Liban, productrice, réalisatrice, animatrice; TV, comédienne, animatrice et productrice, Liban, 59-68. Directrice, rédactrice, 'Chatelaine', Québec. 74-76; adaptrice et traductrice de livres, 76-79; reporter pigiste, magazines libanais et québécois, 59-85. Crée et rédige plusieurs scénarios de documentaires et documentaires-fiction dont *RAMSES II, LA PRINCESSE LOINTAINE, OPHELIE, A BOY FROM SAUDI ARABIA, 15 CIRCLE ROAD, DES JEUX ET DES FORMES'.*

KASTNER, John - see DIRECTORS

KATZ, John Stuart

ACTRA. 199 Marlborough Pl., Toronto, Ont, CAN. (416)922-9630. York U. Film Dept., 4700 Keele St., Downsview, Ont, CAN. (416)667-3729.
Types of Production & Categories: Th Film-Wr; TV Film-Wr.
Genres: Drama-Th&TV; Documentary-TV; Educational-TV.
Biography: Born 1938, Cincinnati, Ohio. Educated at Columbia University and Harvard U., where he earned his doctorate in 67. Has been in Canada since 67; taught at U. of Toronto and York U. for the past 18 years. Has written and edited 4 books on film. *RUBIN* won Museum of Modern Art Award, N.Y.. Has reviewed films on CBC radio and TV; programmer for Festival of Festivals, Toronto; founded and ran distribution company, Beacon Films.
Selective Filmography: *ISAAC LITTLEFEATHERS,* Th, 85, CDN, Co-Wr; *RUBIN,* ED, 74, CDN, Prod/Wr/Dir; *ALPHAVILLE STUDY,* ED, 72, CDN, Co-Dir/Wr; *DOCUMENT,* ED, 71, CDN, Co-Dir/Wr.

KEANE, Laurence - see DIRECTORS

KENT, Laurence - see DIRECTORS

KING, Durnford

DGA, DGC, WGAw. Thalia Productions, 1423 Euclid St., Santa Monica, CA, USA, 90404. (213)394-0877. Fred Shorr, Bloom, Levi, Shorr&Assoc., 800 S. Robertson, Los Angeles, CA, USA, 90035. (213)659-6160.
Types of Production & Categories: TV Film-Wr; TV Video-Dir/Prod.
Genres: Comedy-TV; Variety-TV; Educational-TV; Animation-TV.
Biography: Born 1939, Toronto, Ontario; graduate Ryerson Polytechnical Institute, Communication Arts; worked in Toronto, L.A., Tokyo as producer/director, commercials; Senior Vice President of Creative Affairs, Discovery Int'l. Has won numerous advertising awards in NY, Hollywood, Toronto. Directed *SOMETHING*

(cont/suite)

SCENARISTES/WRITERS

ELSE, Cannes TV Festival winner, Best Music Series; Emmy nomination, *OSCAR PETERSON'S CANADIANA SUITE.*
Selective Filmography: *'GUMMY BEARS'* (1 eps), TV, 86, USA, Wr; *'THE REAL GHOSTBUSTERS'* (1 eps), TV, 86, USA, Wr; *'HEATHCLIFF'* (2 eps), TV, 86, USA, Wr; *'SHE-RA, PRINCESS OF POWER'* (3 eps), TV, 85, USA, Wr; *'GHOSTBUSTERS'* (animation), (4 eps), TV, 85, USA, Wr; *EVENING AT THE IMPROV* (pilot), TV, 81, USA, Wr; *OSCAR PETERSON'S CANADIANA SUITE,* TV, 79, CDN, Prod/Dir; *SUPERSTUNT,* TV, 79, USA, Co-Wr; *SOMETHING ELSE,* TV, 78, USA, Dir; *PREACHER AND THE RABBI,* TV, 77, USA, Dir; *GREASY HEART,* MV, 76, USA, Dir; *TRUE NORTH,* TV, 76, CDN, Dir/Co-Wr.

KLENMAN, Norman

ACTRA, WGAw. 1010 Cypress St., Vancouver, BC, CAN, V6J 3K5. (604)733-2096. CKVU TV, 180 West 2nd Ave., Vancouver, BC, CAN, V5Y 3T9. (604)876-1344. Nancy Colbert, The Colbert Agency, 303 Davenport Rd., Toronto, Ont, CAN, M5R 1K5. (416)964-3302.
Types of Production & Categories: Th Film-Wr/Prod; TV Film-Wr/Prod.
Genres: Drama-Th&TV; Comedy-Th&TV; Action-Th&TV; Science Fiction-Th&TV.
Biography: Born 1923, Brandon, Manitoba. Served 3 years with RCAF; B.A., University of British Columbia, 48. Television, film writer in Canada, England and USA since 50; has written and produced feature films in Canada, USA. One of the founders of City-TV, Toronto, CKVU-TV, Vancouver; senior TV executive, CKVU-TV, 80-86. *PEOPLE OF THE FLY RIVER* won Gold Award, New York Film Fest.; he won the Peabody Award for *THE CITY AT NIGHT.*
Selective Filmography: *'VANCOUVER'* (daily), TV, 86-81, CDN, Co-Exec Prod; *HR,* 'THE WINNERS', TV, 80, CDN, Wr; *THE SWISS CONSPIRACY,* Th, 77, USA, Wr; *FLINT: DEAD ON TARGET,* Th, 76, USA, Wr; *'THE STARLOST'* (Wr-4 eps), (16 eps), TV, 74, CDN/USA, Story Ed; *'THE ALIEN'* (6 eps), TV, 73-70, USA, Wr; *SIX WAR YEARS,* TV, 73, CDN, T'play/Creator; *AN ENEMY OF THE PEOPLE,* TV, 73, CDN, T'play; *'DANNY THOMAS ANTHOLOGY DRAMA'* (1 eps), TV, 71, USA, Wr; *'JERICHO'* (4 eps), TV, 70, USA, Wr; *PEOPLE OF THE FLY RIVER,* TV, 70, CDN, Wr; *'FELONY SQUAD'* (6 eps), TV, 69-66, USA, Wr; *THE SURVIVORS* (mini-series), TV, 69, USA, Staff Wr; *'IRON HORSE'* (6 eps), TV, 67/66, USA, Wr; *'LES CRANE SHOW'* (125 eps), TV, 65/64, USA, Head Wr; *'ON THE SCENE'* (250 eps), TV, 64-60, CDN, Wr; *'FESTIVAL'* (12 eps), TV, 64-56, CDN, Contr Wr; *'STEVE ALLEN SHOW'* (45 eps), TV, 64, USA, Head Wr; *THE CITY AT NIGHT,* TV, 63, CDN, Wr; *'QUEST'* (12 eps), TV, 61/60, CDN, Wr; *'GENERAL MOTORS THEATRE'* (sev eps), TV, 60-56, CDN, Contr Wr; *NOW THAT APRIL'S HERE,* Th, 58, CDN, Scr/Co-Prod; *IVY LEAGUE KILLERS,* Th, 58, CDN, Wr/Co-Prod; *'FORD GRAPHIC'* (100 eps), TV, 57/56, CDN, Head Wr; *'ON THE SPOT'* (26 eps), TV, 54, CDN, Wr/Creator/Story Ed.

KOHANYI, Julius - see DIRECTORS

KOLBER, Sandra

CAPAC. 100 Summit Circle, Westmount, Que, CAN, H3Y 1N8. (514)482-5871. Cemp Investments Ltd., 630 Dorchester Blvd. W., 32nd Fl., Montreal, Que, CAN, H3B 1X5. (514)878-9841.
Types of Production & Categories: Th Film-Wr.
Genres: Drama-Th; Comedy-Th; Animation-TV.
Biography: Born 1934; Canadian citizen. B.A., McGill University, 55. Languages: English, French, Hebrew. Has had 2 books of poetry published: 'Bitter Sweet Lemons & Love', 67, 'All There Is Of Love', 69. Worked for many years as a journalist, story editor for Sagittarius Productions Ltd., New York, 70. One of the first readers for the C.F.D.C., later became Director of Creative Development for

(cont/suite)

Astral Film Productions. She was a founder and until 85, a partner in Canadian Int'l Studios Inc..
Selective Filmography: *GEORGE AND THE STAR,* TV, 84, CDN, Co-Prod; *TELL ME THAT YOU LOVE ME,* Th, 83, CDN/I, Co-Wr.

KROEKER, Allan - see DIRECTORS

LAGER, Martin

ACTRA. 360 Bloor St. E., Ste. 403, Toronto, Ont, CAN, M4W 3M3. (416)961-3923. CTV, 42 Charles St.E., Toronto, Ont, CAN, M4Y 1T5. (416)928-6153.
Types of Production & Categories: Th Film-Wr; TV Film-Wr/Prod; TV Video-Wr.
Genres: Drama-Th&TV; Comedy-Th&TV; Action-Th&TV; Science Fiction-Th&TV.
Biography: Born 1936, Toronto, Ontario. Former professional actor, musician. Playwright, 15 produced plays; 'A Time to Reap' won Best Canadian Play Award, EODL Festival, 73. Was awarded 2 Canada Council grants, 4 Ontario Council for the Arts grants. Taught creative writing, Sir Sanford Fleming College, 73-79. Executive producer, CTV Television, 86, supervising all drama production and co-production.
Selective Filmography: *'THE CAMPBELLS'* (40 eps), TV, 86/85, CDN/USA/GB, Exec Prod; *'PROFILES OF NATURE'* (6 eps), TV, 85/84, CDN, Wr; *SLIM OBSESSION/OUT OF SIGHT, OUT OF MIND,* 'FOR THE RECORD', TV, 83/82, CDN, Wr; *'CITIZENS ALERT'* (2 eps), TV, 82/81, CDN, Wr; *'LITTLEST HOBO'* (Wr-11 eps), (22 eps), TV, 81/80, CDN, Exec Story Ed; *'STONEY PLAIN'* (2 eps), TV, 81, CDN, Wr; *'MATT AND JENNY'* (Wr-11 eps), (26 eps), TV, 79, CDN/GB/D, Exec Story Ed; *KLONDIKE FEVER,* Th, 79, CDN, Co-Scr; *THE SHAPE OF THINGS TO COME,* Th, 78, CDN, Scr; *'SIDESTREET'* (1 eps), TV, 77, CDN, Wr; *DEADLY HARVEST,* Th, 76, CDN, Wr; *WINGS IN THE WILDERNESS,* Th, 75, CDN, Wr; *LIONS FOR BREAKFAST,* Th, 74, CDN, Wr; *'SWISS FAMILY ROBINSON'* (26 eps), TV, 74, CDN/USA, Wr/Assist Story Ed; *'THE STARLOST'* (Wr-6 eps), (16 eps), TV, 73, CDN/USA, Assist Story Ed; *HOBBES AND LOCKE/ROUSSEAU,* 'PHILOSOPHERS', TV, 72, CDN, Wr; *'WORLD RELIGIONS'* (2 eps), TV, 71, CDN, Wr; *'ADVENTURES IN RAINBOW COUNTRY'* (13 eps), TV, 70/69, CDN/GB/AUS, Wr; *WOODLOTS,* ED, 68, CDN, Wr; *LEADERSHIP: RCN OFFICER TRAINING* (6 eps), ED, 67/66, CDN, Wr; *THE OFFERING,* Th, 66, CDN, Wr; *LEADERSHIP: RCAF OFFICER TRAINING* (6 eps), ED, 65/64, CDN, Wr.

LANCTOT, Micheline - voir REALISATEURS

LANGEVIN, Serge

SARDEC. 4328 Melrose, Montréal, Qué, CAN, H4A 2S6. (514)482-3279.
Types de production et Catégories: TV vidéo-Sc.
Types d'oeuvres: Comédie-TV.
Curriculum vitae: Né en 1940. Humoriste, participation aux magazines 'Croc', 'Nous', 'L'Actualité'; publication d'un recueil 'Comment passer à travers ma crise', 85; participation (1 chapitre) au livre 'Unsportsmanlike Conduct', 85.
Filmographie sélective: *'SAMEDI DE RIRE'* (5 eps), TV, 86/85, CDN, Aut.

LASRY, Pierre - see DIRECTORS

LAURIER, Nicole - voir PRODUCTEURS

LAZER, Charles

ACTRA. Lazer Media, 73 Beaconsfield Ave., Toronto, Ont, CAN, M6J 3J1. (416) 530-4767.
Types of Production & Categories: Th Film-Wr; Th Short-Wr; TV Film-Prod/Wr; TV Video-Wr/Dir/Prod.
Genres: Drama-Th&TV; Comedy-Th&TV; Educational-TV; Industrial-Th&TV.
(cont/suite)

Biography: Born 1946; Canadian citizen; B.A., Ph D., Mathematical Sociology, Princeton University. Has published scientific articles. Has been writing, producing for both national Canadian TV Networks, NFB, TV Ontario and major corporate clients.
Selective Filmography: *JUNO AWARDS*, TV, 85, CDN, Co-Wr; *'THE CAMPBELLS'* (1 eps), TV, 85, CDN/USA/GB, Wr; *BACK IN SHAPE*, ED, 85, CDN, Wr/Dir; *PERFECT PARTNERS/PUMP ISLAND SERVICE/WORKING IN HARMONY*, In, 85, CDN, Wr; *WHAT IS SOCIOLOGY?/CRIME AND DEVIANCE/THE FAMILY/POPULATION*, 'SOCIOLOGY', TV, 84, CDN, Wr; *ETHNIC AND MINORITY RELATIONS/URBANIZATION AND URBANISM*, 'SOCIOLOGY', TV, 84, CDN, Wr; *BLOOD CULTURES/CLINICAL MYCOLOGY*, TV, 84, USA, Prod/Dir; *IDENTIFYING COMMON MOLD AND FUNGUS PATHOGENS*, TV, 84, USA, Prod/Dir; *MEET THE QUIGLEYS*, In, 84, CDN, Wr; *CHILDREN TAKE CARE*, TV, 83, CDN, Wr; *'THRILL OF A LIFETIME'* (40 eps), TV, 83-81, CDN/USA, Prod/Wr; *THE DEVIL AT YOUR HEELS*, Th, 82, CDN, Wr; *'HEART OF GOLD'* (3 eps), TV, 82, CDN, Res; *A GIFT OF TIME*, TV, 80, CDN, Wr; *SUPER JUMP*, TV, 79, CDN, Assoc Prod.

LAZURE, Jacques

SARDEC. 47 rue St-Joseph, Ste-Martine, Que, CAN, J0S 1V0. (514)427-2208.
Types de production et Catégories: TV film-Sc; TV vidéo-Sc.
Types d'oeuvres: Drame-TV; Comédie-TV; Comédie musicale-TV; Action-TV.
Curriculum vitae: Né en 1956, St-Isidore de la Prairie, Québec. Education: Baccalauréat en Communications. Prix des jeunes scénaristes, Radio-Québec, 83 et 84; deuxième prix au concours 'La relève du roman québécois', 85. Auteur de nombreux textes pour enfants; membre de la troupe Les Animeries inc..
Filmographie sélective: *LES SOMNAMBULES*, TV, 85, CDN, Sc; *LE COMMANDO DES SANS-SOLEIL*, TV, 84, CDN, Sc.

LECKIE, Keith

ACTRA. 213 Perth Ave., Toronto, Ont, CAN, M6P 3X7. (416)536-5255. The Colbert Agency, 303 Davenport Rd., Toronto, Ont, CAN, M5R 1K5. (416)964-3302.
Types of Production & Categories: TV Film-Wr; TV Video-Wr.
Genres: Drama-TV; Action-TV; Documentary-TV.
Biography: Born 1952, Toronto, Ontario. Education: Ryerson Polytechnical Institute, Degree in Photo-Arts (majoring in Motion Picture). Other film oriented experience: assistant directing, props and set design, location managing, instructor for secondary school filmmaking courses, novelist; journalist.
Selective Filmography: *'SPIRIT BAY'* (4 eps), TV, 86-84, CDN, Wr; *'DANGER BAY'* (2 eps), TV, 86, CDN/USA, Wr; *SPECIAL DELIVERY*, TV, 05, CDN, Wr; *CROSSBAR*, 'ANTHOLOGY', TV, 80, CDN, Wr.

LEDOUX, Paul

ACTRA. 125 Bathurst St., Toronto, Ont, CAN, M5V 2R2. Katherine Martin, 53 Langley Ave., Toronto, Ont, CAN, M4K 1B4. (416)465-4898.
Types of Production & Categories: TV Film-Wr; TV Video-Wr.
Genres: Drama-TV; Comedy-TV; Musical-TV; Children's-TV.
Biography: Born 1949, Halifax, Nova Scotia. B.A., Dalhousie University; Nova Scotia College of Art and Design (video and performance). Chairman, Playwrights Union of Canada; 21 produced plays; playwright in residence, Factory Theatre, Toronto. Winner, Atlantic Film Awards, Best Short Film Script for *STAR REPORTER*.
Selective Filmography: *'THE EDISON TWINS'* (11 eps), TV, 85-83, CDN, Wr; *RUNNING ON EMPTY*, TV, 84, CDN, Wr; *BASES LOADED...*, TV, 84, CDN, Wr; *STAR REPORTER*, MV, 83, CDN, Co-Wr; *'LOOKS AT BOOKS'* (5 eps),
(cont/suite)

WRITERS/SCENARISTES

ED, 81, CDN, Wr; *'FORCEFUL FOLLIES'* (5 eps), ED, 80, CDN, Wr; *'DR. MUSZOSKI'S CYCLOPEDIC SCHOOL...'* (10 eps), ED, 79, CDN, Wr.

LEFEBVRE, Jean Pierre - voir REALISATEURS
LEHMAN, Lewis - see DIRECTORS
LEMAY-ROUSSEAU, Lise

SACD. 249 Simon Saladim, Boucherville, Qué, CAN, J4B 1L5. (514)655-5936. Radio-Québec, 1000 rue Fullum, Montréal, Qué, CAN, H2K 3L7. (514)521-2424.
Types de production et Catégories: l métrage-Sc; TV film-Sc; TV vidéo-Sc.
Types d'oeuvres: Drame-C&TV; Comédie-C; Education-TV; Enfants-TV.
Curriculum vitae: Née en 1937, Frontierville, Québec. Education: Bac., Maitrise. *LE MATOU* remporte le Prix du public au Festival du Film du Québec et au Festival des Films du Monde, Montréal (ainsi que le Prix du jury) .
Filmographie sélective: *'RETRAITE-ACTION'* (20 eps), TV, 85-83, CDN, Sc; *LA MATOU,* C, 85, CDN/F, Sc; *'AGORA'* (3 eps), TV, 84/83, CDN/F/CH, Sc; *'ECOUTE-MOI DONC QUAND JE TE PARLE'* (26 eps), TV, 80, CDN, Sc; *'MOI...'* (17 eps), TV, 79/78, CDN, Sc; *'LES ORALIENS'* (125 eps), TV, 70/69, CDN, Sc; *'AUX YEUX DU PRESENT'* (2 eps), TV, 70/69, CDN, Sc.

LEMELIN, Roger

1 chemin de la Corniche, St-Augustin, Qué, CAN, G3A 1B2. (418)288-2510. 1455 rue Sherbrooke O., PH#3, Montréal, Qué, CAN. (514)288-2510.
Types de production et Catégories: l métrage-Sc; c métrage-Sc.
Types d'oeuvres: Drame-C; Comédie-C.
Curriculum vitae: Né en 1919, St-Sauveur, Québec. Auteur des romans 'Les Plouffe' et 'Le crime d'Ovide Plouffe'.
Filmographie sélective: *LE CRIME D'OVIDE PLOUFFE* (MURDER IN THE FAMILY), C, 83, CDN/F, Co sc; *LES PLOUFFE* (THE PLOUFFE FAMILY), C, 81, CDN, Co sc (**2 GENIE**); *L'HOMME AUX OISEAUX* (THE BIRD FANCIER), C, 52, CDN, Sc.

LENNICK, Michael - see DIRECTORS
LETOURNEAU, Diane - voir REALISATEURS
LICCIONI, Jean-Pierre

SARDEC. 109 MacAuley, St-Lambert, Qué, CAN, J4R 2G8. (514)671-6980.
Types de production et Catégories: c métrage-Sc/Réal; TV film-Sc; TV vidéo/Sc/Réal.
Types d'oeuvres: Comédie-C&TV; Education-TV; Enfants-TV; Animation-TV.
Curriculum vitae: Né en 1942; citoyenneté canadienne et française. Dix ans de réalisation (60 vidéos et courts métrages) et 15 ans de scénarisation (plus de 150 scénarios). *QU'EST-CE QUI M'ARRIVE?* remporte le Prix du Meilleur Scénario de court métrage, Yorkton, 83.
Filmographie sélective: *'LA BANDE A OVIDE'* (60 eps), TV, 86/85, CDN/B, Sc; *BINO-FABULE,* C, 86, CDN/B, Co sc; *'PASSE-PARTOUT II'* (50 eps), TV, 84/83, CDN, Sc; *LA SATANEE QUESTION,* C, 83/82, CDN, Sc; *QUE LA FETE CONTINUE,* TV, 83/82, CDN, Sc; *QU'EST-CE QUI M'ARRIVE?,* C, 83, CDN, Sc; *'FAUT VOIR A SON AFFAIRE'* (13 eps), TV, 81/80, CDN, Réal/Sc; *'SUR LE BOUT DE LA LANGUE'* (20 eps), TV, 81/80, CDN, Sc; *'MANGER COMME DU MONDE'* (13 eps), TV, 79/78, CDN, Sc; *BYE BYE 79,* TV, 79, CDN, Co sc; *'PASSE-PARTOUT I'* (125 eps), TV, 79-77, CDN, Réal.

LIVESLEY, Jack

6 Bartlett Ave., #13, Toronto, Ont, CAN, M6H 3E7. (416)537-9609. TV Ontario, Box 200, Stn Q, Toronto, Ont, CAN, M4T 2T1. (416)484-2600.
Types of Production & Categories: TV Film-Wr/Host; TV Video-Wr/Host.
(cont/suite)

Genres: Documentary-TV; Educational-TV; Children's-TV.
Biography: Born 1928, Brantford, Ontario. Graduate of McMaster University. Wrote, designed, hosted or assisted with 200 television productions; freelance writer, 86. *THE NO NAME SHOW* won a Silver Hugo, Chicago Film Festival.
Selective Filmography: *'QUESTIONS OF CHOICE'* (6 eps), TV, 86, CDN, Wr/Host; *'ACADEMY ON THE SHORT STORY'* (6 eps), TV, 85, CDN, Host/Interv; *THE NO NAME SHOW* (pilot), TV, 84, CDN, Assoc Prod; *'PLAYING SHAKESPEARE'*, TV, 84, CDN, Host/Interv; *'ACADEMY ON COMPUTERS'* (12 eps), TV, 83, CDN, Host/Interv; *'ACADEMY ON PARENTING'* (6 eps), TV, 83, CDN, Host/Wr/Interv; *'ACADEMY ON MORAL PHILOSOPHY'* (7 eps), TV, 82, CDN, Host/Interv.

LOCKE, Jeannine - see PRODUCERS

LONSDALE, Kate

ACTRA. 58 Satok Terrace, West Hill, Ont, CAN, M1E 3N5. (416)281-8893.
Types of Production & Categories: TV Film-Wr; TV Video-Wr.
Genres: Comedy-TV; Musical-TV; Variety-TV; Children's-TV.
Biography: Born 1953, Toronto, Ontario. B.A.A., Radio & TV Arts, Ryerson Polytechnical Institute. Freelance writer in TV as well as advertising for which she has earned Canadian and International awards. Often writes with her husband, Ted Lonsdale.
Selective Filmography: *ACTRA AWARDS* (4 shows), TV, 86-83, CDN, Co-Wr; *'TODAY'S SPECIAL'* (15 eps), TV, 86-81, CDN, Wr; *'MR DRESSUP'* (30 eps), TV, 86-83, CDN, Wr; *MISS CANADA PAGEANT* (3 shows), TV, 86-84, CDN, Co-Wr; *MISS TEEN CANADA PAGEANT* (2 shows), TV, 86/85, CDN, Co-Wr; *HOSPITAL FOR SICK CHILDREN TELETHON* (2), TV, 85, CDN, Co-Wr; *SANTA CLAUS PARADE,* TV, 85, CDN, Wr; *CFTO CELEBRATES 25 SENSATIONAL YEARS,* TV, 85, CDN, Wr; *'LAUGHING MATTERS'* (13 eps), TV, 85, CDN, Contr Wr; *WELCOME HOME* (pilot), TV, 85, CDN, Co-Wr; *'JUST KIDDING'* (22 eps), TV, 85/84, CDN, Co-Wr; *GALLAGER GARDENS* (pilot), TV, 85, CDN, Co-Wr; *GENIE AWARDS,* TV, 83, CDN, Co-Wr; *'WAYNE & SHUSTER'* (14 eps), TV, 83-77, CDN, Contr Wr (ACTRA); *VINCENT PRICE'S DRACULA,* TV, 81, CDN, Co-Wr; *COMMAND PERFORMANCE,* TV, 81, CDN, Co-Wr; *PACIFIC SONG CONTEST,* TV, 80, CDN, Co-Wr; *'THE PALACE PRESENTS'* (26 eps), TV, 80/79, CDN, Co-Wr; *'STAN KANN'* (26 eps), TV, 79, CDN, Co-Wr.

LORD, Jean-Claude - voir REALISATEURS

LOWER, Peter

ACTRA. 243 Waverley Rd., Toronto, Ont, CAN, M4L 3T4. (416)694-4652. CBC, Box 500, Stn A, Toronto, Ont, CAN, M5W 1E6. (416)975-7123.
Types of Production & Categories: TV Film-Wr/Prod.
Genres: Drama-TV; Action-TV; Children's-TV.
Biography: Born 1945, Kingston, Ontario. Several degrees from various universities. Worked as a dramaturge, Playwrights Co-op. Married with 2 expensive children.
Selective Filmography: *THE LAST SEASON,* TV, 86, CDN, Story Ed; *'STREET LEGAL'* (6 eps), TV, 86, CDN, Exec Story Ed; *OAKMOUNT HIGH,* TV, 85, CDN, Prod; *THE EXILE,* TV, 85, CDN, Co-Wr; *SPECIAL DELIVERY,* TV, 85, CDN, Story Ed; *THE BOY NEXT DOOR/TOOLS OF THE DEVIL,* 'FOR THE RECORD', TV, 84, CDN, Story Ed; *SLIM OBSESSION/CHANGE OF HEART/ ROUGH JUSTICE/READY FOR SLAUGHTER,* 'FOR THE RECORD', TV, 83/82, CDN, Story Ed; *THE UNEXPECTED/REASONABLE FORCE,* 'FOR THE RECORD', TV, 82/80, CDN, Co-Wr; *MOVING TARGETS/OUT OF SIGHT, OUT OF MIND/BLIND FAITH,* 'FOR THE RECORD', TV, 82/81, CDN, Story Ed; *THE FRED QUILT INCIDENT,* TV, 78, CDN, Story Ed; *DREAMSPEAKER,* TV, 77, CDN, Story Ed.

WRITERS/SCENARISTES

LUCAS, Steve

ACTRA. 577 Church St. , 2nd Fl., Toronto, Ont, CAN, M4Y 2E4. (416)964-6219.
Types of Production & Categories: TV Film-Wr/Prod.
Genres: Drama-TV; Documentary-Th&TV; Educational-TV.
Biography: Born 1952, Vancouver, British Columbia. B.A. (English, History, Philosophy), University of Toronto. Advertising copywriter for Gordon Hill and Cockfield Brown; freelance articles for 'Cinema Canada', the 'Globe & Mail', 'Quill and Quire', 'Saturday Night'. *AFTER THE AXE* won a Blue Ribbon (New York), Silver Cindy (Chicago), Golden Sheaf (Yorkton) and was nominated for an Oscar, 83.
Selective Filmography: *ALL THE YEARS,* 'BELL CANADA PLAYHOUSE', TV, 84, CDN, T'play; *PITCHMEN,* TV, 84, CDN, Wr; *JAMINI,* Cm, 84, CDN, Wr; *THE TRUESTEEL AFFAIR,* TV, 83, CDN, Wr; *FIRED,* 'ENTERPRISE', TV, 82, USA, Wr; *RIDLEY: A SECRET GARDEN,* TV, 81, CDN, Wr; *AFTER THE AXE,* Th, 81, CDN, Wr/Co-Prod.

LYNN, William

ACTRA, WGAe. 40 Alexander St., PH 4, Toronto, Ont, CAN, M4Y 1B5. (416) 920-0649. Characters, 150 Carlton St., Toronto, Ont, CAN. (416)964-8522.
Types of Production & Categories: TV Film-Wr/Prod; TV Video-Wr/Prod.
Genres: Drama-TV; Comedy-TV; Variety-TV; Musical-TV.
Biography: Born 1938, Toronto, Ontario. Honours B.A., English, McGill University, 60; Gold Medal (Speech), London Academy of Music and Dramatic Art, England, 63. Professor of drama: Rada, Guildhall, Webber Douglas, London, England, 65-67.
Selective Filmography: *'SEEING THINGS'* (4 eps), TV, 86/85, CDN, Co-Wr; *HONKY TONK* (pilot), TV, 84, CDN, Co-Wr; *'JULIE AMATO SHOW'* (50 eps), TV, 82-80, CDN, Co-Wr; *'NELLIE, DANIEL, EMMA AND BEN'* (13 eps), TV, 78, CDN, Co-Wr/Co-Prod; *'MARY AND MICHAEL'* (26 eps), TV, 78/77, CDN, Co-Wr; *NORTHEAST PASSAGE,* TV, 77, CDN, Wr/Prod/Dir; *'TOMMY HUNTER SHOW'* (156 eps), TV, 76-70, CDN, Co-Wr/Prod; *FIT TO PRINT,* TV, 76, CDN, Wr/Prod; *'MIXED DOUBLES'* (26 eps), TV, 76, CDN, Co-Wr; *'FRANKIE HOWERD SHOW'* (13 eps), TV, 75, CDN, Co-Wr/Prod; *'RONNIE PROPHET SHOW'* (20 eps), TV, 75/74, CDN, Co-Wr/Prod; *'WAYNE & SHUSTER'* (10 eps), TV, 71/70, CDN, Contr Wr; *'ED SULLIVAN SHOW'* (30 eps), TV, 70/69, USA, Co-Wr; *'THAT GIRL'* (1 eps), TV, 69, USA, Co-Wr; *'DEAN MARTIN PRESENTS MARTY FELDMAN'* (13 eps), TV, 68, USA/GB, Co-Wr; *'TOBY'* (13 eps), TV, 68, CDN, Co-Wr; *'TOMMY HUNTER'* (26 eps), TV, 68/67, CDN, Co-Wr; *'MAVIS BRAMSTON SHOW'* (26 eps), TV, 67/66, AUS, Co-Wr.

MacGILLIVRAY, William D. - see DIRECTORS

MacGREGOR, Roy

ACTRA. 22 Banting Cres., Kanata, Ont, CAN, K2K 1P4. (613)592-0982. The Ottawa Citizen, Baxter Rd., Ottawa, Ont, CAN. (613)596-3664. Lucinda Vardey Agency, 228 Gerrard St.E., Toronto, Ont, CAN, M5A 2E8. (416)922-0250.
Types of Production & Categories: TV Film-Wr; TV Video-Wr.
Genres: Drama-TV.
Biography: Born 1948, Whitney, Ontario. Educated at Laurentian University; U. of Western Ontario. Has received 4 National Magazine Awards; National Newspaper Award; *TYLER* won the Grand Prix de la Presse, Montreal World Film Festival, 79; *READY FOR SLAUGHTER* won Best TV Drama, Banff Film Festival, 83.
Selective Filmography: *THE LAST SEASON* (3 parts), TV, 86, CDN, T'play; *READY FOR SLAUGHTER,* 'FOR THE RECORD', TV, 83, CDN, Wr; *AN HONORABLE MEMBER,* TV, 82, CDN, Wr; *EVERY PERSON IS GUILTY,* 'FOR THE RECORD', TV, 80, CDN, Co-Wr (**ACTRA**); *CEMENTHEAD,* 'FOR THE RECORD', TV, 80, CDN, Co-Wr; *TYLER,* TV, 79, CDN, Wr (**ACTRA**).

MACINA, Michael

ACTRA. Macinema Inc., 36 Maitland St., G2, Toronto, Ont, CAN, M4Y 1C5. (416)967-7877.
Types of Production & Categories: Th Short-Dir/Prod/Wr/Ed; TV Film-Dir/Prod/ Wr/Ed.
Genres: Drama-Th&TV; Educational-TV; Children's-TV; Industrial-TV.
Biography: Born 1950, Toronto, Ontario; bilingual. M.A., Graduate Drama Centre, University of Toronto; Literature, Theatre, Music studies in France. Ten years as a professional writer, director, actor in theatre; 6 years in film. Extensive work, film, theatre in french in Ontario; many grants and awards as writer/director; Amtec Award of Merit, 81, for *NICKELER LE MONDE*.
Selective Filmography: *'Q.U.E.S.T.'* (6 eps), TV, 86, CDN, Contr Wr; *SOLITUDES*, Th, 86, CDN, Prod/Dir/Ed; *PEPINO*, 'PASSPORT', TV, 86, CDN, Wr/Dir; *MA VIE C'EST A MOI*, '20 ANS EXPRESS', TV, 86, CDN, Dir/Wr; *METALLO BLUES*, Th, 85, CDN, Dir/Wr/Ed; *'POUR L'AMOUR DE MARIE'* (7 eps), TV, 85-82, CDN, Dir/Wr/Ed; *APPARTENANCE*, TV, 84, CDN, Dir/Ed; *LES MOTS DITS*, TV, 83, CDN, Prod; *NICKELER LE MONDE*, TV, 82, CDN, Wr/Prod.

MacKAY, Jed

ACTRA. 91 Summerhill Ave., Toronto, Ont, CAN, M4T 1B1.
Types of Production & Categories: TV Video-Wr/Prod.
Genres: Comedy-TV; Educational-TV; Children's-TV.
Biography: Born Vancouver, British Columbia. Honours B.A., Modern Languages, University of Toronto. Also a composer, lyricist.
Selective Filmography: *'POLKA DOT DOOR'* (Wr-5 eps), (20 eps), TV, 86, CDN, Prod; *'TODAY'S SPECIAL'* (5 eps), TV, 86, CDN, Wr; *'TELEFRANCAIS'* (30 eps), TV, 86/85, CDN, Lyrics; *'STORYLORDS'* (12 eps), TV, 85/84, USA, Wr.

MacLEAN, Janet

ACTRA. R.R. #1, Locust Hill, Ont, CAN, L0H 1J0. (416)683-8838. The Colbert Agency, 303 Davenport Rd., Toronto, Ont, CAN, M5R 1K5. (416)964-3302.
Types of Production & Categories: TV Film-Wr; TV Video-Wr.
Genres: Drama-TV; Comedy-TV; Action-TV; Children's-TV.
Selective Filmography: *HOW I MET MY HUSBAND*, 'POV', TV, 86, CDN, Wr; *DANGER BAY* (3 eps), TV, 86, CDN/USA, Wr; *'PHILIP MARLOWE PRIVATE EYE* (5 eps), TV, 85, CDN, Story Ed; *ABRAHAM GESNER· THE LAMPLIGHTER*, 'CANADIAN DISCOVERIES', ED, 85, CDN, Co-Wr.

MacLEAR, Michael - see PRODUCERS

MacNAUGHTON, Ann M.

ACTRA. 317 Seaton St., Toronto, Ont, CAN, M5A 2T6. (416)964-6238.
Types of Production & Categories: TV Film-Wr; TV Video-Wr.
Genres: Drama-TV; Comedy-TV.
Selective Filmography: *WILD CARD*, TV, 86, CDN, Story Ed; *'THE CAMPBELLS'* (Wr-1 ep), (10 eps), TV, 85, CDN/USA/GB, Exec Story Ed; *MICHAEL AND KITTY/IN THIS CORNER*, TV, 85, CDN, Story Ed; *'SOME HONOURABLE GENTLEMEN'* (9 eps), TV, 85-81, CDN, Story Ed; *CLAUSE MISSION '84*, TV, 84, CDN, Wr; *WHERE THE HEART IS/HIDE AND SEEK*, 'FOR THE RECORD', TV, 84/83, CDN, Story Ed; *CASE OF LIBEL*, TV, 83, USA, Story Ed; *'HOME FIRES'* (16 eps), TV, 81-79, CDN, Story Ed.

MADDEN, Peter

19 Stayner St., #8, Westmount, Que, CAN, H3Z 1W3.

(cont/suite)

Types of Production & Categories: Th Film-Wr.
Genres: Drama-Th; Comedy-Th; Action-Th; Children's-TV.
Biography: Born 1939, Toronto, Ontario. Playwright, plays produced in Montreal and Toronto.
Selective Filmography: 'SESAME STREET' (1 eps), TV, 84, USA, Wr; *BACK ALLEY BLUE,* Th, 78, CDN, Wr; *ONE MAN,* Th, 77, CDN, Co-Wr (**ACTRA/CFA**); *GREAT LITTLE ARTIST,* Th, 77, CDN, Add'l Dial; *CELL 16,* Th, 72, CDN, Wr/Assist Dir/Act.

MANN, Danny

ACTRA, AFTRA, DGA, WGAw, SAG. 925 Gayley Ave. Suite 4, Los Angeles, CA, USA, 90024. (213)208-7550. 44 Charles St. W., #1806, Toronto, Ont, CAN, C4Y 1R7. (416)967-1529. Catherine McCartney, Prendergast Agency, 260 Richmond St.W., Suite 405, Toronto, Ont, CAN, M5V 1W5. (416)922-5308.
Types of Production & Categories: TV Film-Dir/Act/Wr; TV Video-Dir/Act/Wr.
Genres: Comedy-TV; Variety-TV; Documentary-TV; Animation-TV.
Biography: Born 1948, Toronto, Ontario; US-Canadian resident; 15 years in the entertainment business. B.F.A., TV, Film, UCLA; 2 years Journalism, California State University.
Selective Filmography: *NEW LANG SYNE,* TV, 86/85, CDN, Head Wr; *THE NHL AWARDS SPECIAL,* TV, 85, CDN, Wr; *GENIE AWARDS,* TV, 85, CDN, Head Wr; 'ANYTHING FOR MONEY', TV, 84, USA, Prod/Dir/Act; 'THICKE OF THE NIGHT' (sev seg), TV, 83, USA, Prod/Dir/Wr/Act; *THE LOST SATELLITE NETWORK* (2 spec), TV, 83, CDN/USA, Dir/Wr/Act; 'AN EVENING AT THE IMPROV' (2 eps), TV, 82/81, USA, Co-Wr/Act; *THE 3rd ANNUAL AMERICAN IMPORTANCE AWARDS,* TV, 82, USA, Dir; *THE 1st ANNUAL HOCKEY SHTICK,* TV, 81, CDN, Prod/Dir/Wr/Act; *MISS WORLD CANADA,* TV, 80, CDN, Prod/Dir; *WHATTA BUNCHA BANANAS!,* TV, 80, CDN, Dir; *BOO!,* TV, 80, CDN/USA, Dir; *LOTO CANADA,* TV, 80, CDN, Dir; 'THE RENE SIMARD SHOW' (26 eps), TV, 79, CDN, Co-Prod/Dir/Wr/Act; 'THE RENE SIMARD SHOW' (26 eps), TV, 78, CDN, Wr/Act/P Pro Spv.

MANN, Ron - see DIRECTORS

MARKLE, Fletcher - see DIRECTORS

MARR, Leon G. - see DIRECTORS

MARTIN, Bruce

ACTRA. 45 Boswell Ave., Toronto, Ont, CAN, M5R 1M5. (416)964-7490. Stanley Colbert, The Colbert Agency, 303 Davenport Rd., Toronto, Ont, CAN, M5R 1K5. (416)964-3302.
Types of Production & Categories: TV Film-Wr; TV Video-Wr.
Genres: Drama-TV; Action-TV; Documentary-TV; Children's-TV.
Biography: British born; Canadian-British citizenship. Has written many drama and documentary scripts for CBC, CTV, TVO, NFB, independent producers and clients. Awarded medal of Excellence, New York Film Festival.
Selective Filmography: 'HOT SHOTS' (1 eps), TV, 86, CDN, Wr; 'NIGHT HEAT' (4 eps), TV, 86/85, CDN, Wr; *MAGICAL MUSICAL DAYS,* TV, 85, CDN, Wr; *A WHOLE NEW BALLGAME,* TV, 85, CDN, Wr; 'THE EDISON TWINS' (6 eps), TV, 84, CDN, Wr.

MARTIN, Susan - see DIRECTORS
MARTINET, Jean - voir REALISATEURS

MASON, Bruce

2152 Cornwall Ave., Vancouver, BC, CAN, V6K 1B4. (604)731-5487.
Types of Production & Categories: TV Video-Wr.
Genres: Comedy-TV; Variety-TV; Documentary-TV; Educational-TV.
Biography: Born 1946, Vancouver, British Columbia. B.A., Honours English, Simon Fraser University; graduated, BCIT, Broadcast Journalism. Head writer, *VANCOUVER SHOW*, CKVU-TV, live nightly 2 hour news/variety, 3 years; freelance writer: print, television, radio, advertising. Professional musician for 12 years.

MAYEROVITCH, David

ACTRA. 288 Rushton Rd., Toronto, Ont, CAN, M6C 2X5. (416)651-6744.
Types of Production & Categories: TV Video-Wr.
Genres: Drama-TV; Comedy-TV; Variety-TV; Musical-TV.
Biography: Born 1941, Montreal, Quebec. B.A., McGill University, 64. Stage playwright: 'The Maltese Blue Jay', 'Programmed for Passion' (six-part soap opera stage serial). Writer of songs, sketches for revues.
Selective Filmography: *'HANGIN'IN'* (4 eps), TV, 85-83, CDN, Wr; *'KING OF KENSINGTON'* (12 eps), TV, 80-78, CDN, Wr; *'FLAPPERS'* (3 eps), TV, 80-79, CDN, Wr; *'WAYNE & SHUSTER'* (25 eps), TV, 77-71, CDN, Contr Wr; *'FAMOUS JURY TRIALS'* (17 eps), TV, 71, CDN/USA, Wr; *'ED SULLIVAN SHOW'* (12 eps), TV, 70, USA, Co-Wr; *'GOLDDIGGERS IN LONDON'* (10 eps), TV, 70, USA/GB, Contr Wr.

McANDREW, Jack

ACTRA. Meadowbank, PEI, CAN, C0A 1H0. (902)566-2427. Box 2703, Charlottetown, PEI, CAN, C1A 8C3. (902)892-4173.
Types of Production & Categories: TV Video-Wr/Dir/Prod.
Genres: Drama-TV; Variety-TV; Musical-TV; Documentary-TV.
Biography: Born 1933, New Brunswick. Producer, Charlottetown Festival; head of CBC Variety, 75-80; independent, 80-86. Extensive work as trainer and communications consultant, CBC radio and TV; artistic director, Canadian Heritage Festival, 85.
Selective Filmography: *ONE WEEK IN SUMMER*, TV, 85, CDN, Prod/Dir/Wr; *ROCKIN' THE BLUES*, TV, 85, CDN, Prod/Dir/Wr; *'GZOWSKI AND CO'* (1 eps), TV, 85, CDN, Wr; *COAST OF DREAMS*, TV, 84, CDN, Wr; *'FIRST CHOICE ROCKS'* (10 eps), TV, 83, CDN, Prod/Dir; *'ROMANCE'* (5 eps), TV, 82, CDN, Co-Prod/Co-Wr; *CHRISTMAS FANTASY*, TV, 82, CDN/D, Prod/Wr; *LIONA BOYD*, TV, 82, CDN, Prod/Dir/Wr.

McGREEVY, John - see DIRECTORS

McHUGH, Fiona

ACTRA. 766 Markham St., Toronto, Ont, CAN, M6G 2M5. (416)531-6149.
Types of Production & Categories: TV Film-Wr; TV Video-Wr.
Genres: Drama-TV; Documentary-TV; Educational-TV; Children's-TV.
Biography: Born 1945, Dublin, Ireland. B.A., University College, Dublin; Master of Letters, Trinity College, Dublin. Emigrated to Canada, 71; Canadian citizen, 81; speaks English, French and German. Extensive writing and research background, TV and radio; has also written for advertising agencies in field education campaigns, both print and media. Has won 2 Canadian Marketing Awards, 85, 86; the Larry Heywood Award, Canadian Commercial Awards, 84; Gold Medal, Ohio State Award; Gold Medal and Special Jury Gold Medal, Atlanta Int'l Film Fest.; Gold Plaque, Chicago.
Selective Filmography: *ENDING THE NIGHTMARE(PARTS 1&2)/CHILDREN OF ST.NICHOLAS*, 'MAN ALIVE', TV, 86/85, CDN, Wr; *SHROUD OF TURIN*, 'MAN ALIVE', TV, 84, CDN, Wr; *THE INSIDE STORY*, ED, 84, CDN, Wr;

(cont/suite)

HIGH FLIGHT, 'NATURE OF THINGS', TV, 83, CDN, Wr; *VERONICA TENNANT: A DANCER OF DISTINCTION,* TV, 82, CDN, Wr; *'MR. DRESSUP'* (10 eps), TV, 82/81, CDN, Wr; *THE RACE/BORN TO LOVE,* 'THE WINNERS', TV, 80, CDN, Wr; *JOYCE'S 'PORTRAIT OF THE ARTIST AS A YOUNG MAN',* 'EXPLORATIONS IN THE NOVEL', TV, 75, CDN, Wr; *'WRITE ON!'* (sev eps), TV, 75, CDN, Wr; *G.B.S. AND WOMEN,* 'EXPLORATIONS IN DRAMA', TV, 74, CDN, Wr.

McKEOWN, Bob - see PRODUCERS

McLAREN, David

ACTRA. 7-87 Enderby Rd., Toronto, Ont, CAN, M4E 2S6. (416)690-1997.
Types of Production & Categories: TV Film-Wr.
Genres: Drama-TV; Industrial-TV.
Biography: Born Toronto, Ontario. B.A., Queen's and York Universities; several courses in English toward M.A., University of Toronto. Taught screenwriting, Summer Institute of Film, Ottawa, 84-86. Honourable Mention in City TV's 'Toronto Trilogy' Drama Competition. Also has writing credits for radio and the stage.
Selective Filmography: *'VANDERBERG'* (ep #6), TV, 83, CDN, Wr; *BY REASON OF INSANITY,* 'FOR THE RECORD', TV, 81, CDN, Wr.

MELANCON, André - voir REALISATEURS

MENARD, Robert - voir REALISATEURS

MENDELUK, George - see DIRECTORS

MERCER, Michael

ACTRA. 1206 - 1330 Harwood St., Vancouver, BC, CAN, V6E 1S8. (604)684-9781.
Types of Production & Categories: Th Film-Wr; Th Short-Wr; TV Film-Wr; TV Video-Wr.
Genres: Drama-Th&TV; Comedy-Th&TV; Action-Th&TV; Documentary-TV.
Biography: Born 1943, Liverpool, England; naturalized Canadian; bilingual. B.A., Honours English, Sir George Williams University, 67; M.A., University of British Columbia, 72. Served 2 years as Nat'l Chariman, Actra Writers Guild. Full-time freelance writer since 72. Won Actra Award, Best Dramatic Writer (Radio) for 'Freydis', 77; Chalmer's Award for theatre, 'Goodnight Disgrace', 86.
Selective Filmography: *'THE CAMPBELLS'* (5 eps), TV, 86/85, CDN/GB, Wr; *'THE BEACHCOMBERS'* (12 eps), TV, 86-82, CDN, Wr; *DISCOVERY B.C.,* Th, 86, CDN, Wr; *HAIL ALLEY,* Th, 86, CDN, Wr; *THE EXILE,* TV, 85, CDN, Co-Wr; *'DANGER BAY'* (1 eps), TV, 84, CDN/USA, Wr; *'CONSTABLE, CONSTABLE'* (2 eps), TV, 83, CDN, Wr; *SAJO,* Th, 81, CDN, Wr; *WHALE,* TV, 81, CDN, Wr; *'RITTER'S COVE'* (4 eps), TV, 80, CDN/D, Wr; *THE LITTLE BUSINESSMAN,* 'MAGIC LIE', TV, 79, CDN, Wr.

MICHAELS, Lorne - see PRODUCERS

MICHEL, Pauline

CAPAC. 3600 ave. du Parc, #A-1210, Montréal, Qué, CAN, H2X 3R2. (514)845-6900.
Types de production et Catégories: TV film-Sc.
Types d'oeuvres: Variété-TV; Comédie musicale-TV; Education-TV; Enfants-TV.
Curriculum vitae: Née en 1949, Asbestos, Québec. Bac. en Psychologie, Université de Sherbrooke, 65; Licence ès Lettres modernes, Université Laval, 69. Expérience: enseignement (Cégep et Université); publications de romans; 'Les Yeux d'Eau', 'Mirage', receuil de poèmes; auteur-compositeur-interprète de disques; écrit des oeuvres pour radio et spectacles.

(cont/suite)

Filmographie sélective: *'HELLO MOINEAU'* (HELLO COCO), (56 eps), TV, 86-83, CDN/F/CH, Parol; *BEMI, DOSSIC ET COMPAGNIE,* TV, 86, F, Parol; *'TELE-RESSOURCES'* (5 eps), TV, 78/77, CDN, Co sc; *'ANIMAGERIE'* (hebdo), TV, 77/76, CDN, Sc; *'YOU-HOU'* (hebdo), TV, 76, CDN, Sc.

MILLAR, Susan - see PRODUCERS

MITCHELL, Ken
ACTRA. 209 Angus Cres., Regina, Sask, CAN, S4T 6N3. (306)757-6021. Bella Pomer Agency, 22 Shallmar Blvd., PH2, Toronto, Ont, CAN, M5N 2Z8. (416)782-2577.
Types of Production & Categories: Th Film-Wr; Th Short-Dir/Act/Wr; TV Film-Wr/Act; TV Video-Wr/Act.
Genres: Drama-Th&TV; Documentary-Th&TV; Animation-Th.
Biography: Born 1940, Moose Jaw, Saskatchewan. Languages: English, French, Chinese. M.A., University of Saskatchewan. Professor of English, University of Regina since 67; Scottish-Canadian exchange Fellow, 79-80; visiting professor, University of Nanking, China, 80-81. Canadian Authors Association, Best Play Award, 85.
Selective Filmography: *THE MEDICINE LINE,* Th, 86, CDN, Wr/Dir; *THE FRONT LINE,* 'FOR THE RECORD', TV, 85, CDN, Wr; *KEN MITCHELL'S MOOSE JAW,* 'CITYSCAPES', TV, 85, CDN, Act/Wr; *THE SHIPBUILDER,* Th, 85, CDN, Wr; *ST. LAURENT,* Th, 85, CDN, Wr/Act; *THE GREAT ELECTRICAL REVOLUTION,* 'WRITERS AND WRITING', TV, 81, CDN, Act; *THE HOUNDS OF NOTRE DAME,* Th, 80, CDN, Wr; *THIS TRAIN,* TV, 77, CDN, Wr; *STRIKER,* Th, 77, CDN, Wr.

MOHAN, Peter
ACTRA. 291 Oakwood Ave., Toronto, Ont, CAN, M6E 2V3. (416)654-3440.
Types of Production & Categories: Th Film-Wr; TV Film-Wr.
Genres: Drama-TV; Comedy-TV; Action-TV.
Biography: Born 1955.
Selective Filmography: *'NIGHT HEAT'* (6 eps), TV, 86/85, CDN, Co-Wr; *BIG DEAL,* TV, 85, CDN, Co-Wr.

MOHUN, Bruce
ACTRA. 654 Huron St., Toronto, Ont, CAN, M5R 2K9. (416)920-5157.
Types of Production & Categories: TV Film-Wr; TV Video-Wr.
Genres: Drama-TV; Comedy-TV; Variety-TV.
Biography: Born 1952. Graduate Ryerson Polytechnical Institute, Journalism, 80. Winner, City TV, Toronto Trilogy Drama Competition. Worked as a researcher for *LIVE IT UP,* 3 1/2 seasons.
Selective Filmography: *VIDEO BARTENDER,* TV, 85, CDN, Co-Wr; *'LAUGHING MATTERS'* (1 eps), TV, 85, CDN, Wr; *'THE EDISON TWINS'* (1 eps), TV, 85, CDN, Co-Wr; *'HANGIN'IN'* (2 eps), TV, 84, CDN, Co-Wr; *NEIGHBORS,* 'TORONTO TRILOGY', TV, 83, CDN, Wr.

MOORE, Mavor
ACTRA. 3815 W. 27th Ave., Vancouver, BC, CAN, V6S 1R4. (604)222-2502.
Types of Production & Categories: Th Film-Act; TV Film-Wr/Act; TV Video-Wr/Act.
Genres: Drama-Th&TV; Musical-Th&TV; Documentary-Th&TV.
Biography: Born 1919, Toronto, Ontario. B.A., University of Toronto; has received 5 Honorary Doctorates (LL.D., D. Litt.). Playwright, has written over 100 produced plays, musicals and operas; also writes for radio, print (Globe and Mail). First Chief producer, CBC (English language), 52. Recipient of the Order of Canada, Queen's

(cont/suite)

Medal, Centennial Medal, 3 Int'l Peabody Awards, John Drainie Award (82) and a Diplôme d'Honneur from the Canadian Conference of the Arts.
Selective Filmography: *SPOT MARKS THE X,* Th, 85, USA, Act; *THE KILLING FIELDS,* Th, 84, GB, Act; *THE OLYMPICS* (4 parts), TV, 78, CDN, Wr; *BELINDA* (Musical), TV, 76, CDN, Adapt; *THE RONCARELLI AFFAIR,* 'THE PLAY'S THE THING', TV, 74, CDN, Co-Wr; *'PROGRAM X'* (6 eps), TV, 72/71, CDN, Wr; *GETTING IN,* TV, 72, GB, Wr; *THE ARGUMENT,* TV, 72, GB, Wr; *GETTING IN,* TV, 72, CDN, Wr; *THE STORE,* TV, 71, CDN, Wr; *INSIDE OUT,* TV, 71, CDN, Wr; *LOUIS RIEL* (Opera), TV, 69, CDN, Wr; *YESTERDAY THE CHILDREN WERE DANCING/THE PUPPET CARAVAN,* TV, 69/67, CDN, Trans; *THE SON,* TV, 59, CDN, Wr; *THE OTTAWA MAN,* TV, 59, CDN, Wr; *THE MAN WHO CAUGHT BULLETS,* TV, 58, CDN, Wr; *SUNSHINE TOWN* (Musical), TV, 55, CDN, Adapt.

MOORE, Roy

ACTRA. 292 Queen St.W., Toronto, Ont, CAN, M5V 2A1. (416)595-9949. The Colbert Agency, 303 Davenport Rd., Toronto, Ont, CAN, M5R 2K5. (416)964-3302.
Types of Production & Categories: Th Film-Wr; TV Film-Wr.
Genres: Drama-Th&TV; Variety-TV; Musical-TV; Children's-TV.
Biography: Has received 2 Ontario Arts Council Grants for Screenwriting, 79 and 83.
Selective Filmography: *OUT OF SIGHT, OUT OF MIND,* 'FOR THE RECORD', TV, 83, CDN, Story; *RIEL* (2 parts), TV, 79, CDN, Wr (**ANIK**); *CAN I SAVE MY CHILDREN,* TV, 75, USA, Wr; *BLACK CHRISTMAS* (SILENT NIGHT, EVIL NIGHT), Th, 74, CDN, Wr; *SHE CRIED MURDER,* TV, 73, CDN/USA, Wr; *'THE ADVENTURES OF TIMOTHY PILGRIM'* (10 eps), TV, 73, CDN, Wr; *'CUCUMBER'* (pilot), TV, 73, CDN, Wr.

MORENCY, Pierre

SARDEC. 1211 ave.Preston, Sillery, Qué, CAN, G1S 4L1. (418)688-1651.
Types de production et Catégories: TV film-Sc.
Types d'oeuvres: Drame-TV; Documentaire-TV.
Curriculum vitae: Né en 1942 à Lauzon, Québec. Licence ès Lettres, Université Laval, 66. Expérience: chroniqueur et auteur radiophonique; poète et auteur dramatique; animateur de nombreux récitals de poésie. Fonde et dirige la revue 'Inédits', 70. Publications de poèmes dont 'Torrentiel', 78, 'Lieu de naissance' 73.; théâtre: 'Ecoles de mon bazou', 'Les Passeuses', 76 et 'Carbonneau et le chef', 74.
Filmographie sélective: *LA CHOSE LA PLUS DOUCE AU MONDE* (LES PASSEUSES), TV, 83, CDN, Aut; *VISITEURS ET RESIDENTS DE L'ARCTIQUE,* 'CONNAISANCE DU MILIEU', TV, 81, CDN, Textes/Narr.

MURTAGH, Bill

ACTRA. 44 Pintail Cres., Don Mills, Ont, CAN, M3A 2Y7. (416)446-6950.
Types of Production & Categories: TV Film-Wr; TV Video-Wr.
Genres: Drama-TV; Comedy-TV.
Biography: Born 1952, Toronto, Ontario.
Selective Filmography: *'HANGIN' IN'* (20 eps), TV, 85-82, CDN, Wr; *'THE EDISON TWINS'* (1 eps), TV, 85, CDN, Wr.

NAPIER-ANDREWS, Nigel - see DIRECTORS

NASIMOK, Briane

ACTRA. 11 Bertmount Ave., Toronto, Ont, CAN, M4M 2X8. (416)465-5609. Performing Arts Mgmt., 2 College St., Toronto, Ont, CAN. (416)923-5079.
Types of Production & Categories: Th Film-Wr; Th Short-Wr/Dir; TV Video-Wr.
Genres: Drama-Th&TV; Comedy-Th&TV; Variety-TV; Children's-TV.
(cont/suite)

TVONTARIO
Producers and
coproducers of

CANADIAN LITERATURE

BUCK STOPPERS

NEW DIRECTIONS

20 Ans Express

SPEAKING OUT

MOSAÏQUE

THE SCIENCE EDITION

teLYS et le TRILLIUM

TODAY'S SPECIAL

VISTA LOGICIEL VISTA

START YOUR OWN BUSINESS

TAKE A LOOK

POLKA DOT DOOR

The Middle East

FISH IN!

OCTO-PUCE

Hooked on READING

ALL BEING WELL

AUTOMATING THE OFFICE

La Santé Contagieuse

FITNESS OVER Forty

PEOPLE PATTERNS

Realities

ARTSCAPE

MONEY$WORTH

Terrarium

THE FINAL CHAPTER?

LOGICIEL Realities

TVOntario
Truly rewarding television

2180 Yonge Street, Toronto, Ontario. Tel: (416) 484-2600

FUND

Biography: Born 1949, Toronto, Ontario. B.A., University of Toronto. Writer, performer, radio and TV comedy.
Selective Filmography: *'DOWNTOWN SATURDAY NIGHT'* (1 eps), TV, 85, CDN, Contr Wr; *'YAN CAN COOK'* (124 eps), TV, 84, CDN, Co-Wr; *'EVENING AT THE IMPROV'* (5 eps), TV, 83, CDN/USA, Contr Wr; *'IN TORONTO'* (3 eps), TV, 83, CDN, Contr Wr; *SPRING FEVER* (SNEAKERS), Th, 82, CDN, Co-Wr; *'YUK-YUK'S'* (2 eps), TV, 82, CDN, Co-Wr; *'NELLIE, DANIEL, EMMA AND BEN'* (2 eps), TV, 81, CDN, Contr Wr; *TRICIA,* Th, 70, CDN, Wr/Dir.

NATHAN, Deborah A.

ACTRA. 59 Tiverton Ave., Toronto, Ont, CAN, M4M 2M1. (416)469-1948.
Types of Production & Categories: TV Video-Wr.
Genres: Drama-TV.
Biography: Born 1949, Detroit, Michigan; resident of Canada since 74. Worked with playwrights co-op as assistant dramaturge; NDWT Theatre Company as researcher, reader.
Selective Filmography: *'THE CAMPBELLS'* (Co-T'play/Story-1 eps, Wr-1 eps), TV, 85, CDN/USA/GB, Wr; *'HOME FIRES'* (Wr-1 eps), (19 eps), TV, 81-79, CDN, Res.

NEILSEN, Katherine

Lauren Productions Inc., 3 - 1151 Haro St., Vancouver, BC, CAN, V6E 1E3. (604) 683-0001. Ralph Zimmerman, Great North Artists Mgmt., 345 Adelaide St.W., Suite 500, Toronto, Ont, CAN, M5V 1R5. (416)593-2587.
Types of Production & Categories: Th Short-Wr.
Genres: Drama-Th.
Biography: Born 1958.
Selective Filmography: *MAGGIE,* Th, 81, CDN, Wr/Prod/Act.

NEWMAN, Jack

ACTRA. Jack Newman Prod. Ltd., 41 Camberwell Rd., Toronto, Ont, CAN, M6C 3E7. (416)781-0264. The Characters, 150 Carlton St., Toronto, Ont, CAN. (416) 964-8522.
Types of Production & Categories: Th Film-Act; TV Film-Wr/Act; TV Video-Wr/Act.
Genres: Variety-TV; Educational-TV; Children's-TV.
Biography: Born 1946, Landsberg, Germany; Canadian citizen. Languages: English, French, Yiddish. Honours B.A., Psychology; coursework at M.A. level in drama and education; 2 years, law courses. Clio Awards for commercials.
Selective Filmography: *'BIZARRE'* (12 eps), TV, 86-80, CDN/USA, Act; *'CHECK IT OUT!'* (3 eps), TV, 86, CDN/USA, Act; *DEAD OF WINTER,* Th, 86, USA, Act; *MANY HAPPY RETURNS,* TV, 86, USA, Act; *MR. NICE GUY,* Th, 85, CDN, Act; *'SEEING THINGS'* (2 eps), TV, 84/83, CDN, Act; *NEVER TRUST AN HONEST THIEF,* Th, 81, CDN, Act; *'RENE SIMARD SHOW'* (2 eps), TV, 80, CDN, Wr; *ANNE MURRAY: LADIES NIGHT,* TV, 80, CDN, Wr; *'THE EMPLOYMENT FILE'* (12 eps), TV, 79, CDN, Wr; *ALCOHOL, THE DRUG,* ED, 79, CDN, Wr/Narr; *THE JOB SEARCH,* In, 79, CDN, Wr; *'KING OF KENSINGTON'* (4 eps), TV, 78-76, CDN, Act; *'SHH...IT'S THE NEWS'* (12 eps), TV, 76-74, CDN, Act; *'EVERYTHING GOES'* (3 eps), TV, 76-74, CDN, Act.

NEWTON, John

1335 Cypress, Vancouver, BC, CAN, V6J 3L1. (604)738-6482.
Types of Production & Categories: Th Short-Wr/Dir/Prod.
Genres: Drama-Th; Comedy-Th.
Biography: Born 1939, Bakersfield, California; Canadian citizen. Languages: English, Spanish. Teaches filmmaking at University of British Columbia. Won American Film Institute fellowship for *THE MYSTERY OF B.TRAVEN.*
(cont/suite)

Selective Filmography: *THE MYSTERY OF B.TRAVEN,* Th, 77, CDN, Wr/Dir/Ed; *RABBIT HUNT,* Th, 70, USA, Dir/Ed; *MIKE ANGELS,* Th, 66, USA, Wr/Prod.

NICHOL, B.P.

ACTRA. 114 Lauder Ave., Toronto, Ont, CAN, M6H 3E5. (416)654-6639.
Types of Production & Categories: TV Film-Wr; TV Video-Wr.
Genres: Children's-TV; Animation-TV.
Biography: Born 1944, Vancouver, British Columbia. Won the Governor General's Award for poetry, 70 and the Int'l 3-Day Novel Writing Contest, 82. Published 25 books of poetry and prose. Wrote 10 episodes of the TV series *FRAGGLE ROCK;* co-wrote 2 episodes of *THE RACCOONS;* has done series development work for Nelvana, Studio East.

NICHOLLS, Andrew

ACTRA, WGAw. 10120 Dempsey Ave., Mission Hills, CA, USA, 91345. (818)891-0846.
Types of Production & Categories: TV Film-Wr; TV Video-Wr.
Genres: Comedy-TV; Variety-TV; Children's-TV.
Biography: Born 1957, England; Canadian citizen. Professional partner, Darrell Vickers with whom he has written for radio, print; 100's of cartoons , 'Frank & Ernest', 'Ben Wicks'; industrials; special musical and personal appearance material (Alan Thicke, Mickey Rooney); 20 plays; gags for comedians: Joan Rivers, Rodney Dangerfield etc..
Selective Filmography: *'CHECK IT OUT!'* (Co-Wr-7 eps), (22 eps), TV, 86/85, CDN/USA, Co-Story Ed; *'DANGER BAY'* (3 eps), TV, 85, CDN/USA, Co-Wr; *GEORGE CARLIN '2-C',* TV, 85, USA, Co-Wr; *'LOVE BOAT'* (1 eps), TV, 85, USA, Co-Wr; *'BIZARRE',* TV, 85, CDN/USA, Contr Wr; *'THICKE OF THE NIGHT'* (85 eps), TV, 84/83, CDN, Contr Wr; *'FAST COMPANY'* (22 eps), TV, 83, CDN, Co-Wr; *'EVENING AT THE IMPROV'* (3 eps), TV, 82, USA, Contr Wr; *'FLAPPERS'* (3 eps), TV, 81, CDN, Co-Wr.

NICOL, Eric

ACTRA. 3993 W. 36th Ave., Vancouver, BC, CAN, V6N 2S7. (604)261-8070.
Types of Production & Categories: TV Film-Wr; TV Video-Wr.
Genres: Drama-TV; Comedy-TV; Variety-TV; Documentary-TV.
Biography: Born 1919, Kingston, Ontario. B.A., University of British Columbia, 41; 3 years service, RCAF (ground crew); M.A., U.B.C., 48; attended la Sorbonne, 1 year. Wrote radio, TV comedy series for BBC, London; first book published, 48. Returned to Vancouver, 51, columnist, 'The Province'; freelance TV, radio writer. Has published 6 stage plays; 26 books; has won the Leacock Medal for Humor 3 times, for 'The Roving I', 'Shall We Join the Ladies' and ' Girdle Me a Globe'.
Selective Filmography: *MA!,* TV, 84, CDN, Wr.

NIELSEN, Richard - see PRODUCERS

NIMCHUK, Michael John

ACTRA. 554 Merton St., Toronto, Ont, CAN, M4S 1B3. (416)488-3048. Deedee Langford, Ron Francis Agency, 12 Birch St., Toronto, Ont, CAN, M4V 1C8. (416) 968-6808.
Types of Production & Categories: TV Film-Wr.
Genres: Drama-TV; Comedy-TV; Action-TV.
Biography: Born 1934; Canadian citizen. B.A., University of Toronto. Playwright, poet, short story writer; story editor, CBC TV.
Selective Filmography: *THE DAY MY GRANDAD DIED,* TV, 79, CDN, Wr; *THE WEDDING GIFT,* TV, 76, CDN, Wr; *MORTIMER GRIFFIN,* TV, 75, CDN, T'play; *MacIVOR'S SALVATION,* TV, 74, CDN, Wr.

NOEL, Jean-Guy - voir REALISATEURS

NORMAN, Glenn

ACTRA. R.R. #1, Fergus, Ont, , N1M 2W3. (519)843-5187. Ralph Zimmerman, Great North Artists Mgmt., 345 Adelaide St.W., #500, Toronto, Ont, CAN, M5V 1R5. (416)593-2587.
Types of Production & Categories: TV Film-Wr.
Genres: Drama-TV; Comedy-TV; Action-TV; News-TV.
Biography: Born 1948, London, England; Canadian citizen. Educated at De LaSalle College, Toronto. Worked as film editor; freelance aviation writer for int'l magazines; licenced private pilot with 2000 hours experience; amateur astrologer for 25 years. Turned to screenwriting, 81.
Selective Filmography: *THE CAMPBELLS'* (3 eps), TV, 85, CDN/USA/GB, Wr; *FLIER BEWARE,* 'W 5', TV, 85, CDN, Res; *NOTHING BY CHANCE,* Th, 73, USA, Act.

NURSALL, Tom

ACTRA. 100 Oriole Pkwy., #303, Toronto, Ont, CAN, M5P 2G8. (416)487-4603.
Types of Production & Categories: TV Film-Wr; TV Video-Wr.
Genres: Drama-TV; Comedy-TV; Action-TV.
Biography: Born 1957, Edinburgh, Scotland. B.A., English, University of Western Ontario.
Selective Filmography: *THE BOTTS'* (6 eps), TV, 86, CDN/USA/F, Co-Wr; *WHAT THE WORLD'S BEEN WAITING FOR,* TV, 86, CDN, Wr/Act/Co-Prod; *JUST FOR LAUGHS'* (81 eps), TV, 85, CDN, Co-Wr; *'LAUGHING MATTERS'* (3 eps), TV, 85, CDN, Co-Wr.

OBOMSAWIN, Alanis - see DIRECTORS

O'DWYER, Michael J.

CFTA. 4315 Bacchus Cres., Mississauga, Ont, CAN, L4W 2Y2. (416)624-5009. M.J. O'Dwyer Associates Ltd., 884 Queen St.W., Toronto, Ont, CAN, M6J 1G3. (416)536-4991.
Types of Production & Categories: Th Film-Wr; Th Short-Wr; TV Film-Wr; TV Video-Wr.
Genres: Documentary-Th&TV; Educational-Th&TV; Sports-TV.
Biography: Born 1946, Walkerton, Ontario. Diplomas in English, Creative Writing, Public Relations, Business Administration. Background: newspaper, radio, magazine journalist; managing editor, senior communications practitioner. Films he has written have won int'l awards; has also won awards for print writing/editing.
Selective Filmography: *SCHENLEY AWARDS SHOW,* TV, 85, CDN, Wr; *AUDI EXPERIENCE/THE NEW VOYAGEUR/RABBIT RALLYE,* In, 84/83, CDN, Wr; *WHEELS IN MOTION,* TV, 83, CDN, Wr; *NATURAL JOURNEY,* ED, 82, CDN, Wr; *ON TARGET,* ED, 81, CDN, Wr; *GOING FOR GOLD,* ED, 80, CDN, Wr; *SHOTPOINT 260,* In, 79, CDN, Wr; *BATTLEGROUND,* Th, 78, CDN, Wr; *GILLES,* TV, 77, CDN, Wr; *SPEED,* Th, 77, CDN, Wr; *THE MYTHMAKERS,* Th, 76, CDN, Wr.

ORR, James

WGAw. James Orr Productions Inc, 9370 Flicker Way, Los Angeles, CA, USA, 90069. Jim Crabbe, William Morris Agency, 151 El Camino Drive, Beverly Hills, CA, USA, 90212. (213)859-4156.
Types of Production & Categories: Th Film-Wr/Dir.
Genres: Drama-Th.
Biography: Born 1953, Noranda, Quebec; landed U.S. immigrant. B.F.A., Film Production, York University; Directing Fellow, American Film Institute.

(cont/suite)

Selective Filmography: *TOUGH GUYS,* Th, 86, USA, Co-Wr; *BREAKING ALL THE RULES,* Th, 84, CDN, Dir.

ORZARI, Lorenzo

8114 Mirepoix, Montreal, Que, CAN, H1R 2N6. (514)321-0802.
Types of Production & Categories: Th Film-Wr; TV Video-Wr/Dir.
Genres: Drama-Th&TV; Comedy-Th&TV; Action-Th&TV; Horror-Th&TV.
Biography: Born 1955, Rotherham, England; Canadian citizen. Languages: English, French, Italian, some German. Still photographer; co-created comic strips; has written songs, commercials, cable TV scripts and book, 'The Fading Flesh & Other Stories'. Studied directing at McGill University.
Selective Filmography: *UNKNOWN DIMENSIONS* (pilot), TV, 86, CDN, Wr/Dir; *LOVE ME AND DIE,* Th, 85, CDN, Wr; *MONTREAL - JOIE DE VIVRE,* Th, 82, CDN, Wr.

OSBORNE, Jim

ACTRA. 186 Browning Ave., Toronto, Ont, CAN, M4K 1W5. (416)466-1977.
Types of Production & Categories: Th Film-Wr; TV Film-Wr.
Genres: Drama-Th; Horror-TV; Documentary-TV; Educational-TV.
Biography: Born 1943, Foleyet, Ontario. B.A., University of Ottawa, 64; M.A., Theatre Criticism, U. of Alberta, 73. Has had several stage plays produced; story editor, CBC TV drama, 73-76; script consultant on numerous TV productions, 82-86.
Selective Filmography: *YOU WOULDN'T UNDERSTAND,* 'HOOKED ON READING', TV, 85, CDN, Wr; *THE WAR BOY* (POINT OF ESCAPE), Th, 84, CDN, Scr; *STEVIE AND THE DINOSAURS,* ED, 84, CDN, Wr; *A FRONTIER, A HOMELAND/TUKTOYAKTUK: A PIECE OF THE ACTION,* 'LIKE NO OTHER PLACE', ED, 79, CDN, Wr; *SUMMER'S CHILDREN,* Th, 79, CDN, Wr; *WINNIPEG: ALIVE OR DEAD?/WHERE HAVE ALL THE COWBOYS GONE,* 'LIKE NO OTHER PLACE', ED, 78, CDN, Wr; *WITHOUT AN INDUSTRY, WITHOUT A HIGHWAY,* 'LIKE NO OTHER PLACE', ED, 78, CDN, Wr; *50 CENTS OF EVERY DOLLAR/THE PRICE OF POWER,* 'LIKE NO OTHER PLACE', ED, 78, CDN, Wr; *THE COLONIST,* 'IN THEIR SHOES', ED, 78, CDN, Wr; *EYE OF THE BEHOLDER,* TV, 78, CDN, Wr.

OWEN, Don - see DIRECTORS

PALUCK, Richard

ACTRA. Blackbird Productions Ltd., 993 Gale Dr., Tsawwassen, BC, CAN, V4M 2P7. (604)943-6522.
Types of Production & Categories: Th Film-Wr.
Genres: Drama-Th; Comedy-Th.
Biography: Born 1939, Hamilton, Ontario. Extensive background in advertising as writer/creative director; experience as music director/producer for commercials, documentaries.
Selective Filmography: *MELANIE,* Th, 82, CDN, Co-Scr; *A GIFT OF WATER* (PLEASE HELP ME), Th, 75, CDN, Scr/Story.

PARIS, Jacques

SARDEC. 105 Querbes, #14, Outremont, Qué, CAN, H2V 3V8. (514)270-4600.
Types de production et Catégories: l métrage-Sc; c métrage-Sc; TV film-Sc; TV vidéo-Sc.
Types d'oeuvres: Drame-C; Comédie-C&TV; Documentaire-C.
Curriculum vitae: Né en 1929. Cours classique, Université d'Ottawa, spécialisation Economie.; cours de scénarisation, Université Temple et UCLA; aussi professeur de scénarisation à l'UQAM.
(cont/suite)

Filmographie sélective: *ANNAPURNA, C,* 85, CDN, Sc; *LA MER ET SES PRINCES, C,* 84, CDN, Sc; *MARIO, C,* 84, CDN, Sc; *LUCIEN BROUILLARD, C,* 83, CDN, Sc.

PATON, Chris - see DIRECTORS

PAYETTE, Lise

SARDEC, SACD, UDA. 58 Mont Victoria, Hudson Heights, Qué, CAN, J0P 1V0. (514)458-7181.
Types de production et Catégories: TV film-Sc; TV vidéo-Sc.
Types d'oeuvres: Drame-TV.
Curriculum vitae: Née en 1931, Montréal, Québec. Animatrice, radio, TV, *APPELEZ-MOI LISE,* 61-76. Ministre au gouvernement du Québec 76-81; Ministère des Consommateurs, Coopératives et Institutions financières, 76-79; Ministre responsable du Conseil du Statut de la Femme, 76-81. Auteur, scénarios et dialogues. *LA BONNE AVENTURE* remporte le Prix de l'Association des Téléspectateurs.
Filmographie sélective: *'LA BONNE AVENTURE'* (143 eps), TV, 86-82, CDN, Sc/ Dial; *'DES DAMES DE COEUR'* (26 eps), TV, 86, CDN, Sc/Dial; *'BONJOUR DOCTEUR'* (22 eps), TV, 86, CDN, Aut cons; *'L'OR ET LE PAPIER'* (30 eps), TV, 86, CDN/F, Sc/Dial; *LA DEMESURE* (SPECIAL GINETTE RENO), TV, 85, CDN, Aut.

PEARSON, Barry - see PRODUCERS

PEARSON, Peter - see DIRECTORS

PEDERSON, Larry V.

Dew Line Filmworks, P.O. Box 2716, Beverly Hills, CA, USA, 90213-2716. (213) 933-1808.
Types of Production & Categories: Th Short-Dir/Wr/Ed.
Genres: Drama-Th.
Biography: Born 1957, Medicine Hat, Alberta. B.A., Philosophy, University of Alberta; B.A., Film & TV Production, U. of Southern California. Canadian citizen; resident alien, USA. Film censor, Alberta government, 78-80: screened 1100 features annually.
Selective Filmography: *JUXTAPOSITION,* Th, 82, USA, Wr/Dir/Ed.

PELLETIER, Maryse

SARDEC, UDA. 4279 Garnier, Montréal, Qué, CAN, H2J 3R7. (514)526-8447.
Types de production et Catégories: TV film-Sc; TV vidéo-Sc.
Types d'oeuvres: Comédie TV.
Curriculum vitae: Née en 1946, Québec; bilingue. Etudes en Lettres à l'Université Laval; Conservatoire d'Art Dramatique. Dramaturge; adapte aussi ses pièces pour la télévision.
Filmographie sélective: *'TRABOULIDON'* (Aut-20 eps), (40 eps), TV, 86-83, CDN, Scrip éd; *DU POIL AUX PATTES COMME LES CWAC'S,* TV, 85, CDN, Adapt.

PERRON, Clément

SARDEC. Cinéscript Inc., 40 Anselme Lavigne, Dollard-Des-Ormeaux, Qué, CAN, H9A 1N6. (514)684-6037.
Types de production et Catégories: l métrage-Sc/Réal; c métrage-Sc/Réal.
Types d'oeuvres: Drame-C&TV; Documentaire-C&TV.
Curriculum vitae: Né en 1929 dans la Beauce, Québec. Licencié ès Lettres, Université Laval; études en linguistique et cinéma, Académie de Poitière et Institut de Filmologie, Sorbonne, Paris, 55-57. A l'emploi de l'ONF pendant 28 ans comme scénariste, réalisateur, producteur et directeur des programmes français; scénariste

(cont/suite)

pigiste depuis 86. Gagnant de nombreux prix: festivals de Toronto, Chicago, Venise, etc..
Filmographie sélective: *ANN McNEIL,* C, 86, USA, Sc; *PARTIS POUR LA GLOIRE,* C, 75, CDN, Sc/Réal; *CAROLINE,* C, 74, CDN, Co réal; *TAUREAU,* C, 72, CDN, Sc/Réal; *MON ONCLE ANTOINE,* C, 71, CDN, Sc (**CFA**); *JOUR APRES JOUR* (DAY AFTER DAY), C, 63, CDN, Réal.

PINSENT, Gordon - see DIRECTORS

PITTMAN, Bruce - see DIRECTORS

POIRIER, Anne Claire - voir REALISATEURS

POLLACK, Sharon

ACTRA. 319 Manora Dr. N.E., Calgary, Alta, CAN, T2A 4R2. (403)235-1945.
Types of Production & Categories: TV Film-Wr.
Genres: Drama-TV; Documentary-TV.
Biography: Born 1936, Fredericton, New Brunswick. Honorary Doctorate, University of New Brunswick. Writer, stage plays and radio; won the Governor General's Literary Award, drama, for 'Blood Relations'; Actra Award for 'Sweet Land of Liberty' (radio); Chalmer's Award for 'Doc'; *THE PERSON'S CASE* won a Golden Sheaf, Yorkton.
Selective Filmography: *WALSH,* TV, 86, CDN, Wr; *THE KOMOGATA MARU INCIDENT,* TV, 84, CDN, Wr; *THE PERSON'S CASE,* TV, 80, CDN, Wr.

POOL, Léa - voir REALISATEURS

PRICE, Roger - see PRODUCERS

PURDY, Jim

ACTRA. 170 Courcelette Rd., Scarborough, Ont, CAN, M1N 2T2. (416)690-9331.
Types of Production & Categories: TV Film-Wr/Dir; TV Video-Wr/Dir.
Genres: Drama-TV; Documentary-TV; Educational-TV; Children's-TV.
Biography: Born 1949, Toronto, Ontario. Studied English Literature, University of Toronto, 67-69; Film & Theatre Studies, York University, 69-72. Actor, journalist, photographer, painter before co-authoring the book, 'The Hollywood Social Problem Film', published in U.S., 80. Now a freelance writer/director.
Selective Filmography: *WHERE'S PETE?/LEFT OUT,* 'HOME MOVIES', TV, 86/85, CDN, Dir/Wr; *THE DREAM AND THE TRIUMPH,* 'BELL CANADA PLAYHOUSE', TV, 85, CDN, T'play; *'HOME FIRES'* (Co-Creator/Co-Wr-8 eps), (19 eps), TV, 83-80, CDN, Wr; *MORNING MAN,* In, 83, CDN, Wr/Dir; *THE DISEASE IS ARTHRITIS,* In, 82, CDN, Wr; *PLENTY ROOM IN PAKISTAN,* ED, 79, CDN, Wr/Dir.

RASKY, Harry - see DIRECTORS

RAYMOND, Marie-Josée - voir PRODUCTEURS

REDICAN, Dan

ACTRA. 3 Charles St.W., #204, Toronto, Ont, CAN. (416)923-9844.
Types of Production & Categories: TV Film-Wr; TV Video-Wr.
Genres: Comedy-TV; Variety-TV.
Biography: Born 1956, Etobicoke, Ontario. Has worked as standup and sketch comic, puppeteer. Co-writer, 'Frantic Times', which won second prize, radio variety, American Major Armstrong Awards.
Selective Filmography: *'4 ON THE FLOOR'* (13 eps), TV, 85, CDN, Co-Wr/Act.

RENAUD, Bernadette

CAPAC, SARDEC. 6208 Marie-Victorin, C.P.1103, Contrecoeur, Qué, CAN, J0L 1C0. (514)587-5547.
Types de production et Catégories: 1 métrage-Sc; TV film-Sc.

(cont/suite)

Types d'oeuvres: Enfants-C&TV.
Curriculum vitae: Née en 1945, Ascot Corner, Québec. Brevet d'enseignement; 3 ans d'enseignement; 4 ans de secrétariat. Ecrivaine professionnelle pour jeunes depuis 76; 21 albums; 8 livres dont 2 en anglais, 2 en braille. A gagné 2 prix pour son livre 'Emilie la baignoire à pattes'. Conférences auprès de plus de 80,000 jeunes à travers tout le Canada.
Filmographie sélective: *BACH ET BOTTINE,* C, 86, CDN, Sc; *'MICHOU ET PILO'* (8 eps), TV, 85/84, CDN, Sc; *'KLIMBO'* (5 eps), TV, 84-82, CDN, Sc.

RIIS, Sharon

ACTRA. Box 1133, Lac La Biche, Alta, CAN, T0A 2L0. (403)623-4888. Nancy Colbert, The Colbert Agency, 303 Davenport Rd., Toronto, Ont, CAN, M5R 1K5. (416)964-3302.
Types of Production & Categories: Th Film-Wr; TV Film-Wr.
Genres: Drama-Th&TV.
Biography: Born 1947, High River, Alberta. Bachelor of Arts, History, Simon Fraser University, 69. AMPIA award for *A CHANGE OF HEART.*
Selective Filmography: *THE WAKE,* 'DAUGHTERS OF THE COUNTRY', TV, 86, CDN, Wr; *LOYALTIES,* Th, 85, CDN/GB, Scr/Co-Story; *A CHANGE OF HEART,* 'FOR THE RECORD', TV, 83, CDN, Wr; *LATITUDE 55,* Th, 80, CDN, Co-Wr.

RINFRET, Louise

ACTRA, UDA. 4458 De Lorimier, Montréal, Qué, CAN, H2H 2B2. (514)276-7239.
Types de production et Catégories: 1 métrage-Sc/Com; TV film-Com.
Types d'oeuvres: Drame-C&TV.
Curriculum vitae: Née en 1950, Montréal, Québec; bilingue. Comédienne au théâtre, au cinéma et à la télévision. A écrit le roman 'La Dame en Couleurs' d'après le scénario du même nom.
Filmographie sélective: *LE COEUR DECOUVERT,* TV, 86, CDN, Com; *LA DAME EN COULEURS* (OUR LADY OF THE PAINTS), C, 84, CDN, Co sc; *L'OBJET,* C, 83, CDN, Com; *'SESAME STREET'* (pl seg), TV, 79, USA, Com; *NEST OF SHADOWS,* TV, 76, CDN, Com; *'LA PETITE PATRIE;'* (70 eps), TV, 74/73, CDN, Com; *ON N'ENGRAISSE PAS LES COCHONS A L'EAU CLAIRE,* C, 73, CDN, Com; *THE PYX,* C, 73, CDN, Com.

ROBERTSON, George

ACTRA. 158 Glen Rd., Toronto, Ont, CAN, M4W 2W6. (416)928-0073.
Types of Production & Categories: Th Film-Wr; TV Film-Wr; TV Video-Wr.
Genres: Drama-Th&TV; Documentary-Th&TV, Children's TV.
Biography: Born 1922, Regina, Saskatchewan. RCAF, 42-44. Education: Wesley University College, Winnipeg, 44-45. Married, 3 children. Announcer, CJRM, Regina, 39-40; announcer, actor, CBC, Winnipeg, 40-42, 44-45; producer, CBC Int'l Service, 45-46; freelance writer, broadcaster, Montreal, 46-49, Toronto since 49; 1st radio drama, 43; 1st TV drama, 52; writing includes commentary and criticism, CBC's 'Critically Speaking' and 'Canadian Art'; narrator, NFB films; co-founder, Jupiter Theatre, 51; novel, 'Face-Off', 71.
Selective Filmography: *'BACKSTRETCH'* (1 eps), TV, 85, CDN, Wr; *'JUDGE'* (4 eps), TV, 84/83, CDN, Wr; *'THE LAW AND YOU'* (26 eps), TV, 82/81, CDN, Wr/Assoc Prod; *'SNELGROVE SNAIL'* (65 eps), TV, 80-78, CDN, Co-Wr/Assoc Prod; *MATERIALS HANDLING,* In, 78, CDN, Wr; *'THE WINNERS'* (Wr-2 eps), (10 eps), TV, 77, CDN, Story Ed/Co-Creator; *'SIDESTREET'* (2 eps), TV, 76, CDN, Wr; *'HOUSE OF PRIDE'* (52 eps), TV, 75/74, CDN, Head Wr/Story Ed; *ON SITE SAFETY,* In, 74, CDN, Wr; *'THE COLLABORATORS'* (1 eps), TV, 74, CDN, Wr; *FACE-OFF,* Th, 71, CDN, Scr; *'QUENTIN DURGENS, M.P.'*

(cont/suite)

(26 eps), TV, 70-67, CDN, Creator/Wr; *THE ROAD TO CHALDAEA*, TV, 68, CDN, Wr; *MR.MEMBER OF PARLIAMENT*, 'THE SERIAL', TV, 66, CDN, Wr; *'MOMENT OF TRUTH'* (52 eps), TV, 65, CDN, Wr; *'ROOM TO LET'* (50 eps), TV, 65/64, CDN, Wr; *POINT OF IMPACT*, 'SHOW OF THE WEEK', TV, 65, CDN, Wr; *'SCARLETT HILL'* (10 eps), TV, 64, CDN, Wr.

ROGERS, Al

WGAw. 4304 Vantage Ave., Studio City, CA, USA, 91604. (818)762-9161. Al Rogers Productions, 3349 Cahuenga Blvd., Hollywood, CA, USA, 90068. (213)874-3511. Rowland Perkins, CAA, 1888 Century Pk.E., Ste. 1400, Los Angeles, CA, USA, 90067. (213)277-4545.
Types of Production & Categories: TV Film-Wr/Prod; TV Video-Wr/Prod.
Genres: Comedy-TV; Variety-TV; Action-TV; Children's-Th&TV.
Biography: Born 1936, North Sydney, Nova Scotia; Canadian citizen.
Selective Filmography: *'THE COMEDY FACTORY'* (8 eps), TV, 85, USA, Prod/Wr; *AFTER SCHOOL SPECIAL*, TV, 84, USA, Prod/Wr; *'STOCKARD CHANNING SHOW'* (JUST FRIENDS), (26 eps), TV, 83, USA, Prod/Co-Wr; *SUPERSTUNT*, TV, 82, USA, Prod/Wr; *'JOHN DENVER SPECIAL'* (6 eps), TV, 82-80, USA, Prod/Wr **(EMMY)**; *FRANK SINATRA SPECIAL*, TV, 80, USA, Wr; *ADVENTURES OF A YOUNG MAGICIAN IN CHINA*, TV, 80, USA, Prod/Wr; *'FATHER O'FATHER'* (2 eps), TV, 79, USA, Prod/Wr.

ROGERS, Jonathan - see PRODUCERS

ROTHBERG, David

132 Crawford St., Toronto, Ont, CAN, M6J 2V4. (416)927-0930.
Types of Production & Categories: Th Film-Wr; Th Short-Act; TV Film-Wr.
Genres: Drama-Th; Documentary-Th&TV.
Biography: Born 1950, Montreal, Quebec. Worked at City TV, CBC; performed on the stage at W.A.C.. *MY FRIEND VINCE* won Best Picture, University of Knoxville Film Festival and was shown at Museum of Modern Art.
Selective Filmography: *MISDEAL* (BEST REVENGE), Th, 80, CDN, Story/Co-Scr; *MY FRIEND VINCE*, Th, 75, CDN, Wr/Prod/Dir.

ROWE, Peter - see DIRECTORS

RUBBO, Michael

ACTRA. 719 de l'Epee, Montreal, Que, CAN, H2V 3V1. (514)274-3148.
Types of Production & Categories: Th Film-Wr/Dir; TV Film-Wr/Dir.
Genres: Documentary-Th&TV; Children's-Th.
Biography: Born 1938, Melbourne, Australia. Educated Sydney University, B.A. in Anthropology; M.A., Stanford University. Painter, photographer, filmmaker and educator; has taught film at Harvard and Australian Film & TV School. Has won over 30 awards for documentary films including Blue Ribbons, American Film Fest., the Flaherty Award, Atlanta, Columbus, Chicago, Sydney, Mannheim, Melbourne film festivals.
Selective Filmography: *THE PEANUT BUTTER SOLUTION* (LA SOLUTION BEURRE DE PINOTTES), Th, 85, CDN, Dir/Wr; *ONCE IN AUGUST*, TV, 84, CDN, Dir/Wr/Ed; *DAISY: THE STORY OF A FACELIFT*, Th, 82, CDN, Dir/Wr/Ed; *SOLZHENITSYN'S CHILDREN ARE MAKING A LOT OF NOISE IN PARIS*, TV, 79, CDN, Dir/Wr/Ed; *WAITING FOR FIDEL*, TV, 73, CDN, Dir/Wr; *WET EARTH AND WARM PEOPLE*, TV, 72, CDN, Dir/Wr/Ed; *SAD SONG OF YELLOW SKIN*, TV, 70, CDN, Dir/Wr/Ed.

RUSSELL, Paul

ACTRA. 98 Golfview, Toronto, Ont, CAN, M4E 2K4. (416)534-8115.
Types of Production & Categories: TV Film-Wr/Prod; TV Video-Wr/Prod.
Genres: Documentary-TV; Educational-TV; Children's-TV.

(cont/suite)

Biography: Born 1945, Toronto, Ontario. B.A., M.A., University of Toronto. Following art studies in England, held administrative and curatorial positions, Hart House, Art Gallery of Ontario. Critic, journalist: 'Maclean's', 'Toronto Life', 'Toronto Star', 'Time'; has published several books on Canada including 'Queen on Moose Handbook', 85. National editor and adjudicator, *REACH FOR THE TOP*, 82-83.

Selective Filmography: *'REACH FOR THE TOP'* (26 eps), TV, 85, CDN, Wr/ Assoc Prod; *'MEDICAL MALPRACTICE II'* (4 eps), In, 83/82, CDN/USA, Wr/ Dir; *'PRIMARY NURSING'* (12 eps), In, 83/82, CDN, Wr/Dir; *STRESS* (10 films), In, 81, CDN/USA, Prod/Dir; *FITNESS AND LIFESTYLE* (6 films), In, 81, CDN/USA, Prod/Dir; *'MEDICAL MALPRACTICE'* (6 eps), In, 80, CDN, Dir/Wr; *THE MAYA, CHILDREN OF TIME*, TV, 80, CDN/MEX, Wr/Dir; *'DENTISTRY'* (6 eps), In, 79, CDN, Wr/Prod; *'TRIVIA'* (52 eps), TV, 77, CDN, Assoc Prod; *'LORNE GREENE'S LAST OF THE WILD'* (16 eps), TV, 76, CDN/ USA, Wr; *UNTAMED FRONTIER'* (13 eps), TV, 76, CDN, Wr; *'UNTAMED WORLD'* (78 eps), TV, 76-74, CDN/USA, Prod/Wr; *'BEHIND THE SCENES'* (26 eps), TV, 75, CDN, Story Ed; *ELEMENTS OF THE UNKNOWN: THE SEA*, TV, 74, CDN, Wr; *'IMAGES OF CANADA'* (6 eps), TV, 74-72, CDN, Wr/Story Ed; *'LANDMARKS'* (36 eps), TV, 73, CDN, Wr/Dir.

RYLSKI, Nika

ACTRA. 155 Neville Park Blvd., Toronto, Ont, CAN, M4E 3P7. (416)699-4209. Ron Francis Theatrical Mgmt., 12 Birch Ave., Ste. 205, Toronto, Ont, CAN, M4J 3K4. (416)968-6806.
Types of Production & Categories: Th Film-Wr; Th Short-Wr; TV Film-Wr; TV Video-Wr.
Genres: Drama-Th&TV; Comedy-TV; Documentary-TV; Children's-TV.
Biography: Born Buenos Aires, Argentina; Canadian citizen. Languages: English, French, Spanish, Polish. Honours B.A., Political Science, Carleton University. Has written more than 25 radio, TV and film scripts. Best TV Drama Award, Yorkton, for *HONOR THY FATHER*, 77. Has also written stage plays; winner, Eric Harvie Award for Best New Canadian Musical, 82.
Selective Filmography: *MAN OF IRON*, TV, 83, CDN, Wr; *'NUGGETS'* (pilot), (3 eps), TV, 80, CDN, Wr; *STRANGERS*, Th, 77, CDN, Wr; *HONOR THY FATHER*, TV, 76, CDN, Wr; *SUMMERS' MOURNINGS*, TV, 75, CDN, T'play; *THANKS FOR THE RIDE*, TV, 75, CDN, T'play; *LAST OF THE FOUR-LETTER WORDS*, TV, 74, CDN, Wr; *WHEN THE BOUGH BREAKS*, TV, 70, CDN, Wr; *THE FASTEST WORDSLINGER IN THE EAST*, TV, 69, CDN, Wr.

SABOURIN, Marcel

ACTRA, SARDEC, UDA. 224 Boul. Richelieu, Beloeil, Qué, CAN, J3G 4P1. (514)467-3009.
Types de production et Catégories: 1 métrage-Sc/Com; TV film-Com; TV vidéo-Sc/Com.
Types d'oeuvres: Drame-C&TV; Comédie-C&TV; Enfants-C&TV; Animation-C&TV.
Curriculum vitae: Né en 1935, Montréal, Québec. Etudes en théâtre, Collège Ste-Marie; Théâtre du Nouveau Monde et avec Bill Greaves; à Paris avec Jacques Lecoq. A fait beaucoup de théâtre comme comédien et comme auteur; Prix Chalmers pour 'Pleurer Pour Rire'; professeur d'improvisation pendant 7 ans, Ecole Nationale de Théâtre du Canada; parolier d'une trentaine de chansons de Robert Charlebois, Louise Forestier et autres. *J.A. MARTIN PHOTOGRAPHE* gagne 7 prix aux Palmarès du film canadien dont Meilleur Film.
Filmographie sélective: *L'AMOUR AVEC UN GRAND A*, TV, 85, CDN, Com; *COMMENT ACHETER SON PATRON* (mini-serie), TV, 85, CDN, Com; *LAURIER* (mini-serie), TV, 85, CDN, Com; *LA CHOSE LA PLUS DOUCE DU*

(cont/suite)

MONDE, TV, 84, CDN, Com; 'SOS J'ECOUTE' (25 eps), TV, 84, CDN, Com; *DOUX AVEUX,* C, 83, CDN, Com; *'LA BONNE AVENTURE'* (15 eps), TV, 83, CDN, Com; *CORDELIA,* C, 79, CDN, Co sc/Com; *'RIEL'* (4 eps), TV, 78, CDN, Com; *'DUPLESSIS'* (5 eps), TV, 77, CDN, Com; *MOUNTIE, TV,* 77, CDN, Com; *J.A. MARTIN, PHOTOGRAPHE,* C, 76, CDN, Co sc/Com; *TI-MINE, BERNIE PIS LA GANG,* C, 76, CDN, Com; *LE VIEUX PAYS OU RIMBAUD EST MORT,* C, 76, CDN/F, Com; *LES TROUBLES DE JOHNNY,* C, 74, CDN, Co sc/ Com; *DES ARMES ET LES HOMMES,* C, 73, CDN, Com (CFA); *LA MAUDITE GALETTE,* C, 72, CDN, Com; *LE TEMPS D'UNE CHASSE,* C, 72, CDN, Com; *LES CUISINES,* TV, 71, CDN, Sc/Com; *ELIZA'S HOROSCOPE,* TV, 71, CDN, Com; *LE MARTIEN DE NOEL,* C, 71, CDN, Com; *A SOIR ON FAIT PEUR AU MONDE,* C, 71, CDN, Aut comp; *LES SMATTES,* C, 71, CDN, Com; *DEUX FEMMES EN OR,* C, 70, CDN, Com; *ON EST LOIN DU SOLEIL,* C, 70, CDN, Com; *LA CHAMBRE BLANCHE,* C, 69, CDN, Com; *'LES CROQUIGNOLES'* (75 eps), TV, 67-63, CND, Sc/Com; *'LA RIBOULDINGUE'* (75 eps), TV, 67, CDN, Sc/Com; *HENRY V,* TV, 67, CDN, Com; *IL NE FAUT PAS MOURIR POUR CA,* C, 66, CDN, Co sc/Com.

SALEM, Rob

ACTRA. 59 Beech Ave., Toronto, Ont, CAN, M4E 3H3. (416)699-0393. Toronto Star, 1 Yonge St., Toronto, Ont, CAN, M5E 1E6. (416)869-4487. The Revue, 26 Soho St., 4th Fl., Toronto, Ont, CAN, M5T 1Z7. (416)979-9714.
Types of Production & Categories: TV Video-Wr.
Genres: Comedy-TV; Variety-TV.
Biography: Born 1958, Toronto, Ontario. Stand-up comic, Second City workshops, SCTV bits, 76-81. Started at 'Toronto Star', 77, writing for entertainment department, movie reviews, feature interviews, video columnist, co-editor 'What's On' section. Writer/host, *CAPTAIN VIDEO SHOW* (pilot, 85); reporter/writing consultant for CBC's *THE REVUE,* 86.

SALTSMAN, Terry

ACTRA. 59 Anderson Ave., Toronto, Ont, CAN, M5P 1H6. (416)484-6127.
Types of Production & Categories: TV Video-Wr.
Genres: Comedy-TV; Variety-TV.
Biography: Born 1951, Toronto, Ontario. B.A., English, York University, 72; LL.B., Osgoode Hall Law School, 75. Has written humour column for 'Ontario Lawyers Weekly'; worked as advertising copy writer, legal editor.
Selective Filmography: *'HANGIN'IN'* (20 eps), TV, 86-84, CDN, Wr; *'THRILL OF A LIFETIME'* (20 eps), TV, 84, CDN/USA, Story Ed.

SALTZMAN, Deepa - see DIRECTORS

SALUTIN, Rick

ACTRA. 792 Palmerston Ave., Toronto, Ont, CAN, M6G 2R7.
Types of Production & Categories: TV Film-Wr; TV Video-Wr.
Genres: Drama-TV.
Biography: Born 1942, Toronto, Ontario. B.A., Brandeis University; M.A., Columbia University. Chalmers Award (Theatre) for *LES CANADIENS;* former chairman, Guild of Canadian Playwrights.
Selective Filmography: *GRIERSON AND GOUZENKO,* 'SOME HONOURABLE GENTLEMEN', TV, 85, CDN, Wr; *MARIA,* 'HERE TO STAY', TV, 75, CDN, Wr; *1837,* 'FESTIVAL', TV, 74, CDN, Wr.

SALVERSON, George

ACTRA. Matie Molinaro, 44 Douglas Crescent, Toronto, Ont, CAN, M4W 2E7. (416)921-4443.
Types of Production & Categories: Th Film-Wr; Th Short-Wr; TV Film-Wr; TV Video-Wr.

(cont/suite)

Genres: Drama-Th&TV; Comedy-Th&TV; Musical-Th&TV; Documentary-Th&TV.
Biography: Born 1916, St. Catherines, Ontario. Former radio producer turned freelance writer, television, film, radio; 30 years scripting for CBC, NFB and other TV, film, video, stage producers; anchor writer in various film series for TV; contributor to numerous other series; development of musical comedy for TV and adapting it to stage; 4 years, story editor, CBC drama. Has written a thousand plays for radio, TV; several thousand documentaries of various kinds. Has won numerous awards for dramas and documentaries.

SAMUELS, Arthur

ACTRA, WGAw. 4866 Cote des Neiges, #908, Montreal, Que, CAN, H3V 1H1. (514)738-4000.
Types of Production & Categories: Th Film-Wr; TV Film-Wr; TV Video-Wr.
Genres: Drama-Th&TV; Comedy-Th&TV; Documentary-Th&TV; Educational-TV.
Biography: Born 1923, Montreal, Quebec; bilingual. Former actor, radio announcer, V/O narrator; full-time professional writer since 65. Winner, Best Canadian Play Award, Dominion Drama Festival, 68; Writes in English only, but can translate from French; has worked as dialogue coach, script doctor; taught scriptwriting, Concordia University, 79-86; author, 'Words, Sounds and Images'.
Selective Filmography: *'SNOW JOB'* (3 eps), TV, 84/83, CDN, Wr; *BLACK MIRROR,* Th, 80, CDN/F, Scr; *BUSH PILOT,* Th, 78, CDN, Wr; *'SIDESTREET'* (1 eps), TV, 77, CDN, Wr; *ANGUS* (pilot), TV, 76, CDN, Wr; *'KING OF KENSINGTON'* (2 eps), TV, 76-74, CDN, Wr; *'EXCUSE MY FRENCH'* (7 eps), TV, 75/74, CDN, Wr; *OUR SON THE STRANGER,* TV, 73, CDN, Wr; *THE REMARKABLE UPBRINGING OF J.P.McGILECUDDY/ONE MORE FOR THE ROAD,* 'SHOESTRING THEATRE', TV, 73/72, CDN, Wr; *CANADIANS OF OLD,* TV, 73, CDN, Wr; *'ALAN HAMEL COMEDY BAG'* (26 eps), TV, 72, CDN, Co-Wr; *'LET'S CALL THE WHOLE THING OFF'* (26 eps), TV, 72, CDN, Co-Wr; *'LOUIS RIEL'* (2 eps), TV, 71, CDN, Wr; *'ZUT'* (26 eps), TV, 71, CDN, Co-Wr; *'COMEDY CRACKERS'* (26 eps), TV, 70, CDN, Co-Wr; *THE OTHER MAN'S GRASS/LOVE, THE REAL ARTICLE,* 'SHOESTRING THEATRE', TV, 69/68, CDN, Wr; *'COMEDY CAFE'* (26 eps), TV, 69, CDN, Co-Wr; *'TELEVISITS'* (24 eps), TV, 68, CDN, Wr; *THE THINGAMAGIG/THE CENSUS TAKER/DUET FOR A CLEAR, COOL NIGHT,* 'SHOESTRING THEATRE', TV, 66/65, CDN, Wr; *IN SEARCH OF MEDEA,* Th, 64, CDN, Wr/Dir.

SANDOR, Anna

ACTRA. Ziveg Productions Limited, 162 Banff Rd., Toronto, Ont, CAN, M4P 2P7. (416)481-0880. Steve Weiss, William Morris Agency, 151 El Camino Dr., Beverly Hills, CA, USA, 90212. (213)859-4423.
Types of Production & Categories: Th Short-Wr; TV Film-Wr; TV Video-Wr.
Genres: Drama-Th&TV; Comedy-Th&TV; Children's-TV.
Biography: Born 1949, Budapest, Hungary; came to Canada, 57, following Hungarian Revolution; Canadian citizen. Languages: English, Hungarian, some French and German. Graduate of University of Windsor (Theatre, English). Began career as stage and TV actress; started writing, 75; 50 produced TV scripts. Also acts as story consultant and lectures on television and screenwriting. Co-chairperson, Crime Writers of Canada, 85-86. Her works have won numerous international awards.
Selective Filmography: *THE MARRIAGE BED,* TV, 86, CDN, Wr; *'SEEING THINGS'* (9 eps), TV, 86-83, CDN, Co-Wr; *'DANGER BAY'* (1 eps), TV, 86, CDN/USA, Wr; *'HANGIN' IN',* TV, 86-80, CDN, Co-Creator; *CHARLIE GRANT'S WAR,* TV, 84, CDN, Wr **(ACTRA)**; *RUNNING MAN/HIGH CARD,* 'FOR THE RECORD', TV, 82/81, CDN, Wr; *A POLULATION OF ONE,* TV, 80, CDN, Wr; *'KING OF KENSINGTON'* (30 eps), TV, 80-75, CDN, Head Wr.

SAUDER, Peter

85 Rimington Dr., Thornhill, Ont, CAN. (416)669-9547. Nelvana Ltd., 32 Atlantic Ave., Toronto, Ont, CAN, M6K 1X8. (416)588-5571.
Types of Production & Categories: Th Film-Wr; TV Film-Wr.
Genres: Animation-Th&TV.
Biography: Born 1951, Canada. Graduate of 3 year animation program, Sheridan College, 74.
Selective Filmography: *THE CARE BEARS FAMILY* (Wr-7 eps), (13 eps), TV, 86, CDN, Story Ed; *THE CARE BEARS MOVIE II*, Th, 86/85, CDN, Scr; *THE ADVENTURES OF R2D2 AND C3PO'* (Co-Wr-7 eps), (13 eps), TV, 85, CDN/ USA, Assoc Prod/Story Ed; *'EWOKS'* (13 eps), TV, 85, CDN, Assoc Prod; *THE CARE BEARS MOVIE*, Th, 85, CDN, Scr; *STRAWBERRY SHORTCAKE MEETS THE BERRYKINS*, TV, 84, CDN, Wr; *THE GET ALONG GANG*, TV, 84, CDN, Wr; *'INSPECTOR GADGET'* (Wr-1 eps), (64 eps), TV, 83, CDN, Story Ed; *STRAWBERRY SHORTCAKE AND THE BABY WITHOUT A NAME*, TV, 83, CDN, Wr; *THE CARE BEARS AND THE FREEZE MACHINE*, TV, 83, CDN, Wr; *STRAWBERRY SHORTCAKE: A HOUSEWARMING SURPRISE*, TV, 82, CDN, Wr.

SAURIOL, Brigitte - voir REALISATEURS

SAVATH, Philip

ACTRA, WGAw. 1915 West 13th Ave., Vancouver, BC, CAN, V6J 2H5. (604) 734-2935.
Types of Production & Categories: Th Film-Wr; TV Film-Wr; TV Video-Wr/Prod.
Genres: Drama-Th&TV; Comedy-Th&TV; Variety-TV; Children's-TV.
Biography: Born 1946, Brooklyn, New York. Education: B.A., 68. Broadway debut at age 15; emigrated to Canada, 69. Founding director of Homemade Theatre, Toronto; co-creator, Improvisation Olympics; member, Caravan Stage Co.. A&M recording artist with Homemade Theatre.
Selective Filmography: *'SWITCHBACK'* (Contr Wr-28 eps), (56 eps), TV, 86-83, CDN, Prod/Wr; *SAMUEL LOUNT*, Th, 85, CDN, Co-Wr; *BAILEY'S LAW*, TV, 85, CDN, Wr; *'VANCOUVER'* (15/wk), TV, 84/83, CDN, Prod; *SLEEPLESS NIGHTS*, TV, 84, CDN, Wr/Prod; *SUMMER MADNESS*, TV, 84, CDN, Prod; *HOLOCAUST REMEMBERED*, TV, 84, CDN, Wr/Prod; *HIGH SCHOOL CONFIDENTIAL*, TV, 84, CDN, Prod; *WANNA HAVE FUN*, TV, 84, CDN, Prod; *MIDNIGHT MUSIC*, TV, 83, CDN, Wr; *'CARROLL BAKER'S JAMBOREE'* (6 eps), TV, 83/82, CDN, Co-Wr; *'PAUL ANKA SHOW'* (24 eps), TV, 83/82, CDN, Co-Wr; *RISING STARS*, TV, 83, CDN, Wr; *BIG MEAT EATER*, Th, 82, CDN, Co-Wr; *SEE B.C.*, TV, 82, CDN, Wr; *FAST COMPANY*, Th, 78, CDN, Co-Scr; *'HOMEMADE TELEVISION'* (32 eps), TV, 77-75, CDN, Co-Wr; *HOMEMADE THEATRE NIGHT IN CANADA*, TV, 76, CDN, Co-Wr.

SAXTON, John

ACTRA, WGAw. 214 Frontenac St., Kingston, Ont, CAN. (613)547-4286. Writers & Artists Agency, 11726 San Vicente Blvd., #300, Los Angeles, CA, USA, 90049. (213)820-2240.
Types of Production & Categories: Th Film-Wr; TV Film-Wr; TV Video-Wr.
Genres: Drama-Th&TV; Action-Th&TV; Horror-Th; Educational-TV.
Biography: Born in England; Canadian citizen; full-time teacher until 72 when he became a full-time writer.
Selective Filmography: *KATE MORRIS, VICE PRESIDENT*, 'FOR THE RECORD', TV, 83, CDN, Wr; *CLASS OF '84*, Th, 81, CDN/USA, Co-Wr; *HAPPY BIRTHDAY TO ME*, Th, 80, CDN, Story/Co-Scr; *'THE PHOENIX TEAM'* (Wr-3 eps), TV, 79, CDN, Creator/Wr; *THE TIGRESS*, Th, 78, CDN, Wr; *BLACKOUT*, Th, 77, CDN, Wr; *CAN I SAVE MY CHILDREN*, TV, 75, USA, Co-Wr; *'THE GREAT DETECTIVE'* (5 eps), TV, 75, CDN, Wr; *'SIDESTREET'*, TV, 74, CDN, Co-Creator/Story Ed.

SCHECHTER, Rebecca

ACTRA. 50 West Ave., Toronto, Ont, CAN, M4M 2L8. (416)469-5816. CBC, Box 500, Stn.A, Toronto, Ont, CAN, M5W 1E6. (416)975-6710.
Types of Production & Categories: TV Film-Wr.
Genres: Drama-TV; Documentary-TV; Educational-TV.
Biography: Born 1951, Newark, New Jersey; emigrated, 69; Canadian citizenship, 75. Education: University of Chicago, 68-69; York U., Social Sciences, 72-75.
Selective Filmography: *'MARKET PLACE'* (26 eps), TV, 86-84, CDN, Res; *PULLING FLOWERS,* TV, 85, CDN, Co-Wr; *'THE FIFTH ESTATE'* (2 eps), TV, 84, CDN, Res; *NEVER TOO YOUNG,* 'FITNESS AND CHILDREN', TV, 83, CDN, Wr; *FIT TO LAST,* 'EVERYBODY'S CHILDREN', TV, 83, CDN, Res; *SIGNALS, SOUNDS & MAKING SENSE/CHANGING LIMITS,* 'EVERYBODY'S CHILDREN', TV, 80, CDN, Wr; *HEART ATTACK: PRESCRIPTION FOR SURVIVAL,* TV, 79, CDN, Res.

SCOTT, Desmond

ACTRA. 32 Belcourt Rd., Toronto, Ont, CAN, M4S 2T9. (416)489-4028. Pam Friendly, First Artists, 1255 Yonge St., #303, Toronto, Ont, CAN, M4T 1W6. (416)961-7766.
Types of Production & Categories: TV Film-Wr; TV Video-Wr.
Genres: Drama-TV; Documentary-TV; Educational-TV.
Biography: Born 1926, London, England; Canadian citizen. M.A., Cambridge University; London Old Vic Theatre School. Came to Canada, 57. Director, Manitoba Theatre Centre, 59-63; writer, director, actor. Languages: French, some German. Teacher, National Theatre School, many universities, Canada, USA. Sculptor, several one man shows.
Selective Filmography: *LIKE NO OTHER PLACE,* TV, 78, CDN, Wr; *EVERYBODY'S CHILDREN,* TV, 78, CDN, Wr; *'POLICE SURGEON'* (1 eps), TV, 71, CDN/USA, Wr; *THREE SISTERS,* TV, 59, CDN, T'play; *A CURE FOR THE DOCTOR,* TV, 58, CDN, Wr; *THE COCKTAIL PARTY,* TV, 58, CDN, Wr.

SCOTT, Munroe

ACTRA. The Colbert Agency, 303 Davenport Rd., Toronto, Ont, CAN, M5R 1K5. (416)964-3302.
Types of Production & Categories: Th Film-Wr; TV Film-Wr/Dir; TV Video-Wr.
Genres: Drama-TV; Documentary-Th&TV.
Biography: Born 1927, Owen Sound, Ontario. B.A., Queen's University; M.A., Cornell U., major in playwriting. Has written 2 books and a stage play about Dr. Robert McClure; writer of 'The Sound and Light Show' (Ottawa parliament); 100's of educational films and documentaries. Films he has written have won more than 20 nat'l and int'l awards including a Special Jury Award (Canadian Film Awards), 3 Blue Ribbons (American Film Fest.), Gold Medal (Sport Film Fest., Cortina, Italy).
Selective Filmography: *THE SPIRIT PEOPLE,* TV, 86, CDN, Wr; *LAND OF THE MOUNTAIN ELEPHANT,* TV, 84, CDN, Wr; *SIXTEEN DAYS TO TIMBUKTU,* TV, 83, CDN, Wr; *MY PEOPLE ARE DYING,* TV, 80, CDN, Wr; *'THE CANADIAN'* (THE DIEFENBAKER MEMOIRS), (13 eps), TV, 75, CDN, Dir/Wr; *FIRST PERSON SINGULAR* (THE PEARSON MEMOIRS), (13 eps), TV, 73, CDN, Dir/Wr; *THE TENTH DECADE* (THE DIEFENBAKER-PEARSON YEARS), (5 parts), TV, 71, CDN, Dir/Wr; *INSIDE OUT,* Th, 70, CDN, Wr.

SEDAWIE, Gayle Gibson - see PRODUCERS
SEDAWIE, Norman - see PRODUCERS

SEGAL, Matthew

ACTRA. 48 Clinton Street, Toronto, Ont, CAN, M6G 2Y3. (416)536-2000.
Types of Production & Categories: Th Film-Wr; Th Short-Wr; TV Film-Wr; TV Video-Wr.
Genres: Drama-Th&TV; Comedy-TV; Action-TV; Science Fiction-TV.
Biography: Born 1943, Welland, Ontario. Studied Architecture, University of British Columbia. Actor, assistant set designer at the original Theatre Passe Muraille. Story and script editor, CBC TV drama, CTV, 20th Century Fox program development; co-wrote several specials, CBC variety, 76. Taught film & TV writing at Seneca College for 7 years.
Selective Filmography: *'THE CAMPBELLS'* (1 eps), TV, 86, CDN/USA/GB, Wr; *'THE PHOENIX TEAM'* (1 eps), TV, 80, CDN, Story; *'THE COLLABORATORS'* (1 eps), TV, 77, CDN, Wr; *'THE STARLOST'* (1 eps), TV, 74, CDN/USA, Story; *FOXY LADY,* Th, 70, CDN, Co-Wr; *DULCIMA,* Th, 70, CDN, Wr.

SHAPIRO, Paul - see DIRECTORS

SHEER, Tony

ACTRA. 151 Waverley Rd., Toronto, Ont, CAN, M4L 3T4. (416)690-0935.
Troutcake Films Inc., 67 Lee Ave., 3rd Fl., Toronto, Ont, CAN. (416)699-0600.
William Bateman, Nobbs, Woods & Clarke, 70 University Ave., Ste.250, Toronto, Ont, CAN, M5J 2M4. (416)977-1000.
Types of Production & Categories: Th Film-Wr; TV Film-Wr.
Genres: Drama-Th&TV; Comedy-Th&TV; Action-Th&TV; Documentary-TV.
Biography: Born 1937, London, England; Canadian citizen; educated at Arnold School, England; trained as actor at London's E 15 Acting School; worked as an actor in film/TV/stage, England, for 3 years. Came to Canada, 71. Has written over 60 TV dramas and documentaries.
Selective Filmography: *RACE FOR THE BOMB* (mini-series), TV, 86, CDN/F, Co-Wr; *CHINATOWN UNDERGROUND,* TV, 86, USA, Co-Wr; *FOR THOSE I LOVED* (AU NOM DE TOUS LES MIENS), (also 6 eps, TV), Th, 83, CDN/F, Scr; *FINAL EDITION,* 'FOR THE RECORD', TV, 82, CDN, Wr (ACTRA); *MAINTAIN THE RIGHT,* 'FOR THE RECORD', TV, 80, CDN, Wr; *'FISHTALES'* (13 eps), TV, 79, CDN, Wr; *THE FIGHTING MEN,* TV, 78, CDN, Wr (ACTRA); *THE OCTOBER CRISIS,* TV, 76, CDN, Wr; *THE MAN INSIDE,* TV, 76, CDN/USA, Wr; *'SIDESTREET'* (6 eps), TV, 75/74, CDN, Wr; *'ANTHOLOGY'* (8 eps), TV, 74-72, CDN, Wr; *'COLLABORATORS'* (5 eps), TV, 74/73, CDN, Wr.

SHEPPARD, John

ACTRA. 62 Kilkenny Dr., Agincourt, Ont, CAN, M1W 1K1. (416)499-1580.
Barry Perelman Agency, 9200 Sunset Blvd., Ste. 531, Beverly Hills, CA, USA. (213)274-5999.
Types of Production & Categories: Th Film-Wr/Dir; TV Film-Wr/Dir.
Genres: Drama-Th&TV; Comedy-Th; Action-Th; Horror-Th.
Biography: Born 1956, Toronto, Ontario. Education: B.A.A., Journalism, Ryerson Polytechnical Institute.
Selective Filmography: *HIGHER EDUCATION,* Th, 86, CDN, Scr/Dir; *BULLIES,* Th, 85, CDN, Co-Wr; *HIGH STAKES,* Th, 85, CDN, Co-Wr; *'MANIA'* (Dir-1 eps), (4 eps), TV, 85, CDN, Wr; *FLYING,* Th, 84, CDN, Wr; *AMERICAN NIGHTMARE,* Th, 82, CDN, Wr.

SHORT, Michael

ACTRA, WGAw. 243 Cobourg St., Stratford, Ont, CAN, N5A 3G2. (519)273-5340.
Types of Production & Categories: TV Film-Wr; TV Video-Wr.

(cont/suite)

Genres: Comedy-TV; Variety-TV.
Biography: Born 1944, Hamilton, Ontario.
Selective Filmography: *GENIE AWARDS,* TV, 86, CDN, Head Wr; *THE AMAZING ADVENTURES OF HENRY OSGOOD,* TV, 85, CDN/USA, Co-Wr; *JUNO AWARDS* (2 shows), TV, 85/84, CDN, Co-Wr; *MARTIN SHORT'S SPECIAL FOR THE AMERICAS,* TV, 85, CDN/USA, Co-Wr; *THE CANADIAN CONSPIRACY,* TV, 85, CDN/USA, Co-Wr; *'SCTV'* (61 eps), TV, 84-80, CDN, Co-Wr (**ACTRA/2 EMMY**); *'COMEDY TONIGHT'* (13 eps), TV, 83, CDN, Co-Creator/Co-Wr; *'JOHN CANDY'S BIG CITY COMEDY'* (12 eps), TV, 80, CDN/USA, Co-Wr.

SICOTTE, Sylvie

SARDEC. 314 Girouard, C.P. 145, Oka, Qué, CAN, J0N 1E0. (514)479-8714.
Types de production et Catégories: TV vidéo-Sc.
Types d'oeuvres: Drame-TV.
Curriculum vitae: Née en 1936 à Montréal, Québec; bilingue. Licence ès Lettres en littératures française et québécoise, Université de Montréal, 71; Maitrise ès Arts, études française et québécoise, 75. Comédienne à la radio et au théâtre, 58-59; télévision et théâtre, 75-76. Journaliste, 'La Presse', 59-60; plusieurs publications dont 'Infrajour'(73), 'Sur la pointe des dents' (78), 'Non, je n'ai pas dansé nue' (84).
Filmographie sélective: *ENTRE LE SOLEIL ET L'EAU,* 'LES BEAUX DIMANCHES', TV, 80, CDN, Sc.

SIEGEL, Lionel E.

ACTRA, DGA, WGAw. 30 Dorval Rd., Toronto, Ont, CAN, M6P 2B6. (416)533-8994.
Types of Production & Categories: Th Film-Wr; TV Film-Wr/Prod.
Genres: Drama-Th&TV
Biography: Born 1927, Chicago, Illinois; Canadian citizen, 85. Bachelor of Journalism, University of Missouri. Has won 2 Western Heritage Awards, Best Western TV Scripts for episodes of *SIMON* and *RAWHIDE.*
Selective Filmography: *'NIGHT HEAT'* (1 eps), TV, 85, CDN, Wr; *'FROM HERE TO ETERNITY'* (Wr-2 eps/Story Ed-3 eps), (13 eps), TV, 79, USA, Spv Prod; *'SPIDERMAN'* (Wr-2 eps), (22 eps), TV, 78, USA, Prod; *'BIONIC WOMAN'* (Wr-2 eps), (22 eps), TV, 77/76, USA, Exec Prod; *'6 MILLION DOLLAR MAN'* (Wr-4 eps/Story Ed-13 eps), (57 eps), TV, 77-75, USA, Prod; *'THE ULTIMATE IMPOSTER'* (1 eps), TV, 76, USA, Wr/Prod; *'EXO-MAN'* (1 eps), TV, 76, USA, Wr/Prod; *'SIMON'* (1 eps), TV, 75, USA, Wr; *'DEADLY WEEKEND'* (1 eps), TV, 74, USA, Wr; *'KUNG FU'* (1 eps), TV, 70, USA, Wr; *'PEYTON PLACE'* (360 eps), TV, 70-67, USA, Staff Wr; *'RAWHIDE'* (1 eps), TV, 67, USA, Wr; *'MR. NOVAK'* (1 eps), TV, 66, USA, Wr; *'BEN CASEY'* (3 eps), TV, 64, USA, Wr; *'IT'S A MAN'S WORLD'* (4 eps), TV, 64-62, USA, Wr.

SIMONEAU, Yves - voir REALISATEURS

SLADE, Bernard

WGAw. 101 Central Park W., #17F, New York, NY, USA, 10023. Norman Kurland, Broder-Kurland-Webb, 8439 Sunset Blvd., Ste. 402, Los Angeles, CA, USA, 90069. (213)656-9262.
Types of Production & Categories: Th Film-Wr; TV Film-Wr; TV Video-Wr.
Genres: Drama-Th&TV; Comedy-Th&TV.
Biography: Born 1930, Canada. Wrote 20 live and tape TV plays; moved to Los Angeles, 64; worked under contract at Columbia Pictures for 12 years; created 7 TV series, wrote over 100 episodes. Four plays produced on Broadway, 'Same Time Next Year', 'Tribute', 'Romantic Comedy', 'Special Occasions', also in West End of

(cont/suite)

London including 'Fatal Attraction'. Has won Drama Desk Award; Tony, Oscar and WGA nominations.
Selective Filmography: *ROMANTIC COMEDY,* Th, 82, USA, Scr; *TRIBUTE* (UN FILS POUR L'ETE), Th, 80, CDN, Scr; *SAME TIME NEXT YEAR,* Th, 78, USA, Scr; *'EVERYTHING MONEY CAN'T BUY'* (pilot), TV, 74, USA, Wr/ Creator; *'BOBBY SHERMAN SHOW'* (pilot), (2 eps), TV, 73, USA, Wr; *'THE GIRL WITH SOMETHING EXTRA'* (7 eps), TV, 72, USA, Creator/Wr; *'BRIDGET LOVES BERNIE'* (6 eps), TV, 71, USA, Creator/Wr; *'MR DEEDS GOES TO TOWN'* (pilot), (3 eps), TV, 70, USA, Wr/Adapt; *STAND UP AND BE COUNTED,* Th, 68, USA, Wr; *'THE PARTRIDGE FAMILY'* (14 eps), TV, 67, USA, Creator/Wr; *'THE FLYING NUN'* (12 eps), TV, 66, USA, Wr/Adapt; *'LOVE ON A ROOFTOP'* (18 eps), TV, 65, USA, Creator/Story Ed/Wr; *'BEWITCHED'* (18 eps), TV, 65/64, USA, Wr/Story Ed; *A VERY CLOSE FAMILY,* TV, 63, CDN, Wr; *THE BIG COIN SOUND,* TV, 61, CDN, Wr; *RELUCTANT ANGELS,* TV, 61, CDN, Wr; *THE GIMMICK,* TV, 60, CDN, Wr; *DO JERRY PARKER,* TV, 59, CDN, Wr; *THE MOST BEAUTIFUL GIRL IN THE WORLD,* TV, 59, CDN, Wr; *MEN DON'T MAKE PASSES,* TV, 58, CDN, Wr; *THE PRIZE WINNER,* TV, 57, CDN, Wr.

SOBELMAN, David

77 Huntley St., #812, Toronto, Ont, CAN, M4Y 2P3. (416)925-6258.
Types of Production & Categories: Th Film-Wr; TV Video-Wr/Dir/Prod.
Genres: Drama-TV; Action-TV; Horror-TV; Documentary-Th&TV.
Biography: Born 1950, Haifa, Israel; educated in Europe; moved to Canada, 72; Canadian citizen, 77; speaks 4 languages. Graduated York University's Film Dept..
Selective Filmography: *SPACE PIONEERS: A LOW-TECH ROMANCE,* TV, 86, CDN, Wr; *ELEMENTS OF FLIGHT/FIRST IN THE FUTURE,* In, 86/85, CDN, Wr; *'THE SPACE EXPERIENCE'* (6 eps), TV, 86, CDN, Co-Wr; *'ENTERPRISE'* (22 eps), TV, 84/83, CDN, Assoc Prod; *R.C.M.P. ON TRIAL,* TV, 83, CDN, Wr/Dir; *END OF TORONTO,* TV, 83, CDN, Dir/Wr; *TORONTO TRILOGY* (3 shows), TV, 83, CDN, Story Ed; *'SHULMAN FILE'* (22 eps), TV, 83/82, CDN, Assoc Prod; *A VISIT TO CALIFORNIA/CONCORDE SQUARE,* In, 83/82, CDN, Wr; *INWARD PASSAGE* (THE ST.LAWRENCE SEAWAY), Th, 82, CDN, Wr; *'CANADA AM'* (5/week), TV, 81-79, CDN, Story Ed; *'CTV NEWS',* TV, 81, CDN, News Ed.

SOBOL, Ken

ACTRA, CAPAC. R.R. #5, Alexandria, Ont, CAN, K0C 1A0. (613)525-4338.
Philip Spitzer Literary Agency, 1465 Third Ave., New York, NY, USA, 10028. (212)628-0352.
Types of Production & Categories: TV Film-Wr; TV Video-Wr.
Genres: Drama-TV; Documentary-TV; Children's-TV; Animation-TV.
Biography: Born 1938, Cleveland, Ohio; Canadian citizen. Writer for many magazines including 'The Village Voice', 'McCall's', 'New York Magazine', 'This Magazine'; author of 'Babe Ruth and the American Dream' and several children's books including 'The Clock Museum', The Devil and Daniel Mouse', 'Stories from Inside Out'.
Selective Filmography: *'DEAR AUNT AGNES'* (3 eps), TV, 86, CDN, Wr; *'READ ALONG'* (90 eps), TV, 86-75, CDN, Wr; *'TELEFRANCAIS'* (30 eps), TV, 85-79, CDN, Wr; *CHAIRMAN OF THE BOARD,* TV, 82, CDN, Wr; *THE DEVIL AND DANIEL MOUSE,* TV, 78, CDN, T'play; *COSMIC CHRISTMAS,* TV, 77/76, CDN, Wr; *'INSIDE OUT'* (7 eps), TV, 75/74, CDN/USA, Wr (**EMMY**).

SOMCYNSKY, Jean-François

SARDEC. B.P. 500, Succ. A, Ottawa, Ont, CAN, K1N 8T7.
Types de production et Catégories: TV film-Sc.
Types d'oeuvres: Drame-TV.

(cont/suite)

Curriculum vitae: Né en 1943, Paris, France; citoyen canadien. Economiste de formation; Maitrise, Université d'Ottawa, 70. Diplomate de carrière depuis 72. A publié 11 ouvrages de fiction (roman, nouvelles, poésie); 7 nouvelles et 9 pièces radiophoniques. Prix Solaris, 81; 2 Prix Boréal, 82; Prix Esso du Cercle du Livre de France, 83 (tous prix littéraires).
Filmographie sélective: *UN HERITAGE INESPERE,* TV, 78, CDN, Aut; *TON REGARD DANS LE MIROIR,* TV, 73, CDN, Aut.

SPRY, Robin - see DIRECTORS

STANKE, Alain

SARDEC, UDA. 2127 Guy, Montréal, Qué, CAN, H3H 2L9. (514)935-7452.
Types de production et Catégories: TV film-Sc/Prod; TV vidéo-Sc.
Types d'oeuvres: Variété-TV; Documentaire-TV.
Curriculum vitae: Né en 1934, Kaunas, Lithuanie; citoyen canadien. Langues: français, anglais, russe, polonais, allemand, lithuanien. Producteur: Les Productions Stanké Inc. et Les Promotions Audio-Visuelles Stanké-Lamy; éditeur: Les Editions internationales Alain Stanké Ltée.. *CENT ANS DEJA* remporte le Prix Wilderness, 67.
Filmographie sélective: *CARRE BLANC,* C, 85, F, Com/Interv; *'VENEZ DONC CHEZ MOI'* (72 eps), TV, 82/81, CDN, Conc/Interv; *JEAN PAUL LEMIEUX* (version française et anglaise), TV, 81, CDN, Sc/Interv; *RICHARD NIXON,* TV, 78, CDN/F, Prod; *PIERRE E.TRUDEAU: PORTRAIT INTIME,* TV, 77, CDN, Conc/Interv; *CENT ANS DEJA* (IT'S MY BIRTHDAY TOO), TV, 67, CDN, Interv; *'LES INSOLENCES D'UNE CAMERA'* (180 eps), TV, 67-62, CDN, Sc/Anim; *PAS DE VACANCES POUR LES IDOLES,* C, 65, CDN, Com.

STANSFIELD, David

#49, 19th Side Rd, Kettleby, Ont, CAN, L0G 1J0. (416)727-9110. TV Ontario, 2180 Yonge St., Toronto, Ont, CAN. (416)484-2600.
Types of Production & Categories: TV Film-Wr/Prod; TV Video-Wr/Prod.
Genres: Comedy-TV; Variety TV; Documentary-TV; Children's-TV.
Biography: Born 1938, London, England; emigrated to Canada, 67; Canadian citizen, 81; fluent in English, French, German, Arabic. B.A., M.A. in Modern Arabic Studies (First Class Honours B.A. and Middle East Award, 61). Experience in all aspects of educational media; programmed learning, reading machines, computer-assisted instruction, educational films and TV. Has won 12 educational Film & TV Festival awards, Canada, USA.
Selective Filmography: *'ORIGINS'* (12 eps), TV, 86-85, CDN, Co-Prod/Co-Dir/Co-Wr; *'THE MIDDLE EAST'* (14 eps), TV, 85-83, CDN, Co-Prod/Co-Dir/Co-Wr; *'BITS AND BYTES'* (24 eps), TV, 83-81, CDN, Co-Prod/Co-Wr; *GETTING STARTED,* ED, 83, CDN, Co-Prod/Co-Wr; *'IT FIGURES'* (50 eps), TV, 82-79, CDN, Co-Prod/Co-Wr; *'EUREKA'* (30 eps), TV, 81-79, CDN, Co-Prod/Co-Wr; *'PARLEZ-MOI'* (90 eps), TV, 80-76, CDN, Co-Prod/Co-Wr; *'FRENCH FOR CANADIANS'* (sev seg), TV, 80/79, CDN, Co-Prod/Co-Wr; *'THE FRENCH SHOW'* (13 eps), TV, 76, CDN, Co-Wr/Co-Prod.

STERN, Sandor - see DIRECTORS

STEWART, Barbara J.

42A Karen Walk, Waterloo, Ont, CAN, N2L 5X2. (519)886-4924. Advanced Promotions Marketing, 300 Ardelt Ave., Kitchener, Ont, CAN, N2C 2L9. (519)578-5910.
Types of Production & Categories: TV Film-Wr/Dir/Prod.
Genres: Children's-TV.
Biography: Born 1952, Cambridge, Ontario. Has had one book published, 'The Maple Leaf Journal: A Settlement History of Wellesley Township'.

(cont/suite)

Selective Filmography: *THE CHIMNEY SWEEP,* TV, 85, CDN, Wr/Dir/Prod.

STEWART, Gordon - see DIRECTORS

STRANGE, Marc

ACTRA. Rainy River Pictures Inc., 387 Kingswood Rd., Toronto, Ont, CAN, M4E 3P2. (416)690-4991.
Types of Production & Categories: Th Film-Act; TV Film-Wr/Act; TV Video-Wr/ Act.
Genres: Drama-TV; Children's-TV.
Biography: Born Kitchener, Ontario. Thirty years in the entertainment business as writer/actor/director.
Selective Filmography: *'THE BEACHCOMBERS'* (Dir-10 eps/Co-Wr-2 eps), (50 eps), TV, 86-72, CDN, Creator/Wr; *'STREET LEGAL'* (Dir-1 eps), (2 eps), TV, 86, CDN, Wr; *VALENTINE'S REVENGE,* TV, 85, USA, Act; *THE MORNING MAN,* Th, 85, CDN, Act; *ACT OF VENGEANCE,* TV, 85, USA, Act; *'THE CAMPBELLS'* (Co-T'play-1 eps/Wr-1 eps), TV, 85, CDN/GB, Wr; *'DANGER BAY'* (1 eps), TV, 85, CDN/USA, Wr.

SUCH, Peter

ACTRA. 14 Fourth St., Wards Island, Toronto, Ont, CAN, M5J 2B5. (416)367-5424. 312 Adelaide St. W., Ste. 204C, Toronto, Ont, CAN. (416)598-4061. The Colbert Agency, 303 Davenport Rd., Toronto, Ont, CAN, M5R 1K5. (416)964-3302.
Types of Production & Categories: Th Short-Wr; TV Film-Wr; TV Video-Wr.
Genres: Drama-Th&TV; Documentary-Th&TV; Educational-Th&TV; Children's-TV.
Biography: Born 1939, London, England; emigrated to Canada, 53. Began career as a singer, then actor, writer, stage plays, opera; novelist, 5 books; founder, Canadian Studies programmes; professor at York University. Has received Canada Council Awards, Chalmers Award. *FREE DIVE* won 1st Prize, NY Film Fest. (Special U.N. category).
Selective Filmography: *'THE CAMPBELLS'* (1 eps), TV, 85, CDN, Wr; *'HOME FIRES'* (Co-Creator/Co-Wr-8 eps), (16 eps), TV, 82/81, CDN, Co-Story, *FREE DIVE,* TV, 82, CDN, Wr.

SULLIVAN, Kevin - see DIRECTORS

SUTHERLAND, Ian

ACTRA. R.R. #1, Alcove, Que, CAN. The Colbert Agency, 303 Davenport Rd., Toronto, Ont, CAN, M5R 1K5. (416)964-3302.
Types of Production & Categories: Th Film-Wr; TV Film-Wr.
Genres: Drama-Th&TV; Comedy-Th&TV; Action-Th&TV.
Biography: Born 1945, Scotland; landed immigrant, Canada. Attended McGill University. *CERTAIN PRACTICES* won a Genie, 80.
Selective Filmography: *'NIGHT HEAT'* (7 eps), TV, 86/85, CDN, Wr; *CERTAIN PRACTICES/BLIND FAITH/MOVING TARGETS,* 'FOR THE RECORD', TV, 82-79, CDN, Wr; *SUNSPOTS,* TV, 80, CDN, Wr; *IMPROPER CHANNELS,* Th, 79, CDN, Co-Wr; *RITUALS,* Th, 76, CDN, Wr.

SUTHERLAND, Neil - see PRODUCERS

THERIAULT, Denis

5581 Pl.Basile Patenaude, #12, Montréal, Qué, CAN, H1Y 3E3. (514)525-8582.
Types de production et Catégories: TV film-Sc.
Types d'oeuvres: Drame-TV; Comédie-TV.

(cont/suite)

Curriculum vitae: Né en 1959, Sept-Iles, Québec; bilingue. Bac. en Psychologie, Université d'Ottawa; ateliers et stages en théâtre; comédien et professeur de théâtre. Intérêt particulier pour le fantastique et la science fiction.
Filmographie sélective: *VICTOR LE VAMPIRE,* TV, 85, CDN, Sc/Dial; *AIRENEM,* TV, 84, CDN, Sc/Dial.

THICKE, Alan - see PRODUCERS

THOMAS, R. L. - see DIRECTORS

THOMPSON, Judith

ACTRA. 16 Yarmouth Rd., Toronto, Ont, CAN, M6G 1W6. (416)534-3809. Great North Artists Mgmt., 345 Adelaide St.W.,#500, Toronto, Ont, CAN, M5V 1R5. (416)593-2587.
Types of Production & Categories: TV Film-Wr; TV Video-Wr.
Genres: Drama-TV; Comedy-TV.
Biography: Born 1954, Montreal, Quebec. Education: Queen's University, National Theatre School. Playwright, won Governor General's Award for Drama, 84.
Selective Filmography: *TURNING TO STONE,* TV, 85, CDN, Wr; *'AIRWAVES'* (2 eps), TV, 85, CDN, Wr.

THURLING, Peter - see DIRECTORS

TONNEROVA, Maria

271 Orléans, St-Eustache, Qué, CAN, J7P 4Z7. (514)472-6889.
Types de production et Catégories: TV film-Sc.
Types d'oeuvres: Education-TV; Enfants-TV.
Curriculum vitae: Née en 1949, Tchécoslovaquie; citoyenne canadienne depuis 76. Maitrises en sciences humaines et en langues orientales; journaliste, linguiste, interprète, auteur pour enfants (2 livres avec les éditions Héritage). Participation au MIP TV (78 et 79), à la foire du livre à Francfort et au Salon du livre, Montréal.
Filmographie sélective: *'CONTES ORIENTAUX'* (13 eps), TV, 79/78, CDN, Aut; *'CONTES DU TSAR'* (13 eps), TV, 77, CDN, Aut.

TOUGAS, Francine

CAPAC, SARDEC. 4237 rue Fabre, #1, Montréal, Qué, CAN, H2J 3T5. (514) 525-2787.
Types de production et Catégories: TV film-Sc; TV vidéo-Sc.
Types d'oeuvres: Drame-TV; Documentaire-C&TV; Education-TV.
Curriculum vitae: Née en 1952, Dorion, Québec. Conservatoire d'Art dramatique, Montréal (3 ans); comédienne, 73-84. Auteur et interprète de 2 spectacles solos joués à Montréal et au Québec.
Filmographie sélective: *'A PLEIN TEMPS'* (9 eps), TV, 85/84, CDN, Sc; *'LES ENFANTS MAL AIMES'* (3 eps), TV, 84, CDN, Sc/Dial.

TRUCKEY, Don

ACTRA. Storypoint Inc., 728 - 19 Ave.N.W., Calgary, Alta, CAN, T2M 0Z1. (403)289-1570.
Types of Production & Categories: TV Film-Wr; TV Video-Wr.
Genres: Drama-Th&TV; Comedy-TV; Documentary-TV; Educational-TV.
Biography: Born 1955. B.A., English, University of Alberta, 78. Creative writing Award from Rudy Wiebe, University of Alberta, 76. Daily newspaper experience at 'Calgary Herald', 79-86; coverage of criminal courts, politics; now editorial writer and columnist.
Selective Filmography: *'SEEING THINGS'* (1 eps), TV, 86, CDN, Wr; *TOOLS OF THE DEVIL,* 'FOR THE RECORD', TV, 85, CDN, Wr; *NEXT YEAR COUNTRY,* 'THE WAY WE ARE', TV, 85, CDN, Wr; *ROUGH JUSTICE,* 'FOR THE RECORD', TV, 84, CDN, Wr **(ACTRA).**

TRUSS, Adrian
ACTRA. 345 Adelaide St. W., Ste. 506, Toronto, Ont, CAN, M5V 1A6. (416)977-9630. Noble Talent, 2380 Yonge St., Toronto, Ont, CAN. (416)482-6556.
Types of Production & Categories: TV Video-Wr.
Genres: Comedy-TV; Variety-TV.
Biography: Born 1953, London, England; British citizen; landed immigrant, Canada. Writer/performer, 'Second City' reviews (stage), 81-85.
Selective Filmography: *'VARIETY TONITE'* (2 eps), TV, 86, CDN, Contr Wr; *'PET PEEVES'* (4 eps), TV, 86, CDN, Contr Wr.

VARUGHESE, Sugith
ACTRA. The Colbert Agency, 303 Davenport Rd., Toronto, Ont, CAN, M5R 1K5. (416)964-3302.
Types of Production & Categories: Th Short-Wr/Dir; TV Film-Wr; TV Video-Wr.
Genres: Drama-Th&TV; Comedy-TV; Action-TV; Children's-TV.
Biography: Born 1957, Cochin, India; raised in Saskatoon, Saskatchewan; Canadian citizen. B.A., summa cum laude, University of Minnesota; M.F.A., Film, York U.. Also, TV, film actor.
Selective Filmography: *'FRAGGLE ROCK'* (9 eps), TV, 86-83, CDN, Wr; *BEST OF BOTH WORLDS,* TV, 82, CDN, Wr; *THE CRUSH,* Th, 80, CDN, Wr/Dir; *'THE PHOENIX TEAM'* (1 eps), TV, 80, CDN, Wr.

VIALLON, Claudine
3657 West 1st Ave., Vancouver, BC, CAN, V6R 1H1. (604)733-6101.
Types of Production & Categories: TV Film-Wr/Dir; TV Video-Wr/Dir.
Genres: Drama-TV; Documentary-TV; Educational-TV; Children's-TV.
Biography: Born 1948, France; French-Canadian citizenship. Languages: French, English, Spanish. Education: Simon Fraser University; Art School, France. Film Festival Awards at New York, Montreal. Film critic for Radio-Canada, 3 years.
Selective Filmography: *VANCOUVER ON THE MOVE,* TV, 86, CDN, Wr/Co-Dir; *PITOU, PIONNIER,* TV, 85, CDN, Wr/Dir; *PANDOSY, OKANAGAN,* TV, 85, CDN, Wr/Dir; *THE VOYAGERS* (LES VOYAGEURS), TV, 85, CDN, Wr/Dir; *SI ON FAISAIT DES FACES,* TV, 83, CDN, Wr/Dir; *EVOLUTION AT BRACKENDALE,* TV, 80, CDN, Wr/Dir; *BRUJO,* TV, 79, CDN, Co-Wr/Co-Dir; *VIA DOLOROSA,* TV, 79, CDN, Co-Wr/Co-Dir; *TAJIMULTIK,* TV, 79, CDN, Co-Wr/Co-Dir; *THE THREAD,* Th, 75, CDN, Set Des.

VICKERS, Darrell
ACTRA, WGAw. 8600 Rugby Dr., #1, West Hollywood, CA, USA, 90069. (213) 659-3518. 4040 Shadyglade Ave., Studio City, CA, USA, 91604. (818)985-7867.
Types of Production & Categories: TV Film-Wr; TV Video-Wr.
Genres: Comedy-TV; Variety-TV; Children's-TV.
Biography: Born 1957, England; Canadian citizen. Professional partner, Andrew Nicholls with whom he writes for stage: 'Sugar Babies' rewrites, 83-86; gags for comedians: Joan Rivers, Rodney Dangerfield; radio: various comedy series; print: 100's of cartoons: 'Frank and Ernest', 'Ben Wicks'; 100's of industrials; special musical material: over 20 plays; personal appearance material: Alan Thicke, Mickey Rooney, Jim Stafford.
Selective Filmography: *'CHECK IT OUT!'* (Co-Wr-7 eps), (22 eps), TV, 86/85, CDN/USA, Co-Story Ed; *'DANGER BAY'* (3 eps), TV, 85, CDN/USA, Co-Wr; *GEORGE CARLIN '2-C',* TV, 85, CDN, Co-Wr; *'LOVE BOAT'* (1 eps), TV, 85, USA, Co-Wr; *'BIZARRE'* (1 eps), TV, 85, CDN/USA, Contr Wr; *'THICKE OF THE NIGHT'* (85 eps), TV, 84/83, USA, Contr Wr; *'FAST COMPANY'* (22 eps), TV, 83, CDN, Co-Wr; *'EVENING AT THE IMPROV'* (3 eps), TV, 82, USA, Contr Wr; *'FLAPPERS'* (3 eps), TV, 81, CDN, Co-Wr.

WADE, Bryan R.
ACTRA. Great North Artists Mgmt., 345 Adelaide St.W., Suite 500, Toronto, Ont, CAN, M5V 1R5. (416)593-2586.
Types of Production & Categories: TV Video-Wr.
Genres: Drama-TV; Comedy-TV.
Biography: Born 1952; Canadian. Extensive experience as playwright and director in professional theatre.
Selective Filmography: 'HANGIN'IN' (1 eps), TV, 84, CDN, Wr; 'THE GREAT DETECTIVE' (1 eps), TV, 81, CDN, Wr; A BRIEF HISTORY OF THE SUBJECT, 'PEEP SHOW', TV, 75, CDN, Wr.

WAISGLASS, Elaine
ACTRA, WGAw. 644 Huron St., Toronto, Ont, CAN, M5R 2R9. (416)967-5938.
Types of Production & Categories: Th Film-Wr; TV Film-Wr.
Genres: Drama-Th&TV; Documentary-TV; Educational-TV; Children's-TV.
Biography: Canadian citizen with employment and residential papers for Great Britain.
Selective Filmography: A JUDGEMENT IN STONE, Th, 85, CDN, Scr; 'THE EDISON TWINS' (6 eps), TV, 84/83, CDN, Wr.

WALKER, Giles - see DIRECTORS

WALLACE, Clarke
ACTRA. R.R.3, Woodbridge, Ont, CAN, L4L 1A7. (416)851-2623. The Colbert Agency, 303 Davenport Rd., Toronto, Ont, CAN, M5R 1K5. (416)964-3302.
Types of Production & Categories: Th Film-Wr; TV Film-Wr; TV Video-Wr.
Genres: Drama-Th; Variety-TV; Documentary-TV; Children's-TV.
Biography: Born Toronto, Ontario. B.A., Journalism, University of Western Ontario, 62. Author of 5 published books including: 'Empire Inc.' (83), 'Hercules Trust'(82), 'Wanted: Donald Morrison' (77).
Selective Filmography: 'STREET LEGAL' (1 eps), TV, 86, CDN, Wr; THE MORNING MAN, Th, 85, CDN, Wr; SOUTH KOREA, TV, 80, CDN, Wr; SRI LANKA, TV, 80, CDN, Wr; 'THIS LAND' (10 eps), TV, 78-74, CDN, Wr; 'THE PIT STOP' (26 eps), TV, 78/77, CDN, Wr/Co-Host; 'HUMAN JOURNEY' (4 eps), TV, 77-74, CDN, Wr; 'TOMMY HUNTER' (26 eps), TV, 76, CDN, Wr; 'DROP-IN' (60 eps), TV, 74-69, CDN, Wr; 'THIS LAND IS PEOPLE' (52 eps), TV, 69/68, CDN, Wr.

WALLACE, Ratch
ACTRA, WGAw. 50 Hillsboro Ave., #301, Toronto, Ont, CAN, M5R 1S7. (416) 922-0186. First Artists Mgmt., 1255 Yonge St., Toronto, Ont, CAN. (416)961-7766.
Types of Production & Categories: Th Film-Wr/Prod; Th Short-Wr/Prod; TV Film-Wr; TV Video-Wr.
Genres: Drama-Th&TV; Comedy-Th&TV.
Biography: Born 1944, Toronto, Ontario; bilingual. Education: Ryerson Polytechnical Institute, Cinematography; UCLA, Film History. Master of steamship licence (M.O.T.-Canada). Actor in several feature films and TV productions. Nominated twice, Canadian Film Awards.
Selective Filmography: POETRY IN MOTION, Th, 82, CDN, PM/1st AD; THE UNEXPECTED, 'TALES OF THE KLONDIKE', TV, 81, CDN, Co-Wr; RAGTIME SUMMER, Th, 77, CDN/GB, Wr; THE TREE HAS GROWN, In, 75, CDN, Wr; THE HARD PART BEGINS, Th, 73, CDN, Exec Prod; THE MATCH, Th, 72, CDN, Prod/Wr/Dir.

WATSON, John - see PRODUCERS

WRITERS/SCENARISTES

WATSON, Patrick - see PRODUCERS
WAYNE, Paul
ACTRA, WGAw. 5201 Topeka Dr., Tarzana, CA, USA, 91356. (818)344-1070.
Types of Production & Categories: Th Film-Wr; TV Video-Wr/Prod.
Genres: Comedy-Th&TV; Variety-TV.
Biography: Born 1932, Toronto, Ontario; Canadian citizen; permanent resident, USA.
Selective Filmography: *'CHECK IT OUT!'* (13 eps), TV, 85, CDN/USA, Head Wr; *'THREE'S COMPANY'* (65 eps), TV, 78-76, USA, Head Wr; *'EXCUSE MY FRENCH'* (35 eps), TV, 75/74, CDN, Prod (**ACTRA**); *'SONNY AND CHER'* (65 eps), TV, 71, USA, Co-Wr; *ONLY GOD KNOWS,* Th, 69, CDN, Wr; *'SMOTHERS BROTHERS'* (26 eps), TV, 69, USA, Co-Wr (**EMMY**); *THE KING'S PIRATE,* Th, 65, USA, Wr.

WEINTRAUB, William
433 Wood Ave., Westmount, Que, CAN, H3Y 3J4. (514)935-2733.
Types of Production & Categories: Th Film-Wr/Prod; Th Short-Wr/Prod; TV Film-Wr/Dir/Prod.
Genres: Drama-Th&TV; Documentary-Th&TV; Educational-Th&TV.
Biography: Born 1926, Montreal, Quebec. Started career as journalist, 'The Gazette', 'Weekend Magazine', Montreal; joined NFB, 65; has written and/or produced over 100 documentary and dramatic films. Author of 2 novels, 'The Underdogs' and 'Why Rock the Boat?'. Lectured on screenwriting at several universities in Canada.Worked in Kenya for United Nations, instructing African filmmakers. Left the NFB in 86 to do freelance writing and producing.
Selective Filmography: *MORTIMER GRIFFIN AND SHALINSKY/THE SIGHT/ UNCLE T/CONNECTION,* 'BELL CANADA PLAYHOUSE', TV, 85, CDN, Co-Prod; *THE CONCERT MAN,* TV, 82, CDN, Wr; *ARTHRITIS: A DIALOGUE WITH PAIN,* TV, 81, CDN, Prod; *MARGARET LAURENCE: FIRST LADY OF MANAWAKA,* TV, 78, CDN, Prod; *BEKEVAR JUBILEE,* TV, 77, CDN, Prod; *HOLD THE KETCHUP,* Th, 76, CDN, Prod; *SEVEN SHADES OF PALE,* TV, 75, CDN, Prod; *I'VE NEVER WALKED THE STEPPES,* TV, 75, CDN, Prod; *WHY ROCK THE BOAT?,* Th, 74, CDN, Prod/Scr (**CFA**); *THE AVIATORS OF HUDSON STRAIT,* TV, 73, CDN, Wr/Prod; *CHALLENGE FOR THE CHURCH,* TV, 72, CDN, Wr/Dir; *A MATTER OF FAT,* TV, 70, CDN, Wr/Dir (**CFA**); *'STRUGGLE FOR A BORDER'* (9 eps), TV, 69, CDN, Wr; *RECEPTION CENTRE,* ED, 67, CDN, Wr; *CELEBRATION,* Th, 66, CDN, Dir/Prod; *TURN OF THE CENTURY,* TV, 64, CDN, Wr/Prod; *ANNIVERSARY,* Th, 63, CDN, Wr/Prod (**CFA**); *NAHANNI,* Th, 62, CDN, Wr; *'CROSSROADS OF THE WORLD'* (7 eps), TV, 62, CDN, Wr; *VOTE FOR MICHALSKI,* TV, 61, CDN, Wr; *'BETWEEN TWO WARS'* (3 eps), TV, 60, CDN, Wr/Prod; *SALUTE TO FLIGHT,* TV, 59, CDN, Wr; *FIRST NOVEL,* TV, 58, CDN, Wr; *'COMMONWEALTH OF NATIONS'* (13 eps), TV, 57, CDN, Wr; *SASKATCHEWAN TRAVELLER,* TV, 56, CDN, Wr; *IS IT A WOMAN'S WORLD?,* TV, 56, CDN, Wr; *NEW HEARTS FOR OLD,* TV, 55, CDN, Wr.

WEXLER, Gerald
ACTRA. 5378 Esplanade, Montreal, Que, CAN, H2T 2Z7. (514)274-1149.
Types of Production & Categories: Th Film-Wr; Th Short-Wr; TV Film-Wr.
Genres: Drama-Th&TV; Comedy-TV; Educational-TV.
Biography: Born 1950, Montreal, Quebec. B.A., McGill University, English, 71; graduate diploma, Film and TV, Hornsey College of Art, London, England, 73. Film editor, assistant editor on features, documentaries and commercials, 73-80; now concentrates on writing. Has had short stories published in 10 literary magazines and anthologies, 'The Bequest and Other Stories' published, 84.

(cont/suite)

Selective Filmography: *DO YOU KNOW WHAT YOU'RE IN FOR?*, TV, 86, CDN, Wr; *ANGELA'S RETURN*, TV, 85, CDN, Wr; *A GIFT FOR KATE*, TV, 85, CDN, Wr; *UNCLE T/MORTIMER GRIFFIN AND SHALINSKY/BAMBINGER*, 'BELL CANADA PLAYHOUSE', TV, 85/84, CDN, T'play; *OTHER TONGUES*, Th, 83, CDN, Contr Wr; *A RIGHT TO REFUSE*, 'PEOPLE AT WORK', ED, 81, CDN, Wr.

WHEELER, Anne - see DIRECTORS

WHITE, Pete

ACTRA. 11706 126 St., Edmonton, Alta, CAN, T5M 0S2. (403)452-1489. Kicking Horse Prod.Inc., 3630 West 10th Ave., Vancouver, BC, CAN, V6R 2G3. (604)733-4432.
Types of Production & Categories: TV Film-Wr.
Genres: Drama-TV; Action-TV; Documentary-TV; Educational-TV.
Biography: Born 1946, Kaslo, British Columbia. Full time professionel writer since 69; former songwriter with 5 albums of produced material for performer Paul Hann. Co-founder, President, Kicking Horse Productions Ltd, 77-82; advisory committee, Alberta Motion Picture Development Corp., 84-85; Chairman, National Council, Actra Writer's Guild, 86.
Selective Filmography: *STRIKER'S MOUNTAIN*, TV, 85, CDN, Wr; *THE BEACHCOMBERS* (6 eps), TV, 83/82, CDN, Wr; *STONEY PLAIN* (1 eps), TV, 81, CDN, Wr; *THE PARENT PUZZLE* (10 eps), TV, 80, CDN, Wr; *FAMILY AND THE LAW* (10 eps), TV, 79, CDN, Co-Wr; *BARRY BROADFOOT'S PIONEER YEARS* (13 eps), TV, 78, CDN, Co-Wr.

WIEBE, Rudy

ACTRA. c/o English Dept., University of Alberta, Edmonton, Alta, CAN, T6G 2E5. (403)432-4627.
Types of Production & Categories: Th Short-Wr; TV Film Wr.
Genres: Drama-Th&TV.
Biography: Born 1934, Saskatchewan. M.A., Creative Writing, University of Alberta; has taught Creative Writing and English (U. of Alberta) since 67. Author of several books including 'The Temptation of Big Bear', 'The Scorched-Wood People', 'The Mad Trapper', 'My Lovely Enemy'; has also written 3 collections of short stories.
Selective Filmography: *TUDOR KING*, Th, 79, CDN, Story; *SOMEDAY SOON*, TV, 76, CDN, Co-Wr.

WIESENFELD, Joe

ACTRA. 306 Wychwood Ave., Toronto, Ont, CAN, M6C 2T8. (416)654-1597.
Dan Redler & Assoc., 10351 Santa Monica Blvd., #211, Los Angeles, CA, USA, 90025. (213)551-3000.
Types of Production & Categories: Th Film-Wr; Th Short-Wr; TV Film-Wr; TV Video-Wr.
Genres: Drama-Th&TV; Comedy-Th&TV.
Biography: Born 1947, Treysa, Germany; Canadian citizen. Attended University of Manitoba, 2 years. *BOYS AND GIRLS* won an Oscar, 83; *THE PAINTED DOOR* was nominated for an Oscar, 84 and won the Golden Sheaf Award, Yorkton (Best Short Screenplay) and First Channel Golden Sheaf Award (Best Screenplay); *ANNE OF GREEN GABLES* won an Emmy (Best Children's Program) and was also nominated for Outstanding Writing in a Mini-Series or a Special.
Selective Filmography: *BREAKING INTO SONG*, Th, 86, CDN, Wr; *BROTHERS BY CHOICE* (6 eps), TV, 85, CDN, T'play; *GOING TO WAR*, 'BELL CANADA PLAYHOUSE', TV, 85, CDN, T'play; *PRODIGAL*, TV, 85, CDN, Wr; *HOME FREE* (pilot), TV, 85, CDN, Wr; *ANNE OF GREEN GABLES* (mini-series), TV, 85, CDN, Co-T'Play; *CORNET AT NIGHT/THE PAINTED DOOR*, 'BELL

(cont/suite)

CANADA PLAYHOUSE', TV, 83, CDN, T'play; *HOME FROM FAR/BOYS AND GIRLS/DAVID/THE BAMBOO BRUSH,* 'SONS AND DAUGHTERS', TV, 83/82, CDN, T'play; *BY DESIGN,* Th, 80, CDN, Co-Wr; *RECOMMENDATION FOR MERCY,* Th, 75, CDN, Co-Wr; *THE MOURNING SUIT,* Th, 74, CDN, Wr.

WILDEBLOOD, Peter - see PRODUCERS

WILDMAN, Peter

ACTRA. 119 Queensdale Ave., Toronto, Ont, CAN, M4J 1Y5. (416)461-4795. Barb Fogler, 3 Charles St.W., #204, Toronto, Ont, CAN. (416)923-9844.
Types of Production & Categories: TV Film-Wr/Act; TV Video-Wr/Act.
Genres: Drama-TV; Comedy-TV; Musical-TV.
Biography: Born 1954, Peterborough, Ontario. Travelled Fiji, New Zealand for 2 1/2 years. Helped form the Frantics, 79. Has written music and scripts for stage, radio and television.
Selective Filmography: *'OUT OF OUR MINDS'* (13 eps), TV, 85, CDN, Wr; *'4 ON THE FLOOR'* (13 eps), TV, 85, CDN, Co-Wr/Act; *THE NO NAME SHOW,* TV, 84, CDN, Wr/Act.

WILSCAM, Linda

SARDEC, UDA. Habitat 67, #219, Cité du Havre, Montréal, Qué, CAN, H3C 3R6. (514)861-2227.
Types de production et Catégories: TV vidéo-Sc/Com.
Types d'oeuvres: Education-TV; Enfants-TV.
Curriculum vitae: Née en 1949. Etudes en journalisme, théâtre, langues et littérature; diplômée de l'Université McGill et du Conservatoire d'Art Dramatique de Montréal. Travaille comme comédienne; enseigne le théâtre; publie des contes pour enfants et des articles sur le théâtre.
Filmographie sélective: *'ALEXANDRE ET LE ROI'* (44 eps), TV, 80-78, CDN, Aut; *'PICOTINE'* (86 eps), TV, 77-71, CDN, Aut/Com; *'PST PST, AIE-LA - CLIN D'OEIL'* (13 eps), TV, 75/74, CDN, Aut/Com.

WILSON, Sandra - see DIRECTORS

WINNING, David - see DIRECTORS

WOOD, Ted

ACTRA. The Granary, Concession 4, R.R.#1, Pickering, Ont, CAN, L1V 2P8. (416)427-3585. Richard Curtis, Richard Curtis Assoc., 164 East 64th St., New York, NY, USA, 10021.
Types of Production & Categories: TV Film-Wr; TV Video-Wr.
Genres: Drama-TV; Musical-Th&TV; Action-TV; Documentary-TV.
Biography: Born 1931, England. RAF, Aircrew (Flying Boats), 49-53; came to Canada, 54; Toronto policeman, 54-57; advertising writer, creative director, 57-74; freelance writer, 74-86. Has won Gold Lion at Cannes and all major North American Awards for TV advertising. Novelist: 4 crime novels published by Scribner in the US; winner, Scribner Crime Novel Award, 83; books reprinted in Britain, Japan, France, Germany and Holland.
Selective Filmography: *PRECISION BY THE TON,* In, 82, CDN, Wr; *AGING,* 'MAN ALIVE', TV, 77, CDN, Wr; *THE PEOPLE YOU NEVER SEE,* 'THE NATURE OF THINGS', TV, 76, CDN, Wr; *'SIDESTREET'* (1 eps), TV, 75, CDN, Wr; *SUSAN,* 'PEEPSHOW', TV, 75, CDN, Wr; *THE MAN ON FOUR BEAT,* 'GM PRESENTS', TV, 59, CDN, Wr.

WOODLAND, James

Woodland Entertainment, 2404 34th Ave.S.W., Calgary, Alta, CAN, T2T 2L8. (403)249-8006.

(cont/suite)

Types of Production & Categories: Th Film-Wr; Th Short-Wr/Dir; TV Film-Wr/Dir/Prod.
Genres: Comedy-Th&TV; Science Fiction-Th&TV; Documentary-TV; Educational-TV.
Biography: Born 1960, Trenton, Ontario; speaks English, German. Diploma in Film Production, Southern Alberta Institute of Technology, 80.
Selective Filmography: *NUCLEAR FREEZE/ZERO DEGREES,* ED, 86, CDN, Wr/Dir; *NUCLEAR WINTER/DEATH ZONE,* ED, 85, CDN, Wr/Dir; *WOMEN'S RIGHTS,* ED, 85, CDN, Wr/Dir; *SUZIE READER - A TRIBUTE,* TV, 85, CDN, Prod/Wr/Dir; *ALBERTA NATURAL LANDSCAPES,* TV, 85, CDN, Prod/Dir/Wr; *FORCE SASQUATCH SERVICE,* Th, 84, CDN, Co-Wr/Dir; *TOUR DE SASQUATCH,* Th, 84, CDN, Co-Wr/Dir; *APARTMENT ON THE DARK SIDE OF THE MOON,* TV, 84, CDN, 2nd AD; *SNOWBALLS,* Th, 84, CDN, Wr; *SASQUATCH SUMMER,* Th, 83, CDN, Co-Wr/Dir; *DEATH ZONE DRUG SET/OUTSIDE ON THE PLAYGROUND,* 'SCHOOL SMARTS', ED, 82, CDN, Wr/1st AD; *ALCOHOL CORRIDORS/GYM SAFETY TIPS/SCIENCE LABORATORY SAFETY TIPS,* 'SCHOOL SMARTS', ED, 82/81, CDN, Wr.

WOODS, Grahame

ACTRA. R.R. 1, Castleton, Ont, CAN, K0K 1M0. (416)344-7665. Lucinda Vardey, 297 Seaton St., Toronto, Ont, CAN, M5A 2T6. (416)922-0250.
Types of Production & Categories: TV Film-Wr; TV Video-Wr.
Genres: Drama-TV; Comedy-TV.
Biography: Born 1934. Author of over 60 commissioned dramatic productions for Canadian and American networks. Author of the novel 'Bloody Harvest' and the book for the musical 'A Gift to Last'.
Selective Filmography: *9-B,* TV, 86, CDN, Wr; *ANNE'S STORY,* TV, 81, CDN, Wr; *A QUESTION OF THE SIXTH,* TV, 80, CDN, Wr; *WAR BRIDES,* TV, 79, CDN, Wr (ACTRA); *'SIDESTREET'* (1 eps), TV, 75, CDN, Wr; *'THE COLLABORATORS'* (10 eps), TV, 74/73, CDN, Creator/Wr; *'POLICE SURGEON'* (1 eps), TV, 73, CDN/USA, Wr; *VICKY,* TV, 73, CDN, Wr (ACTRA); *THE DISPOSABLE MAN,* TV, 72, CDN, Wr; *KALINSKI'S JUSTICE,* TV, 71, CDN, Wr; *STRIKE!,* TV, 71, CDN, Wr; *WINTER'S DISCONTENT,* TV, 71, CDN, Dir/Wr; *12 1/2 CENTS,* TV, 70, CDN, Wr; *THE MERCENARIES,* TV, 70, CDN, Wr/Cin; *'CORWIN'* (1 eps), TV, 70, CDN, Wr/Cin; *'WOJECK'* (1 eps), TV, 68, CDN, Wr/Cin.

YOUNG, David S.

ACTRA. 34 Marchmount Rd., Toronto, Ont, CAN. (416)656-1692.
Types of Production & Categories: Th Film-Wr; TV Film-Wr; TV Video-Wr.
Genres: Drama-Th&TV; Comedy-TV; Children's-TV.
Biography: Born 1946, Oakville, Ontario. Published 2 novels: 'Incognito' and 'Agent Provocateur'; had 2 plays produced.
Selective Filmography: *'FRAGGLE ROCK'* (12 eps), TV, 86-82, CDN, Wr; *'THE EDISON TWINS'* (12 eps), TV, 86-82, CDN, Wr.

ZARITSKY, John - see DIRECTORS

ZELNIKER, Richard

ACTRA. 21 Tichester Rd., #1209, Toronto, Ont, CAN, M5P 1P3. (416)654-4691. Ralph Zimmerman, Great North Artists Mgmt., 345 Adelaide St.W., #500, Toronto, Ont, CAN. (416)593-2587.
Types of Production & Categories: Th Film-Wr; Th Short-Wr; TV Film-Wr; TV Video-Wr.
Genres: Drama-Th&TV; Comedy-Th&TV; Action-TV; Children's-Th&TV.

(cont/suite)

Biography: Born 1954, Montreal, Quebec. Has written plays for theatre: 'A Test of Will', 85; 'Scorched', 86. *DESTINY'S ANGEL* won an Honourable Mention, American Film Awards, 80.
Selective Filmography: *'CHECK IT OUT!'* (5 eps), TV, 86, CDN/USA, Story Ed/Staff Wr; *BON APPETIT,* Th, 82, USA, Scr; *HEY BABE,* Th, 81, CDN, Story Ed; *'LITTLEST HOBO'* (1 eps), TV, 81, CDN, Wr; *PINBALL SUMMER* (PICK-UP SUMMER), Th, 80, CDN, Scr; *DESTINY'S ANGEL,* Th, 80, CDN, Scr; *A SIMPLE COMPLEX,* Th, 78, CDN, Wr.

ZOLLER, Stephen

New Frontier Films Inc., 618 Adelaide St.W., Toronto, Ont, CAN, M6J 1A9. (416) 361-5798. Donald Kopaloff, 1930 Century Park W., Los Angeles, CA, USA, 90067. (213)203-8430.
Types of Production & Categories: Th Film-Wr/Prod; Th Short-Wr/Prod.
Genres: Drama-Th; Science Fiction-Th; Children's-Th.
Biography: Born 1952, Budapest, Hungary. *SNOW,* awarded at Chicago Film Festival, Genie nomination.
Selective Filmography: *SNOW,* Th, 82, CDN, Co-Prod/Wr; *THE TOMORROW MAN,* Th, 80, CDN, Wr/Co-Prod (**CFTA**); *METAL MESSIAH,* Th, 78, CDN, Co-Prod/Wr.

ZWICKER, Linda

ACTRA. 30 Hillsboro Ave., #1903, Toronto, Ont, CAN, M5R 1S7. (416)967-4103. Elizabeth Bradley, The Colbert Agency, 303 Davenport Rd., Toronto, Ont, CAN, M5R 1K5. (416)964-3302.
Types of Production & Categories: TV Film-Wr.
Genres: Drama-TV.
Biography: Born 1944, Saskatchewan. Background in music, arts administration, theatre production. Wrote 'Panther and Jaguar', 83, which won an Actra Award, Best Radio Program; Actra Award, Best Writer, Original Radio Program for 'Gray Pearls', 86.
Selective Filmography: *TAFIA'S DREAM,* 'SPIRIT BAY', TV, 85, CDN, Wr.

PRODUCERS
★
PRODUCTEURS

A'COURT, Susan - see WRITERS

ADAMS, G. Chalmers
CFTA. 251 Glencairn Ave., Toronto, Ont, CAN, M5N 1T8. 200 King St.W., Ste. 1912, Toronto, Ont, CAN, M5H 3T4. (416)597-8787.
Types of Production & Categories: Th Film-Prod; TV Film-Prod.
Genres: Drama-Th&TV.
Biography: Born Toronto, Ontario. Manager, C.F.D.C. (Toronto), 1969-72; founding President of CAMPP, 72; now a lawyer.
Selective Filmography: *PARTNERS*, Th, 76, CDN, Exec Prod/Prod; *HORSE LATITUDES*, TV, 75, CDN, Exec Prod/Co-Prod; *BRETHREN*, TV, 75, CDN, Exec Prod/Prod; *'SIDESTREET'* (2 eps), TV, 74, CDN, Prod; *THE CANARY*, TV, 74, CDN, Prod; *BETWEEN FRIENDS*, Th, 73, CDN, Exec Prod.

ALEXANDER, Andrew
Second City, 110 Lombard St., Toronto, Ont, CAN, M5C 1M3. (416)863-1162.
Types of Production & Categories: TV Film-Prod.
Genres: Comedy-TV; Experimental-Th&TV.
Biography: Born 1944, London, England. Education: Tri-State College; Ryerson Polytechnical Institute, 65. Owner, Second City Inc., since 74; acquired Chicago Second City, 85. *SCTV* received 13 Emmy nominations and won 2 (writing).
Selective Filmography: *'SCTV'* (195 eps), TV, 84-76, CDN, Creator/Exec Prod; *25th ANNIVERSARY OF SECOND CITY*, TV, 84, CDN, Exec Prod/Prod.

ALLEN, Tom C.
1207-1155 Harwood St., Vancouver, BC, CAN, V6E 1S1. (604)685-9936. Tom C. Allen Productions, 110-1089 West Broadway, Vancouver, BC, CAN, V6H 1E5. (604)731-3931.
Types of Production & Categories: TV Video-Prod.
Genres: Drama-TV; Documentary-TV; Educational-TV; Industrial-TV.
Biography: Born 1944, London, England; Canadian citizen. Certificate in Broadcast Communications (BCIT). Marketing and management skills; television production trainer/ instructor; experienced in technical maintenance and repair (video); has produced/directed 12 industrial videos.
Selective Filmography: *REFLEX CANADA*, In, 85, CDN, Prod; *ROLAND'S JAPAN TOUR*, TV, 84, CDN, Cam; *RAYMOND'S SPRING FEST*, In, 84, CDN, Cam; *MAKING IT*, TV, 84, CDN, Prod/Dir; *DREAM MATES*, In, 83, CDN, Dir.

ALLISON, Robert
CTPDA. 2519 Kline St., Halifax, NS, CAN, B3L 2X6. (902)865-4042. CBC, 1840 Bell Rd., Halifax, N.S., CAN, R3J 3E9. (902)420-4103
Types of Production & Categories: TV Film-Prod; TV Video-Prod.
Genres: Documentary-TV; Current Affairs-TV; News-TV.
Biography: Born 1942, Barrie, Ontario. Education: University of Manitoba, Arts. News reporter for private radio and TV: for CBC Winnipeg, 60-73; CBC Regina, 73-75; CBC Halifax, 75-81. Since 81, senior producer, TV News and current affairs, CBC Halifax.

ALMOND, Paul - see DIRECTORS

AMBURSKI, Henia
CFTA. 42 Manor Rd.E., Toronto, Ont, CAN, M4S 1P8. (416)484-6010. M&M Productions Inc., 189 Dupont St., Toronto, Ont, CAN, M5R 1V6. (416)968-9300.
Types of Production & Categories: TV Film-Prod; TV Video-Prod.
Genres: Documentary-TV; Educational-TV; Children's-TV; Industrial-TV.
Biography: Born 1947, West Germany; grew up in Israel; graduated from Hebrew University, Jerusalem; Canadian citizen. Has been producing film and video since 70.

(cont/suite)

Selective Filmography: *'VID KIDS'* (13 eps), TV, 86, CDN, Co-Prod **(CFTA)**; *THE FRAGILE TREE HAS ROOTS,* TV, 85, CDN, Co-Prod; *STAR SONG,* TV, 84, CDN, Prod; *CELLY AND FRIENDS,* TV, 84, CDN, Co-Prod; *VINCENT PRICE'S DRACULA,* TV, 83, CDN, Co-Prod; *MONEY TO BURN,* TV, 83, CDN, Co-Prod; *WARMING TO WOOD,* TV, 83, CDN, Co-Prod; *SUNSHINE FOR SALE,* TV, 83, CDN, Co-Prod; *TAKING A LEAP,* In, 83, CDN, Co-Prod; *THANKS A LOT,* TV, 82, CDN, Co-Prod; *WATER: FRIEND OR FOE,* TV, 82, CDN, Co-Prod; *THE GREENING OF THE NORTH,* In, 82, CDN, Co-Prod; *YOU DON'T SMOKE EH?/LIVING PROOF,* ED, 81/80, CDN, Co-Prod; *LIBERATION,* TV, 80, CDN, Co-Prod; *SILENCE IS KILLING,* TV, 76/75, CDN, Co-Prod; *A DOVE WITH CLIPPED WINGS,* TV, 75, CDN, Co-Prod.

APOR, Gabor - see DIRECTORS

ARMSTRONG, Mary

APFVQ, ARRFQ. Cinéfort inc., 3603 St-Laurent, Montreal, Que, CAN, H2X 2V5. (514)289-9477.
Types of Production & Categories: TV Film-Prod/Dir.
Genres: Drama-TV; Documentary-TV; Children's-TV; Industrial-TV.
Biography: Born 1953, Winnipeg, Manitoba. Speaks English, French, Spanish. Film Degree, Concordia University. Her films won awards at the American, U.S. Industrial and National Educational Film Festivals.
Selective Filmography: *SEASON ON THE WATER,* 'A LIFE'S WORK', TV, 86, CDN, Co-Prod/1st AD; *WELCOME TO PUBLIC SERVICE,* In, 85, CDN, Wr/Dir; *NON-TRADITIONAL,* In, 83, CDN, Dir/Wr; *MUSIC THERAPY,* ED, 83, CDN, Co-Prod/Dir; *PATIENTS' RIGHTS,* In, 83, CDN, Prod/Dir; *EVERYONE'S BUSINESS,* TV, 82, CDN, Prod/Dir; *YOU COULD SAVE A LIFE,* TV, 80, CDN, Prod/Wr/Dir; *OUR HOUSE,* TV, 78, CDN, Prod/Dir; *NATIVE DOCUMENT,* ED, 78, CDN, Prod/Dir; *AISLIN,* TV, 76, CDN, Prod/Dir.

ARRON, Wayne

Wayne Arron Films Ltd., 26 Tichester Rd., #102, Toronto, Ont, CAN, M5P 1P1. (416)656-6290.
Types of Production & Categories: Th Film-Prod; TV Film-Prod.
Genres: Drama-Th&TV; Action-Th&TV; Documentary-Th&TV.
Biography: Born 1949, Ottawa, Ontario. M.A., B.A., University of Toronto; 10 years experience in film and TV production. *RAOUL WALLENBERG: BURIED ALIVE* won a Certificate of Merit, Academy Awards, Red Ribbon, American Film Festival and a Silver Plaque, Chicago.
Selective Filmography: *'OWL TV'* (10 eps), TV, 85, CDN, Spv Pro Acc't; *THE PARK IS MINE,* TV, 84, CDN/USA, Pro Acc't; *EVERGREEN* (mini-series), TV, 84, USA, Assist Pro Acc't; *RAOUL WALLENBERG: BURIED ALIVE,* Th, 83, CDN, Prod **(GENIE)**; *THE CHINESE* (6 eps), TV, 82/81, CDN, Spv Pro Acc't; *EXPOSURE,* TV, 80, CDN, Prod; *GAS,* Th, 80, CDN, Pro Acc't; *THE FUNNY FARM,* Th, 80, CDN, Pro Acc't; *ARIANE,* TV, 79, CDN, Prod; *HEAD ON,* Th, 79, CDN, Pro Acc't; *TANYA'S ISLAND,* Th, 79, CDN, Pro Acc't; *THE BROOD,* Th, 79, CDN, Pro Acc't; *'PLANET OF PROMISE'* (10 eps), ED, 78, CDN, Pro Acc't; *MUTATION* (M3- THE GEMINI STRAIN), Th, 77, CDN, Assoc Prod; *LIES,* TV, 76, CDN, Exec Prod.

AUBIN, Maurice

CTPDA. 9119-81 Avenue, Edmonton, Alta, CAN, T6C 0W9. CBXT-TV, 8861-75th St., Edmonton, Alta, CAN, T6C 4G8. (403)469-2321.
Types of Production & Categories: TV Video-Prod/Dir.
Genres: Drama-TV; Variety-TV; Documentary-TV; Music Video-TV.

(cont/suite)

PRODUCTEURS/PRODUCERS

Biography: Born 1954, Sudbury, Ontario; bilingual. B.A., Music, University of Ottawa. Has worked in radio, TV and theatre; has also worked as a recording artist, studio musician. *A CHRISTMAS PRESENCE* won the Canadian Music Council Award.
Selective Filmography: *AMPIA AWARDS* (2 shows), TV, 86/85, CDN, Prod; *'A SUMMER'S MUSIC'* (11 eps), TV, 85, CDN, Prod/Dir; *BABY ON THE RADIO,* MV, 85, CDN, Prod/Dir/Wr; *'ROCK WARS'* (1 eps), TV, 84, CDN, Prod; *A CHRISTMAS PRESENCE,* TV, 84, CDN, Prod/Dir; *THEATRE SPORTS SPECTACULAR,* TV, 83, CDN, Prod/Dir; *'STEPPIN' OUT'* (pilot), TV, 83, CDN, Prod/Dir; *SURVIVAL* (4 short films), TV, 82, CDN, 2nd U Dir.

BAILEY, Don - see WRITERS

BARCLAY, Robert - see DIRECTORS

BARDE, Barbara

433 Montrose Ave., Toronto, Ont, CAN, M6E 3H2. (416)532-6708. Why Not Productions Inc., 322 King St.W., Toronto, Ont, CAN, M5V 1J2. (416)591-8598.
Types of Production & Categories: TV Film-Prod/Dir; TV Video-Prod/Dir.
Genres: Drama-TV; Documentary-TV; Educational-TV; Children's-TV.
Biography: Born 1947, St. Paul, Minnesota; Canadian citizen; bilingual. B.A., Journalism and Political Science, Syracuse University; M.A., Mass communications. Eleven years at TV Ontario as director/producer; President, Why Not Productions Inc.; has filmed in Asia, Africa, Latin America. *NORTH OF 60, DESTINY UNCERTAIN* awarded at American Film Festival, 83; *THE AFRICA FILE*, Japan Prize, 75.
Selective Filmography: *'INDONESIA: A GENERATION OF CHANGE'* (4 eps), TV, 86/85, CDN, Prod/Dir; *BRIEFING PROGRAMS FOR CANADIANS WORKING IN INDONESIA* (3 eps), In, 86/85, CDN, Prod/Dir; *ISLANDS IN THE WEB OF TIME: THE QUEEN CHARLOTTES,* TV, 86/85, CDN, Prod/Dir; *'PATHS OF DEVELOPMENT'* (6 eps), TV, 85-83, CDN, Prod/Dir; *'NORTH OF 60, DESTINY UNCERTAIN'* (13 eps), TV, 83-80, CDN, Prod/Dir; *'SEE, HEAR'* (40 eps), TV, 83-78, CDN, Prod/Dir; *'CANADA - THE GREAT EXPERIMENT'* (13 eps), TV, 82-80, CDN, Prod/Dir; *'LIKE NO OTHER PLACE'* (13 eps), TV, 80-77, CDN, Prod/Dir; *'ONE WORLD'* (13 eps), TV, 79/78, CDN, Prod/Dir; *'COPE'* (52 eps), TV, 77-75, CDN, Prod; *'THE AFRICA FILE'* (18 eps), TV, 75-73, CDN, Assoc Prod; *'IT'S NOT SO DIFFICILE'* (26 eps), TV, 73, CDN, Prod; *'CONCEPTS IN ECONOMICS'* (4 eps), TV, 71, CDN, Assoc Prod; *'URBAN SOCIOLOGY'* (3 eps), TV, 71, CDN, Res/Wr; *'THE THIRD WORLD'* (6 eps), TV, 70, CDN, Res; *'URBAN GEOGRAPHY'* (8 eps), TV, 70, CDN, Res/Wr.

BARKER, David

CTPDA. Interlaser Productions, 4598 W. 14th Ave., Vancouver, BC, CAN, V6R 2Y4. (604)224-4549.
Types of Production & Categories: TV Film-Prod/Dir; TV Video-Prod/Dir.
Genres: Documentary-TV; Current Affairs-TV; News-TV.
Biography: Born 1945, London, England; legally able to work in Canada, USA and Common market. Languages: English, French, some German and Swiss-German. Honours B.A., Queen's University. Reporter/editor/writer, news and information, 67-79; producer, news, 80-83; programs and designs interactive videodiscs.
Selective Filmography: *CANADA DAY* (EXPO 86), TV, 86, CDN, Prod/Dir; *'BEST YEARS'* (23 eps), TV, 86/85, CDN, Prod/Dir/Wr; *FEDERAL ELECTION/ B.C. PROVINCIAL ELECTION,* TV, 84/83, CDN, Prod.

BARLOW, David

ACTRA, ATPD, WGAw. 28 Henry Lane Terrace, Toronto, Ont, CAN, M5A 4A1.

(cont/suite)

(416)366-0605. CBC, Box 500, Stn. A, Toronto, Ont, CAN, M5W 1E6. (416)975-7105.
Types of Production & Categories: TV Film-Prod/Wr; TV Video-Prod/Wr.
Genres: Drama-TV; Comedy-TV; Action-TV.
Biography: Born 1946, Hamilton, Ontario. B.A., Queen's University; M.A., Theatre, Northwestern University. Worked as a theatre administrator, stage manager, lighting designer and lighting crew chief, 70-75. Member, Crime Writers of Canada.
Selective Filmography: *'SEEING THINGS'* (Co-Wr-3 eps), (43 eps), TV, 86-81, CDN, Co-Creator/Co-Exec Story Ed/Co-Prod (**ANIK**); *'ANGIE'* (1 eps), TV, 79, USA, Co-Wr; *'KING OF KENSINGTON'* (45 eps), TV, 78-76, CDN, Assoc Prod; *'KING OF KENSINGTON'* (18 eps), TV, 76/75, CDN, Unit M; *THREE'S A CROWD* (pilot), TV, 76, CDN, Unit M; *RIMSHOTS* (pilot), TV, 76, CDN, Assoc Prod; *'PEEP SHOW'* (5 eps), TV, 75, CDN, Unit M.

BARNHOLDEN, Earl

CTPDA. 1590 West 15th Ave., #101, Vancouver, BC, CAN, V6J 2K6. (604)731-9631. Vancouver City College, Dept. of Journalism, 100 West 49th Ave., Vancouver, BC, CAN.
Types of Production & Categories: TV Film-Prod; TV Video-Prod.
Genres: Action-TV; Documentary-TV; Educational-TV; Children's-TV.
Biography: Born 1928, Moose Jaw, Saskatchewan. Worked in wire service, magazine writing, newspaper reporting, radio journalism, 47-57. From 57-84, worked at CBC TV as news and documentary producer with experience in special events and TV election productions. Teaching broadcast journalism, Vancouver Community College, 86; freelance producing.

BAYLIS, Paul

CTPDA. 5885 Spring Garden Rd., #1012, Halifax, NS, CAN, B3H 1Y3. (902) 425-7022. CBC, 1840 Bere Rd. Box 3000, Halifax, NS, CAN, B3J 3E9. (902)420-4151.
Types of Production & Categories: TV Video-Prod/Dir.
Genres: Variety-TV; Educational-TV; Children's-TV; Current Affairs-TV.
Biography: Born 1933, Toronto, Ontario. Education: Radio & TV Arts, Ryerson Polytechnical Institute, 52-53. Joined CBC as announcer, 53-56; production assistant, CBC (Halifax), 56-59; producer/director since 59.
Selective Filmography: *'1ST EDITION'*, TV, 85-84, CDN, Dir; *'REACH FOR THE TOP'* (N.S. & P.E.I.), TV, 85-66, CDN, Prod/Dir; *'MEETING PLACE'*, TV, 83-63, CDN, Prod/Dir; *'REACH FOR THE TOP'* (NATIONAL FINALS), TV, 80-68, CDN, Prod/Dir; *'SINGALONG JUBILEE'*, TV, 75-72, CDN, Prod/Dir; *'ROUNDABOUT'*, TV, 75-70, CDN, Prod/Dir; *'DON MESSER'S JUBILEE'*, TV, 72-69, CDN, Prod/Dir; *'HI SOCIETY'*, TV, 72-60, CDN, Prod/Dir; *'MUSIC HOP'* (LET'S GO), TV, 70-65, CDN, Prod/Dir.

BAYLIS, Robert

APFVQ. 860 Normand St., Laval, Que, CAN, H7P 3Z4. (514)625-5231. 5890 Monkland Ave., Montreal, Que, CAN, H4A 1G1. (514)483-6074.
Types of Production & Categories: Th Film-PM/Prod; TV Film-PM/Prod.
Genres: Drama-Th&TV; Action-Th&TV; Documentary-TV; Animation-Th&TV.
Biography: Born 1935, Montreal, Quebec. Attended university in Canada and US (Political Science, History). Languages: English, French, Italian. Producer/production manager, NFB, 56-68, over 75 documentaries.
Selective Filmography: *LOVE SONGS* (PAROLES ET MUSIQUE), Th, 84, CDN/F, Co-Prod; *MARIA CHAPDELAINE*, Th, 83, CDN/F, Co-Exec Prod; *SILENCE OF THE NORTH,* Th, 80/79, CDN, Co-Prod; *DEATH HUNT,* Th, 80, USA, Co-Prod; *MEATBALLS,* Th, 79, CDN, PM; *AGENCY,* Th, 78, CDN, Assoc Prod; *'THE NEWCOMERS'* (3 eps), TV, 76, CDN, PM; *'MAN OF THE NORTH'* (4 eps), TV, 76, CDN, PM; *CHILD UNDER A LEAF,* Th, 74, CDN, Co-Prod; *TIKI-TIKI,* Th, 69, CDN, PM.

BEARDE, Chris

ACTRA, AFTRA, DGA, WGAw. 2220 Ave. of the Stars, #501, Los Angeles, CA, USA, 90067. (213)277-0800. William Morris Agency, 131 El Camino Dr., Beverly Hills, CA, USA. (213)274-7451.
Types of Production & Categories: TV Video-Prod/Wr.
Genres: Comedy-TV; Variety-TV; Musical-TV; Children's-TV.
Biography: Born in U.K.; emigrated to Canada, 62. Has received 12 Emmy nominations, 4 Writers Guild nominations; won the Golden Globe Award for *SONNY & CHER COMEDY HOUR.*
Selective Filmography: *'FTV'* (36 eps), TV, 86/85, USA, Creator/Exec Prod; *'PUTTIN' ON THE HITS'* (80 eps), TV, 85-81, USA, Creator/Co-Exec Prod; *HYSTERICAL,* MV, 80, USA, Dir; *BOB HOPE IN AUSTRALIA,* TV, 79, USA, Prod; *'THE GONG SHOW'* (120 eps), TV, 78-75, USA, Co-Prod/Creator; *BOB HOPE CHRISTMAS SPECIAL,* TV, 78, USA, Prod; *'BILL COSBY'* (7 eps), TV, 78, USA, Prod; *'BOBBY VINTON'* (48 eps), TV, 77-75, CDN/USA, Prod; *'RAZZLE DAZZLE'* (18 eps), TV, 75, USA/CDN, Co-Prod; *THE JACKSONS* (JACKSON 5 SPECIAL), TV, 75, USA, Co-Prod; *'SONNY & CHER COMEDY HOUR'* (90 eps), TV, 74-71, USA, Co-Prod; *'HUDSON BROTHERS' COMEDY HOUR'* (13 eps), TV, 74, USA, Co-Prod; *'SONNY & CHER SHOW'* (13 eps), TV, 71, USA, Co-Prod; *'ANDY WILLIAMS'* (48 eps), TV, 70/69, USA, Co-Prod; *'RAY STEVENS'* (WHO IS RAY STEVENS), (13 eps), TV, 70, CDN/USA, Co-Prod; *'LAUGH IN'* (48 eps), TV, 69/68, USA, Wr (EMMY); *GRAMMY AWARDS,* TV, 69, USA, Wr; *'WHERE THE GIRLS ARE'* (1 eps), TV, 69, USA, Wr; *'ROMP'* (1 eps), TV, 69, USA, Wr; *ANDY'S COVE CONCERT,* TV, 69, USA, Wr; *'ROCK SCENE'* (1 eps), TV, 68, CDN, Wr; *'LIKE HEP'* (1 eps), TV, 68, USA, Wr; *ELVIS* (SINGER PRESENTS ELVIS), TV, 68, USA, Wr; *'NIGHTCAP'* (60 eps), TV, 67-63, CDN, Wr; *'TOMMY HUNTER'* (sev eps), TV, 67-64, CDN, Wr; *'JULLIETTE'* (1 eps), TV, 67, CDN, Wr; *'IN PERSON'* (13 eps), TV, 67, CDN, Wr; *'SANDRA'* (1 eps), TV, 66, CDN, Wr; *'FRONT & CENTRE'* (13 eps), TV, 63, CDN, Wr; *'NETWORK'* (13 eps), TV, 62, CDN, Wr.

BEAUBIEN, Conrad

Conservision Productions Inc., 8081 Kennedy Rd., Unionville, Ont, CAN, L3R 2E6. (416)477-3821.
Types of Production & Categories: TV Film-Prod/Dir; TV Video-Prod/Dir.
Genres: Drama-TV; Variety-TV; Musical-TV; Educational-TV.
Biography: Born 1947; Canadian; 20 year career in film, TV and music.
Selective Filmography: *'SKETCHES OF OUR TOWN'* (26 eps), TV, 86/85, CDN, Prod/Exec Prod/Dir; *SUN LIFE/AGINCOURT INTERIORS/ALEX COLVILLE,* Cm, 85-82, CDN, Prod/Dir; *NORTHERN AFFAIRS,* ED, 85, CDN, Dir; *ROTO-STATIC/BIRTH OF A CHIP,* In, 85/84, CDN, Prod/Dir; *'DEPT. NATIONAL DEFENSE'* (13 eps), ED, 84, CDN, Dir; *'STRANGE BUT TRUE'* (26 eps), TV, 83, CDN/USA/GB, Co-Prod; *FRED DOBBS GOES TO HOLLYWOOD,* TV, 83, CDN/USA, Exec Prod; *ENERGY, A TIME FOR LEARNING/WHAT'S IT ALL ABOUT,* ED, 82/81, CDN, Prod/Dir; *ADJUSTMENT,* ED, 80, CDN, Dir.

BEAUBIEN, Joseph F.

377 Roslyn Rd., Westmount, Qué, CAN, H3Z 2N7. (514)935-3955.
Types de production et Catégories: l métrage-Prod; TV film-Prod.
Types d'oeuvres: Drame-C; Action-C; Documentaire-TV.
Curriculum vitae: Né en 1938, Montréal, Québec. A étudié le Droit à l'Université McGill. Avocat; conseiller juridique, SDICC (maintenant Telefilm), 70-78; producteur exécutif, longs métrages, 78-84; Président, Vidéo Globe I Inc. depuis 84.
Filmographie sélective: *YOU'VE COME A LONG WAY LADIES* (WOMEN IN SPORTS IN CANADA), TV, 84, CDN, Prod exéc; *HEARTACHES,* C, 81, CDN, Co prod exéc; *UNE JOURNEE EN TAXI,* C, 81, CDN, Co prod exéc; *ATLANTIC CITY,* C, 79, CDN/USA, Co prod exéc; *A NOUS DEUX* (AN ADVENTURE FOR TWO), C, 78, CDN/F, Prod exéc.

PRODUCERS/PRODUCTEURS

BEAUDRY, Hélène

APFVQ. 4745 ave. Grosvenor, Montréal, Qué, CAN, H3W 2L9. Prod. Beaudry-Tremblay inc., 409 rue St-Nicolas, #301, Montréal, Qué, CAN, H2Y 2P4. (514) 288-0036.
Types de production et Catégories: TV film-Prod; TV vidéo-Prod.
Types d'oeuvres: Annonces-TV.
Curriculum vitae: Née à Montréal, Québec; bilingue. Producteur d'émissions TV: *VOUS ETES TEMOIN, PARIS CHANTE, SUR DEMANDE.* Dans le domaine de la publicité, producteur d'annonces pour la radio et la télévision; présidente de la Filmothèque (module de production électronique) de l'Agence BCP Publicité pendant 16 ans. Producteur de plusieurs annonces gagnantes du Coq d'Or du Publicité Club de Montréal; entre autres 'On est 6 millions'(Labatt), 'Venez comme vous êtes'(Air Canada), 'Allo'(Bell Canada) etc..

BEDEL, Jean-Pierre - see DIRECTORS

BELEC, Marilyn A. - see DIRECTORS

BENOIT, Ted

1700 St.Mary's Rd., #7, Winnipeg, Man, CAN. (204)257-6411. Spectra Video Productions Ltd., 1253 Clarence Ave., Bay 3, Winnipeg, Man, CAN, R3T 1T4. (204)452-9832.
Types of Production & Categories: TV Video-Prod.
Genres: Variety-TV; Documentary-TV; Educational-TV; Children's-TV.
Biography: Born 1924. CBC TV producer for 22 years; involved in all facets of TV production. Since opening Spectra Video, 79, has been involved with commercial, documentary and industrial video tape production.
Selective Filmography: *'ATHLETES & INJURY'* (6 eps), ED, 84, CDN, Exec Prod; *'EXPLORATIONS'* (13 eps), ED, 83, CDN, Exec Prod.

BERMAN, Brigitte - see DIRECTORS

BERTOLINO, Daniel

APFVQ, UDA. Les Prods. Via le Monde Inc., 326 rue St-Paul ouest, Montréal, Qué, CAN, H2Y 2A3. (514)285-1658.
Types de production et Catégories: c métrage-Prod/Réal; TV film-Prod/Réal; TV vidéo-Prod/Réal.
Types d'oeuvres: Documentaire-C&TV; Enfants-TV.
Curriculum vitae: Né en 1942; au Canada depuis 67. Fondateur des Productions Via la Monde Inc.. A écrit et réalisé 158 films tournés dans presque tous les pays du globe. Directeur de l'information de l'Unicef au Québec pour l'année de l'enfance, 79; Vice-président de l'APFVQ depuis 82.
Filmographie sélective: *'LEGENDES DU MONDE',* TV, 86-83, CDN, Prod/Co réal; *'LEGENDES INDIENNES',* TV, 82/81, CDN, Prod; *LE PARADIS DES CHEFS,* 'LES GRANDS REPORTAGES', TV, 80, CDN, Réal; *'A COEUR BATTANT',* TV, 79/78, CDN, Réal; *LES AMIS DE MES AMIS,* TV, 79, CDN, Réal; *'LES GRANDS REPORTAGES'* (YASSER ARAFAT), TV, 79, CDN, Prod; *NOSOTROS CUBANOS,* C, 78, CDN, Co réal; *'POSTE FRONTIERE',* TV, 77-74, CDN, Prod/Réal; *'LAISSEZ-PASSER',* TV, 77-74, CDN, Prod/Réal; *AHO - AU COEUR DU MONDE PRIMITIF* (AHO - THE FOREST PEOPLE), C, 76, CDN, Prod **(CFA)**; *LES PRIMITIFS* (4 films), C, 76-72, CDN, Réal.

BITTMAN, Roman

CFTA. 290 Palmerston Ave., Toronto, Ont, CAN, M6J 2J4. (416)962-5652. Mobius, 188 Davenport Rd., Toronto, Ont, CAN, M5R 1J2. (416)964-8484.
Types of Production & Categories: Th Short-Dir/Prod/Wr; TV Film-Dir/Prod/Wr; TV Video-Dir/Prod/Wr.
Genres: Drama-TV; Documentary-TV; Educational-TV.

(cont/suite)

Biography: Born 1941; more than 25 years experience in radio, television film and video production and distribution business in Canada (CBC, NFB, independent); has produced 70 documentaries.
Selective Filmography: *SMOKE RINGS,* TV, 86, CDN, Wr/Dir; *THE SEA IS AT OUR GATES,* TV, 85, CDN, Wr/Dir; *SAFE PASSAGE,* ED, 85, CDN, Wr/Dir; *THE BATTLE OF THE ATLANTIC,* TV, 84, CDN, Prod/Dir; *'ACCESS'* (10 eps), TV, 83, CDN, Prod/Dir/Wr; *JEAN VANIER: HOPE AMONG THE RUINS/ THOMAS MERTON: MONK ON THE RUN,* 'MAN ALIVE', TV, 82/79, CDN, Prod/Dir/Wr; *CASTLES IN THE AIR,* TV, 81, CDN, Prod/Dir/Wr; *THE INVESTMANT PICTURE,* ED, 80, CDN, Prod/Dir/Wr; *CAUGHT BETWEEN, THE ENGLISH IN QUEBEC,* TV, 78, CDN, Prod/Dir/Wr; *THE ECONOMICS OF SEPARATION,* TV, 78, CDN, Prod/Dir/Wr; *BIOSPHERE,* TV, 77, CDN, Exec Prod; *NO ACT OF GOD,* TV, 77, CDN, Exec Prod; *A SENSE OF PLACE,* TV, 76, CDN, Exec Prod/Wr; *THE LAND: A NEW PRIORITY,* TV, 76, CDN, Exec Prod; *A NEW BARGAIN,* TV, 75, CDN, Exec Prod; *RITES AND RITUALS OF NEW GUINEA,* TV, 74, CDN, Dir/Wr; *THE CLUB OF ROME/AND GOD CREATED GREAT WHALES,* 'THE NATURE OF THINGS', TV, 73, CDN, Prod/Dir; *THE JOY OF EFFORT,* TV, 73, CDN, Prod/Dir; *SEALSONG,* TV, 73, CDN, Wr/Prod; *MAN & WOMAN WHAT'S THE DIFFERENCE?/THE BLUE HOLES OF ANDROS,* 'THE NATURE OF THINGS', TV, 72/71, CDN, Prod/ Dir; *STOCKHOLM '72-POLITICS FOR SURVIVAL/THE ICE LOVERS,* 'THE NATURE OF THINGS', TV, 72/71, CDN, Prod/Dir; *LOBSTER AND THE SEA/DECADE SCIENCE REVIEW,* 'THE NATURE OF THINGS', TV, 70, CDN, Prod/Dir; *POPULATION: EVERYBODY'S BABY,* 'THE NATURE OF THINGS', TV, 70, CDN, Prod/Dir; *THE GLOBAL CRISIS (6 eps)/ ENGINEERING (13 eps),* 'THE NATURE OF THINGS', TV, 69/68, CDN, Prod/ Dir.

BLYE, Gary

ACTRA, AFTRA. 11620 Wilshire Blvd., #500, Los Angeles, CA, USA, 90025. (213)657-8740. Gary Blye Enterprises, 85 Richmond St.W., #315, Toronto, Ont, CAN. (416)367-0700. Catherine McCartney, Prendergast Agency, 260 Richmond St.W., #405, Toronto, Ont, CAN, M5V 1W5. (416)922-5308.
Types of Production & Categories: TV Film-Prod; TV Video-Prod.
Genres: Variety-TV; Musical-TV; Documentary-TV; Children's-TV.
Biography: Born 1944, Winnipeg, Manitoba. Graduate, St. John's Tech.; attended Univerity of Manitoba, L.A. Valley College, California State (Northridge), UCLA. Worked as administrative assistant to Col. Tom Parker; TV variety agent/packager, William Morris Agency (Beverly Hills); now independent producer.
Selective Filmography: *MOLSON INDY RACE,* TV, 86, CDN, Prod; *GALA EVENING* (EXPO 86), TV, 86, CDN, Co Prod; *GENIE AWARDS* (2 shows), TV, 86/85, CDN, Co-Prod; *COUNTDOWN TO THE GENIES* (2 shows), TV, 86/85, CDN, Co-Prod; *JUNO AWARDS,* TV, 85, CDN, Co-Prod; *JUNO AWARDS SPECIAL,* TV, 84, CDN, Prod; *POWER OF PURPOSE,* TV, 84, CDN, Prod; *DOLLY PARTON IN LONDON,* TV, 83, USA, Assoc Prod; *HONEYMOON HAVEN,* TV, 83, CDN, Pro Exec; *COLD STORAGE,* TV, 83, CDN, Pro Exec; *'SNOW JOB',* TV, 83/82, CDN, Pro Exec; *NEIL SEDAKA,* TV, 82, CDN, Pro Exec; *DAVID STEINBERG,* TV, 82, CDN, Pro Exec; *OMNIBUS,* TV, 80, USA, Pro Exec; *PSYCHODRAMA,* TV, 79/78, CDN, Exec Prod; *SPECTACULAR EVENING IN PARIS,* TV, 78/77, USA/F, Co-Prod; *OSMONDS SPECIAL,* TV, 74, USA, Assoc Prod; *JACKSON FIVE SPECIAL,* TV, 74, USA, Assoc Prod; *'SONNY & CHER COMEDY HOUR',* TV, 72/71, USA, Assoc Prod; *SUPERSTARS OF ROCK,* TV, 71, USA, Co-Prod.

BOA, Anne

206-1100 W.7th Ave., Vancouver, BC, CAN, V6H 1B4. (604)736-7220. CKVU-TV, 180 West 2nd Ave., Vancouver, BC, CAN. (604)876-1344.
(cont/suite)

Types of Production & Categories: TV Film-Prod; TV Video-Prod/Dir.
Genres: Variety-TV; Documentary-TV; News-TV.
Biography: Born 1953, Toronto, Ontario; bilingual. B.F.A., University of Guelph (Printmaking, Interior Design); B.Ed., Queen's University (Art History, French, English, Physical Education); University of Guanajuato, Mexico (Fine Arts, Spanish, Photography).
Selective Filmography: *'FIRST NEWS'* (VANCOUVER), TV, 86-84, CDN, Prod; *'NEWS ROOM'* (HAMILTON), TV, 83-81, CDN, Prod/Dir; *'VANCOUVER SHOW'*, TV, 81-79, CDN, Report.

BOARD, John

DGC. 326 1/2 Bloor St.W., Toronto, Ont, CAN, M5S 1W5. (416)922-8676.
Types of Production & Categories: Th Film-Prod/1st AD; TV Film-1st Ad.
Genres: Drama-Th&TV; Comedy-Th&TV; Horror-Th.
Biography: Born 1934, Hamilton, Ontario. Education: Trinity College, University of Western Ontario.
Selective Filmography: *THE FLY*, Th, 86, USA, 1st AD; *PIPPI LONGSTOCKING* (2 parts), TV, 85, USA, 1st AD; *OVERNIGHT*, Th, 85, CDN, Co-Prod/1st AD; *A LETTER TO THREE WIVES*, TV, 85, USA, 1st AD; *AGNES OF GOD*, Th, 84, USA, 1st AD; *EVERGREEN* (mini-series), TV, 84, USA, 1st AD; *THE DEAD ZONE*, Th, 83, USA, 1st AD; *MARTIN'S DAY*, Th, 83, CDN/GB, 2nd U Dir; *WHEN WE FIRST MET*, TV, 83, USA, Assoc Prod/1st AD; *WILL THERE REALLY BE A MORNING?*, TV, 82, USA, 1st AD; *VIDEODROME*, Th, 81, CDN, 1st AD; *THE GREY FOX*, Th, 80, CDN, Assoc Prod/1st AD; *THE HOUNDS OF NOTRE DAME*, Th, 80, CDN, 1st AD; *ATLANTIC CITY*, Th, 79, CDN/USA, 1st AD; *HEAD ON*, Th, 79, CDN, 1st AD; *THE BROOD*, Th, 78, CDN, 1st AD/Post PM; *COUP D'ETAT* (POWER PLAY), (STATE OF SHOCK), Th, 77, CDN, 1st AD; *MONKEYS IN THE ATTIC*, Th, 74, CDN, Assoc Prod; *WEDDING IN WHITE*, Th, 73, CDN, 1st AD; *THE MERRY WIVES OF TOBIAS ROUKE*, Th, 71, CDN, Co-Prod/Dir.

BOIRE, Roger

STCQ. 575 Lebrun, Montréal, Qué, CAN, H1L 5C5. (514)352-8995.
Types de production et Catégories: c métrage-Réal/Prod/Mont.
Types d'oeuvres: Drame-C; Comédie-C; Comédie musicale-C; Education-C.
Curriculum vitae: Né en 1948, Montréal, Québec; bilingue. Bac. en Philosophie, U. Q.A.M.; Cinéma, London Film School, Angleterre. Monteur sonore sur plusieurs longs métrages, 85-86.
Filmographie sélective: *IL FAUT CHERCHER POUR APPRENDRE*, C, 81, CDN, Prod/Mont; *HISTOIRE VECUE*, C, 79, CDN, Ass réal; *JEUX DE PORTES*, C, 79, CDN, Prod/Cam; *AU BOUT DU DOUTE*, C, 78, CDN, Cam; *UN GARS BEN CHANCEUX*, C, 77, CDN, Réal; *LA CUEILLETTE DU TABAC D'HIER A DEMAIN*, C, 76, CDN, Prod/Mont.

BOISVERT, Nicole M.

5722 rue Déom, Montréal, Qué, CAN, H3S 2M4.
Types de production et Catégories: l métrage-Prod; c métrage-Prod.
Types d'oeuvres: Drame-C; Horreur-C; Animation-C.
Curriculum vitae: Citoyenne canadienne. Responsable des ventes, achats et de la distribution de films européens au Québec jusqu'en 76; Présidente, Les Productions Agora Inc., 76-83; Présidente, APFVQ, et Vice-présidente, producteur exécutif, SDA Productions Ltée., 82; Présidente directrice-générale, Société générale du cinéma du Québec, 84-85. *POURQUOI L'ETRANGE MONSIEUR ZOLOCK S'INTERESSAIT-IL TANT A LA BANDE DESSINEE?* gagne le Prix Spécial du Jury à Banff.

(cont/suite)

Filmographie sélective: *POURQUOI L'ETRANGE M.ZOLOCK S'INTERESSAIT-IL A LA BANDE DESSINEE?*, C, 83, CDN, Prod dél **(GENIE)**; *HEARTACHES*, C, 81, CDN, Co prod exéc; *AU REVOIR...A LUNDI* (SEE YOU MONDAY), C, 79, CDN/F, Co prod; *BLACKOUT*, C, 77, CDN, Co prod.

BONIN, Claude

APFVQ. Les Films Vision 4 inc., 402 Notre-Dame est, Montréal, Qué, CAN, H2Y 1C8. (514)844-2855.
Types de production et Catégories: 1 métrage-Prod.
Types d'oeuvres: Drame-C; Documentaire-C.
Curriculum vitae: Né en 1948, Montréal, Québec; bilingue.
Filmographie sélective: *HENRI*, C, 86, CDN, Prod; *PELLAN*, C, 86, CDN, Prod; *POUVOIR INTIME*, C, 85, CDN, Prod; *ANNE TRISTER*, C, 85, CDN, Prod assoc; *LA GUERRE DES TUQUES* (THE DOG WHO STOPPED THE WAR), C, 84, CDN, Prod dél; *LES ANNEES DE REVE*, C, 83, CDN, Prod; *LA DIVINE SARAH*, TV, 83, CDN, Prod exéc.

BONIN, Jacques

APFVQ. 1606 blvd. Gouin est, Montréal, Qué, CAN, H2C 1C3. (514)383-5325. 406 rue Notre-Dame est, Montréal, Qué, CAN, H2Y 1C8. (514)282-9662.
Types de production et Catégories: TV film-Prod; TV vidéo-Prod.
Types d'oeuvres: Documentaire-TV; Education-TV; Enfants-TV.
Curriculum vitae: Né en 1951, Montréal, Québec; bilingue. Bac. en Communications (Cinéma et TV), Université du Québec à Montréal.
Filmographie sélective: *HENRI*, Th, 86/85, CDN, Prod assoc; *'TELEGRAMMES'* (22 eps), TV, 86, CDN, Prod; *POUVOIR INTIME*, C, 85, CDN, Prod assoc; *'L'ARGENT DES JEUNES'* (13 eps), TV, 85, CDN, Prod; *'EMPLOI JEUNESSE'* (17 eps), TV, 85, CDN, Prod; *'MEMOIRES D'INSECTES'* (20 eps), TV, 85, CDN, Prod; *'LEURS HERITIERS'* (13 eps), TV, 84, CDN, Prod; *'LA SEXUALITE INACHEVEE'* (13 eps), TV, 84, CDN, Prod; *'ASTROLOGIE AVEC MARYLENE'* (20 eps), TV, 84, CDN, Prod; *'A L'ECOLE DES CHEFS'* (13 eps), TV, 83, CDN, Prod; *'PARLONS MAGAZINES'* (10 eps), TV, 83, CDN, Prod; *'LES THERAPIES'* (13 eps), TV, 83, CDN, Prod; *MUSIQUE OUTRE-MESURE*, TV, 81, CDN, Dir pro/Ass réal; *'MORDICUS'* (10 eps), TV, 80, CDN, Dir pro/Ass réal.

BOUCHARD, Michel - voir REALISATEURS

BOYDEN, Barbara

ACTRA. 165 Shaw St., Toronto, Ont, CAN, M6J 2W6. (416)531-7864. TV Ontario, 2180 Yonge St., Toronto, Ont, CAN. (416)484-2600.
Types of Production & Categories: TH Short-Prod/Wr; TV Film-Prod/Dir/Wr; TV Video-Prod/Dir/Wr.
Genres: Documentary-Th&TV; Educational-TV; Children's-TV.
Biography: Born 1944, Toronto, Ontario. Has spent 81-86 researching/filming documentary on early cameramen in English Canada (turn of the century to mid-40's).
Selective Filmography: *'REPORT CANADA'* (150/year), TV, 86-74, CDN, Prod/Dir; *THE SEAWAY*, 'IT'S YOUR WORLD', TV, 84, CDN, Wr; *KEEP THE BEAT*, 'IT'S MAINLY MUSIC', TV, 84, CDN, Wr; *'MUSIC BOX'* (Co-Wr-pilot/1 eps), (2 eps), TV, 81/80, CDN, Wr; *THE VIEW FROM VINEGAR HILL*, TV, 80, CDN, Prod/Dir/Wr; *'OWL MAGAZINE'* (pilot), TV, 78, CDN, Prod; *THE DOLL FACTORY*, TV, 78, CDN, Co-Prod/Co-Wr; *'GET IT TOGETHER'* (20 eps), TV, 77, CDN, Dir.

BRASSEUR, Raymond

C.P. 742, Station C, Montréal, Qué, CAN, H2L 4L5. JPL Productions Inc., 1600 blvd. de Maisonneuve E., Montréal, Qué, CAN, H2L 4P2. (514)526-2881.

(cont/suite)

Types de production et Catégories: TV film-Prod; TV vidéo-Prod.
Types d'oeuvres: Drame-C&TV; Education-TV; Industriel-C&TV.
Curriculum vitae: Né en 1945; citoyen canadien; bilingue. Vice-président, Directeur général, JPL Productions Inc. depuis 84; employé à JPL depuis 77; à Télé-Métropole depuis 62.
Filmographie sélective: *A MATTER OF CUNNING*, TV, 83, CDN, Co prod; *NEW ORLEANS*, TV, 83, CDN, Co prod; *A PLEIN TEMPS* (pilote), TV, 83, CDN, Prod; *'FAUT VOIR A SON AFFAIRE'* (13 eps), ED, 80, CDN, Prod; *FORANO* (2 ém), TV, 80, CDN, Prod; *'THAT'S IT'* (26 eps), TV, 80, CDN, Prod; *CITY ON FIRE*, C, 79, CDN, Co prod; *CHAUFFEUR, CHAUFFARD*, In, 78, CDN, Prod.

BRAULT, Michel - voir REALISATEURS

BRIND, Bill

SGCT. 130 Pointe Claire Ave., Pointe Claire, Que, CAN, H9S 4M5. (514)694-6681. NFB, P.O.Box 6100, Montreal, Que, CAN, H3C 3H5. (514)283-9497.
Types of Production & Categories: Th Short-Prod/Dir; TV Film-Prod/Dir; TV Video-Prod/Dir.
Genres: Drama-Th&TV; Documentary-Th&TV; Educational-TV.
Biography: Born 1933, London, England; Canadian citizen. Worked for CBC, BBC, NFB and United Nations. Nominated for an Oscar, documentary category, 78 for *HIGH GRASS CIRCUS*. Has worked in U.K., North America, Middle East and Central Europe.
Selective Filmography: *THE WORLD TURNED UPSIDE DOWN*, ED, 85, CDN, Prod; *THE ROAD TO TOTAL WAR/ANYBODY'S SON WILL DO*, 'WAR', TV, 83, CDN, Prod; *THE PROFESSION OF ARMS/THE DEADLY GAME OF NATIONS/GOODBYE WAR*, 'WAR', TV, 83, CDN, Prod; *KEEPING THE OLD GAME ALIVE/NOTES ON NUCLEAR WAR*, 'WAR', TV, 83, CDN, Prod; *DEVIL AT YOUR HEELS*, Th, 83, CDN, Prod (GENIE); *TOMORROW'S ENERGY TODAY*, ED, 81, CDN, Prod; *MY FATHER'S LAND*, ED, 79, CDN, Prod/Dir; *HIGH GRASS CIRCUS*, Th, 78, CDN/GB, Prod; *MY NAME IS FADWA*, ED, 78, CDN, Prod/Dir; *JACK RABBIT*, TV, 75, CDN, Prod/Dir/Ed; *A DREAM OF FREEDOM/THE AWAKENING*, 'PASSAGE WEST', Th, 75, CDN, Prod; *CRY OF THE WILD*, Th, 72, CDN, Prod; *THE SEA*, Th, 70, CDN, Exec Prod; *EXPO 67*, Th, 67, CDN, Dir/Ed; *THE THINGS I CANNOT CHANGE*, ED, 66, CDN, Ed; *THE CHINESE IN BRITAIN*, TV, 65, GB, Dir; *'GRASS ROOTS'* (8 eps), TV, 65, GB, Ed; *'LANDMARKS'* (6 eps), TV, 65, GB, Ed; *'SIX MEN'* (6 eps), TV, 65, GB, Ed; *VOTE, VOTE, VOTE FOR NIGEL BARTON*, TV, 64, GB, Ed; *THE LAST REFUGE*, TV, 64, GB, Ed; *STROKE FOR STROKE*, TV, 64, GB, Ed; *THE SECOND CITY*, TV, 64, GB, Ed.

BRITTAIN, Donald - see DIRECTORS

BROUSSEAU, Pierre

ACTRA, CAPAC, UDA. 65 rue St-Paul O., #515, Montréal, Qué, CAN, H2Y 3S5. (514)287-1063.
Types de production et Catégories: l métrage-Prod/Sc.
Types d'oeuvres: Drame-C; Comédie-C; Action-C.
Curriculum vitae: Né en 1945, Québec; bilingue. Correspondant (radio et revue) au Festival de Cannes; journaliste d'arts et spectacles pendant 15 ans; fondateur de compagnies de disques (OUI-Cine) et gérant d'artistes pop-rock.. Publie 'La vie secrète de Marilyn Monroe' et 'La fantastique histoire du film E.T.'. Devient adjoint au président de Films Mutuels; correspondant au Québec pour le 'Hollywood Reporter' (82-84); critique de cinéma (84-85); sécrétaire du jury au Festival des Films du Monde depuis 81. Publiciste pour films, *LE MATOU, LA GUEPE, KEEPING TRACK, POUVOIR INTIME*, depuis 81; retour à la production, 86.

(cont/suite)

Filmographie sélective: *TANYA'S ISLAND,* C, 79, CDN, Prod/Sc; *APRES-SKI,* C, 71, CDN, Sc; *JAMES BAGATELLE,* C, 69, CDN, Prod/Sc/Réal; *NARCISSUS,* C, 68, CDN, Prod/Sc/Réal.

BROWN, Gary

CTPDA. 30 Prentiss St., Aylmer, Que, CAN, J9H 5V6. (819)684-4469. CBC, 250 Lanark Ave., Ottawa, Ont, CAN. (613)724-1200.
Types of Production & Categories: TV Film-Prod/Dir; TV Video-Prod/Dir.
Genres: Variety-TV; Action-TV; Documentary-TV; Animation-TV.
Biography: Born 1937, Wakefield, Quebec; bilingual. Six years technical experience: camera, audio, switching, lighting; 13 years in TV production as producer, director, stage-site manager; directed 6 film crews for world-wide coverage of 76 Olympic sailing competitions; producer, writer for commercials, English and French.
Selective Filmography: *'NEWSDAY'* (NEWSDAY FINAL), TV, 86-83, CDN, Prod/Dir; *'COUNTRY REPORT',* TV, 79-77, CDN, Prod/Dir; *'MEETING PLACE',* TV, 78-74, CDN, Prod/Dir; *'OPENING OF PARLIAMENT',* TV, 76-74, CDN, Dir; *1976 OLYMPICS* (SAILING EVENTS), TV, 76, CDN, Dir; *'SPORTS PEOPLE PLAY',* TV, 75/74, CDN, Prod/Dir; *'GOING FOR GOLD'* (6 eps), TV, 75, CDN, Prod/Dir; *PROVINCIAL PREMIERS CONFERENCE,* TV, 75, CDN, Dir; *'FOOTBALL HUDDLE',* TV, 74/73, CDN, Dir; *KING HUSSEIN'S VISIT TO CANADA,* TV, 74, CDN, Prod/Dir; *NATO MINISTERS CONFERENCE,* TV, 73, CDN, Dir.

BRUNTON, John

CFTA. Insight Productions Co. Ltd., 333 King St.W., Toronto, Ont, CAN, M5V 1J5. (416)596-8118.
Types of Production & Categories: TV Film-Prod; TV Video-Prod.
Genres: Drama-TV; Comedy-TV; Variety-TV.
Biography: Born 1953, Toronto, Ontario. Background and schooling in business; worked for Insight Productions; took control of the company, 76. *TUCKER AND THE HORSE THIEF* won a Silver Medal, Int'l Film & TV Festival, NY; *MY FATHER, MY RIVAL* a Bronze Medal, NY.
Selective Filmography: *COUNTER PLAY,* TV, 86, CDN, Exec Prod; *'ROCKIT RECORDS'* (pilot), TV, 86, CDN, Exec Prod/Co-Creator; *TUCKER AND THE HORSE THIEF/WORKING FOR PEANUTS/MY FATHER,MY RIVAL,* 'FAMILY PLAYHOUSE', TV, 84, CDN, Exec Prod; *INDIGO!,* TV, 83, CDN, Exec Prod; *HEART OF GOLD* (3 parts), TV, 82, CDN, Prod.

BRYANT, Peter - see WRITERS

BUDGELL, Jack

ATPD. 1 Jean St., Toronto, Ont, CAN, M4W 3A6. (416)929-3403 CBC, Box 500, Stn. A, Toronto, Ont, CAN, M5W 1E6. (416)975-6942.
Types of Production & Categories: TV Video-Prod/Dir.
Genres: Comedy-TV; Variety-TV; Documentary-TV; Children's-TV.
Biography: Born Toronto, Ontario. Education: Technical Studies and Ryerson Radio/TV Production course. Extensive experience in audio production. Credits include production of album 'Rich Little on Broadway' (Columbia).
Selective Filmography: *CBC NEW YEARS SPECIAL,* TV, 85, CDN, Exec Prod; *'COUNTRY WEST'* (6 eps), TV, 85, CDN, Dir; *'FRAGGLE ROCK'* (45 eps), TV, 85, CDN, Line Prod; *'BIZARRE'* (100 eps), TV, 85-82, CDN/USA, Dir; *ACTRA AWARDS* (3 shows), TV, 85-81, CDN, Prod; *'CARROLL BAKER JAMBOREE'* (12 eps), TV, 84, CDN, Exec Prod; *JUNO AWARDS* (5 shows), TV, 83-78, CDN, Prod; *'BOB McLEAN SHOW'* (1400 eps), TV, 82-76, CDN, Exec Prod; *STAGE BAND FESTIVAL,* TV, 80, CDN, Prod; *'JAZZ CANADA'* (12 eps), TV, 80, CDN, Prod/Dir; *MAYNARD FERGUSON CONCERT,* TV, 80, CDN, Prod; *'LOTTO CANADA SPECIALS'* (10 eps), TV, 79/78, CDN, Prod/Dir; *'JULIETTE*

(cont/suite)

& FRIENDS' (350 eps), TV, 78-75, CDN, Prod/Dir; *GOLD ON TAPP,* TV, 78, CDN, Prod.

BURKE, Alan

ATPD. 111 Hilton Ave., Toronto, Ont, CAN, M5R 3E8. (416)533-4463. CBC, Box 500, Stn. A, Toronto, Ont, CAN, M5W 1E6. (416)975-7120.
Types of Production & Categories: TV Film-Prod/Dir.
Genres: Drama-TV; Documentary-TV; Educational-TV; Animation-TV.
Biography: Born 1943, Woodstock, Ontario. Education: B.A.. Produced/directed animation, documentary shorts in London, England for 9 years. Has won awards at New York and Brighton film festivals.
Selective Filmography: *MICHAEL AND KITTY,* TV, 85, CDN, Prod; *IN THIS CORNER,* TV, 85, CDN, Prod; *TILL DEATH DO US PART,* 'THE LAWYERS', TV, 84, CDN, Dir; *WHERE THE HEART IS/HIDE AND SEEK,* 'FOR THE RECORD', TV, 84, CDN, Prod; *OUT OF SIGHT, OUT OF MIND/BY REASON OF INSANITY,* 'FOR THE RECORD', TV, 83/82, CDN, Prod; *YEN FOR YOU/ SHROUD/TRUCKS/TEST TUBE TOWN,* 'THE FIFTH ESTATE', TV, 81/80, CDN, Prod/Dir; *'THE FIFTH ESTATE'* (20 eps), TV, 80, CDN, Prod; *DRUG RESISTANCE,* In, 75, GB, Dir; *LING SUR LING,* In, 75, GB, Prod.

BURNS, Michael

45 Spadina Rd., Toronto, Ont, CAN, M5R 2S9. (416)962-1241. AME Productions, 261 Davenport Rd., Toronto, Ont, CAN, M5R 1K3. (416)961-9977.
Types of Production & Categories: Th Film-Prod; TV Film-Prod; TV Video-Prod.
Genres: Drama-Th; Documentary-Th&TV.
Biography: Born 1947, Toronto, Ontario. Educated at Upper Canada College; Antioch College, Yellow Springs, Ohio (B.A. in Philosophy).
Selective Filmography: *THRESHOLD,* Th, 80, CDN, Co-Prod; *DAYS OF HEAVEN,* Th, 78, USA, Pro Assoc; *WHO IS GURU MAHARAJ-JI?,* 'ROGERS REPORT', TV, 77, CDN, Dir/Prod; *'BARBARA FRUM'* (39 eps), TV, 76, CDN, Prod; *HEARTS AND MINDS,* Th, 75, USA, PM/Assoc Prod; *5 EASY PIECES,* Th, 71/70, USA, PA; *THE LAST PICTURE SHOW,* Th, 71, USA, PA; *HEAD,* Th, 70, USA, Assoc Prod; *'THE MONKEES'* (51 eps), TV, 69-66, USA, Assoc Prod.

BURTON, Robert H.

462 Castlefield Ave., Toronto, Ont, CAN, M5N 1L5. (416)484-6217. 260 Richmond St.W., Ste. 403, Toronto, Ont, CAN, M5V 1W5. (416)591-9360.
Types of Production & Categories: TV Film-Prod/Dir/Wr; TV Video-Prod/Dir/Wr.
Genres: Drama-TV; Comedy-TV; Documentary-TV; Children's-TV.
Biography: Born 1946, USA; Canadian citizen. B.A., University of New Mexico; M.S. Columbia U.. Languages: English, Spanish, French. Has won several NY Int'l Film & TV Festival Awards and CanPro Gold Award for Lorne Greene's *THEY WENT TO FIGHT FOR FREEDOM.*
Selective Filmography: *'DON'T STOP NOW!'* (13 eps), TV, 86, CDN, Prod/Dir; *LATCH KEY KIDS,* ED, 86, CDN, Prod/Wr; *SPACE COMMUNICATIONS,* In, 86, CDN, Prod/Wr; *'TURKEY TV'* (35 eps), TV, 85, CDN/USA, Prod; *THEY WENT TO FIGHT FOR FREEDOM,* TV, 84, CDN, Prod/Dir/Wr; *COSMIC FIRE,* ED, 84, CDN, Prod/Dir/Wr; *'GIVE THE KIDS A CHANCE'* (6 eps), TV, 84, CDN, Prod/Dir/Wr; *CANADA'S NUCLEAR EDGE,* TV, 83, CDN, Prod/Dir/ Wr; *COMMUNICATIONS IS,* In, 83, CDN, Prod; *'BYTEC HYPERION SALES TAPES'* (3 eps), In, 83, CDN, Prod/Dir/Wr; *'CBOT NEWS',* TV, 82, CDN, Prod; *'MORNING MAGAZINE',* TV, 81, CDN, Prod/Dir/Wr; *'HANDS THAT HEAL'* (13 eps), TV, 80/79, CDN, Prod/Dir/Wr; *TWO WOMEN, TWO WORLDS,* 'OF ALL PEOPLE', TV, 74, CDN, Prod/Dir/Wr; *CIGARETTE MONEY,* 'TAKE 60', TV, 73, CDN, Prod/Dir/Wr.

BUSH, Gary

P.O. Box 3887, Vancouver, BC, CAN, V6B 3Z3. (604)689-7190.
Types of Production & Categories: Th Film-Dir; Th Short-Prod/Dir; TV Film-Dir.
Genres: Action-Th&TV; Documentary-Th&TV; Educational-Th&TV; Children's-Th&TV.
Biography: Born 1951, Montreal, Quebec. After attending Sir George Williams University, he was a reporter for the Montreal Star, 68-72. Worked in distribution and production, NFB, 73-81; since then, independent film maker, making the Orient his specialty. *THE ZEN ARCHER* won a Blue Ribbon (American Film Fest.), Chris Award (Columbus, Ohio) and a Golden Sheaf Award (Yorkton); *THE CHILDREN OF SOONG CHING LING* was nominated for an Oscar, won Gold Medal (Houston Int'l Film Festival).
Selective Filmography: *ZEN IN THE ART OF ARM WRESTLING,* Th, 85, CDN, Prod/Dir; *THE CHILDREN OF SOONG CHING LING,* TV, 84, CDN/RC, Prod/Dir; *TOM MAGEE MAN OF IRON,* TV, 83, CDN, Prod/Dir; *THE ZEN ARCHER,* Th, 82, CDN, Prod/Dir (**CFTA**); *THE LONG FIST,* TV, 81, CDN, Prod/Dir; *THE KICKBOXERS,* TV, 79, CDN, Prod/Dir; *BATTLE OF EGO,* TV, 78, CDN, Prod/Dir.

BUTLER, Rick

ACTRA. 50 Stephanie St., #2512, Toronto, Ont, CAN, M5T 1B3. (416)593-1745.
60 Yonge St., Ste. 200, Toronto, Ont, CAN, M5E 1H5. (416)863-6677. Jim Crabbe, William Morris Agency, 151 El Camino Dr., Beverly Hills, CA, USA, 90212. (213)274-7451.
Types of Production & Categories: TV Film-Prod/Wr.
Genres: Drama-TV.
Biography: Born 1946; raised in Truro, Nova Scotia. B.A., Carleton University; M.A., University of Sussex, England. University professor prior to becoming a full-time writer/producer, 79; author of 3 books; producer of 10 record albums distributed by RCA.
Selective Filmography: *MAGGIE AND PIERRE,* TV, 84, CDN, Prod; *BALCONVILLE,* TV, 83, CDN, Prod; *THE MAGIC OF ANIMATION,* TV, 77, CDN, Prod/Wr.

BUTTIGNOL, Rudy

Rudy Inc., 40 Glengarry Ave., Toronto, Ont, CAN, M5M 1C9. (416)489-7115.
Types of Production & Categories: Th Short-Prod/Dir/Wr; TV Film-Prod/Dir/Wr.
Genres: Drama-TV; Documentary-Th&TV; Educational-TV.
Biography: Born 1951, Italy; naturalized as a Canadian citizen, 75; B.F.A., York University. Has produced 45 independent film and video productions (mostly shorts and documentaries) for television, industry and government; worked for the NFB; received numerous grants from the Canada Council, Ontario Arts Council. Co-founder and first Chairman of the Canadian Independent Film Caucus.
Selective Filmography: *SPACE PIONEERS,* TV, 86, CDN, Prod/Dir/Co-Wr; *BANGLADESH, FROM THE RIVER,* TV, 85, CDN, Prod/Dir/Ed; *THE BARTLETTS,* ED, 85, CDN, Prod; *FIRST IN THE FUTURE,* In, 85, CDN, Prod/Dir/Ed/Co-Wr; *NEON: AN ELECTRIC MEMOIR,* Th, 84, CDN, Prod/Dir; *CHRISTINE SUTHERLAND'S BASIC MASSAGE,* Cm, 84, CDN, Co-Prod/Dir; *INWARD PASSAGE,* Th, 83, CDN, Prod/Dir; *AN ARM IN SPACE/UN BRAS SPACIAL,* In, 82, CDN, Prod/Dir/Wr; *SHIPYARD,* TV, 80, CDN, Prod/Dir; *JACK BUSH,* TV, 79, CDN, Prod; *'THE NORGE SERIES'* (4 eps), TV, 79, CDN, Prod; *THE DAIRY,* TV, 78, CDN, Prod/Dir; *TOPPER,* TV, 78, CDN, Prod/Dir; *GRAND CANAL,* TV, 77, CDN, Prod/Dir; *WHERE'S TOPPER,* TV, 76, CDN, Prod/Dir.

CAHILL, T.J. - see WRITERS

CAMPBELL, Harry

373 Glengrove Ave.W., Toronto, Ont, CAN, M5N 1W4. (416)485-8063. Espial Productions Ltd., Box 624, Station K, Toronto, Ont, CAN, M4P 2H1. (416)485-8063.
Types of Production & Categories: TV Film-Prod/Dir.
Genres: Documentary-TV; Educational-TV.
Biography: Born 1919. Entered film production as Head of Foreign Language Unit, NFB. Ottawa, 44. Advisor on educational and instruction material, United Nations Film & Sound Archives, New York, 46-48. Head of Clearing House for Publications, Unesco, 50-56; Chief Librarian, Toronto Public Library, 56-78; film & library consultant, 79-86.
Selective Filmography: *CANADIAN STUDY TOURS IN CHINA,* ED, 86, CDN/ RC, Prod/Dir.

CAMPBELL, Norman - see DIRECTORS

CAMPBELL, Peter

CFTA. The Dreamland Picture Co. Ltd., 10660 - 62nd Ave., Edmonton, Alta. CAN, T6H 1M7. (403)434-8049.
Types of Production & Categories: Th Short-Prod/Dir; TV Film-Prod/Dir; TV Video-Prod/Dir.
Genres: Drama-TV; Documentary-TV; Educational-TV; Children's-TV.
Biography: Born 1951, Sydney, Nova Scotia. Incorporated the Dreamland Picture Company Ltd., 81; produced and directed over 60 films for television.
Selective Filmography: *SYNERGY,* Th, 86, CDN, Prod/Dir; *RAT TALES,* TV, 86, CDN, Prod/Dir; *ALBERTA ENERGY/LIFELINES/CONNECTIONS,* In, 86/85, CDN, Prod/Dir; *TUDOR EDUCATION,* ED, 86, CDN, Dir; *ANOTHER NAKED NIGHT,* TV, 85, CDN, Prod/Dir; *BRIEF ENCOUNTERS,* ED, 85, CDN, Prod/ Dir; *ALBERTA BOUND,* TV, 84, CDN, Dir; *ALL THAT GLITTERS,* TV, 83, CDN, Dir; *KOMPANY!,* Cm, 83, CDN, Prod/Dir; *'ENVIRONMENTAL QUALITY'* (10 eps), ED, 80, CDN, Prod/Dir.

CANELL, Marrin

4700 Bonavista Ave., #210, Montreal, Que, CAN, H3W 2C5. (514)482-2856. NFB, Box 6100, Montreal, Que, CAN, H3C 3H5. (514)283-9517.
Types of Production & Categories: Th Film-Dir/Prod/Ed; Th Short-Dir/Prod/Ed; TV Film-Dir/Prod/Ed; TV Video-Dir/Prod.
Genres: Drama-Th&TV; Variety-TV; Documentary-Th&TV; Educational-Th&TV.
Biography: Born 1943, Montreal, Quebec. Education: Economics, Political Science and Communications, Sir George Williams University; post-graduate work in film and television, Loyola University; Law, University of Montreal. Oscar nomination for *WHISTLING SMITH.*
Selective Filmography: *THE OUTFOXED TIGER/A DOG'S TALE,* 'PARABLES', TV, 86/85, CDN, Prod; *THE REBELLION OF YOUNG DAVID/THE CONCERT STAGES OF EUROPE,* 'BELL CANADA PLAYHOUSE', TV, 85, CDN, Co-Prod; *LEGS OF THE LAME,* 'BELL CANADA PLAYHOUSE', TV, 85, CDN, Co-Prod; *OVERTIME,* TV, 84, CDN, Prod/Dir/Ed; *OTHER TONGUES,* Th, 84, CDN, Prod; *THE VINDICATOR* (THE FRANKENSTEIN FACTOR), Th, 84, CDN, Assoc Prod; *'WAR'* (6 eps), TV, 84-82, CDN, Contr Dir; *BIG AND THE BLUES,* Th, 82, CDN, Prod/Dir/Ed; *THE SWEATER,* Th, 82, CDN, Prod (**BFA**); *THE NEW ESTABLISHMENT,* 'THE CANADIAN ESTABLISHMENT', TV, 81, CDN, Prod/Dir; *MOTHER TONGUE,* TV, 80, CDN, Prod; *PAPERLAND: THE BUREAUCRAT OBSERVED,* TV, 80, CDN, Co-Prod (**GENIE**); *SONG OF THE PADDLE,* TV, 79, CDN, Prod (**CFA**); *SOLZHENITSYN'S CHILDREN ARE MAKING A LOT OF NOISE IN PARIS,* TV, 79, CDN, Prod; *HARMONIUM IN CALIFORNIA,* TV, 79, CDN, Prod; *BOOKMAKERS PROGRESS,* TV, 79, CDN, Prod; *BOW AND ARROW,* Th, 79, CDN, Prod; *IN SEARCH OF THE*

(cont/suite)

BERMUDA PIRATES/THE GREAT LAKES TRIANGLE, 'IN SEARCH OF', TV, 78, USA, Co-Prod; *'NINETY MINUTES LIVE'* (5/wk), TV, 77/76, CDN, Prod; *WHISTLING SMITH,* 'PACIFIC CANADA', TV, 75, CDN, Co-Dir/Ed; *HIS WORSHIP: MR. MONTREAL,* TV, 75, CDN, Prod/Co-Dir/Ed; *HAVE I EVER LIED TO YOU BEFORE,* TV, 75, CDN, Ed; *STRESS: THE WORLD OF HANS SELYE,* ED, 74, CDN, Dir; *KING OF THE HILL,* TV, 74, CDN, Ed; *THE NEW BOYS,* 'WEST', TV, 74, CDN, Ed/Assist Dir; *STATION 10,* TV, 73, CDN, Assist Ed.

CANNING, Bill - see DIRECTORS

CAPPE, Syd

CFTA. S.C. Entertainment Corp., 629A Mount Pleasant Rd., Toronto, Ont, CAN, M4S 2M9. (416)483-0850.
Types of Production & Categories: Th Film-Prod; Th Short-Prod; TV Film-Prod.
Genres: Comedy-Th&TV; Documentary-TV; Educational-TV; Children's-TV.
Biography: Born 1952, Toronto, Ontario. Bachelor degree, Master's, University of Windsor. Producer, theatrical features, educational and TV films through S.C. Entertainment Corporation since 81.
Selective Filmography: *THE PINK CHIQUITAS,* Th, 86, CDN, Exec Prod.

CARMODY, Don

DGC, PGA. Don Carmody Productions, 8275 Mayrand St., Montreal, Que, CAN, H4P 2C8. (514)342-2340.
Types of Production & Categories: Th Film-Prod; TV Film-Prod.
Genres: Drama-Th&TV; Comedy-Th; Horror-Th.
Biography: Born 1951, Providence, Rhode Island; Canadian citizen. Education: Bachelor of Communications, Loyola University; 2 years law, McGill U.. Has owned production company since 78. *PORKY'S* won the Golden Reel Award.
Selective Filmography: *THE ARM,* Th, 86, USA, Co Prod; *JUNIOR,* Th, 85, CDN, Prod/Wr; *THE VINDICATOR* (THE FRANKENSTEIN FACTOR), Th, 84, CDN, Co-Prod; *MEATBALLS III,* Th, 84, CDN, Co-Prod; *PORKY'S II - THE NEXT DAY* (CHEZ PORKY II - LE LENDEMAIN), Th, 83, CDN, Co-Prod; *SPACEHUNTER: ADVENTURES IN THE FORBIDDEN ZONE,* Th, 83, CDN/USA, Line Prod; *THE SURROGATE,* Th, 83, CDN, Co-Prod/Dir/Co-Wr; *'STRANGE TRUE STORIES'* (26 eps), TV, 83, CDN, Co-Prod; *'MEDICAL MARVELS'* (26 eps), TV, 83/82, USA, Co-Prod; *PORKY'S* (CHEZ PORKY), Th, 81, CDN, Co-Prod; *DEATH SHIP,* Th, 79, CDN, Assoc Prod; *TULIPS,* Th, 79, CDN, Prod; *CRUNCH* (THE KINKY COACHES AND THE POM-POM PUSSYCATS), Th, 78, CDN, PM; *DEATH WEEKEND* (THE HOUSE BY THE LAKE), Th, 76, CDN, Assoc Prod; *RABID,* Th, 76, CDN, PM; *THE PARASITE MURDERS* (SHIVERS), Th, 74, CDN, Assoc Prod.

CARTER, Humphrey

CFTA. 66 Sherwood Ave., Toronto, Ont, CAN, M4P 2A7. (416)486-5282. Scollard Productions, 174 Bedford Rd., Toronto, Ont, CAN, M5R 2K9. (416)922-7100.
Types of Production & Categories: TV Film-Prod; TV Video-Prod.
Genres: Drama-TV; Comedy-TV; Action-TV; Commercials-TV.
Biography: Born 1943, Hutton, England; Canadian citizen; bilingual. President and executive producer, Scollard Productions Ltd., 86. Over 500 Canadian commercials produced plus extensive US and European experience; 60 major US and Canadian awards.

CASSON, Barry

NABET. 895 Walfred Rd., Victoria, BC, CAN, V9C 2P1. (604)478-7211.
Types of Production & Categories: Th Short-Prod/Dir/Cin; TV Film-Prod/Dir/Cin; TV Video-Prod/Dir.

(cont/suite)

Genres: Drama-Th&TV; Documentary-Th&TV; Educational-Th&TV; Children's-Th&TV.
Biography: Born 1942, Burnley, Lancashire, England; Canadian citizen. Studied Filmmaking, Columbia College, Hollywood, 78-79; worked with American Film Institute. Former newspaper photographer with numerous awards; also spent 7 years as BC TV news cameraman in Victoria; teaches Film course, Camosun College, Victoria . *CRYSTAL GARDEN* won Bronze Awards at the Houston and New York Film Festivals.
Selective Filmography: *MAKING IT HAPPEN,* Th, 85, CDN, Prod/Dir; *LOST IN THE WOODS/A DAY IN FOREST COMMUNITY,* ED, 82/81, CDN, Prod/Dir; *CRYSTAL GARDEN,* ED, 80, CDN, Dir/Co-Prod/Cin/Wr; *SLICKLICKER,* ED, 78, CDN, Cin; *CRISIS LINE/FROZEN YOGURT PUSHUPS,* Cm, 77, CDN, Prod/Dir; *FLAGPOLE,* ED, 77, CDN, Dir/Cam; *THE MAVERICK NUN,* Th, 76, CDN, Co-Prod/Cin; *AMBULANCE,* ED, 75, CDN, Prod/Dir.

CAULFIELD, Paul

Mirus Communications Inc., 22 Rogers Rd., Brampton, Ont, CAN, L6X 1L8. (416) 457-5117.
Types of Production & Categories: Th Short-Prod/Wr; TV Film-Prod/Dir; TV Video-Prod/Dir.
Genres: Drama-Th&TV; Documentary-TV; Educational-TV; Children's-TV.
Biography: Born 1950, Toronto, Ontario. Journalism Diploma, Humber College; Honours B.A., Film, York University. Editor, 7 years; produced for Film Arts, 3 years; formed Mirus Films, 76, Mirus Communications Inc., 86. His films have won 8 CFTA Awards, Gold Plaque (Chicago), Red Ribbon (American Film Fest.).
Selective Filmography: *GETTING MARRIED, STAYING MARRIED/ MARRIAGE: THE EARLY YEARS,* ED, 85, CDN, Prod; *THE ORDINARY BATH,* ED, 85, CDN, Prod/Dir; *MARGARET LAURENCE,* ED, 85, CDN, Prod/Dir; *THE EDIT,* Th, 84, CDN, Wr/Prod **(GENIE/CFTA)**; *FINDING OUT,* ED, 84, CDN, Prod; *A STORYTELLER'S STORY,* TV, 84, CDN, Prod/Dir; *SKY HIGH,* TV, 84, CDN, Prod; *JOHN DOE,* TV, 82, CDN, Prod; *A HELPING HAND,* 'THE NATURE OF THINGS', TV, 82, CDN, Prod; *HIGHWINDING,* TV, 82, CDN, Prod; *NEW TOMORROW,* TV, 82, CDN, Assoc Prod; *JIMMY AND LUKE,* TV, 82, CDN, Assoc Prod; *THE ONLY CRITIC IS TIME,* TV, 81, CDN, Co-Wr/Co-Prod; *ALLIGATOR SHOES* (LES SOULIERS EN CROCO), Th, 81, CDN, Assoc Prod; *REACHING OUT, LETTING GO,* TV, 80, CDN, Co-Prod/Co-Dir; *A PATH OF HIS OWN,* TV, 79, CDN, Dir/Prod **(CFTA)**; *THE COLOURS OF A POET,* TV, 76, CDN, Prod/Dir; *CREDIT VALLEY ALBUM,* TV, 74, CDN, Prod/Dir; *STEAM,* TV, 73, CDN, Prod/Dir.

CHAMBERLAIN, David

4 Foxden Rd., Don Mills, Ont, CAN, M3C 2A9. (416)445-2749. TV Ontario, 2180 Yonge St., Toronto, Ont, CAN, M4S 2B9. (416)484-2600.
Types of Production & Categories: TV Film-Prod/Dir/Wr; TV Video-Prod/Dir/Wr.
Genres: Documentary-TV; Educational-TV; Children's-TV; Animation-TV.
Biography: Born 1941, St.Thomas, Ontario. Education: University of Western Ontario (Psychology, Geology), 65-68; U. of Toronto, Honours B.A. (Psychology, Anthropology), 71. Has won numerous film awards including: Gold Medals, Houston for *THE FINAL CHAPTER*; Bronze Medal, Blue Ribbon (New York) for *LANDSCAPE OF GEOMETRY*; Bronze Medals (New York and Houston), *N.A.: GROWTH OF A CONTINENT.*
Selective Filmography: *'ORGANIC EVOLUTION'* (6 eps), TV, 86, CDN, Prod; *'ELECTROCHEMISTRY'* (6 eps), TV, 86, CDN, Prod; *'NUCLEAR PHYSICS'* (6 eps), TV, 86, CDN, Prod; *'ELECTRON ARRANGEMENT AND BONDING'* (6 eps), TV, 85, CDN, Prod; *'GEOGRAPHY SKILLS'* (12 eps), TV, 85, CDN, Prod; *'PROTEIN SYNTHESIS'* (6 eps), TV, 85, CDN, Prod; *'STRUCTURE OF THE*

(cont/suite)

ATOM' (6 eps), TV, 85, CDN, Prod; *THE FINAL CHAPTER?,* TV, 85, CDN/J/F, Co-Prod/Wr; *'CHEMICAL EQUILIBRIUM'* (6 eps), TV, 84, CDN, Prod; *'ENERGY FLOW'* (6 eps), TV, 84, CDN, Prod; *'HOMEOSTASIS'* (6 eps), TV, 84, CDN, Prod; *'THE MOLE CONCEPT'* (6 eps), TV, 83, CDN, Prod; *'WAVE-PARTICLE DUALITY'* (6 eps), TV, 83, CDN, Prod; *'LANDSCAPE OF GEOMETRY'* (8 eps), TV, 82, CDN, Prod/Dir; *'N.A.: GROWTH OF A CONTINENT'* (13 eps), TV, 80, CDN, Prod/Dir; *'BREAKTHROUGH'* (9 eps), TV, 78, CDN, Prod; *'CHALLENGE TO SCIENCE'* (15 eps), TV, 77, CDN, Prod; *'MEDIA 77'* (15 eps), TV, 77, CDN, Prod; *'ONTARIO: OUR SCIENCE LAB'* (30 eps), TV, 76, CDN, Prod; *THE LIFE GAME,* TV, 75, CDN/GB, Prod; *'THE STATIONARY ARK'* (13 eps), TV, 75, CDN, Co-Prod; *THE WEATHER MACHINE,* TV, 74, CDN/GB, Prod; *'SCIENCE THE MOTIVATOR'* (9 eps), TV, 73, CDN, Prod; *AND NOT TO YIELD,* TV, 72, CDN, Prod; *'MATHEMATICAL RELATIONSHIPS'* (13 eps), TV, 71, CDN, Prod.

CHAMPAGNE, Edith

ATPD. 39 Austin Ave., Toronto, Ont, CAN, M4M 1V7. (416)466-3103. CBC, 500 Church St., 3rd Fl., Toronto, Ont, CAN, M4Y 2C8. (416)975-5695.
Types of Production & Categories: TV Film-Prod; TV Video-Prod.
Genres: Documentary-TV; Current Affairs-TV; News-TV.
Biography: Born 1953, Winnipeg, Manitoba; bilingual. B.A., University of Manitoba. Has worked for CBC (French & English) for 10 years.
Selective Filmography: *NEWS* (ITEMS: ZUNDEL, MALPRACTICE SUITS, ELDERLY ABUSE), TV, 86-84, CDN, Prod; *'ADOPTION'* (5 eps), TV, 83, CDN, Prod/Pro Coord.

CHAMPAGNE, François

APFVQ, CFTA. 4606 ave. Marcil, Montréal, Qué, CAN, H4A 3A1. (514)487-5384. Les Productions S.D.A., 1221 Hôtel de Ville, Montréal, Qué, CAN, H2X 3A9. (514)866-1761.
Types de production et Catégories: c métrage-Prod; TV film-Prod; TV vidéo-Prod.
Types d'oeuvres: Drame-C&TV; Documentaire-C&TV; Education-C&TV; Industriel-C&TV.
Curriculum vitae: Né en 1941. Etudes en administration, Université McGill; Etudes RIA, Hautes Etudes Commerciales. Vice-président, administrateur, Les Productions S.D.A. Limitée 72-78; Président, administrateur, depuis 78; producteur (projets spéciaux), producteur exécutif (documentaires).
Filmographie sélective: *'A PLEIN TEMPS'* (56 eps), TV, 86-84, CDN, Prod; *LA FAUNE AU QUEBEC I & II/O QUEBEC,* In, 81-78, CDN, Prod; *SOUFFLE DU NORD,* ED, 81, CDN, Prod; *'ECOLOGIE'* (12 eps), ED, 81/80, CDN, Prod; *'ADER'* (42 eps), ED, 81/80, CDN, Prod; *'J'AI UNE HISTOIRE'* (26 eps), ED, 80, CDN, Prod; *CHRONIQUE D'UN ETE,* TV, 80, CDN, Co prod; *HOW TO START A SMALL BUSINESS,* ED, 79, CDN, Prod; *'FRANCAIS III - C'EST A DIRE'* (4 eps), ED, 74, CDN, Prod; *TI-MINE GOULET INC.,* In, 74, CDN, Prod; *'LANGUAGE ARTS'* (3 eps), ED, 73, CDN, Prod; *'LA GEOGRAPHIE'* (4 eps), ED, 73, CDN, Prod; *L'ELECTRICITE/CHURCHILL FALLS/FACE AU DEFI,* In, 72/71, CDN, Prod; *LA MOTONEIGE AU QUEBEC,* ED, 72, CDN, Prod.

CHAREST, Micheline

734 Upper Lansdowne Ave., Montreal, Que, CAN, H3Y 1J7. (514)484-7469. Cinar Films Inc., 1160 Alexandre-de-Seve, #1, Montreal, Que, CAN, H2L 2T8. (514) 521-2045. Cinar Films Inc., 41 East 42nd St., New York, NY, USA, 10017. (212) 286-0695.
Types of Production & Categories: Th Film-Prod; TV Film-Prod; TV Video-Prod.
Genres: Variety-Th&TV; Children's-Th&TV.
Biography: Born 1953, London, England; Canadian citizen. Distributor of features and TV for 7 years.

(cont/suite)

Selective Filmography: *LE MAGICIEN D'OZ* (WIZARD OF OZ), (also 52 eps-TV), Th, 86, CDN, Co-Exec Prod; *THE LAND OF OZ*, Th, 86, CDN, Co-Exec Prod; *OZMA OF OZ*, Th, 86, CDN, Co-Exec Prod; *THE EMERALD CITY OF OZ*, Th, 86, CDN, Co-Exec Prod; *'SIDNEY & ALBERT'* (50 eps), TV, 86, USA, Exec Prod; *'ULTRA-7'* (49 eps), TV, 85, USA, Co-Exec Prod; *PAVLOVA*, TV, 83, CDN/USA, Co-Prod.

CHBIB, Bachar

435 St-Claude, Montreal, Que, CAN, H2Y 3B6. (514)397-1402.
Types of Production & Categories: Th Film-Dir/Prod/Ed; Th Short-Dir/Prod/Wr/Ed.
Genres: Drama-Th; Musical-Th; Documentary-Th; Educational-Th.
Biography: Born 1959, Damascus, Syria; Canadian citizen; B.F.A., Film Production, Concordia University; B.Sc., Microbiology and Immunology, McGill U. *OR 'D'UR* won 1st Prize, Canadian Student Film Festival; *BREAD*, Blue Ribbon, American Film Festival.
Selective Filmography: *EVICTION*, Th, 86, CDN, Dir/Prod/Co-Wr/Co-Ed; *MARIA CARMEN'S SPAIN*, ED, 85, CDN, Dir/Prod; *AMOUR IMPOSSIBLE*, Th, 84, CDN, Dir/Prod/Wr; *MEMOIRS*, Th, 84, CDN, Dir/Prod/Co-Wr/Co-Ed; *OR 'D' UR*, Th, 83, CDN, Dir/Prod/Co-Ed/Co-Wr; *BETSY*, Th, 83, CDN, Dir/Prod/Ed/Wr; *BREAD*, ED, 82, CDN, Prod.

CHERCOVER, Murray

34 Dunbar Rd., Toronto, Ont, CAN, M4W 2X6. CTV, 42 Charles St. E., Toronto, Ont, CAN, M4Y 1T5. (416)928-6000.
Types of Production & Categories: TV Film-Prod.
Genres: Drama-TV; Documentary-TV.
Biography: Born 1929, Montreal, Quebec. Education: Academy of Radio and TV Arts, Toronto; School of Theatre, Neighbourhood Playhouse, New York. Director of theatrical shorts and features, 48-52; producer, director, CBC drama productions: *GENERAL MOTORS PRESENTS, ON CAMERA, PLAYBILL, SPACE COMMAND*, 52-60; executive producer on all productions, CFTO TV, 60; Director of Programming, 61; Vice President of Programming, 61. Chairman of Programming, Independent Television Network, 61; Executive Vice President, General Manager, CTV, 66; President and Chief Operating Officer, 68; President, Managing Director since 69.

CHETWYND, Lionel - see WRITERS

CHETWYND, Robin J.

CFTA, SMPTE. 360 Bloor St. E., Ste. 404, Toronto, Ont, CAN, M4W 3M3. (416) 961-4833. Chetwynd Productions Inc., 214 Gerrard St.E., Toronto, Ont, CAN, M5A 2E6. (416)926-9551.
Types of Production & Categories: Th Film-Prod; TV Film-Prod/Dir/Wr; TV Video-Prod/Dir.
Genres: Variety-TV; Documentary-Th&TV; Industrial-TV; Sports-Th&TV.
Biography: Born 1941, Vancouver, British Columbia. Education: Business Administration, Journalism, Ryerson Polytechnical Institute. Past President, CFTA; Co-Chairman, co-producer, Annual Variety Club of Ontario Telethon, 83-85; Chetwynd Productions Inc. has received more than 250 national and international awards for industrial/sponsored documentary production through 25 years of operation.
Selective Filmography: *SCHWEPPING '86*, In, 86/85, CDN, Prod; *THE GOOD LIFE*, TV, 86/85, CDN, Prod; *GREY CUP*, In, 85, CDN, Prod/Dir; *NO PLACE TO GO*, TV, 85, CDN, Prod; *SCHENLEY AWARDS* (2 shows), TV, 85/84, CDN, Prod; *'CFL STARS OF THE WEEK'* (20 eps), TV, 85, CDN, Prod;

(cont/suite)

KAPTESTING/UNIROYAL, In, 85/84, CDN, Prod; *PLAY YOUR HAND* (JOUE TA BONNE CARTE), In, 85, CDN, Prod; *FINANCIAL SECURITY THROUGH REAL ESTATE/TORONTO*, In, 85/84, CDN, Prod; *WORKING OUT* (QUESTION HUMANITAIRE), In, 84, CDN, Prod; *ST.LAWRENCE SEAWAY 25th ANNIVERSARY*, In, 84, CDN, Prod; *GO CANADA* (French version), (pilot), TV, 84, CDN, Prod/Wr; *AN INSTANT OF TIME*, TV, 84, CDN, Prod/Wr; *OUR CHOICE...THEIR FUTURE*, TV, 83, CDN, Prod; *NEW ZEALAND...NUMBER ONE*, In, 82, CDN, Prod/Dir/Wr; *THE MOLSON STORY/THE NEW VOYAGEUR*, In, 82, CDN, Prod; *SOMEONE IS LISTENING*, TV, 81, CDN, Prod; *LIFELINES*, TV, 80, CDN, Prod; *AURORA...ON TARGET/SHOT POINT 260*, In, 80/79, CDN, Prod; *RUNNERS*, TV, 78, CDN, Prod; *GILLES*, TV, 78, CDN, Prod; *'LABATT CHALLENGE'* (7 eps), TV, 77, CDN, Prod; *THE MYTHMAKERS*, Th, 77, CDN, Prod; *STAMPEDE*, Th, 77, CDN, Prod.

CHILCO, Cathy

CTPDA. 1492 Ross Rd., Vancouver, BC, CAN, V7J 1V2. (604)986-4662. CBC, 700 Hamilton St., Vancouver, BC, CAN, V6B 2R5. (604)662-6199.
Types of Production & Categories: TV Film-Prod; TV Video-Prod.
Genres: Comedy-TV; Variety-TV; Documentary-TV; Children's-TV.
Biography: Born Toronto, Ontario. B.A., University of Toronto. Taught for 2 years; 6 years experience as performer, stage/radio/TV; 9 years as associate producer at TV Ontario.
Selective Filmography: *'VENTURE'* (52 eps), TV, 86/85, CDN, Prod; *'SESAME STREET'* (sev seg), TV, 86-81, USA, Prod; *'FUTURESCAN'* (7 eps), TV, 84, CDN, Prod; *'FABULOUS FESTIVAL'* (7 eps), TV, 84, CDN, Co-Prod; *RICK SCOTT: FEET FIRST*, TV, 84, CDN, Prod; *ANN MORTIFEE: BORN TO LIVE*, TV, 84, CDN, Prod; *SESSIONS*, TV, 83, CDN, Prod; *SUPER VARIETY LIVE WITH DAVID STEINBERG*, TV, 83, CDN, Prod; *RAFFI'S REALLY BIG SHOW*, TV, 82, CDN, Prod; *DAVID STEINBERG PRESENTS THE COMEDIANS*, TV, 82, CDN, Prod; *FLYING FRUIT FLY CIRCUS*, TV, 81, CDN, Prod; *RAFFI, BELUGAS AND FRIENDS*, TV, 81, CDN, Prod; *A SPECIAL PLACE*, TV, 80, CDN, Prod; *'CANADA AFTER DARK'* (daily), TV, 79/78, CDN, Prod; *'90 MINUTES LIVE'* (5/wk), TV, 78/77, CDN, Prod.

CHRISTIE, Keith

110 19th St., #404, West Vancouver, BC, CAN, V7V 3W8. (604)922-0263.
Types of Production & Categories: TV Film-Prod/Dir; TV Video-Prod/Dir.
Genres: Musical-TV; Documentary-TV; Educational-TV; Children's-TV.
Biography: Born 1926, Sydney, Australia. Education: Motion Picture Production, Graphic Art, Stage craft at Sydney College of Art. Has worked for CBC as design director, set designer; producer/director, CBC's first West Coast mobile TV production and colour TV production; now independent producer, director.
Selective Filmography: *THE SINTERKLAAS FANTASY*, TV, 86, CDN, Prod/Dir/Wr/Pro Des; *ANNA IN GRAZ/MICHELANGELO AND THE SHOEMAKER*, MV, 80-78, CDN, Prod/Dir/Wr/Art Dir; *'MEETING PLACE'* (25 eps), TV, 80-70, CDN, Prod/Dir; *MARANATHA/KLEEWYCK*, MV, 75, CDN, Prod/Dir; *'MEDICAL EXPLORERS'* (13 eps), TV, 73, CDN, Prod/Dir/Wr; *'MUSIC TO SEE'* (6 eps), TV, 72, CDN, Prod/Dir; *'SUZUKI ON SCIENCE'* (13 eps), TV, 70, CDN, Prod/Dir; *'ON THE SCENE'* (26 eps), TV, 70/69, CDN, Prod/Dir; *'VACATION TIME'* (26 eps), TV, 70/69, CDN, Prod/Dir; *'THREE LETTER WORD'* (3 eps), TV, 69, CDN, Prod/Dir; *THANK HEAVEN FOR CHRISTMAS/BALLAD AND SONGS*, TV, 66/65, CDN, Prod/Dir.

CLARK, Bob - see DIRECTORS

CLARK, Eliza

36 Maitland, #E2, Toronto, Ont, CAN, M4Y 1C5. (416)961-6512. Visual Productions Ltd., 101 Niagara St., Ste.2, Toronto, Ont, CAN, M5V 1C3. (416)868-1535.
Types of Production & Categories: TV Video-Dir/Prod.
Genres: Variety-TV.
Biography: Born 1963, Toronto, Ontario. B.F.A., York University. Freelance still photographer, writer.
Selective Filmography: *'BACKSTAGE'* (18 eps), TV, 86, CDN, Dir/Prod.

CLARK, Louise

DGC. 663 Huron St., #2, Toronto, Ont, CAN, M5R 2R8. (416)962-5092.
Types of Production & Categories: Th Film-PM/Prod; TV Film-PM/Prod.
Genres: Drama-TV; Comedy-Th; Documentary-Th&TV.
Biography: Born 1954, Sarnia, Ontario. Production manager, associate producer on 35 documentaries since 76; producer/line producer, 85-86. Has worked on many award-winning films.
Selective Filmography: *WORLD DRUM FESTIVAL,* TV, 86, CDN, Line Prod; *'BROTHERS BY CHOICE'* (6 eps), TV, 86, CDN, Co-Prod; *BLUE SNAKE,* TV, 85, CDN, Prod; *MAGNIFICAT,* TV, 85, CDN, Co-Prod; *ALL THAT BACH,* TV, 85, CDN, Co-Prod; *HOCKEY NIGHT,* TV, 84, CDN, PM; *AFTER THE AXE,* Th, 79, CDN, PM.

CLERMONT, Nicolas

ACFTP, APFVQ. Filmline Int'l Inc., 209 rue St-Paul W., 5th Fl., Montreal, Que, CAN, H2Y 2A1. (514)288-5888.
Types of Production & Categories: Th Film-Prod.
Genres: Drama-Th; Children's-Th.
Biography: Born in France; became Canadian resident, 68. Started as producer/director in educational television, Montreal. Co-founder, Can-America Film Corporation, 80; partner in Filmline International Inc. since 84.
Selective Filmography: *WILD THING,* Th, 86, USA, Co-Prod; *TOBY McTEAGUE,* Th, 85, CDN, Prod; *THE BLUE MAN,* Th, 84, CDN, Exec Prod; *THE MOTORCYCLE BOY,* Th, 80, CDN, Prod.

COBLEY, Malcolm

CFTA, DGC. 10 Douglas Cres., Toronto, Ont, CAN, M4W 2E7. (416)861-1446. Malcolm Cobley Assoc. Ltd., 193 Church St., Toronto, Ont, CAN, M5B 1Y7. (416) 362-0302.
Types of Production & Categories: TV Video-Prod/Dir.
Genres: Documentary-TV; Educational-TV; Industrial-TV.
Biography: Born 1940, England; emigrated to Canada, 62. Initial training as an artist, then as a commercials producer; 3 years as staff writer/director for Westminster Films Ltd., Toronto. Operates own business as producer/director/writer of industrial and educational films: documentaries for Saudi Arabian TV, numerous other film/video/print/av projects covering work of Bell Canada Int'l in Saudi Arabia, 78-86. His films have won awards at Mannheim, San Francisco, Columbus and New York film festivals.

COHEN, Annette

ACTRA, CFTA, DGC. 447 Ontario St., Toronto, Ont, CAN, M5A 2V9. (416)920-3745. 25 Imperial St., Ste. 500, Toronto, Ont, CAN, M5P 1C1. (416)483-8018.
Types of Production & Categories: Th Film-Prod/Wr; TV Film-Prod/Wr; TV Video-Prod/Wr.
Genres: Drama-Th&TV.
Biography: Born 1935. Education: B.A., M.A., English, University of Toronto.

(cont/suite)

Selective Filmography: *UNFINISHED BUSINESS,* Th, 83, CDN, Co-Prod; *'ROMANCE'* (6 eps), TV, 82, CDN, Co-Prod; *LOVE* (1 part), Th, 80, CDN, Dir; *THE DOLL FACTORY,* TV, 78, CDN, Co-Prod/Dir/Co-Wr; *ONE PEOPLE, ONE DESTINY,* TV, 77, CDN, Prod/Dir; *NELLIE McCLUNG,* TV, 77, CDN, Wr; *'ROYAL SUITE'* (1 eps), TV, 77, CDN, Wr; *'KING OF KENSINGTON'* (1 eps), TV, 76, CDN, Wr; *THE VISIBLE WOMAN,* ED, 76, CDN, Co-Prod/Co-Dir; *'TRUE NORTH'* (3 seg), TV, 75, CDN, Wr; *'REPORT METRIC'* (100 seg), TV, 75, CDN, Wr.

COHEN, Ronald I.

The Ronald Cohen Film Co., 1155 Dorchester Blvd. W.,#4103, Montreal, Que, CAN. (514)397-1164.
Types of Production & Categories: Th Film-Prod; TV Film-Prod.
Genres: Drama-Th&TV; Comedy-Th&TV.
Biography: Born 1943, Montreal, Quebec; bilingual. B.A., cum laude (Government), Harvard University, 64; B.C.L. (first class honours), McGill U., 68; member, Quebec Bar Association. Taught law, 4 years, McGill U.; Director, Vice President, Consumers Assoc. of Canada, 5 years; Counsel, then Senior Counsel to Quebec Police Commission Inquiry into Organized Crime, 74-77. Started producing feature films, 77; Chairman, Academy of Canadian Cinema & Television, 80-82, 85-86. *TICKET TO HEAVEN* won Best Picture, Taormina Int'l Film Festival, Italy.
Selective Filmography: *RACE FOR THE BOMB* (mini-series), TV, 86/85, CDN/F, Co-Prod; *DRAW!,* TV, 83, CDN/USA, Prod; *CROSS-COUNTRY,* Th, 82, CDN, Exec Prod; *TICKET TO HEAVEN,* Th, 80, CDN, Exec Prod **(GENIE)**; *HARRY TRACY,* Th, 80, CDN, Prod; *RUNNING,* Th, 79, CDN, Co-Prod; *MIDDLE AGE CRAZY,* Th, 78, CDN, Prod; *POWER PLAY* (STATE OF SHOCK), (COUP D'ETAT), Th, 77, CDN/GB, Co-Exec Prod.

COHEN, Sidney M. - see DIRECTORS

COLE, Harold J.

CFTA. Erin Films Ltd., 266 - 66th St., Delta, BC, CAN, V4L 1M8. (604)943-5902.
Types of Production & Categories: Th Film-Prod/Dir/Wr; TV Film-Prod/Dir/Wr; TV Video-Prod/Dir/Wr.
Genres: Drama-Th; Comedy-Th; Horror-Th; Sports-Th&TV.
Biography: Born 1942; Canadian. Over 25 years experience in the motion picture, television and advertising mediums; packages private financing deals with guaranteed distribution; produced/directed/wrote over 300 commercials (won Clio and New York Film Fest. awards), 15 industrial films.
Selective Filmography: *ABDUCTED,* Th, 85, CDN, Prod; *GHOSTKEEPER,* Th, 81, CDN, Prod; *CANADA CUP HOCKEY,* TV, 76, CDN, Prod/Wr; *BUFFALO SABRES* (5 films), Th, 76-72, CDN, Prod/Dir/Wr; *SASKATCHEWAN AIR SHOW,* TV, 72, CDN, Prod/Dir/Wr; *'REACH FOR THE TOP'* (13 eps), TV, 72, CDN, Prod/Dir; *'FOR YOUR INFORMATION'* (150 seg), TV, 72, CDN, Prod/ Dir/Wr; *SABRES READY,* Th, 71, CDN, Prod/Wr.

COLE, Janis

67 Gloucester St., #8, Toronto, Ont, CAN, M4Y 1L8. (416)964-2892. P.O. Box 5613, Stn.A, Toronto, Ont, CAN, M5W 1N8. (416)921-9982.
Types of Production & Categories: Th Film-Prod/Dir.
Genres: Documentary-Th; Educational-TV.
Biography: Born 1954, Chatham, Ontario. Attended Sheridan College, Media Arts Dept., 2 years. Won a Gold Plaque (Chicago), Red Ribbon (American Film Fest.) for *HOOKERS...ON DAVIE*; *P4W: PRISON FOR WOMEN* was Best Film of Festival, Yorkton, and won a Red Ribbon, American Film Festival.

(cont/suite)

Selective Filmography: *THE MAKING OF AGNES OF GOD* (QUIET ON THE SET FILMING AGNES OF GOD), TV, 85, CDN, Co-Prod/Co-Dir/Co-Ed; *HOOKERS...ON DAVIE,* Th, 84, CDN, Co-Prod/Co-Dir/Co-Ed; *P4W: PRISON FOR WOMEN* (P4W), Th, 81, CDN, Co-Prod/Co-Dir/Co-Ed (GENIE); *THIN LINE,* Th, 77, CDN, Co-Prod/Co-Dir/Co-Ed.

COLLETT, Malcolm

2110 Blenheim St., #3, Vancouver, BC, CAN, V6K 4J2. (604)734-8359. Marmalade Animation Ltd., 2040 W. 12th Ave., Vancouver, BC, CAN, V6J 2G2. (604)736-9911.
Types of Production & Categories: TV Film-Dir/An; TV Video-An/Dir/Prod.
Genres: Comedy-TV; Children's-TV; Animation-TV.
Biography: Born 1948, Kidderminster, England; Canadian citizen. Studied at the Emily Carr College of Art, Vancouver. *SNOW WAR* won Best Film (mountain safety), Banff Mountain Film Festival.
Selective Filmography: *TALES OF THE MOUSE HOCKEY LEAGUE,* 'MOUSE SPORTS', TV, 86, CDN, An/Prod/Dir; *MOHAWK OIL/BC LOTTERIES,* Cm, 85, CDN, An/Prod/Dir; *SNOW WAR,* ED, 80, CDN, An/Prod; *'ALBERTA 75th'* (8 eps), TV, 80, CDN, An/Prod.

COOK, R. David

CTPDA. 892 Millbourne Rd.E., Edmonton, Alta, CAN, T6K 2K2. (403)461-8642. CBC, Box 555, Edmonton, Alta, CAN. (403)469-2321.
Types of Production & Categories: TV Film-Prod/Dir; TV Video-Prod/Dir.
Genres: Drama-TV; Variety-TV; Documentary-TV; Sports-TV.
Biography: Born 1941, Medicine Hat, Alberta. B.A., University of Alberta. Private broadcasting experience, 3 1/2 years; 20 years at CBC, 15 of those as producer/ director.
Selective Filmography: *'NEWSDAY'* (Edmonton), TV, 86, CDN, Co-Prod/Co-Dir; *'NATIVE NASHVILLE NORTH'* (13 eps), TV, 86, CDN, Dir; *'FRONT PAGE CHALLENGE'* (3 eps), TV, 86, CDN, Dir; *MATTERS OF CHOICE,* TV, 85, CDN, Prod; *'SPORTS WEEKEND'* (10 seg), TV, 85-75, CDN, Prod/Dir; *'HOURGLASS'/'NEWSDAY'* (Edmonton), TV, 85-75, CDN, Dir; *PRAIRIE CHURCH OF BUSTER GALLOWAY,* TV, 84, CDN, Prod; *PAPAL VISIT,* TV, 84, CDN, Dir; *WILD CAT,* TV, 84, CDN, Co-Prod; *'ON THE ROAD'* (18 eps), TV, 84-82, CDN, Prod/Dir; *TEN DAYS IN AUGUST,* TV, 79, CDN, Dir; *COMMONWEALTH GAMES,* TV, 78, CDN, Dir; *'GREAT CANADIAN ESCAPE'* (2 eps), TV, 77, CDN, Dir; *OLYMPICS* (Fencing), TV, 76, CDN, Dir; *CANADIAN DERBY,* TV, 76/75, CDN, Prod/Dir.

COOPER, Robert

11444 Ayrshire Rd., Los Angeles, CA, USA, 90049. (213)471-7554. Robert Cooper Prods., 954 King St.W., Toronto, Ont, CAN, M6K 1E5. (416)598-3257.
Types of Production & Categories: Th Film-Prod; TV Film-Prod.
Genres: Drama-Th&TV; Comedy-Th&TV; Action-TV; Documentary-TV.
Biography: Born 1944. *THE TERRY FOX STORY* won an ACE Award, Best Dramatic Presentation.
Selective Filmography: *VANISHING ACT,* TV, 86, USA, Prod; *'ADDERLY'* (11 eps), TV, 86, CDN, Co-Exec Prod; *MURDER IN SPACE,* TV, 85, CDN/USA, Prod; *RAPISTS - CAN THEY BE STOPPED?,* 'AMERICA UNDERCOVER', TV, 85, USA, Exec Prod; *BETWEEN FRIENDS,* TV, 83, USA, Co-Prod; *THE GUARDIAN,* TV, 83, CDN/USA, Prod; *THE TERRY FOX STORY,* Th, 82, CDN, Prod (GENIE); *RUNNING,* Th, 79, CDN, Co-Prod; *MIDDLE AGE CRAZY,* Th, 78, CDN, Co-Prod.

COUELLE, Marcia

235 Ave. McDougall, Outremont, Que, CAN, H2V 3P3. (514)271-4933.
Types of Production & Categories: Th Film-Prod; Th Short-Prod; TV Film-Prod; TV Video-Prod.
Genres: Drama-Th&TV; Documentary-Th&TV; Children's-Th&TV.
Biography: Born 1943, Philadelphia, Pennsylvania; US citizen; landed immigrant, Canada. Languages: English, French, Italian. Lived in Italy, 63-68. Began film career in distribution, 69. Co-owner, Vice President, Les Productions Prisma Inc., 74-86. Was on the Board of Directors, Cinémathèque Québécoise, 78-85; President, 84-85. *LES BONS DEBARRAS* won 8 Genie Awards including Best Picture, 80; *COMME LES SIX DOIGTS DE LA MAIN* won le Prix de la Critique Québécoise.
Selective Filmography: *'LIVRE OUVERT'* (OPEN BOOK), (26 eps), TV, 85/84, CDN, Co-Prod; *EARTHWATCH* (EXPO 86), Th, 85, CDN, Co-Prod; *'PROFESSION: ECRIVAIN'* (13 eps), TV, 83, CDN, Co-Prod; *'ZIGZAG'* (6 eps), TV, 83, CDN, Co-Prod; *LE CAHIER NOIR,* 'SECRETS DIPLOMATIQUES', TV, 82, F, Co-Prod; *LE PLUS BEAU JOUR DE MA VIE,* Th, 81, CDN, Co-Prod; *ON EST PAS DES ANGES,* Th, 81, CDN, Co-Prod; *THETFORD AU MILIEU DE NOTRE VIE,* Th, 79, CDN, Co-Prod; *CORRIDORS - PRIS AU PIEGE,* Th, 79, CDN, Co-Prod; *COMME LES SIX DOIGTS DE LA MAIN* (THE BACKSTREET SIX), Th, 78, CDN, Co-Prod; *LES SERVANTES DU BON DIEU,* Th, 78, CDN, Co-Prod; *LES BONS DEBARRAS* (GOOD RIDDANCE), Th, 78, CDN, Co-Prod **(GENIE)**; *MONTREAL,* 'LES GRANDES VILLES DU MONDE', TV, 78, F, Co-Prod; *LE ST-LAURENT,* 'LES GRANDS FLEUVES DU MONDE', TV, 76, F, Co-Prod; *'L'AMOUR QUOTIDIEN'* (13 eps), TV, 75, CDN, Co-Prod.

CRAWLEY, Budge

152 Riverlane, Ottawa, Ont, CAN, K1M 1T1. (613)745-2236.
Types of Production & Categories: Th Film-Prod; Th Short-Prod/Dir; TV Film-Prod.
Genres: Drama-Th&TV; Documentary-Th; Children's-Th&TV; Animation-Th&TV.
Biography: Born 1911, Ottawa, Ontario. Co-founder, Crawley Films, 40; President, Faircrest Films Limited. His films have won 255 awards at film festivals and 70 from the Canadian Film Awards and the Canadian Film and TV Association; 2 Special Achievement Awards from the Academy of Canadian Cinema & Television, 57 and 86.
Selective Filmography: *THE MAN WHO SKIED DOWN EVEREST,* Th, 75, CDN, Prod **(OSCAR)**; *JANIS,* Th, 74, CDN, Prod **(CFA)**; *THE ROWDYMAN,* Th, 72, CDN, Exec Prod; *THE SUN DON'T SHINE ON THE SAME DAWG'S BACK ALL THE TIME,* Th, 70, CDN, Prod/Dir **(CFA)**; *THE ENTERTAINERS,* Th, 67, CDN, Prod **(CFA)**; *GLOBAL VILLAGE,* In, 67, CDN, Prod **(CFA)**; *RETURN TO OZ,* Th, 64, CDN, Prod; *THE LUCK OF GINGER COFFEY,* Th, 64, CDN, Exec Prod **(CFA)**; *'THE TALES OF THE WIZARD OF OZ',* TV, 62, CDN, Prod; *AMANITA PESTILENS,* Th, 62, CDN, Prod; *ABITIBI,* In, 62, CDN, Prod **(CFA)**; *'RCMP',* TV, 60/59, CDN, Prod; *PRESSURE GOLF,* Th, 60, CDN, Prod **(CFA)**; *IT'S PEOPLE THAT COUNT,* Th, 60, CDN, Prod **(CFA)**; *WINTER CROSSING AT L'ILE AUX COUDRES,* Th, 58, CDN, Exec Prod; *'AU PAYS DE LA NEUFVE-FRANCE'* (13 eps), TV, 58, CDN, Prod; *GENERATOR 4,* In, 58, CDN, Prod/Dir **(CFA)**; *LEGEND OF THE RAVEN,* Th, 57, CDN, Exec Prod; *PACKAGED POWER,* In, 51, CDN, Dir; *NEWFOUNDLAND SCENE,* Th, 51, CDN, Prod/Dir **(2 CFA)**; *THE LOON'S NECKLACE,* Th, 48, CDN, DOP/Co-Prod/Co-Dir **(CFA)**.

CULBERT, Bob

ATPD. 16 Oakdene Cres., Toronto, Ont, CAN. (416)465-4114. CBC, 100 Carlton St., 3rd Fl., Toronto, Ont, CAN, M5W 1E6. (416)963-4700.

(cont/suite)

PRODUCERS/PRODUCTEURS

Types of Production & Categories: TV Film-Prod; TV Video-Prod.
Genres: Documentary-TV; Current Affairs-TV.
Biography: Born 1945. Worked at CBC, Winnipeg as executive producer, current affairs, 77-79; CBC, Halifax as area producer overseeing news and current affairs, 79-81; CBC, Toronto, since 81, Senior Editor, *THE JOURNAL*, special responsibilities: features and regional productions.

DALE, Holly - see DIRECTORS

DALEN, Laara

DGC. 546 Marine Dr., Site 1, #23, Gibsons, BC, CAN, V0N 1V0. (604)886-8029.
Types of Production & Categories: Th Film-PM/Prod; Th Short-Prod; TV Film-PM.
Genres: Drama-Th; Industrial-Th&TV; Current Affairs-TV.
Biography: Born British Columbia., B.A., University of British Columbia. Producer of numerous industrial films with Highlight Productions, Vancouver, since 70.
Selective Filmography: *THE VANCOUVER SHOW* (daily), TV, 85, CDN, PM; *SKIP TRACER*, Th, 76, CDN, Prod; *SALLY FEEL GOOD*, Th, 74, CDN, PM.

DALTON, Chris

2879 Forks of Credit Rd., Caledon, Ont, CAN, L0N 1C0. (416)927-5522. Dalton/ Fenske & Friends, 9 New St., Toronto, Ont, CAN, M5R 1P7. (416)967-5588.
Types of Production & Categories: Th Film-Prod; TV Film-Prod.
Genres: Drama-Th&TV.
Biography: Born 1946, Toronto, Ontario. Co-owner, Dalton/Fenske & Friends, commercial producers.
Selective Filmography: *RITES OF SUMMER*, Th, 86, USA, Assoc Prod; *REMO WILLIAMS*, Th, 85, USA, Pro Spv; *RECKLESS DISREGARD*, TV, 84, CDN/ USA, Prod; *20 MINUTE WORKOUT* (120 eps), TV, 83, CDN, Prod; *UTILITIES*, Th, 80, CDN, Co-Prod; *POWER PLAY* (COUP D'ETAT), (STATE OF SHOCK), Th, 77, CDN/GB, Prod; *SEPARATION*, Th, 77, CDN, Prod; *THE CLOWN MURDERS*, Th, 75, CDN, Prod; *ME*, Th, 74, CDN, Co-Prod.

D'AMOUR, Antonio

1196 Van Tassel, Bathurst, NB, CAN. (506)548-3321. Multivision Ltée., 267 ave. King, Bathurst, NB, CAN. (506)548-2189.
Types de production et Catégories: TV vidéo-Prod/Réal/Sc.
Types d'oeuvres: Variété-TV; Action-TV; Documentaire-TV.
Curriculum vitae: Né en 1932. Bac. ès Arts, Collège de Bathurst et Bordeaux (France), Cirtef Communications; B. Ped., Université de Moncton. Enseignant et producteur, 52-75; Président, Comité des médias, Conseil des Ministres de l'Education du Canada, 77-78; conseiller en technique éducative au Ministère de l'Education, N-B, 75-78; producteur et réalisateur à Télé-Acadie et Multivision Ltée..
Filmographie sélective: *VILLES ET VILLAGES* (52 eps), TV, 85-83, CDN, Prod; *COUNTRY CHAUD* (13 eps), TV, 85, CDN, Prod; *HEBDO D'ACADIE* (150 eps), TV, 83-78, CDN, Prod; *L'ILE AU HERON* (14 eps), TV, 83, CDN, Prod/Réal/Aut; *MUSIQUE D'ENTREE* (13 eps), TV, 83, CDN, Prod.

DANE, Lawrence

ACTRA, AFTRA, DGC, SAG. P.O. Box 310, Stn.F, Toronto, Ont, CAN, M4Y 2L7. (416)923-6000.
Types of Production & Categories: Th Film-Wr/Dir/Prod/Act; TV Film-Prod/Dir/ Act.
Genres: Drama-Th&TV; Comedy-Th&TV; Musical-Th; Action-Th&TV.
Biography: Born 1937, Masson, Quebec. Has acted in over 20 movies and over 200 TV shows world-wide as well as producing, directing and writing.

(cont/suite)

Selective Filmography: *HEAVENLY BODIES,* Th, 85, CDN, Dir/Co-Wr; *RITUALS,* Th, 76, CDN, Prod; *ONLY GOD KNOWS,* Th, 73, CDN, Prod; *ROWDYMAN,* Th, 71, CDN, Prod; *ACTION, CUT AND PRINT,* TV, 71, CDN, Prod.

DANYLKIW, John - see PRODUCTION MANAGERS

DARCUS, Jack - see DIRECTORS

DAUPHINEE, Robert

P.O. Box 18, Tantallon, N.S., CAN, B0J 3J0. (902)826-7434. CBC, 1840 Bell Rd., Halifax, N.S., CAN. (902)420-8311.
Types of Production & Categories: TV Video-Prod/Dir.
Genres: News-TV.
Biography: Born 1944, Halifax, Nova Scotia. Began career in electronics; joined CBC as video tape editor, 66. Has worked as a sound engineer, later as switcher and cameraman. Producer/director of *THE MARITIMES TONIGHT* and other news and current affairs shows, 83-86.

DAVID, Pierre

1440 South Sepulveda, Ste. 118, Los Angeles, CA, USA, 90025. (213)478-6100.
Types of Production & Categories: Th Film-Prod.
Genres: Drama-Th; Comedy-Th; Science Fiction-Th; Horror-Th.
Biography: Born 1944, Montreal, Quebec. B.A., University of Montreal. Head of P.R. dept., CJMS radio; President Mutual Productions (concerts) in the 70's; founded Mutual Films (distribution), 72; co-founded New World Mutual Pictures of Canada Ltd., 76; President, Film Plan Int'l, 79; moved to L.A., 83.
Selective Filmography: *MY DEMON LOVER,* Th, 86, USA, Exec Prod; *SCENES FROM A GOLD MINE,* Th, 86, USA, Co-Prod; *HOT PURSUIT,* Th, 85, USA, Prod; *FOR THOSE I LOVED* (AU NOM DE TOUS LES MIENS), Th, 83, CDN/F, Exec Prod; *GOING BERSERK,* Th, 83, CDN/USA, Exec Prod; *OF UNKNOWN ORIGIN,* Th, 82, CDN, Exec Prod; *COVER GIRLS,* Th, 82, CDN, Co-Exec Prod; *VIDEODROME,* Th, 81, CDN, Co-Exec Prod; *SCANNERS,* Th, 80, CDN, Co-Exec Prod; *VISITING HOURS,* Th, 80, CDN, Co-Exec Prod; *THE FUNNY FARM,* Th, 80, CDN, Co-Exec Prod; *DIRTY TRICKS,* Th, 79, CDN, Co-Exec Prod; *HOG WILD,* Th, 79, CDN, Co-Exec Prod; *THE BROOD,* Th, 79, CDN, Co-Exec Prod; *ECLAIR AU CHOCOLAT,* Th, 79, CDN, Prod; *PANIQUE* (PANIC), Th, 76, CDN, Prod; *JE SUIS LOIN DE TOI MIGNONNE,* Th, 76, CDN, Co-Prod; *PARLEZ-NOUS D'AMOUR,* Th, 75, CDN, Exec Prod; *LES AVENTURES D'UNE JEUNE VEUVE,* Th, 75, CDN, Prod; *MUSTANG,* Th, 74, CDN, Exec Prod; *BINGO,* Th, 73, CDN, Prod; *LA MORT D'UN BUCHERON,* Th, 72, CDN, Co-Prod; *LES COLOMBES* (THE DOVES), Th, 72, CDN, Exec Prod.

DAVIDSON, William - see DIRECTORS

DEMERS, Rock

APFVQ. 320 Carré St-Louis, Montréal, Qué, CAN, H2X 1A5. (514)288-5603.
Types de production et Catégories: l métrage-Prod.
Types d'oeuvres: Enfants-C.
Curriculum vitae: Né en 1933. A travaillé dans plusieurs branches de l'industrie dont la production/distribution, programmation. Collabore à l'institution du Festival International du Film et devient le directeur général de 62 à 67; fondateur de Faroun Films (aussi président et directeur exécutif); participe à la formation de l'Institut Québécois du Cinéma, 77-79; co-fondateur de la Cinémathèque Québécoise. Récipiendaire de la Médaille du Gouverneur Général. *LA GUERRE DES TUQUES* remporte la Bobine d'Or, le Grand Prix (Festival du Cinéma Jeune Public, Laon, France), Prix du Public et le Prix Liv Ullman pour la Paix (Chicago).

(cont/suite)

PRODUCERS/PRODUCTEURS

Filmographie sélective: *THE PEANUT BUTTER SOLUTION* (OPERATION BEURRE DE PINOTTES), C, 85, CDN, Co prod; *LA GUERRE DES TUQUES* (THE DOG WHO STOPPED THE WAR), C, 84, CDN, Prod **(CFTA)**.

DENIKE, Brian

ATPD. 144 Albany Ave., #3, Toronto, Ont, CAN, M5R 3C4. (416)532-3190. CBC, 100 Carlton St., 3rd Floor, Toronto, Ont, CAN. (416)975-7920.
Types of Production & Categories: TV Film-Prod/Dir; TV Video-Prod/Dir.
Genres: Documentary-TV; Current Affairs-TV.
Biography: Born 1939, Flin Flon, Manitoba. Education: Carleton University, University of New Brunswick.
Selective Filmography: *'THE JOURNAL'*, TV, 86/85, CDN, Prod; *'MIDDAY'*, TV, 85/84, CDN, Prod; *OLYMPIC GAMES*, TV, 84, CDN, Sr Prod; *OLYMPIC JOURNEY*, TV, 84/83, CDN, Sr Prod; *'THE JOURNAL'*, TV, 83-80, CDN, Sr Ed; *'THE FIFTH ESTATE'*, TV, 80-77, CDN, Sr Prod; *'24 HOURS'* (Winnipeg), TV, 77-74, CDN, Exec Prod.

DENSHAM, Pen

ACTRA, DGA, WGAw. 591 North Cahuenga Blvd., Los Angeles, CA, USA, 90004. (213)463-0044. Insight Group Inc., 1915 Comstock Ave., Los Angeles, CA, USA, 90025. (213)203-8501. Mike Simpson, William Morris Agency, 151 El Camino Dr., Beverly Hills, CA, USA, 90212. (213)859-4100.
Types of Production & Categories: Th Film-Prod/Dir/Wr; Th Short-Prod/Dir/Wr; TV Film-Prod/Dir/Wr.
Genres: Drama-Th&TV; Comedy-Th&TV; Action-Th&TV; Documentary-Th&TV.
Biography: Born 1947, U.K.; emigrated to Canada, 66; Canadian citizen. Formed Insight Productions with John Watson, 70; co-produced, co-wrote, co-directed over 100 films: TV dramas, specials, documentaries, educational films etc.. *IF WISHES WERE HORSES*, winner of 12 int'l awards; his films have won over 70 awards, including 2 Oscar nominations. Received Queen's Silver Jubilee Medal. Moved to L.A., 79.
Selective Filmography: *QUICKSILVER*, Th, 85, USA, 2nd U Co-Dir; *THE ZOO GANG* (WINNERS TAKE ALL), Th, 84, USA, Co-Prod/Co-Dir/Co-Wr; *FLYING TIGERS*, Th, 84, USA, Co-Prod/Co-Wr; *LAST DRAGON II*, Th, 84, USA, Co-Prod/Co-Wr; *BLIND LUCK*, Th, 84, USA, Co-Wr; *ROCKY II*, Th, 80, USA, 2nd U Co-Dir; *DON'T MESS WITH BILL*, TV, 80, CDN, Co-Prod/Co-Dir/Co-Ed; *HOUDINI NEVER DIED (HE JUST VANISHED)*, TV, 79, CDN, Co-Prod/Co-Dir; *IF WISHES WERE HORSES*, TV, 76, CDN, Dir/Wr; *LIFE TIMES NINE*, Th, 74, CDN, Co-Prod.

DESMARAIS, Mario

Arts et Images, 3466 ch. N. Hatley, Rock Forest, Qué, CAN, J1N 1A4. (819)562-5627.
Types de production et Catégories: TV vidéo-Prod/Sc.
Types d'oeuvres: Comédie-TV; Documentaire-TV; Education-TV; Annonces-TV.
Curriculum vitae: Né en 1950, Québec. Formation universitaire. Quatorze ans d'expérience en production et communications.
Filmographie sélective: *'ESTRIE EVIDEMMENT'* (26 eps), TV, 86, CDN, Prod; *DES ENFANTS DE TROP?*, TV, 85, CDN, Prod/Sc; *NEZ DANS LE COURANT*, TV, 84, CDN, Prod; *'DES GENS QUE JE CONNAIS'* (CLEMENCE DESROCHERS), (5 eps), TV, 84, CDN, Prod.

DEVINE, David

CFTA. Devine Videoworks Corp., 5 Sultan St., Toronto, Ont, CAN, M5S 1L6. (416)921-0431.
Types of Production & Categories: TV Film-Prod/Dir; TV Video-Prod/Dir.
Genres: Comedy-TV; Variety-TV; Children's-TV.

(cont/suite)

Biography: Born 1952, Toronto, Ontario. B.A., University of Toronto; M.F.A., UCLA Graduate Film School. Production manager, producer, director for Glen Warren Productions before forming Devine Videoworks.
Selective Filmography: *A YOUNG CHILDREN'S CONCERT WITH RAFFI,* TV, 85, CDN, Prod/Dir; *THE STRAY CATS LIVE,* TV, 84/83, CDN, Prod/Dir; *THE GETAWAY,* MV, 84, CDN, Prod/Dir; *THE MAKING OF STRANGE BREW,* TV, 82, CDN, Prod/Dir; *JEEVES TAKES CHARGE,* TV, 81, CDN/GB, Prod/Dir; *'BIG CITY COMEDY'* (7 eps), TV, 80, CDN/USA, Assoc Prod; *THE JOE-BOB WALKER SHOW,* TV, 79, CDN/USA, Prod/Dir; *'RICH LITTLE SALUTES'* (2 eps), TV, 79, CDN/USA, Assoc Prod.

DEWAR, Stephen W.

27 Tyrrel Ave., Toronto, Ont, CAN, M6G 2G1. (416)651-2530.
Types of Production & Categories: TV Film-Prod/Dir/Wr.
Genres: Documentary-TV; Educational-TV.
Biography: During the course of his career, has worked for NFB, Heritage Films, Mediavision, CTV. Formed Stephen Dewar Productions Ltd., 79; shareholder in Greene & Dewar New Wilderness Productions Inc.. *JET SPEED AT GROUND ZERO* won Best Science Film, Bell Northern Prize, 74.
Selective Filmography: *'LORNE GREENE'S NEW WILDERNESS'* (104 eps), TV, 86-81, CDN, Co-Prod; *'MAN OF THE NORTH'* (Dir-6 eps), (12 eps), TV, 78/77, CDN, Wr; *'LAST OF THE WILD'* (Co-wr-6 eps), (9 eps), TV, 76, CDN/USA, Wr; *'BEHIND THE SCENES WITH JONATHAN WINTERS'* (Co-wr-8 eps), (9 eps), TV, 75, CDN/USA, Wr/Dir; *'GLENN FORD'S FRIENDS OF MAN'* (18 eps), TV, 74/73, CDN/USA, Co-Wr; *'W5'* (sev seg), TV, 71-68, CDN, Dir/Report; *JET SPEED AT GROUND ZERO,* TV, 71, CDN, Dir/Wr.

DEY, Wendy E.

44 Belsize Dr., Toronto, Ont, CAN, M4S 1L4. (416)489-7434. Global TV, 81 Barber Greene Rd., Don Mills, Ont, CAN, M3C 2A2. (416)446-5325.
Types of Production & Categories: TV Video-Prod.
Genres: News-TV.
Biography: Born 1943, Ottawa, Ontario. Education: English, Philosophy, Queen's University; Ontario College of Art; Journalism, Carleton University. Reporter: Ottawa Citizen, Toronto Star; editor, Victoria Times, Toronto Star; Global TV: assignment editor, reporter, producer and executive producer, news and current affairs.
Selective Filmography: *NEWSWEEK/NEWS AT NOON/SATURDAY EDITION,* TV, 86-83, CDN, Exec Prod; *'FIRST NEWS',* TV, 85/84, CDN, Exec Prod/Prod; *'6 O'CLOCK NEWS'/'11 O'CLOCK NEWS'* (NATIONAL EDITION), TV, 85/84, CDN, Exec Prod/Prod; *'EVENING EDITION',* TV, 84/83, CDN, Exec Prod/Prod; *'NEWS AT NOON',* TV, 83-81, CDN, Prod.

DODD, Thomas - see DIRECTORS

DONOVAN, Michael

1533 Granville St., Halifax, NS, CAN. (902)429-6870. Salter Street Films Ltd., 1672 Barrington St., Box 2261, Halifax, NS, CAN, B3J 3C8. (902)420-1577.
Types of Production & Categories: Th Film-Prod.
Genres: Drama-Th&TV; Action-Th.
Biography: Born 1953, Nova Scotia.
Selective Filmography: *DEFCON 4,* Th, 84, CDN, Prod; *SIEGE,* Th, 81, CDN, Prod; *SOUTH PACIFIC 1942,* Th, 80, CDN, Prod.

DRABINSKY, Garth H.

Cineplex Odeon Corporation, 214 King St.W., Suite 600, Toronto, Ont, CAN, M5H 3S6. (416)596-2200.

(cont/suite)

Types of Production & Categories: Th Film-Prod.
Genres: Drama-Th; Comedy-Th; Horror-Th.
Biography: Born 1948, Toronto, Ontario. LL.B. degree, University of Toronto, 73; called to the Bar of Ontario with Honours, 75. Film, TV and theatre producer; lecturer; author of 'Motion Pictures and the Arts in Canada -The Business and the Law'. Co-founder, Pan-Canadian Film Distributors with Nathan A. Taylor, 78; Chairman, President, Chief Executive Officer, Cineplex Odeon Corporation: Cineplex Odeon Theatres; Plitt Theatres; Pan-Canadian Film Distributors; Tiberius Productions and Toronto Int'l Studios. *THE CHANGELING* received 8 Genies, 80.
Selective Filmography: *LOSIN' IT*, Th, 82, USA, Prod; *THE AMATEUR*, Th, 81, CDN, Co-Prod; *TRIBUTE* (UN FILS POUR L'ETE), Th, 80, CDN, Co-Prod; *THE CHANGELING*, Th, 79, CDN, Co-Prod (GENIE); *THE SILENT PARTNER*, Th, 77, CDN, Exec Prod (CFA); *THE DISAPPEARANCE*, Th, 77, CDN, Prod.

DUBRO, James R.

Beacon Hill Prod. Inc., 86 Gloucester St., #402, Toronto, Ont, CAN, M4Y 2S2. (416)922-8706.
Types of Production & Categories: TV Film-Prod.
Genres: Documentary-TV.
Biography: Born 1946, Boston, Massachussetts; Canadian-US citizenship. M.A. with high honours, Columbia University; member, Phi Beta Kappa; teaching fellowship, U. of Toronto, Victoria College, 70-72. Author, 'Mob Rule: Inside the Canadian Mafia'.
Selective Filmography: *THE DECEPTION NETWORK*, TV, 85, CDN, Co-Wr/Co-Dir; *THE INFORMER/BOUNTY HUNTER/TRAITOR IN THE MOUNTIES*, 'THE FIFTH ESTATE', TV, 84/82, CDN, Assoc Prod; *CHINESE GANGS AND MURDERS*, 'THE FIFTH ESTATE', TV, 83-81, CDN, Assoc Prod; *THE KGB CONNECTIONS*, TV, 81, CDN, Co-Prod; *CONNECTIONS: A FURTHER INVESTIGATION*, TV, 79, CDN, Assoc Prod/Res; *CONNECTIONS: AN INVESTIGATION INTO ORGANIZED CRIME*, TV, 77, CDN, Assoc Prod/Res (ANIK); *THE FIFTH ESTATE: THE ESPIONAGE ESTABLISHMENT*, TV, 74, CDN, Res.

DUECK, David B.

CFTA. 295 Wallace Ave., Winnipeg, Man, CAN, R2E 0B1. (204)661-1010. Dueck Film Prods. Ltd., 201 - 1382 Henderson Hwy., Winnipeg, Man, CAN, R2G 1M8. (204)661-2483.
Types of Production & Categories: Th Film-Prod/Dir/Ed; TV Film-Prod/Dir/Ed; TV Video-Ed/Prod.
Genres: Drama-Th&TV; Documentary-Th&TV; Educational-Th&TV; Children's-Th&TV.
Biography: Born 1940, Minto, Manitoba. Graduated from a 3 year theological program, Winkler Bible Institute; B.Sc., Chemistry and Physics and B. Ed. in Administration, University of Manitoba; graduate work in nuclear physics. Has taught Physics and Film Studies, U. of Winnipeg. Active as a distributor since 70; experienced in four-walling films. *AND WHEN THEY SHALL ASK* won awards in Hollywood, Chicago and Toronto.
Selective Filmography: *FAMILIES*, Th, 86, CDN, Prod/Dir; *KOOP EN BUA ENN DIETSCHLAUND*, Th, 85, CDN, Prod/Ed; *WE HAVE POWER*, Cm, 84, CDN, Prod; *PORTAGE PRIDE*, In, 83, CDN, Prod; *AND WHEN THEY SHALL ASK*, Th, 83, CDN, Prod; *HOME FOR THE HOMELESS* (HEIMAT FUER HEIMATLOSE), Th, 81, CDN, Prod/Dir/Ed; *FAMILY LIFE/MENNO'S REIN*, ED, 79/75, CDN, Prod; *INDIAN ARTS AND CRAFTS*, TV, 74, CDN, Prod; *ST. LAURENT SPEAKS*, ED, 73, CDN, Prod/Ed; *GLOBAL PANORAMA*, ED, 71, CDN, Prod/Ed/Dir/DOP; *THE SPIRIT OF 70*, Cm, 70, CDN, Prod/Dir/Ed.

DUNNING, John

Cinépix Inc., 8275 Mayrand, Montreal, Que, CAN, H4P 2C8. (514)342-2340.
Types of Production & Categories: Th Film-Prod.
Genres: Drama-Th; Comedy-Th; Science Fiction-Th; Horror-Th.
Biography: Born Montreal, Quebec; bilingual. Co-founder and Chairman of the Board, Cinépix Inc..
Selective Filmography: *NATIONAL PARK,* Th, 86, CDN, Co-Prod; *MEATBALLS III,* Th, 84, CDN, Co-Prod; *THE VINDICATOR* (FRANKENSTEIN FACTOR), Th, 84, CDN, Co-Prod; *THE SURROGATE,* Th, 83, CDN, Co-Prod; *SPACEHUNTER: ADVENTURES IN THE FORBIDDEN ZONE,* Th, 83, CDN/ USA, Co-Prod; *HAPPY BIRTHDAY TO ME,* Th, 80, CDN, Co-Prod; *MY BLOODY VALENTINE,* Th, 80, CDN, Co-Prod; *YESTERDAY* (GABRIELLE), Th, 79, CDN, Co-Prod/Co-Scr; *MEATBALLS,* Th, 79, CDN, Co-Exec Prod; *HOT DOGS,* Th, 79, CDN, Co-Prod; *BLACKOUT,* Th, 77, CDN, Co-Prod; *RABID,* Th, 76, CDN, Prod; *DEATH WEEKEND* (THE HOUSE BY THE LAKE), Th, 75, CDN, Co-Exec Prod; *THE MYSTERY OF THE MILLION DOLLAR HOCKEY PUCK,* Th, 75, CDN, Co-Prod; *THE PARASITE MURDERS* (SHIVERS), Th, 74, CDN, Co-Prod; *TOUT FEU, TOUT FEMME,* Th, 74, CDN, Co-Prod; *ACROSS THIS LAND WITH STOMPIN' TOM CONNORS,* Th, 73, CDN, Co-Prod; *L'HEPTMARON,* Th, 73, CDN/F, Co-Prod; *KEEP IT IN THE FAMILY,* Th, 72, CDN, Co-Prod; *HAVING A LAUGH,* Th, 71, CDN, Co-Prod; *LE DIABLE EST PARMI NOUS,* Th, 71, CDN, Co-Prod; *LOVE IN A FOUR-LETTER WORLD,* Th, 70, CDN, Co-Prod; *L'AMOUR HUMAIN,* Th, 70, CDN, Co-Prod; *PILE OU FACE,* Th, 70, CDN, Co-Prod; *INITIATION,* Th, 69, CDN, Co-Prod; *VALERIE,* Th, 68, CDN, Co-Prod.

EARL, Morgan

ACTRA, CFTA. 65 Harbour Sq., #2603, Toronto, Ont, CAN, M5J 2L4. (416)862-1346. Painless Productions, 61 St.Nicholas St., Toronto, Ont, CAN, M4Y 1W6. (416)968-9292. Glenn Bickel, CAA, 1888 Century Pk.E., Ste. 1400, Los Angeles, CA, USA, 90067. (213)277-4545.
Types of Production & Categories: TV Film-Prod; TV Video-Prod.
Genres: Comedy-TV; Variety-TV; Musical-TV; Documentary-TV.
Biography: Born 1934; Canadian citizen; bilingual. B. Comm., McGill University. Broadcast producer, 25 years experience: commercials, documentaries, TV specials and series. Winner of 13 Clio awards; Billboard Magazine Award for Best Radio Program, 75.
Selective Filmography: *'4 ON THE FLOOR'* (13 eps), TV, 85, CDN, Prod/Story Ed; *ONE FINE WEEKEND: THE LIGHTHOUSE REUNION,* TV, 82, CDN, Prod.

ECKERT, John M.

CFTA, DGA, DGC. John M. Eckert Prod. Ltd., 385 Carlton St., Toronto, Ont, CAN, M5A 2M3. (416)960-4961.
Types of Production & Categories: Th Film-Prod; TV Film-Prod.
Genres: Drama-Th&TV; Comedy-Th&TV; Action-Th&TV; Horror-Th&TV.
Biography: Canadian citizen. Ryerson Polytechnical Institute, Photographic Arts, Motion Picture major, 68-71.
Selective Filmography: *'DANGER BAY'* (44 eps), TV, 86/85, CDN/USA, Spv Prod; *SILVER BULLET,* Th, 85/84, USA, Assoc Prod; *CAT'S EYE,* Th, 84, USA, Pro Exec; *SPECIAL PEOPLE,* TV, 83, CDN/USA, Prod; *THE DEAD ZONE,* Th, 82, USA, PM; *THE TERRY FOX STORY,* Th, 82, CDN, Assoc Prod; *INCUBUS,* Th, 80, CDN, Prod; *MIDDLE AGE CRAZY,* Th, 78, CDN, Co-Prod; *RUNNING,* Th, 78, CDN, Co-Prod; *POWER PLAY* (COUP D'ETAT), (STATE OF SHOCK), Th, 77, CDN/GB, Assoc Prod; *EQUUS,* Th, 76, USA, 2nd AD; *RITUALS,* Th, 76, CDN, Assist Dir; *SILVER STREAK,* Th, 76, USA, 2nd U Assist Dir; *FIND THE*

(cont/suite)

LADY, Th, 75, CDN, Assist Dir; *SECOND WIND*, Th, 75, CDN, Assist Dir/PM; *THE CLOWN MURDERS*, Th, 75, CDN, Assoc Prod/PM/Assist Dir; *IT SEEMED LIKE A GOOD IDEA AT THE TIME*, Th, 74, CDN, Assist Dir; *LIONS FOR BREAKFAST*, Th, 74, CDN, Assist Dir; *SUDDEN FURY*, Th, 74, CDN, PM/Assist Dir; *BLACK CHRISTMAS* (SILENT NIGHT, EVIL NIGHT), Th, 74, CDN, 2nd AD; *THE HARD PART BEGINS*, Th, 73, CDN, Unit M; *'POLICE SURGEON'* (54 eps), TV, 73/72, CDN, 2nd AD; *HOME FREE*, Th, 72, CDN, Dir/Prod; *THE ROWDYMAN*, Th, 71, CDN, PA/Stills; *THREE FILMS: TORONTO*, Th, 70, CDN, Dir/Prod; *THE DOOR*, Th, 70, CDN, Dir/Prod.

EGOYAN, Atom - see DIRECTORS

ELLIS, Ralph C.

CFTA. 4 Wilfrid Ave., Toronto, Ont, CAN, M4S 2H9. (416)484-9067. Keg Productions Ltd., 1231 Yonge St., Ste. 300, Toronto, Ont, CAN, M4T 2T8. (416) 924-2186.
Types of Production & Categories: Th Film-Prod; TV Film-Prod.
Genres: Drama-Th&TV; Documentary-TV; Children's-TV.
Biography: Born 1924, Milton, Nova Scotia. Served in R.C.A.F., 43-45. Joined NFB as field representative in Halifax, 46; co-ordinator of theatrical distribution, Ottawa, 49-52; assistant regional supervisor, Toronto, 52-54; commercial rep., New York, 54-56. Returned to Canada to specialize in int'l TV program distribution; formed several companies. Received the Jack Chisholm Award, CFTA; films he has produced have won awards at national and int'l film festivals including: Yorkton, Chicago, New York, Cork, Moscow.
Selective Filmography: *'PROFILES OF NATURE'* (65 eps), TV, 86-84, CDN, Prod; *IMAGES OF GALAPAGOS*, TV, 83, CDN, Prod; *'WILD CANADA'* (11 eps), TV, 81-78, CDN, Exec Prod; *'MATT AND JENNY'* (26 eps), TV, 79, CDN/GB/D, Exec Prod **(CFTA)**; *NAHANNI*, 'WILD CANADA', TV, 78, CDN, Exec Prod **(CFTA)**; *WINGS IN THE WILDERNESS*, Th, 75, CDN, Exec Prod; *'TO THE WILD COUNTRY'* (9 eps), TV, 74-72, CDN, Exec Prod; *'WILDLIFE CINEMA'* (26 eps), TV, 74, CDN, Exec Prod; *RETURN OF THE GIANTS*, 'TO THE WILD COUNTRY', TV, 73, CDN, Exec Prod **(CFA)**; *'AUBUDON WILDLIFE THEATRE'* (78 eps), TV, 72-67, CDN, Exec Prod; *'ADVENTURES IN RAINBOW COUNTRY'* (26 eps), TV, 69, CDN/GB/AUS, Exec Prod.

EL-SISSI, Azza

ATPD. 331 Seaton St., Toronto, Ont, CAN, M5A 2T6. (416)923-3166. CBC, P.O. Box 500, Stn. A, Toronto, Ont, CAN, M5W 1E6. (416)975-6574.
Types of Production & Categories. TV Film-Prod/Dir; TV Video-Prod/Dir.
Genres: Drama-TV; Documentary-TV; Educational-TV.
Biography: Born 1942, Cairo, Egypt; Canadian citizen; fluent in English and Arabic. B.Sc. in Electrical Engineering; Dipoma in teaching technologists; graduate studies at University of Toronto, Arts and Science. Worked in Broadcasting since 64 as an engineer, maintenance engineer, video tape editor before joining CBC drama as service producer; with TV current affairs as producer since 78. *THE PRICE TAG* won the Gold Medal, NY Int'l Film Festival.
Selective Filmography: *BACKWARDS TO FRONTWARDS*, TV, 86, CDN, Prod/Dir/Res; *INSIDE OAK RIDGE*, TV, 86, CDN, Prod/Dir/Res; *FOR ALL THE GOOD INTENTIONS*, TV, 84, CDN, Prod/Dir; *'MARKET PLACE'* (2 eps), TV, 83, CDN, Prod/Dir; *THE PRICE TAG* (PREEMIES, THE PRICE TAG), 'THE JOURNAL', TV, 83, CDN, Prod/Dir; *'MAN ALIVE'* (11 eps), TV, 82-78, CDN, Prod/Dir/Wr; *PRETTY BABIES/MEN, SEX AND THE STRAIT JACKET*, 'MAN ALIVE', TV, 82/81, CDN, Prod/Dir; *A GIFT TO LAST* (pilot), TV, 76, CDN, Serv Prod **(ANIK)**.

ENGEL, Fred A.

CTPDA, SMPTE. 1850 St.Denis Pl., West Vancouver, BC, CAN. (604)922-0180.
Types of Production & Categories: TV Film-Prod/Dir; TV Video-Prod/Dir.
Genres: Drama-TV; Documentary-TV; Educational-TV; Religious-TV.
Biography: Born 1931; educated in Winnipeg. **Languages:** English, German.
Experienced pilot, sailor.
Selective Filmography: *'REACH FOR THE TOP'* (120 eps), TV, 85-80, CDN,
Prod/Dir; *'MEETING PLACE'* (24 eps), TV, 85-80, CDN, Prod/Dir;
VANCOUVER SYMPHONY, Cm, 85, CDN, Prod/Dir; *CARING,* TV, 85, CDN,
Prod/Dir; *THE POPE'S VISIT TO CANADA,* TV, 84, CDN, Prod; *WORLD
COUNCIL OF CHURCHES,* TV, 83, CDN, Prod; *'PETS PLEASE'* (13 eps), TV,
82, CDN, Prod/Wr/Dir; *AHOUSAT 'SOUND OF BATTLE',* TV, 70, CDN, Ed;
'MANIPULATORS' (Ed-3 eps), (13 eps), TV, 69, CDN, Spv Ed; *'WATER
PEOPLE'* (2 eps), TV, 68, CDN, Ed; *'HERE AND THERE'* (13 eps), TV, 65,
CDN, Ed.

ENGEL, Paul

AR, CTPDA, SMPTE. CBC/Radio-Canada, 1055 Dorchester East, Montreal, Que,
CAN, H2L 4S5. (514)285-2724. Lillian Campbell, 4065 ave. de Vendome,
Montreal, Que, CAN, H4A 3N2. (514)487-7639.
Types of Production & Categories: TV Film-Prod/Dir; TV Video-Prod/Dir.
Genres: Variety-TV; Documentary-TV; Educational-TV; Sports-TV.
Biography: Born 1949, Tacoma, Washington; emigrated to Canada, 71; Canadian
citizen; bilingual. B.F.A., Concordia University. Began as a freelance photographer;
producer, director of news, current affairs and sports since 79; supervisor, English
news, Radio-Canada International, Montreal, 86.
Selective Filmography: *'COMPASS'* (P.E.I.), TV, 86-84, CDN, Prod/Dir; *GOLD
CUP 85,* TV, 85, CDN, Prod/Dir/Wr; *GOLD CUP PARADE,* TV, 85, CDN, Prod/
Dir; *'NEWSWATCH'* (Montreal), TV, 84-79, CDN, Prod/Dir; *SING NOEL,* TV,
84, CDN, Prod/Dir.

EVANS, Janet

CTPDA. 404 Athlone, Ottawa, Ont, CAN, K1Z 5M5. (613)722-3587.
Types of Production & Categories: Th Short-Dir; TV Film-Dir; TV Video-Prod.
Genres: Drama-TV; Variety-TV; Documentary-Th&TV.
Biography: Born 1939, U.K.; Canadian landed immigrant. Attended Central School,
Stage Management course; worked for Granada TV, BBC London and Glascow in
drama departments. Emigrated to Canada, 66; writer/director, Crawley Films, 67;
CBC Ottawa, writer/broadcaster; contract producer since 77.
Selective Filmography: *'SWITCHBACK'* (30 eps), TV, 86, CDN, Prod; *ICE TIME,*
'THE WAY WE ARE', TV, 85, CDN, Prod/Dir; *LOCAL DRAMA'* (3 eps), TV,
83, CDN, Dir/Prod **(ACTRA)**; *'SCENE FROM HERE'* (52 eps), TV, 81 79, CDN,
Prod; *'COUNTRY REPORT'* (52 eps), TV, 79-77, CDN, Prod; *OTTAWA: THE
NATION'S CAPITAL,* Th, 74, CDN, Dir **(CFA)**.

FALZON, Charles

571 DeLoraine Ave., Toronto, Ont, CAN, M5M 2C7. (416)782-9989. Taffner &
Associates, 9 Prince Arthur Ave., Toronto, Ont, CAN, M5R 1B2. (416)928-2922.
Types of Production & Categories: TV Video-Prod.
Genres: Comedy-TV.
Biography: Born 1956; Canadian citizen. Attended York University; Ryerson Radio
& TV Arts Program. Has distributed programs as Sales Manager for CBC
Enterprises and MCA-TV; 3 years in New York as V.P. Int'l for D.L. Taffner Ltd.
distributing and packaging foreign co-productions. Now President, Taffner &
Associates.
Selective Filmography: *'CHECK IT OUT!'* (22 eps), TV, 86/85, CDN/USA, Pro
Exec.

FANTHAM, Judy

CTPDA. 10E Millrise Lane, Ottawa, Ont, CAN, K2G 4T9. (613)723-1549.
Types of Production & Categories: TV Film-Dir/Prod/Wr; TV Video-Dir/Prod/Wr.
Genres: Documentary-TV; Educational-TV.
Biography: Born 1955, Red Deer, Alberta; Bachelor of Journalism, Carleton University, Ottawa (First Class Honours). Producer in current affairs, CBC, Ottawa, 86.
Selective Filmography: *NETWORKING: THE POWERFUL ALBERTANS,* TV, 85, CDN, Prod/Dir/Wr; *THE STRUGGLE CONTINUES: EDMONTON'S VIETNAMESE,* TV, 85, CDN, Prod/Dir/Wr; *SOME LIKE IT COLD,* 'CITIES', TV, 84, CDN, Prod/Dir/Wr; *THE SURVIVORS,* TV, 84, CDN, Prod/Dir/Wr; *THE CITADEL OPENING,* TV, 84, CDN, Prod/Dir/Wr; *'BUSINESS WATCH',* TV, 83-81, CDN, Prod/Dir/Wr.

FARN, Calla

4 Dumas Court, Don Mills, Ont, CAN, M3A 2N2. (416)445-2552. Global TV, 81 Barber Greene Rd., Don Mills, Ont, CAN. (416)446-5460.
Types of Production & Categories: TV Film-Prod/Wr; TV Video-Prod/Wr.
Genres: Documentary-TV; Educational-TV; News-TV.
Biography: Born 1955, Toronto, Ontario. Has produced *NEWS AT NOON* (Global TV) for 4 years; prior experience as news writer, various newscasts, Global TV.

FEHRENBACH, Del

CTPDA. 214 Vanier Cres., Saskatoon, Sask, CAN, S7L 5H6. CBC, CN Tower, 5th Floor, Saskatoon, Sask, CAN, S7K 1J5. (306)244-1911.
Types of Production & Categories: TV Video-Prod/Dir.
Genres: Variety-TV; Documentary-TV; News-TV; Sports-TV.
Biography: Born Saltcoats, Saskatchewan, 1938.
Selective Filmography: *'SASKATOON TODAY'* (weekly), TV, 86/85, CDN, Prod/Dir; *SINGING CHRISTMAS TREE* (2 shows), TV, 84/83, CDN, Prod/Dir; *'NEWSDAY',* TV, 84-74, CDN, Exec Prod (**ANIK**); *K OF C INDOOR GAMES,* TV, 83/82, CDN, Prod/Dir; *YEAR END NEWS REVIEW,* TV, 83, CDN, Prod/Dir; *SASKATCHEWAN ROUGHRIDERS IS OUR NAME,* TV, 83, CDN, Prod/Dir; *LADIES NORTHERN CURLING PLAYDOWNS,* TV, 82, CDN, Prod/Dir; *ROYAL VISIT,* TV, 80, CDN, Prod/Dir; *30 FROM SASKATOON* (JOHNNY WALKER), TV, 80, CDN, Prod/Dir.

FENSKE, Wayne

CFTA, DGC. 456 Ontario St., Toronto, Ont, CAN, M5A 2W1. (416)964-0194. Dalton/Fenske & Friends, 9 New St., Toronto, Ont, CAN, M5R 1P7. (416)967-5588.
Types of Production & Categories: TV Film-Prod; TV Video-Prod.
Genres: Drama-TV; Variety-TV; Musical-TV; Commercials-TV.
Biography: Born 1947, Toronto, Ontario. Graduate of Ryerson Polytechnical Institute, Radio & TV Arts.
Selective Filmography: *FULL CIRCLE AGAIN,* TV, 84, CDN, Prod; *THE RICH LITTLE SHOW,* TV, 83, CDN, Prod; *SHOCKTRAUMA,* TV, 82, CDN, Prod; *THE MAGIC SHOW,* TV, 80, CDN, Prod.

FERGUSON, Graeme - see DIRECTORS

FERNS, W. Paterson

ACTRA, ACFTP. 78 Manor Rd.E., Toronto, Ont, CAN, M4S 1P8. (416)484-4882. Primedia Productions Ltd., 219 Front St.E., Toronto, Ont, CAN, M5A 1E5. (416) 361-0306.
Types of Production & Categories: TV Film-Prod/Wr; TV Video-Prod.
Genres: Drama-TV; Musical-TV; Documentary-TV; Children's-TV.

(cont/suite)

112

Biography: Born 1945, Winnipeg, Manitoba. Educated at Cambridge University (First Class Honours/Wrenbury Scholar) and Birmingham University (M.Soc. Sc.). President, Banff TV Foundation (84-); past President, CFTA (79-81) and ACFTP (84-85). First recipient of Chetwynd Award . President, Primedia Productions Ltd., Toronto; Primedia Television Inc., Edmonton. His films have won numerous awards including Gold Awards (N.Y., Chicago) for *THE NEWCOMERS*; Gold Plaque (Chicago) for *LYNN SEYMOUR: IN A CLASS OF HER OWN.*

Selective Filmography: *'FRONTIER'* (6 eps), TV, 86, CDN/GB/F/D, Prod/Wr; *HEAVEN ON EARTH*, TV, 86, CDN/GB, Exec Prod; *ONEGIN*, TV, 85, CDN, Exec Prod/Prod; *'DURRELL IN RUSSIA'* (13 eps), TV, 85, CDN/GB, Exec Prod; *COUNTDOWN TO LOOKING GLASS*, TV, 84, CDN/USA, Exec Prod; *BOLD STEPS*, TV, 84, CDN/GB, Prod; *WAITING FOR THE PARADE*, TV, 83, CDN, Prod; *'THE AMATEUR NATURALIST'* (13 eps), TV, 83, CDN/GB, Exec Prod; *MELANCHOLY OF ROMANCE*, 'WRITERS & PLACES', TV, 83, CDN/GB, Exec Prod; *THE TIN FLUTE* (BONHEUR D'OCCASION), (also 5 eps for TV), Th, 82, CDN, Assoc Prod; *COUNTRY CLASSIC*, TV, 82, CDN, Prod; *BILLY BISHOP GOES TO WAR*, TV, 82, CDN/GB, Prod (**ACTRA/CFTA**); *BRIAN MACDONALD'S NEWCOMERS*, TV, 82, CDN, Prod; *'ARK ON THE MOVE'* (13 eps), TV, 81/80, CDN/GB, Exec Prod; *LYNN SEYMOUR: IN A CLASS OF HER OWN*, TV, 79, CDN, Prod; *'PORTRAITS OF POWER'* (26 eps), TV, 79-77, CDN/USA, Exec Prod; *'THE NEWCOMERS'* (LES ARRIVANTS), (7 eps), TV, 78-75, CDN, Prod (**CFTA**); *'CITIES'* (13 eps), TV, 78-76, CDN, Co-Prod (**CFTA**); *HOT POPS*, TV, 77, CDN, Exec Prod; *FROM RUSSIA WITH BRUNO GERUSSI*, TV, 76, CDN, Exec Prod; *'THE STATIONARY ARK'* (13 eps), TV, 75, CDN, Exec Prod (**CFTA**); *KAREN KAIN: BALLERINA*, TV, 75, CDN, Exec Prod; *JUBILEE*, TV, 74, CDN/USA, Exec Prod; *DOSTOEVSKY*, TV, 74, CDN, Prod/Dir; *AN ARK FOR OUR TIME*, TV, 74, CDN, Exec Prod (**CFTA**); *'A THIRD TESTAMENT'* (UN TROISIEME TESTAMENT), (6 eps), TV, 73/72, CDN/USA, Prod/Dir; *IN DISTRESS*, In, 73, CDN, Prod/Dir.

FLOQUET, François

APFVQ. 4753 Meridian, Montréal, Qué, CAN, H3W 2C2. (514)488-3437. 326 St-Paul ouest, Montréal, Qué, CAN, H2Y 2A3. (514)285-1658.
Types de production et Catégories: 1 métrage-Prod/Réal; TV film-Prod/Réal.
Types d'oeuvres: Drame-C; Documentaire-C&TV.
Curriculum vitae: Né en 1939, France; canadien, 67. Doctorat en Géographie, Sorbonne, Paris. Fondation de Productions Via Le Monde Inc., Montréal, 67. Président de l'APFQ, 79. Ouverture de Productions Via Le Monde François Floquet Inc., 84. Il remporte la Médaille d'or et le Prix Spécial du Jury à Atlanta pour *AVENTURE HUMAINE* (épisode Brésil).
Filmographie sélective: *LA GUEPE*, C, 86/85, CDN, Prod; *LES AVENTURES DU GRAND ECRAN*, TV, 85, CDN, Prod/Réal/Cam; *'LE PARADIS DES CHEFS'* (Cam et Réal, 12 ep), (13 eps), TV, 83-79, CDN, Prod; *CHATEAU DE CHAPULTEPES*, 'LES HISTOIRES DE L'HISTOIRE', TV, 81, CDN, Co réal/Cam; *'LES AMIS DE MES AMIS'* (Cam et Réal, 4 ep), (13 eps), TV, 80-77, CDN, Co prod; *LE GRAND DESERT BLANC*, TV, 80, CDN, Réal; *SPECIAL BAIE JAMES*, TV, 79/78, CDN, Prod/Réal; *'AVENTURE HUMAINE'* (2 eps), TV, 77-73, CDN, Co prod/Réal/Cam; *'DES IDEES, DES PAYS, DES HOMMES'* (SURVIVORS), (Réal, 3 ep), (10 eps), TV, 77, CDN, Co prod; *DEFI* (Réal et Cam, 12 ep), (39 eps), TV, 77-74, CDN, Co prod; *AHO AU COEUR DU MONDE PRIMITIF* (AHO...THE FOREST PEOPLE), C, 76, CDN, Co prod/Co réal (**CFA**); *'LES PRIMITIFS'* (cam et Réal, 2 ep), (6 eps), TV, 74-70, CDN, Co prod; *'PLEIN FEU...L'AVENTURE'* (cam, 21 ep), (37 eps), TV, 73-69, CDN, Co prod/Réal; *'DES GOUTS,DES FORMES ET DES COULEURS'* (Cam et Réal, 2 ep), (13 eps), TV, 72, CDN, Prod exéc.

FORTIER, Bob - see DIRECTORS

PRODUCERS/PRODUCTEURS

FOURNIER, Eric
APFVQ. 557 ave. Davaar, Outremont, Qué, CAN, H2V 3A7. (514)277-6271. Les Prod. du Verseau Inc., 4060 Ste-Catherine O., #600, Montréal, Qué, CAN, H3Z 2Z3. (514)935-8521.
Types de production et Catégories: l métrage-Prod; c métrage-Prod; TV film-Prod; TV vidéo-Prod.
Types d'oeuvres: Drame-TV; Comédie musicale-C; Documentaire-TV; Annonces-TV.
Curriculum vitae: Né en 1952, Sherbrooke, Québec. M.B.A, Ecole des Hautes Etudes Commerciales de Montréal. Producteur au Productions du Verseau Inc. depuis 9 ans; nombreuses annonces et films industriels; producteur, *TALK SHOW 4 SAISONS*, 86.
Filmographie sélective: *'MANON'* (46 eps), TV, 86/85, CDN, Prod; *PETRO CANADA*, In, 86, CDN, Prod; *'LES ENFANTS MAL-AIMES'*, TV, 85/84, CDN, Prod; *COCA COLA/ALCAN INSTITUTIONEL*, Cm, 83.82, CDN, Prod; *FANTASTICA*, C, 80/79, CDN/F, Prod.

FOX, Beryl
14 Birch Ave., Toronto, Ont, CAN, M4V 1C9. (416)968-0595.
Types of Production & Categories: Th Film-Prod; Th Short-Prod; TV Film-Prod/Wr; TV Video-Prod/Dir/Wr.
Genres: Drama-Th; Comedy-Th&TV; Documentary-Th&TV.
Biography: Born Winnipeg, Manitoba. B.A., History, University of Toronto. Honours LL.D., University of Western Ontario. Her films have won awards at Atlanta, Vancouver, Columbus and Oberhausen film festivals.
Selective Filmography: *BY DESIGN*, Th, 80, CDN, Prod; *SURFACING*, Th, 79, CDN, Prod; *THE VISIBLE WOMAN*, ED, 76, CDN, Co-Prod/Co-Dir; *'WILD REFUGE'* (26 eps), TV, 75/74, CDN, Co-Prod/Dir/Wr; *TAKE MY HAND*, In, 75, CDN, Prod/Dir/Wr; *'TOWARDS THE YEAR 2000'*, TV, 74-70, CDN, Co-Prod/Dir/Wr; *'HERE COME THE 70'S'* (78 eps), TV, 72-70, CDN, Co-Prod/Dir; *NORTH WITH THE SPRING*, TV, 70, CDN/USA, Prod/Dir/Wr; *IN MEMORIAM: MARTIN LUTHER KING*, TV, 69, USA, Prod/Dir/Wr; *LAST REFLECTIONS ON A WAR*, TV, 68, CDN/USA, Prod/Dir/Wr; *VIEW FROM THE 21st CENTURY*, TV, 68, USA, Prod/Dir/Wr; *SAIGON: PORTRAIT OF A CITY*, TV, 67, USA, Prod/Dir/Wr; *'THIS HOUR HAS SEVEN DAYS'* (52 eps), TV, 66-64, CDN, Dir/Wr; *THE HONORABLE RENE LEVESQUE*, TV, 66, CDN, Prod/Dir/Wr; *MILLS OF THE GODS: VIET NAM*, 'THIS HOUR HAS SEVEN DAYS', TV, 65, CDN, Prod/Dir/Wr (**ANIK/CFA**); *ONE MORE RIVER*, TV, 64, CDN/USA/GB, Co-Prod/Co-Dir; *SUMMER IN MISSISSIPPI*, 'THIS HOUR HAS SEVEN DAYS', TV, 64, CDN, Prod/Dir/Wr (**CFA**); *NFB TORONTO STUDIO*, ED, 64, CDN, Prod; *SINGLE WOMAN-DOUBLE STANDARD*, TV, 63, CDN, Prod/Dir/Wr.

FRANK, Anne
14 Gresham Rd., Toronto, Ont, CAN, M4S 2X9. (416)483-3810. CBC, 790 Bay St., 5th Fl., Toronto, Ont, CAN. (416)975-7144.
Types of Production & Categories: TV Film-Prod.
Genres: Drama-TV.
Biography: B.A., French, Spanish; M.A., Drama, University of Alberta, 72. Story editor, CBC TV drama, 74-75; associate producer, 75-76; producer, 76-86. *A FAR CRY FROM HOME* won a Silver Medal (NY), Chris Statuette (Columbus).
Selective Filmography: *A CHANGE OF HEART*, 'FOR THE RECORD', TV, 83, CDN, Prod; *KATE MORRIS, VICE PRESIDENT/BECOMING LAURA*, 'FOR THE RECORD', TV, 83/82, CDN, Co-Prod; *A FAR CRY FROM HOME/HARVEST*, 'FOR THE RECORD', TV, 80, CDN, Prod; *HOMECOMING/A MATTER OF CHOICE/SEER WAS HERE*, 'FOR THE RECORD', TV, 79/78, CDN, Prod; *DREAMSPEAKER/THE TAR SANDS/HANK*, 'FOR THE RECORD', TV, 77, CDN, Assoc Prod.

PRODUCTEURS/PRODUCERS

FRANKLIN, Elsa
3 Hillcrest Ave., Toronto, Ont, CAN, M4X 1W1. (416)961-6031. My Country Productions Inc., 21 Sackville St., Toronto, Ont, CAN, M5A 3E1. (416)868-1972.
Types of Production & Categories: TV Film-Prod; TV Video-Prod.
Genres: Drama-TV; Documentary-TV.
Biography: Born 1930, Ottawa, Ontario; studied at Queen's University; Academy of Radio Arts and Sciences, Toronto; Neighborhood Playhouse, New York; Martha Graham School of Modern Dance, New York. Founding Director of MCTV, Toronto; Director of McClelland and Stewart since 68; independent television producer for 23 years.
Selective Filmography: 'HERITAGE THEATRE' (26 eps), TV, 85/84, CDN, Prod; 'PIERRE BERTON SHOW REVISITED' (26 eps), TV, 84, CDN, Prod; OUR WORLD, TV, 84, CDN, Co-Creator/Prod; BEGINNINGS, TV, 83, CDN, Wr/Dir/ Prod; I MARRIED THE KLONDIKE, TV, 83, CDN, Co-Creator/Prod; 'THE GREAT DEBATE' (234 eps), TV, 82-73, CDN, Prod; KLONDIKE QUEST, TV, 82, CDN, Prod/Dir; 'FEMALE IMPERATIVE' (24 eps), TV, 79, CDN, Wr/Dir/ Prod; JOSO IN YUGOSLAVIA, TV, 79, CDN, Wr/Dir/Prod; 'UNDER ATTACK' (150 eps), TV, 76-68, CDN, Prod; 'MY COUNTRY' (52 eps), TV, 74, CDN, Prod; LET'S GO, TV, 74/73, CDN, Creator/Prod; SIDE BY SIDE, TV, 74/73, CDN, Creator/Prod; 'A DAY IN THE LIFE OF' (2 eps), TV, 74/73, CDN, Creator/Prod; GALLERY, TV, 74/73, CDN, Creator/Prod; 'PIERRE BERTON SHOW' (3000 eps), TV, 72-64, CDN, Prod; 55 NORTH MAPLE, TV, 71/70, CDN, Exec Prod.

FRASER, Fil
ACTRA. 9027 - 145 Street, Edmonton, Alta, CAN, T5R 0V1. (403)483-6381. Access Network, 16930 - 114 Ave., Edmonton, Alta, CAN, T5M 3S2. (403)451-7272.
Types of Production & Categories: Th Film-Prod; TV Film-Prod; TV Video-Prod.
Genres: Drama-Th&TV; Documentary TV; Educational-TV.
Biography: Born 1932, Montreal, Quebec; bilingual. Broadcaster in radio and TV, on air and in production since 51. Founder, Banff TV Festival, Alberta Film Festival; ran Commonwealth Games Film Festival, 78. Member, Alberta Film Industry Task Force, 78; past Director, National Film Institute, Motion Picture Institute of Canada. Producer of the Year (Alberta Motion Picture Distributors), 76; 2 Best Film Awards (Alberta).
Selective Filmography: THE HOUNDS OF NOTRE DAME, Th, 80, CDN, Prod; LATITUDE 55, Th, 80, CDN, Exec Prod; MARIE ANNE (pilot), TV, 79, CDN, Prod; MARIE ANNE, Th, 77, CDN, Prod; WHY SHOOT THE TEACHER, Th, 76, CDN, Exec Prod.

FROST, F. Harvey - see DIRECTORS

FULMER, T.G.
ACTRA, CTPDA. 5677 Inglis St., Halifax, NS, CAN, B3H 1K2. (902)429-5337. Citadel Communications, 5240 Blowers St., Halifax, NS, CAN, B3J 1J7. (902)421-1326.
Types of Production & Categories: TV Film-Prod/Dir; TV Video-Prod/Dir.
Genres: Comedy-TV; Variety-TV; Documentary-TV; Current Affairs-TV.
Biography: Born 1946. Twenty years of film and broadcasting experience; has worked as a writer/performer for commercials (radio, TV); executive producer, current affairs, CBC Halifax, 78-85. Producer/director, commercials and industrial films for Citadel Communications, 86. Has won National Journalism Awards for films produced/directed for the series INQUIRY.
Selective Filmography: VENTURE GAS/BEYOND REASONABLE DOUBT/LEAD POISONING, 'INQUIRY', TV, 84-82, CDN, Exec Prod/Prod/Dir; BOSTON FISH, 'COUNTRY CANADA', TV, 84, CDN, Prod/Dir; 'INQUIRY' (21 eps), TV, 83, CDN, Exec Prod/Prod/Dir; HEAVY WATER, 'THE JOURNAL', TV, 82,

(cont/suite)

PRODUCERS/PRODUCTEURS

CDN, Prod/Dir; *SCHOONER FEVER/N.S. FOLK ART/BOY SCOUT JAMBOREE*, 'TAKE 30', TV, 80-77, CDN, Prod/Dir; *POWER & POLITICS*, 'INQUIRY', TV, 78, CDN, Prod/Dir (**ACTRA**).

GAD, Ezz E.

10 Grenoble Dr., #1208, Don Mills, Ont, CAN, M3C 1C7. (416)429-0055. Universal Horizons TV Prod., P.O.Box 2007, Stn B, Scarborough, Ont, CAN, M1N 2E5. (416)429-0055. Ajman Ind. Studio, P.O. Box 442, Ajman, UAE, . (971)642-4000.
Types of Production & Categories: TV Video-Prod.
Genres: Documentary-TV; Educational-TV.
Biography: Born 1932, Egypt; Canadian citizen. Languages: English, Arabic. Educated at Cairo University, Ryerson Polytechnical Institute, School of Modern Photography, Centennial College.
Selective Filmography: *'REFLECTIONS ON ISLAM'* (155 eps), TV, 86-83, CDN, Prod/Host; *'ISLAMIC HORIZONS'* (400 eps), TV, 85-83, CDN/UAE, Prod/Host.

GAGNON, Claude - voir REALISATEURS

GARAND, Jean-Marc

90 rue de la Faisanderie, Paris, France, , 75116. (45)049-043. ONF, 15 rue de Berri, Paris, France, , 75008. (43)591-860.
Types de production et Catégories: l métrage-Prod; c métrage-Prod; TV film-Prod.
Types d'oeuvres: Drame-C&TV; Documentaire-C&TV; Education-C&TV; Expérimental-C&TV.
Curriculum vitae: Né en 1934. Producteur/producteur exécutif et directeur de la production française, ONF, 71-84; directeur de la recherche en communications, 68-71; coordonateur de la production de films éducatifs, 66-68. Fondateur du Bureau de Recherche et de Consultation en Education.
Filmographie sélective: *CORDELIA*, C, 79, CDN, Prod; *LA TOILE D'ARAIGNEE*, C, 79, CDN, Co prod; *ARMAND HARDY, MENUISIER/LES CHARBONNIERS*, 'LA BELLE OUVRAGE', C, 78, CDN, Prod exéc; *LA CABANE*, C, 78, CDN, Prod exéc; *JORNALEROS*, C, 78, CDN/MEX, Co prod; *TERRE D'OCCASION*, C, 77, CDN, Prod; *PREMIERE QUESTION SUR LE BONHEUR*, C, 77, CDN/MEX, Co prod; *LES GARS DU TABAC*, C, 77, CDN, Prod; *ETHNOCIDIO* (ETHNOCIDE), C, 76, CDN/MEX, Co prod; *L'INTERDIT*, C, 76, CDN, Prod; *J.A. MARTIN PHOTOGRAPHE*, C, 76, CDN, Prod (**CFA**); *LES JARDINS D'HIVER*, C, 76, CDN, Prod; *RIEN QU'EN PASSANT*, C, 76, CDN, Prod exéc; *AU BOUT DE MON AGE*, C, 75, CDN, Prod; *LE SOLEIL A PAS DE CHANCE*, C, 75, CDN, Prod; *LA PLUS BELLE VIE DU MONDE*, C, 75, CDN, Prod; *A VOTRE SANTE*, C, 74, CDN, Prod; *ABANDONNEE*, C, 74, CDN, Prod exéc; *LES FILLES DU ROY/A QUI APPARTIENT CE GAGE/SOURIS, TU M'INQUIETES*, 'EN TANT QUE FEMMES', TV, 74/73, CDN, Co prod; *FOUGERE ET LA ROUILLE*, C, 74, CDN, Prod; *URBA 2000*, C, 74, CDN, Prod; *SALVADORE ALLENDE GOSSENS*, C, 74, CDN, Prod; *DES ARMES ET LES HOMMES*, C, 73, CDN, Prod; *LES ALLEES DE LA TERRE*, C, 72, CDN, Prod; *LE BONHOMME*, C, 72, CDN, Co prod; *FRANCOISE DUROCHER WAITRESS*, TV, 72, CDN, Co prod; *O OU L'INVISIBLE ENFANT*, C, 72, CDN, Prod.

GARDNER, Derek

Box 3065 VMPO, Vancouver, BC, CAN, V6B 3X6. (604)669-6109.
Types of Production & Categories: TV Film-Prod/Dir; TV Video-Prod/Dir.
Genres: Drama-Th; Documentary-TV; Educational-TV.
Biography: Born 1946, Victoria, British Columbia. Twenty years experience in film and TV. Has won awards for photography; production manager on numerous commercials.

(cont/suite)

Selective Filmography: *'LIES FROM LOTUSLAND'* (39 eps), TV, 86, CDN, Line Prod; *'BROTHERS BY CHOICE'* (6 eps), TV, 85, CDN, 2nd AD; *'NEWSCENTRE'* (Vancouver), TV, 85/84, CDN, Sr Prod; *'VANCOUVER LIFE'* (weekly), TV, 85, CDN, Prod/Dir; *B.C. GOVERNMENT MEDIA CENTRE,* TV, 82, CDN, Prod/Dir; *BY DESIGN,* Th, 80, CDN, 2nd AD; *ISLAND IN JEOPARDY,* TV, 80, CDN, Prod/Dir; *'NEWSCENTRE'* (Vancouver), TV, 79, CDN, Prod/Dir; *'THE NORTHERNERS'* (6 eps), TV, 78, CDN, Co-Prod/Dir; *'THE BEACHCOMBERS'* (1st AD-14 eps/2nd AD-39 eps), TV, 75-71, CDN, Assist Dir.

GENEREUX, René - see DIRECTORS

GERBER, Sig

ATPD. 26 Albertus Ave., Toronto, Ont, CAN, M4R 1J4. CBC, Box 500, Stn. A, Toronto, Ont, CAN, M5W 1E6. (416)975-6716.
Types of Production & Categories: TV Film-Prod/Dir; TV Video-Prod/Dir.
Genres: Drama-TV; Documentary-TV; Current Affairs-TV.
Biography: Born 1940, Germany; Canadian citizen. Languages: English, German. B.A.A., Ryerson Polytechnical Institute. Worked as radio reporter in commercial radio and briefly for German TV before starting career at CBC, 64, as an editor. Studied fine arts, had paintings exhibited. *LIFE BEFORE BIRTH* and *TO BE TRULY HUMAN* both won a Gabriel Award; *READY FOR SLAUGHTER* won Best TV Drama, Banff Int'l TV Festival.
Selective Filmography: *'MARKET PLACE'* (22 eps), TV, 86/85, CDN, Exec Prod; *THE EXILE,* TV, 85, CDN, Exec Prod; *IN THIS CORNER,* TV, 85, CDN, Exec Prod; *OAKMOUNT HIGH,* TV, 85, CDN, Exec Prod; *TURNING TO STONE,* TV, 85, CDN, Exec Prod; *WHERE THE HEART IS/TOOLS OF THE DEVIL/ THE FRONT LINE,* 'FOR THE RECORD', TV, 84, CDN, Exec Prod; *THE BOY NEXT DOOR/CHANGE OF HEART/ROUGH JUSTICE/SLIM OBSESSION,* 'FOR THE RECORD', TV, 84/83, CDN, Exec Prod; *WHO'S IN CHARGE?,* TV, 83, CDN, Dir; *HIDE AND SEEK/I LOVE A MAN IN A UNIFORM/KATE MORRIS,* VP, 'FOR THE RECORD', TV, 83, CDN, Exec Prod; *MOVING TARGETS/OUT OF SIGHT, OUT OF MIND/READY FOR SLAUGHTER,* 'FOR THE RECORD', TV, 82, CDN, Exec Prod; *'TAKE 30'* (weekly), TV, 82-79, CDN, Exec Prod; *'MAN ALIVE'* (30 eps), TV, 78-72, CDN, Prod/Dir; *'MAN ALIVE'* (26 eps), TV, 78, CDN, Exec Prod; *THE QUIET OLYMPICS,* TV, 76, CDN, Prod/Dir; *I AM NOT WHAT YOU SEE,* TV, 76, CDN, Prod/Dir; *TO BE TRULY HUMAN,* TV, 74, CDN, Prod/Dir; *CUBA: FAITH IN REVOLUTION,* TV, 73, CDN, Prod/ Dir; *LIFE BEFORE BIRTH,* TV, 72, CDN, Prod/Dir; *THE BITTERSWEET SOUNDS: BRUCE COCKBURN,* TV, 71, CDN, Prod/Dir.

GIBBONS, Bob - see DIRECTORS

GILBERT, Tony

ACTRA, CTPDA. Togil Communications Inc., 3673 Loraine Ave., North Vancouver, BC, CAN, V7R 4B9. (604)984-7011.
Types of Production & Categories: TV Film-Dir/Prod/Wr; TV Video-Dir/Prod/Wr.
Genres: Variety-TV; Musical-TV; Documentary-TV; Children's-TV.
Biography: Born 1940, Sydney, Australia; Canadian citizen; educated to university level. Twenty years experience in TV production with ABC (Sydney), BBC (London), CBC (Toronto, Vancouver); freelance producer/director/writer in western Canada and Australia since 78. Extensively trained in music; accomplished pianist; experienced private pilot.
Selective Filmography: *CARMEN,* TV, 86, CDN, Prod/Dir; *'WORLDSTAGE 86'* (42 eps), TV, 86, CDN, Prod; *OPENING GALA* (EXPO 86), TV, 86, CDN, Dir; *A GIFT OF MUSIC,* TV, 86, CDN, Prod/Dir; *AIRBORNE,* In, 86, CDN, Dir/Wr; *THE YOUNG PERFORMERS,* TV, 85, CDN, Prod/Dir; *FREE AT LAST*

(cont/suite)

(TRIBUTE TO MARTIN LUTHER KING), TV, 85, CDN, Prod/Dir; *THE MAGIC OF BROADWAY*, TV, 85, CDN, Prod/Dir; *MOZART AT THE GALLERY*, TV, 84, CDN, Prod/Dir; *'FUTURESCAN'* (7 eps), TV, 84, CDN, Dir; *A CELEBRATION OF LIFE* (POPE JOHN PAUL II AT B.C.PLACE), TV, 84, CDN, Dir; *'FABULOUS FESTIVAL'* (6 eps), TV, 84, CDN, Prod/Dir; *SUPER VARIETY LIVE* (DAVID STEINBERG), TV, 83, CDN, Dir; *ANN MORTIFEE: BORN TO LIVE*, TV, 83, CDN, Dir; *THE SEAGRAM POPS*, TV, 83, CDN, Prod/Dir; *'MUSIC CANADA'* (2 eps), TV, 83, CDN, Prod/Dir; *MIRACLES ON CHESTNUT STREET*, TV, 83, CDN, Prod/Dir/Wr; *STARS OF VANCOUVER FOLK FESTIVAL*, TV, 83, USA, Dir; *MARIO BERNARDI: FAREWELL PERFORMANCE*, TV, 82, CDN, Prod/Dir; *'MUSIC IN THE AIR'* (2 eps), TV, 82, CDN, Prod/Dir; *BIG BIRD'S CHRISTMAS SHOW*, TV, 81, CDN, Prod/Dir; *A STUDIO SESSION WITH MITCH*, TV, 81, CDN, Prod/Dir; *VIENNESE FANTASY*, TV, 80, CDN, Prod/Dir; *WHY ME?*, TV, 79, AUS, Dir/Wr; *A GIFT OF MUSIC*, TV, 78, AUS, Prod/Dir; *'THE NORTHERNERS'* (12 eps), TV, 78, CDN, Prod/Wr; *'GREEN DOUBLE DECKER'* (26 eps), TV, 77, CDN, Prod/Dir; *THE MERCHANT OF VENICE*, TV, 77, CDN, Prod (**ACTRA**); *VANCOUVER SYMPHONY IN CONCERT*, TV, 76, CDN, Prod/Dir; *THE MAGIC HEALERS*, TV, 74, CDN, Prod/Dir/Wr.

GILLARD, Stuart - see WRITERS

GINSBERG, Donald

CFTA, DGC. 77 Carlton St., #801, Toronto, Ont, CAN, M5B 2J7. (416)593-0753.
Types of Production & Categories: Th Film-Ed/Prod; Th Short-Ed/Prod; TV Film-Ed/Prod; TV Video-Prod/Dir/Ed.
Genres: Drama-Th&TV; Comedy-Th&TV; Action-Th&TV; Documentary-Th&TV.
Biography: Born London, England; British-Canadian citizen. Producer/director/editor of over 25 dramas and documentaries for the NFB and 100 TV commercials.
Selective Filmography: *'COMEDY TONIGHT'* (13 eps), TV, 85/84, CDN, Creator/Prod/Dir; *TO THE TOP*, Th, 75, CDN, Ed; *MAKING NICKEL*, TV, 75, CDN, Ed (**CFEG**); *SEARCH AND DESTROY*, Th, 74, CDN, Ed (**CFEG**); *'THE COLLABORATORS'* (13 eps), TV, 74, CDN, Ed; *FORTUNE AND MEN'S EYES*, Th, 71, CDN/USA, Co-Prod; *THE EARTH IS MAN'S HOME* (EXPO 67), Th, 67, CDN, Dir/Ed; *NOBODY WAVED GOODBYE*, Th, 64, CDN, Ed; *THE MOST*, TV, 64, CDN, Ed; *TARGET FOR TONIGHT*, Th, 43, GB, Ed.

GIROUX, Nicole

675 Bloomfield, #4, Outremont, Qué, CAN, H2V 3S2. (514)279-4606. Les Films 24 inc., 402 rue Notre-Dame est, Montréal, Qué, CAN, H2Y 1C8. (514)288-6475.
Types de production et Catégories: TV film-Prod.
Types d'oeuvres: Annonces-TV.
Curriculum vitae: Née en 1950. Productrice de films publicitaires; remporte le Coq d'Or pour la campagne de MacDonald, 85.

GLAWSON, Bruce

CFTA. 60 St. Patrick St., #234, Toronto, Ont, CAN, M5T 2X5. (416)979-2558. Cambium Film & Video Prod.Ltd., 141 Gerrard St.E., Toronto, Ont, CAN, M5A 2E3. (416)964-8750.
Types of Production & Categories: TV Film-Prod/Dir/Ed; TV Video-Ed/Prod.
Genres: Variety-TV; Musical-TV; Documentary-TV; Children's-TV.
Biography: Born 1954, Brandon, Manitoba. B.A., Music, Brandon University, 75; recipient of the Silver Medal in music; B.F.A. (Specialized Honours in Film Production), York U., 77. Originally worked as a video and audio switcher/mixer at CBC Winnipeg, Toronto. Formed Cambium Film & Video Productions Ltd., 82. Has won Chris Plaques at Columbus for *CONTACT* and *MICHAEL, A GAY SON* which also won Best Documentary at Yorkton.

(cont/suite)

PRODUCTEURS/PRODUCERS

Selective Filmography: *'SHARON, LOIS AND BRAM'S ELEPHANT SHOW'* (13 eps), TV, 86, CDN, Co-Prod/Ed; *'THE ELEPHANT SHOW'* (pilot), (12 eps), TV, 84, CDN, Co-Prod/Ed; *FOR PAUL,* ED, 83, CDN, Prod/Dir; *SHARON, LOIS AND BRAM AT THE YOUNG PEOPLE'S THEATRE,* TV, 83, CDN, Co-Prod/Co-Dir; *MICHAEL, A GAY SON,* TV, 80, CDN, Prod/Dir; *CONTACT,* TV, 79, CDN, Co-Prod/Co-Dir/Cin.

GODBOUT, Claude

APFVQ. Les Productions Prisma Inc., 5253 ave. du Parc, #330, Montréal, Qué, CAN, H2V 4P2. (514)277-6686.
Types de production et Catégories: l métrage-Prod; TV film-Prod; TV vidéo-Prod.
Types d'oeuvres: Drame-C&TV; Documentaire-C&TV; Enfants-C&TV.
Curriculum vitae: Né en 1941, Montréal, Québec; bilingue. Fondateur et Président directeur-général, Les Productions Prisma Inc.. *LES BONS DEBARRAS* a gagné 8 Prix Génies; *LES SERVANTES DU BON DIEU* fut invité à la Semaine de la Critique, Cannes; *COMME LES SIX DOIGTS DE LA MAIN* remporte le Prix de la Critique Québécoise.
Filmographie sélective: *'LIVRE OUVERT'* (OPEN BOOK), (26 eps), TV, 85/84, CDN, Co prod; *'PROFESSION: ECRIVAIN'* (13 eps), TV, 83, CDN, Co prod; *'ZIGZAG'* (6 eps), TV, 83, CDN, Co prod; *LE CAHIER NOIR,* 'SECRETS DIPLOMATIQUES', TV, 82, F, Co prod; *LE PLUS BEAU JOUR DE MA VIE,* C, 81, CDN, Co prod; *ON EST PAS DES ANGES,* C, 81, CDN, Co prod; *THETFORD AU MILIEU DE NOTRE VIE,* C, 79, CDN, Co prod; *CORRIDORS - PRIS AU PIEGE,* C, 79, CDN, Co prod; *COMME LES SIX DOIGTS DE LA MAIN* (THE BACKSTREET SIX), C, 78, CDN, Co prod; *LES SERVANTES DU BON DIEU,* C, 78, CDN, Co prod; *LES BONS DEBARRAS* (GOOD RIDDANCE), C, 78, CDN, Co prod (GENIE); *MONTREAL,* 'LES GRANDES VILLES DU MONDE', TV, 78, F, Co prod; *LE ST-LAURENT,* 'LES GRANDS FLEUVES DU MONDE', TV, 76, F, Co prod; *'L'AMOUR QUOTIDIEN'* (13 eps), TV, 75, CDN, Co prod; *LES ORDRES,* C, 74, CDN, Prod exéc (2 CFA).

GORD, Ken - see PRODUCTION MANAGERS

GOUGH, Bill - see WRITERS

GOULET, Paul

23 Victor Ave., Toronto, Ont, CAN, M4K 1A7. (416)465-4889. Edmund Glineit, Lilly, McClintock, Bowman, 181 University Ave., Toronto, Ont, CAN. (416)365-8111,
Types of Production & Categories: TV Film-Prod/Wr; TV Video-Prod/Wr.
Genres: Drama-TV; Variety-TV; Documentary-TV.
Biography: Born 1940, Ottawa, Ontario. Honours English and Int'l School of Marketing, Harvard University. Experienced in location work including third world settings.
Selective Filmography: *LEARN THIS POEM OF MINE BY HEART,* TV, 86, CDN, Co-Prod; *TRANSPACIFIC CONTACT,* TV, 85, CDN, Prod/Wr/Dir; *CLAIROL FASHION AWARDS,* TV, 85, CDN, Co-Prod/Wr; *RICH LITTLE AND FRIENDS IN NEW ORLEANS,* TV, 84, CDN, Co-Prod/Co-Wr.

GRANT, Michael - see DIRECTORS

GRAVELLE, Raymond - voir DIRECTEURS-PHOTO

GRAY, Caroline

23 Glebe Rd.E., Toronto, Ont, CAN, M4S 1N7. (416)481-1291. TV Ontario, 2180 Yonge St., Toronto, Ont, CAN, M4S 2B9. (416)484-2600.
Types of Production & Categories: TV Film-Prod/Wr; TV Video-Prod/Wr.
Genres: Documentary-TV; Educational-TV.

(cont/suite)

119

Biography: Born 1953, Khartoum, Sudan. British-Canadian citizenship. Languages: English, German, French; Masters in Philosophy (ABT). Reviewer, book editor.
Selective Filmography: *'FRONTRUNNERS'* (3 eps), TV, 86, CDN, Prod/Contr Wr; *'FAMILY COUNSEL'* (7 eps), TV, 85, CDN, Prod/Contr Wr; *'AUTOMATING THE OFFICE'* (9 eps), TV, 85, CDN, Prod; *'THE ACADEMY ON CONTEMPORARY CANADIAN ART'* (Intros and Extros), (13 eps), TV, 83, CDN, Prod; *'THE ACADEMY ON ADULT LITERACY'* (Intros and Extros), (5 eps), TV, 83, CDN, Prod; *'THE ACADEMY ON CHINA'* (6 eps), TV, 83, CDN, Prod; *'THE ACADEMY ON COMPUTERS'* (12 eps), TV, 83, CDN, Wr.

GREEN, Howard

ACTRA, CTPDA. CBC, 415 Yonge St., 8th Fl., Toronto, Ont, CAN, M5B 2E1. (416)975-3311.
Types of Production & Categories: TV Film-Prod; TV Video-Prod.
Genres: Documentary-TV; Educational-TV; Children's-TV.
Biography: Born 1959, Halifax, Nova Scotia. Bachelor of Journalism, Carleton University. TV news reporter with CTV affiliates in the Maritimes and CBC, Newfoundland and Labrador, 80-83; producer and host of *WHAT'S NEW?*, 83-86 (36 episodes/season).

GREENBERG, Harold

CFTA. Astral Bellevue Pathé Inc., 175 Montpellier Blvd., Montreal, Que, CAN, H4N 2G5. (514)748-6541.
Types of Production & Categories: Th Film-Prod; TV Film-Prod.
Genres: Drama-Th&TV; Horror-Th.
Biography: Born Montreal, Quebec. President, Chief Executive Officer, Astral Bellevue Pathé Inc.; Chairman of the Board, First Choice Canadian Communications Corporation and Premier Choix: TVEC. Has been involved as packager, producer or co-producer of over 35 feature films and TV projects. Received the Presidential Proclamation Award, SMPTE, 85. *PORKY'S* won the Golden Reel Award.
Selective Filmography: *PORKY'S REVENGE,* Th, 84, USA, Exec Prod; *DRAW!,* TV, 83, CDN/USA, Co-Exec Prod; *MARIA CHAPDELAINE,* Th, 83, CDN/F, Prod; *PYGMALION,* TV, 83, CDN, Co-Exec Prod; *PORKY'S II - THE NEXT DAY* (CHEZ PORKY II - LE LENDEMAIN), Th, 82, CDN, Co-Exec Prod; *TELL ME THAT YOU LOVE ME,* Th, 82, CDN/IL, Co-Exec Prod; *MARY AND JOSEPH,* TV, 82, CDN, Co-Exec Prod; *PORKY'S* (CHEZ PORKY), Th, 81, CDN, Exec Prod; *HARD FEELINGS,* Th, 80, CDN, Co-Exec Prod/Prod; *HOT TOUCH* (FRENCH KISS), Th, 80, CDN, Co-Exec Prod/Prod; *TULIPS,* Th, 79, CDN, Co-Exec Prod; *DEATH SHIP,* Th, 79, CDN, Co-Prod; *TERROR TRAIN,* Th, 79, CDN, Prod; *CITY ON FIRE,* Th, 79, CDN, Co-Exec Prod; *A MAN CALLED INTREPID* (mini-series), TV, 78, CDN/GB, Co-Exec Prod; *THE UNCANNY,* Th, 78, CDN/GB, Co-Exec Prod; *IN PRAISE OF OLDER WOMEN,* Th, 77, CDN, Co-Exec Prod; *BREAKING POINT,* Th, 76, CDN/USA, Co-Exec Prod; *THE LITTLE GIRL WHO LIVED DOWN THE LANE,* Th, 76, CDN/F, Co-Exec Prod; *RITUALS,* Th, 76, CDN, Co-Exec Prod.

GREENE, Charles J.

ACTRA. 2800 Olympic Blvd., #201, Santa Monica, CA, USA, 90404. (213)453-0451.
Types of Production & Categories: TV Film-Prod/Wr; TV Video-Prod/Wr.
Genres: Drama-TV; Action-TV; Documentary-TV.
Biography: Born Toronto, Ontario. Education: Undergraduate, MIT (Political Science); Graduate, Sloan School of Management (Systems Analysis). Work history: CTV, CBC, A & M Records, TV Ontario, Mediavision, Heritage

(cont/suite)

Communications. *NEW WILDERNESS* has won numerous awards including 3 Emmys.
Selective Filmography: *'LORNE GREENE'S NEW WILDERNESS'* (104 eps), TV, 86-81, CDN, Co-Prod; *'SURVIVORS'* (5 eps), TV, 78, CDN, Wr; *'LAST OF THE WILD'* (Wr-2 eps), (6 eps), TV, 76, CDN/USA, Co-Wr; *'BEHIND THE SCENES WITH JONATHAN WINTERS'* (5 eps), TV, 75, CDN/USA, Wr; *'GLEN FORD'S FRIENDS OF MAN'* (18 eps), TV, 74/73, CDN/USA, Co-Wr; *AFRICA FILE*, ED, 74, CDN, Wr; *SHOPPERS DRUG MART/CANADIAN TIRE*, In, 73, CDN, Wr; *PROCUL HAREM*, Cm, 72, CDN, Prod/Wr; *'IDEAS'* (5 eps), ED, 71, CDN, Prod/Wr; *'W5'* (52 seg), TV, 71/70, CDN, Wr/Res.

GREENE, David - see DIRECTORS

GREENE, Lorne

2800 Olympic Blvd., Ste. 201, Santa Monica, CA, USA, 90404. (213)453-0451.
Types of Production & Categories: TV Film-Prod/Host.
Genres: Documentary-TV.
Biography: Has been involved in many facets of the entertainment business: radio, stage, film, TV. Early in his career, was anchorman on CBC's *NATIONAL NEWS IN CANADA* and the voice of John Grierson's Oscar award-winning NFB war documentaries. After W.W.II, he established the Academy of Radio Arts, Toronto; appeared in 10 feature films and starred in TV series including *GRIFF, CODE RED, BATTLESTAR GALACTICA* and for 14 years as Ben Cartwright in *BONANZA*. Has received 2 honorary doctorates, Doctor of Law, Doctor of Humane Letters and the Order of Canada, 69. *LORNE GREENE'S NEW WILDERNESS* has won numerous awards including 3 Daytime Emmys, the Int'l Wildlife Festival's Special Recognition Award.
Selective Filmography: *'LORNE GREENE'S NEW WILDERNESS'* (104 eps), TV, 86-81, CDN, Exec Prod/Host.

GULKIN, Harry

APFVQ. Jape Film Services Inc., 111 boul.St-Joseph O., Montreal, Que, CAN, H2T 2P7. (514)277-5307.
Types of Production & Categories: Th Film-Prod; TV Film-Prod.
Genres: Drama-Th&TV; Comedy-Th&TV.
Biography: Born 1927, Montreal, Quebec. Canadian Army Reserve, 42-44; Canadian Merchant Marine, 44-49. Founding President of Motion Picture Institute of Canada, 77-79. Has won numerous awards at nat'l and int'l film festivals including: Gold Medallion, Special Jury Award, Miami Int'l Film Fest. for *JACOB TWO-TWO MEETS THE HOODED FANG*; a Golden Globe and Chris Awards for *LIES MY FATHER TOLD ME*.
Selective Filmography: *BAYO*, Th, 85, CDN, Prod; *THE CHALLENGER*, TV, 79, CDN, Assoc Prod; *TWO SOLITUDES*, Th, 78, CDN, Co-Prod; *JACOB TWO-TWO MEETS THE HOODED FANG*, Th, 75, CDN, Prod; *LIES MY FATHER TOLD ME*, Th, 75, CDN, Co-Prod (**CFA**); *DENNY AND ANN*, TV, 74, CDN, Prod.

GUNNARSSON, Sturla - see DIRECTORS

GZEBB, Ted

292 Sackville St., Toronto, Ont, CAN, M5A 3G2. (416)925-5891. Cornerstone Productions, 3 Church St., Ste. 302, Toronto, Ont, CAN, M5E 1M2. (416)864-0645.
Types of Production & Categories: TV Video-Prod.
Genres: Variety-TV; Educational-TV; Industrial-TV.
Biography: Born 1949, Winnipeg, Manitoba. Degree in Communications, Loyola University, 73; taught for 10 years at Sheridan College. Co-founded Turn Key Studios, 83; became a partner in Cornerstone Productions, 85. Winner of Gold

(cont/suite)

121

CanPro Award for production of 1985 *TELETHON FOR THE HOSPITAL FOR SICK CHILDREN.*
Selective Filmography: *BABN - CONFIDENTIAL,* In, 86, CDN, Prod; *A TOAST TO HOSTING,* In, 86, CDN, Exec Prod; *'STARSCOPES 86'* (12 eps), TV, 85, CDN, Prod; *PURSUIT OF EXCELLENCE - ESSO,* In, 85, CDN, Line Prod; *TELETHON FOR THE HOSPITAL FOR SICK CHILDREN,* TV, 85, CDN, Prod; *TARA,* MV, 85, CDN, Prod.

HAIG, Don

Film Arts, 461 Church St., Toronto, Ont, CAN, M4Y 2C5. (416)962-0181.
Types of Production & Categories: Th Film-Prod; TV Film-Ed/Prod.
Genres: Drama-Th&TV; Documentary-Th&TV; Educational-TV.
Biography: Born 1933, Winnipeg, Manitoba. Began in film at MGM Distribution, Winnipeg; film editor, CBC, 56-63; started own film editing firm, Film Arts, 63. Winner of the Academy of Canadian Cinema & Television's Air Canada Award, 85; Jack Chisholm Award, 85.
Selective Filmography: *BABY JOHN DOE,* TV, 86, CDN, Exec Prod; *ARTIE SHAW: TIME IS ALL YOU'VE GOT,* Th, 85, CDN, Assoc Prod; *SAMUEL LOUNT,* Th, 85, CDN, Exec Prod; *DANCING IN THE DARK,* Th, 85, CDN, Exec Prod; *ALEX COLVILLE: THE SPLENDOR OF ORDER,* TV, 84, CDN, Exec Prod; *UNFINISHED BUSINESS,* Th, 84, CDN, Exec Prod; *ARNOLD SPOHR GALA* (ROYAL WINNIPEG BALLET), TV, 83, CDN, Exec Prod; *ALLIGATOR SHOES* (LES SOULIERS EN CROCO), Th, 81, CDN, Exec Prod; *SUMMER'S CHILDREN,* Th, 79, CDN, Exec Prod; *125 ROOMS OF COMFORT,* Th, 74, CDN, Exec Prod; *MILLS OF THE GODS: VIET NAM,* TV, 65, CDN, Ed (**ANIK**); *SUMMER IN MISSISSIPPI,* TV, 64, CDN, Ed (**ANIK**); *ONE MORE RIVER,* TV, 63, CDN, Ed (**ANIK**).

HAMILTON, Peter Scott

IATSE-667, SMPTE. 2045 Lakeshore Blvd. W., #401, Toronto, Ont, CAN, M8V 2Z6. (416)252-6632. The Partner's Film Co. Limited, 508 Church St., Toronto, Ont, CAN, M4Y 2C8. (416)966-3500.
Types of Production & Categories: Th Short-DOP/Dir/Prod; TV Film-DOP/Dir/Prod.
Genres: Documentary-Th&TV; Educational-Th&TV; Industrial-Th.
Biography: Born 1944, Australia. Worked at ABC TV, Sydney, 62-64; BBC London and Ealing Studios, 64-67; CBC TV, Toronto, 67-68; freelance cameraman, 69-70; independent producer of sponsored films since 70. Inventor of the Pericam snorkel motion control system. Has won many industrial film awards including Gold and Silver Medals (NY), Chris Plaques (Columbus).
Selective Filmography: *PINBALL WIZARD/LAYING RUBBER/THE RUNNERS/RAPID DELIVERY* (EXPO 86), MV, 86, CDN, Co-Prod/DOP; *THE I.C.G. STORY/ONTARIO PAVILION STORY,* In, 85, CDN, Co-Prod/DOP; *I.B.M. MODULE/IN TOUCH WITH THE FOREST/ACCORDING TO PLAN,* In, 85-83, CDN, DOP/Prod/Dir; *I HAD A DREAM - TERRY FOX,* TV, 82, CDN, DOP/Co-Prod; *THE VOLUNTEERS/VOLUNTEERS INSTITUTE/LOOKING GOOD,* In, 81/80, CDN, DOP/Prod; *INSIDE THE BODY/O.F.I.A./THE SECOND REALITY,* In, 81/80, CDN, DOP/Prod/Dir; *FEELING GOOD/THE CHIROPRACTORS/NO ORDINARY MATTERS,* In, 79/78, CDN, DOP/Prod/Dir; *ANATOMY OF PAPER/KOEHRING #1 & #2/SEE HOW THEY RUN,* In, 77-75, CDN, DOP/Prod/Dir; *CMHC HALIFAX/CMHC ONTARIO,* In, 74-73, CDN, DOP/Prod/Dir; *THE BROOMMAKER,* TV, 71, CDN, DOP/Prod/Dir; *PIONEER POWER,* TV, 71, CDN, DOP/Prod/Dir; *A CENTURY OF CRAFTS AND SKILLS,* TV, 71, CDN, DOP/Prod/Dir.

HAMM, Michael

ACTRA. Frame 30 Productions Ltd., 10816A 82 Ave., #202, Edmonton, Alta, CAN, T6E 2B3. (403)439-5322.

(cont/suite)

Types of Production & Categories: TV Film-Prod/Wr; TV Video-Prod/Wr.
Genres: Documentary-TV; Educational-TV; Commercials-TV.
Selective Filmography: *AT THE SPEED OF SIGHT*, TV, 86, CDN, Prod/Wr; *LUSCAR*, In, 85, CDN, Prod/Wr; *MONOPOLY I & II*, Cm, 85, CDN, Prod.

HAMON-HILL, Cindy

Calico Pix, 26 Riverdale Ave., Toronto, Ont, CAN, M4K 1C3. (416)469-8017.
Types of Production & Categories: TV Film-Prod.
Genres: Drama-TV; Documentary-TV; Educational-TV; Children's-TV.
Biography: Born Toronto, Ontario; bilingual. Education: Honours B.A. in Film.
Selective Filmography: *THE NEW NORTH*, TV, 86, CDN, Assoc Prod; *LOST IN THE BARRENS*, TV, 86, CDN, Assoc Prod; *JACK OF HEARTS/ CONNECTION*, 'BELL CANADA PLAYHOUSE', TV, 85, CDN, Co-Prod; *'THE MOVIEMAKERS'* (26 eps), TV, 84/83, CDN, Pro Coord; *'TROUPERS'* (18 eps), TV, 84, CDN, 2nd AD; *GIVE & TAKE*, In, 83, CDN, Pro Coord/Res.

HAMORI, Andras

187 Hudson Dr., Toronto, Ont, CAN, M4T 2K7. (416)485-8497. Alliance Entertainment Corp., 92 Isabella St., Toronto, Ont, CAN, M4Y 1N4. (416)967-1174.
Types of Production & Categories: Th Film-Prod; TV Film-Prod.
Genres: Drama-Th&TV; Comedy-Th&TV; Action-Th&TV.
Biography: Born 1953, Budapest, Hungary; Canadian citizen. Received doctorate from Budapest University, Faculty of Law and Political Science; diploma in Film & Television Journalism. Theatre and film critic for Hungarian magazines and newspapers, London periodicals 'Theatre Quarterly' and 'Theatrefacts'. Worked for Schulz Productions, developing feature films, 81; joined RSL Entertainment Corp., 83; producer, Alliance Entertainment Corp., 86.
Selective Filmography: *'NIGHT HEAT'* (39 eps), TV, 85/84, CDN, Prod; *BIG DEAL*, TV, 85, CDN, Co-Prod; *SEPARATE VACATIONS*, Th, 85, CDN, Assoc Prod; *JOSHUA THEN AND NOW*, Th, 85, CDN, Pro Exec; *HEAVENLY BODIES*, Th, 84, CDN, Assoc Prod; *BEDROOM EYES*, Th, 84, CDN, Assist Prod; *ONE NIGHT ONLY*, Th, 84, CDN, Assist Prod; *PERFECT TIMING*, TV, 84, CDN, Assist Prod; *OVERDRAWN AT THE MEMORY BANK*, TV, 83, CDN/ USA, Assist Prod.

HANSON, Robert G.

CTPDA. Box 57, Stn A, Happy Valley, Goose Bay, Labrador, Nfld, CAN, A0P 1S0. (709)896-5276. CBC, Box 3015, Stn B, Happy Valley, Goose Bay, Labrador, Nfld, CAN, A0P 1E0. (709)896-2911.
Types of Production & Categories: TV Video-Prod/Dir.
Genres: Current Affairs-TV; News-TV.
Biography: Born 1946, Grand Falls, Newfoundland. Producer-director, news and current affairs, segments on *HERE & NOW*, CBC Newfoundland, 85-86.
Selective Filmography: *'SUMMER SCENE'* (4 eps), TV, 84, CDN, Prod/Dir; *'I WELL MINDS THE TIME'* (8 eps), TV, 83, CDN, Prod/Dir.

HARBURY, Martin

ACFTP. Bar Harbour Films Inc., Martin-Paul Prods. Ltd., 12 McMurrich St., Toronto, Ont, CAN, M5R 2A2. (416)968-9375.
Types of Production & Categories: TV Film-Prod; TV Video-Prod/Dir.
Genres: Drama-TV; Documentary-TV; Educational-TV; Children's-TV.
Biography: Born 1945, Worthing, Sussex, England; Canadian-British citizenship; bilingual. Author, 'The Last of the Wild Horses', 84. Experience prior to film business: 2nd Lt., British Army; motor industry; shipping; sales; skipper of sailing

(cont/suite)

charter boat in French West Indies. First 2 1/2 years in film at Insight Productions; many industrial films, videos and PSA's.
Selective Filmography: *THE MAKING OF ANNE OF GREEN GABLES,* TV, 85, CDN, Prod; *HOCKEY NIGHT* (DERRIERE LE MASQUE), TV, 84, CDN, Prod (CFTA); *OPUS II,* TV, 83, CDN, Exec Prod; *CLOWN WHITE* (CHANSON SANS PAROLE), TV, 80, CDN, Prod; *BORN TO RUN,* TV, 79, CDN, Prod; *STALLONE - MILLION TO ONE SHOT ,* TV, 78, CDN, Assoc Prod; *WORLD OF WIZARDS,* TV, 77, CDN, Assoc Prod; *TOLLER,* TV, 76, CDN, Assoc Prod.

HARDING, Stewart

APFVQ. Moving Image Prods. Inc., 106 Florida Dr., Montreal, Que, CAN, H9W 1L9. (514)694-6825.
Types of Production & Categories: Th Film-Prod; TV Film-Prod.
Genres: Drama-TV; Action-Th&TV; Science Fiction-Th; Horror-Th.
Biography: Born 1952, Montreal, Quebec. B.A., Communication Arts, Loyola University, 74. Entered motion picture business as production assistant, 74; rose through production manager, associate producer and line producer positions on theatrical features to producing TV and theatrical films through own company, Moving Image Productions Inc..
Selective Filmography: *HALF A LIFETIME,* TV, 85, CDN, Prod; *IN LIKE FLYNN* (pilot), TV, 85, USA, Co-Prod; *SPACEHUNTER: ADVENTURES IN THE FORBIDDEN ZONE,* Th, 83, CDN/USA, Assoc Prod/Story; *HAPPY BIRTHDAY TO ME,* Th, 80, CDN, Line Prod.

HARRIS, Les - see DIRECTORS

HARVEY, Daniel

7470 Bayard, Montréal, Qué, CAN, H3R 3A9. (514)342-1093. Spectel Vidéo Inc., 355 Ste-Catherine ouest, #301, Montréal, Qué, CAN, H3B 1A5. (514)288-5363.
Types de production et Catégories: TV vidéo-Prod.
Types d'oeuvres: Comédie-TV; Variété-TV; Vidéo clips-TV.
Curriculum vitae: Né en 1950; citoyen canadien; bilingue. Vice-président de Spectel Vidéo Inc. depuis 79. L'émission *RIDEAU* et le vidéo-clip *RUMEURS SUR LA VILLE* remportent des Félix au Gala de l'ADISQ, 85.
Filmographie sélective: *'ROCK ET BELLES OREILLES'* (50 eps), TV, 86, CDN, Prod; *RIDEAU* (2 ém), TV, 86/85, CDN, Prod; *GINETTE RENO/MICHEL LEGRAND AU F.I.J.M.,* TV, 86, CDN, Prod; *TOURNAGE D'ORCHESTRE FANTASTIQUE,* TV, 86, CDN, Prod; *SYMPHONIE FANTASTIQUE AVEC L'ORCHESTRE SYMPHONIQUE DE MONTREAL,* MV, 86, CDN, Prod; *ILS S'AIMENT/DE L'ENFANCE A LA VIOLENCE/LE FEU SAUVAGE DE L'AMOUR,* MV, 86, CDN, Prod; *ANTONIO CARLOS JOBIM AU F.I.J.M.,* TV, 86, CDN, Prod; *J'TE CHERCHE PARTOUT/COCCHEZ OUI COCHEZ NON/ RUMEURS SUR LA VILLE,* MV, 85, CDN, Prod; *DOUBLE VIE/UN CHANTEUR CHANTE/ATTENTION FRAGILE,* MV, 85, CDN, Prod; *JAZZ GREATS,* TV, 85, CDN, Prod; *DU GRAMOPHONE AU LASER,* TV, 85, CDN, Prod; *GILLES VIGNEAULT,* TV, 85, CDN, Prod; *'PLEIN SON'* (15 eps), TV, 85, CDN, Prod; *MOCHE MUZIK,* TV, 85, CDN, Prod; *'EN SCENE'* (66 eps), TV, 84-81, CDN, Prod; *RETROSPECTIVE 5e ANNIVERSAIRE DU F.I.J.M.,* TV, 84, CDN, Prod; *HOMMAGE AU JAZZ FRANCAIS,* TV, 84, CDN, Prod.

HAWKINS, Crawford W.

DGA. 1947 Fulton Ave., West Vancouver, BC, CAN, V7V 1T2. (604)926-8221. Tegra Industries Inc., 916 Davie St., Vancouver, BC, CAN, V6Z 1B8. (604)688-7757.
Types of Production & Categories: TV Film-Prod/Dir; TV Video-Prod/Dir.
Genres: Comedy-TV; Variety-TV; Children's-TV; Commercials-TV.

(cont/suite)

Biography: Born 1933, Brooklyn, New York; US citizen; Canadian landed immigrant. Attended St. Joseph's University, New York U.. Winner of 2 Clio Awards; 2 Hollywood Radio & TV Society Awards and 1 Int'l Film & TV Festival of New York Award.
Selective Filmography: *SWEET DREAMS*, TV, 83, USA, Dir; *SCHOOL FOR SPEED* (pilot), TV, 82, USA, Dir; *PYRAMIDS AND PROPHETS*, TV, 82, USA, Dir; *YOUR CAR AND YOUR MONEY* (pilot), TV, 81, USA, Prod; *UP RIVER*, TV, 79, USA, Prod; *THE NIXON/FROST INTERVIEWS* (6 spec), TV, 77, USA, PM; *'THE NEW MICKEY MOUSE CLUB SHOW'* (165 eps), TV, 77/76, USA, Unit M; *'SOAP'* (13 eps), TV, 76, USA, Unit M.

HAZZAN, Ray

ATPD. 675 Merton St., Toronto, Ont, CAN, M4S 1B4. (416)483-7549. CBC, Box 500, Stn. A, Toronto, Ont, CAN, M5W 1E6. (416)975-6586.
Types of Production & Categories: TV Film-Prod/Dir/Wr; TV Video-Prod/Dir/Wr.
Genres: Documentary-TV; Educational-TV; Children's-TV; Science-TV.
Biography: Born 1931, Alexandria, Egypt; Canadian citizen; speaks English and French. B.A.(Honours), M.A. (Economics, Political Science), Cambridge University, England; Licence ès Lettres, Université de Paris et Lille. Journalist at British United Press; CBC Radio and TV (56-86). Has been head of radio and TV national news; executive producer of *NEWSMAGAZINE*, news specials, children's TV.
Selective Filmography: *ACID RAIN: CLOUDS WITH A SULPHUR LINING*, 'NATURE OF THINGS', TV, 86, CDN, Wr/Dir/Prod; *GREAT LAKES: TROUBLED WATERS*, 'NATURE OF THINGS', TV, 86, CDN, Prod/Dir; *OLD LIKE ME/HEAVENLY METAL/IN THE NAME OF JUSTICE*, 'MAN ALIVE', TV, 85/84, CDN, Dir/Wr/Prod; *THE BIBLE, THE BOMB AND THE PRESIDENT/PARADISE LOST*, 'MAN ALIVE', TV, 84, CDN, Prod/Wr; *VALUES AND BELIEFS*, 'MAN ALIVE', TV, 83, CDN, Prod/Dir/Wr; *FLIGHT SIMULATORS*, 'NATURE OF THINGS', TV, 83, CDN, Prod/Wr/Dir; *THE ELECTRONIC WEB*, TV, 82, CDN, Prod/Dir/Wr.

HEALEY, Barry - see WRITERS

HENAUT, Dorothy Todd - see DIRECTORS

HEROUX, Claude

APFVQ. 3515 Beauséjour, Montréal, Qué, CAN, H4K 1W5. (514)336-7111. Comm. Claude Héroux inc., 444 rue St-Paul est, Montréal, Qué, CAN, H2Y 3V1. (514)842-6633.
Types de production et Catégories: l métrage-Prod; c métrage-Prod.
Types d'oeuvres: Drame-C; Comédie-C; Action-C; Horreur-C.
Curriculum vitae: Né en 1942, Montreal, Québec. Oeuvre dans l'industrie depuis 60; a produit plus de 30 films.
Filmographie sélective: *THE PARK IS MINE*, TV, 84, CDN/USA, Prod exéc; *CLEMENCE ALETTI*, C, 84, CDN, Prod exéc; *AU NOM DE TOUS LES MIENS* (FOR THOSE I LOVED), C, 83, CDN/F, Prod; *GOING BERSERK*, C, 83, CDN/USA, Prod; *OF UNKNOWN ORIGIN*, C, 82, CDN, Prod; *VIDEODROME*, C, 82, CDN, Prod; *DREAMWORLD*, C, 81, CDN, Prod; *GAS*, C, 80, CDN, Prod; *VISITING HOURS*, C, 80, CDN, Prod; *THE FUNNY FARM*, C, 80, CDN, Prod; *SCANNERS*, C, 80, CDN, Prod; *DIRTY TRICKS*, C, 79, CDN, Prod; *HOG WILD*, C, 79, CDN, Prod; *THE BROOD*, C, 79, CDN, Prod; *CITY ON FIRE*, C, 78, CDN, Co prod; *IN PRAISE OF OLDER WOMEN*, C, 77, CDN, Co prod; *THE UNCANNY*, C, 77, CDN/GB, Co prod; *ANGELA*, C, 76, CDN, Co prod; *BREAKING POINT*, C, 76, CDN/USA, Prod; *BORN FOR HELL* (NE POUR L'ENFER), C, 75, CDN/F/I/D, Co prod exéc; *JACQUES BREL IS ALIVE AND WELL AND LIVING IN PARIS*, C, 74, CDN/F, Prod; *Y A PAS DE MAL A SE FAIRE DU BIEN*, C, 74, CDN, Prod; *Y A TOUJOURS MOYEN DE*

(cont/suite)

MOYENNER, C, 74, CDN, Prod; *POUSSE' MAIS POUSSE EGAL, C,* 74, CDN, Prod; *JE T'AIME, C,* 73, CDN, Prod; *J'AI MON VOYAGE, C,* 73, CDN, Prod; *PAR LE SANG DES AUTRES* (POUR UNE POIGNEE DE SALAUDS), C, 73, CDN/F, Co prod; *QUELQUES ARPENTS DE NEIGE* (A FEW ACRES OF SNOW), C, 72, CDN, Prod; *UN ENFANT COMME LES AUTRES,* C, 72, CDN, Prod; *7 FOIS...PAR JOUR* (7 TIMES...A DAY), C, 71, CDN, Co prod.

HEROUX, Denis

28 rue Roskilde, Montréal, Qué, CAN, H2V 2N5. (514)272-0526. Alliance Entertainment Corp., 260 Place Royale, Montréal, Qué, CAN, H2Y 2V1. (514)284-9354.
Types de production et Catégories: l métrage-Prod; TV film-Prod.
Types d'oeuvres: Drame-C&TV; Comédie-C; Action-C; Science-fiction-C.
Curriculum vitae: Né en 1940, Montréal, Québec. Maitrise ès Arts, Université de Montréal; professeur à l'UQAM; auteur de 2 livres. Reçoit le Prix du Mérite de l'Université de Montréal, 82; président du conseil d'administration, Académie du cinéma canadien, 83; décoré Officier de l'Ordre du Canada, 84. Ses films ont remporté plusieurs prix dont le Grand Prix (Festival de Film de Venise) et le Prix du Meilleur Film (Ass. des Critiques de films de Los Angeles) pour *ATLANTIC CITY;* *LA GUERRE DU FEU* remporte 2 Césars, le Gold Scroll Award, BFA, Oscar et 5 Génies; *LES PLOUFFE* remporte 7 Génies et fut projeté lors de l'ouverture de la Quinzaine des Réalisateurs au Festival de Film de Cannes.
Filmographie sélective: *HOLD UP* (QUICK CHANGE), C, 85, CDN/F, Prod exéc; *LE MATOU* (THE ALLEY CAT), C, 85, CDN/F, Prod exéc; *THE PARK IS MINE,* TV, 84, CDN/USA, Prod; *GAZL EL BANAT,* C, 84, CDN/F, Prod exéc; *THE BOY IN BLUE,* C, 84, CDN, Prod exéc; *THE BAY BOY* (UN PRINTEMPS SOUS LA NEIGE), C, 83, CDN/F, Co prod **(GENIE);** *THE BLOOD OF OTHERS* (LE SANG DES AUTRES), C, 83, CDN/F, Co prod; *LE CRIME D'OVIDE PLOUFFE* (MURDER IN THE FAMILY), C, 83, CDN/F, Co prod exéc; *LOUISIANA,* C, 83, CDN/F, Co prod exéc; *LES PLOUFFE,* C. 81, CDN, Co prod exéc; *LA GUERRE DU FEU* (QUEST FOR FIRE), C, 80, CDN/F, Co prod **(CESAR);** *ATLANTIC CITY,* C, 79, CDN/USA, Co prod exéc; *A NOUS DEUX* (AN ADVENTURE FOR TWO), C, 78, CDN/F, Co prod; *L'HOMME EN COLERE* (LABYRINTH), C, 78, CDN/F, Co prod; *VIOLETTE NOZIERE,* C, 77, CDN/F, Co prod; *TOMORROW NEVER COMES,* C, 77, CDN/F, Prod; *BLOOD RELATIVES* (LES LIENS DE SANG), C, 77, CDN/F, Co prod; *THE UNCANNY,* C, 77, CDN/GB, Réal; *THE LITTLE GIRL WHO LIVED DOWN THE LANE,* C, 75, CDN/F, Co prod; *BORN FOR HELL* (NE POUR L'ENFER), C, 75, CDN/F/I/D, Réal; *POUSSE MAIS POUSSE EGAL,* C, 74, CDN, Réal; *JACQUES BREL IS ALIVE AND WELL AND LIVING IN PARIS,* C, 74, CDN/ F, Réal; *J'AI MON VOYAGE,* C, 73, CDN, Réal; *QUELQUES ARPENTS DE NEIGE,* C, 72, CDN, Réal; *UN ENFANT COMME LES AUTRES,* C, 72, CDN, Réal; *7 FOIS...PAR JOUR* (7 TIMES...A DAY), C, 71, CDN, Réal; *L'AMOUR HUMAIN,* C, 70, CDN, Réal; *L'INITIATION,* C, 69, CDN, Réal; *VALERIE,* C, 68, CDN, Réal; *PAS DE VACANCES POUR LES IDOLES,* C, 67, CDN, Réal.

HEROUX, Justine

APFVQ. 28 Roskilde, Outremont, Qué, CAN, H2V 2N5. (514)272-0526. Cinévidéo Inc., 360 Place Royale, Montréal, Qué, CAN, H2Y 2V1. (514)284-9354.
Types de production et Catégories: l métrage-Prod; TV film-Prod.
Types d'oeuvres: Drame-C&TV; Comédie-C&TV; Action-C&TV.
Curriculum vitae: Stagiaire sur plusieurs longs métrages, Paris, 65-66. A l'emploi de Radio-Canada comme script girl, 67-69; puis, elle travaille activement dans le milieu du cinéma comme scripte, et comme 1er assistante réalisatrice; ensuite, directrice de production pour de nombreuses annonces publicitaires et quelques films; productrice, 79. *ATLANTIC CITY* remporte le Grand Prix du Festival de Film de Venise, Meilleur Film, Acteur et Scénario (L.A. Film Critics Assoc.); *LES PLOUFFE*

(cont/suite)

remporte le International Press Award et plusieurs Prix Génies dont Meilleur Scénario en 82.
Filmographie sélective: *LE MATOU* (THE ALLEY CAT), (aussi 6 ém TV), C, 85, CDN/F, Prod; *LE CRIME D'OVIDE PLOUFFE* (MURDER IN THE FAMIY), (aussi 6 ém TV), C, 83, CDN/F, Prod; *LITTLE GLORIA...HAPPY AT LAST,* TV, 82, CDN/USA, Prod; *LES PLOUFFE* (aussi 6 ém TV), C, 81, CDN, Prod; *ATLANTIC CITY,* C, 79, CDN/USA, Prod; *A NOUS DEUX* (AN ADVENTURE FOR TWO), C, 78, CDN/F, Dir pro; *THE UNCANNY,* C, 77, CDN/GB, 1er ass réal; *BLOOD RELATIVES* (LES LIENS DE SANG), C, 77, CDN/F, 1er ass réal; *VIOLETTE NOZIERE,* C, 77, CDN/F, 1er ass réal; *THE LITTLE GIRL WHO LIVED DOWN THE LANE,* C, 75, CDN/F, 1er ass réal; *BORN FOR HELL* (NE POUR L'ENFER), C, 75, CDN/F/I/D, 1er ass réal; *JACQUES BREL IS ALIVE AND WELL AND LIVING IN PARIS,* C, 74, CDN/F, 1er ass réal; *POUSSE MAIS POUSSE EGAL,* C, 74, CDN, 1er ass réal; *SHOW LOTO-QUEBEC,* TV, 74, CDN, Réal; *JE T'AIME,* C, 73, CDN, 1er ass réal; *PORTRAIT D'UN HOMME POLITIQUE,* TV, 73, CDN, Réal; *LA VALLEE DU RICHELIEU,* TV, 73, CDN, Co sc/Co réal; *FINALEMENT,* C, 71, CDN, Scripte; *7 FOIS...PAR JOUR* (7 TIMES...A DAY), C, 71, CDN, Scripte; *DROITS DE REGARD,* TV, 71, CDN, 1er ass réal; *QUELQUES ARPENTS DE NEIGE,* C, 71, CDN, 1er ass réal; *L'AMOUR HUMAIN,* C, 70, CDN, Scripte; *LA FEUILLE D'ERABLE',* TV, 70, CDN, 1er ass réal; *L'INITIATION,* C, 69, CDN, Scripte.

HERTZOG, Larry

Lawrence Hertzog Prod., 686 Richmond St. West, Toronto, Ont, CAN, M6J 1C3. (416)363-2345.
Types of Production & Categories: Th Film-Prod; TV Film-Prod.
Genres: Drama-Th&TV; Comedy-Th&TV; Documentary-TV.
Biography: Born 1933, Hanna, Alberta. Education: University of Alberta; Banff School of Fine Arts. *WHY SHOOT THE TEACHER* won the Golden Reel Award; his television documentaries have won numerous int'l awards at Atlanta, New York, Chicago, Virgin Islands film festivals.
Selective Filmography: *'BIRDS IN PARADISE'* (4 eps), TV, 84, CDN, Prod; *TILL DEATH DO US PART,* Th, 82, CDN, Prod; *FINAL ASSIGNMENT,* Th, 79, CDN, Prod; *WHY SHOOT THE TEACHER,* Th, 76, CDN, Prod; *'POLICE SURGEON'* (78 eps), TV, 75-73, CDN, Assoc Prod; *'CANADA-FIVE PORTRAITS'* (5 eps), TV, 75-72, CDN, Exec Prod; *'WINDOW OF THE WORLD'* (7 eps), TV, 75-72, CDN, Exec Prod; *'HERITAGE'* (6 eps), TV, 75/74, CDN, Exec Prod; *'UNTAMED WORLD'* (120 eps), TV, 75-71, CDN, Exec Prod; *'GEORGE'* (26 eps), TV, 72, CDN, Assoc Prod.

HEYDON, Michael

Much Music, 299 Queen St.W., Toronto, Ont, CAN, M5V 1J9. (416)367-5757.
Types of Production & Categories: Th Short-Ed; TV Video-Ed/Prod.
Genres: Musical-TV; Music Video-TV.
Biography: Born 1950. B.A.A., Radio & TV Arts, Ryerson Polytechnical Institute. Has won CanPro Gold and Silver Awards.
Selective Filmography: *'MUCH MUSIC',* TV, 86-84, CDN, Sr Prod; *I AM A HOTEL,* TV, 84, CDN, Ed; *'CITY LIMITS',* TV, 84/83, CDN, Prod; *'THE NEW MUSIC',* TV, 83/82, CDN, Ed; *BOOZE MOTHERS: DOIN'IT RIGHT ON THE WRONG SIDE OF QUEEN,* TV, 82, CDN, Prod/Wr/Ed/Act; *MASH/NEW GUN,* Cm, 81, CDN, Prod/Dir/Wr/Ed.

HIRSH, Michael

Nelvana Ltd., 32 Atlantic Ave., Toronto, Ont, CAN, M6K 1X8. (416)588-5571.
Types of Production & Categories: Th Film-Prod; TV Film-Prod; TV Video-Prod.
Genres: Children's-Th&TV; Animation-Th&TV.

(cont/suite)

PRODUCERS/PRODUCTEURS

Biography: Co-founder, Vice President, Nelvana Ltd.. Recipient of numerous awards including Wilderness, Chris, a Special Award, Canadian Film Awards, 78; *THE CARE BEARS MOVIE* won the Golden Reel Award, 86.
Selective Filmography: *'THE EDISON TWINS'* (39 eps), TV, 86-83, CDN, Co-Prod; *BURGLAR*, Th, 86, USA, Prod; *MY PET MONSTER*, TV, 86, CDN, Co-Prod; *MAD BALLS*, TV, 86, CDN, Co-Prod; *'THE CARE BEARS FAMILY'* (13 eps), TV, 86, CDN, Co-Prod; *THE CARE BEARS MOVIE II*, Th, 86/85, CDN, Co-Prod; *'EWOKS'* (13 eps), TV, 85, CDN, Co-Prod; *THE CARE BEARS MOVIE*, Th, 85, CDN, Co-Prod; *THE GREAT HEEP*, TV, 85, CDN, Co-Prod; *THE EWOK-DROIDS ADVENTURE HOUR*, TV, 85, CDN, Co-Prod; *STRAWBERRY SHORTCAKE MEETS THE BERRYKINS*, TV, 84, CDN, Co-Prod; *THE GET ALONG GANG*, TV, 84, CDN, Co-Prod; *STRAWBERRY SHORTCAKE AND THE BABY WITHOUT A NAME*, TV, 83, CDN, Co-Prod; *'20 MINUTE WORKOUT'* (120 eps), TV, 83, CDN, Co-Exec Prod; *ROCK & RULE* (RING OF POWER), Th, 83, CDN, Co-Prod; *HERSELF THE ELF*, TV, 83, CDN, Co-Prod; *STRAWBERRY SHORTCAKE: A HOUSEWARMING SURPRISE*, TV, 82, CDN, Co-Prod; *INTERGALACTIC THANKSGIVING* (PLEASE DON'T EAT THE PLANET), TV, 79, CDN, Co-Prod; *THE STAR WARS HOLIDAY SPECIAL* (Cdn inserts), TV, 78, USA, Co-Prod; *ROMIE-0 & JULIE-8*, TV, 78, CDN, Co-Prod; *THE DEVIL & DANIEL MOUSE*, TV, 78, CDN, Co-Prod; *COSMIC CHRISTMAS*, TV, 77/76, CDN, Co-Prod.

HOLENDER, Jacques

ACTT. Nemesis Productions, 21 Howland Ave., Toronto, Ont, CAN, M5R 3B2. (416)927-9546.
Types of Production & Categories: Th Short-Prod/Dir; TV Film-Prod/Dir.
Genres: Documentary-Th&TV.
Biography: Born 1953, Zambia. Studied Fine Arts at University of Cape Town and Film in London, England. Lived and worked in the U.K. for 8 years. Emigrated to Canada, 81; now a Canadian citizen. Has been working as a producer/director since 79; Menesis Productions established in 81. *ECHOES*, winner, Canadian Short Film Showcase, 82.
Selective Filmography: *KODO*, Th, 84, CDN, Prod/Dir/Ed; *TRACES*, Th, 83, CDN, Prod/Dir/Ed; *ECHOES*, Th, 82, CDN, Prod/Dir/Ed.

HOLT, Ralph

Purcell's Cove, Halifax, NS, CAN, B3P 2G6. (902)479-2910. Media Co-operative Prods. Ltd., 5639 Spring Garden Rd., Halifax, NS, CAN, B3J 1G6. (902)422-8586.
Types of Production & Categories: TV Video-Prod.
Genres: Drama-TV; Variety-TV; Educational-TV; Experimental-TV.
Biography: Born in U.K.; early childhood in Germany, Winnipeg; went to school and university in Halifax. *DANCE MAKES WAVES* won an Award of Merit, Atlantic Film Festival.
Selective Filmography: *THE LAMPLIGHTER* (pilot), *'CURIOUS MINDS'*, TV, 85, CDN, Prod; *DANCE MAKES WAVES*, TV, 85, CDN, Prod; *'GENESIS TWO'* (13 eps), TV, 85, CDN, Prod; *GUYSBOROUGH COUNTY*, ED, 85, CDN, Prod.

HOUSE, Bill

Extra Modern Productions, 69 Yorkville, Suite 206, Toronto, Ont, CAN, M5R 1B7. (416)535-7294.
Types of Production & Categories: TV Film-Prod; TV Video-Prod.
Genres: Comedy-TV; Variety-TV; Musical-TV; Documentary-TV.
Biography: Born 1948, Windsor, Ontario. Honours B.A., University of Windsor; M.A., York U. Produced 25 professional theatrical productions, especially at Theatre Second Floor, Toronto. Production manager, Festival of Festivals, 77-81; produced/

(cont/suite)

directed the tributes to Martin Scorsese, Robert Duvall and Warren Beatty, Festival of Festivals.
Selective Filmography: *THE CANADIAN CONSPIRACY,* TV, 85/84, CDN/USA, Co-Prod; *THE MAKING OF SPACEHUNTER,* TV, 84/83, CDN, Prod; *RUMOURS OF GLORY: BRUCE COCKBURN LIVE,* TV, 82, CDN, Prod; *GONGGA SHAN: WHITE PEAK BEYOND THE CLOUDS,* TV, 82, CDN, Prod; *THE LITTLE PAPER THAT GREW,* TV, 81, CDN, Prod.

HOWARD, Duane

DGC. 26 Alcorn Ave., Toronto, Ont, CAN, M4V 1E4. (416)920-3710.
Types of Production & Categories: Th Film-PM/Prod; TV Film-Prod.
Genres: Drama-Th&TV; Comedy-TV; Action-TV; Documentary-TV.
Biography: Born 1940, Morton, Ontario; Canadian citizen; US Green Card. Education: Bachelor of Arts.
Selective Filmography: *HEAVEN ON EARTH,* TV, 86, CDN/GB, Line Prod; *'FRONTIER'* (6 eps), TV, 86, CDN/GB/F/D, Line Prod; *ANNE OF GREEN GABLES - THE SEQUEL* (mini-series), TV, 86, CDN/USA, Line Prod; *LABOUR OF LOVE,* TV, 84, CDN, Assoc Prod; *'TALES OF THE KLONDIKE'* (13 eps), TV, 83/82, CDN, Pro Spv; *'SCTV'* (12 eps), TV, 83/82, CDN, Unit M; *THE KGB CONNECTIONS,* TV, 81, CDN, Pro Spv; *WINNIE,* TV, 81, CDN, Pro Spv; *THE HIGH COUNTRY* (THE FIRST HELLO), Th, 80, CDN, PM; *I, MAUREEN,* Th, 78/77, CDN, Prod; *FISH HAWK,* Th, 78, CDN, Unit M/Loc M; *BIGFOOT,* Th, 76, I, Line Prod; *THE DISSAPEARANCE,* Th, 75, CDN, Unit M/Loc M; *'THE TIMES THEY ARE A CHANGIN'* (13 eps), TV, 75-73, CDN, Prod.

HOWARD, Jeff

R.R. 1, Site 118, C-56, Parksville, BC, CAN, V0R 2S0. (604)248-5446. Jeffrey Howard Prods. Ltd., 893 Shorewood Dr., Parksville, BC, CAN, V0R 2S0. (604) 248-9311.
Types of Production & Categories: Th Short-Dir/Prod/Wr/Ed.
Genres: Documentary-TV; Educational-TV.
Biography: Born 1937, Lamont, Alberta. Has worked in television since 57 starting as host/announcer, becoming film producer/director with Alberta National Communications, 72; founded Jeffrey Howard Productions Ltd., 73; specializes in films for Native people.
Selective Filmography: *SOMEBODY CALLED ERNESTINE,* ED, 86, CDN, Prod/ Dir/Wr/Ed; *NEW DAY NEW HORIZONS/GUNS FOR LIFE,* ED, 83/78, CDN, Prod/Dir/Wr; *THE HOME TEAM,* Cm, 79, CDN, Prod/Dir/Wr/Ed; *PROLINE,* Cm, 78, CDN, Prod/Dir/Ed; *CHIEF DAN GEORGE SPEAKS,* TV, 77, CDN, Prod/Dir/Wr; *TUKUSINUK/YOU'RE HIRED/JOB WANTED/HELP WANTED,* ED, 77-75, CDN, Prod; *NAME OF THE GAME/WHAT DID YOU SAY?/A MATTER OF CHOICE,* ED, 74, CDN, Prod/Dir; *IT WASN'T MY FAULT/ WHO'S IN CHARGE HERE?/HE COMES WITHOUT CALLING,* ED, 74, CDN, Prod/Dir; *MORE POWER TO YOU/I MOVE/MANY VOICES,* ED, 73/72, CDN, Prod/Dir.

HUMPHREY, Jack

ACTRA, WGAw. 1101 Bay St., Ste. 2401, Toronto, Ont, CAN, M5S 2B3. (416) 961-6248.
Types of Production & Categories: TV Film-Wr/Prod.
Genres: Drama-TV; Comedy-TV.
Biography: Born Winnipeg, Manitoba. Writer/producer in radio for 10 years before going into TV; co-author: 'Canadian Inventions'. Won Best Actor Award twice, Dominion Drama Festival.
Selective Filmography: *'HANGIN'IN'* (100 eps), TV, 86-80, CDN, Co-Wr/Exec Prod (**ANIK**); *'SILVER SPOONS'* (22 eps), TV, 86/85, USA, Exec Prod; *'FLAPPERS'* (43 eps), TV, 83-80, CDN, Exec Prod/Co-Wr; *'KING OF KENSINGTON'* (113 eps), TV, 80-75, CDN, Exec Prod/Co-Wr.

PRODUCERS/PRODUCTEURS

HUNTER, John - see WRITERS

ISCOVE, Robert - see DIRECTORS

JACKSON, G. Philip - see DIRECTORS

JACQUES, Alan

1540 W. 13th, #203, Vancouver, BC, CAN, V6J 2G4. (604)732-1582. Showcase Communications Inc., M.P.O. Box 2203, Vancouver, BC, CAN, V6B 3W2. (604) 667-0425.
Types of Production & Categories: TV Film-Prod/Dir; TV Video-Prod.
Genres: Variety-TV; Documentary-TV; Commercials-TV; Industrial-TV.
Biography: Born 1951, Port Alberni, British Columbia. B.Sc., Honours in Biological Sciences, Simon Fraser University. Has produced numerous commercials and industrial films since 81.
Selective Filmography: *MIDNIGHT MUSIC* (12 O'CLOCK ROCK), TV, 83, CDN, Prod; *MARATHON - THE ULTIMATE CHALLENGE,* TV, 82, CDN, Prod/Dir (**CFTA**).

JENSEN, Thea - see DIRECTORS

JEPHCOTT, Samuel C.

ACTRA, BAE, CFTA, DGC. Cyclops Communications Corp., 44 Gibson Ave., Toronto, Ont, CAN, M5R 1T5. (416)922-4038. CFTA, Box 790, Stn. F, Toronto, Ont, CAN, M4Y 2N7. (416)927-8942.
Types of Production & Categories: Th Film-Prod; TV Film-Prod; TV Video-Prod.
Genres: Drama-Th&TV; Comedy-Th; Documentary-TV; Children's-Th.
Biography: Born 1944, England; Canadian citizen. Executive director, CFTA-CAMPP and Governor, Actra Fraternal since 84; Governor, Canadian Conference of the Arts, '86-88; former board member and National Executive Secretary, DGC; Director, CAMPP since 76. Extensive experience in foreign distribution of features and television with Quadrant Films, Nielsen Ferns Int'l and CBC Enterprises.
Selective Filmography: *'THE LAST FRONTIER'* (13 eps), TV, 86/85, CDN, Prod; *THE WARS,* Th, 81, CDN/D, Pro Spv; *'MAN OF THE NORTH'* (7 eps), TV, 78/77, CDN, P Pro Spv; *'THE NEWCOMERS'* (1 eps), TV, 78, CDN, P Pro Spv; *'THE NEW AVENGERS'* (2 eps), TV, 77, CDN/GB/F, PM; *FIND THE LADY,* Th, 76, CDN, Stills; *LOVE AT FIRST SIGHT,* Th, 75, CDN, Pro Acc't; *IT SEEMED LIKE A GOOD IDEA AT THE TIME,* Th, 74, CDN, Assist PM; *A SWEETER SONG* (SNAPSHOTS), Th, 75, CDN, Assoc Prod; *LIONS FOR BREAKFAST,* Th, 74, CDN, PM; *ME,* Th, 74, CDN, PM; *THE HARD PART BEGINS,* Th, 73, CDN, PM; *THE MERRY WIVES OF TOBIAS ROUKE,* Th, 71, CDN, Co-Prod.

JESPERSEN, Rik

495 St. John's Rd., Toronto, Ont, CAN, M6S 2L6. (416)762-7166. City TV, 299 Queen St.W., Toronto, Ont, CAN, M5V 1Z9.
Types of Production & Categories: TV Video-Prod.
Genres: Documentary-TV; News-TV.
Biography: Born 1950, Gravenhurst, Ontario. Diploma in Journalism. Four years at City TV: assignment editor, senior writer, producer. Producer, CBC's *THE JOURNAL,* 83-85; senior producer, City TV news, 86.

JEWISON, Norman - see DIRECTORS

JOHNSON, Richard - see DIRECTORS

JOHNSTON, William

DGC. Lauron Productions Ltd., 56 Shaftesbury Ave., Toronto, Ont, CAN, M4T 1A3. (416)967-6503.
Types of Production & Categories: Th Film-Prod; TV Film-Dir/Prod.
Genres: Drama-Th; Documentary-Th&TV.

(cont/suite)

Biography: Born 1946, Winnipeg, Manitoba; bilingual. London Int'l Film School, England; Institut des Arts de Diffusion, Brussels; Université Paul-Valery, France; B.Sc. University of Manitoba. *THE FAST AND THE FURIOUS* won Red Ribbon, American Film Fest.; *QUILTING: THE PATTERNS OF LOVE*, Chris Plaque, Columbus; *NO SURRENDER* won the Int'l Critics Award, Toronto Festival of Festivals.
Selective Filmography: *LOYALTIES,* Th, 85, CDN/GB, Co-Prod; *NO SURRENDER,* Th, 85, CDN/GB, Co-Prod; *DRASTIC MEASURES,* Th, 84, CDN, Prod; *THE SAGA OF THOSE CRAZY CANUCKS,* TV, 84, CDN, Prod; *THE HEROES OF SUMMER,* TV, 84, CDN, Prod; *BEYOND WORDS,* TV, 84, CDN, Prod; *THE DISABILITY MYTH* (PARTS I, II & III), TV, 84-82, CDN, Prod; *THE FAST AND THE FURIOUS,* TV, 83, CDN, Dir; *THE HEROES OF WINTER,* TV, 83, CDN, Prod; *IT TAKES A CHAMPION,* TV, 83, CDN, Prod; *THREE AGAINST THE WORLD,* TV, 83, CDN, Prod; *THE BEST DOWNHILL RACER,* TV, 82, CDN, Dir; *THIRTEEN MINUTES TO WAIT,* TV, 82, CDN, Dir; *THE DREAM NEVER DIES,* TV, 81, CDN, Dir; *THE BREAKTHROUGH,* TV, 81, CDN, Prod; *OUT ON THE EDGE,* TV, 81, CDN, Prod; *AGAINST ALL ODDS,* TV, 81, CDN, Prod; *THOSE FLYING CANUCKS,* TV, 81, CDN, Prod; *THOSE CRAZY CANUCKS,* TV, 80, CDN, Dir; *EXPORT FOR PROFIT AND SURVIVAL,* TV, 80, CDN, Prod; *STRIPTEASE,* Th, 80, CDN, Prod; *DON'T MESS WITH BILL* (pilot), TV, 80, CDN, Ed; *QUILTING: PATTERNS OF LOVE,* TV, 79, CDN, Dir; *STALLONE: THE MILLION-TO-ONE SHOT,* TV, 78/77, CDN, P Pro Spv/Ed **(CFEG)**.

JONAS, George

ATPD, CAPAC. The Colbert Agency, 303 Davenport Rd., Toronto, Ont, CAN, M5R 1K5. (416)961-8028.
Types of Production & Categories: TV Film-Prod/Dir; TV Video-Prod/Dir.
Genres: Drama-TV; Action-TV; Documentary-TV; Children's-TV.
Biography: Born 1935, Budapest, Hungary; Canadian citizen. Languages: English, German, Hungarian. Education: Academy of Theatre and Film Arts, Budapest. Author of several books including 'Vengeance'. Produced 100, directed 15 dramas, docu-dramas, 69-81; producer, radio, 'Scales of Justice'. Has won an Actra Award, Gabriel Award, Gold Award (NY) for radio shows; many literary awards including Edgar Allan Poe Award for Best Fact Crime Book.
Selective Filmography: *THE HOUSE ON FRONT STREET,* Th, 77, CDN, Prod/Dir; *THE PRINCESS OF TAMBOSO,* TV, 76, CDN, Wr/Prod/Dir; *THE PLAY'S THE THING'* (Dir-2 eps), (12 eps), TV, 74/73, CDN, Prod; *'PURPLE PLAYHOUSE'* (Dir-1 eps), (9 eps), TV, 73/72, CDN, Prod; *'PROGRAM X'* (Dir-8 eps), (60 eps), TV, 72-69, CDN, Prod.

JONES, Donnie see PRODUCTION MANAGERS

JUBENVILL, Ken - see DIRECTORS

KASTNER, John - see DIRECTORS

KAUFMAN, James T.

DGC. 241 Clarke Ave., Montreal, Que, CAN, H3Z 2E3. (514)931-7463.
Types of Production & Categories: Th Film-Prod/1st AD; TV Film-Prod/1st AD; TV Video-Prod/Dir.
Genres: Drama-Th&TV; Action-Th&TV; Children's-Th; Music Video-TV.
Biography: Born 1949, Montreal, Quebec; bilingual. Honours B.Sc., Business, Babson College of Business Administration, Boston, 71. Eastern Canada representative, DGC, 79; National First Vice President and Eastern Canada rep., 80; producer/director, commercials and industrial films.
Selective Filmography: *RACE FOR THE BOMB* (mini-series), TV, 86, CDN/F, Line Prod/1st AD; *CHILDREN OF A LESSER GOD,* Th, 85, USA, 1st AD;
(cont/suite)

EARTHWATCH (EXPO 86), Th, 85, CDN, Line Prod/1st AD; *THE PEANUT BUTTER SOLUTION* (OPERATION BEURRE DE PINOTTES), Th, 85, CDN, Line Prod/1st AD; *NIGHT MAGIC*, Th, 84, CDN/F, Co-Prod; *PEDIGREE SKIWEAR*, MV, 84, CDN, Prod/Dir; *THE SURROGATE*, Th, 83, CDN, 1st AD; *COOK & PEARY: THE RACE TO THE POLE*, TV, 83, USA, 1st AD; *TELL ME THAT YOU LOVE ME*, Th, 83/82, CDN/IL, Co-Prod; *PARADISE*, Th, 81, CDN/ IL, 1st AD/2nd U Dir; *THRESHOLD*, Th, 80, CDN, 1st AD/2nd U Dir; *HOT TOUCH* (FRENCH KISS), Th, 80, CDN, 1st AD/2nd U Dir; *SCANNERS*, Th, 79, CDN, 1st AD; *DIRTY TRICKS*, Th, 79, CDN, 1st AD; *CRUNCH* (THE KINKY COACHES AND THE POM-POM PUSSYCATS), Th, 79, CDN, 1st AD/2nd U Dir; *TOP OF THE HILL*, TV, 79, USA, Assoc Prod/PM; *FAST COMPANY*, Th, 78, CDN, 1st AD; *NAZARETH, A PLACE IN YOUR HEART*, MV, 78, CDN, Dir/Co-Prod; *QUINTET*, Th, 78, USA, Unit M; *'MAN OF THE NORTH'*, TV, 77, CDN, PM; *TELL ME MY NAME*, TV, 77, USA, U Loc M; *WORLD OF DARKNESS*, TV, 77, USA, U Loc M.

KEANE, Laurence - see DIRECTORS

KEATLEY, Philip

CTPDA. 232 West 14th Ave., Vancouver, BC, CAN, V5Y 1X1. (604)879-0071. CBC, 700 Hamilton St., Vancouver, BC, CAN, V6B 4A2. (604)662-6264.
Types of Production & Categories: TV Film-Dir/Prod; TV Video-Dir/Prod.
Genres: Drama-TV; Comedy-TV; Documentary-TV; Children's-TV.
Biography: Born 1929, British Columbia. B.A., University of British Columbia, 51; LAMDA, England. Actor, director in theatre and film; became producer/director CBC, 57; head of Vancouver drama department, 67-78; headed CBC production training program, 78-80; area producer, CBC drama, 85-86. Won American Film Award for *GLORIOUS MUD*.
Selective Filmography: *'BAILEY'S LAW'* (Dir-1 eps), (4 eps), TV, 86, CDN, Prod; *MA!*, TV, 83, CDN, Prod/Dir; *GLORIOUS MUD*, 'HAND AND EYE', TV, 83-81, CDN, Prod/Dir/Wr; *TOUCH WOOD*, 'HAND AND EYE', TV, 83-81, CDN, Prod/Dir; *'THE MAGIC LIE'* (Dir-4 eps), (18 eps), TV, 78-75, CDN, Exec Prod; *'THE BEACHCOMBERS'* (Dir-15 eps/Prod-50 eps), (120 eps), TV, 76-71, CDN, Exec Prod; *'THE MANIPULATORS'* (12 eps), TV, 70, CDN, Exec Prod; *EDUCATION OF PHYLLISTINE/HOW TO BRAKE A QUARTERHORSE, FESTIVAL'*, TV, 68-65, CDN, Prod/Dir; *'CARIBOO COUNTRY'* (22 eps), TV, 67-64, CDN, Prod/Dir.

KEELAN, Matt - see DIRECTORS

KELLNER, Lynne

CTPDA. 44 Mount Royal Cres., Winnipeg, Man, CAN, R3J 2M9. CBC, 541 Portage Ave., Winnipeg, Man, CAN, R3C 2H1. (204)775-8351.
Types of Production & Categories: TV Film-Prod/Dir; TV Video-Prod/Dir.
Genres: Variety-TV; Documentary-TV; Sports-TV.
Biography: Born 1943, Winnipeg, Manitoba.
Selective Filmography: *'BODY TALK'* (47 eps), TV, 86-84, CDN, Prod/Dir; *'SPORTS WEEKEND'* (sev events), TV, 86, CDN, Prod; *CANADIAN NATIONAL DARTS CHAMPIONSHIP*, TV, 86, CDN, Prod/Dir; *CHAI IS A LUCKY NUMBER*, TV, 85, CDN, Prod/Dir; *OPERA IS FOR EVERYBODY*, TV, 85, CDN, Prod/Dir; *WOMEN OF THE YEAR*, TV, 85-83, CDN, Prod/Dir; *RED RIVER EXHIBITION PARADE/SANTA CLAUS PARADE* (yearly), TV, 85-80, CDN, Prod/Dir; *SYMPHONY FOR KIDS*, TV, 84, CDN, Prod/Dir; *MANITOBA MARATHON* (5 specials), TV, 84-79, CDN, Prod/Dir; *LOS ANGELES OLYMPICS*, TV, 84, CDN, Prod; *MEN OF MEDICINE*, TV, 83, CDN, Prod/Dir; *WESTERN CANADA SUMMER GAMES* (2 shows), TV, 83/79, CDN, Exec Prod; *UNIVERSIADE*, TV, 83, CDN, Prod/Dir; *ARNOLD SPOHR GALA* (ROYAL WINNIPEG BALLET), TV, 83, CDN, Prod/Dir; *RUSALKA*

(cont/suite)

DANCERS, TV, 82, CDN, Prod/Dir; *'INTERNATIONAL RAQUETBALL CLASSIC'* (13 eps), TV, 82-79, CDN, Prod.

KELLUM, J.H.

CTPDA. 70 Highland Dr., Wedgewood Pk., St.John's, Nfld, CAN. (709)753-3307. CBC, 95 University Ave., St. John's, Nfld, CAN. (709)737-4164.
Types of Production & Categories: TV Film-Prod/Dir.
Genres: Comedy-TV; Variety-TV; Documentary-TV.
Biography: Born 1943, Southern Ontario. Graduate, Radio & TV Arts, Ryerson Polytechnical Institute. Worked 7 years with CBC, *THIS LAND,* Toronto; 12 years, CBC, St.John's. Writes background music for films.
Selective Filmography: *SEXTON/MALONE COMEDY SHOW* (S & M COMEDY SHOW), (pilot), TV, 85, CDN, Prod/Dir; *'WONDERFUL GRAND BAND'* (Dir-13 eps), (47 eps), TV, 84-80, CDN, Prod; *PIRATES GOLD/CHRISTMAS AT KINGS LANDING/ALL ON A SUMMER'S DAY,* 'RYAN'S FANCY', TV, 82-79, CDN, Prod/Dir; *HOME BOYS HOME,* 'RYAN'S FANCY', TV, 81, CDN, Dir; *PEOPLE OF THE ISLANDS/THE CAPE SHORE IRISH,* 'HERITAGE', TV, 81, CDN, Prod/Dir; *'CANADIAN EXPRESS'* (14 eps), TV, 80-77, CDN, Prod/Dir; *'RYAN'S FANCY'* (39 eps), TV, 77-74, CDN, Prod/Dir; *THE OLDTIMERS' NEWFOUNDLAND,* TV, 75, CDN, Prod/Dir **(ANIK)**; *THE TURKISH EXPERIMENT,* TV, 74, CDN, Prod/Dir; *AIR OF DEATH,* TV, 68, CDN, Comp **(ANIK)**.

KELLY, Peter

ATPD. 78 Lesgay Crescent, Willowdale, Ont, CAN, M2J 2J3. (416)493-2676. CBC, Box 500, Station A, Toronto, Ont, CAN, M5W 1E6. (416)975-7147.
Types of Production & Categories: TV Film-Dir/Prod.
Genres: Drama-TV; Documentary-TV; Children's-TV.
Biography: Born 1929, England; Canadian citizen. Lighting cameraman, England, Iraq, 50-56; NFB, 56-58; DOP, CBC, 58-62. Director, producer, 62-85; currently executive producer, CBC. *FIVE YEARS IN THE LIFE* won the Wilderness Award.
Selective Filmography: *GENTLE SINNERS,* TV, 83, CDN, Exec Prod; *'SOME HONOURABLE GENTLEMEN'* (6 eps), TV, 83, CDN, Exec Prod; *'I MARRIED THE KLONDIKE'* (3 parts), TV, 83/82, CDN, Exec Prod; *'RITTER'S COVE'* (26 eps), TV, 81-79, CDN, Exec Prod; *THE DAWSON PATROL,* TV, 77, CDN, Dir/ Prod; *'FIVE YEARS IN THE LIFE'* (30 eps), TV, 77-71, CDN, Exec Prod; *BALLAD OF THE BICYCLE,* TV, 75, CDN, Dir/Prod; *TO THE SEA IN SHIPS,* TV, 74, CDN, Dir/Prod; *TWO ARCTIC TALES,* TV, 72, CDN, Dir/Prod; *FLIGHT 751,* TV, 70, CDN, Dir/Prod; *THE MAGNIFICENT GIFT,* TV, 70, CDN, Dir/Prod; *THE WHITE CHRISTMAS OF ARCHIE NICOTINE,* 'TO SEE OURSELVES', TV, 70, CDN, Dir; *McQUEEN,* TV, 70, CDN, Dir; *WAS TOM THOMSON MURDERED?,* TV, 69, CDN, Dir/Prod; *AND WE WERE YOUNG,* TV, 68, CDN, Dir/Prod; *ONCE UPON A HUNDRED YEARS,* TV, 67, CDN, Dir/ Prod; *'TELESCOPE'* (Prod-117 eps/Dir-30 eps), TV, 67-63, CDN, Prod/Dir.

KELLY, Tom

ACTRA. Lion's Heart Prods. Inc., 136 Divadale Dr., Toronto, Ont, CAN, M4G 2P4. (416)421-6627. CBC, 790 Bay St., Toronto, Ont, CAN, M5G 1N8. (416)975-6598.
Types of Production & Categories: TV Film-Prod/Dir/Wr; TV Video-Prod/Dir/Wr.
Genres: Drama-TV; Documentary-TV.
Biography: Born 1928, Dublin, Republic of Ireland. B.A., Philosophy, English Literature, Economics. *MAY'S MIRACLE* won a Gold Award (NY), Chris Plaque (Columbus); *SANDRA AND HER KIDS* also won a Chris Plaque.
Selective Filmography: *IN THE CARE OF CRIMINALS/THE INNER HEALER/ BLIND DETERMINATION,* 'MAN ALIVE', TV, 85/83, CDN, Prod/Wr; *THE SWEET LIFE OF JUDY MIX/SANDRA AND HER KIDS,* 'MAN ALIVE', TV,

(cont/suite)

133

83, CDN, Prod/Wr; *MAY'S MIRACLE/DAVID,* 'MAN ALIVE', TV, 83, CDN, Prod/Wr; *'THE FIFTH ESTATE'* (10 segs), TV, 77-75, CDN, Prod/Dir/Wr; *'ADRIENNE AT LARGE'* (sev eps), TV, 75/74, CDN, Prod/Dir/Wr.

KEMENY, John

PGA. 1568 Blue Jay Way, Los Angeles, CA, USA, 90069. (213)855-1457. Alliance Entertainment Corp., 150 S.El Camino Dr., #202, Beverly Hills, CA, USA, 90212. (213)273-4766.
Types of Production & Categories: Th Film-Prod; Th Short-Prod; TV Film-Prod.
Genres: Drama-Th&TV; Action-Th; Documentary-Th&TV; Educational-Th&TV.
Biography: Born in Budapest, Hungary; graduated from Academy of Commerce. Worked at NFB, 57-69. Festival prizes: *ATLANTIC CITY,* Grand Prize (Venice), nominated for 5 Oscars including Best Picture; *THE APPRENTICESHIP OF DUDDY KRAVITZ* Grand Prize (Berlin), Gold Medal and Jury Prize (Atlanta), Silver Mermaid (Sorento); *DON'T LET THE ANGELS FALL,* Interfilm Festival Jury Award (Edinburgh), Best Foreign Feature Film (Ceylon). Received Centennial Medal.
Selective Filmography: *THE BOY IN BLUE,* Th, 84, CDN, Prod; *LE CRIME D'OVIDE PLOUFFE* (MURDER IN THE FAMILY), Th, 83, CDN/F, Co-Exec Prod; *THE BAY BOY* (UN PRINTEMPS SOUS LA NEIGE), Th, 83, CDN/F, Co-Prod **(GENIE)**; *THE BLOOD OF OTHERS* (LE SANG DES AUTRES), Th, 83, CDN/F, Co-Prod; *LOUISIANA,* Th, 83, CDN/F, Co-Prod; *LES PLOUFFE,* Th, 81, CDN, Co-Exec Prod; *LA GUERRE DU FEU* (QUEST FOR FIRE), Th, 80, CDN/F, Co-Prod **(CESAR)**; *ATLANTIC CITY,* Th, 79, CDN/USA, Co-Exec Prod; *ICE CASTLES,* Th, 78, USA, Prod; *SHADOW OF THE HAWK,* Th, 76, CDN, Prod; *WHITE LINE FEVER,* Th, 75/74, USA, Prod; *THE APPRENTICESHIP OF DUDDY KRAVITZ,* Th, 74/73, CDN, Prod **(CFA)**; *THE WORLD OF ENRICO FERMI,* ED, 69/66, USA, Res/Assoc Prod; *THE BEST DAMN FIDDLER FROM CALABOGIE TO KALADAR,* TV, 69, CDN, Prod **(CFA)**; *THE THINGS I CANNOT CHANGE,* TV, 69, CDN, Prod; *DON'T LET THE ANGELS FALL* (SEULS LES ENFANTS ETAIENT PRESENTS), Th, 68, CDN, Prod; *MEMORANDUM* (POUR MEMOIRE), TV, 66, CDN, Prod; *BETHUNE,* TV, 64-62, CDN, Res/Ed/Dir/Wr.

KENT, Laurence - see DIRECTORS

KENT, Patricia - see DIRECTORS

KENT, Paul - see DIRECTORS

KING, Allan - see DIRECTORS

KLEIN, Bonnie - see DIRECTORS

KLENMAN, Norman - see WRITERS

KONYVES, Tom

317 - 527 Commodore Rd., Vancouver, BC, CAN, V5Z 4G5. (604)877-1900. A M Video Productions, 590 West Broadway, Vancouver, BC, CAN, V5Z 1E9. (604) 875-9927.
Types of Production & Categories: TV Video-Prod/Dir.
Genres: Documentary-TV; Educational-TV; Experimental-TV.
Biography: Born 1947, Budapest, Hungary; Canadian citizen; speaks English, French. Published poet.
Selective Filmography: *PROFILE OF AN ARTIST: PNINA GRANIRER,* TV, 86, CDN, Prod; *THE LAST DEBATE: HOFFMAN AND RUBIN,* TV, 86, CDN, Prod; *DANCING IN THE STREET,* TV, 86, CDN, Prod/Dir; *O VANCOUVER!,* In, 86, CDN, Prod/Dir; *CANADIAN-CHINESE ART FESTIVAL,* ED, 86, CDN, Prod/Dir; *CANADIAN-JAPANESE ART FESTIVAL,* ED, 85, CDN, Prod; *BILL VAZAN: COSMOGRAPHE,* TV, 82, CDN, Prod/Dir; *THE BEST OF THE 3rd INT'L MIME FESTIVAL,* ED, 82, CDN, Prod/Dir; *CHRIS BURDEN: AN*
(cont/suite)

STCQ

The only union in Québec representing all freelance movie technicians

Syndicat des Techniciennes et Techniciens du Cinéma du Québec

3449 rue St. Denis, Montréal, Québec,
Canada   H2X 3L1
Téléphone: **(514) 288-4365**

136

INTERVIEW, TV, 82, CDN, Prod/Dir; *LEAVING THE HOUSE: DEBORAH HAY,* TV, 81, CDN, Prod/Dir; *'ART MONTREAL'* (6 eps), ED, 80, CDN, Prod.

KOOL, Allen

ACTRA, CFTA, DGA. Future Films Ltd., 41 Britain St., #101, Toronto, Ont, CAN, M5A 1R7. (416)869-3531.
Types of Production & Categories: Th Film-Prod/Dir; Th Short-Dir; TV Film-Prod/ Dir; TV Video-Prod/Dir.
Genres: Variety-Th&TV; Musical-Th&TV; Music Video-Th&TV.
Biography: Born 1940; Canadian citizen; Education: B.F.A.. President of Future Design & Communication; Futuremax Corporation; Blue Island Management (music mgmt.). *NO* won a Gold Medal, Miami Int'l Film Festival.
Selective Filmography: *IN THE HOUSE/DREAM RADIO,* MV, 86, CDN, Dir; *THE TRUTH ABOUT SHARKS,* TV, 86, CDN, Prod/Dir; *VIDEO QUEEN,* Th, 86, CDN/USA, Co-Prod/Dir; *STRAIGHT SHOT/WATCH OUT/WHY DON'T YOU TAKE IT,* MV, 86, CDN, Dir; *WILD AFRICA,* Th, 86, CDN, Prod/Dir; *I AM YOUR CHILD,* MV, 86/85, CDN, Exec Prod/Co-Prod/Dir; *GREAT WHITE SHARK,* Th, 86, CDN, Prod/Dir; *GREAT WHALES,* TV, 86, CDN, Prod/Dir; *FLOATING OVER CANADA,* TV, 85, CDN, Exec Prod/Co Prod; *SHARK REEF,* Th, 85, CDN, Prod/Dir; *BUTTERFLIES WITH WINGS,* Th, 85, CDN, Prod/Dir; *DEEP CUTS THE KNIFE/WE WERE WILD/TWO CAN PLAY/STAY IN THE LIGHT,* MV, 85, CDN, Dir; *THIS MAN,* Cm, 85, CDN, Dir; *'NATIONAL NEWS'* (CBC), (100 eps), TV, 84/83, CDN, Dir; *'SATURDAY REPORT'/ 'SUNDAY REPORT'* (CBC), (40 eps), TV, 84, CDN, Dir; *SEA NYMPH,* Th, 80, CDN, Co-Prod; *NO,* Th, 79, CDN, Prod; *THE ARABIA INCIDENT,* TV, 78, CDN, Co-Prod; *POINT OF VIEW,* Th, 78, CDN, Prod.

KOTCHEFF, Ted - see DIRECTORS
KOZY-KING, Joyce - see PRODUCTION MANAGERS
KRAMREITHER, Anthony

217 Arnold Ave., Thornhill, Ont, CAN, L4J 1C1. (416)881-5443. Brightstar Films Inc., 22 Front St.W., Toronto, Ont, CAN, M4J 1C4. (416)364-4321.
Types of Production & Categories: Th Film-Prod/Dir.
Genres: Drama-Th&TV; Comedy-Th&TV.
Biography: Born in Vienna, Austria; arrived in Canada, 1954. Acted in television shows and films in Europe and Canada.
Selective Filmography: *CONFIDENTIAL,* Th, 85, CDN, Prod; *DANCING IN THE DARK,* Th, 85, CDN, Prod; *THE MARK OF CAIN,* Th, 84, CDN, Prod; *FLYING,* Th, 84, CDN, Prod; *THRILLKILL,* Th, 83, CDN, Prod/Co-Dir; *FOR LADIES ONLY,* Th, 82, CDN, Prod/Dir; *AMERICAN NIGHTMARE,* Th, 82, CDN, Exec Prod; *HUMONGOUS,* Th, 81, CDN, Prod; *ALL IN GOOD TASTE,* Th, 80, CDN, Prod/Dir; *MONDO I/MONDO II,* Th, 79/78, CDN, Prod/Dir; *SOME DO IT FOR MONEY, SOME DO IT FOR FUN,* Th, 79/78, CDN, Prod/Dir; *DEADLY HARVEST,* Th, 77, CDN, Prod; *GIANT SPIDER INVASION,* Th, 76, CDN, Prod; *A SWEETER SONG* (SNAPSHOTS), Th, 75, CDN, Exec Prod; *LIONS FOR BREAKFAST,* Th, 74, CDN, Prod; *'FAMOUS NOBEL PRIZE WINNERS'* (4 eps), TV, 72, CDN/F/AUS/D, Prod.

KROITOR, Roman

Imax Systems Corporation, 38 Isabella St., Toronto, Ont, CAN, M4Y 1N1. (416) 960-8509.
Types of Production & Categories: Th Film-Prod/Dir.
Genres: Documentary-Th.
Biography: Born 1926, Yorkton, Saskatchewan. M.A., Philosophy, Psychology, University of Manitoba, 49. Began career at NFB; worked for CBC (60's) as producer/director of *CANDID EYE.* Co-founder, Multi Screen Corporation, 67;

(cont/suite)

PRODUCERS/PRODUCTEURS

returned to NFB in 75 to become Executive Producer of Studio B; went back to Imax Systems Corporation where he is now a Director and Vice President.
Selective Filmography: *WE ARE BORN OF STARS,* Th, 85, CDN, Wr/Co-Prod; *SKYWARD,* Th, 84/83, CDN, Prod; *FREEDOM TO MOVE,* Th, 84, CDN, Exec Prod; *HAIL COLUMBIA,* Th, 82, CDN, Co-Prod; *MAN BELONGS TO THE EARTH,* Th, 74, USA, Co-Prod; *CIRCUS WORLD,* Th, 74, USA, Prod/Dir; *TIGER CHILD,* Th, 70, CDN, Prod; *LABYRINTH* (EXPO 67), Th, 67, CDN, Co-Dir; *STRAVINSKY,* TV, 66, CDN, Co-Dir **(CFA)**; *ABOVE THE HORIZON,* Th, 65, CDN, Co-Dir **(CFA)**; *LONELY BOY,* Th, 62, CDN, Co-Dir **(CFA)**; *UNIVERSE,* Th, 60, CDN, Wr/Co-Dir **(2 CFA)**; *PAUL TOMKOWICZ,* Th, 52, CDN, Dir/Co-Wr.

KROONENBURG, Pieter

APFVQ. 656 de Gaspé, Nun's Island, Verdun, Que, CAN, H3E 1H1. Filmline Int'l Inc., 209 St-Paul W., 5th Fl., Montreal, Que, CAN, H2Y 2A1. (514)288-5888.
Types of Production & Categories: Th Film-Prod; TV Film-Prod.
Genres: Drama-Th&TV; Comedy-Th&TV; Action-Th&TV.
Biography: Born 1942, Castricum, Netherlands; went to the Film Academy, Amsterdam. Languages: English, French, Dutch, German. Has lived in Brussels, Rome and Paris, making films, TV series and commercials; moved to Canada, 79.
Selective Filmography: *THE BLUE MAN,* Th, 85, CDN, Prod; *TOBY McTEAGUE,* Th, 85, CDN, Co-Exec Prod; *BREAKING ALL THE RULES,* Th, 84, CDN, Co-Prod; *HOTEL NEW HAMPSHIRE,* Th, 83, USA, Co-Prod; *COOK & PEARY: THE RACE TO THE POLE,* TV, 83, USA, Line Prod; *CROSS-COUNTRY,* Th, 82, CDN, Co-Prod; *HEARTACHES,* Th, 81, CDN, Co-Prod; *THE LUCKY STAR,* Th, 80, CDN, Line Prod; *GIRLS,* Th, 79, CDN, Prod.

KROST, Roy

CFTA. Roy Krost Productions Ltd., 9 Deer Park Cr., #203, Toronto, Ont, CAN, M4V 2C4. (416)964-2838.
Types of Production & Categories: Th Film-Prod; TV Film-Prod; TV Video-Prod.
Genres: Drama-Th; Musical-TV; Educational-TV; Children's-Th&TV.
Biography: Born London, England. Has produced and directed numerous award-winning industrial and educational films: Chris Award (Columbus) for *DON'T TAKE CHANCES*; *THE NUTCRACKER, A FANTASY ON ICE* was nominated for an Emmy, 85.
Selective Filmography: *MAGICAL MUSICAL DAYS,* TV, 85, CDN, Prod/Co-Dir; *MARTIN'S DAY,* Th, 83, CDN/GB, Co-Prod; *NUTCRACKER, FANTASY ON ICE,* TV, 83, CDN, Prod **(CFTA)**; *NIKKI, WILD DOG OF THE NORTH,* Th, 60, CDN, Co-Prod.

LAFFEY, Barbara

ACFTP. Paragon Motion Pictures, 260 Richmond St.W., Ste. 405, Toronto, Ont, CAN, M5V 1W5. (416)977-2929.
Types of Production & Categories: Th Film-PM; TV Film-Prod.
Genres: Drama-TV; Action-TV; Horror-Th&TV.
Biography: Born Chicago, Illinois; landed immigrant, Canada. Attended University of Illinois and Ontario College of Art. Freelance production manager, 1st AD for 10 years; Director of Production, Paragon Motion Pictures since 85.
Selective Filmography: *'ALFRED HITCHCOCK PRESENTS'* (7 eps), TV, 86, CDN, Prod; *'PHILIP MARLOWE PRIVATE EYE'* (6 eps), TV, 86/85, CDN, Line Prod; *THRESHOLD,* Th, 80, CDN, PM; *IMPROPER CHANNELS,* Th, 79, CDN, PM.

LAGAUCHE, Christian - voir REALISATEURS
LAGER, Martin - see WRITERS

LAJOIE, Bernard

3620 Ridgewood, #321, Montréal, Qué, CAN. (514)733-6644. Les Productions Pascal Blais, 640 St-Paul ouest, #200, Montréal, Qué, CAN, H3C 1L9. (514)866-7272.
Types de production et Catégories: TV vidéo-Prod.
Types d'oeuvres: Animation-TV; Annonces-TV.
Curriculum vitae: Né en 1959, Trois-Rivières, Québec; bilingue; Bac. en Administration. Producteur, annonces TV en animation depuis 83; Vice-président, Les Productions Pascal Blais. Animation et effets spéciaux pour le long métrage *THE PEANUT BUTTER SOLUTION.*

LAMB, Duncan

ATPD. 2265 Queen St.E., #32, Toronto, Ont, CAN, M4E 1G3. (416)698-9487. CBC, Box 500, Stn. A, Toronto, Ont, CAN, M5W 1E6. (416)975-7101.
Types of Production & Categories: TV Video-Prod.
Genres: Drama-TV; Comedy-TV.
Biography: Born 1945, England; Canadian citizen. Graduate, Radio & TV Arts, Ryerson Polytechnical Institute, 68.
Selective Filmography: *'SEEING THINGS'* (24 eps), TV, 86-83, CDN, Assoc Prod; *READY FOR SLAUGHTER/MOVING TARGETS/ OUT OF SIGHT OUT OF MIND,* 'FOR THE RECORD', TV, 82, CDN, Assoc Prod; *'HOME FIRES'* (Assoc Prod-15 eps), (5 eps), TV, 82-80, CDN, Prod; *'THE PHOENIX TEAM'* (8 eps), TV, 80, CDN, Pro Coord; *'FOR THE RECORD'* (10 eps), TV, 80-77, CDN, Pro Coord; *RIEL,* TV, 78, CDN, Pro Coord; *'SIDESTREET'* (24 eps), TV, 78-75, CDN, Pro Coord; *BETHUNE,* TV, 76, CDN, Serv Prod; *THE VICTIM/ THE LIE CHAIR/ MICRODRAMAS,* 'PEEP SHOW', TV, 75, CDN, Serv Prod; *OVERLAID,* TV, 75, CDN, Serv Prod; *TURNCOAT,* TV, 75, CDN, Serv Prod.

LAMBERT, Jacques

APFVQ, SMPTE. 3741 rue Prieur est, Montréal Nord, Qué, CAN, H1H 2L7. (514) 328-6029. Lambert, Lepage, Labbé, 3275 rue Prieur est, Montréal nord, Qué, CAN, H1H 2K4. (514)322-0630.
Types de production et Catégories: c métrage-Prod.
Types d'oeuvres: Industriel-TV.
Curriculum vitae: Né en 1940. Langues: français, anglais, portugais. Cofondateur, Lambert, Lepage, Labbé Inc.; Président directeur-général depuis 75.
Filmographie sélective: *LA LAURENTIENNE GENERALE/ENERGIE MINES ET RESSOURCES CANADA,* In, 86/85, CDN, Prod; *MONTREAL REAL ESTATE BOARD/METRO-RICHELIEU,* In, 86, CDN, Prod; *ULTRAMAR MERCIER-LECLERC,* In, 86, CDN, Prod.

LAMY, Pierre

33 rue Jolivent, Beloeil, Qué, CAN, J3G 2C9. (514)467-5514. Régie du Cinéma, 360 rue McGill, Montréal, Qué, CAN, H2Y 2E9. (514)873-6254.
Types de production et Catégories: l métrage-Prod; TV film-Prod.
Types d'oeuvres: Drame-C; Comédie-C; Documentaire-TV.
Curriculum vitae: Né à Montréal, Québec; bilingue. Récipiendaire du Prix Albert Tessier, 81; Prix Air Canada de l'Académie du cinéma canadien, 82.
Filmographie sélective: *LA DAME EN COULEURS* (OUR LADY OF THE PAINTS), C, 85, CDN, Prod; *CONTRECOEUR,* C, 80, CDN, Prod exéc/Prod dél; *'LA TERRE DE L'HOMME'* (3 ém), TV, 80-78, CDN, Prod exéc; *LE SOLEIL SE LEVE EN RETARD,* C, 77, CDN, Prod; *WHO HAS SEEN THE WIND,* C, 76, CDN, Prod exéc; *CHANSON POUR JULIE,* C, 75, CDN, Prod; *THE FAR SHORE,* C, 75, CDN, Prod exéc; *POUR LE MEILLEUR ET POUR LE PIRE,* C, 75, CDN, Prod; *LA TETE DE NORMANDE ST-ONGE,* C, 75, CDN, Prod; *IL ETAIT UNE FOIS DANS L'EST,* C, 74, CDN, Prod exéc; *LES CORPS*

(cont/suite)

CELESTES, C, 73, CDN, Prod exéc; *GINA,* C, 73, CDN, Prod; *KAMOURASKA,* C, 72, CDN/F, Co prod; *LA MORT D'UN BUCHERON,* C, 72, CDN, Prod; *LA MAUDITE GALETTE,* C, 72, CDN, Prod; *LES SMATTES,* C, 72, CDN, Prod; *LA VRAIE NATURE DE BERNADETTE,* C, 72, CDN, Prod exéc; *LES MALES,* C, 70, CDN, Prod; *DEUX FEMMES EN OR,* C, 70, CDN, Prod.

LANG, Robert

104 Bellevue Ave., Toronto, Ont, CAN, M5T 2N9. (416)968-2697. Kensington Communications, 490 Adelaide St.W., #304, Toronto, Ont, CAN, M5V 1T4. (416) 362-9822.
Types of Production & Categories: TV Film-Prod/Dir/Cin.
Genres: Drama-TV; Documentary-TV; Educational-TV.
Biography: Born 1949, Montreal, Quebec. B.A., English and Theatre, Queen's University; Post B.A. Diploma, Communications, Concordia U., 70. Has worked on more than 30 productions in 15 years as director, writer, editor, cinematographer in North America, Europe, Africa and Asia; owned Kensington Communications since 80. Has won awards at Columbus, Yorkton and American film festivals.
Selective Filmography: *FRAGILE HARVEST,* TV, 85, CDN, Prod/Dir; *MOVING THE BANYAN TREE,* TV, 84, CDN, Prod/Dir/Cin; *BANGLADESH FROM THE RIVER,* TV, 84, CDN, Prod/Dir/Cin; *FAMILY BURDEN,* In, 83, CDN, Prod/Dir; *JOE DAVID/SPIRIT OF THE MASK,* TV, 82, CDN, Prod/Dir/Cin; *CHILDHOOD'S END,* TV, 81, CDN, Prod/Dir; *RIDLEY: A SECRET GARDEN,* ED, 81, CDN, Dir; *TAKING CHANCES,* ED, 79, CDN, Dir/Wr; *AN EASY PILL TO SWALLOW,* TV, 78, CDN, Dir/Wr; *POTATOES,* TV, 76, CDN, Dir/Ed; *A GREAT TREE HAS FALLEN,* TV, 73, CDN, Prod/Dir/Cin; *THREE MEN,* TV, 72, CDN, Dir; *'SOCIAL ECONOMIC DISPARITIES'* (12 eps), ED, 72, CDN, Pro Coord.

LANSING, Floyd - see DIRECTORS

LANTOS, Robert

Alliance Entertaiment Corp., 92 Isabella St., Toronto, Ont, CAN, M4Y 1N4. (416) 967-1174.
Types of Production & Categories: Th Film-Prod; TV Film-Prod.
Genres: Drama-Th&TV; Comedy-Th&TV; Musical-Th&TV; Action-Th&TV.
Biography: Born 1949, Budapest, Hungary; emigrated to Uruguay, 58; Canada, 63. B.A., Honours English, McGill University. Co-founder, RSL Entertainment Corporation, 75; partner, producer, Alliance Entertainment Corp. since 85; also theatrical producer. Past Chairman, Academy of Canadian Cinema & Television. *JOSHUA THEN AND NOW* and *NIGHT MAGIC* were both official selections for Cannes.
Selective Filmography: *THE SWORD OF GIDEON* (mini-series), TV, 86, CDN, Prod; *'NIGHT HEAT'* (39 eps), TV, 86-84, CDN, Co-Spv Prod; *SEPARATE VACATIONS,* Th, 85, CDN, Co-Prod; *THE EXECUTION OF RAYMOND GRAHAM,* TV, 85, CDN, Exec Prod; *NIGHT MAGIC,* Th, 84, CDN/F, Co-Prod; *JOSHUA THEN AND NOW,* Th, 84, CDN, Co-Prod; *HEAVENLY BODIES,* Th, 83, CDN, Co-Prod; *BEDROOM EYES,* Th, 83, CDN, Co-Prod; *ONE NIGHT ONLY,* TV, 83, CDN, Co-Prod; *PERFECT TIMING,* TV, 83, CDN, Co-Prod; *OVERDRAWN AT THE MEMORY BANK,* TV, 83, CDN/USA, Co-Prod; *PARADISE,* Th, 81, CDN/IL, Co-Prod; *YOUR TICKET IS NO LONGER VALID,* Th, 79, CDN, Co-Prod; *SUZANNE,* Th, 79, CDN, Co-Prod; *AGENCY,* Th, 78, CDN, Co-Prod; *IN PRAISE OF OLDER WOMEN,* Th, 77, CDN, Co-Prod; *L'ANGE ET LA FEMME,* Th, 77, CDN, Co-Prod.

LAPOINTE, Paul

SGCT. 13 Kerr Rd., TH-2, Toronto, Ont, CAN, M4L 1R2. (416)463-5161. ONF, 65 Adelaide St.E., 2nd Fl., Toronto, Ont, CAN, M5C 1K6. (416)973-2225.
(cont/suite)

PRODUCTEURS/PRODUCERS

Types de production et Catégories: c métrage-Prod; TV film-Prod.
Types d'oeuvres: Drame-C; Documentaire-C&TV.
Curriculum vitae: Né en 1949, Ile d'Orléans, Québec; bilingue. Etudes spécialisées en photographie et cinéma, Ryerson Polytechnical Institute. Chargé de la production française, ONF, Toronto, 80-86.
Filmographie sélective: *PAYS DE SABLE*, C, 86, CDN, Prod; *'20 ANS EXPRESS'* (12 eps), TV, 85, CDN, Prod exéc; *METALLO BLUES*, C, 84, CDN, Prod; *UN GARS D'LA PLACE*, C, 83, CDN, Prod; *LE CERF-VOLANTISTE*, C, 83, CDN, Prod; *UN PERE NOEL D'OCCASION*, C, 82, CDN, Prod; *L'AGE DES PIGEONS*, C, 81, CDN, Prod; *8400 SKIS*, C, 80, CDN, Prod; *'LOISIRS DE L'ACTUEL'* (26 eps), TV, 79, CDN, Rech; *J'AI BESOIN D'UN NOM*, C, 78, CDN, Réal.

LAUGHLIN, Linda
ATPD. 1189 Avenue Rd., Toronto, Ont, CAN, M5N 2G2. CBTL, 500 Church St, Toronto, Ont, CAN, M4Y 2C8. (416)975-5718.
Types of Production & Categories: TV Film-Prod; TV Video-Prod.
Genres: Documentary-TV; Educational-Th&TV.
Biography: Born 1948, Toronto, Ontario. Education: B.A., B.Ed., University of Toronto.
Selective Filmography: *BETTER BUSINESS BUREAU/NO ACCESS/LEGACY OF PAIN/GREY GOLD*, 'MONITOR', TV, 86/85, CDN, Prod; *FACE VALUE/VIAL THREATS*, 'MONITOR', TV, 85, CDN, Prod; *MUCH MOSES*, 'GZOWSKI & CO', TV, 85, CDN, Prod; *WANTED MAN*, 'MONITOR', TV, 84, CDN, Prod (**ANIK**); *POLICE CHASE*, 'THE JOURNAL', TV, 84, CDN, Prod; *FALSE PROMISE*, 'W5', TV, 84, CDN, Prod; *SHELTERED WORKSHOPS*, 'W5', TV, 83, CDN, Res.

LAURIER, Nicole
APFVQ, SARDEC, UDA. Ciné-Doc inc., 906 rue Cherrier, Montréal, Qué, CAN, H2L 1H7. (514)524-9444.
Types de production et Catégories: c métrage-Prod/Réal/Sc; TV film-Prod/Réal/Sc; TV vidéo-Prod/Sc.
Types d'oeuvres: Drame-C&TV; Documentaire-C&TV; Education-C&TV; Enfants-TV.
Curriculum vitae: Née en 1946, Montréal, Québec; bilingue. Maitrise, Sciences politiques, universités de Montréal et McGill; Baccalauréat, Sciences politiques, mineure en théâtre, Université Laval; formation en scénarisation interactive et production de vidéodisque, Université du Nébraska; études littéraires et théâtrales, UQAM; productrice responsable d'une quarantaine de documentaires; auteur de plusieurs articles et scénarios.
Filmographie sélective: *LES INFECTIONS INTRA-ABDOMINALES/COMMUNITY-ACQUIRED*, In, 86, CDN, Prod; *JOB INTERVIEWS: STRATEGIES AND TACTICS/L'ENTREVUE*, ED, 85, CDN, Prod; *AU PAYS DES FRAISES ETERNELLES/APPRENDRE A APPRENDRE*, ED, 85, CDN, Prod/Co réal/Sc; *NOUVEAUX VOISINS, VOISINS LOINTAINS*, ED, 85, CDN, Prod/Co réal/Sc; *LA COOPERATION CANADIENNE AU ZAIRE*, ED, 85, CDN, Prod/Co réal/Sc; *LES JEUNES CONTREVENANTS/OU LA CONNAISSANCE DEVIENT RESPECT*, ED, 84, CDN, Prod; *LA MEDECINE AUSCULTEE*, 'LES BEAUX DIMANCHES', TV, 82, CDN, Sc/Anim; *LE TRAVAIL A TEMPS PARTIEL/RESIDENCE: BIERMANS*, TV, 81, CDN, Rech/Interv; *'MOI AUSSI, JE PARLE FRANCAIS'* (13 eps), TV, 79-77, CDN/F/S, Sc/Rech/Interv; *'CONSOMMATEURS AVERTIS'* (26 eps), TV, 77, CDN, Interv; *'UN MAILLON DE LA CHAINE'* (10 eps), TV, 77/76, CDN, Rech/Interv; *'FEMMES D'AUJOURD'HUI'* (40 eps), TV, 75-73, CDN, Rech/Interv; *'LA SUPERFRANCOFETE'* (8 eps), TV, 74, CDN, Interv; *'KALEIDOSCOPE'* (7 eps), TV, 73, CDN, Rech/Interv.

PRODUCERS/PRODUCTEURS

LAVOIE, Patricia

Voila Productions, 1425 Dorchester W., Ste.400, Montreal, Que, CAN, H3G 1T7. (514)875-5477.
Types of Production & Categories: TV Film-Prod/Dir; TV Video-Prod/Dir.
Genres: Documentary-TV; Educational-TV; Children's-TV; Animation-TV.
Biography: Canadian citizen; bilingual. B.A., Honours, French, Literature, University of Western Ontario and U. of Strasbourg, France; Post B.A. Diploma, Communication Arts, Concordia U..
Selective Filmography: *'SESAME STREET'* (50 seg), TV, 86-72, USA, Dir/Wr; *VIA CANADA*, In, 85, CDN, Prod/Dir; *'NOW!'* (20 eps), TV, 85/84, CDN, Prod/Dir; *FAMILIPRIX/LAISSONS-LES-RIRE/SAVOUPLAIT,* Cm, 85, CDN, Dir; *'MOI AUSSI, J'ECRASE'* (3 eps), TV, 83, CDN, Prod.

LEE, Patrick

227 1/2 Brock Ave., Toronto, Ont, CAN, M6K 2L8. (416)531-3896. Interaxis Visual Systems Inc., 119 Spadina Ave., 10th Fl., Toronto, Ont, CAN, M5V 2L1. (416)598-5300.
Types of Production & Categories: TV Film-Prod; TV Video-Prod.
Genres: Documentary-TV; Educational-TV; Children's-TV.
Biography: Born 1947, London, England; Canadian citizen. B.A., University of Toronto, 68; London Film School, 70. Editor, 72-80; producer, 80-86; also produces videodisks. Taught film production, Niagara College, 80; media, Sheridan College, 85-86. *HEALTHWISE* won a Blue Ribbon, American Film Festival, 81.
Selective Filmography: *SHIELD OF THE HOMELAND,* TV, 84, CDN, Prod; *'WORKING'* (4 eps), ED, 83, CDN, Assoc Prod; *'HEALTHWISE'* (13 eps), ED, 80, CDN, Prod/Dir.

LEEBOSH, Vivienne

CFTA. 9010 Norma Place, Los Angeles, CA, USA, 90069. (213)858-6006. Thomlee Productions, 365 Markham St., Toronto, Ont, CAN, M6G 2K8. (416)922-8700.
Types of Production & Categories: Th Film-Prod; TV Film-Prod.
Genres: Drama-Th&TV; Action-Th&TV; Documentary-TV.
Selective Filmography: *TICKET TO HEAVEN,* Th, 82, CDN, Prod **(GENIE)**; *EVERY PERSON IS GUILTY,* 'FOR THE RECORD', TV, 80, CDN, Prod; *WOMEN IN CUBA,* Th, 78, CDN, Prod.

LEGER, Neil

APFVQ. Téléscène Productions Inc., 360 Place Royale, Montreal, Que, CAN, H2Y 2V1. (514)288-1638.
Types of Production & Categories: Th Film-Prod; TV Film-Prod; TV Video-Prod.
Genres: Action-Th; Documentary-Th&TV; Animation-Th&TV; Commercials-TV.
Biography: Born 1941, St-Isidore de Prescott, Ontario; bilingual. President, Executive producer, Téléscène Productions, Montreal. *COMME LES AUTRES ET UN PEU PLUS* won a Bronze Award (NY); Silver Award for *DOWNHILL ANYWAY YOU CAN*; several awards for commercials.
Selective Filmography: *KEEPING TRACK,* Th, 85, CDN, Exec Prod; *DOWNHILL ANYWAY YOU CAN* (PAR DELA DES PENTES), TV, 84/83, CDN, Prod/Exec Prod; *COMMES LES AUTRES ET UN PEU PLUS,* TV, 81, CDN, Exec Prod; *HOCKEY NIGHT IN CANADA,* TV, 75-71, CDN, Exec Prod; *MONTREAL MATIN/EATON/NATIONAL TYPEWRITER/MAN AND HIS WORLD,* Cm, 68-65, CDN, Exec Prod.

LEIGH, Norman - see CINEMATOGRAPHERS

LEITERMAN, Douglas

Motion Picture Guarantors Inc., 14 Birch Ave., Toronto, Ont, CAN, M4V 1C9. (416)968-0577.
Types of Production & Categories: Th Film-Prod; Th Short-Prod; TV Film-Prod/Dir; TV Video-Prod/Dir/Wr.
Genres: Drama-Th&TV; Comedy-Th&TV; Action-Th&TV; Documentary-Th&TV.
Biography: Born South Porcupine, Ontario. Graduated Economics, Political Science, University of British Columbia; post graduate studies in law and economics as Nieman Fellow, Harvard, 53-54. Parliamentary and overseas correspondent, Southam News Service; reporter, editorial and business writer for the 'Vancouver Province'. Chairman and CEO of Motion Picture Guarantors Inc. since 77; chairman of Hobel Leiterman Communications Ltd., Document Associates Inc. of Toronto and New York, Entertainment Securities Ltd., The Mixing House Ltd., since 68; Board Chairman and CEO, Wired City Communications Ltd., 70-78. Has won 3 Wilderness Awards, 3 Ohio Awards, Gold Award (Atlanta).
Selective Filmography: *BY DESIGN*, Th, 80, CDN, Exec Prod; *SURFACING*, Th, 79, CDN, Exec Prod; *'THE SENSATIONAL SEVENTIES'* (12 eps), TV, 78/77, CDN, Co-Prod; *'HUMAN RESOURCES'* (13 eps), TV, 77, CDN, Co-Prod; *KENNEDY'S DON'T CRY*, Th, 75, CDN, Co-Prod; *'WILD REFUGE'* (13 eps), TV, 75, CDN, Co-Prod; *'YOUTH UNDER THE INFLUENCE'* (13 eps), TV, 75, CDN, Co-Prod; *'TARGET IMPOSSIBLE'* (26 eps), TV, 74, CDN, Co-Prod; *'HERE COME THE SEVENTIES'* (TOWARDS THE YEAR 2000), TV, 73-70, CDN, Co-Prod; *'NORTH AMERICAN SEASONS'* (4 eps), TV, 72, CDN, Co-Prod; *THE CREW*, TV, 69, USA, Dir; *'CBS NEWS'*, TV, 69-66, USA, Prod; *FASTEN YOUR SEATBELTS*, TV, 68, CDN/USA, Dir/Prod; *RESURRECTION CITY*, TV, 68, CDN/USA, Co-Dir/Prod; *THE OLD COLLEGE TRY*, TV, 67, CDN, Dir/Prod (**EMMY**); *DEMOCRATS IN '66*, TV, 66, USA, Dir/Prod; *YOUTH IN SEARCH OF MORALITY*, TV, 66, CDN, Co-Dir/Prod; *'THIS HOUR HAS SEVEN DAYS'* (60 eps), TV, 66-64, CDN, Exec Prod; *STRIKE: MEN AGAINST COMPUTERS*, TV, 65, CDN, Prod; *ONE MORE RIVER*, TV, 64, CDN/USA/GB, Co-Dir/Prod; *THE CHIEF: DIEF*, TV, 63, CDN, Dir/Prod; *THREE ON A MATCH*, TV, 63, CDN, Dir/Prod; *BRITISH GUIANA*, TV, 62, CDN, Dir/Prod; *SERVANT OF ALL*, TV, 62, CDN, Dir/Prod; *BALANCE OF TERROR*, TV, 62, USA, Dir/Prod; *FORTY MILLION SHOES*, 'INTERTEL', TV, 61, CDN, Dir/Prod; *REPORT FROM THE WASTELAND OF TV/U.N. IN PERIL: THE CONGO*, 'THE CRITICAL YEARS', TV, 61/60, CDN, Dir/Prod; *THE AMERICAN PRESIDENCY*, 'THE CRITICAL YEARS', TV, 61, CDN, Dir; *THREE FEET OF EARTH: NUCLEAR EXTINCTION*, TV, 59, CDN, Prod/Dir; *INDIA: REVOLUTION BY CONSENT*, TV, 59, CDN, Prod.

LEUNG, Annette

1339 Meadowlands Dr., #714, Ottawa, Ont, CAN, K2E 7D4. (613)225-6087. CBC, Box 3220, Stn. C, Ottawa, Ont, CAN, K1Y 1E4. (613)724-5006.
Types of Production & Categories: TV Film-Prod; TV Video-Prod.
Genres: Documentary-TV; Current Affairs-TV.
Biography: Born Hong Kong; Canadian citizen. Languages: English, Chinese (Cantonese), some French. B.A., (Sociology), Honours Bachelor of Journalism, Carleton University; Motion Picture Production Program, Algonquin College. Work experience: CBC TV, producer, news and current affairs programs, documentary specials.

LEVENE, Sam

ATPD. 954 Logan Ave., Toronto, Ont, CAN, M4K 3E5. (416)463-6488. CBC, Box 500, Stn. A, Toronto, Ont, CAN, M5W 1E6. (416)975-7139.
Types of Production & Categories: TV Film-Prod; TV Video-Prod.
Genres: Drama-TV; Documentary-TV; Current Affairs-TV.

(cont/suite)

Biography: Born 1936, Kitchener, Ontario. B.A., M.A., Northwestern University, Chicago. Began working in radio and theatre while still a student, then into TV; producer with CBC since mid-60's, current affairs, documentaries, drama. Won a Blue Ribbon, American Film Fest. for *ONE OF OUR OWN*; Silver Award, American F.F., for *A FAR CRY FROM HOME;* Banff Int'l TV Fest., Best Drama Special, *FINAL EDITION;* Chris Bronze Plaque, Columbus, *FRIENDS OF A FEATHER.*
Selective Filmography: *TWELFTH NIGHT,* TV, 85, CDN, Exec Prod/Prod; *ONE FOR THE POT,* TV, 85, CDN, Exec Prod/Prod; *HOME FREE* (pilot), TV, 85, CDN, Prod/Co-Creator; *JOSHUA THEN AND NOW* (TV version), TV, 85, CDN, Pro Exec; *9-B,* TV, 85, CDN, Exec Prod; *TARTUFFE,* TV, 84, CDN, Exec Prod/ Prod; *FRIENDS OF A FEATHER,* TV, 84, CDN, Exec Prod/Prod; *AS YOU LIKE IT,* TV, 83, CDN, Exec Prod/Prod; *'VANDERBERG'* (6 eps), TV, 83/82, CDN, Exec Prod/Prod; *THE TEMPEST,* TV, 82, CDN, Exec Prod/Prod; *TAKEOVER,* TV, 82, CDN, Exec Prod/Prod; *REASONABLE FORCE/BLIND FAITH/BY REASON OF INSANITY,* 'FOR THE RECORD', TV, 82, CDN, Exec Prod; *THE TAMING OF THE SHREW,* TV, 81, CDN, Exec Prod; *FINAL EDITION/ SNOWBIRD/LYON'S DEN,* 'FOR THE RECORD', TV, 81/80, CDN, Exec Prod/ Prod; *RUNNING MAN/A FAR CRY FROM HOME/MAINTAIN THE RIGHT/ ONE OF OUR OWN,* 'FOR THE RECORD', TV, 80/79, CDN, Exec Prod; *THE WINNINGS OF FRANKIE WALLS/EVERY PERSON IS GUILTY,* 'FOR THE RECORD', TV, 80/79, CDN, Exec Prod; *CERTAIN PRACTICES,* 'FOR THE RECORD', TV, 79, CDN, Exec Prod **(GENIE);** *DON'T FORGET, JE ME SOUVIENS/CEMENTHEAD,* 'FOR THE RECORD', TV, 79, CDN, Exec Prod; *'OUR FELLOW AMERICANS'* (Dir-5 eps/Prod-8 eps), (10 eps), TV, 76/75, CDN, Exec Prod; *LETTER FROM PARIS,* 'GALLERY', TV, 75, CDN, Prod/Dir; *'GALLERY'* (30 eps), TV, 75-73, CDN, Exec Prod; *RAILROADS EAST - RAILROADS WEST,* TV, 74, CDN, Prod/Co-Wr; *'TELESCOPE'* (72 eps), TV, 73-70, CDN, Prod; *'MAN ALIVE'* (10 eps), TV, 70/69, CDN, Co-Prod; *'THE WAY IT IS'* (26 eps), TV, 68/67, CDN, Sr Prod; *'THE PUBLIC EYE'* (52 eps), TV, 67-65, CDN, Prod; *'THIS HOUR HAS SEVEN DAYS'* (26 eps), TV, 65/64, CDN, Story Ed; *'THE PIERRE BERTON SHOW'* (390 eps), TV, 64-62, CDN, Assoc Prod.

LEVY, Ira - see DIRECTORS

LILLIE, Ronald

Lauron Productions Ltd., 56 Shaftesbury Ave., Toronto, Ont, CAN, M4T 1A3. **(416)967-6503.**
Types of Production & Categories: Th Film-Prod; Th Short-Prod; TV Film-Prod; TV Video-Prod.
Genres: Drama-Th&TV; Comedy-Th&TV; Action-Th&TV; Documentary-Th&TV.
Biography: Born 1938; Canadian citizen. Education: Radio & TV Arts, Ryerson Polytechnical Institute. *NO SURRENDER* won the Festival of Festivals International Critics Award.
Selective Filmography: *LOYALTIES,* Th, 85, CDN/GB, Co-Prod; *NO SURRENDER,* Th, 85, CDN/GB, Co-Prod; *ISAAC LITTLEFEATHERS,* Th, 84, CDN, Exec Prod.

LINK, André

Cinépix Inc., 8275 Mayrand, Montreal, Que, CAN, H4P 2C8. (514)342-2340.
Types of Production & Categories: Th Film-Prod.
Genres: Drama-Th; Comedy-Th; Science Fiction-Th; Horror-Th.
Biography: Born Montreal, Quebec; bilingual. Co-founder and President of Cinepix Inc.
Selective Filmography: *NATIONAL PARK,* Th, 86, CDN, Co-Prod; *MEATBALLS III,* Th, 84, CDN, Exec Prod; *THE VINDICATOR* (FRANKENSTEIN FACTOR), Th, 84, CDN, Co-Prod; *THE SURROGATE,* Th, 83, CDN, Co-Exec

(cont/suite)

Prod; *SPACEHUNTER: ADVENTURES IN THE FORBIDDEN ZONE*, Th, 83, CDN/USA, Co-Prod; *MY BLOODY VALENTINE*, Th, 80, CDN, Co-Prod; *HAPPY BIRTHDAY TO ME*, Th, 80, CDN, Co-Prod; *YESTERDAY* (GABRIELLE), Th, 79, CDN, Co-Prod; *MEATBALLS*, Th, 79, CDN, Co-Exec Prod; *HOT DOGS*, Th, 79, CDN, Co-Prod; *BLACKOUT*, Th, 77, CDN, Co-Exec Prod; *RABID*, Th, 76, CDN, Co-Exec Prod; *DEATH WEEKEND* (THE HOUSE BY THE LAKE), Th, 75, CDN, Co-Exec Prod; *THE MYSTERY OF THE MILLION DOLLAR HOCKEY PUCK*, Th, 75, CDN, Co-Prod; *THE PARASITE MURDERS* (SHIVERS), Th, 74, CDN, Co-Prod; *TOUT FEU TOUT FEMME*, Th, 74, CDN, Co-Prod; *ACROSS THIS LAND WITH STOMPIN' TOM CONNORS*, Th, 73, CDN, Co-Prod; *L'HEPTMARON*, Th, 73, CDN/F, Co-Prod; *KEEP IT IN THE FAMILY*, Th, 72, CDN, Co-Prod; *HAVING A LAUGH*, Th, 71, CDN, Co-Prod; *LE DIABLE EST PARMI NOUS*, Th, 71, CDN, Co-Prod; *LOVE IN A FOUR-LETTER WORLD*, Th, 70, CDN, Co-Prod; *PILE OU FACE*, Th, 70, CDN, Co-Prod; *L'AMOUR HUMAIN*, Th, 70, CDN, Co-Prod; *INITIATION*, Th, 69, CDN, Co-Prod; *VALERIE*, Th, 68, CDN, Co-Prod.

LOCKE, Jeannine

ATPD. 12 Belmont St., Toronto, Ont, CAN, M5R 1P8. CBC, Box 500, Stn. A, Toronto, Ont, CAN, M5W 1E6. (416)975-6866.
Types of Production & Categories: TV Film-Prod/Dir/Wr.
Genres: Drama-TV; Documentary-TV.
Biography: Born Indian Head, Saskatchewan. M.A., English, University of Saskatchewan. Editorial writer, 'Ottawa Citizen'; staff writer, 'Chatelaine'; London Bureau Chief, 'Toronto Star'; producer/director/writer, CBC. Her films have won awards at Banff, New York and Columbus film festivals.
Selective Filmography: *ISLAND LOVE SONG*, TV, 86, CDN, Prod/Wr; *THE OTHER KINGDOM* (mini-series), TV, 84, CDN, Prod/Wr; *ALL THE DAYS OF MY LIFE*, TV, 82/81, CDN, Prod/Wr; *CHAUTAUQUA GIRL*, TV, 82, CDN, Prod/Wr (**ACTRA**); *YOU'VE COME A LONG WAY KATIE* (mini-series), (Wr-parts 1, 3), TV, 80/79, CDN, Prod; *THE QUIETER REVOLUTION*, TV, 78, CDN, Prod/Dir; *THE CANADIAN MONARCHY*, TV, 77, CDN, Prod/Dir; *THE WOODSWORTH PHENOMENON*, TV, 76, CDN, Prod/Dir; *THE FAMILY PRINCE*, TV, 75, CDN, Prod/Dir; *A CELEBRATION/PERCEPTIONS OF FRANCE/DEFENDING THE PEACEABLE ISLES*, 'PEOPLE OF OUR TIME', TV, 74, CDN, Prod/Dir; *TOO MUCH OF A TERRIBLE BEAUTY/IN REMEMBRANCE: STEWART ALSOR*, 'PEOPLE OF OUR TIME', TV, 74/73, CDN, Prod/Dir; *THE VASSAR GIRL/3 1/2 CHEERS FOR TORONTO/ GUARDIAN OF DREAMS*, 'PEOPLE OF OUR TIME', TV, 73, CDN, Prod/Dir; *GOODBYE JOEY*, TV, 72, CDN, Prod/Dir; *THE GLORY AND THE HOPE*, TV, 71, CDN, Prod/Dir; *HELLO FROM NIAGARA FALLS!*, TV, 71, CDN, Prod/Dir; *TO DIE TODAY*, TV, 70, CDN, Prod/Dir; *NOTHING TO HIDE*, TV, 70, CDN, Prod/Dir; *THE GREEN, THE ORANGE AND THE WHITE*, TV, 70, CDN, Prod/Dir.

LOUBERT, Patrick

Nelvana Ltd., 32 Atlantic Ave., Toronto, Ont, CAN, M6K 1X6. (416)588-5571.
Types of Production & Categories: Th Film-Prod; TV Film-Prod; TV Video-Prod.
Genres: Children's-Th&TV; Animation-Th&TV.
Biography: Co-founder, President, Nelvana Ltd.. Recipient of many awards including Wilderness, Chris, a Special Award at the Canadian Film Awards, 78; *THE CARE BEARS MOVIE* won the Golden Reel Award, 86.
Selective Filmography: 'THE EDISON TWINS' (39 eps), TV, 86-83, CDN, Co-Prod; *MY PET MONSTER*, TV, 86, CDN, Co-Prod; *MAD BALLS*, TV, 86, CDN, Co-Prod; 'THE CARE BEARS FAMILY' (13 eps), TV, 86, CDN, Co-Prod; *THE CARE BEARS MOVIE II*, Th, 86/85, CDN, Co-Prod; 'EWOKS' (13 eps), TV, 85, CDN, Co-Prod; *THE CARE BEARS MOVIE*, Th, 85, CDN, Co-Prod; *THE*

(cont/suite)

GREAT HEEP, TV, 85, CDN, Co-Prod; *THE EWOK-DROIDS ADVENTURE HOUR,* TV, 85, CDN, Co-Prod; *STRAWBERRY SHORTCAKE MEETS THE BERRYKINS,* TV, 84, CDN, Co-Prod; *THE GET ALONG GANG,* TV, 84, CDN, Co-Prod; *'20 MINUTE WORKOUT'* (120 eps), TV, 83, CDN, Co-Exec Prod; *ROCK & RULE* (RING OF POWER), Th, 83, CDN, Co-Prod; *HERSELF THE ELF,* TV, 83, CDN, Co-Prod; *STRAWBERRY SHORTCAKE AND THE BABY WITHOUT A NAME,* TV, 83, CDN, Co-Prod; *STRAWBERRY SHORTCAKE: A HOUSEWARMING SURPRISE,* TV, 82, CDN, Co-Prod; *INTERGALACTIC THANKSGIVING* (PLEASE DON'T EAT THE PLANET), TV, 79, CDN, Co-Prod; *THE STAR WARS HOLIDAY SPECIAL* (Cdn inserts), TV, 78, USA, Co-Prod; *ROMIE-O & JULIE-8,* TV, 78, CDN, Co-Prod; *THE DEVIL & DANIEL MOUSE,* TV, 78, CDN, Co-Prod; *COSMIC CHRISTMAS,* TV, 77/76, CDN, Co-Prod.

LOUNT, Elvira

2090 W. 3rd Ave., Vancouver, BC, CAN, V6J 1L4. (416)738-5217.
Types of Production & Categories: Th Film-Prod; TV Film-Prod.
Genres: Drama-Th&TV; Documentary-TV; Educational-TV.
Biography: Born 1952, Toronto, Ontario. Two-year diploma course in media, Capilano College, 75; Honours B.A. University of London, England (English, Philosophy, History). Coordinator, publicity director for Vancouver Mayor Harcourt's 1980 election campaign; professional belly dancer, 75-82. President, Melkim Productions Ltd.; Director, Moonshine Productions Ltd.. *BABY CLOCK* won a Blue Ribbon (American F.F.), Silver Medal (NY).
Selective Filmography: *SAMUEL LOUNT,* Th, 84, CDN, Prod; *BABY CLOCK,* TV, 81, CDN, Prod/Dir; *QUIET BEACH,* ED, 80, CDN, Prod/Dir; *WOMEN AND THE LAW/CIVIL LIBERTIES/CANADIAN COURT SYSTEM,* TV, 79, CDN, Prod; *SMALL CLAIMS COURT/FAMILY RELATIONS ACT/ UNEMPLOYMENT INSURANCE,* TV, 79/78, CDN, Prod; *WILLS,* TV, 79, CDN, Prod; *BELLY DANCING IMAGES,* TV, 78, CDN, Prod; *LABOUR LAW/ LANDLORD AND TENANT LAW,* TV, 78, CDN, Prod; *TRIDENT - A CANADIAN PERSPECTIVE,* TV, 77, CDN, Prod; *'MENTAL PATIENTS AND THE LAW'* (4 eps), TV, 77, CDN, Prod; *'WOMEN AND THE LAW'* (8 eps), TV, 76, CDN, Prod.

LOWRY, Christopher

46 Wales Ave., Toronto, Ont, CAN, M5T 1J4. (416)368-0407.
Types of Production & Categories: TV Film-Prod/Wr; TV Video-Prod/Dir/Wr.
Genres: Drama-TV; Comedy-TV; Documentary-TV; Educational-TV.
Biography: Born 1955, London, Ontario. Languages: English, French, some Spanish. B.A., Honours English, University of Western Ontario. Began work in film with Insight Productions, Toronto, 79; edited the humour book 'The Best of Playboar', 84. *CHAMBERS: TRACKS AND GESTURES* won a Bronze Award (Houston), Blue Ribbon (American F.F.), Best Film of Festival (Yorkton).
Selective Filmography: *OCTOBER STRANGER,* TV, 85, CDN, Prod/Assoc Dir; *THE PEOPLE WANT MEAT,* MV, 85, CDN, Dir/Prod/Wr; *RANCH,* TV, 85, CDN, Co-Prod/Wr/Ed; *DORIS McCARTHY: HEART OF A PAINTER,* TV, 83, CDN, Assoc Prod; *CHAMBERS: TRACKS AND GESTURES,* TV, 82, CDN, Prod/Co-Wr/Res (**CFTA**); *HEART OF GOLD,* TV, 81, CDN, Res.

MACADAM, William I.

ATPD. 148 Collier St., Toronto, Ont, CAN, M4W 1M3. (416)922-7554.
Types of Production & Categories: TV Film-Prod.
Genres: Documentary-TV.
Biography: Born 1938, London, England; Canadian citizen. Educated at Eaton College, England; moved to Canada, 56. Founded airline on West Coast, 'Trans Mountain Air Services', 62; National Vice President, Progressive Conservative
(cont/suite)

Party, 64-70; ran Robert Stanfield's national campaign, 68. Retired from politics to go into television documentaries. Founded Norfolk Group of Companies, 73. Past Chairman, CFTA.
Selective Filmography: *'TALES OF THE KLONDIKE'* (7 eps), TV, 82-80, CDN, Prod; *LOVE OF LIFE,* TV, 82, CDN, Prod; *SCORN OF WOMEN,* TV, 82, CDN, Prod; *THE KGB CONNECTIONS,* TV, 81, CDN, Exec Prod; *RACE FOR NUMBER ONE,* TV, 81, CDN, Prod; *FINIS,* TV, 81, CDN, Prod; *TALES FROM A TOY SHOP* (3 parts), TV, 81, CDN, Prod; *WINNIE,* TV, 81, CDN, Prod; *THE UNEXPECTED,* 'TALES OF THE KLONDIKE', TV, 81, CDN, Prod; *THE ONE THOUSAND DOZEN,* TV, 80, CDN, Prod; *CONNECTIONS: A FURTHER INVESTIGATION,* TV, 79, CDN, Co-Prod; *THE TOMORROW MAN,* TV, 79, CDN, Co-Prod **(CFTA)**; *CONNECTIONS: AN INVESTIGATION INTO ORGANIZED CRIME,* TV, 77, CDN, Co-Prod **(ACTRA/ANIK)**; *THE FIFTH ESTATE: THE ESPIONAGE ESTABLISHMENT,* TV, 74, CDN, Prod.

MacANDREW, Heather
Asterisk Productions, 110 Spadina Ave., #703, Toronto, Ont, CAN, M5V 2K4. (416)868-1175.
Types of Production & Categories: TV Film-Prod/Wr; TV Video-Prod/Wr.
Genres: Documentary-TV; Educational-TV; Commercials-TV.
Biography: Born 1949. Partner, Asterisk Productions. Her films have won awards at American and Columbus Film Festivals.
Selective Filmography: *THE MAN WE CALL JUAN CARLOS,* TV, 86, CDN, Co-Prod/Wr; *PAPERMAKING IN NEPAL,* 'THE NATURE OF THINGS', TV, 86, CDN, Co-Prod/Wr; *EVERY SECOND COUNTS,* Cm, 86, CDN, Co-Prod/Wr; *ROOTS OF HUNGER, ROOTS OF CHANGE,* TV, 85, CDN, Co-Prod/Wr; *WOMEN AND WATER/MICHAEL GETS WATER/WHAT DO YOU DO WHEN?,* Cm, 84/83, CDN, Co-Prod/Wr; *A MOVEABLE FEAST,* ED, 81, CDN, Co-Prod; *'THE WORLD'S CHILDREN'* (13 eps), TV, 81/80, CDN, Co-Prod.

MacLEAR, Michael
Cineworld Inc., 1300 Yonge St., #504, Toronto, Ont, CAN, M4T 1X3. (416)961-8004.
Types of Production & Categories: TV Film-Prod/Wr; TV Video-Prod/Wr.
Genres: Documentary-TV; Children's-TV.
Biography: Born London, England; Canadian citizen. Former foreign correspondent for CBC, CTV; travelled in 80 countries. President of Cineworld Inc.. *VIETNAM: THE TEN THOUSAND DAY WAR* won best Documentary, Nat'l Education Assoc. of America.
Selective Filmography: *'THE AMERICAN CENTURY'* (6 eps), TV, 86, CDN, Exec Prod/Wr; *'THE CANADIANS'* (4 eps), TV, 86, USA, Exec Prod; *'AMERICAN CAESAR'* (5 eps), TV, 84, CDN, Exec Prod/Wr; *'GOING GREAT'* (52 eps), TV, 82/81, CDN, Exec Prod; *'VIETNAM: THE TEN THOUSAND DAY WAR'* (26 eps), TV, 80, CDN, Exec Prod/Wr; *'MacLEAR'* (60 eps), TV, 78-74, CDN, Wr/Host **(ACTRA)**.

MacMILLAN, Michael
CFTA. Atlantis Films Ltd., 65 Heward Ave., Toronto, Ont, CAN, M4M 2T5. (416) 462-0246.
Types of Production & Categories: TV Film-Prod.
Genres: Drama-TV; Comedy-TV; Science Fiction-TV; Children's-TV.
Biography: Born 1956, Scarborough, Ontario. Films he has produced have won awards at the American, Chicago and Yorkton film festivals.
Selective Filmography: *'AIRWAVES'* (26 eps), TV, 86/85, CDN, Exec Prod; *'REALLY WEIRD TALES'* (3 eps), TV, 86, CDN/USA, Exec Prod; *'RAY BRADBURY THEATRE'* (6 eps), TV, 85/84, CDN, Co-Exec Prod; *'BROTHERS BY CHOICE'* (6 eps), TV, 85, CDN, Exec Prod; *'BELL CANADA PLAYHOUSE'*

(cont/suite)

(26 eps), TV, 85/84, CDN, Exec Prod/Co-Prod; *MIRACLE AT MOREAUX*, TV, 84, CDN, Exec Prod; *'SONS & DAUGHTERS'* (11 eps), TV, 83/82, CDN, Co-Prod; *BOYS & GIRLS*, 'SONS & DAUGHTERS', TV, 82, CDN, Co-Prod **(CFTA/OSCAR)**; *CHAMBERS: TRACKS & GESTURES*, TV, 81, CDN, Exec Prod; *OLDEN DAYS COAT*, TV, 80, CDN, Co-Prod **(BIJOU/CFTA)**.

MACNEE, Rupert

DGC. 1986 Palmerston Pl., Los Angeles, CA, USA, 90027. (213)668-1559.
Types of Production & Categories: TV Film-Dir/Prod; TV Video-Prod.
Genres: Variety-TV; Documentary-TV; Educational-TV.
Biography: Born 1947, England. Educated at Princeton University. Has produced several series for syndication; now living in Los Angeles.
Selective Filmography: *TECHNICAL MARKETING AND PROPOSAL PREPARATION*, ED, 86, USA, Prod; *'OWL TV'* (sev segs), TV, 85, CDN, Dir; *'AN EVENING AT THE IMPROV'* (52 eps), TV, 83-80, USA, Prod; *SUICIDE* (5 parts), TV, 79, CDN, Co-Wr/Co-Ed; *'BEHIND THE SCENES WITH JONATHAN WINTERS'* (Dir-8 eps), (46 eps), TV, 78-76, CDN/USA, Prod; *'FRIENDS OF MAN'* (Dir-8 eps), (45 eps), TV, 75/74, CDN, Co-Prod; *TALK OF THE DEVIL*, TV, 73, CDN, Assoc Prod.

MALO, René

APFVQ. 372 Côte Ste-Catherine, Outremont, Qué, CAN. 440 Place Jacques-Cartier, #3, Montréal, Qué, CAN, H2Y 3B3. (514)878-9181.
Types de production et Catégories: l métrage-Prod; c métrage-Prod.
Types d'oeuvres: Drame-C; Comédie-C.
Curriculum vitae: Né en 1942; bilingue. Fondation de Corporation Image, 70; producteur/réalisateur de plus de 150 courts et moyens métrages. Fonde Les Films René Malo, 74; René Malo Vidéo, 83; distributeur et producteur de films au niveau international; achète Mutual Films, 83, devenant un partenaire dans New World Mutual Pictures. *SONATINE* remporte le Lion d'Argent, Venise, 84; *LE DECLIN DE L'EMPIRE AMERICAIN* gagne le Prix de la Critique Internationale, Cannes, le Prix John Labatt Classic pour le film le plus populaire et le Prix CITY, Meilleur Film Canadien au Festival du Film de Toronto, 86.
Filmographie sélective: *LE DECLIN DE L'EMPIRE AMERICAIN* (DECLINE OF THE AMERICAN EMPIRE), C, 85, CDN, Prod; *HONEYMOON*, C, 84, CDN/F, Prod exéc; *LE RUFFIAN*, C, 83, CDN/F, Prod; *SONATINE*, C, 82, CDN, Prod; *L'HOMME A TOUT FAIRE*, C, 80, CDN, Prod; *PANIQUE*, C, 77/76, CDN, Co prod; *L'ANIMAL*, C, 77, F, Co prod; *L'AILE OU LA CUISSE*, C, 75, F, Co prod.

MANN, Ron - see DIRECTORS

MARGELLOS, James

DGA, DGC. 1341 Duende Lane, Pacific Palisades, CA, USA, 90272. (213)454-1097. Pacific Rim Films Ltd., 43 West 6th Ave., Vancouver, B.C., CAN, V5Y 1K2. (604)873-3921. Gerald Adler, Sy Fischer Co. Agency, 10960 Wilshire Blvd., Los Angeles, CA, USA, 90024. (213)208-0455.
Types of Production & Categories: Th Film-Prod/PM; TV Film-Prod/PM.
Genres: Drama-Th&TV; Comedy-Th&TV; Action-Th&TV; Documentary-Th&TV.
Biography: Born 1946, Revelstoke, British Columbia.
Selective Filmography: *MRS.DELAFIELD WANTS TO MARRY*, TV, 85, USA, PM; *'STIRCRAZY'* (6 eps), TV, 85, USA, PM; *CONTACT*, Th, 84, USA, Prod; *POLICE ACADEMY*, Th, 83, USA, PM; *P.K. AND THE KID*, Th, 82, USA, PM; *MAZES AND MONSTERS*, TV, 81, USA, PM; *RECKLESS*, Th, 81, CDN, PM; *A GREAT RIDE*, Th, 80, USA, Prod; *THE CHANGELING*, Th, 79, CDN, PM; *SEARCH AND DESTROY*, Th, 77, CDN, Prod; *SECOND WIND*, Th, 75, CDN, Prod; *THE INBREAKER*, Th, 74, CDN, Co-Prod; *PAPERBACK HERO*, Th, 73, CDN, Co-Prod; *SLIPSTREAM*, Th, 73, CDN, Prod **(CFA)**; *ANOTHER SMITH*

(cont/suite)

FOR PARADISE, Th, 71, CDN, Prod; *McCABE AND MRS. MILLER,* Th, 71, USA, PM; *BREWSTER McCLOUD,* Th, 71, USA, Assoc Prod; *THAT COLD DAY IN THE PARK,* Th, 69, USA, PM; *THE FOX,* Th, 68, USA, Loc M.

MARKLE, Fletcher - see DIRECTORS

MARKS, Julian
97 Robert St., Toronto, Ont, CAN, M5S 2K5. (416)966-5220.
Types of Production & Categories: TV Film-Prod; TV Video-Prod.
Genres: Drama-Th&TV; Comedy-Th&TV; Action-Th&TV; Horror-Th&TV.
Biography: Born Montreal, Quebec; bilingual. B.A., McGill University; M.A., Sir George Williams U.. Prior to producing, was active as production manager, assistant director, writer and editor.
Selective Filmography: *DOING LIFE,* TV, 86, CDN, Prod; *THE EXECUTION OF RAYMOND GRAHAM,* TV, 85, CDN, Spv Prod; *SEPARATE VACATIONS,* Th, 84, CDN, Assoc Prod; *JOSHUA THEN AND NOW,* Th, 84, CDN, Assoc Prod; *LES CARCASSES,* TV, 83, CDN, Prod.

MARKSON, Morley - see DIRECTORS

MARSHALL, Bill
70 Yorkville Ave., #303, Toronto, Ont, CAN, MR5 1B9. (416)920-6583. Marshall Arts, 9 Sultan St., Toronto, Ont, CAN, M5S 1L6. (416)923-5228.
Types of Production & Categories: Th Film-Prod.
Genres: Drama-Th; Comedy-Th; Action-Th; Horror-Th.
Biography: Born 1939, Scotland; Canadian citizen. Has been executive assistant to mayors of Toronto. Co-founder, Festival of Festivals.
Selective Filmography: *YOU GOTTA COME BACK A STAR,* Th, 86, CDN, Co-Prod; *THE WAR BOY* (POINT OF ESCAPE), Th, 84, CDN, Prod; *HANK WILLIAMS: THE SHOW HE NEVER GAVE,* Th, 81, CDN, Prod; *CIRCLE OF TWO,* Th, 80, CDN, Exec Prod; *MR. PATMAN,* Th, 79, CDN, Co-Prod; *WILD HORSE HANK,* Th, 78, CDN, Co-Prod; *OUTRAGEOUS!,* Th, 77, CDN, Co-Prod; *FLICK* (FRANKENSTEIN ON CAMPUS), Th, 70, CDN, Prod.

MARTIN, Marcia
ACFTP. City-TV, 299 Queen St. W., Toronto, Ont, CAN, M5V 1Z9. (416)367-5757.
Types of Production & Categories: TV Video-Prod.
Genres: Drama-TV; Variety-TV.
Biography: Born 1949, Portland, Maine; Canadian citizen, 85. B.A., Sociology, American University, Washington D.C..
Selective Filmography: *BUTTERBUMP IN THE EIGHTH,* TV, 85, CDN, Prod; *'FASHION TELEVISION'* (4 eps), TV, 85, CDN, Spv Prod; *NEIGHBOURS/ STREET-WISE/GOLDEN PROMISE,* 'TORONTO TRILOGY', TV, 84, CDN, Prod; *I AM A HOTEL,* TV, 84, CDN, Spv Prod; *'TITANS'* (13 eps), TV, 81, CDN, PM.

McANDREW, Jack - see WRITERS

McDOUGALL, Ian
CFTA, DGC. Abaton Pictures Inc., 5 Cottingham Rd., Toronto, Ont, CAN, M4V 1B1. (416)968-2765.
Types of Production & Categories: Th Film-Prod; TV Film-Prod.
Genres: Drama-Th&TV.
Biography: Born 1945, Toronto, Ontario. President, Abaton Pictures. Worked in theatre in England (67-70) before returning to Canada. *ANNE OF GREEN GABLES* won the Golden Gate Award (San Francisco) and the Emily Award (American Film Fest.).

(cont/suite)

PRODUCERS/PRODUCTEURS

Selective Filmography: *ANNE OF GREEN GABLES*, TV, 85, CDN, Co-Prod (EMMY); *RIGHT OF THE PEOPLE*, TV, 85, CDN, Assoc Prod; *'THE EDISON TWINS'* (26 eps), TV, 84/83, CDN, Prod; *'20 MINUTE WORKOUT'* (65 eps), TV, 83, CDN, Exec Prod.

McEWAN, Duncan

ATPD. 196 MacPherson Ave., Toronto, Ont, CAN, M5R 1W8. (416)964-0841. CBC, Box 500, Stn. A, Toronto, Ont, CAN, M5W 1E6. (416)975-7501.
Types of Production & Categories: TV Film-Prod/Dir; TV Video-Prod/Dir.
Genres: Documentary-TV.
Biography: Born 1953, England. B.Sc., University of Toronto, 73. Artistic director, producer, lighting designer, theatre, 74-78. Joined CBC, 76. Manager of Programming & Development, The Star Channel (Pay TV), 82-84; Executive producer, CBC, 84-86.
Selective Filmography: *'VENTURE'* (weekly), TV, 86/85, CDN, Exec Prod; *'THE MEDICINE SHOW'* (Dir/Prod-19 seg), (19 eps), TV, 82-78, CDN, Exec Prod; *COOK COUNTY HOSPITAL,* 'THE FIFTH ESTATE', TV, 80, CDN, Prod/Dir; *'TAKE 30'* (sev items), TV, 78-76, CDN, Prod/Dir.

McEWAN, Maryke

ATPD. 112 Willow Ave., Toronto, Ont, CAN, M4E 3K3. (416)699-1517. CBC, Box 500, Stn. A, Toronto, Ont, CAN, M5W 1E6. (416)975-7114.
Types of Production & Categories: TV Film-Prod.
Genres: Drama-TV.
Biography: Born 1948, Oshawa, Ontario. B.A., English, University of Toronto. *READY FOR SLAUGHTER*, Best TV Drama, Banff Int'l TV Festival.
Selective Filmography: *'STREET LEGAL'* (6 eps), TV, 86, CDN, Exec Prod; *SHELLGAME,* TV, 85, CDN, Prod; *TOOLS OF THE DEVIL,* TV, 84, CDN, Prod; *ROUGH JUSTICE/READY FOR SLAUGHTER/BLIND FAITH,* 'FOR THE RECORD', TV, 83, CDN, Prod; *KATE MORRIS, VICE PRESIDENT,* 'FOR THE RECORD', TV, 83, CDN, Co-Prod.

McGAW, Jack

CFTA. 255A Russell Hill Rd., Toronto, Ont, CAN. (416)968-2202. Documentary Productions Ltd., 61 St. Nicholas St., Toronto, Ont, CAN. (416)968-9292.
Types of Production & Categories: TV Film-Prod; TV Video-Prod.
Genres: Action-TV; Documentary-TV; Educational-TV; Children's-TV.
Biography: Born 1936. Winner of more than 30 film and TV awards world-wide including: Gold, Silver and Bronze Medals, Int'l Film & TV Fest, N.Y. for *LIVE IT UP*; *CHILDREN'S HOSPITAL* was nominated for an Emmy and won a Bronze Medal at the N.Y. Festival.
Selective Filmography: *'LIVE IT UP'* (184 eps), TV, 86-78, CDN, Prod/Host; *THE RED DEER CHALLENGE,* TV, 84, CDN, Prod/Host; *THE FIRST NATIONAL ATTITUDE TEST ON DRINKING DRIVERS,* TV, 83, CDN, Prod/Host; *THE NATIONAL SAFETY DRILL,* TV, 82, CDN, Prod/Dir; *THE KID'S CASE AGAINST VANDALISM,* ED, 81, CDN, Prod; *THE NATIONAL CRIME TEST/ THE NATIONAL DRIVING TEST (1ST & 2ND),* TV, 81-79, CDN, Prod/Host; *THE NATIONAL FIRE DRILL,* TV, 78, CDN, Prod/Host; *YESTERDAY'S CHILDREN,* 'INQUIRY', TV, 78, CDN, Prod/Host (**CFTA**); *THE FAILING STRATEGY/HEAR NO EVIL, SEE NO EVIL,SPEAK NO EVIL,* 'INQUIRY', TV, 77/73, CDN, Prod/Host; *CHILDREN'S HOSPITAL,* 'W5', TV, 76, CDN, Prod/Host; *KEEP OUT OF THE REACH OF ADULTS,* 'INQUIRY', TV, 73, CDN, Prod/Host; *GIVE US THIS DAY OUR DAILY BREAD/TO YOUR HEALTH,* 'INQUIRY', TV, 72, CDN, Prod/Host; *'W5'* (46 eps), TV, 72/71, CDN, Prod/Host.

McGREEVY, John - see DIRECTORS

McKEE, Neill

136 Irving Ave., Ottawa, Ont, CAN, K1Y 1Z4. (613)728-0376. Int'l Dev. Research Centre, P.O. Box 8500, Ottawa, Ont, CAN, K1G 3H9. (613)236-6163.
Types of Production & Categories: TV Film-Prod/Dir.
Genres: Documentary-TV; Educational-TV.
Biography: Born 1945, Elmira, Ontario. After university (68), went to Malaysia with CUSO, worked as a secondary school teacher and made a series of films. Has been making films for Int'l Development ever since. Has won a number of int'l film awards including The World Health Organization Special Prize for *PRESCRIPTION FOR HEALTH.*
Selective Filmography: *TREES OF HOPE/FOOTHOLDS/PRESCRIPTION FOR HEALTH,* ED, 85-83, CDN, Prod/Dir/Cam; *THE MYSTERIOUS MILKFISH/ HARNESSING THE MONSOONS/CHOICES,* ED, 82-80, CDN, Prod/Dir/Cam; *FISH BY-CATCH/AN END TO POUNDING/PODS OF PROTEIN,* ED, 80/79, CDN, Prod/Dir/Cam; *A MESSAGE FROM AFRICAN HEALERS/PANOI THE VILLAGE MIDWIFE,* ED, 79-75, CDN, Prod/Ed; *OYSTER FARMING IN THE TROPICS/PROJECT IMPACT: THE OVERVIEW,* ED, 79/78, CDN, Prod/Dir/ Cam; *WHEN THE HARVEST IS OVER/THOUGHT FOR FOOD/RURAL HEALTH WORKERS,* ED, 78/77, CDN, Prod/Dir/Cam; *CONTINENT IN THE MAKING/CUSO IN GHANA/CUSO IN PAPUA NEW GUINEA,* ED, 72/71, CDN, Prod/Dir/Cam; *CUSO IN EAST & CENTRAL AFRICA/FOUR TIMES CUSO,* ED, 72/71, CDN, Prod/Dir/Cam.

McKEOWN, Bob

ACTRA. McKeown/McGee Films, 11 Alpha Ave., Toronto, Ont, CAN, M4X 1S2. (416)964-3517.
Types of Production & Categories: TV Film-Prod/Dir/Wr; TV Video-Prod/Dir/Wr.
Genres: Documentary-TV; Educational-TV; Commercials-TV.
Biography: Born 1950, Ottawa, Ontario. B.A., Yale University, 71. Member of Ottawa Rough Riders, Canadian Football League, 71-76; journalist and filmmaker since 76.
Selective Filmography: *A MOMENT IN TIME,* TV, 86, CDN, Prod/Dir/Wr; *'THE FIFTH ESTATE'* (30 seg/year), TV, 86-81, CDN, Wr/Host; *LES CANADIENS,* TV, 85, CDN, Prod/Dir/Wr; *ROOTS ALGONQUIN,* Cm, 85, CDN, Prod/Dir/Wr; *ROOTS ATHLETICS,* Cm, 85, CDN, Prod/Dir; *CLEARED FOR TAKE-OFF* (THE U.N. AND CIVIL AVIATION), ED, 84, CDN, Prod/Dir/Wr.

McKEOWN, Brian

ACTRA, CTPDA, DGC. 1492 Ross Rd., North Vancouver, BC, CAN, V7J 1V2. (604)986-4662.
Types of Production & Categories: TV Film-Prod/Dir; TV Video-Prod/Dir
Genres: Drama-TV; Action-TV; Documentary-TV; Children's-Th&TV.
Selective Filmography: *'THE BEACHCOMBERS'* (20 eps), TV, 86/85, CDN, Prod; *'THE BEACHCOMBERS'* (2 eps), TV, 85/82, CDN, Dir; *'MAGEE & COMPANY'* (135 eps), TV, 78-76, CDN, Dir; *'THE FRENCH SHOW'* (8 eps), TV, 77, CDN, Dir; *'THE ADVENTURES OF DORPP'* (20 eps), TV, 71, CDN, Prod/Dir.

McLEAN, Seaton

Atlantis Films Ltd., 65 Heward Ave., Toronto, Ont, CAN, M4M 2T5. (416)462-0246.
Types of Production & Categories: TV Film-Prod.
Genres: Drama-TV; Documentary-TV; Children's-TV.
Biography: Producer, co-owner, Atlantis Films Ltd.. Several films from the *SONS AND DAUGHTERS* and *BELL CANADA PLAYHOUSE* series have won awards at the American, Chicago and Yorkton film festivals.

(cont/suite)

Selective Filmography: *'REALLY WEIRD TALES'* (3 eps), TV, 86, CDN/USA, Prod; *'BELL CANADA PLAYHOUSE'* (25 eps), TV, 85/84, CDN, Co-Prod; *'BROTHERS BY CHOICE'* (6 eps), TV, 85, CDN, Co-Prod; *'AIRWAVES'* (1 eps), TV, 85, CDN, Dir; *THE PAINTED DOOR,* 'BELL CANADA PLAY-HOUSE', TV, 84, CDN, Co-Prod **(CFTA)**; *'SONS AND DAUGHTERS'* (11 eps), TV, 83/82, CDN, Co-Prod; *BOYS AND GIRLS,* 'SONS AND DAUGHTERS', TV, 82, CDN, Co-Prod/Ed **(CFTA/OSCAR)**; *CHAMBERS: TRACKS AND GESTURES,* TV, 82, CDN, Co-Prod; *OLDEN DAYS COAT,* TV, 81, CDN, Co-Prod/Ed **(BIJOU/CFTA)**.

McMANUS, Mike

ACTRA. 102 Confederations Way, Thornhill, Ont, CAN, L3T 5R5. (416)881-0408. TV Ontario, 2180 Yonge St., Toronto, Ont, CAN, M4S 2B9. (416)484-2600. The Characters, 150 Carlton St., Toronto, Ont, CAN, M5A 2K1. (416)964-8522.
Types of Production & Categories: TV Video-Prod.
Genres: Documentary-TV; Educational-TV.
Biography: Born 1935, Montreal, Quebec. Languages: English, French, Italian. Education: B.A., M.Sc.. *ENERGY, SEARCH FOR AN ANSWER,* winner at N.Y. Int'l Film & TV Festival.
Selective Filmography: *'FRONTRUNNERS'* (9 eps), TV, 85, CDN, Exec Prod; *'AUTOMATING THE OFFICE'* (9 eps), TV, 84, CDN, Exec Prod; *'ENERGY: SEARCH FOR AN ANSWER'* (9 eps), TV, 84, CDN, Exec Prod; *'FUTUREWORK'* (9 eps), TV, 84, CDN, Prod; *'BITS AND BYTES'* (12 eps), TV, 83-81, CDN, Exec Prod; *'THE ACADEMY ON COMPUTERS'* (12 eps), TV, 83, CDN, Prod; *'THE ACADEMY ON MORAL PHILOSOPHY'* (7 eps), TV, 82, CDN, Prod; *'THE MORAL QUESTION'* (7 eps), TV, 81, CDN, Prod; *THE TWILIGHT OF THE FAMILY,* TV, 79, CDN, Prod; *'JOURNEYS IN TIME'* (12 eps), TV, 78, CDN, Prod; *'THE EDUCATION OF MIKE McMANUS'* (daily), TV, 78-74, CDN, Exec Prod/Host.

MEDJUCK, Joe

Warner Brothers, 4000 Warner Blvd., Producers Bldg., #7, Rm. 8, Burbank, CA, USA, 91522. (818)954-1771.
Types of Production & Categories: Th Film-Prod; TV Film-Prod.
Genres: Comedy-Th; Children's-TV.
Biography: Born 1943, Fredericton, New Brunswick. Education: McGill University; Ph.D., University of Toronto.
Selective Filmography: *LEGAL EAGLES,* Th, 86, USA, Exec Prod; *'THE REAL GHOSTBUSTERS'* (78 eps), TV, 85, USA, Exec Prod; *GHOSTBUSTERS,* Th, 84, USA, Assoc Prod; *HEAVY METAL,* Th, 82, CDN, Pro Coord; *STRIPES,* Th, 81, USA, Assoc Prod.

MENARD, Robert - voir REALISATEURS

MENDELUK, George - see DIRECTORS

MICHAELS, Joel B.

ACTRA, AFTRA, SAG. Cineplex Odeon Films, 1925 Century Park E., Ste. 300, Los Angeles, CA, USA, 90067. (213)553-5307.
Types of Production & Categories: Th Film-Prod; TV Film-Prod.
Genres: Drama-Th&TV; Comedy-Th.
Biography: Born 1938, Buffalo, New York; American citizen; landed immigrant, Canada. Currently Senior Vice President in Charge of Production, Cineplex Odeon Films.
Selective Filmography: *COURAGE,* TV, 86, USA, Prod; *HAREM* (mini-series), TV, 86, USA, Prod; *BLACK MOON RISING,* Th, 85, USA, Co-Prod; *PHILADELPHIA EXPERIMENT,* Th, 84, USA, Co-Prod; *LOSIN' IT,* Th, 82,

(cont/suite)

154

USA, Exec Prod; *THE AMATEUR*, Th, 81, CDN, Co-Prod; *TRIBUTE* (UN FILS POUR L'ETE), Th, 80, CDN, Co-Prod; *THE CHANGELING*, Th, 79, CDN, Co-Prod (**GENIE**); *THE SILENT PARTNER*, Th, 77, CDN, Co-Prod (**CFA**); *BITTERSWEET LOVE*, Th, 76, USA, Co-Prod.

MICHAELS, Lorne

WGAe. Broadway Video, 1619 Broadway, New York, NY, USA, 10019. (212)265-7621. Sandy Wernick, The Brillstein Co., 9200 Sunset Blvd., Los Angeles, CA, USA. (213)276-6135.
Types of Production & Categories: Th Film-Prod/Wr; TV Video-Prod/Wr.
Genres: Comedy-Th&TV; Variety-TV; Musical-TV.
Biography: Born Toronto, Ontario. Writer/producer, comedy specials, drama, CBC TV, Toronto 69-72.
Selective Filmography: *'SATURDAY NIGHT LIVE'*, TV, 86/85, USA, Exec Prod/Co-Wr; *THREE AMIGOS*, Th, 86, USA, Prod/Wr; *STEVE MARTIN'S BEST SHOW EVER*, TV, 81, USA, Prod; *SIMON AND GARFUNKEL'S CONCERT IN THE PARK*, TV, 81, USA, Exec Prod; *'SATURDAY NIGHT LIVE'*, TV, 80-75, USA, Prod/Co-Wr (**3 EMMY**); *THE RUTLES - ALL YOU NEED IS CASH*, TV, 78, USA, Prod/Wr; *THE PAUL SIMON SPECIAL*, TV, 77, USA, Prod/Wr (**EMMY**); *THE BEACH BOYS SPECIAL*, TV, 76, USA, Prod/Wr; *LILY TOMLIN SPECIAL* (4 shows), TV, 75-72, USA, Prod/Co-Wr (**2 EMMY**); *THE FLIP WILSON SHOW*, TV, 74, USA, Prod/Wr; *THE PERRY COMO SHOW*, TV, 74, USA, Prod/Wr; *ROWAN AND MARTIN'S LAUGH IN*, TV, 69/68, USA, Contr Wr.

MILLAR, Susan

22 Albemarle Ave., Toronto, Ont, CAN, M4K 1H7. (416)465-9644. Soma Film Producers, 43 Britain St., 3rd Fl., Toronto, Ont, CAN, M5A 1R7. (416)868-6012.
Types of Production & Categories: TV Film-Prod/Wr; TV Video-Prod/Wr.
Genres: Drama-TV; Comedy-TV; Documentary-TV; Educational-TV.
Biography: Born 1951, Deep River, Ontario. Bachelor of Journalism, Carleton University, 74. Worked in television journalism for several years; won CFTA, Best Promotional Film, for *CITY WOMAN*, 78; Honourable Mention, American Film Festival *THE TERMINATION INTERVIEW*.
Selective Filmography: *'MONEY SMART'* (13 eps), TV, 85, CDN, Co-Prod/Story Ed; *THE TERMINATION INTERVIEW*, ED, 85, CDN, Co-Prod/Head Wr; *STALKING THE SILENT THIEF*, ED, 85, CDN, Co-Prod/Wr; *TRANSITIONS*, TV, 84, CDN, Co-Prod/Wr; *BRIDGES*, TV, 83, CDN, Co-Prod/Wr; *'STARTING A BUSINESS'* (13 eps), TV, 82, CDN, Co-Prod/Wr; *GOODBYE MR.DICKENS*, TV, 81, CDN, Co-Prod/Wr.

MILLER, Bob

Atlantic Mediaworks, 180 Charlotte St., Fredericton, NB, CAN, E3B 1L2. (506) 458-8806.
Types of Production & Categories: TV Video-Prod/Dir.
Genres: Documentary-TV; Educational-TV; Children's-TV; Commercials-TV.
Biography: Born 1948, Cardiff, Wales; has lived in Canada since 54; Canadian citizen. B.A., B.Ed, M.Ed., University of New Brunswick. Has lectured at U.N.B. in Media; President of Atlantic Mediaworks since 82.
Selective Filmography: *CHOICES*, TV, 86, CDN, Dir; *COME TO THE CITY/ YOU, ME AND THE NDP*, Cm, 86/82, CDN, Dir; *A VISION FULFILLED/ PROJECT POTASH*, In, 85, CDN, Prod/Dir; *PORNOGRAPHY - A DISCUSSION/LISTEN TO THE CHILDREN*, ED, 85, CDN, Prod/Ed; *LET'S GET IT TOGETHER*, ED, 85, CDN, Exec Prod; *EISTEDDFODD/BEFORE IT'S TOO LATE*, ED, 84, CDN, Prod/Dir; *SERVICE TO THE PUBLIC*, In, 84, CDN, Prod; *HOME FOR ALL SEASONS*, TV, 84, CDN, Prod/Dir; *THE NUTRITION CONNECTION*, ED, 84, CDN, Prod/Dir.

MILLS, Michael - see DIRECTORS

MITTON, Susan Young

ACTRA, CTPDA. 6053 Jubilee Rd., Halifax, NS, CAN, B3H 2E3. (902)425-6557.
CBC, P.O. Box 3000, Halifax, NS, CAN, B3H 1E9. (902)420-8311.
Types of Production & Categories: TV Film-Prod/Dir; TV Video-Prod/Dir.
Genres: Drama-TV; Variety-TV; Documentary-Th&TV.
Biography: Born 1951, St.John, New Brunswick. B.A., English, Acadia University.
Has worked in Montreal, P.E.I., Nova Scotia; travelled extensively.
Selective Filmography: *'LAND AND SEA'* (6 eps), TV, 86, CDN, Exec Prod;
'LAND AND SEA' (50 eps), TV, 85-75, CDN, Prod/Dir **(ANIK)**; *'FEELING
GOOD'* (60 eps), TV, 83, CDN, Prod/Dir; *'MacINTYRE FILE'* (8 eps), TV, 77/76,
CDN, Prod/Dir; *'A WAY OUT'* (104 eps), TV, 77-75, CDN, Host/Res; *'STUDIO
13'* (240 eps), TV, 75-73, CDN, Host/Res.

MORIN, Pierre - voir REALISATEURS

MORTIMER, Peter

176 Ava Rd., Toronto, Ont, CAN, M6C 1W5. (416)787-1941. 700 Bay St., Ste.
1800, Toronto, Ont, CAN, M5G 1Z6. (416)598-4587.
Types of Production & Categories: TV Film-Prod/Wr; TV Video-Prod.
Genres: Drama-TV; Musical-TV; Action-TV.
Biography: Born 1937, U.K.; British-Canadian citizenship. Languages: English,
French, Greek. TV and film production experience in U.K.: 6 years with Associated
Rediffusion as producer and executive producer; 3 years with Yorkshire TV as
Deputy Head of Drama, manager of shows for 'Playhouse' including *THE
CARETAKER* which won an Emmy. Experienced in co-productions with foreign
partners; extensive Canadian experience consulting between governments and film
and TV industry and in policy formulation and research.
Selective Filmography: *SUMMER SOUNDS,* TV, 84, CDN, Prod; *'JUST DO IT
YOURSELF'* (26 eps), ED, 78, CDN, Prod; *'KATE'* (26 eps), TV, 71, GB, Prod;
FOR THOSE IN PERIL..., 'HADLEIGH', TV, 70, GB, Wr; *'THE MAIN
CHANCE'* (13 eps), TV, 69, GB, Creator; *'CASTLE HAVEN'* (52 eps), TV, 68,
GB, Prod; *'DOUBLE YOUR MONEY'* (26 eps), TV, 67, GB, Exec Prod; *'READY,
STEADY, GO!'* (26 eps), TV, 64, GB, Pro Coord; *'THIS WEEK'* (26 eps), TV, 63,
GB, Pro Coord.

MULLER, John - see DIRECTORS

MURPHY, Jack F.

3104 Brookdale Dr., Studio City, CA, USA, 91604. (213)654-2820. American
Cinema Marketing, 3575 Cahuenga Blvd. W., Los Angeles, CA, USA, 90068. (213)
850-3300. 1310 Greene Ave., Suite 270, Westmount, Que, CAN, H3Z 2B2.
Types of Production & Categories: Th Film-Prod.
Genres: Drama-Th; Comedy-Th; Action-Th; Science Fiction-Th.
Biography: Born 1943, Montreal, Quebec; Canadian citizen; US resident. Active as
world-wide film distributor, specializing in feature films.
Selective Filmography: *THE DELOS ADVENTURE,* Th, 85, USA, Exec Prod;
PINBALL SUMMER (PICK-UP SUMMER), Th, 79, CDN, Prod; *DARK STAR,*
Th, 74, USA, Assoc Prod; *LES DEUX PIEDS DANS LA MEME BOTTINE* (THE
KLUTZ), Th, 73, CDN, Prod.

MURPHY, Michael D.

CFTA. CineVisa International, 2 College St., #108, Toronto, Ont, CAN, M5G
1K3. (416)927-1724.
Types of Production & Categories: TV Film-Prod/Dir/Wr; TV Video-Prod/Dir/Wr.

(cont/suite)

Genres: Drama-TV; Comedy-TV; Documentary-TV; Educational-TV.
Biography: Born 1951, Windsor, Ontario. Studied Film and TV Production, University of Windsor; 5 years as instructor of photography, film and TV production. Founded Clear Horizon Films, 81; CineVisa Int'l Media Distributors, 84; co-founded P.I.C. Entertainment, 85; President, ViaVideo Communications. Active internationally as export sales agent for Canadian produced TV programs. *WILD GOOSE JACK*, Best Documentary, Nature or Wildlife, American Film Festival and the Canadian Heritage Award, Yorkton.
Selective Filmography: *'CRIME FLASHBACK'* (26 eps), TV, 86, CDN, Prod; *'TO YOUR HEALTH'* (5 eps), ED, 86, CDN, Exec Prod/Prod/Wr; *SCOUTS!*, TV, 85/ 84, CDN, Exec Prod/Prod/Dir/Wr **(CFTA)**; *BRENTWOOD*, ED, 85, CDN, Exec Prod/Prod/Wr; *WILD GOOSE JACK*, TV, 83/82, CDN, Exec Prod/Prod/Dir/Wr **(CFTA)**.

MURRAY, Judith - see DIRECTORS

NADEAU, Jacques

222 ave. McDougall, Outremont, Qué, CAN, H2V 3P2. (514)279-5289. Indéacom inc., 5225 rue Berri, bur. 300, Montréal, Qué, CAN, H2J 2S4. (514)274-6538.
Types de production et Catégories: TV film-Prod; TV vidéo-Prod.
Types d'oeuvres: Documentaire-TV; Education-TV; Enfants-TV; Industriel-TV.
Curriculum vitae: Né en 1939, Montréal, Québec; bilingue. Maitrise, Sciences politiques, Université de Montréal; boursier du gouvernement français, études à l'Institut d'études politiques Université de Grenoble. Président de Idéacom inc. depuis 73.
Filmographie sélective: *AFTER THE CRASH/L'INCONDUITE* (SOUS LE COUP DU CHOC/ON THE ROAD), 'AT THE WHEEL', TV, 86, CDN, Co prod exéc/Co prod; *UNDER THE INFLUENCE/THE ROAD AHEAD* (FACULTES AFFAIBLIES/ROUTES A SUIVRE), 'AT THE WHEEL', TV, 86, CDN, Co prod exéc/Co prod; *LAURENTIENNE GENERALE I & II/IDEAL LTD.*, In, 86/ 85, CDN, Co prod; *AQOCI*, ED, 82, CDN, Co prod; *TVEQ*, In, 82, CDN, Co prod.

NADEAU, Pierre

Habitat 67, #617, Cité du Havre, Qué, CAN, H3C 3R6. (514)861-7865. 1338 Ste-Catherine est, Montréal, Qué, CAN, H2L 2H5. (514)524-2075.
Types de production et Catégories: TV vidéo Prod.
Types d'oeuvres: Documentaire-TV.
Curriculum vitae: Né en 1937. Oeuvre dans le domaine du journalisme depuis bientôt 30 ans. Débute comme animateur à Radio-Canada, 60; remporte le trophée Méritas (meilleur reporter TV) pour *AUJOURD'HUI*, 64; correspondant de Radio-Canada à Paris, 65-68; animateur radio et TV, 68-86. Maintenant animateur et producteur d'émissions d'information à Radio-Canada.
Filmographie sélective: *'DEJA 20 ANS'* (83 eps), TV, 86-83, CDN, Prod/Anim; *'LE POINT'* (journ), TV, 86-84, CDN, Co anim; *'COUSIN CUISINE DES AMERIQUES'* (13 eps), TV, 85, CDN, Prod; *'COUSINS CUISINE'* (13 eps), TV, 85, CDN, Prod.

NAPIER-ANDREWS, Nigel - see DIRECTORS

NEWMAN, Sydney

DGC. 28A Glenilla Rd., Belsize Park, London, GB, NW3 4AN. (011)586-6427.
Types of Production & Categories: Th Short-Prod; TV Film-Prod; TV Video-Prod.
Genres: Drama-Th&TV; Comedy-TV; Documentary-Th&TV.
Biography: Born 1917, Toronto, Ontario. Joined NFB, 41; director/editor, Armed Forces Training Films, War Info. shorts, 42; executive producer in charge of all films (300 documentaries), 47-52; reported to NBC (NY) on TV techniques for NFB, 49-50. Joined CBC, 52, director, supervisor of drama, producer: *GENERAL*

(cont/suite)

MOTORS THEATRE, ON CAMERA, FLIGHT INTO DANGER; ABC TV, England, *ARMCHAIR THEATRE*, 58. Head of Drama Group, BBC TV, 63-68, produced *THE FORSYTHE SAGA, STEVEN D., THE TEA PARTY*; created TV series *THE AVENGERS, ADAM ADAMANT LIVES, DR. WHO.* Exec. producer, Assoc. British Picture Corp., 69. Director, Programs, CRTC, Ottawa 70; Director, CBC, 72-75; Canadian Film Development Corp., 70-75. Special Advisor on Film to Secretary of State, 75-77; Governor, Canadian Conference of the Arts, 78-82; Chief Creative Consultant, CFDC, 82-84. Producer of *THE LITTLE SWEEP* (GB), 86. Received awards from Society of Film & TV Arts, Writers Guild of G.B., Special Recognition Award, SMPTE, 75. Officer, Order of Canada, 81.

NICHOL, Robert L.

Sajo Productions Inc., Box 888, Gibsons, BC, CAN, V0N 1V0. (604)886-3639.
Types of Production & Categories: Th Short-Prod/Dir/Cin; TV Film-Prod/Dir/Cin; TV Video-Prod/Dir/Cin.
Genres: Drama-Th&TV; Documentary-Th&TV; Educational-Th&TV; Children's-Th&TV.
Biography: Born 1936, Brantford, Ontario. Graduate, Ryerson Polytechnical Institute, 60; NFB, Drama training program, 75. Has been on staff at CBC, NFB, private TV stations; now freelance; has worked on 125 films and a number of them have won nat'l and int'l awards for excellence.
Selective Filmography: *RETURN TO SYLVAN,* Th, 86, CDN, Prod/Dir/Wr; *UNDERGROUND RIVER,* TV, 81, CDN, Prod/Dir/Cin; *WONDERLAND,* Th, 80, CDN, Dir/Cin/Wr; *WAR STORY,* TV, 80, CDN, DOP; *CHEWERS OF WOOD,* In, 79, CDN, Prod/Cin/Ed; *GREAT OCEAN GRAND,* In, 79, CDN, Prod/Cin; *THE LION SPEAKS,* Th, 78, CDN, DOP; *STRIKER,* TV, 76, CDN, Dir/Wr; *MASK AND DRUM,* TV, 74, USA, Prod/Dir/Cin; *THAT GANG OF HOODLUMS,* 'CHALLENGE FOR CHANGE', TV, 73, CDN, Dir/Cin/Wr; *FACADE,* Th, 71, CDN, DOP.

NIELSEN, Richard

ACTRA. 219 Front St.E., Toronto, Ont, CAN, M5A 1E8. (416)865-1596.
Types of Production & Categories: Th Film-Prod; TV Film-Prod/Wr.
Genres: Drama-Th&TV; Documentary-TV; Children's-TV.
Biography: Born 1929, Plaster Rock, New Brunswick. Worked at CBC, 61-71 as executive producer on series including: *PUBLIC EYE, DOCUMENT, WEEKEND.* Co-founder, Nielsen-Ferns International Inc., 72; Primedia, 80; Norflick Productions, Ltd., 85. Won the Wendy Michener Award, 70; his films have won numerous awards including Actra, CFTA, Wilderness and an Emmy nomination for *THE NEWCOMERS.*
Selective Filmography: *'THE LITTLE VAMPIRE'* (13 eps), TV, 85, CDN/GB/D, Prod/Wr; *CANADA'S SWEETHEART: THE SAGA OF HAL C.BANKS,* TV, 85, CDN, Co-Wr; *LABOUR OF LOVE,* TV, 84, CDN, Prod/Wr; *QUEBEC/CANADA 1995,* TV, 83, CDN, Co-Prod/Wr; *THE WARS,* Th, 80, CDN/D, Prod; *'CONNECTIONS'* (6 eps), TV, 79-77, CDN, Exec Prod; *'THE NEWCOMERS'* (Prod-3 eps), (7 eps), TV, 77/76, CDN, Exec Prod **(CFTA).**

NIRENBERG, Les

ACTRA, ATPD. 67 Ridge Hill Dr., Toronto, Ont, CAN, M6C 2J5. (416)781-3111.
Types of Production & Categories: TV Film-Prod/Wr; TV Video-Prod/Wr.
Genres: Documentary-TV; Educational-TV.
Biography: Born 1935, Toronto, Ontario. Languages: English, Yiddish.
Selective Filmography: *SOCIAL NETWORK THERAPY,* ED, 86/85, CDN, Prod/Dir; *'VENTURE'* (sev items), TV, 86/85, CDN, Prod/Dir/Wr; *GRAMMER SEATING/SODIUM SULPHUR BATTERIES,* In, 85, CDN, Prod/Dir/Wr; *CAFE,* ED, 85, CDN, Prod/Dir/Wr; *'THE JOURNAL'* (sev items), TV, 85-83, CDN, Prod/Dir/Wr; *MAXIMIZE WITH MULTIPLAN,* In, 83, CDN, Prod/Dir;

(cont/suite)

'QUELQUESHOW', TV, 74-69, CDN, Prod/Host **(ANIK)**; *PROPAGANDA MESSAGE*, Th, 73, CDN, Co-Wr; *LA QUEBECOISE*, 'ADIEU ALOUETTE', TV, 73, CDN, Dir/Wr.

NOVAK, Joseph
CTPDA. 100 Oriole Pkw., #404, Toronto, Ont, CAN, M5P 2G8. CBC, Box 500, Stn. A, Toronto, Ont, CAN, M5W 1E6. (416)975-7800.
Types of Production & Categories: TV Film-Prod; TV Video-Prod.
Genres: Documentary-TV; Current Affairs-TV; News-TV.
Biography: Born 1949, Montreal, Quebec. Education: B.A., MBA. Producer of CBC Information Morning Radio (Ottawa); senior producer, news and current affairs, CBC TV, Ottawa (2 years); producer, *THE JOURNAL*, CBC, Toronto, 86.

NOWLAN, John
CTPDA. 1766 Beech St., Halifax, NS, CAN, B3H 4B6. (902)425-3577. CBC, P.O. Box 3000, Halifax, NS, CAN, B3J 1E9. (902)420-8311.
Types of Production & Categories: TV Film-Prod/Dir.
Genres: Children's-TV; Animation-TV; News-TV.
Biography: Born 1942, Toronto, Ontario. B.Sc., Acadia University. Experience: CBC announcer, radio producer, radio executive producer. Awarded the Centennial Medal, 67; *SWITCHBACK* won the Children's Broadcast Institute Award. Executive producer, Children's TV, Halifax, 85-86; CBC winner of Commonwealth Relations Trust Bursary for study in Britain.
Selective Filmography: *'SWITCHBACK'* (weekly), TV, 85-81, CDN, Exec Prod/Prod/Dir **(ANIK)**; *'SESAME STREET'* (sev seg), TV, 85, USA, Prod; *CHILDREN'S MIRACLE NETWORK TELETHON*, TV, 85, CDN, Exec Prod; *POPE'S TOUR- I.W.K.CHILDREN'S HOSPITAL*, TV, 84, CDN, Prod/Dir; *'COMPASS'* (daily), TV, 81-75, CDN, Exec Prod/Dir.

OBOMSAWIN, Alanis - see DIRECTORS

O'BRIAN, Peter
ACFTP, CFTA. Peter O'Brian Independent Pic., 264 Seaton St., Suite 201, Toronto, Ont, CAN, M5A 2T4. (416)960-6468.
Types of Production & Categories: Th Film-Prod.
Genres: Drama-Th.
Biography: Born 1947, Toronto, Ontario. B.A., Mass Communications and English Literature, Emerson College, Boston. *THE GREY FOX* was nominated as Best Foreign Film, Golden Globe Awards; *MY AMERICAN COUSIN* won the Int'l Critics Award, Festival of Festivals, Toronto, 85.
Selective Filmography: *JOHN AND THE MISSUS*, Th, 86, CDN, Exec Prod/Co-Prod; *ONE MAGIC CHRISTMAS*, Th, 85, CDN/USA, Prod; *DISCOVERY* (EXPO 86), Th, 85, CDN, Prod; *MY AMERICAN COUSIN*, Th, 84, CDN, Prod **(GENIE)**; *THE GREY FOX*, Th, 81/80, CDN, Prod **(GENIE)**; *FAST COMPANY*, Th, 78, CDN, Co-Prod; *BLOOD & GUTS*, Th, 77, CDN, Co-Prod; *OUTRAGEOUS!*, Th, 77, CDN, Assoc Prod; *LOVE AT FIRST SIGHT*, Th, 75, CDN, Prod; *ME*, Th, 74, CDN, Co-Prod.

O'CONNELL, Maura
Salter Street Films Ltd., P.O. Box 2261, Stn. M, Halifax, NS, CAN, B3J 3C8. (902)420-1577.
Types of Production & Categories: Th Film-Prod.
Genres: Drama-Th.
Selective Filmography: *DEFCON 4*, Th, 83, CDN, Co-Prod/Co-Dir; *SIEGE*, Th, 81, CDN, Co-Prod.

OWEN, Don - see DIRECTORS

159

PARK, Alex

131 Silverbirch Ave., Toronto, Ont, CAN, M4E 3L3. (416)690-3545.
Types of Production & Categories: TV Video-Prod.
Genres: Variety-TV; Musical-TV; Documentary-TV.
Biography: Born 1948.
Selective Filmography: *THE SILENT PARTNER,* TV, 86/85, CDN, Prod; *THE SACKVILLE CONCERT,* TV, 85, CDN, Prod; *HEART'S DELIGHT,* TV, 85, CDN, Prod; *TRIBUTE TO MARTIN LUTHER KING,* TV, 85, CDN, Exec Prod; *MAGIC OF BROADWAY,* TV, 85, CDN, Exec Prod; *BALLADE* (2 parts), TV, 85, CDN, Prod/Dir.

PARTINGTON, Lawrence

CFTA. 387 Roehampton Ave., Toronto, Ont, CAN, M4P 1S3. (416)484-6648.
Patterson-Partington Int'l TV, 793 Pharmacy Ave., Scarborough, Ont, CAN, M1L 3K2. (416)752-8850.
Types of Production & Categories: TV Film-Prod/Dir; TV Video-Prod/Dir.
Genres: Sports-TV; Commercials-TV; Industrial-TV.
Biography: Canadian. B.A., Ryerson Polytechnical Institute. Has won 2 Awards of Excellence from the Canadian Public Relations Society.
Selective Filmography: *GAETAN BOUCHER AT THE WORLD SPRINT SPEEDSKATING CHAMPIONSHIPS,* TV, 86, CDN, Prod; *EXPORT A CANADIAN WOMEN'S ALPINE SKI CHAMPIONSHIPS,* TV, 86, CDN, Dir; *MacDONALD DISABLED SKIING CHAMPIONSHIPS,* TV, 85, CDN, Prod/Dir; *JEEP CUP RALLY,* TV, 85, CDN, Prod/Dir/Wr; *CAN-AM AUTO RACE/ BUDWEISER GT AUTO RACE,* TV, 85, CDN, Prod/Dir; *GRAND PRIX DE TROIS-RIVIERES,* TV, 85, CDN, Prod/Dir; *IMSA GT AUTO ENDURANCE RACE* (4 shows), TV, 84-81, CDN, Prod; *RALLYMASTER,* TV, 82, CDN, Prod/ Dir; *CANADIAN GAMES FOR THE PHYSICALLY DISABLED,* TV, 81, CDN, Prod/Dir/Wr.

PATEL, Ishu - see DIRECTORS

PATON, Chris - see DIRECTORS

PATRICK, Bill

City-TV, 299 Queen St.W., Toronto, Ont, CAN, M5V 1Z9. (416)367-5757.
Types of Production & Categories: TV Video-Prod.
Genres: News-TV.
Biography: Born 1952. Audio engineer for Transmedia Services, 75-79; news cameraman (79-80), assignment editor (80-81), director (81-84) for *CITY PULSE* (CITY TV). Associate producer (84-85), producer (85-86) *CITY PULSE TONIGHT.*

PATTERSON, David

25 Nelson St., Montreal West, Que, CAN, H4X 1G2. (514)486-4696. Filmline Int'l Inc., 209 St.Paul St. W., Suite 500, Montreal, Que, CAN, H2Y 2A1. (514)288-5888.
Types of Production & Categories: Th Film-Prod; TV Film-Prod.
Genres: Drama-Th&TV; Action-Th&TV.
Biography: Born 1947, Montreal, Quebec. Education: McGill University. Wrote and produced 500 TV commercials for Eaton's starting in 68; National Advertising Manager, Eaton's, 71-73. Co-founder, Telescene Productions, Montreal, 77; co-founder, Filmline Productions.
Selective Filmography: *WHERE THE DARK STREETS GO,* TV, 86, USA, Co-Prod; *TOBY McTEAGUE,* Th, 85, CDN, Co-Exec Prod; *THE BLUE MAN,* Th, 85, CDN, Exec Prod; *SPEARFIELD'S DAUGHTER* (mini-series), TV, 85, CDN/ USA/AUS, Co-Prod; *CHOICES,* TV, 85, USA, Pro Spv; *BREAKING ALL THE RULES,* Th, 84, CDN, Co-Prod; *HOTEL NEW HAMPSHIRE,* Th, 83, USA, Co-
(cont/suite)

Prod; *COOK & PEARY: THE RACE TO THE POLE*, TV, 83, USA, Co-Prod; *CROSS-COUNTRY*, Th, 82, CDN, Co-Prod; *HEARTACHES*, Th, 81, CDN, Co-Prod.

PAYEUR, Bernadette

4374 Berri, Montréal, Qué, CAN, H2J 2R1. (514)282-0214. ACPAV, 1050 Dorchester est, Ste. 200, Montréal, Qué, CAN, H2L 2L6. (514)849-1381.
Types de production et Catégories: l métrage-Prod; c métrage-Prod.
Types d'oeuvres: Drame-C; Comédie-C.
Curriculum vitae: Née en 1952; bilingue. *LA FEMME DE L'HOTEL* remporte plusieurs prix dont le Prix de la Critique Québécoise, Prix de la Presse Internationale (Montréal), Prix du Public (Créteil, France) et 2 Génies.
Filmographie sélective: *ELVIS GRATTON LE KING DES KINGS*, C, 85, CDN, Prod; *LA FEMME DE L'HOTEL* (WOMAN IN TRANSIT), C, 84, CDN, Prod; *LES VACANCES D'ELVIS*, C, 83, CDN, Prod/Dir pro; *ELVIS GRATTON*, C, 82, CDN, Prod/Dir pro (GENIE).

PAYRASTRE, Georges - see CINEMATOGRAPHERS

PEARCE, Gwyneth

243 Major St., Toronto, Ont., CAN, M5S 2L5. (416)929-0306. Global TV, 81 Barber Greene Rd., Don Mills, Ont, CAN, M3C 2A2. (416)446-5460.
Types of Production & Categories: TV Video-Prod.
Genres: News-TV; Documentary-TV.
Biography: Born 1960, Edmonton, Alberta; bilingual. Honours B.A., University of Toronto; presently studying law. Has been working at Global TV for 7 years; 4 years as producer/writer of the *SATURDAY EVENING EDITION*.

PEARSON, Barry

ACTRA. Poundmaker Productions Ltd., 36 High Park Blvd., Toronto, Ont, CAN, M6R 1M8. (416)535-3752.
Types of Production & Categories: Th Film-Prod/Wr; TV Film-Prod/Wr; TV Video-Prod/Wr.
Genres: Drama-Th&TV; Science Fiction-Th.
Biography: Born Nipawin, Saskatchewan. B.Ed., M.A. University of Saskatchewan. Former Chairman of Actra Writers Guild.
Selective Filmography: *COVERT ACTION*, TV, 86, CDN, Wr/Exec Prod; *ISAAC LITTLEFEATHERS*, Th, 84, CDN, Co-Wr/Co-Prod; *THE LIFE AND TIMES OF EDWIN ALONZO BOYD*, TV, 82, CDN, Co-Wr/Prod; *SPIRIT OF THE RIVER TO CHINA*, 'SPIRIT OF ADVENTURE', TV, 80/79, CDN, Wr/Prod; *MAROONED IN THE LAND GOD GAVE TO CAIN*, 'SPIRIT OF ADVENTURE', TV, 79, CDN, Wr/Prod; *MADELEINE*, 'SPIRIT OF ADVENTURE', TV, 79, CDN, Wr/Dir; *CROSSBAR*, TV, 78, CDN, Assoc Prod; *MUTATION* (M3-THE GEMINI STRAIN), Th, 77, CDN, Wr/Prod; *AMBUSH AT IROQUOIS POINT*, TV, 76, CDN, Wr; *DEATH SENTENCE*, TV, 76, CDN, Wr; *SOMEDAY SOON*, TV, 75, CDN, Wr; *GOING DOWN SLOW*, TV, 74, CDN, Wr; *PAPERBACK HERO*, Th, 73, CDN, Co-Wr; *McLEISH'S WILD HORSES*, TV, 71, CDN, Wr; *'PAUL BERNARD'* (32 eps), TV, 71/70, CDN, Wr; *RODEO RIDER*, TV, 70, CDN, Wr.

PEARSON, Peter - see DIRECTORS

PELLY, Gene

IATSE-667. Genie Productions Inc., 3809 Emerald Dr., North Vancouver, BC, CAN, V7R 3B6. (604)980-2972.
Types of Production & Categories: TV Video-Ed/Prod.
Genres: Commercials-TV; Industrial-Th&TV.
Biography: Born 1942, Vancouver, British Columbia. Producer/editor of industrials and commercials for the past 6 years.

(cont/suite)

Selective Filmography: *SHAWNIGAN LAKE SCHOOL/HYSTAR AEROSPACE/ TEAMSTERS,* In, 86/85, CDN, Prod/Ed/Snd Rec; *GENERAL PAINT,* Cm, 85, CDN, Prod/Ed.

PERLMUTTER, David M.

47 Elgin Ave., Toronto, Ont, CAN, M5R 1G5. (416)968-7255. 980 Yonge St., #404, Toronto, Ont, CAN, M4W 2J5. (416)929-0019.
Types of Production & Categories: Th Film-Prod.
Genres: Drama-Th; Comedy-Th.
Biography: Born 1934, Toronto, Ontario. B. Commerce, University of Toronto; C.A.. Producer or executive producer of several films between 72 and 80 including *THE NEPTUNE FACTOR, SUNDAY IN THE COUNTRY, LOVE AT FIRST SIGHT, BLOOD AND GUTS, FAST COMPANY, TWO SOLITUDES.* Since 80, providing financial consulting services to producers and distributors in the Canadian and US film and television industry including pay, standard broadcast TV productions and theatrical motion pictures.

PERLMUTTER, Renée

47 Elgin Ave., Toronto, Ont, CAN, M5R 1G5. (416)968-7255. Velvet Film Productions Ltd., 980 Yonge St., #404, Toronto, Ont, CAN, M4W 2J5. (416)960-8447.
Types of Production & Categories: Th Film-Prod; TV Video-Prod.
Genres: Drama-Th&TV; Comedy-Th&TV; Variety-TV.
Selective Filmography: *THE HAIRDRESSERS,* TV, 83, USA, Exec Prod/Prod; *HOWIE MANDEL SPECIAL,* TV, 83, USA, Exec Prod/Prod; *LOVE,* Th, 81, CDN, Exec Prod/Prod.

PERZEL, Anthony

Box 603, Canmore, Alta, CAN, T0L 0M0. (403)678-4756.
Types of Production & Categories: TV Film-Prod/Dir/Cin/Ed.
Genres: Documentary-TV; Educational-TV; Animation-TV.
Biography: Born 1946, Venice, Italy; Canadian citizen. Education: Business, Ryerson Polytechnical Institute; 2 year Visual Communication Program and 3 year film apprenticeship, Banff Centre. Artistic and technical advisor, Electronic and Film Media Program, Banff Centre, 86. *LAKE LOUISE - A MOUNTAIN LEGEND* won Best Film, Mountain History, Banff.
Selective Filmography: *LAKE LOUISE - A MOUNTAIN LEGEND,* TV, 84, CDN, Prod/Dir/Cin/Co-Wr; *SIDING 29,* TV, 82, CDN, Prod/Dir/Cin/Ed; *HERITAGE FOR THE FUTURE,* TV, 80, CDN, Prod/Dir/Cin/Ed; *THE METIS,* TV, 79, CDN, Assoc Prod; *THOSE WHO SING TOGETHER,* TV, 78, CDN, Assoc Prod/ Cin/An; *COMPLETING OUR CIRCLE,* TV, 77, CDN, Cin/An.

PETTIGREW, Damien Philip

Stonewall House, Ayer's Cliff, Que, CAN, J0B 1C0. Artcity Films, 10352 Berri, Montreal, Que, CAN, H3L 2G8. (514)389-5811.
Types of Production & Categories: Th Short-Wr/Dir; TV Film-Prod/Dir.
Genres: Drama-Th; Documentary-Th&TV; Educational-TV.
Biography: Born 1958, Magog, Quebec; bilingual. Educated at Bishop's College, Oxford, Glasgow (M.Litt.); awards in creative writing and advanced studies scholarship; graduate, Ecole Nationale Louis Lumière, Paris. Author: 'The Seventh Day', 86.
Selective Filmography: *SVERD SARDUY,* 'CONVERSATIONS AROUND A CAMERA', TV, 85, USA/F, Prod/Dir; *FILM II-BECKETT,* Th, 85, F, Dir; *ITALO CALVINO,* 'CONVERSATIONS AROUND A CAMERA', TV, 84, F/I, Prod/Dir; *40 RANDOM OBSERVATIONS,* Th, 84, CDN, Wr/Dir; *EUGENE IONESCO,* 'CONVERSATIONS AROUND A CAMERA', TV, 83, CDN/F, Prod/Dir.

PICCOLO, John
CTPDA. 134 Home St., Winnipeg, Man, CAN. (204)772-5065. CBC, P.O. Box
160, Winnipeg, Man, CAN, R3C 2H1. (204)775-8351.
Types of Production & Categories: TV Video-Prod.
Genres: Current Affairs-TV; News-TV.
Biography: Born 1951, Italy; Canadian citizen; speaks Italian, English. Has worked
in television news, current affairs, documentaries since 74 as news writer, editor,
producer.
Selective Filmography: *'NEWSDAY'* (Windsor), TV, 85-82, CDN, Prod; *'24
HOURS LATE NIGHT'*, TV, 85, CDN, Prod; *A SACRED GIFT*, TV, 83, CDN,
Prod; *THE FIRST YEAR*, TV, 82, CDN, Prod; *'NEWS FINAL'* (Windsor), TV,
81/80, CDN, Wr/Ed; *'CBC NEWS'* (Vancouver), TV, 79/78, CDN, Wr/Ed;
'NEWSDAY' (Windsor), TV, 78-75, CDN, Wr/Ed; *'NEWS NINE'* (Windsor), TV,
74, CDN, Wr.

PICK, Anne
ACTRA, ATPD. 97 Marion St., Toronto, Ont, CAN, M6R 1E6. (416)531-6162.
CBC, 790 Bay St., 6th Fl., Toronto, Ont, CAN, M5G 1N8. (416)975-6715.
Types of Production & Categories: TV Film-Prod; TV Video-Prod.
Genres: Documentary-TV; Educational-TV; Children's-TV.
Biography: Born 1950, Adelaide, South Australia; Australian citizen; landed
immigrant, Canada. Served cadetship (4 years) as reporter with several newspapers
under auspices of Australian Journalists Assoc.; 6 years experience as a general
reporter, features writer and columnist. Lived in Canada 11 years, worked most of
that time at CBC.
Selective Filmography: *WOMEN & DRUGS/MACROBIOTIC DIET/PROPHY-
LACTIC MASTECTOMIES*, 'MARKET PLACE', TV, 86-84, CDN, Prod/Dir;
*CRIB SAFETY/CANCER & DIET/HERBAL REMEDIES/MEDICAL RATION-
ING*, 'MARKET PLACE', TV, 84-82, CDN, Prod; *MULTI-LEVEL MARKET-
ING*, 'MARKET PLACE', TV, 83, CDN, Prod/Dir; *LAST RIGHTS/HIGH
INTEREST RATES; THE VICTIMS & VICTORS*, 'MARKET PLACE', TV, 82,
CDN, Prod; *GETTING THE LEAD OUT/THE MISSISSAUGA DERAILMENT:
2 YEARS LATER*, 'MARKET PLACE', TV, 82/81, CDN, Prod; *'DREAM
MERCHANTS: IMPACT OF CANADA'S WONDERLAND*, 'NEWSHOUR', TV,
81, CDN, Prod; *BY REASON OF INSANITY/FAT SCAM*, 'LOEB REPORT',
TV, 81/80, CDN, Prod; *IMMIGRATION/ZENOPHOBIA/RACISM/THE BOAT
PEOPLE IN CANADA/ISLAM*, 'CANADIANS', TV, 81, CDN, Prod; *BLACKS:
A CANADIAN HISTORY/THE SPIES/NATIVE INDIANS*, 'CANADIANS',
TV, 81, CDN, Prod.

PLATT, Janice
CFTA. Atlantis Films Ltd., 65 Heward Ave., Toronto, Ont, CAN, M4M 2T5. (416)
462-0246.
Types of Production & Categories: TV Film-Prod.
Genres: Drama-TV; Comedy-TV; Documentary-TV; Children's-TV.
Biography: Born 1953, British Columbia. B.A., Film, Queen's University. Atlantis
films have won awards at the American, Chicago and Yorkton Film Festivals.
Selective Filmography: *'AIRWAVES'* (26 eps), TV, 86/85, CDN, Prod; *'BELL
CANADA PLAYHOUSE'* (26 eps), TV, 86-84, CDN, Co-Prod; *'SONS &
DAUGHTERS'* (11 eps), TV, 83/82, CDN, Co-Prod; *BOYS & GIRLS*, 'SONS &
DAUGHTERS', TV, 82, CDN, Co-Prod (**CFTA/OSCAR**).

POIRIER, Anne Claire - voir REALISATEURS

PRICE, Roger

ACTRA, ACTT. Kid Next Door Productions, 1500 Merivale Rd., Ottawa, Ont, CAN, K2C 3G6. (613)224-1313.
Types of Production & Categories: TV Film-Prod/Dir/Wr; TV Video-Prod/Dir/Wr.
Genres: Drama-TV; Comedy-TV; Science Fiction-TV; Children's-TV.
Biography: Born 1941, Southport, Lancashire, England. Educated in numerous private schools in U.K. and Switzerland. Entered industry, 61, as writer at ATV, Birmingham; later, writer/director, Film Producer's Guild, ABC, BBC, Granada and Thames TV. Came to Canada, 79.
Selective Filmography: *'MORNINGSTAR EVENINGSTAR'* (6 eps), TV, 86, USA, Creator; *'YOU CAN'T DO THAT ON TELEVISION'* (100 eps), TV, 86-79, USA, Creator/Prod/Wr; *'TURKEY TELEVISION'* (65 eps), TV, 85, USA, Creator/Prod/Wr; *UFO KIDNAPPED,* TV, 83, USA, Creator/Prod/Wr; *'DON'T LOOK NOW'* (5 eps), TV, 82, USA, Creator/Prod/Wr; *LET ME PROVE IT,* TV, 82, CDN, Creator/Prod/Wr; *'SOMETHING ELSE'* (10 eps), TV, 81, CDN, Creator/Prod/Wr; *'THE TOMMOROW PEOPLE'* (76 eps), TV, 79-72, GB, Creator/Prod/Dir/Wr; *'WHATEVER TURNS YOU ON'* (14 eps), TV, 79, CDN, Creator/Prod/Wr; *'YOU CAN'T BE SERIOUS'* (7 eps), TV, 78, GB, Creator/Prod/Dir/Wr; *'PAULINE'S PEOPLE'* (13 eps), TV, 78, GB, Creator/Prod/Wr; *'FANFARE'* (26 eps), TV, 77, GB, Creator/Prod/Dir/Wr; *'PAULINE'S QUIRKES'* (6 eps), TV, 76, GB, Creator/Prod/Dir/Wr; *'YOU MUST BE JOKING'* (13 eps), TV, 74, GB, Creator/Prod/Dir/Wr.

PRINGLE, Douglas

ACTRA, AFM. Peak Productions, 7 Neville Park Blvd., Toronto, Ont, CAN, M4E 3P5. (416)690-3478.
Types of Production & Categories: TV Video-Wr/Dir/Prod.
Genres: Musical-Th&TV; Documentary-TV.
Biography: Born 1946, Toronto, Ontario. Extensive career as composer, producer, performer of pop and contemporary music; produced Juno nominee 'Romance at the Roxy', 81 for Michaele Jordana (Best New Vocalist). Staff producer at Global TV, Toronto, 81-85.
Selective Filmography: *FACE TO FACE,* TV, 85, CDN, Prod/Dir; *'THAT'S LIFE'* (100 eps), TV, 84-82, CDN, Prod; *THE FAR SHORE,* Th, 75, CDN, Comp.

PRIZEK, Mario - see DIRECTORS

PUCHNIAK, Tom

AR. 1975 de Maisonneuve W., #2105, Montreal, Que, CAN, H3H 1K4. (514)937-0745. CBC, 1400 Dorchester Blvd. E., Montreal, Que, CAN, H2L 2M2. (514)285-2465.
Types of Production & Categories: TV Film-Prod; TV Video-Prod.
Genres: Documentary-TV.
Biography: Born 1947, Moose Jaw, Saskatchewan; bilingual. Classical studies, Holy Family College, Hartford; 16 years experience as reporter, writer, researcher, producer for CBC radio and TV. Spent 3 years in Whitehorse, Yellowknife as reporter for news service and radio documentaries on northern affairs; producer, network radio series 'Five Nights' and 'Cross Country Check-up'; executive producer, Commonwealth Games radio coverage, 78.
Selective Filmography: *HEALTH AND SAFETY,* TV, 86, CDN, PM; *'STEPPIN' OUT'* (100 eps), TV, 85-82, CDN, Field Prod; *DR.SINGH'S CANADA DAY PARADE,* 'THE CANADIANS', TV, 84, CDN, Prod/Wr; *'QUEBEC REPORT'* (55 eps), TV, 82-80, CDN, Field Prod; *'IN QUESTION'* (26 eps), TV, 80/79, CDN, Res.

PURDY, Brian E.

CFTA. 77 Huntley St., Ste. 2522, Toronto, Ont, CAN, M4Y 2P3. (416)961-1776.
(cont/suite)

PRODUCTEURS/PRODUCERS

Types of Production & Categories: TV Film-Prod/Dir; TV Video-Prod/Dir.
Genres: Variety-TV; Musical-TV; Animation-TV; Industrial-TV.
Biography: Born 1937, Toronto, Ontario. Education: Ryerson Polytechnical Institute; Royal Conservatory of Music. Has produced/directed TV variety shows, industrials and commercials for CFTO, Baker Lovick, Ronalds Reynolds, Lauron Productions. President, producer, Broadcast Productions Inc. since 79.

RADFORD, Tom

Nat'l Screen Institute-Canada, 8540 - 109th St., #202, Edmonton, Alta, CAN, T6G 1E6. (403)439-8461.
Types of Production & Categories: TV Film-Prod/Dir/Wr; TV Video-Prod.
Genres: Drama-TV; Documentary-TV.
Biography: Born 1946, Edmonton, Alberta. B.A., University of Alberta. Founding member, Film Frontiers Ltd, 69; Filmwest Associates Ltd., 72; Great Plains Films Ltd., 78. Set up Northwest Studio of NFB in Edmonton; executive producer, 81-86. Board member, Banff TV Festival, 82-86. Executive Director, National Screen Institute - Canada. His films have won awards at Banff, Yorkton, San Francisco, Hemisfilm and American film festivals.
Selective Filmography: LONG LANCE, TV, 86, CDN, Exec Prod; A CHANGE OF HEART, 'FOR THE RECORD', TV, 83, CDN, Exec Prod; WAR STORY, TV, 82, CDN, Exec Prod; CHINA MISSION - THE CHESTER RONNING STORY, TV, 80, CDN, Co-Wr/Dir; WOOD MOUNTAIN POEMS, TV, 78, CDN, Prod; 'THE RENEWABLE SOCIETY' (26 eps), TV, 76, CDN, Prod; MAN CHOOSES THE BUSH, TV, 75, CDN, Dir; ERNEST BROWN, PIONEER PHOTOGRAPHER, TV, 74, CDN, Wr/Dir; THE COUNTRY DOCTOR, TV, 72, CDN, Wr/Dir.

RASKY, Harry - see DIRECTORS

RAYMOND, Bruce

CFTA. Bruce A. Raymond Prods. Ltd., 353 St. Clair Ave.E., Toronto, Ont, CAN, M4T 1P3. (416)485-3406.
Types of Production & Categories: TV Film-Prod; TV Video-Prod.
Genres: Drama-TV; Documentary-TV; Educational-TV; Children's-TV.
Biography: Born 1925; bilingual Graduated from McGill University. During the 50's, wrote 200 TV documentaries, film scripts and radio programs; head of CBC radio, 60's, then, Head of CBC TV; returned to private enterprise as distributor, producer, 69. SPECIAL PEOPLE won a Christopher Award and the Silver Medal, Houston Int'l Film Festival, 85.
Selective Filmography: 'YOUR HEALTH QUIZ' (6 eps), TV, 85, CDN/USA, Exec Prod; 'PARENTING' (130 eps), TV, 85/84, CDN, Pro Exec; 'FROST OVER CANADA' (10 eps), TV, 83, CDN, Prod; 'BINGO EXPRESS' (65 eps), TV, 83, CDN, Prod; SPECIAL PEOPLE, TV, 83, CDN/USA, Exec Prod; LIVE 'N KICKIN', TV, 83, CDN, Exec Prod; HOOTERS, TV, 83, CDN, Prod; MAGIC OF DAVID COPPERFIELD, TV, 83, CDN/USA, Prod; RICH LITTLE LIFT-OFF, TV, 83, CDN, Exec Prod; 'THE KANGAZOO CLUB' (26 eps), TV, 83/82, CDN, Co-Prod; THE WRECK OF THE MARGESON, TV, 81, CDN, Narr; 'CHANGING WORLDS' (14 eps), TV, 78, CDN, Prod; 'CONNECTION' (16 eps), TV, 77, CDN, Co-Prod; 'ENJOY BEING BEAUTIFUL' (130 eps), TV, 76, CDN, Prod; HER ONE TRUE LOVE, TV, 76, CDN, Exec Prod; MATTHEW MANNING - STUDY OF A PSYCHIC, TV, 75, CDN, Prod; PHILIP: THE IMAGINARY GHOST, TV, 74, CDN, Prod; 'THE WORLD OF GILBERT SULLIVAN' (8 eps), TV, 74, CDN, Prod; 'LAUREL & HARDY' (32 eps), TV, 73, CDN, Prod; 'INNER SPACE' (North Am version), (13 eps), TV, 73, CDN/AUS, Prod; 'ISLAM' (5 eps), TV, 72, CDN/I, Prod; 'THE GORDIE TAPP SHOW' (2 eps), TV, 72, CDN, Prod; 'ALPHABET SOUP' (52 eps), TV, 72/71, CDN, Prod; 'MARC'S MUSIC SHOP' (26 eps), TV, 70, CDN, Prod; McLEAN OF HUDSON'S BAY, TV, 57, CDN/USA, PM; BY-LINE MARGOT, TV, 57, CDN,

(cont/suite)

165

Wr; *'CROSSROADS'* (52 eps), TV, 55/54, CDN, Wr/Host; *MOUNT ROYAL,* TV, 55/54, CDN, Wr; *CINDERELLA,* TV, 55/54, CDN, Wr.

RAYMOND, Donovan B.

620 Jarvis St., #208, Toronto, Ont, CAN, M4Y 2R8. (416)920-8829. Raymond International, 353 St.Clair Ave.E., Toronto, Ont, CAN, M4T 1P3. (416)485-3406.
Types of Production & Categories: TV Video-Prod.
Genres: Educational-TV; Industrial-TV.
Biography: Born 1961, Toronto, Ontario.
Selective Filmography: *DENTU-FICATION,* In, 86, CDN, Prod; *'PARENTING'* (130 eps), TV, 85/84, CDN, Coord Prod; *'YOUR HEALTH QUIZ'* (6 eps), TV, 85, CDN, Prod.

RAYMOND, Marie-Josée

APFVQ, UDA. C.P.40, St-Paul d'Abbotsford, Qué, CAN, J0E 1A0. (514)379-5304. Rose Films Inc., 86 de Brésoles, Montréal, Qué, CAN, H2Y 1V5. (514)285-8901.
Types de production et Catégories: l métrage-Prod/Sc; TV film-Prod/Sc.
Types d'oeuvres: Drame-C&TV; Comédie-C; Documentaire-C.
Filmographie sélective: *BONHEUR D'OCCASION* (THE TIN FLUTE), (aussi 5 ém-TV), C, 82, CDN, Prod/Co sc; *HOT DOGS* (LES CHIENS-CHAUDS), C, 79, CDN, Prod/Co sc; *A SPECIAL DAY* (UNE JOURNEE PARTICULIERE), C, 77, CDN/I, Prod dél; *NIGHT OF THE HIGH TIDE,* C, 76, CDN/I, Prod exéc; *JE SUIS LOIN DE TOI MIGNONNE,* C, 75, CDN, Co prod; *LA POMME, LA QUEUE ET LES PEPINS,* C, 74, CDN, Prod/Co sc; *ALIEN THUNDER,* C, 73, CDN, Prod; *LES CHATS BOTTES,* C, 71, CDN, Prod/Co sc; *DEUX FEMMES EN OR,* C, 69, CDN, Co sc.

RAYMONT, Peter - see DIRECTORS

REED-OLSEN, Joan - see DIRECTORS

REHAK, Peter

CTV, 42 Charles St. E., Toronto, Ont, CAN, M4Y 1T5. (416)928-6332.
Types of Production & Categories: TV Film-Prod; TV Video-Prod.
Genres: News-TV.
Biography: Started career in print journalism as reporter for 'The Windsor Star', 'Vancouver Sun' and 'Canadian Press', 59-62; foreign correspondent (Associated Press), 62-72 and won George Polk Award for Best Reoprting from Overseas, Overseas Press Club and AP Managing Editor's Awards, 68. Ottawa correspondent, 'The Montreal Star', 72-73; Bureau Chief, 'Time', Toronto and Ottawa, 73-76. Vice President, Parliamentary Press Gallery, 75. Senior producer (CBC), *NEWSMAGAZINE, THE NATIONAL,* 76-81; producer, executive producer of *W5* (CTV), 81-86. President of News and Magazine Jury, Monte Carlo TV Festival, 85; member of jury, 83.

REID, Donald W.

ACTRA, CAPAC. Dunblane Farm, R.R. 7, Thamesville, Ont, CAN, N0P 2K0. (519)692-3382. Reid Entertainment Corp., 1500 Don Mills Rd., Ste. 708, Don Mills, Ont, CAN, M3B 3K4. (416)441-9773.
Types of Production & Categories: Th Film-Prod; TV Film-Prod; TV Video-Prod/ Wr.
Genres: Drama-Th&TV; Educational-TV; Children's-TV; Animation-TV.
Biography: Born 1929, Barrie, Ontario. B.A., Economics, University of Western Ontario; Osgoode Hall Law School.
Selective Filmography: *DREAMS OF GOLD,* Th, 86, USA/MEX, Exec Prod; *'THE LAW AND YOU'* (26 eps), TV, 82, CDN, Prod; *'THE ADVENTURES OF SNELGROVE SNAIL'* (200 eps), TV, 81-79, CDN, Prod/Wr/Voice/Comp; *HOME*
(cont/suite)

TO STAY, TV, 78, CDN, Prod; *JUST JESSIE,* Th, 78, CDN, Prod; *TELL ME MY NAME,* TV, 77, CDN, Prod; *'ENCYCLOPEDIA BRITTANICA PRESENTS'* (13 eps), TV, 77, CDN/USA, Prod; *'THE GREAT DEBATE'* (26 eps), TV, 77, CDN, Prod; *'AMERICAN SALESMASTER'* (17 eps), ED, 77, CDN/USA, Prod.

REITMAN, Ivan - see DIRECTORS
REUSCH, Peter - see DIRECTORS
RICHARDSON, Gillian
ACTT, DGC. 93 Ivy Ave., Toronto, Ont, CAN, M4L 2H8. (416)465-3153.
Types of Production & Categories: Th Short-PM/Prod; TV Film-PM/Prod.
Genres: Drama-Th&TV; Action-Th&TV; Science Fiction-Th&TV; Children's-TV.
Biography: Born 1950, Jersey, Channel Islands, Great Britain; British-Canadian citizenship; bilingual. Educated and trained in TV and film production in Britain.
Selective Filmography: *THE FLY,* Th, 86/85, USA, Cont; *LEGS OF THE LAME/ REBELLION OF YOUNG DAVID,* 'BELL CANADA PLAYHOUSE', TV, 85, CDN, Co-Prod; *THE DREAM AND THE TRIUMPH,* 'BELL CANADA PLAYHOUSE', TV, 85, CDN, Co-Prod; *'RAY BRADBURY THEATRE'* (3 eps), TV, 85, CDN, Line Prod/PM; *'BELL CANADA PLAYHOUSE'* (7 eps), TV, 84, CDN, Line Prod/PM; *ISLANDS,* TV, 84, CDN/USA, PM; *'SONS AND DAUGHTERS'* (12 eps), TV, 83, CDN, Line Prod/PM; *THE DEAD ZONE,* Th, 83, USA, Cont; *VIDEODROME,* Th, 81, CDN, Cont; *DEATH BITE* (SPASMS), Th, 81, CDN, Cont; *'KIDSWORLD'* (26 eps), TV, 80, CDN/USA, Assoc Prod/Dir; *KILLER INSTINCT,* Th, 80, CDN, Cont; *THRESHOLD,* Th, 80, CDN, Cont; *BEING DIFFERENT,* Th, 80, CDN, Cont; *HEAD ON,* Th, 79, CDN, Cont; *CRUNCH* (THE KINKY COACHES AND THE POM POM PUSSYCATS), Th, 79, CDN, Cont.

RODGERS, Bob

131 Bloor St.W., #801, Toronto, Ont, CAN, M5S 1R1. (416)924-2946. Bellair Communications, 264 Seaton St., #205, Toronto, Ont, CAN, M5A 2T4. (416)927-1121.
Types of Production & Categories: TV Film-Dir/Prod/Wr; TV Video-Dir/Prod/Wr.
Genres: Drama-Th, Documentary-TV; Educational-TV; Industrial-TV.
Biography: Born 1933, Regina, Saskatchewan. Attended Wayne State U., received B.A., University of Manitoba; M.A., University of Toronto; completed Ph.D. program at U. of T.; thesis research at the Bodleian, Oxford. Taught English, U. of T., McGill before moving into writing, then directing/producing documentary, educational films; associate producer of features, Film Corsortium of Canada; President of Bellair Communications Ltd. Has won IMF and Amtec Awards for several films.
Selective Filmography: *BEHIND THE SCREENS,* 'TRADE SECRETS', TV, 86, CDN, Dir/Wr; *FOUR SEASONS IN A DAY,* In, 85, CDN, Prod; *THE CLOUDED CRYSTAL,* In, 85, CDN, Prod/Dir; *CABBAGETOWN,* 'NEIGHBORHOODS', TV, 85, CDN, Dir/Wr; *HIGH IMPACT WELDING,* In, 84, CDN, Dir/Wr; *UN PREMIER PRIX,* ED, 84, CDN, Prod; *A SENSE OF COMMUNITY,* In, 83, CDN, Dir; *NORTHROP FRYE,* 'THE BIBLE AND LITERATURE', ED, 83-81, CDN, Prod; *THE BREAD WE LIVE BY,* ED, 83, CDN, Prod; *VOICES OF EARLY CANADA,* ED, 81-79, CDN, Prod/Dir; *CHINA: THE CULTURAL REVOLUTION,* ED, 81, CDN, Prod/Dir; *CIRCLE OF TWO,* Th, 80, CDN, Assoc Prod; *FIDDLERS OF JAMES BAY,* TV, 79, CDN, Co-Prod/Dir; *MR. PATMAN,* Th, 79, CDN, Assoc Prod; *LES VOYAGEURS/OIL UNDER ICE,* ED, 79-77, CDN, Prod/Dir; *LEARNING THROUGH PLAY,* ED, 77, CDN, Prod; *TIME OF THE CREE,* TV, 76, CDN, Wr/Dir; *RIVERAIN: A GIFT OF PASSAGE,* TV, 76, CDN, Prod/Wr; *THE N.W.T., ONE THIRD OF CANADA,* TV, 75, CDN, Prod/ Dir; *'THE ABC'S OF CANADIAN FAMILY LIFE'* (7 eps), ED, 75-70, CDN, Prod/Dir; *'CANADIANS IN CONFLICT'* (6 eps), TV, 75/74, CDN, Prod/Dir;

(cont/suite)

'THE MIDDLE AGES' (15 eps), ED, 75-70, CDN, Prod/Dir; *'THE SPLENDID DREAM'* (LABOUR AND THE LEFT IN CANADA), (4 eps), TV, 75/74, CDN, Prod/Dir; *CHURCHILL RIVER DIVERSION,* TV, 73, CDN, Prod/Dir; *GATHERING AT BATOCHE,* TV, 72, CDN, Prod/Dir; *'VICTORIANS'* (13 eps), TV, 72-69, CDN, Prod/Dir; *FLIN FLON STRIKE,* TV, 71, CDN, Prod/Dir; *THE FOURTH WAVE* (IMMIGRATION TO CANADA), TV, 71, CDN, Prod/Dir; *'AS LONG AS THE RIVER SHALL RUN'* (2 eps), TV, 70, CDN, Prod/Dir.

ROGERS, Al - see WRITERS

ROGERS, Jonathan

522 N.Berendo St., Los Angeles, CA, USA, 90004. (213)664-5475.
Types of Production & Categories: TV Film-An/Dir/Prod.
Genres: Animation-TV; Music Video-TV.
Biography: Born 1937, Toronto, Ontario.
Selective Filmography: *'THE GLOFRIENDS'* (26 eps), TV, 86, USA, Prod/Dir; *JEM,* TV, 85, USA, Lay Art; *FACTS OF LICE,* TV, 85, USA, An Svp; *STANLEY THE FLUPPY DOG,* Cm, 85, USA, Ed; *LEVI'S/RAID/GOOD YEAR/STATE LOTTERY/CARTA BLANCA,* Cm, 84, USA, Vid Paint Art; *ROCK & RULE* (RING OF POWER), Th, 83, CDN, Wr/Sc Dir; *ATOMIC DOG,* MV, 82, USA, An; *LET'S PLAY GROWN UPS,* TV, 79, CDN, Prod/Dir/Wr/Voice; *WITCH'S NIGHT OUT/THE BAZOOEY SHOW/MODERATION AT ALL TIMES?,* TV, 79/77, CDN, Prod/Dir/An/Wr; *'SESAME STREET'* (sev seg), TV, 75, USA, Prod/Dir/Wr/An; *THE GIFT OF WINTER/EVOLU,* TV, 74/73, CDN, Prod/Dir/An/Wr.

ROSS, John T.

CFTA. 360 Bloor St.E., #1707, Toronto, Ont, CAN, M4W 3M3. (416)966-3346. Norflicks Productions Ltd,, 219 Front St.E., Toronto, Ont, CAN, M5A 1E8. (416) 865-1596.
Types of Production & Categories: Th Film-Prod; TV Film-Prod; TV Video-Prod.
Genres: Drama-Th&TV; Action-Th&TV; Science Fiction-Th&TV; Children's-Th&TV.
Biography: Born 1930, Quebec City. Education: Bishop's College School, Lennoxville; Middlebury College, Vermont. Founded Robert Lawrence Productions in 55, Eastern Sound Co., VTR Productions Ltd., Cinequip Inc.. Agent for Film Finances Ltd., completion guarantors; President, Actra Fraternal Benefit Society.
Selective Filmography: *'RAY BRADBURY THEATRE'* (3 eps), TV, 85, CDN, Co-Exec Prod; *'THE LITTLE VAMPIRE'* (13 eps), TV, 85, CDN/GB/D, Exec Prod; *'WORLD OF WICKS'* (100 eps), TV, 74, CDN, Prod; *MUSICIANS OF BREMEN,* TV, 71, CDN/USA, Exec Prod; *LEAVING HOME,* TV, 71, CDN, Prod; *FROG PRINCE,* TV, 70, CDN/USA, Exec Prod; *KING OF GRIZZLIES,* Th, 70, CDN/USA, Prod; *'55 NORTH MAPLE'* (130 eps), TV, 69, CDN, Exec Prod; *HEY! CINDERELLA,* TV, 69, CDN/USA, Exec Prod; *'STRATEGY'* (130 eps), TV, 68, CDN, Exec Prod; *CIRCLEVISION 360,* Th, 67, CDN/USA, Prod; *'MOMENT OF TRUTH'* (218 eps), TV, 65, CDN/GB, Exec Prod.

ROTH, Stephen J.

49 Magpie Cres., Toronto, Ont, CAN, M2L 2E6. (416)443-1558. Alliance Entertainment Corp., 92 Isabella St., Toronto, Ont, CAN, M4Y 1N4. (416)967-1174.
Types of Production & Categories: Th Film-Prod; TV Film-Prod.
Genres: Drama-Th&TV; Comedy-Th; Musical-Th; Action-Th&TV.
Biography: Born 1941, Montreal, Quebec. Honours degree, English and Political Science, 63; BCL, (Law), McGill University, 66; admitted to the Bar of the Province of Quebec, 67. Practiced law, specializing in corporate and entertainment matters, 67-77. Co-founder, RSL Films Ltd., 75; President, CEO, Alliance

(cont/suite)

Entertainment Corp., 86. *JOSHUA THEN AND NOW* and *NIGHT MAGIC* were both official selections, Cannes.
Selective Filmography: *'NIGHT HEAT'* (39 eps), TV, 86-84, CDN, Co-Spv Prod; *'HOT SHOTS'* (13 eps), TV, 86, CDN, Spv Prod; *SEPARATE VACATIONS,* Th, 85, CDN, Co-Prod; *BIG DEAL,* TV, 85, CDN, Co-Prod; *NIGHT MAGIC,* Th, 84, CDN/F, Co-Prod; *JOSHUA THEN AND NOW,* Th, 84, CDN, Co-Prod; *HEAVENLY BODIES,* Th, 83, CDN, Co-Prod; *BEDROOM EYES,* Th, 83, CDN, Co-Prod; *ONE NIGHT ONLY,* TV, 83, CDN, Co-Prod; *PERFECT TIMING,* TV, 83, CDN, Co-Prod; *OVERDRAWN AT THE MEMORY BANK,* TV, 83, CDN/USA, Co-Prod; *A MATTER OF CUNNING,* TV, 83, CDN, Co-Prod; *NEW ORLEANS,* TV, 83, CDN, Co-Prod; *SCANDALE,* Th, 82, CDN, Prod; *PARADISE,* Th, 81, CDN/IL, Co-Prod; *YOUR TICKET IS NO LONGER VALID,* Th, 79, CDN, Co-Prod; *SUZANNE,* Th, 79, CDN, Co-Prod; *AGENCY,* Th, 78, CDN, Co-Prod; *IN PRAISE OF OLDER WOMEN,* Th, 77, CDN, Co-Exec Prod; *L'ANGE ET LA FEMME,* Th, 76, CDN, Co-Prod.

ROWE, Peter - see DIRECTORS

ROWLAND, Wade

ATPD. 59 King St., Port Hope, Ont, CAN. (416)885-9774.
Types of Production & Categories: TV Film-Prod/Wr; TV Video-Prod/Wr.
Genres: Documentary-TV; Current Affairs-TV; News-TV.
Biography: Born 1944, Montreal, Quebec. Honours Economics, University of Manitoba. Experience as a journalist; author of several books including 'Making Connections', 'Ark on the Move' (ghost-written for Gerald Durrell), 'Nobody Calls me Mr. Kirck' (co-written with Mr. Kirck).
Selective Filmography: *'MARKET PLACE'* (45 eps), TV, 86-84, CDN, Sr Prod; *'NATIONAL NEWS'* (CTV), (Head Wr-84-79), TV, 84-76, CDN, Prod.

RYAN, John

ACTRA, ACTT, DGC. 158 Gough Ave., Toronto, Ont, CAN, M4K 3P1. (416)463-4232.
Types of Production & Categories: Th Film-Prod/PM; TV Film-Prod/PM.
Genres: Drama-Th&TV; Comedy-Th&TV; Variety-Th&TV; Action-Th&TV.
Biography: Born 1949, London, England; British-Canadian citizenship.
Selective Filmography: *CONFIDENTIAL,* Th, 85, CDN, Co-Prod; *DANCING IN THE DARK,* Th, 85, CDN, Co-Prod; *SPRING FEVER* (SNEAKERS), Th, 82, CDN, PM; *INTRUDER WITHIN,* TV, 81, CDN, Assoc Prod; *THE KIDNAPPING OF THE PRESIDENT,* Th, 79, CDN, Co-Prod; *STONE COLD DEAD,* Th, 79, CDN, Prod; *CHRISTMAS LACE,* TV, 78, CDN, Line Prod; *LOVEY, A CIRCLE OF CHILDREN-PART II,* TV, 78, CDN, PM.

RYLEY, Nancy

ATPD. 145 Albertus Ave., Toronto, Ont, CAN, M4R 1J6. (416)487-4044. CBC, 790 Bay St., 3rd Fl., Toronto, Ont, CAN, M5G 1N8. (416)975-3311.
Types of Production & Categories: TV Film-Prod/Dir.
Genres: Documentary-TV.
Biography: Born 1932, Montreal, Quebec. Education: B.A., B.L.S. Awards: Yorkton Int'l Film Festival, Best TV Feature and Emmy nomination for Outstanding Achievement in News and Documentary Programming for *GREY OWL.*
Selective Filmography: *LAWREN HARRIS* (JOURNEY TOWARDS THE LIGHT), TV, 85, CDN, Prod/Dir; *ERNEST THOMPSON SETON,* TV, 84, CDN, Prod/Dir; *WAYNE NGAN,* TV, 83, CDN, Prod/Dir; *THE WEST COAST ARTISTS: GORDON SMITH AND TONY ONLEY,* TV, 82, CDN, Prod/Dir; *AN EVENING WITH THE PRO ARTE QUARTET,* TV, 81, CDN, Prod/Dir; *HARRY AND FRANCES ADASKIN* (TO PLAY LIKE AN ANGEL), TV, 80, CDN, Prod/Dir; *HARRY ADASKIN,* 'MAN ALIVE', TV, 80, CDN, Prod/Dir;

(cont/suite)

THE PASSIONATE CANADIANS (THE GROUP OF SEVEN - 2 PARTS), TV, 79/78, CDN, Prod/Dir/Wr; *EMILY CARR* (Parts 1 & 2), TV, 75, CDN, Prod/ Dir/Wr (**ACTRA/ANIK**); *GREY OWL,* TV, 73, CDN, Prod/Dir.

SADLER, Richard

APFVQ. Les Films Stock Ltée., 3433 St-Denis, Montréal, Qué, CAN, H2X 3L1. (514)284-0257.
Types de production et Catégories: 1 métrage-Prod; c métrage-Prod; TV film-Prod/Réal; TV vidéo-Prod.
Types d'oeuvres: Drame-C&TV; Action-C&TV; Documentaire-TV; Education-TV.
Curriculum vitae: Né en 1947, Montréal, Québec. Etudes universitaires en philosophie, Université de Montréal. Au cinéma, a occupé les postes de régisseur, éclairagiste et assistant caméraman; fonde sa compagnie, Les Films Stock Ltée., 76.
Filmographie sélective: *FICTION ACCOMPLIE,* TV, 86, CDN, Réal; *DU POIL AUX PATTES COMME LES CWAC'S,* C, 85, CDN, Prod; *ST-LOUIS SQUARE,* C, 84, CDN, Prod; *LETTRE MORTE,* ED, 83, CDN, Prod; *'DISCRIMINATION'* (4 eps), ED, 83, CDN, Prod; *'SUR LE BOUT DE LA LANGUE'* (20 eps), TV, 82, CDN, Prod; *Y A PAS DE MAL A SE FAIRE DU BIEN,* C, 74, CDN/F, Prod assoc; *VALERIE,* C, 68, CDN, Prod assoc/Sc.

SAGER, Ray

DGC. Simcom Limited, 86 Bloor St.W., 5th Fl., Toronto, Ont, CAN, M5S 1M5. (416)961-6278.
Types of Production & Categories: Th Film-Prod; TV Film-Prod.
Genres: Drama-Th&TV; Horror-Th.
Biography: Born 1943, Chicago, Illinois; US citizen; landed immigrant, Canada. B.A., Goodman Theatre School of Drama. Production manager/1st assistant director in US, 70's; 1st AD on 5 features in Canada, 79. Head of Production, Simcom Limited since 85.
Selective Filmography: *THE HAUNTING OF HAMILTON HIGH,* Th, 86, CDN, Spv Prod; *BULLIES,* Th, 85, CDN, Pro Exec; *'MANIA'* (4 eps), TV, 85, CDN, Co-Prod; *FLYING,* Th, 84, CDN, Spv Prod; *THE MARK OF CAIN,* Th, 84, CDN, Spv Prod; *'DANGER BAY'* (5 eps), TV, 84, CDN/USA, Line Prod; *WHEN WE FIRST MET,* TV, 83, USA, Line Prod; *AMERICAN NIGHTMARE,* Th, 82, CDN, Prod.

SAHASRABUDHE, Deepak

Soma Film Producers, 43 Britain St., 3rd Fl., Toronto, Ont, CAN, M5A 1R7. (416) 868-6012.
Types of Production & Categories: TV Film-Prod; TV Video-Prod.
Genres: Drama-TV; Comedy-TV; Documentary-TV; Educational-TV.
Biography: Born 1951, Poona, India; Canadian citizen. B.A., Sociology/ Anthropology, Carleton University, 74.
Selective Filmography: *'MONEY SMART'* (13 eps), TV, 85, CDN, Co-Prod; *THE TERMINATION INTERVIEW,* ED, 85, CDN, Co-Prod; *STALKING THE SILENT THIEF,* ED, 85, CDN, Co-Prod; *TRANSITIONS,* TV, 84, CDN, Co-Prod; *BRIDGES,* TV, 83, CDN, Co-Prod; *'STARTING A BUSINESS'* (13 eps), TV, 82, CDN, Co-Prod; *GOODBYE MR.DICKENS,* TV, 81, CDN, Co-Prod.

SALTZMAN, Deepa - see DIRECTORS

SALTZMAN, Paul

ACTRA, CAPAC, DGC. Sunrise Films Limited, 160 Perth Ave., Toronto, Ont, CAN, M6P 3X5. (416)535-2900.
Types of Production & Categories: TV Film-Prod/Dir.
Genres: Drama-TV; Action-TV; Documentary-TV; Children's-TV.

(cont/suite)

Biography: Born 1943, Toronto, Ontario. Studied Engineering, University of Toronto. Started at CBC as researcher, interviewer, 65-67; NFB, 67; founded Sunrise Films, 73.
Selective Filmography: *'DANGER BAY'* (57 eps), TV, 86-84, CDN/USA, Co-Creator/Exec Prod; *K.Y.T.E.S. HOW WE DREAM OURSELVES,* TV, 85, CDN, Exec Prod; *TRAVELLING LIGHT: THE PHOTOJOURNALISM OF DILIP MEHTA,* TV, 85, CDN/GB, Exec Prod; *VALENTINE'S REVENGE,* TV, 84, USA, Dir/Pro Exec; *WHEN WE FIRST MET,* TV, 83, USA, Prod/Dir; *PARTNERS IN DEVELOPMENT,* In, 83/82, CDN, Dir/Prod/Wr; *SHAO PING THE ACROBAT/YANG-XUN THE PEASANT PAINTER,* 'SPREAD YOUR WINGS', TV, 80, CDN, Co-Dir/Cin; *LAROUSSI AND THE FANTASIA,* 'SPREAD YOUR WINGS', TV, 80, CDN, Co-Dir/Cin; *HASAN THE CARPET WEAVER/CHILD OF GOD,* 'SPREAD YOUR WINGS', TV, 79-76, CDN, Dir; *VALERIE'S WINDOW/JOURNEY FROM ZANZIBAR/CHILD OF THE ANDES,* 'SPREAD YOUR WINGS', TV, 79-76, CDN, Dir; *STEVE'S VIOLIN/ MING-OI THE MAGICIAN/YOSHIKO AND THE PAPER MAKER,* 'SPREAD YOUR WINGS', TV, 79-77, CDN, Dir/Cin; *SEREMA'S MASK/THE MONK'S PARASOL,* 'SPREAD YOUR WINGS', TV, 79-77, CDN, Dir/Cin; *JAFAR'S BLUE TILES/FRANCESCO'S GIFT/THROUGH AMY'S EYES,* 'SPREAD YOUR WINGS', TV, 77, CDN, Cin; *DOLPHI GEORGE: DANCES,* TV, 77, CDN, Prod/Dir; *TO BE A CLOWN,* TV, 76, CDN, Co-Prod/Dir/Co-Wr; *INDIRA GANDHI: THE STATE OF INDIA,* TV, 75, CDN/USA/GB, Prod/Dir/Wr/Interv; *AT 99: A PORTRAIT OF LOUISE TANDY MURCH,* TV, 74, CDN/USA, Co-Prod **(CFA)**; *THE PERLMUTER STORY,* TV, 73, CDN, Co-Prod/Dir/Co-Wr **(3 CFTA)**; *BO DIDDLEY,* TV, 72, CDN, Prod/Dir.

SAMUELS, Maxine

ACTRA. 77 Carlton St., #801, Toronto, Ont, CAN, M5B 2J7. (416)593-0639.
Types of Production & Categories: Th Film-Prod; TV Film-Prod.
Genres: Drama-Th&TV; Action-Th&TV; Documentary-TV; Children's-TV.
Biography: Born 1924, Montreal, Quebec; bilingual; graduated from Sir George Williams University. Has performed as interviewer/host of public affairs TV programs; produced 2 TV series as independent producer; also produced drama programs for CBC, NFB and 100 commercials. Has also designed fashions and costumes. Won an award in Venice for *FOREST RANGERS*; Best TV Commerical, American Commercial Awards, Chicago, 68; honoured by AMPPDC for major contribution to the film industry.
Selective Filmography: *'ADVENTURES IN HISTORY'* (6 eps), TV, 79, CDN, Co-Prod; *OTTAWA VALLEY/SUMMER MOURNINGS,* 'ANTHOLOGY', TV, 74, CDN, Prod; *'SOME OF MY BEST FRIENDS ARE MEN'* (8 eps), TV, 74, CDN, Host/Interv; *THE PYX,* Th, 73, CDN, Exec Prod; *THE CASE OF THE MISSING DIAMONDS* (G.M. PONTIAC), Cm, 68, CDN, Prod; *'THE SEAWAY'* (30 eps), TV, 67/66, CDN, Exec Prod; *'FOREST RANGERS'* (114 eps), TV, 65-62, CDN, Exec Prod; *'TUESDAY CLUB'* (45 eps), TV, 62/61, CDN, Host/Interv; *'MAXINE PRESENTS'* (26 eps), TV, 60, CDN, Prod/Host/Res.

SANDERS, Ed

ATPD. 241 Beatrice St., Toronto, Ont, CAN, M6G 3E9. (416)533-1343. CBC, Box 500, Stn. A, Toronto, Ont, CAN, M5W 1E6. (416)975-6651.
Types of Production & Categories: TV Film-Prod/Dir/Ed.
Genres: Documentary-TV; Educational-TV; Children's-TV.
Biography: Born 1937, Brentford, Middlesex, England. Raised at the Actors Orphanage in Surrey until age 17; spent 7 years on ships, running passenger entertainments; emigrated to Canada, 61; 5 years as an actor. Joined CBC as film editor, 66 and edited over 300 film productions. Became producer, CBC, 80. Won the Gold Award, New York Int'l Film & TV Fest. for *THE MOUNTAIN WAITS.*

(cont/suite)

Selective Filmography: *COTTAGE COUNTRY/RIDING THE WIND/VOYAGE TO LABRADOR,* 'THIS LAND', TV, 85/84, CDN, Prod/Dir; *INWARD BOUND/I CAN SEE CLEARLY/TRAPLINES/THE MOUNTAIN WAITS,* 'THIS LAND', TV, 84-82, CDN, Prod/Dir; *LAND OF SHADOWS/FISH STORIES/FIRE BIRDS,* 'THIS LAND', TV, 82/81, CDN, Prod/Dir; *GREAT LAKES GOLD/ WILDLIFE - THE THRESHOLD,* 'THIS LAND', TV, 81/80, CDN, Prod/Dir.

SARRAZIN, Pierre

CFTA. Pierre Sarrazin Prod. Inc., 9 Olive Ave., Toronto, Ont, CAN, M6G 1T7. (416)535-6740.
Types of Production & Categories: TV Film-Prod/Dir/Wr; TV Video-Prod/Dir/Wr.
Genres: Drama-TV; Comedy-TV; Variety-TV; Documentary-TV.
Biography: Born 1946, Montreal, Quebec. B.A., Loyola College, 68. Received Ontario Arts Council Grant, 80. Winner, Silver Award, N.Y. Int'l Film & TV Festival for *THAT'S LIFE.*
Selective Filmography: *'WOMEN OF THE WORLD'* (7 eps), TV, 86/85, CDN/ USA, Prod/Dir/Wr; *WHAT TO DO WITH MOM AND DAD/A NATION DIVIDED,* 'THE JOURNAL', TV, 85, CDN, Prod/Dir/Wr; *'AMERICAN CENTURY'* (1 eps), TV, 85, CDN, Prod; *JOINED AT THE HIP,* TV, 84, CDN, Prod/Co-Dir; *'THAT'S LIFE'* (390 eps), TV, 84-81, CDN, Prod/Wr/Dir; *CHUCK AND FRAN SHOW* (pilot), TV, 83, CDN, Prod/Dir; *'HOUR GLASS'* (365 eps), TV, 77, CDN, Prod/Dir; *BRETHEN,* Th, 76, CDN, PM.

SAVATH, Philip - see WRITERS

SCHAFER, Joan

Schafer/Thurling Productions, 680 Queen's Quay W., Ste. 503, Toronto, Ont, CAN, M5V 2Y9. (416)593-8652.
Types of Production & Categories: TV Film-Wr/Prod; TV Video-Prod/Dir.
Genres: Drama-TV; Variety-TV; Musical-TV; Documentary-TV.
Biography: Born in Switzerland; Canadian citizen; speaks some German. Educated: Ann Arbor, Michigan; University of Toronto. Vice President of Programming for First Choice Pay TV, 1981-83. *FLOATING OVER CANADA* won at the Atlantic Film Festival.
Selective Filmography: *FLOATING OVER CANADA,* TV, 85, CDN, Prod; *'FRENCH ROCK'* (2 eps), TV, 84, CDN, Co-Wr; *'THE CITY SHOW'* (52 eps), TV, 77-74, CDN, Exec Prod; *'MONEY GAME'* (Dir-60 eps), (156 eps), TV, 74-72, CDN, Prod; *'WORLD OF THE UNEXPLAINED'* (26 eps), TV, 74/73, CDN, Prod/Dir; *FIRE IN THE LAKE,* TV, 74, CDN, Prod/Dir; *'CITY LIGHTS'* (52 eps), TV, 73/72, CDN, Prod/Dir.

SCHECTER, Brian

CTPDA. Multi-Media Productions Ltd., 2329 W. 14th Ave., Vancouver, BC, CAN, V6K 2W2. (604)734-1103.
Types of Production & Categories: TV Film-Prod/Dir; TV Video-Prod/Dir.
Genres: Variety-TV; Action-TV; Documentary-TV; Sports-TV.
Biography: Born 1950, Montreal, Quebec; bilingual. M.A., Carleton University; Institute of Canadian Studies. Twelve years experience working in TV, radio, print (newspaper, magazine writing).
Selective Filmography: *EXPOS BASEBALL,* TV, 85, CDN/USA, Prod; *PACIFETE 85,* 'A GUICHET FERME', TV, 85, CDN, Prod/Dir; *'HOCKEY NIGHT IN CANADA',* TV, 85-78, CDN, Prod/Dir; *SEA FESTIVAL PARADE,* TV, 85-79, CDN, Prod/Dir; *'PACIFIC REPORT',* TV, 85/84, CDN, Prod/Dir; *B.C. LIONS ANNUAL AWARDS NIGHT,* TV, 85-83, CDN, Prod/Dir; *'MIDDAY'* (sev seg), TV, 85, CDN, Prod/Dir; *BASKETBALL/FOOTBALL/HOCKEY/ SWIMMING CHAMPIONSHIPS,* TV, 85/84, CDN, Prod; *INSIDE BASEBALL,* TV, 85, CDN, Prod/Dir; *OLYMPICS,* TV, 84, CDN, Prod/Dir; *'SPORTS*

(cont/suite)

JOURNAL' (61 eps), TV, 84/83, CDN, Prod/Dir; *GREY CUP PARADE,* TV, 83, CDN, Dir; *WORLD STUDENT GAMES,* TV, 83, CDN, Prod; *CANADA SUMMER GAMES,* TV, 81, CDN, Prod/Dir.

SCOTT, Cynthia - see DIRECTORS

SCOTT, Michael J.F.
SGCT. 38 Spruce Hill Rd., Toronto, Ont, CAN, M4E 3G3. (416)973-3013. NFB, 65 Adelaide St. E., Toronto, Ont, CAN, M5C 2P7. (416)973-9110.
Types of Production & Categories: Th Film-Prod/Dir; Th Short-Prod/Dir; TV Film-Prod/Dir.
Genres: Drama-Th&TV; Comedy-Th&TV; Documentary-Th&TV; Animation-Th&TV.
Biography: Born 1942, Winnipeg, Manitoba. Education: Ryerson Polytechnical Institute. Began work at NFB as production assistant, 66; director, 67; director/producer, NFB, Montreal until 76; executive producer, Prairie region, NFB, 76-81 and 84-85; director/producer, Ontario region, 85. His films have won awards at festivals in Berlin, Washington, Montreal, New York, Zagreb; *THE BIG SNIT* was nominated for an Oscar, 85.
Selective Filmography: *THE BIG SNIT,* Th, 85, CDN, Prod **(GENIE)**; *GET A JOB,* Th, 85, CDN, Prod; *CAGES,* 'BELL CANADA PLAYHOUSE', TV, 84, CDN, Dir; *CAPITAL,* 'BELL CANADA PLAYHOUSE', TV, 84, CDN, Prod; *AFTER THE BIG ONE,* TV, 83, CDN, Prod; *TED BARYLUK'S GROCERY,* Th, 82, CDN, Prod; *THE PEDLAR,* TV, 82, CDN, Prod; *THE BOY WHO TURNED OFF,* TV, 81, CDN, Prod; *A WAR STORY,* TV, 81, CDN, Prod; *SOMETHING HIDDEN: A PORTRAIT OF WILDER PENFIELD,* TV, 81, CDN, Prod; *LOVED, HONOURED AND BRUISED,* TV, 80, CDN, Prod; *CHINA MISSION: THE CHESTER RONNING STORY,* TV, 80, CDN, Prod; *W.O.MITCHELL: NOVELIST IN HIDING,* TV, 79, CDN, Prod; *GETTING STARTED,* Th, 79, CDN, Prod; *WOOD MOUNTAIN POEMS,* ED, 79, CDN, Prod; *PRIORY, THE ONLY HOME I'VE GOT,* TV, 78, CDN, Exec Prod; *ONE MAN,* Th, 77, CDN, Prod; *RED DRESS,* TV, 77, CDN, Dir; *FOR GENTLEMEN ONLY,* TV, 76, CDN, Dir **(CFA)**; *WHISTLING SMITH,* 'PACIFIC CANADA', TV, 75, CDN, Prod/Co-Dir **(CFA)**; *STATION 10,* TV, 73, CDN, Dir; *SMALL SMOKE AT BLAZE CREEK,* Th, 71, CDN, Dir, *THAT'S THE PRICE,* ED, 70, CDN, Dir; *RECESS,* Th, 67, CDN, Dir.

SEDAWIE, Gayle Gibson
ACTRA. 19567 Oxnard St., Tarzana, CA, USA, 91356. (818)342-1840.
Types of Production & Categories: TV Film-Prod/Dir/Wr; TV Video-Prod/Dir/Wr.
Genres: Comedy-TV; Variety-TV; Musical-TV; Documentary-TV.
Biography: Born 1936, Toronto Ontario. Attended Royal Academy of Ballet, London, England; graduated Theatre Arts, 76. Dancer, singer, actress, 53-70, then producer, director, writer. *RICH LITTLE'S CHRISTMAS CAROL* won Best Comedy Album, Junos, 79 and Golden Rose of Montreux.
Selective Filmography: *SINGIN' AND DANCIN' TONIGHT,* TV, 84, CDN, Prod/Dir; *AIR FARCE LIVE AT THE BAYVIEW,* TV, 84, CDN, Co-Prod/Co-Dir; *RICH LITTLE COME LAUGH WITH ME,* TV, 84, USA, Co-Prod; *TREASURES,* TV, 82, CDN, Co-Prod/Co-Dir/Co-Wr; *TIME MACHINE,* TV, 82, CDN, Co-Prod/Co-Dir/Co-Wr; *SHOWBIZ BALLYHOO,* TV, 82, CDN, Co-Prod/Co-Dir/Co-Wr; *SHOWBIZ GOES TO WAR,* TV, 80, CDN, Co-Prod/Co-Dir/Co-Wr; *'MARY AND MICHAEL'* (26 eps), TV, 80, CDN, Co-Prod/Co-Wr/Co-Dir; *RICH LITTLE SALUTES* (2 eps), TV, 79, USA, Co-Prod/Co-Dir/Co-Wr; *'MIXED DOUBLES'* (26 eps), TV, 79, CDN, Co-Prod/Co-Dir/Co-Wr; *'CAUGHT IN THE ACT'* (26 eps), TV, 79, CDN, Co-Prod/Co-Dir/Co-Wr; *RICH LITTLE'S CHRISTMAS CAROL,* TV, 78, CDN, Co-Prod **(INT'L EMMY)**; *TUMWATER CARAVAN,* TV, 72, USA, Res; *'SMOTHERS BROTHERS COMEDY'* (3 eps), TV, 70, USA, Act; *'JACKIE RAE SHOW'* (50 eps), TV, 55/54, CDN, Ch/Act; *'MR. SHOW BUSINESS'* (36 eps), TV, 53, CDN, Act/Ch.

SEDAWIE, Norman

ACTRA, DGA, WGAw. 19567 Oxnard St., Tarzana, CA, USA, 91356. (818)342-1840.
Types of Production & Categories: TV Film-Prod/Dir/Wr; TV Video-Prod/Dir/Wr.
Genres: Comedy-TV; Variety-TV; Musical-TV; Documentary-TV.
Biography: Born 1928, Vancouver, British Columbia. Many years as newspaper writer/columnist; television includes over 1500 network programs as director/producer. Winner, Golden Rose of Montreux, Switzerland for *RICH LITTLE'S CHRISTMAS CAROL.*
Selective Filmography: *RICH LITTLE COME LAUGH WITH ME*, TV, 85, USA, Co-Prod; *AIR FARCE LIVE AT THE BAYVIEW*, TV, 84, CDN, Co-Prod/Co-Dir/Co-Wr; *TREASURES*, TV, 82, CDN, Co-Prod/Co-Dir/Co-Wr; *THE TIME MACHINES*, TV, 82, CDN, Co-Prod/Co-Wr/Co-Dir; *SHOWBIZ BALLYHOO*, TV, 82, CDN, Co-Prod/Co-Dir/Co-Wr; *SHOWBIZ GOES TO WAR*, TV, 80, CDN, Co-Prod/Co-Dir/Co-Wr; *'MARY AND MICHAEL'* (26 eps), TV, 80, CDN, Co-Prod/Co-Wr/Co-Dir; *NATIONAL SEX AND MARRIAGE TEST*, TV, 79, USA, Prod/Wr; *'MIXED DOUBLES'* (26 eps), TV, 79, CDN, Co-Prod/Co-Dir/Co-Wr; *'CAUGHT IN THE ACT'* (26 eps), TV, 79, CDN, Co-Prod/Co-Dir/Co-Wr; *RICH LITTLE'S CHRISTMAS CAROL*, TV, 78, CDN, Co-Prod (**INT'L EMMY**); *RICH LITTLE SALUTES* (2 shows), TV, 78, USA, Co-Prod/Co-Dir/Co-Wr; *THE BEAR WHO SLEPT THROUGH CHRISTMAS*, TV, 73, USA, Prod/Wr; *'ORGANIC SPACE RIDE'* (13 eps), TV, 71, USA, Prod/Dir/Wr; *SWISS CONSPIRACY*, Th, 71, USA, Co-Wr; *'SMOTHERS BROTHERS COMEDY'* (12 eps), TV, 70, USA, Prod/Wr; *'PARADE'* (120 eps), TV, 65-60, CDN, Prod/Dir/Wr; *'JACKIE RAE SHOW'* (100 eps), TV, 57-55, CDN, Prod/Dir/Wr; *'MUSIC MAKERS'* (150 eps), TV, 56-52, CDN, Prod/Dir/Wr; *TABLOID*, TV, 55/54, CDN, Prod/Dir/Wr.

SHAFFER, Beverly - see DIRECTORS

SHAVICK, James

P.O. Box 292, Victoria Station, Westmount, Que, CAN, H3Z 2V5. The James Shavick Film Group, 175 Montpellier, Montreal, Que., CAN, H4N 2G5. (514)748-6541.
Types of Production & Categories: Th Film-Prod; TV Film-Prod/Wr; TV Video-Prod/Dir/Wr.
Genres: Drama-Th&TV; Comedy-TV; Musical-TV; Documentary-TV.
Selective Filmography: *OFFENBACH - LE DERNIER SHOW/DIS MOI SI JE DERANGE*, 'LES BEAUX DIMANCHES', TV, 85/84, CDN, Prod; *BEST WISHES, BIG MAMA THORNTON*, TV, 85, CDN, Exec Prod/Ed; *THE UNKNOWN SHOW STARRING THE UNKNOWN COMIC*, TV, 85, CDN, Prod/Wr/Co-Dir; *'THE SEX AND VIOLENCE FAMILY HOUR'* (6 eps), TV, 83, CDN, Prod/Wr; *TILL DEATH DO US PART*, TV, 82, CDN, Co-Prod/Creator; *FINAL ASSIGNMENT*, Th, 80, CDN, Co-Exec Prod; *BLUE LINE BLUES*, TV, 79, CDN, Exec Prod; *TWO SOLITUDES*, Th, 78, CDN, Co-Prod; *BROME COUNTY FAIR/MUNDIN BARNES OF TIBBETTS HILL*, 'COUNTRY CANADA', TV, 74/71, CDN, Prod/Dir; *OUR LAND, OUR PEOPLE*, TV, 73, CDN, Prod/Wr; *WATER, WIND, EARTH AND SUN*, TV, 72, CDN, Prod/Dir; *CLOSED FOR THE WINTER*, Th, 70, CDN, Prod/Dir.

SHERRIN, Robert

114 South Drive, Toronto, Ont, CAN, M4W 1R8. (416)925-8193. CBC, 790 Bay St., 5th Fl., Toronto, Ont, CAN, M5G 1N8. (416)975-7148.
Types of Production & Categories: TV Film-Prod/Dir; TV Video-Prod/Dir.
Genres: Drama-TV; Comedy-TV.
Biography: Born 1935, Kelowna, British Columbia. Bachelor of Architecture, University of British Columbia; B.A., Sir George Williams U.; graduate (directing)

(cont/suite)

National Theatre School of Canada. Fifteen years as theatre director (over 35 professional stage productions in Canada). *SARAH* was nominated for an International Emmy.
Selective Filmography: *SHOWSTOPPER,* TV, 85, CDN, Prod; *LOVE AND LARCENY,* TV, 84, CDN, Prod; *'HOME FIRES'* (31 eps), TV, 83-81, CDN, Prod/Dir; *POPULATION OF ONE,* TV, 80, CDN, Dir; *GROWING UP JEWISH IN SAULT STE MARIE* (3 parts), TV, 79/78, CDN, Prod/Dir; *THE WORDSMITH,* TV, 79, CDN, Prod; *EYE OF THE BEHOLDER,* TV, 78, CDN, Prod; *OTHER PEOPLE'S CHILDREN,* TV, 78, CDN, Prod; *ARTICHOKE,* TV, 77, CDN, Prod; *THE WOLF,* TV, 77, CDN, Prod; *LES BELLES SOEURS,* TV, 76, CDN, Prod; *BETHUNE,* TV, 76, CDN, Prod; *SIX CHARACTERS IN SEARCH OF AN AUTHOR,* TV, 76, CDN, Prod; *SARAH,* TV, 76, CDN, Prod; *OF THE FIELDS LATELY,* TV, 75, CDN, Prod; *SIX WAR YEARS,* TV, 75, CDN, Prod; *ON THE JOB,* TV, 74, CDN, Prod.

SHOSTACK, Murray

1321 Sherbrooke St.W., #E70, Montreal, Que, CAN, H3T 1J4. (514)288-1247.
Types of Production & Categories: Th Film-Prod; TV Film-Prod.
Genres: Drama-Th&TV; Animation-Th&TV.
Biography: Born Montreal, Quebec; bilingual. Bachelor of Commerce, McGill University; Chartered Accountant. President of Canadian International Studios Inc. since 1983.
Selective Filmography: *MILES TO GO...,* TV, 86, CDN, Prod; *GEORGE AND THE STAR,* TV, 85, CDN, Co-Prod; *PAROLES ET MUSIQUE* (LOVESONGS), Th, 85, CDN/F, Co-Exec Prod; *MARIA CHAPDELAINE,* Th, 83, CDN/F, Co-Exec Prod; *DEATH HUNT,* Th, 80, USA, Co-Prod; *SILENCE OF THE NORTH,* Th, 80/79, CDN, Co-Prod; *'MAN OF THE NORTH'* (13 eps), TV, 76, CDN, Prod; *CHRISTMAS MESSENGER,* TV, 75, CDN, Prod; *THE REMARKABLE ROCKET,* TV, 75, CDN, Prod; *CHILD UNDER A LEAF,* Th, 74, CDN, Co-Prod; *THE RAINBOW BOYS,* Th, 73, CDN, Prod; *A HAPPY PRINCE,* TV, 72, CDN, Prod; *THE LITTLE MERMAID,* TV, 72/71, CDN, Prod; *THE SELFISH GIANT,* TV, 71, CDN, Prod; *THE APPRENTICE,* Th, 70, CDN, Prod; *FLEUR BLEUE,* Th, 70, CDN, Prod; *TIKI TIKI,* Th, 69, CDN, Prod; *PINTER PEOPLE,* TV, 68, CDN, Prod.

SHUMAN, Risa

6 Forest Laneway, #2703, Willowdale, Ont, CAN, M2N 5X9. (416)222-6675. TV Ontario, Box 200, Stn. Q, Toronto, Ont, CAN, M4T 2T1. (416)484-2600.
Types of Production & Categories: TV Video-Prod.
Genres: Educational-TV.
Biography: Born 1951, Hamilton, Ontario. Honours B.F.A., Film, York University, 73. Employed at TV Ontario since 73.
Selective Filmography: *'SATURDAY NIGHT AT THE MOVIES'* (26 eps), TV, 86, CDN, Prod; *'FILM INTERNATIONAL'* (6 eps), TV, 86, CDN, Prod/Dir; *'MAGIC SHADOWS'* (24 eps), TV, 86, CDN, Assoc Prod.

SHUMIATCHER, Cal - see EDITORS

SIEGEL, Bonita

ATPD. CBC, 790 Bay St., 5th Fl., Toronto, Ont, CAN, M5G 1N8. (416)975-7113.
Types of Production & Categories: TV Film-Prod; TV Video-Prod.
Genres: Drama-TV.
Biography: Born 1950, Chatham, Ontario. Producer, CBC TV, 80-86. *SLIM OBSESSION* won a Bronze Plaque, Columbus, 84.
Selective Filmography: *SPECIAL DELIVERY,* TV, 85, CDN, Prod; *THE EXILE,* TV, 85, CDN, Prod; *THE CUCKOO BIRD,* TV, 84, CDN, Prod; *SLIM OBSESSION,* 'FOR THE RECORD', TV, 83, CDN, Prod; *'HOME FIRES'* (7

(cont/suite)

eps), TV, 82/81, CDN, Prod; *PASSENGERS,* TV, 80, CDN, Prod; *A POPULATION OF ONE,* TV, 79, CDN, Prod; *SUNSPOTS,* TV, 79, CDN, Prod.

SIEGEL, Lionel E. - see WRITERS

SIMMONDS, Alan Francis - see DIRECTORS

SIMPSON, Peter

Simcom Limited, 86 Bloor St.W., 5th Fl., Toronto, Ont, CAN, M5S 1M5. (416) 961-6278.
Types of Production & Categories: Th Film-Prod; TV Film-Prod.
Genres: Drama-Th&TV; Comedy-Th; Action-Th; Horror-Th.
Biography: Born 1943, Created Simcom Limited, 71, now Chairman and Chief Executive Officer; Chairman, Norstar Releasing Inc., Norstar Home Video and Media Canada Inc..
Selective Filmography: *THE HAUNTING OF HAMILTON HIGH,* Th, 86, CDN, Exec Prod; *HIGHER EDUCATION,* Th, 86, CDN, Exec Prod; *BULLIES,* Th, 85, CDN, Exec Prod; *HIGH STAKES,* Th, 85, CDN, Exec Prod; *'MANIA'* (4 eps), TV, 85, CDN, Exec Prod; *BURTON CUMMINGS: MY OWN WAY TO ROCK,* TV, 84, CDN, Prod; *CURTAINS,* Th, 81, CDN, Exec Prod/Prod; *HANK WILLIAMS: THE SHOW HE NEVER GAVE,* Th, 81, CDN, Co-Exec Prod; *MELANIE,* Th, 80, CDN, Exec Prod; *PROM NIGHT* (LE BAL DE L'HORREUR), Th, 79, CDN, Prod; *THE SEA GYPSIES,* Th, 78, CDN, Exec Prod.

SINELNIKOFF, Michael

AR. 3600 Park Ave., #319, Montreal, Que., CAN, H2Z 3R2. (514)282-0158. CBC/Radio-Canada, 1400 blvd. Dorchester E., Montreal, Que, CAN, H2L 2M2. (514)285-3643.
Types of Production & Categories: TV Film-Prod/Dir; TV Video-Prod/Dir.
Genres: Drama-TV; Musical-TV; Science Fiction-TV; Documentary-TV.
Biography: Born 1928, London, England; Canadian citizen; bilingual. Awards include Louis Jouvet trophy and Final Festival Trophy, Dominion Drama Festival. Professional experience includes 63 half hour dramas, series and specials as producer/director.
Selective Filmography: *PUNCH-DRUNK!,* 'THE WAY WE ARE', TV, 86, CDN, Prod/Dir/Story Ed; *BARNUM,* TV, 86, USA, Act; *CHOICES,* TV, 86, USA, Act; *SPEARFIELD'S DAUGHTER* (mini-series), TV, 85, CDN/USA/AUS, Act; *'GZOWSKI & CO.'* (1 eps), TV, 85, CDN, Dir; *THE FAME GAME,* TV, 84, CDN, Prod; *THE FUN OF BEING WITH OSCAR,* TV, 77, CDN, Dir/Prod (ANIK).

SLAN, Jon

107 Old Forest Hill Rd., Toronto, Ont, CAN, M5P 2R8. Paragon Motion Pictures Inc., 260 Richmond St.W., #405, Toronto, Ont, CAN, M5V 1W5. (416)977-2929.
Types of Production & Categories: Th Film-Prod; TV Film-Prod.
Genres: Drama-Th&TV; Comedy-Th&TV.
Biography: Born 1946, Toronto, Ontario. B.A., York University; M.A., Columbia University; Ph.D., University of Toronto. Lecturer, U. of T. and U. of Western Ontario. Chairman of Superchannel from 82 until its merger with First Choice, 85. President, Paragon Motion Pictures.
Selective Filmography: *'PHILIP MARLOWE PRIVATE EYE'* (6 eps), TV, 86, CDN, Prod; *THRESHOLD,* Th, 80, CDN, Co-Prod; *FISH HAWK,* Th, 79, CDN, Prod; *IMPROPER CHANNELS,* Th, 79, CDN, Exec Prod; *AN AMERICAN CHRISTMAS CAROL,* TV, 79, USA, Prod; *KAVIK THE WOLF DOG,* TV, 78, CDN, Prod; *HIGH-BALLIN',* Th, 77, CDN, Prod; *'TENNIS THE NASTY WAY'* (4 eps), TV, 75, CDN, Prod; *FEARFUL SYMMETRY: NORTHROP FRYE LOOKS AT THE WORLD,* TV, 71, CDN, Prod/Dir; *SATAN'S PIPERS,* TV, 69, CDN, Prod.

SMALLEY, Katherine - see DIRECTORS

SMILEY, Dave
CTPDA. 10927 - 35A Ave., Edmonton, Alta, CAN, T6J 0A2. CBC, Box 555, Edmonton, Alta, CAN. (403)469-2321.
Types of Production & Categories: TV Film-Prod/Dir; TV Video-Prod/Dir.
Genres: News-TV; Sports-TV.
Biography: Born 1938, Toronto, Ontario. Bachelor of Arts in Drama, University of Saskatchewan, 62. TV producer for *SUPPER HOUR NEWSDAY*, 78-86; director/producer of *PAR 27*, a sport series on golf.

SMITH, Arthur
ATPD. 167 Castlefield Ave., Toronto, Ont, CAN, M4R 1G6. (416)489-2699. CBC, 415 Yonge St., 5th Fl., Toronto, Ont, CAN.
Types of Production & Categories: TV Film-Prod/Dir; TV Video-Prod/Dir.
Genres: Comedy-TV; Variety-TV; Sports-TV.
Biography: Born 1959, Montreal, Quebec; bilingual; graduated First in class, Radio & TV Arts, Ryerson Polytechnical Institute, 82. Background in performing, TV and features; announcing.
Selective Filmography: *COMMONWEALTH GAMES* (10 seg), TV, 86, CDN, Sr Prod; *ENCORE, EDINBURGH*, TV, 86, CDN, Sr Prod; *WORLD PROFESSIONAL BODYBUILDING CHAMPIONSHIP*, 'SPORTS WEEKEND', TV, 86, CDN, Prod/Dir; *WORLD JUNIOR HOCKEY CHAMPIONSHIP*, TV, 86, CDN, Prod; *ASPEN WORLDCUP DOWNHILL*, 'SPORTS WEEKEND', TV, 86, CDN, Prod/Dir; *ROTHMAN INTERNATIONAL HORSE RACING*, TV, 85, CDN, Prod; *GREY CUP COUNTDOWN/CALGARY STAMPEDE*, TV, 85, CDN, Prod; *NATIONAL HOCKEY LEAGUE DRAFT*, TV, 85/84, CDN, Prod; *BOXING*, TV, 85, CDN, Prod; *SANTA CLAUS PARADE*, TV, 84, CDN, Prod; *PREVIEW TO L.A. OLYMPICS/LOS ANGELES OLYMPICS* (15 seg), TV, 84, CDN, Prod; *WORLD UNIVERSITY GAMES* (15 segs), TV, 83, CDN, Dir; *HOCKEY NIGHT IN CANADA* (30 eps), TV, 83/82, CDN, Dir.

SMITH, Clive A.
ACTRA, DGC. Nelvana Ltd., 32 Atlantic Ave., Toronto, Ont, CAN, M6K 1X8. (416)588-5571.
Types of Production & Categories: Th Film-Dir/Prod; TV Film-Dir/Prod; TV Video-Dir/Prod.
Genres: Drama-Th&TV; Comedy-Th&TV; Children's-Th&TV; Animation-Th&TV.
Biography: Born in England; emigrated to Canada, 67. Worked on TV commercials; graphic arts. Co-founder, Vice President of Nelvana Ltd.. Recipient of many awards including Graphica, U.S. Industrial Film Fest., Wilderness, Chris, and a Special Award at Canadian Film Awards, 78. *THE CARE BEARS MOVIE* won the Golden Reel Award, 86.
Selective Filmography: *THE EDISON TWINS'* (Dir-2 eps), (39 eps), TV, 86-83, CDN, Exec Prod; *THE CARE BEARS'* (13 eps), TV, 86, CDN, Co-Prod; *THE CARE BEARS MOVIE II*, Th, 86/85, CDN, Co-Prod; *MY PET MONSTER*, TV, 86, CDN, Co-Prod; *MAD BALLS*, TV, 86, CDN, Co-Prod; *THE CARE BEARS MOVIE*, Th, 85, CDN, Co-Prod; *THE GREAT HEEP*, TV, 85, CDN, Dir/Co-Prod; *THE EWOK-DROIDS ADVENTURE HOUR*, TV, 85, CDN, Dir/Co-Prod; *'EWOKS'* (13 eps), TV, 85, CDN, Co-Prod; *STRAWBERRY SHORTCAKE MEETS THE BERRYKINS*, TV, 84, CDN, Co-Prod; *THE GET ALONG GANG*, TV, 84, CDN, Co-Prod; *ROCK & RULE* (RING OF POWER), Th, 83, CDN, Dir; *HERSELF THE ELF*, TV, 83, CDN, Co-Prod; *STRAWBERRY SHORTCAKE AND THE BABY WITHOUT A NAME*, TV, 83, CDN, Co-Prod; *'20 MINUTE WORKOUT'* (120 eps), TV, 83, CDN, Co-Exec Prod; *STRAWBERRY SHORTCAKE: A HOUSEWARMING SURPRISE*, TV, 82, CDN, Co-Prod;

(cont/suite)

INTERGALACTIC THANKSGIVING (PLEASE DON'T EAT THE PLANET), TV, 79, CDN, Dir; *THE STAR WARS HOLIDAY SPECIAL* (animation insert), TV, 78, USA, Dir; *ROMIE-0 & JULIE-8*, TV, 78, CDN, Dir; *THE DEVIL AND DANIEL MOUSE*, TV, 78, CDN, Dir; *COSMIC CHRISTMAS*, TV, 77/76, CDN, Dir.

SMITH, Courtney

Straight Forward Prods. Inc., 2120 Dunbar St., Vancouver, BC, CAN, V6R 3M6. (604)736-7993.
Types of Production & Categories: Th Film-Wr/Prod; TV Film-Wr/Dir/Prod; TV Video-Wr/Dir/Prod.
Genres: Drama-Th; Commercials-TV; Music Video-TV.
Biography: Born 1947, Hamilton, Ontario. Attended University of Alberta and U. of Victoria. Produced 20 TV commercials; advertising copy writer.
Selective Filmography: *ACTION SPEAKS LOUDER THAN WORDS - FOODBANK*, MV, 86, CDN, Wr/Dir/Prod; *TAKE THE PHONE OFF THE HOOK/ON THE ROAD AGAIN*, MV, 85/84, CDN, Wr/Dir/Prod; *FAST COMPANY*, Th, 78, CDN, Co-Scr/Co-Prod.

SMITH, Maurice

121 Cottingham St., Toronto, Ont, CAN, M4V 1B9. 65 Front St. E., Toronto, Ont, CAN, M5E 1B5. (416)362-5907.
Types of Production & Categories: Th Film-Prod/Wr.
Genres: Drama-Th; Comedy-Th; Action-Th; Horror-Th.
Biography: Born 1939, London, England; Canadian.
Selective Filmography: *RECRUITS*, Th, 85, CDN, Prod; *LOOSE SCREWS*, Th, 84, CDN, Prod; *ODD BALLS*, Th, 83, CDN, Prod; *SCREW BALLS*, Th, 82, CDN, Prod; *JULIE DARLING*, Th, 81, CDN/D, Prod/Co-Wr; *DEATH BITE* (SPASMS), Th, 81, CDN, Co-Exec Prod/Co-Prod; *HOW COME NOBODY'S ON OUR SIDE*, Th, 74, USA, Prod; *DELINQUENT SCHOOLGIRLS*, Th, 73, USA, Prod/Co-Wr; *NOVEMBER CHILDREN*, Th, 72, USA, Prod; *LOVE SWEDISH STYLE*, Th, 71, USA, Prod/Dir/Wr; *HARD TRAIL*, Th, 70, USA, Prod; *JEZEBEL* (JOYS OF JEZEBEL), Th, 69, USA, Wr; *DIAMOND STUD*, Th, 69, USA, Assoc Prod/Wr; *CYCLE SAVAGES*, Th, 69, USA, Prod; *SCREAM FREE* (FREE GRASS), Th, 68, USA, Exec Prod; *THE GLORY STOMPERS*, Th, 67, USA, Exec Prod.

SNELL, Peter R.E.

Britannic/British Lion, Pinewood Studios, Iver, Buckinghamshire, GB, , SL0 0NH. (753)651-700.
Types of Production & Categories: Th Film-Prod; TV Film-Prod.
Genres: Drama-Th&TV.
Biography: Born Calgary, Alberta. Degree in Economics, University of British Columbia, then moved to London, England. His early years in the film industry were devoted to the production of Shakespeare films: *THE WINTER'S TALE, JULIUS CAESAR, ANTONY AND CLEOPATRA;* also produced *SOME MAY LIVE, SUBTERFUGE, GOODBYE GEMINI.* Head of Production, 1972, then Managing Director of British Lion Films, responsible for setting up British Lion's U.K. distribution arm and for the production of *DON'T LOOK NOW* and *THE WICKER MAN* which won Grand Prize, Paris Int'l Fest. of Fantasy and Science Fiction Films. Produced *HENNESSY;* joined the Robert Stigwood Group to assist and advise in their feature production programme, when the London office closed, returned to independent production and produced *BEAR ISLAND, MOTHER-LODE* and *HOSTAGE TOWER* (CBS). In 82, he put together and became Chief Executive of Britannic Film and TV Ltd. which has produced *SQUARING THE CIRCLE* (Channel 4); he produced *TURTLE DIARY, LADY JANE* and in 86, *A PRAYER FOR THE DYING.*

P.O. Box 177 Hinton, Alberta: Canada TOEIBO

*Supplying Exotic and Domestic Animals
for Motion Pictures, Television and
Commercial Advertising*

PHONE (403) 865-5542

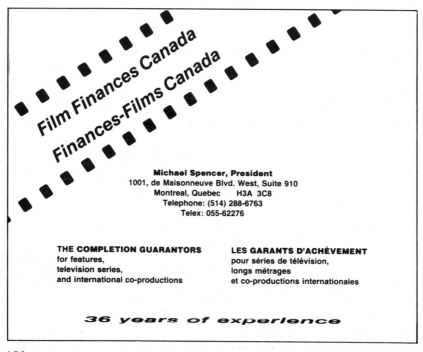

Michael Spencer, President
1001, de Maisonneuve Blvd. West, Suite 910
Montreal, Quebec   H3A 3C8
Telephone: (514) 288-6763
Telex: 055-62276

THE COMPLETION GUARANTORS
for features,
television series,
and international co-productions

LES GARANTS D'ACHÈVEMENT
pour séries de télévision,
longs métrages
et co-productions internationales

36 years of experience

SOBEL, Mark - see DIRECTORS

SOLNICKI, Victor

53 Hillholm Rd., Toronto, Ont, CAN, M5P 1M4. (416)482-0623. 142 Davenport Rd., Toronto, Ont, CAN, M5R 1J2. (416)922-3168.
Types of Production & Categories: Th Film-Prod.
Genres: Drama-Th; Comedy-Th; Horror-Th.
Biography: Born 1938, Paris, France; Canadian citizen; bilingual. B.A., LL.B., University of Toronto. Executive producer and entertainment lawyer.
Selective Filmography: *'PETER USTINOV'S RUSSIA'* (6 eps), TV, 86/85, CDN, Co-Exec Prod; *VIDEODROME*, Th, 81, CDN, Co-Exec Prod; *GAS*, Th, 80, CDN, Exec Prod; *VISITING HOURS*, Th, 80, CDN, Co-Exec Prod; *THE FUNNY FARM*, Th, 80, CDN, Co-Exec Prod; *SCANNERS*, Th, 80, CDN, Co-Exec Prod; *DIRTY TRICKS*, Th, 79, CDN, Co-Exec Prod; *HOG WILD*, Th, 79, CDN, Co-Exec Prod; *THE BROOD*, Th, 79, CDN, Co-Exec Prod.

SOMMERS, Frank G.

Pathway Productions Inc., 360 Bloor St.W., #406, Toronto, Ont, CAN, M5S 1X1. (416)922-7335.
Types of Production & Categories: Th Short-Prod/Dir; TV Video-Prod/Dir.
Genres: Documentary-TV; Educational-TV; Children's-TV.
Biography: Born 1943, Budapest, Hungary; arrived in Canada, 57; Canadian citizen. Graduate of University of Toronto Medical School, now a lecturer there. Psychiatrist with special interest in sexual and marital therapy. Founding President, Physicians for Social Responsibility/Canada. Co-author, 'Curing Nuclear Madness'. President, Pathway Productions Inc.; producer of films on human sexuality including the American Film Festival finalist, *TAKING TIME TO FEEL*.
Selective Filmography: *'MUTUALITY'* (Parts 1-2-3), ED, 84, CDN, Prod/Dir; *'TAKING TIME TO FEEL'* (parts 1-2-3), ED, 78, CDN, Prod/Dir.

SOROSSY, Ivan - see CINEMATOGRAPHERS

SPENCER, Michael

ACTRA, CFTA. 3450 Drummond, #1901, Montreal, Que, CAN, H3G 1Y3. (514) 288-7589. Film Finances Canada, 1001 de Maisonneuve W., #910, Montreal, Que, CAN, H3A 3C8. (514)288-6763.
Types of Production & Categories: Th Film-Prod, Th Short Prod.
Genres: Drama-Th; Documentary-Th.
Biography: Born 1919, London, England; Canadian citizen; bilingual. Educated Rugby School and Oxford University. Cameraman and director, Canadian Army Film and Photo Unit, 41-46; producer, NFB, 46-56; Head of Ottawa Office, 56-60; Director of Planning, NFB, 60-68. Executive Director, Canadian Film Development Corp., 68-78. Producer, Lamy, Spencer Inc., 79-81; Filmline, 81-84. President, Film Finances Canada since 84; President, APFVQ, 81. Member of the Jury, Cannes Film Festival, 80; consultant, Dept. of Communications, Applebaum-Hébert; CFDC, Telefilm Canada, since 79. His films have won awards at nat'l and int'l film festivals including: Silver Statuette (Rome), Silver Medal (Uruguay).
Selective Filmography: *POINT PELEE NATURE SANCTUARY*, ED, 58, CDN, Prod; *WORLD IN A MARSH*, ED, 56, CDN, Prod; *THE SON*, ED, 56, CDN, Prod; *WESTERN WHEAT*, ED, 55, CDN, Prod; *LAND OF THE LONG DAY*, ED, 53, CDN, Prod; *ANGOTEE*, ED, 53, CDN, Prod; *BIRDS OF CANADA*, ED, 50, CDN, Prod.

SPRINGBETT, David - see DIRECTORS

SPRY, Robin - see DIRECTORS

PRODUCERS/PRODUCTEURS

STANSFIELD, David - see WRITERS

STANTON, Bud J.

CTPDA. 8 Caragana Ave., Sherwood Park, Alta, CAN. (403)467-2204.
Types of Production & Categories: TV Film-Cin; TV Video-Prod.
Genres: Documentary-TV; News-TV.
Biography: Born 1947, Ottawa, Ontario; bilingual. Started as film editor, cinematographer, went on to TV directing, producing.
Selective Filmography: *'NEWSDAY'* (CBXT), TV, 86/85, CDN, Sr Prod; *1984 OLYMPICS*, TV, 84, USA, Field Dir; *1983 UNIVERSIADE*, TV, 83, CDN, Prod; *ALBERTA LANDSCAPES/ALBERTA NORTH*, TV, 80, CDN, Cin; *TORONTO JAM* (OPENING SEQUENCE), TV, 79, CDN, Cin; *THE FREESTYLERS*, TV, 78, CDN, Cin; *WEST MEETS WEST*, TV, 77, CDN/J, Cin; *U.S.FOOD MACHINE*, TV, 76, CDN/USA, Cin; *BILLION DOLLAR COW*, TV, 76, CDN, Cin; *THE LONG GOODBYE*, TV, 76, CDN, Cin; *1976 OLYMPICS*, TV, 76, CDN, Cin.

STAROWICZ, Mark

ATPD. CBC, Box 1400, Stn. A, Toronto, Ont, CAN, M5W 1A0. (416)975-7903.
Types of Production & Categories: TV Video-Prod.
Genres: News-TV.
Biography: Born 1946, Nottinghamshire, England; emigrated to Canada, 53. Graduated McGill University, 68 (European diplomatic history, Chinese history). Executive producer, CBC radio: 'Five Nights', 'Commentary', 'As it Happens' 'Sunday Morning' which won an Actra Award (Best Radio Program, 76). As a journalist, has won many awards including the Ohio State Award for radio documentary (73), Canadian Broadcasting League's Award (73); first recipient, CBC President's Award.
Selective Filmography: *'THE JOURNAL'*, TV, 86-82, CDN, Exec Prod (ANIK); *'MIDDAY'*, TV, 86/85, CDN, Exec Prod.

STEELE, Fraser - see DIRECTORS

STEINMETZ, Peter E.

50 Old Mill Rd., #401, Toronto, Ont, CAN, M8X 1G7. (416)239-1825. Peter E. Steinmetz & Assoc., 30 Hazelton Ave., Toronto, Ont, CAN, M5R 2E2. (416)927-7710.
Types of Production & Categories: TV Video-Prod.
Genres: Variety-TV; Musical-TV.
Biography: Born 1941, Toronto, Ontario. B.A., University of Western Ontario, 63; LL.B., University of Toronto, 67; admitted to the Bar of Ontario, 70. Appointed Queen's Counsel, 83. Joined law firm of Cassels, Brock & Blackwell, 70; became a partner, 74, practicing in entertainment law. Established Peter E. Steinmetz & Assoc., 83. Director, President, Academy of Recording Arts and Sciences; Counsel to the Canadian Recording Industry Association and represents numerous independent film, TV and record production companies as well as performing artists and creative talent.
Selective Filmography: *JUNO AWARDS* (3 shows), TV, 86-84, CDN, Exec Prod.

STERN, Steven - see DIRECTORS

STEWART, Gordon - see DIRECTORS

STEWART, Sandy

ATPD. 272 Major St., Toronto, Ont, CAN, M5S 2L6. (416)927-7923.
Types of Production & Categories: TV Film-Prod/Dir; TV Video-Prod/Dir.
Genres: Drama-TV; Documentary-TV; Educational-TV; Children's-TV.
Biography: Born 1930, Calgary, Alberta. Started as radio technician at CFPL, London, 48; CBC radio producer, 52; CBC TV producer, 61; executive producer, 66.

(cont/suite)

Author of 2 histories of broadcasting; President of Canadian Science Writers Association, 86; media adviser to City of Toronto Board of Health.
Selective Filmography: *'REACH FOR THE TOP'* (Dir-sev eps), TV, 86-63, CDN, Exec Prod; *'THE WINNERS'* (3 eps), TV, 81-80, CDN, Exec Prod; *'CANADIAN SHORT STORIES'* (8 eps), TV, 70-67, CDN, Prod/Dir; *THROUGH THE EYES OF TOMORROW INDIANS,* TV, 68, CDN, Dir.

STOHN, J.Stephen

439 Duplex Ave., Toronto, Ont, CAN, M4R 1V3. (416)484-4552. McCarthy & McCarthy, TD Centre, 48th Floor, Toronto, Ont, CAN, M5K 1E6. (416)362-1812.
Types of Production & Categories: Th Film-Prod.
Genres: Drama-Th.
Biography: Born 1948; practicing law in Toronto.
Selective Filmography: *THE CLOWN MURDERS,* Th, 75, CDN, Exec Prod; *ME,* Th, 74, CDN, Exec Prod.

STONEMAN, John - see CINEMATOGRAPHERS

SULLIVAN, Kevin - see DIRECTORS

SUTHERLAND, Neil

ACTRA, CTPDA. 1027 Clyde Ave., West Vancouver, BC, CAN. (604)922-6053. CBC, 700 Hamilton, Vancouver, BC, CAN. (604)662-6266.
Types of Production & Categories: TV Film-Prod/Dir/Wr; TV Video-Prod/Dir/Wr.
Genres: Drama-TV; Variety-TV; Documentary-TV.
Biography: Born 1931, Britain; Canadian citizen. Education: Bachelor of Music, Master of Arts.
Selective Filmography: *'RED SERGE'* (Dir-4 eps), (5 eps), TV, 86/85, CDN, Exec Prod/Wr; *TRIALS OF LORD SELKIRK,* TV, 83, CDN, Prod/Dir/Wr; *MACKENZIE/CAPTAIN VANCOUVER/CAPTAIN COOK,* 'AS FAR AS MAN COULD GO', TV, 82-79, CDN, Prod/Dir/Wr; *THE WORLD OF EMMELICH KALMAN,* TV, 82, CDN, Prod/Dir/Wr; *THE LOOK OF MUSIC,* TV, 80, CDN, Prod/Dir/Wr; *GERSHWIN AND PORGY,* TV, 79, CDN, Prod/Dir/Wr; *SCHUBERT REMEMBERED,* TV, 78, CDN, Prod/Dir/Wr; *THE WORLD OF NOEL COWARD,* TV, 77, CDN, Prod/Dir; *THEY ALL PLAY RAGTIME,* TV, 76, CDN, Prod/Dir/Wr; *THE WORLD OF IVOR NOVELLO,* TV, 75, CDN, Prod/Dir; *THE WORLD OF JACQUES OFFENBACH,* TV, 72, CDN, Prod/Dir/Wr; *THE WORLD OF FRANZ LEHAR,* TV, 70, CDN, Prod/Dir.

SUURALLIK, Aili

ATPD, 114 Cottingham St., Toronto, Ont, CAN, M4V 1C1. (416)920-4139. CBC, Box 500, Stn. A, Toronto, Ont, CAN, M5W 1E6. (416)975-3495.
Types of Production & Categories: TV Film-Prod; TV Video-Prod/Dir.
Genres: Documentary-TV; Educational-TV.
Biography: Born 1946, Stockholm, Sweden; Canadian citizen; Languages: English, Estonian. Education: Ryerson Polytechnical Institute; Ontario College of Education; University of Toronto (Fine Arts); Ontario College of Art (Photography)
Selective Filmography: *THE MAPLE AND THE CROWN,* TV, 85, CDN, Prod/Dir; *JOHN PAUL II IN CANADA,* TV, 85, CDN, Prod; *PAPAL TOUR '84,* TV, 84, CDN, Assoc Prod; *'HAND & EYE'* (7 eps), TV, 84-82, CDN, Assoc Prod.

SWAN, James - see DIRECTORS

SYMANSKY, Adam

SGCT. 63 Chesterfield Ave., Westmount, Que, CAN, H3Y 2M4. (514)489-3582. NFB, Box 6100, Montreal, Que, CAN, H3C 3H5. (514)283-9555.
Types of Production & Categories: Th Film-Prod; Th Short-Prod; TV Film-Prod; TV Video-Prod.

(cont/suite)

Genres: Drama-TV; Documentary-Th&TV; Educational-Th&TV.
Biography: Born 1944. Has won awards for his films at several international film festivals including: Chicago, San Francisco, Melbourne, Los Angeles, New York, Salerno (Italy), Columbus.
Selective Filmography: *THE CHAMPIONS: THE FINAL BATTLE,* TV, 86, CDN, Co-Prod; *CANADA'S SWEETHEART: THE SAGA OF HAL C.BANKS,* TV, 85, CDN, Co-Prod **(ANIK)**; *DEMOCRACY ON TRIAL: THE MORGENTALER AFFAIR,* TV, 84, CDN, Prod/Assist Ed; *CHILDREN'S CRUSADE,* TV, 84, CDN, Prod; *INCIDENT AT RESTIGOUCHE,* TV, 84, CDN, Co-Exec Prod; *FLAMENCO AT 5:15,* Th, 83, CDN, Exec Prod/Co-Prod **(OSCAR)**; *SOMETHING TO CELEBRATE,* TV, 83, CDN, Exec Prod/Prod; *THE AGE OF INVENTION,* Th, 83, CDN, Exec Prod; *GALA,* Th, 82, CDN, Exec Prod; *SEE YOU IN THE FUNNY PAPERS,* TV, 82, CDN, Exec Prod/Prod; *THE KID WHO COULDN'T MISS,* TV, 82, CDN, Exec Prod; *DAISY: THE STORY OF A FACELIFT,* Th, 82, CDN, Exec Prod; *CAPTIVE MINDS, HYPNOSIS AND BEYOND,* Th, 82, CDN, Exec Prod; *THE DEVIL AT YOUR HEELS,* Th, 82, CDN, Co-Prod **(GENIE)**; *FORBES HOME,* Th, 82, CDN, Exec Prod; *WHO WANTS UNIONS,* Th, 82, CDN, Exec Prod; *FOR THE LOVE OF DANCE,* TV, 81, CDN, Prod/Exec Prod; *BUSINESS OF AGING,* Th, 81, CDN, Exec Prod; *ON GUARD FOR THEE* (3 parts), TV, 81, CDN, Prod; *UNDER NEW MANAGEMENT,* TV, 81, CDN, Prod; *THE INHERITANCE,* TV, 80, CDN, Prod; *CANADIAN FEDERATION,* Th, 80, CDN, Prod; *IMAGE MAKERS,* TV, 80, CDN, Prod; *PAPER WHEAT,* TV, 79, CDN, Prod; *YOU'RE UNDER ARREST,* Th, 79, CDN, Prod; *WAGES OF WORK,* Th, 78, CDN, Prod.

SYMCOX, Peter - see DIRECTORS

TAKACS, Tibor - see DIRECTORS

TESTAR, Gerald

643 Plymouth Dr., North Vancouver, BC, CAN, V7H 2H5. (604)929-7769.
Types of Production & Categories: TV Film-Prod/Dir; TV Video-Prod/Dir.
Genres: Drama-TV; Educational-TV.
Biography: Born 1937, Vancouver, British Columbia. Educated at University of British Columbia; M.F.A., Theatre, Pacific U., Oregon; Diploma, BBC Producers Training Program, London. Story editor, CBC drama; educator, Mohawk College, (Hamilton), U. of Victoria (B.C.). Independent producer, educational/industrial productions.

TETREAULT, Louis-Georges

APFVQ, CFTA. 6000 Deacon Rd., K1, Montréal, Qué, CAN, H3S 2T9. (514)342-4643. Les Productions SDA Ltd., 1221 Ave. de l'Hôtel de Ville, Montréal, Qué, CAN, H2X 3A9. (514)866-1761.
Types de production et Catégories: c métrage-Prod; TV film-Prod; TV vidéo-Prod.
Types d'oeuvres: Drame-C&TV; Documentaire-C&TV; Education-C&TV; Enfants-TV.
Curriculum vitae: Né en 1954; bilingue. Bac. en Communications, Université Concordia. Décorateur théâtral; danseur, jazz et classique. Se joint à SDA Productions, 80; présentement Vice-président, SDA Productions Ltd.
Filmographie sélective: *L'ESSOR DE L'AGRICULTURE AU CANADA* (AGRICULTURE ON THE GO), TV, 86, CDN, Prod; *M.NUKE IS A FOOL,* TV, 86, CDN, Prod; *PLUIE D'ETE* (SUMMER RAIN), C, 85, CDN, Prod exéc; *FRANCOMER I & II,* TV, 84/83, CDN, Prod exéc; *TOUCHONS DU BOIS,* TV, 84, CDN, Prod; *CEINTURE DE SECURITE,* TV, 84, CDN, Prod; *CANDU,* In, 84, CDN, Prod exéc; *QUEBEC MOSAIC/CONTES ORAUX,* ED, 84, CDN, Prod; *QUEBEC,* TV, 83, CDN, Prod; *ASSURANCE-VIE DESJARDINS,* In, 83, CDN, Prod; *POISSONS & PECHERIES,* TV, 83, CDN, Prod; *CIDEM-HABITATION/ CIIM,* In, 82, CDN, Prod.

PRODUCTEURS/PRODUCERS

THICKE, Alan
ACTRA, AFTRA, SAG, WGAw. Mike Gursey, Larry Thompson Org., 1888 Century Pk. E., #622, Los Angeles, CA, USA, 90067. (213)478-6100.
Types of Production & Categories: TV Film-Prod/Wr/Act; TV Video-Prod/Wr/Act.
Genres: Drama-TV; Comedy-TV; Variety-TV.
Biography: Born Kirkland Lake, Ontario. B.A., University of Western Ontario. Moved to Los Angeles, 70; has received 4 Emmy nominations.
Selective Filmography: *'GROWING PAINS',* TV, 86/85, USA, Act; *THE CASE OF THE SHOOTING STAR,* TV, 86, USA, Act; *WHO KILLED MARTIN HASTINGS?,* TV, 86, USA, Act; *ANNE MURRAY SPECIALS,* TV, 85-77, USA, Prod/Co-Wr; *THE CALENDAR GIRL MURDERS,* TV, 84, USA, Act; *'THICKE OF THE NIGHT',* TV, 84, USA, Host; *'ALAN THICKE SHOW',* TV, 83-80, USA, Host; *OLIVIA NEWTON JOHN SPECIALS,* TV, 82/81, USA, Prod/Wr; *'BILL COSBY',* TV, 82, USA, Prod/Wr; *RICHARD PRIOR SPECIAL,* TV, 80, USA, Prod/Co-Wr **(WGA)**; *'FERNWOOD TONIGHT',* TV, 79/78, USA, Prod/Co-Wr.

THOMAS, Gayle - see DIRECTORS

THOMAS, R. L. - see DIRECTORS

THOMSON, Andy
CFTA. 50 King St., Port Hope, Ont, CAN, L1A 2R5. (416)885-5920. Norwolf Film Corporation, 437 Sherbourne St., Toronto, Ont, CAN, M4X 1K5. (416)960-6065.
Types of Production & Categories: Th Film-Prod; Th Short-Dir; TV Film-Dir/Prod.
Genres: Drama-Th&TV; Documentary-TV; Educational-TV.
Biography: Born 1946, Montreal, Quebec; Honours B.A., Acadia University, Nova Scotia. Joined NFB, 68 as trainee director; director, 69; producer, 76; executive producer, 83. Left NFB, 86, to become President of Norwolf Film Corporation. *BLACKWOOD* and *THE PAINTED DOOR* were both nominated for an Oscar. *IN SEARCH OF FARLEY MOWAT* won a Chris Plaque, Columbus.
Selective Filmography: *CAGES/JOHN CAT/ALL THE YEARS/THE CAP/THE TRUMPETER,* 'BELL CANADA PLAYHOUSE', TV, 85/84, CDN, Co-Prod; *BAYO,* Th, 85, CDN, Co-Exec Prod; *90 DAYS,* Th, 85, CDN, Exec Prod; *CANADA'S SWEETHEART: THE SAGA OF HAL C BANKS,* TV, 85, CDN, Co-Exec Prod; *FIRST STOP CHINA,* TV, 85, CDN, Exec Prod; *MORTIMER GRIFFIN AND SHALINSKY/THE SIGHT/UNCLE T.,* 'BELL CANADA PLAYHOUSE', TV, 85, CDN, Co-Exec Prod; *THE CONCERT STAGES OF EUROPE/ESSO/LEGS OF THE LAME,* 'BELL CANADA PLAYHOUSE', TV, 85, CDN, Co-Exec Prod; *GOING TO WAR/RED SHOES/HACKER JOHN/ HOTWALKER/CONNECTION,* 'BELL CANADA PLAYHOUSE', TV, 85, CDN, Co-Exec Prod; *THE REBELLION OF YOUNG DAVID/JACK OF HEARTS,* 'BELL CANADA PLAYHOUSE', TV, 85, CDN, Co-Exec Prod; *THE DREAM AND THE TRIUMPH,* 'BELL CANADA PLAYHOUSE', TV, 85, CDN, Co-Exec Prod; *INCIDENT AT RESTIGOUCHE,* TV, 84, CDN, Co-Prod; *A GOOD TREE/THE PAINTED DOOR/BAMBINGER/ONE'S A HEIFER,* 'BELL CANADA PLAYHOUSE', TV, 84, CDN, Co-Prod; *IN SEARCH OF FARLEY MOWAT,* TV, 81, CDN, Prod/Dir; *BLACKWOOD,* Th, 76, CDN, Dir.

THOMSON, Lorraine
ACTRA. 66 Collier St., Ste.6A, Toronto, Ont, CAN, M4W 1L9. (416)964-9579.
Types of Production & Categories: TV Film-Prod/Host; TV Video-Prod/Wr.
Genres: Variety-TV; Musical-TV; Documentary-TV.
Biography: Born 1934; originally a dancer and choreographer; switched to hosting and interviewing. Thirteen seasons as program co-ordinator for *FRONT PAGE CHALLENGE;* produces and writes industrials.

(cont/suite)

Selective Filmography: *PROFILE OF CELIA FRANCA,* TV, 83, CDN, Co-Prod/Host; *GORDON SINCLAIR GALA,* TV, 82, CDN, Prod; *PROFILE OF LUDMILLA CHIARIEFF,* TV, 82, CDN, Co-Prod/Host; *JULIETTE'S RETURN ENGAGEMENT,* TV, 81, CDN, Head Wr; *PROFILE OF GWENETH LLOYD,* TV, 81, CDN, Co-Prod/Host; *ACTRA AWARDS,* TV, 80, CDN, Prod; *JULIETTE'S FAVOURITE THINGS,* TV, 77, CDN, Prod.

TOVELL, Vincent - see DIRECTORS

TRANTER, Barbara

DGC. 118 Bedford Rd., #1, Toronto, Ont, CAN, M5R 2K2. (416)961-0666. Brat Productions Inc., 861 College St., Ste. 302, Toronto, Ont, CAN, M6H 1A1. (416) 535-7294.
Types of Production & Categories: Th Film-Art Dir; Th Short-Wr/Dir; TV Film-Prod; TV Video-Prod.
Genres: Drama-Th&TV; Comedy-Th&TV; Variety-TV; Documentary-Th.
Biography: Born Niagara-on-the-Lake, Ontario. Education: Fine Arts, York University, 72.
Selective Filmography: *THE CANADIAN CONSPIRACY,* TV, 85, CDN/USA, Co-Prod; *PASSION: A LETTER IN 16mm,* Th, 85, CDN, Art Dir; *'OWL TV'* (pilot), TV, 84, CDN, Wr/Dir; *UNFINISHED BUSINESS,* Th, 83, CDN, Co-Art Dir; *HELLO GOODBYE,* TV, 82, CDN, Prod; *PORKY'S* (CHEZ PORKY), Th, 81, CDN, Assist Art Dir; *LOVE,* Th, 80, CDN, Assist Art Dir; *CIRCLE OF TWO,* Th, 80, CDN, Assist Art Dir; *SHE'S A RAILROADER,* Th, 78, CDN, Wr/Dir; *ERNIE,* Th, 77, CDN, Wr/Dir.

VADNAIS, Yvon G.

AR. 8330 DeGaspé, Montréal, Qué, CAN, H2P 2K1. (514)384-0885. Radio-Canada, 1400 blvd. Dorchester est, Montréal, Qué, CAN, H2L 2M2. (514)285-2591.
Types de production et Catégories: TV film-Prod/Réal.
Types d'oeuvres: Documentaire-TV; Affaires publiques-TV; Nouvelles-TV.
Curriculum vitae: Né en 1946; citoyen canadien. Diplôme du Collège Canada. Journaliste (rédacteur/reporter), CFCF Radio-TV; reporter radio-TV, CBC/Radio-Canada.
Filmographie sélective: *TEL QUEL,* TV, 86, CDN, Réal; *'NEWSWATCH',* TV, 85-82, CDN, Prod exéc; *DECISION* (REFERENDUM QUEBEC), TV, 79, CDN, Réal; *REFERENDUM QUESTION,* TV, 79, CDN, Prod/Réal; *'LAPIERRE'* (45 eps), TV, 76, CDN, Prod/Réal; *TWO YEARS TO GO/ONE YEAR TO GO* (OLYMPIC COUNTDOWN), (Prod-1 eps), (2 eps), TV, 75/74, CDN, Journ; *WEEKEND ROUGE* (FIREMEN'S STRIKE), TV, 75, CDN, Prod.

VALCOUR, Pierre

APFVQ. 367 St-Joseph est, Montréal, Qué, CAN, H2T 1J5. (514)521-2908. 1600 De Lorimier, Montréal, Qué, CAN, H2K 3W5. (514)521-1984.
Types de production et Catégories: l métrage-Réal/Prod; c métrage-Sc; TV film-Réal/Prod.
Types d'oeuvres: Drame-C&TV; Documentaire-C&TV; Expérimental-C&TV.
Curriculum vitae: Fondateur et Directeur-général de la Maison Premier Plan; Président de Ciné-Mundo Inc.. Président de l'APFVQ. Officier de l'Ordre de la Paix. Consul Général de la République du Rwanda.
Filmographie sélective: *LE MONDE DES ODEURS,* TV, 86, CDN, Prod; *LES PHARAONS,* TV, 86, CDN, Prod/Réal; *JEUNESSE CANADA MONDE,* TV, 85, CDN, Prod; *GEORGES HENRI LEVESQUE/MARIE VICTORIN,* TV, 84, CDN, Prod; *'PAR LES CHEMINS'* (13 eps), TV, 83, CDN, Prod/Réal; *'LES INTREPIDES'* (6 eps), TV, 82, CDN, Prod; *HISTOIRE DES DECENNIES - 49-59 / 69-79* (6 eps), TV, 81/78, CDN, Prod/Réal; *SPUTUM CYTOLOGY,* C, 80,

(cont/suite)

CDN, Prod; *HISTOIRE DE L'EDUCATION AU QUEBEC*, TV, 79, CDN, Prod/Réal; *HISTOIRE DES JEUNESSES MUSICALES AU CANADA*, TV, 79, CDN, Prod; *LIONEL GROULX - HOMME D'ACTION*, TV, 77, CDN, Prod/Réal; *LES MOUVEMENTS COOPERATIFS AU QUEBEC* (4 ém), TV, 77, CDN, Prod/Réal; *MARIE GUYART, VEUVE MARTIN*, TV, 77, CDN, Réal; *HISTOIRE DES MOUVEMENTS DE JEUNESSE* (4 ém), TV, 76, CDN, Prod/Réal; *PETITE HISTOIRE DES GRANDES COOPERATIVES* (3 ém), TV, 76, CDN, Prod/Réal; *KEBEKOOTUT*, C, 75, CDN, Prod; *JOSEPH CHARBONNEAU* (4 ém), TV, 75, CDN, Prod/Réal; *HISTOIRE DE LA PRESSE AU QUEBEC* (4 ém), TV, 75, CDN, Prod/Réal; *MADININA* (L'ILE DES FLEURS), C, 74, CDN, Prod; *LES ORIGINES DE LA REVOLUTION TRANQUILLE* (2 ém), TV, 74, CDN, Prod/Réal; *ETOOK*, TV, 73, CDN, Prod; *'AMBROISE RACONTE'* (26 eps), TV, 73, CDN, Prod; *LES GRANDS EXPLORATEURS* (6 films), C, 73, CDN, Prod; *BROADBACK*, TV, 73, CDN, Prod.

VALLEE, Jacques

6655 rue du Bouvreuil, Ste-Rose, Laval, Qué, CAN, H7L 4E8. (514)628-2688. ONF, 3155 Côte de Liesse, Montréal, Qué, CAN, H4N 2N4. (514)283-9316.
Types de production et Catégories: l métrage-Prod; c métrage-Prod.
Types d'oeuvres: Documentaire-C; Education-C; Expérimental-C.
Curriculum vitae: Né en 1941, Montréal, Québec. Licencié en Sciences de l'Education; Bac. en pédagogie, Université de Montréal. Travaille à l'ONF, 67-72; scénarisation/réalisation; Productions Carle-Lamy, 72-76; cinéaste conseil pour l'Agence canadienne de dévelopement international, 76-78; membre de la délégation canadienne à la conférence des Nations Unies, 82; producteur exécutif, production française, ONF depuis 80.
Filmographie sélective: *O PICASSO - TABLEAUX D'UNE SUREXPOSITION*, C, 85, CDN, Prod exéc; *'TROIS MILLIARDS'* (7 eps), TV, 85, CDN, Prod exéc; *O PICASSO*, C, 85, CDN, Prod exéc; *L'EMOTION DISSONANTE*, C, 84, CDN, Prod; *LA GRANDE ALLURE*, C, 84, CDN/F, Co prod; *PASSIFLORA*, C, 84, CDN, Prod exéc/Prod; *LE TRAVAIL PIEGE*, C, 84/83, CDN, Prod exéc; *CARNETS DU MAROC: MEMOIRE A REBOURS*, TV, 84/83, CDN, Prod exéc; *MEMOIRES D'UNE ENFANT DES ANDES*, C, 84/83, CDN, Prod exéc; *OUAGADOUGOU...CISSIN ENCORE UNE FOIS*, C, 84/83, CDN, Prod exéc; *BEYROUTH: A DEFAUT D'ETRE MORT*, C, 83, CDN, Prod exéc/Prod; *NO MORE HIROSHIMA* (PLUS JAMAIS HIROSHIMA), C, 83, CDN, Prod (GENIE); *ZARICO*, TV, 83, CDN, Prod exéc/Prod; *MADAME, VOUS AVEZ RIEN* (PLENTY OF NOTHING), C, 82, CDN, Prod exéc/Prod; *LA QUARANTAINE*, C, 82, CDN, Prod exéc/Prod; *LEO GERVAIS, SCULPTEUR*, TV, 82, CDN, Prod exéc/Prod, *POUR DU PAIN*, C, 82, CDN, Prod exéc/Réal; *PLUS JAMAIS D'HIBAKUSHA*, C, 82, CDN, Prod exéc; *DE MAINS ET D'ESPOIR*, C, 82, CDN, Prod exéc; *CISSIN...CINQ ANS PLUS TARD*, C, 82, CDN, Prod exéc; *EL MEXICO DEAL*, C, 81/80, CDN/MEX, Prod exéc; *KLUANE*, TV, 81/80, CDN, Prod exéc.

VAN DER KOLK, Henk

Blanks Inc., 73 Pembrooke St., Toronto, Ont, CAN, M5A 2N9. (416)964-6363.
Types of Production & Categories: Th Film-Prod.
Genres: Drama-Th; Documentary-Th.
Biography: Born Holland; landed immigrant, Canada. Has been producing films for 19 years.
Selective Filmography: *HANK WILLIAMS: THE SHOW HE NEVER GAVE*, Th, 81, CDN, Co-Prod; *CIRCLE OF TWO*, Th, 80, CDN, Prod; *WILD HORSE HANK*, Th, 79, CDN, Co-Prod; *MR. PATMAN*, Th, 79, CDN, Exec Prod; *OUTRAGEOUS!*, Th, 77, CDN, Co-Prod.

VAN DER VEEN, Milton - see DIRECTORS

VEILLEUX, Lucille

APFVQ. 2150 St-Timothée, Montréal, Qué, CAN, H2L 3P6. (514)521-4085. 2109 Montcalm, Montréal, Qué, CAN, H2L 3H8. (514)527-2911.
Types de production et Catégories: l métrage-Prod; c métrage-Prod.
Types d'oeuvres: Drame-C; Documentaire-C&TV; Expérimental-C.
Curriculum vitae: Née en 1953. Licence en Droit, Université Laval; avocate depuis 79. Vice-présidente et administratrice des Productions Vent d'Est depuis 76. *LA TURLUTE DES ANNEES DURES* remporte le Prix Ouimet Molson pour le meilleur long métrage québécois (83) et 2 prix au Festival de Nyon en Suisse; *L'AMIANTE CA TUE* et *LA FUITE* remportent chacun une Gerbe d'Or à Yorkton.
Filmographie sélective: *DU JOUR AU LENDEMAIN,* C, 85, CDN, Prod; *LE REVE DE VOLER,* C, 85, CDN, Prod; *LA FUITE,* C, 85, CDN, Prod; *L'OBJET,* C, 84, CDN, Prod; *LA TURLUTE DES ANNEES DURES,* C, 83, CDN, Prod; *LA MALADIE C'EST LES COMPAGNIES,* C, 79, CDN, Dir pro; *L'AMIANTE CA TUE,* C, 77, CDN, Dir pro; *VOTEZ MAUVE,* C, 76, CDN, Dir pro; *ALTERNANCE,* TV, 75, CDN, Prod.

VERRIER, Hélène

4001 Hingston, Montréal, Qué, CAN, H4A 2J6. (514)486-2077. 335 de Maisonneuve est, Montréal, Qué, CAN. (514)844-1954.
Types de production et Catégories: l métrage-Prod; c métrage-Prod; TV film-Prod; TV vidéo-Prod.
Types d'oeuvres: Drame-C&TV; Comédie-C&TV; Enfants-C&TV; Animation-C&TV.
Curriculum vitae: Née en 1948; bilingue. Productrice d'agence sur plus de 350 annonces, 73-77. *JOUER SA VIE* remporte de nombreux prix dont le Prix de la Presse Internationale et le Film de l'Année, London Film Festival; *UNE GUERRE DANS MON JARDIN* remporte le Prix de la Critique Québécoise.
Filmographie sélective: *UNE GUERRE DANS MON JARDIN,* TV, 85, CDN, Prod; *LA GRANDE ALLURE,* C, 84, CDN/F, Co prod; *MARIO,* C, 83, CDN, Co prod; *LA PLANTE,* C, 83, CDN, Prod; *JOUER SA VIE,* TV, 82, CDN, Prod; *LE JONGLEUR,* C, 81, CDN, Prod; *ST-MALO,* TV, 81, CDN/F, Prod; *'PASSE-PARTOUT',* TV, 79, CDN, Prod assoc.

VIENS, Louise

190 Place Bellevue, Laprairie, Qué, CAN, J5R 4M1. (514)659-0971. Idéacom inc., 5225 rue Berri, bur. 300, Montréal, Qué, CAN, H2J 2S4. (514)274-6538.
Types de production et Catégories: TV film-Prod; TV vidéo-Prod.
Types d'oeuvres: Education-TV; Industriel-TV.
Curriculum vitae: Née en 1952, Montréal, Québec; bilingue. Vice-présidente de Idéacom inc. depuis 73.
Filmographie sélective: *LAURENTIENNE I & II/IDEAL LTD.,* In, 86/85, CDN, Co prod; *AQOCI,* ED, 82, CDN, Co prod; *TVEQ,* In, 82, CDN, Co prod.

WACKO, Wendy

Box 1651, Jasper, Alta, CAN, T0E 1E0. (403)852-4728.
Types of Production & Categories: TV Film-Prod.
Genres: Drama-TV; Documentary-TV; Educational-TV.
Biography: Born 1951. Studied Art at the Ontario College of Art and Central Technical Art School, 69-72.
Selective Filmography: *STRIKER'S MOUNTAIN,* TV, 85, CDN, Exec Prod/Prod; *LUCY WALKER/THE FIRST ASCENT OF MOUNT BLANC/NANGA PARBAT,* 'MOUNTAIN MEN', TV, 85, CDN, Exec Prod/Prod; *THE CLIMB,* Th, 85, CDN/GB, Prod; *CHALLENGE - THE CANADIAN ROCKIES,* TV, 82-79, CDN, Exec Prod/Prod **(CFTA)**; *DORIS McCARTHY - HEART OF A*

(cont/suite)

PAINTER, TV, 82/81, CDN, Exec Prod/Prod; *THE GREAT ROCKY MOUNTAIN RELAY RACE*, TV, 82, CDN, Exec Prod/Prod.

WADE, Tony - see DIRECTORS

WALKER, Brian

570 Wellington St.W., Ste. 11B, Toronto, Ont, CAN, M5V 2X5. (416)363-0880. Nelvana, 32 Atlantic Ave., Toronto, Ont, CAN, M6K 1X8. (416)588-5771.
Types of Production & Categories: Th Film-Prod; TV Film-Prod/Dir.
Genres: Drama-TV; Horror-Th; Documentary-TV; Children's-TV.
Selective Filmography: *'THE EDISON TWINS'* (39 eps), TV, 86-83, CDN, Prod; *PERE MURRAY*, TV, 81/80, CDN, Dir; *MURDER BY PHONE* (BELLS), Th, 80, CDN, Prod; *'SIDESTREET'*, TV, 80-77, CDN, Prod; *CROSSBAR*, TV, 78, CDN, Prod; *'THE COLLABORATORS'*, TV, 76, CDN, Assoc Prod; *'POLICE SURGEON'* (26 eps), TV, 73, CDN, 1st AD; *'THE WHITE OAKS OF JALNA'*, TV, 72, CDN, 1st AD; *FOXY LADY*, Th, 71, CDN, 1st AD/PM; *'ADVENTURES IN RAINBOW COUNTRY'*, TV, 70, CDN/GB/AUS, 1st AD.

WALKER, Giles - see DIRECTORS

WALTON, Lloyd A.

CSC. 7 Harding Blvd., Scarborough, Ont, CAN, M1N 3C8. (416)690-3445.
Types of Production & Categories: Th Short-Dir/DOP; TV Film-Dir/Prod; TV Video-Dir/Prod.
Genres: Drama-Th&TV; Comedy-Th&TV; Documentary-Th&TV; Educational-Th&TV.
Biography: Born 1946, Sault Ste. Marie, Ontario. Graduated Ontario College of Art. Has won 4 Gold Camera Awards and a Silver Screen Award, U.S. Industrial Film Festival.
Selective Filmography: *FUTURES IN WATER*, TV, 84, CDN, Prod/Dir; *SNOW*, ED, 81, CDN, Prod/Dir (BIJOU); *THE LOON, THE NORTH AND YOU*, Th, 77, CDN, Prod/Dir/Cin; *RENDEZ VOUS*, ED, 76, CDN, Prod/Dir/Cin; *SANDUNES/ IMPRINT ON THE LAND*, ED, 76/75, CDN, Prod/Dir/An; *BISCOTDSING*, ED, 73, CDN, Prod/Dir/DOP; *LOGGING IN THE OTTAWA VALLEY*, ED, 73, CDN, Prod/Dir; *PRESSURES ON LAND/AMICH*, ED, 72, CDN, Prod/Dir; *PEACE AND QUIET*, Th, 70, CDN, Prod/Dir/An.

WASIK, Walter

CSC, NABET, SMPTE. 293 Blue Heron Dr., Oshawa, Ont, CAN, L1G 6X7. (416) 576-1030. Walter Wasik Films Ltd., P.O. Box 546, Oshawa, Ont, CAN, L1H 7L9.
Types of Production & Categories: Th Film-DOP/Prod; Th Short-DOP/Prod; TV Video-Prod.
Genres: Drama-Th; Variety-TV; Documentary-Th; Educational TV.
Biography: Born 1930, Ukraine; in Canada since 48; Canadian citizen. Languages: Ukrainian, English, German, Polish, Russian, Slovak. Has owned studio in Oshawa since 50; produces mainly features and his own Ukrainian TV variety show.
Selective Filmography: *DESH - VIDESH*, Th, 79, CDN, Prod; *WHISPERING HIGHLAND*, Th, 77, CDN, Prod; *LESIA*, Th, 75, CDN, Prod; *MARICHKA*, Th, 74, CDN, Prod; *CHRISTMAS TREE*, Th, 73, CDN, Co-Prod; *PROUD RIDER*, Th, 70, CDN, DOP; *I SHALL NEVER FORGET*, Th, 68, CDN, Prod; *CRUEL DAWN*, Th, 65, CDN, Prod; *SHEVCHENKO IN WASHINGTON*, Th, 64, CDN/ USA, Prod; *BANFF/MEXICO*, In, 62/60, CDN, Prod; *SHEVCHENKO'S CENTENNIAL*, TV, 61, CDN, Prod; *CALIFORNIA*, In, 59, CDN/USA, Prod; *CAREER IN PHOTOGRAPHY*, Th, 56, USA, DOP; *HOBO'S DREAM*, Th, 55, USA, Prod.

WATSON, John

DGA, DGC. 619 18th Street, Manhattan Bch., CA, USA, 90266. (213)545-4148.
(cont/suite)

Insight Group Inc., 1915 Comstock Ave., Los Angeles, CA, USA, 90025. (213)203-8501. Mike Simpson, William Morris Agency, 151 El Camino Dr., Beverly Hills, CA, USA, 90212. (213)859-4100.
Types of Production & Categories: Th Film-Dir/Prod/Wr; Th Short-Dir/Prod/Wr; TV Film-Dir/Prod/Wr/Ed.
Genres: Drama-Th&TV; Comedy-Th&TV; Action-Th; Documentary-TV.
Biography: Born 1947, England. M.A., Classics, Cambridge. Emigrated to Canada, 69; Canadian citizen. Formed Insight Productions with Pen Densham, 70. Co-produced, co-wrote and co-directed over 100 films, TV dramas, specials, educational films, documentaries. Won 10 CFEG Awards; 70 nat'l and int'l awards including 2 Oscar nominations. Moved to Los Angeles, 79.
Selective Filmography: *QUICKSILVER*, Th, 85, USA, 2nd U Co-Dir; *THE ZOO GANG* (WINNERS TAKE ALL), Th, 84, USA, Co-Prod/Co-Dir/Wr; *FLYING TIGERS*, Th, 84, USA, Co-Prod/Co-Wr; *LAST DRAGON II*, Th, 84, USA, Co-Prod/Co-Wr; *BLIND LUCK*, Th, 84, USA, Co-Wr; *ROCKY II*, Th, 80, USA, 2nd U Co-Dir; *DON'T MESS WITH BILL*, TV, 80, CDN, Co-Prod/Co-Ed/Co-Dir; *HOUDINI NEVER DIED (HE JUST VANISHED)*, TV, 79, CDN, Co-Prod/Co-Dir; *IF WISHES WERE HORSES*, Th, 76, CDN, Prod/Co-Ed; *LIFE TIMES NINE*, Th, 74, CDN, Co-Prod.

WATSON, Patrick

Goodman & Goodman, Michael Levine, 20 Queen St. W. Ste. 3000, Toronto, Ont, CAN, M5H 1V5. (416)979-2211.
Types of Production & Categories: TV Film-Prod/Wr/Host; TV Video-Prod/Wr/Host.
Genres: Variety-TV; Documentary-TV; Educational-TV.
Biography: First North American filmmaker to film in People's Republic of China. Founded Patrick Watson Enterprises Ltd., 66; co-founded Immedia Inc., Ottawa, 67; anchorman, editor on *THE FIFTY-FIRST STATE*, New York, 77; host, CBS Cable Service, NY, 81. Author of 5 books, 2 of which were Book of the Month Club Selections. Officer of the Order of Canada.
Selective Filmography: *LIVE FROM LINCOLN CENTRE*, TV, 86-8?, USA, Host; *'LAWYERS'* (8 eps), TV, 85, CDN, Host; *COUNTDOWN TO LOOKING GLASS*, TV, 84, CDN/USA, Act; *THE TERRY FOX STORY*, Th, 84, CDN, Act; *'THE WATSON REPORT'* (135 eps), TV, 81-75, CDN, Interv (**ACTRA**); *'TITANS'* (13 eps), TV, 81, CDN, Interv/Wr; *THE CHINESE* (6 parts), TV, 81, CDN, Contr Wr/Host/Narr; *'THE CANADIAN ESTABLISHMENT'* (7 eps), TV, 80, CDN, Contr Wr/Host (**ACTRA**); *FLIGHT: THE PASSIONATE AFFAIR* (4 parts), TV, 78, CDN, Host/Wr; *'WITNESS TO YESTERDAY'* (Wr-6 eps), (36 eps), TV, 76-74, CDN, Interv; *'THIS HOUR HAS SEVEN DAYS'* (Co-Host, 35 eps), (35 eps), TV, 66-64, CDN, Exec Prod; *'INQUIRY'* (120 eps), TV, 64-60, CDN, Prod/Dir; *THE 700 MILLION*, TV, 64, CDN, Prod/Dir; *'CLOSE-UP'* (105 eps), TV, 60-57, CDN, Co-Prod.

WEINBERG, Ronald A.

734 Upper Lansdowne, Montreal, Que, CAN, H3Y 1J7. (514)484-7469. Cinar Films Inc., 1160 Alexandre-de-Sève, Ste. 1, Montreal, Que, CAN, H2L 2T8. (514) 521-2045. Cinar Films Inc., 41 East 42nd St., New York, NY, USA, 10017. (212) 286-0695.
Types of Production & Categories: Th Film-Prod; TV Film-Prod; TV Video-Prod.
Genres: Variety-TV; Children's-Th&TV.
Biography: Born 1951, California, USA; Canadian landed immigrant. Graduated from School of Engineering, Tulane University, New Orleans, 73. Distributor of features and TV for 7 years.
Selective Filmography: *LE MAGICIEN D'OZ* (THE WIZARD OF OZ), (also TV, 52 eps), Th, 86, CDN, Co-Exec Prod; *THE LAND OF OZ*, Th, 86, CDN, Co-Exec Prod; *OZMA OF OZ*, Th, 86, CDN, Co-Exec Prod; *THE EMERALD CITY OF*

(cont/suite)

Congratulations to Glen-Warren's John Botelho on his Emmy nomination for lighting direction.

Nominated for "The Execution of Raymond Graham"
seen live on the CTV and ABC Networks
produced by Alliance Entertainment Corporation.

GLEN·WARREN
PRODUCTIONS LIMITED

OZ, Th, 86, CDN, Co-Exec Prod; *'SIDNEY & ALBERT'* (50 eps), TV, 86, USA, Prod; *'ULTRA-7'* (49 eps), TV, 85, USA, Co-Exec Prod; *PAVLOVA,* TV, 83, CDN/USA, Co-Prod.

WEINSTEIN, Les
Salish Park Productions Inc., 547 Homer St., Vancouver, BC, CAN, V6B 2V7. (604)685-6255.
Types of Production & Categories: TV Film-Prod.
Genres: Drama-TV; Variety-TV; Documentary-TV; Children's-TV.
Biography: Born 1933, Montreal, Quebec. Seven years at Columbia Pictures in distribution; personal manager for The Irish Rovers for 20 years; President, Salish Park Productions Inc..
Selective Filmography: *'PARTY WITH THE ROVERS'* (36 eps), TV, 85-83, CDN, Exec Prod; *HARVEST MOON WITH FRANK MILLS,* TV, 85, CDN, Exec Prod; *ROCKY MOUNTAIN CHRISTMAS WITH FRANK MILLS,* TV, 84, CDN, Exec Prod; *KKID-TV* (pilot), TV, 83, CDN, Exec Prod; *MAGICAL HALLOWEEN PARTY,* TV, 82, CDN, Exec Prod; *CHILDREN OF THE GALE,* TV, 80, CDN, Exec Prod; *BRENDON BEHAN HOLDING FORTH,* TV, 78, CDN, Exec Prod; *SECOND WIND,* Th, 75, CDN, Exec Prod.

WEINTRAUB, William - see WRITERS
WEYMAN, Peter Bay - see DIRECTORS
WHEELER, Anne - see DIRECTORS
WILDEBLOOD, Peter
ACTRA, ATPD. 195 St. Patrick St., #808, Toronto, Ont, CAN, M5T 2Y8. (416) 977-2646. CBC, Box 500, Stn. A, Toronto, Ont, CAN, M5W 1E6. (416)975-7139. Douglas Rae Mgmt Ltd., 28 Charing Cross Rd., London, England, G.B., WC2 H0DB. (01)836-3903.
Types of Production & Categories: TV Film-Prod/Wr; TV Video-Prod/Wr.
Genres: Drama-Th&TV; Musical-TV.
Biography: Born 1923, Alassio, Italy; British subject; Canadian citizen, 81. Education: Radley College, Trinity College, Oxford; speaks English, French, Spanish, some Arabic. Author of 4 books including 'Against the Law'; wrote book and lyrics for 3 stage musicals including ' The Crooked Mile' (Ivor Novello Award for Light Music, GB, 59) Under contract to Granada TV, 58-70 as producer, screenwriter; executive producer (plays), London Weekend TV till 72. Executive-in-Charge (independent production), CBC drama, Toronto, 86.
Selective Filmography: *'BACKSTRETCH'* (Wr-5 eps), (12 eps), TV, 84-82, CDN, Prod **(ANIK)**; *I MARRIED THE KLONDIKE* (3 parts), TV, 83, CDN, Wr; *'THE GREAT DETECTIVE'* (Wr-5 eps), (35 eps), TV, 82 79, CDN, Prod; *LADIES CHOICE,* TV, 82, CDN, Prod; *'A GIFT TO LAST'* (Wr-5 eps), (25 eps), TV, 79-77, CDN, Story Ed; *'FATHER BROWN'* (4 eps), TV, 76, GB, T'play; *'UPSTAIRS DOWNSTAIRS',* TV, 74, GB, Wr; *TEN FROM THE TWENTIES,* TV, 74, GB, T'play; *CRIME OF PASSION,* TV, 73, GB, Wr; *PARABLES,* TV, 73, GB, Wr; *'CROWN COURT',* TV, 72, GB, Prod/Wr; *'BIG BROTHER'* (13 eps), TV, 71, GB, Prod; *'ADVENTURES OF DON QUICK'* (6 eps), TV, 70, GB, Prod; *TESTAMENT OF FRANCOIS VILLON,* TV, 70, GB, Wr/Prod; *THE PEOPLE'S JACK,* TV, 69, GB, Prod/Wr; *PRESENT LAUGHTER,* TV, 68, GB, T'play; *'CINEMA'* (150 eps), TV, 66-64, GB, Prod; *'ROGUES GALLERY'* (10 eps), TV, 64, GB, Wr/Prod; *'THE YOUNGER GENERATION'* (8 eps), TV, 63/62, GB, Prod; *'SIX SHADES OF BLACK'* (6 eps), TV, 62, GB, Prod/Wr; *'THE VERDICT IS YOURS'* (20 eps), TV, 61, GB, Prod/Wr; *'ON TRIAL'* (6 eps), TV, 59, GB, Prod/Wr; *APPOINTMENT WITH COUNT BASIE,* TV, 59, GB, Prod/Wr; *APPOINTMENT WITH DUKE ELLINGTON,* TV, 59, GB, Prod/Wr.

WILLIAMS, Don S. - see DIRECTORS

WINNING, David - see DIRECTORS

WINTONICK, Peter - see EDITORS

WISEMAN, Sheldon

17 Lacewood Court, Nepean, Ont, CAN, K2E 7E2. (613)226-5112. 400 MacLaren St., Ottawa, Ont, CAN, K2P 0M8. (613)238-4455.
Types of Production & Categories: TV Film-Prod.
Genres: Animation-TV.
Biography: Born 1941, Smiths Falls, Ontario. B.A., Queen's University; LL.B., University of Toronto, 66; called to the Bar of Ontario, 68. Legal advisor for various TV specials and series. President of Evergreen Raccoons Marketing Inc. and Gillis-Wiseman Productions Inc..
Selective Filmography: *'THE RACCOONS'* (11 eps), TV, 86, CDN, Exec Prod; *THE RACCOONS - LET'S DANCE*, MV, 84, CDN, Exec Prod; *THE RACCOONS AND THE LOST STAR*, TV, 82, CDN, Exec Prod; *THE RACCOONS ON ICE*, TV, 81, CDN, Exec Prod; *THE CHRISTMAS RACCOONS*, TV, 80, CDN, Exec Prod.

WRIGHT, Paul

ATPD. 7 Sword St., Toronto, Ont, CAN, M5A 3N3. (416)967-0345. CBC, Box 500, Stn. A, Toronto, Ont, CAN, M5W 1E6. (416)975-6644.
Types of Production & Categories: TV Film-Prod/Wr.
Genres: Documentary-TV.
Biography: Born 1924, Winnipeg, Manitoba. Joined CBC, 55. Worked in Winnipeg, Toronto, London (England), Montreal; 10 years as executive producer, documentary specials.
Selective Filmography: *'DEFENCE OF CANADA'* (3 eps), TV, 86, CDN, Exec Prod; *CANADA'S SWEETHEART: THE SAGA OF HAL C. BANKS*, TV, 85, CDN, Co-Exec Prod; *FOR ALL THE GOOD INTENTIONS*, TV, 85, CDN, Exec Prod; *ALL THINGS BRIGHT AND BEAUTIFUL*, TV, 85, CDN, Exec Prod; *THE LIFER AND THE LADY*, TV, 85, CDN, Exec Prod; *20th CENTURY DISEASE*, TV, 83, CDN, Exec Prod; *ON GUARD FOR THEE* (3 parts), TV, 81, CDN, Exec Prod; *THE CHAMPIONS* (Parts I & II), TV, 78, CDN, Co-Exec Prod; *THE DIONNE QUINTUPLETS*, TV, 78, CDN, Exec Prod; *TANKERBOMB*, TV, 78, CDN, Exec Prod (ANIK); *HENRY FORD'S AMERICA*, TV, 76, CDN, Exec Prod (EMMY).

YATES, Rebecca

215 Albany Ave., Toronto, Ont, CAN, M5R 3C7. Cineflics Ltd., 330 Dupont St., #302, Toronto, Ont, CAN, M5R 1V9. (416)967-9183.
Types of Production & Categories: TV Film-Prod/Dir.
Genres: Drama-TV; Children's-TV.
Biography: Born 1950, London, England; emigrated to Canada, 52; Canadian citizen. Honours B.F.A., York University, 74. Has been producing/directing original TV drama in partnership with Glen Salzman since 76. Has won awards from American, Yorkton, Chicago and Teheran Film Festivals.
Selective Filmography: *JEN'S PLACE*, TV, 82, CDN, Co-Prod/Co-Dir; *INTRODUCING...JANET*, TV, 81, CDN, Co-Prod/Co-Dir (**CFTA**); *REACHING OUT*, TV, 80, CDN, Co-Prod/Co-Dir; *CORLETTO & SON*, TV, 80, CDN, Co-Prod/Co-Dir; *NIKKOLINA*, TV, 78, CDN, Co-Prod/Co-Dir; *ANOTHER KIND OF MUSIC*, TV, 77, CDN, Co-Prod/Co-Dir; *HOME FREE*, TV, 76, CDN, Co-Prod/Co-Dir.

YOLLES, Edie - see DIRECTORS

YOSHIMURA, Yuri

APFVQ. 994 ch.de la Montagne, St-Hilaire, Qué, CAN, J3G 4S6. (514)464-7173. Yoshimura-Gagnon, 1600 rue De Lorimier, Montréal, Qué, CAN, H2K 3W5. (514) 521-7103.
Types de production et Catégories: l métrage-Prod; c métrage-Prod.
Types d'oeuvres: Drame-C; Comédie-C; Documentaire-C; Enfants-C.
Curriculum vitae: Née en 1948, Japon; citoyenne japonaise; immigrante reçue; Langues: japonais, anglais, français. Distributrice; s'occupe activement de la promotion du cinéma québécois au Japon. *KEIKO* gagne le Prix Spécial du Jury et le Prix de la Réalisation (Association des réalisateurs de films au Japon); *VISAGE PALE* remporte le Prix de la Presse Internationale, Montréal, 85.
Filmographie sélective: *VISAGE PALE* (PALE FACE), C, 85, CDN, Co prod; *LAROSE, PIERROT ET LA LUCE,* C, 82, CDN, Co prod; *L'HOMME D'AILLEURS,* C, 79, J, Co prod; *KEIKO,* C, 78, J, Co prod; *YIU TO HI,* C, 77, J, Co prod; *GEININ,* C, 75, J, Prod; *ESSAI FILMIQUE SUR MUSIQUE JAPONAISE,* C, 74, J, Prod.

ZARITSKY, John - see DIRECTORS

ZIMMER, Christopher

Imagex Ltd., 1574 Argyle St., Halifax, NS, CAN, B3J 2B3. (902)422-4000.
Types of Production & Categories: TV Film-Prod; TV Video-Prod.
Genres: Drama-TV; Documentary-TV; Sports-TV.
Selective Filmography: *'SPORTSDESK'* (35 seg), TV, 86/85, CDN, Exec Prod; *STARTING RIGHT NOW,* ED, 85, CDN, Prod; *RITA MacNEIL IN JAPAN,* TV, 85, CDN, Prod.

ZIPURSKY, Arnie

CFTA. 1645 Bathurst St., Toronto, Ont, CAN, M5P 3J6. (416)481-9340. Cambium Productions, 141 Gerrard St.E., Toronto, Ont, CAN, M5A 2E3. (416)964-8750.
Types of Production & Categories: TV Film-Ed/Prod; TV Video-Ed/Prod.
Genres: Musical-TV; Documentary-TV; Children's-TV.
Biography: Born 1955, Winnipeg, Manitoba. Diploma in Applied Arts and Science, Capilano College, Vancouver, 75; Honours B.F.A., York University, 78; received Maple Leaf Award for Excellence in Film Studies, 78. Video switcher, CBC Winnipeg, 74-77; editor, CTV, Vancouver, 78.
Selective Filmography: *SHARON, LOIS AND BRAM'S ELEPHANT SHOW'* (26 eps), TV, 85/84, CDN, Co-Prod; *SHARON, LOIS AND BRAM AT YOUNG PEOPLE'S THEATRE,* TV, 83, CDN, Co-Prod/Co-Dir/Ed; *FOR PAUL,* TV, 83, CDN, Assoc Prod/Ed/Comp; *THE VEGETARIAN WORLD,* TV, 83, CDN, Co-Ed/Snd Ed; *MICHAEL, A GAY SON,* TV, 80, CDN, Assist Dir/Ed; *CONTACT,* TV, 79, CDN, Co-Prod/Co-Wr/Co-Ed.

ZLATARITS, Harvey - see EDITORS

ZNAIMER, Moses

City TV, 299 Queen St. W., Toronto, Ont, CAN, M5V 1Z9. (416)367-5757.
Types of Production & Categories: TV Film-Prod; TV Video-Prod.
Genres: Variety-TV; Musical-TV; News-TV.
Biography: Born in Kulab, Tajikistan; grew up in Montreal. Honours B.A., Philosophy and Politics, McGill University; M.A., Government, Harvard U.. Co-founder, President, Chief Executive Officer and Executive Producer of City TV (1972), MuchMusic (84) and MusiquePlus (86). Has worked for CBC radio & TV (65-69) as producer/director/host of several shows including: *CROSS COUNTRY CHECKUP, TWENTY MILLION QUESTIONS, TAKE 30, THE WAY IT IS, REVOLUTION PLUS FIFTY.* Vice President, Helix Investments and T'ang Management Ltd. (69-71); theatrical producer: 'Miss Margarida', 'Travesties' and 'Tamara'.

(cont/suite)

ZOLF, Larry

ATPD. 62 Balsam Ave., Toronto, Ont, CAN, M4E 3B7. (416)690-2900. CBC, 790 Bay St., Toronto, Ont, CAN. (416)975-6641.
Types of Production & Categories: TV Film-Prod; TV Video-Prod.
Genres: Drama-TV; Comedy-TV; Documentary-TV; Current Affairs-TV.
Biography: Born 1934, Winnipeg, Manitoba. Languages: English, German. Education: 1 year Law; completed Masters program in History, University of Toronto. Producer/director, hundreds of documentary items for CBC TV; produced all propaganda for U.S. Democratic Party Gubernatorial race, 66. Won the Wilderness Award for Best TV Journalism for *STRIKE: MEN AGAINST COMPUTERS* which also won a Prize at the Int'l Labour and Industrial Film Fest., Brussels. Awarded the Isbister, Principal Sparling, Marcus Hyman and A.A. Baird Scholarships.
Selective Filmography: *COME TO US,* TV, 75, CDN, Prod/Wr; *STRIKE: MEN AGAINST COMPUTERS,* TV, 66, CDN, Dir/Wr.

ZOLLER, Stephen - see WRITERS

DIRECTORS
★
REALISATEURS

May we have the envelope, please...

If you'd like to join the industry's best and brightest at the Banff Television Festival, please write soon. Or call. Or telex. Then get ready for a very rewarding experience.

You'll screen top programs from around the globe. Share ideas and visions at conferences, seminars and workshops. Enjoy the good times with other talented professionals. All in an incomparable mountain setting.

Sign up for the Banff Television Festival today. Who knows? We may have an envelope with your name on it.

THE 8TH BANFF TELEVISION FESTIVAL
JUNE 7 - 13, 1987

BANFF
TELEVISION FESTIVAL

Write: Box 1020, Banff, Alberta, Canada T0L 0C0
Telephone: (403) 762-3060 Telex: T.V. Fest BNF 03-822804

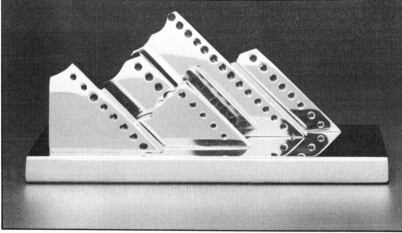

REALISATEURS/DIRECTORS

ADAIR, Trayton
Trayton Adair Productions, 103 Charles St.E., Toronto, Ont, CAN, M4Y 1V2. (416)922-2930.
Types of Production & Categories: TV Film-Dir; TV Video-Dir.
Genres: Commercials-TV.
Biography: Born Saskatoon, Saskatchewan. B.A., University of Saskatoon. Director of 800 commercials since 1974; has won awards including: Toronto Art Directors Association, Broadcasting Executive Society Award, Clio and US Commercials Festival Awards.

ALIANAK, Hrant
ACTRA. 629 Broadview Ave., Toronto, Ont, CAN, M4K 2N3. (416)463-1552.
Ralph Zimmerman, Great North Artists Mgmt., 345 Adelaide St W., Ste.500, Toronto, Ont, CAN. (416)593-2587.
Types of Production & Categories: Th Short-Dir/Wr; TV Film-Dir; TV Video-Dir/Wr.
Genres: Drama-TV; Comedy-TV; Action-Th; Experimental-Th&TV.
Biography: Born 1950; Canadian citizen. Languages: English, French, Armenian. Attented McGill University; York U.. Writer, director in theatre since 72; has worked in Canada, USA, U.K.; actor in TV and films since 80; plays written and directed include: 'Lucky Strike', 'Night', 'Passion and Sin' and 'The Blues'.
Selective Filmography: *MICHAEL AND KITTY,* TV, 85, CDN, Dir; *THE SACRIFICE,* Th, 78, CDN, Dir/Wr; *PARANOID FRACTIONS,* 'MICRODRAMAS', TV, 75, CDN, Dir/Wr.

ALMOND, Paul
DGA, DGC. 1272 Redpath Crescent, Montreal, Que, CAN, H3G 2K1. (514)845-1921.
Types of Production & Categories: Th Film-Dir/Prod; TV Film-Dir; TV Video-Dir/Prod.
Genres: Drama-Th&TV; Comedy-TV; Action-Th&TV; Horror-TV.
Biography: Born 1931, Montreal, Quebec; educated at Bishop's College School, Lennoxville, Quebec; McGill University, Montreal; Balliol College, Oxford, England (B.A., M.A.). Directed and produced over 100 TV dramas in Toronto, London, N.Y., L.A., 54-67. *UPS & DOWNS* won the Bronze Prize, Houston Film Fest..
Selective Filmography: *UPS & DOWNS,* Th, 82, CDN, Wr/Prod/Dir, *JOURNEY,* Th, 72, CDN, Wr/Prod/Dir; *ACT OF THE HEART* (L'ACTE DU COEUR), Th, 70, CDN, Wr/Prod/Dir (CFA); *ISABEL,* Th, 68, CDN, Wr/Prod/Dir.

AMINI, Stephen
DGA, DGC. Shooters Film Company, 95 Berkeley St., Toronto, Ont, CAN, M5A 2W8. (416)862-1955.
Types of Production & Categories: TV Film-Dir/Cam.
Genres: Commercials-TV.
Biography: Born 1950. Director/cameraman on numerous television commercials; awards include Bessies, Clios and a Gold Camera (US Industrial Film Festival) for *AVON INC.*.
Selective Filmography: *AVON INC.,* In, 86, USA, Dir; *HEINZ KETCHUP/QUAKER CHEWY BARS/SUNPAC/CLAIROL CANADA,* Cm, 85/84, CDN, Dir; *WHITEHALL LABS/CANADIAN CANCER SOCIETY/THE BAY/SEARS,* Cm, 84/83, CDN, Dir.

ANDERSON, Michael
ACTT, DGA, DGC. c/o DGC, 3 Church St., Ste. 202, Toronto, Ont, CAN, M5E 1M2. (416)364-0122.
Types of Production & Categories: Th Film-Dir; TV Film-Dir.
(cont/suite)

197

Genres: Drama-Th&TV; Comedy-Th; Action-Th; Science Fiction-Th&TV.
Biography: Born London, England; British-Canadian dual citizenship; fluent English, French, German, Italian. Educated Lycée Corneille, France; Treitschke Schule, Berlin; London Polytechnic. *AROUND THE WORLD IN 80 DAYS*, nominated for 10 Oscars, won 5, including Best Picture and 52 major int'l awards. *THE SHOES OF THE FISHERMAN*, winner Best Picture, the National Board of Review.
Selective Filmography: *THE SWORD OF GIDEON* (mini-series), TV, 86, CDN, Dir; *SEPARATE VACATIONS*, Th, 85, CDN, Dir; *MURDER BY PHONE* (BELLS), Th, 80, CDN, Dir; *THE MARTIAN CHRONICLES*, TV, 79, USA, Dir; *LOGAN'S RUN*, Th, 75, USA, Dir; *CONDUCT UNBECOMING*, Th, 74, GB, Dir; *SHOES OF THE FISHERMAN*, Th, 68, USA, Dir; *THE QUILLER MEMORANDUM*, Th, 66, GB, Dir; *OPERATION CROSSBOW*, Th, 65, GB, Dir; *THE NAKED EDGE*, Th, 61, USA, Dir; *THE WRECK OF THE MARY DEARE*, Th, 60, USA, Dir; *SHAKE HANDS WITH THE DEVIL*, Th, 59, USA, Dir; *BATTLE HELL* (YANGTSE INCIDENT), Th, 56, GB, Dir; *AROUND THE WORLD IN 80 DAYS*, Th, 56, USA, Dir; *THE DAM BUSTERS*, Th, 55, GB, Dir.

APOR, Gabor

12 Cluny Dr., Toronto, Ont, CAN, M4W 2P7. (416)923-9228.
Types of Production & Categories: TV Film-Dir/Prod; TV Video-Dir/Prod.
Genres: Drama-TV; Variety-TV; Documentary-TV; Commercials-TV.
Biography: Hungarian born; Canadian citizen. B.A., Theatre Arts, Budapest, Hungary; studies towards B.Comm., Montreal, Quebec; TV Arts degree, Toronto, Ontario. Producer, director of 3000 commercials; 8 Clio Awards, 3 Gold Lions (Cannes) and many other awards of production excellence. Worked in Toronto, New York; previously Director and Senior V.P. of major advertising agency.
Selective Filmography: *WHAT IS TO BE DONE?*, TV, 84, CDN, Prod/Exec Prod; *'CHALLENGERS'* (13 eps), TV, 81-78, CDN, Dir/Prod/Exec Prod; *'IT'S UP TO YOU!'* (26 eps), TV, 74-72, CDN, Dir/Prod.

ARCAND, Denys

ACTRA, ARRFQ, SARDEC. 4921 Coronet, #12, Montréal, Qué, CAN. (514)341-6139.
Types de production et Catégories: l métrage-Réal/Sc; c métrage-Réal/Sc; TV film-Réal/Sc; TV vidéo-Réal/Sc.
Types d'oeuvres: Drame-C&TV; Documentaire-C&TV.
Curriculum vitae: Né en 1941, Québec. Maitrise en Histoire, Université de Montréal. *LE CONFORT ET L'INDIFFERENCE* gagne le Prix Ouimet-Molson. *LE DECLIN DE L'EMPIRE AMERICAIN* remporte le Prix de la Fédération Internationale de la Presse Cinématographique, Cannes (Quinzaine des Réalisateurs), le Prix John Labatt Classic pour le film le plus populaire et le Prix CITY, Meilleur Film Canadien, Festival du Film de Toronto, 86.
Filmographie sélective: *LE DECLIN DE L'EMPIRE AMERICAIN* (DECLINE OF THE AMERICAN EMPIRE), C, 85, CDN, Réal/Sc; *LE CRIME D'OVIDE PLOUFFE* (Réal, sc-2 ém TV), C, 83, CDN/F, Réal/Co sc; *'EMPIRE INC.'* (3 eps), TV, 83, CDN, Réal; *LE CONFORT ET L'INDIFFERENCE*, C, 80, CDN, Réal; *DUPLESSIS*, TV, 76, CDN, Sc; *GINA*, C, 74, CDN, Réal/Mont/Sc; *REJEANNE PADOVANI*, C, 73, CDN, Réal/Sc; *LA MAUDITE GALETTE*, C, 72, CDN, Réal/Sc; *QUEBEC, DUPLESSIS, ET APRES*, C, 70, CDN, Réal/Mont; *ON EST AU COTON*, C, 69, CDN, Réal.

ARMATAGE, Kay

53 Brunswick Ave., Toronto, Ont, CAN, M5S 2L8. (416)968-3224. University of Toronto, Innis College, Cinema Studies, 2 Sussex Ave., Toronto, Ont, CAN. (416) 978-4671.

(cont/suite)

Types of Production & Categories: Th Short-Dir.
Genres: Drama-Th; Documentary-Th; Experimental-Th.
Biography: Born 1943, Lanigan, Saskatchewan. B.A., Queen's University; Ph.D., University of Toronto. Has written extensively in Canadian publications, including 'Take One' and 'Canadian Forum'. Film reviewer, CBC radio, CTV; programmer, Festival of Festivals. Teaches Cinema and Women's Studies, U of T. *STRIPTEASE* won the Silver Hugo, Chicago Film Fest..
Selective Filmography: *STORYTELLING,* Th, 83, CDN, Dir; *STRIPTEASE,* Th, 80, CDN, Dir; *SPEAK BODY,* Th, 79, CDN, Dir; *BED AND SOFA,* Th, 79, CDN, Dir; *GERTRUDE AND ALICE IN PASSING,* Th, 78, CDN, Dir; *JILL JOHNSTON,* Th, 77, CDN, Dir.

ARMSTRONG, Mary - see PRODUCERS

ARNOLD, Jeffrey

2151 Banbury Rd., #7, North Vancouver, BC, CAN, V7G 1W7. (604)929-3928. Lotus Film Productions, Box 91278, West Vancouver, BC, CAN. Tanya Chasman, Jack Rose Agency, 6430 Sunset Blvd., Suite 1203, Hollywood, CA, USA, 90028.
Types of Production & Categories: TV Video-Dir/Prod/Wr.
Genres: Drama-TV; Comedy-TV; Documentary-TV; Industrial-TV.
Biography: Born 1949, Thunder Bay, Ontario. Worked as cultural consultant and writer with B.C. and Alberta governments; has also written, directed for CBC radio.
Selective Filmography: *NIGHTGAMES,* TV, 86/85, CDN, Dir/Wr/Prod; *COASTAL SEA HOMES,* In, 84, CDN, Dir/Prod/Wr; *COMMONWEALTH GAMES SHOW,* TV, 78, CDN, Wr.

ARSENAULT, Ray

DGC. 236 Balliol St., Toronto, Ont, CAN, M4S 1C5. (416)489-4783. Larry Goldhar, Characters, 150 Carlton St., Toronto, Ont, CAN. (416)964-8522.
Types of Production & Categories: TV Film-Dir; TV Video-Dir.
Genres: Drama-TV; Comedy-TV; Documentary-TV; Industrial-TV.
Biography: Born in U.S.; American citizen; landed immigrant, Canada; Wayne State University; military service, United States Marines. Extensive TV production since 1951; live TV, tape, film, multi-camera, single camera.
Selective Filmography: *WHERE'S WHOOSIT'S* (pilot), TV, 86, CDN, Dir; *THE CLASSIC EGG,* In, 86, CDN, Dir; *THE CHILDREN CARE,* TV, 86, CDN, Dir.

AZZOPARDI, Anthony

345 Bain Ave., Toronto, Ont, CAN, M4J 1B9. (416)466-7379.
Types of Production & Categories: Th Film-Prod; TV Film-Dir/Prod/Wr; TV Video-Dir/Prod.
Genres: Drama-Th&TV; Comedy-TV; Documentary-TV.
Biography: Born 1950; B.F.A., Honours, (Film, Theatre Directing), York University, Toronto, 76.
Selective Filmography: *JOHN KIM BELL,* TV, 84/83, CDN, Dir/Prod; *THE STRONGER,* TV, 82, CDN, Dir/Prod; *THE WORLD OF AHMED FEZ BEN-ZINE,* TV, 82, CDN, Dir/Prod/Wr; *CITY GIRL,* Th, 81, CDN, Co-Prod; *SURFACING,* Th, 79, CDN, Assoc Prod; *TORONTO - THE PEOPLE CITY,* TV, 79, CDN, Dir/Prod.

AZZOPARDI, Mario

DGC. 378 Armadale, Toronto, Ont, CAN, M6S 3X8. (416)762-5960.
Types of Production & Categories: Th Film-Dir; TV Film-Dir.
Genres: Action-Th&TV; Documentary-TV; Children's-TV.
Biography: Born 1950, Malta; emigrated to Canada, 78; Canadian citizen. B.A., Royal University of Malta.

(cont/suite)

DIRECTORS/REALISATEURS

Selective Filmography: *'NIGHT HEAT'* (19 eps), TV, 86/85, CDN, Dir; *'HOT SHOTS'* (pilot), TV, 86, CDN, Dir; *STATE OF SURVIVAL,* Th, 86, CDN, Dir; *'LITTLEST HOBO'* (20 eps), TV, 84-81, CDN, Dir; *'THE EDISON TWINS'* (12 eps), TV, 84/83, CDN, Dir; *NEIGHBOURS/STREET-WISE/GOLDEN PROMISE,* 'TORONTO TRILOGY', TV, 84, CDN, Dir; *DEADLINE,* Th, 80, CDN, Dir.

BARCLAY, Robert
DGC. 129 Walmer Rd., Toronto, Ont, CAN, M5R 2X8. (416)964-1547. Robert Barclay Prod. Inc., P.O. Box 280, Station M, Calgary, Alta, CAN.
Types of Production & Categories: Th Short-Dir; TV Film-Dir/Prod/Wr/Ed; TV Video-Dir/Prod/Wr/Ed.
Genres: Drama-Th&TV; Variety-Th&TV; Documentary-Th&TV.
Biography: Born 1930, Calgary, Alberta. Education: Carleton College, Ottawa. Has made 150 short films and TV programs which have won AMPIA, Can-Pro, Chris and Teddy awards. President, DGC, 78-80. Recently developed a pavilion concept for Expo 86, featuring the world's first 3-D without glasses.
Selective Filmography: *K.D. LANG'S ODYSSEY IN JAPAN,* TV, 85, CDN, Dir/Prod; *DOUBLE PLAY,* TV, 83, CDN, Prod; *STAMPEDE,* TV, 78, CDN, Dir; *STAMPEDE POT POURRI,* TV, 77, CDN, Dir; *'WEEKEND FISHERMAN'* (10 eps), TV, 76, CDN, Dir/Prod; *THE GOLDEN GAMES,* TV, 75, CDN, Dir; *IAN AND SYLVIA ON THE TRAIL OF '98',* TV, 73, CDN, Dir; *STAMPEDE IN SCARLETT,* Th, 73, CDN, Dir/Wr/Ed; *JEAN BELIVEAU,* TV, 72, CDN, Dir/Ed; *WALT DISNEY'S MAGIC CARPET TOUR AROUND THE WORLD,* Th, 71, USA, Dir; *MANITOBA - FESTIVAL COUNTRY,* Th, 70, CDN, Dir/Ed; *HELICOPTER HOLYLAND,* TV, 70, CDN, Dir; *QUEEN GLENDA,* 'TELESCOPE', TV, 69, CDN, Dir; *VIRGINQUEST,* TV, 69, CDN, Dir; *LIGHTFOOT FORWARD,* 'TELESCOPE', TV, 68, CDN, Dir/Ed; *ONE CANADA/TWO NATIONS,* TV, 68, CDN, Dir; *A CENTURY OF CANADIAN MEDICINE,* In, 66, CDN, Dir; *BADMEN OF B.C.,* 'TELESCOPE', TV, 66, CDN, Dir/Ed/Wr; *CANADA '67,* Th, 65, CDN, Dir; *THE DUMBELLS,* TV, 65, CDN, Dir; *SOME ARE SUNFISHERS/WALT DISNEY'S WORLD/GREENE'S BONANZA,* 'TELESCOPE', TV, 64/63, CDN, Dir; *CHUCKWAGON,* Th, 64, CDN, Dir/Ed/Wr; *RIDEAU HALL,* TV, 62, CDN, Dir; *CHILDREN OF PEACE,* TV, 62, CDN, Dir; *THE CHOICE,* Th, 61, CDN, Dir; *LIGHT FOR THE MIND,* Th, 60, CDN, Dir/Ed; *BROKEN DOLL,* Th, 59, CDN, Dir; *MAN OF KINTAIL,* TV, 59, CDN, Dir.

BARDE, Barbara - see PRODUCERS

BARRIE, Scott
ACTRA, DGC. 204 Roxton Rd., Toronto, Ont, CAN, M6J 2Y5. (416)532-2972.
Types of Production & Categories: Th Short-Dir/Prod/Wr; TV Film-Dir/Wr/Ed.
Genres: Drama-TV; Documentary-Th&TV; Children's-TV.
Biography: Born 1951, Collingwood, Ontario. Social Sciences, McMaster University; Hamilton Teacher's College; taught children with learning disabilities. Film Production, Conestoga College. His films have won numerous awards: Yorkton, American, Chicago Film Fest.; twice winner of Canadian Independent Short Film Showcase for *I THINK OF YOU OFTEN, FOOTSTEPS*; 2 Genie nominations, theatrical short films.
Selective Filmography: *'OWL TV'* (10 seg), TV, 86, CDN, Dir; *'THE EDISON TWINS'* (Dir-3 eps/Wr-5 eps/Ed-10 eps), TV, 85-83, CDN, Dir/Wr/Ed; *I THINK OF YOU OFTEN,* Th, 83, CDN, Wr/Dir/Prod; *BOOKWRIGHT,* TV, 83, CDN, Dir/Prod/Cin; *NEWFOUNDLAND SKETCHBOOK,* TV, 83, CDN, Dir/Prod/Cin; *K.C.I. BEYOND THE THREE R'S,* TV, 82, CDN, Dir; *ANNE AND JOEY,* Th, 82, CDN/USA, 1st Assist Cam; *AMERICAN NIGHTMARE,* Th, 82, CDN, 1st Assist Cam; *ROOM FOR CHANGE,* TV, 81, CDN, Fl Dir; *SURFSAILOR,* TV,
(cont/suite)

81, CDN, 2nd U Dir; *PEARLS IN THE ALPHABET SOUP*, TV, 81, CDN, 2nd U Dir; *FLY WITH THE HAWKS*, TV, 81, CDN, Cin; *ICE RIDER*, TV, 80, CDN, Cin; *WINDOW IN THE ICE*, TV, 80, CDN, Cin; *FOOTSTEPS*, Th, 79, CDN, Dir/Wr/Ed (CFEG); *RETURN OF THE SWANS*, TV, 79, CDN, Cin; *GRACIE*, TV, 78, CDN, Dir/Wr.

BATTLE, Murray

369 Sunnyside Ave., Toronto, Ont, CAN, M6R 2R9. (416)531-2519.
Types of Production & Categories: Th Short-Dir; TV Film-Dir; TV Video-Dir.
Genres: Drama-Th; Documentary-Th&TV; Educational-TV.
Biography: Born 1951, Calgary, Alberta. Attended York Universtiy (Film Production).
Selective Filmography: *THE BARTLETTS*, ED, 86, CDN, Dir/Co-Wr; *THE HOSPITAL*, 'HOME MOVIES', TV, 85, CDN, Dir; *SHUTTLE COMMAND*, Th, 85, CDN, Dir; *CAVE AND BASIN*, Th, 85, CDN, Dir; *S2MR/CONNOISSEUR SERVICE/FUEL OF THE FUTURE*, In, 85/84, CDN, Dir.

BAYLIS, Paul - see PRODUCERS

BEAIRSTO, Ric

1133 Barclay St., #401, Vancouver, BC, CAN, V6E 1G8. (604)687-5240. Hy Perspectives Media Group, 1164 Hamilton, Vancouver, BC, CAN, V6B 2S3. (604) 683-2689.
Types of Production & Categories: TV Film-Dir/Wr; TV Video-Dir/Wr.
Genres: Drama-TV.
Biography: Born 1953.
Selective Filmography: *'THE BEACHCOMBERS'* (1 eps), TV, 86, CDN, Dir; *A LIFE OF INDEPENDENCE*, TV, 86, CDN, Wr; *CLOSE TO HOME*, Th, 85, CDN, Dir/Co-Wr.

BEAUBIEN, Conrad - see PRODUCERS

BEAUDIN, Jean

ARRFQ. 23 Laviolette, Outremont, Qué, CAN, H2V 1X6. (514)271-4880.
Types de production et Catégories: l métrage-Réal/Sc; c métrage-Réal/Sc.
Types d'oeuvres: Drame-C; Documentaire-C; Education-C.
Curriculum vitae: Né en 1939 à Montréal, Québec. Diplôme de l'Ecole des Beaux-Arts, Québec; Ecole de Design, Zurich, Suisse. Entre à l'ONF, 64. *J.A. MARTIN PHOTOGRAPHE* remporte 7 prix au Palmarès du film canadien dont le Prix du Meilleur Film; Prix Ecuminik et Palme d'Or pour l'interprétation de Monique Mercure, Cannes.
Filmographie sélective: *L'HOMME A LA TRAINE*, C, 86, CDN, Réal/Co sc; *LE MATOU*, C, 84, CDN/F, Réal; *MARIO*, C, 83, CDN, Réal/Co sc/Co prod; *CORDELIA*, C, 79, CDN, Réal/Co sc/Mont; *UNE JOURNEE DANS LES PARCS NATIONAUX*, C, 79, CDN, Réal; *J.A. MARTIN PHOTOGRAPHE*, C, 76, CDN, Réal/Co sc/Co mont (2 CFA); *JEUX DE LA XXI OLYMPIADE*, C, 76, CDN, Réal dél; *CHER THEO*, C, 75, CDN, Réal/Co sc/Co mont; *TROIS FOIS PASSERA...*, C, 73, CDN, Réal/Mont; *LES INDROGUABLES*, C, 72, CDN, Réal; *STOP*, C, 70, CDN, Réal; *ET POURQUOI PAS?*, C, 69, CDN, Réal; *VERTIGE*, C, 68, CDN, Réal (CFA); *MATHEMATIQUES*, ED, 67, CDN, Réal; *GEOMETRIE*, ED, 66, CDN, Réal.

BEAUDRY, Diane

836 rue McEachran, Outremont, Qué, CAN, H2V 3E1. (514)277-8971. ONF, C.P. 6100, Montréal, Qué, CAN, H3C 3H5. (514)283-9357.
Types de production et Catégories: c métrage-Réal; TV film-Réal.
Types d'oeuvres: Documentaire-C&TV.

(cont/suite)

Curriculum vitae: Née en 1946, Montréal, Québec; bilingue; baccalauréat ès Arts. Directeur exécutif, Festival des Arts, Nouvelle-Ecosse, 72; ONF, production française et anglaise. Représentante de la production française de l'ONF, Décade des Nations-Unies pour la femme, Nairobi, Kenya, 85.
Filmographie sélective: *HISTOIRE A SUIVRE...,* TV, 86, CDN, Réal; *ORDINATEUR EN TETE* (HEAD START, MEETING THE COMPUTER CHALLENGE), TV, 84, CDN, Réal; *LES ARMES A FEU AU CANADA, 400 ANS D'HISTOIRE,* In, 81, CDN, Réal; *THE WAY IT IS,* C, 81, CDN, Prod; *AN UNREMARKABLE BIRTH,* ED, 79-77, CDN, Réal/Prod/Mont; *THE UNBROKEN LINE* (LA NOBLE LIGNEE), In, 78, CDN, Réal; *THREADS,* C, 76, CDN, Prod; *DU COEUR A L'OUVRAGE,* C, 76, CDN, Prod; *MAUD LEWIS, A WORLD WITHOUT SHADOWS,* C, 75, CDN, Réal; *'JUST A MINUTE'* (23 films), C, 75, CDN, Prod; *BALLAD TO CORNWALLIS,* 'ATLANTI-CANADA', TV, 74, CDN, Réal.

BEAUDRY, Jean
ARRFQ, UDA. 5240 Papineau, Montréal, Qué, CAN, H2H 1W2. (514)521-0544. Les Prod. du Lundi Matin, C.P.157, Succ. de Lorimier, Montréal, Qué, CAN, H2H 2N6. (514)526-3925.
Types de production et Catégories: 1 métrage-Réal/Sc/Com/Mont; c métrage-Réal/Mont.
Types d'oeuvres: Drame-C; Documentaire-C.
Curriculum vitae: Né en 1947, Trois-Rivières, Québec; Baccalauréat ès Arts, 67; cours de scénarisation, ACPAV, 83. Metteur en scène et comédien, 65-75; production de diaporamas. *JACQUES ET NOVEMBRE* remporte le Prix Spécial du Jury, Festival international de Tokyo; Prix du Jury Catholique, Mannheim, Allemagne; Meilleur Film étranger (ex aequo), Festival de Belfort, France; primé à la qualité par la Société générale du cinéma du Québec.
Filmographie sélective: *JACQUES ET NOVEMBRE,* C, 84, CDN, Réal/Mont/Sc/Com; *UNE CLASSE SANS ECOLE,* C, 80, CDN, Réal; *MISSION READAPTATION,* C, 80, CDN, Mont; *J'SORS AVEC LUI PIS JE L'AIME,* C, 77, CDN, Réal/Mont/Rech; *LA MAISON QUI EMPECHE DE VOIR LA VILLE,* C, 75, CDN, Com.

BEAUDRY, Michel
ARRFQ. 3822 rue Rivard, Montréal, Qué, CAN, H2L 4H7. (514)288-1942.
Types de production et Catégories: 1 métrage-Mont; c métrage-Réal/Prod/Sc/Mont; TV film-Réal/Prod/Sc/Mont; TV vidéo-Réal/Prod/Sc/Mont.
Types d'oeuvres: Drame-C&TV; Documentaire-C&TV; Education-C&TV; Enfants-C&TV.
Curriculum vitae: Né en 1945, Montréal, Québec; bilingue. Bac., Université de Montréal. Journaliste; a été à l'emploi de plusieurs compagnies de film dont Delta Films, Cinéfilms, Onyx Films; pigiste depuis 74. *HERZBERG* remporte le 1er Prix, Festival de Yougoslavie, 80.
Filmographie sélective: *MANIPULE ET LES JEUX VIDEO,* TV, 86, CDN, Réal; *LA DOUANCE,* TV, 86, CDN, Réal; *ALFRED LALIBERTE,* TV, 85, CDN, Réal; *LE DESIGN,* 'DESSIN TECHNIQUE', TV, 85, CDN, Réal; *POURQUOI?,* TV, 85, CDN, Réal; *NUTRITION AND GROWTH,* TV, 85, CDN, Réal; *LA MAISON DE LA CULTURE,* TV, 84, CDN, Réal; *L'ASSURANCE-VIE DESJARDINS,* TV, 83, CDN, Réal; *LE SYSTEME G,* TV, 83, CDN, Réal; *ENTRE L'ARBRE ET L'ECORCE,* TV, 83, CDN, Réal; *LE PARC INDUSTRIEL, BECANCOUR,* TV, 82, CDN, Réal/Sc; *TERRY FOX, JE CARESSAIS UN REVE,* C, 81, CDN, Adapt; *LE SYSTEME METRIQUE, C'EST PAS SORCIER,* C, 80, CDN, Réal/Sc; *TRAITEMENT ET REHABILITATION,* C, 80, CDN, Sc; *SI REGNE EN METRE,* C, 79, CDN, Prod/Réal/Mont/Mont son; *HERZBERG,* C, 79, CDN, Prod/Mont; *L'AFFAIRE DB,* C, 78, CDN, Sc; *'CODE, UNE NORME'* (7 c métrages), C, 78, CDN, Prod/Réal/Mont; *QUELLE HISTOIRE!* (A LIKELY

(cont/suite)

STORY), C, 77, CDN, Sc/Mont; *'BESOINS FONDAMENTAUX DE L'HOMME'* (6 c métrages), C, 77, CDN, Prod/Réal/Mont; *MESDAMES ET MESSIEURS, LA FETE,* C, 76, CDN, Co réal; *REQUIEM IN PACE,* C, 75, CDN, Sc; *TRUDE SEKELY,* C, 75, CDN, Prod/Réal/Mont; *PROCES SOMMAIRE,* C, 73, CDN, Réal; *C'EST QUOI UN METIER,* C, 73, CDN, Réal/Mont; *QUEBEC, LA BELLE PROVINCE,* C, 72, CDN, Réal/Mont; *THE FTA SHOW,* C, 72, CDN, Mont; *PIERRE LAPORTE,* C, 70, CDN, Co réal/Mont; *'SI JEUNESSE POUVAIT'* (40 eps), TV, 69, CDN, Mont; *'L'EDUCATION A VOTRE SERVICE'* (3 eps), TV, 69, CDN, Mont; *VALERIE,* TV, 69, CDN, Mont son; *'CHIMIE ET PHYSIQUE'* (25 eps), TV, 68, CDN, Réal/Mont.

BEDARD, Jean-Thomas

ASIFA, SGCT. 3744 St-André, Montréal, Qué, CAN, H2L 3V7. (514)598-8862.
ONF, C.P. 6100, Stn A, Montréal, Qué, CAN, H3C 3H5. (514)283-9301.
Types de production et Catégories: c métrage-Réal; TV film-Réal/Sc.
Types d'oeuvres: Documentaire-C&TV; Animation-C.
Curriculum vitae: Né en 1947, Chicoutimi, Québec. Diplôme d'Etudes générales en Histoire de l'Art, Université de Montréal; cours de peinture et de gravure, Ecole des Beaux-Arts de Montréal. Diverses expositions collectives et particulières en peinture, dessin, sérigraphie, photo. Voyage autour du monde, 79-80. Prix du Jury, Festival d'Annecy, France, 80; 1er Prix, Festival de Chicago et Main Award, Festival d'Oberhausen, 80, pour *L'AGE DE CHAISE.*
Filmographie sélective: *LE COMBAT D'ONESIME TREMBLAY,* TV, 85, CDN, Rech/Sc/Réal; *L'AGE DE CHAISE* (CHAIRMEN), C, 79, CDN, Sc/Réal; *CECI EST UN MESSAGE ENREGISTRE* (THIS IS A RECORDED MESSAGE), C, 73, CDN, Sc/Réal; *LA VILLE* (BIG CITY), C, 70, CDN, Réal.

BEDARD, Louis

AR. 680 boul. Desaulniers, #8, St-Lambert, Qué, CAN, J4P 1P6. (514)672-6434.
Types de production et Catégories: TV film-Réal; TV vidéo-Réal.
Types d'oeuvres: Drame-TV; Comédie-TV; Enfants-TV.
Curriculum vitae: Né en 1924, Montréal, Québec; bilingue. Bachelier ès Lettres, Université Laval, Québec; Bac., Université d'Ottawa. Théâtre Les Compagnons, Montréal, 48-49; critique de théâtre et de cinéma; journaliste; publiciste; réalisateur, producteur, Radio-Canada, 53-85. Gagne le Trophée Frigon pour *GRENIER AUX IMAGES.*
Filmographie sélective: *'MONSIEUR LE MINISTRE'* (20 eps), TV, 85/84, CDN, Réal; *'TERRE HUMAINE'* (20 eps), TV, 84/83, CDN, Réal; *'LES GIROUETTES'* (16 eps), TV, 83/82, CDN, Réal; *'BOOGIE-WOOGIE'* (45 eps), TV, 82-80, CDN, Réal; *'A CAUSE DE MON ONCLE'* (45 eps), TV, 80-77, CDN, Réal; *'QUINZE ANS PLUS TARD'* (38 eps), TV, 77/76, CDN, Réal; *'LA P'TITE SEMAINE'* (8 eps), TV, 76/73, CDN, Réal; *'ROSA'* (13 eps), TV, 75, CDN, Réal; *LE GRAND ZEBRE,* 'A GUICHET FERME', TV, 75, CDN, Réal; *MONT JOYE'* (10 eps), TV, 74, CDN, Réal; *'LES FORGES DE ST-MAURICE'* (32 eps), TV, 73/72, CDN, Réal; *'LE PARADIS TERRESTRE'* (37 eps), TV, 71/70, CDN, Réal; *'RUE DES PIGNONS'* (149 eps), TV, 70-66, CDN, Réal; *'DE 9 A 5'* (106 eps), TV, 66-63, CDN, Réal; *'JOIE DE VIVRE'* (39 eps), TV, 63/62, CDN, Réal; *'LA PENSION VELDER'* (77 eps), TV, 62-60, CDN, Réal; *LE TEMPS QU'IL FAIT/LA GRAND' GIGUE/UNE NUIT,* 'THEATRE DU DIMANCHE', TV, 62/61, CDN, Réal; *COMME JE VOUS AIMAIS,* 'THEATRE D'ETE', TV, 61, CDN, Réal; *'JOINDRE LES DEUX BOUTS'* (29 eps), TV, 60/59, CDN, Réal; *DERRIERE LA GRILLE,* 'EN PREMIERE', TV, 59, CDN, Réal; *'EAUX-VIVES ET TEMOIGNAGES'* (49 eps), TV, 59/58, CDN, Réal; *'C'EST LA VIE'* (37 eps), TV, 58/57, CDN, Réal; *M. DAVID A DISPARU/LES CORBEAUX,* 'THEATRE POPULAIRE', TV, 57, CDN, Réal; *'AFFAIRES DE FAMILLE'* (31 eps), TV, 57/56, CDN, Réal; *'GRENIER AUX IMAGES'* (76 eps), TV, 56-54, CDN, Réal; *'TAILLEFER'* (38 eps), TV, 56/55, CDN, Réal; *'KIMO'* (50 eps), TV, 55/54, CDN, Réal.

DIRECTORS/REALISATEURS

BEDEL, Jean-Pierre

CTPDA. 310-1873 Spyglass Place, Vancouver, BC, CAN. (604)874-6757. 37 Ave. Roosevelt, Mantes La Jolie, France, 78200. (333)094-0689.
Types of Production & Categories: Th Short-Dir/Prod; TV Film-Dir/Prod; TV Video-Dir/Prod.
Genres: Variety-TV; Documentary-TV.
Biography: Born 1944, Dammartin En Serve, Yvelines, France; Canadian-French citizen. Raised in France, England, Germany, Spain. B.Sc., Telecommunications, Kent State University, Ohio, 74. French Army, 64-66.
Selective Filmography: *SOMETHING ABOUT PEACE* (TOUT CA POUR LA PAIX), TV, 84, CDN, Dir/Prod; *'CBC NEWS'* (VANCOUVER), (300 eps), TV, 84, CDN, Dir; *'THE VANCOUVER SHOW'* (150 eps), TV, 84/83, CDN, Dir/Prod; *'LAURIER'S PEOPLE'* (30 eps), TV, 84/83, CDN, Dir; *'CBC MIDDAY NEWS'* (200 eps), TV, 83/82, CDN, Dir; *'PILE OU FACE'* (28 eps), TV, 82/81, CDN, Dir/Prod; *'VENDREDI VINGT HEURES'* (18 eps), TV, 82/81, CDN, Dir/Prod; *LE PISSENLIT PAR LA RACINE,* TV, 82, CDN, Dir/Prod; *LE SALON DU LIVRE,* TV, 81, CDN, Dir/Prod; *'CE SOIR'* (200 eps), TV, 81, CDN, Dir; *'A CONTREPOIDS'* (12 eps), TV, 80, CDN, Dir/Prod; *LE JOUR DU SEIGNEUR,* TV, 80, CDN, Dir/Prod; *'ILE DE FRANCE ACTUALITE'* (150 eps), TV, 78/77, F, Dir; *'CE SOIR'* (MANITOBA), TV, 76, CDN, Dir; *THE CHAMP,* TV, 74, USA, Dir/Prod; *L'EAU,* Th, 68, LAO, Dir/Prod; *VOTE 68,* Th, 68, T, Dir/Prod; *DR PIEN,* Th, 68, T, Dir/Prod.

BEECROFT, Stuart

DGC. 106 Dunington Dr., Scarborough, Ont, CAN, M1N 3E3. (416)698-1955. TV Ontario, Box 200, Stn Q, Toronto, Ont, CAN, M4T 2T1. (416)484-2600.
Types of Production & Categories: TV Film-Dir; TV Video-Dir.
Genres: Documentary-TV; Educational-TV; Animation-TV; Experimental-TV.
Biography: Born 1942, Collingwood, Ontario. Seventeen- year technical background (including 9 years as a video-tape editor) beginning at CBC in 64, TVO, 69. *PROPHECY* won a Gold Medal, Chicago Film Festival.
Selective Filmography: *'FISH ON!'* (13 eps), TV, 85, CDN, Prod/Dir; *RIBBON OF STEEL,* TV, 85, CDN, Dir; *UP AND RUNNING,* TV, 84, CDN, Dir; *'OCTO-PUCE'* (12 eps), TV, 83, CDN, Prod/Dir; *'SPEAKING OUT'* (105 eps), TV, 83-80, CDN, Dir; *'BITS AND BYTES'* (12 eps), TV, 82, CDN, Dir; *'FRENCH FOR CANADIANS'* (70 eps), TV, 82-80, CDN, Dir; *'NIGHTMUSIC'* (175 eps), TV, 78-73, CDN, Tech Dir/FX Des; *'WORLD RELIGIONS'* (8 eps), TV, 77, CDN, Ed; *PROPHECY,* TV, 73, CDN, Ed.

BELANGER, Fernand

ARRFQ. 2429 Route 348, Canton de Rawdon, Qué, CAN, J0K 1S0. (514)834-4508. ONF, 3155 Côte de Liesse, Montréal, Qué, CAN. (514)283-9366. Louise Dugal, 4080 Chateaubuan, Montréal, Qué, CAN. (514)525-9988.
Types de production et Catégories: l métrage-Réal/Mont; c métrage-Réal/Mont; TV film-Mont.
Types d'oeuvres: Documentaire-C&TV; Education-C; Enfants-C&TV; Expérimental-C.
Curriculum vitae: Né en 1943, Rivière-du-Loup, Québec; bilingue. Baccalauréat ès Arts. Vingt ans de métier.
Filmographie sélective: *PASSIFLORA,* C, 85, CDN, Co réal/Mont/Sc; *L'EMOTION DISSONANTE,* C, 84, CDN, Réal/Mont/Sc; *L'APRES COURS,* TV, 84, CDN, Réal/Mont; *DEBOUT SUR LEUR TERRE,* C, 82, CDN, Mont; *DE LA TOURBE ET DU RESTANT,* C, 79, CDN, Sc/Réal/Mont; *CONTEBLEU,* C, 76, CDN, Sc/Réal/Mont; *LE VENTRE DE LA NUIT,* C, 75, CDN, Mont; *DEBARQUE MOI AU LAC DES VENTS,* C, 75, CDN, Mont; *OU EST CE QUE TU VAS DE MEME?,* C, 74, CDN, Mont; *LE POIS FOU,* TV, 72, CDN, Sc/Réal/Mont; *TI PEUPE,* C, 70, CDN, Sc/Réal/Mont; *TI COEUR,* C, 69, CDN,
(cont/suite)

Sc/Réal/Mont; *VIA BORDUAS,* C, 68, CDN, Sc/Réal/Mont; *INITIATION,* C, 67, CDN, Sc/Réal/Mont; *MANIC 5,* TV, 67, CDN, Réal.

BELANGER, Ray

DGC. 50 Garnock Ave., Toronto, Ont, CAN, M4K 1M2. (416)463-3629. Venture Film Corp., 69 Front St.E., #205, Toronto, Ont, CAN, M5E 1B5. (416)364-2956.
Types of Production & Categories: TV Film-Dir/Prod.
Genres: Drama-TV; Comedy-TV; Documentary-Th&TV; Educational-TV.
Biography: Born 1950. Previously film editor for 12 years. Awards include CFEG, Best Theatrical Documentary, 82.
Selective Filmography: *'AMERICAN CENTURY'* (2 eps), TV, 85, CDN, Prod; *'FRONTRUNNERS'* (5 eps), TV, 85, CDN, Dir; *THROUGH THE EYES OF OTHERS,* In, 85, CDN, Prod/Dir.

BELEC, Marilyn A.

ACTRA, CFTA. 290 Palmerston Ave., Toronto, Ont, CAN, M6J 2J4. (416)962-5652. Mobius, 188 Davenport Rd., Toronto, Ont, CAN, M5R 1J2. (416)964-8484.
Types of Production & Categories: TV Film-Dir/Prod.
Genres: Drama-TV; Documentary-TV; Educational-Th&TV; Children's-Th&TV.
Biography: Born 1935. Worked in English Production, NFB, Montreal; President of Mobius; has won 20 awards for films she has produced. *TAKING CHANCES* won Best Production, Yorkton; *THE MENOPAUSE STORY,* Chris Plaque, Columbus; *TOM MAGEE - MAN OF IRON,* Blue Ribbon, American Film Festival.
Selective Filmography: *HERE TODAY...WHERE TOMORROW?,* ED, 85, CDN, Prod/Dir; *SAFE PASSAGE,* In, 85, CDN, Prod; *THEOPHYLLINE THERAPY UPDATE,* In, 83, CDN, Prod; *TOM MAGEE - MAN OF IRON,* TV, 83, CDN, Prod **(CFTA);** *THE MENOPAUSE STORY,* ED, 82, CDN, Prod/Dir; *TEEN MOTHER - A STORY OF COPING,* ED, 81, CDN, Prod; *THE INVESTMENT PICTURE,* In, 80, CDN, Co-Prod; *TAKING CHANCES,* ED, 79, CDN, Prod/Dir.

BELL, John

DGC. 2 Sultan St., #505, Toronto, Ont, CAN, M5S 1L7. (416)968-0604. Bell Films Inc., 2725 Tesla Ave., Los Angeles, CA, USA, 90039. (213)665-8690. Jerry Adler, The Sy Fisher Agency, 10960 Wilshire Blvd., #924, Los Angeles, CA, USA, 90024. (213)208-0455.
Types of Production & Categories: TV Film Dir/Prod; TV Video-Dir.
Genres: Drama-TV; Comedy-TV; Variety-TV.
Biography: Born 1949; Canadian citizen; US visa.
Selective Filmography: *'CHECK IT OUT!'* (8 eps), TV, 86/85, CDN/USA, Dir; *SECOND CITY 25th ANNIVERSARY* (L.A./Tor seg), TV, 84, CDN, Dir; *PIERRE ELLIOT TRUDEAU: WE WERE THERE,* TV, 84, CDN, Prod; *OUT OF OUR MINDS,* TV, 84, CDN, Dir; *'SCTV',* TV, 83-81, CDN, Contr Dir.

BENNER, Richard - see WRITERS

BENOIT, Denyse

ARRFQ, SARDEC. 2518 Route 202, Franklin Centre, Qué, CAN, J0S 1E0. (514)827-2483.
Types de production et Catégories: l métrage-Réal/Sc; c métrage-Réal/Sc; TV film-Sc.
Types d'oeuvres: Drame-C&TV.
Curriculum vitae: Née en 1949, Québec. Etudes à l'Ecole des Beaux-Arts, Montréal, 66; diplômée de l'Institut des Arts de Diffusion, Bruxelles, Belgique, 71. Mise en scène de théâtre, comédienne.
Filmographie sélective: *LE DERNIER HAVRE,* C, 85, CDN, Réal/Sc; *L'ETIQUETTE,* TV, 81, B, Sc/Rech; *LA BELLE APPARENCE,* C, 79, CDN, Réal/Sc/Prod; *LA CRUE,* C, 76, CDN, Réal/Sc/Co prod; *LES ENFANTS*

(cont/suite)

D'ABORD, C, 76, CDN, Cast; *LES MALADIES C'EST LES COMPAGNIES,* C, 75, CDN, Rech; *L'AMIANTE CA TUE,* C, 75, CDN, Rech; *UN INSTANT PRES D'ELLE,* C, 74, CDN, Réal/Sc/Prod; *DENYSE BENOIT, COMEDIENNE,* C, 74, CDN, Anim/Comp; *COUP D'OEIL BLANC,* C, 73, CDN, Réal/Sc/Prod.

BERMAN, Brigitte

Bridge Film Prods. Inc., 44 Charles St.W., #2518, Toronto, Ont, CAN, M4Y 1R7. (416)929-0663.
Types of Production & Categories: Th Film-Dir/Prod/Wr; TV Film-Dir/Prod.
Genres: Documentary-Th&TV.
Biography: Born Frankfurt am Main, West Germany; German-Canadian citizenship. Languages: English, German, French. B.A., Queen's University; B. Ed. MacArthur College. *BIX: AIN'T NONE OF THEM PLAY LIKE HIM YET* won a Bronze Hugo (Chicago) and a Merit Award (Athens).
Selective Filmography: *THE MAKING OF CASTAWAY,* TV, 86, GB, Dir; *ARTIE SHAW: TIME IS ALL YOU'VE GOT,* Th, 85-81, CDN, Dir/Prod/Wr/Co-Ed; *'TAKE 30'* (90 eps), TV, 84-81, CDN, Dir/Prod; *'QUARTERLY REPORT',* TV, 81-77, CDN, Co-Dir; *BIX: AIN'T NONE OF THEM PLAY LIKE HIM YET,* Th, 81-77, CDN, Dir/Prod/Co-Wr/Ed; *HOW MUSIC CAME TO THE GARDEN CITY/THE MANY FACES OF BLACK,* 'THIS MONDAY', TV, 77/76, CDN, Dir/Prod; *'IN GOOD COMPANY'* (sev seg), TV, 76/75, CDN, Dir.

BERTOLINO, Daniel - voir PRODUCTEURS

BISSONNETTE, Sophie

ARRFQ. 5354 rue Waverly, Montréal, Qué, CAN, H2T 2X9. (514)271-6180.
Types de production et Catégories: l métrage-Réal/Mont; c métrage-Réal/Prod/Mont.
Types d'oeuvres: Documentaire-C; Education-C.
Curriculum vitae: Née en 1956; bilingue. Baccalauréat en Cinéma/Sociologie, Université Queen's. A été professeur de cinéma. *UNE HISTOIRE DE FEMMES* gagne le Prix de la Critique Québécoise.
Filmographie sélective: *QUEL NUMERO WHAT NUMBER?* (THE ELECTRONIC SWEATSHOP), C, 85-82, CDN, Réal/Rech/Co prod; *LUTTES D'ICI, LUTTES D'AILLEURS,* C, 80, CDN, Réal/Rech/Mont; *UNE HISTOIRE DE FEMMES* (A WIVES' TALE), C, 80-78, CDN, Co réal/Co mont.

BITTMAN, Roman - see PRODUCERS

BLAIS, Pascal

ASIFA. 5045 Claranald, #103, Montréal, Qué, CAN, H3X 2C3. (514)488-5895.
Les Productions Pascal Blais, 640 rue St-Paul ouest, #200, Montréal, Qué, CAN, H3C 1L9. (514)866-7272.
Types de production et Catégories: TV film-Réal/An.
Types d'oeuvres: Animation-TV; Annonces-TV.
Curriculum vitae: Né en 1959, Montréal, Québec; bilingue. Réalisateur et animateur de nombreuses annonces depuis 3 ans; animation et effets spéciaux pour le long métrage *THE PEANUT BUTTER SOLUTION.*

BLANCHARD, André

ARRFQ. 939 Champagnat, Laval, Qué, CAN, H7C 1Z7. (514)661-1685.
Types de production et Catégories: l métrage-Réal/Sc; c métrage-Réal/Sc; TV film-Réal/Sc; TV vidéo-Réal.
Types d'oeuvres: Drame-C&TV; Comédie-C; Documentaire-C&TV.
Curriculum vitae: Né en 1951, Laval, Québec. Direction de la photographie, Institut des Arts de Diffusion, Bruxelles, 70-73. Multi-Média et Noranda, 75-76; Radio-Québec, 79. Diplôme d'Etudes Approfondies, Sorbonne, Paris, 84. *L'HIVER BLEU* gagne le Ducat d'Or, Mannheim et le Prix de la Critique Québécoise.

(cont/suite)

Filmographie sélective: *L'HIVER BLEU* (BLUE WINTER), C, 76, CDN, Réal; *BEAT*, C, 76, CDN, Réal/Sc/Prod.

BLOOMFIELD, George

ACTRA, DGA, DGC, WGAe. 50 Admiral Rd., Toronto, Ont, CAN, M5R 2L5. (416)967-0826.
Types of Production & Categories: Th Film-Dir; TV Film-Dir; TV Video-Dir.
Genres: Drama-Th&TV; Comedy-Th&TV; Variety-TV; Children's-TV.
Biography: Born 1930, Montreal, Quebec. B.A., Master's Degree in Psychology. *FRAGGLE ROCK* won an Int'l Emmy.
Selective Filmography: *'THE CAMPBELLS'* (18 eps), TV, 86/85, CDN/USA/GB, Dir; *FRAGGLE ROCK'* (29 eps), TV, 86-83, CDN, Dir; *'SCTV'*, TV, 79/78, CDN, Dir; *RIEL*, TV, 79, CDN, Dir; *LOVE ON THE NOSE*, TV, 78, CDN, Dir; *CHILD UNDER A LEAF*, Th, 74, CDN, Dir/Wr; *JENNY*, Th, 70, USA, Dir/Wr.

BOCKING, Robert

CFTA, CSC, SMPTE. 75 Hucknall Rd., Downsview, Ont, CAN, M3J 1W1. (416) 636-9587.
Types of Production & Categories: Th Film-Ed; Th Short-Ed; TV Film-Dir/Prod/Ed; TV Video-Dir/Prod/Ed.
Genres: Documentary-Th&TV; Educational-Th&TV; Children's-Th&TV.
Biography: Born 1936, Thunder Bay, Ontario. Edits sound to any format, film or video, in the latest digital audio format; 27 years experience.
Selective Filmography: *'PROFILES OF NATURE'* (39 eps), TV, 86/85, CDN, Snd Ed; *FARMING*, ED, 85, CDN, Prod/Dir/Cam/Ed; *'THE FOUR SEASONS'* (4 eps), ED, 84, CDN, Prod/Dir/Cam/Ed (CSC); *'PROFILES OF NATURE'* (26 eps), TV, 84, CDN, Ed/Snd Ed; *IMAGES OF GALAPAGOS*, TV, 83, CDN, Pro Spv/Ed; *'WILD CANADA'* (13 eps), TV, 80-77, CDN, Snd Ed; *'WILDLIFE CINEMA'* (28 eps), TV, 78-75, CDN, Snd Ed; *'TO THE WILD COUNTRY'* (Pic Ed-6 eps), (13 eps), TV, 78-75, CDN, Snd Ed; *'AUDUBON WILDLIFE THEATRE'* (40 eps), TV, 74-67, CDN, Ed/Snd Ed.

BOISSAY, René

AR 3531 Aylmer, Montréal, Qué, CAN, H2X 2B9. Radio-Canada, 1400 blvd. Dorchester est, Montréal, Qué, CAN, H2L 2M2. (514)285-3735.
Types de production et Catégories: c métrage-Réal/Sc; TV film-Réal.
Types d'oeuvres: Documentaire-TV; Education-TV.
Curriculum vitae: Né en 1929; bilingue. Traversé atlantique à la voile, 70; Président, Cinémathèque Québécoise, 72-74; Directeur, Cinéma-Films à Radio-Canada, 72-79; auteur et réalisateur de films sur l'art français et anglais, 79-85.
Filmographie sélective: *CLARENCE GAGNON* 'LES PEINTRES CANADIENS', (3 eps), TV, 84, CDN, Réal/Sc; *CORNELIUS KRIEGHOFF* 'LES PEINTRES CANADIENS', (3 eps), TV, 82, CDN, Réal/Sc; *'CINEMA D'ICI'* (11 eps), TV, 70, CDN, Réal; *'IMAGES EN TETE'* (hebdo), TV, 69-67, CDN, Réal.

BOKOR, Pierre

SACD, SARDEC. 9309 - 96 rue, Edmonton, Alta, CAN, T6C 3Y6. (403)469-6731. Théâtre Français, 8406 - 91 rue, Edmonton, Alta, CAN, T6C 4G9. (403)469-0829.
Types de production et Catégories: l métrage-Sc/Réal; c métrage-Sc/Réal; TV film-Sc/Réal.
Types d'oeuvres: Drame-C&TV; Comédie-C&TV; Variété-TV; Comédie musicale-TV.
Curriculum vitae: Né en Roumanie, 1940; citoyenneté canadienne. Etudes supérieures en cinéma; licencié ès Arts, Réalisation film, Institut d'Art Théâtral et Cinématographique, Budapest. Langues: français, anglais, hongrois, roumain. A reçu le Cultural Achievement Award (82), le Performing and Creative Arts Award
(cont/suite)

(83), Edmonton; Alberta Achievement Award-Excellence Category, de la province d'Alberta, 84. *APA CA UN BIVOL NEGRU* remporte le Prix des Jeunes cinéastes, Cannes. Réalisation et mise en scène de 73 divers spectacles, 65-86.
Filmographie sélective: *KICSODA ON?*, TV, 85, H, Réal/Co sc; *TUFA DE VENETIA* (RIEN DE RIEN), C, 77, R, Réal/Co sc; *L'ART DE LA CONVERSATION*, TV, 77, R, Réal/Sc; *L'ARTISTE*, TV, 76, R, Réal/Co sc; *HILARIUS*, TV, 76, R, Réal; *D'AUTRES HISTOIRES*, TV, 75, R, Réal/Sc; *POINT D'INTERROGATION*, TV, 75, R, Réal/Co sc; *DES HISTOIRES DE NOTRE CARTIER*, TV, 74, R, Réal/Sc; *LE MOMENT 403*, TV, 74, R, Réal/Co sc; *LOUIS XIX*, TV, 74, R, Réal; *UNE SEULE NUIT DANS LE STUDIO 3*, TV, 73, R, Réal/Co sc; *2 PE CAL, 1 PE MAGAR*, TV, 73, R, Réal; *LE PROFESSEUR ET L'ELEVE*, TV, 72, R, Réal/Co sc; *DON QUIXOTE*, TV, 71, R, Réal/Sc; *PITICUL DIN GRADINA DE VARA*, TV, 71, R, Réal; *APA CA UN BIVOL NEGRU* (L'EAU), C, 70, R, Réal/Co sc.

BOND, Timothy

ACTRA, DGC, WGAe. 44 Palmerston Gardens, Toronto, Ont, CAN, M6G 1V9. (416)535-3870. Scott Yoselow, Phil Gersh Agency, 222 Canon Dr., Beverly Hills, CA, 90210, USA. (212)997-1818.
Types of Production & Categories: Th Film-Dir/Wr; TV Film-Dir/Wr; TV Video-Dir.
Genres: Drama-Th&TV; Comedy-Th&TV; Horror-Th; Educational-TV.
Biography: Born 1942, Ottawa, Ontario; B.A. (English Drama) and B.Sc. (Chemistry and Physics), Carleton University, 65. 20 years of extensive stage directing credits in Canada and abroad.
Selective Filmography: *THE EDISON TWINS'* (9 eps), TV, 86-84, CDN, Dir; *THE CAMPBELLS'* (4 eps), TV, 86/85, CDN/USA/GB, Dir; *GOOD TIMES AT THE RAINBOW BAR AND GRILL*, TV, 86, CDN, Dir; *OAKMOUNT HIGH*, TV, 85, CDN, Dir/Co-Wr; *SPECIAL EDUCATION'* (3 eps), TV, 85/84, CDN, Dir; *JUDGE'* (2 eps), TV, 84, CDN, Dir; *ONE NIGHT ONLY*, Th, 83, CDN, Dir; *TILL DEATH DO US PART*, TV, 81, CDN, Dir/Co-Wr; *HAPPY BIRTHDAY TO ME*, Th, 80, CDN, Co-Scr; *DEADLY HARVEST*, Th, 76, CDN, Dir; *SHE CRIED MURDER*, TV, 73, CDN/USA, Co-Story.

BONIN, Laurier

ARRFQ, SARDEC. 34 France, St-Roch-de-l'Achigan, Qué, CAN, J0K 3H0. (514) 588-4390.
Types de production et Catégories: c métrage-Réal/Sc/Mont; TV film-Réal/Sc/Mont; TV vidéo-Réal/Sc/Mont.
Types d'oeuvres: Drame-C&TV; Documentaire-C&TV; Education-TV; Enfants-C&TV.
Curriculum vitae: Né en 1951, Lanorais; citoyen canadien; bilingue. Cours en cinéma, London Film School; Baccalauréat (Audio-visuel) et Maitrise (Communications), Université de Montréal. Publication: 'L'Utilisation pédagogique de l'image', Université de Montréal, 77. *LA BIOTECHNOLOGIE*, remporte le Prix A.D.A.T.E., 82; *AU BOUT DU DOUTE*, Prix de la Critique Québécoise, 79.
Filmographie sélective: *TELETHON OF STARS*, TV, 85, CDN, Textes; *MAINTENANT'* (pl reportages), TV, 85-82, CDN, Réal/Rech; *INCURSION'* (pl reportages), TV, 84/83, CDN, Réal/Rech; *SCIENCE SPECTRUM'* (18 eps), TV, 84/83, CDN, Réal/Rech; *LA CONQUETE DU CONTINENT INTERIEUR*, TV, 84, CDN, Réal/Sc/Mont; *LES SIX SAISONS ATTICAMEG'* (6 eps), TV, 82, CDN, Mont; *IL FAUT CHERCHER POUR APPRENDRE*, TV, 81, CDN, Sc/Réal; *THE RIDDLE OF THE OLD OWL*, TV, 81, CDN, Sc/Réal; *KINGS AND DESPERATE MEN*, C, 79, CDN, Ass mont; *UN GARS BEN CHANCEUX*, TV, 79, CDN, Mont; *HISTOIRE VECUE*, TV, 79, CDN, Mont; *AU BOUT DU DOUTE*, TV, 78, CDN, Réal/Sc; *L'AGE DES FLEURS*, ED, 77, CDN, Sc/Réal; *LA CUEILLETTE DU TABAC*, TV, 77, CDN, Réal/Sc.

(cont/suite)

BONNIERE, René

DGC. 100 Hazelton Ave., Toronto, Ont, CAN, M5R 2E2. (416)922-6463.
Types of Production & Categories: Th Film-Dir; Th Short-Dir; TV Film-Dir; TV Video-Dir.
Genres: Drama-Th&TV; Comedy-Th&TV; Action-TV; Documentary-TV.
Biography: Born 1928, Lyon, France; Canadian citizen. *FERTILITY RITES* won Gold Medal, New York Film/TV Festival.
Selective Filmography: *'NIGHT HEAT'* (12 eps), TV, 86-84, CDN, Dir; *'THE LITTLE VAMPIRE'* (13 eps), TV, 85, CDN/GB/D, Dir; *ISLANDS,* TV, 84, CDN/USA, Dir; *LABOUR OF LOVE,* TV, 84, CDN, Dir; *HIDE AND SEEK,* 'FOR THE RECORD', TV, 83, CDN, Dir; *S.P.A.,* 'NATURE OF THINGS', TV, 83, CDN, Prod/Dir; *GUIDO/LYPA,* 'NEWCOMERS', TV, 78, CDN, Dir; *FERTILITY RITES,* TV, 76, CDN, Prod/Dir; *LES ANNANACKS,* TV, 62, CDN, Dir; *AMANITA PESTILENS,* Th, 62, CDN, Dir; *'AU PAYS DE NEUFVE FRANCE'* (13 eps), TV, 58, CDN, Dir.

BORRIS, Clay

914 Venezia Ave., Venice, CA, USA, 90291. (213)827-5304. Mike Simpson, William Morris Agency, 151 El Camino Dr., Beverly Hills, CA, USA, 90212. (213) 274-7451.
Types of Production & Categories: Th Film-Dir/Wr; TV Film-Dir/Wr; TV Video-Dir/Wr.
Genres: Drama-Th&TV; Action-Th&TV; Documentary-Th&TV.
Biography: Born 1950, New Brunswick; bilingual. Won Best Director, Mannheim Film Fest. for first feature *ALLIGATOR SHOES* which was also shown in Director's Fortnight, Cannes.
Selective Filmography: *QUIET COOL,* Th, 86, USA, Dir/Co-Wr; *ALLIGATOR SHOES* (LES SOULIERS EN CROCO), Th, 81, CDN, Dir/Wr/Co-Prod/Act; *FAMILY GEOGRAPHY: PARTS 1, 2, 3 AND 4/ SHEILA'S X-MAS/ MISTAWASIS,* 'BROWNDALE', TV, 78-76, CDN, Dir; *ROSE'S HOUSE,* Th, 77, CDN, Wr/Dir; *BUSH CAMPING/ BROWNDALE 10TH ANNIVERSARY,* 'BROWNDALE', TV, 76, CDN, Dir; *FUN AT THE 'EX',* TV, 74, CDN, Dir/Wr; *ONE HAND CLAPPING,* 'OF ALL PEOPLE', TV, 73, CDN, Dir/Wr; *PAPER BOY,* TV, 70-69, CDN, Dir/Wr; *PARLIAMENT STREET,* Th, 67, CDN, Dir/Wr.

BORSOS, Phillip

DGA, DGC. The Radio-Telegraphic Co., 264 Seaton St., Toronto, Ont, CAN, M5A 2T4. (416)960-6468. Michael E. Marcus, CAA, 1888 Century Park E., Ste.1400, Los Angeles, CA, USA, 90067. (213)277-4545.
Types of Production & Categories: Th Film-Dir; Th Short-Dir.
Genres: Drama-Th; Documentary-Th.
Selective Filmography: *ONE MAGIC CHRISTMAS,* Th, 85, CDN/USA, Dir/Exec Prod/Co-Story; *THE MEAN SEASON,* Th, 84, USA, Dir; *THE GREY FOX,* Th, 80, CDN, Dir/Co-Prod (**GENIE**); *NAILS,* Th, 79, CDN, Dir/Prod (**GENIE**); *SPARTREE,* Th, 77, CDN, Dir/Prod (**CFA**); *COOPERAGE,* Th, 76, CDN, Dir/ Prod (**CFA**).

BOUCHARD, Michel

ARRFQ. 6670 ave. de Gaspé, Montréal, Qué, CAN, H2S 2Y2. (514)277-5667.
Types de production et Catégories: l métrage-Réal/Sc; c métrage-Réal/Prod/Sc.
Types d'oeuvres: Drame-C&TV; Comédie-C; Documentaire-TV.
Curriculum vitae: Né en 1949, Montréal, Québec; bilingue. Etudes: Langues (allemand, espagnol, italien), Institut des Arts Appliqués, 67-68.
Filmographie sélective: *LA TERRAPENE* (THE TERRAPIN), TV, 84, CDN, Réal/Prod/Sc; *LES PETITES CRUAUTES* (THE CRIES OF LOVE), TV, 84,
(cont/suite)

209

CDN, Réal/Prod/Sc; *LE TOASTEUR* (THE TOASTER), TV, 82, CDN, Réal/Prod/Sc; *LA BIEN-AIMEE* (THE BELOVED), C, 80, CDN, Réal/Prod/Sc; *LA LOI DE LA VILLE,* TV, 79, CDN, Réal/Rech/Narr; *NOEL ET JULIETTE,* C, 74, CDN, Réal/Sc.

BOUX, Claude

AR. 397 St-Joseph ouest, #19, Montréal, Qué, CAN, H2V 2P1. (514)274-8648. Radio-Canada, 1400 blvd. Dorchester est, Montréal, Qué, CAN, H2L 2M2. (514) 285-3377.
Types de production et Catégories: l métrage-Comp; TV film-Réal; TV vidéo-Réal.
Types d'oeuvres: Comédie musicale-C; Documentaire-TV; Education-TV; Enfants-TV.
Curriculum vitae: Né en 1949, Winnipeg, Manitoba; bilingue. Education: Bac., Maitrise. Réseaux français, anglais de Radio-Canada, 77-85. Musicien et compositeur professionnel depuis 15 ans; chansons, films, enregistrements radio/TV; compositeur de 'Rivière aux Cerises'(Chantal Dupont).
Filmographie sélective: *'TELEJOURNAL'* (quot), TV, 85-83, CDN, Réal; *MUSIC OF THE SPHERES,* C, 83, CDN, Comp; *'McLEAN AT LARGE'* (7 eps), TV, 81, CDN, Réal; *'HEBDO'* (100 eps), TV, 81-78, CDN, Réal; *'REFLETS D'UN PAYS'* (2 eps), TV, 80, CDN, Réal.

BRADSHAW, John R.

ACTRA. 134 Balmoral Ave., Toronto, Ont, CAN, M4V 1J4. (416)922-3801. Gemini Film Productions, 69 Sherbourne St.,Ste.424, Toronto, Ont, CAN, M5A 3X9. (416)862-9031.
Types of Production & Categories: Th Film-Dir/Wr/Ed.
Genres: Drama-Th; Comedy-TV.
Biography: Born 1952, Stratford, Ontario; graduated from Ryerson Film School, 78.
Selective Filmography: *THAT'S MY BABY,* Th, 85, CDN, Co-Dir/Co-Ed/Co-Wr; *ANGELS,* TV, 80, CDN, 1st AD/Assoc Ed; *NOT ANOTHER LOVE STORY,* TV, 78, CDN, Wr/Dir/Prod/Ed; *JIM & MUGGINS TOUR TORONTO,* TV, 78, CDN, Cam.

BRASSARD, André

Centre National des Arts, C.P. 1534, Succ. B, Ottawa, Ont, CAN, K1P 5W1. (613) 996-5051.
Types de production et Catégories: l métrage-Réal; TV film-Réal.
Types d'oeuvres: Drame-C&TV.
Curriculum vitae: Né en 1947, Montréal, Québec; bilingue. Metteur en scène de théâtre depuis 68; a réalisé la 1ère pièce de théâtre au Centre National des Arts, Ottawa, 69 ou il est Directeur Artistique (et metteur en scène) depuis 82. A aussi réalisé des pièces pour la télévision dont *LES BELLES SOEURS* et *SAINTE CARMEN DE LA MAIN.*
Filmographie sélective: *LE SOLEIL SE LEVE EN RETARD,* C, 77, CDN, Réal; *IL ETAIT UNE FOIS DANS L'EST,* C, 74, CDN, Réal/Co sc; *FRANCOISE DUROCHER, WAITRESS,* TV, 72, CDN, Réal (**2 CFA**).

BRAULT, François

ARRFQ. 345 Mercille, St-Lambert, Qué, CAN, J4P 2L3. (514)465-9385. Les Films François Brault, 1600 de Lorimier, #398, Montréal, Qué, CAN, H2K 3W5. (514)523-2127.
Types de production et Catégories: l métrage-Réal/D phot; c métrage-D phot; TV film-Réal/Cam.
Types d'oeuvres: Drame-C; Documentaire-C&TV; Education-TV; Enfants-TV.
Curriculum vitae: Né en 1941; canadien. Professionnel depuis 65; travaille comme caméraman, directeur-photo, réalisateur et/ou producteur.

(cont/suite)

Filmographie sélective: *MIROIR DE LA VIE ET DE LA MORT,* TV, 85/84, CDN, Sc/Réal/Cam; *LA JOURNEE D'UN CURE DE CAMPAGNE,* TV, 83/82, CDN, Réal/Cam; *UNE INSTALLATION A DISPOSER,* TV, 83, CDN, Réal/Cam; *'LES ARTS SACRES DU QUEBEC'* (12 eps), TV, 83-80, CDN, Réal/Cam; *'UN PAYS, UN GOUT, UNE MANIERE'* (13 eps), TV, 79/78, CDN, Réal/Cam; *'MORDICUS',* TV, 79/78, CDN, Cam; *C'ETAIT EN DIRECT,* TV, 78, CDN, Cam; *LA VIE QUI PARLE/LA VIE VA PARLER,* 'POURQUOI PAS MOI?', TV, 77, CDN, Réal/Prod/Cam; *TRICOFIL C'EST LA CLEF,* TV, 76, CDN, Co réal/Sc/Cam; *PARLEZ NOUS D'AMOUR,* C, 76, CDN, D phot/Cam; *'ACTION-SANTE'* (13 eps), TV, 76/75, CDN, Réal/Cam/Prod; *LES EXCLUS,* TV, 75, CDN, Cam; *M'EN REVENANT PAR LES EPINETTES,* C, 74, CDN, Réal/Sc/Cam; *'PRELUDE'* (13 eps), TV, 73/72, CDN, Réal/Conc/Cam/Prod; *SCHLITZ CIRCUS PARADE,* C, 72, CDN, Cam; *FLORALIE OU ES-TU?,* C, 72, CDN, D phot/Cam; *A SOIR ON FAIT PEUR AU MONDE,* C, 69, CDN, Co réal/Cam; *THE MARK OF A CHAMPION,* 'TELESCOPE', TV, 68, CDN, Réal/Cam.

BRAULT, Michel

ARRFQ, APFVQ. 1168 Richelieu, Beloeil, Qué, CAN, J3G 4R3. (514)467-0317. Nanouk Films Ltée., 1600 Delorimier, Montréal, Qué, CAN, H2K 3W5. (514)521-1984.
Types de production et Catégories: l métrage-D phot/Réal; c métrage-D phot/Réal/Prod.
Types d'oeuvres: Drame-C&TV; Documentaire-C&TV.
Curriculum vitae: Né en 1928, Montréal, Québec. Récipiendaire de plusieurs prix dont le Prix de la mise en scène, Cannes, Prix de la Critique Québécoise pour *LES ORDRES*; *LES RAQUETTEURS,* Plaque d'Argent, Dei Popoli, Florence.
Filmographie sélective: *A FREEDOM TO MOVE,* C, 85, CDN, Prod/Réal; *HALF A LIFETIME,* C, 85, CDN, D phot; *LOUISIANA* (LOUISIANE), C, 83, CDN/F, D phot; *M.A. FORTIN,* TV, 82, CDN, D phot/Prod; *ELIA KAZAN, AN OUTSIDER,* C, 81, F, D phot; *LA QUARANTAINE,* C, 81, CDN, D phot; *THRESHOLD,* C, 80, CDN, D phot (GENIE); *'LE SON DES FRANCAIS EN AMERIQUE',* TV, 80-74, CDN, Prod/Réal; *LES BONS DEBARRAS* (GOOD RIDDANCE), C, 78, CDN, D phot (GENIE); *MOURIR A TUE-TETE* (A SCREAM OF SILENCE), C, 78, CDN, D phot; *LES ORDRES,* C, 74, CDN, Réal/Sc (2 CFA), *LE TEMPS D'UNE CHASSE,* C, 72, CDN, D phot; *KAMOURASKA,* C, 72, CDN/F, D phot; *MON ONCLE ANTOINE,* C, 71, CDN, D phot (CFA); *L'ACADIE,* L'ACADIE, C, 71, CDN, Co réal/D phot; *LES ENFANTS DU NEANT,* C, 68, CDN, Réal/D phot; *ENTRE LA MER ET L'EAU DOUCE,* C, 67, CDN, Réal; *POUR LA SUITE DU MONDE,* C, 63, CDN, Co réal/Cam (3 CFA); *A TOUT PRENDRE* (TAKE IT ALL), C, 63, CDN, Cam; *CHRONIQUE D'UN ETE,* C, 61, CDN, Cam, *LES RAQUETTEURS,* C, 58, CDN, Réal/Cam.

BRITTAIN, Donald

471 Clarke Ave., Montreal, Que, CAN, H3Y 3C5.
Types of Production & Categories: Th Film Dir/Prod/Wr; Th Short-Dir/Prod/Wr; TV Film-Dir/Prod/Wr.
Genres: Drama-Th; Documentary-Th&TV.
Biography: Born 1928, Ottawa, Ontario; Queen's University. Journalist, National Press Award, 52; NFB, 54-68; Fuji Group, Japan, 68; independent since 70. *VOLCANO: AN INQUIRY INTO THE LIFE AND DEATH OF MALCOLM LOWRY* was nominated for an Oscar, won Blue Ribbon, American Film Fest.. He has won many other int'l awards including: Grand Prizes, Leipzig and Oberhausen; Chris Plaques, Columbus; First Prize Literature, American Film Awards; John Grierson Award, 78. *CANADA'S SWEETHEART: THE SAGA OF HAL C. BANKS* was named Best Canadian Production, Festival of Festivals, Toronto, 85.

(cont/suite)

Selective Filmography: *THE CHAMPIONS - THE FINAL BATTLE* (Part III), TV, 86, CDN, Dir/Wr/Narr/Co-Prod; *CANADA'S SWEETHEART: THE SAGA OF HAL C. BANKS*, TV, 85, CDN, Dir/Co-Wr/Co-Prod; *THE CHILDREN'S CRUSADE*, TV, 84, CDN, Dir/Wr/Prod; *SOMETHING TO CELEBRATE*, TV, 83, CDN, Dir/Prod/Wr (**ACTRA**); *THE ACCIDENT*, TV, 83, CDN, Dir; *THE HONOURABLE MEMBER*, 'FOR THE RECORD', TV, 82, CDN, Dir; *RUNNING MAN*, 'FOR THE RECORD', TV, 81, CDN, Dir (**CFA**); *THE MOST DANGEROUS SPY*, 'ON GUARD FOR THEE', TV, 81, CDN, Dir/Co-Prod/Wr (**ACTRA**); *A BLANKET OF ICE*, 'ON GUARD FOR THEE', TV, 81, CDN, Dir/Co-Prod/Wr (**ACTRA**); *PAPERLAND: THE BUREAUCRAT OBSERVED*, TV, 79, CDN, Co-Dir/Co-Wr/Co-Prod (**3 GENIE**); *THE DIONNE QUINTUPLETS*, TV, 79, CDN, Dir/Prod; *WHISTLING SMITH*, Th, 79, CDN, Wr; *THE CHAMPIONS* (Parts I & II), Th, 78, CDN, Dir/Wr/Narr/Prod (**2 CFA**); *SMALL IS BEAUTIFUL: IMPRESSIONS OF FRITZ SHUMAKER*, Th, 77, CDN, Dir/Wr; *SECRETS OF THE BERMUDA TRIANGLE*, Th, 77, CDN, Dir/Wr/Co-Prod; *HENRY FORD'S AMERICA*, TV, 76, CDN, Dir/Prod/Wr (**CFA/INT'L EMMY**); *VOLCANO: AN INQUIRY INTO THE LIFE AND DEATH OF MALCOLM LOWRY*, Th, 76, CDN, Co-Dir/Co-Wr/Co-Prod (**3 CFA**); *HIS WORSHIP, MR. MONTREAL*, Th, 75, CDN, Co-Dir/Wr/Co-Prod; *KING OF THE HILL*, Th, 74, CDN, Co-Dir/Wr; *DREAMLAND: A HISTORY OF EARLY CANADIAN MOVIES*, Th, 74, CDN, Dir/Wr (**CFA**); *SAUL ALINSKY WENT TO WAR*, Th, 70, CDN, Co-Dir/Co-Wr; *LABYRINTH* (LABYRINTHE), Th, 67, CDN, Co-Wr; *NEVER A STEP BACKWARD* (LA PRESSE ET SON EMPIRE), Th, 66, CDN, Co-Dir/Wr (**CFA**); *HELICOPTER CANADA*, Th, 66, CDN, Co-Wr; *MEMORANDUM* (POUR MEMOIRE), Th, 65, CDN, Co-Dir/Wr; *LADIES AND GENTLEMEN...MR. LEONARD COHEN*, TV, 65, CDN, Wr/Co-Dir (**CFA**); *BUSTER KEATON RIDES AGAIN*, Th, 65, CDN, Wr; *FIELDS OF SACRIFICE* (CHAMPS D'HONNEUR), Th, 63, CDN, Dir/Wr/Prod (**CFA**); *BETHUNE*, TV, 63, CDN, Wr/Co-Prod; *'CANADA AT WAR'* (13 films), Th, 62, CDN, Dir/Wr.

BROWN, Alastair

ACTRA. 68 Robert St., Toronto, Ont, CAN, M5S 2K3. (416)922-7451.
Types of Production & Categories: Th Film-Dir; TV Film-Dir/Prod; TV Video-Dir/Wr.
Genres: Drama-Th&TV; Action-Th&TV; Documentary-Th&TV; Educational-TV.
Biography: Born 1944, Peterborough, England; Canadian citizen. B.A., English, Trinity College, Dublin. Trained at BBC, London; worked as film director in London, New York, Los Angeles; has over 80 televised documentaries to his credit.
Selective Filmography: *LAST CHANCE*, Th, 86, CDN/AUS, Dir/Wr; *THE PRICE OF VENGEANCE*, TV, 85, CDN, Dir/Co-Wr; *'THE AMATEUR NATURALIST'* (6 eps), TV, 84/83, CDN/GB, Dir; *'ARK ON THE MOVE'* (13 eps), TV, 82/81, CDN, Dir.

BRUNET, François

AR. 221 Champ Doré, St-Mathieu de Beloeil, Qué, CAN, J3G 4S5. (514)464-6332.
Radio-Canada, 1400 blvd. Dorchester est, Montréal, Qué, CAN, H2L 2M2. (514) 285-3622.
Types de production et Catégories: TV film-Réal; TV vidéo-Réal.
Types d'oeuvres: Documentaire-TV; Education-TV; Animation-TV.
Curriculum vitae: Né en 1937, Montréal, Québec. Bac., Collège Jean de Brébeuf; Licence en Droit, Université de Montréal; Barreau (Province de Québec). Depuis 63, au-delà de 400 documentaires dans le domaine de l'information pour Radio-Canada; réalisateur-coordonnateur de l'émission *LE POINT*, 84-86.
Filmographie sélective: *MADE IN KOREA/ COUPABLE D'ETRE VICTIME/ DONNANT - DONNANT*, 'DOCUMENT', TV, 84-83, CDN, Réal; *VIRAGE A*

(cont/suite)

L'OUEST/ L'ETRANGER/ AU BOUT DE MON AGE, 'TEL QUEL', TV, 81-80, CDN, Réal.

BRUYERE, Christian - see WRITERS

BUDGELL, Jack - see PRODUCERS

BUGAJSKI, Richard

391 Royal York Rd., Toronto, Ont, CAN, M8Y 2R4. (416)259-6943. Elizabeth Bradley, The Colbert Agency, 303 Davenport Rd., Toronto, Ont, CAN, M5R 1K5. (416)964-3302.
Types of Production & Categories: Th Film-Dir/Prod/Wr; TV Film-Dir/Wr; TV Video-Dir/Wr.
Genres: Drama-Th&TV; Action-Th&TV; Documentary-TV; Educational-TV.
Biography: Born 1943, Warsaw, Poland; Polish citizen; emigrated to Canada for political reasons, 85. Education: Philosophy, Warsaw University; Directing, Film and Theatre Academy, Lodz. Worked for Commercial Film Studio, 72-74; Warsaw National TV, deputy director-in-chief and director/producer, 74-79; also directed theatre. Worked at Studio X, Poland (headed by Andrzej Wajda), 73-83. Published 2 novels: 'The Interrogation', 'I Confess my Guilt'. Has won several awards including: Best Director, Polish TV Festival, 78; *THE INTERROGATION* won Film of the Year awarded by the Underground Solidarity, 82.
Selective Filmography: *THE INTERROGATION,* Th, 82, PL, Dir/Prod/Wr; *A WOMAN AND A WOMAN,* Th, 80, PL, Co-Dir/Co-Prod/Co-Wr; *CLASSES,* TV, 79, PL, Dir/Wr; *SPANISH BLOOD,* TV, 78, PL, Dir; *TRISMUS,* TV, 78, PL, Dir; *WHEN WILL YOU GIVE ME MY SHARE?,* TV, 77, PL, Dir; *DON CARLOS,* TV, 77, PL, Dir; *THE OTHER SIDE OF THE FLAME,* TV, 76, PL, Dir; *THE BARRIER,* TV, 76, PL, Dir/Co-Wr; *TASTE OF MUSIC,* TV, 76, PL, Dir; *PAUL,* TV, 75, PL, Dir/Wr; *WINCENTY PSTROWSKI STORY,* TV, 75, PL, Dir/Wr; *JOHANN SEBASTIAN BACH,* 'THE COMPOSERS', TV, 75, PL, Dir; *MARATHON,* TV, 73, PL, Dir/Wr.

BURKE, Martyn

ACTRA, DGC, WGAw. 1118 Third St., #303, Santa Monica, CA, USA, 90403. 175 Howland, Toronto, Ont, CAN, M5R 3B7. Rosalie Swedlin, CAA, 1888 Century Park East, #1400, Los Angeles, CA, USA, 90067. (213)277-4545.
Types of Production & Categories: Th Film-Dir/Wr; TV Film-Dir/Wr; TV Video-Dir/Wr.
Genres: Drama-Th&TV; Comedy-Th&TV; Action-Th&TV; Documentary-TV.
Biography: Born in Canada; McMaster University. Vietnam War correspondent and photographer, 66-67; joined CBC, 68. Member of the Authors League; author of 'Laughing War', 80; 'The Commissar's Report', 84.
Selective Filmography: *'WEST 57th'* (1 eps), TV, 85, USA, Dir; *TOP SECRET,* Th, 84, USA, Co-Scr; *THE KGB CONNECTIONS,* TV, 81, CDN, Dir; *THE LAST CHASE,* Th, 80, CDN, Dir/Co-Scr/Co-Prod; *CONNECTIONS: A FURTHER INVESTIGATION,* TV, 79, CDN, Dir/Co-Prod; *CONNECTIONS: AN INVESTIGATION INTO ORGANIZED CRIME,* TV, 77, CDN, Dir/Co-Prod (ACTRA/ANIK); *POWER PLAY (COUP D'ETAT),* (STATE OF SHOCK), Th, 77, CDN/GB, Dir/Scr (CFA); *BACKLOT CANADIANA,* TV, 76, CDN, Prod; *IDI AMIN - MY PEOPLE LOVE ME,* TV, 75, CDN, Dir; *THE CLOWN MURDERS,* Th, 75, CDN, Dir/Wr; *'THE PRESENT TENSE'* (sev eps), TV, 73, CDN, Co-Exec Prod; *CARNIVALS,* Th, 72, CDN, Dir; *SLEEPY GRASS,* TV, 72, CDN, Dir; *CALIFORNIA MOVIE,* Th, 71, CDN, Dir; *THE HOLLYWOOD TEN,* TV, 70, CDN, Dir; *ONE REVOLUTION AROUND THE SUN,* TV, 69, CDN, Dir.

BURTON, Robert H. - see PRODUCERS

BUSH, Gary - see PRODUCERS

BUTTIGNOL, Rudy - see PRODUCERS

CACOPARDO, Max

AR. 149 ave. Balfour, Montréal, Qué, CAN, H3P 1L8. (514)737-2405. Radio-Canada, 1400 blvd. Dorchester est, Montréal, Qué, CAN, H2L 2M2. (514)285-3343.
Types de production et Catégories: TV film-Réal/Sc; TV vidéo-Réal/Sc.
Types d'oeuvres: Documentaire-TV; Education-TV; Enfants-TV; Affaires publiques-TV.
Curriculum vitae: Né en 1932, Italie; réside au Canada depuis 53; citoyen canadien. Langues: italien, français, anglais. Maitrise en Sciences économiques, Université de Montréal. Réalisateur à Radio-Canada depuis 58.; traducteur et scénariste.
Filmographie sélective: *'ECRAN-TEMOIN'* (20 eps), TV, 86, CDN, Réal; *'LES SURTAXES'* (4 eps), TV, 85, CDN, Réal; *'PALME D'OR'* (39 eps), TV, 85, CDN, Réal/Sc; *'LES GRANDS DU CINEMA'* (13 eps), TV, 85, CDN, Prod dél; *'LE PRIX DU SPECTACLE'* (4 eps), TV, 84, CDN, Réal; *'DOSSIER DE PRESSE* (13 eps), TV, 84, CDN, Réal; *'LE POINT',* TV, 83, CDN, Réal; *'SCIENCE - REALITE',* TV, 82, CDN, Réal; *'SALUT SANTE'* (26 eps), TV, 82-78, CDN, Conc/Sc; *'TELEJEANS'* (75 eps), TV, 81-78, CDN, Réal; *SPECIAL PAUL VI,* TV, 78, CDN, Réal; *CAPSULES COJO,* TV, 76, CDN, Réal; *LA TERRE SAINTE A VOL D'OISEAU,* TV, 74, CDN, Réal; *L'ARCHEOLOGIE BIBLIQUE,* TV, 73, CDN, Réal; *SPECIAL JEAN XXIII,* TV, 73, CDN, Réal; *'RENCONTRE'* (40 eps), TV, 73-71, CDN, Réal; *'L'EDUCATION SEXUELLE'* (6 eps), TV, 70, CDN, Réal; *LA VIE DANS L'UNIVERS,* TV, 69, CDN, Réal; *LA PUBLICITE ET LA TELEVISION,* TV, 68, CDN, Réal; *DE GAULLE AU QUEBEC,* TV, 67, CDN, Réal; *DOSSIER ENZO FERRARI,* TV, 67, CDN, Réal; *EXPO-SCOPITONE,* TV, 67, CDN, Réal; *'DOSSIER SARTRE-DE BEAUVOIR'* (7 eps), TV, 67, CDN, Réal; *L'ESPIONNAGE,* TV, 66, CDN, Réal; *'O CANADA'* (4 eps), TV, 64, CDN, Réal; *'CHAMP LIBRE'* (20 eps), TV, 64, CDN, Réal; *QUELQU'UN PARMI VOUS,* TV, 63, CDN, Trad/Adapt; *PAS D'AMOUR,* TV, 63, CDN, Trad; *'CARREFOUR'* (300 eps), TV, 63-61, CDN, Réal; *'CAMERA'* (90 eps), TV, 60-58, CDN, Réal.

CAMPBELL, Norman

ATPD, DGA, DGC. 20 George Henry Blvd., Willowdale, Ont, CAN, M2J 1E2. (416)494-8576. CBC, Box 500, Station A, Toronto, Ont, CAN, M5W 1E6. (416) 975-6877.
Types of Production & Categories: Th Film-Dir; TV Film-Dir/Prod; TV Video-Dir/Prod.
Genres: Drama-TV; Comedy-TV; Variety-Th&TV; Documentary-TV.
Biography: Born 1924, Los Angeles, California; Canadian citizen. B.A., University of British Columbia (Mathematics, Physics), 44. Joined CBC, 52; directed specials in England and the U.S.. Awarded Order of Canada, 79; member Royal Canadian Academy. Has won many awards including the Celia Award from the National Ballet of Canada, Prix René Barthelemy, Monte Carlo; Chris Statuette, Columbus; John Drainie Award.
Selective Filmography: *THE OPERA DIALOGUES OF THE CARMELITES,* TV, 86, CDN, Dir/Prod; *'FRAGGLE ROCK'* (pilot & 5 eps), TV, 85-83, CDN, Dir; *THE RAKE'S PROGRESS* (OPERA), TV, 85, CDN, Dir/Prod; *THE PIRATES OF PENZANCE,* TV, 85, CDN, Dir/Prod; *ONEGIN,* TV, 85, CDN, Dir/Prod; *ANNA BOLENA,* TV, 84, CDN, Dir/Prod; *ROYAL GALA AT ROY THOMSON HALL,* TV, 84, CDN, Dir/Prod; *THE MIKADO,* TV, 83, CDN, Dir/Prod; *ROMEO AND JULIET,* TV, 83, CDN, Dir/Prod; *TAMING OF THE SHREW,* TV, 82, CDN, Dir; *ROY THOMSON HALL OPENING GALA,* TV, 82, CDN, Dir/Prod; *THE MAGIC SHOW,* Th, 80, CDN, Dir; *KAREN KAIN-THE PLEASURE OF YOUR COMPANY,* TV, 79, CDN, Dir/Prod; *EDITH PIAF, JE VOUS AIME,* TV, 79, CDN, Dir/Prod; *TORONTO SYMPHONY IN CHINA,* TV, 78, CDN, Dir/Prod; *LA FILLE MAL GARDEE,* TV, 78, CDN, Dir/Prod; *JOHNNY BELINDA,* TV, 77, CDN, Dir/Prod (**ANIK**); *THE UNSELFISH*

(cont/suite)

GIANT OF STRATFORD, TV, 77, CDN, Dir/Prod; *GISELLE*, TV, 76, CDN, Dir/ Prod (ANIK); *BING CROSBY'S WHITE CHRISTMAS*, TV, 76, USA, Dir; *A SPECIAL OLIVIA NEWTON JOHN*, TV, 76, USA, Dir; *AN EVENING WITH DIANA ROSS*, TV, 76, USA, Dir; *SHE STOOPS TO CONQUER*, TV, 75, CDN, Dir/Prod; *ANDY WILLIAMS CHRISTMAS* (2 years), TV, 74/73, USA, Dir; *'ALL IN THE FAMILY'* (2 eps), TV, 72, USA, Dir; *THE SLEEPING BEAUTY*, TV, 71, CDN, Dir/Prod (EMMY); *CINDERELLA*, TV, 68, CDN, Dir/Prod (EMMY); *BALLERINA*, Th, 65, USA, Dir; *GLENN GOULD, MUSIC FROM THE U.S.S.R.*, 'CONCERT', TV, 61, CDN, Dir/Prod; *THE GERSHWIN YEARS*, TV, 61, USA, Dir.

CAMPBELL, Peter - see PRODUCERS

CANELL, Marrin - see PRODUCERS

CANNING, Bill
SGCT. 473 Marie Therese Ave., Ste-Therese, Que, CAN, J7E 2J2. NFB, 3155 Cote de Liesse Nord, Montreal, Que, CAN, H4M 2M4. (514)283-9499.
Types of Production & Categories: Th Short-Dir/Prod; TV Film-Dir/Prod.
Genres: Action-Th&TV; Documentary-Th&TV; Educational-Th&TV.
Biography: Born 1933, Smiths Falls, Ontario. Has been involved in 100 productions at the NFB. His sport films have won numerous awards. *DIEF* won the Nettie Krysky Award, Yorkton.
Selective Filmography: *MAX WARD*, TV, 84, CDN, Dir; *DIEF*, Th, 81, CDN, Dir; *THE TASTE OF TOMORROW*, TV, 81, CDN, Dir; *WELCOME TO SMITHS FALLS*, TV, 78, CDN, Dir; *CHRIST IS RISEN*, Th, 76, CDN, Dir/Prod; *THE LADY AND THE OWL*, TV, 75, CDN, Dir/Prod; *NIAGARA FOR SALE*, TV, 75, CDN, Dir/Prod; *KING OF THE HILL*, TV, 74, CDN/USA, Dir/Prod; *FOR YOU MR. BELL* (HOMAGE A M. BELL), Th, 72, CDN, Dir/Prod; *TEMPLES OF TIME* (TEMPLES DU TEMPS), Th, 71, CDN, Prod/Dir (CFA); *ANGUS*, Th, 71, CDN, Prod; *THAT'S THE PRICE*, TV, 70, CDN, Prod; *GO WITH US*, TV, 70, CDN, Prod; *DON'T KNOCK THE OX*, Th, 70, CDN, Prod (CFA); *THE DOWRY*, Th, 70, CDN, Prod; *FLIGHT IN WHITE* (ENTRE CIEL ET NEIGE), Th, 69, CDN, Dir/Prod; *NORTH* (LE NORD), Th, 68, CDN, Prod; *WE'RE GONNA HAVE REGRETS*, Th, 68, CDN, Prod; *TO TRACK A SHADOW* (SUIVRE UNE PISTE), TV, 68, CDN, Prod; *BLADES AND BRASS* (LAMES ET CUIVRES), Th, 67, CDN, Dir/Prod; *STRONG AND FREE*, TV, 67, CDN, Dir/Prod; *A TALE OF MAIL* (AU PIED DE LA LETTRE), Th, 67, CDN, Prod; *VALLEY IN A RIVER*, TV, 67, CDN, Prod; *GET WET* (A L'EAU), Th, 66, CDN, Dir/Prod; *WAR II TOTAL WAR* (SECONDE GUERRE MONDIALE - GUERRE TOTALE), TV, 65, CDN, Dir/Prod.

CARDINAL, Roger
DGC. 799 Jean-Bois, Boucherville, Qué, CAN, J4B 3G2. (514)641-2118. Téléscène Productions Inc, 360 Place Royale, Montréal, Qué, CAN, H2Y 2V1. (514)288-1638.
Types de production et Catégories: l métrage-Réal; c métrage-Réal; TV film-Réal.
Types d'oeuvres: Drame-C&TV; Comédie-C; Documentaire-C&TV; Education-C&TV.
Filmographie sélective: *YOU'VE COME A LONG WAY LADIES* (WOMEN IN SPORTS IN CANADA), TV, 84, CDN, Réal; *ETRE INFORME, C'EST ETRE LIBRE*, TV, 84, CDN, Réal; *'MINI DOCS '84'*, TV, 84, CDN, Réal; *DIS LE CANADA, C'EST LOIN DE L'AMERIQUE*, TV, 84, F, Réal; *PIERRE LABELLE, SEUL EN PISTE*, TV, 83, CDN, Réal; *CIVVY STREET*, TV, 81, CDN, Réal; *AU BOULOT GALARNEAU*, TV, 81, CDN, Réal; *LIFE: PART TWO*, TV, 80, CDN, Réal; *SECOND DEBUT*, TV, 80, CDN, Réal; *DOLLARS SANS ORMEAUX*, TV, 79, CDN, Réal; *IRON PLUS*, TV, 78, CDN, Réal; *VOUS AVEZ LE DROIT, LES AUTRES AUSSI*, TV, 77, CDN, Réal; *AIDE-TOI, LE*

(cont/suite)

CIEL T'AIDERA, TV, 77, CDN, Réal; *SMISS,* TV, 75, CDN, Réal; *THE GREATEST SNOW ON EARTH,* TV, 75, CDN, Réal; *MONTREAL, AN OLYMPIC CITY,* C, 75, CDN, Réal; *IN SEARCH OF ACHIEVEMENT,* C, 75, CDN, Réal; *FRANCAIS, SORRY I DON'T,* TV, 74, CDN, Réal; *THE GAME IS THE SAME,* TV, 74, CDN, Réal; *PLUS CA CHANGE, PLUS C'EST PAREIL,* TV, 74, CDN, Réal; *QUEBEC, THE GOOD EARTH,* C, 74, CDN, Réal; *ASTA,* C, 74, CDN, Réal; *BARRIERES ARCHITECTURALES,* TV, 73, CDN, Réal; *L'APPARITION,* C, 71, CDN, Réal; *THE STORM,* C, 70, CDN, Réal; *APRES-SKI,* C, 70, CDN, Réal.

CARLE, Gilles

ARRFQ. 318 Carré St-Louis, Montréal, Qué, CAN. (514)282-1326.
Types de production et Catégories: 1 métrage-Réal/Sc; c métrage-Réal/Sc/Cam/ Prod; TV film-Réal/Sc/Cam/Prod; TV vidéo-Réal/Sc/Cam/Prod.
Types d'oeuvres: Drame-C; Comédie-C; Variété-C&TV; Documentaire-C&TV.
Curriculum vitae: Né en 1929, Maniwaki, Québec; bilingue. Etudes: Belles-Lettres et Beaux-Arts. Plus de 300 films dont 20 longs métrages. *LA VRAIE NATURE DE BERNADETTE, LA MORT D'UN BUCHERON* et *FANTASTICA,* sélections officielles à Cannes; *LA TETE DE NORMANDE ST-ONGE, LES PLOUFFE* et *L'ANGE ET LA FEMME* furent présentés à la Quinzaine des Réalisateurs, Cannes; ses films ont aussi remporté plusieurs prix à des festivals de films internationaux.
Filmographie sélective: *LA GUEPE,* C, 86/85, CDN, Réal/Sc; *O PICASSO,* C, 85, CDN, Réal/Sc; *CINEMA CINEMA,* TV, 84, CDN, Réal/Sc; *LE CRIME D'OVIDE PLOUFFE* (4 eps), TV, 83, CDN/F, Réal/Sc; *MARIA CHAPDELAINE,* C, 83, CDN/F, Réal/Sc; *JOUER SA VIE,* TV, 82, CDN, Réal; *LES PLOUFFE,* C, 81, CDN, Réal/Co sc (**2 GENIE/BIJOU**); *FANTASTICA,* C, 80, CDN, Réal/Sc; *L'AGE DE LA MACHINE,* C, 78, CDN, Réal/Sc (**2 CFA**); *L'ANGE ET LA FEMME,* C, 77, CDN, Réal/Sc; *LA TETE DE NORMANDE ST-ONGE,* C, 75, CDN, Réal/Sc; *A THOUSAND MOONS,* 'FOR THE RECORD', TV, 75, CDN, Réal/Sc; *LES CORPS CELESTES,* C, 73, CDN, Réal/Sc; *LA MORT D'UN BUCHERON,* C, 72, CDN, Réal/Sc; *LA VRAIE NATURE DE BERNADETTE,* C, 72, CDN, Réal/Sc (**2 CFA**); *LES MALES,* C, 70, CDN, Réal/Sc; *RED,* C, 69, CDN, Réal/Sc; *JEUX DE JEROLAS,* TV, 67, CDN, Réal/Sc; *LE VIOL D'UNE JEUNE FILLE DOUCE,* C, 66, CDN, Réal/Sc; *PLACE A OLIVIER GUIMOND,* TV, 66, CDN, Réal/Sc; *LA VIE HEUREUSE DE LEOPOLD Z,* C, 65, CDN, Réal/Sc.

CARRIER, Louis Georges

Radio-Canada, 1400 blvd. Dorchester est, Montréal, Qué, CAN, H2L 2M2. (514) 285-3007.
Types de production et Catégories: 1 métrage-Réal; c métrage-Réal; TV film-Réal; TV vidéo-Réal.
Types d'oeuvres: Drame-C&TV; Variété-TV; Comédie musicale-TV; Documentaire-C&TV.
Curriculum vitae: Né en 1928, Détroit, Michigan; citoyen canadien. Bac., Collège Ste-Marie, Montréal; Maitrise ès Arts en Littérature, Université de Montréal; Théâtre et Littérature, Sorbonne, Paris, France, 52-53.
Filmographie sélective: *LAURIER* (mini-série), TV, 86, CDN, Réal; *JEUX DE HASARD,* TV, 79, CDN/F/B/CH, Réal; *COUP DE SANG,* TV, 78, CDN, Réal; *LE VELO DEVANT LA PORTE,* TV, 77, CDN, Réal; *TCHIN, TCHIN,* TV, 77, CDN, Réal; *HOMMAGE A DENISE PELLETIER,* TV, 76, CDN, Réal; *LE SEA HORSE,* TV, 76, CDN, Réal; *EDNA OU LA CONTRADICTION,* TV, 75, CDN, Réal; *QUI PERD GAGNE,* TV, 74, CDN, Réal; *IL EST UNE SAISON,* TV, 74, CDN, Réal/Co sc; *LE PELICAN,* TV, 74, CDN, Réal; *BYE-BYE 73,* TV, 73, CDN, Réal; *MILLIONNAIRE A FROID,* TV, 73, CDN, Réal; *LE P'TIT VIENT VITE* (THE LITTLE ONE'S COMING FAST), C, 72, CDN, Réal; *DOUBLE SENS,* TV, 71, CDN, Réal; *C'EST TOUJOURS LA MEME HISTOIRE,* TV, 70,

CDN, Réal; *AU RETOUR DES OIES BLANCHES,* TV, 70, CDN, Réal; *LE MISANTHROPE,* C, 64, CDN, Réal; *PAPINEAU,* C, 60, CDN, Réal.

CARRIERE, Bruno

STCQ. Les Films Cinétrie Inc., 4259 de Bullion, Montréal, Qué, CAN, H2W 2E5. (514)288-1915.
Types de production et Catégories: 1 métrage-Réal/Sc; c métrage-Réal/Sc/Cam/ Prod; TV film-Réal/Sc/Cam/Prod; TV vidéo-Réal/Sc/Cam/Prod.
Types d'oeuvres: Drame-C&TV; Action-C&TV; Documentaire-C&TV; Animation-C&TV.
Curriculum vitae: Né en 1953, Cornwall, Ontario; bilingue. Etudes professionnelles en fonderie artistique et sculpture. Ducat d'Or, Mannheim et 6 nominations au Prix Génie pour *LUCIEN BROUILLARD; LE PETIT PAYS* remporte le Prix de la Critique Québécoise, catégorie court métrage.
Filmographie sélective: *LA LECON DES TROIS VOLEURS,* 'LEGENDES DU MONDE', TV, 86, CDN, Réal/Sc/Cam; *L'ESSOR AGRICOLE AU CANADA,* TV, 86, CDN, Réal/Cam; *ALLER-RETOUR,* TV, 86, CDN, Réal/Prod/Conc/Cam; *MUREE VIVE,* 'TRAQUENARD', TV, 85, CDN, Réal/Cam/Co sc; *OPTION QUEBEC CHINE,* TV, 85, CDN, Réal/Cam; *CORENTIN LE VIOLONEUX/LA BUTTE DE COQUILLES/LA FLUTE MERVEILLEUSE,* 'CONTES ET LEGENDES DU MONDE', TV, 84-83, CDN, Réal/Sc/Cam; *GRAVITE ZERO/ LA MARATHONIENNE,* 'ROTOSCOPIE', C, 84, CDN, Réal/Prod/Sc/Cam; *LUCIEN BROUILLARD,* C, 83, CDN, Réal/Co sc; *LE PETIT PAYS,* C, 80, CDN, Prod/Cam.

CASSON, Barry - see PRODUCERS

CAULFIELD, Paul - see PRODUCERS

CHABOT, Jean

ARRFQ. 4166 Laval, Montréal, Qué, CAN. (514)849-7864.
Types de production et Catégories: 1 métrage-Réal; TV film-Réal.
Types d'oeuvres: Drame-C; Comédie-C; Documentaire-C&TV; Education-TV.
Curriculum vitae: Né en 1945, St-Jean-Baptiste de Rouville, Québec. Bac., St-Hyacinthe; Sciences économiques, Université de Montréal. Assistant caméraman, monteur jusqu'en 69; réalisateur indépendant depuis 70.
Filmographie sélective: *LE FUTUR INTERIEUR,* C, 83, CDN, Réal/Sc; *LA FICTION NUCLEAIRE,* C, 78, CDN, Réal/Rech; *UNE NUIT EN AMFRIQUE,* C, 73, CDN, Réal/Sc; *MON ENFANCE A MONTREAL,* C, 70, CDN, Réal/Sc.

CHANTRAINE, Pol

ARRQ. C.P.516, Havre-aux-Maisons, Iles-de-la-Madeleine, Qué, CAN, G0B 1K0. (418)969-2538. Radio-Québec Group/I.M., C.P. 4000, St.Omer, Qué, CAN, G0C 2Z0. (418)364-7081.
Types de production et Catégories: TV vidéo-Réal.
Types d'oeuvres: Documentaire-TV.
Curriculum vitae: Né en 1944, Belgique; citoyen canadien. Auteur de 2 livres; journaliste; Prix des Magazines canadiens, 77, Canadian Business Award, 76.
Filmographie sélective: *UNE REGION D'ELEVAGE/SYNTHESE,* 'CONTOUR ECONOMIQUE D'UNE REGION ELOIGNEE', TV, 85, CDN, Réal/Rech/Textes; *LA MRC DE MATANE/DENIS RIVERIN/GASPE/PABOK,* 'CONTOUR ECONOMIQUE D'UNE REGION ELOIGNEE', TV, 85, CDN, Réal/Rech/Textes; *LE MRC DES ILES DE LA MADELEINE/BONAVENTURE/ D'AVIGNON,* 'CONTOUR ECONOMIQUE D'UNE REGION ELOIGNEE', TV, 85, CDN, Réal/Rech/Textes; *'VIE DE PECHEUR'* (Comp, 3 eps), (13 eps), TV, 85-83, CDN, Réal/Textes; *TANT QUE L'EAU DOUCE DURE,* TV, 79, CDN, Ass réal; *TI-CUL TOUGAS,* C, 74, CDN, 3e Ass réal.

CHAPDELAINE, Gérard

AR. 60 rue de Brésoles, #110, Montréal, Qué, CAN, H2V 1V5. (514)849-2615. Radio-Canada, 1400 blvd. Dorchester est, Montréal, Qué, CAN, H2L 2M2. (514) 285-3188.
Types de production et Catégories: TV film-Réal; TV vidéo-Réal.
Types d'oeuvres: Documentaire-TV; Education-TV; Enfants-TV.
Curriculum vitae: Né en 1927, St-Hyacinthe, Québec. Etudes: Philosophie, Université d'Ottawa; Relations internationales, Université Laval, Québec. Réalisateur à Radio-Canada depuis 55.
Filmographie sélective: *'QUATRE VOIX...UNE PAROLE'* (26 eps), TV, 86/85, CDN, Réal; *'MICRO-MONDE'* (13 eps), TV, 85, CDN, Réal; *SUR LES LIEUX DE LA PASSION,* TV, 84, CDN, Réal; *LES CITES DE JESUS,* TV, 83, CDN, Réal; *'SI TOUS LES GENS DU MONDE'* (36 eps), TV, 83, CDN, Réal; *'MA SOEUR, LA TERRE'* (36 eps), TV, 82, CDN, Réal; *'EN TERRE SAINTE'* (13 eps), TV, 79, CDN, Réal; *'LES PELERINS'* (36 eps), TV, 78, CDN, Réal; *'L'EGLISE EN PAPIER'* (36 eps), TV, 77, CDN, Réal; *'LA BIBLE EN PAPIER'* (36 eps), TV, 76, CDN, Réal; *'L'EVANGILE EN PAPIER'* (36 eps), TV, 75, CDN, Réal; *'FORMAT 60'* (40 eps), TV, 67-65, CDN, Réal; *'AUJOURD'HUI'* (80 eps), TV, 67-65, CDN, Réal; *'LE SEL DE LA SEMAINE'* (39 eps), TV, 67, CDN, Réal; *'PREMIER PLAN'* (hebdo), TV, 63-60, CDN, Réal; *'LE COLOMBIER'* (39 eps), TV, 58, CDN, Réal.

CHAPMAN, Christopher

CSC, DGC. R.R.4, Sunderland, Ont, CAN, L0C 1H0. (705)357-2213. Christopher Chapman Ltd., 415 Merton St., Toronto, Ont, CAN, M4S 1B4. (416)487-3005.
Types of Production & Categories: Th Film-Dir; Th Short-Dir/Prod/Ed; TV Film-Dir/Ed/Cin.
Genres: Documentary-Th.
Biography: Born 1928, Toronto, Ontario. RCAA Medal, 65; Centennial Medal, 67; Jubilee Medal, 77; past President, DGC; member Royal Canadian Academy of Arts. Has won film awards in Salerno, N.Y., Argentina, Czechoslovakia. Has worked in 3D film and Imax.
Selective Filmography: *U.S. PAVILION FILM* (EXPO 86), Th, 86, USA, Dir; *CHICAGO MUSEUM OF SCIENCE AND INDUSTRY,* ED, 86, USA, Dir; *WILDERNESS,* Th, 84, CDN, Dir/Cin/Ed; *KELLY,* Th, 81, CDN, Dir; *PYRAMID OF ROSES,* Th, 82, CDN, Dir/Co-Prod/Ed; *ROME WITH ANTHONY BURGESS,* 'CITIES', TV, 81, CDN, Dir/Ed/Cin; *A SENSE OF HUMUS,* TV, 80, CDN, Dir/Ed/Cin; *VOLCANO,* Th, 73, CDN, Dir/Ed/Cin; *CANADA,* Th, 72, CDN, Dir/Prod/Cin/Ed; *TORONTO THE GOOD,* Th, 71, CDN, Dir/Ed; *FESTIVAL,* Th, 69, CDN, Dir/Prod/Cin/Ed; *A PLACE TO STAND,* Th, 66, CDN, Dir/Prod/Cin/Ed (**OSCAR/CFA**); *EXPEDITION BLUENOSE,* TV, 65, CDN, Dir/Ed/Cin (**CFA**); *LORING AND WYLE,* TV, 63, CDN, Dir/Ed/Cin; *MAGIC MOLECULE,* Th, 62, CDN, Co-Dir/Cin; *THE PERSISTENT SEED,* Th, 61, CDN, Dir/Cin/Ed; *QUETICO,* Th, 56, CDN, Dir/Prod/Cin/Ed (**CFA**); *THE SEASONS,* Th, 52, CDN, Dir/Prod/Cin/Ed (**2 CFA**).

CHAREST, Gaétan

STCQ. 3895 Ed. Montpetit, #1, Montréal, Qué, CAN, H3T 1L1. (514)341-3107.
Types de production et Catégories: c métrage-Mont/Réal/Sc; TV film-Mont/Réal; TV vidéo-Mont/Réal.
Types d'oeuvres: Variété-TV; Documentaire-C&TV; Enfants-TV; Animation-C.
Curriculum vitae: Né en 1951. Etudes en Lettres et Philosophie. Journaliste pigiste; réalisateur d'annonces et de documentaires.
Filmographie sélective: *INVENTEZ,* TV, 86, CDN, Mont; *COLOSSES D'HY,* C, 86, CDN, Sc; *GIVA,* C, 86, CDN, Sc; *ANAMORPHOSIS,* TV, 86, CDN/PL, Co
(cont/suite)

sc; *PEACE AND UNITY*, TV, 86, CDN/USA, Réal; *LA CUISINE DU BONHEUR*, TV, 86, CDN, Réal; *FESTIVAL INTERNATIONAL DES TV COMMUNAUTAIRES*, TV, 84, CDN, Coord pro; *LE GROUPE CHRISTIE*, 'PORTRAIT D'ENTREPRISE', TV, 84, CDN, Réal/Prod exéc; *'TELEJOURNAL'* (160 seg), TV, 84-77, CDN, Mont; *CONFERENCE DARSHAN SINGH*, TV, 83, CDN/USA, Réal; *BON GUIDE...* (BECOMING AN OUTFITTING GUIDE), ED, 83, CDN, Mont.

CHAREST, Louis

ARRQ. 613 rue Mercille, St-Lambert, Qué, CAN, J4P 2M1. (514)672-2092. Radio-Québec, 1000 rue Fullum, Montréal, Qué, CAN, H2K 3L7. (514)521-2424.
Types de production et Catégories: TV film-Réal; TV vidéo-Réal.
Types d'oeuvres: Drame-TV; Comédie-TV; Documentaire-TV.
Curriculum vitae: Né en 1937, Montréal, Québec. Etudes à l'Ecole des Beaux-Arts de Montréal, 57-62; études en musique, Université Laval, Québec. Enseignement en arts, 62-70. Production en télévision depuis 70.
Filmographie sélective: *'LA SOIREE DE L'IMPRO'* (15 eps), TV, 86-82, CDN/F, Réal; *LA DEPRIME*, TV, 84, CDN, Réal; *'L'OBJECTIF'* (16 eps), TV, 81, CDN, Réal; *'NEUF ET DEMI'* (3 eps), TV, 80, CDN, Réal; *'MOI'* (17 eps), TV, 79/78, CDN, Réal.

CHARLEBOIS, Pierre

AR. 236 ave. Metcalfe, Westmount, Qué, CAN, H3Z 2H9. (514)937-5689. Radio-Canada, 1400 blvd. Dorchester est, Montréal, Qué, CAN, H2L 2M2. (514)285-3211.
Types de production et Catégories: TV film-Réal.
Types d'oeuvres: Documentaire-TV; Affaires publiques-TV.
Curriculum vitae: Né en 1934, Montebello, Québec. Langues: français, anglais, espagnol, portugais, italien; A Radio-Canada depuis 61. Président de l'Association des Réalisateurs, 83-86. Membre du Conseil de Presse du Québec. Prix de la Communauté des télévisions francophones, 85, pour *LES GESTIONNAIRES DE LA MORT*.
Filmographie sélective: *QUAND L'AVION BAT DE L'AILE*, TV, 86, CDN, Réal; *LES GESTIONNAIRES DE LA MORT*, TV, 85, CDN, Réal; *CE NE SONT QUE DES BETES*, TV, 85, CDN, Réal; *LE DAILY CAL A BIEN CHANGE*, TV, 84, CDN, Réal; *LES NOIRS AMERICAINS, REVE OU CAUCHEMAR*, TV, 83, CDN, Réal; *REFLEXION SUR UNE PETITE PLANETE* (AGENDA FOR A SMALL PLANET), TV, 80, CDN, Réal; *ADAM, CARLO, CATHERINE, BENOIT...ET DES MILLIONS D'AUTRES*, TV, 77, CDN, Réal; *LE GUATEMALA TREMBLE ENCORE*, TV, 77, CDN, Réal; *'VIEILLIR ET VIVRE'* (19 eps), TV, 76, CDN, Réal; *DES PAYS BAS, SURPEUPLES, MAIS HEUREUX*, TV, 74, CDN, Réal; *'QUI-VIVE'* (24 eps), TV, 73/72, CDN, Réal; *LE REVE*, TV, 69, CDN, Réal; *LES SATELLITES DE COMMUNICATION*, TV, 68, CDN, Réal; *LA RATIONALISATION DE L'ELECTRICITE, 5 ANS APRES*, 'AUJOURD'HUI', TV, 68, CDN, Réal; *LES CANADIENS FRANCAIS ET LA TERRE DES HOMMES*, 'AUJOURD'HUI', TV, 67, CDN, Réal.

CHARTRAND, Alain

ARRFQ, STCQ. Lino Productions Inc., C.P. 31, Katevale, Qué, CAN, J0B 1W0. (819)843-1944.
Types de production et Catégories: l métrage-Réal; c métrage-Réal; TV film-Réal.
Types d'oeuvres: Drame-C; Comédie-C; Documentaire-C&TV; Education-C&TV.
Curriculum vitae: Né en 1946, Montréal, Québec. Etudes: Conservatoire de Musique de la Province de Québec, 63-67. 1er assistant réalisateur sur 22 films, dont 15 longs métrages, 70-86. *L'ETAU-BUS* gagne le Prix du Public, Belfort, 84, et à Clermont Ferrand, France, 85.

(cont/suite)

DIRECTORS/REALISATEURS

Filmographie sélective: *L'ETAU-BUS*, TV, 83, CDN, Réal/Sc (**ANIK**); *ON EST PAS SORTI DU BOIS*, TV, 82, CDN, Réal; *L'ESTRIE EN MUSIQUE*, TV, 81, CDN, Réal; *LES DOUCES*, TV, 80, CDN, Réal; *IMAGES DE L'ESTRIE*, TV, 80, CDN, Réal; *JEUX DE LA XXI OLYMPIADE*, C, 76, CDN, Réal dél; *LA PIASTRE*, C, 74, CDN, Réal/Sc; *ISIS AU 8*, C, 72, CDN, Réal; *ATABOY*, C, 67, CDN, Réal.

CHAYER, Réjean

AR. 6891 Christophe-Colomb, #206, Montréal, Qué, CAN, H2S 2H3. (514)274-4320. Radio-Canada, 1400 blvd. Dorchester est, Montréal, Qué, CAN, H2L 2M2. (514)285-2839.
Types de production et Catégories: TV film-Réal; TV vidéo-Réal.
Types d'oeuvres: Variété-TV; Documentaire-TV.
Curriculum vitae: Né en 1945, Valleyfield, Québec; bilingue. Maitrise, Sciences politiques, Université d'Ottawa. Treize ans d'expérience: 10 en informations, variétés; réalisateur, section dramatique, Radio-Canada, 86.
Filmographie sélective: *'LA BONNE AVENTURE'* (7 eps), TV, 86, CDN, Réal; *'LE PARC DES BRAVES'* (1 eps), TV, 86, CDN, Réal; *'AU JOUR LE JOUR'* (6 eps), TV, 84, CDN, Réal; *CONGRES A LA CHEFFERIE - PARTI LIBERAL DU CANADA*, TV, 84, CDN, Réal/Coord pro; *CONGRES A LA CHEFFERIE - PARTI CONSERVATEUR DU CANADA*, TV, 83, CDN, Réal; *REUNION DU F. M.I. A TORONTO*, TV, 83, CDN, Réal; *SOMMET ECONOMIQUE DE WILLIAMSBURG*, TV, 83, CDN, Réal; *VISITE DU PAPE EN GRANDE-BRETAGNE*, TV, 82, CDN, Réal; *VISITE DU PREMIER MINISTRE CANADIEN EN FRANCE*, TV, 82, CDN, Réal; *SOMMET ECONOMIQUE D'OTTAWA*, TV, 82, CDN, Réal; *'CONSOMMATEUR PLUS'* (4 eps), TV, 81/80, CDN, Réal; *L'IRAN*, 'CE SOIR NATIONAL', TV, 80, CDN, Réal/Coord pro; *DANIEL LAVOIE*, 'VEDETTE EN DIRECT', TV, 79, CDN, Réal; *370e ANNIVERSAIRE DE LA VILLE DE QUEBEC*, 'LES BEAUX DIMANCHES', TV, 78, CDN, Réal; *'FEMMES D'AUJOURD'HUI'* (2 eps), TV, 78, CDN, Réal; *'REFLETS D'UN PAYS'* (3 eps), TV, 78, CDN, Réal; *25 ANS DE RADIO-CANADA*, TV, 77, CDN, Réal.

CHBIB, Bachar - see PRODUCERS

CHETWYND, Lionel - see WRITERS

CHILVERS, Colin

DGA, DGC. P.O. Box 135, Ridgeway, Ont, CAN, L0S 1N0. (416)894-2963. Overview, 11 E. 71st Street, New York, NY, USA, 10021. (212)517-8686. Maureen Moore, London Management, 235 Regent St., London, England, GB, W1A 2JT. (01)493-1610.
Types of Production & Categories: Th Film-Dir SFX; TV Film-Dir.
Genres: Drama-Th; Action-Th; Science Fiction-Th; Commercials-TV.
Biography: Born 1945, England; graduated Hornsey College of Art.
Selective Filmography: *CLIMBING* (NEC COMPUTERS), Cm, 85, USA, Dir (**CLIO**); *THE BAR & DOWNERS GROVE/RUNNING BACK*, MV, 85, CDN, Dir; *WILDERNESS*, Cm, 85, CDN, Dir; *TOUR GUIDE* (BUFFET), Cm, 84, USA, Dir (**CLIO**); *NEW ORLEANS WORLD FAIR/EARTH WIND & FIRE*, Cm, 84/83, USA, Dir; *GODZILLA* (KONICA FILM), Cm, 84, USA, Dir (**CLIO**); *FOLLOW THAT BIRD*, Th, 84, CDN, 2nd U Dir; *SUPERMAN III*, Th, 83, USA/GB, Dir SFX; *CLASS OF '84*, Th, 83, CDN/USA, SFX Spv; *MARCHING BAND* (FRISKIES BUFFET), Cm, 83, USA, Dir (**CLIO**); *SUPERMAN II*, Th, 81, USA/GB, Dir SFX; *THE WARS*, Th, 81, CDN/D, SFX Spv; *CONDOR MAN*, Th, 80, USA, Dir SFX; *INCUBUS*, Th, 80, CDN, SFX Spv; *SATURN III*, Th, 79, USA, SFX Spv; *SUPERMAN*, Th, 78, USA/GB, Dir SFX (**OSCAR**); *SINBAD AND THE EYE OF THE TIGER*, Th, 76, GB, SFX Spv; *THE RITZ*, Th, 76, GB, SFX Spv; *GREAT EXPECTATIONS*, Th, 75, GB, SFX Spv; *LISZTOMANIA*, Th, 75,

(cont/suite)

GB, SFX Spv; *ROCKY HORROR PICTURE SHOW,* Th, 74, USA, SFX Spv; *TOMMY,* Th, 73, GB, SFX Spv; *200 MOTELS,* Th, 70, GB, SFX Spv; *INSPECTOR CLOUSEAU,* Th, 68, GB, SFX Spv.

CHRISTIE, Keith - see PRODUCERS
CIUPKA, Richard - see CINEMATOGRAPHERS
CLAIROUX, Jacques - voir MONTEURS
CLARK, Barry - see WRITERS
CLARK, Bob
DGC, PGA, WGAw. Harold D.Cohen Assoc. Mgmt., 9200 Sunset Blvd., Los Angeles, CA, USA, 90069. (213)550-0570. Mike Marcus, CAA, 1888 Century Park.E., Ste.1400, Los Angeles, CA, USA, 90067. (213)277-4545.
Types of Production & Categories: Th Film-Dir/Prod/Wr.
Genres: Drama-Th; Comedy-Th; Horror-Th.
Selective Filmography: *FROM THE IIIP,* Th, 86, USA, Dir/Co-Prod; *TURK 182,* Th, 85, USA, Dir; *RHINESTONE,* Th, 84, USA, Dir; *A CHRISTMAS STORY,* Th, 83, CDN/USA, Dir/Co-Prod (**GENIE**); *PORKY'S II - THE NEXT DAY* (CHEZ PORKY II-LE LENDEMAIN), Th, 82, CDN, Dir/Co-Prod; *PORKY'S* (CHEZ PORKY), Th, 81, CDN, Dir/Co-Prod; *TRIBUTE,* Th, 80, CDN, Dir/Co-Prod; *MURDER BY DECREE,* Th, 79, CDN, Dir/Co-Prod (**GENIE**); *BREAKING POINT,* Th, 76, CDN/USA, Dir; *BLACK CHRISTMAS* (SILENT NIGHT, EVIL NIGHT), Th, 74, CDN, Dir/Co-Prod; *DEATH DREAM,* Th, 72, CDN, Dir/Prod; *CHILDREN SHOULDN'T PLAY WITH DEAD THINGS,* Th, 71, USA, Dir/Prod.

CLOUTIER, Martin
AR. 365 Markham, Ville Mont-Royal, Qué, CAN. Radio-Canada, 1400 blvd. Dorchester est, Montréal, Qué, CAN, H2L 2M2. (514)285-3377.
Types de production et Catégories: TV film-Réal; TV vidéo-Réal.
Types d'oeuvres: Drame-TV; Documentaire-TV; Animation-TV; Nouvelles-TV.
Curriculum vitae: Né en 1953, Montréal, Québec. Bac., Adm. des Affaires, Université de Moncton, 75. Réalisateur radio, 74-76; réalisateur TV depuis 76; réalisateur-coordonnateur du *TELEJOURNAL* depuis juillet 85.
Filmographie sélective: *VISITE PAPALE* (vues aériennes et papemobile), TV, 84, CDN, Réal; *CAMPAGNE ELECTORALE* (3 em), TV, 84-79, CDN, Co-Field Prod; *REFERENDUM 1980,* 'LA REPONSE', TV, 80, CDN, Co-Field Prod; *LE REVEILLON CHEZ GABRIEL LAFOURNAISE* (UN REVEILLON CHEZ LES METIS EN 1875), TV, 78, CDN, Réal dél.

COHEN, Sidney M.
ATPD. 21 Windsor Court Rd., Thornhill, Ont, CAN, L3T 4Y4. (416)886-3808. CBC, Box 14000, Station A, Toronto, Ont, CAN, M4W 1A0. (416)963-5872. Harvey B. Sindle, 400 Madison Ave., New York, NY, USA, 10017. (212)935-5533.
Types of Production & Categories: TV Video-Dir/Prod.
Genres: Variety-TV; News-TV; Game Shows-TV.
Biography: Born 1947, Montreal, Quebec; bilingual. President, S.P.P.L. Productions. Specializes in live or 'live-to-tape' multi-camera productions demanding little or no post-production.
Selective Filmography: *'MIDDAY'* (400 eps), TV, 86/85, CDN, Dir; *'THRILL OF A LIFETIME'* (100 eps), TV, 86-81, CDN/USA, Dir/Creator; *'CANADA AM'* (200 eps), TV, 84-81, CDN, Dir; *FIRST CANADIAN IN SPACE,* 'CANADA AM', TV, 84, CDN, Dir; *FEDERAL ELECTIONS* (3 specials), TV, 84-72, CDN, Dir; *'GUESS WHAT'* (pilot), (150 eps), TV, 84/83, CDN, Prod/Dir; *'JUST KIDDING'* (pilot), (22 eps), TV, 84/83, CDN, Dir; *'DEFINITION'* (30 eps), TV, 83/82, CDN, Dir; *'JUST LIKE MOM'* (130 eps), TV, 83, CDN, Dir; *POLITICAL CONVENTIONS* (4 specials), TV, 82, CDN, Dir; *'THE MAD DASH'* (pilot), (400

(cont/suite)

eps), TV, 81-79, CDN, Dir/Prod/Creator; *'SAY POWWW'* (pilot), (18 weeks), TV, 80/79, USA, Dir; *THE MORE WE GET TOGETHER,* TV, 80, CDN, Dir/Prod/ Creator; *'THE EDITORS'* (pilot), (50 eps), TV, 79-77, CDN, Dir; *'HEALTH FIELD'* (10 eps), TV, 79, USA, Dir; *'IT'S YOUR MOVE'* (390 eps), TV, 79-74, CDN, Dir/Prod; *'THE ART OF COOKING'* (pilot), (390 eps), TV, 76-74, CDN, Dir/Prod; *LEVESQUE IN NEW YORK,* TV, 76, CDN, Dir/Prod; *'PUPPET PEOPLE'* (pilot), (60 eps), TV, 74-72, CDN, Dir/Prod; *'QUESTION PERIOD'* (50 eps), TV, 72/71, CDN, Dir; *LAPORTE MURDER,* TV, 70, CDN, Dir; *TRUDEAU CONVERSATION,* TV, 70, CDN, Dir.

COLE, Janis - see PRODUCERS

COLLIER, Mike

DGC. 1915 West 35th Ave., Vancouver, BC, CAN, V6M 1H1. (604)266-2878. Yaletown Productions Inc., 304 - 990 Homer St., Vancouver, BC, CAN, V6B 2W7. (604)669-3543.
Types of Production & Categories: TV Film-Ed.
Genres: Drama-TV; Documentary-Th&TV; Educational-Th&TV; Industrial-Th&TV.
Biography: Born 1947, London, England; Canadian citizen. Science Degree from Simon Fraser University. 16 years experience in Vancouver's film industry; created special colour tinting for *McCABE AND MRS. MILLER.* Has won over 30 awards for his films including: Gold Award, Chicago; Silver Screen Awards, U.S. Industrial Film Fest..
Selective Filmography: *THE WORLD IN A CITY,* TV, 85, CDN, Dir/Ed; *AN EXCHANGE OF VALUE,* TV, 84, CDN, Dir **(CFTA)**; *SALMON SPECTACULAR,* TV, 82, CDN, Ed; *'HUCK FINN'* (8 eps), TV, 81, CDN, Ed; *VALLEY OF THE GRIZZLY,* In, 80, CDN, Dir/Ed; *WINTER SURVIVAL,* In, 79, CDN, Dir/Ed; *PACIFIC CELEBRATION,* TV, 78, CDN, Dir/Ed; *THE GIFT OF WATER,* In, 76, CDN, Dir/Ed.

COLLINS, Alan

Nova Productions, 43 Metcalfe St., #20, Toronto, Ont, CAN, M4X 1R7. (416)920-8544.
Types of Production & Categories: TV Film-Dir/Ed; TV Video-Dir.
Genres: Drama-TV; Documentary-TV; Educational-TV; Children's-TV.
Biography: Born 1942; Canadian citizen; emigrated to Canada from England, 68. Film and video editor. Won Best Director, North American Indian Film Fest., *BEAUTY OF MY PEOPLE.*
Selective Filmography: *COVERT ACTION,* TV, 86, CDN, Ed; *CITY BLUES,* TV, 86, CDN, Dir/Ed; *OCTOBER STRANGER,* TV, 85, CDN, Dir; *SPIRIT OF TURTLE ISLAND,* TV, 85, CDN, Dir; *THE BROOD,* Th, 79, CDN, Ed; *BEAUTY OF MY PEOPLE,* TV, 78, CDN, Dir; *LOVE AT FIRST SIGHT,* Th, 75, CDN, Ed **(CFEG)**; *VON RICHTHOFEN AND BROWN,* Th, 72, USA, Ed.

CONDIE, Richard

ASIFA. 118 Lindsay St., Winnipeg, Man, CAN, R3N 1G8. (204)489-8182.
Types of Production & Categories: Th Short-Dir/An/Wr.
Genres: Comedy-Th&TV; Educational-Th&TV; Animation-Th&TV; Experimental-Th.
Biography: Born 1942, Vancouver, British Columbia. B.A., University of Manitoba. *THE BIG SNIT* was nominated for an Oscar and won numerous awards at film festivals including: Montreal, Annecy, San Francisco, Krakow, Hiroshima; *GETTING STARTED* won awards at Krakow, Zagreb and a Bijou Award.
Selective Filmography: *THE BIG SNIT,* Th, 85, CDN, Dir/Wr/An/Co-Prod **(GENIE)**; *PIGBIRD,* TV, 81, CDN, Dir/Wr/An/Voice; *GETTING STARTED,* Th, 79, CDN, Dir/Wr/An/Voice **(BIJOU)**; *W.O.MITCHELL: NOVELIST IN*

(cont/suite)

HIDING, TV, 79, CDN, Comp; *JOHN LAW AND THE MISSISSIPPI BUBBLE,* ED, 78-76, CDN, Dir/An/Co-Wr; *'SESAME STREET'* (sev seg), TV, 75/74, USA, Dir/Wr/An.

COOK, R. David - see PRODUCERS

CORNELLIER, Robert

ARRFQ, ARRQ. 20 rue St-Jean, Val d'Or, Qué, CAN, J9P 5R2. (819)824-6362.
Types de production et Catégories: c métrage-Réal/Prod/Sc; TV film-Réal/Prod/Sc; TV vidéo-Réal/Prod/Mont.
Types d'oeuvres: Drame-C; Documentaire-C&TV.
Curriculum vitae: Né en 1955, Montréal, Québec. Etudes à l'Université Concordia, 76-78. *LA FUITE* remporte le Gerbe d'Or au Yorkton Short Film & Video Festival, 85 et fut la sélection officielle de l'I.N.P.U.T., Montréal, 86.
Filmographie sélective: *'CAMERA UN'* (54 eps), TV, 86-83, CDN, Prod dél/Réal; *LA FUITE,* C, 85, CDN, Réal/Sc; *LA SUITE ABITIBIENNE,* TV, 84, CDN, Réal; *A PROPOS DE LA SUITE...,* TV, 84, CDN, Réal; *POLLUTION A ROUYN NORANDA/PARC AIGUEBELLE,* 'LE POINT', TV, 84, CDN, Réal/Mont; *DANSENDURANCE,* 'LE POINT', TV, 84, CDN, Prod/Mont; *UN CIBO CIRE,* TV, 83, CDN, Réal; *UNE UNIVERSITE INACHEVEE,* TV, 82, CDN, Réal; *LA CABALE,* C, 80, CDN, Prod/Réal/Sc; *UNE AUTRE HISTOIRE DES PAYS D'EN HAUT,* C, 77, CDN, Prod/Réal/Sc.

CORRIVEAU, Raymond

ARRQ. 420 chemin St-Onge, St-Boniface, Qué, CAN, G0X 2L0. (819)535-3619.
Types de production et Catégories: TV film-Réal; TV vidéo-Réal.
Types d'oeuvres: Documentaire-TV; Education-TV; Affaires publiques-TV.
Curriculum vitae: Né en 1950. Bac. en Communications, Université Concordia, 74; Maitrise en Communications, 82; scolarité de Doctorat, Université McGill, 85; rédaction de la thèse de Doctorat, 85. Stages d'études à New York et en France; expositions solo de photographie.
Filmographie sélective: *LE BETE A SEPT TETES,* TV, 81, CDN, Réal; *LE PARMINOU, UN THEATRE DE CORDE A LINGE,* TV, 80, CDN, Réal; *ON NE PERDRA PAS TOUT LE TEMPS,* TV, 80, CDN, Réal; *M'ENTENDEZ-VOUS BIEN?,* TV, 80, CDN, Réal; *UNE PISTE POUR LE PLEIN AIR,* TV, 80, CDN, Réal; *UNE JOURNEE TROP LONGUE,* TV, 79, CDN, Réal; *A LA CAMPAGNE,* TV, 77, CDN, Réal; *CHANGER POUR SURVIVRE,* TV, 77, CDN, Réal; *'AU COEUR DU QUEBEC'* (3 eps), TV, 76, CDN, Réal.

COSMATOS, George P.

DGA, DGC. Rand Holston, CAA, 1888 Century Park East, Los Angeles, CA, USA. (213)277-4545.
Types of Production & Categories: Th Film-Dir/Prod/Wr.
Genres: Drama-Th; Action-Th; Horror-Th; Commercials-TV.
Biography: Born 1941; Canadian citizen; speaks 6 languages fluently; educated at London Film School; University of London (International Affairs). Victoria Film Commissioner; Grand Prize for *OF UNKNOWN ORIGIN,* Paris Film Fest., 83.
Selective Filmography: *COBRA,* Th, 86, USA, Dir; *RAMBO - FIRST BLOOD PART II,* Th, 84, USA, Dir; *OF UNKNOWN ORIGIN,* Th, 82, CDN, Dir; *ESCAPE TO ATHENA* (GOLDEN RAIDERS), Th, 79, GB, Dir/Co-Story; *THE CASSANDRA CROSSING,* Th, 75, GB/D/I, Dir/Co-Wr/Co-Story; *MASSACRE IN ROME,* Th, 73, I/F, Co-Wr/Dir; *BELOVED* (RESTLESS), Th, 69, GB, Prod/Wr/Dir.

COTE, François J.

AR. 4223 Marcil, Montréal, Qué, CAN, H4A 2Z7. (514)481-8385. SDA Productions, 1221 Hôtel de Ville, Montréal, Qué, CAN. (514)866-1761.

(cont/suite)

Types de production et Catégories: TV vidéo-Réal.
Types d'oeuvres: Drame-TV; Education-TV; Enfants-TV; Annonces-TV.
Curriculum vitae: Né en 1946 à Québec. Bac., Université de Montréal, 66.
Monteur de film, 67-69; réalisateur d'annonces, 69-74; directeur de la production, JPL Productions, 74-77; réalisateur pigiste depuis 79; travaille en anglais et en français.
Filmographie sélective: *'A PLEIN TEMPS'* (56 eps), TV, 86-84, CDN, Réal; *'COURT CIRCUIT'* (15 eps), TV, 84/83, CDN, Réal; *'POP CITROUILLE'* (50 eps), TV, 82-80, CDN, Réal; *'DYNAMIQUE DU LECTEUR'* (3 eps), TV, 82, CDN, Réal; *'TELEJEANS'* (15 eps), TV, 80/79, CDN, Réal; *'PASSE-PARTOUT'* (125 eps), TV, 79-77, CDN, Réal.

COWAN, Paul

574 Clermont Ave., Montreal, Que, CAN, H3Y 2P1. (514)484-4194. NFB, Box 6100, Station A, Montreal, Que, CAN, H3C 3H5.
Types of Production & Categories: TV Film-Dir/Wr/Cam.
Genres: Documentary-Th&TV.
Biography: Born 1947. Has worked on films which have won major awards: *FLAMENCO AT 5:15* won an Oscar; *I'LL GO AGAIN,* Yorkton, Best Editing; *GOING THE DISTANCE,* Oscar nomination, 1st Prize, Int'l Torino Sportfilm Festival.
Selective Filmography: *DEMOCRACY ON TRIAL: THE TERRY RYAN AFFAIR,* TV, 86, CDN, Dir/Wr; *AFTER THE CRASH/UNDER THE INFLUENCE,* 'AT THE WHEEL', TV, 85, USA, Dir/Wr/Cam; *DEMOCRACY ON TRIAL: THE MORGENTALER AFFAIR,* TV, 84, CDN, Dir/Cam/Ed/Co-Prod; *ANYBODY'S SON WILL DO/ THE DEADLY GAME OF NATIONS,* 'WAR', TV, 83, USA, Dir/Cam; *FLAMENCO AT 5:15,* Th, 83, CDN, DOP; *THE KID WHO COULDN'T MISS,* TV, 82, CDN, Dir/Wr/Ed/Cam; *STAGES,* TV, 80, CDN, Dir/Wr/Cam; *GOIND THE DISTANCE* (EDMONTON...ET COMMENT S'Y RENDRE), TV, 79, CDN, Dir/Wr/Co-Ed/Cam; *I'LL GO AGAIN,* TV, 78, CDN, Dir/Wr/Ed/Cam; *COACHES,* TV, 76, CDN, Dir/Wr.

CRONENBERG, David

DGC. David Cronenberg Prod., 217 Avenue Rd., Toronto, Ont, CAN, M5R 2J3. (416)961-3432. Mike Marcus, CAA, 1888 Century Park East, Los Angeles, CA, USA, 90067. (213)277-4545.
Types of Production & Categories: Th Film-Dir/Wr.
Genres: Drama-Th.
Selective Filmography: *THE FLY,* Th, 86, USA, Dir/Co-Scr; *THE DEAD ZONE,* Th, 83, USA, Dir; *VIDEODROME,* Th, 82, CDN, Wr/Dir (GENIE); *SCANNERS,* Th, 80, CDN, Dir/Wr; *THE BROOD,* Th, 79, CDN, Dir/Wr; *FAST COMPANY,* Th, 78, CDN, Dir/Co-Scr; *RABID* (RAGE), Th, 76, CDN, Dir; *THE PARASITE MURDERS* (SHIVERS), (THEY CAME FROM WITHIN), Th, 75, CAN, Dir/Wr; *CRIMES OF THE FUTURE,* Th, 70, CDN, Dir/Wr; *STEREO,* Th, 69, CDN, Dir/Wr.

CZURKO, Edward

9 Winfield Ave., Toronto, Ont, CAN, M6S 2J7. (416)762-6732.
Types of Production & Categories: Th Short-Dir/Wr/Cam/Prod; TV Film-Dir/Cam/Prod.
Genres: Drama-Th&TV; Comedy-Th; Documentary-Th&TV; Children's-Th&TV.
Biography: Born 1922, Poland; Canadian citizen. M.A., Fine Arts, Pwstif in Lodz. Writer, director, cinematographer of 30 screen hours of fiction and documentary. In Poland, he won awards for his films at various festivals; freelancing in Canada since 78.
Selective Filmography: *THE YOUTH WITH A VIOLIN,* Th, 82, CDN, Dir/Prod/Cam; *A SIMPLE COMPLEX,* Th, 78, CDN, Co-Wr/DOP; *FLYING TOY,* TV, 78,

(cont/suite)

CDN, Dir/Prod/Cam; *SUMMER JOY*, TV, 78, CDN, Dir/Prod/Cam; *OPTIMIST*, TV, 78, CDN, Dir/Prod/Cam; *LET'S TALK ABOUT COMPUTERS*, Th, 75, PL, Dir/Wr/Cam; *KORAL*, Th, 74, PL, Dir/Wr/Cam; *AND THERE ARE 365 DAYS*, Th, 71, PL, Dir/Wr; *LEON KRUCZKOVSKI*, Th, 70, PL, Dir/Co-Wr; *JOZEF KOSTRZEVSKI*, Th, 69, PL, Dir/Wr/Cam; *THE OLD TOWER*, Th, 67, PL, Dir/Wr/Cam; *SCULPTURE OF RENAISSANCE*, Th, 67, PL, Dir/Wr; *HIGHWAY NUMBER 15*, Th, 65, PL, Dir/Wr.

D'AIX, Alain

APFQ. 5702 Hutchison, Outremont, Qué, CAN, H2V 4B6. (514)270-5215. InformAction, 1151 Alexandre de Sève, Montréal, Qué, CAN, H2L 2T7. (514)524-7569.
Types de production et Catégories: l métrage-Réal; c métrage-Réal; TV film-Réal.
Types d'oeuvres: Documentaire-C&TV; Affaires publiques-TV; Nouvelles-TV.
Curriculum vitae: Né en 1938. Licence ès Lettres, Sorbonne; Maitrise en Psychologie, Université de Montréal. Correspondant de presse en Afrique (AP), 60-64; enseignement en Communications, Université de Montréal. Président, Les Journées du Cinéma Africain au Québec.
Filmographie sélective: *NOUS PRES, NOUS LOIN*, TV, 86, CDN, Réal; *ZONE DE TURBULENCE*, TV, 84, CDN, Co réal; *MERCENAIRES EN QUETE D'AUTEURS*, TV, 83, CDN, Co réal; *VIVRE EN CREOLE*, C, 82, CDN, Co réal; *COMME UN BATEAU DANS LE CIEL*, C, 81, CDN, Réal; *LE DUR DESIR DE DIRE*, C, 81, CDN, Réal; *RASANBLEMAN*, C, 79, CDN, Co réal; *LA DANSE AVEC L'AVEUGLE*, C, 78, CDN, Co réal; *CONTRE CENSURE*, C, 76, CDN, Co réal; *YVONGELISATION*, C, 73, CDN, Co réal; *TAMS TAMS ET BALAFONS*, C, 72, CDN, Réal; *ANYANYA*, C, 71, CDN, Co réal.

DALE, Holly

P.O. Box 5613, Station A, Toronto, Ont, CAN, M5W 1N8. (416)921-9982. Stan Colbert, The Colbert Agency, 303 Davenport Rd., Toronto, Ont, CAN, M5R 1K5. (416)964-3302.
Types of Production & Categories: Th Film-Dir/Prod/Ed; TV Film-Dir/Prod/Ed.
Genres: Drama-Th; Documentary-Th&TV; Educational-Th&TV.
Biography: Born Toronto, Ontario. *HOOKERS ON DAVIE* won the Gold Plaque, Chicago Film Fest., Red Ribbon, American Film Fest.; *P4W: PRISON FOR WOMEN*, Red Ribbon, Yorkton Film Fest. Awards.
Selective Filmography: *THE MAKING OF AGNES OF GOD* (QUIET ON THE SET FILMING AGNES OF GOD), TV, 85, CDN, Co-Dir/Co-Prod/Co-Ed; *DAY IN THE LIFE OF CANADA, THE DOCUMENTARY* (Tor seg), TV, 84, CDN, Dir; *HOOKERS ON DAVIE*, Th, 84, CDN, Co-Dir/Co-Prod/Co-Ed, *P4W: PRISON FOR WOMEN* (P4W), Th, 81, CDN, Co-Dir/Co-Prod/Co-Ed (**GENIE**); *THIN LINE*, Th, 77, CDN, Co-Dir/Co-Prod/Co-Ed.

DALEN, Zale

DGC. 546 Marine Drive, Site 1, #23, R.R.1, Gibsons, BC, CAN, V0N 1V0. (604)886-8029.
Types of Production & Categories: Th Film-Dir/Ed; TV Film-Dir/Ed.
Genres: Drama-Th&TV; Educational-TV; Children's-TV; Industrial-TV.
Biography: Born 1947, Iloilo, Philippine Islands; Canadian citizen; attended Simon Fraser University; married, 3 children. He won the Wendy Michener Award, 77.
Selective Filmography: *MEMORIES* (EXPO 86), Th, 86, CDN, Dir; *'DANGER BAY'* (2 eps), TV, 85, CDN, Dir; *I'D RATHER WALK*, TV, 84, CDN, Dir/Ed; *'THE EDISON TWINS'* (5 eps), TV, 83, CDN, Dir; *OUT OF SIGHT OUT OF MIND*, 'FOR THE RECORD', TV, 82, CDN, Dir; *BORN TO LOVE*, 'THE WINNERS', TV, 81, CDN, Dir; *THE HOUNDS OF NOTRE DAME*, Th, 80, CDN, Dir; *SKIP TRACER*, Th, 76, CDN, Dir/Wr.

DANE, Lawrence - see PRODUCERS

DIRECTORS/REALISATEURS

DANSEREAU, Fernand

ARRFQ. 4228 Delorimier, Montréal, Qué, CAN, H2H 2B1. (514)524-7879.
Types de production et Catégories: l métrage-Réal; c métrage-Réal; TV film-Réal/Sc; TV vidéo-Réal/Sc.
Types d'oeuvres: Drame-C&TV; Documentaire-C&TV.
Curriculum vitae: Né en 1928. Remporte un prix pour *ALFRED J.* au Festival du Film Ouvrier, Vienne; Prix Grierson, 77.
Filmographie sélective: *'LE PARC DES BRAVES'* (pl ep), TV, 86-84, CDN, Sc; *LES DOUX AVEUX,* C, 82, CDN, Réal; *THETFORD AU MILIEU DE NOTRE VIE,* C, 79, CDN, Réal; *'L'AMOUR QUOTIDIEN'* (pl ep), TV, 77/76, CDN, Réal (ANIK); *SIMPLE HISTOIRE D'AMOUR,* TV, 74, CDN, Réal; *ST-JEROME,* C, 66, CDN, Réal; *CA N'EST PAS LE TEMPS DES ROMANS,* TV, 66, CDN, Réal; *LE FESTIN DES MORTS,* C, 65, CDN, Réal; *POUR LA SUITE DU MONDE,* TV, 63, CDN, Prod (CFA); *'TEMPS PRESENT'* (pl ep), TV, 62-60, CDN, Prod; *LES MAINS NETTES,* TV, 58, CDN, Sc; *ALFRED J.,* TV, 56, CDN, Sc.

DANSEREAU, Mireille

ARRFQ. 725 Rockland, Montréal, Qué, CAN, H2V 2Z7. (514)279-9114.
Types de production et Catégories: l métrage-Réal/Sc; TV film-Réal/Sc.
Types d'oeuvres: Drame-C&TV; Documentaire-TV.
Curriculum vitae: Née en 1943, Montréal, Québec. Langues: français, anglais, espagnol. Maitrise, Royal College of Art, Londres; 18 ans de danse classique et jazz. A travaillé à l'ONF, Radio-Canada, Radio-Québec. *LA VIE REVEE* remporte le Prix du Meilleur Film, San Francisco. Elle remporte le Prix Wendy Michener, 72.
Filmographie sélective: *LE SOURD DANS LA VILLE,* C, 86, CDN, Réal; *LE FRERE ANDRE,* TV, 82, CDN, Réal/Sc; *UN PAYS A COMPRENDRE,* TV, 81, CDN, Réal/Sc; *GERMAINE GUEVREMONT,* 'VISAGE', TV, 80, CDN, Réal/Sc; *L'ARRACHE-COEUR,* C, 79, CDN, Réal/Sc; *FAMILLE ET VARIATIONS,* TV, 77, CDN, Réal/Sc; *RAPPELLE-TOI,* TV, 76, CDN, Co réal; *THE BASEMENT,* C, 74, CDN, Co prod; *LE PERE IDEAL,* TV, 74, CDN, Réal; *J'ME MARIE, J'ME MARIE PAS,* 'EN TANT QUE FEMMES', TV, 73, CDN, Réal/Sc; *LA VIE REVEE,* C, 72, CDN, Réal/Sc; *FORUM,* C, 69, GB, Réal; *COMPROMISE,* C, 69, GB, Réal/Sc; *MOI, UN JOUR,* C, 67, CDN, Réal/Sc.

DARCUS, Jack

ACTRA. Exile Productions Ltd., 1848 West 5th Ave., Vancouver, BC, CAN, V6J 1P3. (604)731-2503.
Types of Production & Categories: Th Film-Dir/Prod/Wr.
Genres: Drama-Th.
Biography: Born 1941, Vancouver, British Columbia. Graduate of University of British Columbia (Art History and Philosophy); trained as a visual artist at UBC, Vancouver School of Art. Began career as a painter; several solo exhibitions.
Selective Filmography: *OVERNIGHT,* Th, 85, CDN, Dir/Wr/Prod; *DESERTERS,* Th, 83, CDN, Dir/Wr/Prod; *WOLFPEN PRINCIPLE,* Th, 73, CDN, Dir/Wr; *PROXY HAWKS,* Th, 72, CDN, Dir/Prod/Wr; *GREAT COUPS OF HISTORY,* Th, 70, CDN, Dir/Wr/Prod.

DAVIDSON, William

ACTRA, DGC. 1501 Woodbine Ave., PM26, Toronto, Ont, CAN, M4C 4H1. (416)421-9906.
Types of Production & Categories: Th Film-Dir/Prod/Wr; Th Short-Dir/Prod/Wr; TV Film-Dir/Prod/Wr; TV Video-Dir/Prod.
Genres: Drama-Th&TV; Comedy-Th&TV; Documentary-Th&TV; Educational-TV.
Biography: Born Toronto, Ontario, 1928. Lorne Greene's Academy of Radio Arts, 48; University of Western Ontario, 51. Owner of Klenman-Davidson Productions

(cont/suite)

Ltd., Ivy League Films Ltd., Tower Hill Productions Ltd.; published novel: 'Return to Rainbow Country', 75.
Selective Filmography: *'PROFILES OF NATURE'* (37 eps), TV, 86-84, CDN, Wr; *'NIGHT HEAT'* (2 eps), TV, 86/85, CDN, Wr; *'LITTLEST HOBO'* (5 eps), TV, 80, CDN, Wr; *'MATT AND JENNY'* (Wr-8 eps), (26 eps), TV, 79, CDN/GB/D, Prod; *SHAPE OF THINGS TO COME*, Th, 78, CDN, Prod; *NEVER THE SAME AGAIN*, TV, 75, CDN, Wr; *LIONS FOR BREAKFAST*, Th, 74, CDN, Dir; *'ALMOST HOME'* (9 eps), TV, 74/73, CDN, Wr; *'THE STARLOST'* (16 eps), TV, 73, CDN, Prod; *'THE LAW AND WHERE IT'S AT'* (21 eps), TV, 73-71, CDN, Wr; *'ADVENTURES IN RAINBOW COUNTRY'* (Prod-26 eps/Dir-3 eps/ Wr-4 eps), TV, 69, CDN/GB/AUS, Prod/Dir/Wr; *'FOREST RANGERS'* (Prod-26 eps/Wr-5 eps/Dir-1 ep), TV, 65, CDN, Prod/Wr/Dir; *'TIME OF YOUR LIFE'* (Exec Prod-100 eps/Dir-13 eps), TV, 65-62, CDN, Exec Prod/Dir; *'RAZZLE DAZZLE'* (Exec Prod-600 eps/Dir-200 eps), TV, 64-61, CDN, Exec Prod/Dir; *IVY LEAGUE KILLERS* (THE FAST ONES), Th, 59/58, CDN, Dir/Co-Prod; *NOW THAT APRIL'S HERE*, Th, 58, CDN, Dir/Co-Prod; *A HOME OF THEIR OWN*, Th, 57, CDN, Dir/Co-Prod; *'GRAPHIC'* (26 eps), TV, 57/56, CDN, Dir; *THE HOAX/THE CURLERS*, 'STORIES FROM A SMALL TOWN', TV, 55/54, CDN, Dir; *PREPARE FOR ADVANCEMENT*, Th, 54, CDN, Dir/Wr; *STATION MASTER/COUNTRY AUCTIONEER*, 'FACES OF CANADA', Th, 53, CDN, Dir/Wr.

DAVIS, Bill

DGA, PGA. 330 South Las Palmas Ave., Los Angeles, CA, USA, 90020. (213)935-5289. CAA, 1888 Century Pk.E., Ste. 1400, Los Angeles, CA, USA, 90069. (213) 277-4545.
Types of Production & Categories: TV Film-Dir; TV Video-Dir/Prod.
Genres: Comedy-TV; Variety-TV; Musical-TV.
Biography: Born 1931, Belleville, Ontario; Canadian citizen; US resident. Graduate, Ryerson Polytechnical Institute. Began career, CBC, Toronto prior to broadcast in 52; moved to New York, 65, then Los Angeles, 67. Married, 2 children. TV shows he has directed have won many awards including 2 Silver Rose at Montreux, Christopher Award.
Selective Filmography: *'TV BLOOPERS & PRACTICAL JOKES'* (62 eps), TV, 86-84, USA, Dir; *GLEN CAMPBELL 25th ANNIVERSARY*, TV, 84, USA, Dir; *'PAUL ANKA'*, TV, 84, CDN, Dir; *DEMOCRATIC NATIONAL TELETHON*, TV, 83, USA, Dir; *NATIONAL SNOOP* (pilot), TV, 83, USA, Dir; *JOHNNY CASH SPECIAL*, TV, 83, USA, Dir; *JOEL GREY LIVE*, TV, 83, USA, Dir; *SOLD OUT* (LILY TOMLIN IN VEGAS), TV, 83, USA, Dir (**EMMY**); *THE CARPENTERS SPECIAL*, TV, 82, USA, Dir; *'CHER'*, TV, 82/81, USA, Dir; *JOHN DENVER SPECIAL* (7 shows), TV, 81-76, USA, Dir (**EMMY**); *'THE JACKSONS'*, TV, 79, USA, Prod/Dir; *SUPERSTUNT* (3 shows), TV, 78-76, USA, Prod/Dir; *PUZZLE*, TV, 78, USA, Dir; *FRANK SINATRA AND FRIENDS*, TV, 77, USA, Dir; *MARLO THOMAS* (FREE TO BE YOU AND ME), TV, 76, USA, Dir; *'BARNEY MILLER'*, TV, 75, USA, Dir; *BRASS ARE COMIN'* (HERB ALPERT SPECIAL), TV, 74, USA, Dir; *LILY*, TV, 73, USA, Dir; *'JULIE ANDREWS'*, TV, 73/72, USA, Dir (**EMMY**); *'HEE HAW'*, TV, 72-69, USA, Prod/Dir; *'LENNON SISTERS'*, TV, 69, USA, Dir; *'JONATHAN WINTERS'*, TV, 68, USA, Dir; *'THE SMOTHERS BROTHERS'*, TV, 67, USA, Dir; *'HULLABALOO'*, TV, 66/65, USA, Dir; *'WAYNE & SHUSTER HOUR'*, TV, 65/ 64, CDN, Prod/Dir; *'TOMMY AMBROSE SHOW'*, TV, 62, CDN, Dir/Prod; *'JACK KANE SHOW'*, TV, 62-60, CDN, Dir/Prod; *'PARADE'*, TV, 61, CDN, Prod/Dir; *'MUSIC 60'* (HIT PARADE), TV, 60/59, CDN, Prod/Dir.

DEFALCO, Martin

SGCT. 159 Lakeview Ave., Pointe Claire, Que, CAN, H9S 4B9. (514)697-8875. NFB, Box 6100, Montreal, Que, CAN, H3C 3H5. (514)283-9485.

(cont/suite)

Types of Production & Categories: Th Film-Dir; Th Short-Dir; TV Film-Dir/Wr.
Genres: Drama-Th; Documentary-Th&TV; Educational-TV; Children's-TV.
Biography: Born 1933, Ottawa, Ontario. Two terms as a guest lecturer, Stanford University, California; edited 60 dramatic, documentary, TV and educational films.
Selective Filmography: *THE POLITICS OF PERSUASION,* TV, 83, CDN, Dir/ Wr; *THE GARBAGE MOVIE,* ED, 81, CDN, Dir/Wr; *A GREAT LITTLE ARTIST,* TV, 78, CDN, Dir/Wr; *OTHER SIDE OF THE LEDGES,* TV, 73, CDN, Co-Dir; *COLD JOURNEY,* Th, 71, CDN, Dir/Story; *DON MESSER: HIS LAND AND HIS MUSIC,* Th, 70, CDN, Dir/Prod; *TRAWLER FISHERMAN,* TV, 70, CDN, Dir; *WHAT IN THE WORLD IS WATER,* ED, 68, CDN, Dir; *CHARLIE'S DAY,* ED, 65, CDN, Dir; *NORTHERN FISHERMAN,* TV, 63, CDN, Dir/Wr; *BIRD OF PASSAGE,* ED, 60, CDN, Dir.

DENNIS, Charles

ACTRA, WGAw. Fred Milstein, William Morris Agency, 151 El Camino Dr., Beverly Hills, CA, USA, 90212. (213)859-4423.
Types of Production & Categories: Th Film-Dir/Wr; TV Film-Dir/Wr.
Genres: Drama-Th&TV; Comedy-Th.
Biography: Born 1946, Toronto, Ontario. B.A., University of Toronto. Columnist, 'Toronto Telegram', 64-67. Created series *MARKED PAST TENSE PERSONAL* for Thames TV, England (74-76). Author: 'Shar-li', 'The Dealmakers', 'Bonfire', 'This War is Closed Until Spring', 'A Divine Case of Murder'; has also written for the stage: 'Significant Others', 'Altman's Last Stand', 'Leslie and Lajos'.
Selective Filmography: *'ADDERLY'* (1 eps), TV, 86, CDN, Dir/Wr; *FINDERS KEEPERS,* Th, 84, USA, Co-Scr; *RENO AND THE DOC,* Th, 84, CDN, Dir/Wr/ Act; *COVER GIRLS,* Th, 82, CDN, Wr/Act; *THE JAYNE MANSFIELD STORY,* TV, 80, USA, Wr; *MIRROR, MIRROR,* TV, 80, USA, Co-Wr; *DOUBLE NEGATIVE,* Th, 79, CDN, Co-Wr.

DENSHAM, Pen - see PRODUCERS

DESBIENS, André

AR. 10342 Berri, Montréal, Qué, CAN, H3L 2G8. (514)387-3416. Radio-Canada, 1400 blvd. Dorchester est, Montréal, Qué, CAN, H2L 2M2. (514)285-3001.
Types de production et Catégories: TV film-Réal; TV vidéo-Réal.
Types d'oeuvres: Variété-TV; Documentaire-TV; Affaires publiques-TV.
Curriculum vitae: Né en 1937. Expériences: monteur, régisseur de plateau, divers reportages (actualités, politiques, visites officielles).
Filmographie sélective: *'WINSTON MCQUADE RECOIT'* (hebdo), TV, 80-77, CDN, Réal; *'L'HEURE DE POINTE'* (hebdo), TV, 79/78, CDN, Réal; *'LA SEMAINE VERTE'* (hebdo), TV, 78-74, CDN, Réal.

DESBIENS, Francine

ASIFA, SGCT. 4430 St-André, Montréal, Que, CAN, H2J 2Z4. ONF, 3155 Cote de Liesse, Montréal, Que, CAN, H4N 2N4. (514)283-9295.
Types de production et Catégories: c métrage-Réal/Prod.
Types d'oeuvres: Animation-C.
Curriculum vitae: Née en 1938, Montréal, Québec. Diplômée de l'Institut des Arts Appliqués; prix à Téhéran et Bilbao, *LES BIBITES DE CHROMAGNON.*
Filmographie sélective: *AH! VOUS DIRAIS-JE, MAMAN,* C, 85, CDN, Réal; *L'ART DU CINEMA D'ANIMATION,* TV, 82, CDN, Réal; *VIVRE EN COULEURS,* C, 81, CDN, Prod; *LUNA, LUNA, LUNA,* C, 81, CDN, Prod; *COGNE-DUR,* C, 79, CDN, Prod; *MOI JE PENSE* (THIS IS ME), C, 79, CDN, Prod; *LA PLAGE,* C, 78, CDN, Prod; *DERNIER ENVOL,* C, 77, CDN, Réal; *CHERIE OTE TES RAQUETTES,* C, 75, CDN, Prod; *DU COQ A L'ANE,* C, 73, CDN, Réal; *LES BIBITES DE CHROMAGNON,* C, 71, CDN, Réal; *LE CORBEAU ET LE RENARD,* C, 69, CDN, Réal.

DESCHENES, Clément
ARRQ. B.P. 40, Cascapedia, Co.Bonaventure, Qué, CAN, G0C 1T0. (418)759-3514.
Types de production et Catégories: TV vidéo-Réal/Sc.
Types d'oeuvres: Documentaire-TV.
Curriculum vitae: Né en 1947, St-Jean Port-Joli, Québec. Bac. en Anthropologie et formation en journalisme.
Filmographie sélective: *'INTER ACTION'* (26 eps), TV, 86/85, CDN, Réal; *REGIONALISATION/UTOPIE/GASPE-NORD/MUSEE DE LA GASPESIE,* 'INTER ACTION', TV, 86/85, CDN, Réal; *LES ANCIENS/LA RENCONTRE DE 2 MONDES/LE DRAME MIC MAC,* 'INDIENS DE LA MER', TV, 85/84, CDN, Rech/Interv; *LE PAYS MIC MAC,* 'INDIENS DE LA MER', TV, 85/84, CDN, Rech/Textes/Interv; *LES ANNEES DIFFICILES/LES MIC MAC AUJOURD'HUI,* 'LES INDIENS DE LA MER', TV, 85/84, CDN, Rech/Interv; *LES RELIGIEUSES,* TV, 83, CDN, Sc; *PLACE AUX JEUNES,* TV, 83, CDN, Rech/Interv.

DEVINE, David - see PRODUCERS

DINEL, Pierre
APFVQ, ARRFQ. Les Films D'ici inc., 516 Rivière Nord, St-Roch de l'Achigan, Qué, CAN, J0K 3H0. (514)588-4883.
Types de production et Catégories: c métrage-Réal/Sc; TV film-Réal/Prod/Sc; TV vidéo-Réal/Sc.
Types d'oeuvres: Documentaire-C&TV; Education-C&TV.
Curriculum vitae: Né en 1952, Montréal, Québec; bilingue.
Filmographie sélective: *SAFARI-ZOOPSI,* MV, 86, CDN, Réal; *HORS-MOUANE,* ED, 86, CDN, Réal; *'CITE DES JEUNES'* (1 eps), TV, 85, CDN, Réal; *TERRE DES POISSONS BLANCS,* C, 85, CDN, Sc; *LA RAQUETTE MONTAGNEUSE,* 'METIERS TRADITIONNELS', TV, 84, CDN, Prod dél; *'LES SIX SAISONS ATTIKAMUKS'* (6 eps), TV, 83/82, CDN, Prod/Réal/Sc; *LA TRAPPE,* ED, 83, CDN, Réal; *'CONNAISSANCE DU MILIEU'* (5 eps), TV, 80, CDN, Ass réal; *OUKAIKON, LE TEMPS DES ERABLES,* C, 78, CDN, Prod/Réal; *'PLANETE'* (21 eps), TV, 77, CDN, Rech; *'CINEASTE A L'ECRAN'* (13 eps), TV, 77, CDN, Rech.

DODD, Thomas
ACTT, DGC. 10533 -74 Ave., Edmonton, Alta, CAN, T6E 5M9. (403)433-9042.
Types of Production & Categories: TV Film-Dir/Prod/Wr; TV Video-Dir/Prod/Wr.
Genres: Drama-TV; Documentary-Th&TV; Educational-TV; Children's-TV.
Biography: Born 1944, New Westminster, British Columbia; graduated from BCIT, Communication Studies. Worked at BBC, 8 years, Granada TV, Manchester. *AT THE CROSSROADS* has won Awards of Excellence and Merit: AMPIA, AMTEC, ACE.
Selective Filmography: *ALBERTA BEEF,* In, 86, CDN, Prod/Wr; *THE SALT WOES,* ED, 86, CDN, Dir/Prod/Wr; *THE RIGHT AMOUNT,* TV, 86, CDN, Dir/Prod/Wr; *AT THE CROSSROADS,* TV, 85, CDN, Dir/Prod; *A MATTER OF SOIL/PEST WARS,* ED, 85/83, CDN, Dir/Prod/Wr; *THE WEATHER PICTURE,* ED, 84, CDN, Dir/Prod/Wr; *PRECONDITIONING,* Th, 84, CDN, Dir/Prod/Wr; *IMPROVING THE ODDS,* TV, 83, CDN, Dir/Prod/Wr; *ENERGY FROM THE PEACE,* Th, 80, CDN, Dir/Prod/Wr/Narr; *'ENERGY B.C.'* (4 short films), In, 79-78, CDN, Dir/Prod/Wr; *'THE INVENTORS'* (7 eps), TV, 76, GB, Dir/Prod; *'KIDS AND US',* TV, 76, GB, Dir/Prod; *'SECOND PROFILE'* (10 eps), TV, 75, GB, Dir; *'PERSPECTIVE'* (5 eps), TV, 75, GB, Dir/Prod; *DENIS LOW,* TV, 75, GB, Dir; *'GRANADA REPORTS',* TV, 74, GB, Dir; *WEARDALE,* TV, 74, GB, Dir; *'THE FARMING PROGRAM',* TV, 74, GB, Dir; *'PEBBLE MILLCONE',* TV, 73, GB, Studio Dir; *'JOURNEY THROUGH SUMMER'* (6 eps), TV, 73/72, GB, Dir; *'POINTS WEST',* TV, 71, GB, Dir.

DOLAN, Marianne
DGC. Tumbling CLoud Prod., 133 Hazelton Ave., Toronto, Ont, CAN, M5R 2E4. (416)928-0164.
Types of Production & Categories: Th Short-Dir/Prod/Wr/Ed; TV Video-Dir/Prod/Wr/Ed.
Genres: Documentary-Th&TV; Children's-TV; Experimental-Th&TV; Music Video-TV.
Biography: Born 1942, Marion, Indiana; landed Canadian immigrant, 70; B.A., University of Dallas, Texas, 64. Special interest in long form new age music videos.
Selective Filmography: *SESAME STREET'* (6 seg), TV, 85, CDN, Dir/Ed/Wr; *EXCURSION,* MV, 85, CDN, Dir/Prod/Ed; *'OWL TV'* (15 seg), TV, 84, CDN, Wr; *'THE CANADIANS'* (13 eps), TV, 74, CDN, Ed; *'TODAY SHOW'* (1 seg), TV, 73, USA, Prod/Dir/Ed; *NEWS FEATURES* (100), TV, 73-71, USA, Dir/Wr; *DAMAGES,* Th, 72, USA, Prod/Dir/Wr/Ed; *ZINC OINTMENT,* Th, 71, CDN, Wr/Dir/Ed; *AN AFTERNOON WITH ABBIE HOFFMAN,* Th, 70, USA, Prod/Ed; *THE TEXAS POP FESTIVAL,* Th, 69, USA, Prod/Ed.

DONOVAN, Paul
P.O. Box 2261, Stn. M, Halifax, N.S., CAN, B3J 3L8. (902)423-0646.
Types of Production & Categories: Th Film-Dir/Wr.
Genres: Drama-Th; Comedy-Th; Action-Th; Science Fiction-Th.
Biography: Born 1954, Canada; B.Sc., Physics; graduate of London Film School. Best Script and Critics' Prize, 13th Festival International du Film Fantastique de Paris for *SIEGE.*
Selective Filmography: *DEFCON 4,* Th, 84, CDN, Dir/Wr; *SIEGE* (SELF DEFENSE), Th, 82, CDN, Co-Dir/Wr; *SOUTH PACIFIC 1942* (TORPEDOED), Th, 80, CDN, Dir/Wr.

DORMEYER, James
AR. 3508 Clark, Montréal, Qué, CAN, H2X 2R8. (514)849-7929. Radio-Canada, 1400 blvd. Dorchester est, Montréal, Qué, CAN, H2L 2M2. (514)285-3555.
Types de production et Catégories: TV film-Réal; TV vidéo-Réal.
Types d'oeuvres: Drame-TV; Variété-TV; Enfants-TV; Expérimental-TV.
Curriculum vitae: Né en 1936, Commercy, France; canadien. Langues: français, anglais, espagnol. Baccalauréat en Philosophie; diplôme de l'Institut des Hautes Etudes Cinématographiques, Paris, 59. *PREVERT, ROSE OU BLEU?*, Sélection canadienne pour le Prix Italia et gagne le Golden A Award, New York.
Filmographie sélective: *LE CONTE DE L'OISEAU,* 'LES BEAUX DIMANCHES', TV, 83, CDN, Réal/Conc (ANIK); *A VOIX BASSE,* 'LES BEAUX DIMANCHES', TV, 81, CDN, Réal/Adapt; *PREVERT, ROSE OU BLEU?,* 'L'ENFANCE A VIVRE', TV, 79, CDN, Réal/Conc (ANIK); *NOUS N'IRONS PLUS AU BOIS,* 'L'ENFANCE A VIVRE', TV, 79, CDN, Réal/Conc; *JOURNAL EN IMAGES FROIDES/ LA ROSE DES SABLES/ LE TEMPS DEVANT,* 'SCENARIO', TV, 78-76, CDN, Réal; *CONNEXION,* TV, 75, CDN, Réal/Conc; *LA SUPERFRANCOFETE* (Réal-2 ém/Coord pro-1 ém), TV, 75/74, CDN, Réal/Coord pro; *'TELECHROME'* (hebdo), TV, 74-71, CDN, Réal/Conc; *'GRUJOT ET DELICAT'* (hebdo), TV, 70/69, CDN, Réal; *LE FRANBECOIS,* TV, 69, CDN, Réal; *'AUJOURD'HUI'* (10 eps), TV, 68, CDN, Réal; *'FEMMES D'AUJOURD'HUI'* (3 eps), TV, 68, CDN, Réal; *'DU FEU S'IL VOUS PLAIT'* (3 eps), TV, 68, CDN, Réal; *SPECIAL JEUNESSE OBLIGE,* TV, 67, CDN, Réal; *CINQ JEUNES UN JOUR,* TV, 66, CDN, Réal/Mont.

DUBHE, Thérèse
AR. 6754 Drolet, Montréal, Qué, CAN, H2S 2T2. (514)273-0791. Radio-Canada, 1400 blvd. Dorchester est, Montréal, Qué, CAN, H2L 2M2. (514)285-3020.
Types de production et Catégories: TV vidéo-Réal.

(cont/suite)

Types d'oeuvres: Drame-TV; Education-TV; Enfants-TV.
Filmographie sélective: *'AU JOUR LE JOUR'* (pl seg), TV, 86, CDN, Réal; *'BOBINO'* (quot), TV, 85-75, CDN, Réal; *'CETTE NUIT LA'* (10 eps), TV, 80, CDN, Réal; *'DONALD LAUTREC SHOW'* (1 eps), TV, 70, CDN, Réal.

DUCKWORTH, Martin
ARRFQ, STCQ. 4618 rue Jeanne Mance, Montreal, Que, CAN, H2V 4J4. (514) 849-4060.
Types of Production & Categories: Th Short-Dir/Cam; TV Film-Dir/Cam.
Genres: Drama-Th&TV; Documentary-Th&TV; Educational-TV; Experimental-Th&TV.
Biography: Born 1933, Montreal, Quebec; raised in Halifax, Nova Scotia; B.A., Yale Universtiy; M.A., University of Toronto. Director of Extension at Mt. Allison U., New Brunswick, 58-63; staff cameraman, NFB, 63-70; now freelance cameraman, director. *NO MORE HIROSHIMA* won a Genie and awards at Leipzig, Tokyo, Cracow film festivals.
Selective Filmography: *RETURN TO DRESDEN* (RETOUR A DRESDEN), TV, 86, CDN, Dir/Ed; *CANADIAN ASTRONAUTS,* TV, 85, CDN, Cam; *NO MORE HIROSHIMA* (PLUS JAMAIS HIROSHIMA), Th, 83, CDN, Dir/Cam; *FALASHA,* TV, 83, CDN, Cam; *BACK TO KAMPUCHEA* (ON L'APPELAIT CAMBODGE), TV, 82, CDN, Dir/Cam; *THE NEW SHAMANS,* TV, 82, CDN, Cam; *A TIME TO RISE,* TV, 81, CDN, Cam; *MAGIC IN THE SKY,* TV, 81, CDN, Cam; *BILL LEE,* TV, 81, CDN, Cam; *A WIVES' TALE* (UNE HISTOIRE DE FEMMES), TV, 80, CDN, Co-Dir/Cam; *BLUE LINE BLUES,* TV, 80, CDN, Cam; *CONNECTIONS: AN INVESTIGATION INTO ORGANIZED CRIME,* TV, 79, CDN, Cam; *12,000 MEN,* TV, 78, CDN, Dir/Cam; *L'INTERDIT,* Th, 76, CDN, Cam; *TEMISCAMINGUE, QUEBEC,* TV, 75, CDN, Dir/Cam/Ed; *IL N'Y A PAS D'OUBLI,* TV, 75, CDN, Cam; *LES DEUX COTES DE LA MEDAILLE,* TV, 74, CDN, Cam; *LA RICHESSE DES AUTRES,* Th, 73, CDN, Cam; *ACCIDENT,* Th, 73, CDN, Dir/Cam/Ed; *LE BONHOMME,* Th, 72, CDN, Cam; *CELL 16,* Th, 71, CDN, Dir/Cam/Ed; *PANDORA,* Th, 71, CDN, Cam; *THE WISH,* Th, 70, CDN, Dir/Cam; *HALF-HALF-THREE-QUARTERS-FULL,* Th, 70, CDN, Co-Dir/Cam; *SAD SONG OF YELLOW SKIN,* TV, 70, CDN, Cam; *UNTOUCHED AND PURE,* Th, 70, CDN, Co Dir/Cam; *PASSING THROUGH SWEDEN,* TV, 69, CDN, Dir/Cam; *CHRISTOPHER'S MOVIE MATINEE,* Th, 68, CDN, Cam; *THE ERNIE GAME,* Th, 67, CDN, Cam; *FLIGHT,* Th, 67, CDN, Cam.

DUFFELL, Greg
ACTRA, ACTT. 47 Oakwood Cres., Scarborough, Ont, CAN, M1K 3T7. (416) 755-1741. Lightbox Studios Inc., 345 Adelaide St. W., #300, Toronto, Ont, CAN, M5V 1R5. (416)591-1687.
Types of Production & Categories: Th Film-Dir/An/Wr; TV Film-Dir/An/Wr.
Genres: Animation-Th&TV.
Biography: Born 1955, Toronto, Ontario. Trained at Richard Williams, Animation, London, England, as apprentice in classical character animation. In 73, returned to Canada, worked on TV commercials; corporate films, USA, 76-77; writer, animator, director, Nelvana, Toronto, 77-82. Opened Lightbox Studios, 83.
Selective Filmography: *DARE COOKIES AND CRACKERS/CREST MAGIC GLASS II,* Cm, 85/84, CDN, An/An Dir; *STRANGE ANIMAL,* MV, 85, CDN, An/An Dir; *A CRIMINAL MIND,* MV, 85/84, CDN, An Dir/Co-An; *'INSPECTOR GADGET'* (Wr-4 eps), (64 eps), TV, 83, CDN, Voice; *ROCK & RULE* (RING OF POWER), Th, 83, CDN, Contr Wr/Voice/Seg An Dir; *STRAWBERRY SHORTCAKE: A HOUSEWARMING SURPRISE,* TV, 82, CDN, Co-An; *EASTER FEVER,* TV, 80/79, CDN, Co-An/Seg An Dir/Co-Wr; *INTERGALACTIC THANKSGIVING* (PLEASE DON'T EAT THE PLANET),

(cont/suite)

TV, 79, CDN, Co-An/Co-Wr; *ROMIE-O & JULIE-8,* TV, 78, CDN, Co-An/Voice; *THE DEVIL & DANIEL MOUSE,* TV, 78, CDN, Co-An; *MAGIC OF CYCOLAC,* In, 77/76, USA, Co-An; *COUGAR SHOES,* Cm, 76, CDN, An/Dir; *'UNDERSEA WORLD OF CAPTAIN NEMO'* (5 eps), TV, 76/75, CDN, Co-An; *12 TASKS OF ASTERIX,* Th, 75, F, Co-An.

DUKE, Daryl

DGA, DGC. CKVU-TV, 180 W. 2nd Ave., Vanvouver, BC, CAN, V5Y 3T9. (604) 876-1344. John Burnham, William Morris Agency, 151 El Camino Dr., Beverly Hills, CA, USA, 90212. (213)274-7451.
Types of Production & Categories: Th Film-Dir/Prod; TV Film-Dir/Prod.
Genres: Drama-Th&TV.
Biography: Graduate of University of British Columbia, (English and Philosophy). Began his career at the NFB, then CBC; directed many feature films. Launched the broadcast operations of CKVU-TV, Vancouver, 76 and is currently Chairman of the Board and Chief Executive Officer. *PAYDAY* won the National Society of Film Critics Award; Emmy Award nomination for *THE THORN BIRDS;* Christopher Award, *I HEARD THE OWL CALL MY NAME.*
Selective Filmography: *TAI-PAN,* Th, 85, USA, Dir; *THE THORN BIRDS* (miniseries), TV, 83/82, USA, Dir; *HARD FEELINGS,* Th, 80, CDN, Dir; *THE SILENT PARTNER,* Th, 77, CDN, Dir (**CFA**); *GRIFFIN LOVES PHOENIX,* TV, 75, USA, Dir; *A CRY FOR HELP,* TV, 74, USA, Dir; *FORTY REASONS TO KILL,* 'HARRY O', TV, 74, USA, Dir; *I HEARD THE OWL CALL MY NAME,* TV, 73, USA, Dir/Prod; *NO SIGN OF THE CROSS,* 'BANACEK', TV, 72, USA, Dir; *DOORWAY TO DEATH,* 'CIRCLE OF FEAR', TV, 72, USA, Dir; *'THE BOLD ONES'* (5 eps), TV, 72-69, USA, Dir; *PAYDAY,* Th, 71, USA, Dir; *THE PRESIDENT'S PLANE IS MISSING,* TV, 71, USA, Dir; *THE DAY THE LION DIED,* 'SENATOR', TV, 70, USA, Dir (**EMMY**); *GOD BLESS THE CHILDREN* (pilot), 'THE PSYCHIATRIST', TV, 70, USA, Dir; *WEST COAST ON MY MIND,* TV, 70, CDN, Dir/Prod; *SPIKE IN THE WALL,* 'THE MANIPULATORS', TV, 69, CDN, Dir; *APPLES OF GOLD IN PICTURES OF SILVER,* TV, 69, CDN, Dir; *'QUENTIN DURGENS, M.P.'* (3 eps), TV, 68, CDN, Dir; *THE CANADIANS IN HOLLYWOOD,* TV, 68, CDN, Dir/Prod; *'SUNDAY'* (weekly), TV, 67/66, CDN, Exec Prod/Dir; *'TELESCOPE'* (4 eps), TV, 66/65, CDN, Dir; *'THE LES CRANE SHOW'* (5/week), TV, 65/64, USA, Dir; *'THE STEVE ALLEN SHOW',* TV, 64, USA, Prod; *'QUEST'* (weekly), TV, 64-61, CDN, Exec Prod/Dir.

DUMOULIN, Yves

AR. 370 Banting, St-Bruno, Qué, CAN, J3V 1Y3. (514)653-6321. Radio-Canada, 1400 blvd. Dorchester est, Montréal, Qué, CAN, H2L 2M2. (514)285-3555.
Types de production et Catégories: c métrage-Réal; TV film-Réal; TV vidéo-Réal.
Types d'oeuvres: Drame-TV; Variété-TV; Documentaire-TV; Quiz-TV.
Curriculum vitae: Né en 1930, Montréal, Québec. Réalisateur spécialisé dans les reportages et documentaires, Radio-Canada, 30 ans.
Filmographie sélective: *'AU JOUR LE JOUR'* (50 eps), TV, 85-83, CDN, Réal; *SYLVAIN FORGET/ VIATEUR LAPIERRE,* 'FEMMES D'AUJOURD'HUI', TV, 82/81, CDN, Réal; *BELLE FLEUR/ LA SEPARATION,* 'FEMMES D'AUJOURD'HUI', TV, 75, CDN, Réal.

DUNCAN, Kelly

DGC. 6130 Gleneagles Dr., West Vancouver, BC, CAN, V7W 1W3. (604)921-8260. Kelly Duncan Prod. Inc., 1033 Davie St., #700, Vancouver, BC, CAN, V6E 1M7. (604)684-5714.
Types of Production & Categories: TV Film-Dir.
Genres: Documentary-TV; Educational-TV; Commercials-TV; Industrial-TV.
Biography: Produced hundreds of TV commercials, documentaries and award winning industrial films.

(cont/suite)

Selective Filmography: *CONAIRS WORLD,* In, 86, CDN, Prod/Dir; *ANOTHER MINE, ANOTHER CHALLENGE,* In, 86, CDN, Prod/Dir; *SHIPSHAPER,* In, 85, CDN, Prod/Dir; *COMEWINTER,* In, 84, CDN, Prod/Dir; *THE FOREST STANDS,* In, 84, CDN, Prod/Dir; *ISLANDS IN ICE,* In, 84, CDN, Prod/Dir (CFTA); *WORLD OF PLACER,* In, 84, CDN, Prod/Dir.

DUPONT, Jacques

Convergence Inc., 1463 Préfontaine, Montréal, Qué, CAN, H1W 2N6. (514)521-4521.
Types de production et Catégories: TV vidéo-Réal.
Types d'oeuvres: Education-C&TV; Annonces-TV; Industriel-TV.
Curriculum vitae: Né en 1942, Paris, France; citoyen canadien. Education: Bac. en Philosophie, Paris; Ecole Supérieure de Publicité, Paris; Institut des Hautes Etudes Cinématographiques, Paris. Président fondateur, Log Plus Inc., 78. Conception/réalisation de nombreuses annonces et films éducatifs. Président de Convergence Inc.; consultant et producteur dans les techniques interactives de communications.
Filmographie sélective: *LES DESSOUS DU HASARD,* In, 85, CDN, Prod; *'REPERES'* (sev eps), TV, 80, CDN, Réal; *'SURVILLE'* (32 eps), TV, 77-75, CDN, Réal.

DUSSAULT, Louis

ARRFQ. 6371 St-Dominique, Montréal, Qué, CAN, H2S 3A6. Les Films du Crépuscule, 4503 St-Denis, Ste 1, Montréal, Qué, CAN, H2J 2L4. (514)849-2477.
Types de production et Catégories: l métrage-Réal/Sc; c métrage-Réal/Sc.
Types d'oeuvres: Drame-C; Comédie-C; Documentaire-C.
Curriculum vitae: Né en 1952, Montréal, Québec. Langues: français, anglais, espagnol. 10 ans aux Films du Crépuscule; 12 ans en réalisation de films; 2 ans d'enseignement (cinéma).
Filmographie sélective: *FICTION D'AMOUR,* C, 86, CDN, Prod/Réal/Sc/Mont; *FESTIVAL DU BLE D'INDE,* C, 78, CDN, Rech/Réal; *L'ALTERNATIVE DE BAIE ST-PAUL,* C, 77, CDN, Rech/Réal; *MON GANT ME FAIT MOURIR,* C, 76, CDN, Réal/Sc; *LE ROCKER,* C, 75, CDN, Réal/Sc/Com; *LE FACTEUR,* C, 74, CDN, Réal/Sc.

EASTMAN, Allan

DGC. 32 Salisbury Ave., Toronto, Ont, CAN, M4X 1C4. (416)963-5966. Labyrinth Film & Videoworks, 9 Sultan St., Toronto, Ont, CAN, M5S 1L6. (416)923-5228.
Types of Production & Categories: Th Film-Dir/Prod/Wr/Ed; TV Film-Dir/Prod/Wr/Ed; TV Video-Dir/Prod/Wr/Ed.
Genres: Drama-Th&TV; Comedy-Th&TV; Action-Th&TV.
Biography: Born 1950, Manitoba. Honours B.A., University of Manitoba, 72; M.A., Film School, University of Bristol, 74.
Selective Filmography: *'NIGHT HEAT'* (8 eps), TV, 86/85, CDN, Dir; *RACE FOR THE BOMB* (mini-series), TV, 86, CDN/F, Dir; *'HOT SHOTS'* (1 eps), TV, 86, CDN, Dir; *CRAZY MOON,* Th, 85, CDN, Dir; *'DANGER BAY'* (Dir-12 eps/Wr-1 eps), TV, 85/84, CDN/USA, Dir/Wr; *THE WAR BOY* (POINT OF ESCAPE), Th, 84, CDN, Dir/Ed; *'THE EDISON TWINS'* (2 eps), TV, 84, CDN, Dir; *'LITTLEST HOBO'* (52 eps), TV, 84-79, CDN, Dir; *'THE BEACHCOMBERS'* (15 eps), TV, 80-77, CDN, Dir; *DONNER PASS,* TV, 79, USA, 2nd U Dir; *'GRIZZLY ADAMS'* (3 eps), TV, 78, USA, Dir; *A SWEETER SONG* (SNAPSHOTS), Th, 75, CDN, Dir/Co-Wr; *FOREIGNERS,* TV, 75, CDN/GB/F, Dir/Wr/Ed/Prod; *DEUS EX MACHINA,* TV, 74, CDN/GB, Dir/Wr/Ed/Prod.

EGOYAN, Atom

490 Adelaide St.W., Ste. 102, Toronto, Ont, CAN, M5V 1T3. (416)365-2137.
Types of Production & Categories: Th Film-Dir/Prod/Wr/Ed; Th Short-Dir/Prod/
Wr/Ed; TV Film-Dir.
Genres: Drama-Th&TV.
Biography: Born 1960, Cairo, Egypt; Canadian citizen; graduated University of
Toronto, International Relations, 82. Accomplished classical guitarist. Golden Ducat
Award, Mannheim, for *NEXT OF KIN*.
Selective Filmography: *FAMILY VIEWING*, Th, 86, CDN, Dir/Wr/Prod; *IN THIS
CORNER*, TV, 85, CDN, Dir; *MEN: A PASSION PLAY GROUND*, Th, 85,
CDN, Dir/Cam/Ed; *NEXT OF KIN*, Th, 84, CDN, Dir/Prod/Ed/Wr; *OPEN
HOUSE*, 'CANADIAN REFLECTIONS', TV, 82, CDN, Dir; *PEEP SHOW*, Th,
81, CDN, Dir/Wr/Prod/Ed; *AFTER GRAD WITH DAD*, Th, 80, CDN, Dir/Wr/
Ed/Prod; *HOWARD IN PARTICULAR*, Th, 79, CDN, Dir/Prod/Wr/Ed.

EISENBERG, Nat B.

AFTRA, DGA, DGC. NBE Productions (Canada) Ltd., 217A Church St., Toronto,
Ont, CAN, M5B 1Y7. (416)864-0051.
Types of Production & Categories: TV Film-Dir; TV Video-Dir.
Genres: Educational-TV; Children's-TV; Commercials-TV.
Biography: Born 1921, New York; owner of a Canadian film and videotape
production company; senior member of the DGC. Worked for 20 years in Canada
doing commercials (English & French), children's programming; corporate
industrials and training films.

ELDER, Bruce

Lightworks, 300 St. Clair Ave. W., Ste 401, Toronto, Ont, CAN, M4V 1S4. (416)
921-5970.
Types of Production & Categories: Th Film-Dir/Ed/Wr/Cin; Th Short-Dir/Wr/Ed/
Cin.
Genres: Experimental-Th.
Biography: Born 1947, Hawkesbury, Ontario. Studied philosophy, McMaster
University, University of Toronto; Ryerson Polytechnical Institute (Media). Solo
exhibitions at the Millenium, Museum of Modern Art, N.Y., Los Angeles, London
and Berlin. *THE ART OF WORLDLY WISDOM* won the L.A. Film Critics Award
as Best Independent/Experimental Film.
Selective Filmography: *LAMENTATIONS: A MONUMENT TO THE DEAD
WORLD* (2 parts), Th, 85, CDN, Dir/Cin/Ed; *ILLUMINATED TEXTS*, Th, 82,
CDN, Dir/Cin/Ed; *1857: FOOL'S GOLD*, Th, 81, CDN, Dir/Cin/Ed; *TRACE*, Th,
80, CDN, Dir/Cin/Ed; *SWEET LOVE REMEMBERED*, Th, 80, CDN, Dir/Cin/
Ed; *THE ART OF WORLDLY WISDOM*, Th, 79, CDN, Dir/Cin/Ed; *LOOK! WE
HAVE COME THROUGH!*, Th, 78, CDN, Dir/Cin/Ed; *UNREMITTING
TENDERNESS*, Th, 77, CDN, Dir/Cin/Ed; *PERMUTATIONS AND
COMBINATIONS*, Th, 76, CDN, Dir/Cin/Ed; *BARBARA IS A VISION OF
LOVELINESS*, Th, 76, CDN, Dir/Cin/Ed (CFA); *BREATH/LIGHT/BIRTH*, Th,
75, CDN, Dir/Cin/Ed; *SHE IS AWAY*, Th, 75, CDN, Dir/Cin/Ed.

ELLIOTT, William G.

350 Dennie Ave., Newmarket, Ont, CAN, L3Y 4M7. (416)895-1489. Global TV,
81 Barber Greene Rd., Don Mills, Ont, CAN, M3C 2A2.
Types of Production & Categories: TV Film-Dir/Prod; TV Video-Prod/Dir.
Genres: Drama-TV; Comedy-TV; Variety-TV; Documentary-TV.
Biography: Born 1951, Ontario. Graduate, Broadcasting course, Conestoga College,
73. President, WRAP Television Film Productions Inc..
Selective Filmography: *'JACKPOT'* (130 eps), TV, 86/85, CDN/USA, Dir; *JERRY
LEWIS TELETHON* (9), TV, 86-78, CDN/USA, Dir; *VARIETY CLUB*

(cont/suite)

TELETHON (5), TV, 86-82, CDN, Dir; *CHRISTINE JESSOP CASE/THE JOHNSON-BENTLEY CASE,* 'CITIZEN'S ALERT', TV, 85/84, CDN, Prod/Dir; *TERROR* (parts 1 & 2), TV, 85, CDN, Studio Dir; *YOUNG AND RESTLESS GALA SPECIAL,* TV, 84, CDN/USA, Co-Prod/Dir; *THE NATIONAL FITNESS TEST,* TV, 84, CDN, Dir; *THE GOLDEN AGE OF CANADIAN FIGURE SKATING,* TV, 84, CDN, Dir; *1984 BURSARY AWARDS,* TV, 84, CDN, Dir; *'FROST OVER CANADA'* (6 eps), TV, 83, CDN, Dir; *JOINED AT THE HIP,* TV, 83, CDN, Co-Dir; *'THE KANGAZOO CLUB'* (26 eps), TV, 83, CDN, Dir; *NEIL SEDAKA IN CONCERT,* TV, 82, CDN/USA, Dir; *DAVID STEINBERG IN CONCERT,* TV, 82, CDN/USA, Dir; *WHERE HAS THE LAUGHTER GONE,* TV, 81, CDN/USA, Dir; *'THE QUIZ KIDS'* (44 eps), TV, 81-79, CDN/USA, Dir; *'LIFESTYLES'* (100 eps), TV, 81, CDN/USA, Dir; *DRUG ABUSE SPECIAL,* TV, 81, CDN, Dir; *TALES OF THE HAUNTED* (EVIL STALKS THIS HOUSE), TV, 81, CDN/USA, 1st AD; *'THE TOMMY HUNTER SHOW'* (6 eps), TV, 80, CDN, Dir; *'EASY COUNTRY'* (20 eps), TV, 80/79, CDN, Dir; *'CODE 10-78'* (24 eps), TV, 79-77, CDN, Dir/Prod; *'THE $128,000 DOLLAR QUESTION'* (26 eps), TV, 79, CDN/USA, Dir; *'BLUFF'* (13 eps), TV, 79, CDN, Dir.

EL-SISSI, Azza - see PRODUCERS

ERLICH, Alan

DGC, ATPD. 122 Garfield Ave., Toronto, Ont, CAN, M4T 1E1. (416)483-6665. Tom Korman, Comtemporary Korman, 132 Lasky Drive, Beverly Hills, CA, USA. (213)278-8250.
Types of Production & Categories: TV Film-Dir; TV Video-Dir.
Genres: Drama-TV; Comedy-TV; Documentary-TV.
Biography: Born 1940, Plymouth, England, Canadian citizen. Winner of the 1st Michener Award for journalism, *THE CHARTER REVOLUTION.*
Selective Filmography: *'HANGIN' IN'* (100 eps), TV, 86-80, CDN, Dir; *'STREET LEGAL'* (1 eps), TV, 86, CDN, Dir; *'CHECK IT OUT!'* (16 eps), TV, 86/85, CDN/USA, Dir; *TWELFTH NIGHT,* TV, 85, CDN, Dir; *ONE FOR THE POT,* TV, 85, CDN, Dir; *'LITTLEST HOBO'* (1 eps), TV, 84, CDN, Dir; *TARTUFFE,* TV, 84, CDN, Dir; *BIRDS OF A FEATHER,* TV, 84, CDN, Dir; *'BIRDS IN PARADISE'* (4 eps), TV, 83, CDN/USA, Dir; *MATTER OF CUNNING,* TV, 83, CDN/USA, Dir; *SUNDAY'S CHILD,* TV, 83, CDN, Dir; *'HOME FIRES'* (3 eps), TV, 83/82, CDN, Dir; *'ROMANCE'* (10 eps), TV, 82, CDN, Dir; *VANDALISM,* TV, 82, CDN, Dir; *'FLAPPERS'* (35 eps), TV, 80-78, CDN, Dir; *'KING OF KENSINGTON'* (53 eps), TV, 80-77, CDN, Dir; *'A GIFT TO LAST'* (1 eps), TV, 78, CDN, Dir; *ELECTION '74,* TV, 74, CDN, Dir/Prod; *THE CHARTER REVOLUTION,* TV, 72, CDN, Co-Prod/Dir; *ELECTION '72,* TV, 72, CDN, Dir/Co-Prod; *ELECTION '68,* TV, 68, CDN, Dir.

FALARDEAU, Maurice

AR. 2908 de la Girouette, Ste-Marguerite, Qué, CAN, J0T 2K0. (514)228-4177. Radio-Canada, 1400 blvd. Dorchester est, Montréal, Qué, CAN, H2L 2M2. (514) 285-2846.
Types de production et Catégories: TV film-Réal; TV vidéo-Réal.
Types d'oeuvres: Drame-TV; Comédie-TV; Enfants-TV.
Curriculum vitae: Né en 1931, Montréal, Québec. Réalisateur depuis 28 ans.
Filmographie sélective: *'LA CLE DES CHAMPS'* (20 eps), TV, 86, CDN, Réal; *'POIVRE ET SEL'* (40 eps), TV, 85/84, CDN, Réal; *'LES GIROUETTES'* (40 eps), TV, 84/83, CDN, Réal; *'RACE DE MONDE'* (40 eps), TV, 82-80, CDN, Réal; *'DU TAC AU TAC'* (60 eps), TV, 80-75, CDN, Réal; *'LE GRENIER'* (8 eps), TV, 74, CDN, Réal; *'AVEC LE TEMPS'* (12 eps), TV, 72/71, CDN, Réal; *'PICOTINE'* (24 eps), TV, 71/70, CDN, Réal; *'SOL ET GOBELET'* (75 eps), TV, 70-68, CDN, Réal; *'FANFRELUCHE'* (13 eps), TV, 67/66, CDN, Réal; *'TI-JEAN CARIBOU'* (45 eps), TV, 65/64, CDN, Réal; *'OURAGAN'* (35 eps), TV, 63/62,

(cont/suite)

235

CDN, Réal; *'LA BOITE A SURPRISE'* (104 eps), TV, 61/60, CDN, Réal; *'PROFESSEUR CALCULUS'* (26 eps), TV, 59/58, CDN, Réal; *'BOBINO'* (195 eps), TV, 58/57, CDN, Réal.

FAVREAU, Robert

ARRFQ. 4424 rue Fabre, Montréal, Qué, CAN, H2J 3V3. (514)521-4019.
Types de production et Catégories: 1 métrage-Réal/Sc/Mont; c métrage-Réal/Sc/Mont; TV film-Réal/Sc/Mont.
Types d'oeuvres: Documentaire-C&TV; Education-C&TV.
Curriculum vitae: Né en 1948, Montréal, Québec; bilingue; Baccalauréat ès Arts. Expérience, autre que cinéma: animation, pédagogie.
Filmographie sélective: *FAUX-FUYANTS,* C, 86, CDN, Sc/Réal; *LE MILLION TOUT PUISSANT,* C, 85, CDN, Mont; *LES COULISSES DE L'ENTRAIDE* (TOUCH OF HEALING), C, 84, CDN, Réal/Sc/Mont; *LA VIGIE/HISTOIRES DE BANLIEUE,* 'LES CHOCS DE LA VIE', TV, 82, CDN, Réal/Sc/Mont; *CORRIDORS - PRIS AU PIEGE,* C, 79, CDN, Réal/Sc/Mont; *LA LONGUE MARCHE EN INSTITUTION/UNE CHANCE SUR MILLE,* 'LES EXCLUS', TV, 77, CDN, Réal/Sc/Mont; *LE SOLEIL A PAS D'CHANCE,* C, 75, CDN, Réal/Sc/Mont; *VOUS SAVEZ-CA M. LE MINISTRE?,* TV, 73, CDN, Réal/Mont; *LA FAIM DES CAVES,* C, 73, CDN, Réal/Mont; *CAPABLES D'ETRE UN PEU FOUS,* TV, 73, CDN, Réal/Sc; *Y'ETAND, GASTON,* C, 72, CDN, Réal/Sc; *C'EST PAS L'ARGENT QUI MANQUE,* C, 72, CDN, Réal/Sc.

FEARNLEY, Neill

DGC. 6468 Cypress St., Vancouver, BC, CAN, V6M 3S5. (604)266-1048.
Types of Production & Categories: TV Film-Dir; TV Video-Dir/Prod.
Genres: Drama-TV; Comedy-TV; Commercials-TV.
Biography: Born 1953, Liverpool, England; Canadian-British citizenship. Education: Ryerson Polytechnical Institute, Radio & TV Arts.
Selective Filmography: *'THE BEACHCOMBERS'* (5 eps), TV, 85-83, CDN, Dir.

FEDORENKO, Eugene

76 Durie St., Toronto, Ont, CAN, M6S 3E8. (416)762-6312.
Types of Production & Categories: Th Short-Dir/An.
Genres: Educational-Th; Animation-Th.
Biography: Born 1951, Vilnus, Lithuania; speaks English, Polish, Russian. Attended Ontario College of Art. Film education: NFB. Held animated film workshop for children, 74-84; made 6 flip books jointly with David Suzuki; wrote and animated another flip book, 'Origins'; now experimenting with stereo animation drawing. *EVERY CHILD* has won awards in Varna, Milan, New York, Cracow, Ottawa Film Festivals.
Selective Filmography: *SKYWARD* (1 seg), Th, 85, CDN, Dir/An; *THIS IS AN EMERGENCY* (1 seg), ED, 80, CDN, Dir/An; *MASTERPIECE MYSTERY THEATRE* (OPENING), TV, 80, USA, An; *'MARKET PLACE'* (OPENING), TV, 80, CDN, Dir/An; *EVERY CHILD,* Th, 79, CDN, Dir/An **(GENIE/OSCAR)**.

FERGUSON, Graeme

CSC, DGC, IATSE-644. 1 Hillcrest Ave., Toronto, Ont, CAN, M4X 1W1. (416)922-0549. Imax Systems Corp., 38 Isabella St., Toronto, Ont, CAN, M4Y 1N1. (416)960-8509.
Types of Production & Categories: Th Film-Prod/Dir/Cin; TV Film-Prod/Dir/Cin.
Genres: Documentary-Th; Educational-TV.
Biography: Born 1929, Toronto, Ontario. Began filming with University of Toronto Film Society. Summer student, NFB, 50; worked with Maya Deren. Honours B.A., Political Science and Economics, University of Toronto, 52. National Secretary, World University Service of Canada, 53-55. Worked in India with Arne Sucksderff, 56-58; freelanced in New York, 58-67; Co-founder, President, Imax Systems
(cont/suite)

Corporation since 67. Member, Royal Academy of the Arts; Honorary lifetime member, CSC; Special Achievement Award, Genie Awards, 86; Chetwynd Award. *THE QUESTION OF TV VIOLENCE* won a Chris Award, Columbus.
Selective Filmography: *THE DREAM IS ALIVE*, Th, 85, CDN, Prod/Dir/Co-Cam (**CFTA**); *HAIL COLUMBIA*, Th, 82, CDN, Co-Prod/Dir/Co-Cam; *NISHNAWBE-ASKI*, ED, 77, CDN, Co-Prod/Cam; *OCEAN*, Th, 77, CDN, Prod/Dir/Co-Cam; *SNOW JOB*, Th, 74, CDN, Prod/Dir; *MAN BELONGS TO THE EARTH*, Th, 74, USA, Co-Prod/Dir/Cam; *THE QUESTION OF TV VIOLENCE*, ED, 72, CDN, Dir; *NORTH OF SUPERIOR*, Th, 70, CDN, Prod/Dir/Cam (**CFA**); *IBM CLOSE UP*, In, 68, CDN, Dir; *THE VIRGIN PRESIDENT*, Th, 68, USA, Co-Prod/Dir/ Cam; *POLAR LIFE*, Th, 67, CDN, Prod/Dir/Cam; *THE DAYS OF DYLAN THOMAS*, Th, 65, USA, Dir; *THE LOVE GODDESSES*, Th, 64, USA, Co-Prod; *THE LEGEND OF RUDOLF VALENTINO*, TV, 61, USA, Dir.

FERRAND, Carlos

ARRFQ, STCQ. 1175 St-Marc, Montréal, Qué, CAN, H3H 2E4. (514)931-6584.
Types de production et Catégories: 1 métrage-D phot; c métrage-Réal/D phot; TV film-Réal/Cam; TV vidéo-Réal/Cam.
Types d'oeuvres: Drame-C&TV; Documentaire-C&TV; Expérimental-C&TV.
Curriculum vitae: Né en 1946 à Lima, Pérou; canadien; langues: espagnol, français, anglais. 15 ans de métier. *EPPISURES DE SABLES* remporte le 1er Prix, Int'l TV Association; *EYES ONLY*, 1er Prix, Financial Times of Canada Literary Award. Réalisateur de l'audio visuel (54 projecteurs) pour le pavillon du Québec, Expo 86.
Filmographie sélective: *INVENTEZ*, TV, 86, CDN, Réal/Cam; *FENETRES SUR CA*, C, 86, CDN, Réal/Cam/Comp; *FEMMES HANDICAPEES*, C, 85, CDN, D phot; *A LIFE*, C, 84, CDN, D phot; *VIDEO A LA CHAINE*, TV, 84/83, F, Cam; *THE NEW CINEMA*, TV, 83, CDN, Cam; *CIMARRONES*, C, 82, CDN/PE, Réal/Sc/Cam; *EPPISURES DE SABLES*, TV, 81, CDN, Réal/Cam; *EYES ONLY*, TV, 81, CDN, Réal/Cam; *CEMENTERIO DE ELEFANTES*, C, 74, PE, D phot; *LES INVENTEURS AU QUEBEC*, TV, CDN, Réal/Cam.

FIRUS, Karen

4101 Grace Cr., North Vancouver, BC, CAN, V7R 3Z9. (604)987-3462.
Types of Production & Categories: Th Short-Dir; TV Video-Dir.
Genres: Musical-Th&TV; Experimental-Th; Commercials-TV; Music Video-TV.
Biography: Born 1959, Vancouver, British Columbia. B.A., Film, University of British Columbia; Master of Fine Arts, Film, U.B.C., 86. Awards include CBC Prize for playwriting, 83, Norman McLaren Award, Canadian Student Film Festival for *FASHION 99*, 86.
Selective Filmography: *FASHION 99*, Th, 86, CDN, Dir/Wr/Ed; *B.C. CHILDREN'S HOSPITAL*, Cm, 86, CDN, Art Dir; *CANADA'S WILD PACIFIC SALMON*, In, 85, CDN, Art Dir; *OPEN YOUR HEART - WEST COAST MUSICIANS' AID FOR AFRICA*, MV, 85, CDN, Dir/Ch; *NUCLEAR FOLLIES*, Th, 85, CDN, Art Dir; *WELCOME TO JAPAN*, MV, 85, CDN, Art Dir; *SPECTRUM-SPECTRUM-SPECTRUM*, Th, 81, CDN, Dir/Ch/Co-Ed; *AUDITION!*, ED, 80, CDN, Dir/Wr.

FISCHER, Max

4691 Bonavista Ave., Montreal, Que, CAN, H3W 2C6. (514)482-5827.
Types of Production & Categories: Th Film-Dir/Wr; TV Film-Dir.
Genres: Drama-Th; Comedy-Th; Documentary-Th&TV; Commercials-TV.
Biography: Born 1929, Alexandria, Egypt. Languages: English, French, Italian, Arabic, Dutch, Spanish, Greek. Studies: Literature, Philosophy, History of Art, Egyptology. Worked as a film critic and film historian with the Cinémathèque Française. Director of numerous commercials.
Selective Filmography: *LE PALANQUIN DES LARMES* (mini-series), TV, 86, CDN/F, Dir/Co-Wr; *MAN IN 5A (THE MAN NEXT DOOR)*, Th, 81, CDN, Dir/

(cont/suite)

Co-Scr; *THE LUCKY STAR* (LA BELLE ETOILE), Th, 80, CDN, Dir/Co-Scr (**GENIE**); *DREAMS*, Th, 70, H, Dir/Wr/DOP; *MEWS EN MEIJN*, Th, 65, H, Dir/Wr.

FLOQUET, François - voir PRODUCTEURS

FOLLOWS, Ted

ACTRA. 78 Delaware Ave., Toronto, Ont, CAN, M6H 2T1. (416)535-7513. First Artists Mgmt., 1255 Yonge St., Ste. 303, Toronto, Ont, CAN, M4T 1W6. (416) 961-7766.
Types of Production & Categories: TV Film-Dir; TV Video-Dir.
Genres: Drama-TV; Comedy-TV.
Biography: Born 1926, Ottawa, Ontario. Honours degree in Psychology, University of Toronto, 50. Actor for 40 years in Canada, England and US; stage director; directing for TV since 81.
Selective Filmography: *TO SERVE AND PROTECT* (3 parts), TV, 86/85, CDN, Dir; *'HOOKED ON READING'* (6 eps), TV, 86, CDN, Dir; *'JUDGE'* (11 eps), TV, 84-81, CDN, Dir; *'BACKSTRETCH'* (2 eps), TV, 84, CDN, Dir; *JOEY*, TV, 82, CDN, Dir.

FORCIER, André

ONF, C.P. 6100, Succ. A, Montréal, Qué, CAN, H3C 3H5. (514)283-9000.
Types de production et Catégories: l métrage-Réal/Sc; c métrage-Réal/Sc.
Types d'oeuvres: Drame-C; Documentaire-C.
Curriculum vitae: Né en 1947, Montréal, Québec; bilingue.
Filmographie sélective: *KALAMAZOO*, C, 86, CDN, Réal/Co sc; *AU CLAIR DE LA LUNE*, C, 82, CDN, Réal/Co sc; *L'EAU CHAUDE, L'EAU FRETTE*, C, 76, CDN, Réal/Co sc; *NIGHT CAP*, C, 74, CDN, Réal/Sc; *BAR SALON*, C, 73, CDN, Réal/Co sc; *LE RETOUR DE L'IMMACULEE CONCEPTION*, C, 71, CDN, Réal/Sc; *CHRONIQUES LABRADORIENNES*, C, 67, CDN, Réal/Sc/Prod.

FORGET, Aimé

AR. 160 Tailhandier, Boucherville, Qué, CAN, J4B 2T7. (514)655-8356. Radio-Canada, 1400 blvd. Dorchester est, Montréal, Qué, CAN, H2L 2M2. (514)285-2843.
Types de production et Catégories: TV film-Réal/Prod; TV vidéo-Réal/Prod.
Types d'oeuvres: Drame-TV; Comédie-TV; Action-TV.
Curriculum vitae: Né en 1928, Montréal, Québec. Etudes: art dramatique, théâtre, cinéma, TV. Réalisateur-producteur, TV dramatique depuis 27 ans; de nombreux téléromans et grandes dramatiques dont *QUELLE FAMILLE, GRAND-PAPA, LA BONNE AVENTURE*.

FORTIER, Bob

SGCT. 6151 Cote St-Luc, #319, Hampstead, Que, CAN, H3X 2G4. (514)482-5339. NFB, 3155 Cote de Liesse, Montreal, Que, CAN, H4N 2N4. (514)283-9558.
Types of Production & Categories: Th Film-Dir/Prod/Ed; Th Short-Dir/Ed; TV Film-Dir/Prod/Wr/Ed.
Genres: Drama-TV; Documentary-Th&TV; Educational-TV.
Biography: Born, 1945, New Glascow, Nova Scotia; bilingual.Education: Loyola College, Concordia University, Montreal. *THE LAST RIGHT* won the Grand Prix du Cinéma, Varna.
Selective Filmography: *OUT OF A JOB*, TV, 86, CDN, Dir/Prod/Ed; *ONE STEP AWAY*, TV, 85, CDN, Dir/Prod; *A GIFT FOR KATE*, TV, 85, CDN, Prod; *RUNNING SCARED*, TV, 84, CDN, Dir/Ed/Wr/Prod; *THE LAST RIGHT*, TV, 83, CDN, Dir/Prod/Wr/Ed; *A SINGLE REGRET*, TV, 82, CDN, Dir/Wr/Ed; *THE DEADLY GAME OF NATIONS*, 'WAR', TV, 82, CDN, Ed; *THE DEVIL AT YOUR HEELS*, Th, 82, CDN, Ed/Dir/Co-Prod (**GENIE**); *HARMONIUM IN*

(cont/suite)

CALIFORNIA, TV, 79, CDN, Dir/Ed; *THE MAD CANADIAN,* Th, 76, CDN, Dir/Ed; *METAL WORKERS - ARTISANS DES METAUX,* TV, 76, CDN, Dir/ Ed; *EASTERN GRAPHIC,* 'ATLANTIC', TV, 75, CDN, Ed; *ALL THE YEARS OF HER LIFE,* TV, 74, CDN, Dir/Wr/Ed; *CAVENDISH COUNTRY,* 'WEST', TV, 74, CDN, Ed; *MYTH AND REALITY,* TV, 73, CDN, Dir/Ed; *STATION TEN,* TV, 73, CDN, Ed; *HARD RIDER,* TV, 72, CDN, Ed; *COLD JOURNEY,* Th, 71, CDN, Assist Ed; *SMALL SMOKE AT BLAZE CREEK,* Th, 71, CDN, Ed; *THE CONQUERED DREAM,* TV, 71, CDN, Assist Ed; *ATONEMENT,* TV, 70, CDN, Assist Ed; *END OF A SUMMER DAY,* TV, 69, CDN, Dir/Wr/Ed.

FOURNIER, Claude

ACTRA, SAF, SARDEC. C.P. 40, St-Paul d'Abbotsford, Qué, CAN, J0E 1A0. (514)379-5304. Rose Films Inc., 86 de Brésoles, Montréal, Qué, CAN, H2Y 1V5. (514)285-8901.
Types de production et Catégories: 1 métrage-Réal/Mont/Sc/D phot; c métrage-Réal/ Mont/Sc/D phot; TV film-Réal/Mont/Sc/D phot; TV vidéo-Réal/Mont/Sc/D phot.
Types d'oeuvres: Drame-C&TV; Comédie-C&TV; Action-C&TV; Documentaire-C&TV.
Curriculum vitae: Né en 1931 à Waterloo, Québec. Journaliste, 48-53; publications: 'Les Armes à Faim', 54, 'Le Ciel Fermé', 56. Création du clown 'SOI.', 100 textes, 57-63; ONF, 50-63; puis, longs métrages et films pour la TV.
Filmographie sélective: *UN ORDINATEUR AU COEUR,* 'PAGE TROIS', TV, 85, CDN, Réal/Sc/D phot/Mont; *BONHEUR D'OCCASION* (THE TIN FLUTE), (aussi 5 ém-TV), C, 82, CDN, Co sc/Réal/Cam; *COPS AND OTHER LOVERS,* C, 79, CDN, Réal/Co sc; *THE NEW AVENGERS* (1 eps), TV, 77, CDN/GB/F, Réal; *JE SUIS LOIN DE TOI MIGNONNE,* C, 75, CDN, Réal/Co sc/Cam; *LA POMME, LA QUEUE ET LES PEPINS,* C, 74, CDN, Réal/Dial/Cam; *ALIEN THUNDER,* C, 72, CDN, Réal/Cam; *LES CHATS BOTTES,* C, 71, CDN, Réal/Co sc/Cam; *DEUX FEMMES EN OR,* C, 70, CDN, Réal/Co sc/Cam.

FOURNIER, Jacques

241 Trépanier, Ile Bizard, Montréal, Qué, CAN. (514)282-1505. 318 rue Sherbrooke est, Montréal, Qué, CAN.
Types de production et Catégories: TV film Réal.
Types d'oeuvres: Annonces-TV.
Curriculum vitae: Né en 1953, Sherbrooke, Québec. Président de La Fabrique d'Images Ltéc.. Réalisateur d'annonces publicitaires ayant gagné plusieurs prix dont 2 Certificats d'Excellence du Publicité Club de Montréal et le 1er Prix, Habitas.

FOURNIER, Robert

981 rue des Ormes, Trois-Rivières, Qué, CAN, G8Y 2P5. (819)375-0305
Types de production et Catégories: c métrage-Réal/Prod; TV film-Réal/Prod; TV vidéo-Réal/Prod.
Types d'oeuvres: Documentaire-TV; Animation-TV.
Curriculum vitae: Né en 1953, Trois-Rivières, Québec. Diplôme en photographie professionnelle, Ecole des Arts et Métiers, Trois-Rivières, 72. Prise de vue d'animation et effets spéciaux jusqu'en 79; depuis, réalisateur, producteur.
Filmographie sélective: *PHILIPPE AUBERT DE GASPE/ELIZABETH BEGON,* 'MANUSCRITS', TV, 84, CDN, Réal/Prod/Mont; *MARIE DE L'INCARNATION/NEREE BEAUCHEMIN,* 'MANUSCRITS', TV, 83/82, CDN, Réal/Prod; *ANTOINE GERIN LAVOIE/PAMPHILE LEMAY/OCTAVE CREMAZIE,* 'MANUSCRITS', TV, 83/82, CDN, Co prod; *ALBERT LOZEAU/ LAURE CONAN/LOUIS FRECHETTE/CHARLES GILL,* 'MANUSCRITS', TV, 82-80, CDN, Co prod; *ARTHUR BUIES/OLIVAR ASSELIN,* 'MANUSCRITS', TV, 81/80, CDN, Réal/Prod; *CHEVAUCHEE* (CAVALCADE), TV, 79, CDN, Co réal; *PIERRE GUIMOND: ENTRE FREUD ET DRACULA,* TV, 79, CDN, Cam;

(cont/suite)

DIRECTORS/REALISATEURS

COMMUNAUTE URBAINE DE MONTREAL, In, 79, CDN, Cam; *NOUS VOUS AIMONS EN SANTE,* ED, 79, CDN, Cam; *AU RYTHME DU QUEBEC,* TV, 77, CDN, Cam.

FOURNIER, Roger - voir SCENARISTES

FRANCON, Georges
AR. 1227 Sherbrooke ouest, #63, Montréal, Qué, CAN, H3G 1G1. (514)288-5878. Radio-Canada, 1400 blvd. Dorchester est, Montréal, Qué, CAN, H2L 2M2. (514) 285-2847.
Types de production et Catégories: TV film-Réal; TV vidéo-Réal.
Types d'oeuvres: Documentaire-TV.
Curriculum vitae: Né en 1924, France; canadien; bilingue. Réalisateur, reporter, annonceur, scénariste à la radio et à la télévision.
Filmographie sélective: *CEUX QUI ONT TOURNE LE DOS A LA VIE,* TV, 82, CDN, Réal; *LIVRES D'ARTISTES,* TV, 80, CDN, Réal; *ODANAK,* TV, 79, CDN, Réal; *THEATRE POUR ENFANTS,* TV, 78, CDN, Réal; *MITIARJUK,* TV, 77, CDN, Réal; *LA FIN D'UNE EPOQUE,* 'CANADA RURAL', TV, 70, CDN, Réal; *JOE SMALLWOOD,* TV, 68, CDN, Réal; *ROBERT STANFIELD,* TV, 67, CDN, Réal; *LESTER B. PEARSON,* TV, 67, CDN, Réal; *AUX FRONTIERES DE LA TERRE PROMISE,* TV, 66, CDN, Réal; *ALFRED PELLAN,* TV, 61, CDN, Réal; *'JEUNESSES MUSICALES',* TV, 60, CDN, Réal.

FRASER, Louis
ARRQ. 3471 Chapleau, Montréal, Qué, CAN, H2K 3H7. (514)522-6331. Radio-Québec, 1000 Fullum, Montréal, Qué, CAN, H3K 2L7. (514)521-2424. 437 rue St-Claude, Montréal, Qué, CAN, H2Y 3B6. (514)861-1065.
Types de production et Catégories: TV film-Réal; TV vidéo-Réal.
Types d'oeuvres: Documentaire-TV; Education-TV; Enfants-TV.
Curriculum vitae: Né en 1947.
Filmographie sélective: *RADIO-QUEBEC PAR LUI-MEME,* TV, 85/84, CDN, Réal; *'VENDREDI CHAUD'* (pl ém), TV, 84, CDN, Réal; *VIVRE LE THEATRE,* TV, 83, CDN, Réal; *CONARAC LE ROBOT,* TV, 83, CDN, Mont; *'BOZEJEUNNES'* (pl ém), TV, 82/81, CDN, Réal; *'NEUF ET DEMI'* (7 eps), TV, 81/80, CDN, Réal; *'MOI'* (4 eps), TV, 79, CDN, Réal; *PLANETE,* TV, 79, CDN, Co réal; *L'EXPERIENCE AIDANT'* (12 eps), TV, 76, CDN, Réal.

FRECHETTE, Michel
ASIFA. 367 des Pinsons, Rimouski, Qué, CAN, G5L 7W9. (418)722-6609. Les Entreprises Vidéo Polyfilm, 8, 6e rue est, Rimouski, Qué, CAN, G5L 2H4. (418) 724-2413.
Types de production et Catégories: TV film-Réal; TV vidéo-Réal.
Types d'oeuvres: Documentaire-TV; Animation-TV; Industriel-TV.
Curriculum vitae: Né en 1950, Montréal, Québec. Réalisateur depuis 73; copropriétaire d'une entreprise de production vidéo et film d'animation, 85.
Filmographie sélective: *19 MARS 1980,* TV, 86, CDN, Réal; *LES ACTEURS DU LOISIR,* TV, 86, CDN, Réal; *TELEMAR,* TV, 85, CDN, Réal; *DICKNER INC.,* TV, 85, CDN, Réal; *UNE ADMISSION CHALEUREUSE,* TV, 85, CDN, Réal; *MELINA,* TV, 84, CDN, Réal/Prod; *LES TEMPONAUTES,* TV, 83, CDN, Réal/Sc/Prod; *25 ANS DE TELEVISION,* TV, 79, CDN, Réal; *LE THEATRE D'OCCASION,* TV, 79, CDN, Réal/Sc; *COEUR ATOUT/ FORET Y PENSER/ LA LEGENDE DU PETOUK-PETOUK,* 'TOUT PRES D'ICI', TV, 78/77, CDN, Réal/Sc; *SAMEDI TOUT,* TV, 75, CDN, Réal; *CABRIOLE,* 'ENERSAGE', TV, 75, CDN, Réal/Prod.

FROST, F. Harvey
ACTT, DGC. 20 Blong Ave., Toronto, Ont, CAN, M4M 1P2. (416)463-2223.

(cont/suite)

Types of Production & Categories: Th Film-Dir; TV Film-Dir; TV Video-Dir/Prod.
Genres: Drama-TV; Comedy-TV; Action-TV; Horror-Th.
Biography: Born 1947, London, England; Canadian citizen. B.A., Sociology, Durham University. Produced, directed commercials, 69-78. Emigrated to Canada, 74. Since 78, drama director.
Selective Filmography: *'THE EDISON TWINS'* (1 eps), TV, 85, CDN, Dir; *THE UNKNOWN SHOW*, TV, 85, CDN, Dir; *'FRONTRUNNERS'* (3 eps), TV, 85, CDN, Dir/Co-Wr; *IN GOOD COMPANY*, TV, 84, CDN, Dir; *DIS-MOI SI JE TE DERANGE*, TV, 84, CDN, Assoc Prod; *THE S&V FAMILY SHOW*, TV, 83, CDN, Dir/Co-Prod; *'ROMANCE'* (Dir-15 eps/Co-Prod-11 eps), (9 eps), TV, 82, CDN, Prod; *PASSION OF THE PATRIOTS*, 'SOME HONOURABLE GENTLEMAN', TV, 82, CDN, Dir; *'THE GREAT DETECTIVE'* (9 eps), TV, 81-79, CDN, Dir; *'HOME FIRES'* (1 eps), TV, 80, CDN, Dir; *'HIGH HOPES'* (30 eps), TV, 78, CDN, Dir; *SOMETHING'S ROTTEN*, Th, 78, CDN, Dir.

FRUET, William

DGC. 51 Olive Ave., Toronto, Ont, CAN, M6G 1T7. (416)535-3569.
Types of Production & Categories: Th Film-Dir/Wr; Th Short-Dir/Wr; TV Film-Dir/Wr.
Genres: Drama-Th&TV; Horror-Th; Documentary-Th&TV.
Biography: Born 1933, Lethbridge, Alberta. Began his career in acting; photographer and director on medical films; UCLA FIlm School; sponsored teaching films, California, 60-65; was editor, CBC, Film Arts while also working on screenplays.
Selective Filmography: *'CHASING RAINBOWS'* (5 eps), TV, 86, CDN, Dir; *THE PLAYGROUND*, 'RAY BRADBURY THEATRE', TV, 85, CDN, Dir; *'BROTHERS BY CHOICE'* (6 eps), TV, 85, CDN, Dir; *FULL CIRCLE AGAIN*, TV, 84, CDN, Dir; *FOOL'S NIGHT*, Th, 84, USA, Dir; *'VANDERBERG'* (3 eps), TV, 83, CDN, Dir; *DEATH BITE* (SPASMS), Th, 82, CDN, Dir; *KILLER INSTINCT*, Th, 81, CDN, Dir; *CRIES IN THE NIGHT*, Th, 80, CDN, Dir/Prod; *SEARCH AND DESTROY*, Th, 79, CDN, Dir; *ONE OF OUR OWN*, 'FOR THE RECORD', TV, 79, CDN, Dir; *DEATH WEEKEND* (THE HOUSE BY THE LAKE), Th, 75, CDN, Dir/Wr; *125 ROOMS OF COMFORT*, Th, 74, CDN, Co-Wr; *ITALY*, Th, 74, CDN, Dir/Wr; *BRING WHISKEY AND A SMILE*, Th, 74, CDN, Dir; *SLIPSTREAM*, Th, 73, CDN, Wr; *WEDDING IN WHITE*, Th, 72, CDN, Dir/Wr; *RIP-OFF*, Th, 71, CDN, Wr; *GOIN' DOWN THE ROAD*, Th, 70, CDN, Wr (CFA).

FRUND, Jean-Louis

4100 Grande Coulée, St-Edouard, Maskinongé, Qué, CAN, J0K 2H0. (819)228-9222.
Types de production et Catégories: TV film-Réal.
Types d'oeuvres: Documentaire-TV.
Filmographie sélective: *'CONNAISSANCE DU MILIEU'* (19 films), TV, 86-80, CDN, Réal/Rech/Cam; *LE GRAND HERON*, TV, 78/77, CDN, Réal/Sc; *LA VOLEE DES NEIGES* (L'OIE BLANCHE), In, 75/74, CDN, Sc/Réal; *LA VIE*, TV, 67, CDN, Co réal; *JEAN GAUCHET LAROUCHE*, TV, 66, CDN, Réal/Prod.

FURIE, Sidney J.

DGA. Peter Rawley, ICM, 8899 Beverly Blvd., Los Angeles, CA, USA, 90048. (213)550-4000.
Types of Production & Categories: Th Film-Dir/Prod/Wr.
Genres: Drama-Th.
Biography: Born 1933, Toronto, Ontario. Trained in script writing and directing, Carnegie Institute of Technology, Pittsburgh. Director/writer, CBC-TV, 54; moved

(cont/suite)

on to feature films, directing/writing/producing in Canada, 57; England, 60; USA, 66.
Selective Filmography: *SUPERMAN IV,* Th, 86, USA, Dir; *IRON EAGLE,* Th, 85, USA, Dir/Co-Wr; *PURPLE HEARTS,* Th, 83, USA, Dir/Co-Wr/Prod; *THE ENTITY,* Th, 82, USA, Dir; *THE BOYS IN COMPANY C,* Th, 78, USA, Dir/Co-Wr; *GABLE AND LOMBARD,* Th, 76, USA, Dir; *SHEILA LEVINE IS DEAD AND LIVING IN NEW YORK,* Th, 75, USA, Dir; *LITTLE FAUSS AND BIG HALSY,* Th, 70, USA, Dir; *THE LAWYER,* Th, 70, USA, Dir/Co-Wr; *THE NAKED RUNNER,* Th, 67, GB, Dir; *THE APPALOOSA,* Th, 66, USA, Dir; *THE IPCRESS FILE,* Th, 65, GB, Dir; *WONDERFUL LIFE* (SWINGER'S PARADISE), Th, 64, GB, Dir; *THE LEATHER BOYS,* Th, 64, GB, Dir; *THE BOYS,* Th, 62, GB, Dir/Prod; *THREE ON A SPREE,* Th, 61, GB, Dir; *DURING ONE NIGHT* (NIGHT OF PASSION), Th, 61, GB, Dir/Wr/Prod; *THE YOUNG ONES* (WONDERFUL TO BE YOUNG), Th, 61, GB, Dir; *THE SNAKE WOMAN,* Th, 60, GB, Dir; *DR. BLOOD'S COFFIN,* Th, 60, GB, Dir; *A COOL SOUND FROM HELL* (THE YOUNG AND THE BEAT), Th, 59, CDN, Dir/Wr/Prod; *'HUDSON'S BAY'* (29 eps), TV, 59, CDN, Dir; *A DANGEROUS AGE,* Th, 57, CDN, Dir/Wr/Prod.

GAGLIARDI, Laurent

Les Films de l'Automne Ltée., 3688 ave. Laval, Montréal, Qué, CAN, H2X 3C9. (514)288-5669.
Types de production et Catégories: c métrage-Réal/Prod; TV film-Réal/Prod/Sc; TV vidéo-Réal/Prod/Sc.
Types d'oeuvres: Documentaire-TV; Animation-C&TV.
Curriculum vitae: Né en 1948, Montréal, Québec. Critique de cinéma et écrivain. *CHARLES GILL* de la série *MANUSCRITS* remporte le Prix de l'aide à la création, Festival des Films sur l'Art, 82.
Filmographie sélective: *PAMPHILE LEMAY/ALBERT LOZEAU/ANTOINE GERIN LAJOIE,* 'MANUSCRITS', TV, 84/83, CDN, Réal/Sc/Co prod; *OCTAVE CREMAZIE/LAURE CONAN/LOUIS FRECHETTE/CHARLES GILL,* 'MANUSCRITS', TV, 82-79, CDN, Réal/Sc/Co prod; *CHEVAUCHEE* (CALVACADE), C, 79, CDN, Co réal/Prod; *JACQUES HETU, COMPOSITEUR,* TV, 78, CDN, Réal/Sc; *ANDRE GAGNON,* TV, 77, CDN, Réal/Sc; *UNE ARTISANE: YVONNE LECLERC-DAIGLE,* TV, 76, CDN, Réal/Sc/Prod.

GAGNON, Claude

APFVQ, ARRFQ. 994 chemin de la Montagne, Mont St-Hilaire, Qué, CAN, J3G 4S6. (514)464-7173. Yoshimura-Gagnon Inc., 1600 Delorimier, Montréal, Qué, CAN, H2K 3W5. (514)521-7103.
Types de production et Catégories: l métrage-Réal/Prod/Sc/Mont; c métrage-Réal/Prod/Sc/Mont.
Types d'oeuvres: Drame-C; Comédie-C; Action-C.
Curriculum vitae: Né en 1949, St-Hyacinthe, Québec. A vécu au Japon, 70-79; il y réalisa ses premiers films, puis, retour au Québec. *KEIKO* remporte le Prix de la Réalisation, Association des Réalisateurs du Japon; *VISAGE PALE* gagne le Prix Carlsberg, Festival du Film, Montréal.
Filmographie sélective: *VISAGE PALE,* C, 85, CDN, Réal/Co prod/Sc/Mont; *LAROSE, PIERROT ET LA LUCE,* C, 81, CDN, Réal/Co prod/Sc/Mont; *KEIKO,* C, 78, J, Réal/Co prod/Sc/Mont; *YUI TO HI,* C, 77, J, Réal/Mont; *GEININ,* C, 76, J, Réal/Mont; *ESSAI FILMIQUE SUR MUSIQUE JAPONAISE,* C, 74, J, Réal/Sc.

GEDALOF, Hélène

22 Quarry Point, Box 1169, Hudson, Que, CAN, J0P 1H0. (514)458-2652. Radio-Quebec, 800 rue Fullum, Montreal, Que, CAN, H2K 3L7. (514)521-2424.

(cont/suite)

Types of Production & Categories: TV Film-Dir; TV Video-Dir.
Genres: Drama-TV; Comedy-TV; Musical-TV; Documentary-TV.
Biography: Born 1948, Czechoslovakia; Canadian citizen; bilingual. Degree in Honours Psychology, McGill University, 69; Masters, Psychology, U. of Bordeaux, France, 71. Degree in Communications and Education. Full time director, l'Office de Radio-Télédiffusion du Québec since 76; director since 72. Has worked for Inter-Video and the Minister of Education; professor, UQAM. Has won the Prix Judith Jasmin for *MES PARENTS BUVAIENT*, 83 and *ROLAND HALLE*, 82.
Selective Filmography: *LE REPORTER MASQUE CONTRE CASTAFIORE LIBOIRON*, TV, 86/85, CDN, Dir; *AIRENEM*, TV, 84, CDN, Dir; *DE VIVE VOIX*, TV, 83, CDN, Dir; *VIES-A-VIES*, TV, 82, CDN, Dir; *MES PARENTS BUVAIENT*, TV, 82, CDN, Dir; *ROLAND HALLE*, TV, 82, CDN, Dir; *'BOZEJEUNNES'* (3 eps), TV, 81, CDN, Dir; *'DOSSIERS MEDICAUX'* (4 eps), TV, 80/79, CDN, Dir; *'BABILLART'* (25 eps), TV, 79/78, CDN, Dir; *'LA VIE A DEUX'* (5 eps), TV, 78/77, CDN, Dir; *'LA MAISONNEE'* (20 eps), TV, 77/76, CDN, Dir; *'APPROCHE'* (39 eps), TV, 76/75, CDN, Dir; *'TELE-RESSOURCES'* (20 eps), TV, 75/74, CDN, Dir; *DOSSIERS QUEBEC-QUOI?*, TV, 74, CDN, Dir; *'LA VIE QU'ON MENE'* (13 eps), TV, 74, CDN, Dir; *ČA DES DROITS*, TV, 73, CDN, Dir; *'A MA MANIERE A MOI'* (25 eps), TV, 73/72, CDN, Dir; *'DROIT DE REGARD'* (13 eps), TV, 72, CDN, Dir.

GELINAS, Michel F.

AR, SARDEC. 343 Terrasse St-Denis, Montréal, Qué, CAN, H2X 1E7. (514)845-0531. Radio-Canada, 1400 blvd. Dorchester est, Montréal, Qué, CAN, H2L 2M2. (514)285-2981.
Types de production et Catégories: TV film-Réal; TV vidéo-Réal/Sc.
Types d'oeuvres: Drame-TV; Variété-TV; Documentaire-TV; Affaires publiques-TV.
Curriculum vitae: Né en 1949. Etudes universitaires avec stage de formation à la BBC, Londres; à Radio-Canada, Montréal, depuis 78; organisation et direction de stages internationaux en France et au Sénégal (radio, TV). Langues: français, anglais, italien.
Filmographie sélective: *'TRABOULIDON'* (40 eps), TV, 85-83, CDN, Réal; *'L'AGRESSION SEXUELLE DES JEUNES'* (4 ém), TV, 85, CDN, Réal; *LA JUSTICE ET LES JEUNES*, TV, 85, CDN, Réal/Sc; *'BOF ET CIE'* (20 eps), TV, 83/82, CDN, Réal; *'PIERRE ET CIE'* (15 eps), TV, 82/81, CDN, Réal; *'ALLO BOUBOU'* (45 eps), TV, 82/81, CDN, Réal; *'LES COQUELUCHES'* (39 eps), TV, 80/79, CDN, Réal; *'L'HEURE DE POINTE'* (39 eps), TV, 79/78, CDN, Réal; *HOSTAGES OF HISTORY*, TV, 78, CDN, Field Prod.

GENEREUX, René

CTPDA. 14870 17 Ave., White Rock, BC, CAN, V4A 6V4. (604)531-2166. CBC, 700 Hamilton, Vancouver, BC, CAN, V6B 4A2. (604)662-6262. Genere Communications, 14870 17th Ave., White Rock, BC, CAN, V4A 6V4. (604)531-2166.
Types of Production & Categories: TV Film-Dir/Prod; TV Video-Dir/Prod.
Genres: Variety-TV; Documentary-TV; Educational-TV; Current Affairs-TV.
Biography: Born 1952, St. Paul, Alberta; bilingual. Mount Royal College, Radio and TV Broadcasting and Production, 71-73; B.F.A., TV Production and Management, Eastern Washington University, 77 (Senior Meritus Award). Produced Garaventa (lazer disk) for Expo 86.
Selective Filmography: *THE BEST YEARS'* (pilot), (50 eps), TV, 86/85, CDN, Exec Prod/Dir; *THE ARCTIC SHOW'* (2 eps), TV, 86, CDN, Dir; *VANCOUVER 86*, Th, 86, CDN, Prod; *'NEWSCENTRE'* (Vancouver), TV, 85-82, CDN, Dir; *'CBC EVENING NEWS'* (Calgary), TV, 83-81, CDN, Dir; *MOTHER TERESA COMES TO TOWN*, 'MAN ALIVE', TV, 82, CDN, Assoc Prod; *'OLYMPIC CITY JAZZ'* (2 programs), TV, 82/81, CDN, Dir/Prod.

GERRETSEN, Peter
CFTA, CSC, DGC. Peter Gerretsen Prods. Ltd., 118 Castlefield Ave., Toronto, Ont, CAN, M4R 1G4. (416)484-9671.
Types of Production & Categories: Th Short-Dir/Wr; TV Film-Dir/Wr.
Genres: Drama-Th&TV; Educational-Th&TV.
Biography: Born 1939. Director/writer of commercials, educational, sponsored and dramatic short films since 64. Co-founded own production company, 75. Has won awards of merit and excellence from the Art Directors Club of Ontario, Canadian Film Awards; American, Columbus and New York film festivals.
Selective Filmography: *BABY JOHN DOE,* TV, 86, CDN, Dir/Wr.

GERVAIS, Suzanne
ASIFA, SGCT. 1125 Lajoie, #6, Outremont, Qué, CAN, H2V 1N7. (514)276-8994. ONF, C.P.6100, Succ. A, Montréal, Qué, CAN, H3C 3H5. (514)283-9302.
Types de production et Catégories: c métrage-Réal.
Types d'oeuvres: Animation-C.
Curriculum vitae: Née à Montréal, Québec. Etudes à l'Ecole des Beaux-Arts, Montréal. Peintre et illustrateur; a travaillé presque exclusivement en cinéma d'animation. *CYCLE* remporte des prix aux festivals de San Francisco, Columbus et Lubbock; *PREMIER JOURS,* Festival de Annecy, Columbus, New York, Londres et Ottawa; *TCHOU-TCHOU,* Annecy, New York, Los Angeles et Salerne (Italie).
Filmographie sélective: *TREVE* (STILL POINT), C, 83, CDN, Réal; *PREMIERS JOURS* (BEGINNINGS), C, 80, CDN, Réal; *LA PLAGE,* C, 78, CDN, Réal; *CLIMATS,* C, 75, CDN, Réal; *TCHOU-TCHOU,* C, 72, CDN, Co an; *CYCLE,* C, 71, CDN, Réal.

GIBBONS, Bob
ATPD. 1202 Greening Ave., Mississauga, Ont, CAN, L4Y 1H4. (416)277-4067. CBC, 415 Yonge St., Toronto, Ont, CAN. (416)975-6951.
Types of Production & Categories: TV Film-Dir/Prod; TV Video-Dir/Prod.
Genres: Comedy-TV; Variety-TV; Documentary-TV; Children's-TV.
Biography: Born 1939, London, Ontario. Presently completing B.A. at University of Toronto. 28 years at CBC after several years at various radio stations; experienced television technician: audio, video, camera.
Selective Filmography: *A WORLD OF MUSIC,* TV, 86, CDN, Prod/Dir; *JEUNESSE MUSICALE,* TV, 85, CDN, Dir; *CALGARY CENTRE FOR PERFORMING ARTS GALA OPENING,* TV, 85, CDN, Dir; *INTERNATIONAL GALA CELEBRATION,* TV, 85, CDN, Prod/Dir; *HEART'S DELIGHT: STUART BURROWS SINGS,* TV, 85, CDN, Dir; *'ROCK WARS'* (2 eps), TV, 85, CDN, Prod/Dir; *GENIE AWARDS,* TV, 85, CDN, Dir; *CALGARY CENTRE FOR PERFORMING ARTS VARIETY NIGHT,* TV, 85, CDN, Dir; *THE POPE IN CANADA,* TV, 84, CDN, Dir; *THE QUEEN'S GALA - WINNIPEG,* TV, 84, CDN, Prod/Dir; *INTERNATIONAL MUSIC FESTIVAL SPECIAL,* TV, 84, CDN, Dir; *GALA FOR PREMIER ZHAO OF CHINA,* TV, 84, CDN, Dir; *GALA FOR PRESIDENT REAGAN,* TV, 83, CDN, Dir; *CANADA DAY SPECIAL,* TV, 83, CDN, Dir; *SYMPHONY OF A THOUSAND,* TV, 83, CDN, Dir; *JOY TO THE WORLD,* TV, 83, CDN, Dir; *SUPER VARIETY SPECIAL,* TV, 83, CDN, Dir; *SANTA CLAUS PARADE,* TV, 83, CDN, Prod/Dir; *GENIE AWARDS,* TV, 82, CDN, Prod; *NEW YEAR'S EVE SPECIAL,* TV, 82, CDN, Prod/Dir; *THE BLACK DONNELLYS,* TV, 81, CDN, Prod/Dir; *'FRAGGLE ROCK'* (13 eps), TV, 81, CDN, Loc Dir; *JAZZ CANADA,* TV, 79, CDN, Prod/Dir; *'GENE TAYLOR SHOW'* (150 eps), TV, 78, CDN, Prod/Dir; *'TRIVIA'* (13 eps), TV, 78, CDN, Prod/Dir; *'REACH FOR THE TOP'* (50 eps), TV, 74, CDN, Prod/Dir; *'FRIENDLY GIANT'* (100 eps), TV, 74, CDN, Prod/Dir; *'MR DRESSUP'* (200 eps), TV, 74, CDN, Prod/Dir.

GIBSON, Alan

ACTT, DGA, DGGB. Owaissa-Carcur Productions Ltd, 55 Portland Rd., London, GB, W11 4LR. Hatton & Baker Ltd., 18 Jermyn St., London SW1, GB. (01)439-2971. Stone-Masser, 1052 Carol Dr., Los Angeles, CA, USA. (213)275-9599.
Types of Production & Categories: Th Film-Dir; TV Film-Dir/Wr; TV Video-Dir.
Genres: Drama-Th&TV; Comedy-TV; Science Fiction-TV; Horror-Th.
Biography: Born 1938, London, Ontario; University of Western Ontario; Bristol Old Vic Theatre School, England, 57-59. Directed over 100 TV films and video plays for BBC, ITV since 63. Married with 2 daughters. Grand Prize, N.Y. Film/TV Fest. for *CHURCHILL AND THE GENERALS*; Best Dramatic Script, Banff, *THE FLIPSIDE OF DOMINICK HIDE*.
Selective Filmography: *THE CHARMER* (mini-series), TV, 86, GB, Dir; *MARTIN'S DAY,* Th, 83, CDN/USA, Dir; *HELEN KELLER... THE MIRACLE CONTINUES,* TV, 83, GB/USA, Dir; *WITNESS FOR THE PROSECUTION,* TV, 82, GB, Dir; *THE FLIPSIDE OF DOMINCK HIDE,* 'PLAY FOR TODAY', TV, 81/80, GB, Wr/Dir; *A WOMAN CALLED GOLDA,* TV, 81, USA, Dir; *CHURCHILL AND THE GENERALS,* TV, 79, GB, Dir; *SATANIC RITES OF DRACULA,* Th, 73, GB, Dir; *DRACULA AD 1972,* Th, 71, GB, Dir; *CRESCENDO,* Th, 69, GB, Dir.

GILBERT, Tony - see PRODUCERS

GILLARD, Stuart - see WRITERS

GILLSON, Malca

105 Gloucester St., Toronto, Ont, CAN, M4Y 1M2. (416)920-0732. 65 Adelaide St. E., Toronto, Ont, CAN. (416)369-3012.
Types of Production & Categories: TV Film-Dir/Ed.
Genres: Documentary-TV.
Biography: Born Yorkton, Saskatchewan; studied voice, Royal Conservatory of Music, Toronto; German Lieder, Salzburg, Austria. Founded Baie d'Urfée Little Theatre, Montreal, 61; joined NFB, 54, worked on over 50 productions. *LAST DAYS OF LIVING* won the Gold Plaque, Chicago Int'l Film Festival.
Selective Filmography: *MUSICAL MAGIC: GILBERT AND SULLIVAN IN STRATFORD,* TV, 84, CDN, Dir/Ed; *TIME FOR CARING,* TV, 83, CDN, Dir/ Ed; *SINGING: A JOY IN ANY LANGUAGE,* TV, 83, CDN, Dir/Ed; *REFLECTIONS ON SUFFERING,* TV, 82, CDN, Dir/Ed; *A CHOICE OF TWO,* TV, 81, CDN, Assoc Prod; *THE LAST DAYS OF LIVING,* TV, 81, CDN, Dir/Ed; *IT WASN'T EASY,* TV, 78, CDN, Ed; *ALBERTA GIRLS,* Th, 75, CDN, Dir; *MUSICANADA,* TV, 75, CDN, Dir/Ed; *THE WAR IS OVER,* TV, 75, CDN, Prod; *YOU RE EATING FOR TWO,* TV, 74, CDN, Dir; *NELL AND FRED,* TV, 71, CDN, Ed; *THE QUESTION OF TELEVISION VIOLENCE,* TV, 70, CDN, Ed.

GINSBERG, Donald - see PRODUCERS

GIRARD, Hélène - voir MONTEURS

GIRARD, Simon

ARRQ. 4454 Coolbrook, #6, Montréal, Qué, CAN, H4A 3G2. (514)483-3502. Radio-Québec, 800 rue Fullum, Montréal, Qué, CAN, H2K 3L7. (514)521-2424.
Types de production et Catégories: TV vidéo-Réal.
Types d'oeuvres: Nouvelles-TV.
Curriculum vitae: Né en 1947, Montréal. Licence en Sciences politiques, Université Laval. A fait de l'animation, 3 ans; recherche, 3 ans; journaliste, affaires publiques à Radio-Canada, TV et radio, 4 ans.

(cont/suite)

Filmographie sélective: *ONU DE JEUNES/LIVE AID QUEBECOIS/LORRAINE GUAY/PROCES AU PEROU*, 'NORD-SUD', TV, 86/85, CDN, Réal; *FEMMES DE COOPERANT/PENA GOMEZ/SPECIAL REPUBLIQUE DOMINICAINE*, 'NORD-SUD', TV, 85, CDN, Réal; *ECOLE DE COOPERATION/ ORGANISATION CANADIENNE DE SOLIDARITE*, 'NORD-SUD', TV, 85, CDN, Réal; *LES JUIFS A SOSUA/SACO/LES BATEYS/FORUM-AFRIQUE/ TOTO BISSAINTHE*, 'NORD-SUD', TV, 85, CDN, Réal; *JUMELAGE BURLINGTON-NICARAGUA/LA LEPRE/SOCODEVI/OVA*, 'NORD-SUD', TV, 85, CDN, Réal.

GLAWSON, Bruce - see PRODUCERS

GORDON, Lee

IATSE-873. 4 Deer Park Cres., #2C, Toronto, Ont, CAN, M4V 2C3. (416)920-0350.
Types of Production & Categories: Th Short-Dir/Prod; TV Film-Dir/Prod.
Genres: Drama-Th&TV; Documentary-Th&TV; Educational-Th&TV; Children's-TV.
Biography: Canadian citizen; educated at University of Iowa and Columbia U.. Partner in Westminster Films, Toronto, for 25 years; 200 titles, produced and/or directed by. Has won awards at New York, Prague and American film festivals.
Selective Filmography: *MAXIMIZING PRODUCTION*, ED, 84, CDN/USA, Dir; *IRRIGATION/THE PROFIT PARASITE*, In, 80/79, CDN/USA, Dir; *CANWEL/A WAY OUT*, ED, 74/70, CDN, Prod; *HERE'S LOOKING AT YOU/ ENGINEERING IS FOR PEOPLE*, ED, 74/71, CDN, Dir; *THE LAST ACT OF MARTIN WESTON*, Th, 70, CDN/CS, Prod; *THE TROUBLE WITH WORDS*, ED, 70, CDN, Prod; *PUTTING IT TOGETHER*, ED, 70, CDN, Prod/Dir; *RYE ON THE ROCKS*, In, 69, CDN, Prod (CFA); *AN IRISH TOUCHSTONE*, In, 68, CDN/IRL, Prod/Dir; *NIKKI, WILD DOG OF THE NORTH*, Th, 61, CDN, Co-Prod; *THE LOST MISSILE*, Th, 58, USA, Prod.

GOULET, Stella

ARRFQ. 3013 Boulogne, Ste-Foy, Qué, CAN, G1W 2C4. (418)653-4219. Spirafilm, 56 St-Pierre, Québec, Qué, CAN, G1K 4A1. (418)694-0786.
Types de production et Catégories: c métrage-Réal/Sc/Mont; TV film-Réal/Sc; TV vidéo-Réal/Mont.
Types d'oeuvres: Drame-C&TV; Documentaire-TV; Enfants-TV.
Curriculum vitae: Née en 1947. Baccalauréat Général, mineure en Cinéma et Théâtre, 82. Connaissances en musique et danse folklorique. *PIC ET PIC ET CONTREDANSE* remporte un prix au Palmarès canadien du court métrage indépendant.
Filmographie sélective: *ON JOUE OU ON JOUE PAS?*, TV, 86, CDN, Sc/Co réal/Co mont/Co prod; *ELISE ET LA MER*, TV, 86, CDN, Sc/Réal; *LE GRAND DEFI*, TV, 86, CDN, Sc; *LA TIRELIRE*, TV, 84, CDN, Réal/Co prod/Sc; *LA DIFFERENCE N'A PAS D'IMPORTANCE*, TV, 84, CDN, Co réal/Co mont; *TROIS PETITS TOURS*, TV, 83/82, CDN, Réal/Prod/Mont/Sc; *MELODIE, MA GRAND-MERE*, TV, 83, CDN, Réal/Sc; *LES CHEVAUX D'ACIER*, TV, 83, CDN, Co réal/Co prod/Mont; *PIC ET PIC ET CONTREDANSE*, C, 79/78, CDN, Réal/Co prod.

GRANT, Michael

DGC. 463 Puerto Del Mar, Pacific Palisades, CA, USA, 90272. (213)454-1356.
Types of Production & Categories: Th Film-Dir/Prod.
Genres: Drama-Th.
Biography: Born 1952, Toronto, Ontario; B.A., English and Film, University of Western Ontario.

(cont/suite)

Selective Filmography: *HEAD ON* (FATAL ATTRACTION), Th, 80, CDN, Exec Prod/Co-Prod/Dir; *EMMA ZUNZ*, TV, 79, CDN, Prod; *THE BROTHERS KEEPER*, TV, 78, CDN, Prod/Dir; *RAGTIME SUMMER*, Th, 77, CDN, Assoc Prod.

GREENE, David

DGA, DGC. 142 Adelaide Drive, Santa Monica, CA, USA, 90402. Boz Graham, CAA, 1888 Century Park East, Los Angeles, CA, USA, 90067. (213)277-4545.
Types of Production & Categories: Th Film-Dir/Prod/Wr; TV Film-Dir/Prod/Wr; TV Video-Dir/Prod/Wr.
Genres: Drama-Th&TV; Action-Th&TV; Science Fiction-Th&TV; Horror-Th.
Biography: Born 1921, England; graduated St. Martin's School of Art. Went to New York as an actor with Laurence Olivier in 'Antony and Cleopatra'; joined CBC, Toronto, 52 as director of live dramas on TV; productions included: *OTHELLO*, *HAMLET*, *MACBETH*; *FLIGHT INTO DANGER*, 57. Granted Canadian citizenship.
Selective Filmography: *VANISHING ACT*, TV, 86, USA, Dir; *CIRCLE OF VIOLENCE: A FAMILY DRAMA*, TV, 86, USA, Dir; *GUILTY CONSCIENCE*, TV, 85, USA, Dir; *THIS CHILD IS MINE*, TV, 85, USA, Dir; *FATAL VISION*, TV, 84, USA, Dir; *THE GUARDIAN*, TV, 84, CDN/USA, Dir; *HER REVENGE*, TV, 84, USA, Dir/Prod; *PROTOTYPE*, TV, 83, USA, Dir; *GHOST DANCING*, TV, 83, USA, Dir; *REHEARSAL FOR MURDER*, TV, 83, USA, Dir; *TAKE YOUR BEST SHOT*, TV, 82, USA, Dir; *WORLD WAR III*, TV, 82, USA, Dir/Prod; *THE CHOICE*, TV, 81, USA, Dir/Prod; *HARD COUNTRY*, Th, 81, USA, Dir/Prod; *FRIENDLY FIRE*, TV, 79, USA, Dir (**EMMY**); *VACATION IN HELL*, TV, 79, USA, Dir/Prod; *GRAY LADY DOWN*, Th, 78, USA, Dir; *ROOTS* (mini-series), TV, 77, USA, Co-Dir (**EMMY**); *THE TRIAL OF LEE HARVEY OSWALD*, TV, 77, USA, Dir; *THE COUNT OF MONTE CRISTO*, TV, 76, USA, Dir; *RICH MAN POOR MAN* (mini-series), TV, 76, USA, Co-Dir (**EMMY**); *GODSPELL*, Th, 73, USA, Dir/Scr; *MADAM SIN*, TV, 72, GB, Dir; *I START COUNTING*, Th, 70, GB, Dir; *THE PEOPLE NEXT DOOR*, Th, 70, USA, Dir; *THE PEOPLE NEXT DOOR*, TV, 68, USA, Dir (**EMMY**); *SEBASTIAN*, Th, 68, GB, Dir; *THE SHUTTERED ROOM*, Th, 68, GB, Dir/Scr; *THE STRANGE AFFAIR*, Th, 67, GB, Dir.

GREENWALD, Barry

242 Delaware Ave., Toronto, Ont, CAN, M6H 2T6. (416)536-0655.
Types of Production & Categories: Th Film-Dir/Prod/Ed; Th Short-Dir/Prod/Ed; TV Film-Dir/Prod/Ed; TV Video-Dir/Prod.
Genres: Drama-Th&TV; Documentary-Th&TV; Educational-TV.
Biography: Born 1955, Toronto, Ontario. Film major, Conestoga College; NFB, Directors Training Unit (drama workshop), 76-78. Awards include Palme d'Or, Cannes Film Festival for *METAMORPHOSIS*; Best Documentary Direction (Silver Boomerang), Melbourne Int'l Film Festival for *TAXI!*
Selective Filmography: *PITCHMEN*, Th, 85, CDN, Dir/Co-Ed; *FALASHA: AGONY OF THE BLACK JEWS*, 'MAN ALIVE', TV, 83, CDN, Ed; *TAXI!*, Th, 82, CDN, Dir/Wr; *ARCTIC SPIRITS* (THE NEW SHAMANS), Th, 82, CDN, Ed/Snd Ed; *HOT WHEELS*, Th, 79, CDN, Co-Ed (**CFEG**); *CAREERS FOR EVERYONE*, ED, 77, CDN, Dir/Prod/Ed/Cam; *METAMORPHOSIS*, Th, 75, CDN, Wr/Dir/Prod/Ed (**CFA**); *WILLAMETTE, MORMOT AND PRIEST*, Th, 74, CDN, Dir/Prod; *TANGENTS*, Th, 73, CDN, Prod/Dir/Wr/Cam; *AGAMEMNON THE LOVER*, Th, 71, CDN, Co-Dir/Co-An; *ETUDE*, Th, 70, CDN, Dir/Wr/Ed/Cam.

GRENIER, Henriette

AR. 8950 blvd. Rivard, #201, Brossard, Qué, CAN, J4X 1Y1. (514)465-1303.

(cont/suite)

DIRECTORS/REALISATEURS

Radio-Canada, 1400 blvd. Dorchester est, Montréal, Qué, CAN, H2L 2M2. (514) 285-2888.
Types de production et Catégories: TV film-Réal.
Types d'oeuvres: Variété-TV; Sports-TV.
Curriculum vitae: Née en 1938, Montréal, Québec; bilingue; diplômée de l'Université McGill, Montréal. A Radio-Canada depuis 63; nommée réalisatrice, 77, coordonnatrice, 78; actuellement coordonnatrice des projets spéciaux et coproductions avec les pays francophones (CTF).
Filmographie sélective: *LES INSOLENCES D'UNE CAMERA'* (36 eps), TV, 86, CDN, Coord pro; *GALA DES GRANDES ECOLES,* 'BEAUX DIMANCHES', TV, 85, CDN/F, Coord pro; *SUPER STAR,* 'BEAUX DIMANCHES', TV, 84/83, CDN, Réal; *SI ON CHANTAIT,* 'BEAUX DIMANCHES', TV, 84, CDN/F/L/ CH, Réal/Coord pro; *GALA DES ETOILES DU MAURIER* (DU MAURIER STARS), 'BEAUX DIMANCHES', TV, 84, CDN, Prod dél; *'ALLO BOUBOU'* (quot), TV, 83-78, CDN, Réal/Coord pro; *FETE DE LA ST-JEAN,* TV, 82, CDN, Coord pro; *GALA 25ieme ANNEE TELE JONQUIERE* (AVEC VOUS DEPUIS 25 ANS), 'BEAUX DIMANCHES', TV, 81, CDN, Réal; *'HEURE DE POINTE'* (quot), TV, 78/77, CDN, Réal; *FETE DU CANADA* (LET'S CELEBRATE), TV, 78, CDN, Coord pro.

GRIFFIN, Bruce - see EDITORS

GROULX, Sylvie

ARRFQ, SARDEC. 4396 rue Boyer, Montréal, Qué, CAN, H2J 3E1. (514)524-1420.
Types de production et Catégories: l métrage-Réal; c métrage-Réal; TV vidéo-Réal.
Types d'oeuvres: Documentaire-C&TV.
Curriculum vitae: Née en 1953, Montréal, Québec. Langues: français, anglais, espagnol; Bac. en Communications, Université Concordia, Montréal. Productions indépendantes et ONF; distribution de films, Cinéma Libre Inc.; animatrice à la radio.
Filmographie sélective: *ENTRE DEUX VAGUES,* TV, 85, CDN, Co réal; *LE GRAND REMUE-MENAGE,* C, 78, CDN, Réal/Prod/Rech; *UNE BIEN BELLE VILLE,* C, 76, CDN, Rech.

GUERTIN, Micheline

ARRQ. 391 Hickson, St-Lambert, Qué, CAN, J4R 2N9. (514)465-7768.
Radio-Québec, 800 rue Fullum, Montréal, Qué, CAN, H2K 3L7. (514)521-2424.
Types de production et Catégories: TV vidéo-Réal.
Types d'oeuvres: Drame-TV; Comédie-TV; Variété-TV; Annonces-TV.
Curriculum vitae: Née en 1944 à Montréal, Québec; bilingue. Etudes: Lettres françaises, Costumes de théâtre.
Filmographie sélective: *LES VOISINS,* TV, 86, CDN, Réal; *AU BOUT DE LA NUIT,* TV, 86, CDN, Réal; *VICTOR LE VAMPIRE,* TV, 85, CDN, Réal; *ECAILLE,* TV, 84, CDN, Réal; *JE PERSISTE ET SIGNE...BREL,* TV, 84, CDN, Réal; *'BOZEJEUNNES'* (pl ém), TV, 83-81, CDN, Réal.

GUILBEAULT, Luce

ARRFQ, UDA. 4132 Mentana, Montréal, Qué, CAN, H2L 3S2. (514)524-5948.
Types de production et Catégories: l métrage-Réal/Com; TV film-Com.
Types d'oeuvres: Drame-C&TV.
Curriculum vitae: Née en 1935 à Montréal, Québec. Bac. en Philosophie, Université de Montréal; Conservatoire de la Province de Québec. Réalisatrice, comédienne, théâtre et cinéma; enseignement du théâtre, UQAM, Ecole Nationale de Théâtre du Canada. Fonde Les Reines du Foyer (production cinéma), Montréal, 77.
Filmographie sélective: *'DES DAMES DE COEUR'* (26 eps), TV, 86, CDN, Com; *'LE TEMPS D'UNE PAIX'* (4 eps), TV, 85, CDN, Com; *QUI A TIRE SUR NOS*

(cont/suite)

HISTOIRES D'AMOUR?, C, 85, CDN, Com; *PENSE A TON DESIR*, C, 84, CDN, Com; *ALBEDO*, C, 83, CDN, Com; *LA QUARANTAINE*, C, 82, CDN, Com; *L'ECHANTILLON*, 'CONTREJOUR', TV, 79, CDN, Com; *D'ABORD MENAGERES*, C, 78, CDN, Réal; *MOURIR A TUE-TETE* (A SCREAM OF SILENCE), C, 78, CDN, Com; *SOME AMERICAN FEMINISTS*, C, 77, CDN, Réal; *BARGAIN BASEMENT*, C, 76, CDN, Com (**CFA**); *DENYSE BENOIT, COMEDIENNE*, C, 75, CDN, Réal; *LE TEMPS DE L'AVANT*, 'EN TANT QUE FEMMES', TV, 74, CDN, Com; *MUSTANG*, C, 74, CDN, Com; *PAR UNE BELLE NUIT D'HIVER*, C, 74, CDN, Com; *LA DERNIERE NEIGE*, 'TOUL'MONDE PARLE FRANCAIS', C, 73, CDN, Com; *REJEANNE PADOVANI*, C, 73, CDN, Com; *TENDRESSE ORDINAIRE*, C, 73, CDN, Com; *LE TEMPS D'UNE CHASSE*, C, 72, CDN, Com; *LA MAUDITE GALETTE*, C, 72, CDN, Com; *O.K...LALIBERTE*, C, 72, CDN, Com; *FRANCOISE DUROCHER, WAITRESS*, C, 72, CDN, Com.

GULLIVER, Randy

631 Mortimer Ave., Toronto, Ont, CAN, M4C 2J9. City-TV, 99 Queen St.E., Toronto, Ont, CAN, M5C 2M1. (416)367-5757.
Types of Production & Categories: TV Video-Ed/Dir.
Genres: Documentary-TV; Talk Show-TV.
Biography: Born 1951, Leamington, Ontario. Toured North America extensively, playing with bands 'New Potatoes' and 'Edward Bear'; recorded 4 albums for Capitol Records. Started in film as tape operator, City-TV, 76; master control for 2 years; started directing, 79.
Selective Filmography: *'CITYLINE'* (160 eps), TV, 85, CDN, Dir/Field Prod/Ed; *GROWING UP GAY*, TV, 85, CDN, Wr/Prod/Dir/Ed; *'CITY LIFE'* (200 eps), TV, 84/83, CDN, Dir/Field Prod; *'CITY LIGHTS'* (500 eps), TV, 83-79, CDN, Dir/Ed.

GUNN, John

70 Charles St.E., #15, Toronto, Ont, CAN, M4Y 1T1. (416)924-7494. CITY TV, 99 Queen St.E., Toronto, Ont, CAN, M5C 2M1. (416)367-5757.
Types of Production & Categories: TV Video-Dir.
Genres: Variety-TV.
Biography: Born 1955. Director of on-air promotion and commercial production: City TV/MuchMusic. Awards: New York Film & Television Festival, Broadcast Promotion Assoc. Int'l; Can-Pro; TVB.
Selective Filmography: *'FASHION TELEVISION'* (6 eps), TV, 86/85, CDN, Dir.

GUNNARSSON, Sturla

DGC. 266 Lippincott St., Toronto, Ont, CAN, M5S 2P5. (416)531-7039.
Types of Production & Categories: Th Film-Dir/Prod; Th Short-Dir/Prod; TV Film-Dir/Prod; TV Video-Dir.
Genres: Drama-Th&TV; Documentary-Th&TV.
Biography: Born 1951, Reykjavik, Iceland; Canadian citizen. B.A., English Literature, University of British Columbia, 74. Languages: English, Icelandic, Spanish. He won a Rockefeller Foundation Grant for *AFTER THE AXE* which won a Blue Ribbon (American Film Fest.), Golden Sheaf (Yorkton), Silver Cindy (Chicago) and was nominated for an Oscar; *A DAY MUCH LIKE THE OTHERS* won the Norman McLaren Award and was presented at the Museum of Modern Art (NY) and at Filmex; *FINAL OFFER: BOB WHITE AND THE UNITED AUTO WORKERS FIGHT FOR INDEPENDENCE* won a Rockie and the Prix Italia, 86.
Selective Filmography: *'STREET LEGAL'* (1 eps), TV, 86, CDN, Dir; *'AIRWAVES'* (5 eps), TV, 86/85, CDN, Dir; *THE CANADIANS*, TV, 86, USA, Dir/Prod; *FINAL OFFER: BOB WHITE AND THE UAW'S FIGHT FOR INDEPENDENCE*, Th, 85, CDN, Dir/Co-Prod (**GENIE**); *'BEACHCOMBERS'* (1 eps), TV, 84, CDN, Dir; *THE FRONT LINE*, 'FOR THE RECORD', TV, 84, CDN, Prod; *THE TRUESTEEL AFFAIR*, TV, 83, CDN, Dir; *THE BAMBOO*

(cont/suite)

BRUSH, 'SONS AND DAUGHTERS', TV, 82, CDN, Dir; *FIRED,* 'ENTERPRISE', TV, 82, USA, Dir/Prod; *AFTER THE AXE,* Th, 81, CDN, Dir/ Co-Prod; *COUNTRY MUSIC NITELY,* TV, 79, CDN, Dir/Prod; *B LICENSE,* ED, 78, CDN, Dir/Prod; *A DAY MUCH LIKE THE OTHERS,* Th, 78, CDN, Dir/ Prod.

HALDANE, Don

DGC. 2076 Dickson Rd., Mississauga, Ont, CAN, L5B 1Y6. (416)279-8461.
Types of Production & Categories: Th Film-Dir; TV Film-Dir.
Genres: Drama-Th&TV; Action-TV; Science Fiction-Th; Children's-TV.
Biography: Born 1914, Edmonton, Alberta; graduated Yale Drama School, 41. After war, attended Columbia University and New School of Social Research. Past President of DGC; 25 years as President of Westminster Films. Recipient of Queen's Silver Jubilee Medal.
Selective Filmography: *'THE CAMPBELLS'* (4 eps), TV, 86/85, CDN/USA/GB, Dir; *'THE EDISON TWINS'* (6 eps), TV, 86/85, CDN, Dir; *'THE BEACHCOMBERS'* (12 eps), TV, 86-81, CDN, Dir; *'RED SERGE'* (2 eps), TV, 86, CDN, Dir; *'RITTER'S COVE'* (6 eps), TV, 79/78, CDN, Dir; *'FOR THE RECORD'* (3 eps), TV, 78/77, CDN, Dir; *'SIDESTREET'* (6 eps), TV, 76-74, CDN, Dir; *'SWISS FAMILY ROBINSON'* (7 eps), TV, 75/74, CDN, Dir; *THE REINCARNATE,* Th, 71, CDN, Dir; *'FOREST RANGERS'* (14 eps), TV, 64/63, CDN, Dir; *THE DRYLANDERS,* Th, 62, CDN, Dir; *NIKKI, WILD DOG OF THE NORTH,* Th, 60, CDN/USA, Co-Dir.

HALLEE, Céline

AR. 5877 rue de Terrebonne, Montréal, Qué, CAN, H4A 1B4. Radio-Canada, 1400 blvd. Dorchester est, Montréal, Qué, CAN, H2L 2M2. (514)285-2844.
Types de production et Catégories: TV film-Réal; TV vidéo-Réal.
Types d'oeuvres: Drame-TV; Comédie-TV; Variété-TV; Documentaire-TV.
Curriculum vitae: Née en 1950, Ville-Marie, Québec. Bac. en Musique et Expression dramatique, Université de Montréal et du Québec. 8 ans de mise en scène au théâtre; réalisateur télévision depuis 83; scénariste. Mise en scène de la pièce 'L'Amérique à sec', 86.
Filmographie sélective: *'LA VIE PROMISE'* (26 eps), TV, 85/84, CDN, Réal; *'L'AGENT FAIT LE BONHEUR'* (20 eps), TV, 85, CDN, Réal; *'MONSIEUR LE MINISTRE'* (2 eps), TV, 84/83, CDN, Réal; *'AVIS DE RECHERCHE'* (20 eps), TV, 84/83, CDN, Réal.

HARRIS, Les

ACFTP. 16 Servington Crescent, Toronto, Ont, CAN, M4S 2J3. (416)485-0874. Canamedia Productions Ltd, 511 King St.W., Ste. 301, Toronto, Ont, CAN, M5V 1K4. (416)591-6612.
Types of Production & Categories: TV Film-Dir/Prod; TV Video-Dir/Prod.
Genres: Drama-TV; Comedy-TV; Variety-TV; Documentary-TV.
Biography: Born 1947, England; British-Canadian citizen. Educated in India and England; B.A.(Honours), Economics, Sheffield University. Editor, BBC TV; producer, director, CBC, CTV; TV distributor, consultant; Vice President ACFTP. *ESCAPE FROM IRAN: THE CANADIAN CAPER* won a Silver Medal, New York Film Festival; *THE KING OF FRIDAY NIGHT,* Gold Medal (N.Y.), Silver Hugo (Chicago), Rockie (Banff), The Athens Award, Ohio.
Selective Filmography: *444 DAYS TO FREEDOM: WHAT REALLY HAPPENED IN IRAN,* TV, 85, CDN, Dir/Prod/Ed; *THE KING OF FRIDAY NIGHT,* TV, 85/ 84, CDN, Prod (**2 CFTA**); *AGENTS OF DECEPTION,* TV, 84, CDN, Dir; *'W5'* (50 seg), TV, 84-79, CDN, Dir/Prod; *ESCAPE FROM IRAN: THE INSIDE STORY,* TV, 81, CDN, Dir/Prod; *ESCAPE FROM IRAN: THE CANADIAN CAPER,* TV, 80, CDN, Prod; *CHABOT SOLO* (3 parts), TV, 79, CDN, Dir/Prod.

HARRISON, Jim

831 Richmond St.W., #213, Toronto, Ont, CAN, M6J 3P7. (416)367-5284. Soundhouse, 409 King St.W., Toronto, Ont, CAN, M5V 1K1. (416)598-2260.
Types of Production & Categories: TV Film-Dir/Ed; TV Video-Dir/Ed.
Genres: Drama-TV; Documentary-TV; Sports-TV.
Biography: Born 1941, Britain; Canadian landed immigrant. Studied at London Film School, 70. Moved to Canada, 78.
Selective Filmography: *'SPORTS WEEKEND'* (40 seg), TV, 86-78, CDN, Dir/Ed/ Wr; *'WIDE WORLD OF SPORTS'* (12 seg), TV, 85-80, CDN, Dir/Ed/Wr; *OLYMPIC JOURNEY* (1 seg), TV, 84, CDN, Wr; *SILENCE OF THE NORTH,* Th, 80/79, CDN, Co-Snd Ed; *'COUNTRY CANADA'* (1 eps), TV, 80, CDN, Ed.

HART, Harvey

DGA, DGC. 10 Clarendon, Toronto, Ont, CAN. (416)962-3436. Rohar Productions Ltd., 5 Sultan St., Toronto, Ont, CAN. (416)960-2351. Bill Haber, CAA, 1888 Century Park E., Ste 1400, Los Angeles, CA, USA, 90067. (213)277-4545.
Types of Production & Categories: Th Film-Dir; TV Film-Dir/Prod; TV Video-Dir/ Prod.
Genres: Drama-Th&TV; Comedy-Th&TV; Action-Th&TV; Documentary-Th&TV.
Biography: Born 1928, Toronto, Ontario; University of Toronto, 45-48; dramatic workshop, NYC, 49-50. Co-founder of the Civic Square Theatre, Toronto, 62. President: Rohar Productions, Toronto and California. He won a Golden Globe for *EAST OF EDEN.*
Selective Filmography: *BEVERLY HILLS MADAM,* TV, 85, USA, Dir; *RECKLESS DISREGARD,* TV, 84, CDN/USA, Dir; *MASTER OF THE GAME* (mini-series), TV, 83, USA, Dir; *UTILITIES,* Th, 82, CDN, Dir; *THE YELLOW ROSE* (pilot), TV, 82, USA, Dir; *BORN BEAUTIFUL,* TV, 82, USA, Dir; *EAST OF EDEN* (mini-series), TV, 81, USA, Dir; *THE HIGH COUNTRY* (THE FIRST HELLO), Th, 80, CDN, Dir; *LIKE NORMAL PEOPLE,* TV, 79, USA, Dir; *THE PRINCE OF CENTRAL PARK,* TV, 77, USA, Dir; *CAPTAINS COURAGEOUS,* TV, 77, USA, Dir; *SHOOT,* Th, 76, CDN, Dir; *GOLDENROD,* Th, 76, CDN, Dir (CFA); *'COLUMBO'* (1 eps), TV, 75, USA, Dir; *MURDER OF MERCY,* TV, 74, USA, Dir; *CAN ELLEN BE SAVED,* TV, 74, USA, Dir; *THE PYX,* Th, 73, CDN, Dir; *FORTUNE AND MEN'S EYES,* Th, 71, CDN/USA, Dir; *JUDD FOR THE DEFENSE* (pilot), TV, 70, USA, Dir; *THE SWEET RIDE,* Th, 69, USA, Dir; *THE YOUNG LAWYERS* (pilot), TV, 69, USA, Dir; *DAVID CHAPTER II/ DAVID CHAPTER III,* TV, 68-66, CDN, Dir/Prod; *THE QUARE FELLOW,* TV, 67, CDN, Dir/Prod; *BUS RILEY'S BACK IN TOWN,* Th, 65, USA, Dir; *THE DYBBUK,* TV, 60, CDN, Dir/Prod; *ENEMY OF THE PEOPLE,* TV, 60, CDN, Dir/Prod; *HOME OF THE BRAVE,* TV, 60, CDN, Dir/Prod; *THE CRUCIBLE,* TV, 59, CDN, Dir/Prod; *THE LUCK OF GINGER COFFEY,* TV, 59, CDN, Dir/ Prod.

HAWKINS, Crawford W. - see PRODUCERS

HAZZAN, Ray - see PRODUCERS

HEALEY, Barry - see WRITERS

HEBERT, Pierre

ARRFQ, ASIFA, SGCT. 4607 Marquette, Montréal, Qué, CAN, H2J 3Y3. (514) 527-6855. ONF, C.P. 6100, Montréal, Qué, CAN, H3C 3H5. (514)283-9303.
Types de production et Catégories: c métrage-Réal/An.
Types d'oeuvres: Documentaire-C; Animation-C; Expérimental-C.
Curriculum vitae: Né en 1944, Montréal, Québec. Etudes en Anthropologie. A l'ONF depuis 65; enseigne le cinéma à l'Ecole des Beaux-Arts, Montréal, Université Laval, Québec. Réalisation de séquences pour le spectacle de danse de la compagnie

(cont/suite)

O Vertigo, 86. *CHANTS ET DANSES DU MONDE* remporte le Prix de la Critique Québécoise.
Filmographie sélective: *O PICASSO - TABLEAUX D'UNE SUREXPOSITION,* C, 85, CDN, Réal; *CHANTS ET DANSES DU MONDE ANIME-LE METRO,* C, 85, CDN, Réal; *O PICASSO,* C, 85, CDN, An; *ETIENNE ET SARA,* C, 84, CDN, Réal; *LOVE ADDICT,* C, 84, CDN, Co réal; *L'EMOTION DISSONANTE,* C, 84, CDN, Séq an; *BEYROUTH A DEFAUT D'ETRE MORT,* C, 83, CDN, Des; *PENSE A TON DESIR,* TV, 83, CDN, Des eff sp; *SOUVENIRS DE GUERRE,* C, 82, CDN, Réal; *LA STRATEGIE AMERICAINE,* TV, 82, CDN, Séq an; *ENTRE CHIENS ET LOUP,* C, 78, CDN, Réal; *PERE NOEL! PERE NOEL!,* C, 75, CDN, Réal; *DU COQ A L'ANE,* C, 73, CDN, Co réal; *C'EST PAS CHINOIS,* C, 73, CDN, Co réal; *JE CHANTE A CHEVAL,* C, 72, CDN, Séq an; *NOTIONS ELEMENTAIRES DE GENETIQUE,* C, 71, CDN, Réal; *LE CORBEAU ET LE RENARD,* C, 70, CDN, Co réal; *L'HOMME MULTIPLIE,* C, 69, CDN, Gén an; *AUTOUR DE LA PERCEPTION,* C, 68, CDN, Réal; *JUSQU'AU COEUR,* C, 68, CDN, Gén an; *OPUS 3,* C, 67, CDN, Réal; *POPULATION EXPLOSION,* C, 67, CDN, Réal; *OPHOP,* C, 65, CDN, Réal; *LE REVOLUTIONNAIRE,* C, 65, CDN, Séq an.

HENAUT, Dorothy Todd

SGCT. 5045 Esplanade, Montreal, Que, CAN, H2T 2Y9. (514)276-5333. NFB, Box 6100, Stn. A, Montreal, Que, CAN, H3C 3H5. (514)283-9533.
Types of Production & Categories: Th Film-Prod/Dir; TV Film-Prod/Dir.
Genres: Documentary-Th&TV; Educational-Th&TV.
Biography: Born 1935, Hamilton, Ontario; bilingual. Graduated from the Sorbonne, 54. Founded magazine 'The Craftsman/ l'Artisan', 65; edited newsletter 'Access' (68-74) and created regional community video programmes (72) for 'Challenge for Change', NFB; currently working at Studio D (NFB).
Selective Filmography: *LES TERRIBLES VIVANTES* (FIREWORDS), Th, 86, CDN, Dir; *NOT A LOVE STORY: A FILM ABOUT PORNOGRAPHY* (C'EST SURTOUT PAS DE L'AMOUR), Th, 81, CDN, Prod; *HORSE-DRAWN MAGIC,* TV, 79, CDN, Dir; *SUN, WIND AND WOOD,* TV, 78, CDN, Dir; *TEMISCAMINGUE, QUEBEC,* TV, 76, CDN, Prod; *THE NEW ALCHEMISTS* (ALCHIMIE NOUVELLE), TV, 74, CDN, Dir; *VTR ST-JACQUES,* TV, 69, CDN, Assoc Dir; *OPERATION BOULE DE NEIGE,* TV, 69, CDN, Assoc Dir.

HETU, Donald R.

SARDEC. 1394 Sauvé est, Montréal, Qué, CAN, H2C 2A2. Radio-Canada, 541 ave. du Portage, Winnipeg, Man, CAN. (204)786-0493.
Types de production et Catégories: l métrage-Sc; TV film-Sc; TV film-Réal/Sc.
Types d'oeuvres: Drame-TV; Comédie-C&TV; Variété-TV; Comédie musicale-TV.
Curriculum vitae: Né en 1947, Québec; bilingue. Expérience: publicité, création littéraire; 15 ans de télévision en tant que réalisateur et scénariste.
Filmographie sélective: *'TRES ART'* (42 eps), TV, 86-84, CDN, Réal; *'GENIES EN HERBE'* (20 eps), TV, 86-84, CDN, Réal; *'PILE OU FACE'* (32 eps), TV, 85-83, CDN, Réal; *'MAG OUEST'* (21 eps), TV, 85/84, CDN, Réal; *'DUO DU CLOCHER'* (8 eps), TV, 84/83, CDN, Sc; *'AUTREFOIS A LA RIVIERE ROUGE'* (10 eps), TV, 83/82, CDN, Sc; *PIERROT,* TV, 81, CDN, Sc; *LES JEUNES QUEBECOISES,* C, 78, CDN, Sc.

HILLER, Arthur

DGA, DGC. Phil Gersh, Gersh Agency, 222 N.Canon Dr., Beverly Hills, CA, USA, 90212. (213)274-6611.
Types of Production & Categories: Th Film-Dir/Prod.
Genres: Drama-Th; Comedy-Th; Musical-Th; Action-Th.
Biography: Born 1923, Edmonton, Alberta. M.A., Psychology, University of Toronto. Served on National Board of DGA and Board of Governors, Academy of

(cont/suite)

Motion Picture Arts & Sciences. Chairman, L.A. Student Film Institute; Commander, Sursum Corda (Brussels); Doctor of Letters, London Institute for Applied Research; Doctor Laureate, Imperial Order of Constantine, Lisbon; Flying Officer, R.C.A.F.(overseas) W.W.II. M.E.C.L.A. Award, *MAKING LOVE*; Yugoslav Film Fest. Award, *HOSPITAL*; Golden Globe Award, Oscar nomination for *LOVE STORY*.
Selective Filmography: *OUTRAGEOUS FORTUNE*, Th, 86, USA, Dir; *TEACHERS*, Th, 84, USA, Dir; *AUTHOR! AUTHOR!*, Th, 82, USA, Dir; *MAKING LOVE*, Th, 81, USA, Dir; *THE IN-LAWS* (DON'T SHOOT THE DENTIST), Th, 79, USA, Dir; *SILVER STREAK*, Th, 76, USA, Dir; *MAN IN THE GLASS BOOTH*, Th, 75, USA, Dir; *MAN OF LA MANCHA*, Th, 72, I, Dir/ Prod; *HOSPITAL*, Th, 71, USA, Dir; *PLAZA SUITE*, Th, 70, USA, Dir; *LOVE STORY*, Th, 70, USA, Dir (**DGA**); *OUT OF TOWNERS*, Th, 70, USA, Dir; *'ALFRED HITCHCOCK PRESENTS'* (many eps), TV, 65-55, USA, Dir; *THE AMERICANIZATION OF EMILY*, Th, 64, USA, Dir; *'ROUTE 66'* (many eps), TV, 64-60, USA, Dir; *'NAKED CITY'* (many eps), TV, 63-58, USA, Dir; *'PLAYHOUSE 90'* (sev eps), TV, 61-56, USA, Dir; *'GUNSMOKE'* (many eps), TV, 55, USA, Dir.

HOEDEMAN, Co

SGCT. Dalhousie Mills, R.R. 1, North Lancaster, Ont, CAN, K0C 1Z0. (613)347-3362. ONF, C.P.6100, Succ. A, Montréal, Qué, CAN, H3C 3H5. (514)283-9292.
Types de production et Catégories: c métrage-Réal/Sc.
Types d'oeuvres: Animation-C; Education-C; Enfants-C; Expérimental-C.
Curriculum vitae: Né en 1940, Amsterdam, Pays-Bas; au Canada depuis 65; immigrant reçu. Dix ans d'expérience dans l'industrie du cinéma aux Pays-Bas comme assistant à la caméra et film d'animation; à l'ONF depuis 65 comme animateur et réalisateur de films d'animation; particulièrement spécialisé en animation en volume (puppet films). Education: général, photographie beaux-arts et surtout autodidacte. Membre du conseil de Asifa Canada et Président pendant 4 ans. Ses films ont reçu 57 prix internationaux.
Filmographie sélective: *MASCARADE* (MASQUARADE), C, 84-80, CDN, Réal/An/Sc; *LE TRESOR DES GROTOCEANS* (THE TREASURE OF THE GROTOCEANS), C, 80-77, CDN, Réal/An/Sc; *CO HOEDEMAN ANIMATEUR*, TV, 80/79, CDN, An; *LE CHATEAU DE SABLE* (THE SANDCASTLE), C, 77-75, CDN, Réal/An/Sc; *L'HOMME ET LE GEANT* (THE MAN AND THE GIANT), C, 75/74, CDN, Réal/An; *LUMAAQ*, C, 75/74, CDN, Réal/An; *L'IIIBOU ET LE CORBEAU* (TIIE OWL AND TIIE RAVEN), C, 73/72, CDN, Réal/An; *TCHOU-TCHOU*, C, 72/71, CDN, Réal/Co an/Sc; *L'HIROU ET LE LEMMING*, C, 71/70, CDN, Réal/An; *MATRIOSKA*, C, 70/69, CDN, Réal/An; *ODDBALL* (MABOULE), C, 69/68, CDN, Réal/An/Sc; *LA DERIVE DES CONTINENTS* (CONTINENTAL DRIFT), ED, 68/67, CDN, Réal/An

HOLBROOK, Bob

1865 West 12th Ave., #4, Vancouver, BC, CAN, V6J 2E7. (604)732-8265.
Types of Production & Categories: TV Video-Wr/Dir.
Genres: Educational-TV; Music Video-TV.
Biography: Born 1954, Winnipeg, Manitoba. Studied Media Arts, S.A.I.T., Calgary; Film Production, Algonquin College, Ottawa. Worked on all types of film production since 77 as production assistant, camera assistant, sound/boom man; writing scipts since 80.
Selective Filmography: *HARD TO BE A HERO/SAY YOU'LL SAVE ME*, MV, 86, CDN, Dir/Wr; *'COACH AND PLAY SOCCER'* (Wr-2 eps/Dir-1 eps), ED, 82, CDN, Dir/Wr.

HOLENDER, Jacques - see PRODUCERS

DIRECTORS/REALISATEURS

HOUDE, Jean-Claude

AR. 815 St Jean-Bosco, Ste-Foy, Qué, CAN, G1V 2W8. (418)681-2588. Radio-Canada, 2505 blvd. Laurier, Ste-Foy, Qué, CAN, G1V 2X2. (418)654-1341.
Types de production et Catégories: TV film-Réal; TV vidéo-Réal.
Types d'oeuvres: Education-TV; Sports-TV.
Curriculum vitae: Né en 1930. 30 ans de télévision; 22 ans comme réalisateur.
Filmographie sélective: *'PURE LAINE'* (13 eps), TV, 86, CDN, Prod; *COUPE DU MONDE MONT ST-ANNE,* 'UNIVERS DES SPORTS', TV, 84, CDN, Réal; *JEUX DU CANADA,* TV, 83, CDN, Réal; *JEUX DU QUEBEC* (Réal-6 ans/Coord pro-2 ans), TV, 83-73, CDN, Réal/Coord pro; *'EN MOUVEMENT'* (quot), TV, 81-74, CDN, Réal; *DEFILE DE NUIT, CARNAVAL DE QUEBEC* (4 seg), TV, 80-65, CDN, Réal; *'LES HEROS DU SAMEDI'* (8 seg), TV, 79-74, CDN, Réal; *'SPORT DETENTE'* (150 eps), TV, 77-73, CDN, Réal; *TENNIS COUPE DAVIS,* TV, 74, CDN, Réal; *'LA BOHEME'* (2 eps), TV, 70/69, CDN, Réal; *'COURS UNIVERSITAIRES'* (Maths-52/Musique-26), TV, 64, CDN, Réal.

HOWARD, Jeff - see PRODUCERS

HUNT, Graham

DGC. 71 Charles St. E., #306, Toronto, Ont, CAN, M4Y 2T3. (416)960-1948. Eureka Films Ltd., 31 Mercer St., Toronto, Ont, CAN, M5B 1H2. (416)596-7131.
Types of Production & Categories: TV Film-Dir; TV Video-Dir.
Genres: Children's-TV; Commercials-TV; Music Video-TV.
Biography: Born 1942, England; British-Canadian citizen. Graduate Ryerson Polytechnical Institute, B.F.A. (Communications); P.A.D.I. scuba instructor. Director, producer, writer, many national TV commercials, Canada, Australia; has won numerous awards including N.Y. Art Directors Club, Bessies, Clio's.

HUNTER, John - see WRITERS

IANZELO, Tony

CSC, SGCT. 1140 Dunraven Rd., Montreal, Que., CAN, H3P 2M1. (514)737-4357. NFB, Box 6100, Stn. A, Montreal, Que, CAN, H3C 3H5. (514)283-9524.
Types of Production & Categories: Th Short-Dir/Cam; TV Film-Dir/Cam.
Genres: Drama-Th&TV; Action-Th&TV; Documentary-Th&TV; Educational-Th&TV.
Biography: Born 1935, Toronto, Ontario. Graduate of Ryerson Polytechnical Institute, Radio & TV Arts, 58. Member of the Royal Canadian Academy; his films have won numerous awards at int'l film festivals including Yorkton, Berlin, Brussels, Columbus, San Francisco and Oscar nominations for *BLACKWOOD* and *HIGH GRASS CIRCUS.*
Selective Filmography: *SUTHERLAND,* TV, 86, CDN, Dir/Cam; *TRANSITION,* Th, 86, CDN, Co-Dir; *MAKING TRANSITIONS,* TV, 86, CDN, Dir/Cam; *FROM ASHES TO FOREST,* 'PARKS CENTENNIAL', TV, 85, CDN, Dir/Cam; *SINGING: A JOY IN ANY LANGUAGE,* TV, 82, CDN, Co-Dir/Cam; *THE CONCERT MAN,* TV, 82, CDN, Dir/Cam/Ed; *CHINA: A LAND TRANSFORMED/NORTH CHINA FACTORY/NORTH CHINA COMMUNE,* TV, 80/79, CDN, Co-Dir/Cam; *VIKING VISITORS TO NORTH AMERICA,* ED, 79, CDN, Co-Dir/Cam; *THE MIGHTY STEAM CALLIOPE,* TV, 78, CDN, Dir/Cam; *HIGH GRASS CIRCUS,* TV, 78, CDN/GB, Co-Dir/Cam; *I'LL GO AGAIN* (NOS ATHLETES), TV, 77, CDN, Cam; *LITTLE BIG TOP,* TV, 77, CDN, Co-Dir/Cam; *CREE WAY,* TV, 77, CDN, Dir/Cam; *STRIKER,* TV, 76, CDN, Cam; *BLACKWOOD,* TV, 76, CDN, Co-Dir/Cam; *MUSICANADA,* TV, 75, CDN, Co-Dir/Cam; *THE WHALES ARE WAITING,* ED, 75, CDN, Co-Dir/Cam; *OUR LAND IS OUR LIFE,* TV, 74, CDN, Co-Dir/Cam; *CREE HUNTERS OF MISTASSINI,* TV, 74, CDN, Co-Dir/Cam **(CFA)**; *BATE'S CAR: SWEET AS A NUT,* TV, 74, CDN, Dir/Cam; *GOODBYE SOUSA,* Th, 73, CDN, Dir/Cam **(CFA)**; *HERE IS CANADA,* Th, 72, CDN, Dir/Cam; *TEMPLES OF TIME,* TV,
(cont/suite)

71, CDN, Cam; *DON'T KNOCK THE OX*, Th, 70, CDN, Dir/Cam **(CFA)**; *COLD JOURNEY*, Th, 69, CDN, Cam; *THE BEST DAMN FIDDLER FROM CALABOGIE TO KALADAR*, TV, 69, CDN, Cam **(CFA)**; *SAUL ALINSKY WENT TO WAR*, TV, 69, CDN, Cam; *ANTONIO*, TV, 66, CDN, Dir/Cam.

IPPERSIEL, Fernand

AR. 1025 est, rue Sherbrooke, Montréal, Qué, CAN, H2L 1L4. (514)522-9532.
Types de production et Catégories: TV film-Réal; TV vidéo-Réal.
Types d'oeuvres: Drame-TV; Variété-TV; Documentaire-TV; Enfants-TV.
Curriculum vitae: Né en 1921, Chénéville, Québec. Etudes classiques à Ottawa, 40-42. A débuté comme reporter, annonceur, traducteur et rédacteur d'annonces; réalisateur à Radio-Canada depuis 56-84; réalisateur pigiste depuis 85.
Filmographie sélective: *'AU JOUR LE JOUR'* (50 seg), TV, 84/83, CDN, Réal; *'FEMMES D'AUJOURD'HUI'* (60 eps), TV, 83-75, CDN, Réal; *'CINQ D'* (35 eps), TV, 75-70, CDN, Réal; *'THE TOWN ABOVE'* (78 eps), TV, 70-68, CDN, Réal; *'SHOESTRING THEATRE'* (6 eps), TV, 68-66, CDN, Réal; *'CHEZ HELENE'* (700 eps), TV, 68-61, CDN, Réal; *'LA BOITE A SURPRISE'* (120 eps), TV, 60-57, CDN, Réal.

ISCOVE, Robert

ACTRA, BAE, DGA, DGC. Catherine McCartney, Prendergast Agency, 260 Richmond St.W., Suite 405, Toronto, Ont, CAN, M5V 1W5. (416)922-5308.
Types of Production & Categories: TV Film-Dir/Prod; TV Video-Dir/Prod.
Genres: Drama-TV; Comedy-TV; Variety-TV; Musical-TV.
Biography: Born Toronto, Ontario; scholarship student at Juilliard School of Music, New York; directed and choreographed 'Peter Pan' on Broadway with Sandy Duncan; choreographed over 100 TV variety and music specials. Won the U.S. Advisory Board's Award of Excellence, the Peabody Award and a Rockie for *ROMEO AND JULIET ON ICE*.
Selective Filmography: *'PHILIP MARLOWE PRIVATE EYE'* (4 eps), TV, 86/85, CDN, Dir; *GENIE AWARDS*, TV, 85, CDN, Co-Prod; *JUNO AWARDS*, TV, 85, CDN, Prod; *LOVE AND LARCENY*, TV, 84, CDN, Dir; *'FAERIE TALE THEATRE'* (2 eps), TV, 84, USA, Dir; *ROMEO AND JULIET ON ICE*, TV, 83, USA, Ch/Co-Wr/Prod/Dir **(EMMY)**; *BEST OF BROADWAY*, TV, 83, USA, Dir; *CHAUTAUQUA GIRL*, TV, 82, CDN, Dir; *'MARY TYLER MOORE VARIETY SERIES'* (11 eps), TV, 81, USA, Dir; *CLOWNS*, TV, 77, CDN, Dir/Ch/Co-Wr/Prod **(ACTRA)**; *ANN-MARGRET SMITH TV SPECIAL*, TV, 77, USA, Ch; *THE DUCHESS AND THE DIRTWATER FOX*, Th, 76, USA, Ch; *SILENT MOVIE*, Th, 75, USA, Ch; *JACK-A FLASH FANTASY*, TV, 74, CDN, Dir/Prod/Co-Wr/Ch; *JESUS CHRIST SUPERSTAR*, Th, 73, USA, Ch.

JACKSON, Doug

SGCT. 1540 Summerhill, Ste 307, Montreal, Que, CAN, H3H 1C1. (514)937-6870. NFB, Box 6100, Montreal, Que, CAN, H3C 3H5. (514)283-9665.
Types of Production & Categories: Th Film-Dir/Wr; Th Short-Dir/Wr; TV Film-Dir/Prod/Wr.
Genres: Drama-Th&TV; Comedy-Th&TV; Action-Th&TV; Documentary-Th&TV.
Biography: Born 1940, Montreal, Quebec; bilingual; B.A., Sir George Williams University. Has lectured in film at American Film Institute, University of Oregon, McGill. Semi-pro baseball pitcher and football quarterback. Has won numerous awards including an Oscar nomination, Berlin and London Film Festival Awards for *BLAKE*.
Selective Filmography: *BANSHEE*, 'RAY BRADBURY THEATRE', TV, 86, CDN, Dir; *UNCLE T/BAMBINGER*, 'BELL CANADA PLAYHOUSE', TV, 85/84, CDN, Dir; *THE FRONT LINE*, 'FOR THE RECORD', TV, 84, CDN, Dir; *'EMPIRE INC.'* (eps 1, 3, 4), TV, 83/82, CDN, Dir; *THE ART OF EATING*, Th, 81, CDN, Dir; *WHY MEN RAPE*, TV, 80/79, CDN, Dir/Prod/Wr; *THE*

(cont/suite)

HEATWAVE LASTED 4 DAYS, TV, 74, CDN, Wr/Dir/Prod; *THE SLOANE AFFAIR,* TV, 73, CDN, Dir/Co-Wr/Prod (**3 CFA**); *THE HUNTSMAN,* Th, 72, CDN, Dir/Prod/Wr; *LA GASTRONOMIE,* 'ADIEU ALOUETTE', TV, 72, CDN, Wr/Dir; *NORMAN JEWISON, FILMMAKER,* TV, 71, CDN, Dir/Wr/Prod; *DANNY AND NICKY,* TV, 70/69, CDN, Dir/Wr/Prod; *BLAKE,* Th, 69, CDN, Prod (**CFA**); *RECEPTION,* 'PENITENTIARY SERIES', ED, 68, CDN, Dir/Prod; *'PENITENTIARY SERIES'* (3 short films), ED, 68/67, CDN, Prod; *WHEAT,* In, 66, CDN, Prod; *OPERATIONAL OCEANOGRAPHY,* In, 66, CDN, Prod; *LACROSSE/LEARNING LACROSSE,* In, 65, CDN, Dir/Wr/Prod; *'PENITENTIARY SERIES'* (2 short films), ED, 64/63, CDN, Dir/Wr/Prod; *ECLIPSE AT GRAND MERE,* Th, 63, CDN, Dir/Wr; *THE FIRST STEP,* Th, 63, CDN, Assist Dir; *POWER TO DESTROY,* TV, 60, CDN, Wr; *THE MISTAKE OF HIS LIFE,* TV, 58, CDN, Wr.

JACKSON, G. Philip

Lightscape Motion Picture Co., P.O. Box 6135, Stn. A, Toronto, Ont, CAN, M5W 1P5. (416)465-1098.
Types of Production & Categories: Th Film-Dir/Prod/Ed; TV Film-Dir/Prod/Ed; TV Video-Prod.
Genres: Science Fiction-Th&TV; Documentary-TV; Educational-TV; Experimental-TV.
Biography: Born 1954. Honours B.A., Film, York University. Film editor, Radio-Canada/CBC, 4 years. *THE MUSIC OF THE SPHERES* won Most Promising Feature, Atlantic Film Festival.
Selective Filmography: *PEDESTALS,* TV, 85, CDN, Dir/Co-Prod/Ed; *REFLECTIVE,* TV, 85, CDN, Co-Dir/Co-Prod; *RAIL YARD,* TV, 85, CDN, Dir/Co-Prod/Ed; *SHIFTING,* TV, 85, CDN, Co-Prod/Ed; *COLETTE,* TV, 85, CDN, Co-Prod/Cam; *ROW...ROW,* TV, 85, CDN, Co-Prod/Ed; *WINTERS PAST,* TV, 85, CDN, Co-Prod/Co-Dir; *TRAVELLING SHOT,* TV, 85, CDN, Dir/Prod/Ed; *ETERNAL SPRING,* TV, 85, CDN, Ed; *DISHPAN HANDS,* TV, 85, CDN, Ed; *THE MUSIC OF THE SPHERES,* Th, 84/83, CDN, Prod/Dir/Co-Wr; *CIRCLE OF RECRIMINATION,* ED, 80, CDN, Prod/Ed; *RITES OF PASSAGE,* TV, 80, CDN, Dir/Prod/Ed; *THE SORCERER'S EYE,* TV, 80, CDN, Dir/Prod/Ed.

JARROTT, Charles

ACTT, DGA. Jess Morgan & Co. Inc., 6420 Wilshire Blvd. 19th Fl., Los Angeles, CA, USA, 90048. (213)651-1601. David Shapira, 15301 Ventura Blvd., Ste. 345, Sherman Oaks, CA, USA, 91403. (818)906-0322.
Types of Production & Categories: Th Film-Dir; TV Film-Dir; TV Video-Dir.
Genres: Drama-Th&TV; Comedy-Th&TV; Action-Th&TV; Horror-Th&TV.
Biography: Born 1927, London, England. Educated in England; served in Royal Navy, 39-45. Theatre director, actor, 47-57; director, CBC, 57-59. Has directed over 50 TV dramas. Director of Armchair Theatre, ABC-TV, England, 59-64; BBC, 64-68. Became a Canadian citizen, 58. Won Best Director Award, GB, 62; First Prize, Prix Italia for *SILENT SONG*; Golden Globe Award, *ANNE OF A THOUSAND DAYS.*
Selective Filmography: *WINSTON CHURCHILL,* TV, 86, USA, Dir; *IKE IN GETTYSBURG,* TV, 86, USA, Dir; *THE BOY IN BLUE,* Th, 84, CDN, Dir; *A MARRIED MAN* (5 parts), TV, 82, GB, Dir; *THE AMATEUR,* Th, 81, CDN, Dir; *CONDORMAN,* Th, 81, USA, Dir; *THE LAST FLIGHT OF NOAH'S ARK,* Th, 80, USA, Dir; *THE OTHER SIDE OF MIDNIGHT,* Th, 77, USA, Dir; *THE LITTLEST HORSE THIEVES* (ESCAPE FROM THE DARK), Th, 75, USA, Dir; *THE DOVE,* Th, 74, USA, Dir; *LOST HORIZON,* Th, 72, USA, Dir; *MARY, QUEEN OF SCOTS,* Th, 71, GB, Dir; *ANNE OF A THOUSAND DAYS,* Th, 69, GB, Dir; *MALE OF THE SPECIES,* TV, 68, GB, Dir; *JEKYLL AND HYDE,* TV, 67, CDN, Dir; *CASE OF LIBEL,* TV, 67, USA, Dir; *SILENT SONG,* TV, 67, GB, Dir.

JAVAUX, Pierre

30 rue Compton ouest, Waterville, Qué, CAN, J0B 3H0. (819)837-2548. Arts et
Images, 3466 ch. N. Hatley, Rock Forest, Qué, CAN, J1N 1A4. (819)562-5627.
Types de production et Catégories: TV vidéo-Réal/Sc.
Types d'oeuvres: Comédie-TV; Documentaire-TV; Education-TV; Annonces-TV.
Curriculum vitae: Né en 1947, Ampsin, Belgique; citoyen canadien et belge. Seize
ans d'expérience en production et communications.
Filmographie sélective: *'ESTRIE EVIDEMMENT'* (26 eps), TV, 86, CDN, Réal;
SOLITERRE, MV, 86, CDN, Réal/Sc; *DES ENFANTS DE TROP?,* TV, 85,
CDN, Réal/Sc; *'REFLETS D'UN PAYS'* (8 eps), TV, 85/84, CDN, Réal; *'DES
GENS QUE JE CONNAIS'* (CLEMENCE DESROCHERS), (1 eps), TV, 84,
CDN, Réal; *LE NEZ DANS LE COURANT,* TV, 84, CDN, Réal.

JEAN, Jacques

AR. 4550 Esplanade, Montréal, Qué, CAN, H2T 2Y5. (514)842-3537.
Types de production et Catégories: l métrage-Mont; c métrage-Réal; TV film-Mont;
TV vidéo-Réal.
Types d'oeuvres: Drame-C; Horreur-C; Documentaire-C&TV; Affaires publiques-
TV.
Curriculum vitae: Né en 1948, Amqui, Québec; bilingue. Baccalauréat en 69;
producteur de théâtre; production/réalisation d'annonces publicitaires; expérience en
audio et électronique.
Filmographie sélective: *SCOOP,* C, 84, CDN/F, Prod dél; *HOT WATER*
(JUNIOR), C, 84, CDN, Mont; *'LE CRIME D'OVIDE PLOUFFE'* (2 eps), TV,
83, CDN, Mont; *'LE TELEJOURNAL'* (quot), TV, 83-79, CDN, Réal; *UN
MARIAGE ROYAL,* TV, 83, CDN, Réal; *'CE SOIR'* (quot), TV, 78/77, CDN,
Mont; *CONSTRUCTION DU COMPLEXE OLYMPIQUE,* C, 76, CDN, Réal; *VIE
D'ANGE,* C, 76, CDN, Mont; *BALLAD OF ESKIMOE NELL* (seg can), C, 75,
CDN/AUS, Réal; *HAREM KEEPER,* 75, CDN, Mont; *TOUT FEU TOUT
FEMME,* C, 74, CDN, Mont; *SHE WOLF,* C, 74, CDN, Mont; *ACROSS THIS
LAND,* C, 73, CDN, Ass réal/Mont; *KEEP IT IN THE FAMILY,* C, 73, CDN,
Mont; *LE DIABLE EST PARMI NOUS,* C, 72, CDN, Mont; *LE TEMPS D'UNE
CHASSE,* C, 72, CDN, Ass réal; *LOVING AND LAUGHING,* C, 71, CDN, Mont.

JENSEN, Thea

204 Fulton Ave., Toronto, Ont, CAN, M4K 1Y3. (416)429-7401.
Types of Production & Categories: TV Film-Dir/Prod/Wr; TV Video-Dir/Prod/Wr.
Genres: Documentary-TV.
Biography: Born Trail, British Columbia; tri-lingual (English, French, Spanish);
B.A., French, University of Washington; M.A., Spanish, University of Illinois,
President, Lunatis Communications Inc.. Extensive field production; first person
allowed to shoot in Saudi Arabia in modern times.
Selective Filmography: *THE TEFLON KNEE,* TV, 85, CDN, Dir/Prod; *FOR
RICHER OR POORER,* TV, 84, CDN, Dir/Prod/Wr; *MATTHEW,* TV, 83, CDN,
Dir/Prod; *SUPER BABIES,* TV, 83, CDN, Dir/Prod/Wr; *HERPES,* TV, 83, CDN,
Dir/Prod/Wr; *TIMOTHY FINDLEY,* TV, 83, CDN, Dir/Prod/Wr; *LADY
ORACLE,* TV, 82, CDN, Dir/Prod/Wr; *ADDITIVES OR NEGATIVES?,* TV, 81,
CDN, Co-Dir/Exec Prod; *SWITCHING ON,* TV, 80, CDN, Dir/Prod/Wr; *BIRDS
OF PAY,* TV, 79, CDN, Dir/Prod/Wr; *THE YANKS ARE COMING,* TV, 79,
CDN, Dir/Prod/Wr; *I EXPECT TO BE ASSASSINATED,* 'FORTUNES', TV,
78, CDN, Dir/Prod/Wr; *THE CASE FOR JOINING THE U.S./THE CASE FOR
GOING IN ALONE,* 'FORTUNES', TV, 78, CDN, Exec Prod; *HOW TO MAKE
MILLIONS/ PRICE AND SUPPLY OF OIL/ WRAP-UP ON ECONOMY,*
'FORTUNES', TV, 78, CDN, Dir/Prod/Wr; *WORLD OIL I/ WORLD OIL II/
PETER LOUGHEED,* 'FORTUNES', TV, 77, CDN, Dir/Prod/Wr; *B.C. PEN,* TV,
76, CDN, Dir/Prod/Wr.

JEWISON, Norman

DGA, DGC. Yorktown Productions Ltd., 18 Gloucester St., Toronto, Ont, CAN, M4Y 1L5. (416)923-2787. Larry Auerbach, William Morris Agency, 151 El Camino Drive, Los Angeles, CA, USA, 90210. (213)274-7451.
Types of Production & Categories: Th Film-Dir/Prod; TV Film-Dir.
Genres: Drama-Th; Comedy-Th&TV; Variety-Th&TV.
Biography: Born 1926, Toronto, Ontario; B.A., Victoria College, University of Toronto. Directed at BBC, 50-52; CBC, 52- 58; CBS, 58-61; Universal Studios, 61-64. Named Officer, Order of Canada, 82. Over 30 Oscar nominations for films he has directed; EMMY Award for *TONIGHT WITH HARRY BELAFONTE*; DGA nominations and a Golden Globe Award for *THE RUSSIANS ARE COMING, THE RUSSIANS ARE COMING.*
Selective Filmography: *AGNES OF GOD,* Th, 84, USA, Dir/Prod; *A SOLDIER'S STORY,* Th, 84, USA, Dir/Prod; *ICEMAN,* Th, 83, USA, Exec Prod; *BEST FRIENDS,* Th, 82, USA, Dir/Prod; *ACADEMY AWARDS SHOW,* TV, 81, USA, Prod; *THE DOGS OF WAR,* Th, 80, USA, Exec Prod; *...AND JUSTICE FOR ALL,* Th, 79, USA, Dir/Prod; *F.I.S.T.,* Th, 77, USA, Dir/Prod; *ROLLERBALL,* Th, 74, USA, Dir/Prod; *JESUS CHRIST SUPERSTAR,* Th, 72, USA, Dir/Prod; *BILLY TWO HATS,* Th, 72, USA, Prod; *FIDDLER ON THE ROOF,* Th, 70, USA, Dir/Prod; *THE LANDLORD,* Th, 69, USA, Prod; *GAILY, GAILY,* Th, 68, USA, Dir; *IN THE HEAT OF THE NIGHT,* Th, 67, USA, Dir/Prod **(OSCAR)**; *THE THOMAS CROWN AFFAIR,* Th, 67, USA, Dir/Prod; *THE RUSSIANS ARE COMING, THE RUSSIANS ARE COMING,* Th, 66, USA, Dir/Co-Prod; *THE ART OF LOVE,* Th, 65, USA, Dir; *THE CINCINNATI KID,* Th, 65, USA, Dir/Co-Wr; *SEND ME NO FLOWERS,* Th, 64, USA, Dir; *THE THRILL OF IT ALL,* Th, 63, USA, Dir; *40 POUNDS OF TROUBLE,* Th, 62, USA, Dir.

JOHNSON, Richard

80 Front St.E., #515, Toronto, Ont, CAN, M5E 1T4. (416)868-1362. TV Ontario, 2180 Yonge St., 4th Fl., Toronto, Ont, CAN. (416)484-2700. After Image Video Prod., 80 Front St.E., Ste. 515, Toronto, Ont, CAN, M5E 1T4. (416)868-1362.
Types of Production & Categories: TV Film-Prod; TV Video-Prod/Dir.
Genres: Documentary-TV; Experimental-TV; Educational-TV; Music Video-TV.
Biography: Born 1940, Appleton, Wisconsin; US citizen; landed immigrant, Canada. M.F.A., University of Wisconsin. Has worked at TV Ontario since 69. Won Gold Medal, Los Angeles Film Festival, 71 for film on Jack Nicholson; Gold Medal for Nightmusic Concert *FM.*
Selective Filmography: *'NEW DIRECTIONS FILM'* (2 eps), TV, 86, CDN, Prod/Dir; *'SATURDAY NIGHT AT THE MOVIES'* (208 eps), TV, 86-78, CDN, Prod/Dir; *'THE MOVIE SHOW'* (52 eps), TV, 85-83, CDN, Dir/Prod; *'ROUGH CUTS'* (104 eps), TV, 83-79, CDN, Prod/Dir; *'FILM INTERNATIONAL'* (4 eps), TV, 82, CDN, Prod/Dir; *'ON AIR'* (8 eps), TV, 78, CDN, Prod/Dir; *'AFTER IMAGE'* (16 eps), TV, 78, CDN, Prod/Dir; *'THE COMEDY SHOPPE'* (26 eps), TV, 78, CDN, Prod/Dir; *'NIGHTMUSIC CONCERTS'* (62 eps), TV, 78-76, CDN, Prod/Dir; *'NIGHTMUSIC'* (540 eps), TV, 77-73, CDN, Prod/Dir; *'CALENDAR'* (52 eps), TV, 73-71, CDN, Pro Coord; *'SHOWCASE'* (52 eps), TV, 71-69, CDN, Pro Coord; *'PEOPLE WORTH KNOWING'* (70 eps), TV, 71/70, CDN, Pro Coord; *'MEDIA AND METHODS OF THE ARTIST'* (30 eps), TV, 71/70, CDN, Pro Coord; *'KARATE DOH'* (13 eps), TV, 70, CDN, Pro Coord; *'ONTARIO ART SCENE'* (5 eps), TV, 70/69, CDN, Pro Coord; *'ARTISTS AT THE NATIONAL GALLERY'* (25 eps), TV, 70/69, CDN, Pro Coord; *'THE HISTORY OF AVIATION'* (3 eps), TV, 70/69, CDN, Pro Coord.

JOHNSTON, William - see PRODUCERS

REALISATEURS/DIRECTORS

JUBENVILL, Ken

DGC. 4174 Glenhaven Cr., North Vancouver, BC, CAN, V7G 1B9. (604)929-3817.
1500 - 736 Granville St., Vancouver, BC, CAN, V6Z 1G3. (604)689-9623.
Types of Production & Categories: Th Short-Dir/Prod; TV Film-Dir/Ed; TV Video-Dir.
Genres: Drama-TV; Action-TV; Documentary-TV.
Biography: Born 1937, Dauphin, Manitoba. Began as film editor, 56; began directing while in Australia, 59-63; returned to Canada to produce, direct, edit many commercials and documentaries; director of 50 TV dramas. Won several awards including Gold Camera, US Industrial Film Festival for 4 consecutive years.
Selective Filmography: *'THE BEACHCOMBERS'* (42 eps), TV, 85-71, CDN, Dir; *B.C. AT EXPO 85,* Th, 85/84, CDN, Prod/Dir; *TRANSIT GOIN' TO TOWN,* TV, 85, CDN, Prod/Dir/Ed; *THE GIFT,* TV, 84, CDN, Dir; *LET MUSIC BE THE MESSAGE,* Th, 83, CDN, Dir/Ed; *SUPERMAN III,* Th, 83, USA/GB, 1st AD; *TAKE A GIANT STEP,* TV, 82, CDN, Prod/Dir/Ed; *RODEO/WHITE WATER MAN,* 'STONEY PLAIN', TV, 81, CDN, Dir; *'RITTER'S COVE'* (4 eps), TV, 80/79, CDN, Dir; *'HUCKLEBERRY FINN'* (5 eps), TV, 79, CDN, Dir; *THE SAND BARRIER,* Th, 78, CDN, Prod/Dir/Ed; *'THE BEACHCOMBERS'* (13 eps), TV, 77, CDN, Prod; *A BREAK IN THE ICE,* TV, 75, CDN, Dir/Ed; *TIME OF THE TAR SANDS,* TV, 74, CDN, Dir/Ed; *THE VITAL 2/3rds,* TV, 73, CDN, Dir/Ed; *THE FIRST HARVEST,* TV, 73, CDN, Dir/Ed.

JUTRA, Claude

ARRFQ. 3492 rue Laval, Montréal, Qué, CAN, H2X 3C8. (514)288-2447.
Types de production et Catégories: l métrage-Réal/Sc; TV film-Réal.
Types d'oeuvres: Drame-C; Comédie-C; Documentaire-C&TV; Education-C.
Curriculum vitae: Né en 1930 à Montréal, Québec. Doctorat en Médecine, Université de Montréal, 52; Art dramatique, Théâtre du Nouveau Monde, Montréal, Cours Simon, Paris. ONF, 56; Président-fondateur de l'Association Professionnelle des Cinéastes. 63. *MON ONCLE ANTOINE* a remporté 8 trophées au Palmarès du film canadien dont le meilleur film; ses films ont remporté plusieurs prix dont Chicago Film Fest., Prix de la Presse Internationale, Trophée Frigon; Prix Spécial du jury au Palmarès canadien pour *KAMOURASKA* qui fut aussi le choix officiel de l'Association des critiques français à Cannes.
Filmographie sélective: *LA DAME EN COULEURS* (OUR LADY OF THE PAINTS), C, 85, CDN, Réal/Co sc; *BY DESIGN,* C, 80, CDN, Réal; *SURFACING,* C, 79, CDN, Réal; *THE WORDSMITH,* TV, 78, CDN, Réal; *SEER WAS HERE,* 'FOR THE RECORD', TV, 77, CDN, Réal/Co sc; *DREAMSPEAKER,* 'FOR THE RECORD', TV, 77, CDN, Réal (CFA/ANIK); *ADA,* 'FOR THE RECORD', TV, 77, CDN, Réal/Sc; *THE PATRIARCH,* C, 77, CDN, Réal; *ARTS CUBA,* C, 77, CDN, Réal; *QUEBEC FETE JUIN '75,* C, 75, CDN, Réal; *POUR LE MEILLEUR ET POUR LE PIRE,* C, 75, CDN, Réal/Sc; *KAMOURASKA,* C, 72, CDN/F, Réal/Co sc/Co mont; *MON ONCLE ANTOINE,* C, 71, CDN, Réal (CFA); *MARIE-CHRISTINE,* C, 70, CDN, Réal; *WOW!,* C, 69, CDN, Réal/Sc/Co mont; *AU COEUR DE LA VILLE,* C, 69, CDN, Réal; *COMMENT SAVOIR...,* C, 66, CDN, Réal; *ROULI-ROULANT,* C, 66, CDN, Réal/Mont; *A TOUT PRENDRE* (TAKE IT ALL), C, 63, CDN, Réal/Sc/Mont/Co prod (CFA); *QUEBEC-USA* (L'INVASION PACIFIQUE), C, 62, CDN, Co réal/Mont; *LE NIGER: JEUNE REPUBLIQUE,* C, 61, CDN, Réal/Mont; *LA LUTTE,* C, 61, CDN, Co réal; *FELIX LECLERC, TROUBADOUR,* C, 60, CDN, Réal; *FRED BARRY, COMEDIEN,* C, 60, CDN, Réal; *ANNA LA BONNE,* C, 59, F, Réal; *LES MAINS NETTES,* C, 58, CDN, Réal; *A CHAIRY TALE* (IL ETAIT UNE CHAISE), C, 57, CDN, Com/Co réal (CFA); *JEUNESSES MUSICALES,* C, 56, CDN, Réal/Sc; *PIERROT DES BOIS,* C, 54, CDN, Réal/Sc/Com; *MOUVEMENT PERPETUEL,* C, 49, CDN, Sc/Co réal (CFA).

259

DIRECTORS/REALISATEURS

KACZENDER, George

DGC. 2170 Century Park E., #1608, Los Angeles, CA, USA, 90067. (213)203-0710. Tom Chasin, The Chasin Agency, 190 North Canon Dr., Beverly Hills, CA, USA, 90210. (213)278-7505.
Types of Production & Categories: Th Film-Dir/Prod/Wr/Ed; Th Short-Dir/Prod/Wr/Ed; TV Film-Dir.
Genres: Drama-Th; Action-TV; Documentary-Th; Educational-TV.
Biography: Born 1933. Worked on 75 films at the NFB. *DON'T LET THE ANGELS FALL* won Best Foreign Feature Film, Ceylon; Chris Award, Columbus, Silver Bear, Berlin for *NAHANNI.*
Selective Filmography: *'NIGHT HEAT'* (6 eps), TV, 86/85, CDN, Dir; *CHANEL SOLITAIRE,* Th, 81, USA, Dir; *YOUR TICKET IS NO LONGER VALID,* Th, 80, CDN, Dir; *AGENCY,* Th, 79, CDN, Dir; *IN PRAISE OF OLDER WOMEN,* Th, 78, CDN, Dir/Ed; *U-TURN,* Th, 73, CDN, Dir; *FREUD: THE HIDDEN NATURE OF MAN,* ED, 70, CDN, Dir; *DON'T LET THE ANGELS FALL,* Th, 69, CDN, Dir/Wr; *SABRE AND FOIL,* Th, 69, CDN, Dir; *YOU'RE NO GOOD,* Th, 67, CDN, Dir/Ed; *THE WORLD OF THREE,* Th, 67, CDN, Dir; *THE GAME,* Th, 67, CDN, Dir; *LITTLE WHITE CRIMES,* Th, 67, CDN, Dir; *PHOEBE,* Th, 64, CDN, Dir/Ed.

KANDALAFT, Pierre

Les Films Pierka, 1455 rue de Val-Brillant, Ste-Dorothée, Laval, Qué, CAN, H7Y 1T7. (514)689-2071.
Types de production et Catégories: c métrage-Réal.
Types d'oeuvres: Documentaire-C&TV; Education-C&TV; Industriel-TV.
Curriculum vitae: Né en 1941, Beyrouth, Liban; citoyenneté canadienne. Langues: français, anglais, arabe. Licencié en Sciences politiques, Faculté de Lyon, France; Brevet en Psycho-pédagogie, UQAM; Caméraman TV, Liban; assistant réalisateur, Paris; fonde sa propre compagnie de production au Canada, 79.
Filmographie sélective: *LE SKI EN FETE/ALUPCO/POLYFAB - MAISONS MODULAIRES,* In, 85-83, CDN, Prod/Réal; *CHANGEONS LE MODE D'EMPLOI,* TV, 85, CDN, Prod/Réal; *LES CHEMINS DE L'ESPOIR,* TV, 85, CDN, Prod/Réal; *THE MECHANICAL SERVICE SHOPS/BUDGETING/OWENS CORNING INT'L,* In, 83/82, CDN, Prod/Réal; *A BOY FROM SAUDI ARABIA,* TV, 83, CDN, Co sc; *QUENCHING THE DESERT'S THIRST/ZAMIL SOULE STEEL BUILDINGS,* In, 82/81, CDN, Prod/Réal; *THE ZAMIL GROUP OF COMPANIES/TOOLS AND HEAVY EQUIPMENT,* In, 82, CDN, Prod/Réal; *LIVING IN ARAMCO COMMUNITIES/BATHING YOUR BABY,* In, 82, CDN, Prod/Réal; *WHY ACCIDENTS HAPPEN/SHORTCUTS TO THE END,* In, 82, CDN, Prod/Réal; *EMERGENCY/HAZARDOUS CHEMICALS/INDUSTRIAL MAINTENANCE AT ARAMCO,* In, 82, CDN, Prod/Réal; *SAUDI TRAINING AND CAREER DEVELOPMENT/INFORMATION PLEASE,* In, 82, CDN, Prod/Réal; *AMIANTIT/WATER IN THE DESERT/AMERON PIPES/FIBERGLASS,* In, 80/79, CDN, Prod/Réal; *VENTURE IN SOLID PAINT/SOLID PAINT MARKETING,* In, 77/76, CDN, Prod/Réal; *DO IT YOURSELF WITH SOLID PAINT,* In, 76, CDN, Prod/Réal.

KARDASH, Virlana

1405 1/2 Scott Ave., Los Angeles, CA, USA, 90026. (213)481-0266.
Types of Production & Categories: Th Short-Dir/Ed; TV Film-Ed.
Genres: Drama-Th; Documentary-TV; Educational-TV.
Biography: Born 1959, Winnipeg, Manitoba; General Arts program, University of Toronto; London Int'l Film School, England. Speaks English, French, Ukrainian and Spanish.
Selective Filmography: *A DAY IN THE LIFE OF AMERICA,* TV, 86, USA, Pro Coord; *'PLANET EARTH'* (3 eps), TV, 85, USA, Assist Ed; *SAN FRANCISCO MIME TROUPE,* TV, 84, USA, Assist Ed; *THE MAKING OF LADY HAWKE,*
(cont/suite)

TV, 84, USA, Assist Ed; *JIMMY*, Th, 84, USA, Dir/Ed; *FIRST FASHION SHOW*, Th, 83, GB, 2nd AD; *FRAGMENTS OF TENDERNESS*, Th, 83, GB, 1st AD; *HOSPICE*, TV, 83, GB, Ed; *A DAY TO REMEMBER*, Th, 82, GB, Assist Ed; *GRACE*, Th, 82, GB, Dir/Ed; *THE LOST MAYA*, TV, 82, GB, Assist Ed; *FUNTOWN*, Th, 81, GB, Dir/Ed.

KASTNER, John

ACTRA, ATPD. 48 Claxton Blvd., Toronto, Ont, CAN, M6C 1L8. (416)787-6389. CBC, P.O. Box 500, Station A, Toronto, Ont, CAN. (416)975-6582.
Types of Production & Categories: TV Film-Dir/Prod; TV Video-Dir/Prod.
Genres: Comedy-TV; Documentary-TV.
Biography: Performed in over 100 CBC TV and radio shows as juvenile actor; journalist, 68-71; TV producer at age 20; with his late mother Rose, he wrote the screen story for *THE TERRY FOX STORY*. *THE LIFER AND THE LADY* won the Blue Ribbon, American Film Festival.
Selective Filmography: *PRISON MOTHER, PRISON DAUGHTER*, TV, 86, CDN, Dir/Prod; *THE LIFER AND THE LADY*, TV, 85, CDN, Dir/Prod/Wr; *STREET COMEDY*, TV, 85, CDN, Co-Dir/Co-Prod/Co-Wr; *TURNING TO STONE*, TV, 85, CDN, Prod; *THE PAROLE DANCE*, TV, 84, CDN, Dir/Prod/Wr; *'JUST KIDDING'* (22 eps), TV, 83, CDN, Co-Dir/Co-Prod/Co-Wr; *SHARING THE SECRET* (SELECTED GAY STORIES), TV, 82, CDN, Dir/Prod/Co-Wr; *FIGHTING BACK*, TV, 81, CDN, Dir/Co-Wr/Prod **(INT'L EMMY)**; *FOUR WOMEN*, TV, 78, CDN, Dir/Co-Wr/Prod **(INT'L EMMY)**.

KEANE, Laurence

2090 West 3rd, Vancouver, BC, CAN, V6J 1L5.
Types of Production & Categories: Th Film-Dir/Prod/Wr.
Genres: Drama-Th; Comedy-Th.
Biography: Born 1950, London, England; British-Canadian citizen. B.A., University of British Columbia, 73 (Political Science); Film Studies, Simon Fraser University, 73-74; M.F.A., University of Southern California Cinema Department, 75-77.
Selective Filmography: *SAMUEL LOUNT*, Th, 84, CDN, Dir/Co-Wr/Co-Exec Prod; *BIG MEAT EATER*, Th, 81, CDN, Prod/Co-Wr/Co-Ed.

KEATING, Lulu

2125 Brunswick St., Halifax, NS, CAN, B3K 2Y4. (902)423-3880. Red Snapper Films Ltd., 1574 Argyle St., Halifax, NS, CAN, B3J 2B3. (902)423-9538. THA Distributors Ltd., 1226 Homer St., Vancouver, BC, CAN.
Types of Production & Categories: TV Film-Dir/Wr; TV Video-Dir.
Genres: Drama-TV; Documentary-TV.
Biography: Born 1952, Antigonish, Nova Scotia; bilingual. Education: Saint François Xavier University, N.S., 69-72; Fine Arts Diploma, Vancouver School of Art, 74-76; Ryerson Polytechnical Institute, 76-77. Experience: TV host; actress; Atlantic Filmmaker's Co-operative: film distributor, 79-80, President, 84-86.
Selective Filmography: *WOMEN ENTREPRENEURS*, TV, 86, CDN, Wr/Co-Dir; *STARTING RIGHT NOW*, ED, 85, CDN, Co-Wr/Dir/Co-Ed; *RITA MacNEIL IN JAPAN*, TV, 85, CDN, Dir; *CITY SURVIVAL*, TV, 83, CDN, Prod/Co-Wr/Dir/Ed.

KEATLEY, Philip - see PRODUCERS

KEELAN, Matt

CTPDA. 952 Matthew Brady Blvd., Windsor, Ont, CAN, N8S 3K1. (519)945-8490.
Types of Production & Categories: TV Film-Dir/Prod; TV Video-Dir/Prod.
Genres: Variety-TV; Documentary-TV; Children's-TV; Commercials-TV.
Biography: Born 1930, Windsor, Ontario. 36 years experience: radio, television; 30 years as TV director, producer.

(cont/suite)

Selective Filmography: *FREEDOM FESTIVAL PARADE AND FLAG RAISING* (6 shows), TV, 85-80, CDN, Dir/Prod; *VERY SPECIAL PERSON,* TV, 84, CDN, Dir/Prod; *'AROUND TOWN'* (52 eps), TV, 84, CDN, Dir/Prod; *'THIS IS HOLLYWOOD',* TV, 82-80, CDN, Dir/Prod; *'LEGAL FACTOR'* (4 shows), TV, 81, CDN, Dir/Prod; *'SUMMER FESTIVAL'* (2 eps), TV, 80, CDN, Dir/Prod; *'COLUMBO QUOTES'* (1 eps), TV, 77, CDN, Dir/Prod; *'BOZO THE CLOWN',* TV, 74-66, CDN, Dir/Prod; *'WRESTLING',* TV, 74-68, CDN, Dir/Prod; *'HARNESS RACING',* TV, 73, CDN, Dir/Prod.

KELLNER, Lynne - see PRODUCERS

KELLUM, J.H. - see PRODUCERS

KEMBALL, Harry - see CINEMATOGRAPHERS

KENDALL, Nicholas

DGC. 3880 Point Grey Rd., #201, Vancouver, BC, CAN, V6R 1B4. (604)224-3322. Northern Lights Media Corp., 1020 Mainland St., #113, Vancouver, BC, CAN, V6B 2T4. (604)684-2888.
Types of Production & Categories: TV Film-Dir/Prod/DOP; TV Video-Dir/Prod/DOP.
Genres: Drama-TV; Variety-TV; Documentary-TV; Educational-TV.
Biography: Born 1949, Manchester, England; Canadian. B.A., University of British Columbia (Theatre), 70; Diploma, London Film School, England, 72. Vice President, Northern Lights Media Corp.. Has won several awards for his films including Best Cinematography, Yorkton Int'l Film Fest., *THE LOST PHARAOH*; Blue Ribbon, American Film Fest., Dupont, Columbia University Award for *RAPE: FACE TO FACE.*
Selective Filmography: *'THE FABULOUS FESTIVAL'* (7 eps), TV, 85, CDN, Dir; *VALLEYS IN TRANSITION* (CHANGING VALLEYS), TV, 84, CDN, Dir/DOP; *GIFTED KIDS,* TV, 83, CDN, DOP; *RAPE: FACE TO FACE,* TV, 82, CDN/USA, Co-Dir/DOP; *YESTERDAY'S LOVER,* 'BEACHCOMBERS', TV, 81, CDN, Dir; *HARD OIL,* Th, 80, CDN, Dir/DOP; *THE LOST PHARAOH: THE SEARCH FOR AKHNATON,* TV, 80, CDN, Dir/DOP/Co-Prod; *THE WATCHERS/PEOPLE OF THE FOREST,* 'THIS LAND', TV, 78, CDN, Dir/Prod; *DO IT WITH JOY,* 'PACIFIC WAVE', TV, 77, CDN, Dir/Prod/DOP; *ON TO THE BAY,* TV, 77, CDN, Dir/Prod; *TALA,* Th, 76, CDN, Prod/Dir/DOP; *SURFACE,* Th, 75, CDN, Dir/Prod/DOP; *ICE,* TV, 73, CDN, Dir/DOP/Co-Prod; *BILL AND JOHN,* 'SPROCKETS', TV, 72, CDN, Dir.

KENNEDY, Michael

39 Isabella St., #5, Brampton, Ont, CAN. (416)451-5060.
Types of Production & Categories: Th Film-PM/1st AD; TV Film-Dir/Prod/Wr/Ed.
Genres: Drama-Th&TV; Comedy-Th&TV; Action-Th&TV; Documentary-TV.
Biography: Born 1954. President, Appealing Productions Inc. Administrator/teacher, film and video production, media analysis, Jamia Milia Islamia Mass Communications Research Centre, New Delhi, India, 83-84.
Selective Filmography: *THE SEARCH FOR INTIMACY,* ED, 86, CDN, Dir/Wr; *THE PINK CHIQUITAS,* Th, 86/85, CDN, PM/1st AD; *THE AGING OF NORTH AMERICA,* ED, 85, CDN, Dir/Ed; *'THE STUDY OF FINE ARTS'* (6 eps), In, 85, CDN, Dir/Prod/Wr/Ed; *THE VOLUNTEER,* TV, 83, CDN/IND, Dir/Ed/Prod; *SURFACE TENSION,* TV, 82, CDN, Dir/Prod/Wr/Ed; *THE PARABLE,* TV, 78, CDN, Dir/Prod/Wr/Ed; *JIM AND MUGGINS TOUR TORONTO!,* TV, 78, CDN, Dir/Prod/Ed; *PEOPLE HAVE THEIR STRIFE NOW AND THEN...,* TV, 78, CDN, Dir/Prod/Ed/Cam; *VERITE,* TV, 77, CDN, Dir/Prod/Wr/Ed.

KENT, Laurence

DGC. 37 Palmerston Ave., Montreal, Que, CAN, H3P 1V1. (514)731-5409.
Types of Production & Categories: Th Film-Dir/Prod/Wr; TV Film-Dir.
Genres: Drama-Th&TV; Action-Th.
Biography: Born 1939, Johannesburg, South Africa; Canadian citizen; bilingual.
B.A., University of British Columbia. Has produced/directed/written 19 feature films
in Canada in 23 years; won awards at New York, London, Berlin, Cork, San
Francisco, Buenos Aires, Melbourne, Sydney and Montreal film festivals. Special
Award from the Canadian Film Awards for *SWEET SUBSTITUTE*, 65.
Selective Filmography: *HIGH STAKES*, Th, 85, CDN, Dir; *MEN FROM
ZIMBABOUE*, TV, 82, CDN, Prod/Dir/Co-Wr; *DANCER*, Th, 81, CDN, Co-Wr;
YESTERDAY (GABRIELLE), Th, 79, CDN, Dir; *DREAD*, Th, 78, CDN, Co-Wr;
THE SLAVERS, Th, 77, CDN, Prod/Dir/Wr; *WINTER KILL*, Th, 77, CDN,
Prod/Dir; *CHOCOLATES IN THE SUN*, TV, 75, CDN, Dir; *CRIMINAL
CONVERSATIONS*, TV, 74, CDN, Dir; *KEEP IT IN THE FAMILY*, Th, 73,
CDN, Dir; *COLD PIZZA*, TV, 72, CDN, Dir; *THE APPRENTICE*, Th, 71, CDN,
Dir; *SASKATCHEWAN 45 BELOW*, TV, 69, CDN, Dir; *FACADE*, Th, 68, CDN,
Dir; *HIGH*, Th, 67, CDN, Prod/Dir/Wr; *WHEN TOMORROW DIES*, Th, 65,
CDN, Dir/Prod; *SWEET SUBSTITUTE*, Th, 64, CDN, Dir/Wr/Prod; *THE
BITTER ASH*, Th, 63, CDN, Dir/Prod/Wr.

KENT, Patricia

CTPDA. 85 Harrow St., Winnipeg, Man, CAN, R3M 2X8. (204)452-7211.
Types of Production & Categories: TV Film-Dir/Prod; TV Video-Dir/Prod.
Genres: Drama-TV; Variety-TV; Documentary-TV; Children's-TV.
Biography: Born in the U.K.; Canadian citizen. Production training, Directors
course, BBC TV, 1964-68; Production assistant, CBC, Winnipeg, 68-72; floor
director, variety of productions, 72-76; producer, children's TV programs, 79-85.
Selective Filmography: *CANADA IS YOU*, TV, 85, CDN, Prod; *SESAME
STREET'* (250 seg), TV, 85-79, USA, Dir/Prod/Wr; *THE CAT CAME BACK*,
TV, 80, CDN, Dir/Prod; *JUST KIDDING'* (Winnipeg), (5 eps), TV, 79, CDN,
Exec Prod; *WINGS*, TV, 79, CDN, Assoc Prod; *POINTS WEST'* (27 eps), TV, 78/
77, CDN, Dir/Prod; *TAKE 30'* (8 eps), TV, 78, CDN, Dir/Prod/Wr.

KENT, Paul

ATPD. 18 Unity Road, Toronto, Ont, CAN, M4J 5A4. (416)461-0496. CBC, 500
Church St., 5th Floor, Toronto, Ont, CAN. (416)975-5649.
Types of Production & Categories: TV Film-Prod; TV Video-Dir/Prod/Wr.
Genres: Drama-TV; Documentary-TV; Children's-TV.
Biography: Born 1956, Norwich, England; citizenship, Canadian-British.
Experienced in film financing and marketing; 3 years as V.P. of Production, Norfolk
Communications Ltd.; 2 years Program Executive, First Choice Pay TV.
Selective Filmography: *MONITOR'* (34 eps), TV, 86/85, CDN, Dir/Prod/Wr;
COUNTRY CANADA' (31 eps), TV, 84, CDN, Dir/Prod/Wr; *THE MEDICINE
SHOW'* (8 eps), TV, 82, CDN, Dir/Prod; *TALES FROM A TOY SHOP* (3 parts),
TV, 81, CDN, Pro Coord; *THE KGB CONNECTIONS*, TV, 81, CDN, Pro Coord;
WINNIE, TV, 81, CDN, Pro Coord.

KIEFER, Douglas - see CINEMATOGRAPHERS

KING, Allan

DGC. 461 Church St., Toronto, Ont, CAN, M4Y 2C5. (416)962-0181. Ralph
Zimmerman, Great North Artists Mgmt, 345 Adelaide St. W., Toronto, Ont, CAN.
(416)593-2587. Sam Adams, Triad Artists, 10100 Santa Monica Blvd., Los
Angeles, CA, USA, 90067. (213)556-2727.
Types of Production & Categories: Th Film-Dir/Prod; TV Film-Dir/Prod; TV
Video-Dir/Prod.

(cont/suite)

Genres: Drama-Th&TV; Comedy-Th&TV; Educational-TV; Children's-Th&TV.
Biography: Born 1930, Vancouver, British Columbia. Honours B.A., Philosophy, University of British Columbia; joined CBC, 54; began independent production, Spain, 58; formed Allan King Associates Ltd., Toronto, London, 61. Past President, DGC; Board of Directors, CCA; Chairman of the Mengen Institute. *WHO HAS SEEN THE WIND* won the Grand Prix, Paris Film Fest.; *A MARRIED COUPLE* was shown in Director's Fortnight, Cannes; *WARRENDALE* won the Cannes and New York Critics Awards. He also won awards from San Francisco, Melbourne, Mannheim, Edinburgh, Leipzig, Salerno, Sydney and Vancouver Film Festivals.
Selective Filmography: *THE LAST SEASON,* TV, 86, CDN, Dir; *'PHILIP MARLOWE PRIVATE EYE'* (1 eps), TV, 85, CDN, Dir; *TUCKER AND THE HORSE THIEF,* 'FAMILY PLAYHOUSE', TV, 84, CDN, Dir; *WHO'S IN CHARGE?,* TV, 84, CDN, Prod; *READY FOR SLAUGHTER,* 'FOR THE RECORD', TV, 83, CDN, Dir; *SILENCE OF THE NORTH,* Th, 80/79, CDN, Dir; *ONE NIGHT STAND,* TV, 77, CDN, Dir/Prod **(CFA)**; *WHO HAS SEEN THE WIND,* Th, 76, CDN, Dir/Prod; *RED EMMA,* TV, 74, CDN, Dir/Prod; *BAPTIZING,* TV, 74, CDN, Dir/Prod; *A BIRD IN THE HOUSE,* 'ANTHOLOGY', TV, 74, CDN, Dir; *CAN I COUNT YOU IN/MORTIMER GRIFFIN AND THE JEWISH QUESTION,* 'TO SEE OURSELVES', TV, 73/72, CDN, Dir; *COME ON CHILDREN,* Th, 71, CDN, Dir/Prod; *A MARRIED COUPLE* (UN COUPLE MARIE), Th, 70, CDN, Dir/Prod; *WARRENDALE,* Th, 67, CDN, Dir/Prod **(3 CFA/BFA)**; *CREATIVE PERSONS,* TV, 67, CDN/GB/ USA/D, Exec Prod; *RUNNING AWAY BACKWARDS,* TV, 65, CDN, Dir/Prod; *BJORN'S INFERNO,* 'THIS HOUR HAS SEVEN DAYS', TV, 64, CDN, Dir/ Prod; *LYNN SEYMOUR-A PORTRAIT,* 'QUEST', TV, 64, CDN, Dir/Prod; *THE PEACEMAKERS/THE PURSUIT OF HAPPINESS,* 'THIS HOUR HAS SEVEN DAYS', TV, 63/62, CDN, Dir/Prod/Wr; *A MATTER OF PRIDE,* 'CLOSE-UP', TV, 61, CDN, Dir/Prod/Wr; *JOSEPH DRENTERS-A PORTRAIT,* 'QUEST', TV, 61, CDN, Dir/Prod/Wr; *RICKSHAW/WHERE WILL THEY GO?/ MOROCCO/BULL FIGHT,* 'CLOSE-UP', TV, 60-58, CDN, Dir/Prod; *THE PEMBERTON VALLEY,* 'FESTIVAL', TV, 58, CDN, Dir/Prod; *THE YUKONERS,* TV, 57, CDN, Dir/Prod; *SKIDROW,* 'EXPLORATIONS', TV, 56, CDN, Dir/Prod **(CFA)**.

KING, Durnford - see WRITERS

KINSEY, Nicholas

ARRFQ. Les Productions Cinégraphe Inc, 970 chemin St-Louis, Sillery, Qué, CAN, G1S 1C7. (418)683-2543.
Types de production et Catégories: c métrage-Réal/Cam/prod; TV film-Réal/Cam.
Types d'oeuvres: Drame-TV; Documentaire-C&TV; Education-C&TV; Animation-C.
Curriculum vitae: Né en 1948; langues: français, anglais. Clifton College, Bristol, Angleterre (secondaire); Université du Texas; Université de Heidelberg, Allemagne; Université de Yale, Connecticut; Université du Québec. Prix de l'Excellence à la Création, U.S. Industrial Film Fest., Chicago, *ON REGARDAIT TOUJOURS VERS LA MER.*
Filmographie sélective: *LE PORT DE QUEBEC,* In, 86, CDN, Réal; *LES VIVES DU QUEBEC,* In, 86, CDN, Cam; *POUR UNE FORET NOUVELLE* (FOREST RENEWAL NOW), In, 85, CDN, Réal/Cam; *JE ME SOUVIENS,* TV, 84, CDN, Réal/Cam/Prod; *LA TIREUSE DE CARTES* (MOUVEMENT DESJARDINS), Cm, 84, CDN, Sc/Conc/Réal/Cam; *THE XL SERIES: THE NEW BREED OF MOTORCOACH/VOHL: LA TENACE,* In, 84, CDN, Co sc/Réal/Cam; *FILLES OU FEMMES,* TV, 84, CDN, Prod/Co réal; *LE QUEBEC FORESTIER* (THE FORESTS OF QUEBEC), In, 84, CDN, Réal/Cam; *RISTIGOUCHE 1760,* In, 84, CDN, Réal/Prod; *L'ENTREVUE DE SELECTION,* In, 84, CDN, Réal/Cam; *SK II: UN SYSTEME QUI PROMET/NOTRE IMAGE, C'EST NOUS,* In, 83, CDN,

(cont/suite)

Réal/Cam; *LE PASSAGER*, TV, 83, CDN, Co sc/Réal; *D'LA MORUE POUR DINER?/LE PLAN DES SERVICES*, In, 82/81, CDN, Réal/Cam/Prod; *ON REGARDAIT TOUJOURS VERS LA MER* (WE ALWAYS LOOKED OUT TO SEA), In, 82, CDN, Prod/Réal/Cam; *LES OFFRES DU GOUVERNEMENT/ CHARGEMENT DU PONT NOIR*, In, 82/80, CDN, Cam/Mont; *LES PECHES*, TV, 82, CDN, Cam; *EL ASMAN, P.Q.*, TV, 81, CDN, Cam; *LA P.M.E.*, VOTRE CLIENT, In, 81, CDN, Réal/Cam; *FEUX DE FORETS*, Cm, 81, CDN, Prod; *FAITES LE SAUT AVEC S.L.M.*, In, 81, CDN, Réal/Cam/Mont/Prod; *REGARDS SUR LA GARDE COTIERE CANADIENNE*, In, 80, CDN, Prod; *PORTRAITS D'UNE VILLE: QUEBEC 1900*, TV, 80, CDN, Co réal/Prod/Cam/Mont; *CAPITAINE FANTASTIC*, TV, 79, CDN, Cam/Mont/Dir tech; *LA G.R.C.*, TV, 79, CDN, Cam; *L'ARCHIPEL DE MINGAN*, ED, 78, CDN, Réal/Cam/Sc.

KISH, Albert

SGCT. 241 Melville Ave., Westmount, Que, CAN, H3Z 2J6. (514)933-8065. NFB, Box 6100, Montreal, Que, CAN, H3C 3H5. (514)283-9482.
Types of Production & Categories: Th Short-Dir.
Genres: Documentary-Th; Educational-Th; Experimental-Th.
Biography: Born 1937, Eger, Hungary. Canadian citizen, 62. Senior film editor, CBC, Toronto, 64-67; senior Arts Grant, Canada Council, 73-74. *LOS CANADIENSES* won awards at New York, Mannheim, Chicago, Los Angeles, Melbourne film festivals; *THE AGE OF INVENTION*, Blue Ribbon, N.Y..
Selective Filmography: *AGE OF THE RIVERS*, 'HERITAGE', TV, 85, CDN, Dir/ Ed; *THE AGE OF INVENTION*, Th, 84, CDN, Dir/Ed/Prod; *THE SCHOLAR IN SOCIETY: NORTHROP FRYE/RHYME AND REASON: F.R.SCOTT*, 'CANADIAN WRITERS', TV, 84/83, CDN, Ed; *BREAD*, Th, 83, CDN, Dir/Ed; *THE IMAGE MAKERS*, Th, 80, CDN, Dir/Ed; *PAPER WHEAT*, TV, 79, CDN, Dir/Ed; *HOLD THE KETCHUP*, Th, 77, CDN, Dir/Ed; *BEKEVAR JUBILEE*, Th, 76, CDN, Dir/Ed; *LOS CANADIENSES*, TV, 75, CDN, Dir/Ed/Wr (**BFA**); *OUR STREET WAS PAVED WITH GOLD*, Th, 73, CDN, Dir/Ed; *IN PRAISE OF HANDS*, Th, 73, CDN, Ed; *THIS IS A PHOTOGRAPH*, Th, 71, CDN, Dir/Ed (**CFA**), *BANNER FILM*, Th, 71, CDN, Ed; *ATOMIC JUGGERNAUT*, Th, 71, CDN, Prod/Ed; *BIGHORN*, Th, 70, CDN, Ed; *SEARCH INTO WHITE SPACE*, Th, 70, CDN, Ed; *FREEZE-IN*, Th, 70, CDN, Prod/Ed; *PENCILS*, Th, 70, CDN, Ed; *LOUISBURG*, Th, 69, CDN, Dir/Ed; *TIMEPIECE*, Th, 69, CDN, Dir/Ed; *OCCUPATION*, Th, 69, CDN, Ed; *PORTS CANADA*, Th, 68, CDN, Dir/Ed; *JUGGERNAUT*, Th, 68, CDN, Ed; *FLIGHT IN WHITE*, Th, 68, CDN, Ed.

KLEIN, Bonnie

NFB, Box 6100, Montreal, Que, CAN, H3C 3H5. (514)283-9545.
Types of Production & Categories: Th Short-Dir/Prod; TV Film-Dir/Prod; TV Video-Dir/Prod.
Genres: Documentary-Th&TV.
Biography: Born 1941, Philadelphia, Pennsylvania; Canadian-U.S. citizen; bilingual. B.A., Barnard College; M.A., Film, Communications, Stanford University. Part of original Challenge for Change Program, NFB. Awarded Woman of the Year, Salon de la Femme, 83. Consulting director, Int'l Youth Year Training Program, NFB, 85-86. *DARK LULLABIES* won Best Documentary, Mannheim Film Festival.
Selective Filmography: *A WRITER IN THE NUCLEAR AGE* (A CONVERSATION WITH MARGARET LAURENCE), TV, 86, CDN, Prod; *NUCLEAR ADDICTION: DR.ROSALIE BERTELL ON THE COST OF DETERRENCE*, TV, 86, CDN, Prod; *DARK LULLABIES*, Th, 85, CDN, Co-Prod; *SPEAKING OUR PEACE*, TV, 85, CDN, Co-Dir/Co-Prod; *NOT A LOVE STORY: A FILM ABOUT PORNOGRAPHY*, Th, 81, CDN, Dir; *RIGHT CANDIDATE FOR ROSEDALE*, TV, 79, CDN, Co-Dir/Co-Prod; *PATRICIA'S MOVING PICTURE*, Th, 78, CDN, Dir; *HARMONIE*, TV, 77, CDN, Dir/Prod; *A*

(cont/suite)

WORKING CHANCE (DU COEUR A L'OUVRAGE), TV, 76, CDN, Dir/Prod; *CITIZEN'S MEDICINE* (CLINIQUE DES CITOYENS), TV, 70, CDN, Dir/ Prod; *LA PETITE BOURGOGNE* (LITTLE BURGUNDY), TV, 68, CDN, Dir/ Ed; *ORGANIZING FOR POWER: THE ALINSKY APPROACH*, TV, 68, CDN, Dir/Ed.

KOHANYI, Julius

ACTRA. 36 Lennox St., Toronto, Ont, CAN, M6G 1J5. (416)536-2711. Phil Gersh Agency, 222 North Canon Dr., Beverly Hills, CA, USA, 90210. (213)274-6611.
Types of Production & Categories: Th Film-Dir/Wr; Th Short-Dir/Wr; TV Film-Dir/Prod/Wr; TV Video-Dir/Prod/Wr.
Genres: Drama-Th&TV; Documentary-TV; Educational-TV; Children's-TV.
Biography: Born 1938, Kelowna, British Columbia. Languages: English, Hungarian. Executive producer, CBC TV Drama, 2 years. *SUMMER'S CHILDREN* won the Gold Medal, Best First Feature, Houston Film Festival. Published 1st novel, 'Mahogany Rabbit', 86.
Selective Filmography: *THE WAR BOY*, Th, 84, CDN, Story; *MUSKOKA, A LOOK BACK*, TV, 83, CDN, Dir/Prod; *ROMANTIC LANDSCAPE IN ENGLAND*, TV, 80, CDN, Dir/Prod; *SUMMER'S CHILDREN*, Th, 79, CDN, Dir; *IMPRESSION AND PRE-IMPRESSION IN FRANCE*, TV, 79, CDN, Dir/Prod; *RODIN*, TV, 78, CDN, Dir/Prod/Wr; *I'M ALIVE*, TV, 77, CDN, Dir/Prod/Wr; *GAMES*, TV, 76, CDN, Dir/Prod/Wr; *SKATERS ON THE AMSTEL*, TV, 74, CDN, Dir/Wr; *THE PEASANTS WEDDING*, TV, 74, CDN, Dir/Prod; *HENRY MOORE*, TV, 70, CDN/GB, Dir/Prod; *IMAGES*, Th, 70, CDN, Dir/Wr; *TEDDY*, Th, 70, CDN, Dir/Wr; *THE HERRING BELT*, TV, 64, CDN, Dir/Cam.

KOOL, Allen - see PRODUCERS

KOTCHEFF, Ted

DGA. c/o Teresa Deane, 2516 Via Tejon, #217, Palos Verdes Estates, CA, USA, 90274. Todd Smith, CAA, 1888 Century Park E., Los Angeles, CA, USA, 90067. (213)277-4545.
Types of Production & Categories: Th Film-Dir/Prod/Wr; TV Film-Dir; TV Video-Dir/Wr.
Genres: Drama-Th&TV; Comedy-Th&TV; Action-Th.
Biography: Born 1931, Toronto, Ontario; graduated University of Toronto, English Literature, 52. Worked at CBC, 52-57; went to England, 57, directed TV, theatre, film; returned to Canada to make *THE APPRENTICESHIP OF DUDDY KRAVITZ* which won the Golden Bear, Berlin Film Fest.; moved to Los Angeles, 74. *JOSHUA THEN AND NOW* and *OUTBACK* were both invited entries to the Cannes Film Festival.
Selective Filmography: *JOSHUA THEN AND NOW*, Th, 85, CDN, Dir; *UNCOMMON VALOR*, Th, 83, USA, Dir/Exec Prod; *FIRST BLOOD*, Th, 82, USA, Dir; *SPLIT IMAGE*, Th, 82, USA, Dir/Prod; *NORTH DALLAS FORTY*, Th, 79, USA, Dir/Scr; *SOMEONE IS KILLING THE GREAT CHEFS OF EUROPE*, Th, 78, USA, Dir; *FUN WITH DICK AND JANE*, Th, 76, USA, Dir; *THE APPRENTICESHIP OF DUDDY KRAVITZ*, Th, 74, CDN, Dir; *BILLY TWO HATS*, Th, 73, USA, Dir; *OUTBACK*, Th, 71, AUS, Dir; *EDNA, THE INEBRIATE WOMAN*, TV, 71, GB, Dir; *TWO GENTLEMEN SHARING*, Th, 70, GB, Dir; *LIFE AT THE TOP*, Th, 65, GB, Dir; *TIARA TAHITI*, Th, 62, GB, Dir.

KOTTLER, Les

ATPD. Adderley Productions Inc., 7 Granada Court, Thornhill, Ont, CAN, L3T 4V3. (416)886-3777.
Types of Production & Categories: TV Film-Dir/Prod; TV Video-Dir/Prod.
Genres: Documentary-TV; Educational-TV.

(cont/suite)

Biography: Born 1947, Cape Town, South Africa; emigrated to Canada, 75; Canadian citizen. B.A. (Economics), Diploma in African Government and Law from University of Cape Town. Trained in television at Lord Thomson Foundation , Glasgow, Scotland, 71 (Honour student). Joined CBC, 75-85; producer/director, *TAKE 30, MARKET PLACE, VENTURE*; now freelance.
Selective Filmography: *MISSING*, TV, 85, CDN, Dir/Wr; *NO PLACE TO HIDE*, TV, 85, CDN, Dir/Wr; *THE DISAPPEARING LAND/CHOLESTEROL: MYTH OR FACT*, 'COUNTRY CANADA', TV, 84/83, CDN, Dir/Prod; *THE POISONED GARDEN*, 'THE FIFTH ESTATE', TV, 83, CDN, Dir/Prod; *'OMBUDSMAN'* (45 seg), TV, 80-76, CDN, Dir/Prod; *A TRUE AND FAITHFUL ACCOUNT-THE DIARIES OF MACKENZIE KING*, 'TAKE 30', TV, 75, CDN, Dir/Prod.

KROEKER, Allan

ACTRA, DGC. 237 Glenwood Crescent, Winnipeg, Man, CAN, R2L 1K2. (204) 668-8725.
Types of Production & Categories: Th Short-Dir/Wr/Ed/Cin; TV Film-Dir/Wr; TV Video-Dir/Wr.
Genres: Drama-Th&TV; Action-TV; Documentary-TV; Children's-TV.
Biography: Born 1951, St. Boniface, Manitoba. Honours B.A., Fine Arts, York University, 74. His films have won numerous awards at Yorkton, Columbus, New York, Banff, Can-Pro and Houston film festivals; *TRAMP AT THE DOOR* won 2 Gold Awards (Houston), Silver Medal (NY), Silver Hugo (Chicago), Golden Gate Award (San Francisco), CFTA, Iris Award.
Selective Filmography: *HEAVEN ON EARTH*, TV, 86, CDN/GB, Dir; *RED SHOES*, 'BELL CANADA PLAYHOUSE', TV, 85, CDN, Co-T'Play/Dir; *TRAMP AT THE DOOR*, TV, 85, CDN, T'play/Dir; *THE PRODIGAL*, TV, 84, CDN, T'play/Dir; *IN THE FALL*, TV, 83, CDN, T'play/Dir; *HUNTING SEASON*, TV, 83, CDN, T'play/Dir/Ed; *REUNION*, TV, 82, CDN, T'play/Co-Prod; *THE PEDLAR*, TV, 82, CDN, T'play/Dir; *THE CATCH*, TV, 81, CDN, Dir; *CAPITAL*, TV, 81, CDN, T'play/Dir; *GOD IS NOT A FISH INSPECTOR*, TV, 80, CDN, Dir/DOP/Ed/T'play; *THE STRONGEST MAN IN THE WORLD*, TV, 80, CDN, Cin/Ed (**GENIE**); *TUDOR KING*, Th, 79, CDN, Wr/Dir/DOP/Ed; *HOW MUCH LAND DOES A MAN NEED*, Th, 79, CDN, T'play/Dir/DOP/Ed; *W.O. MITCHELL: NOVELIST IN HIDING*, TV, 79, CDN, Cin.

KROITOR, Roman - see PRODUCERS

KURAMOTO, Ken

DGC. 2130 York Ave., #205, Vancouver, BC, CAN, V6K 1C3. (604)731-2087. Great West Pictures Corp., 1431 Howe St., Vancouver, BC, CAN, V6Z 1R9. (604) 685-5205.
Types of Production & Categories: TV Film-Dir/Cam; TV Video-Dir/Cam.
Genres: Musical-TV; Documentary-TV; Commercials-TV.
Biography: Born 1953, Vancouver, British Columbia. B.F.A., University of British Columbia.
Selective Filmography: *B.C. PAVILION/MR. MIKE'S*, Cm, 86/85, CDN, Cam; *CANADIAN PACIFIC/UNIGLOBE*, In, 86/85, CDN, Cam; *COMMUNITY IN ACTION/B.C. PLACE/RICHLODE*, In, 85, CDN, Cam; *THE GIFT*, TV, 85, CDN, Cam; *GULF TITANIUM/INTERSTRAT RESOURCES/BRICAN RESOURCES*, In, 85, CDN, Prod; *PETRO CANADA/WAGNER ENGINEERING*, In, 85, CDN, Dir/Cam; *SENTIMENTAL JOURNEY*, Cm, 85, CDN, Prod; *CONCERT FOR LIFE*, Cm, 85, CDN, Dir/Cam; *THE WOMBLER*, In, 84, CDN, Dir/Cam; *BUDDY COWAN/MAD MONEY/I DON'T WANNA TALK ABOUT IT*, MV, 84/83, CDN, Dir/Prod; *ANYTHING GOES*, MV, 84, CDN, Dir; *WEST COAST FUSION*, TV, 83, CDN, Prod/Dir; *CELEBRATION OF THE RAVEN*, ED, 81, CDN, Prod/Dir; *'MOA PRESENTS'* (9 eps), TV, 81, CDN, Prod/Dir.

DIRECTORS/REALISATEURS

LABONTE, François

ARRFQ. 470 St-Alexis, #303, Montréal, Qué, CAN, H2Y 2N6. (514)844-2910.
Types de production et Catégories: 1 métrage-Réal/Prod/Mont; c métrage-Réal/Prod/Mont; TV film-Réal/Prod/Mont; TV vidéo-Réal.
Types d'oeuvres: Action-C; Documentaire-C&TV; Enfants-C&TV.
Curriculum vitae: Né en 1949. Commence sa carrière au cinéma comme monteur, 71, puis comme assistant réalisateur, 73. Participe à la fondation de 2 maisons de production, 79-82. En 85, abandonne la production pour se consacrer à la réalisation.
Filmographie sélective: *HENRI,* C, 85, CDN, Réal; *LA NOUVELLE TELEVISION,* In, 85, CDN, Réal/Co sc; *'MEMOIRES D'INSECTES'* (20 eps), TV, 84, CDN, Réal; *'LA SEXUALITE INACHEVEE'* (13 eps), TV, 84, CDN, Réal; *LES ANNEES DE REVE,* C, 83, CDN, Mont/Prod dél; *REVEILLON,* C, 82, CDN, Réal/Co sc/Prod/Mont; *EN PASSANT PAR MASCOUCHE,* C, 81, CDN, Co réal/Co sc/Mont; *LES DOUCES,* C, 80, CDN, Mont; *LE CHATEAU DE CARTES,* C, 79, CDN, Réal/Mont/Prod; *SAMEDI SOIR,* C, 77, CDN, Réal/Sc/Mont; *BABIOLE,* TV, 75, CDN, Réal/Mont/Prod.

LABREQUE, Jean-Claude

1566 Van Horne, Montréal, Qué, CAN, H2V 1L5. (514)271-7694.
Types de production et Catégories: l métrage-Réal/D phot; c métrage-Réal/D phot.
Types d'oeuvres: Drame-C&TV; Documentaire-C&TV.
Curriculum vitae: Né en 1938, Québec. Fondateur de la Société Jeune Cinéma, 61. Directeur de la photographie, réalisateur, opérateur, monteur. Séjour en Italie dans le cadre d'un échange de techniciens, 64. Récipiendaire du Prix Wendy Michener, 69.
Filmographie sélective: *LES ANNEES DE REVE,* C, 83, CDN, Réal; *DESTINATION RIVIERE LA GRANDE,* TV, 82/81, CDN, Réal; *MARIE UGUAY,* TV, 81, CDN, Réal; *LE REVEILLON,* C, 81/80, CDN, D phot/Op; *PAROLES DU QUEBEC,* TV, 80/79, CDN, Co réal; *LA NUIT DE LA POESIE 1980,* C, 80/79, CDN, Co sc; *L'AFFAIRE COFFIN* (THE COFFIN AFFAIR), C, 79, CDN, Réal; *LES MONTAGNAIS,* TV, 79, CDN, Réal/Mont; *JEUX DE LA XXI OLYMPIADE,* C, 76, CDN, Réal; *LA VEILLEE DES VEILLEES,* C, 76, CDN, D phot; *LES VAUTOURS,* C, 74, CDN, Réal/Mont; *MUSTANG,* C, 74, CDN, D phot; *LES CORPS CELESTES,* C, 73, CDN, D phot; *BINGO,* C, 73, CDN, D phot/Dir eff sp; *ESSAI A LA MILLE,* C, 72, CDN, Réal/Mont/D phot **(CFA)**; *LES SMATTES,* C, 71, CDN, Co sc/Réal; *FLEUR BLEUE,* C, 70, CDN, D phot; *UNE BALLE DE GIN,* C, 70, CDN, D phot; *LES MAUDITS SAUVAGES,* C, 70, CDN, D phot/Op; *LES CANOTS DE GLACE,* C, 69, CDN, Réal; *THE ERNIE GAME,* C, 67, CDN, D phot/Op; *A GREAT BIG THING,* C, 66, CDN, D phot/Op; *LA VIE HEUREUSE DE LEOPOLD Z,* C, 65, CDN, D phot/Op; *NOTES FOR A FILM ABOUT DONNA AND GAIL,* C, 65, CDN, D phot/Mont; *60 CYCLES,* C, 64, CDN, Réal/Co mont/D phot **(CSC)**; *LE CHAT DANS LE SAC,* C, 64, CDN, D phot/Op; *MEMOIRE EN FETE,* C, 63, CDN, D phot/Op **(CSC)**; *A TOUT PRENDRE* (TAKE IT ALL), C, 62/61, CDN, D phot/Co op.

LACOSTE, Aurèle

AR. 5925 rue Boyer, Brossard, Qué, CAN, J4Z 2E6. (514)678-3639. Radio-Canada, 1400 blvd. Dorchester est, Montréal, Qué, CAN, H2L 2M2. (514)285-2660.
Types de production et Catégories: TV film-Réal; TV vidéo-Réal.
Types d'oeuvres: Drame-TV; Variété-TV; Documentaire-TV; Education-TV.
Curriculum vitae: Né en 1930, Cochrane, Ontario; Bac. en philosophie, Université d'Ottawa, 52. Annonceur à la radio, 52-54; réalisateur depuis 54, à Radio-Canada depuis 56; affaires publiques (7 ans), variétés (21 ans).

(cont/suite)

REALISATEURS/DIRECTORS

Filmographie sélective: *'AVIS DE RECHERCHE'* (39 eps), TV, 86/85, CDN, Réal; *'LES BEAUX DIMANCHES'* (seg:SUPERSTAR), TV, 85-78, CDN, Réal; *'VEDETTES EN DIRECT'* (60 eps), TV, 78-75, CDN, Réal; *'COQUELUCHES'* (hebdo), TV, 77-75, CDN, Réal; *LA FIN DU VOYAGE,* 'SCENARIO', TV, 77, CDN, Réal; *'BOUBOU'* (hebdo), TV, 75-72, CDN, Réal; *'FORMAT 60'* (hebdo), TV, 70/69, CDN, Réal; *'FORMAT 30'* (hebdo), TV, 70/69, CDN, Réal; *'DU COTE DE QUEBEC'* (75 eps), TV, 69-65, CDN, Réal; *'A LA CARTE'* (hebdo), TV, 63-59, CDN, Réal; *'AROUND THE VALLEY'* (hebdo), TV, 62-59, CDN, Réal; *'SCENARIO'* (36 eps), TV, 62-59, CDN, Réal; *'OPINIONS'* (hebdo), TV, 60-56, CDN, Réal; *'NATION'S BUSINESS'* (75 eps), TV, 59-56, CDN, Réal; *'A LA BONNE FRANQUETTE'* (quot), TV, 56-54, CDN, Réal.

LAFOND, Jean-Daniel

ARRFQ, SARDEC. 218 ave. Bloomfield, Outremont, Qué, CAN, H2V 3R4. (514) 272-9008.
Types de production et Catégories: l métrage-Réal; c métrage-Réal.
Types d'oeuvres: Documentaire-C; Education-C.
Curriculum vitae: Né en 1944, France; citoyen canadien et français. Plusieur années universitaires, auteur de plusieurs ouvrages et études; expérience théâtrale; auteur et réalisateur en radio de création (Radio-Canada, Radio-France).
Filmographie sélective: *LES TRACES DU REVE,* C, 86, CDN, Réal/Sc/Rech; *LA GRANDE ALLURE,* C, 86, CDN/F, Rech; *BEYROUTH, A DEFAUT D'ETRE MORT,* C, 83, CDN, Dial/Adapt; *LA BETE LUMINEUSE,* C, 83, CDN, Adapt; *A CALCULATED EXTINCTION* (ETHONOCIDE DELIBERE), C, 81, CDN, Adapt; *MAN OF THE TUNDRA* (L'HOMME DE LA TUNDRA), C, 81, CDN, Adapt.

LAGAUCHE, Christian

C.W.A.R. TV 1/Actualités, 2175 rue Thierry, Ville Lasalle, Qué, CAN, H8N 1H8. (514)365-1051.
Types de production et Catégories: TV vidéo-Réal/Prod.
Types d'oeuvres: Varlété-TV; Documentaire-TV.
Curriculum vitae: Né en 1946, Montrouge, France; citoyenneté canadienne. Etudes de Droit; journaliste professionnel depuis 69. Chargé de l'enseignement du journalisme TV, Université de Yaounde (Cameroun). Prix du Programming à Banff pour l'émission *ARRET STOP,* 72.
Filmographie sélective: *A LUTA PELA AGUA,* TV, 86, RFC, Réal; *COOKIE DINGLER EN CONCERT,* TV, 86, RFC, Réal; *4e RALLYE NYONG & SANAGA,* TV, 86, RFC, Réal; *TAMANIE LA MODE AFRICAINE* (2 ém), TV, 85, CDN/F, Prod/Journ; *UN TRIBUN DU XXe SIECLE,* TV, 84, CDN, Prod; *ABASSE NDIONNE ECRIVAIN,* TV, 84, CDN, Réal; *GORDON HENDERSSON FORMELY EXILE ONE,* TV, 83, CDN/F, Prod/Réal; *PAROLES: LEOPOLD SEDAR SENGHOR* (2 ém), TV, 83, CDN/F, Prod/Réal; *UN HOMME UN PAYS ABDOU DIOUF,* TV, 83, CDN, Prod/Journ; *SALUT LES IDOLES LES SURFS,* TV, 82, CDN, Prod/Anim; *MADAME LE PRESIDENT,* TV, 81, CDN, Prod/Réal; *BANI SADR OU LE 2e EXIL,* TV, 81, CDN, Prod/Réal/Journ; *SUR PAROLE MICHEL TOURNIER,* TV, 81, CDN/F, Réal; *SADAT-BEGIN ISRAEL,* TV, 81, CDN, Prod/Réal/Journ; *AVEC LES MOUJAHIDINS AFGHANS,* TV, 81, CDN/F, Prod/Journ; *DECOUVERTES 81,* TV, 81, CDN, Prod; *SOUS LE CIEL DE CHYPRE/MONACO/FRANCE/MALTE/BULGARIE,* 'SOUS LE CIEL DE"UNDER THE SKY OF', TV, 80/79, CDN, Prod/Réal; *SOUS LE CIEL DE TUNISIE/YOUGOSLAVIE/GRECE,* 'SOUS LE CIEL DE"UNDER THE SKY OF', TV, 80/79, CDN, Prod/Réal; *'ARRET-STOP'* (36 eps), TV, 72/71, CDN, Prod/Anim.

LAMARRE, Louise

ARRFQ. Les Productions L.L.L., 92 Laurier ouest, Montréal, Qué, CAN, H2T 2N4. (514)276-3970.

(cont/suite)

DIRECTORS/REALISATEURS

Types de production et Catégories: TV film-Réal.
Types d'oeuvres: Comédie-TV; Science-fiction-TV; Documentaire-TV; Annonces-TV.
Curriculum vitae: Née en 1960; bilingue. Baccalauréat (Film Production), Université Concordia, Montréal; Certificat en Etudes cinématographiques, Université Laval, Québec.
Filmographie sélective: *NOUVELLE MEMOIRE* (BEYOND MEMORY), TV, 86, CDN, Réal/Sc; *GROWING WILD*, TV, 86, CDN, Réal; *LOOSE PAGE*, TV, 85, CDN, Sc; *L'ELUE*, TV, 85, CDN, Réal/Prod; *ERROR...ERROR*, 'TECHNOLOGICAL CHANGE', TV, 85, CDN, Réal; *LES COMMUNICATIONS CA SE SOIGNE*, TV, 84, CDN, Réal; *JE ME SOUVIENS DE CHARLEVOIX*, TV, 82, CDN, Sc/Réal/Prod; *LES ANCIENS DOMAINES DE SILLERY*, TV, 81, CDN, Co réal/Mont; *LE VERNISSAGE*, TV, 80, CDN, Sc/Réal/Prod.

LAMOTHE, Arthur

APFVQ, ARRFQ. 194 ave. de l'Epée, Outremont, Qué, CAN, H2V 3T2. (514)277-8787. Ateliers audio-visuels du Qué., 5257 Berri, Montréal, Qué, CAN, H2J 2S7. (514)277-2299.
Types de production et Catégories: l métrage-Réal; c métrage-Réal.
Types d'oeuvres: Drame-C; Documentaire-C; Education-C; Enfants-C.
Curriculum vitae: Né en 1928, Saint-Mont (Gers), France; citoyen canadien. Maitrise en économie politique, Université de Montréal, 58. A travaillé pour Radio-Canada, l'ONF; cofondateur, Festival International du Film de Montréal, l'Association des producteurs de film du Québec; membre fondateur et rédacteur, revues 'Images' et 'Format Cinéma'; Président, ARRFQ, 81-83; Président et fondateur, Ateliers audio-visuels du Québec. Ses films ont remporté plusieurs prix dont le Prix de l'Association québécoise des critiques de cinéma, Sesterce d'Or (Nyon) pour *CARCAJOU ET LE PERIL BLANC*; *LES BUCHERONS DE MANOUANE* remporte le Prix de la Critique Française et le Grand Prix, Festival du Film Canadien.
Filmographie sélective: *EQUINOXE*, C, 86, CDN, Réal; *MEMOIRE BATTANTE*, C, 84/83, CDN, Réal; 'LA TERRE DE L'HOMME' (5 ém), TV, 80-77, CDN, Réal; *C'EST DANGEREUX ICI*, ED, 78, CDN, Réal; *CARCAJOU ET LE PERIL BLANC* (8 films), C, 76-73, CDN, Réal; *LA CHASSE AUX MONTAGNAIS*, ED, 74, CDN, Réal; *A PROPOS DE METHODES*, ED, 73, CDN, Réal; *TE PROMENES-TU SOUVENT SUR UN LAPIN?*, ED, 73, CDN, Réal; *A BON PIED, BON OEIL*, In, 73, CDN, Réal (CFA); *LA ROUTE DU FER*, ED, 72, CDN, Réal; 'LE SYSTEME DE LA LANGUE FRANCAISE' (7 eps), ED, 72, CDN, Réal; *LES GARS D'LAPALME*, ED, 71, CDN, Réal; *LE MONDE DE L'ENFANCE*, ED, 71, CDN, Réal; *LE TECHNICIEN EN ARPENTAGE MINIER*, ED, 71, CDN, Réal; *LA MACHINE A VAPEUR*, ED, 71, CDN, Réal; *LE MEPRIS N'AURA QU'UN TEMPS*, C, 69, CDN, Réal; *ACTUALITE QUEBEC* (5 films), ED, 69, CDN, Réal; 'POUR UNE EDUCATION DE QUALITE' (6 eps), ED, 69, CDN, Réal; *AU-DELA DES MURS*, C, 68, CDN, Réal; *POUSSIERE SUR LA VILLE*, C, 67, CDN, Réal; *LE TRAIN DU LABRADOR*, C, 67, CDN, Réal; *LA MOISSON*, C, 67, CDN, Réal; *CE SOIR-LA, GILLES VIGNEAULT*, C, 66, CDN, Réal; *LA NEIGE A FONDU SUR LA MANICOUAGAN*, C, 65, CDN, Réal; *DE MONTREAL A MANICOUAGAN*, C, 63, CDN, Réal; *LES BUCHERONS DE LA MANOUANE*, C, 62, CDN, Réal.

LANCTOT, Micheline

ARRFQ, UDA. 241 rue Maple, St-Lambert, Qué, CAN, J4P 2S1. (514)465-9014.
Types de production et Catégories: l métrage-Réal/Com/Sc; TV film-Com; TV vidéo-Com.
Types d'oeuvres: Drame-C&TV; Comédie-C&TV; Action-C; Animation-C.

(cont/suite)

271

Curriculum vitae: Née en 1947, Montréal, Québec; bilingue. Etudes classiques et universitaires - lauréate en musique (piano). Débute comme animatrice, ONF, puis chez Potterton Productions; nomination pour un Oscar, *THE SELFISH GIANT*; *L'HOMME A TOUT FAIRE* gagne la Médaille d'Argent, Festival de San Sebastian. *SONATINE*, le Lion d'Argent, 2e Prix au Festival de Venise et Plaque d'Argent, Festival de Figueira da Foz (Portugal). Récipiendaire du Prix d'Excellence de l'Académie du cinéma canadien, 80.
Filmographie sélective: *LA LIGNE DE CHALEUR*, C, 86, CDN, Co sc; *SONATINE*, C, 83, CDN, Sc/Réal (GENIE), *L'HOMME A TOUT FAIRE*, C, 80, CDN, Réal/Sc; *L'AFFAIRE COFFIN* (THE COFFIN AFFAIR), C, 79, CDN, Com; *MOURIR A TUE-TETE* (A SCREAM OF SILENCE), C, 77, CDN, Com; *BLOOD & GUTS*, C, 77, CDN, Com; *FUN WITH DICK AND JANE*, C, 76, USA, Conc gén; *A TOKEN GESTURE*, C, 76, CDN, Réal/An; *THE APPRENTICESHIP OF DUDDY KRAVITZ*, C, 74, CDN, Com; *VOYAGE EN GRANDE TARTARIE*, C, 74, F, Com; *LES CORPS CELESTES*, C, 73, CDN, Com; *NOEL ET JULIETTE*, C, 73, CDN, Com; *SOURIS TU M'INQUIETES*, 'EN TANT QUE FEMMES', TV, 73, CDN, Com; *LA VRAIE NATURE DE BERNADETTE*, C, 72, CDN, Com (CFA); *THE SELFISH GIANT*, TV, 71, CDN, An.

LANG, Robert - see PRODUCERS

LANGLOIS, Yves

ARRFQ. 4609 Henri-Julien, Montréal, Qué, CAN, H2T 2C9. (514)845-3592. Le Vidéographe, 4550 Garnier, Montréal, Qué, CAN, H2J 3S6. (514)521-2116.
Types de production et Catégories: TV film-Réal; TV vidéo-Réal.
Types d'oeuvres: Documentaire-TV; Education-TV; Animation-TV.
Curriculum vitae: Né en 1951, Montréal, Québec. Langues: français, anglais, espagnol, compréhension du créole. Expérience en journalisme et en photographie.
Filmographie sélective: *LA PATRIE DE L'HOMME FIER*, TV, 85, CDN, Réal/Cam/Mont; *LE BATEX*, TV, 85, CDN, Réal; *PEDRO MACHETE*, TV, 85, CDN, Réal; *LAS BRUJAS DE EL CERRITO*, TV, 85, CDN, Réal; *PATACAMAXA PRISE I*, TV, 84, CDN, Réal; *CHAMBELLAN CHAMBELLAN*, TV, 83, CDN, Réal; *NOIRS ET BLANCHES*, TV, 82, CDN, Réal; *UNE HISTOIRE DE LUTTE*, TV, 82, CDN, Réal; *DOMITILA*, TV, 81, CDN, Réal; 'A BAIE COMEAU CE SOIR...', TV, 81, CDN, Réal; *LES PATENTEUX D'ENERGIE*, TV, 81, CDN, Réal; *LA LECON RAYONIER*, TV, 80, CDN, Réal; *JOS H.*, TV, 80, CDN, Co réal; *D'ACADIE EN BOLIVIE*, TV, 79, CDN, Réal; *THE SLIAMMON PROGRAM*, TV, 77, CDN, Réal; *ONE SUCH PROGRAM*, TV, 75, CDN, Réal; 'KEBEC KE CE CA?' (7 eps), TV, 74, CDN, Réal; *L'AFFAIRE DES 5,000*, TV, 73, CDN, Réal; *TEACH-IN SUR LE CHILI*, TV, 73, CDN, Réal.

LANK, Barry

807 Cambridge St., Winnipeg, Man, CAN, R3M 3G3. (204)284-3223. Lank/Beach Productions, 115 Bannatyne Ave. E., 4th Fl., Winnipeg, Man, CAN, R3B 0R3. (204)942-0465.
Types of Production & Categories: Th Short-Dir/Wr; TV Film-Dir.
Genres: Documentary-Th&TV; Commercials-TV.
Biography: Born 1946. Graduate, London School of Film, England, 73; Certificate of Education, University of Manitoba, 71; B.A. (Honours), Sociology, Psychology, U. of Winnipeg, 70. *KELEKIS 50 YEARS IN THE CHIPS* won the Canadian Short Film Showcase; Golden Sheaf Award, Yorkton Film Fest., Chris Plaque, Columbus, *IT'S A HOBBY FOR HARVEY*. Has produced, directed, shot over 100 TV commercials and several industrial films.
Selective Filmography: *NOT A BAD YEAR*, Th, 85, CDN/I, DOP; *MUSCLE*, Th, 84, CDN, Dir/Wr; *KELEKIS 50 YEARS IN THE CHIPS*, Th, 82, CDN, Dir/Cin; *IT'S A HOBBY FOR HARVEY*, Th, 80, CDN, Prod/Dir/Cin.

LANSING, Floyd

CTPDA, DGC. Lansing Productions, 1355 West 4th Avenue, #210, Vancouver, BC, CAN. (604)738-6494.
Types of Production & Categories: TV Film-Dir/Prod; TV Video-Dir/Prod.
Genres: Drama-TV; Comedy-TV; Variety-TV; Sports-TV.
Biography: Born 1951, High River, Alberta. Diploma: Television, Stage and Film Arts, S.A.I.T., Calgary. Producer, director for 12 years. 4 Gold Medals, Can-Pro, for live variety, music shows, dramas, sports. Won the National Award of Excellence (School Board) for *BACK TO BASICS*.
Selective Filmography: *LIFE AFTER DARK*, TV, 86, CDN, Prod/Dir; *SLEEPLESS NIGHTS*, TV, 84, CDN, Dir; *NUT CRACKER*, TV, 83, CDN, Prod/Dir; *IN-MOTION*, TV, 83, CDN, Dir; *SUPER SUNDAY* (HEART), TV, 82, CDN, Dir; *WORLD POPULAR SONG FESTIVAL*, TV, 82, CDN, Prod/Dir; *L.R.B.*, TV, 80, CDN, Prod/Dir; *DISCOTHON*, TV, 80, CDN, Prod/Dir; *CONFESSIN' THE BLUES*, TV, 80, CDN, Prod/Dir; *THE ROUGHEST AND TOUGHEST*, TV, 79, CDN, Prod/Dir; *BACK TO BASICS*, TV, 78, CDN, Prod/Dir.

LAPOINTE, Nicole

ARRQ. 3919 St-Jean, Jonquière, Qué, CAN, G7X 3J5. (418)542-0534.
Radio-Québec, 100 St-Joseph sud, Alma, Qué, CAN, G8B 7A6. (418)668-6191.
Types de production et Catégories: TV vidéo-Réal.
Types d'oeuvres: Documentaire-TV; Quiz-TV.
Curriculum vitae: Née en 1953. Etudes en Arts, Université du Québec à Chicoutimi.
Filmographie sélective: *L'INDUSTRIE DE LA FORME*, TV, 86, CDN, Réal; *LE SUICIDE*, TV, 86, CDN, Réal; *QUI A PEUR DE L'INFORMATIQUE*, TV, 86, CDN, Réal; *CAPSULE ANALPHABETE*, TV, 86, CDN, Réal; *'A CAUSE DES MOTS'* (20 eps), TV, 86/85, CDN, Réal; *LES INSTITUTIONS PSYCHIATRIQUES*, TV, 85, CDN, Réal; *LA PREMIERE FOIS* (PROSTITUTION JUVENILE), TV, 85, CDN, Réal; *'LE VILLAGE DE LA PAIX'* (2 eps), TV, 85, CDN, Réal; *'L'ENJEU'* (13 eps), TV, 85/84, CDN, Réal; *CAPSULE SANTE*, TV, 85, CDN, Réal.

LAPORTE, Gaston

AR. 150 Rive-Berlioz, Ste 620, Montréal, Qué, CAN, H3E 1K3. (514)768-0542.
Radio-Canada, 1400 blvd. Dorchester est, Montréal, Qué, CAN, H2L 2M2. (514) 285-2809.
Types de production et Catégories: TV film-Réal; TV vidéo-Réal/Prod.
Types d'oeuvres: Drame-TV; Variété-TV; Documentaire-TV; Sports-TV.
Curriculum vitae: Né en 1933, Montréal, Québec; bilingue. Connaissances particulières: finance, budgetisation, étude de marché et génie civil; 25 ans dans le domaine des communications.
Filmographie sélective: *DEMISSION DU PREMIER MINISTRE DU CANADA*, TV, 85/84, CDN, Réal/Coord pro; *VISITE DE JEAN PAUL II AU CANADA* (100 hrs), TV, 84, CDN, Réal/Coord pro; *40e ANNIVERSAIRE DU DEBARQUEMENT EN NORMANDIE*, TV, 84, CDN, Réal/Coord pro; *SOMMET ECONOMIQUE DE LONDRES*, TV, 84, CDN, Réal/Coord pro; *CONGRES A LA CHEFFERIE DU PARTI LIBERAL DU CANADA*, TV, 84, CDN, Réal/Coord pro; *INVESTITURE DU GOUVERNEUR GENERAL DU CANADA*, TV, 84, CDN, Réal/Coord pro; *'LE TEMPS DE VIVRE'* (54 eps), TV, 83-81, CDN, Réal; *SOIREE DES ELECTIONS FEDERALES* (3 ém), TV, 80-74, CDN, Réal; *SOIREE DU REFERENDUM QUEBECOIS*, TV, 80, CDN, Réal/Coord pro; *'L'ENJEU'* (12 eps), TV, 80/79, CDN, Réal/Coord pro; *DIMANSHOW SOIR/ FAUT VOIR CA* 'LES BEAUX DIMANCHES', (22 eps), TV, 79-75, CDN, Réal; *FETES DU 1er JUILLET* (2 ém), TV, 79/78, CDN, Réal; *25e ANNIVERSAIRE DE LA TELEVISION DE RADIO-CANADA*, TV, 77, CDN, Réal/Coord pro; *LA 2000e DE 'FEMMES D'AUJOURD'HUI'*, TV, 76,

(cont/suite)

CDN, Réal/Coord pro; *JEUX OLYMPIQUES DE MONTREAL* (ATHLETISME), TV, 76, CDN, Réal; *'LA SOIREE DU HOCKEY'* (120 eps), TV, 74-71, CDN, Réal; *'PRENEZ LE VOLANT'* (60 eps), TV, 73-71, CDN, Réal; *'DONALD LAUTREC SHOW'* (24 eps), TV, 70, CDN, Réal.

LARRY, Sheldon

DGA. 1330 N. Harper Ave., #201, Los Angeles, CA, USA, 90046. (213)650-1004. 143 W. 21st St., New York, NY, USA, 10011. (212)243-7174. Alan Berger, William Morris Agency, 151 El Camino Dr., Beverly Hills, CA, USA, 90212. (213) 274-7451.
Types of Production & Categories: Th Film-Dir; TV Film-Dir; TV Video-Dir.
Genres: Drama-Th&TV; Comedy-TV; Action-TV.
Biography: Born 1948, Toronto, Ontario; bilingual. Graduated 1st Class Honours, York University. Worked for BBC, over 100 credits, 68-76; has directed theatre: New York Shakespeare Festival, Playwrights Horizons, Mark Taper Forum, L.A.. Has won Humanitas, ACE and Newman Awards.
Selective Filmography: *'REMINGTON STEELE'* (sev eps), TV, 86-84, USA, Dir; *'HILL STREET BLUES'* (sev eps), TV, 86-84, USA, Dir; *'KNOTS LANDING'* (sev eps), TV, 86-83, USA, Dir; *'ST ELSEWHERE'* (sev eps), TV, 86/85, USA, Dir; *A MATTER OF MINUTES*, 'TWILIGHT ZONE', TV, 86, USA, Dir; *O.S.S.* (pilot), TV, 85, USA, Dir; *BEHIND ENEMY LINES*, TV, 85, USA, Dir; *HOME* (pilot), TV, 85, USA, Dir; *FIRST STEPS*, TV, 84, USA, Dir; *POPULAR NEUROTICS*, 'AMERICAN PLAYHOUSE', TV, 84, USA, Dir; *'LOVING FRIENDS AND PERFECT COUPLES'* (sev eps), TV, 83, USA, Dir; *TERMINAL CHOICE*, Th, 82, CDN, Dir; *SECRET OF CHARLES DICKENS*, TV, 81, USA, Dir (**EMMY**); *ROCKING CHAIR REBELLION*, TV, 81, USA, Dir; *A GOREY HALLOWEEN*, TV, 80, USA, Dir; *'MISS PEACH'* (sev eps), TV, 80/79, USA, Dir; *'MONTY PYTHON'S FLYING CIRCUS'* (sev eps), TV, 76/75, GB, Dir.

LASRY, Pierre

465 Dufferin Rd., Montreal, Que, CAN, H3X 2Z1. (514)484-9374. NFB, Box 6100, Montreal, Que, CAN, H3C 3H5. (514)283-9617.
Types of Production & Categories: Th Film-Prod; Th Short-Dir/Prod/Wr; TV Film-Dir/Wr.
Genres: Drama-Th; Documentary-Th&TV.
Biography: Born 1938; raised and educated in Morocco, emigrated to Canada, 57. Completed his education at Sir George Williams University, Montreal; New York City College; Lee Strasberg Directors Studio (Filmmaking), 62. Spent 7 years in N.Y. editing features, directing industrial films and commercials. Films he has directed have won various awards including Silver Medal (Venice Film Fest.), Blue Ribbon (American Film Fest.) Chris Bronze Plaque (Columbus, Ohio).
Selective Filmography: *THE DIFFERENCE*, TV, 86, CDN, Dir/Wr; *CAPTIVE MINDS: HYPNOSIS AND BEYOND* (LES PRISONS DE L'ESPRIT), Th, 84/83, CDN, Dir/Wr/Ed; *UNEMPLOYMENT: VOICES FROM THE LINE*, Th, 80, CDN, Dir/Wr/Ed; *NICARAGUA EARTHQUAKE*, Th, 79, CDN, Dir/Wr/Ed; *HEALING*, Th, 77, CDN, Dir/Wr/Ed; *THE WALLS CAME TUMBLING DOWN*, Th, 76, CDN, Co-Dir/Res/Ed; *'CORPORATION'* (6 short films), Th, 72, CDN, Ed; *LAURETTE*, Th, 69, CDN, Dir/Wr/Ed; *MRS CASE*, Th, 69, CDN, Dir/Wr/Ed; *THE DRIFTER*, Th, 66, USA, Prod.

LAVALLEE, François

AR. 10630 des Prairies, Montréal, Qué, CAN, H2B 2K6. Radio-Canada, 1400 blvd. Dorchester est, Montréal, Qué, CAN, H2L 2M2. (514)285-2986.
Types de production et Catégories: TV vidéo-Réal.
Types d'oeuvres: Sports-TV.
Curriculum vitae: Né en 1950, Richelieu, Québec; bilingue. Education: cours classique jusqu'en Belles Lettres.

(cont/suite)

Filmographie sélective: *FOOTBALL CANADIEN* (58 eps), TV, 85-83, CDN, Réal; *FOOTBALL AMERICAIN* (75 eps), TV, 85-80, CDN, Réal; *SUPER BOWL XV, XVI, XVII, XVIII, XIX,* TV, 85-81, CDN, Réal; *JEUX DU CANADA* (32 eps), TV, 85-83, CDN, Réal; *REPECHAGE L.N.H.* (2 eps), TV, 85/84, CDN, Réal; *COUPE GREY,* TV, 84/83, CDN, Réal; *JEUX OLYMPIQUES,* TV, 84, CDN, Réal.

LAVOIE, Patricia - see PRODUCERS

LAVUT, Martin

ACTRA, DGC, WGA. 367 Sackville St., Toronto, Ont, CAN, M5A 3G5. (416) 929-9677. Ralph Zimmerman, Great North Artists Mgmt, 345 Adelaide St. W., Toronto, Ont, CAN, M4V 1R5. (416)593-2587.
Types of Production & Categories: Th Film-Dir/Wr; Th Short-Dir/Prod/Wr; TV Film-Dir/Wr; TV Video-Dir.
Genres: Drama-Th&TV; Documentary-TV; Children's-TV.
Biography: Born 1939, Montreal, Quebec. Has worked at NFB; writer, director, Foster and J.Walter Thompson Advertising Agencies; directed over 30 commercials (awards); actor, Second City; night club comic: Maclean's Magazine, Young Canadians Issue, Canadian Comic of the Year.
Selective Filmography: *THE MARRIAGE BED,* TV, 86, CDN, Dir; *'PHILIP MARLOWE PRIVATE EYE'* (1 eps), TV, 85, CDN, Dir; *RED RIVER,* TV, 85, CDN, Dir; *CHARLIE GRANT'S WAR,* TV, 84, CDN, Dir; *'FRAGGLE ROCK'* (1 eps), TV, 84, CDN, Dir; *MAGGIE AND PIERRE,* TV, 83, CDN, Dir; *RUMOURS OF GLORY: BRUCE COCKBURN LIVE,* TV, 82, CDN, Dir; *'LANDSCAPE OF GEOMETRY'* (12 eps), TV, 82, CDN, Dir; *JANIE CANUCK,* 'THE WINNERS', TV, 82, CDN, Dir; *WAR BRIDES,* TV, 80, CDN, Dir; *THE WINNINGS OF FRANKIE WALLS/ CERTAIN PRACTICES,* 'FOR THE RECORD', TV, 80/79, CDN, Dir; *NORTHERN LIGHTS,* TV, 80, CDN, Dir; *THIS WILL DO FOR TODAY,* TV, 77, CDN, Dir/Wr/Prod; *SAM, GRACE, DOUG AND THE DOG,* TV, 76, CDN, Dir; *TOGETHERNESS,* TV, 75, CDN, Dir; *'OF ALL PEOPLE'* (3 eps), TV, 75, CDN, Dir; *MELONY,* TV, 74, CDN, Dir/Wr; *MIDDLE GAME,* TV, 74, CDN, Dir; *ORILLIA: OUR TOWN,* TV, 74, CDN, Dir/Wr/Co-Prod; *WITHOUT A HOBBY, IT'S NO LIFE,* TV, 73, CDN, Dir/Wr/Prod; *THE LIFE GAME,* TV, 70, CDN, Dir/Wr/Co-Prod; *JENNY,* Th, 70, USA, Co-Wr; *AT HOME,* Th, 68, CDN, Dir/Wr/Prod **(CFA)**; *LENI RIEFENSTAHL, HITLER'S CAMERA,* TV, 65, CDN, Dir; *MARSHALL McLUHAN,* TV, 65, CDN, Dir.

LEBLANC, Pierre

AR. 246 rue Dominion, Moncton, NB, CAN, E1C 6H3. (506)854-2554.
Types de production et Catégories: TV film-Réal; TV vidéo-Réal.
Types d'oeuvres: Variété-TV; Documentaire-TV.
Curriculum vitae: Né en 1941, Moncton, Nouveau-Brunswick; bilingue. Bac., Université Laval, Québec; études en chant, piano, orgue, direction de chorale, chant grégorien. Réalisateur, radio, 66-75; réalisateur TV, Radio-Canada,75-85; indépendant depuis 85.
Filmographie sélective: *'A VOTRE SERVICE'* (hebdo), TV, 86, CDN, Réal; *'COUNTRY CHAUD'* (13 eps), TV, 85, CDN, Réal; *SI ON CHANTAIT/ CONCERT DU BICENTENAIRE,* 'LES BEAUX DIMANCHES', TV, 84, CDN, Réal; *'LA BASTRINGUE'* (45 eps), TV, 84-82, CDN, Réal; *PORTRAIT D'UN JOCKEY (RON TURCOTTE),* 'REFLETS D'UN PAYS', TV, 82, CDN, Réal; *'PISTROLI'* (59 eps), TV, 80-77, CDN, Réal; *UN TOURISTE NOMME CHAMPLAIN/ SHOW-CHAUD,* 'LES BEAUX DIMANCHES', TV, 80-78, CDN, Réal; *25 ANS ENSEMBLE/ EN ACADIE POUR RESTER,* 'LES BEAUX DIMANCHES', TV, 77/76, CDN, Réal; *'ENCORE DEBOUT'* (52 eps), TV, 77-75, CDN, Réal.

LEDUC, Jacques

ARRFQ, SGCT. 4408 de Mentana, Montréal, Qué, CAN, H2J 3B3. (514)765-9876. O.N.F., 3155 Côte de Liesse, Montréal, Qué, CAN, H4N 2N4. (514)283-9338.
Types de production et Catégories: l métrage-Réal; c métrage-Réal/Cam.
Types d'oeuvres: Drame-C; Documentaire-C; Expérimental-C.
Curriculum vitae: Né en 1941, Montréal, Québec; bilingue. Caméraman, assistant réalisateur, ONF, 66; rédacteur à la revue 'Objectif', 60-67; réalisateur depuis 66; fondateur de la revue 'Format Cinéma', 81. Photographe, expose à la Cinémathèque Québécoise.
Filmographie sélective: *LES INQUIETUDES DE DIANE/LES ATTENTES/ CHARADE CHINOISE,* TV, 86, CDN, Réal; *VOYAGE EN AMERIQUE SUR UN CHEVAL EMPRUNTE,* C, 86, CDN, Cam; *HAITI - QUEBEC,* TV, 85, CDN, Cam; *LE DERNIER GLACIER,* C, 84/83, CDN, Co réal/Co cam; *LE TRAVAIL PIEGE,* TV, 82, CDN, Cam; *BEYROUTH: A DEFAUT D'ETRE MORT,* C, 82, CDN, Cam; *TORNGAT,* C, 82, CDN, Cam; *ALBEDO,* C, 82, CDN, Réal/Sc; *MADAME, VOUS AVEZ RIEN,* C, 81, CDN, Cam; *DU GRAND LARGE AUX GRANDS LACS,* C, 80, CDN, Cam; *DEBOUT SUR LEUR TERRE,* C, 80, CDN, Cam; *DOUCE ENQUETE SUR LA VIOLENCE,* C, 79, F, Co aut; *'CHRONIQUE DE LA VIE QUOTIDIENNE'* (8 eps), C, 78-75, CDN, Réal; *ULTIMATUM,* C, 74, CDN, Cam; *ALGERIA,* C, 73, CDN, Réal; *TENDRESSE ORDINAIRE,* C, 73, CDN, Réal; *ON EST LOIN DU SOLEIL,* C, 70, CDN, Réal; *TOTAL SERVICE,* C, 69, CDN, Co réal; *LA OU AILLEURS,* C, 69, CDN, Co réal; *CAP D'ESPOIR,* C, 69, CDN, Réal; *MON AMIE PIERRETTE,* C, 67, CDN, Cam; *NOMININGUE,* C, 67, CDN, Réal.

LEDUC, Lucile

AR. 2250 Papineau, #PH 402, Montréal, Qué, CAN, H2K 4J6. (514)523-7181. Radio-Canada, 1400 blvd. Dorchester est, Montréal, Qué, CAN, H2L 2M2. (514) 285-2845.
Types de production et Catégories: TV vidéo-Réal.
Types d'oeuvres: Drame-TV.
Curriculum vitae: Née en 1928, Verdun, Québec; bilingue. Cours de photographie; 6 ans d'art dramatique. *LA BONNE AVENTURE* remporte le Prix de l'Association nationale des téléspectateurs.
Filmographie sélective: *'DES DAMES DE COEUR'* (4 eps), TV, 86, CDN, Réal; *'LA BONNE AVENTURE'* (48 eps), TV, 85-82, CDN, Réal; *'BOOGIE-WOOGIE 47'* (40 eps), TV, 81/80, CDN, Réal; *'CAROLINE'* (26 eps), TV, 79, CDN, Réal; *'GRAND-PAPA'* (40 eps), TV, 78/77, CDN, Réal; *MONSIEUR ZERO,* TV, 76, CDN, Réal.

LEFEBVRE, Jean Pierre

ARRFQ. 1313 chemin Guthrie, C.P.260, Bedford, Qué, CAN, J0J 1A0. (514)248-3295.
Types de production et Catégories: l métrage-Réal/Sc.
Types d'oeuvres: Drame-C; Comédie-C; Documentaire-C; Expérimental-C.
Curriculum vitae: Né en 1941, Montréal, Québec; bilingue. Maitrise en Littérature française, Université de Montréal, 62. Critique de cinéma, 58-67; publication: 'Parfois quand je vis', et plusieurs autres. *LES FLEURS SAUVAGES* gagne le Prix de la Critique internationale, Cannes, Plaque d'Argent, Fest. Int'l de Figueira da Foz, Portugal. *IL NE FAUT PAS MOURIR POUR CA* remporte le Prix de la Critique Québécoise et le Prix du Meilleur Film étranger, Hyères, France. Il remporte aussi le Prix Wendy Michener en 70.
Filmographie sélective: *LE JOUR S...,* C, 83, CDN, Réal/Co sc; *AU RYTHME DE MON COEUR,* C, 83/82, CDN, Réal/Sc/Comp; *LES FLEURS SAUVAGES,* C, 82, CDN, Réal/Sc; *AVOIR 16 ANS,* C, 79, CDN, Réal/Co sc; *LE VIEUX PAYS OU RIMBAUD EST MORT,* C, 77, CDN, Réal/Co sc; *LE GARS DES VUES,* C,
(cont/suite)

76, CDN, Réal/Co sc; *L'AMOUR BLESSE*, C, 75, CDN, Réal/Sc; *LES DERNIERES FIANCAILLES*, C, 73, CDN, Réal/Sc; *ON N'ENGRAISSE PAS LES COCHONS A L'EAU CLAIRE* (PIGS ARE SELDOM CLEAN), C, 73, CDN, Réal/Sc; *ULTIMATUM*, C, 73-71, CDN, Réal/Sc; *LES MAUDITS SAUVAGES*, C, 71, CDN, Réal/Sc; *Q-BEC MY LOVE*, C, 69, CDN, Réal/Sc; *LA CHAMBRE BLANCHE*, C, 69, CDN, Réal/Sc; *JUSQU'AU COEUR*, C, 68, CDN, Réal/Sc; *MON AMIE PIERRETTE*, C, 67, CDN, Réal/Sc; *IL NE FAUT PAS MOURIR POUR CA* (DON'T LET IT KILL YOU), C, 66, CDN, Réal/Co sc; *MON OEIL*, C, 66, CDN, Réal/Sc; *PATRICIA ET JEAN-BAPTISTE*, C, 66, CDN, Réal/Sc; *LE REVOLUTIONNAIRE*, C, 65, CDN, Réal/Sc; *L'HOMOMAN*, C, 64, CDN, Réal/Sc.

LEHMAN, Lewis

ACTRA, DGA. 1638 Bathurst St., Toronto, Ont, CAN, M5P 3J5. (416)781-5326.
Types of Production & Categories: Th Film-Dir/Prod/Wr; TV Film-Dir/Prod/Wr; TV Video-Dir/Prod/Wr.
Genres: Drama-Th&TV; Science Fiction-Th; Horror-Th; Documentary-Th.
Biography: Born 1933, Boston, Massachussetts; attended Boston University. Founded Charles Playhouse, Boston; worked at MPO Productions and Cannon Films, NY. Past President, DGC. Has written 'The Lady With the Alligator Purse', 85 (play) and 'Love Song', 84 (novel).
Selective Filmography: *SUMMER SOUNDS* (SALOME BEY/LEROY SIBBLES HOUR), TV, 85/84, CDN, Dir; *THE PIT*, Th, 81, CDN, Dir; *PHOBIA*, Th, 80, CDN, Co-Scr; *'SEARCH AND RESCUE'* (26 eps), TV, 80, CDN/USA, Prod; *KILLERS OF THE WILD*, Th, 75, CDN, Wr; *SOUTH OF HELL MOUNTAIN*, Th, 74, USA, Dir/Wr; *ALL TOGETHER NOW*, Th, 74, USA, Dir/Wr; *THE GOLDEN BOY PLAYS HIS OYSTER SHELL*, Th, 73, USA, Wr; *NIGHT OF THE WOLF*, Th, 73, USA, Wr; *OVER THERE*, Th, 73, USA, Wr.

LEITERMAN, Richard - see CINEMATOGRAPHERS

LENNICK, Michael

441 Wellesley St. E., Toronto, Ont, CAN, M4X 1H8. (416)921-5603.
Types of Production & Categories: Th Short-Dir/Wr; TV Film-Dir/Prod/Wr; TV Video-Dir/Prod/Wr.
Genres: Comedy-Th&TV; Science Fiction-Th&TV; Documentary-TV; Children's-TV.
Biography: Born 1952. Visual effects supervisor on many films. *SPACE MOVIE* won First Prize, Cinemagic amd Top Prize, First Choice-Great Canadian Shorts Competition, 86.
Selective Filmography: *'OWL TV'* (20 eps), TV, 86-84, CDN, Dir/Wr; *DIFFERENT WORLDS* (EXPO 86), Th, 86, CDN, Wr; *THE NEW MAGICIANS*, 'VISTA', TV, 85, CDN, Dir/Wr/Prod; *NO PLEASURE/ PAINLESS*, MV, 84/83, CDN, VFX Des; *'ROCKET BOY'* (4 eps), TV, 84, CDN, VFX Des; *HEAD OFFICE*, Th, 84, USA, VFX Des; *'COMEDY JAM'* (2 eps), TV, 84, CDN, Wr; *SPACE MOVIE*, TV, 83, CDN, Dir/Wr/Prod/VFX Des; *'FILM MAGIC'* (22 seg), TV, 83, CDN, Dir/Wr/Prod; *THE DEAD ZONE*, Th, 83, CDN, VFX Des; *'KIDBITS'* (6 eps), TV, 82, CDN, Dir/Wr; *VIDEODROME*, Th, 82, CDN, VFX Des; *'THE ALL NIGHT SHOW'* (302 eps), TV, 81/80, CDN, Dir; *VIRUS*, Th, 80/79, J, VFX Des; *THE LAST CHASE*, Th, 80, CDN, VFX Des; *COMICON*, TV, 76, CDN/USA, Dir/Wr.

LESAUNIER, Daniel

5025 rue St-André, Montréal, Qué, CAN, H2J 3A5. (514)277-3583.
Types de production et Catégories: l métrage-Réal; c métrage-Réal; TV film-Réal.
Types d'oeuvres: Comédie-C&TV; Documentaire-C&TV; Education-C&TV.

(cont/suite)

Curriculum vitae: Né en 1950, Paris, France; éducation en France et au Québec. Bac. en Communications, UQAM, 76. Réalisateur d'une douzaine de documentaires pour Radio-Québec, 76-81; réalise les nouvelles, Radio-Canada, 82-83. Réalisateur indépendant; travaille maintenant comme producteur. Prix spécial du Jury et Premier prix documentaire en 78 au Festival du Jeune Cinéma de Montréal pour *DEUX POUCES EN HAUT DE LA CARTE.*
Filmographie sélective: *GRELOT ROUGE ET SANGLOT BLEU*, TV, 86, CDN, Prod; *UN CAS DE POLLUTION A BAIE-COMEAU*, 'CONTRE-CHAMP', TV, 84, CDN, Réal; *PIERRE HARVEY/SKI DE FOND (COUPE MONDIALE) (CHAMPIONAT CANADIEN)*, 'UNIVERS DES SPORTS', TV, 84, CDN, Réal; *FERMETURE DE SHEFFERVILLE*, 'PREMIERE PAGE', TV, 84, CDN, Réal; *LE JOUR DU SEIGNEUR A SEPT-ILES*, 'LE JOUR DU SEIGNEUR', TV, 84, CDN, Réal; *HABITANT GLORIEUX*, C, 82, CDN, Co réal; *RADIO-QUEBEC COTE-NORD*, TV, 81, CDN, Réal; *L'ARCHIPEL DE MINGAN*, TV, 81, CDN, Réal; *LUCE DEMERS SHEFFERVILLE*, TV, 81, CDN, Réal; *GASTON ISABEL HAUTERIVE*, TV, 81, CDN, Réal; *THERESE P.GAGNON BAIE COMEAU*, TV, 81, CDN, Réal; *LE TEMPS DE LA MANIC*, TV, 80, CDN, Prod/Réal; *CLARK CITY*, TV, 78, CDN, Réal; *L'ENRACINEMENT*, TV, 78, CDN, Réal; *CE QUE TU VERRAS ICI TU NE LE VERRAS PAS AILLEURS*, TV, 78, CDN, Réal; *VIVRE AU PRIMAIRE*, TV, 77, CDN, Réal; *UN MONDE A RAPROCHER*, TV, 77, CDN, Réal; *J'ETAIS VENU POUR UN AN*, TV, 77, CDN, Réal; *DEUX POUCES EN HAUT DE LA CARTE*, C, 76, CDN, Prod/Réal.

LESS, Henry

Henry Less Productions, 1196 Queen St. W., Toronto, Ont, CAN, M6J 1J6. (416) 532-1116.
Types of Production & Categories: TV Film-Dir/Prod; TV Video-Dir/Prod.
Genres: Musical-TV; Documentary-TV; Children's-TV; Industrial-TV.
Biography: Born 1947. Has won 2 Gold Camera Awards, US Industrial Film Festival for *TALKTO* and *DOMINOS.*
Selective Filmography: *'DIFFERENT WORLDS'*, TV, 86, CDN, Dir/Wr/Ed; *TALKTO*, In, 84, CDN, Dir/Prod; *DOMINOS*, In, 83, CDN, Dir/Prod; *THE HAWK EXPRESS*, TV, 81, CDN, Prod; *GINO VANELLI*, TV, 79, CDN, Prod (CFTA).

LETOURNEAU, Diane

ARRFQ, SGCT. 3474 ave. Laval, Montréal, Qué, CAN, H2X 3C8. (514)289-9526. O.N.F., 3155 côte de Liesse, Montréal, Qué, CAN, H4N 2N4. (514)283-9353.
Types de production et Catégories: l métrage-Réal/Sc; c métrage-Réal/Sc.
Types d'oeuvres. Documentaire-C&TV.
Curriculum vitae: Née en 1942, Sherbrooke, Québec.
Filmographie sélective: *UNE GUERRE DANS MON JARDIN*, TV, 85, CDN, Réal/Sc; *C'EST PAS MOI, C'EST L'AUTRE*, C, 83, CDN, Réal/Sc; *EN SCENE*, C, 82, CDN, Réal/Sc; *LA PASSION DE DANSER*, C, 81, CDN, Réal/Sc; *LE PLUS BEAU JOUR DE MA VIE*, C, 80, CDN, Réal/Sc; *LES STATUES DE MONSIEUR BASILE*, C, 79, CDN, Réal/Sc; *LES SERVANTES DU BON DIEU*, C, 78, CDN, Réal/Sc; *LES ENFANTS DU QUEBEC*, C, 78, CDN, Rech; *LES OISEAUX BLANCS DE L'ILE D'ORLEANS*, C, 77, CDN, Réal/Sc; *RENE LEVESQUE, UN VRAI CHEF*, TV, 76, CDN, Rech/1er ass réal; *LIVRAISON SPECIALE APRES-DEMAIN*, TV, 76, CDN, Rech; *SURVILLE*, TV, 76, CDN, Rech; *JEUX DE LA XXI OLYMPIADE*, C, 76, CDN, Coord pro; *VIEILLIR SEULE A MONTREAL*, TV, 75, CDN, Rech/1er ass réal; *TI-DRE LE RAMONEUR*, C, 75, CDN, 1er ass réal; *AU BOUT DE MON AGE*, C, 74, CDN, Rech/1er ass réal/Ass mont; *LES JARDINS D'HIVER*, C, 74, CDN, Rech/1er ass réal/Ass mont; *A VOTRE SANTE*, C, 73, CDN, Rech/1er ass réal/Ass mont.

DIRECTORS/REALISATEURS

LEVY, Ira

DGC. 69 Marchmount Rd., Toronto, Ont, CAN, M6G 2A8. (416)532-3878. Breakthrough Films & TV Inc., 67 Mowat Ave., Ste. 331, Toronto, Ont, CAN, M6K 3E3. (416)534-2307.
Types of Production & Categories: TV Film-Dir/Prod; TV Video-Dir/Prod.
Genres: Drama-TV; Comedy-TV; Documentary-TV; Educational-TV.
Biography: Born 1952, Hamilton, Ontario. B.A., University of Toronto; graduate, London Int'l Film School, England. *THE BREAKTHROUGH* won Golden Sheaf, Yorkton and Red Ribbon, American Film Festival.
Selective Filmography: *CONSERVING KINGDOM,* TV, 86, CDN, Dir; *MEMORIES OF PARADISE,* TV, 85, CDN, Prod/Dir; *HEROES OF SUMMER,* TV, 84, CDN, Dir; *'SUMMER OLYMPIC MOMENTS'* (18 eps), TV, 84, CDN, Prod/Dir; *'WINTER OLYMPIC MOMENTS'* (10 eps), TV, 84, CDN, Prod/Dir; *THREE AGAINST THE WORLD,* TV, 83, CDN, Dir; *TWO WAY STREET,* TV, 83, CDN, Prod/Dir; *THE FAST AND THE FURIOUS,* TV, 82, CDN, Dir; *'THE ALPINE SKI SCHOOL'* (5 eps), TV, 82, CDN, Dir; *AGAINST ALL ODDS* (MALGRE TOUT), TV, 81, CDN, Prod/Dir; *INSIDE BASEBALL* 'INSIDE SPORTS', (2 eps), TV, 81, CDN, Prod/Dir; *I DON'T LIKE MONDAYS,* TV, 81, CDN, Prod/Dir; *VANPOOLING - EN ROUTE,* TV, 81, CDN, Dir; *THE SPITFIRES,* TV, 81, CDN, Dir; *THE BREAKTHROUGH,* TV, 80, CDN, Dir/Co-Prod; *NOW I CAN SPEAK,* TV, 80, CDN, Prod/Dir; *WOODSIDE,* TV, 80, CDN, Prod; *THE LETTER,* TV, 80, CDN, Prod.

LIIMATAINEN, Arvi

DGC. 10543 125th St., Edmonton, Alta, CAN, T5N 1T4. (403)488-2607. Kicking Horse Prod. Ltd., 11930 100 Ave., Edmonton, Alta, CAN, T5K 0E6. (403)482-6441.
Types of Production & Categories: Th Short-Dir; TV Film-Dir/Prod.
Genres: Drama-TV; Documentary-TV; Educational-TV; Industrial-TV.
Biography: Born 1949, Finland; Canadian citizen. Worked in motion picture industry since 68. President of Alberta Motion Picture Industries Association (AMPIA), 80-82; Advisory Committee member for Alberta Motion Picture Development Corporation, 82-84.
Selective Filmography: *'HAMILTON'S QUEST'* (3 eps), TV, 86, CDN, Dir; *GOOD TIMES AT THE RAINBOW BAR & GRILL,* TV, 86, CDN, Co-Prod; *'THE BEACHCOMBERS'* (6 eps), TV, 85-82, CDN, Dir; *STRIKER'S MOUNTAIN,* TV, 85, CDN, Line Prod; *GREAT DAYS IN THE ROCKIES,* Th, 84/83, CDN, Dir; *BRIDGE TO TERABITHIA,* 'WONDERWORKS', TV, 84, CDN, Co-Prod/PM; *ISAAC LITTLEFEATHERS,* Th, 84, CDN, Assoc Prod/PM; *'STONEY PLAIN'* (3 eps), TV, 83/82, CDN, Dir; *GAME PLAN,* TV, 83, CDN, Prod/Dir; *LATITUDE 55,* Th, 80, CDN, 1st AD.

LORD, Jean-Claude

ARRFQ. 311 rue Notre-Dame, Saint-Lambert, Qué, CAN, J4P 2K2. (514)466-2602.
Types de production et Catégories: l métrage-Réal/Sc; TV film-Réal.
Types d'oeuvres: Drame-C; Horreur-C.
Curriculum vitae: Né en 1943, Montréal, Québec. Critique de film pour la télévision québécoise, 69-72; chroniqueur de film, 71-74.
Filmographie sélective: *'LANCE ET COMPTE'* (HE SHOOTS, HE SCORES), (13 eps), TV, 86/85, CDN, Réal; *TOBY McTEAGUE,* C, 85, CDN, Réal; *THE VINDICATOR* (FRANKENSTEIN FACTOR), C, 84, CDN, Réal; *DREAMWORLD,* C, 81, CDN, Réal; *VISITING HOURS,* C, 80, CDN, Réal; *ECLAIR AU CHOCOLAT,* C, 78, CDN, Réal/Sc/Mont; *PANIQUE* (PANIC), C, 77/76, CDN, Co prod/Réal/Sc/Mont; *PARLEZ-NOUS D'AMOUR,* C, 76/75, CDN, Co prod/Réal/Sc/Mont; *BINGO,* C, 74/73, CDN, Co prod/Réal/Co sc/Mont; *LES COLOMBES* (THE DOVES), C, 72, CDN, Co prod/Réal/Sc/Mont; *TROUBLE-FETE,* C, 63, CDN, 1er ass réal.

LORD, Roger

ARRQ. 227 boul. Riel, Hull, Qué, CAN, J8X 5X9. (819)770-0785. Radio-Québec, 227 boul. St-Joseph, Hull, Qué, CAN, J8X 3X5. (819)771-1243.
Types de production et Catégories: c métrage-Réal; TV film-Réal; TV vidéo-Réal.
Types d'oeuvres: Drame-TV; Documentaire-TV; Education-TV; Enfants-TV.
Curriculum vitae: Né en 1946.
Filmographie sélective: *'BLOC-NOTES'* (122 eps), TV, 86-84, CDN, Réal; *CHOEUR ET CORDES PASCALS,* TV, 86, CDN, Réal; *'CITE DES JEUNES'* (7 eps), TV, 85, CDN, Réal/Prod dél; *'LES 100 COUPS DE THEATRE'* (6 eps), TV, 84, CDN, Réal/Prod dél; *'CONTOUR'* (38 eps), TV, 83, CDN, Réal; *'A TIRE D'AILE'* (78 eps), TV, 82/81, CDN, Réal; *'ACTUALITE'* (jour), TV, 80-77, CDN, Réal.

LORRAIN, Lise

CTPDA. 5 Edgett Ave., Moncton, NB, CAN, E1C 7A9. (506)855-6084. Radio-Canada, 250 rue Archibald, Moncton, NB, CAN, E1C 8N8. (506)853-3061.
Types of Production & Categories: TV Video-Dir/Prod/Ed.
Genres: Variety-TV; Documentary-TV; News-TV.
Biography: Born 1960, Gravelbourg, Saskatchewan; bilingual. Education: Mount Royal College, Calgary, Broadcasting; Royal Conservatory, Toronto, Music Studies; Trinity College, England, Music Studies. Experience: Radio-Canada, Moncton; CBC/Radio-Canada, Regina.
Selective Filmography: *'COURTE POINTE'* (30 eps), TV, 85/84, CDN, Dir; *'NEWSDAY FINAL'* (REGINA), (10 eps), TV, 85-83, CDN, Dir; *EASTER SEALS TELETHON* (1 seg), TV, 85, CDN, Dir; *'PLAINE PERSPECTIVE'* (16 eps), TV, 84, CDN, Prod; *'ARTISTES D'ICI',* TV, 84, CDN, Prod; *'CE SOIR'* (REGINA), (daily), TV, 84/83, CDN, Dir.

LOW, Colin

SGCT. 4844 Grosvenor Ave., Montreal, Que, CAN. (514)481-7116. NFB, 3155 Côte de Liesse, Montreal, Que, CAN. (514)283-9548.
Types of Production & Categories: Th Short-Dir/Prod; TV Film-Dir/Prod.
Genres: Action-Th; Documentary-Th; Educational-Th; Animation-Th.
Biography: Born 1926, Cardston, Alberta; studied graphic arts, Banff, Calgary. Head of Animation Dept., NFB, 50-62; producer, Challenge for Change series, 70-72; executive producer, Unit C, 72-75; Director, Regional Production, 75-78. Over 100 producer, executive producer and designer credits. Cannes TV Award for *DAYS OF WHISKEY GAP*; Oscar nomination for *UNIVERSE*; John Grierson Award, 72. Co-director of the first 3-D IMAX film for Expo 86, *TRANSITIONS*.
Selective Filmography: *TRANSITIONS* (EXPO 86), Th, 85, CDN, Co-Dir; *CONTOUR CONNECTION,* ED, 83, CDN, Dir; *PETE STANDING ALONE,* TV, 82, CDN, Dir; *ATMOS,* Th, 79, CDN, Dir; *THE SEA,* TV, 71, CDN, Prod/Des; *THE WINDS OF FOGO,* Th, 70, CDN, Dir; *FARMERSVILLE* (30 films), ED, 69, CDN, Co-Dir; *FOGO ISLAND* (28 films), 'CHALLENGE FOR CHANGE', TV, 68, CDN, Dir/Prod; *LABYRINTH,* Th, 67, CDN, Co-Dir/An Co-Des; *THE HUTTERITES/DAYS OF WHISKEY GAP,* 'CANDID EYE', TV, 63-62, CDN, Dir; *CIRCLE OF THE SUN,* Th, 61, CDN, Dir (CFA); *HORS D'OEUVRES,* Th, 61, CDN, Dir (CFA); *UNIVERSE,* Th, 60, CDN, Co-Dir (2 CFA); *CITY OUT OF TIME,* Th, 58, CDN, Dir; *CITY OF GOLD,* Th, 56, CDN, Co-Dir (2 CFA); *GOLD,* Th, 56, CDN, Dir (CFA); *THE JOLIFOU INN,* Th, 55, CDN, Dir; *CORRAL,* Th, 53, CDN, Dir; *L'AGE DU CASTOR,* Th, 53, CDN, Dir (CFA); *ROMANCE OF TRANSPORTATION,* Th, 52, CDN, An Svp.

LYNCH, Paul

DGC, DGA. Questcan Inc., 1720 Pacific Ave., Suite 303, Los Angeles, CA, USA,

(cont/suite)

90291. (213)392-2621. Barry Perelman Agency, 9200 Sunset Blvd., Suite 531, Hollywood, CA, USA. (213)274-5999.
Types of Production & Categories: Th Film-Dir; TV Film-Dir.
Genres: Drama-Th&TV; Action-Th; Horror-Th&TV; Documentary-TV.
Biography: Born 1946, Liverpool, England; Canadian citizen. Former magazine photographer and advertising art director/designer. Special skill: corporate design.
Selective Filmography: *'BLACKE'S MAGIC'* (sev eps), TV, 86, USA, Dir; *'MURDER SHE WROTE'* (sev eps), TV, 86, USA, Dir; *'TWILIGHT ZONE'* (1 eps), TV, 85, USA, Dir; *BULLIES,* Th, 85, CDN, Dir; *MARIONETTES INC.,* 'RAY BRADBURY THEATRE', TV, 84, CDN, Dir; *FLYING,* Th, 84, CDN, Dir; *CROSS-COUNTRY,* Th, 82, CDN, Dir; *DARKROOM,* TV, 81, USA, Dir; *HUMONGOUS,* Th, 81, CDN, Dir; *PROM NIGHT* (LE BAL DE L'HORREUR), Th, 79, CDN, Dir; *BLOOD & GUTS,* Th, 77, CDN, Dir; *THE HARD PART BEGINS,* Th, 73, CDN, Dir.

MacDONALD, Ramuna

ASIFA. 212 James St., Ottawa, Ont, CAN, K1R 5M7. (613)230-9769. Doomsday Studios Ltd., 1672 Barrington St., Halifax, NS, CAN, B3J 2A2. (902)422-3494.
Types of Production & Categories: Th Short-Dir/Ed; TV Film-Dir/Prod/Ed.
Genres: Drama-Th&TV; Comedy-Th&TV; Documentary-Th&TV; Animation-Th&TV.
Biography: Canadian. B.A., B.Sc., special courses, Nova Scotia College of Art & Design. Interim Acting Director, Atlantic Film and Video Festival, 84. *SPIRITS OF AN AMBER PAST* won Chris Bronze Plaque, Columbus; Best Editing Award, Atlantic Film Fest. for *SARAH JACKSON.*
Selective Filmography: *SUCCESS* (pilot), TV, 86, CDN, Exec Prod; *NOBODY'S PERFECT,* TV, 86, CDN, Dir/Prod/Wr; *SARAH JACKSON,* TV, 80, CDN, Dir/Ed; *GOD'S ISLAND,* Th, 80, CDN, Dir/Ed; *SPIRITS OF AN AMBER PAST,* TV, 78, CDN, Dir/Co-Ed.

MacGILLIVRAY, William D.

Picture Plant Limited, P.O. Box 2465, Stn. M, Halifax, NS, CAN, B3J 3E8. (902) 423-3901.
Types of Production & Categories: Th Short-Dir/Prod/Wr; TV Film-Dir/Prod/Wr; TV Video-Dir/Prod/Wr.
Genres: Drama-Th&TV; Documentary-Th&TV.
Biography: Born 1946. Founding member, 1st President, Atlantic Filmmakers' Co-operative, the Atlantic Independent Film and Video Association.
Selective Filmography: *LIFE CLASSES,* TV, 86, CDN, Dir/Wr/Exec Prod; *LINDA JOY,* Th, 85, CDN, Dir/Wr/Prod; *ABRAHAM GESNER,* TV, 85, CDN, Dir; *ALISTAIR MacLEOD,* TV, 84, CDN, Dir/Wr/Prod; *STATIONS,* TV, 81, CDN, Dir/Wr/Prod/Ed; *THE AUTHOR OF THESE WORDS,* Th, 80, CDN, Dir/Wr/Prod; *AERIAL VIEW,* Th, 79, CDN, Dir/Wr/Prod/Ed; *BREAKDOWN,* Th, 77, CDN, 2nd AD; *7:30 A.M.,* Th, 71, CDN, Dir/Wr; *TALKAUTOBANDEN,* Th, 70, CDN, Dir/Co-Wr/Cin.

MACINA, Michael - see WRITERS

MacKAY, Bruce

SGCT. 100 Ballantyne South, Montreal West, Que, CAN, H4X 2B3. (514)484-5668. NFB, 3155 Cote de Liesse, Montreal, Que, CAN, H3C 3C5. (514)283-9570.
Types of Production & Categories: Th Short-Dir/Wr/Ed; TV Film-Dir/Prod/Ed.
Genres: Drama-Th&TV; Documentary-Th&TV; Educational-Th&TV; Children's-Th&TV.
Biography: Born 1945, Montreal,Quebec; bilingual. Produced playwright and song writer, singer with 2 albums. *GULF STREAM* won the Grand Prize, Rio de Janiero Science Film Festival.

(cont/suite)

Selective Filmography: *EDGE OF ICE*, TV, 85, CDN, Prod/Ed; *STARBREAKER*, Th, 85, CDN, Dir/Co-Ed/Wr; *UNCERTAIN FUTURES*, TV, 84, CDN, Snd Des; *MOZAMBIQUE: COMMUNAL VILLAGE*, TV, 81, CDN, Prod; *GULF STREAM*, TV, 81, CDN/USA, Prod/Dir/Ed; *NORTHERN COMPOSITION*, TV, 79, CDN, Prod/Dir/Ed; *SAIL AWAY*, TV, 79, CDN/USA, Dir/Prod/Ed; *ENERGY CONSERVATION*, Cm, 76, CDN, Dir/Ed; *STILL IN ONE PIECE ANYWAY*, TV, 75, CDN, Dir/Ed/Comp; *A CASE OF EGGS*, Th, 74, CDN, Ed/Comp; *'WEST'*, TV, 73, CDN, Theme Comp; *THIS RIEL BUSINESS*, TV, 73, CDN, Ed; *CRY OF THE WILD*, Th, 72, CDN, Theme Comp/Act; *THE PEARLY YEATS*, Th, 71, CDN, Dir/Ed/Comp; *BLOOD SUGAR*, TV, 71, CDN, Snd Des/Theme Comp; *GARDEN*, Th, 71, CDN, Comp; *PERCEPTION: STRUCTURE OR FLOW*, ED, 71, CDN, Comp; *HALF-HALF-THREE-QUARTERS-FULL*, Th, 70, CDN, Comp; *IF HE IS DEVOURED, I WIN*, Th, 70, CDN, Comp; *A ONE-TWO MANY WORLD*, Th, 70, CDN, Comp; *HALF-MASTED SCHOONER*, Th, 69, CDN, Dir/Ed/Comp/Act; *THE RISE AND FALL OF THE GREAT LAKES*, Th, 68, CDN, Comp/Act; *EACH DAY THAT COMES*, TV, 66, CDN, Comp; *NOTES FOR A FILM ABOUT DONNA AND GAIL*, Th, 66, CDN, Comp/Act; *NO REASON TO STAY*, TV, 66, CDN, Comp/Act; *HIGH STEEL* (CHARPENTIER DU CIEL), Th, 65, CDN, Comp/Act.

MALLET, Marilu

ARRFQ. 743 Davaar, Outremont, Qué, CAN, H2V 3B3. (514)272-0292. ONF, 3155 Côte-de-Liesse, Montréal, Qué, CAN, H4N 2N4.
Types de production et Catégories: c métrage-Réal/Prod/Mont; TV film-Réal/Mont.
Types d'oeuvres: Drame-C&TV; Documentaire-C&TV.
Curriculum vitae: Née en 1945, Santiago, Chili; naturalisée canadienne; vit au Québec depuis 73. Maitrise en Cinéma, Université de Montréal, 85; Ecole d'Etudes Cinématographiques de l'O.C.I.C., Santiago, Chili, Initiation au cinéma, 67-69; Architecture, Université du Chili, 64-69. *JOURNAL INACHEVE* remporte le Prix de la Critique Québécoise et le Prix Spécial, Festival de Biarritz, France.
Filmographie sélective: *MEMOIRES D'UNE ENFANT DES ANDES* (ANDAHAYLILLAS), C, 85, CDN, Réal/Rech; *JOURNAL INACHEVE* (UNFINISHED DIARY), C, 83, CDN, Réal/Prod/Mont, *HOMMAGE A JORDI BONET/ PIERRE ET LE CAPITAINE*, 'PLANETE', TV, 80, CDN, Réal/Mont; *LES BORGES*, C, 79, CDN, Réal/Rech.

MALTBY, Michael

Maltby Films Ltd., 2 Brighton Ave., Toronto, Ont, CAN, M4M 1P4. (416)465-4996.
Types of Production & Categories: TV Film-Dir; TV Video-Dir.
Genres: Documentary-TV; Educational-TV; Animation-Th; Industrial-TV.
Biography: Born 1942, Toronto, Ontario. B.A., History, Carleton University, 66. Seven years as radio and television director/producer, CBC public affairs; specialty: technology films, corporate communications.
Selective Filmography: *THE ESTONIANS: FOR THE RECORD*, ED, 84, CDN, Wr/Prod; *THE ANIMATED NETWORK*, ED, 82, CDN, Wr/Prod; *THE DIGITAL CONNECTION* (L'ABC DU NUMERIQUE), ED, 81, CDN, Dir/Wr; *LEAVING SOMETHING OVER*, ED, 80, CDN, Prod; *THE ELECTRONIC TELEPHONE* (LE TELEPHONE ELECTRONIC), In, 79, CDN, Dir/Wr; *LIGHT CONVERSATIONS* (DES COMMUNICATIONS ECLAIREES), In, 78, CDN, Dir/Wr (CFTA); *'THE STATIONARY ARK'* (L'ARCHE IMMOBILE), (13 eps), TV, 76, CDN, Dir/Co-Prod (CFTA).

MANATIS, Janine

ACTRA. 97 Bellefair Ave., Toronto, Ont, CAN, M4L 3T7. (416)691-1010. Debbie Peck, ACI, 88 Spruce St., Toronto, Ont, CAN, M5A 2J1. (416)925-2488.

(cont/suite)

Types of Production & Categories: Th Film-Dir/Wr; Th Short-Dir/Act; TV Film-Dir/Act.
Genres: Drama-Th; Documentary-Th&TV.
Biography: U.S. citizen; Canadian landed immigrant. Trained, Actor's Studio, New York as actor, director.
Selective Filmography: *INTENSIVE CARE*, TV, 85, USA, Act; *HOTEL NEW HAMPSHIRE*, Th, 84, USA, Act; *TEEN MOTHER: A STORY OF COPING*, Th, 83, CDN, Dir/Co-Wr; *BREAKING OUT*, Th, 82, CDN, Dir; *IN A FAR COUNTRY*, 'TALES OF THE KLONDIKE', TV, 81, CDN, Dir; *AFTER THE AXE*, Th, 79, CDN, Act; *I, MAUREEN*, Th, 78, CDN, Dir/Wr; *OTTAWA VALLEY*, TV, 76, CDN, Dir; *THE TIMES THEY ARE 'A CHANGING'* (3 eps), TV, 75, CDN, Dir/Prod.

MANKIEWICZ, Francis

269 Carré St-Louis, Montréal, Qué, CAN, H2X 1A3. (514)288-5131. Great North Artists Mgmt., 345 Adelaide St. W., Ste. 500, Toronto, Ont, CAN, M5V 1R5. (416)593-2587.
Types de production et Catégories: l métrage-Réal/Sc; c métrage-Réal; TV film-Réal; TV vidéo-Réal.
Types d'oeuvres: Drame-C&TV; Documentaire-C&TV; Education-C&TV; Annonces-TV.
Curriculum vitae: Né en 1944, Chang-Hai, Chine; citoyen canadien; Baccalauréat en Sciences (Géologie), Université de Montréal; London School of Film Techniques, Angleterre (2 ans). Caméraman pigiste, Angleterre, 68; *LE TEMPS D'UNE CHASSE* a été invité au Festival du Film de Cannes, a remporté un prix au Fest. du Film de Venise et un Prix Spécial aux Palmarès du film canadien; *LES BONS DEBARRAS* a remporté 8 Génies dont Meilleur Film, a aussi été sélectionné comme entrée officielle du Canada aux Academy Awards.
Filmographie sélective: *THE SIGHT*, 'BELL CANADA PLAYHOUSE', TV, 85, CDN, Réal; *LES BEAUX SOUVENIRS*, C, 80, CDN, Réal; *LES BONS DEBARRAS* (GOOD RIDDANCE), C, 78, CDN, Réal **(GENIE)**; *I WAS DYING AWAY*, ED, 77, CDN, Réal; *A MATTER OF CHOICE*, 'FOR THE RECORD', TV, 77, CDN, Réal; *UNE AMIE D'ENFANCE*, C, 77, CDN, Réal; *POINTE PELEE*, C, 76, CDN, Réal; *EXPROPRIATION*, TV, 75, CDN, Réal; *PROCES CRIMINEL/ORIENTATION/CAUSE CIVILE*, ED, 74, CDN, Réal; *LES ALLEES DE LA TERRE*, C, 73, CDN, Prod exéc; *VALENTIN*, TV, 73, CDN/CH/F, Réal; *LE TEMPS D'UNE CHASSE*, C, 72, CDN, Réal/Sc.

MANN, Danny - see WRITERS

MANN, Ron

Sphinx Productions Ltd., 41 Riderwood Dr., Willowdale, Ont, CAN, M2L 2E7. (416)445-7492. The Colbert Agency, 303 Davenport Rd., Toronto, Ont, CAN, M5R 1K5. (416)964-3302.
Types of Production & Categories: Th Film-Dir/Prod/Wr; Th Short-Dir/Prod/Wr; TV Film-Dir/Prod/Wr.
Genres: Documentary-Th; Animation-Th; Experimental-Th.
Biography: Born 1958, Toronto, Ontario; B.A., University of Toronto. Films he has produced and/or directed have won numerous prizes including Silver Hugo, Chicago, *IMAGINE THE SOUND*; Gold Plaque, Chicago, *POETRY IN MOTION*.
Selective Filmography: *MARCIA RESNICK'S BAD BOYS*, Th, 85, CDN, Prod/Dir; *NEW CINEMA*, TV, 84, CDN, Assoc Prod; *LISTEN TO THE CITY*, Th, 84, CDN, Prod/Dir/Co-Wr; *ECHOES WITHOUT SAYING*, TV, 83, CDN, Prod/Dir; *POETRY IN MOTION*, Th, 82, CDN, Prod/Dir; *IMAGINE THE SOUND*, Th, 81, CDN, Co-Prod/Dir; *SSSHHH!*, Th, 80, CDN, Prod/Dir; *FEELS SO GOOD*, Th, 80, CDN, Prod/Co-Dir; *THE ONLY GAME IN TOWN*, Th, 79, CDN, Co-Prod/Co-Dir/Co-Wr; *DEPOT*, Th, 78, CDN, Co-Prod/Co-Dir; *FLAK*, Th, 76, CDN, Prod/Dir/Wr/DOP.

MARCOUX, Royal

AR. 740 Victoria, Longueuil, Qué, CAN, J4H 2K3. (514)677-3147. Radio-Canada, 1400 blvd. Dorchester est, Montréal, Qué, CAN, H2L 2M2. (514)285-2011.
Types de production et Catégories: TV film-Réal; TV vidéo-Réal.
Types d'oeuvres: Comédie-TV; Variété-TV; Documentaire-TV.
Curriculum vitae: Né en 1944, Thetford-Mines, Québec. Baccalauréat ès Arts, Université de Sherbrooke; stage en technique télévisuelle, Ryerson Polytechnical Institute.
Filmographie sélective: *'LE 101 OUEST, AV. DES PINS'* (24 eps), TV, 85/84, CDN, Réal; *SUPER STAR,* 'LES BEAUX DIMANCHES', TV, 85, CDN, Réal; *'ALLO BOUBOU'* (80 eps), TV, 84-82, CDN, Réal; *'DU TAC AU TAC'* (8 eps), TV, 82/81, CDN, Réal; *'L'OBSERVATEUR'* (24 eps), TV, 81-78, CDN, Réal; *'L'HEURE DE POINTE'* (65 eps), TV, 78/77, CDN, Réal; *'MESDAMES ET MESSIEURS'* (15 eps), TV, 77/76, CDN, Réal; *'LISE LIB'* (22 eps), TV, 76/75, CDN, Réal; *'APPELEZ-MOI LISE'* (85 eps), TV, 75-72, CDN, Réal.

MARION, Jean-Claude

AR. 3542 Marcil, Montréal, Qué, CAN, H4A 2Z3. (514)483-1755. Radio-Canada, 1400 blvd. Dorchester est, Montréal, Qué, CAN, H2L 2M2. (514)285-2894.
Types de production et Catégories: TV film-Réal.
Types d'oeuvres: Documentaire-TV.
Curriculum vitae: Né en 1940, Marionville, Ontario. Bac. avec spécialisation en Sciences politiques, Université d'Ottawa. Langues: français, anglais, allemand. Trois ans de réalisation radio; réalisateur TV, CBOFT, Ottawa, 66-75; directeur de la radio des Forces Canadiennes en Europe (R.F.A.), 75-82; retour à la réalisation TV, Montréal.
Filmographie sélective: *INCESTE - SORTIE DE SECOURS,* TV, 86, CDN, Réal; *'ICI RADIO-CANADA'* (14 eps), TV, 86, CDN, Réal; *NEW YORK - SORTIES DE SECOURS,* 'DELINQUENCE JUVENILE', TV, 85/84, CDN, Réal; *'AU JOUR LE JOUR'* (pl seg), TV, 85-82, CDN, Réal; *LES ENFANTS DU CANCER,* 'AU JOUR LE JOUR', TV, 84, CDN, Réal; *L'INDUSTRIE DU BOEUF DU CANADA/ LA G.R.C.,* 'DOSSIERS', TV, 75-73, CDN, Réal; *'CONSOMMATEURS AVERTIS'* (20 eps), TV, 72/71, CDN, Réal; *'SUR LE VIF'* (quot), TV, 70-66, CDN, Réal/Prod dél.

MARKLE, Fletcher

ACTRA, AFTRA, DGA, DGC, PGA, WGAw 351 Congress Place, Pasadena, CA, USA, 91105. (818)799-6907.
Types of Production & Categories: Th Film-Dir; Th Short-Wr/Narr; TV Film-Dir/Prod/Wr; TV Video-Dir/Prod/Wr.
Genres: Drama-Th&TV; Comedy-TV; Documentary-Th&TV.
Biography: Born 1921, Winnipeg, Manitoba; still a Canadian citizen. Served in 2nd World War with R.C.A.F., 42-45. George Foster Peabody Award (radio drama), 48. Writer-in-Residence, University of Toronto, 74-75. *THE INCREDIBLE JOURNEY* won the Boxoffice Blue Ribbon Award; *V-1: THE STORY OF THE ROBOT BOMB* was nominated for an Oscar and was Picture of the Month, November, 44 (War Activities Committee).
Selective Filmography: *'THAT'S HOLLYWOOD'* (2 eps), TV, 78, USA, Prod/Wr; *THE OLYMPICS: A TELEVISION HISTORY OF THE GOLDEN GAMES* (4 parts), TV, 76/75, CDN, Prod; *'THE PLAY'S THE THING'* (10 eps), TV, 74/73, CDN, Exec Prod; *'TELESCOPE'* (300 eps), TV, 69-63, CDN, Prod/Contr Dir/Wr/Host; *'FESTIVAL'* (8 eps), TV, 69-63, CDN, Wr; *'JULIA'* (2 eps), TV, 69, USA, Dir; *THE INCREDIBLE JOURNEY,* Th, 62, CDN, Dir; *'FATHER OF THE BRIDE'* (10 eps), TV, 62, USA, Dir; *'HONG KONG'* (8 eps), TV, 61, USA, Prod/Contr Dir; *'THRILLER'* (8 eps), TV, 60, USA, Prod/Contr Dir; *'RENDEZVOUS'* (8 eps), TV, 59, GB, Dir; *'TALES OF THE VIKINGS'* (6 eps), TV, 58, GB, Dir; *'GEORGE SANDERS' MYSTERY THEATRE'* (13 eps), TV, 57, USA, Dir/Prod;
(cont/suite)

285

'BUCKSKIN' (4 eps), TV, 56, USA, Dir; *'M SQUAD'* (6 eps), TV, 56, USA, Dir; *'FRONT ROW CENTER'* (10 eps), TV, 55, USA, Dir/Prod; *'LIFE WITH FATHER'* (118 eps), TV, 55-53, USA, Prod/Contr Dir; *'STUDIO ONE'* (39 eps), TV, 53/52, USA, Prod; *THE MAN WITH A CLOAK,* Th, 52, USA, Dir; *NIGHT INTO MORNING,* Th, 51, USA, Dir; *JIGSAW,* Th, 48, USA, Dir/Co-Wr; *V-1: THE STORY OF THE ROBOT BOMB,* Th, 44, CDN/GB, Wr/Narr.

MARKSON, Morley

Morley Markson & Assoc. Ltd., 2900 Bathurst St., Ste. 208, Toronto, Ont, CAN, M6B 3A9. (416)784-1229.
Types of Production & Categories: Th Film-Dir/Prod; TV Video-Dir/Prod.
Genres: Drama-Th; Comedy-Th; Documentary-Th&TV.
Biography: Born Toronto, Ontario. Producer, director and designer of 'From Out of the Depths' (a.v.) presented at the Toronto Holocaust Memorial Museum. *BREATHING TOGETHER - REVOLUTION OF THE ELECTRIC FAMILY* was the French Critics Selection, Cannes.
Selective Filmography: *THE LIVING TRADITION,* TV, 86, CDN, Dir/Co-Prod; *OFF YOUR ROCKER,* Th, 80, CDN, Co-Dir/Co-Wr; *MONKEYS IN THE ATTIC,* Th, 74, CDN, Dir/Prod/Co-Wr; *BREATHING TOGETHER - REVOLUTION OF THE ELECTRIC FAMILY,* Th, 71, CDN, Dir/Prod; *TRAGIC DIARY OF ZERO THE FOOL,* Th, 70, CDN, Dir/Prod; *MAN AND COLOR - KALEIDOSCOPE* (EXPO 67), Th, 67, CDN, Dir/Prod.

MARR, Leon G.

ACTRA, DGC. Ikon Kino Films, 101 MacLean Ave., Toronto, Ont, CAN, M4E 2Z8. (416)691-1215.
Types of Production & Categories: Th Film-Dir/Wr; TV Film-Dir/Prod.
Genres: Drama-Th&TV.
Biography: Born 1948, Toronto, Ontario. Graduate of Ryerson Polytechnical Institute, Photographic Arts. *DANCING IN THE DARK* was invited to Directors Fortnight, Cannes, 86.
Selective Filmography: *DANCING IN THE DARK,* Th, 85, CDN, Dir/Scr; *FLOWERS IN THE SAND,* TV, 80, CDN, Dir/Co-Prod; *CLARE'S WISH,* TV, 79, CDN, Dir/Co-Prod.

MARTIN, Maude

AR. 105 ave. Querbes, #17, Outremont, Qué, CAN. (514)272-7647. Radio-Canada, 1400 blvd. Dorchester est, Montréal, Qué, CAN, H2L 2M2. (514)285-2073.
Types de production et Catégories: TV vidéo-Réal.
Types d'oeuvres: Drame-TV; Comédie-TV.
Curriculum vitae: Née en 1944, Montréal, Québec; bilingue. A travaillé comme assistante réalisatrice à Radio-Canada pendant 12 ans; réalisatrice depuis 9 ans.
Filmographie sélective: *'POIVRE ET SEL'* (37 eps), TV, 86-83, CDN, Réal; *'DES DAMES DE COEUR'* (8 eps), TV, 86, CDN, Réal; *'METRO-BOULOT-DODO'* (22 eps), TV, 83/82, CDN, Réal; *'CHEZ DENYSE'* (40 eps), TV, 82-80, CDN, Réal; *'CAROLINE'* (13 eps), TV, 80/79, CDN, Réal; *'GRAND'PAPA'* (10 eps), TV, 79, CDN, Réal; *'A CAUSE DE MON ONCLE'* (10 eps), TV, 78, CDN, Réal.

MARTIN, Mike

33 Eastmount Ave., Toronto, Ont, CAN, M4K 1V3. (416)469-9719. City-TV, 299 Queen St. W., Toronto, Ont, CAN, M5V 1Z9. (415)367-5757.
Types of Production & Categories: TV Video-Dir/Ed.
Genres: News-TV.
Biography: Born 1959, Bracebridge, Ontario. Education: Community College Degree in Television.
Selective Filmography: *'CITY PULSE/CITY PULSE TONITE/CITY LINE'* (daily), TV, 86, CDN, Dir; *'CITY PULSE'* (daily), TV, 86-80, CDN, Ed.

MARTIN, Susan

ACTRA, DGC, IATSE-776, WGAw. 13B St. Mathias Pl., Toronto, Ont, CAN, M6J 2N4. (416)868-0807. 1837 N. Garfield Pl., #F, Hollywood, CA, USA, 90028. (213)463-3743.
Types of Production & Categories: Th Film-Dir/Wr/Ed; TV Film-Dir/Wr/Ed.
Genres: Drama-Th&TV; Comedy-Th&TV; Variety-TV; Children's-TV.
Biography: Born Baltimore, Maryland; Canadian citizen. Attended Ontario College of Art, 2 years; Goddard College (Vermont), York University and UCLA Film School. Films she has worked on have won awards at New York, San Francisco, Chicago and Berlin film festivals.
Selective Filmography: *'DANGER BAY'* (1 eps), TV, 86, CDN/USA, Dir; *'AIRWAVES'* (Wr-2 eps), (3 eps), TV, 86/85, CDN, Dir; *'FRAGGLE ROCK'* (Co-Wr-1 eps), (5 eps), TV, 85, CDN, Dir; *THE OVALTINE CAFE,* Th, 85, USA, Co-Wr; *ROSEDALE,* 'NEIGHBOURHOODS', TV, 84, CDN, Dir; *PARALLEL TRACKS,* 'FOR THE RECORD', TV, 83, CDN, Co-Wr; *THE GLITTER DOME,* TV, 83, CDN/USA, Ed; *IS ANYONE HOME ON THE RANGE,* TV, 83, USA, Ed; *THRESHOLD,* Th, 80, CDN, Ed; *FIRST FAMILY,* Th, 80, USA, Ed; *BLOW JOB* (short film), 'SATURDAY NIGHT LIVE', TV, 78, USA, Dir; *BLACK STALLION,* Th, 78, USA, Co-Ed; *DAYS OF HEAVEN,* Th, 77, USA, Co-Ed; *FLAKES* (pilot), TV, 77, USA, Ed; *BEACHBOYS SPECIAL,* TV, 76, USA, Co-Ed; *BYPASS,* Th, 75, USA, Dir; *POCO A POCO,* Th, 75, USA, Dir; *HEARTS AND MINDS,* Th, 75, USA, Ed; *TOUT VA BIEN,* Th, 72, F, Co-Ed; *WARNING: EARTHQUAKE,* TV, 70, USA, Dir; *PUNISHMENT PARK,* Th, 70, USA, Prod.

MARTINET, Jean

AR. 46 Dufferin, Hampstead, Qué, CAN. (514)487-3764. Radio-Canada, 1400 blvd. Dorchester est, Montréal, Qué, CAN, H2L 2M2. (514)285-3620.
Types de production et Catégories: TV film-Réal/Sc.
Types d'oeuvres: Documentaire-TV; Animation-C.
Curriculum vitae: Né en 1923, Latour de Salvagny, France; citoyen canadien. Expérience: 31 ans de réalisation.
Filmographie sélective: *'HORIZONS 2000'* (26 eps), TV, 82/81, CDN, Réal/Sc; *'AUX FRONTIERES DU CONNU'* (120 eps), TV, 80-77, CDN, Réal/Sc; *'LA FLECHE DU TEMPS'* (130 eps), TV, 75-71, CDN, Réal; *'ATOME ET GALAXIES'* (180 eps), TV, 70-65, CDN, Réal; *'ORIENTATION'* (39 eps), TV, 61/60, CDN, Réal/Sc; *'LE ROMAN DE LA SCIENCE'* (117 eps), TV, 59-57, CDN, Réal.

MATTHEWS, Bill

DGA. 130 Eardley Rd., Aylmer, Que, CAN, J9H 5C9. (819)684-8698.
Types of Production & Categories: TV Film-Dir; TV Video-Dir.
Genres: Variety-TV; Documentary-TV; Animation-TV; News-TV.
Biography: Born Montreal, Quebec, 1947; bilingual. Has worked in Canada, USA, Great Britain, France, Italy, China, Japan, Hong Kong; directing 15 years; total 21 years in business.
Selective Filmography: *'ENTERTAINMENT TOMATO'* (3 eps), TV, 86, CDN, Dir; *1984 DEMOCRATIC CONVENTION,* TV, 84, USA, Dir; *1984 REPUBLICAN CONVENTION,* TV, 84, USA, Dir; *'NITELINE',* TV, 84/83, USA, Dir; *'SPACE SHUTTLE CHALLENGER'* (8 eps), TV, 84/83, USA, Dir; *'WORLD NEWS TONIGHT',* TV, 84-83, USA, Dir; *AMERICA'S CUP,* TV, 83, USA, Dir; *'THE JOURNAL'* (175 eps), TV, 82-80, CDN, Dir; *FEDERAL ELECTIONS,* TV, 80/79, CDN, Dir; *OH WHAT A FEELING,* TV, 80, CDN, Dir.

McANDREW, Jack - see WRITERS

DIRECTORS/REALISATEURS

McCOWAN, George

DGA. Mark Lichtman, Shapiro-Lichtman Agency, Century City, Los Angeles, CA, USA, 90048. (213)859-8877.
Types of Production & Categories: Th Film-Dir; TV Film-Dir; TV Video-Dir.
Genres: Drama-Th&TV; Comedy-Th&TV.
Biography: Born in Winnipeg, Manitoba. B.A., University of Toronto. Canadian citizen, American resident. Has directed hundreds of episodes for TV series and movies for TV, USA and Canada. *RUN SIMON RUN* won the Cowboy Hall of Fame Award.
Selective Filmography: *'SEEING THINGS'* (43 eps), TV, 86-81, CDN, Dir; *'HART TO HART'* (10 eps), TV, 84-82, USA, Dir; *'STARSKY AND HUTCH'* (20 eps), TV, 79-75, USA, Dir; *'CHARLIE'S ANGELS'* (15 eps), TV, 79-75, USA, Dir; *'STREETS OF SAN FRANCISCO'* (20 eps), TV, 75-71, USA, Dir; *'CANNON'* (40 eps), TV, 75-71, USA, Dir; *THE MAGNIFICENT SEVEN RIDE,* Th, 72, USA, Dir; *CARTER'S ARMY,* TV, 70, USA, Dir; *FACE-OFF,* Th, 70, CDN, Dir; *FROGS,* Th, 70, USA, Dir; *'F.B.I.'* (20 eps), TV, 69-67, USA, Dir; *BALLAD OF ANDY CROCKER,* TV, 69, USA, Dir; *RUN SIMON RUN,* TV, 69, USA, Dir; *'RUN FOR YOUR LIFE'* (6 eps), TV, 69-67, USA, Dir.

McGREEVY, John

ACTRA, CFTA, DGC. 36 Roxborough St.E., Toronto, Ont, CAN, M5R 2X7. (416)922-8625.
Types of Production & Categories: TV Film-Dir/Prod/Wr; TV Video-Dir/Prod.
Genres: Drama-TV; Documentary-TV.
Biography: Has won several television awards including 2 Gold Medals, New York Int'l Film Fest. for *CITIES;* Emmy nomination for *HOPE ABANDONED.*
Selective Filmography: *PEN '86,* TV, 86, CDN, Prod/Dir; *'PETER USTINOV'S RUSSIA'* (6 eps), TV, 85, CDN, Prod/Co-Exec Prod/Dir/Wr; *QUEBEC/CANADA 1995,* TV, 84, CDN, Dir/Co-Prod; *'AMERICAN CAESAR',* TV, 84, CDN, Dir/ Prod; *'QUINTET: VISIONS OF FIVE'* (1 seg), TV, 84, CDN, Dir/Prod; *'CITIES'* (13 parts), TV, 79-76, CDN, Dir/Co-Prod/Wr; *BEAVERBROOK- THE LIFE AND TIMES OF MAX AITKEN,* TV, 76, CDN, Dir/Wr/Prod **(ACTRA)**; *'PEOPLE OF OUR TIME'* (18 eps), TV, 75/74, CDN, Dir/Prod; *MANDELSTAM'S WITNESS,* TV, 75, CDN, Prod; *HOPE AGAINST HOPE,* TV, 75, CDN, Prod; *HOPE ABANDONED,* TV, 75, CDN, Prod; *THREE WOMEN ON HUMAN VALUES,* 'MAN ALIVE', TV, 73, CDN, Dir/Prod/Wr; *BECKET / LUTHER / CROMWELL / MARY STEWART / RIEL,* 'MAN ALIVE', TV, 73-71, CDN, Dir/Prod.

McKEE, Neill - see PRODUCERS

McKEOWN, Bob - see PRODUCERS

McKEOWN, Brian - see PRODUCERS

McLAREN, Norman

ONF, Box 6100, Montreal, Que, CAN, H3C 3H5. (514)283-9252.
Types of Production & Categories: Th Short-Dir/An.
Genres: Drama-Th; Documentary-Th; Animation-Th; Experimental-Th.
Biography: Born Stirling, Scotland, 1914. Studied at the Glasgow School of Arts; joined Glasgow Film Society, then worked at the General Post Office Film Unit, London, where he began his professional apprenticeship under John Grierson. In 41, he began to work at the National Film Board, Ottawa. He has over 60 films to his credit; has received prestigious State Honours and Honorary Degrees from a number of universities; many film awards at int'l festivals including Venice, Berlin, for *BEGONE DULL CARE;* Melbourne, Atlanta, Columbus, *BALLET ADAGIO;* Cannes, Edinburgh, Berlin, *BLINKITY BLANK;* San Francisco, Barcelona, Melbourne, *SYNCHROMY;* Oscar nominations for *A CHAIRY TALE* and *CHRIST-*

(cont/suite)

MAS CRACKER. Several Special Awards at the CFA's and a Special Achievement Award from the Academy of Canadian Cinema. He is now retired.
Selective Filmography: *NARCISSUS,* Th, 81, CDN, Dir; *ANIMATED MOTIONS* (5 parts), Th, 78-76, CDN, Dir; *PINSCREEN,* Th, 73, CDN, Co-Dir/Ed; *BALLET ADAGIO,* Th, 72, CDN, Dir; *SYNCHROMY,* Th, 71, CDN, Dir/An/Comp; *SPHERES,* Th, 69, CDN, Co-An; *PAS DE DEUX,* Th, 67, CDN, Dir (**BFA**); *MOSAIC,* Th, 65, CDN, Co-Dir; *CANON,* Th, 64, CDN, Dir (**CFA**); *CHRISTMAS CRACKER,* Th, 63, CDN, Co-Dir; *LINES HORIZONTAL,* Th, 61, CDN, Co-Dir/Co-An (**CFA**); *LINES VERTICAL,* Th, 60, CDN, Co-Dir/Co-An; *OPENING SPEECH,* Th, 60, CDN, Dir; *SHORT AND SUITE,* Th, 59, CDN, Dir/Co-An; *MAIL EARLY FOR CHRISTMAS,* Th, 59, CDN, An; *LE MERLE,* Th, 58, CDN, Dir/Co-An; *A CHAIRY TALE* (IL ETAIT UNE CHAISE), Th, 57, CDN, Co-Dir (**BFA/CFA**); *RYTHMETIC,* Th, 56, CDN, Co-Dir (**BFA**); *BLINKITY BLANK,* Th, 55, CDN, An (**BFA**); *NEIGHBOURS,* Th, 52, CDN, Dir/An/Comp/Prod (**OSCAR**); *AROUND IS AROUND,* Th, 51, CDN/GB, An; *BEGONE DULL CARE,* Th, 49, CDN, Dir; *FIDDLE-DE-DEE,* Th, 47, CDN, Dir/An; *A LITTLE PHANTASY ON A 19TH CENTURY PAINTING,* Th, 46, CDN, Dir/An; *HOPPITY POP,* Th, 46, CDN, An; *KEEP YOUR MOUTH SHUT,* Th, 44, CDN, Dir; *LOOPS,* Th, 40, GB, An; *DOTS,* Th, 40, GB, An; *LOVE ON THE WING,* Th, 38, GB, Dir/An; *HELL UNLIMITED,* Th, 36, GB, Co-Dir/Co-An/Co-Prod.

MELANCON, André
Ruisseau-Nord, St-Ours sur le Richelieu, Qué, CAN, J0G 1P0. (514)785-5586.
Types de production et Catégories: l métrage-Réal/Sc; c métrage-Réal/Sc.
Types d'oeuvres: Comédie-C; Enfants-C.
Curriculum vitae: Né en 1942, Rouyn, Québec. Etudes: Université de Montréal, Institut de Psychologie. Scénariste et réalisateur depuis 72; gagne le Prix de la Critique Québécoise, *COMME LES SIX DOIGTS DE LA MAIN*; Golden Reel Award, Moscou pour *LA GUERRE DES TUQUES.*
Filmographie sélective: *BACH ET BOTTINE,* C, 86, CDN, Réal/Partic sc; *CECI EST MON CORPS,* TV, 86, CDN, Réal; *LA GUERRE DES TUQUES* (THE DOG WHO STOPPED THE WAR), C, 84, CDN, Réal; *ZIG ZAGS,* TV, 82, CDN, Réal/Sc; *L'ESPACE D'UN ETE,* TV, 80, CDN, Réal; *LA PAROLE AUX ENFANTS,* TV, 79, CDN, Réal; *COMME LES SIX DOIGTS DE LA MAIN,* TV, 78, CDN, Réal/Sc; *LES VRAIS PERDANTS,* TV, 77, CDN, Réal; *PARTIS POUR LA GLOIRE,* C, 75, CDN, Com (**CFA**); *LE VIOLON DE GASTON,* TV, 74, CDN, Réal/Sc; *LES TACOTS,* TV, 73, CDN, Réal/Sc; *TAUREAU,* C, 73, CDN, Com; *LES OREILLES MENE L'ENQUETE,* TV, 73, CDN, Réal/Sc; *DES ARMES ET LES HOMMES,* TV, 72, CDN, Réal/Sc (**CFA**).

MENARD, Robert
APFVQ. 296 rue St-Paul O., Montréal, Qué, CAN, H2Y 2A3. (514)844-8611.
Types de production et Catégories: l métrage-Réal/Prod/Sc; c métrage-Réal/Prod/Sc; TV film-Réal/Prod/Sc.
Types d'oeuvres: Drame-C; Comédie-C&TV.
Curriculum vitae: Né en 1947. Education: Génie civil, Université de Montréal. Prix d'Excellence du Publicité Club (Place Laurier); 7 nominations au Prix Génie pour *UNE JOURNEE EN TAXI* qui a aussi été sélectionné par le Festival du Film de Toronto et pour représenter le Canada au Festival Int'l du Film de Manille. Secrétaire-trésorier de l'APFQ, 79-82; Directeur exécutif, 78.
Filmographie sélective: *EXIT,* C, 86, CDN, Prod/Réal; *'UN AMOUR DE QUARTIER'* (26 eps), TV, 85/84, CDN, Réal/Co sc; *LES CREATIONS JOSEPH ET LEONARD* (pilote), TV, 85, CDN, Prod; *UNE JOURNEE EN TAXI,* C, 81, CDN/F, Prod/Réal; *L'ARRACHE-COEUR,* C, 79, CDN, Prod; *L'AFFAIRE COFFIN* (THE COFFIN AFFAIR), C, 79, CDN, Prod; *BEAUX BECS DU*

(cont/suite)

DIRECTORS/REALISATEURS

QUEBEC (pilote), TV, 78, CDN, Réal/Prod; *ECLAIR AU CHOCOLAT,* C, 78, CDN, Prod; *PARLEZ-NOUS D'AMOUR,* C, 76, CDN, Prod dél; *PORTRAITS DE FEMMES,* C, 75, CDN, Réal/Prod/Sc; *SPECIAL MAGNUM,* C, 75, CDN/I, Prod dél; *LES AVENTURES D'UNE JEUNE VEUVE,* C, 74, CDN, Prod dél; *MUSTANG,* C, 74, CDN, Prod dél.

MENDELUK, George

World Classic Pix Inc., 6263 Tapia Dr., Malibu, CA, USA, 90265. (213)457-9911. Jonathan Krane, Mgmt Co. Entertainment, 1888 Century Pk.E., Ste. 1616, Los Angeles, CA, USA, 90067. (213)553-6741.
Types of Production & Categories: Th Film-Dir/Prod/Wr; Th Short-Dir/Prod/Wr; TV Film-Dir/Prod/Wr; TV Video-Dir/Prod/Wr.
Genres: Drama-Th&TV; Comedy-Th&TV; Variety-TV; Children's-Th&TV.
Biography: Born 1948, Augsburg, Germany; Canadian citizen; resident alien USA. B.A., English and Humanities, York University. Speaks English, Ukranian and French. Trained in production at the CBC. Currently resides in California. Chris Award, Columbus Film Fest., *CHRISTMAS LACE.*
Selective Filmography: *'NIGHT HEAT'* (3 eps), TV, 86/85, CDN, Dir; *'HOT SHOTS'* (2 eps), TV, 86, CDN, Dir; *LOVERBOY,* Th, 84, CDN, Dir; *DOIN' TIME,* Th, 83, USA, Prod/Dir/Wr; *THE KIDNAPPING OF THE PRESIDENT,* Th, 79, CDN, Co-Prod/Dir; *STONE COLD DEAD,* Th, 79, CDN, Prod/Dir/Scr; *CHRISTMAS LACE,* TV, 78, CDN, Co-Prod/Dir/Co-Wr; *JUST ANOTHER DAY,* 'SIDESTREET', TV, 78, CDN, Dir; *MIGUEL'S NAVIDAD,* TV, 77, MEX, Dir; *'TAKE 30'* (sev eps), TV, 77-74, CDN, Prod/Dir; *CHRISTMAS TREE,* TV, 73, CDN, Dir/Prod/Dir; *'DAVID CLAYTON THOMAS SHOW'* (sev eps), TV, 73, CDN, Wr; *ROUNDELAY,* TV, 72, CDN, Wr; *THE HART AND LORNE TERRIFIC HOUR,* TV, 71, CDN, Wr.

METCALFE, Bill

Box 4215, South Edmonton, Alta, CAN, T6E 4T2. (403)432-0074.
Types of Production & Categories: TV Film-Dir/DOP; TV Video-Dir/DOP.
Genres: Commercials-TV; Industrial-TV.
Biography: Born 1951, Toronto, Ontario. Education: Ryerson Polytechnical Institute. Director/cinematographer working in retail commercials and sponsored films since 73 (Leon's, Safeway, Woolworth's, City of Edmonton); has won TVB awards; background in film to tape post-production.

METHE, Jacques

DGC, STCQ. 4560 Hampton, Montréal, Qué, CAN, H4A 2L4. (514)487-3907.
Types de production et Catégories: TV vidéo-Réal.
Types d'oeuvres: Drame-C; Variété-TV.
Curriculum vitae: Né en 1949, Québec. Etudes: Sciences, Mathématiques, Université Laval; connaissances en informatique; Langues: français, anglais, espagnol.
Filmographie sélective: *FESTIVAL D'ETE DE QUEBEC* (CONCERT AMADEUS), TV, 85, CDN, Réal; *ORCHESTRE SYMPHONIQUE DE QUEBEC,* TV, 85, CDN, Réal; *ORCHESTRE SYMPHONIQUE DE TROIS-RIVIERES,* TV, 85, CDN, Réal; *HONEYONEYMOON,* C, 85, CDN, 1er ass réal; *THE BOY IN BLUE,* C, 84, CDN, 1er ass réal; *AU PIED DE LA LETTRE,* C, 83, CDN, Réal; *LE SOLEIL SE LEVE EN RETARD,* C, 75, CDN, 1er ass réal; *LES VAUTOURS,* C, 74, CDN, 1er ass réal; *LES BEAUX DIMANCHES,* C, 74, CDN, 1er ass réal; *GINA,* C, 74, CDN, 1er ass réal; *NOEL ET JULIETTE,* C, 73, CDN, 1er ass réal; *REJEANNE PADOVANI,* C, 72, CDN, 1er ass réal.

MIHALKA, George

2030 Lambert Closse, Montreal, Que, CAN, H3H 1Z8. (514)937-4047.
Types of Production & Categories: Th Film-Dir/Wr; Th Short-Dir/Wr; TV Film-Dir/Wr; TV Video-Dir/Wr.

(cont/suite)

Genres: Drama-Th&TV; Documentary-Th&TV; Educational-Th&TV; Commercials-Th&TV.
Biography: Born 1952, Budapest, Hungary; emigrated to Canada, 61. B.A., English Literature, Sir George Williams University. Teaching: Faculty of Fine Arts, Concordia University, Montreal. Formed a company, SFC Corporation, 79. Has written and/ or directed numerous documentaries, educational films and hundreds of commercials.
Selective Filmography: *THE BLUE MAN*, Th, 85, CDN, Dir; *HUMBUG*, Th, 82, CDN, Wr; *SCANDAL* (SCANDALE), Th, 81, CDN, Dir; *OLD HIPPIES*, Th, 81, CDN, Co-Wr; *MY BLOODY VALENTINE*, Th, 80, CDN, Dir; *PINBALL SUMMER*, Th, 79, CDN, Dir.

MILLER, Bob - see PRODUCERS

MILLS, Michael

ACTRA, CAPAC, CFTA, SMPTE. Michael Mills Productions, 4492 St.Catherine W., Montreal, Que, CAN, H3Z 1R7. (514)931-7117.
Types of Production & Categories: Th Short-Prod/Dir/An; TV Film-Prod/Dir.
Genres: Children's-Th&TV; Animation-Th&TV; Commercials-TV.
Biography: Born 1942, London, England; became Canadian citizen, 73. Producer/ director/animator, London, 59-66; NFB, Canada, 66-69; Joined Potterton Productions, 69; formed Michael Productions Ltd., 74. Animator/director of award winning commercials; *EVOLUTION* won over 35 prizes at various international film festivals including New York (American Film Fest.), London, San Francisco, Melbourne; it was also nominated for an Oscar. *HISTORY OF THE WORLD IN THREE MINUTES FLAT* won a Golden Bear Award (Berlin), a Blue Ribbon (American F. F.) and was nominated for an Oscar.
Selective Filmography: *CONSTANT ACCELERATION/UNIFORM MOTION* (EXPO 86), Th, 86/85, CDN, Prod/Dir; *CIRCULAR MOTION/OCCILATORY MOTION* (EXPO 86), Th, 86/85, CDN, Prod/Dir; *HISTORY OF THE WORLD IN THREE MINUTES FLAT*, Th, 80, CDN, Prod/Dir/Wr; *THE HAPPY PRINCE*, TV, 74, CDN, Co-Prod/Dir/Wr; *MAN THE POLLUTER*, Th, 73, CDN, Dir/An; *EVOLUTION*, Th, 72, CDN, Prod/Dir/Wr/An (CFA); *TIKI TIKI*, Th, 69, CDN, An.

MINNIS, Jon

7098 Boyer St., Montreal, Que, CAN, H2S 2J8. (514)279-5444. Michael Mills Prod., 4492 St.Catherine St.W., Westmount, Que, CAN, H3Z 1R7. (514)931-3164.
Types of Production & Categories: Th Short-Dir/Prod/Wr/An.
Genres: Comedy-Th; Animation-Th.
Biography: Born 1950, Birmingham, England; Canadian citizen, 78. Attended Sheridan College, Int'l Summer School of Animation, 81-83. Directs and animates spots for TV; involved in writing and storyboarding for animation and live action; freelance cartoonist. *CHARADE* won the Canadian Independent Short Film Showcase (84), Best First Film: Toronto, Annecy, Hiroshima Int'l Festivals of Animation.
Selective Filmography: *CHARADE*, Th, 83, CDN, Prod/Dir/Wr/An (2 CFTA/ OSCAR).

MITTON, Susan Young - see PRODUCERS

MOORE-EDE, Carol

ATPD. 156 Winchester St., Toronto, Ont, CAN, M4X 1B6. (416)962-9139. CBC, Box 500, Station A, Toronto, Ont, CAN, M5W 1E6. (416)979-3244.
Types of Production & Categories: TV Film-Dir/Prod; TV Video-Dir/Prod.
Genres: Drama-TV; Musical-TV; Documentary-TV; Experimental-Th&TV.

(cont/suite)

DIRECTORS/REALISATEURS

Biography: Born 1943, Tunbridge Wells, England; Canadian citizen; bilingual. B.A. Art and Architecture, University of Toronto; post-graduate, University of Paris; Film Animation, Vancouver School of Art. Author: 'Canadian Architecture 1960-70' which won Best Canadian Book of The Year, 71, 'The Lives and Works of Canadian Artists'; photographer; TV and magazine writer, reviewer.
Selective Filmography: *GOING TO WAR,* 'BELL CANADA PLAYHOUSE', TV, 85, CDN, Dir; *THE CANADIAN BRASS VIDEO SHOW,* 'THURSDAY NIGHT', TV, 85, CDN, Prod/Dir; *WHERE THE HEART IS,* 'FOR THE RECORD', TV, 84, CDN, Dir; *BUT I'M JUST A KID* (VIDEO SHOW), (CONCERT), TV, 84, CDN, Dir; *THY SERVANT ARTHUR/ A FLUSH OF TORIES/ KING'S GAMBIT,* 'SOME HONOURABLE GENTLEMEN', TV, 84/83, CDN, Dir; *VERONICA TENNANT; A DANCER OF DISTINCTION,* 'SPECTRUM', TV, 83, CDN, Dir/Prod; *GETTING INTO THE ACT; THEATRE FOR THE YOUNG,* TV, 82, CDN, Dir/Prod; *'HOME FIRES'* (1 eps), TV, 82, CDN, Dir; *DRAK:CIRCUS UNIKUM,* TV, 81, USA, Dir; *PUPPETS, MASKS & MEN,* TV, 81, USA, Dir; *DRAK; SLEEPING BEAUTY,* TV, 81, USA, Dir; *HERE COME THE PUPPETS,* TV, 81, CDN/USA, Dir/Prod; *'A GIFT TO LAST'* (1 eps), TV, 80, CDN, Dir; *JOURNEYS THROUGH ILLUSION* (MERMAIDS & MANTICORES), TV, 80, CDN, Dir/Prod; *THE GARDEN & THE CAGE,* TV, 79, CDN, Dir/Prod; *CYRUS EATON: THE PROPHET FROM PUGWASH,* TV, 78, CDN, Dir/Prod; *'IMAGES OF CANADA'* (Prod-5 eps/Dir-4 eps), TV, 78-74, CDN, Dir/Prod.

MOREAU, Michel

APFVQ, ARRQ. 643 ave.Stuart, Outremont, Qué, CAN, H2V 3H2. (514)271-6529.
Types de production et Catégories: l métrage-Réal; c métrage-Réal; TV film-Réal.
Types d'oeuvres: Documentaire-C&TV; Education-C&TV; Enfants-C.
Curriculum vitae: Né en 1931, France; citoyen canadien. Etudes classiques; études en graphisme; Maitrise en Psychologie. Rédacteur, concepteur en publicité; réalisateur de films fixes et diapositives. Création de l'équipe de films éducatifs français à l'ONF (responsable de la production). Réalisation pour la SGME de films sur la formation des professeurs; enseignement à l'UQAM (psychologie et audio-visuel). Fondation de la compagnie Educfilm.
Filmographie sélective: *LE MILLION TOUT-PUISSANT,* C, 85, CDN, Réal; *'CHOCS DE LA VIE'* (5 eps), TV, 83/82, CDN, Réal; *EN PASSANT PAR MASCOUCHE,* ED, 81, CDN, Réal; *LES TRACES D'UN HOMME,* TV, 81, CDN, Réal; *LE DUR METIER DE FRERE,* TV, 80, CDN, Co réal; *PREMIERES PAGES DU JOURNAL D'ISABELLE,* TV, 80, CDN, Co réal; *ENFANTS DU QUEBEC,* TV, 79, CDN, Réal/Prod/Sc; *UNE NAISSANCE APPRIVOISEE,* ED, 79, CDN, Réal; *'L'ENVERS DU JEU'* (4 eps), ED, 78, CDN, Co réal; *'LES EXCLUS'* (5 eps), TV, 77-75, CDN, Réal; *TROIS CENTS SOURDS,* ED, 75, CDN, Réal; *LES DEBILES LEGERS/LE COMBAT DES SOURDS,* ED, 74, CDN, Réal; *LA LECON DES MONGOLIENS/A L'AISE DANS MA JOB,* ED, 72, CDN, Réal.

MORETTI, Pierre

ASIFA. 49 Montée du Moulin, Laval-des-Rapides, Qué, CAN. (514)667-7898.
Types de production et Catégories: c métrage-Réal/Prod.
Types d'oeuvres: Documentaire-C; Animation-C; Expérimental-C.
Curriculum vitae: Né en 1931, Montréal, Québec; bilingue; cours classique, études en design. Dix ans comme concepteur visuel en spectacle et théâtre; 21 ans comme réalisateur et producteur à l'ONF. Plusieurs prix en graphisme et en cinéma documentaire et animation dont la Médaille d'Argent au Festival de Venise pour *BRONZE.*
Filmographie sélective: *BIOSCOPE,* C, 83, CDN, Réal; *VARIATIONS GRAPHIQUES SUR TELIDON,* C, 81, CDN, Réal; *DEMON ET MERVEILLES,*

(cont/suite)

C, 77, CDN, Prod; *L'HOMME ET LE GEANT*, C, 75, CDN, Prod; *LUMAAN*, C, 75, CDN, Prod; *LE MARIAGE DU HIBOU*, C, 75, CDN, Prod; *CLIMATS*, C, 75, CDN, Prod; *MODULO*, C, 74, CDN, Réal; *LE HIBOU ET LE CORBEAU*, C, 73, CDN, Prod; *CECI EST UN MESSAGE ENREGISTRE*, C, 73, CDN, Prod; *TCHOU-TCHOU*, C, 73, CDN, Prod; *AIR*, C, 72, CDN, Prod; *L'OEIL*, C, 72, CDN, Prod; *LE BLEU PERDU*, C, 72, CDN, Prod; *L'OEUF*, C, 72, CDN, Prod; *META-DATA*, C, 71, CDN, Prod; *LE HIBOU ET LE LEMMING*, C, 71, CDN, Prod; *N'AJUSTEZ PAS*, C, 70, CDN, Réal; *BRONZE*, C, 70, CDN, Réal; *CERVEAU GELE*, C, 70, CDN, Réal; *UN ENFANT...UN PAYS*, C, 67, CDN, Réal.

MORIN, Pierre

AR. 44 Academy Rd., #11, Westmount, Qué, CAN, H3Z 1N6. (514)989-9192. Radio-Canada, 1400 blvd. Dorchester est, Montréal, Qué, CAN, H2L 2M2. (514) 285-2366.
Types de production et Catégories: TV film-Réal/Prod; TV vidéo-Réal/Prod.
Types d'oeuvres: Comédie musicale-TV; Documentaire-TV; Danse-TV.
Curriculum vitae: Né en 1932. Réalisateur à Radio-Canada depuis 56; spécialité: ballet, danse, opéra, musique (concerts, récitals). *LE MANDARIN MERVEILLEUX* remporte le Prix Iris et représente le Canada dans les ambassades à travers le monde.
Filmographie sélective: *BALLET EDDY TOUSSAINT DE MONTREAL*, TV, 85, CDN, Réal/Prod; *THE TAYLOR COMPANY: RECENT DANCES* (OEUVRES RECENTES DE LA TAYLOR COMPANY), TV, 84, CDN/USA, Réal/Prod; *PAVLOVA*, TV, 83, CDN/USA, Réal/Prod/Adapt; *QUAND 1200 ENFANTS S'ACCORDENT...*, TV, 83, CDN, Réal/Prod/Adapt; *PILOBOLUS*, TV, 81, CDN, Réal/Prod; *LE MANDARIN MERVEILLEUX* (THE MIRACULOUS MANDARIN), TV, 81, CDN, Réal/Prod (**ANIK**); *THE MEDIUM*, TV, 79, CDN, Réal/Prod; *NEW YORK CITY BALLET* (2 ém), TV, 79/78, CDN, Prod/Réal; *LES GRANDS BALLETS CANADIENS*, TV, 78, CDN, Réal/Prod; *LES BALLETS JAZZ*, TV, 77, CDN, Réal/Prod; *LA BELLE HELENE*, TV, 76, CDN, Réal/Prod; *LOVES* (Les Grands Ballets Canadiens), TV, 75, CDN, Réal/Prod; *L'HEURE ESPAGNOLE*, TV, 75, CDN, Réal/Prod; *MESSE POUR LE TEMPS PRESENT* (Maurice Béjart et le Ballet du XXe Siècle), TV, 72, CDN, Réal/Prod/Adapt; *LA FILLE DE MADAME ANGOT*, TV, 69, CDN, Réal/Prod; *LE PAUVRE MATELOT*, TV, 66, CDN, Réal/Prod; *LE BARBIER DE SEVILLE*, TV, 65, CDN, Réal/Prod (**INT'L EMMY**); *IL TABARRO*, TV, 64, CDN, Réal/Prod.

MORRIS, Ian

DGC. 969 Wayne Drive, Newmarket, Ont, CAN, L3Y 2W9. (416)895-9979.
Types of Production & Categories: Th Short-Dir; TV Film-Dir/Prod; TV Video-Dir/Prod.
Genres: Documentary-TV; Educational-TV; Children's-TV.
Biography: Born 1937, India; Canadian citizen. Languages: English, German, French. Studied TV Design, Fine Arts and Architecture, Art College, London (2 years). Worked at BBC, 4 years; Ontario Educational Communications Authority, 10 years. Children's novelist and short story writer. *BEFORE AND AFTER SURGERY* won the creative Excellence Award, American Film Fest..
Selective Filmography: *'BEFORE AND AFTER SURGERY'* (12 eps), ED, 81/80, CDN, Dir; *'POLKA DOT DOOR'* (250 eps), TV, 80-71, CDN, Dir/Prod; *'SPEAKING OUT'* (34 eps), TV, 80-77, CDN, Dir/Prod; *'KIDSWORLD'* (52 eps), TV, 80/79, CDN, Dir; *'COPE'* (12 eps), TV, 78, CDN, Dir/Prod; *'READALONG'* (23 eps), TV, 78-76, CDN, Dir; *'TELL ME A STORY'* (46 eps), TV, 77-74, CDN, Dir/Prod; *'TURN ON'* (15 eps), TV, 76, CDN, Dir/Prod; *'REPORT METRIC'* (33 eps), TV, 75/74, CDN, Dir; *'MORE THAN ONE WAY'* (7 eps), TV, 74, CDN, Dir/Prod.

MOWAT, Kenneth R.

SMPTE. Box 11335, Stn. H, Ottawa, Ont, CAN, K2H 7V1. (613)836-3003. Mowat Film Productions, 1572 Carling Ave., Ottawa, Ont, CAN.
Types of Production & Categories: Th Short-Dir/Ed/Wr/DOP; TV Film-Dir/Ed/Wr/DOP.
Genres: Documentary-Th&TV; Educational-TV.
Biography: Born 1937, Ottawa, Ontario. Worked at Crawley Films for 2 years after high school; moved to Hollywood, made documentaries, 56-75, then returned to Ottawa. Continues making documentaries (over 100), writing, photographing and editing each subject himself; films for businesses, associations and government departments.

MULLER, John

CFTA. 42 Manor Rd.E., Toronto, Ont, CAN, M4S 1P8. (416)484-6010. M&M Film Productions Ltd., 189 Dupont St., Toronto, Ont, CAN, M5R 1V6. (416)968-9300.
Types of Production & Categories: Th Film-Prod; Th Short-Prod/Dir; TV Film-Prod/Dir; TV Video-Prod/Dir.
Genres: Drama-TV; Variety-TV; Documentary-Th&TV; Educational-TV.
Biography: Born 1942, Holland; came to Canada, 78, to develop a TV series with Marshall McLuhan; Canadian citizen, 82. Graduate of San Francisco State, UCLA and the University of Amsterdam. Produced films in Europe. *THE FRAGILE TREE HAS ROOTS*, winner at Columbus Film Festival.
Selective Filmography: *'VID KIDS'* (13 eps), TV, 85, CDN, Co-Prod/Dir (**CFTA**); *THE FRAGILE TREE HAS ROOTS*, TV, 85, CDN, Dir/Co-Prod; *STAR SONG*, TV, 84, CDN, Dir/Exec Prod; *CELLY AND FRIENDS*, TV, 84, CDN, Dir/Co-Prod; *VINCENT PRICE'S DRACULA*, TV, 83, CDN, Dir/Co-Prod; *MONEY TO BURN*, TV, 83, CDN, Co-Prod; *WARMING TO WOOD*, TV, 83, CDN, Co-Prod; *SUNSHINE FOR SALE*, TV, 83, CDN, Co-Prod; *TAKING A LEAP*, In, 83, CDN, Dir/Co-Prod; *THANKS A LOT*, TV, 82, CDN, Dir/Co-Prod; *WATER FRIEND OR FOE*, TV, 82, CDN, Co-Prod; *THE GREENING OF THE NORTH*, In, 82, CDN, Dir/Co-Prod; *YOU DON'T SMOKE EH?/LIVING PROOF*, ED, 81/80, CDN, Dir/Co-Prod; *LIBERATION*, TV, 80, CDN, Dir/Co-Prod; *SILENCE IS KILLING*, TV, 76/75, CDN, Dir/Co-Prod; *A DOVE WITH CLIPPED WINGS*, TV, 75, CDN, Dir/Co-Prod.

MULLINS, Ronald G.

RGM Productions Inc., 357 East 22nd St., North Vancouver, BC, CAN, V7L 3C8. (604)986-7932.
Types of Production & Categories: TV Film-Dir/Prod; TV Video-Dir/Prod/PM.
Genres: Drama-TV; Variety-TV; Children's-TV; Commercials-TV.
Biography: Born 1943. Directed, produced over 2500 commercials over the past 20 years.
Selective Filmography: *'FAMILY THEATRE'* (sev eps), TV, 85, CDN, PM; *CANADA IN AN INFORMATION AGE*, TV, 85, CDN, Dir/Prod; *BATHING YOUR BABIES*, TV, 85, CDN, Dir/Prod; *'THE MINIKINS'* (sev eps), TV, 84, CDN, Dir; *THE VANCOUVER SHOW*, TV, 84, CDN, Prod; *'NUGGETTS'* (sev eps), TV, 83/82, CDN, Dir; *'MACPHERSON'* (sev eps), TV, 82, CDN, Dir; *'HOUR MUSIC'* (sev eps), TV, 82, CDN, Dir; *'CANADIAN EXPRESS'* (sev eps), TV, 82/81, CDN, Dir/Prod; *THE ORIGINAL CASTE*, TV, 82, CDN, Dir/Prod.

MURPHY, Michael D. - see PRODUCERS

MURRAY, Judith

AR. 4960 Hingston Ave., Montreal, Que, CAN, H3X 3R2. (514)488-2621. Radio-Canada, 1400 Dorchester E., Montreal, Que, CAN, H2L 2M2. (415)285-2067.
Types of Production & Categories: TV Film-Dir/Prod; TV Video-Dir/Prod.
(cont/suite)

REALISATEURS/DIRECTORS

Genres: Variety-TV; Documentary-TV; Educational-TV.
Biography: Born 1945, Toronto, Ontario; bilingual. B.A., Chatham College, Pennsylvania, 67; 1 year, Sorbonne, France as part of undergraduate degree, 66; 1 year, special TV and Radio Training, Ryerson Polytechnical Institute, Toronto, 68.
Selective Filmography: *THE ECONOMIST AND THE CONDUCTOR/H. GORDON GREEN*, 'GZOWSKI AND CO', TV, 86/85, CDN, Dir/Prod; *DO YOU KNOW WHAT YOU'RE IN FOR?*, 'THE WAY WE ARE', TV, 86, CDN, Dir/ Prod; *'CANADANCE'* (1 seg), TV, 85, CDN, Dir/Prod; *ROGER LEMELIN'S QUEBEC CITY*, 'CITYSCAPES', TV, 85, CDN, Dir/Prod; *'GOOD ROCKIN' TONIGHT'* (4 seg), TV, 85/84, CDN, Dir/Interv; *RE-CREATING THE GARDEN*, 'SEEING IT OUR WAY', TV, 84, CDN, Dir/Prod; *MONTREALER FERNANDO SANTOS*, 'THE CANADIANS', TV, 84, CDN, Dir/Prod; *GASPE - 3 FAMILIES*, TV, 84, CDN, Dir/Prod; *'STEPPIN' OUT'* (weekly), TV, 84-82, CDN, Dir/Prod (ANIK); *'FIRST EDITION'* (4 seg), TV, 82/81, CDN, Dir/Prod; *'CONSUMERSCOPE'* (76 eps), TV, 81-79, CDN, Dir/Prod; *ROBERT STANFIELD*, 'SEEING FOR OURSELVES', TV, 77, CDN, Dir/Prod/Wr; *ASBESTOS*, TV, 77, CDN, Dir/Prod; *HUSBANDS*, TV, 76, CDN, Dir/Prod; *A WOMAN'S PLACE*, TV, 76, CDN, Dir/Prod; *THE OCTOBER CRISIS*, TV, 76/ 75, CDN, Assoc Prod; *THE MONTREAL ELECTION SPECIAL*, TV, 74, CDN, Prod; *THIS CITY IS FOR SALE*, TV, 74, CDN, Prod/Res.

NAPIER-ANDREWS, Nigel

ATPD. 1756 Angela Cres., Mississauga, Ont, CAN, L5J 1B9. (416)822-4132. Napier-Andrews Comm. Ltd., 98 Dupont St., Toronto, Ont, CAN, M5R 1V2. (416) 968-1932.
Types of Production & Categories: TV Film-Dir/Wr; TV Video-Dir/Prod/Wr.
Genres: Drama-TV; Comedy-TV; Variety-TV; Documentary-TV.
Biography: Born 1942, Buckinghamshire, England; Canadian. Author of 'How To Eat Well and Stay Single', 74, 'This Is The Law?', 76. Principal in Napier-Andrews Communications Limited and Scott-Atkison Only Int'l Inc.. Instructor, Media Arts faculty, Sheridan College.
Selective Filmography: *ACTRA AWARDS*, TV, 86/85, CDN, Exec Prod; *JEFF HEALEY*, MV, 86, CDN, Dir; *'HERITAGE THEATRE'* (26 eps), TV, 85, CDN, Dir; *ACTRA AWARDS* (4 shows), TV, 84-78, CDN, Prod; *'THE MUSIC GAME'* (14 eps), TV, 82, CDN, Dir/Wr; *McLEAN AT LARGE'* (107 short films), TV, 82/ 81, CDN, Field Dir/Wr; *SHARK REEF*, TV, 80, USA, Dir/Wr; *'SUMMER FESTIVAL'* (55 eps), TV, 80, CDN, Exec Prod, *'BEYOND REASON'* (125 eps), TV, 79-77, CDN, Prod; *'BOB McLEAN SHOW'* (165 eps), TV, 79-77, CDN, Prod/ Dir; *'FEMALE IMPERATIVE'* (13 eps), TV, 79, CDN, Dir; *'HIGH HOPES'* (27 eps), TV, 78, CDN, Dir; *'MIXED DOUBLES'* (9 eps), TV, 77, CDN, Dir; *'STAY TUNED!'* (12 eps), TV, 76, CDN, Dir/Prod; *'THIS IS THE LAW'* (175 eps), TV, 76-71, CDN, Dir/Prod/Wr; *'FRED DAVIS SHOW'* (45 eps), TV, 72, CDN/GB, Dir; *'ELWOOD GLOVER'S LUNCHEON DATE'* (460 eps), TV, 71-69, CDN, Dir/ Prod.

NEWLAND, Marv

Int'l Rocketship Ltd., 1227 Richards St., Vancouver, BC, CAN, V6B 3G3. (604) 681-2716.
Types of Production & Categories: Th Film-Dir; Th Short-Dir/Prod.
Genres: Comedy-Th; Variety-Th; Musical-Th; Animation-Th.
Biography: Born 1947, South Korea. Graduate, Art Center College of Design, Los Angeles, 69. Staff designer, Spungbuggy Works, L.A., 69-70; freelance animation designer, director, Toronto, 71-72. Crawley Films (Ottawa), Phos-Cine (New York): commercials, educational and theatrical films. Founder of Rocketship International Ltd., Vancouver, 74. His films have won prizes at various film festivals including Int'l Animation Fest., Toronto (Jury Prize) for *ANIJAM*; Silver Hugo, Chicago,

(cont/suite)

Best Children's (Annecy) for *DRY NOODLES*; Canadian Short Film Showcase winner, *THE BUTTERFLY*, 83.
Selective Filmography: *LUPO THE BUTCHER*, Th, 86, CDN, Prod; *HOORAY FOR SANDBOX LAND*, ED, 85, CDN, Prod/Dir; *DRY NOODLES*, Th, 85, CDN, Prod; *ANIJAM*, Th, 84, CDN, Prod/Dir; *THE BUTTERFLY*, Th, 83, CDN, Prod; *POINTS*, Th, 83, CDN, Prod; *SING BEAST SING*, Th, 80, CDN, Prod/Dir; *BAMBI MEETS GODZILLA*, Th, 69, USA, Prod/Dir/An.

NICHOL, Robert L. - see PRODUCERS

NICOL, Normand

ARRQ. 7841 Yves Prévost, Anjou, Qué, CAN, H1K 1V5. (514)352-6699.
Radio-Québec, 1000 rue Fullum, Montréal, Qué, CAN, H2K 3L7. (514)521-2424.
Types de production et Catégories: TV vidéo-Réal.
Types d'oeuvres: Education-TV; Enfants-TV.
Curriculum vitae: Né en 1934, Montmagny, Québec. Education: Ingénieur en Electronique. Expérience professionnelle: affaires publiques, émissions pour enfants et publicité. Gagnant d'un certificat d'excellence de la publicité française, 85.
Filmographie sélective: *'PUBLICITE MAISON'* (500 eps), TV, 86/85, CDN, Réal; *'MAYA L'ABEILLE'* (95 eps), TV, 86-84, CDN, Réal; *'PINOCCHIO'* (49 eps), TV, 86/85, CDN, Réal; *'CINE-CADEAU'* (31 eps), TV, 85-83, CDN, Réal; *'PIERRE NADEAU RENCONTRE...'* (155 eps), TV, 83/82, CDN, Réal; *'LES LUNDIS DE PIERRE NADEAU'* (37 eps), TV, 82/81, CDN, Réal; *ELECTION 81*, TV, 81, CDN, Réal; *LES DEBATS A L'ASSEMBLEE NATIONALE (370)/ SOMMET ECONOMIQUE (3)*, TV, 81-77, CDN, Réal; *'A LA MESURE DE LA TERRE'* (37 eps), TV, 77/76, CDN, Réal; *TELECONFERENCE MONTREAL-PARIS* (3 ém), TV, 75, CDN, Réal; *'PRODUCTION ANIMALE'* (100 eps), TV, 75-73, CDN, Réal; *'PRODUCTION VEGETALE'* (50 eps), TV, 72/71, CDN, Réal; *'LES 100 TOURS DE CENTOUR'* (24 eps), TV, 71, CDN, Réal; *'GESTION AGRICOLE'* (39 eps), TV, 71/70, CDN, Réal; *'LES ORALIENS'* (45 eps), TV, 69-60, CDN, Réal.

NICOLLE, Douglas

104 - 1112 Broughton St., Vancouver, BC, CAN. (604)685-7679. Spectra Communications, #310 - 319 West Pender St., Vancouver, BC, CAN, V6B 1T4. (604)682-4366.
Types of Production & Categories: Th Short-Dir; TV Film-Dir; TV Video-Dir.
Genres: Drama-Th&TV; Documentary-Th&TV; Commercials-TV; Industrial-TV.
Biography: Born 1952, Vancouver, British Columbia. Honours B.A., Philosophy, Simon Fraser University. Spent 2 years as news, public affairs editor, CBC, Vancouver; 10 years in partnership, Spectra Media.
Selective Filmography: *LADIES OF THE LOTUS*, Th, 86, CDN, Dir; *THE LAGOONS/CANADIAN SOLUTIONS/ALCOHOL, TOMORROWS FUEL*, In, 86/85, CDN, Dir; *MR. MIKE'S/SIRLOINER*, Cm, 85, CDN, Dir; *VANCOUVER: A PORTRAIT BY ARTHUR ERICKSON*, TV, 84, CDN, Dir; *SEE HOW WE RUN/YOUNG OFFENDERS/HYPOTHERMIA*, ED, 84/83, CDN, Dir; *IMAGES B.C.*, TV, 84, CDN, Dir; *SKI CROSS COUNTRY*, TV, 83, CDN, Dir.

NOEL, Jean-Guy

ARRFQ, SARDEC. 4263 rue Boyer, Montréal, Qué, CAN, H2J 3C8. (514)521-0538.
Types de production et Catégories: 1 métrage-Réal/Prod/Sc; c métrage-Réal/Prod/Sc; TV film-Sc.
Types d'oeuvres: Drame-C; Comédie-C; Action-C&TV.
Curriculum vitae: Né en 1945 à Montréal, Québec. Baccalauréat ès Arts, Collège St-Laurent, Montréal, 66; Philosophie, Université de Louvain, Belgique, 67-68; études à l'Institut National des Arts du Spectacle, Belgique, 68-69. Assistant réalisateur,

(cont/suite)

Radio-Télévision Belge, 69; conseiller à la scénarisation, ONF, 78. *TI-CUL TOUGAS* remporte le Grand Prix de la Critique Québécoise et plusieurs autres.
Filmographie sélective: *L'AMELANCHIER,* TV, 84, CDN, Adapt; *LABRADOR 1905,* TV, 84, CDN, Co sc; *CAMELEON,* C, 84, CDN, Réal/Co sc; *LE LION EN CAGE* (3 films), C, 83/82, CDN, Réal/Sc/Prod; *GRIEF 81,* C, 81, CDN, Réal; *CONTRECOEUR,* C, 80/79, CDN, Réal/Co sc; *FLEUR DE MAI,* C, 77, CDN, Réal/Sc; *TI-CUL TOUGAS,* C, 75, CDN, Réal/Sc; *TU BRULES...TU BRULES,* C, 73, CDN, Réal/Sc; *ELLE ETAIT UNE FOIS...UNE AUTRE FOIS,* C, 71, CDN, Réal/Sc/Prod; *ZEUZERE DE ZEGOUZIE,* C, 70, CDN, Réal/Sc/Prod/Com.

NOVAK, Allan

721 Manning Ave., Toronto, Ont, CAN, M5G 2W5. (416)534-1222. Suite One Video Inc., 299 Queen St. W., 5th Fl., Toronto, Ont, CAN. (416)440-0148.
Types of Production & Categories: TV Video-Dir/Wr/Ed.
Genres: Comedy-TV; Children's-TV.
Biography: Born 1959, Winnipeg, Manitoba. B.F.A, Specialized Honours, Film and Videotape, York University. Casting director, Film Extra Services, 79-82. Co-founder and principal of Suite One Video Inc..
Selective Filmography: *'VID KIDS'* (Co-Ed-13 eps), (13 eps), TV, 86/85, CDN, Dir; *IN FASHION,* TV, 86, CDN, Ed; *GM RECORD BREAKERS,* In, 86, CDN, Dir/ Prod; *PARTY TIME 85,* MV, 85, CDN, Dir; *CALIFORNIA DREAM,* TV, 85, CDN, Dir; *THE RISE AND FALL OF TONY TROUBLE,* TV, 83, CDN, Dir/Wr; *BABBLE ON,* TV, 82, CDN, Dir/Ed; *MONDO YORK,* Th, 82, CDN, Dir/Wr.

NOWLAN, John - see PRODUCERS

OBOMSAWIN, Alanis

ACTRA, CAPAC, UDA. 1635 Selkirk Ave., Montreal, Que, CAN, H3H 1C7. (514)933-0987. NFB, Box 6100, Montreal, Que, CAN, H3C 3H5. (514)283-9536.
Types of Production & Categories: Th Short-Dir/Prod/Wr; TV Film-Dir/Prod/Wr.
Genres: Variety-Th; Documentary-Th&TV; Educational-Th&TV; Children's-Th&TV.
Biography: Born 1932; raised on the Odanak Reserve. Writes and sings her own songs. Received the Order of Canada, 83; Arts and Humanities Education Award, 82. *MOTHER OF MANY CHILDREN* won Best Documentary, American Indian Film Fest. and Grand Prize, Dieppe, France.
Selective Filmography: *INCIDENT AT RESTIGOUCHE* (LES EVENEMENTS DE RESTIGOUCHE), Th, 84, CDN, Dir/Co-Prod/Wr; *GABRIEL GOES TO THE CITY,* TV, 79, CDN, Dir/Prod/Wr; *'SOUNDS FROM OUR PEOPLE'* (6 eps), TV, 79, CDN, Dir/Prod/Wr; *AMISK,* TV, 77, CDN, Dir/Co-Prod; *OLD CROW,* TV, 77, CDN, Dir/Prod/Wr; *MOTHER OF MANY CHILDREN* (MERE DE TANT D'ENFANTS), TV, 76, CDN, Dir/Prod/Wr; *CHRISTMAS AT THE MOOSE FACTORY,* TV, 71, CDN, Dir.

OWEN, Don

38 Nasmith Ave., Toronto, Ont, CAN, M5A 3J3. (416)929-5678. Zebra Films, R.R. 1 Locust Hill, Glenstreams, Ont, CAN, L0H 1J0. (416)294-5163.
Types of Production & Categories: Th Film-Dir/Prod/Wr/Ed; Th Short-Dir/Prod/ Wr/Ed; TV Film-Dir/Prod/Ed; TV Video-Dir.
Genres: Drama-Th&TV; Comedy-Th&TV; Action-Th&TV; Documentary-Th&TV.
Biography: Born 1935, Toronto, Ontario. Studied English and Anthropology, University of Toronto. Began in film as a grip, has worked in all departments, eventually directing, editing, producing, NFB; moving on to freelance. *YOU DON'T BACK DOWN* won the Robert Flaherty Award; *RUNNER,* First Prize, Tours; *HIGH STEEL,* the Golden Bear, Berlin.
Selective Filmography: *TURN-ABOUT,* Th, 86, CDN, Prod/Dir/Wr; *UNFINISHED BUSINESS,* Th, 84/83, CDN, Dir/Wr/Co-Prod; *'THE JOURNAL'*

(cont/suite)

(3 seg), TV, 82, CDN, Dir; *TANYA'S MOSCOW PUPPETS,* TV, 81, CDN, Dir/
Wr; *HOLSTEIN,* Th, 77, CDN, Dir/Wr/Ed; *'ONTARIO TOWNS AND
VILLAGES'* (19 short films), TV, 77-72, CDN, Dir/Prod/Ed; *PARTNERS,* Th, 76,
CDN, Dir/Co-Wr/Co-Prod; *'THE COLLABORATORS'* (3 eps), TV, 74, CDN,
Dir; *NOT FAR FROM HOME,* TV, 73, CDN, Dir/Prod/Ed; *CANADA: THE ST.
LAWRENCE,* TV, 73, CDN, Dir/Prod; *COWBOY AND INDIAN,* Th, 72, CDN,
Dir/Ed; *COUGHTRY IN IBIZA,* TV, 71, CDN, Dir; *RICHLER OF ST.
URBAIN,* TV, 71, CDN, Dir; *SNOW IN VENICE,* 'TELESCOPE', TV, 70, CDN,
Dir; *GALLERY: A VIEW OF TIME,* Th, 69, USA, Dir/Ed/Co-Prod; *THE ERNIE
GAME* (ERNIE), Th, 67, CDN, Wr/Dir (CFA); *A FURTHER GLIMPSE OF
JOEY,* TV, 67, CDN, Dir; *LADIES AND GENTLEMEN: MR. LEONARD
COHEN,* TV, 66, CDN, Co-Dir; *NOTES FOR A FILM ABOUT DONNA AND
GAIL,* Th, 66, CDN, Dir/Wr; *HIGH STEEL* (CHARPENTIER DU CIEL), Th,
65, CDN, Wr/Ed/Dir (CFA); *YOU DON'T BACK DOWN,* Th, 65, CDN, Dir;
NOBODY WAVED GOODBYE (DEPART SANS ADIEUX), Th, 64, CDN, Dir/
Wr/Co-Prod (BFA); *TORONTO JAZZ,* Th, 63, CDN, Dir/Ed; *RUNNER* (LE
COUREUR), Th, 62, CDN, Dir/Ed.

PAAKSPUU, Kalli

471 Main St., Toronto, Ont, CAN, M4C 4Y1. (416)691-5449.
Types of Production & Categories: Th Short-Dir/Prod/Wr; TV Film-Dir/Prod/Wr;
TV Video-Dir/Prod/Ed.
Genres: Drama-Th&TV; Documentary-Th&TV; Educational-TV; Experimental-Th.
Biography: Born 1952, Vancouver, British Columbia. Graduate of University of
British Columbia Film program; M.A., U. of Toronto. Founding member, President
of Womenfilm/Womenart. Her films have been awarded grants from the Ontario
Arts Council, Canada Council and the Secretary of State. *OCTOBER ALMS* won
the Bronze Award, New York Int'l Film & TV Festival.
Selective Filmography: *I NEED A MAN LIKE YOU,* TV, 86, CDN, Co-Dir/Co-
Prod; *SET IN MOTION,* TV, 82, CDN, Dir/Prod; *MAYPOLE CARVING,* ED, 81,
CDN, Dir/Wr/Prod/Ed; *CEREMONIES OF INNOCENCE,* ED, 80, CDN, Dir/
Prod/Ed/Cam; *THE FIRST DAY OF SCHOOL/THE CHILD'S CONCEPTION
OF AGE,* ED, 79/78, CDN, Dir/Cam/Ed; *OCTOBER ALMS,* TV, 78, CDN, Dir/
Prod/Wr; *PASSAGE,* Th, 78, CDN, Wr/Prod/Dir; *SACRED CIRCLE,* ED, 76,
CDN, Snd Rec/Wr/Ed; *SOLSTANZ,* TV, 75, CDN, Dir/Prod/Cam.

PACHECO, Bruno-Lazaro

City of Dark Productions Inc., 1245 Nelson St., #21, Vancouver, BC, CAN, V6E
1J5. (604)681-8178.
Types of Production & Categories: Th Short-Dir/Wr; TV Film-Dir/Prod/Wr/Ed.
Genres: Drama-TV; Documentary-Th&TV; Educational-TV; Experimental-
Th&TV.
Biography: Born 1957, Madrid, Spain; speaks English, Spanish, French, Italian.
B.A., Simon Fraser University (Film). *HATE TO LOVE* was shown at Film
Festivals in Montreal, Toronto, Bilbao, Yorkton and invited to Directors Fortnight
in Cannes, 83; it won Best Experimental Film (Toronto and Edmonton), Silver
Plaque (Chicago).
Selective Filmography: *THE TRAVELLER AND THE MASK,* TV, 86, CDN,
Prod/Wr/Dir; *SWING SPAN,* TV, 85, CDN, Wr/Dir; *SENTENCING DILEMMA,*
'CRIMINAL JUSTICE', ED, 85, CDN, Prod/Wr/Dir/Ed; *HATE TO LOVE,* Th,
82, CDN, Wr/Dir/Ed.

PALMER, John

Cameron and Palmer Prod. Inc., 80 Wellesley St.E., #701, Toronto, Ont, CAN,
M4Y 1H3. (416)967-7455. Ronda Cooper, Characters Talent, 150 Carlton St.,
Toronto, Ont, CAN, M5A 2K1. (416)964-8522.
Types of Production & Categories: Th Film-Wr/Dir.

(cont/suite)

Genres: Drama-Th; Comedy-Th.
Biography: Born 1943, Sydney, Nova Scotia. Has written, directed extensively for the stage, Canada, Britain and USA. *MONKEYS IN THE ATTIC* won Best Foreign Film, Toulon Film Festival, France.
Selective Filmography: *MONKEYS IN THE ATTIC,* Th, 74, CDN, Co-Wr; *ME,* Th, 74, CDN, Dir.

PAQUET, Denis
ARRQ. 59 rue Montcalm, Val D'Or, Qué, CAN. (819)825-8640. Radio-Québec, 1032, 3e avenue, Val D'Or, Qué, CAN. (819)825-5132.
Types de production et Catégories: TV film-Réal; TV vidéo-Réal.
Types d'oeuvres: Documentaire-TV; Annonces-TV; Industriel-TV.
Curriculum vitae: Né en 1955, Ville-Marie, Québec; bilingue. Bac. spécialisé en Communications, Université Concordia. Cinq ans d'expérience à la télévision éducative, documentaire. *REAL CAOUETTE, L'HOMME* reçoit une mention d'honneur, Prix Judith Jasmin, 84.
Filmographie sélective: *JOUR DE DANSE,* TV, 86, CDN, Réal; *LE DEUXIEME SOUFFLE,* TV, 85, CDN, Réal; *'CITE DES JEUNES',* TV, 85, CDN, Réal; *LA VILLE OUVERTE,* TV, 85, CDN, Réal; *LES ZEC/KATIMAVIK/LA BASE DE PLEIN-AIR DU LAC MOURRIER,* 'CA VAUT LE VOYAGE', TV, 84, CDN, Réal; *'CAMERA UN',* TV, 84/83, CDN, Réal; *LE PARTAGE DES EAUX,* TV, 83, CDN, Réal; *REAL CAOUETTE, L'HOMME,* TV, 83, CDN, Réal; *SUR LE BOUT DES DOIGTS,* TV, 82, CDN, Réal; *UNE ECOLE QUI S'APPARTIENT,* TV, 82, CDN, Réal; *LES PONTS COUVERTS DU SILENCE,* C, 81, CDN, Réal.

PARE, Constance
AR. 1741 Rang du Nord, St-Raymond de Portneuf, Qué, CAN. (418)337-4372.
Types de production et Catégories: TV film-Réal; TV vidéo-Réal.
Types d'oeuvres: Drame-TV; Variété-TV; Enfants-TV; Affaires publiques-TV.
Curriculum vitae: Née en 1946, St-Anne de Beaupré, Québec. Baccalauréat en Pédagogie; Baccalauréat ès Arts; réalisatrice TV depuis 8 ans.
Filmographie sélective: *QUILICO ET PELLIGNINI,* 'LES BEAUX DIMANCHES', TV, 85, CDN, Réal; *'REFLETS D'UN PAYS'* (1 eps), TV, 85, CDN, Réal; *MUSIQUE JEUNESSE,* TV, 85, CDN, Réal; *'GENIES EN HERBE'* (115 eps), TV, 85-81, CDN, Réal; *LES ETHNIES D'ICI,* TV, 84, CDN, Réal; *'QUEBEC MER ET MONDE'* (40 seg), TV, 84, CDN, Réal; *ORCHESTRE DE RADIO-CANADA,* TV, 82, CDN, Réal; *'FELIX ET CIBOULETTE'* (51 eps), TV, 81, CDN, Réal; *EVA ET EVELYNE,* 'LES BEAUX DIMANCHES', TV, 80, CDN, Réal; *'QUEBEC MAGAZINE'* (200 eps), TV, 80/79, CDN, Réal; *AU TEMPS DES GOELETTES,* 'REFLETS D'UN PAYS', TV, 78, CDN, Réal; *'CONTRE CHAMP'* (60 eps), TV, 78/77, CDN, Réal.

PARENT, Karl
AR. 906 Henri-Bourassa est, Montréal, Qué, CAN, H2C 1E9. (514)384-7538. Radio-Canada, 1400 blvd. Dorchester est, Montréal, Qué, CAN, H2L 2M2. (514) 285-3343.
Types de production et Catégories: TV film-Réal; TV vidéo-Réal.
Types d'oeuvres: Documentaire-TV; Education-TV; Enfants-TV.
Curriculum vitae: Né en 1941; bilingue. A l'emploi de Radio-Canada depuis 74; réalisateur à la télévision éducative de l'Ontario. Enseignement aux universités de Dakar, Port-au-Prince et Montréal. *JUSTE UN REVE DU PASSE* fut sélectionné pour INPUT 83; *DE SCHEHERAZADE A SELIMA* gagne le Prix Madea à Tokyo; Prix Judith Jasmin pour *TORONTO UNLIMITED*; *LE SAHARA ALGERIEN,* Plaque de Bronze, Columbus.
Filmographie sélective: *LES PARENTS BATTUS PAR LEURS ENFANTS,* TV, 86, CDN, Réal; *LES JEUNES ET LE CHOMAGE,* TV, 86, CDN, Réal;

(cont/suite)

DIRECTORS/REALISATEURS

'L'AUSTRALIE AU DELA DES KANGOUROUS' (4 eps), TV, 85, CDN, Réal; *BHOPAL/LES SIKHS ET LE PUNDJAB/L'ISLAM A NEW YORK,* 'LE POINT', TV, 85, CDN, Réal; *TORONTO UNLIMITED,* TV, 84, CDN, Réal; *GRENADE APRES L'INVASION AMERICAINE,* TV, 84, CDN, Réal; *LA FAMINE AU SAHEL,* TV, 84, CDN, Réal; *LES EGLISES ELECTRONIQUES,* TV, 83, CDN, Réal; *LE SUICIDE,* TV, 83, CDN, Réal; *...JUSTE UN REVE DU PASSE* (STE-MARIE AU PAYS DES HURONS), TV, 82, CDN, Réal; *LES PUNKS,* TV, 82, CDN, Réal; *BEN BELLA,* TV, 82, CDN, Réal; *IL Y A AUSSI DES NEGRES NOIRS* (VINGT ANS D'INDEPENDANCE EN AFRIQUE), TV, 81, CDN, Réal; *LES JUIFS A PARIS,* TV, 81, CDN, Réal; *L'ITALIE ROUGE ET NOIRE,* TV, 81, CDN, Réal; *LE P.Q. APRES LE REFERENDUM,* TV, 80, CDN, Réal; *LEOPOLD SENGHOR,* TV, 80, CDN, Réal; *EINSTEIN,* TV, 79, CDN/CH, Réal/Sc; *RACES HUMAINES,* TV, 79, CDN, Réal; *LA DOULEUR,* TV, 79, CDN, Réal; *SOEUR EUGENE EN PROVENCE,* TV, 78, CDN, Réal; *ENERGIE SOLAIRE ET EOLIENNE,* TV, 77, CDN, Réal; *ACTUALITE 24,* TV, 76, CDN, Réal; *DE SCHEHERAZADE A SELIMA/ LE SAHARA ALGERIEN/ FEZ,* 'DOSSIER AFRIQUE', TV, 75, CDN, Réal; *L'ALGERIE INDEPENDANTE/ LES MOURIDES,* 'DOSSIER AFRIQUE', TV, 75, CDN, Réal; *'LES GRANDS DEBATS CANADIENS'* (6 eps), TV, 74, CDN, Réal; *'AUTOUR DU MONDE PAR LE CONTE'* (12 eps), TV, 73, CDN, Réal.

PARKER, Fred

201 Rushton Rd., Toronto, Ont, CAN, M6G 3J2. CBC, Box 500, Station A, Toronto, Ont, CAN, M5W 1E6. (416)975-7819.
Types of Production & Categories: TV Video-Dir/Prod.
Genres: News-TV.
Biography: Born 1955, Montreal, Quebec; educated in Ottawa and Toronto. Joined CBC as a film assistant, later a production assistant, then director. In December, 84, made senior director, producer, CBC National News.

PATEL, Ishu

SCGT. 113 Lepage, Dorval, Que, CAN, H9S 3E5. NFB, 3155 Cote de Liesse, Montreal, Que, CAN, H3C 3H5. (514)283-9634.
Types of Production & Categories: Th Short-An/Dir/Prod; TV Film-Dir/An.
Genres: Educational-Th&TV; Children's-Th&TV; Animation-Th&TV; Experimental-Th.
Biography: Born 1942, India. Received training at the Faculty of Fine Arts in Baroda; post graduate training in graphic design, typography, photography and exhibition design, National Institute of Design, Ahmedabad, India; advanced graphic design course, Switzerland. After winning a Rockefeller Scholarship, 70, he came to the NFB to explore the art of animation; since then, has directed, produced several int'l award-winning shorts: *PARADISE, THE BEAD GAME, AFTERLIFE.*
Selective Filmography: *THE TALISMAN,* TV, 86/85, CDN, Dir/Prod; *'SESAME STREET'* (60 seg), TV, 85-75, USA, An/Dir/Wr; *PARADISE,* Th, 84, CDN, Creator/Dir/An/Prod; *A SPECIAL LETTER,* Th, 82, CDN, Prod; *SOUND COLLECTOR,* Th, 82, CDN, Prod; *TOP PRIORITY,* Th, 81, CDN, An/Dir/Prod; *TOURNEE TITLES,* Th, 81, CDN, An/Dir; *THIS IS ME,* TV, 80, CDN, An; *OTTAWA FESTIVAL LOGO,* Th, 80, CDN, An/Dir; *AFTERLIFE* (APRES LA VIE), Th, 79, CDN, Creator/Des/An/Dir **(CFA)**; *THE BEAD GAME* (HISTOIRE DE PERLES), Th, 78, CDN, Creator/Des/An/Dir **(BFA)**; *INCOME TAX CLIPS,* Cm, 76, CDN, An/Dir; *PERSPECTRUM,* Th, 75, CDN, Creator/Des/An/Dir; *CONCEPTION & CONTRACEPTION/ABOUT VD/ABOUT PUBERTY & RE-PRODUCTION,* 'SEX EDUCATION', ED, 73/72, CDN, Creator/An/Dir/Des; *HOW DEATH CAME TO EARTH,* ED, 71, CDN, An/Dir; *ILLUSTRATIVE WORDS,* ED, 69, IND, An/Dir.

PATON, Chris
CTPDA. 7201 Granville St., #203, Vancouver, BC, CAN, V6P 4X6. (604)261-7090.
Types of Production & Categories: TV Film-Dir/Prod/Wr; TV Video-Dir/Prod/Wr.
Genres: Comedy-TV; Variety-TV; Documentary-TV; Current Affairs-TV.
Biography: Born in Edmonton, Alberta. In television production for 25 years. Educated in General Arts. Fully competent in field of design and layout; early experience in television commercials as a performer, writer.
Selective Filmography: *MASK '86,* TV, 86/85, CDN, Prod; *FONYO: THE ROAD TO MILE ZERO,* TV, 85, CDN, Dir/Prod; *'VANCOUVER LIFE'* (52 eps), TV, 85/84, CDN, Prod/Wr; *'THE CANADIANS'* (10 eps), TV, 84/83, CDN, Dir/Prod/Wr; *'THE ELECTRIC THEATRE'* (2 eps), TV, 82/81, CDN, Dir/Prod/Wr; *'ONE OF A KIND'* (22 eps), TV, 81/80, CDN, Dir/Prod/Wr; *'CELEBRATE VANCOUVER'* (5 eps), TV, 81/80, CDN, Dir/Prod; *'THE NICE SHOW'* (46 eps), TV, 80-78, CDN, Dir/Prod/Wr; *'HOURGLASS'* (daily), TV, 79-76, CDN, Exec Prod; *'BARBARA FRUM'S JOURNAL'* (13 eps), TV, 75, CDN, Dir; *'MARKETPLACE'* (26 cps), TV, 75/74, CDN, Dir; *'SECOND CAREERS'* (26 eps), TV, 75/74, CDN, Dir/Prod; *'INSIDE-OUTSIDE'* (26 eps), TV, 74/73, CDN, Dir; *'TORONTO TONIGHT'* (sev seg), TV, 74/73, CDN, Dir.

PATTERSON, Carol - see CINEMATOGRAPHERS

PAYER, Roch Christophe
1 rue du Hameau, C.P. 733, St-Gabriel de Brandon, Qué, CAN, J0K 2N0. (514) 835-5364.
Types de production et Catégories: c métrage-Réal/Mont; TV vidéo-Réal/Mont.
Types d'oeuvres: Drame-C; Comédie-C; Documentaire-TV; Education-TV.
Curriculum vitae: Né en 1955, St-Hubert, Québec Baccalauréat en Production cinématographique, Université Concordia, Montréal.
Filmographie sélective: *JEUNE SAIT PAS LIRE* (ETRE ANALPHABETE A 20 ANS), TV, 85, CDN, Réal; *BI-ENERGIE,* In, 84, CDN, Co réal; *UNIVERSIADE,* TV, 83, CDN, Réal/Mont; *ART JAPONAIS CONTEMPORAIN,* TV, 83, CDN, Réal/Mont; *L'AGE D'OR A VELO,* TV, 83, CDN, Co réal/Mont; *INSIMINATION,* TV, 82, CDN, Mont; *JEPEN* (MUSI MUVICCI), TV, 82, CDN, Mont; *LES BIENHEUREUX* (LES SAINTS), TV, 82, CDN, Co réal/Mont; *EMPLOI CANADA,* TV, 81, CDN, Réal; *PUGWASH,* TV, 81, CDN, Mont; *TIM SIKEA,* TV, 81, CDN, Réal/Mont; *...DE CHICAGO,* TV, 81, CDN, Co réal/Mont; *RENCONTRE,* C, 80, CDN, Réal; *COUP DE SANG,* TV, 80, CDN, Réal; *ISABELLE* (TELEPATHIE), C, 80, CDN, Dir pro, *LEOPOLD GERVAIS,* SCULPTEUR, C, 80, CDN, Ing son; *WHAT'S HAPPENING HERE,* C, 80, CDN, Ing son; *I 4 FINE POINTE,* C, 79, CDN, Réal; *LIBRE SERVICE* (3 films), C, 78, CDN, Réal.

PAYETTE, Denise
C.P. 115, St-Adolphe de Dudswell, Qué, CAN. (819)887-6692. Arts et Images, 3466 ch. N. Hatley, Rock Forest, Qué, CAN, J1N 1A4. (819)562-5627.
Types de production et Catégories: TV vidéo-Réal.
Types d'oeuvres: Education-TV; Industriel-TV.
Curriculum vitae: Née en 1947, Montréal, Québec. Formation univeristaire; 14 ans d'expérience en réalisation.
Filmographie sélective: *UN PROGRAMME A VIVRE/GENS DU NORD, GENS DU SUD/EVALUATION,* ED, 85, CDN, Réal; *ENVIRONNEMENT PHYSIQUE/ Y'AVAIT PLEIN DE COULEURS/AU FIL DES JOURS,* ED, 85/84, CDN, Réal; *A PARTIR D'UNE QUESTION/LA VIE QU'ILS MENAIENT/L'AGAPE,* ED, 84, CDN, Réal; *VIENS VOIR COMMENT J'ECRIS/IL ETAIT UNE FOIS,* ED, 83, CDN, Réal; *INTERVENIR C'EST PREVENIR/A PARTIR D'UNE FLEUR,* ED, 83, CDN, Réal.

PEARSON, Peter

20 ave. Holton, Westmount, Qué, CAN, H3Y 2E8. Téléfilm Canada, Tour de la Banque Nationale, 600 de la Gauchetière O., Montréal, Qué, CAN, H3B 4L2. (514)283-8540.
Types of Production & Categories: Th Film-Dir/Wr; Th Short-Dir/Wr; TV Film-Dir/Prod/Wr; TV Video-Dir/Wr.
Genres: Drama-Th&TV; Documentary-Th&TV; Current Affairs-TV.
Biography: Born 1938, Toronto, Ontario. Languages: French, English, Italian.
Education: Centro Sperimentale di Cinematografia, Rome; University of Toronto, Political Science; Ryerson Polytechnical Institute, Toronto, TV Production. Associate professor, Film Studies, Queen's University. Past President, DGC. Director of Broadcast Funds, Telefilm Canada, 83-85; currently Executive Director, Telefilm Canada. Films he has directed have won awards at numerous international film festivals.
Selective Filmography: *HEAVEN ON EARTH*, TV, 86, CDN/GB, Co-Wr; *QUEBEC ECONOMY IN CRISIS*, 'THE JOURNAL', TV, 82, CDN, Prod/Dir; *NATIONAL CRIME TEST*, TV, 82, CDN, Dir/Wr; *SNOWBIRD*, 'FOR THE RECORD', TV, 81, CDN, Dir/Co-Wr; *THE UNEXPECTED*, 'TALES OF THE KLONDIKE', TV, 81, CDN, Dir; *THE CHAIRMAN: A PORTRAIT OF PAUL DESMARAIS*, 'THE CANADIAN ESTABLISHMENT', TV, 81, CDN, Dir/Prod/Wr; *THE CHALLENGERS* (6 films), In, 78, CDN, Dir; *THE TAR SANDS*, 'FOR THE RECORD', TV, 77, CDN, Dir/Co-Wr; *KATHY KARUKS IS A GRIZZLY BEAR*, 'FOR THE RECORD', TV, 77, CDN, Dir; *ONE MAN*, Th, 77, CDN, Co-Wr **(ACTRA/CFA)**; *INSURANCE MAN FROM INGERSOLL*, TV, 76, CDN, Dir/Co-Wr **(ACTRA)**; *SIDESTREET* (2 eps), TV, 76, CDN, Dir; *ONLY GOD KNOWS*, Th, 74, CDN, Dir; *ALONG THESE LINES*, Th, 74, CDN, Prod/Dir **(CFA)**; *PAPERBACK HERO*, Th, 73, CDN, Dir; *ADVENTURES IN RAINBOW COUNTRY* (pilot), TV, 71, CDN/GB/AUS, Dir; *SEASONS IN THE MIND*, Th, 70, CDN, Dir/Wr; *IF I DON'T AGREE, MUST I GO AWAY?*, TV, 70, CDN/USA, Prod/Dir/Wr; *SAUL ALINSKY WENT TO WAR*, Th, 69, CDN, Co-Dir/Co-Wr; *THE DOWRY*, Th, 69, CDN, Dir/Wr; *THE BEST DAMN FIDDLER FROM CALABOGIE TO KALADAR*, TV, 69, CDN, Dir **(3 CFA)**; *WHATEVER HAPPENED TO THEM ALL?*, TV, 66, CDN, Dir/Prod/Wr; *THIS HOUR HAS SEVEN DAYS* (41 seg), TV, 66-64, CDN, Prod/Story Ed; *THIS BLOOMING BUSINESS OF BILINGUALISM*, TV, 66, CDN, Dir/Prod/Wr; *MASTROIANNI*, TV, 65, CDN, Dir/Wr; *TORONTO FILE* (sev eps), TV, 63/62, CDN, Story Ed.

PELLETIER, Bernard

ARRQ. 111 Chadbourne, Noranda, Qué, CAN, J9X 1B8. (819)762-8516.
Types de production et Catégories: TV vidéo-Réal.
Types d'oeuvres: Documentaire-TV; Education-TV; Affaires publiques-TV.
Curriculum vitae: Né en 1951; bilingue. Bac. en Journalisme et Information, Université Laval, 76; Master's, Media Studies, Université Concordia. Expérience: journaliste pigiste; reporter, radio et TV (Radio-Nord); professeur de langues, Tchad (Afrique). Se consacre à la réalisation depuis 85.
Filmographie sélective: *CAMERA UN* (Journ-6 ém), (pl ém), TV, 86-84, CDN, Réal; *ASKIGWASH 1 ET 2*, TV, 85, CDN, Réal; *CAMERA UN* (6 eps), TV, 85/84, CDN, Journ; *POLLUTION A ROUYN NORANDA*, 'LE POINT', TV, 85/84, CDN, Journ/Co réal; *A PIERRE FENDRE*, TV, 84, CDN, Réal; *CONNEXION* (4 eps), TV, 84, CDN, Réal.

PELLETIER, Vic

APFVQ, ARRFQ. C.P. 45, St-Luc de Matane, Matane, CAN, G0J 2X0. (418)562-5302.
Types de production et Catégories: TV film-Réal/Prod; TV vidéo-Réal.

(cont/suite)

Types d'oeuvres: Documentaire-TV; Education-TV.
Curriculum vitae: Né en 1948. Professeur de cinéma au Cégep de Matane depuis 76.
Filmographie sélective: *'CITE DES JEUNES'* (1 eps), TV, 85, CDN, Réal; *LES OISEAUX DE LA GASPESIE,* TV, 84, CDN, Réal; *LES RELIGIEUSES,* TV, 84, CDN, Réal; *LES GRANDS VOILIERS,* TV, 84, CDN, Réal; *LES FETES 84,* TV, 84, CDN, Réal; *L'ART ENVIRONNEMENTAL,* TV, 84, CDN, Réal; *'PRESENCE AMERINDIENNE EN GASPESIE'* (6 eps), TV, 84, CDN, Réal; *CARTIER, REVU ET CORRIGE,* TV, 83, CDN, Réal; *MIGUASHA,* TV, 83, CDN, Réal; *UNE SAISON AUX LOTS RENVERSES,* TV, 79, CDN, Réal/Prod; *LES BUCHERONNES,* TV, 76, CDN, Réal/Prod; *CE QUE GENS PENSENT,* TV, 75, CDN, Réal/Prod.

PERRIS, Anthony

130 S. Adams St., Suite 2, Glendale, CA, USA, 91205. (818)241-1407. Brian Gaffikin/APA Comm., 1633 Sunset Drive, Santa Monica, CA, USA, 95401. (213) 450-3599.
Types of Production & Categories: Th Short-Dir/Wr; TV Film-Dir; TV Video-Dir.
Genres: Drama-TV; Action-TV; Documentary-Th&TV; Educational-TV.
Biography: Born 1939, Athens, Greece; citizenship: Canadian-American-Greek. Languages: English, Greek, Afrikaans. Education: Matriculation, South Africa. Former production assistant to George Stevens, 59-65, Hollywood. *HONOUR THY FATHER* won Best Drama, Yorkton Int'l Film Fest.; Hoyts Theatres Film Award for *BEING.*
Selective Filmography: *SPECIAL ATHLETES,* TV, 80, USA, Dir; *'LITTLEST HOBO'* (1 eps), TV, 79, CDN, Dir; *'RITTER'S COVE'* (1 eps), TV, 79, CDN, Dir; *SCOOP,* 'FOR THE RECORD', TV, 77, CDN, Dir; *HONOUR THY FATHER,* 'HERE TO STAY', TV, 76, CDN, Dir; *'TO SEE OURSELVES'* (sev eps), TV, 74-72, CDN, Dir; *'THE COLLABORATORS'* (1 eps), TV, 74, CDN, Dir; *BEING,* Th, 72, CDN, Dir/Wr; *JUST ONCE,* Th, 68, CDN, Dir; *WHEREVER THERE ARE CHILDREN,* Th, 68, CDN, Dir; *THE GREATEST STORY EVER TOLD,* Th, 65/64, USA, PA.

PERRON, Clément - voir SCENARISTES

PESANT, Raymond

AR. 3550 Jeanne Mance, #1416, Montréal, Qué, CAN, H2X 3P7. (514)622-9435. Radio-Canada, 1400 blvd. Dorchester est, Montréal, Qué, CAN, II2L 2M2. (514) 285-2991.
Types de production et Catégories: c métrage-Réal; TV film-Réal; TV vidéo-Réal.
Types d'oeuvres: Comédie-TV; Documentaire-TV; Education-TV; Enfants-TV.
Curriculum vitae: Né en 1943 à Montréal, Québec. Education: Ecole dramatique, régisseur, metteur en scène. Régisseur, Télé-Métropole (3 ans); tournée européenne de théâtre, Monaco, 65. Danseur folklorique, Feux-Follets, 62-65.
Filmographie sélective: *'AU JEU'* (130 eps), TV, 86-83, CDN, Réal; *'QUEBEC 1534-1984'* (20 seg), TV, 85/84, CDN, Réal; *'BOBINO'* (12 eps), TV, 85-73, CDN, Réal; *'JEUX COMMONWEALTH'* (40 seg), TV, 84-73, CDN, Réal; *'HEROS DU SAMEDI'* (20 seg), TV, 80-70, CDN, Réal; *'UNIVERS DES SPORTS'* (12 eps), TV, 80-70, CDN, Réal; *'OLYMPIQUE 76'* (125 seg), TV, 76/75, CDN, Réal; *'VIRGINIE'* (hebdo), TV, 76-71, CDN, Réal; *'ANIMAGERIE'* (hebdo), TV, 74-69, CDN, Réal; *'SESAME STREET'* (65 seg), TV, 72/71, CDN, Réal.

PETRIE, Daniel M.

DGA, DGC, SAG. D. Petrie Productions Inc, 13201 Haney Pl., Los Angeles, CA, USA, 90049. (213)451-9157. Fred Spector, CAA, 1888 Century Park E., #1400, Los Angeles, CA, USA, 90067. (213)277-4545.

(cont/suite)

Types of Production & Categories: Th Film-Dir/Wr; TV Film-Dir.
Genres: Drama-Th&TV.
Biography: Born in Nova Scotia. B.A., Saint Francis Xavier University, Nova Scotia, later awarded an Honorary Doctorate of Literature; M.A., Columbia U. Has taught at Northwestern U., Creighton U. (head of Theatre Dept.). Won the Peabody Award for *SYBIL*; Special Award, Cannes Film Festival for *RAISIN IN THE SUN*.
Selective Filmography: *HALF A LIFETIME*, TV, 85, USA, Dir; *THE EXECUTION OF RAYMOND GRAHAM*, TV, 85, CDN, Dir; *THE BAY BOY* (LE PRINTEMPS SOUS LA NEIGE), Th, 83, CDN/F, Dir/Wr (**GENIE**); *THE DOLLMAKER*, TV, 83, USA, Dir (**DGA**); *SIXPACK*, Th, 83, USA, Dir; *FORT APACHE, THE BRONX*, Th, 79, USA, Dir; *RESURRECTION*, Th, 78, USA, Dir; *THE BETSY*, Th, 77, USA, Dir; *HARRY TRUMAN: PLAIN SPEAKING*, TV, 77, USA, Dir; *SYBIL*, TV, 76, USA, Dir; *ELEANOR AND FRANKLIN, THE WHITE HOUSE YEARS*, TV, 76, USA, Dir (**EMMY**); *ELEANOR AND FRANKLIN*, TV, 75, USA, Dir (**EMMY**); *LIFEGUARD*, Th, 74, USA, Dir; *BUSTER AND BILLIE*, Th, 73, USA, Dir; *'THE MAN AND THE CITY'*, TV, 72, USA, Dir; *HEC RAMSEY*, TV, 71, USA, Dir; *SILENT NIGHT, LONELY NIGHT*, TV, 69, USA, Dir; *RAISIN IN THE SUN*, Th, 60, USA, Dir.

PETTIGREW, Damien Philip - see PRODUCERS

PINSENT, Gordon

ACTRA, SAG. 130 Carlton St., PH 8, Toronto, Ont, CAN, M5A 2K1. (416)926-8778.
Types of Production & Categories: Th Film-Dir/Act/Wr; TV Film-Dir/Act; TV Video-Wr/Act.
Genres: Drama-Th&TV.
Biography: Born 1930, Grand Falls, Newfoundland. Education: Grand Falls Academy; Honorary Doctorate of Laws, University of Prince Edward Island, 75. Officer, Order of Canada.
Selective Filmography: *JOHN AND THE MISSUS*, Th, 86, CDN, Scr/Dir/Act; *THE EXILE*, TV, 85, CDN, Dir; *AND MILES TO GO*, TV, 85, CDN, Wr/Act; *'AIRWAVES'* (2 eps), TV, 85, CDN, Dir; *READY FOR SLAUGHTER*, 'FOR THE RECORD', TV, 83, CDN, Act; *THE LIFE AND TIMES OF EDWIN ALONZO BOYD*, TV, 83, CDN, Act; *ONCE*, TV, 80, CDN, Dir; *'A GIFT TO LAST'* (Wr-18 eps/Act-21eps), TV, 80-76, CDN, Creator/Wr/Act (**ACTRA**); *A FAR CRY FROM HOME*, TV, 80, CDN, Dir; *SILENCE OF THE NORTH*, Th, 80/79, CDN, Act; *ESCAPE FROM IRAN: THE CANADIAN CAPER*, TV, 80, CDN, Act; *KLONDIKE FEVER*, Th, 79, CDN, Act (**GENIE**); *WHO HAS SEEN THE WIND*, Th, 76, CDN, Act; *HORSE LATITUDES*, TV, 75, CDN, Act; *THE HEATWAVE LASTED FOUR DAYS*, TV, 74, CDN, Act; *MICHAEL IN THE MORNING*, TV, 73, CDN, Wr; *THE ROWDYMAN*, Th, 71, CDN, Wr/Act (**ACTRA/CFA**); *'QUENTIN DURGENS, M.P.'* (30 eps), TV, 68-65, CDN, Act.

PITTMAN, Bruce

Chrysalis Productions, 191 Logan Ave., Toronto, Ont, CAN, M4M 2N2. (416)469-0459.
Types of Production & Categories: Th Film-Dir/Wr/Ed; TV Film-Dir/Prod/Wr/Ed; TV Film-Dir/Prod/Wr.
Genres: Drama-Th&TV; Action-TV; Horror-Th; Children's-TV.
Biography: Born 1950, Toronto, Ontario. Has directed films which have won awards at film festivals including: Silver and Gold Plaques, Chicago, Chris Award, Columbus; *THE PAINTED DOOR* received an Oscar nomination.
Selective Filmography: *CONFIDENTIAL*, Th, 86, CDN, Wr/Dir/Ed; *THE SCREAMING WOMAN*, 'RAY BRADBURY THEATRE', TV, 86, CDN, Dir; *THE HAUNTING OF HAMILTON HIGH*, Th, 86, CDN, Dir; *MARK OF CAIN*, Th, 85, CDN, Dir; *LEGS OF THE LAME*, 'BELL CANADA PLAYHOUSE', TV,

(cont/suite)

85, CDN, Dir/T'play; *THE PAINTED DOOR*, 'BELL CANADA PLAYHOUSE', TV, 85, CDN, Dir; *'MOVIEMAKERS'* (25 eps), TV, 84, CDN, Dir/Prod; *CORNET AT NIGHT/ I KNOW A SECRET/ DAVID*, 'SONS AND DAUGHTERS', TV, 83/82, CDN, Dir; *OLDEN DAYS COAT*, TV, 81, CDN, Dir; *'WORLD ACCORDING TO NICHOLAS'* (4 eps), TV, 80, CDN, Dir/Co-Wr/Ed/ Prod; *'TALKING FILM'* (60 eps), TV, 80-77, CDN, Dir/Prod; *'SATURDAY NIGHT AT THE MOVIES'* (114 eps), TV, 77-74, CDN, Dir/Prod; *RITUAL*, TV, 73, CDN, Dir/Ed/Prod/Cam; *KILLER BEES*, TV, 73, USA, Loc M; *FRANKENHEIMER*, TV, 71, CDN, Dir/Cam/Ed/Prod.

PLOUFFE, Jean-Paul

AR. 461 31e Ave., Lasalle, Qué, CAN, H8P 2W9. (514)364-1648. Radio-Canada, 1400 blvd. Dorchester est, Montréal, Qué, CAN, H2L 2M2. (514)285-3198.
Types de production et Catégories: TV film-Réal; TV vidéo-Réal.
Types d'oeuvres: Documentaire-TV.
Curriculum vitae: Né en 1933, Montréal, Québec; bilingue. Baccalauréat en Sciences politiques.
Filmographie sélective: *'LA SEMAINE VERTE'* (6 eps), TV, 86-83, CDN, Réal; *TRAVAUX CORRECTEURS A LA BAIE JAMES/ RADISSON VILLE OUVERTE*, 'BAIE JAMES', TV, 85, CDN, Réal; *CHASSE A L'OIE/ LES INSECTES PIQUEURS*, 'BAIE JAMES', TV, 85, CDN, Réal; *RELOCALISATION DE FORT-GEORGES A CHISASIBI*, 'BAIE JAMES', TV, 85, CDN, Réal; *VISITE JEAN-PAUL II*, TV, 84, CDN, Réal; *LE MER ET SES PRINCES*, TV, 83, CDN/F, Réal; *INDUSTRIE DU SPORT PROFESSIONNEL/ BILAN INFLATION*, 'CONSOMMATEUR PLUS', TV, 80-78, CDN, Réal; *OLYMPIQUE 76* (Seg:HALTEROPHILIE), TV, 76, CDN, Réal.

POIRIER, Anne Claire

SGCT. 1120 Bernard O., #7, Montréal, Qué, CAN, H2V 1V3. (514)270-2020. ONF, C.P. 6100, Montréal, Qué, CAN, H3C 3H5. (514)283-9342.
Types de production et Catégories: l métrage-Réal/Prod/Sc; c métrage-Réal/Prod/Sc.
Types d'oeuvres: Drame-C; Documentaire-C.
Curriculum vitae: Née en 1932, St Hyacinthe, Québec. Licenciée en Droit de l'Université de Montréal, 58; Conservatoire d'Art Dramatique de Montréal (Théâtre). ONF, assistante réalisatrice, 60; mère de famille; tient une chronique et collabore à *FEMMES D'AUJOURD'HUI* (R-C), 64-65; productrice à l'ONF, 70; productrice exécutive et Chef de studio à la production française et responsable du programme Société Nouvelle, 75-78; retourne à la réalisation. Récipiendaire de l'Ordre du Québec, 85.
Filmographie sélective: *LA QUARANTAINE*, C, 82, CDN, Réal/Co sc; *MOURIR A TUE-TETE* (A SCREAM OF SILENCE), C, 78, CDN, Réal/Co sc/Prod; *FAMILLE ET VARIATIONS*, C, 77, CDN, Prod; *RAISON D'ETRE*, C, 77, CDN, Prod; *LA MALADIE*, C, 77, CDN, Prod; *LA THERAPIE*, C, 77, CDN, Prod; *QUEBEC A VENDRE*, C, 77, CDN, Prod; *SHAKTI*, C, 76, CDN, Prod; *SURTOUT L'HIVER*, TV, 76, CDN, Prod; *LES HERITIERS DE LA VIOLENCE*, C, 76, CDN, Prod; *LA P'TITE VIOLENCE*, C, 76, CDN, Prod; *LE TEMPS DE L'AVANT*, 'EN TANT QUE FEMMES', TV, 75, CDN, Réal/Sc/Co prod; *A QUI M'APPARTIENT CE GAGE?/ J'ME MARIE, J'ME MARIE PAS*, 'EN TANT QUE FEMMES', TV, 74/73, CDN, Prod; *SOURIS TU M'INQUIETES/ LES FILLES C'EST PAS PAREIL*, 'EN TANT QUE FEMMES', TV, 74/73, CDN, Prod; *LES FILLES DU ROY*, 'EN TANT QUE FEMMES', TV, 74/73, CDN, Réal/Sc/Co prod; *DE MERE EN FILLE*, C, 67-65, CDN, Réal/Sc; *LA FIN DES ETES*, C, 63, CDN, Réal/Co sc/Mont; *JOUR APRES JOUR*, C, 62, CDN, Mont; *NOMADE DE L'OUEST*, C, 62, CDN, Réal; *30 MINUTES*, MR. PLUMMER, C, 62, CDN, Réal/Sc/Mont; *QUEBEC-USA*, C, 60, CDN, Ass mont; *VOIR MIAMI*, C, 60, CDN, Ass réal.

(cont/suite)

POOL, Léa

SARDEC. 5964 Hutchison, Outremont, Qué, CAN, H2V 4C1. (514)273-9351.
Types de production et Catégories: l métrage-Réal/Sc; TV vidéo-Réal.
Types d'oeuvres: Drame-C; Documentaire-TV.
Curriculum vitae: Née à Soglio, Suisse; immigrante au Canada, 1975. Diplôme ès Arts, Université du Québec, 78. Réalisatrice de documentaires et d'émissions de variétés, Radio-Québec. Prix: Festival de Sceaux, France pour *STRASS CAFE*; Prix de la Presse (Festival Int'l du Film du Monde), Prix d'Excellence (Festival de Toronto), Prix Ouimet-Molson, nominations au César et au Prix Génie pour *LA FEMME DE L'HOTEL*.
Filmographie sélective: *ANNE TRISTER,* C, 85, CDN, Réal/Sc; *'PLANETE'* (10 eps), TV, 84-80, CDN, Réal; *MINISTERE DE L'EDUCATION* (6 films), ED, 84-80, CDN, Réal; *LA FEMME DE L'HOTEL* (WOMAN IN TRANSIT), C, 84, CDN, Réal/Sc; *STRASS CAFE,* C, 80, CDN, Réal/Sc/Mont/Prod.

POTTERTON, Gerald

R.R.3 Brome Lake, Cowansville, Que, CAN, J2K 3G8. (514)263-3282. Potterton-LaRoque Films Inc., 1604 Pine Ave. West, Ste.5, Montreal, Que, CAN, H3G 1B4. (514)931-5753.
Types of Production & Categories: Th Film-Dir/Wr; Th Short-Dir/Wr; TV Film-Dir/Wr.
Genres: Drama-Th; Comedy-Th; Animation-Th&TV.
Biography: Born 1931, London, England; Canadian citizen; bilingual. Studied Art, Hammersmith Art College, London; 2 years service (R.A.F.). Assistant animator on *ANIMAL FARM*; emigrated to Canada. NFB, 54-68: animator, director, writer. Formed Potterton Productions, 68; worked in London, New York and Los Angeles. Member, Royal Canadian Academy. *PINTER PEOPLE* won the Gold and Silver Hugos, Chicago; *RAILRODDER*, the Prix Femina, Belgium and a Special Award, Berlin.
Selective Filmography: *THE GHOST SHIP,* TV, 86, CDN, Dir; *GEORGE AND THE STAR* (GEORGE ET L'ETOILE), TV, 85, CDN, Dir/Wr; *MELPOMENUS JONES,* Th, 83, CDN, Dir; *HEAVY METAL* (METAL HURLANT), Th, 81, CDN, Dir; *RAGGEDY ANN,* Th, 77, USA, Co-Dir; *THE REMARKABLE ROCKET,* TV, 75, CDN, Dir; *THE RAINBOW BOYS,* Th, 73, CDN, Dir/Wr; *TIKI-TIKI,* Th, 70, CDN, Dir/Wr; *PINTER PEOPLE,* 'EXPERIMENTS IN TELEVISION', TV, 68, CDN, Dir; *RAILRODDER,* Th, 65, CDN, Dir/Wr; *CHRISTMAS CRACKER,* Th, 63, CDN, Co-Dir/Wr; *MY FINANCIAL CAREER,* Th, 62, CDN, Dir/An Des.

PREFONTAINE, Michel

5825 Du Rocher, Outremont, Qué, CAN, H2V 3Y5. (514)495-8671.
Types de production et Catégories: l métrage-Réal/Prod; TV vidéo-Réal/Prod.
Types d'oeuvres: Drame-C; Comédie-TV; Variété-TV; Documentaire-C.
Curriculum vitae: Né en 1947, St-Hyacinthe, Québec; bilingue. Bac., études en cinéma à Londres (2 ans). Réalisateur/producteur depuis 13 ans.
Filmographie sélective: *HUGHES AUFRAY,* TV, 86, CDN, Prod/Réal; *'MADE IN QUEBEC',* TV, 86, CDN, Réal; *WAITER,* TV, 85, CDN, Prod/Réal; *'LAUTREC 85',* TV, 85, CDN, Réal; *MEDIUM BLUES,* C, 84, CDN, Prod/Réal/Co sc.

PRIZEK, Mario

ACTT, ATPD. 51 Alexander ST., #1517, Toronto, Ont, CAN, M4Y 1B3. (416) 923-7490.
Types of Production & Categories: TV Film-Dir/Prod/Wr; TV Video-Dir/Prod/Wr.
Genres: Drama-TV; Variety-TV; Experimental-TV.

(cont/suite)

Biography: Born 1922, Edmonton, Alberta. B.A, Honours, University of British Columbia; scholarships, diplomas, Banff School of Fine Arts. 4 years active service with RCAF, Bomber Command, W.W.II (2 years overseas) as radar technician. Fluent in 8 languages; has done translations from French, Italian, Polish, German, Russian, Spanish. Published poetry, stories, criticism. 34 years in radio and TV; producer, director: BBC, Granada TV (G.B.), PBS (U.S.), Clasart Films (W. Germany); joined CBC, 51.
Selective Filmography: *L'ILE INCONNU*, 'CANADANCE', TV, 85, CDN, Dir/ Exec Prod/Prod; *CATULLI CARMINA*, 'MUSICAMERA', TV, 80, CDN, Dir/ Wr; *MUSIC IN OUR TIME* (4 shows), 'MUSICAMERA', TV, 77-73, CDN, Dir/ Prod; *THE LOST CHILD*, 'MUSICAMERA', TV, 76, CDN, Dir/Prod; *THE BEAR/LA SERVA PADRONA*, 'FESTIVAL', TV, 75/73, CDN, Dir/Prod; *BARYSHNIKOV*, TV, 74, CDN, Dir; *BROTHERS IN THE BLACK ART/ VOLPONE*, 'FESTIVAL', TV, 74/69, CDN, Dir/Prod; *MICHELANGELI*, TV, 70, CDN, Dir/Prod; *GLENN GOULD PLAYS BEETHOVEN*, TV, 70, CDN, Dir/Prod; *LADY WINDERMERE'S FAN/ AN IDEAL HUSBAND*, 'FESTIVAL', TV, 67/ 66, CDN, Dir/Prod; *CONVERSATIONS WITH GLENN GOULD* (THE WELL-TEMPERED LISTENER), (2 shows), TV, 66, CDN/USA, Dir/Prod; *THE TAMING OF THE SHREW/ THE DUCHESS OF MALFI*, 'FESTIVAL', TV, 66/ 61, CDN, Dir/Prod/Adapt; *GALILEO/ THE THREE SISTERS*, 'FESTIVAL', TV, 63/61, CDN, Dir/Prod; *FIRST LOVE*, 'PLAYDATE', TV, 63, CDN, Dir/ Prod; *SOUTH/ PENELOPE*, 'TELEVISION PLAYHOUSE', TV, 60/59, CDN, Dir; *THE TRIAL OF GOVERNOR WALL*, TV, 60, GB, Dir; *HEDDA GABLER*, 'FORD STARTIME', TV, 60, CDN, Dir/Prod; *QUEEN AFTER DEATH/ A MONTH IN THE COUNTRY*, 'FOLIO', TV, 58, CDN, Dir/Prod; *PEER GYNT*, 'FOLIO', TV, 57, CDN, Dir; *THE UNBURIED DEAD/ GIANNI SCHICHI*, 'FOLIO', TV, 57/56, CDN, Dir/Prod.

PURDY, Jim - see WRITERS

PYKE, Roger

DGC. 58 Cartier Crescent, Richmond Hill, Ont, CAN, L4C 2N2. (416)884-5957. Roger Pyke Prods. Ltd., 314 Jarvis St., # 103B, Toronto, Ont, CAN, M5B 2C5. (416)591-6860.
Types of Production & Categories: Th Film-Ed; Th Short-Ed; TV Film-Dir/Ed; TV Video-Dir.
Genres: Drama-Th&TV; Comedy-Th&TV; Documentary-TV; Educational-TV.
Biography: Born 1940, London, England; Canadian; languages: English, French, Spanish. Graduated Ryerson Polytechnical Institute, 63. Has worked in London (BBC), Berlin, Guatemala, Nicaragua, N.Y. and L.A.. Has directed or edited many int'l award winning films.
Selective Filmography: *WINGS OF EAGLES*, Th, 86, CDN, Dir; *THESE FEW YEARS*, In, 86, CDN, Prod/Dir; *CANADIAN CONNECTION*, TV, 85, CDN, Dir/ Prod; *CRUDE AWAKENING*, TV, 84, CDN, Dir; *ENERGY-SEARCH FOR AN ANSWER*, TV, 84, CDN, Dir; *FALASHA - EXILE OF THE BLACK JEWS*, Th, 83, CDN, Ed; *THE GREAT BACK ATTACK*, TV, 83, CDN, Ed; *DREAM CITIES*, TV, 82, CDN, Ed; *FREEMAN PATTERSON: THE REVEALING EYE*, TV, 82, CDN, Ed; *BRING'EM ON*, Th, 82, CDN, Dir; *THE PLAYING FIELDS OF BROCK*, Th, 82, CDN, Dir; *GILBERTO'S DREAM* (LE REVE DE GILBERTO), TV, 80, CDN, Dir; *JOURNEY FROM ZANZIBAR*, TV, 79, CDN, Ed; *CHILD OF THE ANDES/ HASSAN THE CARPET WEAVER*, 'SPREAD YOUR WINGS', TV, 77, CAN, Ed; *INDIRA GANDHI: THE HERITAGE OF POWER*, ED, 76, CDN, Ed.

RACHED, Tahani

ARRFQ. 923 Marie Anne Est, Montréal, Qué, CAN, H2J 2B2. (514)723-1921.
ONF, 3155 Côte de Liesse, Montréal, Qué, CAN, H4N 2N4. (514)283-9344.
Types de production et Catégories: c métrage-Réal; TV film-Réal; TV vidéo-Réal.
(cont/suite)

Types d'oeuvres: Documentaire-C&TV.
Curriculum vitae: Née en 1947, Le Caire, Egypte; réside au Canada depuis 66, citoyenneté canadienne; trilingue; arabe, français, anglais. Met sur pied un centre de production vidéo en Tunisie auprès de la Fédération des Cinéastes Amateurs Tunisiens, 76.
Filmographie sélective: *RENDEZ-MOI MON PAYS,* TV, 86, CDN, Réal; *HAITI - QUEBEC,* TV, 85, CDN, Réal; *BEYROUTH A DEFAUT D'ETRE MORT,* C, 83, CDN, Réal; *LA PHONIE FURIEUSE,* C, 82, CDN, Réal; *AUTOUR DU PAIN/ LES CHRETIENS DU MOYEN-ORIENT,* 'PLANETE ARABE', TV, 81/80, CDN, Réal; *JE SUIS CROYANT/ DE PURE RACE/ CARTE D'IDENTITE,* 'PLANETE ARABE', TV, 81/80, CDN, Réal; *LES VOLEURS DE JOBS,* C, 79, CDN, Réal; *LES FRERES ENNEMIS,* TV, 79, CDN, Réal.

RACINE, Pierre - voir MONTEURS

RADFORD, Tom - see PRODUCERS

RAKOFF, Alvin

ACTT, DGC, WGGB. 1 The Orchard, Chiswick, London, GB, W4 1JZ. (01)994-1269. John Redway & Associates, 16 Berners St., London, England, GB, W1P 3DD. (01)637-1612.
Types of Production & Categories: Th Film-Dir/Prod/Wr; TV Film-Dir/Prod/Wr; TV Video-Dir/Prod/Wr.
Genres: Drama-Th&TV; Action-Th&TV.
Biography: Born 1937, Toronto, Ontario; graduate of University of Toronto. On staff at BBC, London, 4 years; seconded to French TV in Paris; worked in Germany, Spain, Italy, USA etc...
Selective Filmography: *'PARADISE POSTPONED'* (12 parts), TV, 86/85, GB, Dir; *THE FIRST OLYMPICS - ATHENS, 1896,* TV, 85, USA/GB, Dir; *MR HALPERN AND MR JOHNSON,* TV, 83, GB, Dir; *'DISRAELI'* (ep 10), TV, 82, GB, Dir; *A VOYAGE ROUND MY FATHER,* TV, 81, GB, Dir/Prod (INT'L EMMY); *DIRTY TRICKS* (ACCROCHE-TOI...J'ARRIVE), Th, 79, CDN, Dir; *CITY ON FIRE,* Th, 79, CDN, Dir; *ROMEO AND JULIET,* 'SHAKESPEARE', TV, 78, GB, Dir; *THE KITCHEN,* TV, 77, GB, Dir; *KRUMNAGEL,* Th, 77, GB, T'play; *THE DAME OF SARK,* TV, 76, GB, Dir; *IN PRAISE OF LOVE,* TV, 75, GB, Dir/Adapt; *THE NICEST MAN IN THE WORLD,* TV, 75, GB, Dir.

RANCOURT, Daniel

ARRFQ. 1029 Girouard, Montréal, Qué, CAN, H4A 3B9. (514)489-4549.
Types de production et Catégories: c métrage-Réal/Sc; TV film-Réal/Sc.
Types d'oeuvres: Comédie-C; Documentaire-C; Enfants-C&TV.
Curriculum vitae: Né en 1955, Montréal, Québec. Etudes en Production Cinéma au Collège Algonquin, Ottawa, 77-79. Professeur de photographie, 84.
Filmographie sélective: *'VINGT ANS EXPRESS'* (2 eps), TV, 86, CDN, Rech/Sc/ Ass réal; *L'ACTEUR, LA VOISINE,* C, 82, CDN, Réal/Sc; *LES AVENTURES DE TETE DE BOIS* (pilote), TV, 81, CDN, Ass réal; *LES BLEUS...LA NUIT...,* C, 80, CDN, Réal/Sc; *MECANIQUE MATINALE,* C, 80, CDN, Ass réal; *PREMEDITATIONS,* C, 78, CDN, Co cam; *MONTREAL, T'SE VEUT DIRE!,* C, 75, CDN, Sc/Cam.

RANIERI, Nik

1420 Crescent St., #206, Montreal, Que, CAN, H3G 2B7. (514)842-2436. Pascal Blaise Inc., 612 William St., Montreal, Que, CAN.
Types of Production & Categories: Th Short-Dir/An; TV Film-Dir/An.
Genres: Animation-Th&TV.
Biography: Born 1961, Toronto, Ontario. College education. *COMMON PROBLEMS* won the Canadian Independent Short Film Showcase.

(cont/suite)

Selective Filmography: *RUSH: THE BODY ELECTRIC,* MV, 85, CDN, An; *UNITED WAY,* Cm, 85, CDN, An; *'THE RACCOONS'* (5 eps), TV, 85, CDN, An; *COMMON PROBLEMS,* Th, 83, CDN, Dir/An.

RASKY, Harry

ACTRA, DGA, WGA. CBC, Box 500, Station A, Toronto, Ont, CAN, M5W 1E6. (416)975-6888.
Types of Production & Categories: Th Film-Dir/Prod/Wr; TV Film-Dir/Prod/Wr; TV Video-Dir/Prod/Wr.
Genres: Drama-Th&TV; Variety-Th&TV; Documentary-Th&TV.
Biography: Born 1928, Toronto, Ontario. Education: University of Toronto. Has worked as a journalist, author, lecturer, host-interviewer. Granted Honorary Degree by University of Toronto. Won many awards for his films including Int'l Critics Prize, Montreal for *ARTHUR MILLER ON HOME GROUND*; Grand Prize, NY TV/Film Fest., an Oscar nomination for *HOMAGE TO CHAGALL: THE COLOURS OF LOVE*; Academy Award Certificate of Merit for *STRATASPHERE.* Selected as Top Non-Fiction Director by the TV Directors Guild of America, 86.
Selective Filmography: *KARSH, THE SEARCHING EYE,* TV, 86, CDN, Dir/Prod/Wr; *THE MYSTERY OF HENRY MOORE,* TV, 84, CDN, Dir/Prod/Wr; *RAYMOND MASSEY: ACTOR OF THE CENTURY,* TV, 82, CDN, Dir/Prod/Wr; *STRATASPHERE,* TV, 82, CDN, Dir/Prod/Wr; *BEING DIFFERENT,* Th, 82, CDN, Dir/Prod/Wr; *THE SPIES WHO NEVER WERE,* TV, 81, CDN, Dir/Prod/Wr; *THE MAN WHO HID ANNE FRANK,* TV, 80, CDN, Dir/Prod/Wr; *THE SONG OF LEONARD COHEN,* TV, 79, CDN, Dir/Prod/Wr; *ARTHUR MILLER ON HOME GROUND,* Th, 79, CDN, Dir/Prod/Wr; *TRAVELS THROUGH LIFE WITH LEACOCK,* TV, 76, CDN, Dir/Prod/Wr; *HOMAGE TO CHAGALL: THE COLOURS OF LOVE,* Th, 75, CDN, Dir/Prod/Wr; *NEXT YEAR IN JERUSALEM,* TV, 73, CDN, Dir/Prod/Wr (ACTRA); *TENNESSEE WILLIAMS' SOUTH,* TV, 73, CDN, Dir/Prod/Wr; *AN INVITATION TO THE ROYAL WEDDING,* TV, 73, CDN/USA, Dir/Prod/Wr; *THE WIT AND WORLD OF G. BERNARD SHAW,* TV, 72, CDN/GB, Dir/Prod/Wr; *UPON THIS ROCK,* Th, 71, USA, Dir/Wr; *THE LEGEND OF SILENT NIGHT,* TV, 69, USA, Co-Dir/Prod/Wr; *ZOOS OF THE WORLD,* TV, 68, USA, Dir; *HALL OF KINGS,* TV, 67, USA, Dir/Wr/Prod (EMMY); *CUBA AND CASTRO TODAY,* TV, 65, USA, Dir/Prod/Wr; *THE NOBEL PRIZE,* TV, 64, USA, Dir/Prod; *ELEANOR ROOSEVELT: FIRST LADY OF THE WORLD,* 'PERSPECTIVE ON GREATNESS', TV, 63, USA, Dir/Prod/Wr; *MAHATMA: THE GREAT SOUL,* 'PERSPECTIVE ON GREATNESS', TV, 62, USA, Dir/Prod/Wr; *THE LION AND THE CROSS,* 'THE 20th CENTURY', TV, 61, USA, Dir/Wr (EMMY); *PANAMA: DANGER ZONE,* 'WHITE PAPER', TV, 60, USA, Dir/Wr; *'U.N. IN ACTION',* TV, 59-55, USA, Dir/Prod; *BANDWAGON '56,* TV, 56, USA, Prod/Wr; *'NEWSMAGAZINE'* (100 films), TV, 55-52, CDN, Dir/Prod/Wr.

RASTELLI, Maryse

CTPDA. 35 Moncion, Hull, Qué, CAN, J9A 1K4. (819)770-9788. Radio-Canada, B.P. 3220, Succ. A, Ottawa, Ont, CAN, K1E 1Y4. (613)724-5240.
Types de production et Catégories: TV film-Prod; TV vidéo-Réal/Prod.
Types d'oeuvres: Drame-TV; Variété-TV; Documentaire-TV.
Curriculum vitae: Née en 1937, Longuyon, France; canadienne par naturalisation; bilingue. Baccalauréat en Philosophie, cours à Cambridge et universités St-Paul et Ottawa. Réalisatrice à Radio-Canada depuis 74.
Filmographie sélective: *FABIENNE THIBEAULT/ PETER PRINGLE ET NICOLE CROISILLE,* 'LES BEAUX DIMANCHES', TV, 85, CDN, Réal; *BAL DE NEIGE,* TV, 85, CDN, Réal; *'AU JOUR LE JOUR'* (pl seg), TV, 85-83, CDN, Réal; *'LA BETE...OU LE CAPRICE DU TEMPS'* (2 eps), TV, 83, CDN, Réal;

(cont/suite)

EDITH BUTLER/ M.P. BELLE, 'LES BEAUX DIMANCHES', TV, 82, CDN, Réal; *'JEUNES VIRTUOSES'* (3 eps), TV, 80, CDN, Réal; *'PULSION'* (26 eps), TV, 79-76, CDN, Réal; *'LES BEAUX DIMANCHES'* (Prod dél-8 ém/Réal-3 ém), TV, 78/77, CDN, Réal/Prod dél.

RAWI, Ousama

ACTT, DGA, IATSE-667. Rawifilm Inc., 567 Queen St.W., Toronto, Ont, CAN, M5V 2B6. (416)366-7881.
Types of Production & Categories: Th Film-Dir/DOP; TV Film-Dir/DOP.
Genres: Drama-Th&TV; Comedy-Th; Action-Th; Commercials-TV.
Biography: British-Canadian citizenship. Entered film industry in U.K., 65; started as newsreel, TV drama and commercials cameraman, then feature film DOP. Started directing commercials, 79; first feature, 86. Has won numerous awards including Clios and awards at NY, Cannes and U.K. commercials festivals.
Selective Filmography: *A JUDGEMENT IN STONE,* Th, 86, CDN, Dir; *CHARLIE MUFFIN,* TV, 79, GB, DOP; *STORY OF PRINCESS GRACE,* TV, 78, USA, DOP; *GIRL IN BLUE VELVET,* Th, 78, F, DOP; *ZULU DAWN,* Th, 78, USA, DOP; *POWER PLAY* (STATE OF SHOCK), (COUP D'ETAT), Th, 77, CDN/GB, DOP; *BOVVER BOOTS,* TV, 77, GB, DOP; *SKY RIDERS,* Th, 76, USA, DOP; *HUMAN FACTOR,* Th, 76, USA, DOP; *RACHEL'S MAN,* Th, 74, GB, DOP; *ALFIE DARLING,* Th, 74, GB, DOP; *BLACK WINDMILL,* Th, 73, USA, DOP; *GOLD,* Th, 73, GB, DOP; *THE 14* (WILD LITTLE BUNCH), Th, 72, GB, DOP; *PULP,* Th, 71, GB, DOP.

RAYMONT, Peter

3 Hingham St., Cambridge, Mass, USA, 02138. (617)864-1509. WGBH TV, 125 Western Ave., Boston, Mass, USA, 02134. (617)492-2777.
Types of Production & Categories: Th Film-Dir/Prod; TV Film-Dir/Prod/Wr/Nar; TV Video-Dir/Prod/Wr/Nar.
Genres: Action-Th&TV; Documentary-Th&TV; Educational-TV.
Biography: Born 1950, Ottawa, Ontario. B.A., Film, Politics, Economics, Queen's University. Worked at CBC, NFB. Producer, radio documentaries for CBC's 'Sunday Morning'; writer of magazine articles for 'Globe & Mail', 'Canadian Business'. Winner, Red Ribbon, American Film Fest., Gold Plaque, Chicago for *MAGIC IN THE SKY; ON TO THE POLAR SEA: A YUKON ADVENTURE,* winner at Yorkton.
Selective Filmography: *AT THE BRINK,* 'THE NUCLEAR AGE', TV, 86, USA/J, Prod/Dir/Wr; *WITH OUR OWN TWO HANDS,* Th, 85, CDN, Dir/Prod; *'VENTURE'* (weekly), TV, 85, CDN, Prod/Report; *THE BROKERS,* Th, 84, CDN, Dir/Prod/Narr; *ON TO THE POLAR SEA: A YUKON ADVENTURE,* Th, 83, CDN/USA, Dir/Co-Prod/Co-Wr; *PRISONERS OF DEBT,* Th, 82, CDN, Dir/ Narr; *FALASHA - AGONY OF THE BLACK JEWS,* Th, 82, CDN, Dir/Co-Wr/ Narr; *FALASHA - EXILE OF THE BLACK JEWS,* Th, 82, CDN, Loc Dir; *THE FORGOTTEN REFUGEES,* Th, 82, CDN, Loc Dir; *ARCTIC SPIRITS,* Th, 82, CDN, Dir/Prod/Wr; *SHIFTING SANDS: INSIDE THE PASSIONS OF THE MIDDLE EAST,* Th, 82, CDN, Co-Wr; *MAGIC IN THE SKY,* Th, 81, CDN, Dir/ Wr/Prod **(CFTA)**; *HISTORY ON THE RUN,* Th, 79, CDN, Dir/Prod/Wr/Narr; *THE ART OF THE POSSIBLE,* Th, 78, CDN, Dir/Wr/Ed/Narr; *FLORA: SCENES FROM A LEADERSHIP CONVENTION,* Th, 77, CDN, Dir/Wr/Ed/ Narr; *REFLECTIONS ON A LEADERSHIP CONVENTION,* Th, 77, CDN, Dir/ Wr/Ed/Narr; *NATSIK HUNTING,* Th, 76, CDN, Prod; *WE JUST WON'T TAKE IT,* Th, 76, CDN, Ed; *GRIERSON'S DOCUMENTARY PHILOSOPHY: THE WORKING CLASS ON FILM,* Th, 75, CDN, Co-Dir/Ed; *LUMSDEN,* Th, 75, CDN, Dir/Wr/Narr; *SIKUSILARMIUT,* Th, 75, CDN, Dir/Wr/Narr; *THE FOREST WATCHERS,* Th, 74, CDN, Dir/Wr/Narr; *RIVER, PLANET EARTH,* Th, 74, CDN, Dir; *THE INNOCENT DOOR,* Th, 73, CDN, Assoc Prod/Ed; *THE COLDSPRING PROJECT,* Th, 73, CDN, Assoc Prod/Ed; *HAVE YOU EVER BEEN NORTH OF PRINCESS STREET?,* Th, 71, CDN, Dir/Prod/Ed.

REED-OLSEN, Joan

12 Hazel Ave., Toronto, Ont, CAN, M4E 1C5. (416)694-0589. TV Ontario, Box 200, Stn. Q, Toronto, Ont, CAN, M4T 2T1. (416)484-2600.
Types of Production & Categories: TV Film-Dir/Prod; TV Video-Dir/Prod.
Genres: Documentary-TV.
Biography: Born 1923, Toronto, Ontario; Norwegian-Canadian citizenship; lived in Norway for 25 years; speaks English and Norwegian. Worked as freelance writer, broadcaster in Norway; returned to Canada, 70; research, writing, hosting, directing, producing documentaries, TV Ontario, 71-86.
Selective Filmography: *MUSKOKA ROAD SHOW/CREATURES OF ASPEN VALLEY/MASTERSN GAMES,* 'PEOPLE PATTERNS', TV, 86/85, CDN, Prod/Dir; *FESTIVAL OF THE SOUND/SHERRY, ISLAY AND CHARLOTTE,* 'PEOPLE PATTERNS', TV, 85, CDN, Prod/Dir; *BLACK THEATRE CANADA/ THE OSBORNES REVISITED/THE POETRY SWEATSHOP,* 'PEOPLE PATTERNS', TV, 85, CDN, Prod/Dir; *IN THE SPIRIT OF SHARING/ FESTIVAL OF THANKSGIVING,* 'PEOPLE PATTERNS', TV, 84, CDN, Prod/Dir; *NORTHWINDS FOLK FESTIVAL/IT'S MORE THAN JUST A GAME,* 'PEOPLE PATTERNS', TV, 84, CDN, Prod/Dir; *NEW TO THE VALLEY/ PEOPLE MAKE THE VALLEY/WOOD,* 'PEOPLE PATTERNS', TV, 84, CDN, Prod/Dir; *TODAYS TREES TOMORROW/TALL TREES MADE TALL SHIPS/ SOUTH PARKDALE,* 'PEOPLE PATTERNS', TV, 84/83, CDN, Prod/Dir; *CONFUSED, HURT AND ANGRY/DREAMS, MYTHS AND MEMORIES/ LINKING,* 'PEOPLE PATTERNS', TV, 84/83, CDN, Prod/Dir; *ST.LAWRENCE TOWN/SACRED HOME OF THE MANITOU/WATERWAY/HELP,* 'PEOPLE PATTERNS', TV, 83, CDN, Prod/Dir; *THE END WAS JUST THE BEGINNING/FROM THE OUTSIDE,* 'PEOPLE PATTERNS', TV, 83, CDN, Prod/Dir; *GREEN GROWS SUDBURY/YOU KNOW WHEN THE SINGING STARTS,* 'PEOPLE PATTERNS', TV, 83, CDN, Prod/Dir; *BALANCING THE CYCLE,* 'PEOPLE PATTERNS', TV, 83, CDN, Prod/Dir.

REISENAUER, George

DGC. 744 Huron St., Toronto, Ont, CAN, M4V 2W3. (416)962-0678.
Types of Production & Categories: TV Film-Dir.
Genres: Documentary-TV; Educational-TV; Commercials-TV.
Biography: Born 1947, Prague, Czechoslovakia; Czech and English. Educated to grade 12 level in Prague; studied photography, then film-making at Ryerson Polytechnical Institute, Toronto, 70-74. Has been producing TV commercials, short films, industrials and documentaries since 66.

REITMAN, Ivan

DGA. Warner Bros., 4000 Warner Blvd, Producers Bldg.#7, Room 8, Burbank, CA, USA, 91522. (818)954-1771. Michael Ovitz, CAA, 1888 Century Park E,, Ste. 1400, Los Angeles, CA, USA, 90067. (213)277-4545.
Types of Production & Categories: Th Film-Dir/Prod.
Genres: Comedy-Th; Horror-Th.
Biography: Born 1947, Komano, Czechoslovakia; Canadian citizen. Attended McMaster University, where he set up a film society. Upon graduation, started New Cinema of Canada; producer for Cinépix Inc.; produced Broadway shows. Received Special Award from the Academy of Canadian Cinema, 84.
Selective Filmography: *LEGAL EAGLES,* Th, 86, USA, Dir/Prod; *GHOSTBUSTERS,* Th, 84, USA, Dir/Prod; *SPACEHUNTER: ADVENTURES IN THE FORBIDDEN ZONE,* Th, 83, CDN/USA, Prod; *HEAVY METAL,* Th, 82, CDN, Prod; *STRIPES,* Th, 81, USA, Dir; *MEATBALLS,* Th, 79, CDN, Dir; *NATIONAL LAMPOON'S ANIMAL HOUSE,* Th, 78, USA, Co-Prod; *RABID,* Th, 76, CDN, Exec Prod; *DEATH WEEKEND* (THE HOUSE BY THE LAKE), Th, 75, CDN, Prod; *THE PARASITE MURDERS* (SHIVERS), (THEY CAME FROM WITHIN), Th, 73, CDN, Prod; *CANNIBAL GIRLS,* Th, 72, CDN, Dir/ Prod; *FOXY LADY,* Th, 71, CDN, Dir/Prod.

RENAUD, France Y.Y.

SARDEC. 4216 Rivard, Montréal, Qué, CAN, H2J 2M8. (514)842-5546.
Types de production et Catégories: c métrage-Réal; TV vidéo-Sc.
Types d'oeuvres: Documentaire-C; Enfants-TV; Expérimental-C.
Curriculum vitae: Née en 1950, Montréal, Québec. Séjours en France et 1 an en Afrique du Nord. Langues: français, anglais, espagnol. Carrière connexe de photographie (expositions). Collaboratrice à des revues d'art et écriture de Québec.
Filmographie sélective: *'TRABOULIDON'* (1 eps), TV, 85, CDN, Sc; *HISTOIRE DE LA POMME,* C, 82, CDN, Réal; *LES JEUX SONT FAITS,* C, 79, CDN, Réal; *PIQUEZ SUR LA LIGNE BRISEE,* C, 76, CDN, Réal.

REUSCH, Peter

DGC. Yacht Nordic V, Vancouver, BC, CAN. Peter Reusch Pictures Ltd., 703-1875 Robson St., Vanvouver, BC, CAN, V6G 1E5. (604)688-1772.
Types of Production & Categories: TV Film-Dir/Prod.
Genres: Drama-TV; Action-TV; Documentary-Th&TV; Educational-TV.
Biography: Born 1930, Hamburg, Germany; lived in Canada since 55. After graduation from art college, worked as art director, photo-journalist, special effects cameraman; DOP on many feature films, TV series, TV commercials and documentary films. Opened film/video production houses in Vancouver and Seattle, 73.
Selective Filmography: *CANADIAN COAST GUARD* (EXPO 86), Th, 86, CDN, Dir/Prod; *THE LEADING EDGE,* TV, 85, CDN, Dir/Prod/Cam/Ed; *UNITY CANADA,* TV, 84, CDN, Dir/Prod/Cam/Ed; *VACATION,* TV, 84, CDN, Dir/Prod/Cam/Ed; *A VISIT TO PURDY'S,* TV, 83, CDN, Dir/Prod/Cam/Ed; *IT'S YOUR MONEY,* TV, 82, USA, Dir/Prod/Cam.

RICH, Ron

ACTT, DGA, DGC. 91 Post Road, Don Mills, Ont, CAN, M3B 1J3. (416)446-1886. Partners Film Company, 508 Church St., Toronto, Ont, CAN. (416)966-3500.
Types of Production & Categories: TV Film-Dir.
Genres: Drama-Th&TV; Variety-TV; Action-TV; Commercials-TV.
Biography: Born 1940, London, England; British citizen; landed immigrant, Canada; H1 status, USA. Graduate of the Wimbledon College of Art, St. Martins School of Art, England. Began his professional career in advertising. Started as a film director, 71, winning a Lion d'Argent, Cannes, with his first commercial, later winning awards all over the world including: Lion d'Or (Cannes), Gold Award (US TV Commercial Fest.), Tokyo Silver, Hollywood Broadcast Award.
Selective Filmography: *BOARDWALK* (BLACK'S PHOTOGRAPHY), Cm, 85, CDN, Dir; *TELEPHONE* (DENTYNE GUM), Cm, 85, CDN, Dir; *NEW STAR* (TEXACO), Cm, 85, CDN, Dir; *GOING OUT* (HOCHTALER), Cm, 84, CDN, Dir; *MESS* (LESTOIL), Cm, 84, USA, Dir; *DESERT* (LEVI STRAUSS), Cm, 84, CDN, Dir (**CMA/TVB**); *EARLY MORNING* (VELOUR), Cm, 84, CDN, Dir (**TVB/CLIO**); *NO CAFFEINE* (DR. PEPPER), Cm, 84, USA, Dir; *TOUCH ME* (JOHNSON'S BABY POWDER), Cm, 83, CDN, Dir (**TVB/CLIO**); *CHEW-CHEW* (HERSHEY), Cm, 83, CDN, Dir; *FREEDOM IN MARRIAGE* (SUNDAY TIMES), Cm, 80, GB, Dir; *MARILYN* (SUNDAY TIMES), Cm, 80, GB, Dir (**CLIO**).

RICHARDS, Gladys

DGC. 110 Erskine Ave., #409, Toronto, Ont, CAN, M4P 1Y4. (416)489-1522. TV Ontario, 2180 Yonge St., Toronto, Ont, CAN, M4T 2T1. (416)484-2600.
Types of Production & Categories: TV Film-Dir; TV Video-Dir.
Genres: Drama-TV; Documentary-TV; Educational-TV.

(cont/suite)

Biography: Born St.John's, Newfoundland. Fifteen years as producer/director at TV Ontario. Recipient of Career Education Citation, 85 from Ontario School Counsellors Association; has also won awards for programs at various film festivals including: Columbus, Chicago, New York and Houston Film Festivals.
Selective Filmography: *'GOOD WORK'* (50 eps), TV, 86-81, CDN, Prod/Dir; *PORTRAIT OF THE ARTIST AS A YOUNG MAN,* TV, 77, CDN, Prod/Dir; *REQUIEM FOR LITERACY,* TV, 76, CDN, Prod/Dir.

RICHER, Simon

AR. C.P.71, Lacolle, Qué, CAN, J0J 1J0. (514)294-2544. Radio-Canada, 1400 blvd. Dorchester est, Montréal, Qué, CAN, H2L 2M2. (514)285-3191.
Types de production et Catégories: TV film-Réal/Sc; TV vidéo-Réal/Sc.
Types d'oeuvres: Documentaire-TV; Education-TV; Religion-TV.
Curriculum vitae: Né en 1929, Montréal, Québec. Langues: français, anglais, italien.
Filmographie sélective: *LA CRECHE DE NOEL,* ED, 82, CDN, Réal; *LES CROIX DE CHEMINS,* ED, 80, CDN, Réal/Sc; *'LA SEMAINE VERTE'* (50 seg), TV, 74, CDN, Sc; *'LES TRAVAUX ET LES JOURS'* (300 seg), TV, 73-55, CDN, Réal.

ROBERTSON, David M.

DGC. 1677 Sargent Court, Los Angeles, CA, USA, 90026. (213)482-1344. Barry Perelman Agency, 9200 Sunset Blvd., Ste.531, Los Angeles, CA, USA, 90069. (213)274-5999.
Types of Production & Categories: Th Film-Dir/1st AD/PM; TV Film-Dir/1st AD.
Genres: Drama-Th&TV; Action-Th; Horror-Th; Children's-TV.
Biography: Born 1941, Scotland; British-Canadian citizen; US resident alien (Green Card). Education: Art School; Creative Writing, University of Toronto Extension; Theatre Drama, U. of British Columbia Extension.
Selective Filmography: *THE HAUNTING OF HAMILTON HIGH,* Th, 86, CDN, 1st AD; *HOSTAGE: DALLAS,* Th, 85, USA, 1st AD; *LIMOUSINE* (MY CHAUFFEUR), Th, 85, USA, 1st AD; *LETTING GO,* TV, 85, USA, 1st AD; *FRIDAY THE 13th PART V,* Th, 85, USA, 1st AD; *'MANIA'* (1 eps), TV, 85, CDN, Dir; *THE RETURN OF THE LIVING DEAD,* Th, 84, USA, 1st AD; *DOIN' TIME,* Th, 83, USA, 1st AD/2nd U Dir; *'THE EDISON TWINS',* TV, 83, CDN, 1st AD; *'SEEING THINGS',* TV, 83, CDN, 1st AD; *I WON'T DANCE,* Th, 82, CDN/F, Assoc Prod; *'CAGNEY AND LACEY',* TV, 81, USA, 1st AD; *FIREBIRD 2015,* Th, 80, CDN, Dir; *PHOBIA,* Th, 80, CDN, 1st AD; *YESTERDAY* (GABRIELLE), Th, 79, CDN, Line Prod; *AN AMERICAN CHRISTMAS CAROL,* TV, 79, USA, 1st AD; *TOM AND JO ANN,* TV, 78, CDN/USA, PM; *HOME TO STAY,* TV, 78, CDN/USA, PM; *NEVER TRUST AN HONEST THIEF,* Th, 77, CDN, PM; *WORLD OF DARKNESS,* TV, 77, USA, PM; *TELL ME MY NAME,* TV, 77, USA, PM; *BREAKING POINT,* Th, 76, CDN/USA, PM; *WAR BETWEEN THE TATES,* TV, 75, USA, PM; *MAHONEY'S LAST STAND,* Th, 75, CDN, PM; *BLACK CHRISTMAS* (SILENT NIGHT, EVIL NIGHT), Th, 74, CDN, PM.

RODGERS, Bob - see PRODUCERS

ROGERS, Jonathan - see PRODUCERS

ROLLASON, Steve

DGC. 50 Buckland Way, Brampton, Ont, CAN, L6V 3P4. J & J Television Ent., 4432 Beacon Lane, Mississauga, Ont, CAN, L5C 4B6. (416)451-0790.
Types of Production & Categories: TV Video-Dir.
Genres: Documentary-TV; Industrial-TV.
Biography: Born 1951, Toronto, Ontario. Received top Honour Student Award, College. Media experience: City TV, Film House, National Advertising, Panasonic, Sony; Vice President of J. & J. Television Entertainment.

(cont/suite)

Selective Filmography: *CROWD MANAGEMENT/CROWD CONTROL/CRIME SCENE MANAGEMENT/T.R.U. TEAM,* In, 85/84, CDN, Dir; *TRANSPORT TRUCK INSPECTION/DIRECTING TRAFFIC/COMPUTER SERVICES,* In, 84, CDN, Dir; *FINGER PRINTING/DEATH NOTIFICATION/A.L.E.R.T./ YOUNG OFFENDERS,* In, 84/83, CDN, Dir; *B.O.S.S./BATON/HAND CUFFS/ FOREIGN WEAPONS,* In, 83, CDN, Dir; *SEARCH AND SEIZURE/FORM X-37/VEHICLE REGISTRATION/HOUSE SEARCH.* In, 82, CDN, Dir; *CONSIDER THE SOURCE/THE O.P.P. ACADEMY/TELECOMMUNI-CATION.* In, 82/81, CDN, Dir; *SEARCH OF A PERSON,* In, 81, CDN, Dir; *ALF NEILSEN/A TASTE OF DISBELIEF,* In, 74/70, CDN, Dir.

ROWE, Peter

ACTRA. 35 Cardiff Rd., Toronto, Ont, CAN, M4P 2N8. (416)487-8222. Rosebud Films Ltd., 35 Cardiff Rd., Toronto, Ont, CAN, M4P 2N8. (416)483-3161.
Types of Production & Categories: Th Film-Dir/Prod; TV Film-Dir/Prod; TV Video-Dir/Prod.
Genres: Drama-TV; Comedy-TV; Action-TV; Documentary-TV.
Biography: Born 1947, Winnipeg, Manitoba. Specialty: maritime subject matter. He won Best Director, Yorkton Film Fest., for *HORSE LATITUDES.*
Selective Filmography: *THE ARCHITECT OF FEAR,* Th, 86, CDN, Dir; *'THE CAMPBELLS'* (4 eps), TV, 86, CDN/USA/GB, Dir; *LOST!,* Th, 85, CDN, Dir/ Prod/Wr; *'THE EDISON TWINS'* (2 eps), TV, 85/84, CDN, Dir; *ADVENTURES ON SHARK REEF,* TV, 84, CDN, Wr/Cin; *'VANDERBERG'* (3 eps), TV, 83, CDN, Dir; *MICRONESIA: THE WINDS OF CHANGE,* TV, 83, CDN, Dir; *REASONABLE FORCE/ FINAL EDITION,* 'FOR THE RECORD', TV, 83-81, CDN, Dir; *TAKEOVER* (pilot), 'VANDERBERG', TV, 81, CDN, Dir; *1000 DOZEN,* 'TALES OF THE KLONDIKE', TV, 80, CDN, Dir; *THE SPIRIT OF ADVENTURE,* TV, 79, CDN, Dir/Prod; *HORSE LATITUDES,* TV, 75, CDN, Dir/Wr/Ed; *THE NEON PALACE* (A 50'S TRIP, A 60'S TRIP), Th, 70, CDN, Dir/Wr **(CFA)**.

ROZEMA, Patricia

785 Queen St.E., #1, Toronto, Ont, CAN, M4M 1H5. (416)461-8874.
Types of Production & Categories: Th Short-Dir/Prod/Wr; TV Video-Dir/Wr.
Genres: Drama-Th; Documentary-TV.
Biography: Born 1958. Languages: English, Dutch. B.A. (Honours), Calvin College, Michigan (English and Philosophy, Journalism minor), 81; Dean's list for scholastic achievement.
Selective Filmography: *PASSION: A LETTER IN 16mm,* Th, 85, CDN, Dir/Wr/ Prod; *'THE JOURNAL'* (sev seg), TV, 83-82, CDN, Assoc Prod.

RUBBO, Michael - see WRITERS

RYLEY, Nancy - see PRODUCERS

SALTZMAN, Deepa

Sunrise Films Limited, 160 Perth Ave., Toronto, Ont, CAN, M6P 3X5. (416)535-2900.
Types of Production & Categories: TV Film-Dir/Prod/Wr.
Genres: Documentary-TV.
Biography: Born 1949, Amritsar, India; Canadian citizen. Degree in Philosophy from the University of New Delhi. Writer for youth section of the New Delhi 'Statesman'. Executive Vice President of Sunrise Films Limited since 73. Her films have won numerous awards at International Film Festivals including Chicago, San Francisco, American Film Fest., Nyon, Krakow, Columbus.
Selective Filmography: *TRAVELLING LIGHT: THE PHOTOJOURNALISM OF DILIP MEHTA,* TV, 86, CDN/GB, Dir; *K.Y.T.E.S. HOW WE DREAM*

(cont/suite)

OURSELVES, TV, 85, CDN, Prod/Dir; *THE ANNEX,* 'TORONTO NEIGHBORHOODS', TV, 84, CDN, Dir/Wr; *REASONABLE FORCE,* 'FOR THE RECORD', TV, 82, CDN, Act; *KURTIS IN HOLLYWOOD,* 'SPREAD YOUR WINGS', TV, 81, CDN, Co-Prod/Co-Wr; *CHILD OF THE ANDES/ YOSHIKO THE PAPERMAKER,* 'SPREAD YOUR WINGS', TV, 79/78, CDN, Co-Prod/Wr/Snd Rec; *SERMA'S MASK/THE MONK'S PARASOL,* 'SPREAD YOUR WINGS', TV, 79, CDN, Wr/Co-Prod/Snd Rec; *WHAT'S THE WEATHER LIKE UP THERE?,* TV, 77, CDN, Dir/Prod; *FRANCESCO'S GIFT,* 'SPREAD YOUR WINGS', TV, 77, CDN, Co-Prod/Snd Rec; *TO BE A CLOWN,* TV, 76, CDN, Co-Prod/Co-Wr; *HASAN THE CARPET WEAVER/ CHILD OF GOD,* 'SPREAD YOUR WINGS', TV, 76, CDN, Co-Prod/Co-Wr/Snd Rec; *INDIRA GANDHI: THE HERITAGE OF POWER,* ED, 75, CDN, Co-Prod; *AT 99: A PORTRAIT OF LOUISE TANDY MURCH,* TV, 74, CDN/USA, Dir/Co-Prod (CFA); *FATHER BILL MACKEY: SON OF BELOVED BHUTAN,* TV, 74, CDN, Co-Wr/Co-Ed/Snd Rec; *THE PERLMUTER STORY,* TV, 73, CDN, Co-Wr/Assist Ed.

SALTZMAN, Paul - see PRODUCERS

SALZMAN, Glen

215 Albany Ave., Toronto, Ont, CAN, M5R 3C7. Cineflics Ltd., 330 Dupont St., #302, Toronto, Ont, CAN, M5R 1V9. (416)967-9183.
Types of Production & Categories: TV Film-Dir/Prod.
Genres: Drama-TV; Children's-TV.
Biography: Born 1951, Montreal, Quebec. Honours B.F.A., York University, 74. Since 76, has been directing/producing original TV drama with partner Rebecca Yates. Has won awards at film festivals including: American, Yorkton, Columbus, Childfilm.
Selective Filmography: *JEN'S PLACE,* TV, 82, CDN, Co-Dir/Co-Prod; *INTRODUCING...JANET,* TV, 81, CDN, Co-Dir/Co-Prod (CFTA); *REACHING OUT,* TV, 80, CDN, Co-Dir/Co-Prod; *CORLETTO & SON,* TV, 80, CDN, Co-Dir/ Co-Prod; *NIKKOLINA,* TV, 78, CDN, Co-Dir/Co-Prod; *ANOTHER KIND OF MUSIC,* TV, 77, CDN, Co-Dir/Co-Prod; *HOME FREE,* TV, 76, CDN, Co-Dir/Co-Prod.

SANCHEZ-ARIZA, José

ARRFQ. 3 Armstrong Dr., Dollard Des Ormeaux, Qué, CAN, H9G 1B6. (514)620-6441.
Types de production et Catégories: c métrage-Réal/Prod.
Types d'oeuvres: Drame C; Documentaire-C&TV; Annonces-TV.
Curriculum vitae: Né en 1943, Puerto Plata, République Dominicaine; citoyenneté espagnole, immigrant reçu; langues: espagnol, anglais, français. Education: Ecole Supérieure de Cinéma, Théâtre et TV de Lodz, Pologne.
Filmographie sélective: *SAHARA LA DETERMINATION D'UN PEUPLE,* C, 76, E, Réal/D phot/Prod; *SEMINARISTE,* C, 70, PL, Réal/Sc; *DESERTEURS,* TV, 69, S, Réal/Sc; *OLYMPIQUE DE MEXICO,* C, 68, MEX, Co réal; *LE CHAT EST MORT DE FAIM,* C, 68, PL, Réal/Sc; *LALKA 594,* C, 67, PL, Réal/Sc; *ENTRACTE,* C, 66, PL, Réal/Sc; *PASSAGE A NIVEAU,* C, 66, PL, Réal/Sc; *TIR A LA CIBLE,* C, 66, PL, Réal/Sc; *BARRO,* C, 64, MEX, D phot; *BREAD AND PUPPETS,* C, 64, USA, Cam; *QUAND LA NUIT TOMBE,* C, 64, MEX, Réal/Sc.

SANDERS, Ed - see PRODUCERS

SARETZKY, Eric

22 McMurrich St., Toronto, Ont, CAN, M5R 2A2. (416)964-2876. Box 5248, Stn. A, Toronto, Ont, CAN, M5W 1N5. (416)928-9000.
Types of Production & Categories: Th Film-Dir/Prod/DOP.
Genres: Drama-Th; Documentary-Th&TV; Dance-Th&TV.

(cont/suite)

Biography: Born Johannesburg, South Africa; Canadian citizen; American Field Service Scholar. Degree in Physics, Mathematics, Philosophy and English Literature, University of Witwatersrand, Johannesburg; numerous exhibitions of photography; Helped motivate the development of the super-16 Cooke 5:1 lens and use of the format in Canada. Founder of a non-racial Nat'l School of the Arts and Nat'l Film Institute for South Africa. Won Special Gold Jury Prizes for *A PRIVATE WORLD* at Chicago and Houston Int'l Film Festivals.

Selective Filmography: *SONGS OF HOPE*, Th, 86, CDN/GB, Dir/Prod/DOP/Wr; *A PRIVATE WORLD*, Th, 81, CDN, Dir/Prod/DOP.

SARIN, Vic

CSC, IATSE-667. 84 Hillsdale Ave.E., Toronto, Ont, CAN, M4S 1T5. (416)484-8415. CBC, 790 Bay St., 4th Fl., Toronto, Ont, CAN, M5G 1N8. (416)975-7602.

Types of Production & Categories: Th Film-DOP; TV Film-Dir/DOP.

Genres: Drama-Th&TV; Comedy-TV; Musical-TV; Documentary-Th&TV.

Biography: Born 1941, Srinagar, Kashmir; Canadian citizen. Languages: English, Hindi, Urdu. Diploma in TV Techniques, Sydney Technical School, Australia; 2 years of Fine Arts, University of Melbourne.

Selective Filmography: *ISLAND LOVE SONG*, TV, 86, CDN, Dir/DOP; *THE LAST SEASON*, TV, 86, CDN, DOP; *DANCING IN THE DARK*, Th, 85, CDN, DOP; *LOYALTIES*, Th, 85, CDN/GB, DOP; *TIMES AND TRAVEL OF HENRY OSGOOD*, TV, 85, USA, DOP; *TURNING TO STONE*, TV, 85, CDN, DOP; *CHARLIE GRANT'S WAR*, TV, 85, CDN, DOP (**ANIK**); *THE SUICIDE MURDERS*, TV, 85, CDN, DOP; *GURKHAS OF NEPAL*, TV, 85, CDN, Dir/Cam; *THE OTHER KINGDOM* (mini-series), TV, 84, CDN, Dir/DOP; *LOVE AND LARCENY*, TV, 84, CDN, DOP; *NAMUMKIN*, Th, 83, CDN/I, DOP; *THE ACCIDENT*, TV, 83, CDN, DOP; *CHAUTAUQUA GIRL*, TV, 82, CDN, DOP (**ANIK/CSC**); *RUMOURS OF GLORY: BRUCE COCKBURN LIVE*, TV, 82, CDN, DOP; *A FAR CRY FROM HOME*, TV, 82, CDN, DOP; *PASSENGER*, TV, 82, CDN, Dir; *HEARTACHES*, Th, 81, CDN, DOP; *ANNE'S STORY*, TV, 81, CDN, DOP; *TYLER*, TV, 80, CDN, DOP; *YOU'VE COME A LONG WAY KATIE* (mini-series), TV, 80/79, CDN, DOP/Dir; *WAR BRIDES*, TV, 80, CDN, DOP (**BIJOU**); *CROSSBAR*, TV, 80, CDN, DOP; *FOUR WOMEN*, TV, 80, CDN, Cam; *RIEL*, TV, 79, CDN, DOP; *THE FIGHTING MEN*, TV, 79, CDN, DOP; *THE WORDSMITH*, TV, 79, CDN, DOP; *COMING AND GOING*, TV, 79, CDN, Cam; *LOVE ON THE NOSE*, TV, 75, CDN, DOP (**ANIK**); *NAKED PEACOCK*, Th, 75, CDN, DOP.

SARRAZIN, Pierre - see PRODUCERS

SAURIOL, Brigitte

ARRFQ. 4519 rue Resther, Montréal, Qué, CAN, H2J 2V2. (514)522-2507.

Types de production et Catégories: l métrage-Réal/Sc; c métrage-Réal/Sc; TV film-Réal/Sc; TV vidéo-Réal/Sc.

Types d'oeuvres: Drame-C&TV; Comédie-C; Variété-C&TV.

Curriculum vitae: Née en 1945.

Filmographie sélective: *L'EAU NOIRE*, C, 86, CDN/F, Réal/Sc; *REIN QU'UN JEU* (JUST A GAME), C, 83, CDN, Réal/Sc; *BLEUE BRUME*, C, 82, CDN, Réal/Sc; *'UNE VILLE QUE J'AIME'* (l eps), TV, 81, B, Réal/Sc; *L'ABSENCE*, C, 75, CDN, Réal/Sc; *LE LOUP BLANC*, C, 73, CDN, Réal/Sc.

SAVOIE, Marc

4702 rue Des Erables, Montréal, Qué, CAN, H2H 2C9. (514)598-7030.

Types de production et Catégories: TV film-Réal; TV vidéo-Réal.

Types d'oeuvres: Documentaire-TV; Nouvelles-TV.

(cont/suite)

Curriculum vitae: Né en 1954, Edmundston, Nouveau-Brunswick; bilingue. Etudes : Communications à l'U.Q.A.M., Montréal. Co-récipiendaire du Prix aux Médias, B'nai Brith, Canada, 84.
Filmographie sélective: *L'ILE DE SABLE - L'OASIS DE L'ATLANTIQUE,* TV, 85, CDN, Réal/Sc; *'CE SOIR ATLANTIQUE'* (quot), TV, 85-82, CDN, Réal; *LE RACISME AU CANADA,* 'LE POINT', TV, 84, CDN, Réal; *'REFLEXION'* (40 eps), TV, 82/81, CDN, Réal.

SCANLAN, Joseph L.

DGA, DGC. 149 South Rodeo Dr., Beverly Hills, CA, USA, 90212. (213)275-2911. Mitchell Kaplan, Kaplan/Stahler Agency, 8383 Wilshire Blvd., #923, Beverly Hills, CA, USA, 90211. (213)653-4483.
Types of Production & Categories: Th Film-Dir; TV Film-Dir.
Genres: Drama-Th&TV; Comedy-TV; Action-TV.
Selective Filmography: *'ADDERLY'* (1 eps), TV, 86, CDN, Dir; *'KNOT'S LANDING'* (7 eps), TV, 86, USA, Dir; *'FALCON CREST'* (1 eps), TV, 86, USA, Dir; *'HOT SHOTS'* (2 eps), TV, 86, CDN, Dir; *'NIGHT HEAT'* (1 eps), TV, 86, CDN, Dir; *'LOVING FRIENDS' AND PERFECT COUPLES'* (40 eps), TV, 83/82, USA, Dir; *SPRING FEVER* (SNEAKERS), Th, 82, CDN, Dir; *'MATT AND JENNY'* (10 eps), TV, 79/78, CDN/GB/D, Dir; *OUR MAN FLINT,* TV, 78, USA, Dir; *'SEARCH AND RESCUE'* (10 eps), TV, 78, CDN/USA, Dir.

SCHULZ, Bob

DGC. 56 Russell Hill Rd., Toronto, Ont, CAN, M4V 2T2. (416)961-6160. Schulz Productions, 41 Peter St., Toronto, Ont, CAN, M5V 2G2. (416)593-5969.
Types of Production & Categories: Th Film-Dir; TV Film-Dir/Prod; TV Video-Dir/ Prod.
Genres: Drama-Th&TV; Comedy-Th&TV; Action-Th&TV; Commercials-TV.
Biography: Born 1931; came to Canada as a Hungarian refugee; graduate of Academy of Cinematography, Budapest. Has directed in over 30 countries. Formed Schulz Productions which has associates in N.Y., Chicago. Has won all major awards for TV commercials; directed over 3,500.
Selective Filmography: *DAN HILL/OHM,* MV, 84/83, CDN, Dir; *EUROPEAN WORLD CUP SOCCER CHAMPIONSHIP,* TV, 84, CDN, Exec Prod; *FALCON'S GOLD* (ROBBERS OF THE SACRED MOUNTAIN), Th, 82, CDN, Dir; *ACTRA'S LIVE COMMAND PERFORMANCE,* TV, 81, CDN, Dir; *GROWN UP TOMORROW,* TV, 81, CDN, Dir; *NEAR AND FAR,* TV, 80, CDN, Prod; *EXPLODING THE MYTH,* TV, 80, CDN, Co-Dir/Prod; *THE GLOVE,* TV, 79, CDN, Dir; *HOUSE ON FRONT STREET,* TV, 79, CDN, Dir; *1976 CANADA CUP HOCKEY,* TV, 76, CDN, Prod; *AVE LUNA,* TV, 73, CDN, Dir; *COME AWAY, COME AWAY,* TV, 72, CDN, Dir.

SCOTT, Cynthia

51 Windsor Ave., Montreal, Que, CAN, H3Y 2L9. (514)481-0823. NFB, Box 6100, Montreal, Que, CAN, H3C 3H5. (514)283-9533.
Types of Production & Categories: Th Film-Dir; Th Short-Dir/Prod; TV Film-Dir/ Prod; TV Video-Dir/Prod.
Genres: Drama-Th&TV; Variety-Th&TV; Documentary-Th&TV.
Biography: Born 1939, Winnipeg, Manitoba. B.A., University of Manitoba; also studied music and art. Producer, director for CBC, Toronto for 8 years. Married, 1 child. Member, Royal Canadian Academy. Her films have won many awards including Golden Sheaf for *FLAMENCO AT 5:15;* other awards from film festivals: San Francisco, New York, Salerno, Krakow.
Selective Filmography: *A CHRONIC PROBLEM,* 'DISCUSSIONS IN BIOETHICS', TV, 85, CDN, Dir; *JACK OF HEARTS,* 'BELL CANADA PLAYHOUSE', TV, 85, CDN, Dir; *FLAMENCO AT 5:15,* Th, 84/83, CDN, Dir/ Co-Prod/Co-Ed **(OSCAR)**; *GALA,* Th, 82, CDN, Co-Dir; *FOR THE LOVE OF*

(cont/suite)

DANCE, TV, 81, CDN, Co-Dir; *FIRST WINTER,* TV, 81/80, CDN, Co-Wr; *DON ARIOLI FITNESS AND NUTRITION* (11 clips), TV, 79/78, CDN, Prod; *LISTEN, LISTEN, LISTEN,* TV, 76, CDN, Prod; *SCOGGIE,* 'ATLANTIC CANADA', TV, 74, CDN, Dir; *SOME NATIVES OF CHURCHILL,* 'WEST', TV, 73, CDN, Dir; *'WEST'* (12 eps), TV, 73, CDN, Co-Prod; *THE UNGRATEFUL LAND,* 'ADIEU ALOUETTE', TV, 72, CDN, Dir **(CFA).**

SCOTT, Michael J.F. - see PRODUCERS
SEDAWIE, Gayle Gibson - see PRODUCERS
SEDAWIE, Norman - see PRODUCERS
SEGUIN, Jean-Gaétan
ARRQ. 632 ave. Outremont, Montréal, Qué, CAN, H2V 3M7. (514)276-6867.
Radio-Québec, 1000 rue Fullum, Montréal, Qué, CAN, H2K 3L7. (514)521-2424.
Types de production et Catégories: TV vidéo-Réal.
Types d'oeuvres: Variété-TV; Documentaire-TV; Education-TV; Expérimental-TV.
Curriculum vitae: Né en 1940, Montréal, Québec. Etudes en linguistique et en psychologie. Un des idéateurs de la série *LES ORALIENS*; à Radio-Québec depuis 71; a participé à Input 81; travaille surtout sur les émissions culturelles.
Filmographie sélective: *L'UNIVERS DE ARMAND VAILLANCOURT/CARBONE 14/L'ECRAN HUMAIN,* TV, 86, CDN, Réal; *L'UNIVERS DE 6 PEINTRES ACTUELS,* TV, 86, CDN, Réal; *L'UNIVERS DE JEAN-GUY MOREAU/ MICHEL LEMIEUX/MARGIE GILLIS,* TV, 85/84, CDN, Réal; *L'UNIVERS DE CHARLES DUTOIT/JULIETTE HUOT/LUCIEN FRANCOEUR,* TV, 84, CDN, Réal; *FOUS...COMME DANS FOUFOUNES,* TV, 83, CDN, Réal; *TO BE OR NOT TO BE,* TV, 82, CDN, Réal; *DEMI-TOUR,* TV, 81, CDN, Réal; *'NEUF ET DEMI'* (30 eps), TV, 81, CDN, Prod dél; *'L'ENVERS DU DECOR'* (37 eps), TV, 80-78, CDN, Réal; *'MOI, MES CHANSONS'* (27 eps), TV, 77/76, CDN, Réal.

SEGUIN, Roger J.
CTPDA. 1557 Sunvalley Dr., Windsor, Ont, CAN, N9C 3R1. (519)966-2953.
Types of Production & Categories: TV Video-Dir.
Genres: Variety-TV; Sports-TV.
Biography: Born 1939, Windsor, Ontario; bilingual: Education: Communications, University of Detroit.
Selective Filmography: *JUNIOR A HOCKEY,* TV, 85/84, CDN, Dir; *SYMPHONY CANADA,* TV, 84, CDN, Dir.

SELZNICK, Arna
79 Blantyre Ave., Scarborough, Ont, CAN, M1N 2R6. (416)698-9888. Nelvana, 32 Atlantic Ave., Toronto, Ont, CAN, M6K 1X8. (416)588-5571.
Types of Production & Categories: Th Film-Dir; TV Film-Dir.
Genres: Musical-Th&TV; Action-TV; Children's-Th&TV; Animation-Th&TV.
Biography: Born 1948, Toronto, Ontario. Working graphic artist and illustrator; teacher/designer of a course on storyboarding, Ryerson Polytechnical Institute, 83. **Main focus of professional attention:** concept design, story development and film direction for feature films, specials and series work for TV in both animation and live action.
Selective Filmography: *THE CARE BEARS MOVIE II,* Th, 86/85, CDN, Sr Spv Lay; *THE GREAT HEEP,* TV, 85, CDN, Spv St'board; *'EWOKS'* (26 eps), TV, 85, CDN, Spv St'board; *THE CARE BEARS MOVIE,* Th, 85/84, CDN, Dir; *A FREEDOM TO MOVE,* Th, 84, CDN, St'board; *ON TO THE POLAR SEA: A YUKON ADVENTURE,* Th, 84, CDN, Illustr; *STRAWBERRY SHORTCAKE AND THE BABY WITHOUT A NAME,* TV, 83, CDN, Dir; *'INSPECTOR GADGET'* (64 eps), TV, 83, CDN, Sr Spv St'board; *HERSELF THE ELF,* TV, 83/ 82, CDN, Spv Lay; *STRAWBERRY SHORTCAKE AND THE HOUSEWARMING SURPRISE,* TV, 82, CDN, Spv Lay; *ROCK & RULE* (RING OF POWER), Th, 82-80, CDN, Lay Art.

SENECAL, Gilles

AR. 223 bas de la rivière sud,, Rg.5, St-Césaire, Qué, CAN, J0L 1T0. (514)469-4189. Radio-Canada, 1400 blvd. Dorchester est, Montréal, Qué, CAN, H2L 2M2. (514)285-2608.
Types de production et Catégories: TV film-Réal/Prod; TV vidéo-Réal/Prod.
Types d'oeuvres: Variété-TV; Documentaire-TV; Enfants-TV; Religion-TV.
Curriculum vitae: Né en 1926. Etudes: faculté de Médecine, Université de Montréal (1 an) et à Paris; pédiâtrie, Hôpital des Enfants Malades de Paris, 3 ans. Réalisateur à Radio-Canada depuis 56. Ses films ont remportés plusieurs prix aux festivals de films internationaux.
Filmographie sélective: *'MONSIEUR LE MINISTRE'* (15 eps), TV, 86/85, CDN, Réal; *'LA VIE PROMISE'* (hebdo), TV, 84/83, CDN, Réal; *TU REVES ADRIENNE*, 'LES BEAUX DIMANCHES', TV, 83, CDN, Réal; *CATHERINE PROVOST, FILLE DU ROY*, TV, 82, CDN, Réal; *C'EST A CAUSE D'ELLE*, TV, 82, CDN, Réal; *'RACE DE MONDE'* (11 eps), TV, 81, CDN, Réal; *ENTRE LE SOLEIL ET L'EAU*, 'LES BEAUX DIMANCHES', TV, 80, CDN, Réal (ANIK); *'POP CITROUILLE'* (10 eps), TV, 80, CDN, Réal; *'PSST-PSST AIE LA!'* (76 eps), TV, 80/79, CDN, Réal; *LA MEMOIRE CASSEE* (4 seg), 'SCENARIO', TV, 78, CDN, Réal; *LE QUATRIEME AGE*, 'SCENARIO', TV, 77, CDN, Réal; *FRANCOIS*, 'LES BEAUX DIMANCHES', TV, 76, CDN, Réal; *'TOUR DE TERRE'*, TV, 73-64, CDN, Réal; *'LA SOURIS VERTE'* (60 eps), TV, 70-67, CDN, Co réal/Prod; *'VIENS VOIR'* (hebdo), TV, 67/66, CDN, Co réal/Prod; *'DANS TOUS LES CANTONS'* (15 eps), TV, 64-61, CDN, Co réal/Prod; *'COUCOU'* (hebdo), TV, 63-59, CDN, Réal/Prod; *'LA BOITE A SURPRISE'* (15 eps), TV, 59/58, CDN, Co réal; *'FILS DE DIEU'* (39 eps), TV, 59/58, CDN, Réal; *'BOBINO'* (13 eps), TV, 58/57, CDN, Co réal; *'LA VIE QUI BAT'* (30 eps), TV, 57/56, CDN, Réal.

SENS, Al

ASIFA. 2018 York Ave., Vancouver, BC, CAN, V6J 1E6. (604)733-6635. Al Sens Animation Ltd., 1020 Mainland St., Vancouver, BC, CAN, V6B 2T4. (604)681-9728.
Types of Production & Categories: Th Short-Dir/An; TV Film-Dir/An.
Genres: Educational-Th&TV; Children's-Th&TV; Animation-Th&TV; Experimental-Th&TV.
Biography: Born 1933, Vancouver, British Columbia. Attended Vancouver School of Art. *ACTING OUT*, Canadian Independent Short Film Showcase winner.
Selective Filmography: *PACIFIC CONNECTION*, ED, 83/82, CDN, An; *BACKSTAGE AT A NURSERY RHYME*, Th, 83, CDN, Dir/An; *ACTING OUT*, Th, 83, CDN, Dir/An; *THE FUNNY COW*, Th, 81, CDN, Dir/An; *AN INTERVIEW WITH IVAN SHUSIKOV*, Th, 80, CDN, Dir/An; *PROBLEMS ON AN IMAGINARY FARM*, Th, 79, CDN, Dir/An; *A HARD DAY AT THE OFFICE*, Th, 78, CDN, Dir/An; *PHYSICAL FITNESS: A NEW PERSPECTIVE*, ED, 77, CDN, Dir/An; *LA VACHE HISTOIRE*, ED, 73, CDN, An; *THE TWITCH*, Th, 73, CDN, Dir/An; *DIALECTICAL MATERIALISM*, ED, 71/70, CDN, Dir/An; *MAN AND MACHINE*, Th, 69, CDN, Dir/An; *HENRY*, ED, 68/67, CDN, Dir/An; *THE BROTHERHOOD*, Th, 67, CDN, Dir/An; *THE PLAYGROUND*, Th, 64/63, CDN, Dir/An; *THE SEE HEAR TALK THINK DREAM AND ACT FILM*, Th, 63-61, CDN, Dir/An; *THE SORCERER*, Th, 61/60, CDN, Dir/An; *THE PUPPET'S DREAM*, Th, 60/59, CDN, Dir/An.

SHAFFER, Beverly

508 Lansdowne, Westmount, Que, CAN, H3Y 2V2. (514)932-1347. NFB, Box 6100, Montreal, Que, CAN, H3C 3H5. (514)283-9533.
Types of Production & Categories: TV Film-Dir/Prod.
Genres: Documentary-TV; Educational-TV; Children's-TV.

(cont/suite)

DIRECTORS/REALISATEURS

Biography: Born 1945, Montreal, Quebec. Languages: English, French, Hebrew, Yiddish. Education: B.A., McGill University, Hebrew University, Jerusalem; M.Sc., Boston University (Film). *I'LL FIND A WAY* won 1st Prize and Grand Prize at the Child Film Festival (Winnipeg), 1st Prize, Tempere Festival, Finland; *BENOIT* won at the Yorkton Film Festival.
Selective Filmography: *BREAKING THE SILENCE,* TV, 86/85, CDN, Dir; *WHO WILL DECIDE,* 'DISCUSSIONS IN BIOETHICS', TV, 85, CDN, Dir; *I WANT TO BE AN ENGINEER* (NOUS SOMMES LES INGENIEURES), TV, 83, CDN, Dir; *JULIE O'BRIAN/IT'S JUST BETTER/THE WAY IT IS/VERONICA/ BENOIT,* 'CHILDREN OF CANADA', TV, 81-78, CDN, Dir/Prod; *I'LL FIND A WAY,* 'CHILDREN OF CANADA', TV, 78, CDN, Dir/Prod **(OSCAR)**; *GURDEEP SINGH BAINS/KEVIN ALEE/BEAUTIFUL LENNARD ISLAND,* 'CHILDREN OF CANADA', TV, 77, CDN, Dir/Prod; *MY NAME IS SUSAN LEE/MY FRIENDS CALL ME TONY,* 'CHILDREN OF CANADA', TV, 76, CDN, Dir/Prod.

SHANDEL, Tom F.

WTVS, 1 Yonge St., #1801, Toronto, Ont, CAN, M5E 1E5. (416)364-1166.
Types of Production & Categories: Th Film-Dir/Prod; TV Film-Dir/Prod/Wr; TV Film-Dir/Prod/Wr.
Genres: Drama-Th&TV; Documentary-Th&TV; Educational-Th&TV; Experimental-Th&TV.
Biography: Born 1938, Winnipeg, Manitoba. B.A., University of British Columbia; Film, Stanford U.. Dupont Columbia Award for *RAPE: FACE TO FACE.* Executive producer, Canadian and Int'l operations, WTVS (Detroit public TV), 86.
Selective Filmography: *WINNERS/LOSERS,* 'ECONOMY', TV, 86, CDN, Dir/ Wr; *WALLS,* Th, 84, CDN, Dir/Co-Prod; *BITTER MEDICINE,* 'QUARTERLY REPORT', TV, 83, CDN, Dir/Wr; *RAPE: FACE TO FACE,* TV, 82, CDN/USA, Co-Dir/Co-Prod; *LOTOMANIA,* TV, 80, CDN, Dir/Wr.

SHAPIRO, Paul

ACTRA, DGC. 50 Allen Ave., Toronto, Ont, Can, M4M 1T4. (416)461-5053. Martin-Paul Prod. Ltd., 12 McMurrich St., Toronto, Ont, Can, M5R 2A2. (416) 968-9375.
Types of Production & Categories: TV Film-Dir/Wr.
Genres: Drama-TV; Comedy-TV; Action-TV; Children's-TV.
Biography: Born 1955, Regina, Saskatchewan. Ryerson Polytechnical Institute, Photoarts, Film major, 72-75; NFB, directors' training units, 76-78; classical violin, Royal Conservatory of Music, Regina, Sask.(6 years); 15 years guitar training, music composition. Playwright: 'The True Story of Frankenstein', 82. *HOCKEY NIGHT* won a CFTA.
Selective Filmography: *MIRACLE AT MOREAUX,* TV, 85, CDN, Dir/Co-T'Play; *THE UMPIRE,* TV, 84, CDN, Dir/Co-Wr; *HOCKEY NIGHT,* TV, 84, CDN, Dir/ Co-Wr; 'THE EDISON TWINS' (5 eps), TV, 84-83, CDN, Dir/Co-Wr; *R.W.,* 'SONS AND DAUGHTERS', TV, 82, CDN, Dir/Co-Wr; *CLOWN WHITE,* TV, 80, CDN, Dir/Co-Wr; *THE UNDERSTUDY,* TV, 75, CDN, Dir/Co-Wr; *LIFE TIMES NINE* (Seg:THE TANK), Th, 74, CDN, Dir/Wr.

SHATALOW, Peter

FS Systems, 396 Dundas St. E., Toronto, Ont, CAN, M5A 2A5. (416)960-0679.
Types of Production & Categories: Th Film-Dir/Wr; TV Film-Dir/Wr; TV Video-Dir/Wr.
Genres: Variety-TV; Documentary-Th&TV.
Biography: Born Brussels; Canadian. Attended Seneca College. Joined CBC as film editor; in mid 70's, formed own production company. *CHALLENGE: THE CANADIAN ROCKIES* won CFTA.

(cont/suite)

Selective Filmography: *THE MAKING OF LA CAGE,* TV, 85, CDN, Dir/Wr; *THE PAPAL VISIT: BEHIND THE SCENES,* TV, 84, CDN, Wr; *CAROLINE,* 'SONS AND DAUGHTERS', TV, 83, CDN, Dir; *HEART OF AN ARTIST,* TV, 83, CDN, Dir/Wr; *'HEART OF GOLD'* (3 eps), TV, 82, CDN, Dir/Wr; *CHALLENGE: THE CANADIAN ROCKIES,* Th, 81, CDN, Dir/Wr/Ed; *LAROUSSI AND THE FANTASIA,* 'SPREAD YOUR WINGS', TV, 81, CDN, Co-Dir/Ed; *BLACK ICE,* Th, 80, CDN, Dir/Ed.

SHEBIB, Don

DGC. Evdon Films Ltd., 312 Wright Ave., Toronto, Ont, CAN, M6R 1L9. (416) 536-8969. John Bornham, William Morris Agency, 151 El Camino Dr., Beverly Hills, CA, USA. (213)859-4271.
Types of Production & Categories: Th Film-Dir/Prod/Ed; Th Short-Dir/Ed/Cam; TV Film-Dir/Ed/Cam.
Genres: Drama-Th&TV; Comedy-Th; Action-Th; Documentary-TV.
Biography: Born 1938, Toronto, Ontario. B.A., University of Toronto, 60; M.F.A., UCLA, 65.
Selective Filmography: *'THE EDISON TWINS'* (8 eps), TV, 86/85, CDN, Dir; *'NIGHT HEAT'* (1 eps), TV, 86, CDN, Dir; *THE CLIMB,* Th, 85, CDN/GB, Dir; *RUNNING BRAVE,* Th, 83, CDN/USA, Dir; *SLIM OBSESSION,* 'FOR THE RECORD', TV, 83, CDN, Dir; *HEARTACHES,* Th, 81, CDN, Dir; *FISH HAWK,* Th, 79, CDN, Dir; *FIGHTING MEN,* 'FOR THE RECORD', TV, 77, CDN, Dir; *SECOND WIND,* Th, 75, CDN, Dir/Ed **(CFA)**; *WE'VE COME A LONG WAY TOGETHER,* TV, 75, CDN, Dir/Ed; *BETWEEN FRIENDS,* Th, 73, CDN, Dir; *BORN HUSTLER,* TV, 72, CDN, Dir; *RIP-OFF,* Th, 71, CDN, Dir; *GOIN' DOWN THE ROAD,* Th, 70, CDN, Dir/Ed/Prod **(CFA)**; *GOOD TIMES BAD TIMES,* TV, 68, CDN, Dir/Cam/Prod/Snd Ed **(2 CFA)**; *SAN FRANCISCO SUMMER,* TV, 67, CDN, Dir/Ed/Cam; *SATAN'S CHOICE,* Th, 65, CDN, Dir/Ed/Cam; *SURFIN',* TV, 64, CDN, Dir/Ed.

SHEKTER, Louise

46 Muriel Ave., Toronto, Ont, CAN, M4J 2X9. (416)469-3104. French Media Solutions, 67 Mowat, #242, Toronto, Ont, CAN, M6K 3E3. (416)537-4270.
Types of Production & Categories: Th Short-Dir; TV Film-Dir.
Genres: Documentary-Th&TV; Educational-TV; Children's-TV.
Biography: Born 1950, Montreal, Quebec; bilingual. Active as a translator/writer; specializes in Audio Visual and broadcast work; experience in all aspects of dubbing production; musical background. *MAKING A DIFFERENCE* won awards at the American, San Francisco and Yorkton Film Festivals.
Selective Filmography: *CA ME TROTTE DANS LA TETE,* TV, 86, CDN, Dir; *'PAYS EN DEVELOPPEMENT'* (6 eps), TV, 86, CDN, Prod/Dir; *LE COEUR A SES RAISONS,* ED, 85, CDN, Dir/Prod; *MAKING A DIFFERENCE,* Th, 84, CDN, Dir/Prod **(CFTA)**; *JOURNEY OF DISCOVERY,* Th, 84, CDN, Res.

SHERRIN, Robert - see PRODUCERS

SHILTON, Gilbert

ACTRA, DGA, DGC, WGAw. Michael Neidors, Perry & Neidors, 315 S. Beverly Dr., Beverly Hills, CA, USA, 90212. (213)553-0171.
Types of Production & Categories: TV Film-Dir.
Genres: Drama-TV; Action-TV.
Biography: Born 1945; raised and educated in Montreal; Has worked for TV stations in Montreal, Toronto; worked in L.A. for CBS, Metromedia, 75-79; self employed as a director, writer since.
Selective Filmography: *SPEARFIELD'S DAUGHTER* (mini-series), TV, 85, CDN/USA/AUS, Dir; *'V'* (3 eps), TV, 85/84, USA, Dir; *'DANGER BAY'* (Dir-5 eps/Wr-1 eps), TV, 84, CDN/USA, Dir/Wr; *ARM'S RACE,* 'BLUE THUNDER', TV,

(cont/suite)

84, USA, Dir; *'THE A-TEAM'* (3 eps), TV, 84/83, USA, Dir; *'THIS IS THE LIFE'* (2 eps), TV, 84/83, USA, Dir; *SECOND THUNDER* (pilot), 'BLUE THUNDER', TV, 83, USA, Dir; *'MAGNUM P.I.'* (Dir 1 eps), (sev eps), TV, 82-79, USA, Assoc Prod.

SIEGEL, Lois

2182 Prud'homme, Montreal, Que, CAN, H4A 3H2. (514)481-0611.
Types of Production & Categories: Th Short-Dir/Prod/Ed; TV Film-Dir/Prod/Ed.
Genres: Drama-Th; Documentary-Th&TV; Experimental-Th.
Biography: Born 1946, Milwaukee, Wisconsin; Canadian citizen; bilingual. B.Sc. (Honours in English), Journalism; Masters in Comparative and English Literature, Ohio University.
Selective Filmography: *BAD NEWS BANANAS,* Th, 84, CDN, Dir/Ed; *A 20th CENTURY CHOCOLATE CAKE,* Th, 83, CDN, Dir/Prod/Ed; *EXTREME CLOSE-UP* (UN PROFOND REGARD), TV, 80, CDN, Dir/Prod/Ed; *ARENA,* TV, 79, CDN, Dir/Ed; *STUNT FAMILY* (LES CASCADEURS), TV, 78, CDN, Dir/Ed; *DIALOGUE OF AN ANCIENT FOG* (DIALOGUE D'UNE BRUME ANTIQUE), Th, 78, CDN, Dir/Ed; *RECIPE TO COOK A CLOWN,* Th, 78, CDN, Dir/Prod/Ed; *SOLITUDE,* Th, 78, CDN, Dir/Ed/Cam; *BRANDY ALEXANDER,* Th, 76, CDN, Dir/Prod/Ed; *BOREDOM,* Th, 76, CDN, Dir/Prod/Ed; *FACES,* Th, 76, CDN, Dir/Prod/Ed/Cam; *PAINTING WITH LIGHT,* Th, 74, CDN, Dir/Ed; *DREAMS,* Th, 73, CDN, Co-Dir/Ed; *THE PERFORMANCE,* Th, 73, CDN, Dir/Prod/Ed/Cam; *PARALYSIS,* Th, 72, CDN/USA, Co-Dir/Prod/Ed; *SPECTRUM IN WHITE,* Th, 71, USA, Dir/Prod/Ed.

SIMARD, Cheryl

Peartree House Productions Inc, 2 Jean St., Toronto, Ont, CAN, M4W 3A7. (416) 921-3793. Paul Simmons, 125 Dupont Ave., Toronto, Ont, CAN. (416)920-1500.
Types of Production & Categories: TV Film-Dir/Prod; TV Video-Dir/Prod.
Genres: Drama-TV; Comedy-TV; Documentary-TV; Educational-TV.
Biography: Born 1946, Quebec City; bilingual. Studied at Marymount College. Has been directing since 75. Cordon Bleu diploma, London; La Varenne Diploma, Paris.
Selective Filmography: *PETRO CANADA/GM LEO/GULF,* In, 86/85, CDN, Dir; *'C'EST TON DROIT'* (39 eps), TV, 85-83, CDN, Prod/Dir/Wr; *'A VOTRE SERVICE'* (64 eps), TV, 85/84, CDN, Dir.

SIMMONDS, Alan Francis

CFTA, DGC. 27 Oakview Ave., Toronto, Ont, CAN, M6P 3J3. (416)763-4529. Big Meadow Prods., 6565 Sunset Blvd., Ste. 400, Hollywood, CA, USA, 90028. (213) 456-2788. Spiro Skouras, Herb Tobias & Associates, 1901 Ave. of the Stars, #840, Los Angeles, CA, USA, 90067. (213)277-6211.
Types of Production & Categories: Th Film-Prod; TV Film-Dir; TV Video-Dir.
Genres: Drama-Th&TV; Action-Th&TV; Documentary-TV; Children's-TV.
Biography: Born 1942, London, England. Graduate of Ryerson Polytechnical Institute (Communications and Fine Arts), 65.
Selective Filmography: *'DANGER BAY'* (10 eps), TV, 86, CDN/USA, Dir; *STRIKER'S MOUNTAIN,* TV, 85, CDN, Dir; *'THE EDISON TWINS'* (7 eps), TV, 85/84, CDN, Dir; *'THE BEACHCOMBERS'* (5 eps), TV, 85-82, CDN, Dir; *'LITTLEST HOBO'* (6 eps), TV, 84/83, CDN, Dir; *'LORNE GREENE'S NEW WILDERNESS'* (sev eps), TV, 83, CDN, Dir; *'THE HITCHIKER'* (sev eps), TV, 83, CDN/USA, Line Prod; *HARRY TRACY,* Th, 80, CDN, Line Prod; *TICKET TO HEAVEN,* Th, 80, CDN, Line Prod; *HEAD ON* (FATAL ATTRACTION), Th, 79, CDN, Co-Prod.

SIMONEAU, Guy

ARRFQ, STCQ. 4374 boul. St-Laurent, Montréal, Qué, CAN, H2W 1Z5. (514) 288-5022.
Types de production et Catégories: l métrage-Réal; c métrage-Réal; TV film-Réal; TV vidéo-Réal.
Types d'oeuvres: Documentaire-C&TV; Vidéo clips-C&TV.
Curriculum vitae: Né en 1952 à Québec. Intérêts: musique, (opéra, rock), vidéo clips.
Filmographie sélective: *MADAME/LOUISE FORESTIER/UZEB/ BELGAZOU/ MARC DROUIN/ THE BOX,* MV, 86-84, CDN, Réal/Conc; *LES CONTES DES 1001 NEZ,* TV, 86, CDN, Réal; *LA SYMPHONIE FANTASTIQUE,* C, 86, CDN, Réal/Conc; *E—ROCK,* TV, 84, CDN, Réal/Conc; *ON N'EST PAS DES ANGES,* C, 82, CDN, Réal/Co aut; *PLUSIEURS TOMBENT EN AMOUR,* C, 80, CDN, Réal/Prod **(GENIE);** *JE SUIS EN MEME TEMPS MAUDIT ET CLASSIQUE,* TV, 78, CDN, Réal/Prod.

SIMONEAU, Yves

ARRFQ. 5046 rue Clark, Montréal, Qué, CAN, H2T 2T8. (514)271-7593.
Types de production et Catégories: l métrage-Réal/Sc; c métrage-Réal/Sc.
Types d'oeuvres: Comédie-C; Action-C&TV; Documentaire-C&TV; Education-TV.
Curriculum vitae: Expérience professionnelle: Radio-Canada, Radio-Québec; réalisation et montage d'une trentaine d'annonces; caméraman; responsable d'un atelier aux Rencontres Internationales du Jeune Cinéma, Cannes, 76. *POURQUOI L'ETRANGE MONSIEUR ZOLOCK S'INTERESSAIT-IL TANT A LA BANDE DESSINEE?* remporte un Prix Génie et un Prix Spécial du Jury, Banff.
Filmographie sélective: *LES FOUS DE BASSAN,* C, 86, CDN/F, Réal; *POUVOIR INTIME,* C, 83, CDN, Réal/Co aut; *POURQUOI L'ETRANGE M. ZOLOCK S'INTERESSAIT-IL A LA BANDE DESSINEE?,* C, 83, CDN, Réal/Sc; *LES YEUX ROUGES* (LES VERITES ACCIDENTELLES), C, 82, CDN, Réal/Sc; *LE GENIE DE L'INSTANT,* C, 82/81, CDN, Réal/Sc; *LES CELEBRATIONS,* C, 78, CDN, Réal/Mont.

SINGH, Hardev

31 Longboat Ave., Toronto, Ont, CAN, M5A 4C9. (416)365-1632. Cdn. Filmmakers Dist. Centre, 67A Portland St., Toronto, Ont, CAN, M5V 2M9. (416) 593-1808.
Types of Production & Categories: Th Short-Dir.
Genres: Drama-Th; Documentary-Th.
Biography: Born 1934, India; Canadian citizen. Artist, has had 50 one-man shows and participated in numerous other international exhibitions in Europe, India, North America. Has made short films in Italy, Poland, India and Canada.
Selective Filmography: *HOLOCAUST - SIKHS,* Th, 86, CDN, Dir; *THE SIKHS,* ED, 79, CDN, Dir/Prod; *MY SCROLLS,* Th, 73, CDN, Dir; *REGIONAL PROGRAM,* ED, 72, CDN, Dir; *EYES,* Th, 68, PL, Dir.

SKAGEN, Peter

9102 - 168th Street, Surrey, BC, CAN, V3S 5X7. (604)576-2747. Gossamer Films, 314 N. Pender St., Vancouver, BC, CAN, V6B 1T3. (604)683-0313.
Types of Production & Categories: Th Short-Dir/Prod/Wr.
Genres: Industrial-Th.
Biography: Born 1957, Calgary, Alberta; Canadian-US citizen. B.A., University of Calgary; M.A., Film, California State U. of Northridge.
Selective Filmography: *THE ROAD TO THE FUTURE,* In, 86, CDN, Dir/Prod/ Wr; *WEDGE CLAMP/CONCERT RESOURCES,* In, 86, CDN, Dir/Wr; *C'MON ABOARD,* In, 86, CDN, Wr; *RANGER MACHINERY,* In, 85, CDN, Dir/Prod; *CANADIAN SOLUTIONS,* In, 85, CDN, Dir/Prod/Wr.

SMALLEY, Katherine

ATPD. 368 Brunswick Ave., Toronto, Ont, CAN, M5R 2Y9. (416)961-8907. CBC, Box 500, Station A, Toronto, Ont, CAN, M5W 1E6. (416)975-6588.
Types of Production & Categories: TV Film-Dir/Prod; TV Video-Dir/Prod.
Genres: Documentary-TV; Educational-TV; Experimental-TV.
Biography: Born 1946, Oakville, Ontario; bilingual. Havergal College, Toronto, 63; Laval University, Quebec, French Language Certificate, 64; B.A. (Honours), Political Science and Philosophy, McGill University, 67. CBC, 70-86; consultation and programming, United Nations Conference on Human Settlements. She has won various awards including Gold Medal, N.Y. Int'l Film Fest. for *ALL THAT GLISTENS*.
Selective Filmography: *GLIMPSE OF HEAVEN - EASTER IN THE SOVIET UNION*, TV, 86, CDN, Prod/Dir; *PROFILE OF THE AGA KHAN*, 'MAN ALIVE', TV, 86, CDN, Dir/Prod; *RETURN TO POLAND WITH SAUL RUBINEK*, TV, 86, CDN, Prod/Dir; *PORNOGRAPHY/ ETHIOPIA/ SHRINE UNDER SIEGE*, 'MAN ALIVE', TV, 84, CDN, Dir/Prod; *ONE FOOT IN HEAVEN*, TV, 84, CDN, Dir/Prod; *ALL THAT GLISTENS/ AGAINST OBLIVION*, 'MAN ALIVE', TV, 83, CDN, Dir/Prod; *THE SHROUD OF TURIN*, TV, 82, CDN, Dir/Prod; *LEAVING EARLY/ SAINTS OR SUBRERSIRES/ EL SALVADOR*, 'MAN ALIVE', TV, 81, CDN, Dir/Prod; *SOAPS: THE LOVE BUSINESS/ MISSION FROM CHINA*, 'MAN ALIVE', TV, 80, CDN, Dir/Prod; *DOES FAITH KILL?/ A LEGACY OF HATE*, 'MAN ALIVE', TV, 79, CDN, Dir/Prod; *POLITICS AND THE POPE/ LISTEN TO THE CHILDREN*, 'MAN ALIVE', TV, 78, CDN, Dir/Prod; *MUST FREEDOM FAIL*, TV, 78, CDN, Dir/Prod; *A CHURCH UNDER THE CROSS/NO EASY WALK TO FREEDOM/ FIELDS OF VISION*, 'MAN ALIVE', TV, 77, CDN, Dir/Prod; *THE GOOD LIFE*, TV, 76, CDN, Dir/Prod; *SAINTS IN OUR TIME?/ A SPACE TO BE*, 'MAN ALIVE', TV, 75, CDN, Dir/Prod.

SMITH, Clive A. - see PRODUCERS

SNOW, Michael

Isaacs Gallery, 832 Yonge St., Toronto, Ont, CAN, M4W 2H1. (416)923-7301.
Types of Production & Categories: Th Film-Dir/Ed/Wr/Cin; Th Short-Dir/Wr/Ed/ Cin.
Genres: Experimental-Th.
Biography: Born 1929, Toronto, Ontario. Ontario College of Art, 52; received an Honorary degree from Brock University, 74. Began his film career at George Dunning's Graphic Associates, Toronto, 55-56; based in New York in the 60's. Also painter, sculptor and musician; solo exhibitions world-wide. Recipient of a Toronto Arts Award, 86.
Selective Filmography: *SO IS THIS*, Th, 83, CDN, Dir/Wr/Ed/Cin; *PRESENTS*, Th, 81, CDN, Dir/Wr/Ed/Cin; *BREAKFAST/TABLE TOP DOLLY*, Th, 76-72, CDN, Dir/Wr/Ed/Cin; *RAMEAU'S NEPHEW BY DIDEROT THANX TO DENNIS YOUNG BY WILMA SHODEN*, Th, 74, CDN, Dir/Wr/Ed/Cin; *LA REGION CENTRALE*, Th, 71, CDN, Dir/Wr/Ed/Cin; *SIDE SEAT PAINTINGS SLIDES SOUND FILM*, Th, 70, USA, Dir/Wr/Ed/Cin; *BACK AND FORTH*, Th, 69, USA, Dir/Wr/Ed/Cin; *ONE SECOND IN MONTREAL*, Th, 69, USA, Dir/ Wr/Ed/Cin; *DRIPPING WATER*, Th, 69, USA, Co-Dir/Wr/Ed/Cin; *WAVELENGTH*, Th, 67, USA, Dir/Wr/Ed/Cin; *STANDARD TIME*, Th, 67, USA, Dir/Wr/Ed/Cin; *SHORT SHAVE*, Th, 65, USA, Dir/Wr/Ed/Cin; *NEW YORK EYE AND EAR CONTROL*, Th, 64, USA, Dir/Wr/Ed/Cin; *A TO Z*, Th, 56, CDN, Dir/Wr/Ed/Cin.

SOBEL, Mark

DGA, DGC, PGA. P.O. Box 8601, Universal City, CA, USA, 91608. (818)763-5428. Cinecan Film Prod., 154 Munro Blvd., Willowdale, Ont, CAN, M2P 1C8.

(cont/suite)

(416)444-9360. Eisenbach Agency, 9000 Sunset Blvd., Los Angeles, CA, USA, 90069. (213)273-0801.
Types of Production & Categories: Th Film-Dir/Prod; TV Film-Dir/Prod.
Genres: Drama-Th&TV; Action-Th.
Biography: Born in Canada; USA resident. Chicago Int'l Film Fest. Award for *CHRISSY AND ME.*
Selective Filmography: *SWEET REVENGE,* Th, 86, USA, Dir; *ACCESS CODE,* Th, 84, USA, Dir/Prod; *WELCOME HOME JELLY BEAN,* TV, 84, USA, Pro Exec; *LOOKING GOOD,* 'HERE'S BOOMER', TV, 81, USA, Dir; *CHRISSY AND ME,* TV, 80, USA, Dir/Prod; *'HARPER VALLEY PTA',* TV, 80, USA, Assoc Prod; *MON AME,* TV, 75, CDN, Dir/Prod.

SPRINGBETT, David

72 Coolming Rd., Toronto, Ont, CAN, M6J 3E9. (416)536-8496. Asterisk Productions, 110 Spadina Ave., #703, Toronto, Ont, CAN, M5V 2K4. (416)868-1175.
Types of Production & Categories: Th Short-Prod; TV Film-Dir/Prod; TV Video-Dir/Prod.
Genres: Documentary-Th&TV; Educational-Th&TV; Children's-Th&TV.
Biography: Born 1944; Canadian; educated at University of Manitoba. Specializes in documentary production in developing countries and difficult environments. Awards include Blue Ribbon, Red Ribbons (3) from American Film Festival; Bronze Chris Award, Audubon Environmental Film Festival.
Selective Filmography: *ROOTS OF HUNGER, ROOTS OF CHANGE,* TV, 85, USA, Co-Prod/Dir; *MICHAEL GETS WATER/WOMEN & WATER,* Cm, 84/83, USA, Dir/Ed; *WHAT DO YOU DO WHEN...,* Cm, 83, CDN, Dir/Ed; *OLD HOUSE, NEW HOUSE,* ED, 82, CDN, Prod; *'WORLD'S CHILDREN'* (Dir-7 eps), (13 eps), TV, 80/79, CDN, Co-Prod; *BLACK ICE,* Th, 79, CDN, Prod.

SPRY, Robin

ACTRA, APFVQ, ARRFQ, DGA, DGC. 5330 Durocher, Montreal, Que, CAN, H2V 3Y1. (514)277-1503. Telescene Productions Ltd., 360 Place Royale, Montreal, Que, CAN, H2Y 2V1. (514)288 1638.
Types of Production & Categories: Th Film-Dir/Prod/Wr; TV Film-Dir/Prod.
Genres: Drama-Th; Comedy-Th; Action-Th; Documentary-Th&TV.
Biography: Born 1939, Toronto, Ontario. Attended Oxford University and London School of Economics where he headed a film unit. Joined NFB, 65; directed first feature, 68-69; has directed numerous commercials in both French and English
Selective Filmography: *KEEPING TRACK,* Th, 85, CDN, Dir/Co-Prod/Co-Wr; *STRESS AND EMOTIONS,* 'THE BRAIN', TV, 84/83, CDN, Dir/Wr/Prod; *'THE JOURNAL'* (sev seg), TV, 83/82, CDN, Dir/Prod; *TO SERVE THE COMING AGE,* ED, 83, CDN, Dir/Wr; *WINNIE,* TV, 81, CDN, Dir; *SUZANNE,* Th, 80, CDN, Dir; *DON'T FORGET/JE ME SOUVIENS/DRYING UP THE STREETS,* 'FOR THE RECORD', TV, 79/78, CDN, Dir; *ONE MAN,* Th, 77, CDN, Dir/Co-Wr (**CFA**); *FACE,* Th, 75, CDN, Co-Prod/Ed/Dir (**CFA**); *DOWNHILL,* Th, 73, CDN, Dir/Co-Prod; *REACTION: A PORTRAIT OF A SOCIETY IN CRISIS,* Th, 73, CDN, Dir/Co-Prod; *ACTION: THE OCTOBER CRISIS OF 1970* (LES EVENEMENTS D'OCTOBRE 1970), Th, 70, CDN, Dir/ Co-Prod (**CFA**); *PROLOGUE,* Th, 69, CDN, Dir; *FLOWERS ON A ONE WAY STREET,* Th, 67, CDN, Dir/Wr; *RIDE FOR YOUR LIFE,* Th, 67, CDN, Dir/Wr; *ILLEGAL ABORTION,* Th, 66, CDN, Dir/Wr; *LEVEL 4350,* Th, 66, CDN, Dir/ Wr; *THE MINER,* Th, 66, CDN, Dir/Wr; *CHANGE IN THE MARITIMES,* Th, 66, CDN, Dir/Wr; *YOU DON'T BACK DOWN,* Th, 65, CDN, Wr.

STEELE, Fraser

Stainless Productions Ltd., P.O. Box 151, Stn. J, Toronto, Ont, CAN, M4J 4Y1. (416)465-4906.

(cont/suite)

Types of Production & Categories: TV Film-Dir/Prod/Wr; TV Video-Dir/Prod/Wr.
Genres: Drama-TV; Documentary-TV; Educational-TV.
Biography: Born 1949, Montreal, Quebec. Honours B.A., Film and English Literature, Sir Geoege Williams University. Directing and producing since 77.
Selective Filmography: *'THE FIFTH ESTATE'* (2 seg), TV, 86, CDN, Dir/Prod; *'AUTOMATING THE OFFICE'* (9 eps), TV, 85, CDN, Dir; *'FUTUREWORK'* (10 eps), TV, 84, CDN, Dir; *RODGERS AND SALAZAR,* 'WORLD'S GREATEST ATHLETES', TV, 83, CDN, Dir/Prod/Wr; *INSIDE TV NEWS,* TV, 82, CDN, Dir/Prod; *'TURNING POINT'* (8 eps), TV, 81, CDN, Dir/Prod; *'BEYOND THE FRIDGE'* (13 eps), TV, 78/77, CDN, Prod; *KING KONCERT: THE BOFFO WORLD OF DONALD K. DONALD,* TV, 77, CDN, Dir/Prod/Wr; *THE BATTLE FOR MONTREAL,* TV, 77, CDN, Dir/Prod.

STERN, Sandor

DGA, PGA, WGAw. 474 Peck Dr., Beverly Hills, CA, USA, 90212. (213)556-0788. Jamson Productions Inc., 9116 1/2 Pico Blvd., Los Angeles, CA, USA, 90035. (213)275-0180. Broder, Kurland & Webb, 8439 Sunset Blvd., #402, Los Angeles, CA, USA, 90069. (213)656-9262.
Types of Production & Categories: Th Film-Wr; TV Film-Dir/Prod/Wr; TV Video-Dir/Wr.
Genres: Drama-Th&TV; Comedy-Th&TV; Variety-TV; Horror-Th&TV.
Biography: Born 1936, Timmins, Ontario. B.A. and M.D., University of Toronto. Practiced medicine for 5 years in Toronto. Has written, directed TV movies, series since 60. Winner of NAACP image Award (80), Best Screeplay for *FAST BREAK.*
Selective Filmography: *ASSASSIN,* TV, 86, USA, Dir/Wr/Exec Prod; *JOHN AND YOKO: A LOVE STORY,* TV, 85, USA/GB, Dir/Wr; *PASSIONS,* TV, 84, USA, Dir/Co-Wr; *CUTTER TO HOUSTON,* TV, 83, USA, Dir/Wr; *MEMORIES NEVER DIE,* TV, 82, USA, Dir/Co-Wr; *MUGGABLE MARY: STREET COP,* TV, 81, USA, Dir/Wr; *TO FIND MY SON,* TV, 80, USA, Wr; *THE SEEDING OF SARAH BURNS,* TV, 79, USA, Dir/Co-Wr; *THE AMITYVILLE HORROR,* Th, 78, USA, Scr; *FAST BREAK,* Th, 78, USA, Wr; *KILLER ON BOARD,* TV, 77, USA, Prod/Wr; *RED ALERT,* TV, 76, USA, Wr.

STERN, Steven

DGA, DGC, WGAw. 4321 Clear Valley Dr., Encino, CA, USA, 91436. (818)788-3607. Elliot Webb, Broder/Kurland/Webb, Sunset Blvd., Los Angeles, CA, USA, 90069. (213)656-9262.
Types of Production & Categories: Th Film-Dir/Wr; TV Film-Dir/Prod/Wr.
Genres: Drama-Th; Comedy-Th; Variety-TV; Action-Th.
Biography: Born 1937, Timmins, Ontario. Graduate of Ryerson Polytechnical Institute, Radio & TV Arts. Winner of over 40 writing and directing awards for commercials: Cannes, Venice, New York, etc.. *NEITHER BY DAY NOR BY NIGHT* won the Grand Peace Prize, European Critics Award, Int'l Writers Guild Award.
Selective Filmography: *MANY HAPPY RETURNS,* TV, 86, USA, Dir/Prod; *ROLLING VENGEANCE,* Th, 86, USA, Dir/Prod; *TERROR IN THE SKY,* TV, 85, USA, Dir; *YOUNG AGAIN,* TV, 85, USA, Dir/Wr/Prod; *THE PARK IS MINE,* TV, 84, CDN/USA, Dir; *THE UNDERGRADS,* TV, 84, USA, Dir/Prod; *OBSESSIVE LOVE,* TV, 84, USA, Dir; *GETTING PHYSICAL,* TV, 84, USA, Dir; *DRAW!,* TV, 83, CDN/USA, Dir; *UNCOMMON LOVE,* TV, 83, USA, Dir; *DEVIL AND MAX DEVLIN,* Th, 83, USA, Dir; *A SMALL KILLING,* TV, 82, USA, Dir; *PORTRAIT OF A SHOWGIRL,* TV, 82, USA, Dir; *MAZES AND MONSTERS,* TV, 82, USA, Dir; *AMBUSH MURDERS,* TV, 81, USA, Dir; *FORBIDDEN LOVE,* TV, 81, USA, Dir; *PROFESSIONAL DATE,* TV, 81, USA, Dir; *YOUNG LOVE FIRST LOVE,* TV, 80, USA, Dir; *MIRACLE ON ICE,* TV, 80, USA, Dir; *ANATOMY OF A SEDUCTION,* TV, 80, USA, Dir; *FAST*

(cont/suite)

FRIENDS, TV, 80, USA, Dir; *RUNNING*, Th, 79, CDN, Dir/Wr; *THE YOUNG DOCTORS*, TV, 79, USA, Dir; *GHOST OF FLIGHT 401*, TV, 78, USA, Dir; *GETTING MARRIED*, TV, 78, USA, Dir; *ESCAPE FROM BOGEN COUNTY*, TV, 78, USA, Dir; *'JESSICA NOVAK'*, TV, 78, USA, Dir; *McCLOUD*, TV, 77, USA, Dir; *'QUINCY'* (pilot), TV, 77, USA, Dir; *'SERPICO'* (3 eps), TV, 77, USA, Dir.

STEWART, Gordon

ATPD. 157 Forest Hill Rd., Toronto, Ont, CAN, M5P 2N2. (416)482-1733. CBC, Box 500, Station A, Toronto, Ont, CAN, M5W 1E6. (416)975-6680.
Types of Production & Categories: TV Film-Dir/Prod/Wr; TV Video-Prod.
Genres: Documentary-TV.
Biography: Born 1940, London, England; Canadian citizen. Former reporter: newspaper, TV and radio in Canada, US, Africa and Europe.
Selective Filmography: *GREAT BALLS OF FIRE*, TV, 86, CDN, Dir/Prod/Wr; *MISTRESS TO THE MOB*, TV, 86, CDN, Dir/Prod/Wr; *WAKE UP, DOC/FAT CITY/THE WRIGHT STUFF/THE INFORMER*, 'THE FIFTH ESTATE', TV, 85-84, CDN, Dir/Prod/Wr; *MEGA MALL*, TV, 85, CDN, Dir/Prod/Wr; *SHRINKING FREUD/HIT MAN/TRAITOR IN THE MOUNTIES*, 'THE FIFTH ESTATE', TV, 84-82, CDN, Dir/Prod/Wr; *ALCOHOLIC HEAVEN/THE TICO WAY/MANDELA/UPSTAIRS DOWNSTAIRS*, 'THE FIFTH ESTATE', TV, 82/81, CDN, Dir/Prod/Wr; *ZAPPED/GETTING LANDED/BAD FRIENDS/ SURVIVAL*, 'THE FIFTH ESTATE', TV, 81/80, CDN, Dir/Prod/Wr; *HEBRON*, 'THE FIFTH ESTATE', TV, 81, CDN, Wr; *GET UP AND GO/CANADIAN BRASS!/RAGE AGAINST THE SHAH*, 'THE FIFTH ESTATE', TV, 79/78, CDN, Dir/Prod/Wr; *RANGER'S GAMBLE/PLANE LANGUAGE/ SHAHANSHAH/DEATH AT 100 BELOW*, 'THE FIFTH ESTATE', TV, 78-75, CDN, Dir/Prod/Wr; *AIRLINES AT WAR*, TV, 77, CDN, Prod/Dir/Wr; *BLACK TIDE RISING*, 'ADRIENNE AT LARGE', TV, 74, CDN, Dir/Prod/Wr; *OIL AND ISLAM - THE SAUDI EXPLOSION*, 'TAKE 30', TV, 74, CDN, Dir/Prod/ Wr; *MAN IN THE STORM*, 'MAN ALIVE', TV, 72, CDN, Dir/Prod/Wr; *PROFILE: HELEN SUZMAN/BABY AND THE BUBBLE*, 'TAKE 30', TV, 71, CDN, Dir/Prod/Wr; *TANZANIA. GREAT BLACK HOPE*, 'NEWSMAGAZINE', TV, 69, CDN, Dir/Prod/Wr.

STOLLER, Bryan M.

B.M.S. Film Productions, 4660 Kester Ave., Ste. 225, Sherman Oaks, CA, USA, 91403. (818)986-5588. Lee Dinstman, Contemp. Korman Artists, 132 Lasky Dr., Beverly Hills, CA, USA, 90212. (213)278-8250.
Types of Production & Categories: Th Film-Dir/Wr; TV Film-Dir.
Genres: Drama-Th; Comedy-TV; Science Fiction-Th; Documentary-Th.
Biography: Born 1960, Peterborough, Ontario; attended the American Film Institute as a director fellow; won 11 international film awards including Gold Award, Bronze Award, Houston Film Fest..
Selective Filmography: *THE BITTEREST PILL*, 'TALES FROM THE DARK SIDE', TV, 86, USA, Dir; *HANDS ACROSS AMERICA* (3 seg), TV, 86, USA, Dir; *THE FROG PRINCE*, 'TV BLOOPERS & PRACTICAL JOKES', TV, 85, USA, Dir/Wr/Ed/Prod; *THE SHADOW OF MICHAEL/ENCOUNTER WITH AN E.T./DON'T WALK/HYDRANTS*, 'FOUL-UPS, BLEEPS & BLUNDERS', TV, 84, USA, Dir/Wr/Ed/Prod; *INCREDIBLE BULK/THE KARATE GUY/*, 'FOUL-UPS, BLEEPS & BLUNDERS', TV, 84, USA, Dir/Wr/Ed/Prod; *GREENLIGHT*, MV, 84, USA, Dir/Wr/Ed; *STORYTIME*, TV, 83, USA, Dir/Wr; *JUST LIKE MAGIC*, TV, 82, USA, Dir/Wr; *THE MAKING OF SLAPSTICK*, TV, 82, USA, Dir/Wr; *JUST JOKING*, TV, 82, USA, Dir/Wr/Ed/Prod.

STONEMAN, John - see CINEMATOGRAPHERS

STREET, Bill

937 Parthia Crescent, Mississauga, Ont, CAN, L4Y 2K9. (416)277-2685.
Types of Production & Categories: TV Film-Dir.
Genres: Documentary-TV; Educational-Th&TV; Sports-TV.
Biography: Born Ottawa, Ontario. Sound department, Briston Films Ltd., Montreal, 55-59, Chetwynd Films Ltd., Toronto, 60; picture editing, 62; became director/producer, 65.
Selective Filmography: *ON CAMERA '81 AND '82*, In, 83-80, CDN, Dir; *SOME OF THOSE NEWCOMERS*, TV, 82, CDN, Dir; *ON COMPUTER AND TELEVISION*, In, 80, CDN, Ed; *SMALL IS BEAUTIFUL* (pilot), TV, 80, CDN, Ed; *I'VE GOT A STORY* (pilot), TV, 79, CDN, Dir; *RAVAGES OF DAVID*, TV, 79, CDN, Ed; *GREY CUP '77*, TV, 77, CDN, Ed (**CFTA**); *CANADIAN PARACHUTE JUMPING CHAMPIONSHIP*, TV, 76, CDN, Dir; *HERITAGE CANADA*, TV, 75, CDN, Dir; *MARCIA LONGA*, TV, 75, CDN, Dir; *THE STANLEY CUP* (3 times), TV, 70-60, CDN, Dir; *'INSTRUCTIONAL HOCKEY'* (9 eps), ED, 69, CDN, Dir; *LIFE IS WORTH THE LIVING*, In, 67, CDN, Dir/Prod (**CFA**); *GRAND PRIX CANADA*, TV, 67, CDN, Dir; *PLAYER'S 200* (SPORTS CAR RACING), TV, 65-62, CDN, Dir.

SUISSA, Danièle J.

APFVQ. 3638 ave. Laval, Montréal, Qué, CAN, H2X 3C9. (514)284-2026.
3 Thèmes Inc, 3640 ave. Laval, Montréal, Qué, CAN, H2X 3C9. (514)284-2026.
Types of Production & Categories: Th Film-Dir; Th Short-Dir; TV Film-Dir; TV Video-Dir/Prod.
Genres: Drama-Th&TV; Commercials-TV.
Biography: Born 1940, Casablanca, Morocco; Canadian citizen, in Canada since 68. Paris Conservatory of Dramatic Arts, 60-62. Training with the BBC, multiple camera direction, 80. Creation of 3 Thèmes Inc., 81. President, APFVQ, 83-84. Has directed over 200 commercials; won a Coq d'Or; directed 30 theatre plays (French, English).
Selective Filmography: *THE MORNING MAN*, Th, 85, CDN, Dir; *EVANGELINE DEUSSE/DIVINE SARAH*, 'OF LOVE AND THEATRE', TV, 84, CDN, Dir/Prod; *KATE MORRIS, VICE-PRESIDENT*, 'FOR THE RECORD', TV, 83, CDN, Dir; *'JUDGE'* (6 eps), TV, 83-81, CDN, Dir; *HEY JO*, TV, 75, CDN, Dir; *SUMMER MORNINGS*, TV, 74, CDN, Dir.

SULLIVAN, Kevin

ACTRA, DGC. Sullivan Films, 17 Madison Ave., Toronto, Ont, CAN, M5R 2S2. (416)928-2982.
Types of Production & Categories: Th Short-Dir/Prod/Wr; TV Film-Dir/Prod/Wr.
Genres: Drama-Th&TV.
Biography: Born 1955, Toronto, Ontario; bilingual; B.Sc. (Honours), University of Toronto. Owner of Sullivan Films Inc.. *MEGAN CARIE*, winner, Canadian Short Film Showcase. *ANNE OF GREEN GABLES* won the Golden Gate Award (San Francisco) and the Emily Award (American Film Fest.).
Selective Filmography: *ANNE OF GREEN GABLES - THE SEQUEL* (mini-series), TV, 86, CDN/USA, Exec Prod/Prod/Dir/Wr; *ANNE OF GREEN GABLES*, TV, 85, CDN, Dir/Co-T'Play/Co-Prod (**EMMY**); *WILD PONY*, TV, 83, CDN, Dir/T'play/Co-Prod (**CFTA**); *KRIEGHOFF*, TV, 81, CDN, Dir/Prod/Wr; *MEGAN CARIE*, Th, 80, CDN, Dir; *THE FIR TREE*, TV, 79, CDN, Dir/Prod/Wr.

SUTHERLAND, Neil - see PRODUCERS

SUTHERLAND, Paul

ACTRA, DGC. Quantum Creative Ltd., 50 Vicora Linkway, Don Mills, Ont, CAN, M3C 1B1. (416)423-7070. Characters, 150 Carlton St., 2nd Fl., Toronto, Ont, CAN. (416)964-8522.
Types of Production & Categories: TV Film-Dir/Prod; TV Video-Dir/Prod.
Genres: Drama-TV; Documentary-TV; Educational-TV; Children's-TV.
Biography: Born 1930, Toronto, Ontario. Educated at University of Toronto, Ryerson. Experience: CBC, Riverbank Productions, Foster Advertising (copywriter, producer, director), IBM Canada (industrials); video disk and commercials for interactive kiosks; Quantum Creative Ltd.. Has won IBA outstanding Achievement Award.

SWAN, James

ATPD. 136 Waverley Rd., Toronto, Ont, CAN, M4L 3T3. (416)690-4572. CBC, Box 500, Station A, Toronto, Ont, CAN. (416)975-7164.
Types of Production & Categories: TV Film-Dir/Prod; TV Video-Dir/Prod.
Genres: Drama-TV; Comedy-TV; Musical-TV; Horror-TV.
Biography: Born 1941, Gainsborough, Great Britain; British-Canadian citizenship. Fifteen years of stage experience as performer, director, designer, stage manager (mainly in England); dialect coach, story editor, CBC.
Selective Filmography: *9B,* TV, 85, CDN, Dir/Prod; *AND MILES TO GO,* TV, 85, CDN, Prod; *THE JOB,* TV, 84, CDN, Dir; *THE REGIMENT,* TV, 84, CDN, Dir; *'HOME FIRES'* (8 eps), TV, 83, CDN, Prod; *ONCE,* TV, 80, CDN, Prod; *'A GIFT TO LAST'* (Dir eps #15-18-21), (18 eps), TV, 80-78, CDN, Assoc Prod.

SYMCOX, Peter

AR. 220 Olivier Ave., #307, Westmount, Que, CAN, H3Z 2C5. (514)937-8362. Radio-Canada, 1400 est, bd. Dorchester, Montreal, Que, CAN, H2L 2M2. (514) 285-2388. Robert Lombardo Assoc. Inc., 61 West 62nd, New York, NY, USA, 10023. (212)586-4453.
Types of Production & Categories: TV Video-Dir/Prod.
Genres: Musical-Th&TV.
Biography: Born 1925, England, Canadian citizen; languages: French, English, Italian. M.A. in English Literature, Oxford University. Stage actor for opera in Canada, USA and Central America. President, International Jury, Golden Prague TV Festival, Czechoslovakia, 80. Currently senior music producer/ director for French and English networks (CBC). Teaches master's classes in stage directing for opera and stage deportment for singers; articles published in 'The Opera Quarterly', 'Opera Canada', 'Montreal Star'.
Selective Filmography: *SOIREE VIENNOISE,* TV, 85, CDN, Dir/Prod; *PORTRAIT OF MARIA PELLEGRINI,* TV, 83, CDN, Dir/Prod; *PORTRAIT OF JOSEPH ROULEAU,* TV, 84, CDN, Dir/Prod; *MUSIC FOR PIANOS,* TV, 84, CDN, Dir/Prod; *ANDRE LAPLANTE,* TV, 84, CDN, Dir/Prod; *DUOS D'AMOUR,* TV, 84, CDN, Dir/Prod; *LA VOIX HUMAINE,* TV, 83, CDN, Dir/ Prod; *PORTRAIT OF LOUIS QUILICO,* TV, 83, CDN, Dir/Prod; *JEROME HINES: PORTRAIT,* TV, 83, CDN, Dir/Prod; *WAGNER: DIE VALKYRIE,* TV, 82, CDN, Dir/Prod; *MADAMA BUTTERFLY,* TV, 81, CDN, Dir/Prod; *MACBETH,* TV, 79, CDN, Dir/Prod; *THE BURNING FIERY FURNACE,* TV, 78, CDN, Dir/Prod; *MAUREEN FORRESTER/ ROBERTA PETERS / GRACE BUMBRY,* 'PORTRAIT', TV, 77, CDN, Dir/Prod; *SHIRLEY VERRETT/ PIERRE DUVAL,* 'PORTRAIT', TV, 77, CDN, Dir/Prod; *'LES BEAUX DIMANCHES'* (sev eps), TV, 76, CDN, Dir/Prod; *THE WORLD YOUTH ORCHESTRA: 20th ANNIVERSARY,* 'JEUNESSES MUSICALES', TV, 65, CDN, Dir/Prod.

TABORSKY, Vaclav

DGC. 56 Church St., Willowdale, Ont, CAN, M2N 4E9. (416)222-3385. York University, Film/Video Dept., 4700 Keele St., North York, Ont, CAN, M3J 1P3. (416)667-3729.
Types of Production & Categories: Th Film-Dir/Wr; Th Short-Dir/Wr; TV Film-Dir/Wr.
Genres: Comedy-Th&TV; Documentary-Th; Educational-TV.
Biography: Born 1928, Prague, Czechoslovakia; Canadian. Graduate of FAMU. Directed, wrote feature films, TV comedies, 80 documentaries and educational films. Won the Golden Lion, Venice for *MUD COVERED CITY*; Silver Lion, Venice for *ESCAPE IN THE WIND.* Currently Associate Professor, Film Dept., York University.
Selective Filmography: *MIRACULOUS PUZZLE,* Th, 67, CZ, Dir/Prod/Co-Wr; *ESCAPE IN THE WIND,* Th, 65, CZ, Dir/Prod/Co-Wr; *MUD COVERED CITY,* Th, 63, CZ, Dir/Wr.

TAKACS, Tibor

DGC. New Frontier Films Inc., 618 Adelaide St. W., Toronto, Ont, CAN, M6J 1A9. (416)361-5798. Donald Kopaloff, 1930 Century Park W., Los Angeles, CA, USA, 90067. (213)203-8430.
Types of Production & Categories: Th Film-Dir/Prod/Ed; Th Short-Dir/Prod/Ed.
Genres: Drama-Th&TV; Science Fiction-Th&TV; Horror-Th&TV.
Biography: Born 1954, Budapest, Hungary; Canadian citizen. *SNOW* won an award at Chicago and was the Official Entry at Berlin Film Festival.
Selective Filmography: *THE GATE,* Th, 86, CDN, Dir; *SNOW,* Th, 82, CDN, Co-Prod/Ed/Dir; *THE TOMORROW MAN,* TV, 79, CDN, Dir/Co-Prod/Ed **(CFTA)**; *METAL MESSIAH,* Th, 78, CDN, Dir/Co-Prod/Ed.

TEODORESCO, Marius

ARRQ. 2100 Côte Vertu, Ville St-Laurent, Qué, CAN, H4R 1N7. (514)337-5952. Radio-Québec, 800 rue Fullum, Montréal, Qué, CAN, H2K 3L7. (514)521-2424.
Types de production et Catégories: TV film-Réal; TV vidéo-Réal.
Types d'oeuvres: Documentaire-TV; Education-TV.
Curriculum vitae: Né en 1925, Bucarest, Roumanie; citoyenneté canadienne; parle français, roumain et italien. Etudes: Institut d'Art Cinématographique, Bucarest. A réalisé 3 longs métrages en Roumanie. Diplôme pour l'Excellence de la Création, Festival International de Chicago pour le film *POUR UN CERTAIN SOURIRE,* 75.
Filmographie sélective: *CHANTAL GAGNON/DOMINIQUE BERTRAND/ MONIQUE MERCIER/ROBERT LAPALME,* 'L'UNIVERS DE...', TV, 86/85, CDN, Réal; *PAUL LAYONNET/FRANCOIS BARBEAU,* 'L'UNIVERS DE...', TV, 85, CDN, Réal; *UNE FENETRE SUR L'EDEN,* TV, 84, CDN, Réal; *TOUT EST FUTUR,* TV, 83, CDN, Réal; *MICHELINE BEAUCHEMIN/JACQUES DE TONNACOUR/NAIM KHATAM,* 'VISAGE', TV, 82, CDN, Réal; *GUIDO MOLINARI,* 'PLANETE', TV, 82, CDN, Réal; *L'ETERNITE DEVANT SOI,* TV, 81, CDN, Réal; *LE CARDINAL LEGER/PIERRE GAVREAU/ANNE HEBERT,* 'VISAGE', TV, 80/79, CDN, Réal; *FERNAND LEDUC/LUDMILLA CHIRIAEFF,* 'VISAGE', TV, 79, CDN, Réal; *DE PINOCCHIO A G.I.JOE,* TV, 76, CDN, Réal; *LE SOLEIL D'AILLEURS,* TV, 75, CDN, Réal; *'CA N'A PLUS L'AIR D'UNE ECOLE'* (2 eps), TV, 74, CDN, Réal; *'COMMENT RACONTER CES CHOSES?'* (3 eps), TV, 74, CDN, Réal; *'SI ON S'Y METTAIT'* (3 eps), TV, 73, CDN, Réal; *LA SEVE QUI BOUT,* TV, 73, CDN, Réal; *VALSE-HESITATION,* TV, 73, CDN, Réal; *POUR UN CERTAIN SOURIRE,* TV, 73, CDN, Réal; *LE NOUVEAU MODELE,* TV, 73, CDN, Réal; *LE PARAVENT,* TV, 73, CDN, Réal; *LE VENT DANS LES VOILES,* TV, 73, CDN, Réal; *PARTICIPE PRESENT,* TV, 73, CDN, Réal.

You work hard to be the best...
Sometimes you achieve it.
Congratulations to all
Genie winners.

PRIX GENIE AWARDS
Academy of Canadian Cinema & Television
Académie canadienne du cinéma
et de la télévision

TERRY, Chris

DGC. 604 King St.W., Toronto, Ont, CAN, M5V 1M6. (416)368-9805. The Imaginators, P.O. Box 1061, Stn. F, Toronto, Ont, CAN, M4Y 2T7. (416)922-1600.
Types of Production & Categories: TV Film-Dir/DOP; TV Video-Dir/DOP.
Genres: Drama-TV; Musical-TV; Documentary-TV; Children's-TV.
Biography: Born 1952, Upminster, Essex, U.K.; Canadian citizen. Honours B.F.A., York University, 73. Has taught extensively at Ontario College of Art (Film instructor); owns small production facility. Won Heinz Music Video Award (Video Culture 85) for *PERFECT WORLD, HAVE A GOOD LOOK.*
Selective Filmography: *'VID KIDS'* (13 eps), TV, 86/85, CDN, Dir; *'QTV'* (2 eps), TV, 86/85, CDN, Dir; *OPEN UP THE SKIES/WITH A LITTLE HELP FROM MY FRIENDS*, MV, 85, CDN, Dir; *HANLAN'S POINT/HANDSOME NED*, MV, 85, CDN, DOP; *MAKE ME DO ANYTHING YOU WANT/HIDING FROM LOVE*, MV, 85, CDN, Dir; *HAVE A GOOD LOOK/SOMEONE TO HOLD/ HEAVY MENTAL BREAKDOWN*, MV, 85/84, CDN, Prod/Dir/DOP; *EVIL INVADERS*, MV, 85, CDN, Dir/DOP; *NEON: AN ELECTRIC MEMOIR*, TV, 84, CDN, Co-Cin; *ROGER WHITTAKER*, Cm, 84, CDN, Dir; *NEW GIRL NOW*, MV, 84, CDN, Dir/Co-Prod; *PUPPY HEAVEN*, In, 84, CDN/USA, Dir/Prod/ DOP; *MUSKOKA, A LOOK BACK*, TV, 83, CDN, DOP/Assoc Prod; *BALLAD OF HANDSOME NED*, MV, 83, CDN, DOP; *THE CLOG*, TV, 83, , Prod/Dir/DOP; *THAT KIND OF MAN*, MV, 83, CDN, Prod/Dir; *PLEASURE CARRIAGES*, In, 83, CDN, Prod/Dir/Cin; *AN EPISODE UNDER THE REIGN OF TERROR*, TV, 82, CDN, Prod/Dir/DOP/Wr; *FREELOADING*, Th, 81, CDN, Co-Dir; *PERU, THE HIDDEN EMPIRE*, TV, 80, CDN, Prod/Dir/Ed/Cin.

TESSIER, Jean

ARRFQ. 919 ave. Cartier, Québec, Qué, CAN, G1R 2R8. (418)522-3675. Spirafilm, 56 rue St-Pierre, Québec, Qué, CAN, G1K 4A1. (418)694-0786.
Types de production et Catégories: l métrage-Réal/Sc/Cam/Prod; TV vidéo-Prod.
Types d'oeuvres: Drame-C; Documentaire-C&TV; Education-C&TV; Enfants-C&TV.
Curriculum vitae: Né en 1950; bilingue. Majeure en sociologie, mineure en Etudes cinématographiques, Université Laval, Québec, 77; Maitrise en Création littéraire/Cinéma, 83.
Filmographie sélective: *EN DERNIERES PAGES*, C, 83, CDN, Réal/Sc/Prod/Cam; *MELODIE, MA GRAND-MERE*, TV, 83, CDN, Prod; *C'EST PAS MON GENRE*, TV, 81, CDN, Prod.

TETREAULT, Roger

AR. 2145 Barclay, Montréal, Qué, CAN, H3S 1J4. (514)738-3438.
Types de production et Catégories: c métrage-Réal; TV film-Réal; TV vidéo-Réal.
Types d'oeuvres: Drame-TV; Documentaire-C&TV; Education-TV; Enfants-TV.
Curriculum vitae: Né en 1941, Farnham, Québec; bilingue. Baccalauréat ès Arts; classe de réalisation, Institut des Hautes Etudes Cinématographiques, Paris; études musicales (piano), physique nucléaire et archéologie.
Filmographie sélective: *'LES ENFANTS MAL-AIMES'* (3 eps), TV, 84, CDN, Réal; *'VIVRE EN PRISON'* (3 eps), TV, 80, CDN, Réal; *'LA SCIENCE EN QUESTION'* (30 eps), TV, 78/77, CDN, Réal; *A L'AUTRE BOUT DE MON AGE*, C, 75, CDN, Réal.

THEBERGE, André

SGCQ, 335 boul.de Maisonneuve est, Montréal, Qué, CAN, H2X 1K1. (514)844-1954.
Types de production et Catégories: 1 métrage-Réal/Sc/Mont; c métrage-Réal/Sc/ Mont; TV film-Réal/Sc/Mont.

(cont/suite)

Types d'oeuvres: Drame-C; Documentaire-C&TV.
Curriculum vitae: Né en 1945, Kamouraska, Québec. Bac. ès Arts, Collège de Saint-Laurent, 65; Licence ès Lettres, Université de Montréal, 69 (Certificat d'Etudes Cinématographiques). Langues: français, anglais, allemand, danois. Présentement Directeur de l'aide à la création et à la production, Société Générale du Cinéma du Québec.
Filmographie sélective: *LA PETITE NUIT,* C, 83, CDN, Réal; *CA PEUT PAS ETRE L'HIVER, ON N'A MEME PAS EU D'ETE,* C, 80, CDN, Mont; *LE RESEAU,* C, 79, CDN, Mont/Mont son; *LES QUAIS,* C, 79, CDN, Mont/Mont son; *LA NUIT DES CLAIRONS,* C, 79, CDN, Mont; *LA BELLE APPARENCE,* C, 78, CDN, Mont/Mont son; *JEANNE MOREAU,* 'VISAGE', TV, 78, CDN, Sc; *PAPETERIE SAINT-GILLES,* C, 78, CDN, Mont; *LA QUADRILLE ACADIENNE,* C, 78, CDN, Mont/Mont son; *QUICKSILVER,* 'TELEPLAY', TV, 76, CDN, Réal/Sc; *CLOSE CALL,* 'PEEP SHOW', TV, 75, CDN, Réal; *UN FAIT ACCOMPLI,* 'TOUL'MONDE PARLE FRANCAIS', C, 74, CDN, Réal/Sc; *LA DERNIERE NEIGE,* 'TOUL'MONDE PARLE FRANCAIS', C, 73, CDN, Réal/Sc/Mont; *L'ACCIDENT,* C, 73, CDN, Sc; *LES ALLEES DE LA TERRE,* C, 72, CDN, Réal/Sc; *QUESTION DE VIE,* C, 69, CDN, Réal/Sc/Mont; *TERELEUR,* C, 67, CDN, Réal/Co sc/Mont.

THEOBALD, Geoff

4391 Capilano Rd., North Vancouver, BC, CAN, V7R 4J8. (604)987-2518.
Types of Production & Categories: TV Video-Dir/Prod.
Genres: Drama-TV; Comedy-TV; Variety-TV; Game Shows-TV.
Biography: Born 1934, British Columbia. Stage and TV actor before 60, still active as voice-over narrator. Vice President and Creative Director of 2 advertising agencies; writer, producer, director of award winning film and video commercials.
Selective Filmography: *'PITFALL'* (sev eps), TV, 81/80, CDN, Dir; *'LET'S MAKE A DEAL'* (sev eps), TV, 81/80, CDN, Dir; *'STAN KANN'* (sev eps), TV, 79-77, CDN, Dir/Prod; *HANDEL'S MESSIAH,* TV, 79, CDN, Dir; *'COSMOPOLITAN KITCHEN'* (sev eps), TV, 77, CDN, Dir; *CELEBRITY REVUE,* TV, 76, CDN, Dir/Pro Spv; *'MANTRAP'* (sev eps), TV, 71/70, CDN, Dir; *'WINDFALL'* (sev eps), TV, 70-63, CDN, Dir; *WORKSHOP 30,* TV, 65, CDN, Dir/Prod; *TIDES AND TRAILS,* TV, 60, CDN, Dir/Prod; *AUDITION,* TV, 60, CDN, Dir/Prod.

THIBAULT, Gilles

AR. 3218 Cherrier, Ile Bizard, Qué, CAN, H9C 1E2. (514)620-1186. Radio-Canada, 1400 blvd. Dorchester est, Montréal, Qué, CAN, H2L 2M2. (514)285-3242.
Types de production et Catégories: TV film-Réal; TV vidéo-Réal.
Types d'oeuvres: Documentaire-TV; Nouvelles-TV.
Curriculum vitae: Né en 1937, Hull, Québec; bilingue. Etudes: Académie de Lasalle, Ottawa, Université d'Ottawa. Vice-président national de l'Association des Réalisateurs de Radio-Canada. Prix Wilderness pour la série *DOSSIER.*
Filmographie sélective: *SOMMET ECONOMIQUE* (6 ém), TV, 85-78, CDN, Réal/Coord pro; *CONGRES POLITIQUES* (12 ém), TV, 85-73, CDN, Réal/Coord pro; *CONFERENCE DES PREMIERS MINISTRES,* TV, 85-73, CDN, Réal/Coord pro; *BUDGET FEDERAL,* TV, 85-74, CDN, Réal/Coord pro; *VISITE DU PAPE,* TV, 84/83, CDN, Co réal; *ELECTIONS* (12 ém), TV, 84-72, CDN, Réal/Coord pro; *VISITE DU PRESIDENT REAGAN,* TV, 84, CDN, Réal/Coord pro; *VISITE ROYALE* (6 ém), TV, 83-76, CDN, Réal/Coord pro; *CONSTITUTION A WESTMINSTER,* TV, 82, CDN, Réal; *COMMISSION PEPIN-ROBARTS* (7 ém), TV, 81/80, CDN, Réal; *COUR SUPREME,* TV, 81, CDN, Réal; *UNE QUESTION DE PAYS,* 'TEL QUEL', TV, 80, CDN, Réal/Coord pro; *FUNERAILLES D'ETAT,* TV, 79-72, CDN, Réal/Coord pro; *INSTALLATION GOUVERNEUR GENERAL,* TV, 79-74, CDN, Réal/Coord pro;

(cont/suite)

HABITAT FORUM, TV, 76, CDN, Réal; CONFERENCE COMMONWEALTH, TV, 75, CDN, Réal; VISITE TRUDEAU A PARIS, TV, 74, CDN, Réal; REEDUCATION (6 ém), 'DOSSIER', TV, 72-69, CDN, Réal; INDUSTRIE PETROLE/ DEVELOPPEMENT REGIONAL (5 ém), 'DOSSIER', TV, 72-69, CDN, Réal; 'LES ANNEES '80' (17 eps), TV, 69/68, CDN, Prod dél; 'CANADA EXPRESS' (31 eps), TV, 67/66, CDN, Prod dél; 'SEXTANT' (100 eps), TV, 65-63, CDN, Réal.

THIBAULT, Louis-Claude

3535 Papineau, #1513, Montréal, Qué, CAN, H2K 4J9. (514)526-0667. 2300 Florian, Montréal, Qué, CAN, H2K 2P5. (514)522-2145.
Types de production et Catégories: TV film-Réal; TV vidéo-Réal/Prod.
Types d'oeuvres: Drame-C&TV; Documentaire-C&TV; Annonces-TV.
Curriculum vitae: Né en 1944 à Valleyfield, Québec. Expérience professionnelle: journaliste, 70-73; concepteur, 73-75; producteur/réalisateur, 75-86. A reçu des mentions honorables pour des annonces publicitaires.
Filmographie sélective: ATAR / KENNER / IDEAL TOY / TYCO / SLINKY ACTIVISION, Cm, 86-82, USA, Prod/Réal; IRWIN TOY/TREMBLAY FOURRURES, Cm, 86-82, CDN, Réal/Prod; DA GIOVANI/VILLE MARIE PONTIAC BUICK/UNI TOTAL/FORD ESCORT, Cm, 86/85, CDN, Réal; AECQ, In, 85, CDN, Réal; FIVA, C, 84, CDN, Prod/Réal; AU VOLEUR, TV, 83, CDN, Réal; ECHEC AU FEU, TV, 82, CDN, Réal; LES UNS LES AUTRES/LES FEMMES ET LES ENFANTS D'ABORD, 'L'ULTIME CREATURE', TV, 80, CDN, Réal/Mont; HOMMES ET FEMMES/L'ETERNELLE JEUNESSE, 'L'ULTIME CREATURE', TV, 80, CDN, Réal/Mont; MEN AND WOMEN, 'BEING HUMAN', TV, 80, CDN, Réal; LA CORRIVEAU, C, 79, CDN, Prod/Réal.

THIBAULT, Norman

ARRFQ. 4076 rue Cartier, Montréal, Qué, CAN, H2K 4G4. (514)523-7450. Feedback Audio-Visuel inc., 5269 rue Marquette, Montréal, Qué, CAN, H2J 3Z4. (514)526-1187.
Types de production et Catégories: TV vidéo-Réal/Prod/Sc/Mont.
Types d'oeuvres: Drame-TV; Documentaire-TV; Education-TV.
Curriculum vitae: Né en 1957, Montréal, Québec. Bac.- Diplôme de Droit (L.L.B.), Sciences juridiques. QUI VEUT LA VIE remporte le Premier Prix à AMTEC et le Prix d'Excellence au Vidéo Culture Canada.
Filmographie sélective: MOZAMBIQUE 85, TV, 85, CDN, Réal/Prod/Mont/Sc; PROBLEMES-SOLUTIONS, TV, 85, CDN, Réal/Prod/Mont/Sc; PREVENTION, TV, 85, CDN, Réal/Prod/Mont/Sc; LE COMITE, TV, 85, CDN, Réal/Prod/Sc/Mont; LES ELLES COUPEES, TV, 85, CDN, Réal/Prod/Sc/Mont; LES MARCHANDS DISENT, TV, 84, CDN, Réal/Prod/Sc/Mont; QUI VEUT LA VIE, TV, 83, CDN, Réal/Prod/Sc/Mont; JOE, TV, 82, CDN, Réal/Prod/Sc; LA FETE, TV, 81, CDN, Co réal; LA LUTTE DE DAVID CONTRE GOLIATH, TV, 80, CDN, Réal; COMMONWEALTH PLYWOOD: UNE LUTTE POUR LA DIGNITE, TV, 77, CDN, Co réal.

THOMAS, Gayle

ASIFA. 113 Lepage, Dorval, Que, CAN, H9S 3E5. (514)631-4498. NFB, 3155 Cote de Liesse, Montreal, Que, CAN, H3C 3H5. (514)283-9629.
Types of Production & Categories: Th Short-Dir/Prod/Wr/An; TV Film-Dir/Prod/Wr/An.
Genres: Educational-Th&TV; Children's-Th&TV; Animation-Th&TV; Experimental-Th&TV.
Biography: Born 1944, Montreal, Quebec; bilingual. B.F.A., Sir George Williams University, 68; 1 year at Ecole des Beaux Arts; 3 years drafting at Montreal Institute of Technology, (evenings). Worked as draftswoman, Bell Canada, 63-64;

(cont/suite)

joined NFB, 70. Her films have won numerous awards including Chris Bronze Plaque, Columbus; 1st Prize, Films for Youth Festival, Portugal.
Selective Filmography: *THE BOY AND THE SNOW GOOSE*, TV, 84, CDN, Dir/Prod/Wr/An (**ACTRA**); *THE MAGIC FLUTE* (LA FLUTE MAGIQUE), Th, 77, CDN, An/Dir/Prod/Wr; *A SUFI TALE* (UN CONTE DE SUFI), Th, 77, CDN, An/Dir/Prod/Wr; *KLAXON*, ED, 75, CDN, An/Dir/Prod; *IT'S SNOW*, Th, 74, CDN, An/Prod/Dir/Creator; *TAXATION CLIPS*, TV, 74, CDN, Co-Dir.

THOMAS, R. L.

ACTRA, DGC, WGAw. 9010 Norma Place, Los Angeles, CA, USA, 90069. (213) 858-6006. Thomlee Productions Inc., 365 Markham St., Toronto, Ont, CAN, M6G 2K8. (416)922-8700. David Wardlow, Camden Artists, 409 N. Camden Drive, Ste. 202, Beverly Hills, CA, USA, 90210. (213)278-6885.
Types of Production & Categories: Th Film-Dir/Wr; TV Film-Dir/Prod/Wr.
Genres: Drama-Th&TV; Documentary-TV.
Biography: Born Saohuiz, Maranhao, Brazil; Canadian citizen; U.S. resident. He won a Special Award, Canadian Film Awards, 77; *TYLER* won the Int'l Critics Award, Montreal Film Fest.; Ace Award for *THE TERRY FOX STORY*.
Selective Filmography: *THE CROWD*, 'BRADBURY THEATRE', TV, 84, CDN, Dir; *THE TERRY FOX STORY*, Th, 82, CDN, Dir; *TICKET TO HEAVEN*, Th, 80, CDN, Dir/Co-Scr; *EVERY PERSON IS GUILTY*, 'FOR THE RECORD', TV, 79, CDN, Co-Wr (**ACTRA**); *THEY'RE DRYING UP THE STREETS*, 'FOR THE RECORD', TV, 78, CDN, Prod (**ACTRA**); *TYLER*, TV, 77, CDN, Dir/Prod; *DREAMSPEAKER*, 'FOR THE RECORD', TV, 76, CDN, Prod (**CFA**).

THORNE, John

CTPDA. 8049 Argyle St., Vancouver, BC, CAN. (604)324-1302.
Types of Production & Categories: TV Film-Dir/Prod; TV Video-Dir/Prod.
Genres: Drama-TV; Comedy-TV; Educational-TV; Children's-TV.
Biography: Born 1922, Punnichy, Saskatchewan. M.A., Northwestern University, 52. Taught at the Summer School of Theatre, U. of British Columbia, directed stage productions. Director, producer, CBC, 54-85.
Selective Filmography: *'THE BEACHCOMBERS'*, TV, 85-80, CDN, P Prod; *'MON AMI'*, TV, 78-76, CDN, Dir/Prod; *'MUSIC TO SEE'*, TV, 70, CDN, Dir/Prod; *'SHOESTRING THEATRE'*, TV, 70, CDN, Dir/Prod.

THURLING, Peter

DGC. Schafer/Thurling Productions, 680 Queen's Quay W., Ste. 503, Toronto, Ont, CAN, M5V 2Y9. (416)593-8652.
Types of Production & Categories: TV Film-Dir/Wr; TV Video-Dir/Wr.
Genres: Drama-TV; Musical-TV; Documentary-TV.
Selective Filmography: *FLOATING OVER CANADA*, TV, 85, CDN, Dir/Wr (**ACTRA**); *GOPHER BROKE*, TV, 79, CDN, Dir/Wr; *BREAKDOWN*, TV, 78, CDN, Dir; *'TARGET: IMPOSSIBLE'* (26 eps), TV, 74/73, CDN, Dir; *'HERE COME THE SEVENTIES'* (TOWARDS THE YEAR 2000), (100 eps), TV, 73-70, CDN, Dir/Wr; *'THE SEASONS'* (3 eps), TV, 70/69, CDN, Dir/Wr.

TICHENOR, Harold - see PRODUCTION MANAGERS

TILL, Eric

DGC. 62 Chaplin Crescent, Toronto, Ont, CAN, M5P 1A3. (416)488-4068.
Types of Production & Categories: Th Film-Dir; TV Film-Dir.
Genres: Drama-Th&TV; Comedy-Th; Horror-Th&TV; Documentary-Th.
Biography: Born 1929, London, England; Canadian citizen. Came to Canada as a manager with the National Ballet of Canada, 54; directed first TV program at CBC, 57. Has since directed feature films in Canada and England and award-winning TV dramas.

(cont/suite)

Selective Filmography: *TURNING TO STONE,* TV, 85, CDN, Dir; *GLENN GOULD: A PORTRAIT,* TV, 85, CDN, Co-Dir; *'HOME FIRES'* (sev eps), TV, 83, CDN, Dir; *SHOCKTRAUMA,* TV, 83, CDN, Dir; *GENTLE SINNERS,* TV, 83, CDN, Dir; *CASE OF LIBEL,* TV, 83, USA, Dir; *IF YOU COULD SEE WHAT I HEAR,* Th, 82, CDN, Dir/Co-Prod; *MARY AND JOSEPH,* TV, 82, CDN, Dir; *EYE OF THE BEHOLDER,* Th, 80, CDN, Dir; *IMPROPER CHANNELS,* Th, 79, CDN, Dir; *MAD SHADOWS,* TV, 79, CDN, Dir; *WILD HORSE HANK,* Th, 78, CDN, Dir; *'THE NEWCOMERS'* (3 eps), TV, 78-76, CDN, Dir; *BETHUNE,* TV, 77, CDN, Dir; *ALL THINGS BRIGHT AND BEAUTIFUL* (IT SHOULDN'T HAPPEN TO A VET), Th, 76, GB, Dir; *THE FIRST NIGHT OF PYGMALION,* TV, 75, CDN, Dir; *THE NATIONAL DREAM* (8 parts), TV, 74, CDN, Co-Dir; *FREEDOM OF THE CITY,* Th, 74, CDN, Dir/Prod; *FOLLOW THE NORTH STAR,* TV, 72, CDN, Dir; *TALKING TO A STRANGER,* TV, 71, CDN, Dir/ Prod; *A FAN'S NOTES,* Th, 70, CDN, Dir; *THE WALKING STICK,* Th, 70, GB, Dir; *'FESTIVAL'* (17 eps), TV, 69-63, CDN, Dir; *HOT MILLIONS,* Th, 68, GB, Dir; *A GREAT BIG THING,* Th, 66, CDN, Dir.

TOSONI, Joan

Joan Tosoni Productions Inc., 111 Latimer Ave., Toronto, Ont, CAN, M5N 2M3. (416)484-6468.
Types of Production & Categories: TV Film-Dir; TV Video-Dir.
Genres: Variety-TV; Documentary-TV.
Selective Filmography: *'THE TOMMY HUNTER SHOW'* (weekly), (85-80, Dir), TV, 86/85, CDN, Prod/Dir; *EASTER SEAL SUPERTHON,* TV, 86, CDN, Dir; *ACTRA AWARDS* (yearly), TV, 86-83, CDN, Dir; *TRIBUTE TO THE CHAMPIONS,* TV, 86, CDN, Dir; *COUNTRY WEST* (pilot), TV, 85, CDN, Dir; *DU MAURIER SEARCH FOR THE STARS,* TV, 84, CDN, Dir; *ETHIOPIA REPORT: OUR CHILDREN ARE DYING,* TV, 84, CDN, Dir; *CHILDREN RUNNING OUT OF TIME,* TV, 83, CDN, Dir; *'HONKY TONK'* (16 eps), TV, 82/81, CDN, Dir; *JUNO AWARDS,* TV, 82, CDN, Dir; *'THE BOB McLEAN SHOW'* (daily), TV, 81, CDN, Dir; *'FRONT PAGE CHALLENGE'* (weekly), TV, 81, CDN, Dir.

TOUSIGNANT, Richard

267 rue Principale est, St-Anaclet, Qué, CAN, G0K 1H0. Les Entreprises Vidéo Polyfilm, 8, 6e rue est, Rimouski, Qué, CAN, G5L 2H4. (418)724-2413.
Types de production et Catégories: TV vidéo-Réal
Types d'oeuvres: Animation-TV; Annonces-TV; Industriel-TV.
Curriculum vitae: Né en 1960, St-Hyacinthe, Québec. Directeur artistique et choréographe pour ensemble folklorique, 78-83; formation à New York, Montréal et Mexico. Scénariste, annonces publicitaires en animation, 82; recherchiste et concepteur de textes, 85; réalisateur, 86.
Filmographie sélective: *BERNIER BONGO,* TV, 86, CDN, Réal; *LES BENÉVOLES/INFIRMIERES ET INFIRMIERS DE LA REGION 01,* Cm, 86, CDN, Réal; *PLAN DE DEVELOPEMENT DES RESSOURCES HUMAINES,* In, 86, CDN, Réal; *REPARATIONS DES NAVIRES,* In, 86, CDN, Co réal/Sc; *LES SITES HISTORIQUES/BRACONNAGE,* Cm, 83, CDN, Réal.

TOVELL, Vincent

ACTRA. 190 St.George St., Toronto, Ont, CAN, M5R 2N4. (416)925-4006.
Types of Production & Categories: TV Film-Dir/Prod; TV Video-Dir/Prod.
Genres: Drama-TV; Documentary-TV; Educational-TV.
Biography: Born 1922, Toronto, Ontario; bilingual. B.A., M.A., University of Toronto, Columbia U. (N.Y.). Director, Hart House Theatre, 46-48; producer, director, announcer, writer, United Nations radio/TV/film, 50-53; producer, CBC, New York, 53-57, Toronto, 57-85. Elected: Royal Canadian Academy of Arts;

(cont/suite)

Centennial Medal, 67; Queen's Jubilee Medal, 78. Has won various television awards including CFA, Anik, Wilderness.
Selective Filmography: *GLENN GOULD: A PORTRAIT,* TV, 85, CDN, Exec Prod/Co-Prod/Co-Dir; *'HAND AND EYE'* (7 eps), TV, 84, CDN, Exec Prod/Co-Prod/Co-Dir; *THE OWL AND THE DYNAMO: GEORGE GRANT,* TV, 79, CDN, Prod/Dir; *THE MASSEYS,* TV, 78, CDN, Exec Prod/Prod/Co-Dir; *MUST FREEDOM FAIL,* TV, 78, CDN, Prod/Dir; *'IMAGES OF CANADA'* (10 eps), TV, 76-70, CDN, Exec Prod/Co-Prod/Co-Dir.

TREMBLAY, Robert

94 A rue Bourget, Montréal, Qué, CAN, H4C 2M2. (514)931-4528.
Types de production et Catégories: 1 métrage-Réal/Prod/Sc/Mont; c métrage-Réal/Prod/Sc/Mont.
Types d'oeuvres: Documentaire-C; Education-C; Enfants-C.
Curriculum vitae: Né en 1946, Pointe au Pic, Québec. Bac. spécialisé en information culturelle, UQAM. Réalisateur et monteur depuis 70; producteur pour les Films d'Aventures Sociales du Québec depuis 74.
Filmographie sélective: *BRUNO,* C, 86, CDN, Co prod/Mont; *POW WOW TE MORT OU BEN J'JOUE PU* (LES MEDES), C, 80, CDN, Prod/Réal/Sc/Mont; *DU MAUVAIS COTE DE LA CLOTURE,* C, 79, CDN, Mont; *BELLE FAMILLE,* C, 78, CDN, Prod/Réal/Sc/Mont; *TOUTE MA VIE AU SERVICE DES RICHES,* C, 78, CDN, Prod/Réal/Sc/Mont; *A MAISON,* C, 78, CDN, Co mont; *TOUL QUEBEC AU MONDE SUA JOBBE* (LE QUEBEC SUA JOBBE), C, 75, CDN, Prod/Réal/Sc/Mont.

TRUDEL, Yvon

AR. 6, 21e Avenue, Melocheville, Qué, CAN. (514)429-4865. Radio-Canada, 1400 blvd. Dorchester est, Montréal, Qué, CAN, H2L 2M2. (514)285-2842.
Types de production et Catégories: TV vidéo-Réal.
Types d'oeuvres: Drame-TV.
Curriculum vitae: Né en 1934 à Montréal, Québec. Trente et un ans à Radio-Canada, 19 ans comme réalisateur, TV drame.
Filmographie sélective: *'LE TEMPS D'UNE PAIX'* (100 eps), TV, 85-80, CDN, Réal; *LE TEMPS D'UNE PAIX* (SPECIAL NOEL), TV, 81, CDN, Réal (ANIK); *'TERRE HUMAINE'* (60 eps), TV, 80/79, CDN, Réal; *'RUE DES PIGNONS'* (hebdo), TV, 78-70, CDN, Réal; *'LES BELLES HISTOIRES DES PAYS D'EN HAUT'* (hebdo), TV, 69-66, CDN, Réal.

TUCKER, Paul - see PRODUCTION MANAGERS

VAITIEKUNAS, Vincent

DGC. 263 Spring Garden Ave., Willowdale, Ont, CAN, M2N 3H1. (416)223-4297. York University, Film/Video Dept., 4700 Keele St., North York, Ont, CAN, M3J 1P3. (416)736-5149.
Types of Production & Categories: Th Film-Wr; Th Short-Dir; TV Film-Dir.
Genres: Drama-Th&TV; Documentary-Th&TV; Educational-Th&TV; Children's-Th&TV.
Biography: Born in Lithuania; Canadian citizen; professional filmmaker in Canada since 1958. Winner of film awards including Bronze Medal, Silver Medal, N.Y. Int'l Film Festival. Currently Associate Professor, York University Film/Video Dept.. Winner of the Ontario Federation of University Faculty Associations Award for Excellence in University Teaching.
Selective Filmography: *ONTARIO SURPRISE,* Th, 79, CDN, Dir; *FINE ARTS AT YORK,* ED, 77, CDN, Dir/Wr/Prod/Ed; *'THE WHITE OAKS OF JALNA'* (ep #10), TV, 71, CDN, Dir; *CANADA AT 8:30,* Th, 70, CDN, Dir/Ed; *MULTIPLICITY,* Th, 70, CDN, Dir/Wr/Co-Prod/Ed; *THE SUN DON'T SHINE*

(cont/suite)

ON THE SAME DAWG'S BACK ALL THE TIME, Th, 69, CDN, Dir **(CFA)**; *MR. FILM-FLAM,* 'McQUEEN', TV, 69, CDN, Dir; *THE WANT OF A SUITABLE PLAYHOUSE* (SHAW FESTIVAL), Th, 68, CDN, Dir/Wr/Prod/Ed; *EXPLORE - EXPO 67,* Th, 67, CDN, Dir/Ed; *MOTION,* Th, 66, CDN, Dir/Ed; *'THIS HOUR HAS SEVEN DAYS'* (sev seg), TV, 66/65, CDN, Co-Dir/Ed; *'MR. PIPER'* (sev eps), TV, 63, CDN, Dir.

VALCOUR, Pierre - voir PRODUCTEURS

VAN DER VEEN, Milton

10 Tangreen Ct., #2606, Willowdale, Ont, CAN, M2M 4B9. (416)223-4714. Miscellaneous Productions, Manfred's Meadow, R.R. #1, Grand Valley, Ont, CAN, L0N 1G0. (519)925-5306.
Types of Production & Categories: TV Film-Prod/Dir/Wr; TV Video-Prod/Dir/Wr.
Genres: Drama-TV; Documentary-TV; Educational-TV; Children's-TV.
Biography: Born 1945, Netherlands; Canadian citizen. Project officer at TV Ontario since 73; producer/director, children's programming since 78. *THE SCIENCE ALLIANCE* won prizes at Columbus, American Film Festivals and the Ohio State Award.
Selective Filmography: *'TAKE A LOOK'* (Wr-5 eps), (20 eps), TV, 86/85, CDN, Prod/Dir; *'THE COMPUTER ROOM'* (Dir-sev segs), (10 eps), TV, 85/84, CDN, Prod/Wr; *WHAT IS PCEmas?,* In, 85, CDN/USA, Dir/Wr; *'PCEmas'* (8 eps), In, 85, CDN/USA, Dir/Wr; *'IT'S YOUR WORLD'* (Wr-5 eps), (20 eps), TV, 84/83, CDN, Prod/Dir; *'ARTSCAPE'* (8 eps), TV, 83/82, CDN, Prod/Dir; *'THE SCIENCE ALLIANCE'* (Wr-8 eps), (10 eps), TV, 82-80, CDN, Prod/Dir; *'THE BODY WORKS'* (Dir-22 eps), (40 eps), TV, 80-78, CDN, Prod; *'KIDSWORLD'* (52 eps), TV, 79/78, CDN, Prod.

VERGARA, Eduardo

AR. 66 Maple Grove Village, Moncton, NB, CAN, E1A 4R2. (506)853-3061. CBC/Radio-Canada, 250 Archilbald, Moncton, NB, CAN, E1C 8M8. (506)388-4805.
Types de production et Catégories: TV vidéo-Réal.
Types d'oeuvres: Variété-TV, Affaires publiques-TV.
Curriculum vitae: Né en 1942, Santiago, Chili; citoyen canadien. Langues: espagnol, français, anglais, portugais. Réalisateur, affaires publiques, Radio-Canada, Moncton pour l'émission *CE SOIR,* 85-86.

VIALLON, Claudine - see WRITERS

VON PUTTKAMER, Peter

175 W. 10th, #303, Vancouver, BC, CAN, V5Y 1R7. (604)874-6925. Gryphon Productions Ltd., 3154 Travers Ave., West Vancouver, BC, CAN, V7V 1G3. (604) 922-7025.
Types of Production & Categories: Th Short-Dir/Ed; TV Video-Dir/Ed/Cin.
Genres: Drama-Th; Documentary-TV; Educational-TV.
Biography: Born 1957, Bonn, West Germany; Canadian citizen; languages: English, German, French. B.A., Film & TV, University of British Columbia. Has produced video programs for Health and Welfare Canada; formed Gryphon Productions, 83.
Selective Filmography: *C.P.-A DAY AT A TIME,* In, 86, CDN, Prod/Dir/Ed; *THE HONOUR OF ALL: THE STORY OF ALKALI LAKE,* TV, 86/85, CDN, DOP/Ed; *AMERICAN MYTH AND THE IMAGE OF INDIANS,* ED, 85, USA, DOP/Ed; *SHARING INNOVATIONS THAT WORK,* ED, 85, CDN, Wr/DOP/Ed; *A CARAVAN FOR YOUTH,* ED, 85, CDN, Prod/Dir/Ed/Wr; *ALL NIGHT LONG,* MV, 84, CDN, Dir/Ed; *FINDING A NEW PATH,* ED, 84, CDN, Prod/Dir/Wr/DOP; *IN THE HEART OF THE CEDAR,* ED, 83/82, CDN, Dir/Ed/Wr/DOP; *THE ENVIRONMENTAL HEALTH OFFICER/ASBESTOS HAZARD CONTROL,* In, 82/81, CDN, Dir/Wr/Ed/Cin; *SUICIDE-A COMMUNITY'S*

(cont/suite)

CONCERN/THE COMMUNITY HEALTH REPRESENTATIVE, ED, 81/80, CDN, Wr/Dir/Ed/Cin; *OWEEKENO: IN TOUCH WITH THE PAST,* ED, 80, CDN, Dir/Wr/Ed/Cin; *AH, C'EST BON,* Th, 80, CDN, An; *SEABIRD, LANDBIRD,* Th, 80, CDN, Dir/Ed; *ROOFSPACE,* Th, 79, CDN, Dir/Ed.

WADE, Tony

CTPDA, DGC. 3102 Fromme Rd., North Vancouver, BC, CAN, V7K 2C9. (604) 986-9708. CBC, 700 Hamilton St., Vancouver, BC, CAN.
Types of Production & Categories: TV Film-Dir/Prod; TV Video-Dir/Prod.
Genres: Drama-TV; Documentary-TV; Educational-TV.
Biography: Born 1948, England; grew up as Air Force brat in Germany, Cyprus, Denmark etc... Educated at Wellington College, Berkshire, U.K.; emigrated to Canada, 67, Canadian citizen. Since 67, TV producer, director in Canada, US, Australia. President, Tojo Motion Pictures Inc..
Selective Filmography: *'PACIFIC REPORT'* (26 eps), TV, 86/85, CDN, Exec Prod; *THE VOYAGE OF THOMAS CROSBY V,* TV, 85, CDN, Dir/Prod; *'CORELLI'* (25 eps), TV, 84, CDN, Dir/Prod; *'PACIFIC REPORT'* (75 eps), TV, 83-80, CDN, Dir/Prod; *'THE JOURNAL'* (2 seg), TV, 83, CDN, Prod; *THE LEGEND OF THE SILVER RAVEN,* TV, 82, CDN, Dir/Prod; *'SKYWAYS'* (20 eps), TV, 80, AUS, Assoc Prod; *'THE SULLIVANS'* (47 eps), TV, 79, AUS, Dir/1st AD; *'THINKABOUT'* (8 eps), TV, 78, CDN/USA, Dir; *'RENEWABLE SOCIETY'* (12 eps), TV, 77, CDN, Dir; *PEOPLE OF AMIDA,* TV, 77, CDN, Dir; *'COME ALIVE'* (daily), TV, 76, CDN, Exec Prod; *'BARRY BROADFOOT'S PIONEER YEARS'* (13 eps), TV, 76, CDN, Exec Prod; *'IN THE SHADOW OF LIBERTY'* (12 eps), TV, 76, CDN/USA/AUS, Dir; *'THE CANADIAN WEST'* (26 eps), TV, 74/73, CDN, Dir/Prod.

WALKER, Giles

SGCT. 4039 Grand Blvd., Montreal, Que, CAN, H4B 2X4. (514)483-3270. NFB, Box 6100, Montreal, Que, CAN, H3C 3H5. (514)283-9536.
Types of Production & Categories: Th Film-Dir/Prod/Wr; Th Short-Dir; TV Film-Dir/Prod/Wr.
Genres: Drama-Th&TV; Comedy-Th&TV; Documentary-TV; Children's-TV.
Biography: Born 1946, Dundee, Scotland; Canadian citizen. B.A., University of New Brunswick, 70; M.A. Stanford University Film School, 72. Worked at the NFB since 72. His films have won awards including: Red Ribbon, Blue Ribbon, American Film Fest., Silver Hugo, Chicago Film Fest.; *BRAVERY IN THE FIELD* was nominated for an Oscar, won a Silver Plaque, Chicago Film Fest.. *90 DAYS* received 6 Genie nominations, Gold Plaque (Chicago), Gold Ducat (Mannheim), Gold Toucan (Rio de Janiero).
Selective Filmography: *90 DAYS,* Th, 85, CDN, Dir/Co-Wr/Prod; *JACK OF HEARTS,* 'BELL CANADA PLAYHOUSE', TV, 85, CDN, Co-Prod; *THE CONCERT STAGES OF EUROPE/A GOOD TREE,* 'BELL CANADA PLAYHOUSE', TV, 84, CDN, Dir; *THE MASCULINE MYSTIQUE,* Th, 84, CDN, Dir/Wr/Prod; *DAISY: THE STORY OF A FACELIFT,* Th, 82, CDN, Prod; *I LIKE TO SEE WHEELS TURN,* TV, 81, CDN, Dir/Prod; *HARVEST,* 'FOR THE RECORD', TV, 80, CDN, Dir; *TWICE UPON A TIME,* Th, 79, CDN, Dir; *BRAVERY IN THE FIELD,* TV, 78, CDN, Dir/Wr **(GENIE)**; *I WASN'T SCARED,* TV, 77, CDN, Dir/Co-Wr; *THE SWORD OF THE LORD,* TV, 76, CDN, Dir/Wr; *NO WAY THEY WANT TO SLOW DOWN,* TV, 75, CDN, Dir; *DESCENT,* Th, 75, CDN, Dir; *FRESHWATER WORLD,* TV, 74, CDN, Dir; *A RIGHT TO SURVIVE,* TV, 73, CDN, Dir/Prod/Wr; *DOWN TO THE SEA,* TV, 72, CDN/USA, Dir/Prod/Wr.

WALTON, Lloyd A. - see PRODUCERS

WARREN, Mark

AFTRA, DGA. 3528 10th Ave., Los Angeles, CA, USA, 90018. Mew Prod./BNW Prod.Consultants, 1954 Roscomare Rd., Los Angeles, CA, USA, 90024. (213)476-1462. Sue Goldin Talent, 6380 Wilshire Blvd., #1600, Los Angeles, CA, USA, 90048. (213)852-1441.
Types of Production & Categories: Th Film-Dir; TV Film-Dir/Prod; TV Video-Dir/Prod.
Genres: Drama-Th&TV; Comedy-Th&TV; Variety-TV; Action-TV.
Biography: Born 1938. Directed and/or produced *JULIETTE, IN PERSON,THE WORLD OF MUSIC*, CBC, 62-68; then in U.S., TV series and specials.NAACP Image Award winner for *THE NEW BILL COSBY SHOW*; LAPD Commendation for *GET CHRISTIE LOVE*.
Selective Filmography: *'THE COMEDY FACTORY'* (sev eps), TV, 85, CDN/USA, Dir; *'BENSON'* (sev eps), TV, 84/83, USA, Dir; *'SNOW JOB'* (12 eps), TV, 84/83, CDN, Dir; *'BIG CITY COMEDY'*, TV, 82, CDN/USA, Dir; *THE 5th ANNUAL RHYTHM & BLUES AWARDS*, TV, 82, USA, Dir/Prod; *TWO IN A BOX*, TV, 82, USA, Dir/Prod; *'DIAHANN CARROLL'*, TV, 81, USA, Dir; *SAMMY DAVIS JR., LIVE FROM ACAPULCO*, TV, 80, USA, Dir/Prod; *BLACK ACHIEVEMENT AWARDS*, TV, 80, USA, Dir/Prod; *'SAMMY & CO'*, TV, 78-76, USA, Dir; *CRUNCH* (THE KINKY COACHES AND THE POM-POM PUSSYCATS), Th, 78, CDN, Dir; *'WHAT'S HAPPENING'*, TV, 77/76, USA, Dir; *'SANFORD & SON'* (sev eps), TV, 77-72, USA, Dir; *'DINAH SHORE AND HER NEW BEST FRIENDS'*, TV, 76, USA, Dir; *AN ONLY SON*, TV, 76, USA, Dir; *'GET CHRISTIE LOVE'* (sev eps), TV, 75/74, USA, Dir; *'CHER'*, TV, 75, USA, Dir; *'JOEY & DAD'*, TV, 75, USA, Dir; *A TRIBUTE TO MARTIN LUTHER KING*, TV, 75, USA, Dir/Prod; *'ROWAN & MARTIN'S LAUGH-IN'*, TV, 73-70, USA, Dir (**EMMY**); *'THE NEW BILL COSBY SHOW'*, TV, 73, USA, Dir; *'THE BURNS & SCHREIBER COMEDY HOUR'*, TV, 73, USA, Dir; *COME BACK CHARLESTON BLUE*, Th, 73, USA, Dir; *THE BEST ON RECORD* (GRAMMY AWARDS), TV, 69, USA, Dir.

WATSON, John - see PRODUCERS

WAXMAN, Al

ACTRA, DGA, DGC, SAG. c/o The Brillstein Co., 9200 Sunset Blvd., Ste 428, Los Angeles, CA, USA, 90069. (213)275-6135. Catherine McCartney, Prendergast Agency, 260 Richmond St.W., Suite 405, Toronto, Ont, CAN, M5V 1W5. (416) 922-5308.
Types of Production & Categories: Th Film-Dir/Act; TV Film-Dir/Act; TV Video-Dir/Act.
Genres. Drama Th&TV; Comedy-Th&TV; Action-Th&TV.
Biography: Born 1935, Toronto, Ontario. B.A., University of Western Ontario; London School of Film Technique, England; Neighborhood Playhouse School of Theatre, N.Y.; Actors Studio, N.Y.; N.Y. School of Motion Picture Production. Directed over 100 commercials, documentaries and industrials. Awarded the Queen's Silver Jubilee Medal.
Selective Filmography: *'CAGNEY AND LACEY'* (Dir-5 eps), (96 eps), TV, 86-81, USA, Act; *'MOMENTS IN TIME'* (26 eps), TV, 86, USA, Host; *'NIGHT HEAT'* (1 eps), TV, 85, CDN, Dir; *'THE EDISON TWINS'* (1 eps), TV, 85, CDN, Dir; *'DANGER BAY'* (1 eps), TV, 85, CDN/USA, Dir; *'LITTLEST HOBO'* (3 eps), TV, 84/83, CDN, Dir; *COP, 'FOR THE RECORD'*, TV, 81, CDN, Dir; *CLASS OF '84*, Th, 81, CDN/USA, Act; *DEATH BITE* (SPASMS), Th, 81, CDN, Act; *'KING OF KENSINGTON'* (111 eps), TV, 80-75, CDN, Act (**ACTRA**); *'THE PHOENIX TEAM'* (1 eps), TV, 80, CDN, Dir; *THE ABORTION ISSUE, 'THE MORAL QUESTION'*, TV, 80, CDN, Dir; *ATLANTIC CITY*, Th, 79, CDN/USA, Act; *THE WINNINGS OF FRANKIE WALLS, 'FOR THE RECORD'*, TV, 79, CDN, Act (**ACTRA**); *WILD HORSE HANK*, Th, 78, CDN, Act; *'SIDESTREET'* (1 eps), TV, 78, CDN, Dir.

DIRECTORS/REALISATEURS

WEINTHAL, Eric

DGC. Hania Productions Inc., 1598 Bathurst St., Ste. 312, Toronto, Ont, CAN, M5P 3H9. (416)787-7433.
Types of Production & Categories: Th Film-Dir/Wr.
Genres: Drama-Th; Comedy-TV; Variety-TV; Action-TV.
Biography: Born 1958, Montreal, Quebec. B.A., University of Toronto, 79 (Cinema). Plays guitar, sings, acts in theatre, TV. Co-composed the film score and songs for his first feature film.
Selective filmography: *WAY DOWN INSIDE*, MV, 86, CDN, Dir/Ed/Comp/Sing; *TIMING*, Th, 85, CDN, Dir/Wr/Co-Prod/Ed; *'CHECK IT OUT!'* (2 eps), TV, 85, CDN/USA, Assoc Dir; *'COMEDY FACTORY'* (8 eps), TV, 85, CDN, P Pro Spv; *'SNOW JOB'* (54 eps), TV, 85-82, CDN, P Pro Spv; *'BIZARRE'* (48 eps), TV, 84-81, CDN/USA, Pro Assoc; *DAVID STEINBERG IN CONCERT*, TV, 82, CDN/USA, Pro Assoc; *'LITTLEST HOBO'* (24 eps), TV, 80/79, CDN, 3rd AD.

WELDON, John

ASIFA, SGCT. 4338 Kensington, Montreal, Que, CAN, H4B 2W3. (514)484-2753.
NFB, Box 6100, Stn. A, Montreal, Que, CAN, H3C 3H5. (514)283-9631.
Types of Production & Categories: Th Short-Dir.
Genres: Animation-Th&TV.
Biography: Born 1945, Belleville, Ontario. Wrote 'Genius is a Four Letter Word', 67(Green & Gold Revue); 'Pipkin Papers', a comic book, 69. NFB animation department, 70-86. Developed Weldon Animaster System, computer animation software. *REAL INSIDE* won a Silver Hugo, Chicago.
Selective Filmography: *GIORDANO*, 'CHARTER', TV, 85, CDN, Wr; *ELEPHANTRIO*, TV, 85, CDN, Co-Dir; *PIECE OF THE ACTION*, TV, 84, CDN, Co-Dir; *REAL INSIDE*, Th, 84, CDN, Co-Dir; *ICE*, 'VIGNETTES', TV, 84, CDN, Prod; *LOG DRIVER'S WALTZ*, 'VIGNETTES', TV, 80, CDN, Dir; *SPECIAL DELIVERY*, Th, 79, CDN, Co-Dir (**OSCAR**); *SPINNOLIO*, Th, 77, CDN, Dir (**CFA**).

WEYMAN, Peter Bay

Close Up Film Productions Ltd., 44 Dewson St., Ste. 4, Toronto, Ont, CAN, M6H 1G7. (416)534-7114.
Types of Production & Categories: TV Film-Dir/Prod/Wr/Ed.
Genres: Musical-TV; Documentary-TV.
Biography: Born 1954, Toronto, Ontario. M.F.A., Film Production, York University; Honours B.A. in Cultural Studies and Comparative Development Studies. *THE LEAHYS: MUSIC MOST OF ALL* won Best Foreign Student Film Award, Academy of Motion Picture Arts & Sciences, L.A., 85. Has travelled extensively in Asia; won several schorlarships for his academic work; assistant co-ordinator for the Canadian Images Film Festival.
Selective Filmography: *AGAINST REASON: A PORTRAIT OF JACK McCLELLAND*, TV, 86/85, CDN, Co-Prod/Dir/Wr/Ed; *THE LEAHYS: MUSIC MOST OF ALL*, TV, 84/83, CDN, Prod/Dir/Wr/Co-Ed.

WHEELER, Anne

ACTRA, DGC. 10904 - 126th St., Edmonton, Alta, CAN, T5M 0P3. (403)451-0219.
Types of Production & Categories: Th Film-Dir/Prod/Wr/Ed; Th Short-Dir/Prod/Wr/Ed; TV Film-Dir/Prod/Wr/Ed.
Genres: Drama-Th&TV; Documentary-Th&TV; Educational-Th&TV; Children's-Th&TV.
Biography: Born 1946, Edmonton, Alberta. Filmwest Associates Ltd., 70-75; freelance writer, director, actor, 75-78; NFB, 78-83; independent producer, director,
(cont/suite)

writer since 83. Awards include 5 AMPIA; *A WAR STORY* won a Blue Ribbon, American Film Fest., Flanders Film Fest..

Selective Filmography: *LOYALTIES*, Th, 85, CDN/GB, Dir/Co-Prod/Co-Story; *TO SET OUR HOUSE IN ORDER/ONE'S A HEIFER*, 'BELL CANADA PLAYHOUSE', TV, 84, CDN, Dir/Wr; *A CHANGE OF HEART*, 'FOR THE RECORD', TV, 83, CDN, Dir; *FROM BEARS TO BARTOK*, TV, 82, CDN, Prod; *CHILDREN OF ALCOHOL*, TV, 82, CDN, Prod/Ed; *A WAR STORY*, Th, 81, CDN, Dir/Wr/Prod; *BYRON HARMON*, Th, 80, CDN, Prod; *PRIORY, THE ONLY HOME I'VE GOT*, Th, 79, CDN, Prod (GENIE); *NEVER A DULL MOMENT*, TV, 79, CDN, Prod; *TEACH ME TO DANCE*, 'ADVENTURES IN HISTORY', TV, 78, CDN, Dir; *TRIANGLE ISLAND*, TV, 77, CDN, Prod; *WELFARE WORKERS*, 'CHALLENGE FOR CHANGE', TV, 77, CDN, Cin; *KRAJINA*, TV, 76, CDN, Ed; *RED DRESS*, 'ADVENTURES IN HISTORY', TV, 76, CDN, Ed; *AUGUSTA*, TV, 76, CDN, Dir/Ed; *HAPPILY UNMARRIED*, TV, 76, CDN, Dir/Prod/Ed; *GREAT GRAND MOTHER*, TV, 75, CDN, Dir/Wr; *MARIA CAMPBELL*, TV, 74, CDN, Cin; *LITTLE STARTLERS*, TV, 74, CDN, Cin; *A GRAIN OF TRUTH*, TV, 74, CDN, Cin; *THREE MINUTES TO LIVE*, TV, 74, CDN, Ed; *BRUCE COCKBURN*, TV, 74, CDN, Ed; *EVERY SATURDAY NIGHT*, 'WEST', TV, 74, CDN, Assist Dir.

WHITE, Helene B.

ACTRA. 1135 Sifton Blvd. S. W., Calgary, Alta, CAN, T2T 2K8. (403)243-6819.
HBW/TOTH Co-Productions, 902 - 11th Ave. S.W., #312, Calgary, Alta, CAN, T2R 0E7. (403)228-1900.
Types of Production & Categories: Th Short-Dir; TV Film-Dir/Prod; TV Video-Dir/Prod.
Genres: Comedy-TV; Documentary-Th&TV; Educational-Th&TV.
Biography: Born 1945, Alberta. B.F.A., Drama, University of Calgary, 73; Film Production and Entertainment Law, UCLA; Visual Arts, Banff Centre, Alberta College of Art. President of HBW/Toth Co-Productions and Film Productions Inc. Wrote 'Echoes in the Attic', stage production, 74-75. *LADY IN MOTION* and *CONNECTING* won Bronze Medals, Int'l Film & TV Fest., NY.
Selective Filmography: *'CONNECTING'* (9 eps), TV, 85, CDN, Dir/Co-Prod; *FREEDOM OF CHOICE*, Th, 83, CDN, Dir; *LADY IN MOTION*, TV, 82, CDN, Dir/Wr/Prod.

WIELAND, Joyce

Isaacs Gallery, 832 Yonge St., Toronto, Ont, CAN, M4Y 2H1. (416)923-7301.
Types of Production & Categories: Th Film-Dir/Prod/Wr/Ed.
Genres: Experimental-Th.
Biography: Born 1931, Toronto, Ontario. Studied Commercial Art, Central Technical School, Toronto, 55-57. Animator, George Dunning's Associates; worked in New York, 62-69; filmmaker and artist; numerous solo art and film exhibitions around the world. Received the Order of Canada, 83. 2 awards for *RAT LIFE AND DIET IN NORTH AMERICA*, 3rd Independent Filmmakers Fest., New York.
Selective Filmography: *PEGGY'S BLUE SKYLIGHT*, Th, 85, CDN/USA, Dir/Wr/Ed/Prod; *BIRDS AT SUNRISE*, Th, 85, CDN, Dir/Wr/Ed/Prod; *A AND B IN ONTARIO*, Th, 84, CDN, Co-Dir/Co-Wr/Co-Ed/Co-Prod; *THE FAR SHORE*, Th, 75, CDN, Dir/Co-Wr/Co-Prod (CFA); *SOLIDARITY*, Th, 73, CDN, Dir/Wr/Ed/Prod; *PIERRE VALLIERES*, Th, 72, CDN, Dir/Wr/Ed/Prod; *DRIPPING WATER*, Th, 69, USA, Co-Dir/Co-Wr/Co-Ed/Co-Prod; *LA RAISON AVANT LA PASSION* (REASON OVER PASSION), Th, 69, USA, Dir/Wr/Ed/Prod; *SAILBOAT*, Th, 68/67, USA, Dir/Wr/Ed/Prod; *1933*, Th, 68/67, USA, Dir/Wr/Ed/Prod; *HANDTINTING*, Th, 68/67, USA, Dir/Wr/Ed/Prod; *RAT LIFE AND DIET IN NORTH AMERICA*, Th, 68, USA, Dir/Wr/Ed/Prod; *BILL'S HAT*, Th, 67, USA, Dir/Wr/Ed/Prod; *BARBARA'S BLINDNESS*, Th, 67, USA, Dir/Wr/Ed/Prod; *WATER SARK*, Th, 65/64, USA, Dir/Wr/Ed/Prod; *PATRIOTISM, PART*

(cont/suite)

ONE, Th, 64, USA, Dir/Wr/Ed/Prod; *PATRIOTISM, PART TWO,* Th, 64, USA, Dir/Wr/Ed/Prod; *LARRY'S RECENT BEHAVIOR,* Th, 63, USA, Dir/Wr/Ed/Prod; *ASSAULT IN THE PARK,* Th, 59, CDN, Co-Dir/Co-Wr/Co-Ed/Co-Prod; *TEA IN THE GARDEN,* Th, 58, CDN, Co-Dir/Co-Wr/Co-Ed/Co-Prod.

WILLIAMS, Don S.

ACTRA, CTPDA, DGC. Donness Productions Ltd., 1863 Layton Drive, North Vancouver, BC, CAN, V7H 1Y1. (604)929-2766.
Types of Production & Categories: Th Film-Dir; TV Film-Dir/Prod; TV Video-Dir/Prod.
Genres: Drama-Th&TV; Comedy-TV; Variety-TV; Documentary-TV.
Biography: Born 1938, Edmonton, Alberta. Stage, film and videotape director, choreographer; past President, DGC; past President and a founder of CTPDA; TV films he's directed and/or produced have won 2 Wilderness Awards and an Ohio State Award.
Selective Filmography: *'THE BEACHCOMBERS',* TV, 86-81, CDN, Exec Prod; *CHUNG CHUCK,* TV, 85, CDN, Dir/Exec Prod; *'CONSTABLE, CONSTABLE'* (2 pilots), TV, 83, CDN, Dir/Exec Prod; *'MAYONNAISE'* (3 pilots), TV, 83, CDN, Dir/Exec Prod; *LAST CALL,* TV, 83, CDN, Dir/Exec Prod; *'THE BUSH PILOT COMPANY'* (3 pilots), TV, 83, CDN, Dir; *'THE BEACHCOMBERS'* (30 eps), TV, 81-71, CDN, Dir; *'RITTER'S COVE'* (7 eps), TV, 80/79, CDN, Dir; *'HUCKLEBERRY FINN AND HIS FRIENDS'* (4 eps), TV, 79, CDN, Dir; *'NELLIE, DANIEL, EMMA AND BEN'* (2 eps), TV, 79, CDN, Dir; *LITTLE JUDGE BIGMOUTH,* TV, 79, CDN, Dir/Prod; *'DEADLINE'* (2 eps), TV, 78, CDN, Dir/Prod; *BOBBING FOR THE BIG APPLE,* TV, 78, CDN, Dir/Prod; *BALLET IN THE PARK,* TV, 77, CDN, Dir/Prod; *TELEVISION DANCE THEATRE,* TV, 77, CDN, Dir/Prod; *LEONA,* TV, 77, CDN, Dir/Prod; *MENNO'S REINS,* Th, 76, CDN, Dir; *MOSES,* TV, 76, CDN, Dir/Prod; *THE LARSENS,* TV, 76, CDN, Dir/Prod; *RAISINS AND ALMONDS,* TV, 75, CDN, Dir; *THE ECSTASY OF RITA JOE* (BALLET), TV, 74, CDN, Dir/Prod; *CORNET AT NIGHT,* TV, 74, CDN, Dir/Prod; *SETON'S MANITOBA,* TV, 73, CDN, Prod; *TRIAL OF POLLY UPDATE,* 'INDUSTRIAL REVOLUTION TRILOGY',* TV, 73, CDN, Dir/Prod **(CFA)**; *LA LEGENDE DU VENT,* TV, 73/72, CDN, Dir/Prod/Ch; *THE ECSTASY OF RITA JOE* (MULTI-MEDIA BALLET), Th, 72, CDN, Dir; *'SESAME STREET'* (16 seg), TV, 72, CDN, Dir; *WORLD OF WORDS,* TV, 72, CDN, Dir/Prod; *NISK'U,* TV, 70/69, CDN/USA, Dir/Prod; *DEATH OF A NOBOBY,* TV, 68, CDN, Dir/Prod.

WILLIAMS, Douglas

DGC. 98 Fulton Ave., Toronto, Ont, CAN, M4K 1X8. (416)423-8714. Stanley Colbert, The Colbert Agency, 303 Davenport Rd., Toronto, Ont, CAN, M5R 1K5. (416)964-3302.
Types of Production & Categories: TV Film-Dir; TV Video-Dir.
Genres: Drama-TV; Comedy-TV; Action-TV; Science Fiction-TV.
Selective Filmography: *THE WEE WONDERS* (pilot), TV, 86, USA, Dir; *'FRAGGLE ROCK'* (4 eps), TV, 85-83, CDN, Dir; *OVERDRAWN AT THE MEMORY BANK,* TV, 83, CDN/USA, Dir; *BEST OF BOTH WORLDS,* TV, 82, CDN, Dir; *'THE PHOENIX TEAM'* (2 eps), TV, 80, CDN, Dir.

WILSON, Sandra

2576 W. 6th Avenue, Vancouver, BC, CAN, V6K 1W5. (604)734-4688. Joan Scott, Writers & Artists, 11726 San Vincente Blvd., #300, Los Angeles, CA, USA, 90049. (213)820-2240. Ralph Zimmerman, Great North Artists Mgmt., 345 Adelaide St. W.,Ste. 500, Toronto, Ont, CAN, M5V 1R5. (416)593-2587.
Types of Production & Categories: Th Film-Dir/Wr; Th Short-Dir/Wr; TV Film-Dir/Wr.
Genres: Drama-Th&TV; Documentary-TV; Educational-TV.

(cont/suite)

Biography: Born 1947, Penticton, British Columbia; B.A. in English and History, Simon Fraser University, 69. *MY AMERICAN COUSIN* received the Int'l Critics Choice Award, Festival of Festivals, Toronto, 85; won 6 Genie Awards including Best Picture, 86; *HE'S NOT THE WALKING KIND* won at Yorkton, Blue Ribbon (New York), Chris Statuette (Columbus).

Selective Filmography: *MY AMERICAN COUSIN,* Th, 85, CDN, Co-Prod/Wr/Dir (**2 GENIE**); *GOING ALL THE WAY,* Th, 80, CDN, Dir/Ed/Co-Prod; *MOUNT CHOPAKA EASTER SUNDAY JACKPOT RODEO,* TV, 79, CDN, Dir; *GROWING UP AT PARADISE,* Th, 77, CDN, Dir/Prod/Ed; *PEN-HI GRAD,* Th, 74, CDN, Dir; *RAISING THE GILHAST POLE,* Th, 73, CDN, Dir/Ed; *HE'S NOT THE WALKING KIND,* Th, 72, CDN, Dir; *THE BRIDAL SHOWER,* Th, 71, CDN, Dir/Wr/Prod/Ed; *PENTICTON PROFILE,* Th, 70, CDN, Dir/Ed; *GARBAGE,* Th, 69, CDN, Prod/Dir/Ed.

WINDSOR, Chris

New Caledonia Motion Pic.Inc., 102 Abbeywood Trail, Don Mills, Ont, CAN, M3B 3B5. (416)444-7784.

Types of Production & Categories: Th Film-Dir/Wr; Th Short-Dir; TV Video-Dir/Prod/Ed.

Genres: Drama-Th&TV; Comedy-Th&TV; Documentary-TV; Educational-TV.

Biography: Born 1949, England; Canadian citizen. B.A., Bristol University, English Literature. Languages: English, French, Spanish. Moved to Canada, 71. Joined Simon Fraser University Film Workshop; worked at Access Alberta, 75-78, edited over 70 films. Won the Norman McLaren Award for *TRAPPER DAN*; *SCHOOLING, FACES OF YESTERDAY* won the AMTEC Award.

Selective Filmography: *BIG MEAT EATER,* Th, 81, CDN, Dir/Co-Wr; *'APPRENDRE EN FRANCAIS'* (11 eps), TV, 80/79, CDN, Dir/Prod; *URBAN CANADA,* TV, 78, CDN, Ed; *ATHABASCA UNIVERSITY,* TV, 78, CDN, Ed; *INFORMATION FOR THE HANDICAPPED* (2 parts), TV, 78, CDN, Ed; *FESTIVAL '78,* TV, 78, CDN, Ed; *THE CAR SHOW* (pilot), TV, 78, CDN/USA, Assoc Prod; *'SCHOOLING, FACES OF YESTERDAY'* (10 eps), TV, 78, CDN, Ed; *'E.Q.C.-THE WAY TO GO'* (10 eps), TV, 77, CDN, Ed; *ONDEKOZA,* TV, 77, CDN, Ed; *RETIREMENT IN VICTORIA,* TV, 76, CDN, Ed; *MENNONITES,* TV, 76, CDN, Ed; *JEHOVAH'S WITNESSES,* TV, 76, CDN, Ed; *U.F.O.'S OVER ALBERTA* (2 parts), TV, 76, CDN, Dir/Prod/Wr; *ABE ANGHIK-INUIT ARTIST,* TV, 76, CDN, Ed; *MORMONS-ZION BUILDERS OF ALBERTA,* TV, 76, CDN, Ed; *WHO IS ALEX?,* TV, 75, CDN, Ed; *'SKI CROSS COUNTRY'* (10 eps), TV, 75, CDN, Ed; *TRAPPER DAN,* Th, 74, CDN, Dir/Wr.

WINKLER, Donald

SGCT. 4305 Esplanade, Montreal, Que, CAN, H2W 1T1. (514)842-1674. NFB, Box 6100, Montreal, Que, CAN, H3C 3H5. (514)283-9495.

Types of Production & Categories: Th Short-Dir; TV Film-Dir.

Genres: Documentary-Th&TV; Educational-TV; Experimental-Th.

Biography: Born 1940, Winnipeg, Manitoba; B.A., Honours, University of Manitoba; Woodrow Wilson Fellowship; post graduate, Yale Drama School. Films he has directed have won numerous awards including Moscow, Atlanta, Chicago for *TRAVEL LOG.*

Selective Filmography: *POET: IRVING LAYTON OBSERVED,* TV, 86, CDN, Dir; *A TALL MAN EXECUTES A JIG,* TV, 86, CDN, Dir; *THE SCHOLAR IN SOCIETY: NORTHROP FRYE IN CONVERSATION,* TV, 84, CDN, Dir; *F.R. SCOTT: RHYME AND REASON,* TV, 82, CDN, Dir/Wr; *EARLE BIRNEY: PORTRAIT OF A POET,* TV, 81, CDN, Dir/Wr; *BOOKMAKER'S PROGRESS,* TV, 79, CDN, Dir/Wr; *TRAVEL LOG,* Th, 78, CDN, Dir/Wr/Stills; *IN PRAISE OF HANDS,* TV, 74, CDN, Dir; *ONE MAN'S GARDEN,* TV, 74, CDN, Dir/Wr; *BANNER FILM,* Th, 72, CDN, Dir; *DOODLE FILM,* Th, 70, CDN, Dir/Wr/Ed.

WINNING, David

Groundstar Pictures Inc., 3308 - 24th Street N.W., Calgary, Alta, CAN, T2M 3Z7. (403)282-4906.
Types of Production & Categories: Th Film-Dir/Prod/Wr; Th Short-Dir/Wr; TV Video-Dir.
Genres: Drama-Th; Comedy-TV; Action-Th; Horror-Th.
Biography: Born 1961, Calgary, Alberta.
Selective Filmography: *FLASH FRAME,* Th, 86, CDN, Prod/Dir/Co-Wr; *STORM,* Th, 85, CDN, Prod/Dir/Wr; *'PROFILE'* (25 eps), TV, 82, CDN, Dir; *ALL STAR COMEDY* (pilot), TV, 82, CDN, Dir/Act; *RAT PATROL,* Cm, 80, CDN, Dir/Wr; *SEQUENCE,* Th, 80, CDN, Dir/Wr.

WOODLAND, James - see WRITERS

WRIGHT, Charles R.D.

3886 W. 11th Ave., Vancouver, BC, CAN, V6R 2K9. (604)224-7734. CKVU TV, 180 West 2nd Ave., Vancouver, BC, CAN, V5Y 3T9. (604)876-1344.
Types of Production & Categories: TV Video-Dir/Prod/Wr.
Genres: Variety-TV; Musical-TV; Documentary-TV; Children's-TV.
Biography: Born 1961, Hamilton, Ontario. Worked in Queensland, Australia, as TV producer/director for 18 months. Has performed as keyboardist for several bands.
Selective Filmography: *'VANCOUVER LIVE'* (daily), TV, 86-84, CDN, Dir; *2nd ANNUAL VANCOUVER AWARDS,* TV, 86, CDN, Dir; *'LAURIER'S PEOPLE'* (13 eps), TV, 85, CDN, Dir; *THE WEBB BROTHERS,* 'TWO ANNIVERSARIES', TV, 83, AUS, Prod/Dir/Wr; *'TELECLUB'* (52 eps), TV, 82, AUS, Prod/Dir; *'FIRST NEWS'* (Vancouver-daily), TV, 81-79, CDN, Dir.

WYNNE, Cordell

DGC. 1592 Vernon St., Halifax, NS, CAN, B3H 3M7. (902)429-1536. Salter Street Films, Box 2261, Station M, Halifax, NS, CAN, B3J 3C8. (902)420-1577.
Types of Production & Categories: Th Film-PM/Line Prod; TV Film-Dir/Ed; TV Video-Dir.
Genres: Drama-TV; Comedy-TV; Action-Th; Science Fiction-Th.
Biography: Born 1950, Vancouver, British Columbia. Bachelor of Fine Arts. Editor, cameraman, researcher on many commercials, industrials and documentaries. *STAR REPORTER* won awards at the Atlantic Film Festival.
Selective Filmography: *'SUCCESS'* (pilot), TV, 85, CDN, Dir; *NEVER SURRENDER,* MV, 85, CDN, PM; *DREAMBOATS,* TV, 85, CDN, Dir; *ANGELA'S RETURN,* TV, 85, CDN, Dir; *SAMUEL LOUNT,* Th, 84, CDN, PM; *DEFCON 4,* Th, 84, CDN, Line Prod; *'PREDICTIONS'* (39 eps), TV, 83, CDN, Dir; *STAR REPORTER,* TV, 82, CDN, Dir/Wr/Prod; *SIEGE,* Th, 81, CDN, Unit M; *YOU LAUGH LIKE A DUCK,* TV, 80, CDN, Dir/Co-Prod; *RUBBER MADNESS,* TV, 80, CDN, Dir.

YALDEN-TOMSON, Peter

60 De Grassi St., Toronto, Ont, CAN, M4M 2K3. (416)466-6630. McWaters Vanlindt, 495 King St. E., Toronto, Ont, CAN, M5A 1L9. (416)366-9158. Martin Givertz, 1 Yorkdale Pl., Toronto, Ont, CAN. (415)789-4175.
Types of Production & Categories: Th Short-Dir; TV Film-Dir.
Genres: Drama-Th&TV.
Biography: Born 1937, Cleveland, Ohio; moved to Canada, 41; Canadian as of 51. Educated in Canada, U.S., Spain, Switzerland; speaks English, French, Spanish. Many commercial Awards for industrial short films, USA.
Selective Filmography: *SHELLGAME,* TV, 85, CDN, Dir; *TOOLS OF THE DEVIL/ ROUGH JUSTICE,* 'FOR THE RECORD', TV, 84/83, CDN, Dir;

(cont/suite)

CLOWNS OF CHRISTMAS, TV, 80, CDN, Dir; *FOUR TO FOUR,* TV, 78, CDN, Dir.

YATES, Rebecca - see PRODUCERS

YOLLES, Edie
CSC. Gemini Film Prod. Ltd., 69 Sherbourne St., Ste.424, Toronto, Ont, CAN, M5A 3X7. (416)862-9031.
Types of Production & Categories: Th Film-Dir/Prod/Wr/Ed; TV Film-Dir/Prod/ Wr/Ed.
Genres: Drama-Th&TV; Comedy-Th&TV; Documentary-Th&TV; Educational-Th&TV.
Biography: Graduated Ryerson Polytechnical Institute, Toronto; Gold Medal in Sociology, University of Toronto; Diploma in Town Planning; painting and sculpture, Ontario College of Art. *ANGELS* won Red Ribbon (American Film Fest.), Chris Statuette (Columbus), Diploma of Merit and Medal (Mifed, Milan), Gold Medal (Int'l Film & TV Fest., NY).
Selective Filmography: *THAT'S MY BABY!,* Th, 85, CDN, Co-Dir/Co-Ed/Co-Wr/ Prod; *ANGELS,* TV, 79, CDN, Dir/Ed/Prod.

YOUNG, Donna
ATPD. 242 Woodfield Rd., Toronto, Ont, CAN, M4L 2W7. (416)466-8450.
Types of Production & Categories: TV Video-Dir.
Genres: Current Affairs-TV.
Biography: Born 1952, Winnipeg, Manitoba. Education: University of Manitoba, Arts, English.
Selective Filmography: *'CBLT MORNING'* (daily), TV, 85/84, CDN, Dir; *'NEWSHOUR/NEWSFINAL'* (daily), TV, 84-80, CDN, Dir; *PROVINCIAL ELECTION,* TV, 84, CDN, Pro Coord; *LEADERSHIP CONVENTION,* TV, 84, CDN, Pro Coord.

YOUNG, Stephen
CFTA. 1297 Walnut St., Victoria, BC, CAN, V8T 1N5. (604)385-2480. Pastiche Productions Ltd., 14 Bastion Sq., Victoria, BC, CAN, V8W 1H9. (604)384-6263.
Types of Production & Categories: TV Film-Prod/Dir; TV Video-Prod/Dir.
Genres: Drama-TV; Documentary-TV; Educational-Th&TV; Children's-TV.
Biography: Born 1943, England; came to Canada in 56. Began his carreer in broadcasting in 62; has been involved with several aspects of the industry including sales, marketing and producing.
Selective Filmography: *ROOT ROT DISEASE,* In, 85, CDN, Prod; *CANADA BRITISH COLUMBIA F.R.D.A./ DECISIONS,* ED, 85, CDN, Prod; *WORKING WELL,* In, 85, CDN, Prod/Dir; *OLY'S,* Cm, 85, CDN, Prod/Dir; *TREASURE HUNTERS,* TV, 85, CDN, Tech Dir; *WOODGROVE CENTRE/QUALICUM INN/U.I. FORD MERCURY,* Cm, 84/83, CDN, Dir; *DEATH FROM SEX,* MV, 84, CDN, Dir; *SCRAPBOOK,* TV, 83, CDN, Dir; *TOM HARRIS CHEV-OLDS/ BEACH GARDEN RESORT/GRANITE INDUSTRIES,* Cm, 83-80, CDN, Dir; *DAVID BARRETT ADRESS TO THE PROVINCE,* TV, 82, CDN, Dir.

ZARITSKY, John
K.A. Productions Inc., 49 Cavell Ave., Toronto, Ont, CAN, M4J 1H5. (416)466-8202.
Types of Production & Categories: Th Film-Dir/Prod; TV Film-Dir/Prod/Wr.
Genres: Drama-TV; Variety-Th&TV; Documentary-TV.
Biography: Born 1943, St-Catherines, Ontario; bilingual. B.A., Trinity College, University of Toronto. National Newspaper Award, 70; Ford Foundation Fellowship, Washington Journalism Centre, 70. Awards for *JUST ANOTHER MISSING KID* include: Gold Medal, N.Y. Film Fest.; Gold Medal, Hemisfilm;

(cont/suite)

Rockie, Banff Int'l; Blue Ribbon, American Film Fest.. *I'LL GET THERE SOMEHOW* won the Wilderness Award, Bronze Plaque, Columbus.
Selective Filmography: *THE REAL STUFF*, TV, 86, CDN, Exec Prod/Prod/Dir/ Wr; *TEARS ARE NOT ENOUGH*, Th, 85, CDN, Dir/Prod; *RAPISTS - CAN THEY BE STOPPED?*, 'AMERICA UNDERCOVER', TV, 85, USA, Dir/Prod/ Wr; *THE BOY NEXT DOOR*, 'FOR THE RECORD', TV, 84, CDN, Prod; *I'LL GET THERE SOMEHOW*, TV, 84, CDN, Dir/Prod/Wr; *BJORN BORG*, 'CHAMPIONS', TV, 83, CDN, Dir/Prod/Wr; *JUST ANOTHER MISSING KID*, 'THE FIFTH ESTATE', TV, 81, CDN, Dir/Prod/Wr (**ACTRA/OSCAR**); *CARING FOR CHRYSLER/ CHARITY BEGINS AT HOME/ THE LOSER'S GAME*, 'THE FIFTH ESTATE', TV, 80-77, CDN, Dir/Prod/Wr; *GORD S./ I DID NOT KILL BOB NEVILLE/ BETSY'S LAST CHANCE*, 'THE FIFTH ESTATE', TV, 78-76, CDN, Dir/Prod/Wr; *THE MAKING OF A MARTYR/ STEELTOWN STAR*, 'THE FIFTH ESTATE', TV, 76, CDN, Dir/Prod/Wr.

ZIELINSKA, Ida Eva

ASIFA. 1225 St.Marc St., #401, Montreal, Que, CAN, H3H 2E7. (514)932-5856. Spiral Studios Inc., 3170 Place de Ramezay, Montreal, Que, CAN, H3Y 2B5. (514) 932-0396.
Types of Production & Categories: Th Short-Dir/Prod/Wr/An.
Genres: Comedy-Th&TV; Documentary-Th&TV; Animation-Th&TV; Music Video-TV.
Biography: Born 1957, Warsaw, Poland; grew up in India, Egypt, USA, Canada; Canadian citizen. Languages: English, French, Polish, some Spanish. B.F.A, Magna Cum Laude, Concordia University, 80; enrolled in Masters of Educational Technology program, Concordia U., 86. Background in painting, graphics, music, writing, animation and special effects. Founder (81) and President, Spiral Studios Inc. and Ida Eva Publishing (music publishing).
Selective Filmography: *UCOPAN BARBADOS PROJECT*, In, 86, CDN, Prod/Wr/ Dir; *TRESPASS*, Th, 85, CDN, Wr/Prod/Dir/Des; *ODDBALLS*, Th, 84, CDN, VFX Des; *SCREWBALLS*, Th, 83, CDN, VFX Des; *AGENCY*, Th, 79, CDN, Co-An/VFX Des; *OLD ORCHARD BEACH P.Q.*, Th, 79, CDN, An; *CENTRE DU REMBOURREUR*, Cm, 79, CDN, Wr/Dir/Des/An; *HEADS OR TAILS*, Th, 78, CDN, Wr/Prod/Dir.

ZIELINSKI, Rafal

43 Albany Ave., Toronto, Ont, CAN, M5R 3C2. (416)535-7942. Vision Pictures, 3170 Ramezay Pl., Montreal, Que, CAN, H3Y 2B5. (514)932-0396. 8033 Sunset Blvd., #640, Los Angeles, CA, USA, 90046. (213)654-3241.
Types of Production & Categories: Th Film-Dir.
Genres: Drama-Th; Comedy-Th; Action-Th.
Biography: Born 1954, Warsaw, Poland. Studied and lived in U.S., Europe, Middle East and India; B.Sc., M.I.T. (Art and Design), 74. Directed and produced documentaries and commercials, Montreal. President of Vision Pictures. *MICHEL PELLUS*, entry at Cannes, 79; Silver Medal, Moscow Film Festival, Australian Film Fest..
Selective Filmography: *RECRUITS*, Th, 85, CDN, Dir; *VALET GIRLS*, Th, 85, USA, Dir; *LOOSE SCREWS*, Th, 84, CDN, Dir; *HEY BABE*, Th, 82, CDN, Dir/ Co-Prod; *SCREWBALLS*, Th, 82, CDN, Dir; *MICHEL PELLUS*, Th, 79, CDN, Dir/Prod.

PRODUCTION
MANAGERS
★
REGISSEURS

REGISSEURS/PRODUCTION MANAGERS

ARBEID, Gerry

ACTT, DGA, DGC. 95 Pears Ave., Toronto, Ont, CAN, M5R 1S9. (416)960-8007.
Types of Production & Categories: Th Film-PM/1st AD; Th Short-PM/1st AD; TV Film-PM/1st AD; TV Video-PM/1st AD.
Genres: Drama-Th&TV; Comedy-Th&TV; Science Fiction-Th&TV; Horror-Th&TV.
Biography: Born 1934, London, England; Canadian and American resident (Green Card). Entered film industry, 53; has worked in various capacities on over 70 feature films; also, 8 years of film editorial experience; consultant to insurance and bonding companies including Lloyds London.
Selective Filmography: *ALTER EGO,* TV, 85, USA, Assist Dir; *MYSTERY HAUNTED CASTLE,* Th, 84, USA, Assist Dir; *BEDROOM EYES,* Th, 83, CDN, PM; *HEAVENLY BODIES,* Th, 83, CDN, PM; *OVERDRAWN AT THE MEMORY BANK,* TV, 83, CDN/USA, PM; *BETWEEN FRIENDS,* TV, 83, USA, PM; *CURTAINS,* Th, 81, CDN, PM; *HANK WILLIAMS: THE SHOW HE NEVER GAVE,* Th, 81, CDN, Post PM; *MELANIE,* Th, 80, CDN, PM; *TRIBUTE* (UN FILS POUR L'ETE), Th, 80, CDN, PM; *THE KIDNAPPING OF THE PRESIDENT,* Th, 79, CDN, PM; *AN AMERICAN CHRISTMAS CAROL,* TV, 79, USA, PM; *FISH HAWK,* Th, 79, CDN, PM; *YESTERDAY* (GABRIELLE), TV, 79, CDN, Line Prod; *KAVIK THE WOLF DOG,* TV, 78, CDN, PM; *'SUCCESS IN REAL ESTATE'* (12 eps), ED, 77, CDN, Prod; *DISAPPEARANCE,* Th, 77, CDN/GB, Prod; *GOLDENROD,* Th, 76, CDN, Co-Prod; *BLACK CHRISTMAS* (SILENT NIGHT, EVIL NIGHT), Th, 74, CDN, Co-Prod; *NEPTUNE FACTOR,* Th, 72, CDN, PM; *MURPHY'S ESTATE,* Th, 71, CDN, Assist Dir.

BARKER, Nicholas

STCQ. 687 Querbes, #5, Outremont, Qué, CAN. (514)279-5855. Pyrate Communications, 451 St. Sulpice, Studio L, Montréal, Qué, CAN, H2Y 2V9. (514) 284-0761.
Types de production et Catégories: TV film-Rég/Prod; TV vidéo-Rég/Prod.
Types d'oeuvres: Documentaire-TV; Education-TV; Annonces-TV.
Curriculum vitae: Né en 1948, Angleterre; citoyen canadien. producteur d'agence pour annonces, TV et radio; rédacteur (scénarios) et concepteur; régisseur/directeur de production sur maintes annonces, documentaires et films éducatifs.

BIRD, Christopher

DGC. 1 - 2559 Bloor St.W., Toronto, Ont, CAN, M6S 1S2. (416)767-7412. Seabird Prod., 314 Jarvis St., Suite 101, Toronto, Ont, CAN, M5B 2C5. (416)979-3225.
Types of Production & Categories: TV Film-PM/1st AD; TV Video-PM/1st AD.
Genres: Musical-TV; Documentary-TV; Children's-TV.
Biography: Born 1942, London, England; British-Canadian citizen. Stage manager, Canadian Equity; musician/artist; production manager/1st assistant director on numerous commercials and industrial films, 79-86.
Selective Filmography: *THE CHIMNEY SWEEP,* TV, 85, CDN, PM/1st AD; *'VID KIDS'* (13 eps), TV, 85, CDN, PM/1st AD; *MORGENTALER: IN CONVERSATION,* TV, 85, CDN, PM/1st AD; *RONNIE HAWKINS SPECIAL,* TV, 80, CDN, PM/1st AD; *GINO VANELLI IN CONCERT,* TV, 79, CDN, PM/1st AD.

BRAIDWOOD, Tom

DGC. 21431 Stonehouse Ave., Maple Ridge, BC, CAN, V2X 3Z5. (604)463-9650.
Types of Production & Categories: Th Film-PM; Th Short-PM; TV Film-PM; TV Video-PM.
Genres: Drama-Th; Documentary-Th&TV; Educational-Th&TV; Experimental-Th&TV.

(cont/suite)

Biography: Born 1948, Vancouver, British Columbia. B.A., Theatre, University of British Columbia, 71; M.A., Film Studies, U.B.C., 75. Resident actor/writer/ director, Tamahnous Theatre Co., 72-78; author; film lecturer, Simon Fraser U.. Executive Director, Pacific Cinematheque, 82-85.
Selective Filmography: *AND AFTER TOMORROW...,* ED, 86, CDN, PM; *EMMA,* ED, 85, CDN, PM; *'DANGER BAY'* (1 eps), TV, 85, CDN/USA, 1st AD; *SEED,* Th, 85, CDN, PM; *MY AMERICAN COUSIN,* Th, 84, CDN, PM; *WALLS,* Th, 84, CDN, Assoc Prod/PM; *LOW VISIBILITY,* Th, 83, CDN, Assoc Prod/PM; *DESERTERS,* Th, 82, CDN, Assoc Prod/PM; *MARATHON,* Th, 81, CDN, PM; *TAPESTRY ARTIST,* ED, 81, CDN, Prod/Dir; *RIGHT TO FIGHT,* ED, 81, CDN, Dir; *SKIP TRACER,* Th, 78, CDN, 1st AD; *LIMITED ENGAGEMENT,* Th, 76, CDN, Dir; *INSIDE THE REFLECTION,* Th, 74, CDN, Dir; *WIND FROM THE WEST,* Th, 73, CDN, Prod/Dir.

BUCHSBAUM, Don

834 4th St., Santa Monica, CA, USA, 90403. (213)394-3494.
Types of Production & Categories: Th Film-PM/1st AD; TV Film-PM/1st AD.
Genres: Drama-Th&TV; Comedy-Th; Action-Th&TV.
Biography: Born 1934, New York City; lived in Canada, 70-83; landed immigrant. In charge of production, Introvision, Los Angeles, 86.
Selective Filmography: *MAFIA PRINCESS,* TV, 85, USA, 1st AD; *BLACKOUT,* TV, 84, USA, 1st AD; *RUNNING BRAVE,* Th, 83, CDN/USA, PM; *HEARTACHES,* Th, 81, CDN, PM/1st AD; *SPRING FEVER* (SNEAKERS), Th, 80, CDN, PM; *SCANNERS,* Th, 80, CDN, PM; *HOG WILD,* Th, 79, CDN, PM; *YESTERDAY* (GABRIELLE), Th, 79, CDN, PM; *WHO HAS SEEN OUR CHILDREN,* TV, 78, USA, PM; *FIGHTING MEN,* 'FOR THE RECORD', TV, 77, CDN, 1st AD; *'THE NEW AVENGERS'* (4 eps), TV, 77, CDN/GB/F, PM; *JUST JESSIE,* Th, 77, CDN, Assoc Prod; *MARIA,* TV, 75, CDN, Assoc Prod; *'FOR THE RECORD',* TV, 75/74, CDN, 1st AD; *THE APPRENTICESHIP OF DUDDY KRAVITZ,* Th, 74, CDN, PM; *KEEP IT IN THE FAMILY,* Th, 73, CDN, PM; *WEDDING IN WHITE,* Th, 72, CDN, PM.

CARR, Warren H.

DGC. 691 W. 32nd Ave., Vancouver, BC, CAN, V5Z 2J8. (604)872-4777.
Types of Production & Categories: Th Film-PM; TV Film-PM; TV Video-Dir.
Genres: Drama-Th&TV; Action-Th&TV; Documentary-TV; Educational-TV.
Selective Filmography: *ROXANNE,* Th, 86, USA, PM; *THE BOY WHO COULD FLY,* Th, 85, USA, PM; *GOING FOR THE GOLD: THE BILL JOHNSON STORY,* TV, 85, CDN, PM; *YEAR OF THE DRAGON,* Th, 85/84, USA, 2nd AD; *THE STEPFATHER,* Th, 85, USA, PM; *THE CLAN OF THE CAVE BEAR,* Th, 84, USA, 2nd AD; *SECRETS OF A MARRIED MAN,* TV, 84, USA, 2nd AD; *LABATT 1984 ROCK EXPRESS AWARD,* TV, 84, CDN, Assoc Prod; *THE GLITTER DOME,* TV, 83, CDN/USA, 2nd AD; *DRAW!,* TV, 83, CDN/USA, Wran; *ICEMAN,* Th, 83, USA, 2nd AD; *SPACEHUNTER: ADVENTURES IN THE FORBIDDEN ZONE,* Th, 83, CDN/USA, U Loc M; *THE ETERNAL HARVEST: WATER,* 'RESOURCE REVIEW', TV, 81/80, CDN, Dir; *THE MARITIME MUSEUM OF BC,* 'GALLERIES AND MUSEUMS', TV, 79, CDN, Dir.

CLARK, Louise - see PRODUCERS

CLAYTON, Christopher

IATSE-667. 612 Bay Ave., Kelowna, BC, CAN, V1Y 7J9. (604)762-2391.
Types of Production & Categories: TV Film-PM; TV Video-PM.
Genres: Drama-TV; Comedy-TV; Action-TV; Documentary-TV.

(cont/suite)

Biography: Born 1958, Blackpool, England. Education: 2 years military (surveillance photography); pilot. President, founder of Exposure Enterprises, The Interior Film Production Film Association (B.C.) and Pacific Film Productions Vancouver Ltd..
Selective Filmography: *MEMBERS OF THE ORCHESTRA,* TV, 86, CDN, Stills; *TRIAL & ERROR,* TV, 86, CDN, Op; *RENFIELDS DETOURS,* TV, 86, CDN, PM; *HATS,* TV, 86, CDN, PM; *THE ACCIDENT,* TV, 85, CDN, Op; *SOLO,* Th, 85, USA, Stills; *HAILSTORM,* Th, 84, USA, Stills.

CUDDY, Janet

DGC. 44 Grace St., Toronto, Ont, CAN, M6J 2S2. (416)530-0409.
Types of Production & Categories: Th Film-PM/Unit M; TV Film-PM.
Genres: Drama-Th&TV; Horror-Th.
Biography: Born 1958, Ottawa, Ontario. Studied at Queen's University, Kingston, Ontario and Concordia, Montreal. Speaks French, English, Italian.
Selective Filmography: *'KAY O'BRIEN'* (13 eps), TV, 86, USA, PM; *PIPPI LONGSTOCKING* (2 parts), TV, 85, USA, PM; *THE CARE BEARS MOVIE,* Th, 85, CDN, Unit M; *SKYWARD,* Th, 84, CDN/J, Unit M; *A MATTER OF SEX,* TV, 83, CDN/USA, Assist PM; *WILL THERE REALLY BE A MORNING?,* TV, 82, USA, Pro Coord; *JEN'S PLACE,* TV, 82, CDN, PM; *VIDEODROME,* Th, 81, CDN, Assist PM; *VISITING HOURS,* Th, 80, CDN, Assist PM.

DALE, Miles

Demilo Productions Ltd., 158 Albany Ave., #3, Toronto, Ont, CAN, M4W 1R6. (416)588-2809.
Types of Production & Categories: Th Film-Prod; TV Film-PM; TV Video-PM.
Genres: Drama-Th&TV; Comedy-TV; Variety-TV; Musical-TV.
Biography: Born 1960, Toronto, Ontario; has U.S. and European visas. Worked as a radio programmer (CITR-FM) while at University of British Columbia.
Selective Filmography: *EASTER SEALS TELETHON,* TV, 86, CDN, Line Prod; *TIMING,* Th, 85, CDN, Co-Prod; *THE EXECUTION OF RAYMOND GRAHAM,* TV, 85, CDN, Pro Spv; *'THE COMEDY FACTORY'* (8 eps), TV, 85, CDN/USA Assoc Prod; *FASHION TELEVISION,* TV, 85, CDN, Assoc Prod; *GENIE AWARDS,* TV, 85, CDN, Pro Coord; *JUNO AWARDS,* TV, 84, CDN, PM; *ANNE MURRAY IN QUEBEC,* TV, 84, CDN, PM; *'OFFICE GIRLS'* (45 eps), TV, 83, CDN, PM; *ROMEO AND JULIET ON ICE,* TV, 83, USA, PM; *HONEYMOON HAVEN,* TV, 83, CDN, PM; *COLD STORAGE,* TV, 83, CDN, PM.

DALEN, Lyara - see PRODUCERS

DANYLKIW, John

DGC. 8 Geneva Ave., Toronto, Ont, CAN, M5A 2J8. (416)964-0725. Heartstar Productions Ltd., 439 Wellington St.W., 4th Fl., Toronto, Ont, CAN, M5V 1E7. (416)596-8305.
Types of Production & Categories: Th Film-PM; TV Film-PM/Prod; TV Video-PM/Prod.
Genres: Drama-Th&TV; Action-Th&TV; Documentary-TV; Children's-Th&TV.
Biography: Born 1949; Canadian citizen; bilingual. B.A., Communication Arts, Loyola College, Montreal. President, Heartstar Productions Ltd., Toronto, 79-86; producer of many national and int'l commercials.
Selective Filmography: *APOLOGY,* TV, 85, USA, Pro Spv; *ALEX, THE LIFE OF A CHILD,* TV, 85, USA, Pro Spv; *ROCKABYE,* Th, 85, USA, Pro Spv; *THE UNDERGRADS,* TV, 85, USA, Pro Spv; *MIRACLE AT MOREAUX,* TV, 85, CDN, Line Prod/PM; *YOUNG AGAIN,* TV, 85, USA, Pro Spv; *AGNES OF GOD,* Th, 84, USA, PM; *THE WIZARD OF OZ* (animation), Th, 83, CDN, P Pro Spv; *DR. DOOLITTLE* (pilot), TV, 82, CDN/USA, P Pro Spv; *ONE FINE WEEKEND - LIGHTHOUSE REUNION,* TV, 82, CDN, Line Prod; *'THE LANDSCAPE OF*

(cont/suite)

GEOMETRY', TV, 81, CDN, Prod/Pro Spv; *B.C. A SPECIAL CHRISTMAS*, TV, 81, CDN, Prod/Pro Spv; *UTILITIES*, Th, 80, CDN, PM; *TUKIKI*, TV, 79, CDN, Prod/PM; *THE SHAPE OF THINGS TO COME*, Th, 79, CDN, Assoc Prod; *THE NEW MISADVENTURES OF ICHABOD CRANE*, TV, 79/78, CDN, Prod/PM; *OH HEAVENLY DOG*, Th, 79, USA, PM; *'CURIOUS GEORGE'*, TV, 79, CDN, Prod/PM; *THE LITTLE BROWN BURRO*, TV, 77, CDN, Prod/PM.

DE GRANDPRE, Sylvie

STCQ. 564 Birch, St-Lambert, Qué, CAN, J4P 2N1. (514)672-6837. 86 De Brésoles, Montréal, Qué, CAN, H2Y 1V5. (514)285-8901.
Types de production et Catégories: l métrage-Rég; TV film-Rég; TV vidéo-Rég.
Types d'oeuvres: Drame-C&TV; Comédie-TV.
Curriculum vitae: Née en 1950; bilingue. A travaillé comme assistante et directrice de production pour diverses compagnies: cinéma, télévision et annonces publicitaires.
Filmographie sélective: *PAGE 3* (UN ORDINATEUR AU COEUR), (pilote), TV, 85, CDN, Dir pro; *BONHEUR D'OCCASION* (THE TIN FLUTE), (aussi 5 ep-TV), C, 82, CDN, Dir pro; *BLACK MIRROR*, C, 80, CDN, Dir pro; *UNE JOURNEE PARTICULIÈRE*, C, 77, CDN/I, Dir pro; *THE NIGHT OF THE HIGH TIDE*, C, 76, CDN/I, Ass pro; *JE SUIS LOIN DE TOI MIGNONNE*, C, 75, CDN, Ass pro.

DUNDAS, Sally

DGC. 190 Crawford St., Toronto, Ont, CAN, M6J 2V6. (416)531-1461. Imax Systems Corporation, 38 Isabella St., Toronto, Ont, CAN, M4Y 1N1. (416)960-8509.
Types of Production & Categories: Th Film-PM; TV Film-PM.
Genres: Drama-Th&TV; Documentary-Th; Children's-TV.
Biography: Born 1953, England; British-Canadian citizen; educated in England. Freelance production manager since 73; Senior Production Executive, First Choice, 82-83; on staff at Imax Systems Corporation, 86.
Selective Filmography: *'THE EDISON TWINS'* (26 eps), TV, 85/84, CDN, PM; *SKYWARD*, Th, 84/83, CDN, PM; *FREEDOM TO MOVE*, Th, 84, CDN, Pro Exec; *TICKET TO HEAVEN*, Th, 80, CDN, PM; *ESCAPE FROM IRAN: THE CANADIAN CAPER*, TV, 80, CDN, PM; *CLOWN WHITE* (CHANSON SANS PAROLE), TV, 80, CDN, PM; *HEAD ON*, Th, 79, CDN, PM; *SUMMER'S CHILDREN*, Th, 79, CDN, PM; *I MISS YOU HUGS AND KISSES*, Th, 77, CDN, PM; *THE SHOE FITS*, TV, 76, CDN, Assoc Prod.

GILROY, Grace

DGC. Kicking Horse Productions Ltd., 11930 100th Ave., Edmonton, Alta, CAN, T5K 0K5. (403)482-6441.
Types of Production & Categories: Th Film-PM; TV Film-PM.
Genres: Drama-Th&TV; Action-Th&TV; Horror-Th.
Biography: Born Edmonton, Alberta. Partner in Kicking Horse Productions Ltd. since 1977.
Selective Filmography: *I'LL TAKE MANHATTAN* (mini-series), TV, 86, USA, Pro Spv; *THE CASE OF THE NOTORIOUS NUN*, TV, 86, USA, PM; *KANE & ABEL* (mini-series), TV, 85/84, USA, PM; *A NICE, PLEASANT, DEADLY WEEKEND*, TV, 85, USA, PM; *A LETTER TO THREE WIVES*, TV, 85, USA, PM; *LOYALTIES*, Th, 85, CDN, PM; *EVERGREEN* (mini-series), TV, 84, USA, PM; *APRIL FOOL*, Th, 84, USA, PM.

GORD, Ken

DGC. 39 Havelock St., Toronto, Ont, CAN. (416)534-6117.
Types of Production & Categories: Th Film-PM/Prod; TV Film-PM/Prod.
Genres: Drama-Th&TV; Comedy-Th; Action-Th; Science Fiction-Th.
Biography: Born 1949, Toronto, Ontario. Educated at University of Toronto, 67-69. Has filmed in the Orient, India, USA.

(cont/suite)

Selective Filmography: *A JUDGEMENT IN STONE*, Th, 86, CDN, PM; *MR. NICE GUY*, Th, 85, CDN, PM; *RECRUITS*, Th, 85, CDN, Pro Spv; *BUSTED UP*, Th, 84, CDN, PM; *LOOSE SCREWS*, Th, 84, CDN, PM; *'FIRST CLASS WITH PATRICK MacNEE'* (2 eps), TV, 83, CDN, Co-Prod; *DEADLY EYES* (THE RATS), Th, 82, CDN, PM; *THE HIGH COUNTRY* (THE FIRST HELLO), Th, 80, CDN, Co-Prod; *STARSHIP INVASIONS*, Th, 77, CDN, Co-Prod; *POINT OF NO RETURN*, Th, 75, CDN, Co-Prod/PM; *DREAM ON THE RUN*, TV, 73, CDN, Co-Prod/PM.

GRAY, Bob
DGC. 4309 Patterdale Dr., North Vancouver, BC, CAN, V7R 4L6. (604)381-6414.
Types of Production & Categories: Th Film-PM; TV Film-PM.
Genres: Drama-Th&TV; Action-Th.
Biography: Born in England; Canadian citizen. Production manager, CBC, 60-72; spent 2 years in Kenya; now freelance.
Selective Filmography: *BACKFIRE*, Th, 86, CDN, PM; *CROSSINGS* (mini-series), (in Paris), TV, 86, USA, Pro Spv; *'LOVE BOAT'* (25 eps), TV, 86-83, USA, Unit PM; *EUREKA*, Th, 83, GB, PM; *THE LAST DESPERADO*, Th, 81, USA, PM; *A MAN, A WOMAN AND A BANK*, Th, 79, CDN, PM; *LA MENACE* (THE THREAT), Th, 79, CDN/F, PM; *SHADOW OF THE HAWK*, Th, 76, CDN, PM; *RUSSIAN ROULETTE*, Th, 76, GB, PM.

GRAY, Nick
DGC. 147 Gough Ave., Toronto, Ont, CAN, M4K 3N9. (416)465-9155.
Types of Production & Categories: Th Film-PM/Prod; TV Film-PM/Prod.
Genres: Drama-Th; Action-TV; Children's-Th&TV.
Biography: Born 1955, Toronto, Ontario. B.A., Film Theory, Queen's University.
Selective Filmography: *NIAGARA - MIRACLES, MYTHS AND MAGIC*, Th, 86, CDN, Prod; *'PHILIP MARLOWE PRIVATE EYE'* (6 eps), TV, 86, CDN, PM; *ANNE OF GREEN GABLES* (mini-series), TV, 85, CDN, PM; *TUCKER AND THE HORSE THIEF/WORKING FOR PEANUTS/MY FATHER,MY RIVAL, 'FAMILY PLAYHOUSE'*, TV, 84, CDN, Co-Prod; *'THE EDISON TWINS'* (26 eps), TV, 84/83, CDN, PM; *BLOOD RELATIONS*, TV, 83, CDN, PM; *HUMONGOUS*, Th, 81, CDN, PM; *JULIE DARLING*, Th, 81, CDN, 1st AD; *ALLIGATOR SHOES* (LES SOULIERS EN CROCO), Th, 80, CDN, Line Prod; *THE LIFE AND TIMES OF EDWIN ALONZO BOYD*, Th, 80, CDN, 1st AD.

HACKETT, Jonathan
DGC. 212 Crawford St., Toronto, Ont, CAN, M6J 2V6. (416)535-1835.
Types of Production & Categories: Th Film PM; TV Film-PM/1st AD; TV Video-PM/1st AD.
Genres: Children's-Th&TV; Commercials-TV.
Biography: Born in England; Canadian citizen. Started in film business in 1970; worked mostly as key grip till 80; 1st assistant director/production mamager on numerous commercials, 81-84; commercials producer, 85-86.
Selective Filmography: *'ADDERLY'* (PM-3 eps), (8 eps), TV, 86, CDN, Line Prod; *FOLLOW THAT BIRD*, Th, 84, USA, PM.

IVESON, Gwen
DGC. 64 Langley Ave., Toronto, Ont, CAN, M4K 1B5. (416)466-9436. Telefilm Canada, 130 Bloor St. W., Toronto, Ont, CAN, M5S 1N5. (416)973-6436.
Types of Production & Categories: Th Film-PM/Prod; TV Film-PM/Prod.
Genres: Drama-Th&TV; Science Fiction-Th; Documentary-Th&TV; Current Affairs-TV.
Biography: Born 1937, Victoria, British Columbia. Manager, Business Affairs-Toronto, Telefilm Canada, since 83.

(cont/suite)

Selective Filmography: *A MATTER OF SEX,* TV, 83, CDN/USA, Co-Prod/PM; *WILL THERE REALLY BE A MORNING?,* TV, 82, USA, PM; *VIDEODROME,* Th, 82, CDN, PM; *VISITING HOURS,* Th, 80, CDN, PM; *SILENCE OF THE NORTH,* Th, 80/79, CDN, PM; *THE BROOD,* Th, 78, CDN, PM; *ONE NIGHT STAND,* TV, 77, CDN, Assoc Prod; *WHO HAS SEEN THE WIND,* Th, 76, CDN, Assoc Prod; *'THE FIFTH ESTATE'* (35 eps), TV, 76/75, CDN, PM; *A MARRIED COUPLE,* Th, 68, CDN, Assoc Prod; *WARRENDALE,* Th, 67, CDN, PM; *'THIS HOUR HAS 7 DAYS'* (35 eps), Th, 65/64, CDN, Pro Coord.

JONES, Dennis

DGA, DGC. 9708 Beverlywood St., Los Angeles, CA, USA, 90034. (213)559-1476. Prometheus Productions Inc., 1900 Ave. of the Stars, #2270, Los Angeles, CA, USA, 90067. (213)277-1900. Jim Leonard, Leonard and Zeitsoff, 11845 W. Olympic Blvd., #645, Los Angeles, CA, USA, 90064. (213)312-8660.
Types of Production & Categories: Th Film-PM/Prod; TV Film-PM/Prod.
Genres: Drama-Th&TV; Comedy-Th&TV; Action-Th&TV; Science Fiction-Th&TV.
Biography: Born 1943, Grimsby, Lincolnshire, England; emigrated to Canada in 55, Canadian citizen; to US, 73 (Green Card). B.A., Economics, University of Toronto, 66; Radio & TV Arts, Ryerson Polytechnical Insitute, 70.
Selective Filmography: *SHORT CIRCUIT,* Th, 86/85, USA, Co-Prod; *BACK TO THE FUTURE,* Th, 85/84, USA, PM; *MRS. SOFFEL,* Th, 84/83, USA, Assoc Prod/PM; *BUCKAROO BANZAI,* Th, 83, USA, Assoc Prod/PM; *TWILIGHT ZONE - THE MOVIE,* Th, 82, USA, PM; *POLTERGEIST,* Th, 81, USA, PM; *RICH AND FAMOUS,* Th, 81/80, USA, PM; *FUN AND GAMES,* TV, 80, USA, PM; *FREEDOM ROAD,* TV, 79, USA, PM; *LOVE FOR RENT,* TV, 79/78, USA, PM; *SEIZURE: THE STORY OF KATHY MORRIS,* TV, 78, USA, PM; *LETTERS FROM FRANK,* TV, 78, CDN, 1st AD; *INDIANS* (4 parts), TV, 77, USA, PM; *AWAKENING LAND* (3 parts), TV, 77, USA, 1st AD; *BLACK OAK CONSPIRACY,* Th, 76, USA, 1st AD; *OUTLAW BLUES,* Th, 76, USA, 1st AD; *THE AMAZING DOBERMANS,* Th, 76, USA, 1st AD; *GUMBALL RALLY,* Th, 76/75, USA, 2nd AD; *TRACKDOWN,* Th, 75, USA, 1st AD; *BOBBY JOE ANT THE OUTLAW,* Th, 75, USA, 1st AD; *DEATH RACE 2000,* Th, 75, USA, 1st AD; *ALIEN THUNDER,* Th, 72, CDN, Props; *F.C.E.DILLON,* In, 72, USA, Prod/Dir; *'HERE COME THE SEVENTIES'* (TOWARDS THE YEAR 2000), (52 eps), TV, 72-70, CDN, Assoc Prod/PM.

KELLY, Barbara

DGC. Screen Mgmt. Services Inc., 32 Barton Ave., Toronto, Ont, CAN, M6G 1P1. (416)535-4104.
Types of Production & Categories: Th Film-PM; TV Film-PM.
Genres: Drama-Th&TV; Comedy-Th&TV.
Selective Filmography: *AMERIKA* (mini-series), TV, 86, USA, PM; *DEADLY BUSINESS,* TV, 85, USA, PM; *MAFIA PRINCESS,* TV, 85, USA, PM; *PERRY MASON RETURNS,* TV, 85, USA, PM; *ELENI* (in Canada), Th, 85, USA/GB, PM; *DAVIES AND HEARST,* TV, 84, USA, PM; *FULL CIRCLE AGAIN,* TV, 84, CDN, U Loc M; *HEARTSOUNDS,* TV, 84, USA, U Loc M; *'SCTV'* (16 eps), TV, 84/83, CDN, Loc M; *COUGAR,* TV, 83, USA, U Loc M; *BETWEEN FRIENDS,* TV, 83, USA, U Loc M; *INTELLIGENT UNIVERSE,* TV, 83, CDN, U Loc M; *JEN'S PLACE,* TV, 82, CDN, U Loc M; *FRANK AND FEARLESS,* TV, 82, USA, U Loc M; *UTILITIES,* Th, 82, CDN, U Loc M; *CLASS OF '84,* Th, 81, CDN/USA, U Loc M; *CORLETTO & SON,* TV, 80, CDN, U Loc M; *OH HEAVENLY DOG,* Th, 79, USA, Unit M.

KIMBER, Les

ACTRA, DGC, IATSE. R.R. #4, Calgary, Alta, CAN, T2M 4L4. (403)239-1060.
(cont/suite)

Types of Production & Categories: Th Film-PM; TV Film-PM; TV Video-PM.
Genres: Drama-Th&TV; Comedy-Th; Action-Th; Horror-Th&TV.
Biography: Born 1942, Calgary, Alberta.
Selective Filmography: *'THE HITCHIKER'* (13 eps), TV, 85, CDN/USA, PM; *THE JOURNEY OF NATTY GANN,* Th, 84, USA, Assoc Prod; *FINDERS KEEPERS,* Th, 84, USA, PM; *SUPERMAN III* (in Canada), Th, 83, USA/GB, PM; *MOTHERLODE,* Th, 80, USA, PM/Assoc Prod; *DEATH HUNT,* Th, 80, USA, PM; *SKI LIFT TO DEATH,* TV, 79, USA, PM; *TOUCHED BY LOVE,* TV, 78, USA, PM; *AMBER WAVES,* TV, 78, USA, PM; *SUPERMAN,* Th, 78, USA/GB, Unit PM; *ORCA,* Th, 75, USA, Unit PM; *DAYS OF HEAVEN,* Th, 75, USA, PM; *BUFFALO BILL AND THE INDIANS,* Th, 74, USA, PM; *BLACK HARVEST,* Th, 73/72, USA, PM; *PIONEER WOMAN,* Th, 70, USA, PM.

KOZY-KING, Joyce

DGC. 27 Summerhill Ave., Toronto, Ont, CAN, M4T 1A9. (416)968-3133.
Types of Production & Categories: Th Film-PM/Prod; TV Film-PM/Prod; TV Video-PM/Prod.
Genres: Drama-Th&TV; Comedy-Th&TV; Variety-TV; Action-Th&TV.
Biography: Born Winnipeg, Manitoba; of Ukrainian descent. Has worked at CBC, Toronto, 60's; began freelancing as script supervisor, switching to production manager and producer in the 70's. Has on occasion been hired as 'The Broom'; worked in USA, Europe and Middle East.
Selective Filmography: *THE ARM,* Th, 86, USA, PM; *THE SWORD OF GIDEON* (mini-series), TV, 86, CDN, PM; *ALTER EGO,* TV, 85, USA, PM; *MURDER IN SPACE,* TV, 85, CDN/USA, Pro Spv; *BEER,* Th, 84, USA, PM; *'LOVING FRIENDS AND PERFECT COUPLES'* (61 eps), TV, 84/83, USA, Prod; *THE GUARDIAN,* TV, 83, CDN/USA, Pro Spv; *MAGIC PLANET,* TV, 83, CDN/USA, PM; *THE TERRY FOX STORY,* Th, 82, CDN, PM; *IF YOU COULD SEE WHAT I HEAR,* Th, 82, CDN, Assoc Prod; *THE SINS OF DORIAN GREY,* TV, 81, USA, PM; *CASTLE ROCK,* TV, 81, USA, Assoc Prod; *THE LAST CHASE,* Th, 80, CDN, PM; *NOTHING PERSONAL,* Th, 79, CDN, PM; *DOUBLE NEGATIVE,* Th, 79, CDN, PM.

LABERGE, Pierre

STCQ. 1898 Leclaire, Montréal, Qué, CAN, H1V 2Z8. (514)259-3528. Communications Claude Héroux, 444 St-Paul est, Montréal, Qué, CAN. (514)842-6633.
Types de production et Catégories: l métrage-Dir pro/Loc M; c métrage-Rég; TV film-Rég.
Types d'oeuvres: Drame-C&TV; Enfants-C&TV.
Filmographie sélective: *'LANCE ET COMPTE'* (HE SHOOTS, HE SCORES), (13 eps), TV, 86/85, CDN, Rég; *MOLLY-O,* TV, 85, I, Dir pro; *CLAIRE LE JOUR ET LA NUIT,* C, 85, CDN, Loc M; *THE PEANUT BUTTER SOLUTION* (OPERATION BEURRE DE PINOTTES), C, 85, CDN, Loc M; *TAMING OF THE DEMONS,* ED, 85, CDN, Rég; *JOSHUA THEN AND NOW,* C, 84, CDN, Loc M; *NEW YEAR'S EVE,* C, 84, CDN, Rég; *ST-LOUIS SQUARE,* C, 83, CDN, Rég; *ONCE UPON A TIME IN AMERICA,* C, 83, USA/I, Loc M; *LES PLOUFFE,* C, 81, CDN, Rég gén.

LECLERC, François

STCQ. 3981 boul.St-Laurent, Ste.800B, Montréal, Qué, CAN, H2W 1Y5. (514) 842-7071.
Types de production et Catégories: l métrage-Rég; c métrage-Rég; TV film-Rég.
Types d'oeuvres: Drame-C&TV; Comédie-C&TV; Action-C&TV; Science-fiction-C&TV.

(cont/suite)

Curriculum vitae: Né en 1956, Montréal, Québec. Bac. en Communications, Université Concordia, Montréal, 79. Membre du conseil de direction du STCQ depuis mars 85.
Filmographie sélective: *DU PAIN ET DES JEUX,* C, 86/85, CDN, Prod; *CHOICES,* TV, 85, USA, Rég; *SPEARFIELD'S DAUGHTER* (mini-series), TV, 85, CDN/USA/AUS, Rég; *MIRACLE AT MOREAUX,* TV, 85, CDN, Rég; *THE VINDICATOR* (THE FRANKENSTEIN FACTOR), C, 84, CDN, Rég; *MEATBALLS III,* C, 84, CDN, Rég; *THE LEADING EDGE,* C, 84, CDN, Rég; *VAS-Y STEPHANE,* C, 84, CDN, Cast; *SONATINE,* C, 83, CDN, Rég; *LE RUFFIAN,* C, 83, CDN, Ass décor; *LE SKI AU QUEBEC,* In, 83, CDN, Rég; *LE PARC DE LA MAURICIE,* In, 83, CDN, Dir pro; *VICTOR, LA TERRE EST PLATE?,* TV, 83, CDN, Rég; *LITTLE GLORIA HAPPY AT LAST...* (2 ém), TV, 82, CDN/USA, Ass décor; *SCANDALE* (SCANDAL), C, 82, CDN, Rég; *DEAD RINGER,* C, 81, CDN, Rég/Ass réal; *LA GUERRE DU FEU* (QUEST FOR FIRE), C, 80, CDN/F, Ass réal; *HARD FEELINGS,* C, 80, CDN, Rég; *HOT TOUCH,* C, 80, CDN, Rég; *TERROR TRAIN,* C, 80, CDN, Rég; *TULIPS,* C, 79, CDN, Rég.

MacDONALD, Michael

DGC. 93 Westminster Ave., Toronto, Ont, CAN, M6R 1N3. (416)534-9666.
Types of Production & Categories: Th Film-PM/Loc M/Unit M; TV Film-PM/Loc M/Unit M.
Genres: Drama-Th&TV; Comedy-Th&TV; Action-Th&TV; Science Fiction-Th&TV.
Biography: Born 1949, Toronto, Ontario. Worked at Al Guest Animation Group as animator and special effects cameraman; freelanced in live action and animation, 69-77; has been actively working in features.
Selective Filmography: *DEAD OF WINTER,* Th, 86, USA, Assoc Prod/PM; *ONE MAGIC CHRISTMAS,* Th, 85, CDN/USA, Assoc Prod; 'THE EDISON TWINS' (18 eps), TV, 84, CDN, PM; *YOUNGBLOOD,* Th, 84, USA, PM; *MRS. SOFFEL,* Th, 84, USA, Unit M; 'THE EDISON TWINS' (18 eps), TV, 83, CDN, Loc M; *WHEN WE FIRST MET,* TV, 83, USA, Loc M; *A CHRISTMAS STORY,* Th, 83, CDN/USA, Unit M/Loc M; *IN DEFENSE OF KIDS,* TV, 82, USA, Unit M/Loc M; *HUMONGOUS,* Th, 82, CDN, Unit M/Loc M; *KELLY,* Th, 81, CDN, Unit M/Loc M; *ESCAPE FROM IRAN: THE CANADIAN CAPER,* TV, 80, CDN, Co-Loc M; *DEATH HUNT,* Th, 80, USA, Unit M/Loc M; *SILENCE OF THE NORTH,* Th, 80/79, CDN, Unit M/Loc M; *THE NOSE JOB,* TV, 80, CDN, Unit M/Loc M; *OLIVE FREDERICKSON'S 80th BIRTHDAY,* TV, 80, CDN, PM; *DOUBLE NEGATIVE,* Th, 79, CDN, PA; *SHAPE OF THINGS TO COME,* Th, 79, CDN, 3rd AD; *MEATBALLS,* Th, 79, CDN, Unit M/Loc M; *RED LIGHT - GREEN LIGHT,* Th, 70, CDN, Cam; *PARLIAMENT ST.,* Th, 69, CDN, Cam.

MAITLAND, Scott

IATSE-44, IATSE-156, IATSE-873, ACTRA, DGA, DGC. P.O. Box 1079, Murphy's, CA, USA, 95247. (209)728-2731.
Types of Production & Categories: Th Film-PM/1st AD; TV Film-PM/1st AD.
Genres: Drama-Th&TV; Comedy-Th; Action-Th&TV; Horror-Th.
Biography: Born Sudbury, Ontario; bilingual; US Green Card. Specializes in distant locations.
Selective Filmography: *CONVICTED,* TV, 86, USA, PM; *EYE OF THE TIGER,* Th, 86, USA, PM; *SILENT WITNESS,* TV, 85, USA, PM; *SHATTERED SPIRITS,* TV, 85, USA, PM; *LIBERTY* (mini-series), TV, 85, USA, PM; *DEADLY FORCE,* TV, 85, USA, PM; *MRS. SOFFEL,* Th, 84, USA, 1st AD; *CAT'S EYE,* Th, 84, USA, 2nd Unit PM/1st AD; *DAVIES AND HEARST,* TV, 84, USA, 1st AD; *DEADLY MESSAGES,* TV, 84, USA, 1st AD; *PETALUMA PRIDE,* Th, 83, USA, 1st AD; *CLASS,* Th, 83, USA, PM; *JAWS 3-D* (underwater seq), Th, 83, USA, 1st AD; *ZOO GANG,* Th, 83, USA, PM; *NEVER CRY WOLF,*

(cont/suite)

Th, 82, USA, 1st AD; *THIEF,* Th, 81, USA, 1st AD; *HARRY TRACY,* Th, 80, CDN, 1st AD; *RAGING BULL,* Th, 80, USA, 1st AD; *CENTENNIAL* (miniseries), (last 6 eps), TV, 79/78, USA, 1st AD; *TEXAS RANGERS,* TV, 79, USA, 1st AD; *KING OF COMEDY,* Th, 79, USA, 1st AD; *YEAR OF THE HORSE,* TV, 78, USA, PM; *'HAWAII 5-0'* (26 eps), TV, 78, USA, 1st AD; *BUFFALO SOLDIERS,* TV, 77, USA, PM; *JAWS II,* Th, 77, USA, 1st AD; *WHICH WAY IS UP?,* Th, 77, USA, 1st AD; *SCOTT FREE,* TV, 76, USA, PM.

MARGELLOS, James - see PRODUCERS

MARTINELLI, Gabriella

DGC. 4609 Woodburn Rd., West Vancouver, BC, CAN, V7S 2W5. (604)922-0718. Independent Pictures Inc., 264 Seaton St., Toronto, Ont, CAN, M5A 2T4. (416) 960-6468. Independent Pictures Inc., 1227 Richards St., Vancouver, BC, CAN, V6B 3G3. (604)687-8905.
Types of Production & Categories: Th Film-PM/Prod; TV Film-PM.
Genres: Drama-Th; Variety-TV; Documentary Th.
Biography: Born 1949, Italy; Canadian citizen. Studied Art, Art History, Carleton University. Producer, production manager on hundreds of commercials before entering feature film industry, 84.
Selective Filmography: *JOHN AND THE MISSUS,* Th, 86, CDN, Assoc Prod/PM; *DISCOVERY* (EXPO 86), Th, 86/85, CDN, Co-Prod/PM; *WESTERN CANADA LOTTERY CHRISTMAS,* TV, 84, CDN, PM; *MY AMERICAN COUSIN,* Th, 84, CDN, Pro Coord; *WALLS,* Th, 84, CDN, Pro Coord.

NADEAU, Mario

STCQ. 920 Gilford, Montréal, Qué, CAN, H2J 1P2. (514)523-4695.
Types de production et Catégories: l métrage-Rég; TV film-Rég.
Types d'oeuvres: Drame-C; Comédie-C; Action-C; Enfants-C.
Curriculum vitae: Né en 1950 à Mont Joli, Québec.
Filmographie sélective: *STREET SMART,* C, 86, USA, Unit M; *THE MORNING MAN,* C, 85, CDN, Unit M; *HENRI,* C, 85, CDN, Rég; *QUI A TIRE SUR NOS HISTOIRES D'AMOUR,* C, 85, CDN, Rég; *L'UNE DE MIEL* (HONEYMOON), C, 85, F, Rég; *'UN AMOUR DE QUARTIER'* (13 eps), TV, 84, CDN, Rég; *LA GUERRE DES TUQUES* (THE DOG WHO STOPPED THE WAR), C, 84, CDN, Rég; *LA FEMME DE L'HOTEL* (WOMAN IN TRANSIT), C, 83, CDN, Rég; *LES ANNEES DE REVE,* C, 83, CDN, Rég; *MARIA CHAPDELAINE,* C, 83, CDN/F, Rég gén; *RIEN QU'UN JEU* (ONLY A GAME), C, 82, CDN, Rég; *LE FUTUR INTERIEUR,* C, 81, CDN, Dir pro; *'LES TRANSISTORS'* (7 eps), TV, 81, CDN, Rég; *'LES FILS DE LA LIBERTE'* (6 eps), TV, 80, CDN/F, Rég; *LES CHIENS CHAUDS* (HOT DOGS), C, 79, CDN, Rég; *YESTERDAY* (GABRIELLE), C, 79, CDN, Rég; *KINGS AND DESPERATE MEN,* C, 77, CDN, Assist Unit M; *TOMORROW NEVER COMES,* C, 77, CDN/GB, Unit M; *'THE NEWCOMERS'* (LES ARRIVANTS), (7 eps), TV, 77, CDN, Assist Unit M; *JACOB TWO TWO MEETS THE HOODED FANG,* C, 75, CDN, Assist Unit M; *PARLEZ NOUS D'AMOUR,* C, 75, CDN, Ass pro; *SPECIAL MAGNUM,* C, 75, CDN/I, Ass pro; *IL ETAIT UNE FOIS DANS L'EST,* C, 74, CDN, Ass pro; *TOUT FEU TOUT FEMME,* C, 74, CDN, Ass pro; *SWEET MOVIE,* C, 73, CDN/F, Ass pro.

RICHARDSON, Gillian - see PRODUCERS

ROBERTSON, David M. - see DIRECTORS

ROBINSON, Gord

DGC. 535 St. Clements Ave., Toronto, Ont, CAN, M5N 1M3. (416)485-6098.
Types of Production & Categories: Th Film-PM/1st AD; TV Film-PM/1st AD.
Genres: Drama-Th&TV; Comedy-Th; Action-Th; Horror-Th.

(cont/suite)

Selective Filmography: *RAD THE MOVIE,* Th, 86, GB, 1st AD; *'NIGHT HEAT'* (2 eps), TV, 85, CDN, PM; *APRIL FOOL,* Th, 84, CDN/USA, 1st AD; *RECKLESS DISREGARD,* TV, 84, CDN/USA, PM; *FULL CIRCLE AGAIN,* TV, 84, CDN, PM; *COUGAR,* TV, 83, USA, PM/1st AD; *SHOCKTRAUMA,* TV, 83, CDN, PM/1st AD; *FRANK AND FEARLESS,* TV, 82, USA, PM/1st AD; *DEATH BITE* (SPASMS), Th, 81, CDN, Co-Prod/PM; *MAGIC SHOW,* TV, 81, CDN, PM; *MEATBALLS,* Th, 79, CDN, 1st AD; *AN AMERICAN CHRISTMAS CAROL,* TV, 79, USA, U Loc M; *'MATT AND JENNY'* (26 eps), TV, 79, CDN/GB/D, PM; *THE SHAPE OF THINGS TO COME,* Th, 78, CDN, 1st AD; *SEPARATION,* Th, 77, CDN, 1st AD; *A QUIET DAY IN BELFAST,* Th, 74/73, CDN/GB, 1st AD; *'SALTY'* (10 eps), TV, 74, CDN, 1st AD; *SHE CRIED MURDER,* TV, 73, CDN/USA, 1st AD; *FOLLOW THE NORTH STAR,* TV, 72, CDN, 1st AD; *RACE HOME TO DIE,* Th, 72, CDN, PM; *FACE-OFF,* Th, 71, CDN, 1st AD; *WHEN MICHAEL CALLS,* TV, 71, USA, 1st AD; *ROCK ONE/ROCK TWO,* TV, 71, CDN, Assoc Prod; *THE CROWD INSIDE,* TV, 70, CDN, 1st AD; *FLICK* (FRANKENSTEIN ON CAMPUS), Th, 70, CDN, 1st AD.

ROSS, Brian

DGC. 134 Dewbourne Ave., Toronto, Ont, CAN, M6C 1Y9. (416)783-1997.
Types of Production & Categories: Th Film-PM/1st AD; TV Film-PM/1st AD; TV Video-PM/1st AD.
Genres: Drama-Th&TV; Comedy-Th&TV; Action-Th; Horror-Th.
Biography: Born 1945. Over 20 years experience in film and video tape; responsible for assisting in film and video bylaws of Toronto. Production supervisor for over 2000 commercials world wide; producer of short films in the Arctic and South Seas; extensive travel. Experienced as production manager, unit location manager and 1st AD, theatrical, made for TV movies and commercials.

RYAN, John - see PRODUCERS

SHEPHERD, David

964 Avenue Rd., Toronto, Ont, CAN, M5P 2K8. (416)488-1526.
Types of Production & Categories: Th Film-PM/1st AD; TV Film-PM/1st AD.
Genres: Drama-Th&TV; Comedy-Th&TV; Horror-Th.
Biography: Worked at CBC, 62-71; production manager/1st assistant director on documentaries and commercials, 71-78; freelancing since 78.
Selective Filmography: *EASY PREY,* Th, 86, USA, 1st AD; *POPEYE DOYLE* (pilot), TV, 86, USA, 1st AD; *'FRONTIER'* (6 eps), TV, 86, CDN/GB/F/D, 1st AD; *ANNE OF GREEN GABLES - THE SEQUEL* (mini-series), TV, 86, CDN/USA, PM; *FOLLOW THAT BIRD,* Th, 84, USA, 1st AD; *THE GUARDIAN,* TV, 83, CDN/USA, 1st AD; *STRANGE INVADERS,* Th, 82, USA, 1st AD; *DEADLY EYES* (THE RATS), Th, 82, CDN, 1st AD; *DEATH BITE* (SPASMS), Th, 81, CDN, 1st AD; *BILL COSBY HIMSELF,* TV, 81, USA, 1st AD; *IF YOU COULD SEE WHAT I HEAR,* Th, 80, CDN, PM; *PHOBIA,* Th, 79, CDN, PM; *NEVER TRUST AN HONEST THIEF,* Th, 79, CDN, 1st AD; *TITLE SHOT,* Th, 79, CDN, 2nd AD; *MEATBALLS,* Th, 79, CDN, 2nd AD; *SHAPE OF THINGS TO COME,* Th, 78, CDN, 2nd AD.

SHRIER, Barbara

STCQ. 812 Gilford, Montreal, Que, CAN, H2J 1N9. (514)526-4766.
Types of Production & Categories: Th Film-PM/Loc M/Unit M; Th Short-PM/Loc M/Unit M; TV Film-PM/Loc M/Unit M; TV Video-PM/Loc M/Unit M.
Genres: Drama-Th&TV; Action-Th&TV; Documentary-TV; Children's-Th&TV.
Biography: Born 1955, Montreal, Quebec. B.A., McGill University (Communications), 77. Languages: French, English, Mandarin, Hebrew. Extensive travels through South East Asia, Middle East, Australia, Europe, Caribbean, USA and Canada. STCQ Vice President.

(cont/suite)

Selective Filmography: *'WILLIAM TELL'* (6 eps), TV, 86, USA/F, PM; *CHOICES,* TV, 85, USA, Loc M; *SPEARFIELD'S DAUGHTER* (mini-series), TV, 85, CDN/ USA/AUS, Loc M; *HYUNDAI INTERNATIONAL,* Cm, 85, USA, Line Prod; *MIRACLE AT MOREAUX,* TV, 85, USA, 2nd AD; *PROVIGO/CIL/CMPC-QUEBEC GOV'T/BANQUE NATIONALE,* Cm, 85, CDN, PM/1st AD; *LA LAURENTIENNE/DOVE/LE PERMANENT/SUPER LOTO,* Cm, 85/84, CDN, PM/1st AD; *THE LEADING EDGE,* Th, 84, CDN, Pro Coord/Res; *SECRET WEAPONS,* TV, 84, USA, 2nd AD; *MULTICULTURALISM/MacDONALD'S/ BELL CANADA,* Cm, 84/83, CDN, PM/1st AD; *THE BOY IN BLUE,* Th, 84, CDN, Art Dept Coord; *VICTOR, LA TERRE EST PLATE?,* Th, 83, CDN, Co-Prod; *SKI QUEBEC,* Th, 83, CDN, PM/1st AD; *THE MAN IN 5A* (THE MAN NEXT DOOR), Th, 82, CDN, Art Dept Coord; *QUEST FOR FIRE* (LA GUERRE DU FEU), Th, 80, CDN/F, Pro Coord; *DIONNE WARWICK LIVE,* TV, 80, USA, Unit M; *ATLANTIC CITY,* Th, 79, CDN/USA, Pro Coord; *1976 OLYMPICS,* TV, 76, USA, Res/Wr.

ST-ARNAUD, Michèle

STCQ. 4589 De La Roche, Montréal, Qué, CAN, H2J 3J5. (514)527-3182.
Types de production et Catégories: l métrage-Rég; TV film-Rég.
Types d'oeuvres: Drame-C; Comédie-C; Documentaire-C&TV; Annonces-TV.
Curriculum vitae: Née en 1954, Ste-Foy, Québec. Etudes en administration, UQAM.
Longs séjours à l'étranger: 2 ans en Afrique, 4 ans en Europe.
Filmographie sélective: *IMAGE PAR IMAGE,* C, 86/85, CDN, Rég; *POUVOIR INTIME,* C, 85, CDN, Rég; *PECHINEY,* In, 84, F, Dir pro; *'PETITS CONTES CRUELS'* (2 eps), TV, 84, CDN, Rég; *COGEMA,* In, 84, F, Dir pro; *LA DIVINE SARAH,* TV, 83, CDN, Ass rég; *MARC-AURELE FORTIN,* TV, 82, CDN, Dir pro; *THE MAN IN 5 A* (THE MAN NEXT DOOR), C, 82, CDN, Rég; *ALERTE A GENTILLY,* In, 82, CDN, Rég; *LE GRIEF,* C, 81, CDN, Rég; *LES BEAUX SOUVENIRS,* C, 80, CDN, Rég; *THE SQUAD,* C, 79, CDN, 2c ass réal; *LE DANSEUR,* C, 79, CDN, 2e ass réal; *LES BONS DEBARRAS* (GOOD RIDDANCE), C, 78, CDN, Ass rég.

STONEHOUSE, Marilyn

Bedroom Window Prods. Ltd., 1123 North 23rd St., Wilmington, NC, USA, 28405.
(919)343-3576.
Types of Production & Categories: Th Film-PM; TV Film-PM; TV Video-PM.
Genres: Drama-Th&TV; Comedy-Th&TV; Action-Th&TV.
Selective Filmography: *FROM THE HIP,* Th, 86, USA, PM; *MAXIMUM OVERDRIVE,* Th, 85, USA, PM; *LETTING GO,* TV, 85, USA, PM; *HEAD OFFICE,* Th, 85/84, USA, PM; *INTO THE LOOKING GLASS DARKLY,* TV, 84, CDN/USA, PM; *MARTIN'S DAY,* Th, 83, CDN/GB, PM; *FOLLOW THE PARADE,* TV, 83, CDN, PM; *QUEBEC/CANADA 1995,* TV, 83, CDN, PM; *A CHRISTMAS STORY,* Th, 83, CDN/USA, PM; *WHEN ANGELS FLY,* TV, 82, CDN/USA, PM; *STRANGE INVADERS,* Th, 82, USA, PM; *CLASS OF '84,* Th, 81, CDN/USA, PM; *THE AMATEUR,* Th, 81, CDN, PM; *MUM, THE WOLFMAN AND ME,* TV, 80, USA, PM; *MR. PATMAN,* Th, 79, CDN, PM; *HIGH POINT,* Th, 79, CDN, PM; *KLONDIKE FEVER,* Th, 79, CDN, PM; *TORN BETWEEN TWO LOVERS,* TV, 79/78, USA, PM; *SHAPE OF THINGS TO COME,* Th, 78, CDN, PM; *LOST AND FOUND,* Th, 78, GB, PM; *HIGH-BALLIN',* Th, 77, CDN, PM; *THE SILENT PARTNER,* Th, 77, CDN, PM; *'SEARCH AND RESCUE'* (18 eps), TV, 77/76, CDN/USA, PM; *EMMETT OTTER AND HIS JUGBAND CHRISTMAS,* TV, 75, CDN/USA, PM; *MUPPET MUSICIANS OF BREMEN,* TV, 75, CDN, PM; *THE FROG PRINCE,* TV, 75, CDN, PM; *'POLICE SURGEON'* (78 eps), TV, 74-71, CDN, PM; *WHEN MICHAEL CALLS,* TV, 72, USA, PM; *'DR. SIMON LOCKE'* (26 eps), TV, 71/70, CDN/USA, PM; *FORTUNE AND MEN'S EYES,* Th, 71, CDN/USA, PM.

THATCHER, Tony

DGC. 1970 Woodview Ave., Pickering, Ont, CAN, L1V 1L6. (416)286-2065.
Types of Production & Categories: Th Film-PM/1st AD; TV Film-PM/1st AD.
Genres: Drama-Th&TV; Comedy-Th&TV; Action-Th&TV; Horror-Th&TV.
Biography: Born 1943, Oxford, England; British citizenship; landed immigrant, Canada, 68.
Selective Filmography: *DEAD OF WINTER,* Th, 86, USA, 1st AD; *'STREET LEGAL'* (3 eps), TV, 86, CDN, 1st AD; *DEADLY BUSINESS,* TV, 85, USA, 1st AD; *'SEEING THINGS'* (24 eps), TV, 85-82, CDN, 1st AD; *GENTLE SINNERS,* TV, 83, CDN, 1st AD; *IN DEFENCE OF KIDS,* TV, 82, USA, PM; *THE KIDNAPPING OF THE PRESIDENT,* Th, 79, CDN, PM.

TICHENOR, Harold

DGC. Box 116, Errington, BC, CAN, V0R 1V0. (604)248-6010. Cinetel Film Prod. Ltd., P.O. Box 2129, Parksville, BC, CAN, V0R 2S0. (604)248-9123.
Types of Production & Categories: Th Film-PM; TV Film-Dir/Prod/PM/Ed; TV Video-Dir/Prod/PM.
Genres: Drama-Th&TV; Documentary-TV; Educational-TV; Children's-TV.
Biography: Born 1946, Philadelphia, USA; Canadian citizen. Received original training for career in music. Attended University of Alaska, major: Biological Sciences, 63-66. Produced anthropologic-science films until 66; freelance cameraman, Vancouver, 67; media producer for University of Lethbridge, 67-72; formed own company, independent production since 72. Over 60 directing, editing credits; many film festival awards.
Selective Filmography: *'DANGER BAY'* (44 eps), TV, 86/85, CDN, PM; *HOAX,* TV, 86, CDN, PM; *TO KILL A WOPPINGBIRD,* In, 85, CDN, Prod/Dir; *'FREE TO FLY'* (3 eps), TV, 84, CDN, Assoc Prod; *THE NEVERENDING STORY,* Th, 83, D, PM; *SENTIMENTAL REASONS,* Th, 82, CDN, Assoc Prod/Co-Ed; *INUPIATUN,* TV, 81, CDN, Prod/Dir; *LATITUDE 55,* Th, 80, CDN, PM; *THE SNOW WAR,* ED, 80, CDN, Prod/Dir; *GYROS: HANDLE WITH CARE,* In, 79, CDN, Prod/Dir; *KATEI SEIKATSU,* ED, 78, CDN, Prod/Dir; *NEXT TIME AROUND,* In, 78, CDN, Ed.

TUCKER, Paul

DGA, DGC. 8268 Marmont Lane, Los Angeles, CA, USA, 90069. (213)654-9228. CBS-MTM Studios, Studio City, CA, USA, 91604. (818)760-5561. Jerome S.Klein & Co., 4565 Sherman Oaks Ave., Sherman Oaks, CA, USA, 91403. (818)783-4450.
Types of Production & Categories: Th Film-PM; TV Film-PM/Dir.
Genres: Drama-Th&TV; Comedy-Th&TV; Action-Th&TV; Science Fiction-Th&TV.
Biography: Born 1950, Bristol, England; Canadian-British citizen; resident alien, USA (Green Card). Working as production executive, CBS-TV, 86.
Selective Filmography: *IF TOMORROW COMES* (mini-series), TV, 86/85, USA, Pro Exec; *ADAMS APPLE/R.E.L.A.X./BLUE SKIES* (pilots), TV, 86, USA, Pro Exec; *'TWILIGHT ZONE'* (Dir-2 eps), (24 eps), TV, 86/85, USA, Pro Exec; *'FOLEY SQUARE'* (13 eps), TV, 86/85, USA, Pro Exec; *STARK/ STARK II/ BLIND JUSTICE/CHILDREN OF ALCOHOLICS,* TV, 85, USA, Pro Exec; *ONE TERRIFIC GUY/CLASSIFIED LOVE/FOLLOWING FOOTSTEPS,* TV, 85, USA, Pro Exec; *LOVE MARY/FIRST STEPS/NORTHBEACH,* TV, 85, USA, Pro Exec; *BROTHERLY LOVE,* TV, 84, USA, PM; *CONSENTING ADULT,* TV, 84, USA, PM; *BILLY GRIER,* TV, 84, USA, PM; *SECRETS,* TV, 84, USA, PM; *FIRST BLOOD,* Th, 82, USA, PM; *STAR 80,* Th, 82, USA, PM; *THE GOLDEN SEAL,* Th, 82, USA, PM; *THE GREY FOX,* Th, 80, CDN, PM; *OUT OF THE BLUE,* Th, 80, CDN, PM; *SKI LIFT TO DEATH,* TV, 79, USA, 2nd AD; *SUPERMAN,* Th, 78, USA/GB, Unit M; *WILD HORSE HANK,* Th, 78, CDN, 2nd AD.

CATERING

90 Russell Crescent
Oshawa, Ontario
728-5348

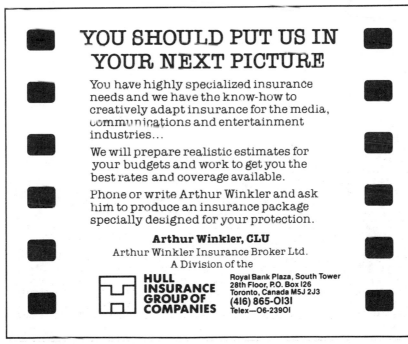

YOU SHOULD PUT US IN YOUR NEXT PICTURE

You have highly specialized insurance needs and we have the know-how to creatively adapt insurance for the media, communications and entertainment industries...

We will prepare realistic estimates for your budgets and work to get you the best rates and coverage available.

Phone or write Arthur Winkler and ask him to produce an insurance package specially designed for your protection.

Arthur Winkler, CLU
Arthur Winkler Insurance Broker Ltd.
A Division of the

HULL INSURANCE GROUP OF COMPANIES

Royal Bank Plaza, South Tower
28th Floor, P.O. Box 126
Toronto, Canada M5J 2J3
(416) 865-0131
Telex—06-23901

364

CINEMATOGRAPHERS
★
DIRECTEURS-PHOTO

ALLEN-WOOLFE, Nicholas

ACTT, CSC, IATSE. 70 Langford Ave., Toronto, Ont, CAN, M4J 3E5. (416)469-1424. Eureka Films, 31 Mercer St., Toronto, Ont, CAN. (416)596-7131.
Types of Production & Categories: Th Film-DOP; Th Short-DOP; TV Film-DOP.
Genres: Drama-Th&TV; Musical-TV; Horror-Th&TV; Commercials-TV.
Biography: Born 1944, Wiltshire, England. Entered industry in London, 61 as clapper boy; worked as focus puller, operator before becoming lighting cameraman at age 22. Came to Canada, 68, worked in TV series, documentaries, commercials. Worked as freelance and contract DOP for most major production houses in 70's and 80's. Has won 4 Bessie Awards.
Selective Filmography: *DIET COKE/CHIC JEANS,* Cm, 86, USA, Light Cam; *INFORMATION,* MV, 85, CDN, Light Cam; *WHOSE LOVE?,* MV, 85, CDN, Light Cam (**CSC**); *MOLSON BEER/DEL MONTE/SUNLIGHT/TAB/HONDA,* Cm, 85-83, CDN, Light Cam; *CARLSBERG LIGHT/7 UP,* Cm, 82/78, CDN, Light Cam (**2 CSC**).

ALLIN, Norman C.

CSC, CUPE. Norman Allin Productions Ltd., 1 Shadetree Cres., Etobicoke, Ont, CAN, M9C 1W9. (416)621-5463.
Types of Production & Categories: TV Film-DOP.
Genres: Drama-TV; Comedy-TV; Documentary-TV; Educational-TV.
Biography: Born 1926, Yorkshire, England; Canadian citizen, 54. Forty-four years experience as DOP on over 200 TV productions. Nominated 9 times, Canadian Film Awards; Bill Hilson Award; numerous 1st, 2nd, 3rd awards for films. President of CSC for 7 years; Vice-president, 3 years. Wildlife artist in both watercolor and black-and-white sketches.
Selective Filmography: *9B,* TV, 86, CDN, DOP; *VOICES IN THE WIND,* 'NATURE OF THINGS', TV, 85, CDN, DOP; *BACH MAGNIFICAT,* TV, 84, CDN, DOP; *ON MY OWN,* TV, 83, CDN, DOP.

AMIGUET, Philippe

STCQ. 630 Querbes, #12, Outremont, Qué, CAN, H2V 3W7. (514)274-5896.
Types de production et Catégories: c métrage-D phot; TV film-D phot; TV vidéo-Réal/D phot.
Types d'oeuvres: Drame-C; Documentaire-C&TV; Education-C&TV; Nouvelles-TV.
Curriculum vitae: Né en 1943, Suisse; citoyenneté canadienne. Etudes en Suisse jusqu'au Bac.; école de photographie, Suisse. Reporter et journaliste, Agence Interpresse, Genève et Paris; Agence Scope, Lausanne et Milan; Agence Les Reporters Associés, Montréal. Journaliste: magazines 'Affaires', 'La Presse Plus', 'Journal Les Affaires'. Réalisateur de films industriels depuis 85.
Filmographie sélective: *AU NOM DE DIEU,* C, 86, CDN, D phot; *CULINAR,* In, 85, CDN, Réal; *'CONDUIS-TOI BIEN'* (20 ém), In, 85, CDN, Réal; *'DEFI MONDIAL'* (6 eps), TV, 84, CDN/F, D phot; *CAFE,* TV, 83, CDN, Cam; *LE CHASSEUR DE FANTOMES,* 'LEGENDES DU MONDE', TV, 82, CDN, D phot; *LES AVENTURES DE TETE DE BOIS,* TV, 81, CDN, D phot; *FOUCCRAY/JOVY/GOINEAU & BOUSQUET/FOURRURES LABELLE/VALBAR,* Cm, 81-74, CDN, D phot; *SERVICE A TABLE,* ED, 79, CDN, D phot; *LES PETITS MARCHANDS DE BONHEUR,* TV, 78, CDN, D phot/Co réal/Sc; *'SI ON S'Y METTAIT'* (9 eps), TV, 75, CDN, D phot; *'PRODUCTION HORTICOLE'* (13 eps), TV, 74, CDN, D phot; *TORNGAT,* C, 73, CDN, D phot; *MONTREAL, JOUR VERSUS NUIT,* TV, 73, CDN, D phot; *LES JEUX SONT FAITS,* TV, 71, CDN, D phot; *PIZZAGONE,* C, 70, CDN, Réal/Sc; *ACTION,* C, 70, CDN, Cam; *REACTION,* C, 70, CDN, Cam.

ARCHAMBAULT, Noel

3450 West 43rd Ave., Vancouver, BC, CAN, V6N 3J7. (604)261-4515.

(cont/suite)

Types of Production & Categories: Th Short-DOP/Cam; TV Film-Cam/Ed.
Genres: Drama-Th; Documentary-Th&TV; Educational-Th&TV.
Biography: Born 1961, Vancouver, British Columbia. B.A., Film, Simon Fraser University. *ROOM FOR RENT* won the Norman McLaren Award, Best Canadian Student Film.
Selective Filmography: *374-HAIL THE CONQUERING HERO,* TV, 86, CDN, Snd Ed/Gaf; *TRANSITIONS,* Th, 86, CDN, 1st Assist Cam; *SMILE AND DIAL,* TV, 86, CDN, Cam; *SWINGSPAN,* TV, 86, CDN, 2nd U Cam; *THE OUTFITTER,* In, 85, CDN, DOP/Ed; *ENVIRONMENTS WORTH PROTECTING,* In, 85, CDN, Cam/Snd Ed; *THE MAGIC QUILT,* TV, 85, CDN, 1st Assist Cam; *CHILD'S PLAY,* TV, 84, CDN, DOP; *GEORGE NORRIS IN DEPTH,* Th, 84, CDN, Dir/Ed/Prod; *ROOM FOR RENT,* Th, 83, CDN, DOP.

BAIRD, Douglas

2050 Nelson St., #604, Vancouver, BC, CAN, V6G 1N6. (604)681-3035.
Types of Production & Categories: TV Film-Cam; TV Video-Cam.
Genres: Documentary-TV; Educational-TV; News-TV; Sports-TV.
Biography: Born 1952, Calgary, Alberta. Honours B.Sc., Kinesiology, University of Waterloo. Producer/director of educational sports films and industrials; location sound recordist for 10 years. Certified diver and underwater photographer. Cameraman on one of the three crews working for foreign broadcasters at Expo 86 as part of the Canadian Host Broadcaster system.
Selective Filmography: *'GOOD ROCKIN' TONIGHT'* (12 eps), TV, 86/85, CDN, Cam; *WORLDSTAGE 86* (EXPO), TV, 86, CDN, Cam; *'GZOWSKI & CO.'* (2 eps), TV, 85, CDN, Cam; *'VENTURE'* (1 eps), TV, 85, CDN, Cam; *'MIDDAY'* (2 eps), TV, 85, CDN, Cam; *'MARKETPLACE'* (1 eps), TV, 85, CDN, Cam; *'PACIFIC REPORT'* (2 eps), TV, 85, CDN, Cam; *'NEWSHOUR'* (BCTV), TV, 85-80, CDN, Cam; *'WIDE WORLD OF SPORTS'* (50 eps), TV, 79-74, CDN, Cam.

BAL, Walter

IATSE. 278 MacPherson Ave., Toronto, Ont, CAN, M4V 1A3. (416)926-1936.
Partners Film Co., 508 Church St., Toronto, Ont, CAN, M4Y 2C8. (416)966-3500.
Types of Production & Categories: Th Film-DOP; TV Film-Dir/DOP.
Genres: Drama-Th&TV; Comedy-TV; Action-TV; Children's-TV.
Biography: Born 1939, Djakarta, Indonesia; Dutch citizenship; Canadian landed immigrant. Languages: English, French, Dutch, German, some Spanish. Underwater camera specialist. DOP/cameraman/operator on over 40 feature films, mainly in France; over 500 commercials in Europe and North America; 150 commercials as cameraman/director. Has won many awards for commercials including: Cannes, Hollywood, Bronze, Silver and Gold Lions, Coq d'Or.
Selective Filmography: *BOBO JACCO,* Th, 78, F, Dir; *'J.Y. COUSTEAU'S UNDERWATER WORLD'* (5 eps), TV, 75-70, F, DOP/Cam; *STATE OF SIEGE,* Th, 74, F, Op; *DAY FOR NIGHT,* Th, 72, F, Op.

BEAUCHEMIN, François

SGCT. 8426 Drolet, Montréal, Qué, CAN, H2P 2H7. (514)389-7381. ONF, 3155 Côte de Liesse, Montréal, Qué, CAN, H3C 3H5. (514)283-9364.
Types de production et Catégories: l métrage-D phot; c métrage-Cam; TV film-D phot; TV vidéo-D phot.
Types d'oeuvres: Drame-C&TV; Comédie-C&TV; Action-C&TV; Documentaire-C&TV.
Curriculum vitae: Né en 1943, Noranda, Québec; bilingue. Etudes à l'Ecole de Cinéma, Institut National des Arts du Spectacle, Bruxelles, Belgique (3 ans). Caméraman vidéo, Radio-Québec, 68-71; pigiste, caméraman et directeur-photo, 71-82; à l'ONF depuis 82. *TI-CUL TOUGAS* gagne le Prix de la Critique Québécoise.
(cont/suite)

Filmographie sélective: *IMAGE PAR IMAGE*, C, 86, CDN, D phot; *PRODIGAL*, TV, 85, CDN, D phot; *PLACE AUX JEUNES*, TV, 85, CDN, D phot; *L'INCONDUITE*, 'PRENDRE LA ROUTE', TV, 85, CDN, D phot; *LE DRAME D'ISIDORE TREMBLAY* (PIEKOUAGAMI), TV, 84, CDN, D phot; *L'HIVER LES BLES*, TV, 84, CDN, D phot; *L'EMOTION DISSONANTE*, TV, 84, CDN, D phot; *DE MAINS ET D'ESPOIR*, TV, 83, CDN, D phot; *QUITTE OU DOUBLE*, C, 81, CDN, D phot; *EN PLEIN COEUR*, C, 81, CDN, D phot; *'VIVRE ICI... MAINTENANT'* (13 eps), TV, 81, CDN, D phot; *UNE VIE EN PRISON* (3 parties), TV, 80, CDN, D phot; *CONTRE-COEUR*, C, 79, CDN, D phot; *LE CHATEAU DE CARTES*, C, 79, CDN, D phot; *ENSOLEILLE AVEC PASSAGE NUAGEUX*, C, 79, CDN, D phot; *'VIVRE SA VIE'* (13 eps), TV, 78, CDN, D phot; *CHEMIN DE FER DU MALI*, TV, 77, CDN, Cam; *MARATHON*, 'DEFI', TV, 77, CDN, Cam; *JEUX DE LA XXI OLYMPIADE*, C, 76, CDN, Co cam; *20 ANS APRES*, TV, 75, CDN, D phot; *LA PIASTRE*, C, 74, CDN, D phot; *TI-CUL TOUGAS*, C, 74, CDN, D phot; *LE MONDE S'EN VIENT A QUEBEC*, C, 74, CDN, Cam; *PEPINIERES / REBOISEMENT*, TV, 73, CDN, Cam; *EN GAROUINE AVEC PHILIPPE GAGNON*, TV, 73, CDN, Cam; *TU BRULES...TU BRULES...*, C, 72, CDN, D phot; *VIEWPOINT*, TV, 72, CDN, D phot; *BULLDOZER*, C, 71, CDN, D phot; *'TRIBULLE'* (13 eps), TV, 71, CDN, D phot.

BELLEMARE, Rénald

STCQ. Imagidé Inc., 4210 ave. l'Hôtel de Ville, Montréal, Qué, CAN, H2W 2H2. (514)849-5816.
Types de production et Catégories: TV film-Aut comp; TV vidéo-Cam/Mont.
Types d'oeuvres: Documentaire-C&TV; Education-C&TV; Expérimental-C&TV.
Curriculum vitae: Né en 1954, Montréal, Québec. Langues: français, anglais, espagnol. Bac. spécialisé en communications. Directeur-photo et caméraman, film et vidéo; conception visuelle de spectacles de scène; producteur de film et vidéo, Imagidé inc.. Plusieurs tournages et voyages à l'étranger: Afrique, Amérique centrale et du sud, Asie, Europe.
Filmographie sélective: *FAVELADAS*, TV, 86, CDN, Cam; *ETHIOPIA: CANADIAN AID*, TV, 86, CDN, Cam; *LES CONTES DES MILLE ET UN NEZ*, TV, 85, CDN, Cam; *FEMME SANS FRONTIERES*, TV, 85, CDN, Cam; *'COUSIN CUISINE'* (13 eps), TV, 85, CDN, D phot/Cam; *LE REVE EVEILLE*, MV, 85, CDN, Prod/Réal/Cam/Mont; *PETITE FILLE* (BELGAZOU), MV, 85, CDN, D phot; *C'EST COMME UNE PEINE D'AMOUR*, TV, 85/84, CDN, Cam; *ROCK AT CHOUKA 4*, TV, 84, CDN, Réal/Cam/Mont; *MICHEL LEMIEUX*, *L'OEIL RECILAPGEABLE*, TV, 84, CDN, Réal/Cam/Mont; *'LE CHOC DES AMERIQUES'* (6 eps), TV, 84/83, CDN, Cam/Mont; *MARGIE GILLIS: NEW DREAMS*, TV, 84, CDN, Cam; *EL SALVADOR*, *LA GUERRE CIVILE ET LES ELECTIONS 82*, TV, 82, CDN, Mont; *LES BLEUS...LA NUIT*, TV, 81, CDN, Prod/Cam; *CHARLEVOIX, PAYS DU HUITIEME JOUR*, TV, 80, CDN, Prod/Cam; *FOCUS ON KARL STEINER*, TV, 80, CDN, Cam; *CA PARLE AU DIABLE*, TV, 79, CDN, Réal/Prod/Cam.

BELZILE, Jocelyn

1430 De La visitation, #6, Montréal, Qué, CAN, H2L 3B8. (514)598-7256. Radio-Canada, 1400 blvd. Dorchester est, Montréal, Qué, CAN, H2L 2M2. (514)285-3426.
Types de production et Catégories: TV film-D phot.
Types d'oeuvres: Drame-TV; Variété-TV; Documentaire-TV; Vidéo clips-TV.
Curriculum vitae: Né en 1927, Trois-Pistoles, Québec; bilingue. Education: Humanités, latin, grec, Collège de l'Assomption. Monteur film à Radio-Canada.
Filmographie sélective: *HENRYK SZERING/MARIA PELLEGRINI/KENNETH GILBERT*, 'LES BEAUX DIMANCHES', TV, 86/85, CDN, D phot; *'STEPPIN' OUT'* (120 eps), TV, 86-82, CDN, D phot (**ANIK**); *CHARLES DUTOIT/GERALD*

(cont/suite)

CINEMATOGRAPHERS/DIRECTEURS-PHOTO

GODIN, 'GZOWSKY & CO', TV, 85, CDN, D phot; *GASPE 3 FAMILIES,* TV, 84, CDN, D phot.

BENISON, Peter

CAMERA, CSC, STCQ. 2297 Oxford Ave., Montreal, Que, CAN, H4A 2X7. (514)484-0714. 1 Bellhaven Rd., Toronto, Ont, CAN, M4L 3J4. (416)698-4482.
Types of Production & Categories: Th Film-DOP; Th Short-DOP; TV Film-DOP; TV Video-DOP.
Genres: Drama-Th&TV; Comedy-Th&TV; Action-Th&TV; Documentary-Th&TV.
Biography: Born 1950. B.Sc., McGill University. 71.
Selective Filmography: *OKLAHOMA SMUGGLERS,* Th, 86, CDN/USA, DOP; *'WOMEN OF THE WORLD'* (7 eps), TV, 86/85, CDN/USA, DOP; *BRADOR/ PANASONIC/IRVING OIL/AMERICAN DREAM,* Cm, 86-83, CDN, DOP; *AIR CANADA / CN / ALCAN / GENERAL   ELECTRIC / IBM / AVON / VIA / BELL CANADA,* In, 86-72, CDN, DOP; *'NIGHT HEAT'* (2 eps), TV, 85, CDN, DOP; *'NATIONAL GEOGRAPHIC'* (2 eps), TV, 85, CDN, DOP; *WAYNE BISCAYNE/ BEAU GESTE,* MV, 85/84, CDN, DOP; *MEATBALLS III,* Th, 84, CDN, DOP; *JOSHUA THEN AND NOW,* Th, 84, CDN, 2nd U DOP; *THE JUGGLER,* TV, 83, CDN, DOP; *HOTEL NEW HAMPSHIRE,* Th, 83, USA, 2nd U DOP; *THE SURROGATE,* Th, 83, CDN, 2nd U DOP; *ONCE UPON A TIME IN AMERICA,* Th, 83, USA/I, 2nd U DOP; *BABE,* Th, 82, CDN, 2nd U DOP; *UPS & DOWNS,* Th, 81, CDN, DOP; *DREAMWORLD,* Th, 81, CDN, 2nd U DOP; *GAS,* Th, 80, CDN, 2nd U DOP; *NAZARETH,* MV, 78, CDN, DOP.

BERGTHORSON, Barry

CAMERA, IATSE-667. 1 Fitzroy Terrace, Toronto, Ont, CAN, M5T 2K3. (416) 597-2200.
Types of Production & Categories: TV Film-DOP; TV Video-DOP.
Genres: Drama-TV; Musical-TV; Documentary-TV.
Biography: Born 1938.
Selective Filmography: *PETER USTINOV'S RUSSIA* (6 eps), TV, 85, CDN, DOP; *KING OF FRIDAY NIGHT,* TV, 84, CDN, DOP; *OVERDRAWN AT THE MEMORY BANK,* TV, 83, CDN/USA, DOP; *WAITING FOR THE PARADE,* TV, 83, CDN, DOP; *THE COUNTRY WIFE,* TV, 83, CDN, DOP.

BERUBE, Gilles

STCQ. 19 ch. de la Seigneurie, C.P. 1184, Lac Beauport, Qué, CAN, G0A 2C0. (418)849-9449.
Types de production et Catégories: TV film-Cam; TV vidéo-Cam.
Types d'oeuvres: Comédie-TV; Documentaire-TV; Education-TV.
Curriculum vitae: Né en 1951, St-Raymond de Portneuf, Québec. Langues: français, Anglais, Espagnol. Baccalauréat ès Arts, mineure en cinéma, journalisme et photographie, Université Laval.
Filmographie sélective: *SI TAUDIS, SITOT DEMOLIES,* TV, 85, CDN, D phot/ Cam/Mont; *PLUIE D'ETE,* TV, 84, CDN, Phot plat/Mach; *DIVINE SUR MER,* TV, 84, CDN, Cam; *L'ABOITEAU DE LA SEIGNEURIE DE KAMOURASKA,* In, 83, CDN, D phot/Cam/Mont; *HISTOIRE D'UN CHAMBREUR,* TV, 82, CDN, Ass cam; *LE MARIAGE ET PIS APRES,* ED, 78, CDN, Rech/Cam/Co mont/Co réal; *VOTEZ MAUVE,* C, 77, CDN, Phot plat; *L'AGE DORT,* TV, 76, CDN, Ass cam/Phot plat.

BONILLA, Peter

IATSE-644. 17806 Porto Marina Way, Pacific Palisades, CA, USA, 90272. (213)454-8909.
Types of Production & Categories: Th Film-DOP; Th Short-DOP; TV Film-DOP; TV Video-DOP.
Genres: Drama-Th&TV; Action-Th; Documentary-Th&TV; Educational-TV.

(cont/suite)

Biography: Born 1949, Montreal, Quebec; Canadian citizen. Languages: French, English, Spanish. B.A. (Cum Laude), UCLA Film School, 74. Certified scuba diver.
Selective Filmography: *AEROBICIDE*, Th, 85, USA, DOP; *RABBIT*, Th, 85, USA, DOP; *THE LAW OF NATURE*, TV, 85, USA, DOP; *PAPARAZZI*, MV, 85, USA, DOP; *HOUR CLOCKS*, Cm, 85, USA, DOP; *THE FOLLOWER*, ED, 84, USA, DOP; *COLD WARRIORS*, TV, 84, USA, DOP; *THE STOCK MARKET*, ED, 84, USA, DOP; *'ENTERTAINMENT TONIGHT'* (5 eps), TV, 83, USA, Co-Cam; *ALZHEIMER'S DISEASE*, ED, 82, USA, DOP; *BUILDING AGAIN*, Th, 82, USA, DOP; *NEW YORK NIGHTS*, Th, 81, USA/GB, DOP; *MAN FROM AFRICA*, Th, 81, USA/TT, DOP.

BORREMANS, Guy

STCQ. 5899 Hutchison, Montréal, Qué, CAN, H2V 4B7. (514)495-2367.
Types de production et Catégories: l métrage-D phot; c métrage-D phot/Réal.
Types d'oeuvres: Drame-C; Documentaire-C&TV.
Curriculum vitae: Né en 1934, Dinant, Belgique: citoyen canadien depuis 60. A vécu et travaillé à New York, San Francisco, Paris, Londres, Amsterdam, Mexico; photographe de presse et photo-journaliste, 53; ex-correspondant pour Paris-Match; débute dans le cinéma en 56; participe au mouvement cinéma-vérité, ONF, 61. Constructeur et navigateur de voilier. Connaisance particulière de l'Afrique. A remporté plusieurs prix dont le Prix de la Critique Québécoise pour *LE JOURNAL INNACHEVE* et *24h OU PLUS*. Spécialisé en caméra portée.
Filmographie sélective: *MARIA CHAPDELEINE*, C, 83, CDN/F, Cam 2e éq; *NATURPLY*, In, 81, CDN, Prod/Réal/Cam; *LES PLOUFFE*, C, 81, CDN, Cam 2e éq; *JOURNAL INNACHEVE*, C, 80, CDN, D phot; *LE SOULIER*, C, 79, CDN, D phot; *LE REVENANT*, C, 79, CDN/SN, D phot; *PAKUASHIPU/MISTASHIPU*, 'CARCAJOU ET LE PERIL BLANC', TV, 79-72, CDN, D phot; *LA BARRIERE/LE PASSAGE DES TENTES AUX MAISONS*, 'CARCAJOU ET LE PERIL BLANC', TV, 79-72, CDN, D phot; *24h OU PLUS*, C, 78, CDN, D phot; *KOUCHIBOUGUAC*, C, 77, CDN, Réal; *CHISSIBI* (JOB'S GARDEN), TV, 71, CDN, D phot; *LE MEPRIS N'AURA QU'UN TEMPS*, TV, 70, CDN, D phot; *NO HARVEST FOR THE REAPER*, TV, 68, USA, D phot; *DIMANCHE D'AMERIQUE*, C, 65, CDN, D phot; *PLRCE ON THE ROCKS*, C, 64, CDN, D phot; *L'HOMME VITE*, C, 63, CDN, Réal; *TORONTO JAZZ*, C, 63, CDN, D phot; *JOUR APRES JOUR*, C, 62, CDN, D phot; *BUCHERONS DE LA MANOUANE*, C, 62, CDN, D phot; *GOLDEN GLOVES*, C, 61, CDN, D phot; *LA FEMME-IMAGE*, C, 59, CDN, Prod/Réal/Cam.

BOTELHO, John

NABET-79. 123 Copperwork Sq., Scarborough, Ont, CAN. Glen-Warren Productions Ltd., Box 9, Toronto, Ont, CAN, M4A 2M9. (416)291-7571.
Types of Production & Categories: TV Video-DOP.
Genres: Drama-TV; Variety-TV; Children's-TV.
Biography: Born 1951, Portugal; landed immigrant, Canada. Has worked for CFTO TV for 18 years. Received an Emmy nomination for *THE EXECUTION OF RAYMOND GRAHAM*, 86.
Selective Filmography: *TELETHON FOR SICK CHILDREN'S HOSPITAL* (2 shows), TV, 86/85, CDN, Light Cam; *THE EXECUTION OF RAYMOND GRAHAM*, TV, 85, CDN, Light Cam; *GROWN UPS*, TV, 85, USA, Light Cam; *ALL MY SONS*, TV, 85, USA, Light Cam; *'LITTLEST HOBO'*, TV, 84-79, CDN, Light Cam.

BRAULT, François - voir REALISATEURS

BRAULT, Michel - voir REALISATEURS

CINEMATOGRAPHERS/DIRECTEURS-PHOTO

BROOKS, Robert

CSC, CFTA, IATSE-667, SMPTE. 34 Cheval Dr., Don Mills, Ont, CAN, M3B 1R6. (416)445-5334. 214 Gerrard St.E., Toronto, Ont, CAN, M5A 2E6. (416)926-9459.
Types of Production & Categories: Th Film-DOP; TV Film-DOP; TV Video-DOP.
Genres: Drama-Th&TV; Documentary-Th&TV; Educational-Th&TV.
Biography: Born 1929, Regina, Saskatchewan. Entered film industry with Associate Screen News, 47; joined Chetwynd Films Ltd. as DOP and Head of Camera Dept., 56; began freelancing, started Robert Brooks Associates Ltd., 69; shot the first 35mm Eastman Color negative in Canada, 55. Has worked on many award-winning films: won the Bill Hilson Award, 76.
Selective Filmography: *A PLACE FOR ALL SEASONS - TORONTO/C.S.A. - A PART OF YOUR LIFE*, In, 86, CDN, DOP; *THE STRAW BULL/BUTT OUT*, In, 86, CDN, DOP; *BEAT THE STREET/STAYING YOUNG, STAYING HAPPY/ HART HAVEN*, 'PEOPLE PATTERNS', TV, 86, CDN, DOP; *TOMORROW'S EDGE*, In, 86, CDN, DOP; *EVINRUDE/JOHNSON*, Cm, 85, CDN, DOP; *THE GOOD LIFE*, In, 85, CDN, DOP; *KNIGHTS AND CASTLES*, TV, 85, CDN, DOP; *ANIMAL FEVER*, TV, 85, CDN, DOP; *MONSTERS AND THINGS THAT GO BUMP*, TV, 85, CDN, DOP; *SPIES AND DETECTIVES*, TV, 85, CDN, DOP; *FAMILY AND FRIENDS*, TV, 85, CDN, DOP; *TODD'S BIRTHDAY*, TV, 85, CDN, DOP; *STEVIE AND THE DINOSAURS*, TV, 84, CDN, DOP; *GO, JEAN GUY, GO*, TV, 82, CDN, DOP; *LOVERBOY*, TV, 82, CDN, DOP; *THE MAKING OF THE TERRY FOX STORY*, TV, 82, CDN, DOP; *VARIATIONS OF A THEME*, In, 81, CDN, DOP **(CSC)**; *AURORA ON TARGET*, In, 80, CDN, DOP; *GILLES VILLENEUVE*, TV, 78, CDN, DOP; *DEADLY HARVEST*, Th, 76, CDN, DOP; *A SWEETER SONG*, Th, 75, CDN, DOP; *BACHMAN TURNER OVERDRIVE*, TV, 75, CDN, DOP; *LIONS FOR BREAKFAST*, Th, 74, CDN, DOP; *TROOPING THE COLOUR-PPCLI*, Th, 55, CDN, DOP.

BURSTYN, Thomas

CSC, IATSE-667, STCQ. 562 Spadina Ave., Toronto, Ont, CAN, M5S 2J9. (416) 922-3195. Suzanne Depoe, Creative Technique, P.O. Box 311, Stn.F, Toronto, Ont, CAN, M4Y 2L7. (416)466-4173.
Types of Production & Categories: Th Film-DOP; TV Film-DOP.
Genres: Drama-Th&TV; Action-Th&TV; Documentary-Th&TV; Commercials-TV.
Biography: Born 1954. Awards: Ace Award, Best Cinematography for *THE HITCHIKER*; *IF BRAINS WERE DYNAMITE YOU WOULDN'T HAVE ENOUGH TO BLOW YOUR NOSE* won a Gold Plaque, Chicago Int'l Film Festival.
Selective Filmography: *NATIVE SON*, TV, 86, USA, DOP; *'THE HITCHIKER'* (11 eps), TV, 85/84, CDN/USA, DOP; *MR.WRONG*, Th, 84, NZ, DOP; *'RAY BRADBURY THEATRE'* (2 eps), TV, 84, CDN, DOP; *HONDA/FORD SIERRA*, Cm, 83, NZ, DOP; *LOST TRIBE*, Th, 81, NZ, DOP; *IF BRAINS WERE DYNAMITE YOU WOULDN'T HAVE ENOUGH TO BLOW YOUR NOSE*, TV, 74, CDN, DOP.

CARON, Michel

STCQ. 3713 rue Ste-Famille, Montréal, Qué, CAN, H2X 2L7. (514)845-8918.
Types de production et Catégories: l métrage-D phot; c métrage-D phot.
Types d'oeuvres: Drame-C; Documentaire-C.
Curriculum vitae: Né en 1946, Montréal, Québec. Bac. ès Arts, Ecole des Beaux-Arts. Directeur-photo pigiste au cinéma depuis 15 ans.
Filmographie sélective: *LA LIGNE DE CHALEUR*, C, 86, CDN, D phot; *HENRI*, C, 85, CDN, D phot; *LE MATOU (THE ALLEY CAT)*, C, 85, CDN/F, Cadr; *CAFFE ITALIA*, C, 84, CDN, D phot; *'EMPIRE INC.'* (6 eps), TV, 83, CDN, Cadr; *CHER MONSIEUR L'AVIATEUR*, C, 82, CDN, D phot; *VOYAGEUR*, C, 82, CDN, D phot.

DIRECTEURS-PHOTO/CINEMATOGRAPHERS

CARRIERE, Bruno - voir REALISATEURS

CASEY, Bill
CSC. Bill Casey Productions Inc., 4256 Westhill, Montreal, Que, CAN, H4B 2S7. (514)487-0730.
Types of Production & Categories: TV Film-Cam; TV Video-Cam.
Genres: Documentary-TV; Children's-TV; Commercials-TV; Industrial-TV.
Biography: Born 1947, Montreal, Quebec; bilingual. B.A., Communication Arts, Loyola University, 68. Cameraman, photographer for CN Railways (15 films), 68-72; freelance cameraman since 72. Formed Bill Casey Productions Inc., 76. *CN 50 YEARS LATER* won a Gold Camera Award, Chicago.
Selective Filmography: *'NATIONAL NEWS'*, TV, 86-76, CDN, Cam; *ROAD TO PATRIATION*, TV, 84, CDN, Co-Cam; *I LIKE TO SEE THE WHEELS TURN*, TV, 82, CDN, Cam; *'THE FIFTH ESTATE'* (6 seg), TV, 81, CDN, Cam; *COACHES*, TV, 75, CDN, Cam; *CN - 50 YEARS LATER*, In, 72, CDN, Cam.

CAYLA, Eric
STCQ. 4543 Christophe Colomb, Montréal, Qué, CAN, H2J 3G7. (514)526-9971.
Types de production et Catégories: c métrage-D phot; TV film-D phot; TV vidéo-D phot.
Types d'oeuvres: Drame-C&TV; Action-C&TV; Documentaire-C&TV; Expérimental-C&TV.
Curriculum vitae: Né en 1957, Sorel, Québec; citoyenneté canadienne et française; bilingue. Education: Arts et Lettres, Champlain College; Communications, Université Loyola; Cinematography, American Film Institute, L.A..
Filmographie sélective: *'A PLEIN TEMPS'* (10 eps), TV, 86/85, CDN, D phot; *'MANON'* (13 eps), TV, 86/85, CDN, Cam; *MOCHE MUSIK* (ROCH ET BELLES OREILLES), TV, 86, CDN, D phot; *LE FEU SAUVAGE DE L'AMOUR*, MV, 86, CDN, D phot; *'TELECLIP'* (13 eps), TV, 86, CDN, D phot; *EXPO 86*, Cm, 86, CDN, D phot; *A L'ECOUTE/BLITZ*, Cm, 86/83, CDN, D phot; *'A PLEIN TEMPS'* (50 eps), TV, 85/84, CDN, Cam; *'DEFI MONDIAL'* (6 eps), TV, 85, CDN/F, Cam; *LE REVE DE VOLER*, C, 85, CDN, Cam; *L'ELUE*, C, 85, CDN, D phot; *EVANGELINE DEUSSE*, TV, 84, CDN/F, Cam; *DOUBLE DOLLAR/MON PRET A PARTIR*, Cm, 84/83, CDN, Cam; *JOANNIE AND THE WHALES*, C, 83, USA, Cam; *A DOLLAR A MILE*, C, 83, USA, D phot; *IN ANOTHER LIFE*, C, 83, USA, D phot; *LE NOYAU*, C, 83/82, CDN, D phot; *LAURE CONAN*, 'MANUSCRITS', TV, 83/82, CDN, D phot; *NEW ORLEANS*, TV, 82, CDN/USA, Cam; *A MATTER OF CUNNING*, TV, 82, CDN, Cam; *BIG MAMA THORTON*, TV, 82, CDN, D phot; *LA SECURITE A BICYCLETTE/ L'ECOLOGIE*, In, 82/81, CDN, D phot/Réal; *A LEAP OF A THOUSAND YEARS*, C, 81, CDN, D phot; *THESE STRANGERS, OUR FRIENDS*, C, 81/80, CDN, D phot; *KLUANE*, TV, 80, CDN, D phot; *FABULOUS YUKON*, C, 79, CDN, D phot.

CHAMPION, Marc
CSC, CST, SMPTE. 2 Sultan St., #406, Toronto, Ont, CAN, M5S 1L7. (416)967-4253.
Types of Production & Categories: Th Film-DOP; TV Film-DOP; TV Video-DOP.
Genres: Drama-Th&TV; Action-Th; Commercials-TV; Music Video-TV.
Biography: Born in France; Canadian citizen; bilingual. Graduated from Ecole Nationale de Cinématographie and the Institut des Hautes Etudes Cinématographiques, Paris. Worked in France, 46-67, in Canada since then. DOP on numerous features and award-winning commercials shot around the world. Has won 2 craft awards for Best Cinematograhy for commercials 'Canada Dry'(81) and 'Cadbury'(84); *SLIPSTREAM* won Best Canadian Cinematography, L.A. Film Festival.

(cont/suite)

Selective Filmography: *ANNE OF GREEN GABLES - THE SEQUEL* (miniseries), TV, 86, CDN/USA, DOP; *SAMUEL LOUNT,* Th, 85, CDN, DOP; *'FRONTIER'* (6 eps), TV, 85, CDN/GB/F/D, DOP; *THE HOUSE OF DIES DREAR,* TV, 84, USA, DOP; *HELIX/TRIUMPH/LARRY GOWAN,* MV, 84, CDN, DOP; *OUT OF THE BLUE,* Th, 80, CDN, DOP; *WHY SHOOT THE TEACHER,* Th, 76, CDN, DOP; *PARTNERS,* Th, 76, CDN, DOP; *SLIPSTREAM,* Th, 73, CDN, DOP; *SUNDAY IN THE COUNTRY,* Th, 73, CDN, DOP; *THE HEART FARM,* Th, 70, CDN, DOP.

CHAPMAN, Christopher - see DIRECTORS

CHENTRIER, Bernard

STCQ. 121 Rang Ste-Julie, St. Guillaume, Qué, CAN, J0C 1L0. (819)396-3063.
Types de production et Catégories: 1 métrage-D phot.
Types d'oeuvres: Drame-C; Horreur-C; Annonces-TV.
Curriculum vitae: Né en 1937 à Paris; citoyen canadien. Vingt-huit ans de cinéma à Montréal; a débuté chez Niagara Films; recyclage en tournage vidéo, annonces, 82.
Filmographie sélective: *'LANCE ET COMPTE'* (HE SHOOTS, HE SCORES), (13 eps), TV, 86/85, CDN, D phot/Cadr; *143 JOURS DE TOURNAGE,* C, 86, CDN, D phot; *CLEMENCE ALETTI,* TV, 83, CDN, D phot; *LE DOSSIER NOIR,* TV, 82, CDN/F, D phot; *BLACKOUT,* C, 78, CDN, D phot 2e éq; *'JO GAILLARD',* TV, 75-73, F, D phot; *LE GRAND THEATRE DE QUEBEC,* TV, 73, CDN, D phot/Cadr; *POUSSE, MAIS POUSSE EGAL,* C, 73, CDN, D phot; *J'AI MON VOYAGE,* C, 72, CDN, D phot/Cadr; *QUELQUES ARPENTS DE NEIGE,* C, 72, CDN, D phot/Cadr; *TRANSPORTS ET COMMUNICATIONS,* C, 71, CDN, D phot/Cadr; *BUREAU DES INVENTEURS,* C, 71, CDN, D phot/Cadr; *'LA FEUILLE D'ERABLE'* (8 eps), TV, 70, CDN, D phot; *RED,* C, 69, CDN, D phot/ Cadr (CFA); *LE VIOL D'UNE JEUNE FILLE DOUCE,* C, 66, CDN, D phot/ Cadr.

CHMURA, Andy

IATSE-667, STCQ. 783 Fisher St., Hemmingford, Que, CAN, J0L 1H0. (514)247-2119.
Types of Production & Categories: Th Film-DOP; Th Short-Cam; TV Film-Cam; TV Video-Cam.
Genres: Drama-Th&TV; Comedy-Th&TV; Action-Th&TV; Science Fiction-Th&TV.
Biography: Born 1946, Italy; British-Canadian citizenship. Languages: English, French, Polish. Education: university studies in Biochemistry. Experienced in helicopter and car stunt filming.
Selective Filmography: *STREET SMART,* Th, 86, USA, Op; *DEADLY BUSINESS,* TV, 85, USA, Op; *ACT OF VENGEANCE,* Th, 85, USA, Op; *PERRY MASON RETURNS,* TV, 85, USA, Op; *HOLD UP,* Th, 85, CDN/F, DOP; *SECRET WEAPONS,* TV, 84, USA, Op; *THE BOY IN BLUE,* Th, 84, CDN, Op; *HEARTSOUNDS,* TV, 84, USA, Op; *THE GUARDIAN,* TV, 83, CDN/USA, Op; *COOK & PEARY: THE RACE TO THE POLE,* TV, 83, USA, Op; *THE TERRY FOX STORY,* Th, 82, CDN, Op; *QUEST FOR FIRE* (LA GUERRE DU FEU), Th, 80, CDN/F, Op.

CHOW, Wang

CSC. 416 Runnymede Rd., Toronto, Ont, CAN, M6S 2Y8. (416)762-5448.
Types of Production & Categories: TV Film-DOP; TV Video-DOP.
Genres: Documentary-TV; Educational-TV; Industrial-TV; News-TV.
Biography: Born 1953, China; Canadian citizen. Languages: Chinese, English. Education: Degree from Ryerson Polytechnical Institute. DOP, specializes in lighting and camera operating on industrial, documentary and educational subjects.
Selective Filmography: *CHINESE CAFES IN RURAL SASKATCHEWAN,* TV, 85, CDN, DOP.

CIUPKA, Richard

CSC, DGC, IATSE-667. 71 Cornwall St., Montreal, Que, CAN, H3P 1M6. (514) 738-9996.
Types of Production & Categories: Th Film-DOP/Dir; TV Film-DOP.
Genres: Drama-Th&TV; Comedy-Th&TV; Action-Th&TV; Commercials-TV.
Biography: Born 1950, Liege, Belgium; Canadian citizen. Languages: English, French, Polish. Education: Cours Classique and Electronic Diploma. Worked 4 years in camera special effects with Wally Gentleman. Directed numerous commercials, 83-86; DOP on over 400.
Selective Filmography: *HOLD-UP*, Th, 85, CDN/F, DOP; *SECRET WEAPONS*, TV, 84, USA, DOP; *HEARTSOUNDS*, TV, 84, USA, DOP; *THE GUARDIAN*, TV, 83, CDN/USA, DOP; *THE BLOOD OF OTHERS* (LE SANG DES AUTRES), Th, 83, CDN/F, DOP; *THE TERRY FOX STORY*, Th, 82, CDN, DOP; *CURTAINS*, Th, 81, CDN, Dir; *MELANIE*, Th, 80, CDN, DOP; *ATLANTIC CITY*, Th, 79, CDN/USA, DOP (CSC/BSC); *DIRTY TRICKS*, Th, 79, CDN, DOP; *AN AMERICAN CHRISTMAS CAROL*, TV, 79, USA, DOP; *YESTERDAY* (GABRIELLE), Th, 79, CDN, DOP; *IT RAINED ALL NIGHT THE DAY I LEFT*, Th, 78, CDN/IL/F, DOP; *VIOLETTE NOZIERE*, Th, 77, CDN/F, DOP/Op; *ANGELA*, Th, 76, CDN, Op; *BLOOD RELATIVES* (LES LIENS DE SANG), Th, 76, CDN/F, Op.

COQUILLON, John

ACTT, IATSE-667, IATSE-659. CCA Personal Management, 4 Court Lodge, 48 Sloane Square, London SW1, GB. (01)730-8857.
Types of Production & Categories: Th Film-DOP; TV Film-DOP.
Genres: Drama-Th&TV; Comedy-Th&TV; Action-Th&TV; Horror-Th&TV.
Selective Filmography: *CHRISTMAS PRESENT*, TV, 86, USA, DOP; *LACE II* (mini-series), TV, 85, GB/USA, DOP; *CLOCKWISE*, Th, 85, GB, DOP; *HYPER SAPIEN*, Th, 85, USA, DOP; *LAST PLACE ON EARTH*, TV, 84, GB, DOP; *YELLOW PAGES*, Th, 84, GB, DOP; *OSTERMAN WEEKEND*, Th, 83, USA, DOP; *MASTER OF THE GAME* (mini-series), TV, 83, USA, DOP; *IVANHOE*, TV, 82, GB/USA, DOP; *THE WARS*, Th, 81, CDN/D, DOP; *THE AMATEUR*, Th, 81, CDN, DOP; *BERKELEY SQUARE*, Th, 80, GB, DOP; *FINAL ASSIGNMENT*, Th, 80, CDN, DOP; *MISDEAL* (BEST REVENGE), Th, 80, CDN, DOP; *THE CHANGELING*, Th, 79, CDN, DOP (GENIE); *MR. PATMAN*, Th, 79, CDN, DOP; *WESTERN FRONT*, TV, 78, USA, DOP; *39 STEPS*, Th, 77, GB/USA, DOP; *FOUR FEATHERS*, Th, 76, GB/USA, DOP; *ABSOLUTION*, Th, 76, GB/USA, DOP; *CROSS OF IRON*, Th, 74, GB/USA, DOP; *WILBY CONSPIRACY*, Th, 73, USA, DOP; *PAT GARRETT AND BILLY THE KID*, Th, 72, USA, DOP; *TRIPLE ECHOE*, Th, 72, GB, DOP; *STRAW DOGS*, Th, 71, GB/USA, DOP; *WUTHERING HEIGHTS*, Th, 70, GB/USA, DOP; *CRY OF THE BANSHEE*, Th, 69, GB/USA, DOP; *SCREAM AGAIN*, Th, 68, GB/USA, DOP; *OBLONG BOX*, Th, 68, GB/USA, DOP; *WITCHFINDER GENERAL*, Th, 67, GB/USA, DOP.

COWAN, Paul - see DIRECTORS

CRONE, David

CSC, IATSE-667. 23 Leacrest Rd., Toronto, Ont, CAN, M4G 1E4. (416)421-3388. Crone Films Ltd., 400 Walmer Rd., Toronto, Ont, CAN, M5P 2X7. (416)924-9044.
Types of Production & Categories: Th Film-Cam.
Genres: Drama-Th; Action-Th; Documentary-Th; Children's-Th.
Biography: Born 1954; Canadian citizen. Graduated University of Western Ontario. Steadicam specialist, operator on numerous feature films.
Selective Filmography: *DEAD OF WINTER*, Th, 86, USA, St'cam; *APOLOGY*, TV, 85, USA, Op; *UNNATURAL CAUSES*, Th, 85, USA, Op; *AGNES OF GOD*, Th, 84, USA, St'cam/2nd U Op; *ONE MAGIC CHRISTMAS*, Th, 85, CDN/USA, 2nd

(cont/suite)

Cam op/St'cam; *THE JOURNEY OF NATTY GANN,* Th, 85, USA, St'cam; *RUNAWAY,* Th, 84, USA, Op; *CLAN OF THE CAVE BEAR,* Th, 84, USA, Op; *MRS. SOFFEL,* Th, 84, CDN, St'cam; *BLACKOUT,* Th, 77, CDN, St'cam/2nd U DOP.

CRONE, Robert

CSC, DGC, IATSE-667. 400 Walmer Rd., Toronto, Ont, CAN, M5P 2X7. (416) 924-9044.
Types of Production & Categories: Th Film-DOP; TV Film-Dir/Prod; TV Video-Dir/Prod.
Genres: Drama-Th; Documentary-TV; Educational-Th&TV.
Biography: Born 1932, Toronto, Ontario. Education: Bob Jones University, South Carolina; Television Workshop of New York (Gold Camera Award). President AMPPLC. Recipient of Canada Medal and the Air Canada Award, Academy of Canadian Cinema, 81. Steadicam operator on 45 feature films, 80-86; pilot, instrument rated.
Selective Filmography: *AMERIKA* (mini-series), TV, 86, USA, St'cam; *THE GIRL WHO SPELLED FREEDOM,* TV, 86, USA, Op/St'cam; *'MIAMI VICE'* (sev eps), TV, 86/85, USA, St'cam; *HUNTERS,* Th, 85, CDN, DOP/St'cam; *PERRY MASON RETURNS,* TV, 85, USA, 2nd Op/St'cam; *INDESTRUCTIBLE MAN,* TV, 85, USA, 2nd Op/St'cam; *STEPFATHER,* TV, 85, USA, 2nd U DOP/2nd Op/St'cam; *NOBODY'S CHILD,* TV, 85, USA, 2nd U DOP/Op/St'cam; *MRS. DELAFIELD WANTS TO MARRY,* TV, 85, USA, 2nd U DOP; *PAPAL VISIT* (world-wide), TV, 84, CDN, Cam; *EVERGREEN* (mini-series), TV, 84, USA, St'cam; *RECKLESS DISREGARD,* TV, 84, CDN/USA, St'cam; *'WORLD'S GREATEST ATHLETES',* TV, 83/82, CDN, Dir; *SPEAKING THROUGH SPIRITS,* TV, 83, CDN, DOP; *PRIME MINISTER'S SPEECH TO THE NATION* (6 seg), TV, 82, CDN, Prod; *THESE THINGS WE SHARE,* TV, 82, CDN, Dir; *ANGLICAN WORLD CONFERENCE* (13 shows), TV, 60, CDN, Prod; *'CLOSE UP'* (27 eps), TV, 59/58, CDN, Dir; *'LANDS AND FORESTS'* (40 eps), TV, 58-56, CDN, Prod; *DOUKHOBOR,* TV, 58, CDN, Dir.

CZURKO, Edward - see DIRECTORS

DELACROIX, Yves

STCQ. 4591 Des Erables, Montréal, Qué, CAN, H2H 2E1. (514)524-7627.
Types de production et Catégories: c métrage-D phot; TV film-D phot; TV vidéo-D phot.
Types d'oeuvres: Documentaire-C&TV; Education-C&TV; Enfants-C&TV; Industriel-C&TV.
Curriculum vitae: Né en 1936; citoyen canadien; bilingue. Bac., Sciences humaines, Louvain, Belgique. Radio-Canada, 60-64; réalisateur de films industriels et annonces; directeur-photo et caméraman sur maintes annonces et documentaires depuis 66.

DE VOLPI, David

47 Dobie Ave., Mount Royal, Que, CAN, H3P 1R9. (514)738-4409. NFB, 3155 Cote de Liesse, Montreal, Que, CAN, H3C 3H5.
Types of Production & Categories: Th Film-DOP; Th Short-DOP; TV Film-DOP.
Genres: Drama-Th&TV; Documentary-TV; Children's-Th&TV; Experimental-Th&TV.
Biography: Born 1942, Montreal, Quebec. Attended Loyola College. Began at the NFB, 64, assistant cameraman. Apart from dramas, main skill lies in special effects work, especially blue screen.
Selective Filmography: *OTHER TONGUES,* Th, 85, CDN, DOP; *RUNNING SCARED,* TV, 85, CDN, DOP; *TO SET OUR HOUSE IN ORDER/A GOOD TREE,* 'BELL CANADA PLAYHOUSE', TV, 85/84, CDN, DOP; *OUT OF A*

(cont/suite)

JOB, TV, 85, CDN, DOP; *NARCISSUS,* Th, 84, CDN, DOP; *FIRST STOP CHINA,* TV, 84, CDN, Cin; *STARBREAKER,* Th, 83, CDN, DOP; *THE FIRST WINTER,* TV, 82, CDN, DOP; *REVOLUTION'S ORPHAN,* Th, 78, CDN, DOP; *THE RED DRESS,* TV, 78, CDN, DOP; *BREAKDOWN,* TV, 77, CDN, DOP; *HAPPINESS IS LOVING YOUR TEACHER,* TV, 77, CDN, DOP.

DOSTIE, Alain

STCQ. 1903 Lionel-Groulx, Montréal, Qué, CAN, H3J 1J2. (514)932-4159.
Types de production et Catégories: l métrage-D phot; c métrage-D phot; TV film-D phot; TV vidéo-D phot.
Types d'oeuvres: Drame-C&TV; Comédie-C; Documentaire-C.
Curriculum vitae: Né en 1943, Québec. Bac. en Pédagogie, Université de Montréal, 63. Assistant caméra à partir de 63; caméraman, ONF, 67-74; pigiste depuis 74.
Filmographie sélective: *ELVIS GRATTON LE KING DES KINGS,* C, 85, CDN, D phot; *LES ANNEES DE REVE,* C, 83, CDN, D phot; *'EMPIRE INC.'* (6 eps), TV, 82, CDN, D phot; *AU PAYS DE ZOM,* C, 80, CDN, D phot; *LE SOLEIL SE LEVE EN RETARD,* C, 75, CDN, D phot; *GINA,* C, 74, CDN, D phot; *POUR LE MEILLEUR ET POUR LE PIRE,* C, 74, CDN, D phot; *LES VAUTOURS,* C, 74, CDN, D phot; *TENDRESSE ORDINAIRE,* C, 72, CDN, D phot; *REJEANNE PADOVANI,* C, 72, CDN, D phot; *QUEBEC, DUPLESSIS ET APRES,* C, 71/70, CDN, Cam; *LA MAUDITE GALETTE,* C, 71, CDN, D phot; *LE MARTIEN DE NOEL,* C, 70, CDN, D phot; *ON EST LOIN DU SOLEIL,* C, 70, CDN, D phot; *ON EST AU COTON,* C, 69/68, CDN, Cam.

DUCKWORTH, Martin - see DIRECTORS

DUFAUX, Guy

ARRFQ, STCQ. 200 de Gaspé, #310, Ile des Soeurs, Verdun, Qué, CAN, H3E 1E6. (514)768-9549.
Types de production et Catégories: l métrage-D phot; c métrage-D phot/Réal; TV film-D phot.
Types d'oeuvres: Drame-C&TV; Comédie-C&TV; Action-C&TV; Documentaire-C&TV.
Curriculum vitae: Né en 1943, Lille, France; citoyen canadien. Etudes aux Beaux-Arts à Marseille, France; émigration au Canada, 65. Monteur et caméraman aux Cinéastes Ass.; ONF, 66-70; directeur fondateur des Productions Prisma, 70-77; Président du Syndicat National du Cinéma, 69-70; Président de l'ARRFQ, 75-76; Directeur du Conseil d'Administration de l'Institut Québécois du Cinéma.
Filmographie sélective: *SCALP,* C, 85, CDN, D phot; *LE DECLIN DE L'EMPIRE AMERICAIN* (DECLINE OF THE AMERICAN EMPIRE), C, 85, CDN, D phot; *EQUINOXE,* C, 85, CDN, D phot; *POUVOIR INTIME,* C, 85, CDN, D phot; *'UN AMOUR DE QUARTIER'* (13 eps), TV, 84, CDN, D phot; *LE JOUR S, C,* 83, CDN, D phot; *DE L'AUTRE COTE DE LA GLACE,* C, 83, CDN, Co réal; *SONATINE,* C, 82, CDN, D phot; *'ZIGZAG'* (5 eps), TV, 82, CDN, D phot; *FUTUR INTERIEUR,* C, 81, CDN, D phot; *LA MER DE BEAUFORT,* TV, 81, CDN, Réal/Cam; *LES FLEURS SAUVAGES,* C, 81, CDN, D phot; *L'EQUIPE DES GRANDS DEFIS,* In, 81, CDN, Phot/Réal; *LES PIEGES DE LA MER,* C, 80, CDN/F, Cam; *'L'AGE DE L'ENERGIE'* (13 eps), TV, 79, CDN, Cam; *PRIS AU PIEGE,* C, 79/78, CDN, Co réal/Cam/Mont; *CORRIDORS,* C, 79/78, CDN, Cam/Co réal; *AVOIR 16 ANS,* C, 77, CDN, Phot; *LA PECHE,* TV, 77, CDN, Réal; *COMME LES SIX DOIGTS DE LA MAIN,* C, 77, CDN, Cam; *LE VIEUX PAYS OU RIMBAUD EST MORT,* C, 76, CDN/F, D phot; *LE FLEUVE ST-LAURENT,* TV, 76, CDN/F, Réal; *'L'AMOUR QUOTIDIEN'* (13 eps), TV, 75, CDN, Cam; *'LES JOUEURS'* (3 eps), TV, 74, CDN, Réal; *LES DERNIERES FIANCAILLES,* C, 73, CDN, Cam; *LES SMATTES,* C, 71, CDN, D phot.

DUNK, Bert

IATSE-644, IATSE-659, IATSE-667, ASC, CSC. 44 Charles St.W., #3303, Toronto, Ont, CAN, M4Y 1R8. (416)961-6857. Ray Gosnell, Smith/Gosnell Agency Inc., 3872 Las Flores Canyon Rd., Malibu, CA, USA, 90265. (213)456-6641.
Types of Production & Categories: Th Film-DOP; TV Film-DOP.
Genres: Drama-Th&TV; Comedy-Th&TV; Action-Th&TV; Music Video-TV.
Biography: Born 1944, Regina, Saskatchewan. Studied Photography, Germaine School of Photography, New York. Started as assistant cameraman in N.Y.; operator, then freelance DOP; DOP on numerous commercials and music videos.
Selective Filmography: *THE RULING PASSION,* TV, 86, USA, DOP; *PERRY MASON RETURNS,* TV, 85, USA, DOP; *ILLUSIONS,* TV, 85, USA, DOP (**CSC**); *CLASS OF '84,* Th, 82, CDN/USA, DOP; *IF YOU COULD SEE WHAT I HEAR,* Th, 82, CDN, 2nd U Cam; *'CAGNEY & LACEY'* (pilot), TV, 81, USA, DOP (**CSC**); *INCUBUS,* Th, 81, CDN, DOP; *HANK WILLIAMS: THE SHOW HE NEVER GAVE,* Th, 81, CDN, DOP; *ESCAPE FROM IRAN: THE CANADIAN CAPER,* TV, 80, CDN, DOP; *HARD FEELINGS,* Th, 80, CDN, 2nd U Cam; *MURDER BY PHONE* (BELLS), Th, 80, CDN, 2nd U Cam; *PHOBIA,* Th, 80, CDN, 2nd U Cam; *KLONDIKE FEVER,* Th, 79, CDN, DOP; *HIGH POINT,* Th, 79, CDN, DOP; *KAVIK THE WOLF DOG,* TV, 78, CDN, DOP; *HIGH-BALLIN',* Th, 77, CDN, 2nd U Cam; *'THE NEWCOMERS'* (1 eps), TV, 76, CDN, DOP; *'SEARCH AND RESCUE',* TV, 76, CDN/USA, DOP; *BREAKING POINT,* Th, 76, CDN/USA, 2nd U Cam; *SECOND WIND,* Th, 75, CDN, 2nd U Cam; *'WITNESS TO YESTERDAY',* TV, 74, CDN, DOP; *SHE CRIED MURDER,* TV, 73, CDN/USA, 2nd U Cam.

EARNSHAW, Philip

CSC. 177 Geoffrey St., Toronto, Ont, CAN, M5R 1P6. (416)536-5241.
Types of Production & Categories: TV Film-DOP; TV Video-DOP.
Genres: Drama-TV; Documentary-TV; Educational-TV; Children's-TV.
Biography: Born 1951, Hamilton, Ontario. Honours degree in Fine Arts, York University, 75. Worked for 3 years as a photo-journalist and news cameraman; staff cameraman, Global TV news, 75-78; freelance DOP, director, producer, industrial and educational films which have won awards at int'l film festivals.
Selective Filmography: *'OWL TV'* (20 eps), TV, 86/85, CDN, DOP; *'KIDS OF DEGRASSI STREET'* (26 eps), TV, 85/84, CDN, DOP; *REBECCA,* Cm, 85, CDN, DOP; *THE PASSION,* TV, 82, CDN, Dir.

ENNIS, Bob

CSC, IATSE-667. 1518 Norton Crt., North Vancouver, BC, CAN. (604)929-5355. Argus Productions, 853 Hamilton St., Vancouver, BC, CAN, V6B 2R7. (604)687-4707.
Types of Production & Categories: Th Film-DOP; TV Film-DOP.
Genres: Drama-Th&TV; Musical-TV; Action-Th&TV; Documentary-TV.
Biography: Born 1943, Calgary, Alberta. Director, producer of commercials and short documentaries. Has won the Governor General's Award; Gold Camera Award, Chicago.
Selective Filmography: *'DANGER BAY'* (22 eps), TV, 86, CDN/USA, DOP; *PORTRAITS OF CANADA* (EXPO 86), Th, 85, CDN, DOP; *'RITTER'S COVE'* (13 eps), TV, 81/80, CDN, DOP; *LATITUDE 55,* Th, 80, CDN, DOP; *UP RIVER,* TV, 79, USA, DOP; *TANKER BOMB,* TV, 78, CDN, DOP (**ANIK**); *MULTIPLICITY,* Th, 70, CDN, DOP (**CFA**).

EVDEMON, Nikos

CSC. 72 Southwood Dr., Toronto, Ont, CAN, M4E 2T9. (416)690-6644.
Types of Production & Categories: Th Film-DOP; Th Short-DOP; TV Film-DOP.
(cont/suite)

Genres: Drama-Th&TV; Comedy-TV; Action-TV; Documentary-TV.
Biography: Born 1949, Salonika, Greece; Canadian citizen; speaks English, German, Greek. **Education:** Academy for Film and TV, Berlin, West Germany.
Selective Filmography: *SEEING THINGS'* (42 eps), TV, 86-82, CDN, DOP; *THE MARRIAGE BED,* TV, 86, CDN, DOP; *ONE FOOT IN HEAVEN,* 'MAN ALIVE', TV, 84, CDN, DOP (ANIK); *BEYOND OBLIVION/METAL,* 'HAND AND EYE', TV, 83, CDN, DOP; *BEST OF BOTH WORLDS,* TV, 82, CDN, DOP; *MAY'S MIRACLE/DAVID,* 'MAN ALIVE', TV, 81-79, CDN, DOP; *TAKE OVER* (pilot), 'VANDERBERG', TV, 81, CDN, DOP; *FINAL EDITION/ RUNNING MAN/HARVEST/THE WINNINGS OF FRANKIE WALLS,* 'FOR THE RECORD', TV, 80/79, CDN, DOP; *MOVING MOUNTAINS,* In, 80, CDN, DOP; *LYON'S DEN,* TV, 79, CDN, DOP; *COMING OUT ALIVE,* TV, 79, CDN, DOP; *TORONTO JAM* (pilot), TV, 79, CDN, DOP; *NORTHERN LIGHTS* (pilot), TV, 79, CDN, DOP; *KILROY IS HERE* (pilot), TV, 79, CDN, DOP; *ONE OF OUR OWN/CERTAIN PRACTICES/JE ME SOUVIENS,* 'FOR THE RECORD', TV, 79/78, CDN, DOP; *'SIDESTREET'* (8 eps), TV, 78/77, CDN, DOP; *'PEEPSHOW'* (3 eps), TV, 76, CDN, DOP; *PEOPLES PROBLEM,* TV, 75, CDN, DOP; *'OUR FOLKS NEXT DOOR'* (9 eps), TV, 75, CDN, DOP; *THE LAST BATTLE,* 'NEWS MAGAZINE', TV, 74, CDN, DOP (ANIK); *ME,* Th, 74, CDN, DOP; *THE YELLOW LEAF,* Th, 70, CDN, DOP.

FERGUSON, Graeme - see DIRECTORS

FERRAND, Carlos - voir REALISATEURS

FERRON, Gilbert

SMPTE, STCQ. 1060 rue Ste-Angèle, Trois-Rivières, Qué, CAN, G9A 1M9. (819) 378-6457.
Types de production et Catégories: c métrage-Cam; TV film-Cam; TV vidéo-Réal/ Cam.
Types d'oeuvres: Drame-C&TV; Variété-TV; Science-fiction-C; Documentaire-C&TV.
Curriculum vitae: Né au Québec. Education: mincure en cinéma, Université du Québec à Trois-Rivières; Institut des Arts de Diffusion, Bruxelles.
Filmographie sélective: *'VIVRE A...'* (Réal-3 eps), (9 eps), TV, 86, CDN, Cam; *'LE PLAISIR DE LIRE'* (5 eps), TV, 86, CDN, Cam; *'DOSSIERS MEDICAUX'* (2 eps), TV, 86, CDN, Cam; *'CONTACT'* (50 eps), TV, 86-84, CDN, Cam; *ARRETE DE ME PRENDRE,* C, 85, CDN, Cam; *LES MOTOS DU DIMANCHE,* TV, 85, CDN, Réal; *ENFIN PAQUE,* TV, 85, CDN, Cam; *LA VOYANCE DEMYTHIFIEE/LA SEXUALITE DEMYTHIFIEE,* TV, 85, CDN, Cam; *L'AVENIR AU MASCULIN/L'AVENIR AU FEMININ,* TV, 85, CDN, Cam; *AU RYTHME DU MONDE,* TV, 85, CDN, Cam; *SALUT JEAN LAPRISE,* TV, 85, CDN, Cam; *NELLIGAN - FORGUES,* TV, 85, CDN, Cam; *LE POUVOIR ROSE,* TV, 85, CDN, Cam; *'ENTRE LES LIGNES'* (13 eps), TV, 83, CDN, Cam; *'LES RACONTAGES DE LOUIS CARON'* (12 eps), TV, 82, CDN, Cam; *'LES ENFANTS DE LA MARGE'* (3 eps), TV, 82, CDN, Cam; *LE FIL QUI CHANTE,* C, 81, CDN, Cam; *SURSIS,* C, 81, CDN, Cam; *LA BETE A SEPT TETES,* TV, 80, CDN, Cam; *LE GUEUX ET LE REVENANT,* C, 79, CDN, Cam; *AU ROYAUME DU BINGO,* C, 78, CDN, Ing son; *RIBO, OU LE SOLEIL SAUVAGE,* C, 76, CDN, Cam/Ing son; *GOBITAL,* C, 75, CDN, Cam; *SPASMES ET PULSIONS,* C, 74, CDN, Cam/Mont; *C'EST PAS POUR DEMAIN,* C, 72, CDN, Cam.

FIKS, Henri

CSC, IATSE-667, STCQ. 66 Hampton Ave., Toronto, Ont, CAN, M4K 2Y6. (416) 466-8739.
Types of Production & Categories: Th Film-DOP; Th Short-DOP; TV Film-DOP.
(cont/suite)

Genres: Drama-Th&TV; Comedy-Th&TV; Documentary-Th&TV; Educational-Th&TV.
Biography: Born 1938, Paris, France; Canadian citizen, 68. Languages: English, French, Spanish. Licensed Ultralight pilot. Has specialized in 2nd unit cinematography. *A FINE LINE* won a Silver Hugo, Chicago; *LIFE MACHINE,* Gold Medal, New York; *WHISTLING SMITH,* Oscar nomination.
Selective Filmography: *ARROW BRIGADE,* Cm, 85, CDN, DOP; *MRS. SOFFEL,* Th, 84, USA, 2nd U DOP; *'LANDSCAPE OF GEOMETRY'* (8 eps), ED, 83, CDN, DOP; *MARTIN'S DAY,* Th, 83, CDN/GB, 2nd U DOP; *A FINE LINE,* ED, 81, CDN, DOP; *LIFE MACHINE,* 'CAMERA & SONG', ED, 76, GB, DOP; *WHISTLING SMITH,* TV, 76, CDN, DOP.

FILLINGHAM, Tom

IATSE-667. 2668 York Ave., Vancouver, BC, CAN, V6K 1E5. (604)736-9601.
Types of Production & Categories: Th Film-Prod/1st AD; TV Film-DOP.
Genres: Drama-Th&TV; Documentary-TV; Educational-TV.
Biography: Born 1949, Noranda, Quebec; bilingual. B.A., major in sociology.
Selective Filmography: *'HIS HIGHNESS THE AGA KHAN'* (5 eps), In, 85, CDN/F, DOP; *FOCUS ON KOREA,* In, 85, CDN/USA/SKO, DOP; *'STIR CRAZY'* (6 eps), TV, 85, USA, 2nd U DOP/Op; *'DANGER BAY'* (1 eps), TV, 85, CDN, 2nd U DOP; *SAMUEL LOUNT,* Th, 84, CDN, Op.

GANDER, Mogens

CSC. R.R. #5, Madoc, Ont, CAN, K0K 2K0. (613)473-2891.
Types of Production & Categories: Th Film-DOP; TV Film-DOP.
Genres: Drama-Th&TV; Documentary-Th&TV; Educational-Th&TV.
Biography: Born 1933, Denmark; Canadian citizen; speaks English, Danish. Initial employment at NFB; freelance cameraman for CBC and independent producers, Toronto; produced, directed and acted in many documentaries, TV commercials and CBC drama.
Selective Filmography: *THE MAN THAT WOULD DIE,* TV, 75, USA, 2nd U DOP; *THE CHICAGO SEVEN,* Th, 72, USA, DOP; *THE LONG WAY HOME,* Th, 66, CDN, DOP.

GEORGE, Laszlo

CSC, IATSE-644, IATSE-667. 80 Greenbrook Dr., Toronto, Ont, CAN, M6M 2J9. (416)920-1696. 8616 E. Worthington Dr., San Gabriel, CA, USA, 91775. (213)271-1686.
Types of Production & Categories: Th Film-DOP; TV Film-DOP.
Genres: Drama-Th&TV; Action-Th&TV.
Biography: Born Budapest, Hungary. Graduated from Academy of Film and Dramatic Arts, Budapest. Came to Canada, 57; Canadian citizen; US Green Card. Languages: Hungarian, English.
Selective Filmography: *ROLLING VENGEANCE,* Th, 86, USA, DOP; *BETRAYAL OF TRUST,* TV, 86, USA, DOP; *STRANGER IN MY BED,* TV, 86, USA, DOP; *VANISHING ACT,* TV, 86, USA, DOP; *MANY HAPPY RETURNS,* TV, 86, USA, DOP; *MASTERPIECE OF MURDER,* TV, 85, USA, DOP; *'STIR CRAZY'* (6 eps), TV, 85, USA, DOP; *YOUNG AGAIN,* TV, 85, USA, DOP; *A LETTER TO THREE WIVES,* TV, 85, USA, DOP; *A NICE, PLEASANT, DEADLY WEEKEND,* TV, 85, USA, DOP; *MURDER IN SPACE,* TV, 85, CDN/USA, DOP; *THE UNDERGRADS,* TV, 84, USA, DOP; *THE PARK IS MINE,* TV, 84, CDN/USA, DOP; *THE BEAR,* Th, 84, USA, DOP; *DRAW!,* TV, 83, CDN/USA, DOP (CSC); *MAZES AND MONSTERS,* TV, 82, USA, DOP; *FALCON'S GOLD* (ROBBERS OF THE SACRED MOUNTAIN), Th, 82, CDN, DOP; *PAROLE,* TV, 82, USA, DOP; *CIRCLE OF TWO,* Th, 80, CDN, DOP; *RUNNING,* Th, 79, CDN, DOP (CSC); *NOTHING PERSONAL,* Th, 79, CDN,

(cont/suite)

Co-DOP; *SILENT SKY,* Th, 77, CDN, DOP (**CFTA**); *HOMER,* Th, 68, USA, DOP.

GIMMI, William

IATSE-644, IATSE-667. Eagle Lake, Ont, CAN, K0M 1M0. (705)754-2055.
Types of Production & Categories: TV Film-DOP.
Genres: Commercials-TV.
Biography: Born 1930. Director of photography on hundreds of commercials; has won numerous national and international awards.

GONZALES, Angel

IATSE-667. 75 Carolbreen Square, Scarborough, Ont, CAN, M1V 1J1. (416)293-6822.
Types of Production & Categories: Th Short-DOP; TV Film-DOP; TV Video-Prod.
Genres: Drama-Th&TV; Action-Th; Documentary-Th&TV; Educational-Th&TV.
Biography: Born 1950, Mexico City; Canadian landed immigrant. Languages: Spanish, English. B.A.A., Photo Arts, Ryerson Polytechnical Institute, 78.
Selective Filmography: *POLICE ACADEMY III,* Th, 85, USA, 2nd Op; *REMO WILLIAMS,* Th, 85, USA, Op; *VICTIMS* (GUATEMALAN REFUGEES), TV, 85, MEX, Prod; *ELECTIONS 85,* TV, 85, MEX, Prod; *RAMBO: FIRST BLOOD PART II,* Th, 84, USA, 2nd U Op; *THE FALCON AND THE SNOWMAN,* Th, 84, USA, Assist Cam; *UNDER COVER OF THE NIGHT,* MV, 84, GB, Op; *CORUNA,* Th, 82, E, DOP; *'ROSES'* (2 eps), TV, 81, MEX, DOP; *NAVY SCHOOL,* Th, 78, MEX, DOP.

GORDON, Barry O.

CSC. 778 N. Holliston, Pasadena, CA, USA, 91104. (818)794-2228. United Artists Communications, 6380 Wilshire Blvd., #1111, Los Angeles, CA, USA, 90048. (213)655-3200.
Types of Production & Categories: Th Film-DOP/Cam; Th Short-DOP/Cam.
Genres: Documentary-Th; Experimental-Th; Industrial-Th.
Biography: Born 1920, Elora, Ontario. Has been DOP since 38; cameraman, WW II. Consulting cinematographer, advisor on numerous omnimax and omnivision films; technical director on Broadway musical, 'The Happy Time'. He was technical producer and won a Special Award, Canadian Film Awards (Dynamic Frame, Multi Image) for *A PLACE TO STAND* which also won an Oscar. Film Consultant, Ontario Pavilion, Expo 86, has worked in research and development, United Artists Communications since 78.
Selective Filmography: *TUTANKHAMEN,* Th, 79, USA, DOP/Cam; *CLEVELAND, ED,* 75, USA, DOP/Cam; *STANDING UP COUNTRY,* Th, 74, USA, DOP/Cam; *GARDEN ISLE,* Th, 74, USA, DOP/Cam; *CAPTURE THE SUN,* Th, 73, USA, DOP/Cam; *WORLD IN MOTION,* In, 71, USA, Ed; *HARMONY OF NATURE AND MAN,* Th, 70, USA, Cam/Ed; *NUMBER ONE BUSH,* In, 69, USA, DOP/Cam.

GRATTAN, James D.

CFTA, CSC, IATSE-734. 695 Victoria Ave., Westmount, Que, CAN, H3Y 2S2. (514)486-3565. Grattan Communications Int'l, 4606 Ste-Catherine W., Montreal, Que, CAN, H3Z 1S3. (514)932-1463.
Types of Production & Categories: TV Film-DOP/Dir/Prod; TV Video-DOP/Dir/Prod.
Genres: Documentary-TV; Educational-TV; Industrial-Th.
Biography: Born 1936, Montreal, Quebec. Has been in the field of film, video TV and corporate productions since 58.
Selective Filmography: *THIS IS YOUR LIFE,* TV, 86, CDN, Dir/DOP; *PRO-TIPS,* TV, 86, CDN, DOP; *CBS HILTON* (GOLF TOURNAMENT), TV, 86, USA, Dir/DOP; *PRICE/DAXION,* In, 85, CDN, DOP; *PRESIDENT RETIRES,* In, 85,
(cont/suite)

CDN, Dir/DOP; *THE FUTURE IS NOW*, In, 85, CDN, Prod/Dir/DOP; *DON KING - HILTON*, TV, 85, USA, DOP; *BAHAMA VINTAGE SPEED WEEK*, TV, 85, CDN, Dir/DOP; *DURAFLEX - ESSO*, In, 85, CDN, Prod; *SKOAL BANDIT*, In, 85, CDN, Prod/Dir; *AIR CANADA EXPRESS*, TV, 85, CDN, Dir/DOP; *COMPUTERIZING HOCKEY*, TV, 84, CDN, DOP; *G.E. FACTORY / BROMONT/FTD CONVENTION*, In, 84, USA, DOP; *CATCH THE SPIRIT*, TV, 84, CDN, Prod/Dir/DOP.

GRAVELLE, Raymond
SMPTE. 818 de LaGauchetière est, Montréal, Qué, CAN, H2L 2N2. (514)844-8304. Les Prods. LaGauchet inc., 816 de LaGauchetière est, Montréal, Qué, CAN, H2L 2N2. (514)845-8186.
Types de production et Catégories: TV film-D phot/Prod; TV vidéo-D phot/Prod.
Types d'oeuvres: Documentaire-TV; Education-TV; Enfants-TV.
Curriculum vitae: Né en 1947, Ottawa, Ontario; bilingue. Bac., cours en gestion et administration. Rédacteur, CBOFT, Ottawa; caméraman pour CBC/Radio-Canada à la colline parlementaire; caméraman, journaliste, TVA et CTV en Chine; caméraman et administrateur, bureau de CTV à Washington. Fonde et dirige Les Productions LaGauchet inc., Montréal depuis 77.
Filmographie sélective: *JEUNES STARS*, TV, 86, CDN, Prod; *CREATIONS D'ENFANTS*, TV, 86, CDN, Prod/Réal; *ERYTHREE*, TV, 85, CDN, Prod; *LA FAMILLE*, TV, 85, CDN, D phot; *MOUVEMENT DANSE*, TV, 85, CDN, Prod assoc; *ROSE LATULIPPE*, TV, 84, CDN, Prod; *SANTE TROPIQUE*, ED, 84, CDN, Prod; *LG4...UN CONTE*, In, 83, CDN, D phot; *'LEVIS RIDE AND TIE'* (4 eps), TV, 82, USA, D phot; *LA BAIE JAMES CE N'EST PAS LA RUE STE-CATHERINE*, ED, 82, CDN, D phot.

GREGG, Kenneth W.
CSC, CUPE. 4235 Sherwoodtowne Blvd.,#1507, Mississauga, Ont, CAN, L4Z 1W3. (416)848-2029. CBC, 790 Bay St., 4th Floor, Toronto, Ont, CAN. (416)975-7606.
Types of Production & Categories: TV Film-DOP; TV Video-DOP.
Genres: Drama-Th&TV; Musical-TV; Documentary-TV; Educational-TV.
Biography: Born 1928, Winnipeg, Manitoba. Graduated, top marks from the Royal Canadian Air Force School of Photography, 49; served as photographer for 5 years. Joined CBC, Winnipeg, 54, stills photographer, film editor and cinematographer; contracted, 58, senior cinematographer, TV news, sports, documentaries and dramas for 13 years, then transferred to CBC, Toronto. Awarded CBC President's Award, 82.
Selective Filmography: *KARSH - THE SEARCHING EYE*, TV, 86, CDN, DOP; *OAKMOUNT HIGH*, TV, 85, CDN, DOP; *IN THIS CORNER*, TV, 85, CDN, DOP; *THE EXILE*, TV, 85, CDN, DOP; *SPECIAL DELIVERY*, TV, 85, CDN, DOP; *THE MYSTERY OF HENRY MOORE*, TV, 84, CDN, DOP; *THE BOY NEXT DOOR*, 'FOR THE RECORD', TV, 84, CDN, DOP; *GENTLE SINNERS*, TV, 83, CDN, DOP; *'VANDERBERG'* (3 eps), TV, 83, CDN, DOP; *RAYMOND MASSEY - ACTOR OF THE CENTURY*, TV, 82, CDN, DOP; *I MARRIED THE KLONDIKE* (3 parts), TV, 82, CDN, DOP; *STRATASPHERE* (TERESA STRATAS), TV, 82, CDN, DOP; *THE SPIES WHO NEVER WERE*, TV, 81, CDN, DOP; *AGE OF CLASS*, TV, 80, CDN, DOP; *THE SONG OF LEONARD COHEN*, TV, 79, CDN, DOP; *'THE MUSIC OF MAN'* (8 eps), TV, 78, CDN, DOP; *THEY'RE DRYING UP THE STREETS*, 'FOR THE RECORD', TV, 77, CDN, DOP; *ONE NIGHT STAND*, TV, 77, CDN, DOP; *THE MAN INSIDE*, TV, 75, CDN, DOP; *THE PASSIONATE CANADIANS*, TV, 75, CDN, DOP; *HOMAGE TO CHAGALL - THE COLOURS OF LOVE*, Th, 75, CDN, DOP; *DEEDEE*, TV, 74, CDN, DOP (**CFA**); *A BIRD IN THE HOUSE*, TV, 73, CDN, DOP (**CFA**); *NEXT YEAR IN JERUSALEM*, TV, 73, CDN, DOP (**CFA**); *'CHILDREN OF THE WORLD'* (6 eps), TV, 72, CDN, DOP; *SPRINGHILL*, TV,

(cont/suite)

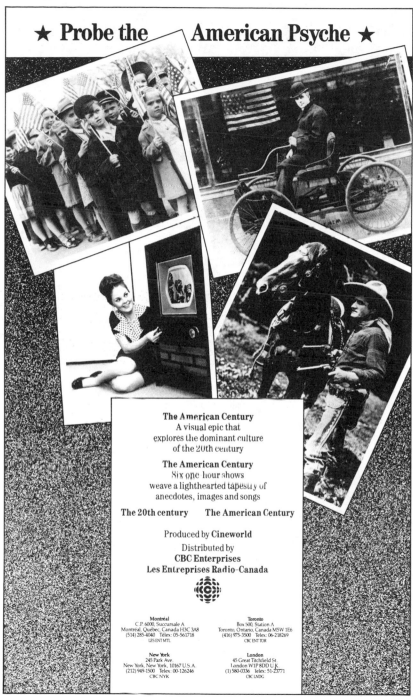

ALBERT J. DUNK

DIRECTOR OF PHOTOGRAPHY C.S.C., A.S.C.

FEATURE FILMS

Highpoint
Class of 1984 • Incubus
Hank Williams – The Show He Never Gave
Jack London's "Klondike Fever"

TV MOVIES

The Ruling Passion – (NBC)
Perry Mason Returns – (NBC) • Illusion – (CBS)
Cagney and Lacey – (CBS) • Escape from Iran – (CBS)
The Courage of Kavik – (NBC)

TV SERIES

Police Surgeon • New Comers • Witness to Yesterday
Search and Rescue

AWARDS

1982	CSC Award for Cinematography for Best TV Drama CAGNEY AND LACEY
1983	CSC Award for Cinematography for Best TV Drama ILLUSIONS
1984	GOLD New York Art Directors Show, – CLIO
	– SILVER Toronto Art Directors Show, CLIO
1985	– Chicago Film Festival

Phone: Toronto (416) 961-6857
Los Angeles, Agent (213) 456-6641

384

72, CDN, DOP; *NISKU, TV,* 70, CDN, DOP **(ANIK)**; *DEATH OF A NOBODY,* TV, 69, CDN, DOP; *ONCE UPON A MARSH,* TV, 66, CDN, DOP **(ANIK)**.

GREGORY, Colin

NABET. The Video Stylists, 52 Barr St., Regina, Sask, CAN, S4R 6N1. (306)924-0621.
Types of Production & Categories: TV Film-DOP/Cam; TV Video-DOP/Cam.
Genres: Drama-TV; Documentary-Th&TV; Educational-Th&TV.
Biography: Born 1951, Christchurch, New Zealand; citizen of Canada and New Zealand. B.A. (Photography and Theatre Arts), University of Saskatchewan. Has won numerous awards including an Award of Merit from INTERCOM: the Chicago Int'l Film Fest.. Proficient with a wide range of film and video cameras, specializes in Betacam.
Selective Filmography: *DISTANT BATTLES,* ED, 85, CDN, DOP; *ILFULL BLINDNESS,* In, 85, CDN, DOP; *NICE GUY,* TV, 84, CDN, DOP; *TO BUILD A BETTER BURGER/PRAIRIE BIG WHEEL,* 'THE ACHIEVERS', TV, 84/83, CDN, Prod/Dir; *THE LAST TIME,* MV, 84, CDN, DOP; *REGINA BROADCAST CENTER SPECIAL,* TV, 83, CDN, DOP; *PROEM,* TV, 83, CDN, DOP/Dir; *REGINA MANIFESTO,* ED, 83, CDN, Ed; *A DUCK IN THE WILDERNESS,* 'THE ACHIEVERS', TV, 82, CDN, Prod/Dir; *REQUIEM FOR ROSIE,* ED, 78, CDN, DOP/Dir.

GRIFFIN, John

CSC. 28 Butternut St., Toronto, Ont, CAN, M4K 1T7. (416)463-4337.
Types of Production & Categories: Th Film-DOP; TV Film-DOP.
Genres: Documentary-TV.
Biography: Born 1938, Ontario. Education: Radio & TV Arts, Ryerson Polytechnical Institute.
Selective Filmography: *A JOURNEY BACK/JUST ANOTHER MISSING KID,* 'THE FIFTH ESTATE', TV, 85/83, CDN, DOP; *RAPISTS - CAN THEY BE STOPPED?,* 'AMERICA UNDERCOVER', TV, 85, USA, DOP; *I'LL GET THERE SOMEHOW,* TV, 84, CDN, DOP; *RENE SIMARD AU JAPON,* Th, 75, CDN, DOP; *A THIRD TESTAMENT* (7 parts), TV, 73, CDN, DOP.

HAMILTON, Peter Scott - see PRODUCERS

HEBB, Brian R.R.

CSC. 483 Euclid Ave., Toronto, Ont, CAN, M6G 2T1. (416)923-7102.
Types of Production & Categories: Th Film-DOP; TV Film-DOP.
Genres: Drama Th&TV; Documentary-TV.
Biography: Born 1949, Halifax, Nova Scotia. Attended Photographic Art School, England. Photographer: commercial, fashion, portraits, travel. Employed as DOP, CBC, 69-85. Has also directed and produced 5 short dramas for TV.
Selective Filmography: *'AIRWAVES'* (13 eps), TV, 86/85, CDN, DOP; *OVERNIGHT,* Th, 85, CDN, DOP; *SHELL GAME,* TV, 85, CDN, DOP; *CUCKOO BIRD,* TV, 84, CDN, DOP; *TOOLS OF THE DEVIL/THE FRONT LINE/ROUGH JUSTICE,* 'FOR THE RECORD', TV, 84/83, CDN, DOP; *THE BROKERS,* TV, 84, CDN, Cin; *I DECLARE,* TV, 84, CDN, Cin; *SUSAN NELLES,* 'MAN ALIVE', TV, 84, CDN, Cin; *KATE MORRIS, VICE-PRESIDENT/READY FOR SLAUGHTER/MOVING TARGETS,* 'FOR THE RECORD', TV, 83/82, CDN, DOP; *TRAINS,* TV, 83, CDN, Cin; *'VANDERBERG'* (3 eps), TV, 82, CDN, DOP; *ALL THE DAYS OF MY LIFE,* TV, 82, CDN, DOP; *BATEMAN,* 'TAKE 30', TV, 82, CDN, Cin; *AIR WARS,* TV, 82, CDN, Cin; *BLIND FAITH/BECOMING LAURA,* 'FOR THE RECORD', TV, 81, CDN, DOP; *HUMONGOUS,* Th, 81, CDN, DOP; *WOMEN AT WAR,* TV, 81, CDN, Cin; *ONCE,* TV, 80, CDN, DOP **(ANIK)**; *PASSENGERS,* TV, 80, CDN, DOP; *THE JULY GROUP,* TV, 80, CDN, DOP; *MERCHANTS OF*

(cont/suite)

GRAIN, TV, 80, CDN, Cin; *SUNSPOTS,* TV, 79, CDN, DOP; *STONEWARS,* 'CANADIAN ESTABLISHMENT', TV, 79, CDN, Cin; *SOMETHING'S ROTTEN,* Th, 78, CDN, DOP.

HERRINGTON, David

IATSE-667. 29 Bruce Farm Dr., Willowdale, Ont, CAN, M2H 1G4. (416)733-2034.
Types of Production & Categories: Th Film-DOP; TV Film-DOP.
Genres: Drama-Th&TV; Children's-TV; Commercials-TV.
Biography: Born 1948, London, England; Canadian-British citizenship. Worked at Film House as chief timer, 72-74; technical director, 75-78. Camera assistant, focus puller on various features, 78-84; DOP on 100 commercials since 84, winning 10 awards including Bronze Lion at Cannes, Bessie. Nominated for an Emmy for *PIPPI LONGSTOCKING.*
Selective Filmography: *A JUDGEMENT IN STONE,* Th, 86, CDN, DOP; *KAY O'BRIEN'* (13 eps), TV, 86, USA, DOP; *PIPPI LONGSTOCKING* (2 parts), TV, 85, USA, DOP; *DEADLY BUSINESS,* TV, 85, USA, DOP; *URGENT/EMO PHILLIPS,* MV, 85, USA, DOP.

HIGGINSON, Edward B.

CSC, IATSE-667, SMPTE. 1838 Stonepath Cr., Mississauga, Ont, CAN, L4X 1X9. (416)625-1643. E. Higginson Productions Ltd., 330 Adelaide St.W., Toronto, Ont, CAN, M5V 1R4. (416)593-0556.
Types of Production & Categories: Th Film-DOP; TV Film-DOP; TV Video-DOP.
Genres: Drama-Th&TV; Documentary-TV; Children's-TV; Music Video-TV.
Biography: Born 1935, Toronto, Ontario. Contracted, CBC, worldwide news/documentaries, 60-71; contracted, CTV, 71-76.
Selective Filmography: *COVERT ACTION,* TV, 86, CDN, DOP; *TERRITORIAL/ MAKE ME DO,* MV, 85, CDN, DOP; *ISAAC LITTLEFEATHERS,* Th, 84, CDN, DOP; *THE LIFE AND TIMES OF EDWIN ALONZO BOYD,* TV, 82, CDN, DOP; *KEEPING THE PEACE,* TV, 75, CDN, DOP (**CSC**).

HORVATH, Stefan

IATSE-667, SMPTE. 4 Killarney Rd., Toronto, Ont, CAN, M5P 1L8. (416)481-0259.
Types of Production & Categories: Th Film-DOP; Th Short-DOP; TV Film-DOP.
Genres: Drama-Th; Documentary-Th; Industrial-Th&TV; Dance-Th&TV.
Biography: Born 1929, Timisoara, Romania; Canadian citizen. Languages: Hungarian, Romanian, Russian, English, German and French. Attended VGIK Unional State Film Art Institute, Moscow, 49-54. Professor for 13 years, Institute for Film and Theatrical Arts (I.L. Caragiale), Bucharest, Romania. Has won awards for science fiction films at Edinburgh, Trieste, Mamaia, Paris; for TV ballet at Adelaide. Co-creator of Transcolor, a special colour effect invention (Romania).
Selective Filmography: *RUNNING BRAVE,* Th, 83, CDN/USA, 2nd U DOP/2nd U Cam; *MANOR GARDENS/YEAR OF THE CHILD AND FAMILY IN B.C.,* Cm, 79, CDN, Dir/Cam/Ed; *THE STORY OF LOVE,* Th, 77, R, DOP; *THE FANTASTIC COMEDY,* Th, 75, R, DOP; *THE DESPERATES* (AN AUGUST IN FLAMES), Th, 74, R, DOP; *CAPTAIN JOHN'S ARROW,* Th, 73, R, DOP; *ON A CERTAIN HAPPINESS,* Th, 73, R, Cam; *BIHOR UNDER THE SUN,* TV, 72, R, DOP; *TAKE-OFF,* Th, 72, R, DOP; *THE HAPPY PRINCE,* TV, 70, R, DOP; *THE GIRL WITH THE MATCHES,* TV, 69, R, DOP; *THE SILENT FRIENDS* (DOGS TO THE RESCUE), TV, 69, CDN/R, DOP; *IN ROMANIA,* ED, 68, CDN/R, DOP; *THE CYCLISTS ARE COMING,* Th, 67, R, DOP; *THE LEGEND OF SKYLARK,* TV, 66, R, DOP; *FAUST XX,* Th, 65, R, DOP; *TITANIC VALSE,* Th, 64, R, DOP; *STEPS TO THE MOON,* Th, 63, R, DOP; *CODINE,* Th, 62, R/F, 2nd U DOP; *A BOMB STOLEN,* Th, 61, R, DOP; *THE BUMPKINS,* Th, 60, R, DOP; *THE CARNIVAL STORY,* Th, 58, R, DOP; *TWO*
(cont/suite)

LOTTERY TICKETS, Th, 57, R, DOP; *THE MILL OF GOOD LUCK,* Th, 56, R, Cam; *AFTER THE COMPETITION,* Th, 55, R, Cam.

HOSKING, Brian W.

Cinescene Films, 318 Rushton Rd., Toronto, Ont, CAN, M6C 2X9. (416)653-8839.
Types of Production & Categories: TV Film-Cin; TV Video-Cin.
Genres: Documentary-TV; Educational-TV; News-TV.
Biography: Born 1934, Australia; Canadian citizen. Travelled and filmed world-wide including 2 years in Hong Kong as Far East cameraman for CBC news, 71-73; with news dept. for 5 years; filmed 5 documentaries in the Arctic.
Selective Filmography: *THE FIFTH ESTATE',* TV, 86-81, CDN, Cin; *JUST ANOTHER MISSING KID,* 'THE FIFTH ESTATE', TV, 81, CDN, Add'l Phot; *FIGHTING BACK,* TV, 81, CDN, Cin.

HUNTER, Don

Don Hunter Photography, P.O. Box 1939, Gibsons, BC, CAN. (604)886-3049.
Types of Production & Categories: TV Film-DOP.
Genres: Drama-TV; Documentary-TV; Children's-TV; Musical-TV.
Biography: Born 1943, St. Thomas, Ontario. Graduate New York Institute of Photography, 65; Brooks Institute of Photography (Motion Picture Production), 76. DOP on 60 TV dramas; camera operator: 25 TV dramas, 25 commercials, 160 documentary films; 5 years of TV news and public affairs filming; 7 years staff photographer on a daily newspaper.
Selective Filmography: *THE BEACHCOMBERS'* (Op-7 eps), (31 eps), TV, 85-81, CDN, DOP; *'CONSTABLE, CONSTABLE',* TV, 84, CDN, DOP; *SEA OTTERS,* 'NATURE OF THINGS', TV, 84, CDN, Cam; *LEGEND OF THE SILVER RAVEN,* TV, 82, CDN, DOP; *LITTLE JUDGE BIGMOUTH,* TV, 79, CDN, DOP; *STEPANSSON,* 'THE WINNERS', TV, 78, CDN, DOP/Op; *DEADLINE I & II,* TV, 78/77, CDN, DOP; *LE REVEILLON CHEZ LE VIEUX AUX LABOUCANNE,* TV, 78, CDN, DOP; *STARBUCK VALLEY WINTER,* 'MAGIC LIE', TV, 77, CDN, DOP/Op; *PUP TENT,* TV, 77, CDN, DOP/Op; *THE RESIDENTS,* TV, 77, CDN, Cam; *WUTTUNEE* (2 parts), TV, 77, CDN, Cam; *LEONA,* TV, 77, CDN, DOP; *KOREA/SRI LANKA,* 'CHILDREN OF THE WORLD', TV, 76, CDN, Cam; *SHOE STRING/THREE TO GET READY,* ED, 76/75, CDN, Cam; *THE LARSENS,* TV, 76, CDN, DOP/Op; *MOSES/LA LEGENDE DU VENT,* 'MUSICAMERA', TV, 76/72, CDN, DOP/Op; *WINTERPEG,* 'MUSICAMERA', TV, 75, CDN, Cam; *MENO'S REINS,* TV, 75, CDN, DOP; *RAISINS AND ALMONDS,* TV, 74, CDN, DOP; *THE ECSTASY OF RITA JOE* (2 parts), TV, 74, CDN, DOP/Op; *CORNET AT NIGHT,* 'TO SEE OURSELVES', TV, 73, CDN, DOP/Op.

HURTEAU, Paul

4870 Côte des Neiges, #809, Montréal, Qué, CAN, H3V 1H3. (514)738-8456.
Types de production et Catégories: TV film-D phot; TV vidéo-D phot/Réal.
Types d'oeuvres: Variété-TV; Comédie musicale-TV; Education-TV; Annonces-TV.
Curriculum vitae: Né en 1952, Montréal, Québec. Etudes en Communications, Université Concordia, 73-76; Campus Loyola, 76-82 Photographe, films industriels, annonces, portraits, 79-83; réalisateur, directeur-photo, annonces et documentaires.
Filmographie sélective: *LA BAIE,* Cm, 86, CDN, D phot; *BELL CANADA/LES CAISSES DESJARDINS,* In, 86, CDN, Réal/D phot; *R.I.O.,* In, 86, CDN, Réal/D phot; *STEINBERG/G.M./FER PLUS/LOIS,* Cm, 86/85, CDN, D phot; *'A LIVRE OUVERT'* (36 eps), TV, 86, CDN, D phot; *BANQUE DE MONTREAL/SKI/GAS METROPOLITAIN,* In, 86, CDN, D phot; *LES GENS DE L'AVENIR/JEAN COUTU,* Cm, 85, CDN, Réal/D phot; *ZACHARIE RICHARD/MARTINE ST-CLAIR/ROMANTIQUE MACHINE,* MV, 85, CDN, D phot; *NICOLE MARTIN/ CHIFFON/LUCIEN FRANCOEUR,* MV, 85, CDN, D phot; *'LAUTREC 85'* (18 eps), TV, 85, CDN, D phot; *C.M.P.C. MINES/EXPORTATIONS/*
(cont/suite)

HABITATIONS/AGRICULTURES/VILLES, Cm, 85, CDN, D phot; *METRO,* In, 85, CDN, D phot.

HUTTON, Joan

CSC, IATSE. High Road Prod., 67 Strathcona Ave., Toronto, Ont, CAN, M4J 1G9. (416)461-3089.
Types of Production & Categories: TV Film-DOP; TV Video-DOP.
Genres: Documentary-TV; Educational-Th&TV; Children's-TV.
Biography: Born 1942, Toronto, Ontario. Education: Ryerson Polytechnical Institute.
Selective Filmography: *THE BIRTH OF LANGUAGE/SEE-SAW MARGERY DAW/BREAKING THE SILENCE,* ED, 86/85, CDN, DOP; *DOCTOR, LAWYER, INDIAN CHIEF/PRIME TIME,* ED, 85, CDN, DOP; *OLYMPIC PROFILES,* TV, 84, CDN, DOP; *DO IT OR DIE,* TV, 83, CDN, DOP; *GRAND PRIX 83,* TV, 83, CDN, DOP; *HERE'S TO THE COWBOY,* TV, 82, CDN, DOP; *SCHOONER GRAND PRIX,* TV, 82, CDN, DOP; *SQUAMISH DAYS,* TV, 82, CDN, DOP; *WITCHES AND HEALERS/WALL OF WITHROW,* ED, 80/79, CDN, DOP; *C.N.I.B. BALLET,* Cm, 79, CDN, DOP; *WITCHES,* ED, 76, CDN, Dir; *THE SPRING AND FALL OF NINA POLANSKI,* Th, 75, CDN, DOP.

IANZELO, Tony - see DIRECTORS

IRWIN, Mark

CSC, CAMERA, NABET-15. Ovation Visual Productions Ltd, 223 Chaplin Cres., Toronto, Ont, CAN, M5P 1B1. (416)964-6858. Gerald K.Smith, P.O. Box 7430, Burbank, CA, USA, 91510. (213)849-5388.
Types of Production & Categories: Th Film-DOP; Th Short-DOP; TV Film-DOP.
Genres: Drama-Th; Science Fiction-Th; Horror-Th; Documentary-TV.
Biography: Born 1950; Canadian citizen; green card, USA; British working papers. Received 2 Genie nominations.
Selective Filmography: *THE FLY,* Th, 86, USA, DOP; *'RAY BRADBURY THEATRE'* (4 eps), TV, 85, CDN, DOP; *THE PROTECTOR,* Th, 84, USA, DOP; *YOUNGBLOOD,* Th, 84, USA, DOP; *SPECIAL PEOPLE,* TV, 83, CDN/ USA, DOP; *THE DEAD ZONE,* Th, 83, USA, DOP **(CSC)**; *VIDEODROME,* Th, 82, CDN, DOP **(CSC)**; *DEATH BITE* (SPASMS), Th, 81, CDN, DOP; *KILLER INSTINCT* (CHATWILL'S VERDICT), Th, 80, CDN, DOP; *SCANNERS,* Th, 80, CDN, DOP; *NIGHT SCHOOL,* Th, 80, USA, DOP; *CRIES IN THE NIGHT* (FUNERAL HOME), Th, 79, CDN, DOP; *TANYA'S ISLAND,* Th, 79, CDN, DOP; *THE BROOD,* Th, 79, CDN, DOP; *FAST COMPANY,* Th, 78, CDN, DOP; *MUTATION* (M3- THE GEMINI STRAIN), Th, 77, CDN, DOP; *BLOOD & GUTS,* Th, 77, CDN, DOP.

JEFFREY, James

7148-85th St., Edmonton, Alta, CAN. (403)466-3512.
Types of Production & Categories: Th Short-DOP; TV Film-DOP/Dir.
Genres: Drama-TV; Action-TV; Documentary-TV; Educational-TV.
Biography: Born 1951, Melville, Saskatchewan. B.A.A., Ryerson Polytechnical Institute, 74. Five years as staff cinematographer, CBC. Formed Viewfinder Prods. Ltd., Edmonton, 82. Travelled extensively, 84-86, in Nicaragua, West Indies, Europe.
Selective Filmography: *ELK ISLAND,* ED, 85, CDN, Dir/Cam; *OUR OWN TWO HANDS,* TV, 85, CDN, DOP; *BOOM AND BUST,* 'ECONOMIC SERIES', TV, 85, CDN, DOP; *OIL AND GAS,* In, 85, CDN, DOP; *MAKING IT WORK,* ED, 85, CDN, DOP; *LONG LANCE,* TV, 85, CDN, DOP; *BISON SAGA,* TV, 84, CDN, DOP; *THIS IS ONLY A TEST / LIFE LINE,* ED, 84, CDN, DOP; *HISTORIC SITES,* TV, 83, CDN, DOP; *KALEIDOSCOPE,* TV, 83, CDN, DOP; *SARI KURRI,* TV, 83, SF, DOP; *COCA-COLA,* Cm, 83, CDN, DOP; *HARRIOT'S*

(cont/suite)

390

HATS, TV, 83, CDN, DOP; *SOAPS,* TV, 82, CDN, DOP; *UAW,* TV, 82, CDN, DOP; *SANDERSON,* 'NBC SPORTS', TV, 82, USA, DOP.

JOBIN, Daniel

STCQ. 4136 St-Christophe, Montréal, Qué, CAN, H2L 3Y2. (514)527-2884.
Types de production et Catégories: l métrage-D phot; c métrage-D phot; TV film-D phot; TV vidéo-D phot.
Types d'oeuvres: Drame-C&TV; Action-C&TV; Science-fiction-C&TV; Annonces-TV.
Curriculum vitae: Né en 1949, Québec; bilingue. Etudes à l'INSAS, Bruxelles, 70-73. Douze ans assistant caméraman; 4 ans directeur-photo et cadreur. Inventeur du Panaflasher acheté par Panavision (disponible début 87).
Filmographie sélective: *COKE DIETE,* Cm, 86, CDN, D phot; *MONSIEUR LEON,* TV, 86, CDN, D phot; *LES FOUS DE BASSAN,* C, 86, CDN/F, D phot 2e éq; *TRANSIT,* TV, 86, CDN, D phot; *FOG AREA/AIR/METEOR STUDIO/ EXHIBITION,* MV, 85, CDN, D phot; *TROUBLE,* C, 85, CDN, D phot; *LE CHAT,* C, 85, CDN, D phot; *LUNE DE MIEL,* C, 85, CDN/F, Cadr 2e éq; *THE MORNING MAN,* C, 85, CDN, Cadr 2e éq; *POUVOIR INTIME,* C, 85, CDN, Cadr 2e éq; *LE TRAIN,* TV, 84, CDN, D phot; *LA FEMME DE L'HOTEL* (WOMAN IN TRANSIT), C, 84, CDN, Co D phot.

KEMBALL, Harry

311 - 2080 Maple St., Vancouver, BC, CAN, V6J 4P9. (604)738-1240.
Types of Production & Categories: TV Film-DOP/Dir/Prod; TV Video-DOP/Dir/ Prod.
Genres: Drama-TV; Documentary-TV; Animation-TV; Commercials-TV.
Biography: Born 1936, Cranbrook, British Columbia. Education: Master of Science. Has shot animation for Hanna Barbera; developed slit-scans, graphics for slit-scans, claymation (3-D animation); writes jingles.
Selective Filmography: *THE HAPPY TIGER,* TV, 86, CDN, DOP/Co-Prod; *DRACULA,* TV, 85, CDN, DOP/Dir; *CONVICT AND THE SCREW,* TV, 85, CDN, DOP/Dir; *STARR BRETT,* MV, 85, CDN, DOP/Dir; *YOUNG AT HEART/TRU-VALUE OPTICAL/EAGLE BASEBALL,* Cm, 84, CDN, DOP/Dir/ Prod/Wr; *MIDGI,* In, 84, CDN, DOP/Dir/Prod/Wr; *EAGLE DROID-3/SAM EAGLE/KEMBALL'S JEWELLERY,* Cm, 79-77, CDN, DOP/Dir/Prod/Wr; *MAN, WOMAN AND THE PAPERBAG CATHOLIX,* TV, 75, CDN, DOP/Dir/ Prod/Wr; *EAGLE FORD,* Cm, 72, CDN, DOP/Dir/Prod/Wr; *AMEN,* TV, 71, CDN, DOP; *EAGLE SPECIAL PEOPLE/MUSGROVE FORD RANGER/BLOCK BROS.,* Cm, 71-69, CDN, DOP/Dir/Prod/Wr; *BLOCK BROS. WITH GLENN FORD,* Cm, 70, CDN, DOP/Dir; *WATER BEAM,* ED, 66, CDN, DOP/Dir.

KENDALL, Nicholas - see DIRECTORS

KIEFER, Douglas

CSC, CAMERA-81. DWK Film Productions Ltd., 181 Wychwood Ave., #2, Toronto, Ont, CAN, M6C 2T4. (416)656-6774.
Types of Production & Categories: Th Film-DOP; Th Short-DOP; TV Film-DOP/ Dir.
Genres: Drama-Th&TV; Documentary-Th&TV; Educational-TV; Children's-TV.
Biography: Born 1938, Dundas, Ontario. Attended Ryerson Polytechnical Institute. Worked in NFB camera department, 65-85; presently freelance DOP.
Selective Filmography: 'EDISON TWINS' (26 eps), TV, 85, CDN, DOP; *TUCKER AND THE HORSE THIEF/WORKING FOR PEANUTS/MY FATHER,MY RIVAL,* 'FAMILY PLAYHOUSE', TV, 84, CDN, DOP; *'AUTOMATING THE OFFICE'* (9 eps), TV, 84, CDN, DOP; *UNFINISHED BUSINESS,* Th, 83, CDN, DOP; 'WAR' (7 eps), TV, 83-80, CDN, DOP/Dir; *SOMETHING TO CELEBRATE,* TV, 82, CDN, DOP; *ATMOS,* Th, 79, CDN, DOP/Dir; *'IN*

(cont/suite)

SEARCH OF...' (2 eps), TV, 78, USA, DOP; *SMALL IS BEAUTIFUL,* TV, 77, CDN, DOP/Dir; *ONE MAN,* Th, 77, CDN, DOP; *VOLCANO...AN INQUIRY INTO THE LIFE AND DEATH OF MALCOLM LOWRY,* Th, 76, CDN, DOP; *WAITING FOR FIDEL,* TV, 74, CDN, DOP; *PROLOGUE,* Th, 68, CDN, DOP.

KINSEY, Nicholas - voir REALISATEURS

LABREQUE, Jean-Claude - voir REALISATEURS

LADOUCEUR, Serge

STCQ. 409 ave. du Mont-Royal O., #3, Montréal, Qué, CAN, H2V 2S6. (514)271-2700.
Types de production et Catégories: l métrage-D phot; c métrage-D phot; TV film-D phot; TV vidéo-D phot.
Types d'oeuvres: Drame-C&TV; Variété-TV; Action-C; Documentaire-C&TV.
Curriculum vitae: Né en 1952; bilingue. Etudes; Univeristé Loyola et London International Film School.
Filmographie sélective: *'LANCE ET COMPTE'* (HE SHOOTS, HE SCORES), (13 eps), TV, 86/85, CDN, 2e cam; *LE GRAND DEFI,* C, 86, CDN, D phot; *HELLO, MV,* 86, CDN, D phot; *MOLSON EXPORT,* Cm, 85, CDN, Cadr; *VISAGE PALE,* C, 84, CDN, D phot; *LG4 - PLUS QUE DE L'ENERGIE,* In, 83, CDN, D phot; *OF UNKNOWN ORIGIN,* C, 82, CDN, D phot 2e éq; *L'OBESITE/ L'INFERTILITE,* 'DOSSIER SANTE', TV, 82, CDN, D phot; *LE REVE ASSASIN* (DEATH OF A ONE-NIGHT-STAND), C, 81, CDN, D phot; *IL FAUT CHERCHER POUR APPRENDRE,* ED, 81, CDN, D phot; *'THE WALSH INSTRUMENTATION TRAINING PROGRAM'* (30 eps), ED, 81/80, CDN, D phot; *LOGAN ROAD RENEWAL,* C, 79, USA, D phot; *RUEL-MALENFANT,* C, 79, CDN, D phot/Dir art; *5...4...3...D'EUX,* TV, 77, CDN, Réal/Cadr; *MOUVEMENT DANSE,* C8, 3, CDN, D phot/Prod.

LANGEVIN, Gordon

IATSE-667. Facet Photographic Ltd., 59 Campbell Ave., Toronto, Ont, CAN, M6P 3T9. (416)531-6455.
Types of Production & Categories: TV Film-DOP; TV Video-DOP.
Genres: Drama-Th&TV; Action-Th&TV; Documentary-Th&TV; Commercials-TV.
Biography: Born 1948, Toronto, Ontario; bilingual. Education: Photographic Arts. Camera operator for 2 years; focus puller, 15 years; over 30 features and series as assistant cameraman; DOP on numerous TV commercials.
Selective Filmography: *'STINGRAY'* (7 eps), TV, 86, USA, Op; *THE CASE OF THE SHOOTING STAR,* TV, 86, USA, Op; *EASY PREY,* TV, 86, USA, Op; *POLICE ACADEMY III,* Th, 85, USA, Op; *PERRY MASON RETURNS,* TV, 85, USA, Op; *A CHRISTMAS STORY,* Th, 83, CDN/USA, Focus Pull; *DEFCON 4,* Th, 84, CDN, Focus Pull; *STRANGE INVADERS,* Th, 83, USA, Focus Pull; *MURDER BY PHONE* (BELLS), Th, 83, CDN, Focus Pull; *STRANGE BREW,* Th, 82, CDN/USA, Focus Pull; *'CAGNEY AND LACEY'* (pilot), TV, 82, USA, Focus Pull; *CLASS OF '84,* Th, 81, CDN/USA, Focus Pull; *THE WARS,* Th, 81, CDN/D, Focus Pull; *PORKY'S* (CHEZ PORKY), Th, 81, CDN, Focus Pull; *LOVE,* Th, 80, CDN, Focus Pull; *TRIBUTE* (UN FILS POUR L'ETE), Th, 80, CDN, Focus Pull; *'MATT AND JENNY'* (20 eps), TV, 80/79, CDN, Focus Pull; *TORN BETWEEN TWO LOVERS,* TV, 79/78, USA, Focus Pull; *MEATBALLS,* Th, 79, CDN, Focus Pull; *THE FAMILY MAN,* TV, 79, USA, Focus Pull; *LOST AND FOUND,* Th, 78, GB, Focus Pull; *RAGTIME SUMMER,* Th, 77, CDN, Focus Pull; *'SEARCH AND RESCUE'* (13 eps), TV, 77/76, CDN/USA, Focus Pull; *WORLD OF DARKNESS,* TV, 77, USA, Focus Pull; *'WITNESS TO YESTERDAY'* (13 eps), TV, 76/75, CDN, Focus Pull; *GOLDENROD,* Th, 76, CDN, Focus Pull; *SHOOT,* Th, 76, CDN, Focus Pull; *WAR BETWEEN THE TATES,* TV, 75, USA, Focus Pull.

LARUE, Claude

CSC, STCQ. 5 rue Faucher, #2, St-Roch-de-l'Achigan, Qué, CAN, J0K 3H0. (514)588-5116.
Types de production et Catégories: l métrage-D phot; c métrage-D phot; TV film-D phot/Réal/Prod; TV vidéo-D phot.
Types d'oeuvres: Drame-C; Documentaire-C&TV; Education-C; Enfants-C&TV.
Curriculum vitae: Né en 1940, Montréal, Québec. Caméraman, directeur-photo pigiste depuis 71.
Filmographie sélective: *SUCRE D'AMOUR,* C, 84, CDN/F, D phot; *LA CONQUETE DU CONTINENT INTERIEUR,* TV, 84, CDN, D phot; *LE PASSAGER,* TV, 83, CDN, D phot; *LA CRECHE DU VILLAGE,* TV, 83, CDN, D phot; *LES YEUX ROUGES,* C, 81, CDN, D phot; *'LES AVENTURES DE VIRULYSSE'* (26 eps), TV, 81, CDN, D phot; *L'ODYSSEE DE LA PACIFIQUE,* C, 80, CDN/F, Cam; *'ECOLOGIE'* (6 eps), TV, 80, CDN, D phot; *'BONJOUR MONSIEUR NOE'* (13 eps), TV, 79, CDN, D phot; *'CINQ MILLIARDS D'HOMMES'* (12 eps), TV, 79, CDN, D phot; *SITUATION ENERGETIQUE DU QUEBEC,* TV, 79, CDN, Réal/Cam; *MAITRE DE L'UNGAVA,* TV, 78, CDN, D phot; *LE DERNIER VOYAGE,* TV, 78, CDN, D phot; *LA FEE MAJUSCULE,* TV, 78, CDN, D phot; *'L'OMBRE DU SOLEIL'* (5 eps), ED, 77, CDN, D phot; *QUEBEC WHOLE DIFFERENT MORNING,* C, 76, CDN, D phot; *PROJET MINIER FIER, LAKE PORT-CARTIER,* In, 76, CDN, D phot/Réal; *DU SKI POUR TOUT L'MONDE,* TV, 76, CDN, Prod/Réal; *'LES ENFANTS DU CANADA'* (5 eps), TV, 76, CDN, Cam; *BAIE TRINITE,* TV, 75, CDN, Prod/Réal; *VALSE A TROIS,* C, 74, CDN, D phot; *RESPECT DE L'UNIVERS,* TV, 74, CDN, D phot/Réal; *BINGO,* C, 73, CDN, D phot; *LES COLOMBES* (THE DOVES), C, 72, CDN, D phot; *L'APPARITION,* C, 72, CDN, D phot; *LES JEUX D'ETE DU QUEBEC,* TV, 72, CDN, D phot; *MOTO-NEIGE,* C, 70, CDN, D phot/Réal; *COMMUNAUTE NOUVELLE,* C, 70, CDN, D phot; *TI COEUR,* C, 69, CDN, D phot.

LAVALETTE, Philippe

STCQ. 760 ave. Champagneur, Outremont, Qué, CAN, H2V 3P8. (514)276-5728.
Types de production et Catégories: l métrage-D phot; c métrage-D phot/Réal; TV film-D phot/Réal; TV vidéo-D phot/Réal.
Types d'oeuvres: Drame-C&TV; Comédie musicale-C&TV; Documentaire-C&TV; Industriel-C&TV.
Curriculum vitae: Né en 1949, Paris, France; citoyen canadien. Licencié en Biologie. *LES COLERES DE L'HIDALGO* remporte le Grand Prix, Festival du Film d'Auteur, Belfort, France; *LA SYNTAXE DU REGARD,* le Grand Prix de l'URTI, Bruxelles.
Filmographie sélective: *PLEIN FEUX SUR LA RONDE,* In, 86, CDN, Réal; *'LE CHASSEUR DE POLE'* (2 eps), TV, 86, CDN/F, Réal/Cam; *ROBERT BARTSON,* TV, 86, CDN, D phot; *JUSTE UNE IMAGE,* C, 86, CDN, D phot; *LAVAL: TOUT UN POTENTIEL* (EXPO 86), In, 85, CDN, Réal/Cam; *BEAUJOLAIS NOUVEAU,* TV, 85, CDN, Réal/Cam; *JUSTICE BLANCHE,* TV, 85, CDN, D phot; *ZONE DE TURBULENCE,* TV, 85, CDN, D phot; *NOUS PRES, NOUS LOIN,* C, 85, CDN/F, D phot; *LA GRANDE TRAVERSEE,* C, 84, CDN/F, D phot; *2 TEMPS, 3 MOUVEMENTS,* In, 83, CDN, Cam/Réal; *LA MER ET SES PRINCES,* TV, 83, CDN, D phot; *MERCENAIRES EN QUETE D'AUTEURS,* C, 82, CDN, D phot; *AROCAND MICHELIS,* C, 81, F, Réal; *'RECOURS'* (30 eps), TV, 81/80, CDN, D phot; *LES CULTURALIES,* TV, 80, CDN, D phot; *SHOCKING,* TV, 80, CDN, D phot; *NOUS SOMMES PLUSIEURS BEAUCOUP DE MONDE,* TV, 80, CDN, D phot; *LA GIGUE DE L'OURS,* C, 79, F, Réal; *LA SYNTAXE DU REGARD,* C, 77, F, Réal; *L'AUGE,* C, 75, F, D phot; *LES COLERES DE L'HIDALGO,* C, 72, F, Réal.

CINEMATOGRAPHERS/DIRECTEURS-PHOTO

LAVERDIERE, Jim

CSC. 32 Killarney Gardens, Pointe-Claire, Que, CAN, H9S 4X8. (514)695-4781.
Types of Production & Categories: TV Video-Cam.
Genres: Documentary-TV; Educational-TV.
Biography: Born 1954, Quebec City; bilingual. Courses in Motion Picture
Production, Algonquin College, Ottawa. Shoots news, public affairs (Radio-Canada,
CBC), documentaries, industrial and educational films.

LECLERC, Martin

SGCT. 209 Larivée, Vaudreuil, Qué, CAN, J7V 5V5. (514)455-2328. ONF, 3155
Côte de Liesse, Montréal, Qué, CAN, H4N 2N4. (514)283-9362.
Types de production et Catégories: l métrage-Cam; c métrage-D phot; TV film-Cam.
Types d'oeuvres: Drame-C&TV; Documentaire-C; Education-C.
Curriculum vitae: Né en 1945, Montréal, Québec. Etudes collégiales à Montréal et
en France; études en photographie, Famous Photographers School, USA. Formation
d'assistant caméraman, ONF, Montréal, 71; assistant permanent, 75; caméraman
officiel, 79.
Filmographie sélective: *L'HOMME A LA TRAINE*, 'BIO ETHIQUE', TV, 86,
CDN, Cadr; *JEUNESSE EN DIRECT*, TV, 85, CDN, Cam; *PAYS DE SABLE*,
TV, 85, CDN, Cam; *LA FAMILLE LATINO*, TV, 85, CDN, Cam; *FAMILLE EN
DELIRE*, TV, 85, CDN, Cam; *UNE GUERRE DANS MON JARDIN*, C, 85,
CDN, 2e cam; *LA GRANDE ALLURE*, C, 84, CDN/F, Cam; *ANTICOSTIE*, TV,
84, CDN, Co cam; *LES TRACES DU REVE*, TV, 84, CDN/F, Cam; *ZARICO*,
TV, 83, CDN, Cam; *COULEUR ENCERCLEE*, C, 83, CDN, Cam; *GARDE
PINET*, TV, 83/82, CDN, Cam; *LES VOILES BAS ET EN TRAVERS*, TV, 83,
CDN/F, Cam; *LA BETE LUMINEUSE* (THE SHIMMERING BEAST), TV, 83/
82, CDN, Cam; *DE L'AUTRE COTE DE LA GLACE*, TV, 83, CDN, Cam;
AMUSE-GUEULE, TV, 82, CDN, Cam; *LEO GERVAIS, SCULPTEUR*, TV, 81,
CDN, Ass cam; *CANOT A RENALD ET A THOMAS*, 'ARTISANTS', TV, 81/
80, CDN, Ass cam; *MARIE UGUAY*, TV, 81, CDN, Ass cam/2e cam; *LES
VOITURES DU DIMANCHE*, TV, 81/80, CDN, Ass cam; *STATUES DE M.
BASILE*, TV, 81/80, CDN, Ass cam; *KLUANE*, TV, 80, CDN, Ass cam;
ELLESMERE, TV, 76, CDN, Cam/Ing son; *OLYMPIQUES*, TV, 76, CDN, ; *TI-
MINE*, BERNIE PIS LA GANG, C, 75, CDN, 1er ass cam; *LES
AVIRONNEUSES*, TV, 75, CDN, Réal; *LA GAMMICK*, C, 73, CDN, 1er ass
cam; *TENDRESSE ORDINAIRE*, C, 71, CDN, 2e ass cam.

LEDUC, Jacques - voir REALISATEURS

LEHMAN, Douglas E.

CSC, IATSE-667, SMPTE. 27 Breckenridge Ave., Dollard Des Ormeaux, Que,
CAN, H9G 1E9. (514)626-0036. The Group Productions Ltd., 5101 de
Maisonneuve W., Montreal, Que, CAN, H4A 1Z1. (514)487-5616.
Types of Production & Categories: TV Film-DOP; TV Video-DOP.
Genres: Drama-TV; Comedy-TV; Documentary-TV; Commercials-TV.
Biography: Born 1936, Kitchener, Ontario. Thirteen years experience, CKCO-TV,
CFCF-TV, film and tape cinematographer; seventeen years as a partner in a
production house in Montreal as DOP. Five years experience editing, mostly off-line
VCR; experience with Arrivision 3D system.
Selective Filmography: *SECRET INTERNATIONAL/VISIONS 84-85/MILLION
DOLLAR BEAUTIES*, Cm, 85-83, CDN, DOP; *FLORIDA RAIL COMMISSION
VISIT/MASS TRANSIT/SMOOTHEST RIDE ON RAIL* (BOMBARDIER), In,
85/83, CDN, DOP/Ed; *GENFOOT* (HANG 10), Cm, 85, CDN, Ed; *SEAGRAM'S
SAMPLING PROGRAM*, In, 84, CDN, DOP.

LEIGH, Norman

IATSE-644, IATSE-667, NABET-531, DGA. Stage One Inc., 19 Nirvana Ave.,
Great Neck, NY, USA, 11023. (516)487-3659.

(cont/suite)

Types of Production & Categories: Th Film-DOP/Prod; TV Film-DOP; TV Video-Dir.
Genres: Drama-Th; Comedy-Th; Action-Th; Educational-TV.
Biography: Born New York; American citizen; landed immigrant, Canada. DOP/director on hundreds of commercials.
Selective Filmography: *CHIEF ZABU*, Th, 86, USA, Prod; *DEADLY FORCE*, Th, 83, USA, DOP; *MAID IN AMERICA*, TV, 82, USA, DOP; *TODAY'S FBI*, TV, 82, USA, DOP; *LOVE* (2 parts), Th, 80, CDN, DOP; *MATING SEASON*, TV, 80, USA, DOP; *BIG BLONDE*, TV, 80, USA, DOP; *'OMNI - NEW FRONTIERS'* (6 eps), TV, 79, CDN/USA, Dir; *SCHIZOID*, Th, 79, USA, DOP; *THE BRINKS JOB*, Th, 78, USA, DOP; *THE WIZ*, Th, 77, USA, Gaf; *NETWORK*, Th, 76, USA, Gaf; *SAVAGE WEEKEND*, Th, 72, USA, Line Prod; *TOUCH-ME-NOT* (THE HUNTED), Th, 71, USA/S/D/F, Prod; *MIDNIGHT COWBOY*, Th, 69, USA, Gaf; *THE CAVE*, Th, 69, I, Prod; *CHARLY*, Th, 68, USA, Gaf.

LEITERMAN, Richard

IATSE-667, IATSE-659, ACTT, CSC, DGC. 14 Birch Ave., Toronto, Ont, CAN, M4V 1C9. (416)928-9029. Suzanne Depoe, Box 311, Stn. F, Toronto, Ont, CAN, M4V 2L7. (416)466-4173.
Types of Production & Categories: Th Film-DOP; Th Short-Dir/DOP; TV Film-DOP; TV Video-Dir.
Genres: Drama-Th&TV; Action-Th; Documentary-Th&TV; Educational-TV.
Biography: Born 1935, Dome Mines, Ontario. Worked as a cameraman, London, England, 61-69; returned to Toronto, 69; filmed documentaries for CBC, ABC, CBS, BBC NET. Working knowledge of French and Spanish; filmed commercials in Canada. Nominated twice for an Emmy; various other film awards.
Selective Filmography: *THE CLIMB*, Th, 85, CDN/GB, DOP; *RAD*, Th, 85, USA, DOP; *TRIBUTE*, In, 85, CDN, Dir/DOP; *STRIKER'S MOUNTAIN*, TV, 85, CDN, DOP; *MY AMERICAN COUSIN*, Th, 84, CDN, DOP; *'PROBATION'* (9 eps), TV, 84, GB, Dir/DOP; *QUINTET: VISIONS OF FIVE* (1 seg), TV, 84, CDN, Dir; *JUNO AND AVOS*, TV, 84, GB, DOP; *HE'S FIRED, SHE'S HIRED*, TV, 84, USA, DOP; *COUGAR*, TV, 83, USA, DOP; *A CHANGE OF HEART*, 'FOR THE RECORD', TV, 83, CDN, DOP; *HEART OF AN ARTIST*, TV, 82, CDN, Dir/DOP; *THE GREAT ROCKY MOUNTAIN RELAY RACE*, TV, 82, CDN, Dir/DOP; *UTILITIES*, Th, 82, CDN, DOP; *MOTHERLODE*, Th, 81, USA, DOP; *TICKET TO HEAVEN*, Th, 80, CDN, DOP; *SILENCE OF THE NORTH*, Th, 80/79, CDN, DOP (GENIE); *JOSEPHINE*, Th, 80, CDN, Dir/DOP; *SURFACING*, Th, 79, CDN, DOP; *WILD HORSE HANK*, Th, 78, CDN, DOP; *'WILDERNESS'* (6 eps), TV, 78, CDN, Dir/DOP; *WHO HAS SEEN THE WIND*, Th, 76, CDN, DOP; *RECOMMENDATION FOR MERCY*, Th, 74, CDN, DOP; *THE FAR SHORE*, Th, 74, CDN, DOP (CFA); *WEDDING IN WHITE*, Th, 72, CDN, DOP; *BETWEEN FRIENDS*, Th, 72, CDN, DOP; *RIP-OFF*, Th, 71, CDN, DOP; *GOIN'DOWN THE ROAD*, Th, 70, CDN, DOP; *A MARRIED COUPLE*, Th, 69, CDN, DOP/Assoc Dir.

LENTE, Miklos

CAMERA, DGC. 79 Laurentide Dr., Don Mills, Ont, CAN, M3A 3E2. (416)445-2442.
Types of Production & Categories: Th Film-DOP/Dir; TV Film-DOP; TV Video-DOP.
Genres: Drama-Th&TV; Comedy-Th&TV; Action-Th&TV.
Biography: Born 1930, Hungary; Canadian citizen. Thirty years experience in film production; DOP on numerous commercials in Canada, USA. Won a Certificate of Merit, CSC Awards, for *SCRIBE*.
Selective Filmography: *DOING LIFE*, TV, 86, CDN, DOP; *'NIGHT HEAT'* (39 eps), TV, 86-84, CDN, DOP; *BIG DEAL*, TV, 85, CDN, DOP; *BEDROOM EYES*,

(cont/suite)

Th, 83, CDN, DOP; *ODDBALLS,* Th, 83, CDN, Dir/DOP; *SCREWBALLS,* Th, 82, CDN, DOP; *JULIE DARLING,* Th, 81, CDN, DOP; *HAPPY BIRTHDAY TO ME,* Th, 80, CDN, DOP; *YOUR TICKET IS NO LONGER VALID,* Th, 79, CDN, DOP; *SUZANNE,* Th, 79, CDN, DOP; *AGENCY,* Th, 79, CDN, DOP; *IN PRAISE OF OLDER WOMEN,* Th, 77, CDN, DOP (CSC/GENIE); *ONTARIO/ SUMMERTIDE,* Th, 75, CDN, DOP; *'SALTY'* (24 eps), TV, 74, CDN, DOP; *THE EXECUTION OF PRIVATE SLOVIK* (in Canada), Th, 73, USA, 2nd U DOP/Op; *THE INBREAKER,* Th, 73, CDN, DOP; *U-TURN,* Th, 72, CDN, DOP; *ANOTHER SMITH FOR PARADISE,* Th, 71, CDN, DOP; *INSIDE OUT,* Th, 70, CDN, DOP; *'ADVENTURES IN RAINBOW COUNTRY'* (13 eps), TV, 69, CDN/GB/AUS, 2nd U Cam/2nd U Dir; *SCRIBE,* Th, 66, CDN, DOP.

LHOTSKY, Antonin

CSC, CAMERA. 675 Echo Dr., Ottawa, Ont, CAN, K1S 1P2. (613)234-7385.
Types of Production & Categories: TV Film-Cin; TV Video-Cin.
Genres: Drama-Th&TV; Documentary-Th&TV; Commercials-TV.
Biography: Born 1942, Prague, Czechoslovakia; Canadian citizen. Languages: English, Czech, French. Graduated from Film Academy, Prague, 65. Worked in Paris for O.R.T.F. (service de la recherche); came to Canada, 67, worked for S.P.E.A.C. (special effects), Montreal; set up film and TV unit for the National Museum of Man; taught film making, Algonquin College, Ottawa, 74-81. Cinematographer on over 50 commercials, 80-85.
Selective Filmography: *THE SECRET,* TV, 85, CDN, Cin; *THE TAMING OF THE DEMONS* (EXPO 86), Th, 85, CDN, Cin; *ACT OF GOD,* TV, 84, CDN, Cin; *YEAR OF THE TALL SHIPS,* In, 84, CDN, Cin; *MARRAKECH,* ED, 83, CDN, Cin; *THE RIGHT TIME, THE RIGHT PLACE,* In, 82, CDN, Cin; *ENERGY PI,* ED, 82, CDN, Cin; *A VISIT TO THE BANK OF CANADA,* In, 81, CDN, Cin.

LLOYD-DAVIES, Scott R.

ACTT, IATSE-659, IATSE-667, DGA. 34 - 25th Ave., Venice, CA, USA, 90291. (213)823-5533. Boardwalk Pictures, 46 Power St., Toronto, Ont, CAN, M5A 3A6. (416)362-3155.
Types of Production & Categories: TV Film-Dir/Cam.
Genres: Commercials-TV; Industrial-TV.
Biography: Born 1944, Deadwood, South Dakota; landed immigrant, Canada. Attended Chouinard Art Institute, Los Angeles. Has worked in the film business since 64; primiraly as DOP for the last 12 years. Has won awards for TV commercials including Clios, Cannes and New York Festival Awards.
Selective Filmography: *AMERICAN AIRLINES/MITSUBISHI/REEBOK,* Cm, 86, USA, Cam/Dir; *PORSCHE 9285,* In, 86, USA, Cam/Dir; *TWINNING'S TEA,* Cm, 86, GB, Cam/Dir; *MOSLON 200th/CN RAILWAYS,* Cm, 85, CDN, Cam/Dir.

LUPTON, Doug

7938 Edson Ave., Burnaby, BC, CAN. (604)437-8887.
Types of Production & Categories: TV Film-Cam; TV Video-Cam.
Genres: Documentary-TV; Educational-TV; Industrial-TV; Sports-TV.
Biography: Born 1951, Vancouver, British Columbia. Education: College Diploma, Arts.
Selective Filmography: *ROOM WITH A VIEW,* TV, 86, CDN, DOP; *LOOKING FOR OUR PAST,* 'DISCOVERING B.C.', ED, 85, CDN, Cam; *SKI KIMBERLY/ KWIK HOLE - A REVOLUTION IN DRILLING,* In, 85, CDN, Cam; *THE SWIFTSURE YACHT RACE,* TV, 85, CDN, Cam.

MAGDER, Zale

Magder Film Productions, 793 Pharmacy Ave., Scarborough, Ont, CAN, M1L 3K2. (416)752-8850.

(cont/suite)

Types of Production & Categories: Th Film-DOP/Prod; TV Film-DOP.
Genres: Drama-Th&TV.
Biography: President, Magder Film Productions and Magder Entertainment Corp. of America.
Selective Filmography: *SHOCKTRAUMA,* TV, 83, CDN, DOP; *FRANK AND FEARLESS,* TV, 83, CDN, DOP; *TERMINAL CHOICE,* Th, 83, CDN, DOP/Prod; *THE SINS OF DORIAN GREY,* TV, 81, USA, DOP; *TIME TO QUIT,* TV, 81, CDN, DOP; *THE FAMILY MAN,* TV, 79, USA, DOP; *MUM, THE WOLFMAN AND ME,* TV, 79, USA, DOP; *WAR BETWEEN THE TATES,* TV, 77, USA, DOP; *TELL ME MY NAME,* TV, 77, USA, DOP; *SHOOT,* Th, 75, CDN, DOP.

MAKIN, Harry

CSC, IATSE-644, IATSE-667, DGC. c/o Paul Robinson, 2150 S.E. 17th Street, #101, Fort Lauderdale, Fl, USA, 33316. (305)764-8855.
Types of Production & Categories: Th Film-DOP; TV Film-DOP.
Genres: Drama-Th&TV; Comedy-Th&TV; Action-Th&TV; Science Fiction-Th&TV.
Biography: Born Winnipeg, Manitoba. Started with CBC Winnipeg; 2 years in Ghana, West Africa as film director for Ghana TV on loan from Canadian External Aid, to set up and train Ghanaians for film production. Has worked in features, TV drama series, TV commercials, winning many awards.
Selective Filmography: *IF YOU COULD SEE WHAT I HEAR,* Th, 82, CDN, DOP; *HARD FEELINGS,* Th, 80, CDN, DOP; *PETER USTINOV'S LENINGRAD,* 'CITIES', TV, 78, CDN, DOP; *BEAVERBROOK - THE LIFE AND TIMES OF MAX AITKEN,* TV, 76, CDN, DOP (ANIK); *GOLDENROD,* Th, 76, CDN, DOP; *MAHONEY'S LAST STAND,* Th, 75, CDN, DOP; *'THE NATIONAL DREAM'* (8 eps), TV, 74, CDN, DOP (CSC); *'SWISS FAMILY ROBINSON'* (26 eps), TV, 74, CDN, DOP; *A QUIET DAY IN BELFAST,* Th, 74/73, CDN/GB, DOP; *MY PLEASURE IS MY BUSINESS,* Th, 74, CDN/USA, DOP; *IT SEEMED LIKE A GOOD IDEA AT THE TIME,* Th, 74, CDN, DOP; *SHE CRIED MURDER,* TV, 73, CDN/USA, DOP; *'POLICE SURGEON'* (26 eps), TV, 72/71, CDN, DOP; *GROUSE COUNTRY,* TV, 72, CDN, DOP (ANIK); *THE NEPTUNE FACTOR,* Th, 72, CDN/USA, DOP; *THE CROWD INSIDE,* Th, 70, CDN, DOP; *A FAN'S NOTES,* Th, 70, CDN, DOP; *'ADVENTURES IN RAINBOW COUNTRY'* (26 eps), TV, 69, CDN/GB/AUS, DOP; *'THE ACTIONEER'* (13 eps), TV, 68, CDN, DOP; *'QUENTIN DURGENS, M.P.'* (13 eps), TV, 67, CDN, DOP.

MATTER, Armin

IATSE-667. 3904 - 15A St. S.W., Calgary, Alta, CAN, T2T 4C7. (403)243-5688.
Types of Production & Categories: TV Film-DOP.
Genres: Drama-TV; Action-Th&TV; Documentary-TV; Commercials-TV.
Biography: Born 1944, Bern, Switzerland; Canadian citizen. Education: Motion Picture Studies, Ryerson Polytechnical Institute. Languages: English, French, German. DOP on hundreds of commercials and documentaries.
Selective Filmography: *'HAMILTON'S QUEST',* TV, 86, CDN, Op; *RAD - THE MOVIE,* Th, 85, USA, Op; *THIRTEEN MINUTES TO WAIT,* TV, 81, CDN, DOP; *THE DREAM NEVER DIES,* TV, 80, CDN, DOP.

McLACHLAN, Robert

CSC. 1075 Marigold Place, North Vancouver, BC, CAN. (604)980-9025. 1101 - 207 W. Hastings St., Vancouver, BC, CAN. (604)681-6543.
Types of Production & Categories: Th Film-DOP; Th Short-DOP/Cam; TV Film-DOP/Cam; TV Video-Cam.
Genres: Drama-Th&TV; Action-Th&TV; Horror-Th&TV; Documentary-Th&TV.

(cont/suite)

Biography: Born 1956, San Francisco, California; Canadian citizen. Studied Art, University of British Columbia; Film and Communications, San Francisco U. Canadian cycling champion, Canada Games Gold Medalist, 73. Founded Omni Film Productions Ltd., 79; shot and directed 300 commercials, TV films, documentaries and experimental films; extensive world-wide experience as cameraman (many rugged, remote locations).
Selective Filmography: *CANADA'S WILD PACIFIC SALMON/CARING FOR THE FUTURE/CAMP GOODTIMES*, In, 86/85, CDN, Cam/Co-Dir; *YUKON - CANADA'S LAST FRONTIER*, TV, 86/85, CDN, Cam/Co-Dir; *WHICH WAY TO CARNEGIE HALL?*, TV, 86, CDN, Cam; *KANGAROOS UNDER FIRE*, TV, 86/85, CDN, Cam; *BUILDING TRADES*, Cm, 86, CDN, Cam; *CLEAN WATER*, Cm, 86, USA, Cam/Dir; *ABDUCTED*, Th, 85, CDN, DOP/Op; *YUKON HERITAGE*, Cm, 84, CDN, Co-Dir/Cam/DOP; *PICTURES*, TV, 83, CDN, Dir/Cam; *AN EGG STORY*, TV, 80, CDN, Dir/Cam; *HOT TIPS*, TV, 78, CDN, Dir/Cam; *OLD FASHIONED STYLE*, In, 77/76, CDN, Dir/Cam.

METTLER, Peter

25 Aylesbury Rd., Islington, Ont, CAN, M9A 2M3. (416)233-8321. Grimthorpe Film Inc., 14 Grimthorpe Rd., Toronto, Ont, CAN, M6C 1G3. (416)653-2088.
Types of Production & Categories: Th Short-DOP; TV Film-DOP/Dir.
Genres: Drama-Th&TV; Musical-TV; Documentary-Th&TV; Dance-Th&TV.
Biography: Born 1958, Toronto, Ontario; Canadian-Swiss citizen; speaks English, Swiss-German, German, French. Education: Film, Ryerson Polytechnical Institute; Acting, New School of Drama. Travelled extensively in Europe, North Africa, Asia.
Selective Filmography: *PHOENIX FIRE MYSTERY*, TV, 86/85, CDN/USA, DOP; *DIVINE SOLITUDE*, Th, 86-84, CDN, DOP; *A TRIP AROUND LAKE ONTARIO*, TV, 85/84, CDN, DOP; *PASSION: A LETTER IN 16mm*, Th, 85, CDN, DOP; *YOU DON'T NEED*, MV, 85, CDN, DOP; *EASTERN AVENUE*, Th, 85, CDN, DOP/Dir/Prod; *KNOCK KNOCK*, Th, 85/84, CDN, DOP; *'GENERATION ON HOLD'* (2 eps), TV, 84, CDN, DOP/Dir; *COMING APART*, TV, 84, CDN, DOP; *GUARDIAN*, In, 84, CDN, Dir/Prod; *GEORGETOWN BOYS*, ED, 84, CDN, DOP; *NEXT OF KIN*, Th, 84, CDN, DOP; *NION IN THE KABARET DE LA VITA*, TV, 84, CDN, DOP; *I.I.I.*, Th, 83, CDN, DOP; *DAVID ROCHE TALKS TO YOU ABOUT LOVE*, Th, 82, CDN, DOP; *MAKING A DIFFERENCE*, TV, 82, CDN, DOP; *OPEN HOUSE*, TV, 82, CDN, DOP; *SCISSERE*, Th, 82, CDN, DOP/Dir/Wr/Ed; *GREGORY*, Th, 81, CDN, DOP/Dir/Wr/Ed; *BLACK RAGE*, TV, 81, CDN, Snd Rec; *LANCALOT FREELY*, Th, 80, CDN, DOP/Dir/Wr/Ed.

MIGNOT, Pierre

STCQ. 4735 Meridian, Montréal, Qué, CAN, H3W 2C2. (514)482-1616.
Types de production et Catégories: l métrage-D phot; c métrage-D phot; TV film-D phot.
Types d'oeuvres: Drame-C&TV; Comédie-C; Action-C; Documentaire-C.
Curriculum vitae: Né en 1944, Montréal, Québec; bilingue. Assistant caméraman, caméraman, ONF, 67-79; directeur de la photographie, pigiste depuis 79. Honoré Grand Montréalais en cinéma, 83.
Filmographie sélective: *EXIT*, C, 86, CDN, D phot; *FOOL FOR LOVE*, C, 85, USA, D phot; *ANNE TRISTER*, C, 85, CDN, D phot; *LAUNDROMAT*, TV, 84, USA, D phot; *THE BOY IN BLUE*, C, 84, CDN, D phot; *SECRET HONOR*, C, 84, USA, D phot; *MARIO*, C, 84, CDN, D phot (**GENIE**); *STREAMERS*, C, 83, USA, D phot; *MARIA CHAPDELAINE*, C, 83, CDN/F, D phot (**GENIE**); *COME BACK TO THE 5 & DIME, JIMMY DEAN, JIMMY DEAN*, C, 82, USA, D phot; *LUCIEN BROUILLARD*, C, 82, CDN, D phot; *UNE JOURNEE EN TAXI*, C, 81, CDN, D phot; *LE TOASTER*, TV, 81, CDN, D phot; *DE JOUR EN JOUR*, TV, 80, CDN, D phot; *LA BIEN-AIMEE*, TV, 80, CDN, D phot; *L'AFFAIRE COFFIN* (THE COFFIN AFFAIR), C, 79, CDN, D phot; *CORDELIA*, C, 79,

(cont/suite)

CDN, D phot; *J.A. MARTIN, PHOTOGRAPHE*, C, 76, CDN, D phot (CFA); *UNE NUIT EN AMERIQUE*, C, 75, CDN, D phot; *CHER THEO*, C, 75, CDN, D phot.

MORITA, George

IATSE-667, IATSE-644, CSC, DGC. Partners Film Company Ltd., 508 Church St., Toronto, Ont, CAN, M4Y 2C8. (416)966-3500.
Types of Production & Categories: TV Film-DOP/Dir; TV Video-DOP/Dir.
Genres: Commercials-TV.
Biography: Born Chemainus, British Columbia. Attended Ryerson Polytechnical Institute. Has worked for Batten Films, Clenman Davidson Productions, The Guest Group, Rabko TV; now at Partners Film Company Ltd.. DOP on numerous documentaries and music specials, CBC; DOP/director on commercials (since 65) which have won Bessies, Clios and awards at Cannes.

MORRIS, Reginald H.

ACTT, IATSE-644, IATSE-667, CSC. 255 Bamburgh Circle, #308, Scarborough, Ont, CAN, M1W 3T6. (416)497-9266. Miller Agency, 4425 Riverside Dr., Ste. 200, Burbank, CA, USA, 91505. (213)849-2363.
Types of Production & Categories: Th Film-DOP; Th Short-DOP; TV Film-DOP; TV Video-DOP.
Genres: Drama-Th&TV; Comedy-Th&TV; Action-Th&TV; Science Fiction-Th&TV.
Biography: Born 1918, Ruislip, Middlesex, England; Canadian citizen. Combat cameraman during WW II, being twice 'Mentioned in Despatches'. Emigrated to Canada, 55, after 20 years in the British film industry. Has won 2 Bronze Awards at the Int'l Film & TV Festival, New York; the Mulholland Award for *ESSAY ON SCIENCE*; 3 Genie nominations.
Selective Filmography: *POPEYE DOYLE* (pilot), TV, 86, CDN/USA, DOP; *'THE HITCHIKER'* (6 eps), TV, 85, CDN/USA, DOP; *TURK 182*, Th, 85, USA, DOP; *YES CONCERT*, TV, 84, USA, DOP; *A CHRISTMAS STORY*, Th, 83, CDN/USA, DOP; *PORKY'S II - THE NEXT DAY* (CHEZ PORKY II - LE LENDEMAIN), Th, 82, CDN, DOP; *PORKY'S* (CHEZ PORKY), Th, 81, CDN, DOP; *LOVE* (4 parts), Th, 80, CDN, DOP; *MURDER BY PHONE* (BELLS), Th, 80, CDN, DOP; *TRIBUTE*, Th, 80, CDN, DOP; *PHOBIA*, Th, 79, CDN, DOP; *MIDDLE AGE CRAZY*, Th, 79, CDN, DOP; *SHAPE OF THINGS TO COME*, Th, 78, CDN, DOP; *MURDER BY DECREE*, Th, 78, CDN, DOP; *MARIE-ANNE*, Th, 77, CDN, DOP; *GRANDPA AND FRANK*, TV, 77, USA, DOP; *EMPIRE OF THE ANTS*, Th, 76, USA, DOP; *WELCOME TO BLOOD CITY*, Th, 76, CDN/GB, DOP; *FOOD FOR THE GODS*, Th, 75, USA, DOP; *SECOND WIND*, Th, 75, CDN, DOP (CSC); *BLACK CHRISTMAS* (SILENT NIGHT, EVIL NIGHT), Th, 74, CDN, DOP (CSC); *WHEN MICHAEL CALLS*, TV, 72, USA, Co-DOP; *A NAME FOR EVIL* (THE GROVE), Th, 70, USA, DOP; *KING OF THE GRIZZLIES*, TV, 69, USA, DOP; *HEY! CINDERELLA*, TV, 68, USA, DOP.

NICOLLE, Victor W.

DGC. 2817 W. 29th Ave., Vancouver, BC, CAN, V6L 1Y2. (604)733-6905.
Types of Production & Categories: Th Short-DOP; TV Video-DOP/Wr.
Genres: Documentary-Th&TV; Educational-TV.
Biography: Born 1955, Vancouver, British Columbia. B.A., Psychology, Simon Fraser University.
Selective Filmography: *LADIES OF THE LOTUS*, Th, 86, CDN, DOP; *VANCOUVER - A PORTRAIT BY ARTHUR ERICKSON*, TV, 85, CDN, DOP/Wr; *WEIGHT TRAINING - YOUR KEY TO FITNESS/SEE HOW WE RUN*, ED, 85/84, CDN, DOP/Wr; *HYPOTHERMIA - NATURE'S COLD KILLER/SKI CROSS COUNTRY*, ED, 83/82, CDN, DOP/Wr.

NOWAK, Dan

3015 Gilmore Div., Burnaby, BC, CAN. (604)433-1494.
Types of Production & Categories: TV Film-Cam.
Genres: Documentary-TV; Commercials-TV; Industrial-TV; Music Video-TV.
Biography: Born 1959, British Columbia.
Selective Filmography: *BRILLIANT ORANGE/POISONED/GO FOUR THREE,*
MV, 86/85, CDN, Cam; *TWO ARTISTS,* TV, 86, CDN, Cam;
REGENERATION, Th, 86, CDN, Assist Cam/2nd U Cam; *CLEOPATRA'S
SECRET,* Cm, 85, CDN, Cam; *CLOSE TO HOME,* Th, 85, CDN, Assist Dir;
MEAT BIPRODUCT, MV, 85, CDN, Dir/Ed; *AMBULANCE,* In, 85, CDN, SFX
Makeup; *BATTERED WIVES,* TV, 85, CDN, SFX Makeup; *THE SHAME I
FEEL/ROMANCE/PART OF THE NOISE,* MV, 84, CDN, Cam.

OHASHI, Rene

CSC, CAMERA. 564 Palmerston Ave., Toronto, Ont, CAN, M6G 2P7. (416)536-4680.
Types of Production & Categories: TV Film-DOP; TV Video-DOP; Th Film-DOP.
Genres: Drama-Th&TV; Documentary-Th&TV.
Biography: Born 1952, Toronto, Ontario. Honours B.F. A., Film Production.
Selective Filmography: *'PHILIP MARLOWE PRIVATE EYE'* (6 eps), TV, 85,
CDN, DOP; *ANNE OF GREEN GABLES,* TV, 85, CDN, DOP; *MIRACLE AT
MOREAUX,* TV, 85, CDN, DOP; *NEVER SURRENDER/WE RUN/RISE UP,*
MV, 85, CDN, DOP; *'THE EDISON TWINS'* (39 eps), TV, 84/83, CDN, DOP;
HOCKEY NIGHT, TV, 84, CDN, DOP; *LISTEN TO THE CITY,* Th, 84, CDN,
DOP; *KODO* (HEARTBEAT DRUMMERS OF JAPAN), Th, 84, CDN, DOP;
SUNGLASSES AT NIGHT/MELODY, MV, 83, CDN, DOP; *THANKS FOR
THE RIDE,* TV, 82, CDN, DOP; *R.W.,* 'SONS AND DAUGHTERS', TV, 82,
CDN, DOP; *GONGGA SHAN: WHITE PEAK BEYOND THE CLOUDS,* TV, 82,
CDN, DOP; *'VISIONS'* (13 eps), TV, 81, CDN, DOP; *JEN'S PLACE,* TV, 81,
CDN, DOP; *INTRODUCING...JANET,* TV, 81, CDN, DOP; *CLOWN WHITE,*
TV, 80, CDN, DOP; *'HEAD START'* (13 eps), TV, 79, CDN, DOP.

ORIEUX, Ron

CSC, IATSE-667. 3075 W. 39th Ave., Vancouver, BC, CAN, V6N 2Z7. (604)266-9368.
Types of Production & Categories: Th Film-DOP; Th Short-DOP; TV Film-DOP.
Genres: Drama-Th&TV; Action-Th&TV; Documentary-TV.
Biography: Born 1942, St. Boniface, Manitoba. University of British Columbia
graduate in Civil Engineering; Bachelor af Arts (English, Sociology). Seventeen
years experience as a documentary cameraman/director; 10 years experience
shooting TV commercials, TV dramas, feature films.
Selective Filmography: *'BROTHERS BY CHOICE'* (6 eps), TV, 85, CDN, DOP;
DISCOVERY (EXPO 86), Th, 85, CDN, DOP; *TRAMP AT THE DOOR,* TV, 84,
CDN, DOP; *SHADOW PLAY,* Th, 84, CDN, DOP; *THE PRODIGAL,* TV, 83,
CDN, DOP; *THE HOUNDS OF NOTRE DAME,* Th, 80, CDN, DOP; *THE
GREY FOX,* Th, 80, CDN, Op; *NAILS,* Th, 79, CDN, DOP; *SKIP TRACER,* Th,
79, CDN, DOP.

OSTRIKER, David M.

CSC. 101 Belsize Dr., Toronto, Ont, CAN, M4S 1L3. Avalon Classics Inc., 59 St.
Nicholas St., Toronto, Ont, CAN, M4Y 1W6. (416)486-5768.
Types of Production & Categories: Th Film-DOP; TV Film-DOP; TV Video-DOP/
Prod.
Genres: Drama-Th&TV; Documentary-TV; Educational-TV; Industrial-Th&TV.
Biography: Born 1947, New York City; Canadian-US citizen. Attended and later
taught at New York University.

(cont/suite)

Selective Filmography: *TWICE PROMISED LAND,* TV, 86, CDN, Prod; *'NEW WORDS OF LIBERATIONS'* (6 eps), TV, 86, CDN, Prod; *AGENTS OF DECEPTION,* TV, 84, CDN, DOP/Prod; *SCORN OF WOMEN,* TV, 82, CDN, DOP; *THE KGB CONNECTIONS,* TV, 81, CDN, DOP; *THE INTRUDER,* Th, 79, CDN, DOP; *BRETHREN,* Th, 79, CDN, DOP; *'SOMETHING VENTURED'* (13 eps), TV, 76, CDN, DOP; *'HERE COME THE SEVENTIES'* (39 eps), TV, 71-69, CDN, DOP; *WOODSTOCK* (helicopter shots), Th, 68, USA, Co-Cam.

PATTERSON, Carol

CFTA, CSC. 387 Roehampton Ave., Toronto, Ont, CAN, M4P 1S3. (416)484-6648. Patterson-Partington Int'l, 793 Pharmacy Ave., Scarborough, Ont, CAN, M1L 3K2. (416)752-8850.
Types of Production & Categories: TV Film-DOP/Dir/Prod; TV Video-DOP/Dir/Prod.
Genres: Documentary-TV; Commercials-TV; Industrial-TV.
Biography: Canadian citizen; bilingual. B.A., University of Toronto.
Selective Filmography: *C.A.R.T RACING SERIES WITH JACQUES VILLENEUVE,* TV, 85, CDN, Dir/Wr; *HUSKY WORLD DOWNHILL/EXPORT A WOMENS ALPINE SKI CHAMPIONSHIPS,* TV, 85, CDN, Prod/Dir/Wr; *CANADA'S CUP YACHT RACING* (2 shows), TV, 84/81, CDN, Dir/DOP; *HUSKY WORLD DOWNHILL* (2 shows), TV, 84/83, CDN, Dir/DOP/Wr; *CANADIAN WINDSURFING CHAMPIONSHIPS/BROOKS 10K RUN FOR WOMEN,* TV, 84/83, CDN, Dir/Prod/Wr; *SHUR GAIN'S TOP PRODUCERS,* In, 82, CDN, Dir/DOP; *PROMOSCOPE,* In, 82, CDN, Dir; *THANKS A BILLION,* In, 81, CDN, Dir/Prod; *ON TOP OF THE WORLD* (SUR LE TOIT DU MONDE), TV, 80, CDN, Dir/DOP.

PAYRASTRE, Georges

3657 West 1st Ave., Vancouver, BC, CAN, V6Z 1H1. Okexnon Films Inc., Box 33961, Stn. D, Vancouver, BC, CAN, V6J 4L7. (604)733-6101.
Types of Production & Categories: Th Short-Dir/Cam/Prod; TV Film-Dir/Cam/Prod.
Genres: Drama-Th; Documentary-TV; Educational-TV; Children's-TV.
Biography: Born 1944, Paris, France; French-Canadian citizen. Languages: English, French. Spanish. Education: Simon Fraser University Film School; Bachelor of Mathematics, France. Numerous credits as cameraman on TV productions (film and tape).
Selective Filmography: *VANCOUVER ON THE MOVE,* TV, 86, CDN, Prod/Co-Dir/Cam; *PITOU, PIONNIER,* TV, 85, CDN, Prod/Cam; *PANDOSY, OKANAGAN,* TV, 85, CDN, Prod/Cam; *THE VOYAGERS,* TV, 85, CDN, Prod/Cam; *SI ON FAISAIT DES FACES,* TV, 83, CDN, Cam; *EVOLUTION A BRACKENDALE,* TV, 80, CDN, Cam; *BRUJO,* TV, 76, CDN, Prod/Co-Dir/Cam; *FIVE DAYS WITHOUT NAME,* TV, 76, CDN, Prod/Dir/Cam; *VIA DOLOROSA,* TV, 76, CDN, Prod/Co-Dir/Cam; *THE THREAD,* Th, 75, CDN, Dir/Cam.

PEARCE, Adrian Mike

P.O.Box 10, Site 302, R.R.3, Onoway, Alta, CAN, T0E 1V0. (403)967-2065. #5 Lakewood Dr., R.R.3, Onoway, Alta, CAN, T0E 1V0. (403)480-2078.
Types of Production & Categories: TV Film-DOP; TV Video-DOP.
Genres: Drama-TV; Action-TV; Documentary-TV; Educational-TV.
Biography: Born 1953, Sarnia, Ontario. Worked for London Free Press; took 3 year creative cinematography program, Humber College. Bureau cameraman, CTV, Edmonton; assignments from Gulf of Mexico to North Pole. Past Vice President, Alberta News Photographers Association. Received National Journalism Award for *RUMOURS OF P.I.P. FRAUD.*

(cont/suite)

CINEMATOGRAPHERS/DIRECTEURS-PHOTO

Selective Filmography: *'LIVING TO LEARN'* (13 eps), TV, 86, CDN, DOP; *RUMOURS OF P.I.P FRAUD*, TV, 84, CDN, DOP; *THE MOONIES* (MOON WEBS), (2 eps), TV, 79, CDN, DOP; *SEX CULTS*, TV, 79, CDN, DOP; *GINO VANELLI*, Cm, 77, CDN/USA, Assist Cam.

POULSSON, Andreas

12 Windsor Ave., Westmount, Que, CAN, H3Y 2L6. (514)481-3133. NFB, 3155 Cote de Liesse Rd., Montreal, Que, CAN, H3C 3H5. (514)283-9567.
Types of Production & Categories: Th Film-DOP; Th Short-DOP; TV Film-DOP.
Genres: Drama-Th&TV; Documentary-Th&TV; Educational-Th&TV.
Biography: Born 1944, Oslo, Norway; Canadian citizen. Languages: English, Danish, some French and German. Cinematographer on documentaries and drama, 13 years. *HENRY FORD'S AMERICA* won an Emmy, 77. Has shot over 40 documentaries; DOP on 19 dramas.
Selective Filmography: *JACK OF HEARTS/REBELLION OF YOUNG DAVID/ CONNECTION*, 'BELL CANADA PLAYHOUSE', TV, 85, CDN, DOP; *HOTWALKER/ESSO/CONCERT STAGES OF EUROPE/UNCLE T/THE SIGHT*, 'BELL CANADA PLAYHOUSE', TV, 85, CDN, DOP; *MORTIMER GRIFFIN AND SHALINSKY*, 'BELL CANADA PLAYHOUSE', TV, 85, CDN, DOP; *CANADA'S SWEETHEART: THE SAGA OF HAL C.BANKS*, TV, 84, CDN, DOP; *CAGES/ONE'S A HEIFER/JOHN CAT*, 'BELL CANADA PLAYHOUSE', TV, 84, CDN, DOP; *THE PAINTED DOOR*, 'BELL CANADA PLAYHOUSE', TV, 84, CDN, Op; *RIVER JOURNEY*, Th, 83, CDN, DOP; *ONCE IN AUGUST - MARGARET ATWOOD*, ED, 83, CDN, DOP; *IN THE FALL*, TV, 82, CDN, DOP; *REUNION*, TV, 82, CDN, DOP; *HUNTING SEASON*, TV, 82, CDN, DOP; *THE PEDLAR*, TV, 81, CDN, DOP; *SOMETHING HIDDEN: A PORTRAIT OF WILDER PENFIELD*, TV, 81, CDN, DOP; *AFTER THE AXE*, TV, 80, CDN, DOP; *CO HOEDEMAN, ANIMATOR*, TV, 80/79, CDN/NL, DOP; *NEW DENMARK*, Th, 79, CDN/DK, DOP; *HISTORY ON THE RUN*, TV, 79, CDN, DOP; *CHALLENGER*, TV, 78, CDN, DOP; *GOPHER BROKE*, ED, 78, CDN, Op; *THE UNBROKEN LINE*, ED, 78, CDN, DOP; *SOLZHENITSYN'S CHILDREN ARE MAKING A LOT OF NOISE IN PARIS*, Th, 78, CDN, DOP; *THE CHAMPIONS*, TV, 78, CDN, DOP.

PRECIOUS, Ronald J.

IATSE-667. 3866 West 13th Ave., Vancouver, BC, CAN, V6R 2S8. (604)224-4240. 27 William Cragg Drive, Donwsview, Ont, CAN, M3M 1T8. (416)241-6757.
Types of Production & Categories: TV Film-DOP.
Genres: Drama-TV; Action-TV; Documentary-TV; Educational-TV.
Biography: Born 1946, Toronto, Ontario. Education: Film program, York University; Film workshop, Simon Fraser U.. Has experience in aerial and still photography and sound recording.
Selective Filmography: *ECOLOGY IN ACTION*, TV, 85, CDN, DOP; *SLAVES OF THE HARVEST*, TV, 84, CDN, DOP; *'THE LAST SAILORS'* (3 eps), TV, 83, CDN/GB, DOP; *RITES OF SPRING*, TV, 79, CDN/USA, DOP; *GREENPEACE: VOYAGES TO SAVE THE WHALES*, TV, 77, CDN, DOP/Co-Dir/Co-Prod (CFA).

PROTAT, François

STCQ. 1568 Van Horne, Outremont, Qué, CAN, H2V 1L5. (514)273-9552.
Types de production et Catégories: 1 métrage-D phot.
Types d'oeuvres: Drame-C; Comédie musicale-C; Documentaire-C.
Curriculum vitae: Né à Paris, France; citoyenneté française et canadienne. Education: Bac. en Sciences; cours en cinéma, Ecole Nationale du Cinéma, Paris. Directeur de la photographie sur 500 annonces et 35 longs métrages. *LES ORDRES* remporte le prix de la mise en scène, Cannes.

(cont/suite)

Filmographie sélective: *JOSHUA THEN AND NOW,* C, 85, CDN, D phot (GENIE); *LE CRIME D'OVIDE PLOUFFE,* C, 83, CDN/F, D phot; *RUNNING BRAVE,* C, 83, CDN/USA, D phot; *BETWEEN FRIENDS,* C, 83, USA, D phot; *LES PLOUFFE,* C, 81, CDN, D phot; *FANTASTICA,* C, 80, CDN, D phot; *AU REVOIR...A LUNDI* (SEE YOU MONDAY), C, 79, CDN/F, D phot; *LA TETE DE NORMANDE ST-ONGE,* C, 75, CDN, D phot; *LES ORDRES,* C, 74, CDN, D phot.

REUSCH, Peter - see DIRECTORS

RINDSEM, Dennis E.

CSC, NABET. 27 Columbine Ave., Toronto, Ont, CAN, M4L 1P4. (416)694-5760.
Types of Production & Categories: TV Film-Cin; TV Video-Cam.
Genres: Drama-TV; Action-TV; Documentary-TV; Children's-TV.
Biography: Born 1942; Canadian citizen. B.A., English, University of Waterloo; Ontario Teaching Certificate, Toronto Teacher's College. DOP on numerous commercials and industrial films.
Selective Filmography: *'THE LAST FRONTIER'* (2 eps), TV, 85, CDN, Cin; *REINCARNATION,* TV, 85, CDN, Cin; *'W5'* (10 eps), TV, 85/84, CDN, Cin; *'LIVE IT UP'* (3 segs), TV, 85, CDN, Cin; *'LIFETIME'* (5 eps), TV, 85, CDN, Cam; *SEARCH FOR PIPPI LONGSTOCKING,* TV, 85, USA, Cam; *WHAT'S COOKING,* TV, 85, CDN, Cam; *JERRY LEWIS TELETHON,* TV, 85, CDN, Cam; *BEYOND REALISM: D.P. BROWN,* TV, 84, CDN, Cin; *OSTEOPOROSIS,* TV, 84, CDN, Cin; *'THE JOURNAL'* (sev segs), TV, 84/83, CDN, Cin; *'THRILL OF A LIFETIME'* (4 eps), TV, 84, CDN, Cam; *'JUST KIDDING'* (3 eps), TV, 84, CDN, Cam; *'REALITIES'* (5 segs), TV, 84, CDN, Cam; *'PIZZAZZ'* (1 eps), TV, 84, CDN, Cam; *SKIN PEELING,* TV, 84, CDN, Cin; *DOG SCHOOL,* TV, 84, CDN, Cin; *YOUNG ENTREPRENEUR,* TV, 84, CDN, Cin; *ROBERT CAMPEAU,* 'LES ENTREPRENEURS', TV, 83, CDN, Cin; *PEOPLE PATTERNS,* 'WILDERNESS', TV, 83, CDN, Cin; *NEVER TOO YOUNG,* TV, 83, CDN, Cin; *'COMEDY TONIGHT'* (3 eps), TV, 83, CDN, Cin; *ASPIRIN,* 'THE NATURE OF THINGS', TV, 83, CDN, Cin; *FUN AND PROFIT,* TV, 82, CDN, Cin; *MONDO STRIP,* TV, 82, CDN, Cin; *DUTY TO PROVIDE,* TV, 82, CDN, Cin.

ROUVEROY, Robert

CSC, IATSE-667, SMPTE. 2 Ardsley St., Streetsville, Ont, CAN, L5N 1G2. (416) 858-8954.
Types of Production & Categories: Th Short-DOP; TV Film-DOP; TV Video-DOP.
Genres: Drama-TV; Documentary-Th&TV; Industrial-Th&TV.
Biography: Born Bandung, Indonesia; in Canada since 56; Canadian citizen. Languages: English, French, German, Dutch, Bahasa Indonesia. Started in 47 as cameraman on features in Indonesia; *FRIEDA* won the Prague Peace Prize, 56. Past President, CSC, 81-85; membership chairman, 86. Has published CSC Directory and newsletter since 79. *THE HUMAN JOURNEY* won 4 prizes at Atlanta Film Festival, 3 at New York, 3 at Chicago. *SWEET WILLIAM* won at MIFED, Italy, 83. Cameraman (industrials), for the Magna Group, 86.
Selective Filmography: *WHERE THERE'S A WHEEL,* TV, 85, CDN, DOP; *VALENTINE'S REVENGE,* TV, 84, USA, DOP; *SWEET WILLIAM,* ED, 82, CDN, DOP; *MEATBALLS,* Th, 79, CDN, 2nd U DOP; *'THE HUMAN JOURNEY'* (6 eps), TV, 74-71, CDN, DOP.

ROY, Maurice

STCQ. 4458 Hôtel de Ville, Montréal, Qué, CAN, H2W 2H5. (514)849-4942.
Types de production et Catégories: TV film-D phot; TV vidéo-D phot.
Types d'oeuvres: Variété-TV; Documentaire-C&TV; Education-C&TV; Annonces-TV.

(cont/suite)

Curriculum vitae: Né en 1947.
Filmographie sélective: *UNIPRIX* (NOEL), Cm, CDN, D phot/Cadr; *TAPIS ROUGE A PARIS*, MV, 85, CDN/F, D phot/Cadr; *TAPIS ROUGE - CONCERTO POUR PICASSO*, TV, 85, CDN/F, Cadr; *CIRQUE DU SOLEIL*, TV, 85, CDN, D phot/Cadr; *MANIPULE* (LES JEUX VIDEO), TV, 85, CDN, D phot/Cadr; *LITHOPROBE/CHAMPS TIR BFC*, In, 85, CDN, D phot/Cadr; *OFFENBACH*, TV, 85, CDN, Cadr; *CHANSONS AMOUR/ LES FAMILLES*, 'MADE IN QUEBEC', TV, 85, CDN, Cadr; *'FESTIVAL JUSTE POUR RIRE'* (7 eps), TV, 85, CDN, Cadr; *DANIEL LAVOIE/ CLAUDE DUBOIS*, 'PLEIN SON', TV, 85, CDN, Cadr; *LE BOTIN ORANGE/SANTE NATURELLE/DACIA/EVAN JOANNES*, Cm, 85, CDN, D phot/Cadr; *BANQUE ROYALE* (2 films), In, 85, CDN, D phot/Cadr; *DESSINS TECHNIQUES* (INTRODUCTION), In, 85, CDN, D phot/Cadr; *UZEB/ TONY BENNET/ MILES DAVIS*, 'FESTIVAL JAZZ DE MONTREAL', TV, 85, CDN, Cadr; *RIDEAU* (LA RELEVE), TV, 85, CDN, Cadr; *LOTO QUEBEC/BO JEANS/T-FAL/MARCHE LAVAL*, Cm, 85/84, CDN, D phot/Cadr; *'SAMEDI DE RIRE'* (17 eps), TV, 85, CDN, Cadr; *DEBUT DU VOYAGE - CAP ESPOIR*, C, 84, CDN, D phot/Cadr; *A MATTER OF CUNNING*, TV, 84, CDN, Cadr.

RUCK, Wolf

Wolf Ruck Productions, 1720 Lincolnshire Blvd., Mississauga, Ont, CAN, L5E 2S7. (416)278-0296.
Types of Production & Categories: Th Short-Prod/Dir/Cin; TV Film-Cin/Snd Rec.
Genres: Drama-TV; Action-Th&TV; Documentary-TV; Educational-Th&TV.
Biography: Born 1946, Augsburg, West Germany; Canadian citizen; languages: English, German, working knowledge of French, Spanish, Italian. B.P.H.E. Degree, University of Toronto, 69. Independent filmmaker, freelance cinematographer, sound recordist since 76; translator, author, photographer, illustrator of 3 sports books (McGraw-Hill). Member of Canadian Olympic Canoeing team, Mexico, 68.
Selective Filmography: *FREEWHEELIN'*, TV, 85, CDN, Prod/Dir/Cin/Ed; *LOST!*, Th, 85, CDN, 1st Assist Cam/2nd U Cam; *TURNING TO STONE*, TV, 85, CDN, Assist Cam/2nd U Cam; *FINAL OFFER*, TV, 84, CDN, Snd Rec; *THE FRONT LINE*, 'FOR THE RECORD', TV, 84, CDN, Snd Rec; *HEART/WATER WEEDS/CYCLOSPORIN - A*, 'THE NATURE OF THINGS', TV, 84-82, CDN, Snd Rec; *THIS IS CROSS COUNTRY* (LE SKI DE FOND, C'EST CA!), TV, 83, CDN, Prod/Dir/Snd Rec/Cin; *ORCHIDS*, 'THE NATURE OF THINGS', TV, 82, CDN, Cin; *TELIDON*, 'THE NATURE OF THINGS', TV, 82, CDN, Add'l Phot; *MEDICARE*, 'QUARTERLY REPORT', TV, 82, CDN, Snd Rec; *WORLD CUP SOCCER / MATURITY / QUEEN'S PLATE / MENNEN CUP SQUASH*, 'SPORTSWEEKEND', TV, 82, CDN, Cin; *SALVATION ARMY*, 'MAN ALIVE', TV, 82, CDN, Snd Rec; *U.F.F.I./CAR MAINTENANCE/TONY GABRIELLE*, 'TAKE 30', TV, 82/81, CDN, Snd Rec; *'MARKETPLACE'* (8 seg), TV, 82/81, CDN, Snd Rec; *'COUNTRY CANADA'* (1 eps), TV, 82, CDN, Snd Rec; *'THIS LAND'* (1 eps), TV, 82, CDN, Snd Rec; *WINNING!* (GAGNER!), Th, 80, CDN, Prod/Dir/Cin; *MADELEINE DE VERCHERES/SPIRIT OF THE RIVER TO CHINA*, 'SPIRIT OF ADVENTURE', TV, 80/79, CDN, 2nd U Cam; *MAROONED IN THE LAND GOD GAVE TO CAIN*, 'SPIRIT OF ADVENTURE', TV, 79, CDN, 2nd U Cam; *PADDLES UP!* (VA, MON CANOT, VA!), TV, 78, CDN, Prod/Dir/Cin.

SAAD, Robert

IATSE-667. 496 Soudan Ave., Toronto, Ont, CAN, M4S 1X3. (416)481-5429.
Types of Production & Categories: Th Film-DOP; TV Film-DOP; TV Video-DOP.
Genres: Comedy-Th&TV; Action-Th&TV; Horror-Th&TV; Documentary-Th&TV.
Biography: Born 1936, Haifa, Israel; came to Canada, 67. Languages: English, French, Arabic, Italian. Spent most of his childhood in Lebanon and Egypt;

(cont/suite)

attended Jesuit school and worked his way up from apprentice to camera operator at studio Nahas in Cairo, Egypt.
Selective Filmography: *POLICE ACADEMY IV,* Th, 86, USA, DOP; *THE RETURN OF BILLY JACK,* Th, 86, USA, DOP; *POLICE ACADEMY III,* Th, 85, USA, DOP; *ONE MAGIC CHRISTMAS,* Th, 85, CDN/USA, Op; *BEER,* Th, 84, USA, Op/2nd U DOP; *EVERGREEN* (mini-series), TV, 84, USA, Op; *HE'S FIRED, SHE'S HIRED,* TV, 84, USA, Op; *MARTIN'S DAY,* Th, 83, CDN/GB, Op; *POLICE ACADEMY* (Uncr. DOP/8 wks), (2 wks), Th, 83, USA, 2nd U DOP; *A MATTER OF SEX,* TV, 83, CDN/USA, Op; *STRANGE INVADERS,* Th, 82, USA, Op; *STRANGE BREW,* Th, 82, CDN/USA, Op; *THE AMATEUR* (Op-2 wks), Th, 81, CDN, 2nd Cam op; *MOTHERLODE,* Th, 81, USA, Op; *ESCAPE FROM IRAN: THE CANADIAN CAPER,* TV, 80, CDN, Op; *MISDEAL* (BEST REVENGE), Th, 80, CDN, Op; *TICKET TO HEAVEN,* Th, 80, CDN, Op; *UTILITIES,* Th, 80, CDN, Op; *LOVE* (2 parts), TV, 80, CDN, Op; *SILENCE OF THE NORTH,* Th, 80/79, CDN, Op; *TORN BETWEEN TWO LOVERS,* TV, 79, USA, Op; *'MATT AND JENNY'* (16 eps), TV, 79, CDN/GB, 2nd U DOP; *CIRCLE OF CHILDREN,* TV, 78, USA, 2nd Cam op; *'THE FIFTH ESTATE',* TV, 78/77, CDN, DOP; *'SEARCH AND RESCUE'* (18 eps), TV, 77, CDN/USA, 2nd U DOP; *DEATH WEEKEND* (THE HOUSE BY THE LAKE), Th, 75, CDN, DOP; *'WITNESS TO YESTERDAY'* (13 eps), TV, 75, CDN, DOP; *THE PARASITE MURDERS* (SHIVERS), Th, 75, CDN, DOP; *THE HARD PART BEGINS,* Th, 73, CDN, DOP; *THE RAINBOW BOYS,* Th, 72, CDN, DOP.

SALE, Tim
IATSE-667. 96 - 1947 Pendrell St., Vancouver, BC, CAN, V6G 1T5. (604)687-0610.
Types of Production & Categories: Th Short-Cam; TV Film-Cam.
Genres: Drama-Th; Educational-Th; Children's-Th; Commercials-TV.
Biography: Born 1950, England; Canadian citizen; attended Simon Fraser University Film Workshop; British Columbia Institute of Technology, Biomedical Electronics (1st year). Cameraman on numerous commercials, 78-83.
Selective Filmography: *PARTNERS IN ENTERPRISE/GRANVILLE ISLAND MARKET/SUPERNATURAL B.C.,* Cm, 86-83, CDN, Cam; *MOHAWK OIL/B.C. TEL,* Cm, 84, CDN, Cam; *A SENSE OF TOUCH/BODY TALKING/KIMBERLY,* ED, 84/83, CDN, Cam; *RAINFOREST,* ED, 83, CDN, Cam; *MARATHON,* Th, 83, CDN, Cam; *SPARTREE,* Th, 77, CDN, Co-Cam (CFA); *COOPERAGE,* Th, 77, CDN, Cam.

SARETZKY, Eric - see DIRECTORS

SARIN, Vic - see DIRECTORS

SAROSSY, Paul
1183 Islington Ave., Toronto, Ont, CAN, M8Z 4S8. (416)233-9928.
Types of Production & Categories: Th Short-DOP/Dir.
Genres: Documentary-Th&TV.
Biography: Born 1963, Barrie, Ontario. B.F.A., Film, York University. Won CBC Telefest Award, 83 and 85 for *GET HAPPY* and *STATE OF MIND;* CSC Student Award for *FRUSTRATION.*
Selective Filmography: *STATE OF THE HEART,* MV, 86, CDN, DOP; *STATE OF MIND,* ED, 85, CDN, Dir/DOP; *FRUSTRATION,* Th, 85, CDN, Dir/DOP; *GUARDIAN ANGELS,* ED, 84, CDN, Dir/DOP; *GET HAPPY,* Th, 83, CDN, Dir/DOP.

SEALE, Neil
CSC, IATSE-667. Multi-Craft Productions, 43 Spruce Hill Rd., Toronto, Ont, CAN, M4E 3G2. (416)699-8389.
Types of Production & Categories: Th Film-Cam; TV Film-Cam; TV Video-Cam.
(cont/suite)

Genres: Drama-Th&TV; Comedy-Th&TV; Documentary-TV; Music Video-TV.
Biography: Born 1951, Barbados, West Indies; Canadian citizen. Education: Electrical Engineering, McMaster University, 70-72. Lighting designer, occasional set designer for theatre productions. Won a CSC Award for Outstanding Service, 86.
Selective Filmography: *AMERIKA* (mini-series), TV, 86, USA, Op; *TERI-ANN*, MV, 86, CDN, Cam; *DEAD OF WINTER*, Th, 86, USA, 2nd U Cam; *ALTER EGO*, TV, 85, USA, 2nd U Cam; *POLICE ACADEMY III*, Th, 85, USA, Op; *TEARS FOR FEARS* (CANADIAN CONCERT), MV, 85, CDN/GB, Op; *ONE MAGIC CHRISTMAS*, Th, 85, CDN/USA, 1st Assist Cam; *BEER*, Th, 84, USA, 2nd Cam op; *DAVIES AND HEARST*, TV, 84, USA, 2nd Cam op; *HE'S FIRED, SHE'S HIRED*, TV, 84, USA, 1st Assist Cam; *HEARTSOUNDS*, TV, 84, USA, 1st Assist Cam; *THEATRE IN THE ROUGH*, In, 84, CDN, Cam; *THE GUARDIAN*, TV, 83, CDN/USA, 1st Assist Cam; *COUGAR*, TV, 83, USA, 1st Assist Cam; *STRANGE BREW*, Th, 82, CDN/USA, 1st Assist Cam; *THE TERRY FOX STORY*, Th, 82, CDN, 1st Assist Cam; *SHOCKTRAUMA*, TV, 82, CDN, 1st Assist Cam; *TERMINAL CHOICE*, Th, 82, CDN, 1st Assist Cam; *THE SINS OF DORIAN GRAY*, TV, 81, USA, 1st Assist Cam; *ESCAPE FROM IRAN: THE CANADIAN CAPER*, TV, 80, CDN, 1st Assist Cam; *HARD FEELINGS*, Th, 80, CDN, 1st Assist Cam; *INCUBUS*, Th, 80, CDN, 1st Assist Cam; *TICKET TO HEAVEN*, Th, 80, CDN, 1st Assist Cam; *MUM, THE WOLFMAN AND ME*, TV, 80, USA, 1st Assist Cam.

SECKERESH, Josef

CSC, IATSE-667. 2601 Bathurst St., #601, Toronto, Ont, CAN, M6B 2Z5. (416) 784-1428.
Types of Production & Categories: Th Film-DOP; Th Short-DOP; TV Film-DOP.
Genres: Action-Th&TV; Documentary-Th&TV; Educational-Th&TV; Children's-Th&TV.
Biography: Born 1925, Hungary; Canadian citizen. Languages: English, Hungarian. Graduated from Theatrical Art and Movie Academy College, Budapest and worked for Budapest Film Studio. For 23 years, has been involved with 300 films shot internationally.
Selective Filmography: *THE SEARCH FOR SANTA CLAUS*, TV, 82, CDN, DOP; *'CHAMPION CURLING'* (6 eps), TV, 81, CDN, DOP; *FREELOADING*, Th, 81, CDN, DOP; *'BANG BANG'* (6 eps), TV, 81, CDN, DOP; *SUMMER'S CHILDREN*, Th, 79, CDN, DOP; *A WAY OUT*, TV, 78, CDN, DOP; *KING OF BLADES*, Th, 78, CDN, DOP; *OLD TORONTO*, TV, 78, CDN, DOP; *A SUMMER PLACE*, TV, 74, CDN, DOP.

SOROSSY, Ivan

CSC. 1183 Islington Ave., Toronto, Ont, CAN, M8Z 4S8. (416)233-9928. City-TV, 299 Queen St.W., Toronto, Ont, CAN, M5V 1Z9. (416)367-5757.
Types of Production & Categories: TV Video-DOP/Prod.
Genres: Documentary-TV; Educational-TV; Commercials-TV.
Biography: Born 1926, Hungary; Canadian citizen. Studied at Ontario College of Art, 52. DOP, CKVR TV (Barrie) for 15 years; producer/DOP, City-TV commercials department, Toronto, 86.
Selective Filmography: *I AM A HOTEL*, TV, 84, CDN, 2nd U DOP; *'SHOWBIZ'* (200 eps), TV, 80-72, CDN, Prod; *'FACES OF SMALL PLACES'* (100 eps), TV, 78-74, CDN, Prod.

STONE, Barry

CSC. 51A Tecumseth Ave., Toronto, Ont, CAN, M5V 2X6. (416)361-0714. 780 King St.W., Toronto, Ont, CAN, M5V 1N6. (416)860-1265.
Types of Production & Categories: TV Film-DOP.
Genres: Drama-TV; Industrial-Th&TV; Music Video-TV.

(cont/suite)

Biography: Born 1945, England; Canadian citizen. Languages: English, French, Spanish.
Selective Filmography: *'MAX HAINES CRIME FLASHBACK'* (pilot), TV, 86, CDN, DOP; *ME AND JOEY/GO FOR SODA/MIMI ON THE BEACH,* MV, 86-84, CDN, DOP; *PIZZA PIZZA-WE LOVE IT,* Cm, 85, CDN, DOP; *THE BETTER WAY,* In, 85, CDN, DOP (CSC); *LADY BEAR,* TV, 84, CDN, DOP; *VIEW FROM A PORTRAIT,* TV, 83, CDN, DOP.

STONEMAN, John

IATSE-667, ACTRA, CFTA, CSC. Mako Films Ltd., 25 St. Mary St., Ste. 101, Toronto, Ont, CAN, M4Y 1R3. (416)960-3228.
Types of Production & Categories: Th Film-DOP/Dir; TV Film-Prod/Dir/Wr/DOP.
Genres: Drama-Th; Documentary-TV; Educational-TV.
Biography: Born in England; Canadian citizen. Masters degree in Zoology. Specialist in underwater photography; scuba diver with over 9000 dives recorded in all oceans. Producer, over 80 films which have won 100 int'l awards including: Gold Medals (Festival of the Americas), Silver Medals (NY); also awarded for environmental and conservation work. President of Mako Films Ltd..
Selective Filmography: *'THE LAST FRONTIER'* (48 eps), TV, 86-83, CDN, Exec Prod/Dir/Wr/DOP (2 CFTA); *THE LAST GIANTS: A QUEST FOR SURVIVAL,* TV, 83, CDN, Prod/Dir/Wr/Cin; *THE DEAD ZONE* (underwater seq), Th, 83, USA, Cin; *MARTIN'S DAY* (underwater seq), Th, 83, CDN/GB, Cin; *SHARK!,* TV, 82, CDN, Prod/Dir/Wr/Cin; *MYTHICAL MONSTERS OF THE DEEP,* TV, 82, CDN, Prod/Dir/Wr/Cin; *LORD OF THE SEA,* TV, 82, CDN/GB, Prod/Dir/Wr/DOP; *SENTINEL OF THE SEA,* TV, 81, CDN, Prod/Dir/Wr/DOP; *DEFENDERS OF THE SEA,* TV, 81, CDN, Prod/Dir/Wr/DOP; *CORAL REEF ECOLOGY* (underwater seq), 'NATURE OF THINGS', TV, 80, CDN, Cin; *SANCTUARY OF THE SEA,* TV, 80, USA, Prod/Dir/Wr/Cin; *GHOST SHIPS,* TV, 80, USA, Prod/Dir/Wr/Cin; *SEA NYMPH,* Th, 80, CDN, Dir/Cin/Co-Prod; *THE FRAGILE SEA,* TV, 79, CDN, Prod/Dir/Wr/Cin; *INCIDENT AT NORTHAMPTON* (underwater seq), Th, 79, CDN, Cin; *THE LAST FRONTIER,* TV, 79, CDN, Dir/Cin; *NO,* Th, 79, CDN, Dir/Cin; *SURFACING* (underwater seq), Th, 79, CDN, Cin; *NOMADS OF THE DEEP,* Th, 79, CDN, Prod/Dir/Cin; *THE ARABIA INCIDENT,* TV, 78, CDN, Dir/Cin/Co-Prod; *WHERE SHIPWRECKS ABOUND,* TV, 77, CDN, Dir/Cin/Wr; *WRECK,* TV, 76, CDN, Wr/Cin; *THE INDIAN OCEAN* (Cin-underwater seq), TV, 76, GB, Dir; *THE SAVAGE SEA,* TV, 75, CDN, Dir/Prod/Cin; *SONG OF THE WHALE,* TV, 75, CDN, Dir/Prod/Cin; *THE CORAL REEF* (Cin-underwater seq), TV, 74, GB, Dir; *SHARKS' TREASURE,* Th, 74, USA, 2nd U Dir; *TEN MAN STAR,* TV, 74, GB, Dir/Cin; *SEA SANCTUARY,* TV, 73, GB, Dir/Cin.

STRINGER, Richard A.

CAMERA, CSC. 196 Hallam St., Toronto, Ont, CAN, M6H 1X7. (416)533-6085.
Types of Production & Categories: TV Film-DOP/Prod; TV Video-DOP/Prod.
Genres: Drama-TV; Musical-TV; Documentary-TV; Educational-TV.
Biography: Born 1944; Canadian citizen. Graduate of Ryerson Polytechnical Institute, 67. Nineteen years experience on award-winning films. Toronto is his home base; also active member of the Winnipeg film community; has worked on many locations across Canada and the Far North; extensive international travel. Specializes in hand-held operation; extensive aerial experience, innovative lighting and camera rigs; has produced several films.
Selective Filmography: *PAPERMAKING,* 'NATURE OF THINGS', TV, 86, CDN, DOP; *MANITOBA TOURISM/DANBY MICROWAVE OVENS/TRANSPORT CANADA SAFETY,* Cm, 85/84, CDN, DOP; *HEART AND SOUL,* 'HERITAGE CANADA', ED, 85, CDN, Cam; *THE TERMINATION INTERVIEW,* ED, 85, CDN, DOP; *THE GREAT CIRCUS OF CHINA/JOB CREATION,* Cm, 84, CDN,

(cont/suite)

Prod; *SYSTEMS OF EXCELLENCE*, ED, 84, CDN, DOP; *LET'S DANCE*, TV, 83, CDN, DOP; *FOR YOUR BENEFIT*, ED, 83, CDN, DOP; *CANADA 1*, TV, 83, CDN, Cam; *FAMOUS PEOPLE PLAYERS IN CHINA*, TV, 82, CDN, Cam; *OLD HOUSE, NEW HOUSE*, ED, 82, CDN, DOP; *BEECH HALL/THE COUNTRY IS ALIVE*, 'MAN ALIVE', TV, 82/76, CDN, DOP; *ANNE MURRAY*, '20/20', TV, 82, CDN, Cam; *THE HAWK*, TV, 80, CDN, Cam; *CANADA'S TECHNOLOGICAL CAPABILITIES*, ED, 80, CDN, DOP; *THE WORLD'S CHILDREN* (4 eps), ED, 80, CDN, DOP; *MOTION, ALGOMA STEEL*, In, 79, CDN, DOP; *GINO VANELLI*, TV, 79, CDN, Cam; *BUSH PILOT*, ED, 78, CDN, DOP; *FIRE IN 1117*, In, 78, CDN, DOP; *FIDDLERS OF JAMES BAY*, ED, 78, CDN, Cam; *THE McINTYRE BLOCK*, ED, 76, CDN, DOP; *TO SERVE OURSELVES*, ED, 74, CDN, Prod; *ANDEAN JOURNEY*, TV, 73, GB, DOP; *RECESS 10:15-10:30*, TV, 72, CDN, Prod.

TARKO, Mihai Gabor

IATSE-667. 62 Wellesley St.W., #1903, Toronto, Ont, CAN, M5S 2X3. (416)966-3403. Schulz Productions, 41 Peter St., Toronto, Ont, CAN. (416)593-5969.
Types of Production & Categories: Th Film-DOP; TV Film-DOP/Dir.
Genres: Drama-Th; Musical-TV; Documentary-TV; Commercials-TV.
Biography: Born 1952, Arad, Romania; Canadian citizen. Languages: English, Italian, Hungarian, Romanian, French. Education: Faculty of Dramatic Arts, Cinematography and Television, I.L. Caragiale, Bucharest; Faculty of Physics, University of Bucharest. Cinematographer on 300 commercials in Canada and US.
Selective Filmography: *ROGER EDWARDS/ROGER EDWARDS CONVERTIBLES II*, MV, 86/85, CDN, Dir/Cin; *FORD EATON'S/SEA QUEEN*, MV, 86/85, CDN, Cin; *CRUISE*, Th, 80, R, DOP; *WINTER STARS*, Th, 80, R, DOP; *THE PALE LIGHT OF SORROW*, Th, 79, CDN, DOP; *DEATH ARRIVES ON TAPE*, Th, 78, R, DOP.

TERRY, Chris - see DIRECTORS

THOMAS-d'HOSTE, Michel

4850 Côte des Neiges, #106, Montréal, Qué, CAN, H3V 1G5. (514)735-3994.
Types de production et Catégories: l métrage-Cam; TV film-Cam; TV vidéo-Cam.
Types d'oeuvres: Drame-C; Documentaire-C&TV; Enfants-TV.
Curriculum vitae: Né en 1927, Paris, France. Au service cinéma des Armées Françaises, 47-48; photographe et caméraman de reportage, Société Familiale Thomas-d'Hoste et Cie., 49-53; assistant caméraman, Oméga Productions, Montréal, 54-57; caméraman, TV, 57-62; ONF, 62-79; caméraman pigiste, séries film et vidéo pour TV depuis 80.
Filmographie sélective: *'PALME D'OR'*, TV, 85, CDN, Cam; *ET-DU-FILS*, C, 72, CDN, Cam; *L'EXIL*, C, 70, CDN, Cam; *LABYRINTHE* (EXPO 67), C, 67, CDN, Cam; *LE GRAND ROCK*, C, 67, CDN, Cam; *'AU PAYS DE NEUFVE FRANCE'* (13 eps), TV, 58, CDN, Cam.

THOMSON, Brian

CSC, IATSE. 48 Brunswick Ave., Toronto, Ont, CAN, M5R 2Z6. (416)963-4470.
Types of Production & Categories: TV Film-DOP/Dir; TV Video-DOP.
Genres: Commercials-TV; Music Video-TV.
Biography: Canadian citizen. DOP/director for 10 years on many award-winning commercials and music videos. Won the CSC Award for 'Air Canada' commercial.

TOUGAS, Kirk

1986 West First Ave., #2, Vancouver, BC, CAN, V6J 1G6. (604)736-4861.
Types of Production & Categories: Th Film-Cin; TV Film-Cin.
Genres: Drama-Th; Documentary-Th&TV; Educational-Th&TV; Experimental-Th.

(cont/suite)

Biography: Born 1949. His films and photographs have been exhibited at the Vancouver Art Gallery and the Grierson Seminars, Canada; Cinémathèque Française, Musée d'Art Moderne, Centre George Pompidou and the Centre National de la Photographie in Paris. Has had his one-man show, Issue des Récits exhibited in Paris, Nice and Avignon.
Selective Filmography: *RETURN TO DEPARTURE,* Th, 85, CDN, Prod/Cin; *WINNERS/LOSERS,* TV, 85, CDN, Cin; *THE THREE WATCHMEN,* Th, 84, CDN, Cin; *SINGLE FATHERS,* ED, 84, CDN, Cin; *LOW VISIBILITY,* Th, 84, CDN, Co-Cin; *BITTER MEDICINE: PART II, MEDICARE IN CRISIS,* Th, 82, CDN, Co-Cin; *RAPE: FACE TO FACE,* TV, 82, CDN, Light Dir; *BUY BUY VANCOUVER,* TV, 81, CDN, Cin; *A TIME TO RISE,* Th, 80, CDN, Co-Cin; *LETTER FROM VANCOUVER,* Th, 73, CDN, Prod; *POLITICS OF PERCEPTION,* Th, 73, CDN, Prod; *FEMINIST PORTRAIT,* Th, 72, CDN, Prod/ Cin; *LOIN DU QUEBEC/FAR FROM QUEBEC,* Th, 71, CDN, Prod/Cin.

TREMBLAY, Jean-Charles

STCQ. 4932 rue St-Denis, Montréal, Qué, CAN, H2J 2L6. (514)844-7291.
Types de production et Catégories: l métrage-D phot; c métrage-D phot; TV film-D phot.
Types d'oeuvres: Drame-C&TV; Action-TV; Documentaire-TV; Annonces-TV.
Curriculum vitae: Né en 1941, Sherbrooke, Québec; bilingue. Bac. en Lettres, Université de Montréal; Certificat d'Etudes cinématographiques, U. de Montréal. Directeur de la photographie et opérateur depuis 77. Beaucoup de travail à l'étranger: USA, Amérique Latine, et du Sud, Europe, Afrique, Artique.
Filmographie sélective: *'SAMEDI DE RIRE'* (20 eps), TV, 86/85, CDN, Co cam; *QUI A TIRE SUR NOS HISTOIRES D'AMOUR,* C, 85, CDN, D phot; *THE INVESTIGATION,* In, 85, CDN, D phot; *BOMBARDIER,* Cm, 85-83, CDN, Cam; *C'EST COMME UNE PEINE D'AMOUR,* TV, 84, CDN, Co cam; *O RAGE ELECTRIQUE,* C, 84, CDN, D phot; *C.C.M.,* In, 84, CDN, D phot; *'LES ENFANTS MAL-AIMES'* (3 eps), TV, 84, CDN, D phot; *LAURE GAUDREAULT,* TV, 83, CDN, D phot; *LA PETITE NUIT,* TV, 83, CDN, D phot; *L'ACTEUR LA VOISINE,* TV, 82, CDN, D phot; *'LA CLE DES BOIS'* (12 eps), TV, 82, CDN, Cam; *'LE TEMPS DES CHOIX'* (11 eps), TV, 82/81, CDN, Cam; *PIWI,* TV, 81, CDN, D phot; *'LES FILS DE LA LIBERTE'* (6 eps), TV, 80, CDN/F, Cadr; *LA PASSION DE DANSER,* TV, 80, CDN, D phot; *LE PLUS BEAU JOUR DE MA VIE...,* TV, 80, CDN, D phot; *ALEXANDRE,* TV, 79, CDN, D phot; *LA CUISINE ROUGE,* TV, 79/78, CDN, D phot; *MONTREAL,* 'LES GRANDES VILLES DU MONDE', TV, 78, CDN/F, Cam; *VOLER DANS LES REGLES,* TV, 78, CDN/F, Cam; *LES SERVANTES DU BON DIEU,* TV, 78, CDN, D phot; *'EN PAYS DE CONNAISSANCE'* (13 eps), TV, 77, CDN, D phot; *ANASTASIE OH! MA CHERIE,* TV, 77, CDN, D phot; *L'AMOUR BLESSE,* C, 75, CDN, D phot.

VAMOS, Thomas

STCQ. 893 Stuart, Outremont, Qué, CAN, H2V 3H7. (514)274-1564.
Types de production et Catégories: l métrage-D phot/Réal; c métrage-D phot/Réal; TV film-D phot.
Types d'oeuvres: Drame-C&TV; Action-C; Documentaire-C.
Curriculum vitae: Né en 1938, Hongrie; citoyen canadien. Etudes cinématographiques (4 ans), Ecole Supérieure du Cinéma et Théâtre, Budapest. Travaille en Hongrie comme directeur-photo sur de nombreux courts et longs métrages, mais en particulier avec Istvan Szabo. Au Canada depuis 65; travaille à l'ONF comme directeur-photo et réalisateur, 65-81; pigiste depuis 81 (longs métrages et annonces).
Filmographie sélective: *THE GATE,* C, 86, CDN, D phot; *OPERATION YPSILON,* TV, 86, CDN/F, D phot; *THE PEANUT BUTTER SOLUTION* (OPERATION BEURRE DE PINOTTES), C, 85, CDN, D phot; *LA DAME EN*

(cont/suite)

COULEURS, C, 83, CDN, D phot; *LA PLANTE,* C, 82, CDN, Réal; *LE JONGLEUR,* C, 81, CDN, Réal; *L'ENFANT FRAGILE,* C, 78, CDN, Réal; *LES HERITIERS DE LA VIOLENCE,* C, 77, CDN, Réal; *HIS MOTHER,* C, 76, CDN, D phot; *LA FLEUR AUX DENTS,* C, 75, CDN, Réal; *O.K...LALIBERTE,* C, 73, CDN, D phot; *IXE-13,* C, 72, CDN, D phot; *L'EXIL,* C, 71, CDN, Réal; *Q-BEC MY LOVE,* C, 70, CDN, D phot; *MON ENFANT C'EST MONTREAL,* C, 70, CDN, D phot; *LA CHAMBRE BLANCHE,* C, 69, CDN, D phot; *ST-DENIS DANS LE TEMPS,* C, 69, CDN, D phot; *OU ETES-VOUS DONC?,* C, 68, CDN, D phot; *JUSQU'AU COEUR,* C, 68, CDN, D phot; *KID SENTIMENT,* C, 67, CDN, D phot.

VAN DER LINDEN, Paul

IATSE-667. 33 Bowden St., Toronto, Ont, CAN, M4K 2X3. (416)466-0663.
Types of Production & Categories: Th Film-DOP; Th Short-DOP; TV Video-DOP.
Genres: Drama-Th&TV; Comedy-Th; Action-Th; Documentary-Th.
Biography: Born 1941, Amsterdam, Netherlands; Dutch citizen; landed immigrant status in Canada since 66; speaks English, French, Dutch. Education: Latin School, Amsterdam (Barlevs Gymnasium). Operator for Wesscam Camera systems (helicopter).
Selective Filmography: *THE BLUE MAN,* Th, 85, CDN, DOP; *THE PURACON FACTOR,* Th, 85, CDN, DOP; *CIRCOKRAFT,* In, 85, CDN, DOP; *RIEN QU'UN JEU,* Th, 83, CDN, DOP; *THE RIVER TO CHINA,* Th, 81, CDN, DOP; *QUEST FOR FIRE* (LA GUERRE DU FEU), Th, 80, CDN/F, 2nd U DOP; *THE LAST CHASE,* Th, 80, CDN, DOP; *'LITTLEST HOBO'* (12 eps), TV, 80, CDN, DOP; *KELLY,* Th, 81, CDN, DOP; *NIGHT FLIGHT,* Th, 79, CDN, DOP; *WILLIE HEAPS,* Th, 79, CDN, DOP; *WINSTON CHURCHILL,* Th, 79, CDN, DOP; *KINGS AND DESPERATE MEN,* Th, 78, CDN, DOP; *QUINTET,* Th, 77, USA, Op; *THE HOUSE ON FRONT STREET,* Th, 77, CDN, DOP; *WHY ROCK THE BOAT?,* Th, 76, CDN, Op; *KING SOLOMON'S TREASURE,* Th, 76, CDN/GB/ZA, DOP; *LIES MY FATHER TOLD ME,* Th, 75, CDN, DOP; *IL ETAIT UNE FOIS DANS L'EST,* Th, 72, CDN, DOP; *ELIZA'S HOROSCOPE,* Th, 71, CDN, DOP **(CFA)**; *TOU FEU TOUT FEMME,* Th, 69, CDN, DOP; *HIGH,* Th, 68, CDN, DOP.

VANHERWEGHEM, Robert

STCQ. 2518 Rte.202, Franklin Centre, Qué, CAN, J0S 1E0. (514)827-2483.
Types de production et Catégories: l métrage-D phot; c métrage-D phot; TV film-D phot.
Types d'oeuvres: Drame-C; Comédie-C; Action-C; Documentaire-C.
Curriculum vitae: Né en 1948, Belgique. Ecole Technique de Photographie, Diplôme A2 (64-67); Etudes Techniques supérieures de cinéma, Diplôme A1; 3 ans d'étude à temps plein en direction photo cinéma (67-71).
Filmographie sélective: *LE DERNIER HAVRE,* C, 85, CDN, D phot/Co réal; *LES LIMITES DU CIEL,* C, 84, CDN, D phot; *LA FUITE,* C, 83, CDN, D phot; *L'OBJET,* C, 83, CDN, D phot; *L'ILE BIZARRE,* C, 83, CDN, D phot; *LA TURLUTTE DES ANNEES DURES,* C, 82, CDN, D phot; *L'ETIQUETTE DANS LA TETE,* C, 82, B, D phot; *'CINEASTES A L'ECRAN'* (26 eps), TV, 82/81, CDN, D phot; *'RECOURS'* (8 eps), TV, 81-79, CDN, D phot; *PARMI LES MASQUES,* C, 81, CDN, D phot; *LA CABALLE,* C, 80, CDN, D phot; *CA NE PEUT PAS ETRE L'HIVER... ON A MEME PAS EU D'ETE,* C, 79, CDN, D phot; *LA BELLE APPARENCE,* C, 79, CDN, D phot/Co réal; *UNE HISTOIRE A SE RACONTER,* C, 79, CDN, D phot; *L'AMIANTE CA TUE,* C, 79, CDN, D phot; *LA CRUE,* C, 76, CDN, Co réal/Co sc/D phot/Cadr; *LUTINEIGE,* C, 75, CDN, D phot.

VERZIER, René

4543 Henri-Julien, Montréal, Qué, CAN, H2T 2C7. (514)845-1410.

(cont/suite)

Types de production et Catégories: l métrage-D phot; TV film-D phot.
Types d'oeuvres: Drame-C; Comédie-C; Action-C; Science-fiction-C.
Curriculum vitae: Né en 1934, Casablanca, Maroc; citoyen canadien depuis 66. Reporter personnel du Roi Mohammed V et Hassan II, Maroc, 57-65. Directeur-photo sur plusieurs documentaires et 2 films au Maroc. Reçoit un prix photographie pour *THE NEWCOMERS* et *THE SEVENTEEN SUMMER*.
Filmographie sélective: *THE MORNING MAN,* C, 85, CDN, D phot; *TOBY McTEAGUE,* C, 85, CDN, D phot; *THE VINDICATOR* (FRANKENSTEIN FACTOR), C, 84, CDN, D phot; *RECKLESS DISREGARD,* TV, 84, CDN/USA, D phot; *JOY,* C, 83, CDN, D phot; *OF UNKNOWN ORIGIN,* C, 82, CDN, D phot; *CROSS-COUNTRY,* C, 82, CDN, D phot; *DEADLY EYES* (THE RATS), C, 82, CDN, D phot; *VISITING HOURS,* C, 80, CDN, D phot; *DEATH SHIP,* C, 79, CDN, D phot; *DOUBLE NEGATIVE,* C, 79, CDN, D phot; *FISH HAWK,* C, 79, CDN, D phot; *CITY ON FIRE,* C, 78, CDN, D phot; *SEARCH AND DESTROY,* C, 78, CDN, D phot; *HIGH-BALLIN',* C, 77, CDN, D phot; *TWO SOLITUDES,* C, 77, CDN, D phot; *RABID,* C, 76, CDN, D phot; *RITUALS,* C, 76, CDN, D phot; *THE LITTLE GIRL WHO LIVED DOWN THE LANE,* C, 75, CDN/F, D phot; *MUSTANG,* C, 74, CDN, D phot; *JACQUES BREL IS ALIVE AND WELL AND LIVING IN PARIS,* C, 74, CDN/F, D phot; *PAR LE SANG DES AUTRES,* C, 73, CDN, D phot; *THE PYX,* C, 72, CDN, D phot; *LA MORT D'UN BUCHERON,* C, 72, CDN, D phot; *LA VRAIE NATURE DE BERNADETTE,* C, 72, CDN, D phot; *LE DIABLE EST PARMI NOUS,* C, 71, CDN, D phot; *LES MALES,* C, 70, CDN, D phot; *L'INITIATION,* C, 69, CDN, D phot; *VALERIE,* C, 68, CDN, D phot.

VOLKMER, Werner

4151 Northcliffe Ave., Montreal, Que, CAN. (514)484-2856. Aquilon Film Inc., P.O. Box 370, Victoria Stn., Westmount, Que, CAN. (514)484-8213.
Types of Production & Categories: Th Short-DOP/Dir/Prod.
Genres: Documentary-Th; Educational-Th.
Biography: Born 1944, West Germany; Canadian citizen, 76. Languages: German, English, working knowledge of French. Diploma in Advertising and Visual Communication, Academy of Art, Kassel, West Germany, 68. Art Director for advertising agencies, West Germany, 68-70; Designer, art director, advertising, Montreal, 70-75; partner in Aquilon Film Inc., Montreal, since 75. His films have won numerous awards at film festivals including: Gold Award (Chicago), Silver Medal (N.Y.), Chris Statuette (Ohio), Bronze Award (Houston) for *SPIRIT OF THE LAND*
Selective Filmography: *R.A.M.P.,* ED, 85, CDN, Prod/Cam; *THE OWL AND THE PUSSYCAT,* Th, 85, CDN, Cam; *IN GOOD COMPANY,* In, 84, CDN, Cam/Dir; *THE MAKING OF CANADIAN WHISKY/BIRDSTRIKES,* ED, 83/81, CDN, Prod/Cam; *SPIRIT OF THE LAND,* ED, 82, CDN, Cam/Prod **(CFTA)**; *THE LAST OF THE CF 100,* In, 82, CDN, Dir/Cam; *POWER BEHIND THE WINGS,* ED, 80, CDN, Dir/Cam.

WALKER, John

CSC. 730 Euclid Ave., Toronto, Ont, CAN, M6G 2T9. (416)531-3252. 490 Adelaide St.W., #304, Toronto, Ont, CAN. (416)368-1338.
Types of Production & Categories: Th Film-Prod/Dir; Th Short-Cin; TV Film-Dir/DOP.
Genres: Drama-TV; Musical-TV; Documentary-Th&TV; Children's-TV.
Biography: Born 1952, Montreal, Quebec. Has had many photographic exhibitions of his work; received numerous Canada and Ontario Arts Council Grants. *CHAMBERS - TRACKS AND GESTURES* won many awards including CFTA, Golden Sheaf and Blue Ribbon, American Film Festival.

(cont/suite)

Selective Filmography: *YOU CALL ME COLOURED*, TV, 85, CDN, Dir/Cin; *CANADA DAY*, Th, 85, CDN, Dir/Cin; *'THE EDISON TWINS'*, TV, 85, CDN, Cin; *WILLS*, ED, 85, CDN, Dir/Cin; *MULTICULTURALISM*, TV, 85, CDN, Dir/Cin; *THE LIFE AND WORK OF PAUL STRAND*, Th, 84, CDN, Prod/Dir; *MAKING OVERTURES*, TV, 84, CDN, Dir/Cin; *A FRAGILE TREE*, TV, 84, CDN, Dir/Cin; *NEON: AN ELECTRIC MEMOIR*, Th, 84, CDN, Co-Cin; *THE FIRST CANADIAN ASTRONAUT*, TV, 84, CDN, Dir/Cin; *AMERICA AND LEWIS HINE*, TV, 83, USA, DOP; *ON TO THE POLAR SEA: A YUKON ADVENTURE*, TV, 83, CDN, Dir/Cin; *SENSE OF MUSIC*, TV, 83, CDN, Dir/Cin; *START OF LIFE*, TV, 83, CDN, Dir/Cin; *INWARD PASSAGE*, Th, 82, CDN, Co-Cin; *CHAMBERS: TRACKS AND GESTURES*, TV, 82, CDN, Dir/Cin (CSC); *ALL YOU REALLY HAVE TO DO*, TV, 81, CDN, Co-Cin; *THE FOOD CONNECTION*, ED, 79, CDN, Cin; *TREE POWER*, ED, 79, CDN, Cin; *ATOMIC CLOCK*, Th, 78, CDN, Cin; *CELTIC SPIRITS*, TV, 77, CDN, Co-Cin; *ELLIOT LAKE - SCENES FROM A MINING TOWN*, Th, 76, CDN, DOP; *SONG FOR A MINER*, Th, 75, CDN, DOP.

WANNAMAKER, Tony

12 Don Way E., Ste. 409, Don Mills, Ont, CAN. (416)447-8629. City TV, 299 Queen St.W., Toronto, Ont, CAN, M5V 1Z9. (416)367-5757.
Types of Production & Categories: TV Film-Cam; TV Video-DOP/Cam.
Genres: Variety-TV; Educational-TV; Music Video-TV; News-TV.
Biography: Born 1958; Canadian citizen. Graduated High Honours, Radio and TV Broadcasting, Seneca College, 81.
Selective Filmography: *'MUCH MUSIC'* (sev seg), TV, 86-84, CDN, Cam; *'NEW MUSIC'* (sev seg), TV, 86-81, CDN, Cam; *NO CONTEST - THE CATHY EVELYN SMITH STORY*, TV, 86, CDN, Co-Cam; *'ENTERTAINMENT TONIGHT'* (sev seg), TV, 86/85, USA, Cam; *GLASS TIGER/KID CREOLE AND THE COCONUTS* (Concert simulcast), TV, 86/85, CDN, Co-Cam; *TRINIDAD CARNIVAL*, 'NEW MUSIC', TV, 85, CDN, Cam; *'A.K.A.'* (14 eps), TV, 85, CDN, DOP/Op; *THE GOLDEN PROMISE*, 'TORONTO TRILOGY', TV, 83, CDN, 2nd U Cam; *'CITY LIMITS'* (Field Cam), (40 eps), TV, 83, CDN, Cam; *'CITY PULSE'* (sev seg), TV, 81, CDN, Cam; *'STREET KIDS'* (5 parts), TV, 81, CDN, Cam.

WEGODA, Ron

CSC, IATSE. Apex Films Ltd., 1260 Dr. Penfield Ave., #1102, Montreal, Que, CAN, H3G 1B6. (514)845-6731.
Types of Production & Categories: TV Film-Cam; TV Video-Cam.
Genres: Drama-Th&TV; Action-Th&TV; Documentary-Th&TV; News-Th&TV.
Biography: Born 1929, England; Canadian citizen. Wide experience working for all major TV networks as cameraman; currently on contract to CBC-TV, news.
Selective Filmography: *3 BLUE PANTHERS*, Th, 67, D/I, 2nd U Op; *WAIT UNTIL DARK*, Th, 66, USA, 2nd U Op; *'RADISSON'* (TOMAHAWK), (20 eps), TV, 58-56, CDN, Op; *'LA VIE QUI BAT'* (9 eps), TV, 56, CDN, Op.

WESTMAN, Tony

IATSE-659, IATSE-667. 2621 Panorama Dr., North Vancouver, BC, CAN. (604) 929-7858.
Types of Production & Categories: Th Film-DOP; Th Short-Dir/Cam; TV Film-DOP.
Genres: Drama-Th&TV; Comedy-Th&TV; Action-Th&TV; Documentary-Th&TV.
Biography: Born 1946, Seattle, Washington; Canadian citizen; bilingual. B.A., Anthropology and Political Science, Simon Fraser University. Married, 2 children. Special skill: diving, underwater cinematography. Has won awards for best cinematography, Yorkton; Oscar nomination for *GOING THE DISTANCE*.

(cont/suite)

Selective Filmography: *BETRAYAL OF TRUST,* TV, 86, USA, Op; *SPOT MARKS THE X,* TV, 86, USA, Op; *VANISHING ACT,* TV, 86, USA, Op; *A NICE, PLEASANT, DEADLY WEEKEND,* TV, 85, USA, Op; *'THE HITCHIKER'* (13 eps), TV, 85, CDN/USA, Op; *ROCKY IV,* Th, 85, USA, Op; *'DANGER BAY'* (12 eps), TV, 84, CDN/USA, 2nd U DOP; *DESERTERS,* Th, 83, CDN, DOP; *CHILDREN OF SOONG CHING LING,* Th, 83, CDN/USA/RC, DOP; *'WORLD WAR II'* (13 eps), TV, 83, CDN/GB, Dir; *HOPPY,* TV, 83, CDN, DOP; *FROM BEARS TO BARTOK,* TV, 82, CDN, DOP; *THE GOLDEN SEAL,* Th, 82, USA, 2nd U DOP; *MOTHERLODE,* Th, 81, USA, 2nd U DOP; *GOING THE DISTANCE,* Th, 79, CDN, DOP/Dir; *GRANVILLE,* Th, 79, CDN, Dir/Cam; *BELUGA BABY,* Th, 78, CDN, Dir/Cam; *FAMILY DOWN THE FRASER,* TV, 78, CDN, Dir; *PAPER TIGERS AND DRAGONS,* TV, 78, CDN, DOP; *MENTAL PATIENTS ASSOCIATION,* In, 78, CDN, DOP; *CARAVANERS,* TV, 77, CDN, DOP; *SALMON PEOPLE,* TV, 77, CDN, Dir/Cam; *MAN WHO CHOOSES THE BUSH,* TV, 76, CDN, DOP; *BABY THIS IS FOR YOU,* Th, 75, CDN, DOP; *SOCCER,* Th, 75, CDN, DOP; *THE SUPREME KID,* Th, 74, CDN, DOP; *POTLATCH,* TV, 74, CDN, DOP; *PLEASURE FAIR,* TV, 72, CDN, DOP; *STOP THE CITY,* TV, 71, CDN, DOP.

WILDER, Don

55 Harbourside, #2118, Toronto, Ont, CAN, M5J 2L1. (416)361-0099.
Types of Production & Categories: Th Film-DOP; TV Film-DOP.
Genres: Drama-Th; Comedy-Th; Documentary-Th&TV.
Biography: Canadian citizen. Producer/director on hundreds of commercials in 60's; worked at NFB on many award-winning films; has directed numerous documentaries.
Selective Filmography: *LOST!,* Th, 85, CDN, Assoc Prod; *SPRING FEVER* (SNEAKERS), Th, 80, CDN, DOP/Assoc Prod; *MEATBALLS,* Th, 79, CDN, DOP; *WHO WILL SAVE OUR CHILDREN,* TV, 78, USA, DOP; *I MISS YOU HUGS AND KISSES,* Th, 77, CDN, DOP; *CHILD UNDER A LEAF,* Th, 74, CDN, DOP; *ONLY GOD KNOWS,* Th, 74, CDN, DOP; *PAPERBACK HERO,* Th, 73, CDN, DOP (CFA); *COOL MILLION* (pilot), TV, 73, USA, DOP; *WHEN MICHAEL CALLS,* TV, 72/71, USA, Co-DOP; *FACE-OFF,* Th, 71, CDN, DOP; *NAHANNI,* Th, 63, CDN, Dir/Cam (2 CFA); *YOU CAN GO A LONG WAY,* ED, 62, CDN, Dir/Cam; *ONE DAY'S POISON,* TV, 59, CDN, Cam; *FIRST AID FOR AIR CREW,* In, 56, CDN, Cam; *THE STRATFORD ADVENTURE,* Th, 55, CDN, Cam.

Second unit and second camera on:
The Fly, The Believers,
Heaven on Earth, Edison Twins,
Night Heat, Hot Shots

In Quality
and Service

SECOND to NONE!

(416) 277-2111

CSC.

416

ART DIRECTORS
★
DIRECTEURS ARTISTIQUES

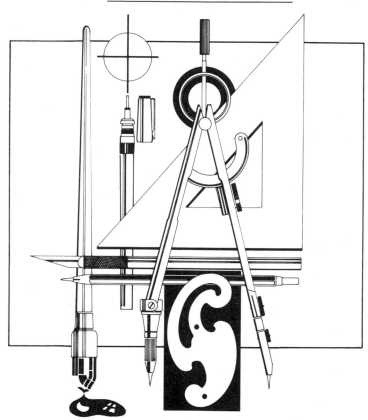
418

AMES, Paul

ABS (GB), CUPE. 951 Logan Ave., Toronto, Ont, CAN, M4K 3E3. (416)463-3878. CBC, Box 500, Stn. A, Toronto, Ont, CAN, M5W 1E6. (416)975-7009.
Types of Production & Categories: TV Film-Art Dir; TV Video-Art Dir.
Genres: Drama-TV; Variety-TV; Educational-TV; News-TV.
Biography: Born 1949, London, England; British-Canadian citizenship. Diploma in Film & TV Design, Medway College of Design, England. Awarded the M.S.I.A. in TV design from the Society of Artists & Industrial Designers; I.O.S. Diploma for Film & TV Art Direction, 84, Toronto. Worked for London Weekend TV, BBC, Thames, ETV (London), TV Ontario, CBC.
Selective Filmography: 'ROMANTIC ROCK' (weekly), TV, 86, CDN, Set Des; *THE LAST SEASON*, TV, 86, CDN, Art Dir; *AND MILES TO GO*, TV, 85, CDN, Art Dir; *THE SUICIDE MURDERS*, TV, 85, CDN, Set Des; 'VIDEO HITS' (daily), TV, 85, CDN, Set Des; 'CBLFT NEWS', TV, 85, CDN, Set Des; 'TELE OBJECTIVE' (2 eps), TV, 85, CDN, Set Des; 'ROMANCE' (5 eps), TV, 82, CDN, Art Dir; *MOVING TARGETS*, TV, 82, CDN, Art Dir; 'BACKSTRETCH' (12 eps), TV, 82, CDN, Art Dir; *A MATTER OF CHOICE/ FINAL EDITION/RUNNING MAN/ M.P.*, 'FOR THE RECORD', TV, 81-78, CDN, Art Dir; *ACTRA COMMAND PERFORMANCE*, TV, 81, CDN, Set Des; 'THE PHOENIX TEAM' (1 eps), TV, 81, CDN, Art Dir; *YOU'VE COME A LONG WAY KATIE* (mini-series), TV, 80/79, CDN, Art Dir.

BASARABA, Catherine

DGC. 550 Ontario St., #513, Toronto, Ont, CAN, M4X 1X3. (416)923-8442.
Types of Production & Categories: TV Video-Art Dir.
Genres: Drama-TV; Variety-TV; Children's-TV; Industrial-TV.
Biography: Born 1954, Montreal, Quebec. Education: Ontario College of Art, Interior Design, 72-74; Bachelor of Applied Arts and Interior Design, Ryerson Polytechnical Institute, 79. Worked as a restaurant designer, 79-80; began working in TV, 80; assistant art director for 'Tour of the Universe, Space Port 2019' at the CN Tower.
Selective Filmography: 'STREET LEGAL' (6 eps), TV, 86, CDN, Assist Art Dir; 'OWL TV' (13 eps), TV, 86/85, CDN, Assist Art Dir; *ALL-ONTARIO NIGHT RALLY*, TV, 85, CDN, Art Dir; *ROCHE TELECONFERENCE*, In, 85, CDN, Set Des; *GREAT IDEAS INCENTIVE PROGRAM*, In, 85, CDN, Set Des; 'TODAY'S SPECIAL' (20 eps), TV, 84, CDN, Art Dir; *SALOME BEY AND FAMILY*, TV, 84, CDN, Set Des; 'NIGHT HEAT' (pilot), TV, 84, CDN, Assist Art Dir; *COUNTDOWN TO LOOKING GLASS*, TV, 84, CDN, Assist Art Dir; *HEARTSOUNDS*, TV, 84, USA, Assist Art Dir; *KATE MORRIS, VICE PRESIDENT/ROUGH JUSTICE*, 'FOR THE RECORD', TV, 83, CDN, Assist Art Dir; *GENTLE SINNERS*, TV, 83, CDN, Assist Art Dir; *MAGIC SKATES*, TV, 82, CDN/USA, Assist Art Dir; *SEARCH FOR STARS*, TV, 81, CDN, Assist Art Dir; 'ROYAL CANADIAN AIR FARCE' (10 eps), TV, 80, CDN, Assist Art Dir.

BEETON, William

384 Crawford St., Toronto, Ont, CAN, M6J 2V9. (416)531-3271.
Types of Production & Categories: Th Film-Pro Des; TV Film-Art Dir; TV Video-Art Dir/Pro Des.
Genres: Drama-Th&TV; Comedy-TV; Variety-TV; Horror-Th.
Biography: Born 1935, Toronto, Ontario. Educated at various art schools. Employed at CBC, 58, first in special effects, then design department; established freelance production design/art direction company, 79.
Selective Filmography: *THE GATE*, Th, 86, CDN, Pro Des; *THE EXECUTION OF RAYMOND GRAHAM*, TV, 85, CDN, Pro Des; *GROWN UPS*, TV, 85, USA, Art Dir; 'CHECK IT OUT!', TV, 85, CDN/USA, Pro Des; *THE BOY IN BLUE*, Th, 84, CDN, Pro Des; *PYGMALION*, TV, 83, CDN, Pro Des; *ROUGH JUSTICE/*
(cont/suite)

KATE MORRIS, VICE PRESIDENT, 'FOR THE RECORD', TV, 83, CDN, Art Dir; *'FRAGGLE ROCK'*, TV, 82, CDN, Art Dir; *UTILITIES*, Th, 81, CDN, Pro Des; *MISDEAL* (BEST REVENGE), Th, 80, CDN, Pro Des; *BLIND FAITH*, 'FOR THE RECORD', TV, 80, CDN, Art Dir; *RIEL*, TV, 79, CDN, Pro Des (ANIK); *SURFACING*, Th, 79, CDN, Art Dir; *STRANGERS AT THE DOOR*, 'ADVENTURES IN HISTORY', TV, 78, CDN, Art Dir; *ADA*, 'FOR THE RECORD', TV, 77, CDN, Art Dir; *'A GIFT TO LAST'*, TV, 76, CDN, Pro Des (ANIK); *EMMETT OTTER AND HIS JUGBAND CHRISTMAS*, TV, 75, CDN/USA, Art Dir; *'THE HOUSE OF PRIDE'*, TV, 75/74, CDN, Pro Des; *MAHONEY'S LAST STAND*, Th, 75, CDN, Art Dir; *THE FROG PRINCE*, TV, 75, CDN, Des; *THE TRAVELING MUSICIANS*, TV, 73, CDN, Des.

BOLTON, Michael

IATSE-891. 3441 W. 35th Ave., Vancouver, BC, CAN, V6N 3N3. (604)261-6732.
Types of Production & Categories: Th Film-Art Dir; Th Short-Art Dir; TV Film-Art Dir; TV Video-Art Dir.
Genres: Drama-Th&TV; Comedy-Th&TV; Action-Th&TV; Science Fiction-Th&TV.
Biography: Born 1945; Canadian citizen. Started in television at CBC Vancouver, 68; art director, drama and variety series including: *THE IRISH ROVERS, THE BEACHCOMBERS, FOR THE RECORD*; freelance since 80.
Selective Filmography: *ASTRO & SON*, TV, 86, USA, Pro Des; *STRANGER IN MY BED*, TV, 86, USA, Pro Des; *TRIPWIRE*, Th, 86, USA, Art Dir; *I-MAN*, TV, 85, USA, Pro Des; *FIRE WITH FIRE*, Th, 85, USA, Art Dir; *LOVE MARY*, TV, 85, USA, Art Dir; *RAINBOW WAR* (EXPO 86), ED, 85, USA, Art Dir; *THE JOURNEY OF NATTY GANN*, Th, 84, USA, Art Dir; *RUNAWAY*, Th, 84, USA, Art Dir; *THE GLITTER DOME*, TV, 83, CDN/USA, Art Dir; *DRAW!*, TV, 83, CDN/USA, Art Dir; *ICEMAN*, Th, 83, USA, Art Dir; *THE GOLDEN SEAL*, Th, 82, USA, Set Dec; *STAR 80*, Th, 82, USA, Art Dir; *EUREKA*, Th, 82, GB, Props; *MOTHERLODE*, Th, 81, USA, Art Dir; *HARRY TRACY*, Th, 80, CDN, Art Dir; *UP RIVER*, TV, 79, USA, Art Dir; *ELEMENT OF RISK*, TV, 79, USA, Set Des.

BONNIERE, Claude

DGC. 100 Hazelton Ave., Toronto, Ont, CAN, M5R 2E2. (416)922-6463.
Types of Production & Categories: Th Film-Art Dir/Pro Des; TV Film-Art Dir/Pro Des.
Genres: Drama-Th&TV; Comedy-Th; Children's-Th&TV.
Biography: Born 1932, Paris, France; French-Canadian citizen. Languages: English, French, Spanish. Educated at Ecole des Arts Appliqués, Paris; Ecole du Musée du Louvre. Has travelled extensively. Has been an art director since 62.
Selective Filmography: *'OWL TV'*, TV, 86-84, CDN, Pro Des; *MAFIA PRINCESS*, TV, 85, USA, Pro Des; *LABOUR OF LOVE*, TV, 84, CDN, Pro Des; *MY MOTHER WAS NEVER A KID*, TV, 82, CDN/USA, Pro Des (D EMMY); *PARADISE*, Th, 81, CDN/IL, Pro Des; *CIRCLE OF TWO*, Th, 80, CDN, Pro Des; *LOVE*, Th, 80, CDN, Pro Des; *YOUR TICKET IS NO LONGER VALID*, Th, 79, CDN, Pro Des; *CRUNCH* (THE KINKY COACHES AND THE POM-POM PUSSYCATS), Th, 79, CDN, Pro Des.

BRODIE, Bill

ACTT, DGC. 18 Nursewood Rd., Toronto, Ont, CAN, M4E 3R8. (416)699-3016.
Lynn Kinney, Credentials, 25 St. Mary St., #1410, Toronto, Ont, CAN, M4Y 1R2. (416)967-1179.
Types of Production & Categories: Th Film-Art Dir/Pro Des; TV Film-Art Dir/Pro Des.
Genres: Drama-Th&TV; Comedy-Th&TV; Action-Th; Science Fiction-Th.
Biography: Born 1931, Ottawa, Ontario; Canadian-British citizen. Directed/co-produced *TERRY WHITMORE FOR EXAMPLE*, invited to

(cont/suite)

DIRECTEURS ARTISTIQUES/ART DIRECTORS

Director's Fortnight, Cannes, 69; received Quality Award, Swedish Film Institute, 69.
Selective Filmography: *ONE MAGIC CHRISTMAS*, Th, 85, CDN/USA, Pro Des; *BEER*, Th, 84, USA, Pro Des; *THE UNDERGRADS*, TV, 84, USA, Pro Des; *DRAW!*, TV, 83, CDN/USA, Pro Des; *THE GREY FOX*, Th, 80, CDN, Pro Des (GENIE); *SILENCE OF THE NORTH*, Th, 80/79, CDN, Pro Des; *AGENCY*, Th, 79, CDN, Pro Des; *SUPERMAN*, Th, 78, USA/GB, Spv Art Dir; *JOSEPH ANDREWS*, Th, 76, GB, Art Dir; *BARRY LYNDON*, Th, 74, GB, Art Dir; *MALACHIS' COVE*, Th, 73, GB, Art Dir; *ALICE IN WONDERLAND*, Th, 72, GB, Art Dir; *TERRY WHITMORE FOR EXAMPLE*, Th, 69, GB/S, Dir/Co-Prod; *PEACE GAME*, Th, 68, S, Art Dir; *PRIVILEDGE*, Th, 66, GB, Art Dir/Pro Des; *MODESTY BLAISE*, Th, 65, GB, Assist Art Dir; *SERGEANT MUSGRAVE'S DANCE*, TV, 61, GB, Des; *THE SQUARE*, TV, 61, GB, Des; *FANCY TALES OF NEW YORK*, TV, 61, GB, Des; *ZOO STORY*, TV, 60, GB, Des; *A MEMBER OF THE WEDDING*, TV, 60, GB, Des; *THE CRUCIBLE*, TV, 59, GB, Des; *DEATH OF A SALESMAN*, TV, 57, GB, Des; *FORTUNE MY FOE*, TV, 53, CDN, Des.

BROMLEY, Karen

DGC. 385 Carlton St., Toronto, Ont, CAN, M5A 2M3. (416)960-4962.
Types of Production & Categories: Th Film-Art Dir/Pro Des; TV Film-Art Dir/Pro Des; TV Video-Art Dir/Pro Des.
Genres: Drama-Th&TV; Action-Th&TV; Science Fiction-Th&TV; Horror-Th&TV.
Biography: Born Brandon, Manitoba. Studied Architecture and Interior Design, University of Manitoba. Has worked in professional theatre in Ontario and US; extensive video work including CTV public affairs. Experienced in electronic effects, models, projection systems, mattes and film effects.
Selective Filmography: *SPECIAL PEOPLE*, TV, 83, CDN/USA, Pro Des; *A MATTER OF SEX*, TV, 83, CDN/USA, Pro Des; *SOMETHING'S AFOOT*, TV, 82, USA, Pro Des; *WILL THERE REALLY BE A MORNING?*, TV, 82, USA, Pro Des; *ROMANCE* (30 eps), TV, 82, CDN, Pro Des; *THE SINS OF DORIAN GRAY*, TV, 81, USA, Pro Des; *HARRY TRACY*, Th, 80, CDN, Pro Des; *MUM, THE WOLFMAN AND ME*, TV, 80, USA, Pro Des; *TITLE SHOT*, Th, 79, CDN, Pro Des; *MIDDLE AGE CRAZY*, Th, 78, CDN, Pro Des; *CIRCLE OF CHILDREN*, TV, 78, USA, Pro Des; *SEPARATION*, TV, 77, CDN, Art Dir; *POWER PLAY* (COUP D'ETAT), (STATE OF SHOCK), Th, 77, CDN/GB, Art Dir; *OUTRAGEOUS!*, Th, 77, CDN, Art Dir; *TELL ME MY NAME*, TV, 77, USA, Art Dir; *WORLD OF DARKNESS*, TV, 76, USA, Art Dir; *RITUALS*, Th, 76, CDN, Art Dir; *WHY SHOOT THE TEACHER*, Th, 76, CDN, Art Dir; *FIND THE LADY*, Th, 75, CDN, Art Dir; *SECOND WIND*, Th, 75, CDN, Art Dir; *SUDDEN FURY*, Th, 74, CDN, Art Dir; *BLACK CHRISTMAS* (SILENT NIGHT, EVIL NIGHT), Th, 74, CDN, Art Dir; *LAST OF THE FOUR-LETTER WORDS*, TV, 74, CDN, Art Dir; *POLICE SURGEON* (104 eps), TV, 74-71, CDN, Art Dir; *WEDDING IN WHITE*, Th, 72, CDN, Art Dir (CFA).

CHARLES, David Orin

IATSE-873. 2144 Gerrard St.E., Toronto, Ont, CAN, M4E 2C2. (416)690-4400.
Types of Production & Categories: Th Film-Art Dir; TV Film-Art Dir; TV Video-Art dir.
Genres: Drama-TV; Comedy-Th&TV; Educational-TV; Commercials-TV.
Biography: Born 1944, Toronto, Ontario. Architecture Degree, University of Hawaii and New Mexico State U., 66; taught theatre arts, Connecticut and Penn State U.; B.Ed., M.A., U. of Toronto, 85. In professional theatre since age 12; employed on over 30 films and 700 commercials. Early experience in acting, radio and newspaper journalism.
Selective Filmography: *CASE OF LIBEL*, TV, 83, USA, Assist Art Dir; *I AM A HOTEL*, TV, 83, CDN, Assist Art Dir; *MEATBALLS*, Th, 79, CDN, Pro Des; *GILBERT* (4 eps), TV, 79, CDN/USA, Pro Des.

CHICK, Russell David

CUPE. 73 Courcelette Rd., Scarborough, Ont, CAN, M1N 2S9. (416)699-3437.
CBC, Box 500, Stn. A, Toronto, Ont, CAN, M5W 1E6. (416)975-7013.
Types of Production & Categories: TV Film-Pro Des; TV Video-Art Dir.
Genres: Drama-TV; Variety-TV; Children's-TV; News-TV.
Biography: Born 1948, London, England; emigrated to Canada, 72. Studied at
Camberwell Art College and Wimbledon Art College (Theatre Design). Resident
designer for London Theatre Co.. Graduate, London School of TV/Stage Make-up
Design and CBC Institute of Scenography. Emmy award nomination for Boston TV
Design.
Selective Filmography: *'SESAME STREET'* (sev seg), TV, 86, USA, Art Dir;
ISLAND LOVE SONG, TV, 86, CDN, Pro Des; *'FRAGGLE ROCK',* TV, 86-84,
CDN, Art Dir; *TURNING TO STONE,* TV, 86, CDN, Art Dir; *'HOME FIRES'*
(31 eps), TV, 83-80, CDN, Art Dir; *'THE JOURNAL'/'MIDDAY',* TV, 84, CDN,
Pro Des/Art Dir; *THE OTHER KINGDOM* (mini-series), TV, 84, CDN, Pro Des;
PRODUCTION MATTING, ED, 84, CDN, Co-Prod; *SUNDAY WITH PATRICK
WATSON,* TV, 84, CDN, Art Dir; *A SENSE OF MISSION,* TV, 83, CDN, Art
Dir; *NON MERCI,* TV, 82, CDN, Art Dir; *'THE JOURNAL'/'THE NATIONAL
NEWS',* TV, 82/81, CDN, Pro Des; *'THE SATURDAY-SUNDAY REPORT',* TV,
82, CDN, Pro Des; *GENIE AWARDS,* TV, 80, CDN, Art Dir; *'THE GREAT
DETECTIVE'* (4 eps), TV, 79, CDN, Set Des; *THE REFERENDUM,* TV, 79,
CDN, Set Des; *COMING OUT ALIVE,* TV, 79, CDN, Art Dir; *'A GIFT TO
LAST'* (4 eps), TV, 79, CDN, Art Dir; *THE STOWAWAY,* TV, 78, CDN, Art Dir;
'THE TOMMY HUNTER SHOW' (8 eps), TV, 78, CDN, Set Des.

DAVIS, David

DGC. 281 Booth Ave., Toronto, Ont, CAN, M4M 2M7. (416)466-2703. Gerald K.
Smith, P.O. Box 7430, Burbank, CA, USA, 91501. (213)849-5388.
Types of Production & Categories: Th Film-Art Dir; Th Short-Art Dir; TV Film-
Art Dir.
Genres: Drama-Th&TV; Action-Th&TV; Children's-TV.
Biography: Born 1945, Wales; British citizenship; Canadian landed immigrant. M.
A., Fine Arts, Chelsea School of the Arts; graduate scholarship, Yale University.
Ten years experience in all aspects of theatre art direction.
Selective Filmography: *COURAGE,* TV, 86, USA, Art Dir; *ACT OF
VENGEANCE,* Th, 85, USA, Art Dir; *SEPARATE VACATIONS,* Th, 85, CDN,
Assist Art Dir; *EVERGREEN* (mini-series), TV, 84, USA, Art Dir **(EMMY)**;
HEAVENLY BODIES, Th, 83, CDN, Assist Art Dir; *BEDROOM EYES,* Th, 83,
CDN, Assist Art Dir; *DRAW!,* TV, 83, CDN/USA, Assist Art Dir; *SPECIAL
PEOPLE,* TV, 83, CDN/USA, Assist Art Dir; *A MATTER OF SEX,* TV, 83,
CDN/USA, Assist Art Dir; *FALCON'S GOLD* (ROBBERS OF THE SACRED
MOUNTAIN), Th, 82, CDN, Pro Des; *WILL THERE REALLY BE A
MORNING?,* TV, 82, USA, Assist Art Dir; *THE SINS OF DORIAN GRAY,* TV,
81, USA, Assist Art Dir; *HARRY TRACY,* Th, 80, CDN, Assist Art Dir; *KOZA
DEREZA,* Th, 80, CDN, Art Dir.

DESKIN, Andrew

DGC, IATSE-873. Sundance Film Services, 1 Albemarle Ave., Toronto, Ont, CAN,
M4K 1H6. (416)463-7047.
Types of Production & Categories: Th Film-Art Dir; Th Short-Art Dir; TV Film-
Art Dir; TV Video-Art Dir.
Genres: Drama-Th&TV; Comedy-Th&TV; Action-Th&TV; Horror-Th&TV.
Biography: Born 1951. B.F.A., Concordia University, 76.
Selective Filmography: *OKLAHOMA SMUGGLERS,* Th, 86, CDN/USA, Art Dir;
OVERNIGHT, Th, 85, CDN, Art Dir; *BULLIES,* Th, 85, CDN, Props; *'MANIA'*
(4 eps), TV, 85, CDN, Props; *FLYING,* Th, 84, CDN, Art Dir; *HEARTSOUNDS,*
TV, 84, USA, Props; *THE KILLING FIELDS* (in Canada), Th, 84, GB, Props;
[cont/suite]

MULTIPLE CHOICE IN
TORONTO

Complete the following by choosing the most appropriate statement.

I'm shooting my next production in Toronto because ....

a. ☐ Toronto's Film Liaison provides a comprehensive service that is fast, efficient and free

b. ☐ Toronto is the third-largest film and video production centre in North America

c. ☐ Toronto's locations adapt to time and place

d. ☐ all of the above

For the correct answer and a lot more, contact:

Naish McHugh
Toronto Film Liaison
City of Toronto Planning and Development Department
18th Floor, East Tower, City Hall
Toronto, Ontario M5H 2N2
Telephone (416) 392-7570

AFC

In Any Vision
Calgary Has It All!

On 'Finders Keepers' starring Lou Gossett Jr, Beverley D'Angelo and Michael O'Keefe; Director Richard Lester answered the question

WHY CALGARY?

"Well, it's my third time in Calgary, and I was very well treated and very happy on 'Superman III'. The co-operation we had from the Alberta Government and the City of Calgary was marvelous. From the police to the townspeople, everyone was so generous in allowing us to come in and interfere with their lives. It seemed to be a wonderful place to shoot.

You have a wide variety of scenery within an hour's drive of Calgary and plenty of hotel rooms for a crew. I enjoy working with the Canadian members of the crew. I know many of the people in each grade. It made for a nice homecoming and you don't have to introduce yourself on the first day of shooting. There are many reasons, certainly economics cannot be ruled out. It is considerably cheaper without any loss of quality".

Calgary has no retail sales or accommodation tax, and has regular air service to most major cities in the U.S.

For further information on shooting in Calgary contact:

David Crowe, Manager, Film Industry Office
Calgary Economic Development Authority
P.O. Box 2100, Station M
Calgary, Alberta T2P 2M5
Telephone (403) 268-2771

WW

THRILLKILL, Th, 83, CDN, Art Dir; *BETWEEN FRIENDS,* TV, 83, USA, Props; *TORONTO TRILOGY* (3 parts), TV, 83, CDN, Art Dir; *IMAGE IN REVERSE,* Th, 82, CDN, Art Dir; *AMERICAN NIGHTMARE,* Th, 82, CDN, Art Dir; *SKULLDUGGERY,* Th, 82, USA, Props; *DEATH BITE* (SPASMS), Th, 81, CDN, Props; *HEARTACHES,* Th, 80, CDN, Props; *'TALES OF THE KLONDIKE'* (1 eps), TV, 80, CDN, Props; *IMPROPER CHANNELS,* Th, 79, CDN, Props; *PINBALL SUMMER,* Th, 79, CDN, Props; *THE INTRUDER,* Th, 79, CDN, Props.

DURAND, Fernand

STCQ. 161 rg du Petit St-Esprit, St-Léonard D'Aston, Qué, CAN, J0C 1M0. (819) 399-2956.

Types de production et Catégories: l métrage-Dir art; c métrage-Dir art; TV film-Dir art; TV vidéo-Dir art.

Types d'oeuvres: Drame-C&TV; Comédie-C&TV; Education-C&TV; Expérimental-C&TV.

Curriculum vitae: Né en 1939, Montréal, Québec. Etudes en dessin industriel et décoration intérieure, 57-60; étudie aussi la peinture, gravure et sculpture au Musée des Beaux-Arts, Montréal. Depuis 70, a travaillé aux décors de 193 annonces, 68 courts métrages et 30 longs métrages.

Filmographie sélective: *REBEL HIGH,* C, 86, CDN/USA, Dir art; *'TIME OF YOUR LIFE'* (3 eps), TV, 85, CDN, Dir art; *LE MATOU* (THE ALLEY CAT), (aussi 6 ém-TV), C, 84, CDN/F, Ass dir art; *'LES RACONTAGES DE LOUIS CARON'* (12 eps), TV, 82, CDN, Dir art; *TERRASSE 45* (3 ém), TV, 82, CDN, Décor; *'ENTRE LES LIGNES'* (6 eps), TV, 82, CDN, Dir art; *LA BETE A SEPT TETE,* TV, 81, CDN, Dir art; *LES YEUX ROUGES,* C, 81, CDN, Eff sp; *VIRUS,* C, 80/79, J, Décor; *ODYSSEY OF THE PACIFIC* (L'EMPEREUR DU PEROU), C, 80, CDN/F, Dir art; *FINAL ASSIGNMENT,* C, 79, CDN, Ass dir art; *NIGHT FLIGHT,* TV, 78, CDN/USA, Dir art; *'LA LETTRE DE LA NOUVELLE FRANCE'* (13 eps), TV, 77, CDN, Dir art; *LIES MY FATHER TOLD ME,* C, 74, CDN, Acces; *TI-CUL TOUGAS,* C, 74, CDN, Dir art; *BINGO,* C, 73, CDN, Décor; *MOUSIE,* TV, 73, CDN, Acces; *UN NOUVEAU ROI,* ED, 72, CDN, Décor/Acces; *DROGUE,* C, 72, CDN, Dir art; *THE PYX,* C, 72, CDN, Acces; *PHILIDOR,* ED, 71, CDN, Com/Décor/Acces; *TIENS-TOI BIEN APRES LES OREILLES A PAPA,* C, 71, CDN, Acces; *L'AMOUR HUMAIN,* C, 70, CDN, Décor; *PILE OU FACE,* C, 70, CDN, Décor; *YOU KNOW IT AIN'T EASY,* C, 70, CDN, Acces; *LA TERRE A BOIRE,* C, 64, CDN, Acces.

FLANNERY, Seamus

ACTT, DGC. 550 Jarvis St, #113, Toronto, Ont, CAN, M4Y 1N6. (416)921-7639.

Types of Production & Categories: Th Film-Pro Des; Th Short-Pro Des; TV Film-Pro Des; TV Video-Pro Des.

Genres: Drama-Th&TV; Musical-Th&TV; Action-Th&TV; Science Fiction-Th&TV.

Biography: Born Eire, England; Canadian citizen. Educated at St. Paul's, London (England) and Ontario College of Art. Was manager of design department for BBC1, BBC2. Has won awards from BISFA, US Industrial, San Francisco and Cannes film festivals; Kraft Best Art Director, Berlin; 2 Genie nominations.

Selective Filmography: *'THE CAMPBELLS'* (49 eps), TV, 86/85, CDN/USA/GB, Pro Des; *'NIGHT HEAT'* (24 eps), TV, 85/84, CDN, Pro Des; *SALAD DAYS,* TV, 83, GB, Pro Des; *'EMMERDALE FARM'* (12 eps), TV, 83, GB, Pro Des; *MURDER BY PHONE* (BELLS), Th, 83, CDN, Pro Des; *CANADA DAY CELEBRATIONS* (2 shows), TV, 79/78, CDN, Des; *HIGH POINT,* Th, 79, CDN, Pro Des; *KLONDIKE FEVER,* Th, 79, CDN, Pro Des; *FISH HAWK,* Th, 79, CDN, Pro Des; *KAVIK THE WOLF DOG,* TV, 78, CDN, Pro Des; *ANGELA,* Th, 78, CDN, Pro Des; *BETHUNE,* TV, 78, CDN, Pro Des; *JACOB TWO TWO*

(cont/suite)

MEETS THE HOODED FANG, Th, 75, CDN, Pro Des; *PARTNERS*, Th, 75, CDN, Pro Des; *WICKER MAN*, Th, 73, GB, Pro Des; *UP THE FRONT*, Th, 72, GB, Pro Des; *UP POMPEII*, Th, 71, GB, Pro Des; *UP THE CHASTITY BELT*, Th, 71, GB, Pro Des; *YOU CAN'T WIN THEM ALL*, Th, 70, USA, Pro Des; *WHATEVER HAPPENED TO WHAT'S HIS NAME*, Th, 68, GB, Pro Des; *MAROC 7*, Th, 67, GB, Pro Des; *'DANGER MAN'* (SECRET AGENT), (12 eps), TV, 66, GB, Pro Des; *DROP DEAD DARLING*, Th, 66, GB/USA, Pro Des; *HE WHO RIDES THE TIGER*, Th, 65, GB, Pro Des; *INADMISSABLE EVIDENCE*, Th, 65, GB, Pro Des; *REPULSION*, Th, 65, GB, Pro Des; *'MARY BARTON'* (8 eps), TV, 64, GB, Pro Des; *SANDS OF KALAHARI*, Th, 64, GB/USA, Pro Des; *TIGER AT THE GATES*, TV, 63, GB, Pro Des; *SMALL WORLD OF SAMMY LEE*, Th, 62, GB/USA, Pro Des.

FREED, Reuben

DGC. 139 Hogarth Ave., Toronto, Ont, CAN, M4K 1K5. (416)463-5085. Suzanne Depoe, Box 311. Stn.F, Toronto, Ont, CAN, M4V 2L7. (416)466-4173.
Types of Production & Categories: Th Film-Art Dir; Th Short-Art Dir; TV Film-Art Dir; TV Video-Art Dir.
Genres: Drama-Th&TV; Comedy-Th&TV; Action-Th&TV; Horror-Th&TV.
Biography: Born 1949, Johannesburg, South Africa; Canadian-US citizen; bilingual. Education: graduate architect. Extensive travel in Southern Africa, Europe, USA and Canada; has had photographs published in S. Africa and U.K.; set up and taught course for black architectural draughtsmen (S. Africa).
Selective Filmography: *'KAY O'BRIEN'* (13 eps), TV, 86, USA, Art Dir; *PATER NOSTER*, Th, 86, CDN, Pro Des; *A JUDGEMENT IN STONE*, Th, 86, CDN, Pro Des; *SPEARFIELD'S DAUGHTER* (mini-series), TV, 85, CDN/USA/AUS, Pro Des; *WORLDS APART*, TV, 85, CDN, Art Dir; *APRIL FOOL*, Th, 84, USA, Art Dir; *HE'S FIRED, SHE'S HIRED*, TV, 84, USA, Art Dir; *A CHRISTMAS STORY*, Th, 83, CDN/USA, Pro Des; *PAJAMA TOPS*, TV, 83, USA, Pro Des; *IN DEFENCE OF KIDS*, TV, 82, USA, Pro Des; *PORKY'S II - THE NEXT DAY*, Th, 82, CDN, Pro Des; *PERRY COMO'S CHRISTMAS IN QUEBEC*, TV, 81, USA, Art Dir; *PORKY'S* (CHEZ PORKY), Th, 81, CDN, Pro Des; *BY DESIGN*, Th, 80, CDN, Pro Des; *'TALES OF THE KLONDIKE'* (6 eps), TV, 80, CDN, Pro Des; *TRIBUTE* (UN FILS POUR L'ETE), Th, 80, CDN, Art Dir; *THE HIGH COUNTRY* (THE FIRST HELLO), Th, 80, CDN, Pro Des; *PROM NIGHT* (LE BAL DE L'HORREUR), Th, 79, CDN, Pro Des; *YESTERDAY* (GABRIELLE), Th, 79, CDN, Art Dir; *AN AMERICAN CHRISTMAS CAROL*, TV, 79, USA, Art Dir; *THE CHANGELING*, Th, 79, CDN, Art Dir; *WHO WILL SAVE THE CHILDREN*, TV, 78, USA, Art Dir; *BLOOD & GUTS*, Th, 77, CDN, Art Dir.

GAUTHIER, Vianney

STCQ. 1280 est St-Zotique, Montréal, Qué, CAN, H2S 1N7. (514)272-2923.
Types de production et Catégories: l métrage-Dir art; c métrage-Dir art; TV film-Dir art; TV vidéo-Dir art.
Types d'oeuvres: Drame-C; Comédie-C; Enfants-C&TV; Animation-C.
Curriculum vitae: Né en 1944, Montréal, Québec; bilingue. Diplôme en esthétique, option décoration intérieure, Institut des Arts Appliqués de Montréal, 66; boursier du Québec pour une année de perfectionnement en France, 68-69. *J.A. MARTIN PHOTOGRAPHE* remporte Meilleure direction artistique, Festival du Film de Cork.
Filmographie sélective: *IMAGE PAR IMAGE*, C, 86/85, CDN, Dir art; *QUI A TIRE SUR NOS HISTOIRES D'AMOUR*, C, 85, CDN, Dir art; *THE PEANUT BUTTER SOLUTION* (LA SOLUTION BEURRE DE PINOTTES), C, 85, CDN, Dir art; *ANNE TRISTER*, C, 85, CDN, Dir art; *'UN AMOUR DE QUARTIER'* (13 eps), TV, 84, CDN, Décor; *CINEMA CINEMA*, TV, 84, CDN, Décor; *LA FEMME DE L'HOTEL* (WOMAN IN TRANSIT), C, 83, CDN, Dir art; *LA DAME EN COULEURS* (OUR LADY OF THE PAINTS), C, 83, CDN, Décor;

(cont/suite)

LES ANNEES DE REVE, C, 83, CDN, Dir art; *POURQUOI L'ETRANGE M. ZOLOCK S'INTERESSAIT-IL A LA BANDE DESSINEE?,* C, 83, CDN, Décor; *'VIRULYSSE'* (26 eps), TV, 82, CDN, Décor; *DESIRE,* TV, 81, CDN, Décor; *PROPRIETE PRIVEE,* C, 81, CDN, Décor; *UNE JOURNEE EN TAXI,* C, 81, CDN, Décor; *LA BIEN-AIMEE,* C, 79, CDN, Dir art; *L'AFFAIRE COFFIN* (THE COFFIN AFFAIR), C, 79, CDN, Dir art; *SUZANNE,* C, 79, CDN, Dir art; *A CONTRECOEUR,* C, 79/78, CDN, Conc vis; *CORDELIA,* C, 79, CDN, Dir art; *JALOUSIE,* C, 78, CDN, Décor; *TWO SOLITUDES,* C, 77, CDN, Dir art; *KING SOLOMON'S TREASURE,* C, 77/76, CDN/GB/ZA, Dir art; *J.A. MARTIN PHOTOGRAPHE,* C, 76, CDN, Dir art (CFA); *JACOB TWO-TWO MEETS THE HOODED FANG,* C, 75, CDN, Ass eff sp; *L'ESPOIR,* C, 74, CDN, Décor; *CHER THEO,* C, 74, CDN, Dir art; *LA GAMMICK,* C, 73, CDN, Décor; *SOURIS TU M'INQUIETES,* 'EN TANT QUE FEMMES', TV, 73, CDN, Décor; *TAUREAU,* C, 72/71, CDN, Décor; *IXE-13,* C, 71, CDN, Conc vis.

GRAHAM, Marlene

DGC, NABET. 394 Bloor St.W., #2, 3rd Fl., Toronto, Ont, CAN, M5S 1X4. (416) 960-5126. P.O. Box 725, Stn. P, Toronto, Ont, CAN.
Types of Production & Categories: TV Film-Art Dir; TV Video-Art Dir.
Genres: Drama-Th&TV; Action-Th&TV; Experimental-Th&TV.
Selective Filmography: *THE RULING PASSION,* TV, 86, USA, Set Dec; *THE GATE,* Th, 86, CDN, Set Dec; *PIPPI LONGSTOCKING* (2 parts), TV, 85, USA, Art Dir; *THE CANADIAN CONSPIRACY,* TV, 85, CDN/USA, Art Dir; *THE UMPIRE,* TV, 84, CDN, Art Dir; *HOCKEY NIGHT,* TV, 84, CDN, Assist Art Dir; *CLASS OF '84,* Th, 81, CDN/USA, 2nd Assist Art Dir; *TICKET TO HEAVEN,* Th, 80, CDN, 2nd Assist Art Dir.

HACKBORN, Robert

CUPE, DGC. 219 Lord Seaton Rd., Willowdale, Ont, CAN, M2P 1L2. (416)225-2145. CBC, Box 500, Stn. A, Toronto, Ont, CAN, M5W 1E6. (416)975-7008.
Types of Production & Categories: TV Film-Art Dir; TV Video-Art Dir.
Genres: Drama-TV; Variety-TV; Musical-TV; Children's-TV.
Biography: Born 1928; Canadian citizen; graduate of Ontario College of Art. Has developed and used in-camera (film) glass matte shots and other special visual effects for which he has twice been nominated for the CBC President's Award. Lectures at York University and Ryerson Polytechnical Institute.
Selective Filmography: *EASTER SEAL SUPERTHON,* TV, 86, CDN, Art Dir; *SHAKESPEARE'S TWELFTH NIGHT - STRATFORD,* TV, 85, CDN, Des; *OAKMOUNT HIGH,* TV, 85, CDN, Art Dir; *S.H.C.,* 'FIFTH ESTATE', TV, 85, CDN, Des/VFX Des; *MICHAEL AND KITTY,* TV, 85, CDN, Art Dir; *CANADA'S SWEETHEART: THE SAGA OF HAL C. BANKS,* TV, 84, CDN, Art Dir; *'FRAGGLE ROCK'* (31 eps), TV, 84/83, CDN, Art Dir; *I LOVE A MAN IN A UNIFORM,* 'FOR THE RECORD', TV, 83, CDN, Art Dir; *ACTRA AWARDS,* TV, 82, CDN, Art Dir; *RICH LITTLE'S ROBIN HOOD,* TV, 82, CDN/USA, Art Dir/VFX Des; *I MARRIED THE KLONDIKE,* TV, 81, CDN, Des/VFX Des; *ROYAL CANADIAN AIR FARCE,* TV, 80, CDN, Art Dir/VFX Des; *KISS ME BETTER,* TV, 80, CDN, Art Dir; *A ROSEN BY ANY OTHER NAME,* TV, 79, CDN, Art Dir; *'MUSIC OF MAN'* (ep #6), TV, 78, CDN, Art Dir; *TODAY I AM A FOUNTAIN PEN,* TV, 78, CDN, Art Dir; *'THE GREAT DETECTIVE'* (1 eps), TV, 77, CDN, Art Dir; *HEDDA GABLER,* TV, 77, CDN, Art Dir; *THE DUMBELLS,* TV, 76, CDN, Art Dir; *SIX WAR YEARS,* TV, 75, CDN, Art Dir; *THE MARRIAGE CIRCUS,* TV, 75, CDN, Art Dir; *PARADISE LOST,* TV, 75, CDN, Art Dir; *GINETTE RENO SPECIAL,* TV, 74, CDN, Art Dir; *HEAD, GUTS AND SOUNDBONE DANCE,* TV, 74, CDN, Art Dir; *WAYNE & SHUSTER COMEDY,* TV, 73, CDN, Art Dir; *ANNE MURRAY SPECIALS* (2), TV, 72, CDN, Art Dir; *THREE LITTLE INDIANS,* TV, 71, CDN, Art Dir; *'MAN ALIVE'* (1 eps), TV, 71, CDN, Art Dir; *MISS TEEN CANADA,* TV, 71, CDN, Art Dir; *YOU OWE ME ONE HONEYMOON,* TV, 70, CDN, Art Dir.

HALL, Tony

DGC. 33 Foxbar Rd., Toronto, Ont, CAN, M4V 2G5. (416)961-8662.
Types of Production & Categories: Th Film-Art Dir/Pro Des; TV Film-Art Dir/Pro Des.
Genres: Drama-Th&TV.
Biography: Canadian citizen; Bachelor of Architecture, University of Toronto, 66. From 60-67, urban planning and architectural work with various firms in Toronto and Helsinki, Finland; began in film production at Allan King Associates, Toronto, 67; has also been freelancing in architecture (period and restoration), 79-85.
Selective Filmography: *NIAGARA - MIRACLES, MYTHS AND MAGIC,* Th, 86, CDN, Pro Des; *MANY HAPPY RETURNS,* TV, 86, USA, Art Dir; *'PHILIP MARLOWE PRIVATE EYE'* (6 eps), TV, 85, CDN, Pro Des; *YOUNG AGAIN,* TV, 85, USA, Art Dir; *ONE MAGIC CHRISTMAS,* Th, 85, CDN/USA, Art Dir; *BEER,* Th, 84, USA, Art Dir; *LOVE AT FIRST SIGHT,* Th, 75, CDN, Art Dir; *THREE CARD MONTE,* Th, 77, CDN, Pro Des; *THE MOURNING SUIT,* Th, 75, CDN, Pro Des; *HORSE LATITUDES,* TV, 75, CDN, Art Dir/Co-Prod; *ALONG THESE LINES,* Th, 74, CDN, Pro Des; *PAPERBACK HERO,* Th, 73, CDN, Art Dir; *THE NEON PALACE,* Th, 70, CDN, Art Dir/Assoc Prod.

HERRIOTT, Arthur

DGC. 92 Glen Rd., Toronto, Ont, CAN, M4W 2V6. (416)921-6667.
Types of Production & Categories: TV Film-Art Dir; TV Video-Art Dir.
Genres: Drama-TV; Variety-TV; Musical-TV; News-TV.
Biography: Born 1941, London, England; Canadian citizen. Educated at Ealing College of Art. Exhibition and display designer, 59-71; projects include the War Museum (Ottawa) and POD-5 Pavilion (Ontario Place). Production designer/art director, CBC since 71; on contract (6 months), head of design dept. of TV network, Sydney, Australia. *DREAMWEAVER* won the Rose d'Or, Montreux, 80.
Selective Filmography: *'STREET LEGAL'* (6 eps), TV, 86, CDN, Art Dir; *9-B,* TV, 86, CDN, Art Dir; *NHL AWARDS,* TV, 86-84, CDN, Art Dir; *THE SUICIDE MURDERS,* TV, 85, CDN, Art Dir; *THE CANADIAN BRASS,* TV, 85/76, CDN, Art Dir; *THE BOY NEXT DOOR/OUT OF SIGHT, OUT OF MIND,* 'FOR THE RECORD', TV, 84/82, CDN, Art Dir; *CHARLIE GRANT'S WAR,* TV, 84, CDN, Art Dir (**ANIK**); *FEDERAL ELECTION COVERAGE,* TV, 84-78, CDN, Art Dir; *'VANDERBERG'* (6 eps), TV, 83, CDN, Art Dir; *ANNE'S STORY,* TV, 83, CDN, Art Dir; *DON CHERRY SPORTS SHOW,* TV, 82, CDN, Art Dir; *THE ACCIDENT,* TV, 81, CDN, Art Dir; *GENIE AWARDS,* TV, 81, CDN, Art Dir; *JUNO AWARDS,* TV, 81, CDN, Art Dir; *THE RIVALS,* TV, 80, CDN, Art Dir; *DREAMWEAVER,* TV, 79, CDN/D, Art Dir; *DINAH CHRISTIE,* TV, 79, CDN, Art Dir; *THE SHIRLEY BASSEY SPECIAL,* TV, 78, AUS, Art Dir; *'DOCTORS DOWN UNDER'* (6 eps), TV, 78, AUS/GB, Art Dir; *THE NORMAN GLINSTON SHOW,* TV, 78, AUS, Art Dir; *THE JEANNIE LITTLE SHOW,* TV, 78, AUS, Art Dir; *ONE NIGHT STAND,* TV, 77, CDN, Art Dir; *CLOWNS,* TV, 77, CDN, Art Dir; *BURTON CUMMINGS,* TV, 77, CDN, Art Dir; *OSCAR PETERSON,* TV, 75, CDN, Art Dir; *JACK,* TV, 74, CDN, Art Dir; *THE NATIONAL DREAM,* TV, 73, CDN, Art Dir; *HERE WE ALL ARE,* ED, 73, CDN, Art Dir.

HOLMES, Gerald

DGC, IATSE-873. 46 Chine Dr., Scarborough, Ont, CAN, M1M 2K7. (416)264-4081.
Types of Production & Categories: Th Film-Art Dir; TV Film-Art Dir; TV Video-Art Dir.
Genres: Drama-Th&TV; Action-Th&TV; Science Fiction-Th.
Biography: Born 1935, London, England; emigrated to Canada, 67; became a citizen, 80. Graduate of Campbell School of Art, London. Has worked as theatre stage manager in West End; entered art dept., Thames TV; also did set dressing and special effects for Hammer Films and Assoc. British Pathé.

(cont/suite)

DIRECTEURS ARTISTIQUES/ART DIRECTORS

Selective Filmography: *'NIGHT HEAT'* (26 eps), TV, 86/85, CDN, Art Dir; *LETTING GO,* TV, 85, USA, Art Dir; *STARCROSSED,* TV, 84, USA, Art Dir; *RECKLESS DISREGARD,* TV, 84, CDN/USA, Art Dir; *'LITTLEST HOBO'* (72 eps), TV, 84-81, CDN, Art Dir; *'LOVING FRIENDS AND PERFECT COUPLES'* (80 eps), TV, 83/82, USA, Art Dir; *'MATT AND JENNY'* (26 eps), TV, 79, CDN/GB/D, Art Dir; *THE SHAPE OF THINGS TO COME,* Th, 78, CDN, Pro Des; *LOST AND FOUND,* Th, 78, USA, Set Dr; *WILD HORSE HANK,* Th, 77, CDN, Art Dir; *'SEARCH AND RESCUE'* (sev eps), TV, 77, CDN/USA, Art Dir; *THE SILENT PARTNER,* Th, 77, CDN, Set Dr; *GOLDENROD,* Th, 76, CDN, Art Dir; *EQUUS,* Th, 75, USA/GB, Set Dr; *'POLICE SURGEON'* (sev eps), TV, 75-72, CDN, Art Dir; *'SWISS FAMILY ROBINSON'* (sev eps), TV, 74, CDN, Art Dir; *THE FAR SHORE,* Th, 74, CDN, Set Dr; *THE PAPER CHASE,* Th, 73, USA, Set Dr; *WHEN MICHAEL CALLS,* TV, 72, USA, Set Dr; *'WALKER STREET'* (sev eps), TV, 71, CDN, Art Dir; *'DORP'* (sev eps), TV, 71, CDN, Art Dir; *'ADVENTURES IN RAINBOW COUNTRY'* (sev eps), TV, 69, CDN/GB/AUS, Art Dir.

HUDOLIN, Richard

DGA, IATSE-210. 12141 Jasper Ave., #604, Edmonton, Alta, CAN, T5N 3X8. (403)482-1370.
Types of Production & Categories: Th Film-Art Dir; TV Film-Art Dir.
Genres: Drama-Th&TV; Action-Th&TV; Documentary-Th.
Biography: Born Thunder Bay, Ontario. Educated at Ontario College of Art. Won an Ampia Award for art direction on *THE HOUNDS OF NOTRE DAME.*
Selective Filmography: *VANISHING ACT,* TV, 86, USA, Art Dir; *HYPER SAPIEN,* Th, 85, USA, Art Dir; *LOYALTIES,* Th, 85, CDN, Art Dir; *PORTRAITS OF CANADA* (EXPO 86), Th, 85, CDN, Art Dir; *ISAAC LITTLEFEATHERS,* Th, 84, CDN, Art Dir; *FINDERS KEEPERS,* Th, 84, USA, Assist Art Dir; *SUPERMAN III,* Th, 83, USA/GB, Assist Art Dir; *FIREBIRD 2015,* Th, 80, CDN, Art Dir; *LATITUDE 55,* Th, 80, CDN, Art Dir; *THE HOUNDS OF NOTRE DAME,* Th, 80, CDN, Art Dir.

JOLY, Jocelyn

4287 Esplanade, Montréal, Qué, CAN, H2W 1T1. (514)845-2617.
Types de production et Catégories: l métrage-Dir art/Pro des; c métrage-Dir art; TV film-Dir art/Pro des.
Types d'oeuvres: Drame-C&TV; Comédie musicale-C; Science-fiction-C&TV; Enfants-C.
Filmographie sélective: *TOBY McTEAGUE,* C, 85, CDN, Pro des; *SECRET WEAPONS,* TV, 04, USA, Pro des; *'THE HITCHIKER'* (10 eps), TV, 84, CDN/USA, Pro des; *LE CRIME D'OVIDE PLOUFFE* (aussi 6 cm TV), C, 83, CDN/F, Dir art; *MARIA CHAPDELAINE,* C, 83, CDN/F, Dir art **(GENIE)**; *'LES FILS DE LA LIBERTE'* (5 eps), TV, 81/80, CDN/F, Dir art; *FANTASTICA,* C, 80, CDN, Dir art; *FINAL ASSIGNMENT,* C, 80, CDN, Pro des; *'THE NEWCOMERS'* (LES ARRIVANTS), (3 eps), TV, 77, CDN, Pro des; *LES LEGENDES DU QUEBEC,* TV, 77, CDN, Dir art; *L'AGE DE LA MACHINE,* C, 77, CDN, Dir art **(CFA)**; *BLACKOUT,* C, 76, CDN, Pro des; *LA TETE DE NORMANDE ST-ONGE,* C, 75, CDN, Dir art; *CHRISTMAS MESSENGER,* TV, 75, CDN, Dir art; *CHILD UNDER A LEAF,* C, 74, CDN, Pro des; *SWEET MOVIE,* C, 74, CDN/F, Pro des; *LES BEAUX DIMANCHES,* C, 73, CDN, Dir art; *LES CORPS CELESTES,* C, 73, CDN/F, Dir art; *LA VRAIE NATURE DE BERNADETTE,* C, 72, CDN, Dir art; *KAMOURASKA,* C, 72, CDN/F, Décor; *LA MORT D'UN BUCHERON,* C, 72, CDN, Dir art; *PERRY TO THE NORTH POLE,* TV, 70, USA, Pro des; *LES FRONTIERES DU POSSIBLE,* TV, 70, CDN/F, Dir art; *ACT OF THE HEART* (L'ACTE DU COEUR), C, 70, CDN, Ass dir art; *DEUX FEMMES EN OR,* C, 69, CDN, Ass dir art; *RED,* C, 69, CDN, Ass dir art.

KEYWAN, Alicia

DGC. 178 Jarvis St., #806, Toronto, Ont, CAN, M5B 2K7. (416)362-8703.
Types of Production & Categories: Th Film-Art Dir; TV Film-Art Dir; TV Video-Art Dir.
Genres: Drama-Th&TV; Variety-TV; Educational-TV.
Biography: Born 1950. B.E.S.; B.Arch., University of Waterloo, U of Illinois, 75. Received Canada Council Award, 84.
Selective Filmography: *DEAD OF WINTER,* Th, 86, USA, Art Dir; *'RAY BRADBURY THEATRE'* (3 eps), TV, 85, CDN, Art Dir; *ONE MAGIC CHRISTMAS,* Th, 85, CDN/USA, Assist Art Dir; *YOUNGBLOOD,* Th, 84, USA, Art Dir; *UTILITIES,* Th, 80, CDN, Art Dir; *MISDEAL* (BEST REVENGE), Th, 80, CDN, Assist Art Dir; *SILENCE OF THE NORTH,* Th, 80/79, CDN, Co-Art Dir.

KROEGER, Wolf

David Gersh, The Gersh Agency, 222 N. Canon Dr., Ste. 201, Beverly Hills, CA, USA, 90210. (213)274-6611.
Types of Production & Categories: Th Film-Art Dir/Pro Des; TV Film-Pro Des.
Genres: Drama-Th&TV; Comedy-Th; Action-Th.
Selective Filmography: *THE SICILIAN,* Th, 86, USA, Pro Des; *LADYHAWKE,* Th, 85, USA, Pro Des; *YEAR OF THE DRAGON,* Th, 85/84, USA, Co-Prod Des; *STREAMERS,* Th, 83, USA, Pro Des; *THE BAY BOY* (UN PRINTEMPS SOUS LA NEIGE), Th, 83, CDN/F, Art Dir; *FIRST BLOOD,* Th, 82, USA, Pro Des; *SPLIT IMAGE,* Th, 82, USA, Pro Des; *POPEYE,* Th, 80, USA, Pro Des; *HEALTH,* Th, 80, USA, Pro Des; *QUINTET,* Th, 79, USA, Pro Des; *THE EXECUTION OF PRIVATE SLOVIK,* TV, 74, USA, Pro Des.

LEBRUN, Luc

CUPE. 18 Norice St., Nepean, Ont, CAN, K29 2X5. (613)225-1774. CBC, 250 Lanark Ave., Ottawa, Ont, CAN. (613)724-5354.
Types of Production & Categories: TV Video-Art Dir.
Genres: Drama-TV; Variety-TV; Musical-TV; Current Affairs-TV.
Biography: Born 1953, Ottawa, Ontario; bilingual. Studied Visual Arts, Sheridan College. Production designer (TV) since 70's. Often recognized by Central Design Committee for exceptional work on various projects.
Selective Filmography: *MASTER PETER'S PUPPET SHOW,* TV, 86, CDN/GB, Pro Des; *INTERPARLIAMENTARY UNION GALA,* TV, 85, CDN, Pro Des; *GRAND PIANOS,* TV, 85, CDN, Pro Des; *HDTV COLLOQUIUM,* In, 85, CDN/USA/J/GB, Art Dir; *'ROCK WARS'* (3 eps), TV, 85, CDN, Pro Des; *JON VICKERS,* TV, 84, CDN, Pro Des; *'FAME GAME'* (3 eps), TV, 84, CDN, Pro Des; *'LAWYERS'* (5 eps), TV, 84, CDN, Pro Des; *SYMPHONY OF A THOUSAND,* TV, 83, CDN, Pro Des; *'PULSION'* (25 eps), TV, 80-76, CDN, Pro Des; *'CAFE HIBOU'* (15 eps), TV, 80-78, CDN, Pro Des; *'TODAY FROM ONTARIO'* (30 eps), TV, 80/79, CDN, Pro Des; *'90 MINUTES LIVE'* (5 eps), TV, 78, CDN, Pro Des; *RADIO IN THE 80'S,* In, 78, CDN, Art Dir; *GINETTE RENO,* TV, 76, CDN, Pro Des.

LONGMIRE, Susan

DGC. 66 Hampton Ave., Toronto, Ont., CAN, M4K 2Y6. (416)465-7275. Chutney & Various Inc., 419 Coxwell Ave., Toronto, Ont., CAN, M4L 3B9. (416)463-5975.
Types of Production & Categories: Th Film-Art Dir/Pro Des; TV Film-Art Dir/Pro Des; TV Video-Art Dir.
Genres: Drama-Th; Comedy-TV; Horror-Th; Children's-TV.
Biography: Born 1943, Kingston, Ontario. B.A., Fine Arts and Art History, University of Toronto. Former scenic artist, film and theatre set designer in England and Canada. Display booth design, Best Booth, CBA, 84.

(cont/suite)

Selective Filmography: *ANNE OF GREEN GABLES - THE SEQUEL* (mini-series), TV, 86, CDN/USA, Art Dir; *PIPPI LONGSTOCKING* (2 parts), TV, 85, USA, Pro Des; *'SHARON, LOIS AND BRAM'S ELEPHANT SHOW'* (13 eps), TV, 85, CDN, Art Dir; *'SCTV'* (8 eps), TV, 85, CDN, Set Des; *TICKET TO HEAVEN*, Th, 80, CDN, Pro Des; *SILENCE OF THE NORTH*, Th, 80/79, CDN, Co-Art Dir; *CRIES IN THE NIGHT* (FUNERAL HOME), Th, 80, CDN, Art Dir; *RUNNING*, Th, 78, CDN, Art Dir.

McCROW, William

ACTT. 204 W.Frederick St., Rhinelander, Wisconsin, USA, 54501. (715)369-1565.
Types of Production & Categories: Th Film-Art Dir/Pro Des; Th Short-Art Dir; TV Film-Art Dir/Pro Des; TV Video-Art Dir.
Genres: Drama-Th&TV; Comedy-Th&TV; Musical-Th&TV; Science Fiction-Th&TV.
Biography: Born 1912, Princeton, Ontario; Canadian citizen. Languages: English, French, German. Associate, Ontario College of Art, Painting and Design; won the Lieutenant Governor's Medal upon graduation. His architectural credits include: Windrush Project, Kleinberg; Graphic Associates Studio; many private residences. First Director of Design, CBC TV, Toronto, 51-54; art director, production designer, CBC, 55-61; Telefis, Eireann, Dublin, Eire (also theatre designer), 61-64; BBC 1, BBC 2, ABC TV, Assoc. Rediffusion (now London Weekend TV), London, 64-68. Has worked on features in Canada and Europe.
Selective Filmography: *LES PLOUFFE*, Th, 81, CDN, Pro Des (**GENIE**); *CITY ON FIRE*, Th, 79, CDN, Pro Des; *'THE NEWCOMERS'* (3 eps), TV, 77, CDN, Pro Des; *THE THIRD WALKER*, Th, 78, CDN, Pro Des; *KINGS AND DESPERATE MEN*, Th, 77, CDN, Pro Des; *THE SQUEEZE*, Th, 76, GB, Pro Des; *OPERATION DAYBREAK* (PRICE OF FREEDOM), Th, 75/74, GB/CS, Pro Des; *LEGEND OF THE CHRISTMAS MESSENGER*, TV, 74, CDN, Pro Des; *DRACULA*, Th, 74, GB, Art Dir; *HOME*, TV, 73, GB, Art Dir; *FAMILY LIFE*, Th, 71, GB, Art Dir; *RUNNING SCARED*, Th, 71, GB, Art Dir; *UNMAN, WITTERING AND ZIGO*, Th, 70, GB, Art Dir; *THE BODY*, Th, 69, GB, Art Dir; *KES*, Th, 68, GB, Art Dir.

MURRAY, Graeme

IATSE-891. 12274 Gardiner St., Crescent Beach, BC, CAN, V4A 3C7. (604)538-3035.
Types of Production & Categories: Th Film-Pro Des; TV Film-Pro Des; TV Video-Pro Des.
Genres: Drama-Th&TV; Variety-TV; Musical-TV; Action-Th.
Biography: Born 1945.
Selective Filmography: *'BROTHERS BY CHOICE'* (6 eps), TV, 85, CDN, Pro Des; *THE BOY WHO COULD FLY*, Th, 85, USA, Art Dir; *BROTHERLY LOVE*, TV, 84, USA, Pro Des; *CONSENTING ADULT*, TV, 84, USA, Pro Des; *'DANGER BAY'* (13 eps), TV, 84, CDN/USA, Pro Des; *WALLS*, Th, 84, CDN, Pro Des; *THE GIFT*, TV, 83, CDN, Pro Des; *ICEMAN*, Th, 83, USA, Art Dir; *NEVER CRY WOLF*, Th, 82, USA, Pro Des; *PACKIN' IT IN*, TV, 82, USA, Pro Des.

OUELLETTE, Réal

STCQ. 4130 Drolet, Montréal, Qué, CAN, H2W 2L4. (514)843-8291.
Types de production et Catégories: l métrage-Dir art; c métrage-Dir art; TV film-Dir art.
Types d'oeuvres: Drame-C&TV; Comédie-C&TV; Comédie musicale-C; Action-C.
Curriculum vitae: Né en 1943, Trois-Rivières, Québec; bilingue. Education: Ecole Nationale de Théâtre. A fait les décors et les costumes d'une quarantaine de pièces de théâtre; enseigne décors et costumes de théâtre au niveau du Cégep et à l'Ecole Nationale de Théâtre.

(cont/suite)

Filmographie sélective: *LE MATOU* (THE ALLEY CAT), (aussi 6 ém TV), C, 85, CDN/F, Décor; *FUN PARK,* C, 84, CDN, Décor; *CARAVANE,* C, 82, CDN, Décor; *MASSABIELLE,* C, 81, CDN, Dir art; *LES PLOUFFE* (aussi 6 ém TV), C, 81, CDN, Chef décor; *BABE,* C, 79, CDN, Dir art; *FINAL ASSIGNMENT,* C, 79, CDN, Décor; *NIGHT FLIGHT,* C, 78, CDN, Décor; *LA CUISINE ROUGE,* C, 78, CDN, Dir art; *L'EAU CHAUDE L'EAU FRETTE,* C, 77, CDN, Décor; *THE APPRENTICESHIP OF DUDDY KRAVITZ,* C, 76, CDN, Décor; *KAMOURASKA,* C, 72, CDN/F, Ass dir art; *ET DU FILS,* C, 72, CDN, Cos/ Acces; *ELYZA'S HOROSCOPE,* C, 70, CDN, Ass décor; *THE CIRCUS,* C, 68, CDN, Acces.

PARCHER, Milton

Production Design, 419 St. Clair Ave. E., Toronto, Ont, CAN, M4T 1P6. (416)482-1994.
Types of Production & Categories: Th Film-Art Dir; TV Film-Art Dir; TV Video-Art Dir.
Genres: Drama-Th&TV; Variety-TV; Action-TV; Children's-TV.
Biography: Born 1940, Canada. Has worked in TV since 63 as graphics and set designer, art director and production designer; comprehensive knowledge of Ultimatte and Glass shots.
Selective Filmography: *'SEEING THINGS'* (15 eps), TV, 86/85, CDN, Art Dir; *DORITOS/ARCTIC POWER,* Cm, 86, CDN, Set Des; *BLUE CROSS/EASTERN AIRLINES,* Cm, 86/85, USA, Set Des; *LOVE AND LARCENY,* TV, 84, CDN, Art Dir; *'VENTURE',* TV, 84, CDN, Des; *L.A. OLYMPICS,* TV, 84, CDN, Set Des; *GENTLE SINNERS,* TV, 83, CDN, Art Dir; *MAGIC PLANET,* TV, 83, CDN/USA, Art Dir; *JUNO AWARDS,* TV, 83, CDN, Art Dir; *MEETING PLACE,* TV, 83, CDN, Set Des; *A FAR CRY FROM HOME/BY REASON OF INSANITY/P-1,* 'FOR THE RECORD', TV, 82-80, CDN, Art Dir; *'CANADA CONFIDENTIAL'* (2 eps), TV, 81, CDN, Art Dir; *'THE GREAT DETECTIVE'* (2 eps), TV, 81, CDN, Art Dir; *STRAWBERRY ICE,* TV, 81, CDN, Pro Des **(ANIK)**; *JONATHAN WINTER'S SALUTE TO BASEBALL,* TV, 80, CDN, Art Dir; *FLIP WILSON'S SALUTE TO FOOTBALL,* TV, 79, CDN, Art Dir; *THE WORDSMITH,* TV, 78, CDN, Art Dir **(GENIE)**; *'THE BEACHCOMBERS'* (7 eps), TV, 76/75, CDN, Art Dir; *THE NEW QUIZ KIDS,* TV, 76/75, CDN, Set Des; *'SIDESTREET'* (6 eps), TV, 76, CDN, Art Dir; *SUNDAY IN THE COUNTRY,* Th, 75, CDN, Art Dir; *'THE WHITE OAKS OF JALNA',* TV, 72/71, CDN, Assist Art Dir; *THE MERCENARIES,* TV, 70, CDN, Art Dir.

PRESTON, Earl

DGC. P.O. Box 450, Mont Tremblant, Que, CAN, J0T 1Z0. (819)425-7458.
Types of Production & Categories: Th Film-Art Dir/Pro Des; TV Film-Art Dir/Pro Des.
Genres: Drama-Th&TV.
Biography: Born 1926, Buffalo, New York; Canadian citizen. Education: University of Toronto, Ontario College of Art. Theatre set designer in London (England), Toronto, Montreal. Set designer, variety/drama, CBC TV, Toronto, 55-56; art director, studio manager, NFB, 56-58; freelance since 69. Artist (serigraph, lithograph, painting, drawing), has taken part in many group exhibitions; member, Print and Drawing Council of Canada; Conseil Québécois de l'Estampe.
Selective Filmography: *JOHN AND THE MISSUS,* Th, 86, CDN, Pro Des/Art Dir; *ALEX, THE LIFE OF A CHILD,* TV, 85, USA, Art Dir; *HAPPY BIRTHDAY TO ME,* Th, 80, CDN, Pro Des; *DIRTY TRICKS,* Th, 79, CDN, Art Dir; *L'HOMME EN COLERE* (LABYRINTH), Th, 78, CDN/F, Art Dir; *REVOLUTION'S ORPHAN,* TV, 78, CDN, Pro Des; *THE WAR IS OVER,* Th, 77, CDN, Pro Des; *BLACK STALLION,* Th, 77, USA, Co-Art Dir; *WAR BETWEEN THE TATES,* TV, 76, USA, Pro Des; *SHOOT,* Th, 75, CDN, Art Dir; *WHY ROCK THE*

(cont/suite)

Our locations run hot and cold.

Considering that British Columbia is four times the size of Texas and has climates that range from rain forest to desert, it's hardly surprising how many films have located here.

In fact, in the past few years, we've been a stand-in for everything from Cambodia to New York City, and from prehistoric America to an uncharted planet far, far away.

Our Film Commission has a solid network of relationships throughout the province, to get you into any area you need. And with our sophisticated transport system, out again too. (After all, life on a glacier is no picnic.)

Call us directly at (604) 660-2732 for scouting information, photo presentations and any other assistance that you require.

We promise your reception will be anything but lukewarm.

Hot Property

Super, Natural British Columbia

British Columbia Film Commission, #802 - 865 Hornby Street, Vancouver, British Columbia, Canada V6Z 2G3

Member of **AFC** ASSOCIATION OF FILM COMMISSIONERS

433

BOAT?, Th, 74, CDN, Pro Des; *THE PYX*, Th, 72, CDN, Art Dir; *FORTUNE AND MEN'S EYES*, Th, 71, CDN/USA, Art Dir.

PRITCHARD, Anne

DGC. 3629 Ave. Laval, Montreal, Que, CAN, H2X 3E1. (514)288-3999.
Types of Production & Categories: Th Film Art Dir/Cos.
Genres: Drama-Th.
Selective Filmography: *JOSHUA THEN AND NOW*, Th, 84, CDN, Art Dir (GENIE); *BEST FRIENDS*, Th, 82, USA, Art Dir; *FANTASTICA*, Th, 80, CDN, Cos (GENIE); *THRESHOLD*, Th, 80, CDN, Art Dir; *A MAN, A WOMAN AND A BANK*, Th, 79, CDN, Art Dir/Cos; *ATLANTIC CITY*, Th, 79, CDN/USA, Art Dir (GENIE); *BLOOD RELATIVES* (LES LIENS DE SANG), Th, 77, CDN/F, Art Dir/Cos; *THE DISAPPEARANCE*, Th, 77, CDN, Art Dir/Cos; *OBSESSION*, Th, 76, USA, Art Dir/Cos; *THE FAR SHORE*, Th, 76, CDN, Art Dir (GENIE); *WHO HAS SEEN THE WIND*, Th, 76, CDN, Art Dir/Cos; *JE SUIS LOIN DE TOI MIGNONNE*, Th, 75, CDN, Art Dir/Cos; *THE APPRENTICESHIP OF DUDDY KRAVITZ*, Th, 74, CDN, Art Dir/Cos; *ALIEN THUNDER*, Th, 72, CDN, Art Dir/Cos; *JOURNEY*, Th, 72, CDN, Cos; *ACT OF THE HEART* (L'ACTE DU COEUR), Th, 70, CDN, Art Dir/Cos (CFA); *LES MALES*, Th, 70, CDN, Art Dir/Cos.

PROULX, Michel

8337 ave. de Gaspé, Montréal, Qué, CAN, H2P 2K2. (514)387-9868.
Types de production et Catégories: l métrage-Dir art; TV film-Dir art.
Types d'oeuvres: Drame-C; Action-C; Documentaire-C&TV.
Curriculum vitae: Né en 1946, Montréal, Québec; bilingue. Etudie à l'Institut des Arts Appliqués, Montréal et un an à l'Institut des Arts Décoratifs, Paris. Directeur artistique à la pige pour longs métrages; a aussi fait les décors pour maintes annonces.
Filmographie sélective: *LES FOUS DE BASSAN*, C, 86, CDN/F, Dir art; *KALAMAZOO*, C, 86, CDN, Dir art; *POUVOIR INTIME*, C, 85, CDN, Dir art; *KEEPING TRACK*, C, 85, CDN, Dir art; *COOK & PEARY: THE RACE TO THE POLE*, TV, 83, USA, Dir art; *LE RUFFIAN*, C, 83, CDN/F, Dir art; *CROSS-COUNTRY*, C, 82, CDN, Dir art; *DREAMWORLD*, C, 81, CDN, Dir art; *THE LUCKY STAR* (LA BELLE ETOILE), C, 80, CDN, Dir art; *VISITING HOURS*, C, 80, CDN, Dir art; *AU REVOIR...A LUNDI* (SEE YOU MONDAY), C, 79, CDN/F, Dir art; *LES BONS DEBARRAS* (GOOD RIDDANCE), C, 78, CDN, Dir art; *ECLAIR AU CHOCOLAT*, C, 78, CDN, Dir art; *PANIQUE*, C, 77/76, CDN, Dir art; *PARLEZ-NOUS D'AMOUR*, C, 76, CDN, Dir art; *POUR LE MEILLEUR ET POUR LE PIRE*, C, 75, CDN, Dir art; *LES ORDRES*, C, 74, CDN, Dir art; *GINA*, C, 74, CDN, Dir art.

ROZON, Gilbert

87 McCulloch, Outremont, Qué, CAN, H2V 3L8. Les Films Rozon Inc., 63 rue Prince-Arthur est, Montréal, Qué, CAN, H2X 1B4. (514)845-3155.
Types de production et Catégories: TV vidéo-Dir art.
Types d'oeuvres: Comédic-TV; Variété-TV.
Curriculum vitae: Né en 1954, Québec; bilingue. Avocat, membre du Barreau.
Filmographie sélective: *'JUSTE POUR RIRE'* (JUST FOR LAUGHS), (22 eps), TV, 85-83, CDN, Dir art.

SARAFINCHAN, Lillian

DGC, IATSE-873. 7 Astley Ave., Toronto, Ont, CAN, M4W 3B3. (416)923-4939.
Types of Production & Categories: Th Film-Pro Des; TV Film-Art Dir.
Genres: Drama-Th&TV; Comedy-Th; Variety-TV; Action-Th&TV.
Biography: Born 1935, Vegreville, Alberta. Education: Banff School of Fine Arts; Ontario College of Art; Associate Fellow, Stong College, York University, 69-77. As
[cont/suite]

an artist, has had may solo exhibitions in Canada, USA; group exhibitions in Kiev, Lvov, Uzhgorod, Ukraine. Has designed for Royal Ontario Museum, various theatres, schools.
Selective Filmography: *DANCING IN THE DARK,* Th, 85, CDN, Pro Des; *'PHILIP MARLOWE PRIVATE EYE'* (2 eps), TV, 85, CDN, Loc M; *HEAD OFFICE,* Th, 84, USA, Loc M; *CHARLIE GRANT'S WAR,* TV, 83, CDN, Assist Des; *SUNDAY IN THE COUNTRY,* Th, 73, CDN, Assist Art Dir; *THE MERRY WIVES OF TOBIAS ROUKE,* Th, 71, CDN, Art Dir; *THE CROWD INSIDE,* Th, 70, CDN, Art Dir.

SAURIOL, Gaudeline

STCQ. 362 Labadie, #1, Montréal, Qué, CAN, H2V 2J8. (514)273-6081.
Types de production et Catégories: l métrage-Dir art; TV film-Dir art.
Types d'oeuvres: Drame-C&TV.
Curriculum vitae: Née à Montréal, Québec; bilingue. Education: Ecole des Métiers Commerciaux, Montréal. Aussi Directeur artistique sur des douzaines d'annonces.
Filmographie sélective: *TRANSIT,* TV, 86, CDN, Dir art; *LE SOURD DANS LA VILLE,* C, 86, CDN, Dir art; *LE DECLIN DE L'EMPIRE AMERICAIN* (THE DECLINE OF THE AMERICAN EMPIRE), C, 85, CDN, Dir art; *ANNE TRISTER,* C, 85, CDN, Dir art; *LA FEMME DE L'HOTEL* (WOMAN IN TRANSIT), C, 84, CDN, Dir art; *CAFFE ITALIA,* C, 84, CDN, Dir art; *RIEN QU'UN JEU* (JUST A GAME), C, 83, CDN, Dir art.

SCHMIDT, Phil

406-1347 Nicola St., Vancouver, B.C., CAN, V6G 2G1. (604)669-0196.
Types of Production & Categories: Th Film-Art Dir; TV Film-Art Dir.
Genres: Drama-Th; Commercials-TV.
Biography: Born 1947, Wadena, Saskatchewan. Education: Bachelor of Fine Arts.
Selective Filmography: *MY AMERICAN COUSIN,* Th, 84, CDN, Art Dir/Assoc Prod.

SMITH, Roy Forge

ACTT, DGC. 284 Indian Rd., Toronto, Ont, CAN, M6R 2X2. (416)767-2534.
Types of Production & Categories: Th Film-Pro Des; TV Film-Pro Des; TV Video-Pro Des.
Genres: Drama-Th&TV; Comedy-Th&TV; Action-Th&TV; Horror-Th&TV.
Biography: Born 1929, London, England. Studied Architecture, Architectural Association School; degree in Art & Design, Hammersmith, London. Post-war national service as cameraman in Fleet Air Army and Navy. Worked in West End theatres; after college, started at BBC London; came to Canada, 57, worked at CBC Toronto and Ottawa until 63; since then, freelanced in Canada and England.
Selective Filmography: *S & M COMIC BOOK,* TV, 86, CDN, Pro Des; *DEADLY BUSINESS,* TV, 85, USA, Pro Des; *TUCKER AND THE HORSE THIEF/ WORKING FOR PEANUTS,* 'FAMILY PLAYHOUSE', TV, 84, CDN, Pro Des; *DARK BUT FULL OF DIAMONDS,* TV, 84, CDN, Pro Des; *MRS. SOFFEL,* Th, 84, USA, Art Dir; *'SCTV',* TV, 83, CDN, Pro Des; *LOOSE ENDS,* Th, 82, CDN, Pro Des; *MELANIE,* Th, 81, CDN, Pro Des; *CLOWN WHITE,* TV, 80, CDN, Pro Des; *THE LAST CHASE,* Th, 80, CDN, Pro Des; *CRIES IN THE NIGHT* (FUNERAL HOME), Th, 79, CDN, Pro Des; *YESTERDAY* (GABRIELLE), Th, 79, CDN, Pro Des; *RUNNING,* Th, 78, CDN, Pro Des; *'THE NEWCOMERS'* (2 eps), TV, 78, CDN, Pro Des; *THE HOUND OF THE BASKERVILLES,* Th, 77, GB, Pro Des; *JABBERWOCKY,* Th, 76, GB, Pro Des; *DEATH WEEKEND* (THE HOUSE BY THE LAKE), Th, 75, CDN, Pro Des; *MONTY PYTHON & THE HOLY GRAIL,* Th, 74, GB, Pro Des.

SPIER, Carol

DGC. 29 Langley Ave., Toronto, Ont, CAN, M4K 1B4. (416)465-2515. 1 Dupont St., #8, Toronto, Ont, CAN, M5R 1V3. (416)537-7095.

(cont/suite)

Types of Production & Categories: Th Film-Art Dir/Pro Des; TV Film-Art Dir/Pro Des; TV Video-Pro Des.
Genres: Drama-Th&TV; Comedy-Th&TV; Science Fiction-Th&TV; Horror-Th&TV.
Biography: Born 1948, Daysland, Alberta. Education: Interior Design, Faculty of Architecture, University of Manitoba.
Selective Filmography: *THE BELIEVERS,* Th, 86, USA, Art Dir; *THE FLY,* Th, 86, USA, Pro Des; *ANNE OF GREEN GABLES,* TV, 85, CDN, Pro Des; *AGNES OF GOD,* Th, 84, USA, Art Dir; *FOLLOW THAT BIRD,* Th, 84, USA, Pro Des; *OVERDRAWN AT THE MEMORY BANK,* TV, 83, CDN/USA, Pro Des; *THE DEAD ZONE,* Th, 83, USA, Pro Des; *RUNNING BRAVE,* Th, 83, CDN/USA, Pro Des; *VIDEODROME,* Th, 82, CDN, Pro Des; *ESCAPE FROM IRAN: THE CANADIAN CAPER,* TV, 80, CDN, Pro Des; *THE FUNNY FARM* (COMICS), Th, 80, CDN, Pro Des; *GAS,* Th, 80, CDN, Pro Des; *SCANNERS,* Th, 80, CDN, Pro Des; *EXPOSURE,* TV, 80, CDN, Art Dir; *THE BROOD,* Th, 79, CDN, Art Dir; *HOG WILD,* Th, 78, CDN, Pro Des; *FAST COMPANY,* Th, 78, CDN, Pro Des; *SEARCH AND DESTROY,* Th, 78, CDN/USA, Art Dir; *RIEL,* TV, 78, CDN, Assist Art Dir; *'SEARCH AND RESCUE'* (18 eps), TV, 78, CDN/USA, Art Dir; *I MISS YOU HUGS AND KISSES,* Th, 77, CDN, Art Dir; *WHY SHOOT THE TEACHER,* Th, 76, CDN, Assist Art Dir; *EQUUS,* Th, 75, USA/GB, Assist Art Dir; *FIND THE LADY,* Th, 75, CDN, Assist Art Dir; *THE MOURNING SUIT,* Th, 74, CDN, Assist Art Dir.

STEER, Kim

1934 William St., No.1, Vancouver, BC, CAN, V5L 2K8. (604)245-2863. 1149 Homer St., #204, Vancouver, BC, CAN, V6Z 1W1. (604)669-1333.
Types of Production & Categories: Th Film-Art Dir.
Genres: Drama-Th; Action-Th.
Biography: Born 1953, Vancouver, British Columbia. Worked as an animator and graphic artist after graduating from Capilano College; freelance interior designer since 80.
Selective Filmography: *ABDUCTED,* Th, 85, CDN, Art Dir; *SAMUEL LOUNT,* Th, 84, CDN, Art Dir.

TRANTER, Barbara - see PRODUCERS

WATKINS, Ted

DGC. 86 Strathcona Ave., Toronto, Ont, CAN, M4J 1G8. (416)466-2553.
Types of Production & Categories: Th Film-Art Dir; TV Film-Art Dir; TV Video-Art Dir.
Genres: Drama-Th&TV; Comedy-TV; Action-Th&TV; Horror-Th.
Biography: Born 1936, U.K.. Settled in Toronto, 59; became involved in art community and theatre; subsequently worked in film and TV; began art directing, 63.
Selective Filmography: *'TRIBUTE TO THE CHAMPIONS'* (2 eps), TV, 86/85, CDN, Art Dir; *FEAR STALKER,* Th, 85, CDN, Art Dir; *'BIZARRE'* (120 eps), TV, 85-81, CDN/USA, Art Dir; *COUNTDOWN TO LOOKING GLASS,* TV, 84, USA, Art Dir; *DECISION 84* (NATIONAL ELECTION), TV, 84, CDN, Art Dir; *SUNDAYS CHILD,* TV, 83, CDN, Art Dir; *CLASS OF '84,* Th, 82, CDN/USA, Art Dir; *HYANNIS AFFAIR,* TV, 82, CDN, Art Dir; *HANK WILLIAMS: THE SHOW HE NEVER GAVE,* Th, 81, CDN, Art Dir; *INCUBUS,* Th, 80, CDN, Pro Des; *HOT TOUCH* (FRENCH KISS), Th, 80, CDN, Pro Des; *TULIPS,* Th, 79, CDN, Art Dir; *HAPPY BIRTHDAY GEMINI,* Th, 79, CDN/USA, Art Dir; *STONE COLD DEAD,* Th, 78, CDN, Art Dir; *THE INTRUDER,* Th, 78, CDN, Art Dir; *SOMETHING'S ROTTEN,* Th, 77, CDN, Art Dir; *OUTRAGEOUS!,* Th, 77, CDN, Art Dir; *RAGTIME SUMMER,* Th, 76, CDN, Art Dir; *A QUIET DAY IN BELFAST,* Th, 73, CDN/GB, Art Dir.

(cont/suite)

438

EDITORS
★
MONTEURS

Film Arts
Film Arts

16/35 post-production
Television and feature
production

461 Church Street

Toronto - Canada

M4Y 2C5

Telephone : 416-962-0181

APPLEBY, George

DGC. R.R.1, Zephyr, Ont, CAN, L0E 1T0. (416)473-2379.
Types of Production & Categories: Th Film-Ed; TV Film-Ed/Dir; TV Video-Ed.
Genres: Drama-Th&TV.
Biography: Born 1939, Toronto, Ontario; grew up in South America; languages: English, Spanish. Won the Wilderness Award for *WOJECK*, 66.
Selective Filmography: *'REALLY WEIRD TALES'* (2 eps), TV, 86, CDN/USA, Ed; *'DANGER BAY'* (4 eps), TV, 86, CDN/USA, Ed; *'RAY BRADBURY THEATRE'* (3 eps), TV, 86/85, CDN, Ed; *'THE HITCHIKER'* (2 eps), TV, 85, CDN/USA, Ed; *MIRACLE AT MOREAUX*, TV, 85, CDN, Ed; *THE EXILE*, TV, 85, CDN, Ed; *FAMILY THERAPY - ANOREXIA*, TV, 84, CDN, Dir; *TUCKER AND THE HORSE THIEF*, 'FAMILY PLAYHOUSE', TV, 84, CDN, Ed; *INCUBUS*, Th, 80, CDN, Ed; *NOTHING PERSONAL*, Th, 79, CDN, Ed; *WILD HORSE HANK*, Th, 78, CDN, Ed **(CFEG)**; *OUTRAGEOUS!*, Th, 77, CDN, Ed; *THE SILENT PARTNER*, Th, 77, CDN, Ed **(CFA)**; *LIFE AMONG THE HURONS*, TV, 76, CDN, Dir; *RITUALS*, Th, 76, CDN, Ed **(CFEG)**; *CASTLEGUARD CAVE - JOURNEY UNDER THE ICE*, TV, 75, CDN, Prod; *'FLIM FLAM'* (26 seg), TV, 75, CDN, Dir; *PARTNERS*, Th, 75, CDN, Ed; *THE FAR SHORE*, Th, 75, CDN, Ed; *DEAR JOE*, TV, 74, CDN, Dir/Prod; *RECOMMENDATION FOR MERCY*, Th, 74, CDN, Ed; *'WORLD RELIGIONS'* (3 parts), TV, 73, CDN, Dir; *'THE WHITE OAKS OF JALNA'* (12 eps), TV, 71, CDN, Ed; *THE REINCARNATE*, Th, 71, CDN, Ed; *'ADVENTURES IN RAINBOW COUNTRY'* (7 eps), TV, 70, CDN/GB/AUS, Spv Ed; *'ANTHOLOGIES/SHORT STORIES'* (15 eps), TV, 68, CDN, Ed **(CFEG)**; *'HATCH'S MILL'* (8 eps), TV, 67, CDN, Ed; *ISABEL*, Th, 67, CDN, Ed **(CFA)**; *'WOJECK'* (6 eps), TV, 66, CDN, Ed; *'SEAWAY'* (8 eps), TV, 65, CDN, Ed; *'FOREST RANGERS'* (34 eps), TV, 64/63, CDN, Ed.

ARCAND, Michel

STCQ. 4321 Berri, Montréal, Qué, CAN, H2J 2P9. (514)523-3948.
Types de production et Catégories: l métrage-Mont/Mont son; c métrage-Mont; TV film-Mont/Mont son; TV vidéo-Mont.
Types d'oeuvres: Drame-C&TV; Comédie-TV; Comédie musicale-C; Documentaire-C&TV.
Curriculum vitae: Né en 1949, Valdor (Abitibi), Québec. Plongée sous-marine 3 étoiles CMAS; photographie sous-marine pour le journal 'La Plongée'. Musicien claviériste et synthétiseur ayant fait beaucoup de scéances et de bandes pour le Musée d'Art Contemporain.
Filmographie sélective: *LA GUEPE*, C, 86, CDN, Mont; *EXIT*, C, 86, CDN, Mont/Mont son; *ANNE TRISTER*, C, 85, CDN, Mont/Mont son; *NIGHT MAGIC*, C, 85, CDN/F, Mont; *UN AMOUR DE QUARTIER'* (13 eps), TV, 84, CDN, Mont; *LA FEMME DE L'HOTEL* (WOMAN IN TRANSIT), C, 84, CDN, Mont/Mont son; *MARIA CHAPDELAINE*, C, 83, CDN/F, Co mont; *LA MARATHONIENNE*, TV, 83, CDN, Comp; *LUCIEN BROUILLARD*, C, 82, CDN, Mont/Mont mus; *SALUT SANTE II*, TV, 82, CDN, Mont; *'LES TRANSISTORS'* (4 eps), TV, 82/81, CDN, Mont; *'VIVRE ICI ET MAINTENANT'* (3 eps), TV, 81, CDN, Mont/Mont son; *LES FILS DE LA LIBERTE*, TV, 81/80, CDN/F, Mont/Mont mus; *HISTOIRE DE FEMME*, C, 80, CDN, Mont; *RUELLE MALENFANT*, C, 79, CDN, Mont/Mont son; *MOUCHE A FEU*, C, 79, CDN, Mont; *LE METRO*, TV, 79/78, CDN, Mont/Mont son; *VIVRE SA VIE*, TV, 78, CDN, Mont/Mont son; *LA LETTRE DE LA NOUVELLE FRANCE*, TV, 78, CDN, Mont; *LE PRIX D'UNE VIE*, TV, 78, CDN, Mont; *GESTES*, C, 78, CDN, Mont/Mont son; *PANDORE*, TV, 77, CDN, Mont/Mont son; *'QUARTIER'* (3 eps), TV, 77, CDN, Mont/Mont son; *RAISON D'ETRE*, C, 77, CDN, Mont son; *COMME DES CHIENS EN PACAGE*, C, 76, CDN, Mont son; *QUEBEC, QUEBEC*, C, 74, CDN, Mont son; *DES VILLES, UN FLEUVE*, C, 74, CDN, Mont son; *MUSTANG*, C, 74, CDN, Ass mont; *CORPS A CORPS*, TV, 73, CDN, Mont/Mont son; *'LES JOUEURS'* (13 eps), TV, 73, CDN, Mont son.

EDITORS/MONTEURS

BACKUS, Barry

169 Seaton St., Toronto, Ont, CAN, M5A 2T5. (416)928-1426. Film Arts, 461 Church St., Toronto, Ont, CAN, M4Y 2C5. (416)962-0181.
Types of Production & Categories: Th Short-Dir; TV Film-Ed.
Genres: Documentary-Th&TV; Educational-TV; Children's-TV; Animation-TV.
Biography: Born 1951, Sudbury, Ontario. Education: Faculty of Engineering, Carleton University, 70/71; Photo Arts and Motion Pictures, Ryerson Polytechnical Institute, 75.
Selective Filmography: *'WHEELED WARRIORS'* (Snd Ed-7 eps), (8 eps), TV, 86/85, USA, FX Ed; *'MASKED HEROES'* (Snd Ed-3 eps), (8 eps), TV, 86/85, USA, FX Ed; *'THE FIFTH ESTATE'* (8 eps), TV, 86-80, CDN, Ed; *PROCEED WITH CAUTION*, In, 86, CDN, Ed; *TURNING TO STONE*, TV, 86, CDN, FX Ed; *BABY JOHN DOE*, TV, 86, CDN, FX Ed; *'KID VIDEO'* (6 eps), TV, 86, USA, FX Ed; *'HULK HOGAN'* (2 eps), TV, 86, USA, FX Ed; *RAPISTS - CAN THEY BE STOPPED?*, 'AMERICA UNDERCOVER', TV, 85, USA, Snd Ed; *SPIRIT OF BATOCHE - THE METIS*, TV, 85, CDN, Ed; *THE VIRGIN*, TV, 84, CDN, Ed; *DAN P. BROWN* (BEYOND REALITY), TV, 84, CDN, Ed; *GATHERING*, TV, 84, CDN, Ed; *HIGH IMPACT WELDING*, In, 84, CDN, Ed; *'INSPECTOR GADGET'* (3 eps), TV, 83, CDN, Ed; *'COUNTRY CANADA'* (4 eps), TV, 83/81, CDN, Ed; *FEVRIER/63*, Th, 83, CDN, Snd Ed; *NEVER DID LIKE THAT RAIN*, MV, 83, CDN, Ed; *'COUNTRY CANADA'* (1 eps), TV, 82, CDN, Dir/Prod/Wr; *'LES ENTREPRENEURS'* (5 eps), TV, 82, CDN, Ed; *C'EST L'ENFANT QUI COMPTE*, TV, 81, CDN, Ed; *'LIFESTYLES FOR FITNESS AND HEALTH'* (7 eps), In, 81, CDN, Ed; *'DENTISTRY TO-DAY'* (13 eps), ED, 80, CDN, Ed; *THE WORDSMITH*, TV, 79, CDN, Snd Ed; *'DOCUMENT'* (4 eps), TV, 79, CDN, Ed; *'DOSSIER'* (2 eps), TV, 79, CDN, Ed; *EASTER RABBIT*, TV, 79, CDN, Ed; *THE GLASS ORCHESTRA*, Th, 78, CDN, Dir/Wr; *PRE-CON*, In, 76, CDN, Dir.

BARCLAY, John

354 Euclid Ave., Toronto, Ont, CAN, M6J 2K2. (416)927-0955. Triune Productions Inc., 24 Ryerson Ave., Ste. 304, Toronto, Ont, CAN, M5T 2P3. (416) 362-9120.
Types of Production & Categories: Th Short-Prod/Dir; TV Film-Ed; TV Video-Ed/Dir.
Genres: Drama-Th&TV; Comedy-TV; Educational-TV; Commercials-TV.
Biography: Born 1956, Pembroke, Ontario. Honours B.F.A in Film Production, York University, 80. *BAY STREET TAP*, winner, Canadian Independent Short Film Showcase, 83; Canada Council Film Production Grant, 84. Founding member, Triune Acting Ensemble.
Selective Filmography: *THE DIPLOMAT*, 'MOTLEY TALES', TV, 86, CDN, Ed; *LITTLE PEOPLE*, Cm, 85, CDN, Ed; *TECHNOLOGY TODAY/A BETTER WAY*, In, 85, CDN, Ed; *'EARTH ODYSSEY'* (13 eps), TV, 83, CDN, Ed; *DANCING FEET*, TV, 83, CDN, Assoc Prod; *BAY STREET TAP*, Th, 82, CDN, Co-Prod/Co-Dir; *JACK HAS IT MADE*, 'MOTLEY TALES', TV, 82, CDN, Dir; *'THERE'S NO PLACE LIKE HOME'* (12 eps), ED, 78, CDN, Assist Dir.

BEAUDOIN, Jean

STCQ. Baude Films, 5169 ave. King Edward, Montréal, Qué, CAN, H4V 2J8. (514)488-1855.
Types de production et Catégories: l métrage-Mont; c métrage-Réal/Mont; TV film-Mont; TV vidéo-Réal/Mont.
Types d'oeuvres: Drame-TV; Comédie musicale-TV; Documentaire-C&TV; Education-C&TV.
Curriculum vitae: Né en 1959.
Filmographie sélective: *'LES FORCES ARMEES CANADIENNES'* (CANADIAN ARMED FORCES), (16 eps), TV, 86/85, CDN, Mont/Sup p pro; *MISTER NUKE IS A FOOL*, MV, 86, CDN, Mont/Sup p pro; *LA LAURENTIENNE MUTUELLE*
(cont/suite)

D'ASSURANCE, In, 86, CDN, Réal/Mont/Cam; *PROGRAMME D'ESSAIS D'AUTOBUS ARTICULES URBAINS,* TV, 86, CDN, Mont/Réal/Sc; *A DASH OF EXCELLENCE,* In, 86, CDN, Mont/Sup p pro; *'TOUCHONS DU BOIS'* (3 eps), TV, 85, CDN, Mont/Sup p pro; *'POUR UNE CHANSON'* (6 eps), TV, 84, CDN, Mont; *SUR LES CHEMINS DE MA MAISON,* TV, 84, CDN, Mont; *ENERGY FOR TOMORROW,* TV, 84, CDN, Mont; *GARDE A L'AFFICHE,* C, 83, CDN, Mont; *FRANCOMER II,* TV, 83, CDN, Mont/Sup p pro; *'PROPOS D'ECOLOGIE'* (6 c métrages), C, 83, CDN, Mont; *A MATTER OF CUNNING,* TV, 83, CDN, Mont; *'ADER'* (25 eps), TV, 82, CDN, Mont.

BELANGER, Fernand - voir REALISATEURS

BENWICK, Rick

DGC, IATSE-212. 904 - 2nd Ave.N.W., Calgary, Alta, CAN, T2N 0E6. (403)283-5032.
Types of Production & Categories: Th Film-Ed; Th Short-Ed; TV Film-Ed; TV Video-Ed.
Genres: Drama-Th&TV; Science Fiction-Th; Horror-Th; Commercials-TV.
Biography: Born 1948, Alberta. B.A.A., Motion Picture Studies, Ryerson Polytechnical Institute. Picture, sound editor on 48 documentary films, 205 commercials, 77-86.
Selective Filmography: *HYPER SAPIEN,* Th, 85, USA, Ed; *YEAR OF THE DRAGON,* Th, 84, USA, Assist Ed; *FINDERS KEEPERS,* Th, 84, USA, Assist Ed; *WILD PONY,* TV, 83, CDN, Ed/Dial Ed; *LE RUFFIAN,* Th, 82, CDN/F, Assist Ed; *GHOSTKEEPER,* Th, 81, CDN, Assist Ed; *TOUCHED BY LOVE,* Th, 80, USA, Assist Ed; *WILD HORSE HANK,* Th, 78, CDN, Assist Ed.

BERNER, Tom

Film Arts, 461 Church St., Toronto, Ont, CAN, M4Y 2C5. (416)962-0181.
Types of Production & Categories: Th Film-Ed; TV Film-Ed.
Genres: Drama-Th&TV; Musical-TV; Action-Th&TV; Documentary-Th&TV.
Biography: Born 1943, Toronto, Ontario. Editor for 20 years; post production supervisor/editor at Film Arts since 63.
Selective Filmography: *ISLAND LOVE SONG,* TV, 86, CDN, Ed; *TURNING TO STONE,* TV, 85, CDN, Ed; *DANCING IN THE DARK,* Th, 85, CDN, Ed; *THE OTHER KINGDOM* (mini-series), TV, 84, CDN, Ed; *'NATURE OF THINGS'* (2 eps), TV, 83/82, CDN, Ed; *CHAUTAUQUA GIRL,* TV, 82, CDN, Ed; *A PATH OF HIS OWN,* TV, 80, CDN, Ed (CFTA); *YOU'VE COME A LONG WAY KATIE* (mini-series), TV, 80/79, CDN, Ed; *DIEPPE 1942,* TV, 79, CDN, Ed; *THE QUIETER REVOLUTION,* TV, 78, CDN, Ed; *THE FAMILY PRINCE,* TV, 75, CDN, Ed; *'PEOPLE OF OUR TIME'* (8 eps), TV, 74/73, CDN, Ed; *'THIS HOUR HAS SEVEN DAYS'* TV, 65/64, CDN, Co-Ed.

BOCKING, Robert - see DIRECTORS

BOYER, Claire

SGCT. 819 ave. de l'Epée, Outremont, Qué, CAN, H2V 3V2. (514)271-6471.
ONF, C.P.6100, Montréal, Qué, CAN, H3C 3H5. (514)283-9371.
Types de production et Catégories: l métrage-Mont; c métrage-Réal.
Types d'oeuvres: Drame-C; Documentaire-C.
Curriculum vitae: Née en 1928, Montréal, Québec; bilingue. Cours lettres-sciences, cours post-scolaires en philosophie et littérature française, cours de coupe et de sculpture sur bois.
Filmographie sélective: *MEMOIRE D'UNE ENFANT DES ANDES,* C, 85, CDN, Mont; *LES ILLUSIONS TRANQUILLES,* C, 84, CDN, Mont; *LA DAME EN COULEURS* (OUR LADY OF THE PAINTS), C, 84, CDN, Mont; *LA GRANDE ALLURE,* C, 84, CDN/F, 2e Mont; *LEO GERVAIS, SCULPTEUR,* TV, 83, CDN, Réal/Mont; *UNE INSTALLATION A DISPOSER,* C, 83, CDN, Mont; *CHEMIN*

(cont/suite)

FAISANT, C, 81, CDN, Mont; *LE COQ DU CLOCHER,* C, 80, CDN, Réal/Mont; *GENS D'ABITIBI,* C, 79/78, CDN, Mont; *C'ETAIT UN QUEBECOIS EN BRETAGNE, MADAME,* C, 76, CDN, Mont; *CAP D'ESPOIR,* C, 75, CDN, Co mont; *L'INTERDIT,* C, 75, CDN, Ass mont son; *LE RETOUR A LA TERRE,* C, 74, CDN, Mont; *SOURIS TU M'INQUIETES,* 'EN TANT QUE FEMMES', TV, 73, CDN, Mont/Mont son; *J'ME MARIE, J'ME MARIE PAS,* 'EN TANT QUE FEMMES', TV, 73, CDN, Mont; *LE BONHOMME,* C, 72, CDN, Mont; *MON ONCLE ANTOINE,* C, 71, CDN, Co mont; *ST-URBAIN DE TROYES,* C, 71, CDN, Ass mont; *DANS NOS FORETS,* C, 71, CDN, Ass mont; *QUESTION DE VIE,* C, 69, CDN, Ass mont; *WOW,* C, 68, CDN, Ass mont; *PARCS ATLANTIQUES,* C, 66, CDN, Rég; *COMMENT SAVOIR...,* C, 65, CDN, Rég; *LE REGNE D'UN JOUR,* C, 65, CDN, Rég.

BROWN, Les

DGC. 51 Garnock Ave., Toronto, Ont, CAN, M4K 1M1. (416)465-1339. 409 King St.W., Toronto, Ont, CAN. (416)598-2260.
Types of Production & Categories: TV Film-Ed.
Genres: Drama-TV; Documentary-TV; Educational-TV; Children's-TV.
Biography: Born 1939, Boston, Massachusetts; Canadian citizen; knowledge of French, German, Russian, Italian, Spanish. Graduate of Harvard and U.S.C.. Winner of the Bell Northern Award for *JET SPEED AT GROUND ZERO.*
Selective Filmography: *PRISON MOTHER, PRISON DAUGHTER,* TV, 86, CDN, Ed; *'PHILIP MARLOWE PRIVATE EYE'* (2 eps), TV, 85, CDN, Ed; *VALENTINE'S REVENGE,* TV, 84, USA, Ed; *THE LIFER AND THE LADY,* TV, 84, CDN, Ed; *FOR ALL THE GOOD INTENTIONS,* TV, 84, CDN, Ed; *'VANDERBERG'* (6 eps), TV, 83, CDN, Ed; *FINAL EDITION/EVERY PERSON IS GUILTY,* 'FOR THE RECORD', TV, 82, CDN, Ed; *HUNTERS OF CHABUT,* TV, 82, CDN/USA, Ed **(D EMMY)**; *JET SPEED AT GROUND ZERO,* 'TARGET THE IMPOSSIBLE', TV, 73, CDN, Ed.

BRUNJES, Ralph

DGC. 17 Donalbain Crescent, Thornhill, Ont, CAN, L3T 3S3. (416)889-3370. Inverclyde Film Prods. Ltd., 409 King St. W., Toronto, Ont, CAN. (416)598-2260.
Types of Production & Categories: Th Film-Ed; TV Film-Ed.
Genres: Drama-Th&TV; Comedy-Th&TV; Action-Th&TV; Horror-Th.
Biography: Born 1944, Dunoon, Scotland; Canadian citizen. Twenty years experience (hundreds of documentaries, dramas, specials).
Selective Filmography: *THE LAST SEASON,* TV, 86, CDN, Ed; *'AIRWAVES'* (13 eps), TV, 86, CDN, Spv Ed; *'REALLY WEIRD TALES'* (1 eps), TV, 86, CDN/ USA, Ed; *OAKMOUNT HIGH,* TV, 85, CDN, Ed; *THE PLAYGROUND,* 'RAY BRADBURY THEATRE', TV, 85, CDN, Ed; *AND MILES TO GO,* TV, 85, CDN, Ed; *LOVE AND LARCENY,* TV, 84, CDN, Ed; *GENTLE SINNERS,* TV, 83, CDN, Ed; *OVERDRAWN AT THE MEMORY BANK,* TV, 83, CDN/USA, Spv Snd Ed; *A MATTER OF SEX,* TV, 83, CDN/USA, Co-Ed; *UTILITIES,* Th, 82, CDN, P Pro Spv; *FALCON'S GOLD* (ROBBERS OF THE SACRED MOUNTAIN), Th, 82, CDN, Ed; *DEATH BITE* (SPASMS), Th, 81, CDN, Ed; *I MARRIED THE KLONDIKE* (3 parts), TV, 81, CDN, Spv Ed; *ONCE,* TV, 80, CDN, Ed; *KILLER INSTINCT* (CHATWILL'S VERDICT), Th, 80, CDN, Ed; *CRIES IN THE NIGHT* (FUNERAL HOME), Th, 79, CDN, Ed **(CFEG)**; *ONE OF OUR OWN,* TV, 79, CDN, Ed; *A WORLD OF DARKNESS,* TV, 77, CDN, Ed; *GOLDENROD,* Th, 76, CDN, Co-Ed.

BUCHAN, Bob

53 Isleworth Ave., Toronto, Ont, CAN, M4E 1J6. (416)698-4815. Flickers, 59 Mutual St., Toronto, Ont, CAN, M5B 2A9. (416)368-4594.
Genres: Commercials-TV.
Biography: Born 1947. Fifteen years experience in film: feature, drama, documentary, 70-75; mostly commercials and short films since 75.

CASTELYN, Chris

DGC. 155 Balliol St., Ste. 1001, Toronto, Ont, CAN, M4S 1C4. (416)486-1507.
Types of Production & Categories: TV Film-Ed; TV Video-Ed.
Genres: Drama-TV; Documentary-TV; Educational-TV; Industrial-TV.
Biography: Canadian citizen; languages: English, French, German, Dutch.
Education: Arts & Sciences, Data Processing and Architectural Design, McGill
University and Sir George Williams U.. Films he has edited have won numerous
awards including: Blue Ribbons (N.Y.), Hugo (Chicago).
Selective Filmography: *MORE THAN MEETS THE EYE/AN OUNCE OF
PREVENTION,* 'VISTA', TV, 85/84, CDN, Ed; *'SKETCHES OF OUR TOWN'*
(13 eps), TV, 84, CDN, Ed; *PIONEERS OF THE FUTURE,* 'VISTA', TV, 83,
CDN, Ed; *'STRANGE BUT TRUE'* (24 eps), TV, 83, CDN/USA/GB, Ed;
'VISIONS' (13 eps), TV, 83/82, CDN, Ed; *'MASTER CLASS'* (4 eps), TV, 82,
CDN, Ed; *'KIDSWORLD',* TV, 82-78, CDN, Ed; *'TEN-THOUSAND-DAY WAR'*
(4 parts), TV, 82, CDN/USA, Ed; *'GARDENS OF MAN'* (13 eps), TV, 81, CDN/
F/GB, Ed; *'PORTRAITS OF POWER'* (26 eps), TV, 80, CDN/USA, Ed; *THE
MANNIKIN,* 'DARK AND DANGEROUS', TV, 79, CDN/GB, Ed; *'CAMERA
AND SONG'* (4 eps), TV, 78, CDN, Ed; *'PLANET OF MAN'* (13 eps), TV, 77,
CDN/USA, Ed; *IT'S ONLY ROCK'N ROLL,* TV, 77, CDN/USA, Ed; *'SEARCH
FOR VALUES'* (15 eps), TV, 76, CDN/USA, Ed; *'THEMES IN LITERATURE'*
(6 eps), TV, 76, CDN/USA, Ed; *'RUSSIAN REVOLUTION'* (3 eps), TV, 76,
CDN/USA, Ed; *'TO BE A WOMAN'* (6 eps), TV, 76, CDN/USA, Ed;
'CHILDREN'S CLASSICS' (4 eps), TV, 76, CDN/USA, Ed.

CEREGHETTI, Jean-Pierre

STCQ. 317 rue Rivermere, St-Lambert, Qué, CAN, J4R 2G3. (514)672-3296.
Types de production et Catégories: l métrage-Mont; c métrage-Mont; TV film-Mont.
Types d'oeuvres: Drame-C&TV; Action-TV; Documentaire-TV; Animation-C.
Curriculum vitae: Né en 1946, Binche, Belgique; au Canada depuis 73; bilingue.
Etudes: Beaux-Arts, Musique, Cinéma, TV (I.A.D., Bruxelles), Philosophie.
Filmographie sélective: *LES SOMNAMBULES,* TV, 86, CDN, Mont; *LE MATOU*
(THE ALLEY CAT), C, 85, CDN/F, Sup mont; *DU REVE AU DEFI* (SOFATI-
SOCONAV-QUEBEC), TV, 84, CDN, Mont; *COMMUNICATIONS*
(L'ORDINATEUR), TV, 83, CDN, Mont; *MALADIES HEREDITAIRES* (LES
GRANDES MALADIES), TV, 83, CDN, Mont; *OBESITE/INFERTILITE,*
'DOSSIER SANTE', TV, 83, CDN, Mont; *UN W.E. HEUREUX,* TV, 82, CDN,
Réal; *J.DE TONNANCOURT/PAUL DAVID/MAURICE PROULX,* 'VISAGE',
TV, 82/81, CDN, Mont; *LES SONS/LE CONTE/LE CANCER,* 'DOSSIER', TV,
82-79, CDN, Mont; *FERDINAND RIONDI/MICHELINE BEAUCHEMIN/
CARDINAL LEGER,* 'VISAGE', TV, 81/80, CDN, Mont; *DE JOUR EN JOUR,*
TV, 80, CDN, Sup mont; *'MORDICUS'* (13 eps), TV, 80, CDN, Mont; *PIERRE
GAUVREAU/PAUL LOYONNET,* 'VISAGE', TV, 79, CDN, Mont; *ANNE
HEBERT,* TV, 79, CDN, Mont; *JEAN NARRACHE,* TV, 79, CDN, Mont; *'LES
COLLECTIONNEURS'* (13 eps), TV, 78, CDN, Mont; *HABITAT,* TV, 78, CDN/
F/B, Mont; *'SCIENCE EN QUESTION'* (16 eps), TV, 77, CDN, Mont;
'SURVILLE' (17 eps), TV, 76, CDN, Mont; *TINTIN ET LE LAC AUX
REQUINS,* C, 73, B, Sup mont; *LUCKY LUKE,* C, 72, B/F, Mont.

CHAPMAN, Christopher - see DIRECTORS

CHAREST, Gaétan - voir REALISATEURS

CLAIROUX, Jacques

ARRFQ, SARDEC. 339 che. de la Rabsatelière E., St-Bruno-de-Montarville, Qué,
CAN, J3V 1Z6. (514)653-7746.
Types de production et Catégories: TV film-Mont/Réal; TV vidéo-Réal.
Types d'oeuvres: Variété-TV; Documentaire-TV; Expérimental-TV.
Curriculum vitae: Né en 1945, Verdun, Québec. Onze ans comme monteur à Radio-
Canada. Publication: 'Coeur de Hot-Dog'.

(cont/suite)

Filmographie sélective: *LG4 - PLUS QUE DE L'ENERGIE,* TV, 84, CDN, Mont; *DU QUETEUX AU JOUEUR D'ORGUE DE BARBARIE,* TV, 83, CDN, Réal/Prod; *QUAND 1200 ENFANTS S'ACCORDENT...,* TV, 81, CDN, Mont/Sc; *'OPTION CEGEP'* (30 eps), TV, 81-79, CDN, Réal; *77 JUIN,* C, 79, CDN, Mont/Réal; *TRISTAN UND ISOLDE,* TV, 77, CDN, Mont; *LA SUPERFRANCOFETE,* TV, 76, CDN, Mont; *RAOUL DUGUAY,* TV, 75, CDN, Mont.

CLANCEY, Patrick

NABET 57. 14 Appomattox, Irvine, CA, USA, 92720. (714)551-2195. ABC, 4151 Prospect Ave., Hollywood, CA, USA, 90027. (213)557-7777.
Types of Production & Categories: TV Video-Ed.
Genres: Drama-TV; Comedy-TV; Variety-TV; Commercials-TV.
Biography: Born 1956, Vancouver, British Columbia. Staff editor, ABC TV, Hollywood since 80.
Selective Filmography: *PHASE III/CAN YOU FEEL IT?/MOONLIGHTING CAMPAIGN,* Cm, 85, USA, Ed; *I THOUGHT IT WAS YOU,* MV, 79, USA, Ed; *'THE ALAN HAMEL SHOW'* (200 eps), TV, 77/76, CDN, Ed; *'THE ROLF HARRIS SHOW'* (26 eps), TV, 77, CDN, Ed; *THE TOMMY BANKS SHOW* (pilot), TV, 76, CDN, Ed.

COLE, Stan

IATSE-771, IATSE-776. 26 Cranbrooke Ave., Toronto, Ont, CAN, M5M 1M4. (416)483-7034.
Types of Production & Categories: Th Film-Ed; TV Film-Ed; TV Video-Ed.
Genres: Drama-Th&TV; Comedy-Th; Musical-Th; Action-Th&TV.
Biography: Born 1936, Toronto, Ontario.
Selective Filmography: *FROM THE HIP,* Th, 86, USA, Ed; *TURK 182,* Th, 85, USA, Ed; *RHINESTONE,* Th, 84, USA, Ed; *A CHRISTMAS STORY,* Th, 83, CDN/USA, Ed; *'THE HITCHIKER'* (pilot), TV, 83, CDN/USA, Ed; *PORKY'S II - THE NEXT DAY* (CHEZ PORKY II - LE LENDEMAIN), Th, 82, CDN, Ed; *PORKY'S* (CHEZ PORKY), Th, 81, CDN, Ed; *PHOBIA,* Th, 80, CDN, Ed; *MURDER BY DECREE,* Th, 79, CDN, Ed **(GENIE)**; *WHY SHOOT THE TEACHER,* Th, 76, CDN, Ed; *JACOB TWO-TWO MEETS THE HOODED FANG,* Th, 75, CDN, Ed; *BLACK CHRISTMAS* (SILENT NIGHT, EVIL NIGHT), Th, 74, CDN, Ed **(CFA)**; *'SALTY'* (12 eps), TV, 73, CDN, Ed; *NEPTUNE FACTOR,* Th, 71, CDN, Ed.

COLLIER, Mike - see DIRECTORS

COLLINS, Alan - see DIRECTORS

CORRIVEAU, André

STCQ. 590 Labonté, Longueuil, Qué, CAN, J4H 2R3. (514)679-3098.
Types de production et Catégories: l métrage-Mont; c métrage-Mont.
Types d'oeuvres: Drame-C; Comédie-C; Action-C; Documentaire-C.
Curriculum vitae: Né en 1946, Longueuil, Québec; bilingue. Diplômé de l'Institut des Hautes Etudes Cinématographiques, Paris, 68.
Filmographie sélective: *HENRI,* C, 86, CDN, Mont; *POUVOIR INTIME,* C, 85, CDN, Mont; *C'EST COMME UNE PEINE D'AMOUR,* TV, 84, CDN, Mont; *LA GUERRE DES TUQUES* (THE DOG WHO STOPPED THE WAR), C, 84, CDN, Mont **(GENIE)**; *BONHEUR D'OCCASION* (THE TIN FLUTE), C, 82, CDN, Mont; *LES YEUX ROUGES,* C, 82, CDN, Mont; *LA QUARANTAINE,* C, 82, CDN, Mont; *LES BEAUX SOUVENIRS,* C, 81, CDN, Mont; *L'AFFAIRE COFFIN* (THE COFFIN AFFAIR), C, 80, CDN, Mont; *MOURIR A TUE-TETE* (A SCREAM OF SILENCE), C, 79, CDN, Mont; *LES BONS DEBARRAS* (GOOD RIDDANCE), C, 78, CDN, Mont **(GENIE)**; *'COMME LES SIX*

(cont/suite)

DOIGTS DE LA MAIN' (20 eps), TV, 77, CDN, Mont; *LE SOLEIL SE LEVE EN RETARD,* C, 75, CDN, Mont; *L'EAU CHAUDE L'EAU FRETTE,* C, 75, CDN, Mont; *IL ETAIT UNE FOIS DANS L'EST,* C, 74, CDN, Mont; *NOEL ET JULIETTE,* C, 73, CDN, Mont; *LE MARTIEN DE NOEL,* C, 70, CDN, Mont.

DANDY, Michael

51 Alexander St., #1119, Toronto, Ont, CAN, M4Y 1B3. (416)920-6644. Film Arts, 461 Church St., Toronto, Ont, CAN, M4Y 2C5. (416)962-0181.
Types of Production & Categories: Th Short-Ed/Snd Ed; TV Film-Ed/Snd Ed.
Genres: Drama-TV; Musical-TV; Documentary-Th&TV; Educational-TV.
Biography: Born 1955, Toronto, Ontario. Edited *TRIBUTE TO MARTIN SCORSESE* for the Festival of Festivals, 82.
Selective Filmography: *'THE FIFTH ESTATE'* (8 eps), TV, 86-83, CDN, Ed; *ROOTS ATHLETICS,* Cm, 86/85, CDN, Ed; *LES CANADIENS,* TV, 85, CDN, Co-Ed/Snd Ed/Snd Rec; *COMPANY OF ADVENTURERS,* TV, 85, CDN, Ed; *MINOMEN HARVEST,* Th, 85, CDN, Ed/Snd Ed; *CLEARED FOR TAKE-OFF,* Tn, 85-83, CDN, Ed/Snd Rec.

DE BAYSER, Eric

STCQ. 1303 Bernard O., #2, Outremont, Qué, CAN, H2V 1W1. (514)276-5914.
Types de production et Catégories: l métrage-Mont; c métrage-Mont; TV film-Mont/Réal.
Types d'oeuvres: Drame-C&TV; Comédie-C&TV; Documentaire-C&TV.
Curriculum vitae: Né en 1937, Paris, France; immigré au Canada, 61; citoyen français et canadien. ONF, 63-73, plus de 77 films. Remporte le Prix du Meilleur Film Canadien au Festival du Film de Vancouver, 67 pour *LA TELEVISION EST LA.* Carte professionnelle de monteur à Paris.
Filmographie sélective: *LE CHOIX D'UN PEUPLE,* C, 85, CDN, Mont son; *FREEDOM TO MOVE,* C, 85, CDN, Mont; *ENVOYEZ D'L'AVANT NOS GENS,* 'LE SON DES FRANCAIS EN AMERIQUE', TV, 75, CDN, Mont; *DENIS VANIER,* 'LA VIE QU'ON MENE', TV, 74, CDN, Mont; *LES FILLES DU ROY,* 'EN TANT QUE FEMMES', TV, 74/73, CDN, Mont; *ETES-VOUS SEULS?,* 'TEMOIGNAGE P', TV, 73, CDN, Mont; *THE NETSILIK ESKIMO TODAY,* 'NETSILIK', C, 72, CDN/USA, Sup mont; *VOUDOU-HAITI 1972,* TV, 72, F, Mont; *CONTENEURS,* C, 71, CDN, Mont; *LES ROCHASSIERS,* C, 69, CDN, Mont; *VERTIGE,* C, 68, CDN, Mont; *LA TELEVISION EST LA,* C, 67, CDN, Mont/Co réal; *REGARDS SUR L'OCCULTISME,* C, 65, CDN, Sc; *PERCE ON THE ROCKS,* C, 64, CDN, Mont; *LA FIN DES ETES,* C, 63, CDN, Mont.

DESJARDINS, Jacques

SARDEC. 6436 ave. Faribault, #4, Montréal, Qué, CAN, H1N 1G6. (514)254-0522. Montage Eclair Inc., 1276 rue Amherst, Montréal, Qué, CAN. (514)849-2241.
Types de production et Catégories: c métrage-Mont/Sc; TV film-Mont/Sc.
Types d'oeuvres: Drame-C&TV; Documentaire-TV.
Curriculum vitae: Né en 1955, Montréal, Québec; bilingue. Certificat en Gestion d'entreprise. Monteur pigiste pour la TV, 79-86: émissions spéciales, *LE POINT, REPERES, TELEMAG, PREMIERE PAGE, SECOND REGARD, LA SEMAINE VERTE, AU JOUR LE JOUR, FEMME D'AUJOURD'HUI, L'OBSERVATEUR,* etc..
Filmographie sélective: *ON PEUT SE DEBROUILLER SEUL,* TV, 79, CDN, Mont/Sc/Réal/Prod; *BETONVILLE,* C, 77/76, CDN, Mont/Sc/Réal/Prod.

DUPUIS, François

APFVQ, ARRFQ, STCQ. 1069, Rte. 219, Hemmingford, Qué, CAN, J0L 1H0. (514)247-2579. ACPAV, 1050 Dorchester E., Montréal, Qué, CAN, H2L 2L6. (514)849-1381.

(cont/suite)

EDITORS/MONTEURS

Types de production et Catégories: l métrage-Mont/Prod; c métrage-Réal; TV film-Mont.
Types d'oeuvres: Drame-C&TV; Documentaire-C&TV; Education-TV.
Curriculum vitae: Né en 1947. *RAILI MINKANEN* gagne le Wilderness Award; meilleur film expérimental, Yorkton, pour *LES OISEAUX NE MEURENT PAS DE FAIM.*
Filmographie sélective: *LE DERNIER HAVRE,* C, 86, CDN, Mont; *O PICASSO,* C, 85, CDN, Prod; *PLUIE D'ETE,* C, 84, CDN, Mont; *POURQUOI L'ETRANGE M ZOLOCK S'INTERESSAIT-IL A LA BANDE DESSINEE?,* C, 83, CDN, Mont; *LES CANDIDATS,* C, 81, CDN, Prod; *EN PLEIN COEUR,* TV, 81, CDN, Réal/Co sc; *T'ETAIS BELLE AVANT,* TV, 80, CDN, Mont; *COGNE-DUR,* C, 79, CDN, Mont; *LES OISEAUX NE MEURENT PAS DE FAIM,* C, 79, CDN, Réal/Sc; *LA FICTION NUCLEAIRE,* C, 78, CDN, Mont; *LES BORGES,* TV, 77, CDN, Mont; *LA CRUE,* C, 76, CDN, Mont; *JOS CARIBOU,* C, 75, CDN, Mont; *LES AVENTURES D'UNE JEUNE VEUVE,* C, 74, CDN, Mont; *JUSTE POUR PARTIR LE MONDE,* TV, 74, CDN, Mont; *ANNE HEBERT,* TV, 74, CDN, Mont; *RAILI MINKANEN,* TV, 73, CDN, Mont; *LE SYSTEME DE LA LANGUE FRANCAISE,* TV, 72, CDN, Mont; *SERGIO LEONE,* TV, 72, CDN, Mont; *JACQUES FERRON QUI ETES-VOUS?,* TV, 71, CDN, Ass mont; *300 MILLIONS POUR L'AUTOROUTE,* C, 71, CDN, Mont/Réal; *LES GARS DE LAPALME,* C, 71, CDN, Mont/Co réal; *SPECIAL DELIVERY,* C, 71, CDN, Mont/Réal.

ELDRIDGE, Scott

DGC. 12 Lynwood Ave., Toronto, Ont, CAN, M4V 1K2. (416)960-1258.
Types of Production & Categories: TV Film-Ed.
Genres: Documentary-TV; Music Video-TV.
Biography: Born 1956. B.A., University of Windsor, 78.
Selective Filmography: *LOST SOMEWHERE INSIDE YOUR LOVE/GOOD OLD ROCK AND ROLL,* MV, 86/85, CDN, Ed/Dir; *TAKE ME AS I AM,* MV, 84, CDN, Ed/Dir; *INTRODUCING ASHLEY AND KIMBERLY,* TV, 83, CDN, Ed.

ERICKSON, Jim

197 St. Clarens Ave., Toronto, Ont, CAN, M6H 3W2. (416)534-0384. Suite One Video Inc., 2180 Yonge St., Main Floor, South Tower, Toronto, Ont, CAN, M4S 2B9. (416)440-0148.
Types of Production & Categories: Th Film-Ed; TV Film-Ed; TV Video-Ed.
Genres: Drama-TV; Documentary-TV; Animation-Th; Commercials-TV.
Biography: Born 1956. Honours B.A., Motion Picture Production. Partner at Suite One Video Inc..
Selective Filmography: *FOOLING AROUND WITH SCIENCE* 'OWL TV', (10 eps), TV, 86/85, CDN, Ed; *'VID KIDS'* (26 eps), TV, 86/85, CDN, Co-Ed; *'MATH WORKS'* (2 eps), TV, 85, CDN, Ed; *THE CARE BEARS MOVIE,* Th, 85, CDN, Ed; *'ROCKET BOY'* (5 eps), TV, 85/84, CDN, Ed; *BICYGULL,* TV, 84, CDN, Ed/Dir/Comp; *'EARTH ODYSSEY'* (2 eps), TV, 84, CDN, Wr.

FANFARA, Stephan

DGC. 70 Cambridge Ave., #633, Toronto, Ont, CAN, M4K 2L5. (416)461-7010. Rock 'N' Reel Motion Pictures, 14 Bulwer St., Toronto, Ont, CAN, M5T 2V3. (416)597-0404.
Types of Production & Categories: Th Film-Ed; TV Film-Ed; TV Video-Ed.
Genres: Drama-Th&TV; Comedy-TV; Action-Th; Music Video-TV.
Biography: Born 1950.
Selective Filmography: *PRESENCE OF THE HEART,* MV, 86, CDN, Ed; *RECRUITS,* Th, 85, CDN, Ed; *WAVE BABIES,* MV, 85, CDN, Ed/Prod; *LOOSE SCREWS,* Th, 84, CDN, Ed; *THE HIGHWAY,* TV, 83, CDN, Ed; *JIMMY AND*

(cont/suite)

LUKE, TV, 82, CDN, Ed/Prod; *THE AMATEUR,* Th, 81, CDN, Ed; *LOVE* (3 parts), Th, 80, CDN, Ed; *HAPPY BIRTHDAY GEMINI,* Th, 79, CDN/USA, Ed.

FAVREAU, Robert - voir REALISATEURS

FULLER, Michael

271 Silverbirch Ave., Toronto, Ont, CAN, M4E 3L6. (416)698-5047. Film Arts, 461 Church St., Toronto, Ont, CAN, M4Y 2C5. (416)962-0181.
Types of Production & Categories: Th Film-Ed/Dir; Th Short-Ed/Dir; TV Film-Ed/Dir.
Genres: Drama-TV; Documentary-Th&TV; Educational-TV; Children's-TV.
Biography: Born 1949, London, Ontario. B.A., English, Philosophy, Film, Queen's University, 70. Worked extensively as cameraman; professional musician with film recording experience, 70-74. Films he has edited have won major awards at Chicago and New York Film Festivals.
Selective Filmography: *GREAT LAKES SALMON ADVENTURE,* Th, 86, CDN, Dir/Ed; *'THE FIFTH ESTATE'* (125 eps), TV, 86-76, CDN, Ed; *LES CANADIENS,* TV, 85, CDN, Co-Ed; *THE BEACH WITH JOHN SEWELL,* 'NEIGHBOURHOODS', TV, 84, CDN, Dir/Wr; *THE BROKERS,* TV, 84, CDN, Ed; *NIGHTSHIFT,* MV, 84, CDN, Ed; *ALBERTO SALAZAAR & BILL ROGERS,* 'THE WORLD'S GREATEST ATHLETES', TV, 83, CDN, Ed; *MAGIC IN THE SKY,* TV, 82, CDN, Ed; *ICE FLIGHT,* TV, 78, CDN, Dir/Ed/Cam/Wr; *'UP CANADA'* (weekly), TV, 74-72, CDN, Assist Ed/Ed; *DENE,* TV, 72, CDN, Dir/Co-Prod/Ed/Cam.

GIBB, Alan

110 Erskine Ave., #808, Toronto, Ont, CAN, M4P 1Y5. Film Images Inc., 2 College St., Suite 304, Toronto, Ont, CAN, M5G 1K3. (416)928-9687.
Types of Production & Categories: TV Film-Ed/Prod.
Genres: Drama-TV; Documentary-TV; Educational-TV; Children's-TV.
Biography: Born 1947, Lisburn, Northern Ireland; British citizen, Canadian landed immigrant. Education: Journalism, Centennial College. Nine years at CBC; partner, Film Images Inc.. *GOLD: THE HEMLO STORY* won a Silver Medal, N.Y.; *WILD GOOSE JACK,* Blue Ribbon, American Film Festival.
Selective Filmography: *'INDONESIA: A GENERATION OF CHANGE'* (6 eps), TV, 86, CDN, Dir; *'MARKET PLACE'* (38 eps), TV, 85/76, CDN, Ed; *MR. NEVER LEARN MEETS THE FIREFIGHTER,* 'MR. NEVER LEARN MEETS...', TV, 85, CDN, Ed/Prod; *SCOUTS!,* TV, 85, CDN, Ed; *GOLD: THE HEMLO STORY,* TV, 84, CDN, Ed; *QUEST FOR THE CITY OF DAVID,* TV, 84, CDN, Ed; *EVERYBODY,* TV, 84, CDN, Ed; *WILD GOOSE JACK,* TV, 83, CDN, Ed; *A QUESTION OF CONFIDENCE,* TV, 83, CDN, Ed; *THE CABBAGETOWN KID/SKI PREVIEW,* 'SPORTS WEEKEND', TV, 83/82, CDN, Ed/Prod; *WINE/THE GRASSLANDS,* 'COUNTRY CANADA', TV, 83/82, CDN, Ed; *'THE WINNERS'* (3 eps), TV, 81, CDN, Ed; *'JUST ASK INC.'* (13 eps), TV, 81, CDN, Ed; *DOROTHY LIVESAY THE WOMAN I AM,* TV, 80, CDN, Ed; *'THE PHOENIX TEAM'* (2 eps), TV, 80, CDN, Ed; *'NATURE OF THINGS'* (4 eps), TV, 79, CDN, Ed; *MUSIC OF MAN: PREVIEW,* TV, 79, CDN, Ed; *THE OTHER SIDE OF RIEL,* TV, 79, CDN, Ed; *'MAN ALIVE'* (3 eps), TV, 79, CDN, Ed; *CONN SMYTHE,* TV, 78, CDN, Ed; *'MONEY MAKERS'* (26 eps), TV, 78, CDN, Ed; *'OMBUDSMAN'* (5 eps), TV, 77, CDN, Ed; *'WHAT'S NEW'* (26 eps), TV, 76, CDN, Ed; *GUN CONTROL,* TV, 75, CDN, Ed; *'AWAY OUT'* (5 eps), TV, 74, CDN, Ed.

GILLSON, Malca - see DIRECTORS
GINSBERG, Donald - see PRODUCERS

GIRARD, Hélène

STCQ. 650 de l'Epée, Outremont, Qué, CAN, H2V 3T8. (514)276-5126.
Types de production et Catégories: l métrage-Mont/Réal; c métrage-Mont/Réal; TV vidéo-Mont/Réal.
Types d'oeuvres: Drame-C&TV; Documentaire-C&TV; Education-C&TV.
Curriculum vitae: Née en 1945. Bac., Collège Français, Montréal; B.Sc., Anthropologie, Université de Montréal. Langues: français, anglais, espagnol. Organisatrice du premier Festival 'La Femme et le Film', 73.
Filmographie sélective: *SPEAKING OF NAIROBI,* TV, 86, CDN, Mont; *SI JAMAIS TU PARS,* TV, 85, CDN, Mont; *J'OSAIS PAS RIEN DIRE,* TV, 85, CDN, Mont; *FALLAIT QUE CA CHANGE,* TV, 85, CDN, Mont/Ass réal; *ZONE DE TURBULENCE,* TV, 84, CDN, Mont; *ORDINATEUR EN TETE* (HEAD START: MEETING THE COMPUTER CHALLENGE), TV, 84, CDN, Mont; *BATEAU BLEU, MAISON VERTE,* TV, 84, CDN, Rech; *COUTE QUE COUTE,* C, 83, CDN, Réal; *POSSESSION,* C, 83, CDN, Mont; *UN BEBE TOUT NEUF,* TV, 82, CDN, Réal; *J'AVIONS 375 ANS,* TV, 82, CDN, Mont/Mont son; *'RECOURS'* (2 eps), TV, 81, CDN, Mont/Mont son; *'LES FILS DE LA LIBERTE'* (6 eps), TV, 81, CDN/F, Mont son; *SUZANNE,* C, 79, CDN, Co mont; *'FREDERIC'* (10 eps), TV, 79, CDN, Co mont; *DON'T FORGET - JE ME SOUVIENS,* 'FOR THE RECORD', TV, 78, CDN, Mont; *FUIR,* C, 78, CDN, Réal/Co mont; *J.A. MARTIN PHOTOGRAPHE,* C, 76, CDN, Co mont **(CFA)**; *LA P'TITE VIOLENCE,* TV, 76, CDN, Réal/Mont; *LES FILLES C'EST PAS PAREIL,* 'EN TANT QUE FEMMES', TV, 74, CDN, Réal/Mont/Rech.

GRADIDGE, Havelock

DGC. R.R.1, Zephyr, Ont, CAN, L0E 1T0. (416)473-2379.
Types of Production & Categories: Th Film-Ed; Th Short-Ed; TV Film-Ed; TV Video-Ed.
Genres: Drama-Th&TV; Documentary-TV; Educational-TV.
Biography: Born 1933, South Africa; moved to Canada, 57; Canadian citizen.
Selective Filmography: *'CANADIAN HISTORY'* (12 eps), TV, 86, CDN, Ed; *'ONTARIO LOYALISTS'* (4 eps), TV, 85/84, CDN, Ed; *'NEWS FROM ZOOS'* (26 eps), TV, 81/80, CDN, Ed; *'WHAT WILL THEY THINK OF NEXT'* (104 eps), TV, 80-76, CDN, Ed; *'ON THE LEVEL'* (6 eps), TV, 79, CDN, Ed; *'THINK ABOUT IT'* (6 eps), TV, 79, CDN, Ed; *'BEST KEPT SECRETS'* (5 eps), TV, 78, CDN, Ed; *'LIKE NO OTHER PLACE'* (10 eps), TV, 78, CDN, Ed; *'FRED AND HARRY'* (13 eps), TV, 77, CDN, Ed; *LIFE AMONG THE HURONS,* TV, 76, CDN, Ed; *FESTIVALS NORTH,* TV, 76, CDN, Ed; *CASTLEGUARD CAVE - JOURNEY UNDER THE ICE,* TV, 75, CDN, Ed; *'ONTARIO SCENE'* (6 eps), TV, 75, CDN, Ed; *IGLOOLIK,* TV, 75, CDN, Ed; *PORTRAIT OF THE ARTIST AS A YOUNG MAN,* 'EXPLORATIONS IN THE NOVEL', TV, 75, CDN, Ed **(CFEG)**; *DEAR JOE,* TV, 74, CDN, Ed; *'MANY WORLDS OF CHILDHOOD'* (6 eps), TV, 74, CDN, Ed; *'IN THEIR SHOES'* (6 eps), TV, 73, CDN, Ed; *'THE QUALITY OF LIFE'* (26 eps), TV, 71, CDN, Ed **(CFEG)**; *THE CROWD INSIDE,* Th, 71, CDN, Ed; *'ADVENTURES IN RAINBOW COUNTRY'* (13 eps), TV, 70/69, CDN/GB/AUS, Ed.

GREENWALD, Barry - see DIRECTORS

GRIFFIN, Bruce

31 Alexander St., #114, Toronto, Ont, CAN, M4Y 1B2. (416)924-0854. Film Arts, 461 Church St., Toronto, Ont, CAN, M4Y 2C5. (416)962-0181.
Types of Production & Categories: TV Film-Ed/Prod/Dir.
Genres: Drama-TV; Comedy-TV; Documentary-TV.
Biography: Born 1955, Canada. B.A. in English and Dramatic Arts. Experience as a musician; working knowledge of most musical instruments. *WHO KILLED J.F.K.?* won an editing Award at Yorkton Film Festival.

(cont/suite)

Selective Filmography: *'THE FIFTH ESTATE'* (67 eps), TV, 86-82, CDN, Ed; *PROFILE: OFRA HARNOY,* 'GZOWSKI & CO', TV, 85, CDN, Ed/Dir/Prod; *OFRA HARNOY: THE MUSIC INSIDE/FROM GRAPE TO GLASS,* 'CANADIAN REFLECTIONS', TV, 85/83, CDN, Ed/Dir/Prod; *VIDPRO DISPLAY SYSTEM,* In, 85, CDN, Ed/Dir/Wr/Prod; *WHO KILLED J.F.K.?/ SECRET TESTS,* 'FIFTH ESTATE', TV, 84/83, CDN, Ed.

GULKIN, Cathy

DGC. 56 Wellesley St.E., Unit 15, Toronto, Ont, CAN, M4Y 1G2. (416)920-5347.
Types of Production & Categories: Th Short-Ed; TV Film-Ed.
Genres: Drama-TV; Variety-TV; Documentary-TV; Educational-TV.
Biography: Born 1954, Montreal, Quebec. Languages: English, French, some Spanish; graduate, London Int'l Film School, England. *ALL OF OUR LIVES* won a Blue Ribbon, American Film Festival.
Selective Filmography: *HEALING SCIENCE AND COMPASSION,* Th, 86, CDN, Ed; *I NEED A MAN LIKE YOU TO MAKE MY DREAMS COME TRUE,* Th, 86, CDN, Ed; *WOMEN AND DRUGS/CRIB DESIGN,* 'MARKET PLACE', TV, 86, CDN, Ed; *THE BEST TIME OF MY LIFE,* Th, 85, CDN, Ed; *NORTH OF 60,* TV, 84, CDN, Ed; *A SAFE PLACE/ RACISM,* 'MULTICULTURALISM', TV, 84, CDN, Ed; *YES WE CAN,* Th, 84, CDN, Ed; *TORONTO: FOUR FACES,* TV, 83, CDN, Ed; *ALL OF OUR LIVES,* Th, 83, CDN, Ed; *FITNESS ON TRIAL,* TV, 83, CDN, Ed; *LITTLE BY LITTLE,* TV, 83, CDN, Ed; *BREAKING THE SILENCE,* Th, 83, CDN, Ed; *NEVER TOO YOUNG,* TV, 82, CDN, Ed; *THE FAST AND THE FURIOUS,* TV, 82, CDN, Ed; *DON'T TAKE IT EASY/ N'Y ALLEZ PAS LENTEMENT,* TV, 82, CDN, Ed; *GOOD MONDAY MORNING,* Th, 82, CDN, Ed; *HEART OF GOLD,* TV, 82/81, CDN, Ed; *HOUDAILLE: DAYS OF COURAGE DAYS OF RAGE,* Th, 81, CDN, Ed; *THOSE FLYING CANUCKS,* TV, 81, CDN, Ed; *MOVING MOUNTAINS,* Th, 81, CDN, Ed; *BREAKTHROUGH,* TV, 80, CDN, Ed; *'REAL PEOPLE'* (15 seg), TV, 80, CDN/USA, Ed; *'SPEAK UP AMERICA'* (5 seg), TV, 80, CDN/USA, Ed; *LE DETROIT,* TV, 79, CDN, Ed; *PAUL HORN IN CHINA,* Th, 79, CDN, Ed; *HOUDINI NEVER DIED (HE JUST VANISHED),* TV, 79, CDN, Ed; *'DOSSIER'* (3 eps), TV, 78, CDN, Ed.

GULLIVER, Randy - see DIRECTORS

HALL, Ray

IATSE-891. 2886 West 32nd Ave., Vancouver, BC, CAN, V6L 2B6. (604)263-0247. Petra Film Prod. Assoc., 1149 Hornby St., Ste. 204, Vancouver, BC, CAN, V6Z 1B1. (604)669-1333.
Types of Production & Categories: Th Film-Ed; Th Short-Ed/Snd Ed; TV Film-Ed/ Dir; TV Video-Ed.
Genres: Drama-Th&TV; Documentary-Th&TV; Educational-TV; Children's-TV.
Biography: Born 1932, Norfolk Island, Australia; Canadian citizen, 62. Languages: English, French, German. Attended High School in New Zealand; University of British Columbia. President, BCFIA. Professor, Film Studies program, U.B.C.. *DANCE AND KIDS* won a Blue Ribbon, American Film Festival, N.Y..
Selective Filmography: *DIFFERENCES,* TV, 86, CDN, Ed/Snd Ed; *NORTH WEST TERRITORIES* (EXPO 86), Th, 86, CDN, Ed/Snd Ed; *DANCE AND KIDS,* TV, 85, CDN, Ed/Snd Ed; *JACKS OR BETTER,* TV, 82, CDN, Ed/Prod; *ON TOP OF THE WORLD,* TV, 80, CDN, Dir; *SING BEAST SING,* Th, 80, CDN, Ed/Snd Ed; *NAILS,* Th, 79, CDN, Ed/Snd Ed (**CFEG**); *ONE CYCLIST,* TV, 79, CDN, Prod; *ONE TREE,* TV, 79, CDN, Dir; *SPARTREE,* Th, 77, CDN, Ed/Snd Ed (**CFA**); *B.T.O.,* TV, 76, CDN, Ed/Snd Ed (**CFEG**); *HOW TO BREAK A QUARTER HORSE,* TV, 65, CDN, Ed/Snd Ed; *TORCH TO TOKYO,* TV, 64, CDN, Ed/Snd Ed.

HANNIGAN, Teresa

1303 King St. W., Toronto, Ont, CAN, M6K 1G9. (416)534-2203. Nelvana, 32 Atlantic Ave., Toronto, Ont, CAN, M6K 1X8. (416)588-5571.
Types of Production & Categories: TV Film-Ed.
Genres: Drama-TV; Documentary-TV; Children's-TV; Animation-TV.
Biography: Born 1957, Kingston, Ontario. Graduated in Media Arts, Sheridan College, 80. Currently studying part-time at University of Toronto towards B.A..
Selective Filmography: *THE EDISON TWINS'* (16 eps), TV, 86/85, CDN, Ed; *'THE FIFTH ESTATE'* (2 seg), TV, 85, CDN, Ed; *ON TO THE POLAR SEA - A YUKON ADVENTURE,* TV, 85/84, CDN, Snd Ed; *THE OTHER KINGDOM* (mini-series), (2 eps), TV, 84, CDN, Co-Ed; *'INSPECTOR GADGET'* (64 eps), TV, 83, CDN, Mus Ed/Dial Ed; *CHAUTAUQUA GIRL,* TV, 82, CDN, Snd Ed/ Assist Ed.

HART, Roger

SGCT. 40 chemin des Perches, Lac Marois, Que, CAN, J0R 1B0. (514)224-2339. NFB, P.O.Box 6100, Montreal, Que, CAN, H3C 3H5. (514)283-9549.
Types of Production & Categories: Th Short-Ed; TV Film-Ed/Dir.
Genres: Documentary-Th&TV.
Biography: Born 1934, Ottawa, Ontario.
Selective Filmography: *MOBILITY,* TV, 86, CDN, Dir/Ed; *FIRST STOP CHINA* (SUR LES SCENES DE L'ORIENT), TV, 85, CDN, Ed/Snd Rec; *CHILDREN'S CRUSADE,* TV, 84, CDN, Ed; *SOMETHING TO CELEBRATE,* TV, 83, CDN, Ed/Co-Prod; *'ON GUARD FOR THEE'* (3 eps), TV, 82, CDN, Ed/Co-Prod; *TEST PILOT,* Th, 82, CDN, Prod; *CHALLENGER* (INDUSTRIAL ROMANCE), TV, 81, CDN, Ed/Co-Dir; *THE LAND* (A NEW PRIORITY), TV, 79, CDN, Dir/Ed; *A NEW BARGAIN,* TV, 78, CDN, Ed/Dir; *ENCOUNTER ON URBAN ENVIRONMENT,* TV, 77, CDN, Ed/Dir.

HEYDON, Michael - see PRODUCERS

HILTON, Jack

IATSE-879, IATSE-776. Kinemagic Pictures Ltd., Color Bars Prods. Inc., 2931 Second St., #1, Santa Monica, CA, USA, 90405. (213)392-1303.
Types of Production & Categories: Th Short-Ed/Snd Ed; TV Film-Ed; TV Video-Ed.
Genres: Drama-Th&TV; Action-TV; Documentary-TV; Experimental-Th&TV.
Biography: Born 1952, Vancouver, British Columbia. Has done a variety of jobs including film processing, grip, gaffer, construction; started Kinemagic Pictures Ltd., Vancouver, 79.
Selective Filmography: *ROCKY IV,* Th, 85, USA, Assist Ed; *RAPPIN',* Th, 85, USA, 1st Assist Ed; *RUNAWAY,* Th, 84, CDN/USA, Assist Ed; *HARDBODIES,* Th, 84, USA, 1st Assist Ed; *THE CHOICE,* TV, 84, USA, Snd Ed; *THE MATCHMAKER,* TV, 84, USA, Ed; *THE BEST CHRISTMAS PAGEANT EVER,* TV, 83, USA, Assist Ed; *THE HAUNTING PASSION,* TV, 83, USA, Assist Ed; *THE DESERTER,* TV, 83, CDN, Assist Snd Ed; *MOTHERLODE,* Th, 80, USA, 1st Assist Ed; *LATITUDE 55,* Th, 80, CDN, Assist Ed; *OUT OF THE BLUE,* Th, 80, CDN, 1st Assist Ed; *BEAR ISLAND,* Th, 80/79, CDN/GB, Assist Ed; *AMERICAN PIE,* TV, 75, CDN, Ed/Dir/Prod.

HOWARD, Chris

SMPTE. 31 Evans Ave., Toronto, Ont, CAN, M6S 3V7. (416)766-0846. Suite One Video Inc., 299 Queen St. W., 5th Fl., Toronto, Ont, CAN, M5V 1Z9. (416)440-0148.
Types of Production & Categories: TV Film-Ed/Wr; TV Video-Ed/Wr.
Genres: Variety-TV; Documentary-TV; Children's-TV; Commercials-TV.
Biography: Born 1954, Windsor, Ontario; Masters degree (English Literature). Has had poetry and short stories published. Edited over 1000 television commercials.
(cont/suite)

Selective Filmography: *'OWL TV'* (Dir-5 eps), (20 eps), TV, 86/85, CDN, Spv Ed; *'VID KIDS'* (13 eps), TV, 85, CDN, Co-Ed; *'EARTH ODYSSEY'*, TV, 84, CDN, Wr; *COMMAND PERFORMANCE,* TV, 83, CDN, Spv Ed; *'HEARTBEAT',* TV, 83, CDN, Ed/Wr.

IRVINE, Frank

IATSE-881. 1415 Lamey's Mill, #10, Vancouver, BC, CAN, V6H 3W1. (604)738-8831. Petra Film Productions, 1149 Hornby St., #204, Vancouver, BC, CAN, V6Z 1W1. (604)669-1333.
Types of Production & Categories: Th Film-Ed; Th Short-Ed; TV Film-Ed.
Genres: Drama-Th&TV; Comedy-Th&TV; Action-Th&TV; Documentary-TV.
Biography: Born 1938, Edmonton, Alberta. Editor on over 60 documentaries, 62-79; commercials and industrials, 79-85.
Selective Filmography: *'THE BEACHCOMBERS'* (71 eps), TV, 86-70, CDN, Ed; *MEGADREAM,* TV, 86, CDN, Ed; *MY KIND OF TOWN,* Th, 85, CDN, Ed/Act; *HIGH STAKES,* Th, 85, CDN, Ed; *MARATHON,* TV, 83, CDN, Ed; *LAST CRIME,* TV, 82, USA, Ed; *THE GREY FOX,* Th, 80, CDN, Ed; *'RITTER'S COVE'* (13 eps), TV, 80/79, CDN, Ed; *MAN FROM PETROLAN,* TV, 80, CDN, Ed; *LOTOMANIA,* TV, 80, CDN, Ed; *ENERGY CRISIS,* TV, 69, CDN, Ed; *CANADA'S WATER FOR SALE,* TV, 68, CDN, Ed.

JALBERT, Pierre

MPEG-776, SAG. 2642 N. Beverly Glen Blvd., Los Angeles, CA, USA, 90077. (213)475-3733.
Types of Production & Categories: Th Film-Ed/Act/Dir; TV Film-Cin/Snd Rec.
Genres: Drama-Th&TV; Comedy-Th&TV; Action-Th&TV; Documentary-Th&TV.
Biography: Born 1925, Quebec City; educated at Laval University. Captain of Canadian Olympic Ski Team, 48; trained and worked for NFB, 44-45; trained at Epinay Studios, Paris; portrayed 'Caje' in *COMBAT,* 61-68.
Selective Filmography: *A FINE MESS,* Th, 85, USA, Dial Ed/Dial Dir; *PORTRAITS OF CANADA* (EXPO 86), Th, 85, CDN/USA, Dial Ed/Dial Dir; *'WILDSIDE',* TV, 85, USA, Dial Ed; *MY SCIENCE PROJECT,* Th, 85, USA, Dial Ed; *'COVER UP',* TV, 84, USA, Dial Ed; *DARK ECHOES,* Th, 83, USA/YU, Spv Ed; *SOMETHING WICKED THIS WAY COMES,* Th, 82, USA, Dial Ed; *BLOODLINE,* Th, 81, USA, Dial Ed; *DIRTY TRICKS,* Th, 80, CDN, Ed; *FINAL ASSIGNMENT,* Th, 80, CDN, Ed; *SKI LIFT TO DEATH,* Th, 79, USA, Act/2nd U Dir; *CONCORDE,* Th, 79, USA, Act; *GOODBYE CRUEL WORLD,* Th, 79, USA, Act; *SHOGUN,* TV, 78, USA, Dial Ed **(EMMY)**; *GREASE,* Th, 78, USA, Dial Ed; *STAR TREK THE MOTION PICTURE,* Th, 77, USA, Dial Ed; *MIKEY AND NICKY,* Th, 76/75, USA, Ed; *GRIZZLY ADAMS,* Th, 74, USA, Ed; *BLACK CAESAR,* Th, 73, USA, Ed; *43 - PETTY STORY,* Th, 72, USA, Ed/ Act/Dir; *THE GODFATHER,* Th, 71/70, USA, Ed/Dial Ed; *SKI BUM,* Th, 70, USA, Act/2nd U Dir; *'MISSION IMPOSSIBLE',* TV, 69, USA, Act; *'COMBAT',* TV, 61-68, USA, Act; *MUTINY ON THE BOUNTY,* Th, 61, USA, Dial Ed; *AN AMERICAN IN PARIS,* Th, 60, USA, Dial Ed; *BEN HUR,* Th, 60, USA, Dial Ed; *BLACKBOARD JUNGLE,* Th, 55, USA, Assist Ed.

JEAN, Jacques - voir REALISATEURS

KARDASH, Virlana - see DIRECTORS

KAREN, Debra

Final Cut Enterprises Ltd, 5207 Globert, Montreal, Que, CAN, H3W 2E6. (514) 489-0657.
Types of Production & Categories: Th Film-Ed; TV Film-Ed.
Genres: Drama-Th&TV; Comedy-Th; Action-Th; Horror-Th.
Biography: Born 1952, Montreal, Quebec; bilingual. B.A., Magna cum Laude, Communication Arts, Concordia University.

(cont/suite)

Selective Filmography: *SPEARFIELD'S DAUGHTER* (mini-series), TV, 85, CDN/
USA/AUS, Ed; *THE VINDICATOR* (FRANKENSTEIN FACTOR), Th, 84,
CDN, Ed; *LOVERBOY*, Th, 84, CDN, Ed; *TEETH* (MAMA-DRACULA), Th,
83, CDN/B, Ed; *HAPPY BIRTHDAY TO ME*, Th, 80, CDN, Ed; *FINAL
ASSIGNMENT*, Th, 79, CDN, Ed; *YESTERDAY* (GABRIELLE), Th, 79, CDN,
Ed; *CRUNCH* (THE KINKY COACHES AND THE POM-POM PUSSYCATS),
Th, 78, CDN, Ed; *MEATBALLS*, Th, 78, CDN, Ed; *BLACKOUT*, Th, 77, CDN,
Ed; *RABID*, Th, 76, CDN, Ed; *DEATH WEEKEND*, Th, 75, CDN, Ed.

KERLANN, Hervé

STCQ. 4291 Clark, Montréal, Qué, CAN, H2W 1X2. (514)849-1586.
Types de production et Catégories: 1 métrage-Mont/Mont son; c métrage-
Mont/Mont son; TV vidéo-Mont.
Types d'oeuvres: Drame-C; Comédie-C; Documentaire-TV; Education-TV.
Curriculum vitae: Né en 1953, Rabat, Maroc; bilingue. Deug d'Anglais, Université
de Bordeaux, France; Bac., Communications, UQAM, Montréal. Réalisateur de
vidéos pédagogiques et sociaux; scénariste, fictions.
Filmographie sélective: *NOUS PRES NOUS LOIN*, C, 86, CDN, Mont; *LE
MATOU* (THE ALLEY CAT), C, 85, CDN/F, 1er ass mont; *JUSTICE
BLANCHE*, C, 85, CDN, Mont; *ADRAMELECH*, C, 85, CDN, Mont; *L'ELUE*, C,
85, CDN, Mont; *DEMIE-JOUR*, C, 84, CDN, Mont; *LA MER ET SES
PRINCES*, C, 84, CDN, Mont son; *PAS FOU COMME ON LE PENSE*, C, 83,
CDN, Mont; *TEETH* (MAMA-DRACULA), C, 83, CDN/B, Mont son/Mont mus;
POSSESSION, C, 83, F, Ass mont/Mont mus; *MAN IN 5A* (THE MAN NEXT
DOOR), C, 82, CDN, 1er ass mont; *ODYSSEY OF THE PACIFIC*
(L'EMPEREUR DU PEROU), C, 81, CDN/F, 1er ass mont; *CAMPAGNE
ALCAN*, TV, 80, CDN, 1er ass mont; *HAPPY BIRTHDAY TO ME*, C, 80, CDN,
2e ass mont; *YES ANGLOPHONE* (LES ANGLAIS DU YES), TV, 80, CDN,
Réal/Prod; *LA PLANIFICATION*, ED, 79, CDN, Réal; *L'HOMME EN COLERE*
(LABYRINTH), C, 78, CDN/F, 2e ass mont.

KISH, Albert - see DIRECTORS

KRAVSHIK, Marty

12 Crestland Ave., Toronto, Ont, CAN, M4C 3L1. (416)425-3167. Reel Ideas Inc.,
217A Church St., Toronto, Ont, CAN, M5B 1Y7. (416)863-0898.
Types of Production & Categories: TV Film-Ed; TV Video-Ed.
Genres: Documentary-TV; Commercials-TV; Industrial-TV.
Biography: Born 1951, Toronto, Ontario. On-line video editor for 3 years; has edited
over 1500 commercials in 11 years; won various awards. Also produced and edited
several industrials (Xerox, Esso).

LAHTI, James

DGC. 194 Howland Ave., Toronto, Ont, CAN, M5R 3B6. (416)537-6123.
Types of Production & Categories: TV Film-Ed; TV Video-Ed.
Genres: Drama-TV; Action-TV; Children's-TV.
Biography: Born in Northern Ontario. B.F.A., Film, York University. Film and tape
editor since 76; has also edited music videos, sponsored films and dozens of
documentaries.
Selective Filmography: *ANNE OF GREEN GABLES - THE SEQUEL*, TV, 86,
CDN/USA, Co-Ed; *'ADDERLY'* (2 eps), TV, 86, CDN, Ed; *'SPIRIT BAY'* (1 eps),
TV, 86, CDN, Ed; *ANNE OF GREEN GABLES*, TV, 85, CDN, Co-Ed; *HOCKEY
NIGHT*, TV, 84, CDN, Ed; *COMING APART*, TV, 84, CDN, Ed; *THE UMPIRE*,
TV, 84, CDN, Ed; *INTRODUCING...JANET*, TV, 81, CDN, Co-Ed; *REACHING
OUT*, TV, 80, CDN, Co-Ed; *CLOWN WHITE*, TV, 80, CDN, Co-Ed.

LANGE, Bruce
DGC. 13B St. Mathias Place, Toronto, Ont, CAN, M6J 2N4. (416)868-0870.
1837 N. Garfield Pl., #F, Hollywood, CA, USA, 90028. (213)463-3743.
Types of Production & Categories: Th Film-Ed.
Genres: Drama-Th; Comedy-Th; Action-Th; Horror-Th.
Biography: Born 1951, Jasper, Alberta; B.Sc., Dalhousie University, Nova Scotia.
Selective Filmography: *THE ARM*, Th, 86, USA, Assoc Ed; *AGNES OF GOD*, Th, 84, USA, Assoc Ed; *ABDUCTED*, Th, 85, CDN, Ed; *BLUE SNAKE*, TV, 85, CDN, Ed; *MRS. SOFFEL*, Th, 84, USA, Assist Ed; *THE GLITTER DOME*, TV, 83, CDN/USA, 2nd Assist Ed; *MARTIN'S DAY*, Th, 83, CDN/GB, Assist Ed; *STRANGE BREW*, Th, 82, CDN/USA, Assist Ed; *THE AMATEUR*, Th, 81, CDN, Assist Ed; *PURE ESCAPE*, Th, 80, CDN, Assist Ed; *HOT TOUCH* (FRENCH KISS), Th, 80, CDN, Assist Ed; *PHOBIA*, Th, 80, CDN, Assist Ed; *KLONDIKE FEVER*, Th, 79, CDN, Assist Ed; *THE SHAPE OF THINGS TO COME*, Th, 79, CDN, Assist Ed.

LASRY, Pierre - see DIRECTORS

LAWRENCE, Stephen
ACTT, DGC. Merlin Films Inc., 1088 Kipling Ave., Etobicoke, Ont, CAN, M9B 3M2. (416)233-3570.
Types of Production & Categories: Th Film-Ed/Snd Ed; Th Short-Ed/Snd Ed; TV Film-Ed/Snd Ed; TV Video-Ed/Snd Ed.
Genres: Drama-Th&TV; Comedy-Th&TV; Action-Th&TV; Documentary-TV.
Biography: Born in the United Kingdom; British-Canadian citizen. Started in film business in 1966 with National Screen Services; freelance since 70.
Selective Filmography: *OKLAHOMA SMUGGLERS*, Th, 86, CDN/USA, Ed/Mus Ed; *'DANGER BAY'* (31 eps), TV, 85/84, CDN/USA, Spv Ed; *AGENTS OF DECEPTION*, TV, 84, CDN, Spv Ed; *GOLD LUST*, TV, 84, CDN, Spv Ed; *FOR ONE NIGHT ONLY*, Th, 83, CDN, Snd Ed; *G.M.84*, In, 83, CDN, Ed/Dir; *A MATTER OF SEX*, Th, 83, CDN/USA, Snd Ed; *FALCON'S GOLD* (ROBBERS OF THE SACRED MOUNTAIN), Th, 82, CDN, Snd Ed; *TILL DEATH DO US PART*, Th, 81, CDN, Ed; *'TALES OF THE KLONDIKE'* (6 eps), TV, 81, CDN, Ed; *DOUBLE NEGATIVE*, Th, 79, CDN, Snd Ed; *'MATT AND JENNY'* (10 eps), TV, 79, CDN/GB/D, Ed; *'A MAN CALLED INTREPID'* (3 eps), TV, 79/78, CDN/GB, Snd Ed; *SEPARATION*, TV, 78, CDN, Snd Ed; *'THE NEW AVENGERS'* (1 eps), TV, 77, CDN, Ed; *MUST FREEDOM FAIL*, TV, 77, CDN, Ed; *VALDY: FOLKSINGER DELUXE*, TV, 76, CDN, Ed/Snd Ed; *'SWISS FAMILY ROBINSON'* (11 eps), TV, 75, CDN, Ed; *'POLICE SURGEON'* (4 eps), TV, 74/73, CDN, Ed.

LEACH, David
DGC. 387 Scarborough Rd., Toronto, Ont, CAN, M4E 3N1. (416)694-4490.
Types of Production & Categories: TV Film-Ed/Dir.
Genres: Drama-TV; Documentary-TV; Educational-TV; Commercials-TV.
Biography: Born 1952, Montreal, Quebec; bilingual. Educated at McGill University and York U.; graduated in 74 with Honours B.A in film. Musician for 20 years, recording, composing.
Selective Filmography: *RACE AGAINST THE WIND*, TV, 86, CDN, Ed; *ROOTS OF HUNGER, ROOTS OF CHANGE*, TV, 85, CDN/USA, Ed/Assoc Prod; *LIFE INSURANCE*, 'MONEY SMART', TV, 85, CDN, Dir; *P & L INSURANCE*, 'MONEY SMART', TV, 85, CDN, Ed/Dir; *'A MODERN COUNTRY'* (3 eps), TV, 84, CDN, Ed; *THE JUGGLER*, TV, 83, CDN, Ed; *I MARRIED THE KLONDIKE* (3 parts), TV, 82, CDN, Ed.

LOWER, Tony
ACTT, DGC. 30 Bathford Crescent, Willowdale, Ont, CAN, M2J 2S4. (416)222-9316.

(cont/suite)

EDITORS/MONTEURS

Types of Production & Categories: Th Film-Ed/Snd Ed/Mus Ed; Th Short-Ed/Snd Ed/Mus Ed; TV Film-Ed/Snd Ed/Mus Ed.
Genres: Drama-Th&TV; Comedy-Th&TV; Variety-Th&TV; Action-Th&TV.
Biography: Born 1930, Watford, Hertfordshire, England; Canadian citizen
Selective Filmography: *EASY PREY*, TV, 86, USA, Ed; *MANY HAPPY RETURNS*, TV, 86, USA, Ed/Mus Ed; *'DANGER BAY'*, TV, 85, CDN/USA, Ed; *'PHILIP MARLOWE PRIVATE EYE'* (1 eps), TV, 85, CDN, Ed; *RECKLESS DISREGARD*, TV, 84, CDN/USA, Ed/Mus Ed; *BEDROOM EYES*, Th, 84, CDN, Ed; *RUNNING BRAVE*, Th, 83, CDN/USA, Ed; *THE WARS*, Th, 81, CDN/D, Ed; *HARD FEELINGS*, Th, 80, CDN, Ed/Mus Ed; *THE HOUNDS OF NOTRE DAME*, Th, 80, CDN, Ed/Mus Ed; *BEAR ISLAND*, Th, 78, CDN/GB, Ed; *A MAN CALLED INTREPID* (mini-series), TV, 78, CDN/GB, Ed; *'BEHIND THE SCENES'*, TV, 78-75, CDN, P Pro Spv; *IT SEEMED LIKE A GOOD IDEA AT THE TIME*, Th, 74, CDN, Ed/Mus Ed; *SUNDAY IN THE COUNTRY*, Th, 73, CDN, Ed/Mus Ed; *BETWEEN FRIENDS*, Th, 72, CDN, Ed; *WEDDING IN WHITE*, Th, 72, CDN, Ed/Mus Ed; *SLIPSTREAM*, Th, 72, CDN, Ed/Mus Ed; *RIP-OFF*, Th, 71, CDN, Ed; *NORTH OF SUPERIOR*, Th, 70, CDN, Snd Ed; *'McQUEEN'*, TV, 69, CDN, Ed; *QUENTIN DURGENS, M.P.'*, TV, 68/67, CDN, Ed; *DULCIMA*, TV, 68, CDN, Ed; *CALIFORNIA DREAMING*, TV, 68, CDN, Ed/Mus Ed; *'WOJECK'*, TV, 67/66, CDN, Ed; *'THE THIRD MAN'*, TV, 59, GB, Ed; *THE AFRICAN QUEEN*, Th, 51, USA, Assist Ed; *STAIRWAY TO HEAVEN*, Th, 46, GB, Assist Ed.

MacKAY, Bruce - see DIRECTORS

MacLAVERTY, Michael

DGC. 431 Kingston Rd., Toronto, Ont, CAN, M4L 1V2. (416)690-6405.
Types of Production & Categories: Th Film-Ed; TV Film-Ed; TV Video-Ed.
Genres: Drama-Th&TV; Variety-TV; Action-Th&TV; Horror-Th&TV.
Biography: Born 1947, England; emigrated to Canada, 64; Canadian citizen, 78. Started in film business, 67.
Selective Filmography: *LAST CHANCE*, TV, 86, CDN/AUS, Ed; *NIAGARA STRIP*, TV, 86, CDN, Spv Ed; *BODY COUNT*, TV, 86, CDN, Spv Ed; *MARK OF THE BEAST*, TV, 86, CDN, Spv Ed; *VIRGIN PARADISE*, TV, 86, CDN, Spv Ed; *NIGHT TRACKERS*, TV, 86, CDN, Ed; *'MANIA'*, TV, 85, CDN, Ed; *PRICE OF VENGEANCE*, TV, 85, CDN, Spv Ed; *MARKED FOR DEATH*, TV, 85, CDN, Spv Ed; *THE TOWER*, TV, 85, CDN, Spv Ed; *THE HIGHJACKING OF STUDIO 4*, TV, 85, CDN, Spv Ed; *DEATH IN HOLLYWOOD*, TV, 85, CDN, Spv Ed; *SHOCK CHAMBER*, TV, 85, CDN, Spv Ed; *'JUST JAZZ'* (52 eps), TV, 85/84, CDN, Spv Ed; *'NIAGARA REPERTORY THEATRE'* (24 eps), TV, 84/83, CDN, Ed/Spv Ed; *FLY WITH THE HAWK*, TV, 84, CDN, Spv Ed; *LADY BEAR*, TV, 84, CDN, Spv Ed; *BLUE MURDER*, TV, 84, CDN, Spv Ed; *DEADLY PURSUIT*, TV, 84, CDN, Spv Ed; *THE BORROWER*, TV, 84, CDN, Spv Ed; *THE EDGE*, TV, 83, CDN, Spv Ed; *THE CHRONICLE OF 1812*, TV, 83, CDN, Spv Ed; *SURVIVAL 1990*, TV, 83, CDN, Spv Ed; *CURTAINS*, Th, 82, CDN, Ed; *FIREBIRD 2015*, Th, 80, CDN, Ed; *TANYA'S ISLAND*, Th, 80, CDN, Ed; *THE KIDNAPPING OF THE PRESIDENT*, Th, 79, CDN, Ed; *JUST JESSIE*, Th, 79, CDN, Ed; *RUNNING*, Th, 78, CDN, 1st Assist Ed; *RAGTIME SUMMER*, Th, 78, CDN/GB, 1st Assist Ed.

MANNE, M.C.

ACTRA, IATSE-873. 546 Old Orchard Gr., Toronto, Ont, CAN, M5M 2G9. (416) 781-3837.
Types of Production & Categories: Th Film-Ed; TV Film-Ed/Dir/Wr.
Genres: Drama-Th&TV; Comedy-Th&TV; Documentary-TV; Educational-TV.
Biography: Born 1931; speaks English, French, German and Spanish.

(cont/suite)

Selective Filmography: *'MAN ALIVE'* (19 eps), TV, 86-67, CDN, Ed; *THE FATAL ITCH*, TV, 86, CDN, Ed; *'THE FIFTH ESTATE'* (25 eps), TV, 85-80, CDN, Ed; *'QUARTERLY REPORT'* (16 eps), TV, 84-79, CDN, Spv Ed; *'IMAGES OF CANADA'* (4 eps), TV, 82-69, CDN, Ed; *SUMMER'S CHILDREN*, Th, 79, CDN, Ed; *OBIT: GORDON SINCLAIR*, TV, 77, CDN, Ed/Co-Dir; *SONGS AND TALES OF YESTERDAY*, TV, 77, CDN, Ed/Wr; *ALONG THE WHOOPUP TRAIL*, TV, 76, CDN, Ed/Wr; *SLOPES OF THE ROCKIES*, TV, 75, USA, Ed; *RUFFLED GROUSE RIDDLE*, TV, 75, USA, Ed; *DANCE OF THE WHOOPING CRANE*, TV, 75, USA, Ed; *CARPATHIAN TALES*, TV, 75, CDN, Ed/Wr; *PASTORALE*, TV, 75, CDN, Ed/Wr; *'POLICE SURGEON'* (10 eps), TV, 74-72, CDN, Ed; *AFRICAN IMPRESSIONS*, TV, 74, USA, Ed; *SO LITTLE TIME*, TV, 74, USA, Ed; *RHYTHM OF THE MARSH*, TV, 73, USA, Ed; *'CANADIAN SHORT STORIES'* (6 eps), TV, 72-69, CDN, Ed; *THE ROWDYMAN*, Th, 71, CDN, Ed; *A FAN'S NOTES*, Th, 70, CDN, Ed; *THE ONLY WAY OUT IS DEAD*, Th, 70, CDN, Ed; *HOMER*, Th, 69, CDN, Ed; *'McQUEEN'* (6 eps), TV, 69, CDN, Ed; *'QUENTIN DURGENS, M.P.'* (4 eps), TV, 69, CDN, Ed; *'CORWIN MD'* (6 eps), TV, 69, CDN, Ed; *DENNY*, TV, 69, CDN, Ed; *THE MERCENARIES*, TV, 68, CDN, Ed; *THE PAPER PEOPLE*, TV, 68, CDN, Ed; *WHERE ONCE THE MAYA GLORIED AND DRANK DEEP*, TV, 67, CDN, Ed/Dir/Wr.

MARTIN, Mike - see DIRECTORS

MARTIN, Susan - see DIRECTORS

MATTIUSSI, Roger

DGC. Millennium Films, 577 Church St., Toronto, Ont, CAN, M4Y 2E4. (416) 964-6219.
Types of Production & Categories: TV Film-Ed; TV Video-Ed.
Genres: Drama-TV; Comedy-TV; Action-TV; Documentary-TV.
Biography: Born 1951, Vancouver, British Columbia. Had a number of poems published; has edited over 75 films, from animation to documentaries; a number of these films have won international awards.
Selective Filmography: *'AIRWAVES'* (4 eps), TV, 86/85, CDN, Ed; *AT THE BRINK*, 'THE NUCLEAR AGE', TV, 86, USA, Ed; *'ADDERLY'* (2 eps), TV, 86, CDN, Ed; *SHOWSTOPPERS*, TV, 85, CDN, Ed/Snd Ed; *THE CROWD*, 'RAY BRADBURY THEATRE', TV, 85, CDN, Ed; *THE FRONT LINE*, 'FOR THE RECORD', TV, 84, CDN, Ed/Snd Ed; *ALL THE YEARS*, 'BELL CANADA PLAYHOUSE', TV, 84, CDN, Ed; *WHITE LIES/ AN OUNCE OF CURE*, 'SONS AND DAUGHTERS', TV, 84/83, CDN, Ed; *'SPIRIT BAY'* (1 eps), TV, 83, CDN, Ed; *THANKS FOR THE RIDE*, TV, 82, CDN, Ed; *AFTER THE AXE*, TV, 81, CDN, Ed/Narr, *'THE PHOENIX TEAM'* (3 eps), TV, 80, CDN, Snd Ed; *A POPULATION OF ONE*, TV, 80, CDN, Snd Ed; *'LITTLEST HOBO'* (20 eps), TV, 80/79, CDN, Snd Ed; *MAINTAIN THE RIGHT*, 'FOR THE RECORD', TV, 79, CDN, Snd Ed; *MAPLE SYRUP TIME*, TV, 78, CDN, Ed/Pro Spv; *LEGENDES DU QUEBEC* (BEWARE OF THE DEVIL), TV, 77, CDN, Ed.

MAZUR, Lara

152 Linden Ave., Winnipeg, Man, CAN, R2K 0N1. (204)661-1687.
Types of Production & Categories: Th Film-Ed; TV Film-Ed; TV Video-Ed.
Genres: Drama-Th&TV; Documentary-Th&TV; Educational-Th&TV.
Biography: Born 1948, Winnipeg, Manitoba. B.F.A., University of Manitoba, 69. Art teacher, instructor, 71-79; film jury, Manitoba Arts Council, 84-85. Has won awards for music, art; films she has edited have won numerous awards including: Genie, CanPro, Actra, Rockie, Iris.
Selective Filmography: *LITTLE WOMEN/THE WAKE/IKWE*, 'DAUGHTERS OF THE COUNTRY', TV, 86/85, CDN, Ed; *GET A JOB*, Th, 86, CDN, Ed; *HEAVEN ON EARTH*, TV, 86, CDN/GB, Ed; *TRAMP AT THE DOOR*, TV, 85,

(cont/suite)

CDN, Ed/Cont; *SYSTEMS OF EXCELLENCE,* In, 84, CDN, Ed/Snd Ed; *CAGES,* 'BELL CANADA PLAYHOUSE', TV, 84, CDN, Ed/Snd Ed; *THE PRODIGAL,* TV, 84, CDN, Ed/Cont; *IT'S HARD TO GET IT HERE,* Th, 84, CDN, Ed; *IN THE FALL,* TV, 83, CDN, Ed/Snd Ed/Cont; *INTERCONNECTIONS,* Th, 83, CDN, Ed/Snd Ed; *REUNION,* TV, 82, CDN, Ed/Snd Ed/Cont; *THE PEDLAR,* Th, 82, CDN, Ed/Snd Ed; *SOLUTIONS: A FILE ON CANADIAN TECHNOLOGY,* In, 81, CDN, Co-Ed/Snd Ed; *BEGINNINGS,* TV, 80, CDN, Ed/Snd Ed.

McCLELLAN, Gordon

DGC. 96 Chelsea Ave., Toronto, Ont, CAN, M6P 1C3. (416)531-7974. Film Arts, 461 Church St., Toronto, Ont, CAN, M4Y 2C5. (416)962-0181.
Types of Production & Categories: Th Film-Ed; TV Film-Ed.
Genres: Drama-Th&TV; Documentary-Th&TV.
Biography: Born 1949, Ottawa, Ontario; graduated Queen's University, Film Program, 71; film editor since 71. Edited *JUST ANOTHER MISSING KID* which won an Oscar; *ALEX COLVILLE: THE SPLENDOR OF ORDER* won Best Editing, Atlantic Film Fest., Best Documentary at Houston, Yorkton, Atlantic Film Festivals and a CFTA.
Selective Filmography: *THE RIGHT STUFF,* TV, 86, CDN, Ed/2nd U Dir; *'SPIRIT BAY'* (2 eps), TV, 86, CDN, Ed; *TEARS ARE NOT ENOUGH,* Th, 85, CDN, Ed/Assoc Prod; *RAPISTS - CAN THEY BE STOPPED?,* 'AMERICA UNDERCOVER', TV, 85, USA, Ed; *MICHAEL AND KITTY,* TV, 85, CDN, Ed; *ALEX COLVILLE: THE SPLENDOR OF ORDER,* TV, 84, CDN, Ed; *THE BOY NEXT DOOR/ WHERE THE HEART IS,* 'FOR THE RECORD', TV, 84, CDN, Ed; *I'LL GET THERE SOMEHOW,* TV, 84, CDN, Ed; *HIDE AND SEEK/ I LOVE A MAN IN A UNIFORM/ BY REASON OF INSANITY,* 'FOR THE RECORD', TV, 83-81, CDN, Ed; *BJORN BORG,* 'CHAMPIONS', TV, 83, CDN, Ed; *OSCAR PETERSON: WORDS AND MUSIC,* TV, 82, CDN, Ed; *NEW TOMORROW,* TV, 82, CDN, Ed; *JUST ANOTHER MISSING KID,* 'THE FIFTH ESTATE', TV, 81, CDN/USA, Ed; *ALLIGATOR SHOES* (LES SOULIERS EN CROCO), Th, 81, CDN, Ed; *'THE FIFTH ESTATE'* (60 eps), TV, 80-75, CDN, Ed.

McLEOD, David

McLeod Film Assoc. Inc., 4277 Esplanade, #2, Montreal, Que, CAN, H2W 1T1. (514)843-8140.
Types of Production & Categories: TV Film-Ed/Dir; TV Video-Ed/Dir.
Genres: Commercials-TV; Industrial-TV.
Biography: Born 1950, Montreal, Quebec; bilingual. Studied at the University of Alberta; Communication Arts, Loyola College. Fourteen years experience as editor/ director on industrials and commercials; experience in the use and production of interactive video disc format.
Selective Filmography: *A LOOK BEHIND THE SCENES,* TV, 85, CDN, Ed/Dir; *BELL CANADA,* In, 85, CDN, Ed; *AIR CANADA/DIRECT FILM,* Cm, 85, CDN, Ed; *CAYMAN ISLANDS ROYAL VISIT,* TV, 84, CDN, Ed/Dir; *IN STEP,* TV, 82, CDN, Ed/Dir; *BUMPS WITHOUT BRUISES,* TV, 81, CDN, Ed/Dir; *THE FUTURE OF CITIES,* TV, 76, USA, Ed; *SKI EAST FOR THE FUN OF IT,* TV, 75, CDN, Ed; *BEHIND THE BROOM IN BERNE,* TV, 74, CDN, Ed.

MERRITT, Judith

SCGT. 3730 Coloniale Ave., Montreal, Que, CAN, H2X 2Y6. (514)849-1561. NFB, Box 6100, Montreal, Que, CAN, H3C 3H5. (514)283-9474.
Types of Production & Categories: TV Film-Ed/Dir.
Genres: Documentary-Th&TV.
Biography: Born 1937; educated in London, England; came to Canada, 54. Married, has children. Received professional training at the NFB.

(cont/suite)

Selective Filmography: *THE APPRENTICESHIP OF MORDECAI RICHLER,* TV, 86, CDN, Ed; *FORT WILLIAM,* ED, 86, CDN, Ed; *HEALTH AND SAFETY,* TV, 86, CDN, Ed; *AFTER THE CRASH,* 'AT THE WHEEL', TV, 85, CDN, Ed; *GOODBYE WAR/ANYONE'S SON WILL DO,* 'WAR', TV, 84, CDN, Ed/Co-Dir; *SEE YOU IN THE FUNNY PAPERS,* TV, 83, CDN, Ed; *ARTHRITIS: A DIALOGUE WITH PAIN,* TV, 83, CDN, Ed; *THE LOST PHARAOH: THE SEARCH FOR AKHENATEN,* TV, 82, CDN, Ed; *LOVED, HONOURED AND BRUISED,* TV, 81, CDN, Ed; *MOTHER TONGUE,* TV, 80, CDN, Ed; *'CANADA VIGNETTES'* (Dir-2 eps), (4 eps), TV, 78, CDN, Ed; *HOTTEST SHOW ON EARTH,* TV, 77, CDN, Ed; *PAINTINGS OF THE 1930'S,* TV, 77, CDN, Ed; *THE VACANT LOT,* TV, 76, CDN, Ed/Dir; *CRAZY QUILT,* TV, 76, CDN, Ed.

MONTPETIT, Jean-Guy

STCQ. 3711 Drolet, Montréal, Qué, CAN, H2X 3H7. (514)845-4837.
Types de production et Catégories: 1 métrage-Mont/Mont son; TV film-Mont; TV vidéo-Mont.
Types d'oeuvres: Drame-C&TV; Comédie-C&TV; Enfants-C&TV; Animation C&TV.
Curriculum vitae: Né à Québec en 1951. Etudes: Baccalauréat en Journalisme, Université Laval, Québec.
Filmographie sélective: *GETTING TO WORK* (pilote), TV, 86, CDN, Mont; *CAP LUMIERE* (pilote), TV, 86, CDN, Mont; *TRANSIT,* TV, 86, CDN, Mont; *ANNE McNEIL,* C, 86, CDN, Mont; *THE PEANUT BUTTER SOLUTION* (LA SOLUTION BEURRE DE PINOTTES), C, 85, CDN, Mont; *GEORGE AND THE STAR* (GEORGES ET L'ETOILE), TV, 85, CDN, Mont; *'LES ENFANTS MAL-AIMES'* (6 eps), TV, 84, CDN, Mont son; *LOUISIANA,* C, 83, CDN/F, Mont; *MARIA CHAPDELAINE,* C, 83, CDN/F, Mont son; *MAN IN 5A* (THE MAN NEXT DOOR), C, 82, CDN, Mont; *LES PLOUFFE,* C, 81, CDN, Mont son; *QUEST FOR FIRE* (LA GUERRE DU FEU), C, 80, CDN/F, Mont 2e éq; *THE LUCKY STAR* (LA BELLE ETOILE), C, 80, CDN, Mont son (GENIE); *GIRLS,* C, 80, F, Ass mont; *IT RAINED ALL NIGHT THE DAY I LEFT,* C, 79, CDN/IL/F, Ass mont; *LE CRABE-TAMBOUR,* C, 78, F, Ass mont.

MORNINGSTAR, Michael

Morningstar Films, 76 Ferrier Ave., Toronto, Ont, CAN, M4K 3H4. (416)469-1729.
Types of Production & Categories: TV Film-Ed/Prod/Dir.
Genres: Documentary-TV.
Biography: Born 1954, Niagara Falls, Ontario. Education: Theatre & Film, Brock University; Film Production, York University.
Selective Filmography: *'THE FIFTH ESTATE'* (30 eps), TV, 86-83, CDN, Ed; *DREAM MERCHANTS/ THE FASTEST MAN ON WHEELS,* 'THE FIFTH ESTATE', TV, 82/81, CDN, Assoc Prod; *A.J.CASSON - THE ONLY CRITIC IS TIME,* TV, 80, CDN, Dir/Prod/Wr.

NICHOLSON, David

DGC. 167 Roehampton Ave., Toronto, Ont, CAN, M4P 1P9. (416)483-9769.
Types of Production & Categories: Th Film-Ed; TV Film-Ed.
Genres: Drama-Th&TV; Comedy-Th&TV; Action-Th&TV.
Biography: Born Nova Scotia. Attended Mount Allison and Dalhousie Universities (pre-med).
Selective Filmography: *'PHILIP MARLOWE PRIVATE EYE'* (1 eps), TV, 86, CDN, Ed; *UNFINISHED BUSINESS,* Th, 83, CDN, Ed; *KELLY,* Th, 81, CDN, Spv Ed; *CIRCLE OF TWO,* Th, 80, CDN, Ed; *RUNNING,* Th, 79, CDN, Ed; *SUDDEN FURY,* Th, 75, CDN, Ed; *'GEORGE',* TV, 74, CDN, Spv Ed.

NOLD, Werner

SGCT. 3675 Côte Terrebonne, St-Louis de Terrebonne, Qué, CAN, J0N 1N0. (514)471-2604. ONF, 3155 Côte de Liesse, Montréal, Qué, CAN, H3C 3H5.
Types de production et Catégories: l métrage-Mont; c métrage-Mont; TV film-Mont.
Types d'oeuvres: Drame-C; Documentaire-C&TV.
Curriculum vitae: Né en 1933, Suisse; arrive au Canada, 55. A l'emploi de l'ONF depuis 61; monteur de plus de 60 films documentaires et 20 fictions. Devient membre de l'Ordre du Canada, 84.
Filmographie sélective: *CINEMA, CINEMA,* TV, 85, CDN, Co réal; *O PICASSO,* C, 85, CDN, Mont; *MARIO,* C, 84, CDN, Mont; *ZEA,* C, 82, CDN, Mont; *UN MONOLOGUE NORD SUD,* TV, 82, CDN, Mont; *DISTORSIONS,* TV, 81, CDN, Mont; *DERRIERE L'IMAGE,* C, 78, CDN, Mont; *JEUX DE LA XXI OLYMPIADE,* C, 76, CDN, Sup mont; *TI-MINE, BERNIE PIS LA GANG,* C, 76, CDN, Mont; *LA FLEUR AUX DENTS,* C, 75, CDN, Mont; *LA GAMMICK,* C, 74, CDN, Mont; *O.K....LALIBERTE,* C, 73, CDN, Mont; *LE TEMPS D'UNE CHASSE* (ONCE UPON A HUNT), C, 72, CDN, Mont; *IXE 13,* C, 71, CDN, Mont; *L'EXIL,* C, 71, CDN, Mont; *PREAMBULE,* C, 69, CDN, Réal/Mont; *ST-DENIS DANS LE TEMPS...,* C, 69, CDN, Mont; *AVEC TAMBOURS ET TROMPETTES,* C, 67, CDN, Mont; *COMMENT SAVOIR* (KNOWING TO LEARN), C, 66, CDN, Mont; *LA VIE HEUREUSE DE LEOPOLD Z,* C, 65, CDN, Mont; *LA FLEUR DE L'AGE: LES ADOLESCENTES,* C, 65, CDN, Mont; *POUR LA SUITE DU MONDE,* C, 64, CDN, Mont; *PATINOIRE* (THE RINK), C, 63, CDN, Mont.

PARISEAU, Marcel

AR. 1856 André Vimont, Laval, Qué, CAN. (514)667-7615. Radio-Canada, 1400 blvd. Dorchester est, Montréal, Qué, CAN, H2L 2M2. (514)285-2860.
Types de production et Catégories: TV film-Mont; TV vidéo-Réal.
Types d'oeuvres: Documentaire-TV; Education-TV; Enfants-TV.
Curriculum vitae: Né en 1939, Montréal, Québec; bilingue. A remporté le Prix du RTNDA (national et est du Canada) pour le montage de *ONE YEAR TO GO.*
Filmographie sélective: *'THE CITY AT SIX'* (pl eps), TV, 80, CDN, Réal (**ANIK**); *THIS LAND IS NOT FOR SALE,* TV, 78, CDN, Mont; *ONE YEAR TO GO,* TV, 75, CDN, Mont.

PATE, Brent

77 Quebec Ave., #626, Toronto, Ont, CAN. (416)766-3607. The Magnetic North Corp., 70 Richmond St.E., Toronto, Ont, CAN. (416)365-7622.
Types of Production & Categories: TV Video-Ed.
Genres: Comedy-TV; Children's-TV; Commercials-TV; Music Video-TV.
Biography: Born 1957, London, Ontario. Education: TV Broadcasting, Fanshawe College.
Selective Filmography: *WINTARIO/ESSO/WOODIES/KRAFT/CRISPY CRUNCH/ PORK,* Cm, 86, CDN, Ed; *PROJECT LEAPFROG,* In, 86, CDN, Ed; *'THE LITTLE VAMPIRE'* (13 eps), TV, 86, CDN/GB/D, Ed; *MADAME,* MV, 86, CDN, Ed; *TEXACO/KLONDIKE DAYS/TRAPPERS BASEBALL/SILVER-WING TRAVEL,* Cm, 85, CDN, Ed; *BUTT-OUT,* In, 85, CDN, Ed; *BOPOLINA/ POLLY-ANNE,* MV, 85, CDN, Prod/Dir/Ed; *GOOD FRIENDS,* MV, 85, CDN, Ed; *'SCTV'* (Re-edit for syndication), (160 eps), TV, 85/84, CDN, Co-Ed; *'NATIVE HERITAGE'* (26 eps), TV, 85, CDN, Ed; *APARTMENT ON THE DARK SIDE OF THE MOON,* TV, 84, CDN, Ed; *'RENDEZVOUS'* (13 eps), TV, 84, CDN, Ed; *BONNIE DOON,* Cm, 84, CDN, Ed; *'LIVING TODAY'* (26 eps), TV, 84, CDN, Ed.

PATERSON, Sally

DGC. 321 Crawford St., Toronto, Ont, CAN, M6J 2V7. (416)588-4213.
Types of Production & Categories: Th Film-Ed; TV Film-Ed; TV Video-Ed.
Genres: Drama-Th&TV; Comedy-Th&TV; Documentary-Th&TV.
Biography: Born 1946, England; Canadian citizen. Taught film editing at Toronto Film Cooperative; President of Canadian Film Editors Guild, 83. Editor on many award-winning films.
Selective Filmography: 'STREET LEGAL' (3 eps), TV, 86, CDN, Ed; OVERNIGHT, Th, 85, CDN, Ed; 'AIRWAVES' (4 eps), TV, 85, CDN, Ed; 'DANGER BAY' (6 eps), TV, 85, CDN/USA, Ed; CLASS OF PROMISE, TV, 85, CDN, Ed; 'AMERICAN CAESAR' (3 eps), TV, 84, CDN, Ed; 'GOING GREAT' (26 eps), TV, 82/81, CDN, Ed; CHAMBERS: TRACKS AND GESTURES, TV, 82, CDN, Ed (CFEG); HANK WILLIAMS: THE SHOW HE NEVER GAVE, Th, 81, CDN, Ed; THE CHINESE (6 parts), TV, 81, CDN, Ed; 'SPREAD YOUR WINGS' (4 eps), TV, 81/80, CDN, Ed; EXPORT FOR PROFIT AND SURVIVAL, TV, 80, CDN, Ed; QUILTING: PATTERNS OF LOVE, TV, 79, CDN, Ed; THE KEEPER, Th, 76, CDN, Ed/Cont; THE SUPREME KID, Th, 75, CDN, Ed/Cont; WOLFPEN PRINCIPLE, Th, 74, CDN, Snd Ed; POTLATCH, TV, 74, CDN, Ed; PLEASURE FAIR, TV, 72, CDN, Ed; HOMER, Th, 69, CDN, Assist Ed; ISABEL, Th, 68, CDN, Assist Ed.

PAYER, Roch Christophe - voir REALISATEURS

PILON, France

STCQ. 3942 Berri, Montréal, Qué, CAN, H2L 4H1. (514)849-5091.
Types de production et Catégories: l métrage-Mont; c métrage-Mont; TV film-Mont/Sc.
Types d'oeuvres: Drame-C&TV; Documentaire-C&TV; Education-C&TV; Enfants-C&TV.
Curriculum vitae: Née en 1947, Kapuskasing, Ontario; bilingue. Baccalauréat ès Arts, Collège St-Maurice, Québec. A participé à des jury pour l'Institut Québécois du Cinéma.
Filmographie sélective: PELLAN, C, 86, CDN, Sc/Rech/Mont; TOUTES LES PHOTOS FINISSENT PAR SE RESSEMBLER, C, 85/84, CDN, Mont; BATEAU BLEU, MAISON VERTE, C, 85/84, CDN, Mont; MARC-AURELE FORTIN, 1888-1970, TV, 83-81, CDN, Mont/Sc; CES ETRANGERS NOS AMIS, C, 80, CDN, Mont; 'PORTRAITS D'UN ETE' (2 eps), TV, 80/79, CDN, Mont; LA POINTE DU MOULIN, C, 79, CDN, Mont; THETFORD, AU MILIEU DE NOS VIES, C, 78, CDN, Mont; CLARA, D'AMOUR ET DE REVOLTE, C, 78, CDN, Mont; LA TRADITION DE L'ORGUE AU QUEBEC, C, 78, CDN, Mont; 'UN PAYS, UN GOUT, UNE MANIERE' (10 eps), TV, 77/76, CDN, Mont; 'PASSE DEFINI' (5 eps), TV, 76, CDN, Mont, 'L'AMOUR QUOTIDIEN' (6 eps) TV, 75, CDN, Mont; AUTOPSIE D'UNE EXCLUSION, 'LES EXCLUS', TV, 75, CDN, Mont; HISTOIRE DE PECHE, C, 74, CDN, Mont; PRE-NATAL, TV, 74, CDN, Mont; ON PEUT VAINCRE LE CANCER, TV, 74, CDN, Mont; PAREIL COMME, TV, 74, CDN, Mont; VIVRE A LA QUATRIEME DIMENSION, TV, 73, CDN, Mont; UNE NUIT EN AMERIQUE, C, 73, CDN, Mont; LA TRAPPE, TV, 72, CDN, Mont; TRAVELLING BLUES, C, 71, CDN, Mont.

PINDER, Chris

DGC. 150 Kenilworth Ave., Toronto, Ont, CAN, M4L 3S6. (416)690-3262.
Types of Production & Categories: TV Film-Ed/Snd Ed.
Genres: Drama-Th&TV; Documentary-Th&TV; Educational-TV; Industrial-TV.
Biography: Born in Canada; bilingual. Honours B.A., English Language and Literature, Glendon College, York University, 1971. Editor on award-winning documentaries.

(cont/suite)

Selective Filmography: *LANGUAGE: A POINT OF DEPARTURE,* TV, 86, CDN, Ed; *'DURRELL IN RUSSIA'* (4 eps), TV, 85, CDN, Snd Ed; *BY OUR OWN HANDS,* TV, 85, CDN, Snd Ed; *VALENTINE'S REVENGE,* TV, 85, USA, 1st Assist Snd Ed; *WHERE THE HEART IS,* 'FOR THE RECORD', TV, 84, CDN, 1st Assist Snd Ed; *'THE OLYMPIANS'* (6 eps), TV, 84, CDN, Ed; *LISTEN TO THE CITY,* Th, 84, CDN, 1st Assist Ed; *SUNSHINE FOR SALE,* In, 84, CDN, Snd Ed; *THEOPHYLLINE THERAPY,* In, 83, CDN, Ed; *RAOUL WALLENBERG: BURIED ALIVE,* Th, 83, CDN, Snd Ed; *'THE CHINESE'* (4 eps), TV, 82, CDN, Snd Ed; *REACTOR SAFETY,* In, 82, CDN, Snd Ed; *'TEN-THOUSAND-DAY WAR'* (4 parts), TV, 82, CDN/USA, Snd Ed; *THE BATTLE OF BEECH HALL,* 'MAN ALIVE', TV, 81, CDN, Ed; *MELANIE,* Th, 81, CDN, 2nd Assist Ed; *POLICE STRESS,* 'ON THE JOB', In, 81, CDN, Snd Ed; *AFTER THE AXE,* TV, 80, CDN, 1st Assist Ed; *WORLD ON PARADE* (pilot), In, 80, CDN, Ed; *'CASH FOR LIFE LOTTERY'* (8 eps), TV, 79, CDN, Ed; *IT'S IN EVERY ONE OF US,* In, 79, CDN, Ed; *CAN CANADA COMPETE,* In, 78, CDN, Ed.

POLLINGTON, Mike

SMPTE. 3504 Rubens Crt., Burlington, Ont, CAN, L7N 3K4. (416)681-0044. Editcomm Inc., 100 Lombard St., Suite 104, Toronto, Ont, CAN, M5C 1M3. (416) 864-1780.
Types of Production & Categories: TV Video-Ed.
Genres: Documentary-TV; Educational-TV; Commercials-TV; Industrial-TV.
Biography: Born 1962, Hamilton, Ontario. Graduated from Mohawk College, Television Broadcasting Diploma, 83.
Selective Filmography: *'OPEN ROADS'* (13 eps), TV, 86, CDN, Ed; *'THE REAL FISHING SHOW'* (26 eps), TV, 86, CDN, Co-Ed; *TEXACO NEWS AND VIEWS,* In, 85, CDN, Ed; *PROFESSIONALISM,* 'OUTERBRIDGE BARRISTERS AND SOLICITORS', ED, 85, CDN, Ed; *CITADEL FOR 86/THE NEW BLACK & DECKER/HISTORY OF IMPERIAL OPTICAL,* In, 85, CDN, Ed; *POULAN CHAIN SAWS/ART GALLERY OF ONTARIO,* Cm, 85, CDN, Ed; *SHIPPING BY CP TRUCKS/G.M. MAGAZINE,* In, 85/84, CDN, Ed; *PRINTING* (16 films), In, 85/84, CDN/USA, Ed.

POTHIER, Marcel

2911 chemin Côte Ste-Catherine, Montréal, Qué, CAN, H3T 1C2. (514)738-5106. 1151 Alexandre de Sève, Montréal, Qué, CAN. (514)522-9828.
Types de production et Catégories: l métrage-Mont/Mont son; TV film-Mont/Mont son; c métrage-Mont/Mont son.
Types d'oeuvres: Drame-C&TV; Variété-TV; Action-C; Documentaire-C&TV.
Curriculum vitae: Né en 1948, St-Hyacinthe, Québec. Etudes classiques. Début de formation cinéma, Onyx Films (Montréal), 69-72. Boursier du Conseil des Arts, stage à Paris en bruitage et postsyncro au Studio de Boulogne, 77. Plusieurs nominations aux Prix Génies.
Filmographie sélective: *HENRI,* C, 86, CDN, Conc son; *LE MILLION TOUT PUISSANT,* TV, 86, CDN, Mont son; *ANNAPURNA,* TV, 85, CDN, Conc son; *THE VINDICATOR* (FRANKENSTEIN FACTOR), C, 84, CDN, Sup mont son; *LA FEMME DE L'HOTEL* (WOMAN IN TRANSIT), C, 84, CDN, Bruit; *LES ANNEES DE REVE,* C, 83, CDN, Sup mont son/Bruit; *SONATINE,* C, 83, CDN, Bruit; *RIEN QU'UN JEU,* C, 83, CDN, Mont/Sup mont son/Bruit; *LES YEUX ROUGES,* C, 82, CDN, Bruit; *BLEUE BRUME,* TV, 82, CDN, Mont son/Conc son; *UNE JOURNEE EN TAXI,* C, 81, CDN/F, Mont/Mont son/Prod assoc; *VISITING HOURS,* C, 81, CDN, Conc son; *HEARTACHES,* C, 81, CDN, Sup mont son; *L'AFFAIRE COFFIN* (THE COFFIN AFFAIR), C, 79, CDN, Mont son; *L'ARRACHE COEUR,* C, 79, CDN, Mont/Mont son; *L'ANGE GARDIEN,* C, 78, CDN/F, Mont son/Bruit; *L'EAU CHAUDE L'EAU FRETTE,* C, 78, CDN, Mont son; *PANIQUE* (PANIC), C, 77, CDN, Mont son; *'MAN OF THE*

(cont/suite)

NORTH', TV, 77, CDN, Sup mont; *THE LITTLE GIRL WHO LIVED DOWN THE LANE*, C, 76, CDN/F, Mont son; *THE FAR SHORE*, C, 75, CDN, Mont son; *MUSTANG*, C, 75, CDN, Mont son; *LES VAUTOURS*, C, 74, CDN, Mont son; *JACQUES BREL IS ALIVE AND WELL AND LIVING IN PARIS*, C, 74, CDN/F, Mont son; *THE CHRISTMAS MESSENGER*, TV, 74, CDN, Sup mont; *THE APPRENTICESHIP OF DUDDY KRAVITZ*, C, 73, CDN, Mont son; *ALIEN THUNDER*, C, 73, CDN, Mont son; *LA MORT D'UN BUCHERON*, C, 72, CDN, Mont son; *QUELQUES ARPENTS DE NEIGE*, C, 72, CDN, Mont son; *LA VRAIE NATURE DE BERNADETTE*, C, 72, CDN, Mont son.

PROCTOR, Goody

DGC. 6959 Marine Drive, Vancouver, BC, CAN. Action Cuts, 1260 Hornby Street, Vancouver, BC, CAN.
Types of Production & Categories: TV Film-Ed.
Genres: Variety-Th&TV; Documentary-Th&TV; Commercials-TV; Music Video-TV.
Biography: Born in Germany, 1946; emigrated to Canada, 51; Languages: English, German, some French. Editor for 15 years. Has won Clio Awards, Bessie and Creative Excellence Award for rock video of 'Parachute Club'.
Selective Filmography: *AT THE FEET OF THE MOON*, MV, 85, CDN, Ed; *THE REHEARSAL*, MV, 84, CDN/USA, Ed/Spv Ed.

PYKE, Roger - see DIRECTORS

RACINE, Pierre

STCQ. Les Promotions Multivisions, 492 ouest, rue Arago, Québec, Qué, CAN, G1K 2J8. (418)683-5481.
Types de production et Catégories: c métrage-Mont; TV film-Mont/Réal; TV vidéo-Mont/Prod/Réal.
Types d'oeuvres: Documentaire-C&TV; Education-C&TV; Industriel-C&TV.
Curriculum vitae: Né à Québec; bilingue.
Filmographie sélective: *LE GASODUC*, C, 84, CDN, Mont/Réal/Prod; *WHERE IS THE PUCK*, C, 83, CDN, Mont/Prod; *FESTIVAL D'ETE DE QUEBEC* (5 films), TV, 82, CDN, Mont/Réal/Prod; *MACFOR*, C, 80, CDN, Prod/Réal; *FESTIVAL DE ST-ANDRE*, TV, 78, CDN, Mont/Réal; *CLUB MED DE L'EUTERA*, C, 77, CDN, Mont/Réal; *URAKEN CANADA*, C, 76, CDN, Mont; *'NOUVELLES GOUVERNEMENTALES'* (200 clips), TV, 75-72, CDN, Mont; *CANIAPISCAU*, C, 75, CDN, Mont/Réal; *TUKTU*, C, 75, CDN, Mont; *VOYAGE SUB-ARCTIQUE*, C, 75, CDN, Mont; *LA PECHE A 4 CELCIUS*, C, 75, CDN, Mont; *L'AVENIR EST AU NORD*, C, 75, CDN, Mont; *CHENO*, C, 75, CDN, Mont; *FORET ECOLE DE VIE*, C, 73, CDN, Mont; *CONTROLE DE LA CHASSE A L'ORIGNAL*, TV, 74, CDN, Mont; *CAGE THORAXIQUE*, C, 74, CDN, Mont, *MLCP* (49 ém), TV, 73/72, CDN, Mont.

RAVOK, Brian

DGC. 111 Davisville Ave., PII 18, Toronto, Ont, CAN, M4S 1G5. (416)485-3100.
Types of Production & Categories: Th Film-Ed/Snd Ed; Th Short-Ed/Snd Ed; TV Film-Ed/Snd Ed; TV Video-Ed/Snd Ed.
Genres: Drama-Th; Comedy-Th; Documentary-Th&TV; Commercials-TV.
Biography: Born 1942, England; naturalized Canadian; bilingual. Started at BBC; emigrated to Montreal under contract to Onyx Film Inc. as supervising editor, 74; TV Ontario, then freelance, 77; has edited many commercials, documentaries, docudramas since 64. Supervising editor on animation series in Korea (K.K. DIC), 85; Japan (K.K. DIC), 86.
Selective Filmography: *SCREWBALLS*, Th, 83, CDN, Ed; *MELANIE*, Th, 81, CDN, Ed; *PROM NIGHT* (LE BAL DE L'HORREUR), Th, 79, CDN, Ed; *SOMETHING'S ROTTEN*, Th, 77, CDN, Ed; *QUEBEC THE GOOD EARTH*, Th, 75, CDN, Ed **(CFEG)**.

RODECK, Ken

Box 1347, Stonewall, Man, CAN. (204)467-8327. Rode Pictures, 411 Hammond Bldg, 63 Albert St, Stonewall, Man, CAN. (204)947-9037.
Types of Production & Categories: Th Film-Snd Ed; Th Short-Ed; TV Film-Ed; TV Video-Ed.
Genres: Drama-Th&TV; Documentary-Th&TV; Educational-TV; Animation-Th&TV.
Biography: Born 1951, Winnipeg, Manitoba; graduate of Banff School of Fine Arts, Film and Television Production. Six years with NFB, Winnipeg. Won Best Sound (Zagreb) for *GETTING STARTED.*
Selective Filmography: *SCIENCE FAIR KIDS,* TV, 86/85, CDN, Ed/Snd Ed; *LITTLE WOMEN,* 'DAUGHTERS OF THE COUNTRY', TV, 86/85, CDN, Snd Ed; *THE OLD BELIEVERS,* TV, 85, CDN, Ed; *THE AMAZING CREATION OF AL SIMMONS,* Th, 85, CDN, Ed/Snd Ed; *ROCKY ROULETTE,* TV, 85, CDN, Ed; *TRAMP AT THE DOOR,* TV, 84, CDN, Snd Ed; *THE BIG SNIT,* Th, 84, CDN, Snd Ed; *A POPLAR STORY,* TV, 84, CDN, Ed; *WILD BOUNTY,* TV, 84, CDN, Ed; *CONSERVATION FOR PROFIT,* In, 84, CDN, Ed; *THE PRODIGAL,* TV, 83, CDN, Snd Ed; *STEAM SCHEMES AND NATIONAL DREAMS,* TV, 83, CDN, Snd Ed; *WE HAVE POWER,* TV, 83, CDN, Ed; *PORTAGE PRIDE,* TV, 83, CDN, Ed; *YOU CAN'T GET IT HERE,* TV, 82, CDN, Snd Ed; *CAF COLOURS PRESENTATION,* TV, 82, CDN, Ed; *MUSCLE,* Th, 82, CDN, Ed; *IT'S A HOBBY FOR HARVEY* (THE WHISTLER), Th, 81, CDN, Ed; *KELEKIS 50 YEARS IN THE CHIPS,* Th, 81, CDN, Ed; *GRAIN ELEVATOR,* TV, 81, CDN, Snd Ed; *PIGBIRD,* TV, 80, CDN, Snd Ed; *STATUE,* TV, 80, CDN, Snd Ed; *GETTING STARTED,* TV, 80, CDN, Snd Ed; *LOVED, HONOURED AND BRUISED,* TV, 80, CDN, Snd Ed; *CAPITAL,* TV, 80, CDN, Snd Ed/Assist Ed; *RICE HARVEST,* TV, 80, CDN, Snd Ed; *THE STRONGEST MAN IN THE WORLD,* Th, 80, CDN, Snd Ed; *TUDOR KING,* Th, 79, CDN, Snd Ed/Assist Ed; *W.O.MITCHELL: NOVELIST IN HIDING,* TV, 79, CDN, Snd Ed.

ROTUNDO, Nick

83 Arlington Ave., Toronto, Ont, CAN, M6G 3Z2. (416)654-1277.
Types of Production & Categories: Th Film-Ed/Snd Ed/Mus Ed; Th Short-Ed/Prod; TV Film-Ed.
Genres: Drama-Th; Horror-Th.
Biography: Born 1954, Toronto, Ontario; speaks English, French, Italian. Honours B.F.A., Film Studies, York University, 78. Photographer, musician.
Selective Filmography: *THE HAUNTING OF HAMILTON HIGH,* Th, 86, CDN, Ed; *BULLIES,* Th, 85, CDN, Spv Ed/Mus Ed; *HIGH STAKES,* Th, 85, CDN, Spv Ed/Mus Ed; *THE BLUE MAN,* Th, 85, CDN, Ed; *FLYING,* Th, 84, CDN, Spv Ed/Mus Ed; *THRILLKILL,* Th, 83, CDN, Ed/Mus Ed; *CROSS-COUNTRY,* Th, 82, CDN, Ed/Snd Ed/Mus Ed; *HUMONGOUS,* Th, 81, CDN, Ed/Mus Ed/Snd Ed.

ROY, Rita

2255 Old Orchard, Montreal, Que, CAN, H4A 3A7. (514)484-5383. NFB, Box 6100, Montreal, Que, CAN, H3C 3H5. (514)283-9475.
Types of Production & Categories: Th Film-Ed; Th Short-Ed; TV Film-Ed/Dir.
Genres: Drama-Th&TV; Comedy-Th&TV; Variety-Th&TV; Educational-TV.
Biography: Born 1937, Bourlamaque, Quebec; bilingual. Education: Arts and Languages, Cinematography, Concordia University, McGill U., Sorbonne. Lived in Europe, 5 years; worked for CBC Ottawa, 1 year; joined NFB, 72.
Selective Filmography: *THE DREAM & THE TRIUMPH/MORTIMER GRIFFIN & SHALINSKY,* 'BELL CANADA PLAYHOUSE', TV, 86/85, CDN, Ed; *THE JOB OFFER,* TV, 86, CDN, Ed; *REBELLION OF YOUNG DAVID/THE TRUMPETTER/UNCLE T.,* 'BELL CANADA PLAYHOUSE', TV, 85, CDN, Ed; *CRITICAL CHOICE/HAPPY BIRTHDAY,* 'BIOETHICS', TV, 85, CDN, Ed; *CANADA'S SWEETHEART: THE SAGA OF HAL C.BANKS,* TV, 85, CDN, Ed;

(cont/suite)

ALL ABOUT BEARS, TV, 84, CDN, Ed/Dir; *BAYO*, Th, 84, CDN, Assist Ed; *BAMBINGER*, 'BELL CANADA PLAYHOUSE', TV, 84, CDN, Co-Ed; *THE TIN FLUTE* (Assist Ed-BONHEUR D'OCCASION), (5 eps), TV, 82, CDN, Ed; *THE TIN FLUTE* (Spv Assist Ed-BONHEUR D'OCCASION), Th, 82, CDN, Assist Ed; *THE CHEMISTRY OF FIRE* (LA CHIMIE DU FEU), TV, 82, CDN, Ed/Dir; *ONE OUT OF THREE IS A FISHBOAT*, TV, 82, CDN, Ed; *UNE FOIS SUR TROIS C'EST UN BATEAU DE PECHE*, TV, 81, CDN, 1st AD/Ed; *PAPER WHEAT*, TV, 80, CDN, Dir/Ed; *THE INHERITANCE*, TV, 79, CDN, Assist Ed/Res; *THE BLACKSMITH/FROM FLAX TO LINEN*, 'VIGNETTES', TV, 78, CDN, Dir/Ed; *OUR DAILY BREAD/LE MER S'AVANCE SUR NOS TERRES/THE WEAVER*, 'VIGNETTES', TV, 78, CDN, Ed.

RUSSELL, Robin

DGC. 98 Golfview Ave., Toronto, Ont, CAN, M4E 2K4. (416)920-9605.
Types of Production & Categories: Th Short-Ed; TV Film-Ed; TV Video-Ed.
Genres: Drama-TV; Comedy-TV; Documentary-TV; Educational-TV.
Biography: Born 1954. Honours B.A., Queen's University, 78.
Selective Filmography: *DEAD OF WINTER*, Th, 86, USA, 1st Assist Ed; *COURAGE*, TV, 86, USA, 1st Assist Ed; *THE BELIEVERS*, Th, 86, USA, 1st Assist Ed; *THE RETURN OF BILLY JACK*, Th, 86, USA, 1st Assist Ed; *ONE MAGIC CHRISTMAS*, Th, 85, CDN, Assist Ed; *STARCROSSED*, TV, 84, USA, Assist Ed; *BEER*, Th, 84, USA, 2nd Assist Ed; *MAKING IT YOUNG/ YOUTH STRESS*, 'YOUTH LIFESKILLS', TV, 84/83, CDN, Ed; *STRESS MANAGEMENT/ HEART DISEASE/ NEW HEALTH PROFESSIONALS*, 'SURVIVAL OF THE FITTEST', TV, 84, CDN, Ed; *LOONS 1984*, TV, 84, CDN, Ed; *EGG MARKETING BOARD FILM*, In, 84, CDN, Ed; *WELLNESS IN THE WORKPLACE/ EMPLOYEE FITNESS*, 'SURVIVAL OF THE FITTEST', TV, 83, CDN, Ed; *'LIVE IT UP'* (13 eps), TV, 82, CDN, Assist Ed; *'THE CHINESE'* (6 eps), TV, 82/81, CDN, Assist Ed.

SANDERS, Ron

DGC. 181 Carlaw Ave., Toronto, Ont, CAN, M4M 2S1. (416)465-3031. Dark Horse Productions, 69 Front St. E., Toronto, Ont, CAN, M5E 1B5. (416)368-7616. Smith/Gosnell Agency, 3872 Las Flores Canyon Rd., Malibu, CA, USA, 90265. (213)456-6641.
Types of Production & Categories: Th Film-Ed; TV Film-Ed.
Genres: Drama-Th&TV; Action-Th; Science Fiction-Th; Horror-Th.
Biography: Born 1945, Winnipeg, Manitoba. B.A., (English, Political Science, History), St. John's College, University of Manitoba.
Selective Filmography: *THE FLY*, Th, 86, USA, Spv Ed; *STRIKER'S MOUNTAIN*, TV, 85, CDN, Ed; *'PHILIP MARLOWE PRIVATE EYE'* (2 eps), TV, 85, CDN, Ed; *THE PARK IS MINE*, TV, 84, CDN/USA, Ed; *FIRESTARTER*, Th, 83, USA, Ed; *THE DEAD ZONE*, Th, 83, USA, Ed; *VIDEODROME*, Th, 82, CDN, Ed; *SCANNERS*, Th, 81, CDN, Ed; *TITLE SHOT*, Th, 79, CDN, Ed; *FAST COMPANY*, Th, 78, CDN, Ed; *BLOOD & GUTS*, Th, 77, CDN, Ed/Snd Ed.

SAUNDERS, Peter

ACTT, DGC. 22 Close ave., #809, Toronto, Ont, CAN, M6K 2V4. (416)536-1360. Keg Productions, 1231 Yonge St., Toronto, Ont, CAN. (416)924-2186.
Types of Production & Categories: Th Film-Ed/Dir/Wr; Th Short-Dir/Prod/Wr/Ed; TV Film-Ed/Dir/Wr.
Genres: Drama-Th&TV; Comedy-Th&TV; Variety-Th&TV; Documentary-Th&TV.
Biography: Born 1930, London, England; landed immigrant, Canada, 82. Has been in the film industry since 45. Has had 10 short stories and 'The Serbian Triangle', his first novel, published. Has worked in the Middle East, Africa, various European

(cont/suite)

countries, Canada and the U.S.. Supervising editor for many British series including: *INTERNATIONAL DETECTIVE, GLENCANNON, GHOST SQUAD*. Co-writer and director of 6 episodes of *SWALLOWS AND AMAZONS*; has directed over 50 commercials.

Selective Filmography: *THE MAN WHO LOVED BIRDS,* TV, 86, CDN, Ed; *'PROFILES OF NATURE'* (11 eps), TV, 85, CDN, Ed; *HEAVENLY BODIES,* Th, 84, CDN, Dial Ed; *PAROLE DANCE,* TV, 84, CDN, Ed; *BIRDS IN PARADISE,* Th, 83, CDN/USA, 1st AD; *CABIN FEVER,* Th, 83, CDN, 1st AD; *'LORNE GREENE'S NEW WILDERNESS'* (9 eps), TV, 83/82, CDN, Ed; *LIGHT ON A DARK CONTINENT,* Th, 81/80, GB, Ed/Dir/Wr; *NORTH SEA OIL,* Th, 80, GB, Dir; *TEN SECONDS TO KNOCKDOWN,* Th, 79, GB, Dir; *PYRENE PROTECTS,* Th, 79, GB, Dir; *HOUSEWIVES CHOICE,* Th, 78, GB, Dir; *THE LONELY PLACES,* Th, 76, GB, Dir; *TARGO FLORIO,* TV, 74, GB/I, Dir; *PARKER PEN,* Th, 73, F, Dir; *ROCKET TO THE MOON,* Th, 67, GB, 2nd U Dir; *THE AFRICAN QUEEN,* Th, 51, USA, Assist Ed.

SAUVE, Alain

SGCT. 9728 De La Roche, Montréal, Qué, CAN, H2C 2N7. (514)388-5808. ONF, 3155 Côte de Liesse, Montréal, Qué, CAN, H4N 2N4. (514)283-9366.
Types de production et Catégories: c métrage-Réal/Sc/Mont; TV film-Mont; TV vidéo-Mont.
Types d'oeuvres: Drame-C&TV; Documentaire-C&TV; Education-TV; Enfants-C&TV.
Curriculum vitae: Né en 1947, Montréal, Québec. Bac. en Sciences, Collège du Mont St-Louis; Comptabilité, Administration, Ecole des Hautes Etudes Commerciales. Administrateur de production, ONF, 68-71; cinéaste pigiste, 71-79; monteur, réalisateur, 79-85. Stage de montage film et video assisté par ordinateur sur système Editroid, Montréal, 86.
Filmographie sélective: *LA POLITIQUE AU FEMININ,* TV, 86, CDN, Mont son; *RENDEZ-VOUS: 10h.30* (SCULPTURE D'IVOIRE), TV, 85, CDN, Sup mont/ Mont son/Réal; *LE VIEILLARD ET L'ENFANT,* TV, 85, CDN, Mont son; *RETOUR A DRESDE,* TV, 85, CDN, Mont son; *KASPAR,* C, 85, CDN, Bruit; *RIOPELLE,* TV, 84, CDN, Mont/Mont son; *HIBAKUSHA* (PLUS JAMAIS HIBAKUSHA), TV, 83, CDN, Mont son/Bruit; *LA PLANTE,* C, 82, CDN, Bruit/ Conc son; *LA QUARANTAINE,* C, 82, CDN, Mont son; *DEMO-RIOPELLE,* TV, 81, CDN, Mont/Mont son; *LES TERRES-NEUVIENS FRANCAIS,* TV, 81, CDN, Mont/Mont son; *LES PIEGES DE LA MER* (CALYPSO), C, 81, CDN, Mont/Mont son; *LE JONGLEUR,* C, 81, CDN, Mont son; *ON EST RENDU DEVANT LE MONDE,* C, 80, CDN, Mont son; *LE PAYS DE LA TERRE SANS ARBRE,* TV, 80, CDN, Mont son; *GENS D'ABITIBI,* TV, 80, CDN, Mont son; *40e ANNIVERSAIRE DE L'ONF,* C, 79, CDN, Mont son; *'LES ENFANTS DES NORMES'* (8 eps), TV, 79, CDN, Mont son; *DES ASTRES ET DESASTRES,* TV, 78, CDN, Mont/Mont son/Réal/Sc; *VINGT-SIX FOIS DE SUITE,* TV, 78, CDN, Mont/Réal; *'CHRONIQUE DE LA VIE QUOTIDIENNE'* (4 eps), TV, 77, CDN, Mont/Mont son; *JEUX DE LA XXI OLYMPIADE,* C, 76, CDN, Mont; *AIMEZ-VOUS LES CHIENS?,* TV, 74, CDN, Ass mont/Mont son; *SI TU ES SAGE...,* TV, 74, CDN, Mont/Réal; *PARTIS POUR LA GLOIRE,* C, 74, CDN, Ass cam; *LA GAMMICK,* C, 74, CDN, Ass mont/Mont son; *POUR UNE CULTURE,* C, 73, CDN, Mont/Mont son/Réal/Sc; *LA TETE A PAPINEAU,* TV, 73, CDN, Mont; *PARA-COMMANDO,* C, 71, CDN, Mont/Co réal; *LE MARSIEN,* C, 70, CDN, Réal/Sc.

SCHREINER, Reinhard

DGC. 1231 24th St., #4, Santa Monica, CA, USA, 90404. (213)453-6555. 5253 Clark St., #2, Montreal, Que, CAN, H2T 2V3. (514)270-8898.
Types of Production & Categories: Th Film-Ed; TV Film-Ed.
Genres: Drama-Th; Comedy-Th; Action-Th&TV; Documentary-TV.

(cont/suite)

Biography: Born 1952.
Selective Filmography: *THE SPYING PIZZA,* Th, 85, USA, Ed/Snd Ed; *THE RHYTHMATIST* (TALKING DRUMS), TV, 85, USA/GB, Ed/Snd Ed; *BLUE ICE,* Th, 84, USA, Ed; *CUBA, PLAYING TO WIN,* TV, 84, USA, Snd Ed; *E.T. PHONE DOME,* TV, 83, CDN, Ed; *DANTE'S INFERNO,* Th, 82, CDN, Ed.

SHUMIATCHER, Cal

IATSE-891. 2345 W.8th Ave., Vancouver, BC, CAN, V6K 2A8. (604)736-6779.
Petra Film Productions, 1149 Hornby St., #204, Vancouver, BC, CAN, V6Z 1W1. (604)669-1333.
Types of Production & Categories: Th Short-Ed/Snd Ed/Prod; TV Film-Snd Ed.
Genres: Drama-Th&TV; Comedy-TV; Documentary-Th&TV; Animation-Th&TV.
Biography: Born 1957, Calgary, Alberta. B.A., Film & TV, University of British Columbia , 81. *NO VACANCY* won a Gold Jury Award, Houston.
Selective Filmography: *MY AMERICAN COUSIN,* Th, 85, CDN, Foley; *MY KIND OF TOWN,* Th, 85, CDN, Prod/Snd Ed; *HOORAY FOR SANDBOXLAND,* TV, 85, CDN, Ed/Snd Ed; *ANIJAM,* Th, 84, CDN, Ed/Snd Ed; *THE LITTLE TOWN THAT DID,* TV, 84, CDN, Prod/Ed; *NO VACANCY,* Th, 83, CDN, Prod/Ed; *BIG MEAT EATER,* Th, 81, CDN, Assist Snd Ed.

SKOGLAND, Kari

197 Chaplin Crescent, Toronto, Ont, CAN, M5P 1B1. (416)483-5736. The Editors Film & Video, 127 John St., Toronto, Ont, CAN, M5V 2E2. (416)597-1137.
Types of Production & Categories: Th Short-Ed; TV Film-Ed; TV Video-Ed.
Genres: Documentary-Th&TV; Commercials-TV; Music Video-TV.
Biography: Born 1959. Co-owner, The Editors Film and Video. Awards include: Marketing, TVB, Art Directors Club, Cannes, various U.S. TV commercials awards.
Selective Filmography: *LABATT'S/ CADBURY'S/ SCHWEPPS/ POWELL/ MOLSONS/ GENERAL FOODS,* Cm, 85, CDN, Spv Ed; *PROCTOR & GAMBLE/ CANADIAN PACIFIC/ QUAKER/ KRAFT FOODS LTD.,* Cm, 85/84, CDN, Spv Ed; *KLEENEX/ EFFEM FOODS/ GENERAL MOTORS/ AMERICAN STANDARD/ HONDA,* Cm, 85/84, CDN, Spv Ed; *DYNATEC,* 'FRONTRUNNERS', TV, 85, CDN, Ed; *DESTINY'S ROAD,* Th, 84, CDN, Spv Ed; *TORONTO TRANSIT COMMISSION/ DAD'S COOKIES/ ANDRES' WINES,* Cm, 84, CDN, Spv Ed.

SLIPP, Marke

DGC. 107 Lorelei Close, Edmonton, Alta, CAN, T5X 2E7. (403)457-0780. Pegasus Productions Ltd., 11930 - 100 Ave., Edmonton, Alta, CAN, T5K 0K5. (403)488-2287.
Types of Production & Categories: Th Film-Ed; Th Short-Ed; TV Film-Ed/Dir; TV Video-Dir.
Genres: Drama-Th&TV; Variety-TV; Documentary-TV; Educational-TV.
Biography: Born 1949, Sackville, New Brunswick. Started film career at 7 doing commercials; began editing career, 69, Toronto; freelancer on a variety of productions; worked for Canawest Productions, Vancouver as staff editor. Established Pegasus Productions Ltd., Edmonton, 78.
Selective Filmography: *RISE & SHINE,* TV, 86, CDN, Ed; *AT THE CROSSROADS,* TV, 86, CDN, Ed; *TURN IT OFF,* TV, 85, CDN, Ed; *FROZEN MUSIC,* TV, 85, CDN, Dir; *A MATTER OF SOIL,* ED, 84, CDN, Ed; *TO THE ENDS OF THE EARTH,* TV, 84, CDN/USA, Ed; *SQUADRON 417,* TV, 84, CDN, Ed/Dir/Prod; *PEST WARS,* TV, 83, CDN, Ed; *'ALBERTA ARTISTS',* TV, 83, CDN, Ed; *TRANSITIONS,* TV, 83, CDN, Ed; *SNOWBIRDS 81,* Th, 82, CDN, Ed; *RIDING MOUNTAIN NATIONAL PARK/PRINCE ALBERT NATIONAL PARK,* TV, 82, CDN, Ed/Prod; *DEMOCRATIC CROSSING,* TV, 81, CDN, Ed; *RCMS STORY,* TV, 81, CDN, Ed; *IT ALL COUNTS, 'A MATTER*
(cont/suite)

OF TIME', TV, 80, CDN, Ed; *'SACRED CIRCLE'* (part 1), TV, 80, CDN, Ed; *LATITUDE 55*, Th, 80, CDN, Ed; *DO WHAT YA WANT, MAMA*, TV, 79, CDN, Prod/Ed **(CFEG)**; *ONE WAY TICKET*, TV, 79, CDN, Ed; *PARALLELS*, Th, 79, CDN, Ed; *PRIORY: THE ONLY HOME I'VE GOT*, TV, 78, CDN, Snd Ed; *NEVER A DULL MOMENT*, Th, 78, CDN, Ed; *JAZZ - MILT JACKSON*, TV, 77, CDN, Ed; *MUSIC THERAPY*, TV, 76, CDN, Ed/Dir; *'COME ALIVE'* (daily), TV, 75/74, CDN, Ed; *THE WAY OF WOOD*, TV, 72, CDN, Ed; *PROUD RIDER*, Th, 70, CDN, Snd Ed; *'ADVENTURES IN RAINBOW COUNTRY'* (26 eps), TV, 69, CDN/GB/AUS, Assist Ed.

SLOAN, Anthony

143 Harrison St., Toronto, Ont, CAN, M6J 2A5. (416)532-6772. Triune Productions, 24 Ryerson Ave., #304, Toronto, Ont, CAN, M5T 2P3. (416)362-9120.
Types of Production & Categories: Th Short-Prod/Dir; TV Film-Ed; TV Video-Dir.
Genres: Drama-TV; Comedy-Th&TV; Musical-TV; Documentary-TV.
Biography: Born 1958, Montreal, Quebec. B.F.A., Specialized Honours Degree in Film Production, York University, 80; awarded the Famous Players Theatres Maple Leaf Award for Outstanding Achievement. Member of Triune Acting Ensemble. *BAY STREET TAP*, winner, Independent Short Film Showcase, 80.
Selective Filmography: *THE DIPLOMAT*, *'MOTLEY TALES'*, TV, 86, CDN, Dir; *AMNESTY INTERNATIONAL*, Cm, 86, CDN, DOP; *THE MIGHTY QUINN*, *'MAN ALIVE'*, TV, 85, CDN, Snd Ed; *ALL THAT BACH*, TV, 85, CDN, Ed; *MAKING OVERTURES*, TV, 84, CDN, Ed; *COWBOYS DON'T CRY*, TV, 84, CDN, Snd Ed; *THRILLKILL*, Th, 83, CDN, 1st Assist Cam; *BAY STREET TAP*, Th, 82, CDN, Co-Prod/Co-Dir; *DOOR DESH*, Th, 81, CDN/IND, Assist Cam/ Assist Ed.

STRAUGHAN, Brent

GCFC, NABET. R.R.#1, Ashburn, Ont, CAN, L0B 1A0. (416)655-4867.
Types of Production & Categories: Th Short-Dir/Comp; TV Video-Ed.
Genres: Musical-Th; Current Affairs-TV; News-TV.
Biography: Born 1946, Edmonton, Alberta. B.Sc., Zoology, University of Washington, Seattle, 68; M.A., Communications, Simon Fraser U., 73. Entertainment editor (tape), CTV's *NATIONAL NEWS* and *CANADA A.M.*, 82-86. Has 2 albums out 'Mystery Mama Plays the Golden Oldies' and 'Enfilony'.
Selective Filmography: *ENFILONY: FUGITIVE WOODS/ALL THESE THINGS I POSSESS/SKATE WITH ME*, Th, 78, CDN, Comp/Dir/DOP.

STREET, Bill - see DIRECTORS

TABORSKY, Dagmar

DGC. 56 Church Ave., Willowdale, Ont, CAN, M2N 4E9. (416)222-3385.
Types of Production & Categories: Th Film-Ed/Dir; TV Film-Ed/Dir.
Genres: Drama-TV; Documentary-Th&TV; Educational-Th&TV.
Biography: Born Prague, Czechoslovakia. Worked as an editor, director in public affairs department in Prague TV. Directed, edited (in Canada) many programs for Museum of Man and Radio-Quebec. *VIANOCE - THE SLOVAK-CANADIAN CHRISTMAS* won the Blue Ribbon, American Film Fest.; *ENERGY* was named Best Show of the Decade by Time magazine.
Selective Filmography: *TAMING OF THE DEMONS* (EXPO 86), Th, 86, CDN, Ed; *ENERGY* (multiscreen), Th, 82, CDN/USA, Ed; *'ETHNICS'* (6 short films), TV, 80, CDN, Ed/Dir; *'CANADIAN INDIANS'* (4 short films), Th, 79, CDN, Ed/ Dir; *VIANOCE - THE SLOVAK-CANADIAN CHRISTMAS*, Th, 78, CDN, Ed/ Dir/Wr.

Academy of Canadian Cinema & Television
Académie canadienne du cinéma et de la télévision

En reconnaissance du succès
exceptionnel et des accomplissements
des artistes responsables de la
production de nos émissions de
télévision francophones et anglophones.

Joignez-vous à la fête!

Félicitations à tous les lauréats!

PRIX GENIE AWARDS
Academy of Canadian Cinema & Television
Académie canadienne du cinéma et de la télévision

TATE, Christopher
DGC, IATSE-210. 11930 - 100 Ave., Edmonton, Alta, CAN, T5K 0K5. (403)488-2390. 222 Cranbrooke Ave., Toronto, Ont, CAN, M5M 1M7. (416)489-4897.
Types of Production & Categories: Th Short-Ed; TV Film-Ed.
Genres: Drama-Th&TV; Documentary-Th&TV; Children's-Th&TV.
Biography: Born 1951.
Selective Filmography: *'LAUGHING MATTERS'*, TV, 85, CDN, Key Grip; *BRIDGE TO TERABITHIA*, 'WONDERWORKS', TV, 84, CDN, Snd Ed; *ISAAC LITTLEFEATHERS*, Th, 84, CDN, Snd Mix; *ANOTHER NAKED NIGHT*, TV, 84, CDN, Ed; *AMBER VALLEY*, Th, 83, CDN, Ed; *GREAT DAYS IN THE ROCKIES*, Th, 83, CDN, Ed; *RUNNING BRAVE*, Th, 83, CDN/USA, Grip; *OIL SPILL*, 'BUSH PILOTS', TV, 82, CDN, Ed; *SPIRIT OF THE HUNT*, Th, 82, CDN, Ed; *ALL THAT GLITTERS*, TV, 82, CDN, Ed; *CHINA MISSION*, Th, 80, CDN, Ed; *BANFF FESTIVAL*, TV, 80, CDN, Ed; *LATITUDE 55*, Th, 80, CDN, Boom; *PRIORY, THE ONLY HOME I'VE GOT*, Th, 78, CDN, Ed; *FAST COMPANY*, Th, 78, CDN, Boom.

THEBERGE, André - voir REALISATEURS

THOMPSON, Don
3432 Dieppe Dr., Vancouver, BC, CAN, V5M 4C7. (604)435-4007. ADD Video Productions, 550 Cambie St., Vancouver, BC, CAN, V6B 2N7. (604)687-3937.
Types of Production & Categories: TV Video-Ed/Prod.
Genres: Musical-TV; Documentary-TV; Sports-TV.
Biography: Born 1962. Strong news/news magazine background; works in model, fashion industry including fashion videos.
Selective Filmography: *WONDER WHY THEY'RE LONELY*, MV, 85, CDN, Ed; *CHALLENGE OF CHANGE*, TV, 85, CDN, Ed/Co-Prod; *SWIFTSURE 85*, TV, 85, CDN, Tech Dir; *DISCOVERY*, TV, 84, CDN, Prod; *THE FIFTH ESTATE* (1 eps), TV, 84, CDN, Snd Rec; *NORTH AMERICAN WKA KICKBOXING*, TV, 84, CDN, Ed; *UNDERSTANDING THE STOCKMARKET* (10 eps), TV, 83, CDN, Dir.

THOMPSON, Jane
DGC. 170 Lippincott St., Toronto, Ont, CAN, M5S 2P1. (416)964-7949.
Types of Production & Categories: Th Short-Ed.
Genres: Drama-TV; Documentary-Th.
Biography: Born 1952, Montreal, Quebec; B.A. in Film Studies, Queen's University. Film editor 73-82; developed and managed post production unit at Schulz Productions, 81-85; NFB Dramalab 85 as director for Ontario. *BEGINNINGS* won the Silver Plaque, Chicago Film Festival.
Selective Filmography: *BUSH PILOT: REFLECTIONS ON A CANADIAN MYTH*, Th, 80, CDN, Ed; *BEGINNINGS*, TV, 80, CDN, Prod.

TILDEN, Annette
1666 Queen St. E., #32, Toronto, Ont, CAN, M4L 1G3. (416)699-1829. Unicorn Concepts, 19 Mercer St., Toronto, Ont, CAN, M5V 1H2. (416)591-1737.
Types of Production & Categories: TV Film-Ed.
Genres: Drama-TV; Documentary-TV; Educational-TV; Children's-TV.
Biography: Born 1940, Harriston, Ontario; graduated Radio & TV Arts, Ryerson Polytechnic Institute; University of Toronto. Twenty years film experience; started Unicorn Concepts, 83.
Selective Filmography: *'OWL TV'* (sev segs), TV, 86-84, CDN, Ed; *THE SIMULATOR CHALLENGE*, ED, 84/83, CDN, Co-Ed; *JUDGEMENT II*, ED, 83, CDN, Ed; *HOCKEY NIGHT IN CANADA FEATURES* (29 seg), TV, 82-76, CDN, Ed; *COMPANIONS*, ED, 82, CDN, Ed; *SAFETY ALOFT*, ED, 81, CDN, Ed; *SPECIAL OLYMPICS*, Th, 81, CDN, Ed; *'SPORT FISHING'* (13 eps), TV,

(cont/suite)

81/80, CDN, Ed; *SPORTS HALL OF FAME INDUCTEES*, ED, 80, CDN, Ed; *'PERSONAL SPACES'* (13 eps), TV, 79/78, CDN, Ed; *MAPLE LEAFS' GOLDEN ANNIVERSARY/NATIONAL ASSEMBLY*, ED, 79/77, CDN, Ed; *'FISH TALES'* (13 eps), TV, 78/77, CDN, Co-Ed; *GOLD FOR THE GODS*, TV, 76, CDN, Ed; *BAD PAINT STORY*, 'MARKET PLACE', TV, 76, CDN, Ed; *'COUNTRY CANADA'* (4 seg), TV, 76/75, CDN, Ed; *'SIDESTREET'* (1 eps), TV, 75, CDN, Ed; *NEW CANADIANS AT SCHOOL*, TV, 75, CDN, Ed; *OUT OF SCHOOL LEARNING*, TV, 75, CDN, Ed; *BEYOND THE CLASSROOM*, ED, 74, CDN, Ed; *'POLICE SURGEON'* (5 eps), TV, 74, CDN, Ed; *PANASONIC TOWER*, In, 74, CDN, Ed; *JOURNEY TO CATARAQUI*, TV, 73, CDN, Ed; *ALGOMA FALL FESTIVAL*, TV, 73, CDN, Dir; *BEYOND THE SOUTH POLE*, TV, 73, CDN, Ed.

TINGLEY, Cameron

DGC. 74 Ellsworth Ave., Toronto, Ont, CAN, M6G 2K3. (416)654-6297.
Types of Production & Categories: Th Short-Ed/Snd Ed; TV Film-Ed/Snd Ed; TV Video-Ed/Snd Ed.
Genres: Documentary-Th&TV; Educational-Th&TV; Industrial-Th.
Biography: Born 1953, London, Ontario. Education: Film Production, Conestoga College. Has own film and video editing equipment.
Selective Filmography: *'PROFILES OF NATURE'* (55 eps), TV, 86-84, CDN, Ed; *WELLINGTON COUNTY COURTHOUSE*, ED, 84, CDN, Ed; *CELLY AND FRIENDS*, TV, 84, CDN, Ed/Snd Ed; *ROCK, ICE AND OIL*, TV, 83, CDN, Ed; *SAFE STRANGERS*, ED, 82, CDN, Ed/Snd Ed; *CANADA: ON THE LEADING EDGE OF SCIENCE*, TV, 82, CDN, Snd Ed; *CANADA: COAST AND COAST/ THE HOUSE NEXT DOOR*, ED, 81, CDN, Ed/Snd Ed; *'WILD CANADA'* (3 eps), TV, 80, CDN, Ed; *JASON AND THE CHAMPS*, ED, 79, CDN, Ed/Snd Ed; *THE IMBALANCE OF NATURE*, TV, 77, CDN, Ed/Snd Ed; *A MIDNIGHT SNACK*, TV, 75, CDN, Ed/Snd Ed; *THE FOREST CITY*, In, 74, CDN, Ed; *HEAVEN ONLY KNOWS*, TV, 73, CDN, Ed/Snd Ed.

TOUSSAINT, Jurgen

DGC. 19 Smithfield Drive, Toronto, Ont, CAN, M8Y 3M1. (416)251-6801. Jatco Film Services Inc., 266 Adelaide St. W., Toronto, Ont, CAN. (416)591-6761.
Types of Production & Categories: TV Film-Ed.
Genres: Documentary-TV; Educational-TV; Commercials-TV.
Biography: Born 1941, Berlin, Germany. Languages: English, German. Educated in Germany, emigrated to Canada, 66; German citizenship. Trained in Canada; self employed since 78; founded Jatco Film Services Inc., 78; editor on numerous commercials and industrial films.

VAN DYKE, Archie

58 Parklea Dr., Toronto, Ont, CAN, M4G 2J6. (416)423-0538. The Editors Film & Video, 127 John St., Toronto, Ont, CAN, M5V 2E2. (416)597-1137.
Types of Production & Categories: TV Film-Ed; TV Video-Ed.
Genres: Documentary-TV; Commercials-TV.
Biography: Born 1947, Netherlands; Canadian citizen. Entered commercial film editing in 66 on apprenticeship level to become editor for commercial production companies; has worked on many shorts, documentaries and award-winning commercials.

VAN VELSEN, Hans

DGC. 642 Sheppard Ave. E., #1214, Willowdale, Ont, CAN, M2K 1B9. (416)223-2699. 181 Carlaw Ave., Toronto, Ont, CAN, M4M 2S1. (416)469-2040.
Types of Production & Categories: Th Film-Ed; TV Film-Ed.
Genres: Drama-Th&TV; Comedy-TV; Documentary-TV; Commercials-TV.
Biography: Born 1926, Holland; has worked in Canada since 56. Has been editing commercials since 79.

(cont/suite)

Selective Filmography: *'MATT AND JENNY'* (6 eps), TV, 79, CDN/GB/D, Ed; *'SEARCH AND RESCUE'* (7 eps), TV, 76, CDN/USA, Ed; *'SWISS FAMILY ROBINSON'* (5 eps), TV, 75/74, CDN, Ed; *'GEORGE'* (15 eps), TV, 74, CDN, Ed; *'POLICE SURGEON'* (18 eps), TV, 70-67, CDN, Ed; *'THE COLLABORATORS'* (5 eps), TV, 68, CDN, Ed; *'DR. SIMON LOCKE'* (16 eps), TV, 66, CDN/USA, Ed; *'FOREST RANGERS'* (17 eps), TV, 62, CDN, Ed; *'HUDSON'S BAY'* (4 eps), TV, 60, CDN, Ed; *ROSES IN DECEMBER*, Th, 58, CDN, Ed.

WALLIS, Rit

STCQ, DGC. 4818 Park Ave., Montreal, Que, CAN, H2V 4E6. (514)270-7454. 122 Edgewood Ave., Toronto, Ont, CAN, M4L 3H1. (416)465-3313.
Types of Production & Categories: Th Film-Ed; TV Film-Ed; TV Video-Ed.
Genres: Drama-Th&TV; Action-Th; Science Fiction-Th&TV; Horror-Th.
Biography: Graduated with High Honours (Cinema and TV), John Abbott College. Two-year apprenticeship at Cinepix Inc., 1978-80.
Selective Filmography: *HALF A LIFETIME,* TV, 86, CDN, Ed; *THE GATE,* Th, 86, CDN, Ed; *MURDER IN SPACE,* TV, 85, CDN/USA, Ed; *THE BOY IN BLUE,* Th, 84, CDN, Ed; *THE SURROGATE,* Th, 83, CDN, Ed; *OVERDRAWN AT THE MEMORY BANK,* TV, 83, CDN/USA, Ed; *'THE LAST SAILORS'* (6 eps), TV, 82, CDN/GB, Ed/P Pro Spv; *SCANDALE,* Th, 82, CDN, P Pro Spv/Co-Ed; *'ARAMCO'* (3 eps), In, 82, CDN, Ed/Snd Ed; *TWENTY-NINE,* Th, 82, USA, Ed; *MY BLOODY VALENTINE,* Th, 81, CDN, Ed/P Pro Spv; *HOT TOUCH* (FRENCH KISS), Th, 81, CDN, Dial Ed; *YESTERDAY* (GABRIELLE), Th, 79, CDN, P Pro Spv.

WARREN, Jeff

DGC. 507 Glengarry Ave., Toronto, Ont, CAN, M5M 1G2. (416)782-7445.
Types of Production & Categories: Th Film-Ed; TV Film-Ed; TV Video-Ed.
Genres: Drama-TV; Documentary-Th&TV; Educational-TV; Children's-TV.
Biography: Born 1950; Canadian. Attended Ryerson Polytechnical Institute, Photographic Arts. Has been a full-time editor since 72; edited award-winning dramas, documentaries and educational programs: *FINAL OFFER - BOB WHITE AND THE UNITED AUTO WORKERS FIGHT FOR INDEPENDENCE* won a Genie and the Prix Italia, 86.
Selective Filmography: *WHERE'S PETE?,* TV, 86, CDN, Ed; *FINAL OFFER: BOB WHITE AND THE UAW'S FIGHT FOR INDEPENDENCE,* Th, 85, CDN, Ed/Snd Ed; *'BRILLIANT CAREERS'* (6 eps), TV, 84, CDN, Ed; *SOLIDARITY,* TV, 84, CDN, Ed; *'GOING GREAT'* (20 eps), TV, 83, CDN, Ed; *'AMERICAN CAESAR'* (2 eps), TV, 83, CDN, Ed; *NATIONAL SAFETY DRILL,* TV, 82, CDN, Ed; *KIDS CASE AGAINST VANDALISM,* ED, 82, CDN, Ed; *FIT TO LAST,* TV, 82, CDN, Ed; *PRETTY BABIES,* TV, 82, CDN, Ed; *NATIONAL CRIME TEST,* TV, 81, CDN, Ed; *DAVID LINCOLN,* TV, 81, CDN, Ed; *AWAY FROM HOME,* TV, 81, CDN, Ed; *ESCAPE FROM IRAN: THE INSIDE STORY,* TV, 81, CDN, Ed; *ESCAPE FROM IRAN: THE CANADIAN CAPER,* TV, 80, CDN, Ed (CFEG); *UPPER REACHES,* TV, 80, CDN, Ed; *BELONGING: A FILM ABOUT ADOPTION,* TV, 80, CDN, Ed; *THE YANKS ARE COMING,* TV, 79, CDN, Ed; *'W5'* (sev seg), TV, 79-77, CDN, Ed; *ESSIAC,* TV, 78, CDN, Ed; *'MacLEAR'* (23 eps), TV, 77-74, CDN, Ed; *'WORLD OF WICKS'* (6 eps), TV, 73, CDN, Ed; *'LIFELINES'* (4 eps), TV, 73, CDN, Ed; *'WILD REFUGE'* (3 eps), TV, 72, CDN/USA, Ed; *'HERE COME THE SEVENTIES'* (2 eps), TV, 71, CDN, Ed.

WEBSTER, Ion

DGC, STCQ. 80 Quebec Ave., Toronto, Ont, CAN, M6P 4B7. (416)762-9485.
Types of Production & Categories: Th Film-Ed; TV Film-Ed; TV Video-Ed.
(cont/suite)

Genres: Drama-Th&TV; Comedy-Th; Documentary-TV.
Biography: Born 1950, Ottawa, Ontario. Languages: English, French, working knowledge of Greek, Russian. Travelled in Europe, the USSR and the Far East.
Selective Filmography: *JEUNESSE'* (2 eps), TV, 86, CDN, Ed; *MATERIAL GIRL,* 'DISCUSSIONS IN BIOETHICS', TV, 85, CDN, Ed; *THE PRODIGAL,* 'LIFESTUDIES', TV, 85, CDN, Ed; *ALICE MUNRO/AL PURDY/MICHEL TREMBLAY/JANICE RAPOPORE,* 'CANADIAN LITERATURE', TV, 85, CDN, Dir; *CONSEIL DES ARTS DE L'ONTARIO/ORLEANS/ALCIDE,* 'MOSAIQUE', TV, 85, CDN, Ed; *MR. NICE GUY,* Th, 85, CDN, Ed; *TORONTO/POINTE-AUX-ROCHES/NOELVILLE/FESTIVAL/ROCKLAND,* 'MOSAIQUE', TV, 84, CDN, Ed; *CORNWALL,* 'MOSAIQUE', TV, 84, CDN, Ed; *THE FUTURE OF WORK,* TV, 84, CDN, Ed; *GAMBLING A LIFETIME,* TV, 83, CDN, Ed; *TERMINAL CHOICE* (CRITICAL LIST), Th, 82, CDN, Add'l Ed; *'CURIOUS GEORGE',* TV, 81, CDN, Snd Ed; *HARRY TRACY,* Th, 80, CDN, Co-Ed; *THRESHOLD,* Th, 80, CDN, Mus Ed; *TICKET TO HEAVEN,* Th, 80, CDN, Assist Ed; *PINBALL SUMMER,* Th, 79, CDN, Ed; *NIGHT FLIGHT,* TV, 78, CDN, Ed; *L'HOMME EN COLERE* (LABYRINTH), Th, 78, CDN, Assist Ed; *TEACH ME TO DANCE,* TV, 78, CDN, Ed; *THE WAR IS OVER,* TV, 77, CDN, Ed; *ANGELA,* Th, 76, CDN, Assist Ed.

WESLAK, Steve

DGC. 181 Carlaw Ave., Toronto, Ont, CAN, M4M 2S1. (416)469-2961. North Star Films, 65 Front St.E., Toronto, Ont, CAN. (416)364-1548.
Types of Production & Categories: Th Film-Ed; TV Film-Ed; TV Video-Ed.
Genres: Drama-Th; Documentary-TV; Educational-TV; Children's-TV.
Biography: Born 1947; working in film business since 69; staff editor, CBC, 70-72; Kingcroft Films, Sydney, Australia, 72-74; now freelance, working in Toronto.
Selective Filmography: *THE FLY,* Th, 86, CDN, Co-Ed; *'DURRELL IN RUSSIA'* (6 eps), TV, 85, CDN/GB, Ed; *A FRAGILE TREE HAS ROOTS,* TV, 85, CDN, Ed; *'OFFICE AUTOMATION'* (5 eps), TV, 84, CDN, Ed; *'FUTUREWORK'* (5 eps), TV, 84, CDN, Ed; *'THE AMATEUR NATURALIST'* (6 eps), TV, 83, CDN/GB, Ed; *HOME FEELING, STRUGGLE FOR A COMMUNITY,* TV, 82, CDN, Ed; *'ARK ON THE MOVE'* (13 eps), TV, 81, CDN/GB, Ed; *THE LAST CHASE,* Th, 80, CDN, Ed; *CONNECTIONS: A FURTHER INVESTIGATION,* TV, 79, CDN, Spv Ed; *CONNECTIONS: AN INVESTIGATION INTO ORGANIZED CRIME,* TV, 77, CDN, Spv Ed; *LIGHT CONVERSATIONS,* In, 76, CDN, Ed; *'THE STATIONARY ARK'* (L'ARCHE IMMOBILE), (13 eps), TV, 75, CDN, Sr Ed; *'THE AFRICA FILE'* (10 eps), TV, 75, CDN, Snd Ed; *'WILD COUNTRY'* (2 eps), TV, 74, AUS, Ed; *'WEEKEND'/'MIDWEEK',* TV, 72-70, CDN, Staff Ed.

WHITE, Bryon

DGC. 230 Heath St. W., #116, Toronto, Ont, CAN, M5P 1N8. (416)488-0550. Robert Cooper Prod., 954 King St.W., Toronto, Ont, CAN, M6K 1E5. (416)598-3257.
Types of Production & Categories: Th Film-Ed; TV Film-Ed; TV Video-Ed.
Genres: Drama-Th&TV; Commercials-TV.
Biography: Born 1952, Toronto, Ontario; Bachelor of Science; pioneered use of electronic film editing system on *MURDER IN SPACE*; acts as a consultant/liaison with PFA and editors. Distribution manager, Robert Cooper Productions, 84-85.
Selective Filmography: *'PHILIP MARLOWE PRIVATE EYE'* (1 eps), TV, 86, CDN, Ed; *PLAYING THE ODDS,* TV, 86, CDN, PM; *'HOT SHOTS'* (13 eps), TV, 86, CDN, P Pro Spv; *MURDER IN SPACE,* TV, 85, CDN/USA, P Pro Spv; *RAPISTS - CAN THEY BE STOPPED?,* 'AMERICA UNDERCOVER', TV, 85, USA, PM; *LAS ARADAS,* TV, 84, CDN, Ed/Snd Ed; *A MATTER OF SEX,* TV, 83, CDN/USA, Co-Ed; *KELLY,* Th, 81, CDN, Ed; *CIRCLE OF TWO,* TV, 80, CDN, Assist Ed/Mus Ed; *THUNDER,* TV, 79, CDN, Ed/Snd Ed.

WILKINSON, Mairin

DGC. 194 Howland Ave., Toronto, Ont, CAN, M5R 3B6. (416)537-6123.
Types of Production & Categories: Th Film-Ed; TV Film-Ed; TV Video-Ed.
Genres: Drama-Th&TV; Documentary-TV; Children's-TV.
Biography: Born in England; landed immigrant, Canada. Education: York
University Film Program. Film and tape editor since 77; also edits music videos,
sponsored films and documentaries.
Selective Filmography: *ANNE OF GREEN GABLES - THE SEQUEL,* TV, 86,
CDN/USA, Co-Ed; *'ADDERLY'* (1 eps), TV, 86, CDN, Ed; *'SPIRIT BAY'* (1 eps),
TV, 86, CDN, Ed; *ANNE OF GREEN GABLES,* TV, 85, CDN, Co-Ed; *ISAAC
LITTLEFEATHERS,* Th, 84, CDN, Ed; *JEN'S PLACE,* TV, 82, CDN, Ed;
INTRODUCING...JANET, TV, 81, CDN, Co-Ed; *CLOWN WHITE,* TV, 80,
CDN, Co-Ed; *CORLETTO & SON,* TV, 80, CDN, Ed; *REACHING OUT,* TV, 80,
CDN, Co-Ed.

WILLIAMSON, Neil

CFTA, SMPTE. 2 Castle View Ave., Toronto, Ont, CAN, M5R 1Y9. (416)929-
9874. Editcomm Inc., 100 Lombard St., Ste. 104, Toronto, Ont, CAN, M5C 1M3.
(416)864-1780.
Types of Production & Categories: TV Video-Cam/Ed.
Genres: Variety-TV; Action-TV; Documentary-TV; Educational-TV.
Biography: Born 1955, Toronto, Ontario. Educated at York University (Film
Production); Paris American Academy, France (Photography). Switcher/editor/
cameraman, Multilingual TV, Toronto, 80-82; worked at CBC, 83; currently staff
editor, Editcomm, Toronto.
Selective Filmography: *ONTARIO MINISTRY OF NATURAL RESOURCES:
IMAGES,* In, 85, CDN, Ed; *EDITCOMM,* In, 85, CDN, Ed/Dir/Wr; *'THE
NATIONAL',* TV, 83, CDN, Ed; *'THE ALL NIGHT SHOW',* TV, 81/80, CDN,
Sw.

WINTONICK, Peter

DGC. Cinergy Films, 4299 de l'Esplanade, #5, Montreal, Que, CAN, H2W 1T1.
(514)844-2130.
Types of Production & Categories: Th Film-Ed/Dir; TV Film-Ed; TV Video-Ed/
Prod/Dir
Genres: Drama-Th&TV; Documentary-Th&TV; Educational-TV; Experimental-Th.
Biography: Born 1953, Trenton, Ontario Degree in Film Production, Algonquin
College; studied journalism, Carleton University. Fifteen years as film and video
editor/producer; writes for 'Cinema Canada'; programmer, film series/festivals.
THE NEW CINEMA won the Blue Ribbon, American Film Festival.
Selective Filmography: *THE MEDIA PROJECT,* TV, 86, CDN, Prod/Dir; *THE
JOURNEY,* Th, 86, CDN, Prod; *FILMMAKER PEACEMAKER,* TV, 85, CDN,
Ed/Dir/Prod; *THE NEW CINEMA,* TV, 84, CDN, Ed/Dir/Prod; *WIM
WENDERS: AN INTERVIEW,* TV, 84, CDN, Ed/Dir/Prod; *LISTEN TO THE
CITY,* Th, 84, CDN, Assoc Prod/Act; *UNCERTAIN FUTURE,* Th, 84, CDN, Ed;
THE BAY BOY (UN PRINTEMPS SOUS LA NEIGE), Th, 83, CDN/F, Co-Ed;
POETRY IN MOTION, Th, 83, CDN, Ed/Assoc Prod; *DOCTOR TILLEY AND
HIS GUINEA PIGS,* Th, 83, CDN, Ed/Assoc Prod; *BABE,* Th, 82, CDN, Add'l
Ed; *SUZANNE,* Th, 81, CDN, Add'l Ed; *YOUR TICKET IS NO LONGER
VALID,* Th, 81, CDN, Ed; *AGENCY,* Th, 79, CDN, Co-Ed; *IN PRAISE OF
OLDER WOMEN,* Th, 78, CDN, Co-Ed; *REVOLUTION'S ORPHAN,* TV, 78,
CDN, Ed; *HIS MOTHER,* TV, 77, CDN, Co-Ed.

WISMAN, Ron

DGC. 41 Cheston Rd., Toronto, Ont, CAN, M4S 2X4. (416)486-9339.
Types of Production & Categories: Th Film-Ed; Th Short-Ed; TV Film-Ed.
Genres: Drama-Th&TV; Comedy-Th; Science Fiction-Th; Horror-Th.
Biography: Born 1943. Has been associated with many award-winning
documentaries and commercials over the past 20 years.
Selective Filmography: *THE SWORD OF GIDEON* (mini-series), TV, 86, CDN,
Ed; *ROLLING VENGEANCE,* Th, 86, USA, Ed; *YOUNG AGAIN,* TV, 85, CDN,
Ed; *SEPARATE VACATIONS,* Th, 85, CDN, Ed; *THE CLIMB,* Th, 85, CDN/
GB, Ed; *JOSHUA THEN AND NOW* (also 4 eps-TV), Th, 84, CDN, Ed; *THE
UNDERGRADS,* TV, 84, USA, Ed; *DRAW!,* TV, 83, CDN/USA, Ed; *SPECIAL
PEOPLE,* TV, 83, CDN/USA, Ed; *A MATTER OF SEX,* TV, 83, CDN/USA, Spv
Ed; *THE TERRY FOX STORY,* Th, 82, CDN, Ed **(GENIE)**; *DEADLY EYES*
(THE RATS), Th, 82, CDN, Ed; *THE SINS OF DORIAN GRAY,* TV, 81, USA,
Ed; *HARRY TRACY,* Th, 80, CDN, Ed; *TICKET TO HEAVEN,* Th, 80, CDN,
Ed **(CFEG/GENIE)**; *THE HIGH COUNTRY* (THE FIRST HELLO), Th, 80,
CDN, Ed/P Pro Spv; *AN AMERICAN CHRISTMAS CAROL,* TV, 79, USA, Ed;
FISH HAWK, Th, 79, CDN, Ed; *PLAGUE* (MUTATIONS), Th, 78, CDN, P Pro
Spv; *CEMENT HEAD,* 'FOR THE RECORD', TV, 78, CDN, Ed; *TYLER,* 'FOR
THE RECORD', TV, 78, CDN, Ed **(CFEG)**; *THREE CARD MONTE,* Th, 77,
CDN, Ed; *FULL CIRCLE* (THE HAUNTING OF JULIA), Th, 77, CDN/GB, Ed;
GOLDENROD, Th, 76, CDN, Co-Ed; *SHOOT,* Th, 76, CDN, Ed; *KILLERS OF
THE WILD,* Th, 75, CDN, Ed/Snd Ed; *ALONG THESE LINES,* Th, 74, CDN, Ed
(CFTA); *THE VIOLIN,* Th, 74, CDN, Ed; *ONLY GOD KNOWS,* Th, 74, CDN,
Ed; *THE PYX,* Th, 73, CDN, Ed.

WITHROW, Stephen

282 Pacific Ave., Toronto, Ont, CAN, M6P 2P9. (416)767-7133. S.C.
Communications, 629A Mt. Pleasant Rd., Toronto, Ont, CAN, M4S 2M9. (416)
483-0850.
Types of Production & Categories: Th Film-Ed; TV Film-Ed.
Genres: Drama-Th; Comedy-TV; Documentary-TV; Educational-TV.
Biography: Born 1953, Toronto, Ontario. B.A.A., Motion Picture Studies, Ryerson
Polytechnical Institute, 78.
Selective Filmography: *BEYOND RETIREMENT,* 'AGING: THE HIDDEN
AGENDA', ED, 85, CDN/USA, Ed/Dir; *HOW STREETPROOF ARE YOU?/
CAREER PLANNING,* 'YOUTH LIFESKILLS', ED, 84, CDN, Ed/Dir; *THE
FITNESS FORMULA,* 'SURVIVAL OF THE FITTEST', ED, 84, CDN/USA,
Ed/Snd Ed; *UNDERSTANDING ADOLESCENCE,* 'YOUTH LIFESKILLS', ED,
84, CDN, Ed/Snd Ed; *PRODUCTIVITY AND PERFORMANCE BY ALEX K.,*
Th, 84, CDN, Ed/Snd Ed; *THAT'S MY BABY,* Th, 83, CDN, Co-Ed; 'SMALL
BUSINESS' (2 eps), ED, 83, CDN, Ed; *BY DESIGN,* Th, 80, CDN, 1st Assist Ed;
'THE SENSATIONAL 70'S' (Assist Ed-9 eps), (2 eps), TV, 80/79, , Ed/Snd Ed;
SURFACING, Th, 79, CDN, 1st Assist Ed.

WOLINSKY, Sidney

DGC, IATSE-776, MPEG. 3935 Alla Rd., Los Angeles, CA, USA, 90066. (213)
827-1253. Norman Kurland, 8439 Sunset Blvd., #402, Los Angeles, CA, USA,
90069. (213)656-9262.
Types of Production & Categories: Th Film-Ed.
Genres: Drama-Th; Comedy-Th.
Biography: Born 1946, Winnipeg, Manitoba. B.A., English, American Literature,
Brandeis University, 69; M.A. Film, San Francisco State University, 74.
Selective Filmography: *HOWARD THE DUCK,* Th, 86, USA, Co-Ed; *ONE MAGIC
CHRISTMAS,* Th, 85, CDN/USA, Ed; *BEST DEFENSE,* Th, 84, USA, Ed;
TERMS OF ENDEARMENT, Th, 83, USA, Add'l Ed; *MY TUTOR,* Th, 83, USA,
Ed; *YOUNG DOCTORS IN LOVE,* Th, 82, USA, Add'l Ed.

WRATE, Eric
SMPTE. 200 Silverbirch Ave., Toronto, Ont, CAN, M4E 3L5. (416)694-0827. Post Production Services Ltd., 19 Mercer St., Toronto, Ont, CAN, M5V 1H2. (416)591-1609.
Types of Production & Categories: Th Film-Ed; TV Film-Ed; TV Video-Ed.
Genres: Drama-Th&TV; Comedy-Th&TV; Documentary-TV; Children's-Th&TV.
Biography: Born London, England; Canadian citizen. Owner, Post Production Services Ltd.. Trained in the British film industry working with directors such as Alfred Hitchcock and John Boultin.
Selective Filmography: *'PHILIP MARLOWE PRIVATE EYE'* (1 eps), TV, 86, CDN, Ed; *SPECIAL DELIVERY,* TV, 85, CDN, Ed; *SHELL GAME* (pilot), TV, 85, CDN, Ed; *CUCKOO BIRD,* TV, 85, CDN, Ed; *'KIDS OF DEGRASSI STREET'* (6 eps), TV, 85, CDN, Ed; *BRIDGE TO TERABITHIA,* 'WONDERWORKS', TV, 84, CDN, Ed; *SHOCKTRAUMA,* TV, 83, CDN, Spv Ed; *IF YOU COULD SEE WHAT I HEAR,* Th, 82, CDN, Ed; *HIGH POINT,* Th, 79, CDN, Ed; *A MAN CALLED INTREPID* (mini-series), TV, 78, CDN/GB, Spv Ed; *KAVIK THE WOLF DOG,* TV, 78, CDN, Ed; *HIGH-BALLIN',* Th, 77, CDN, Ed; *'THE NEW AVENGERS'* (2 eps), TV, 77, CDN/GB/F, Ed; *'THE NEWCOMERS'* (2 eps), TV, 77, CDN, Ed **(CFEG)**; *SECOND WIND,* Th, 75, CDN, Ed.

ZANDER, Ildy
25 Bedford Rd., #706, Toronto, Ont, CAN, M5R 2K1. (416)922-2800.
Types of Production & Categories: Th Short-Ed/Prod; TV Film-Ed; TV Video-Ed/Prod.
Genres: Drama-Th&TV; Documentary-Th; Educational-TV; Industrial-TV.
Biography: Born 1944, Budapest, Hungary; Canadian citizen; B.A., University of Toronto; speaks English, French and Hungarian, has working knowledge of German and Spanish.
Selective Filmography: *IBM* (20 videos), In, 85-75, CDN, Ed/Prod; *MENOPAUSE,* TV, 82, CDN, Ed; *BROOKE: A NEW GENERATION,* Th, 81, CDN, Ed/Prod; *THE JULY GROUP,* TV, 80, CDN, Ed; *COMING HOME ALIVE,* TV, 79, CDN, Ed; *RAISING CANE,* ED, 78, CDN, Ed/Assoc Prod; *THE FIGHTING MEN* (re-cut for Th release), Th, 78, CDN, Ed; *SILENT SKY,* Th, 77, CDN, Ed; *PAPERBACK HERO,* Th, 71, CDN, Assist Ed; *THE ROWDYMAN,* Th, 71, CDN, Assist Ed; *A FAN'S NOTES,* Th, 70, CDN, Assist Ed.

ZIPURSKY, Arnie - see PRODUCERS

ZLATARITS, Harvey
DGC. 26 Delaware Ave., Toronto, Ont, CAN, M6H 2S7. (416)535-9476. Int'l Learning & Ent., 106 Dupont St., Toronto, Ont, CAN, M5R 1V2. (416)923-9067.
Types of Production & Categories: Th Film-Ed; TV Film-Ed/Prod; TV Video-Ed/Prod.
Genres: Variety-TV; Documentary-Th&TV; Educational-TV; Children's-TV.
Biography: Born 1946, Regina, Saskatchewan; Bachelor of Environmental Studies, University of Manitoba; Film Arts, Ryerson Polytechnical Institute. Also works as cameraman, architectural designer, draughtsman, still photographer.
Selective Filmography: *'QUEST'* (13 eps), TV, 85, CDN, P Pro Spv/Prod; *'CELEBRATIONS'* (5 eps), TV, 85, CDN, P Pro Spv/Prod; *STAR SONG,* TV, 84, CDN, Ed; *OLYMPIC MOMENTS,* TV, 84, CDN, Ed; *'DISABILITY MYTH'* (parts I & II), TV, 84/83, CDN, Ed; *'ALPINE SKI SCHOOL'* (5 eps), TV, 83, CDN, Ed; *THE HAWK,* Th, 82, CDN, Ed **(BIJOU/CFEG)**; *DEADLINE,* Th, 81, CDN, Ed; *GINO,* TV, 80, CDN, Ed **(CFEG)**.

COMPOSERS
★
COMPOSITEURS

AIREY, Paul

4018 West 37th Ave., Vancouver, BC, CAN, V6N 2W7. (604)266-7266. Avenue Music Productions, 104-1090 Homer St., Vancouver, BC, CAN, V6B 2W9. (604) 688-8728.

Types of Production & Categories: Th Film-Comp; Th Short-Comp; TV Film-Comp; TV Video-Comp.

Genres: Documentary-Th&TV; Educational-Th&TV.

Biography: Born 1957, Vancouver, British Columbia. B.A., University of British Columbia; Performance (Music) degree A.R.C.T., University of Toronto. Studied 4 years music composition and arranging under Stephen Chatman and Elliot Weisgarber. Has composed numerous scores for planetariums resulting in an album, 'The Mystery of the SS433' and an EP, 'Horizons' from the 'Canada in Space' planetarium show. Also composes jingles.

Selective Filmography: *CATCH THE SPIRIT,* ED, 85, CDN, Comp; *SUPERNATURAL SKIES,* Th, 85, CDN, Comp; *CANADA IN SPACE,* Th, 85, CDN, Comp; *GORDON SOUTHAM OBSERVATORY,* ED, 85, CDN, Comp; *SOUTHLANDS RIDING CLUB,* TV, 85, CDN, Comp; *BAD DREAMS,* Th, 85, CDN, Comp; *INSTANT METRIC,* ED, 84, CDN, Comp; *MUSILLUSION,* Th, 84, CDN, Comp; *SPACE SHUTTLE,* TV, 84, CDN, Comp; *CHARTING THE COSMOS,* Th, 83, CDN, Comp; *CANCER RESEARCH,* ED, 83, CDN, Comp; *GOURMET GETAWAY,* TV, 83, CDN, Comp; *THE MYSTERY OF SS433,* Th, 82, CDN, Comp; *PLANETS,* Th, 81, CDN, Comp.

APPLEBAUM, Louis

AFM, CAPAC, GCFC. Affiliated Arts Co.Ltd., 400 Walmer Rd., #629, Toronto, Ont, CAN, M5P 2X7. (416)924-7856.

Types of Production & Categories: Th Film-Comp; Th Short-Comp; TV Film-Comp; TV Video-Comp.

Genres: Drama-Th&TV; Comedy-Th&TV; Action-Th&TV; Documentary-Th&TV.

Biography: Born 1918, Toronto, Ontario. Education: University of Toronto; New York U.. Music direction, NFB, 41-46; composed over 200 scores, 41-53; worked in NY for all radio and TV networks and United Nations Radio, 46-50; feature and avant garde films, Hollywood, 45-46; back to Canada, 50, freelance film composer; first music director, composer, Stratford Festival, 53. Has composed scores for theatre in Canada, USA, England. Executive director, Ontario Arts Council, 71-79; Chairman, Federal Cultural Policy Review Committee, 79-82. Won the Canadian Music Council Award for *THE MASSEYS.*

Selective Filmography: *KARSH - THE SEARCHING EYE,* TV, 85, CDN, Comp/Cond; *THE MYSTERY OF HENRY MOORE,* TV, 84, CDN, Comp/Cond; *RAYMOND MASSEY,* TV, 83, CDN, Comp/Cond; *ARTHUR MILLER: ON HOME GROUND,* TV, 79, CDN, Comp/Cond; *THE MASSEYS* (2 parts), TV, 78, CDN, Co-Comp/Cond; *TYRONE GUTHRIE, THE UNSELFISH GIANT,* TV, 78, CDN, Comp/Cond; *SARAH,* TV, 76, CDN, Comp/Cond; *JOURNEY WITHOUT ARRIVAL,* TV, 76, CDN, Comp/Cond (**ANIK**); *HOMAGE TO CHAGALL: THE COLOURS OF LOVE,* Th, 75, CDN, Comp/Cond; *NEXT YEAR IN JERUSALEM,* TV, 74, CDN, Comp/Cond; *'THE NATIONAL DREAM'* (8 eps), TV, 74, CDN, Comp/Cond; *TENNESSEE WILLIAMS' SOUTH.* TV, 73, CDN, Comp/Cond; *FOLLY ON THE HILL,* TV, 73, CDN, Comp/Cond; *THE DISCOVERERS,* TV, 72, CDN, Comp/Cond; *WIT AND WISDOM OF G.B. SHAW,* TV, 72, CDN, Comp/Cond; *THE JOURNALS OF SUSANNA MOODIE,* TV, 71, CDN, Comp/Cond; *BONJOUR CANADA,* TV, 69, CDN, Comp/Cond; *ATHABASCA,* TV, 68, CDN, Comp (**CFA**); *'CBC NEWS',* TV, 67, CDN, Theme Comp; *'SEAWAY'* (26 eps), TV, 65, CDN, Comp; *'GRAPHIC'* (54 eps), TV, 58-56, CDN, Comp; *OEDIPUS REX,* Th, 57, USA, Comp/Cond; *WALK EAST ON BEACON,* Th, 52, USA, Comp/Cond; *WHISTLE AT ETON FALLS,* Th, 51, USA, Comp/Cond; *TERESA,* Th, 51, USA, Comp/Cond; *DREAMS THAT MONEY CAN BUY,* Th, 48, USA, Comp/Cond; *LOST BOUNDARIES,* Th, 48,

(cont/suite)

COMPOSERS/COMPOSITEURS

USA, Comp/Cond; *STORY OF G.I.JOE,* Th, 45, USA, Comp/Cond; *TOMORROW THE WORLD,* Th, 44, USA, Comp/Cond.

BAKER, Michael Conway

CLC, GCFC. 1163 W. 26th Ave., Vancouver, BC, CAN, V6H 2A6. Glenn Morley, 47 Huntley St., Toronto, Ont, CAN. (416)929-9324.
Types of Production & Categories: Th Film-Comp; Th Short-Comp; TV Film-Comp; TV Video-Comp.
Genres: Drama-Th&TV; Action-Th&TV; Documentary-Th&TV; Educational-Th&TV.
Biography: Born 1941, West Palm Beach, Florida; Canadian citizenship, 70. B.Music, University of British Columbia, 65; London College of Music (A.L.C.M.); M.A., Western Washington U., 71. Taught music and special courses in film music, U.B.C.; also taught for the Vancouver School Board. Has written over 70 concert works in various forms: symphony, concerto, chamber music.
Selective Filmography: *DISCOVERY* (EXPO 86), Th, 86, CDN, Comp; *THE EMERGING NORTH,* Th, 86, CDN, Comp; *JOHN AND THE MISSUS,* Th, 86, CDN, Comp; *'A PLANET FOR THE TAKING'* (8 eps), TV, 85, CDN, Comp; *ONE MAGIC CHRISTMAS,* Th, 85, CDN/USA, Comp; *OVERNIGHT,* Th, 85, CDN, Comp; *LOYALTIES,* Th, 85, CDN/GB, Comp; *I'LL GET THERE SOMEHOW,* TV, 84, CDN, Comp; *THE BOY NEXT DOOR,* 'FOR THE RECORD', TV, 84, CDN, Comp; *DANIEL IZZARD, ARTIST,* TV, 83, CDN, Comp; *DESERTERS,* Th, 83, CDN, Comp; *GLORIOUS MUD,* TV, 83, CDN, Comp; *TOUCH WOOD,* TV, 83, CDN, Comp; *MAGGIE,* Th, 82, CDN, Comp; *WOMEN TODAY,* TV, 82, CDN, Comp; *THE GREY FOX,* Th, 80, CDN, Comp (**GENIE**); *NAILS,* Th, 80, CDN, Comp (**GENIE**); *HARRISON'S YUKON,* TV, 79, CDN, Comp; *FAMILY DOWN THE FRASER,* TV, 78, CDN, Comp; *FLASHPOINT,* TV, 77, CDN, Comp.

BARNES, Milton

GCFC. Ari-Mic-Dan Music, 192A Lowther Ave., Toronto, Ont, CAN, M5R 1E8. (416)961-9925.
Types of Production & Categories: Th Film-Comp; TV Film-Comp; TV Video-Comp.
Genres: Drama-Th&TV; Documentary-Th&TV; Children's-Th&TV; Animation-Th&TV.
Biography: Born 1931, Toronto, Ontario. Languages: English, French, German. Education: Royal Conservatory of Music; Vienna Academy of Music, Austria; Berkshire Music Centre, Tanglewood, USA; Chigiana Music School, Italy. Full time composer for concert hall, theatre, dance and film.
Selective Filmography: *'THE EDISON TWINS'* (sev eps), TV, 86-84, CDN, Orch/Cond; *'SHARON, LOIS AND BRAM'S ELEPHANT SHOW',* TV, 85, CDN, Orch/Arr; *THE CARE BEARS MOVIE II,* Th, 86/85, CDN, Orch/Arr/Cond; *THE GREAT HEEP,* TV, 85, CDN, Orch; *THE CARE BEARS MOVIE,* Th, 85, CDN, Orch/Arr/Cond; *READY FOR SLAUGHTER,* 'FOR THE RECORD', TV, 83, CDN, Comp/Cond; *STRAWBERRY ICE,* TV, 82, CDN, Orch; *SPIRIT OF THE HUNT,* TV, 82, CDN, Comp/Cond; *'PORTRAITS OF POWER'* (sev eps), TV, 80/79, CDN, Cond; *BLOOD & GUTS,* Th, 77, CDN, Comp/Cond; *THE BETRAYAL,* TV, 76, CDN, Comp/Cond.

BELL, Allan Gordon

AFM, GCFC. Synergy Music Productions Ltd., 222 Ranchlands Court N.W., Calgary, Alta, CAN, T3E 1N9. (403)239-8068.
Types of Production & Categories: Th Short-Comp; TV Film-Comp; TV Video-Comp.
Genres: Drama-TV; Action-Th&TV; Documentary-Th&TV; Educational-Th&TV.

(cont/suite)

Biography: Born 1953, Calgary, Alberta. Education: B.A., M. Music (composition), University of Alberta; film music synchronization with Earl Hagen. Commissions: Canada Council, CBC, Alberta Culture. Created works for soloists, chamber ensembles, orchestra, electronic media; arranger for numerous recording projects and commercials.
Selective Filmography: *'CONNECTING'* (13 eps), TV, 85, CDN, Comp; *LORAM '85*, In, 85, CDN, Comp; *LEON'S*, Cm, 85, CDN, Comp; *ALBERTA AGRICULTURE*, In, 84, CDN, Comp; *CATHERINE BURGESS: SCULPTOR IN STEEL*, Th, 83, CDN, Comp; *FREEDOM OF CHOICE*, Th, 83, CDN, Comp; *A FILM ABOUT JUSTICE*, ED, 82, CDN, Comp; *'STONEY PLAIN'* (13 eps), TV, 81, CDN, Comp.

BHATIA, Amin

115-723 57th Ave.S.W., Calgary, Alta, CAN. (403)259-0071.
Types of Production & Categories: Th Film-Comp; TV Film-Comp; TV Video-Comp.
Genres: Drama-Th; Science Fiction-TV; Horror-TV; Documentary-TV.
Biography: Born 1961. Has twice won the Roland Int'l Synthesizer Tape Competition; four certificates of excellence, CLIO Awards, 4 AMPIA Awards.
Selective Filmography: *3 MINUTES TO LIVE*, In, 86, CDN, Comp; *STORM*, Th, 85, CDN, Comp; *APARTMENT ON THE DARK SIDE OF THE MOON*, TV, 84, CDN, Comp; *FUGITIVES IN THE WIND*, TV, 83, CDN, Comp; *WHY CAN'T IT BE FUN*, TV, 83, CDN, Comp; *ROMOX SOFTWARE/MISTER TIME/ ROCKY MOUNTAIN BREWERIES*, Cm, 83/82, CDN, Comp; *LORAM CONSTRUCTION*, In, 83, CDN, Comp; *'WEEKEND'* (13 eps), TV, 82, CDN, Comp; *PAYDAY*, ED, 82, CDN, Comp.

BOUX, Claude - voir REALISATEURS

BRONSKILL, Richard

ACTRA, AFM, CAPAC, GCFC. 828 N.Sweetzer Ave., Los Angeles, CA, USA, 90069. (213)653-3986. Great North Artists Mgmt., 345 Adelaide St.W., #500, Toronto, Ont, CAN, M5V 1R5. (416)593-2586. Gerald K. Smith, Box 7430, Burbank, CA, USA, 91510. (213)849-5388.
Types of Production & Categories: Th Film-Comp; Th Short-Comp; TV Film-Comp; TV Video-Comp.
Genres: Drama-TV; Comedy-TV; Action-TV; Documentary-TV.
Biography: Born 1951, Ottawa, Ontario. B.Music, University of Toronto, 73; Master of Music, 77. Secretary, Treasurer, Guild of Canadian Film Composers, 84-86; record producer; conductor; orchestrator, arranger; editor.
Selective Filmography: *GRIERSON AND GOUZENKO/SAM HUGHES'S WAR/ KING'S GAMBIT*, 'SOME HONOURABLE GENTLEMEN', TV, 85-83, CDN, Comp; *AND MILES TO GO*, TV, 85, CDN, Comp; *9B*, TV, 85, CDN, Comp; *CAROLINE*, 'SONS AND DAUGHTERS', TV, 83, CDN, Comp; *THY SERVANT ARTHUR/PASSION OF THE PATRIOTS*, 'SOME HONOURABLE GENTLEMEN', TV, 83/82, CDN, Comp; *NORTH OF 60: DESTINY UNCERTAIN*, TV, 82, CDN, Theme Comp; *TERRY FOX TRIBUTE*, TV, 82, CDN, Comp; *ANDRE L'ARCHEVEQUE*, In, 82, CDN, Comp; *ONCE*, TV, 80, CDN, Comp.

COHEN, Leonard

28 Vallieres, Montreal, Que, CAN, H2W 1C2. Marty Machat, Machat & Machat, Paramount Bldg., 1501 Broadway, 30th Floor, New York, NY, USA, 10036. (212) 840-2200.
Types of Production & Categories: Th Film-Comp; TV Video-Comp.
Genres: Musical-Th&TV; Documentary-Th.
Biography: Born 1934, Montreal, Quebec; bilingual. B.A., McGill University. Composer, lyricist, novelist, poet.

(cont/suite)

Selective Filmography: *NIGHT MAGIC,* Th, 85, CDN/F, Lyrics (**GENIE**); *DANCE ME TO THE END OF LOVE,* MV, 84, USA, Comp; *I AM A HOTEL,* TV, 84, CDN, Comp; *BIRD ON THE WIRE,* Th, 78, GB, Comp.

COLLIER, Ron

CLC, GCFC. 28 Confederation Way, Thornhill, Ont, CAN, L3T 5R5. (416)731-7276. Humber College - Music Dept., Humber College Blvd., Rexdale, Ont, CAN. (416)657-3111.
Types of Production & Categories: Th Film-Comp; Th Short-Comp; TV Film-Comp; TV Video-Comp.
Genres: Drama-Th&TV; Musical-Th; Documentary-Th&TV; Educational-Th&TV.
Biography: Born 1930, Coleman, Alberta; moved to Vancouver, 43; to Toronto, 51. Studied with Gordon Delamont; formed the Ron Collier Quintet, concerts at Stratford, Massey Hall, etc.. Trombonist, CBC TV, radio. Recorded album with Duke Ellington, 'Collages', 69. Quit playing in 70 to do more composing and conducting; resident composer at Humber College since 72. Won the Big Band Open Class in the Canadian Stage Band Festival, 3 times (75-82-86).
Selective Filmography: *INDONESIAN OPENING CEREMONIES,* In, 77, CDN, Comp; *BACK TO BEULAH,* TV, 74, CDN, Comp; *PAPERBACK HERO,* Th, 73, CDN, Comp; *FOLLOW THE NORTH STAR,* TV, 72, CDN, Comp; *FACE-OFF,* Th, 71, CDN, Comp; *'TALKING TO A STRANGER'* (4 eps), TV, 71, CDN, Comp; *A WAY OUT/A PLACE TO ...?/YOU TAKE THE CREDIT,* ED, 71-69, CDN, Comp; *THE SHIELD PROJECT/GROWING/DOWNSTREAM/LIFE LINES/RYE ON THE ROCKS,* In, 71-68, CDN, Comp; *PLANED, DIPPED OR FANCY/SHEBANDOWAN - A SUMMER PLACE,* In, 71, CDN, Comp; *A FAN'S NOTES,* Th, 70, CDN, Comp; *SEVEN CRITERIA/CALL ME,* In, 67, CDN, Comp; *SILENT NIGHT, LONELY NIGHT,* TV, 65, CDN, Comp; *HEAR ME TALKIN' TO YA,* TV, 64, CDN, Comp.

CULLEN, Patricia

11 Camden St., Toronto, Ont, CAN, M5V 1V2. (416)862-7579. Robert Light Agency, 6404 Wilshire Blvd., Ste.800, Los Angeles, CA, USA, 90048. (213)651-1777.
Types of Production & Categories: Th Film-Comp; TV Film-Comp; TV Video-Comp.
Genres: Drama-Th; Documentary-TV; Children's-Th&TV; Animation-Th&TV.
Biography: Born 1951.
Selective Filmography: *THE CARE BEARS MOVIE II,* Th, 86/85, CDN, Comp; *'EWOKS'* (13 eps), TV, 85, CDN, Comp; *'THE EDISON TWINS'* (26 eps), TV, 85-83, CDN, Comp; *THE GREAT HEEP,* TV, 85, CDN, Comp; *THE CARE BEARS MOVIE,* Th, 85, CDN, Comp; *STRAWBERRY SHORTCAKE MEETS THE BERRYKINS,* TV, 84, CDN, Comp; *'MR. MICROCHIP'* (13 eps), TV, 83, CDN, Comp; *ROCK & RULE* (RING OF POWER), Th, 83, CDN, Comp; *STRAWBERRY SHORTCAKE AND THE BABY WITHOUT A NAME,* TV, 83, CDN, Comp; *UNFINISHED BUSINESS,* Th, 82, CDN, Co-Comp; *UPS & DOWNS,* Th, 82, CDN, Co-Comp; *STRAWBERRY SHORTCAKE: A HOUSEWARMING SURPRISE,* TV, 82, CDN, Comp; *AFTER THE AXE,* Th, 81, CDN, Comp; *'NORTH AMERICA: GROWTH OF A CONTINENT'* (26 eps), TV, 80, CDN, Comp; *'PORTRAITS OF POWER'* (26 eps), TV, 79, CDN/USA, Comp.

DALE, James

AFM. 86 South Dr., Toronto, Ont, CAN, M4W 1R6. (416)961-1259. One 'B' Management, 6239 W. 6th St., Los Angeles, CA, USA, 90036. (213)933-2404.
Types of Production & Categories: Th Film-Comp; Th Short-Comp; TV Film-Comp; TV Video-Comp.
(cont/suite)

Genres: Drama-Th&TV; Comedy-Th&TV; Variety-Th&TV; Musical-Th&TV.
Biography: Born 1935, London, England; classically trained; emigrated to Canada, 47. Trained with Gordon Delamont in composition and orchestration. Has worked in TV and film since 63; moved to L.A., 69-75; now works out of Toronto. Has composed for many TV series including David Steinberg, Ken Berry, Ray Stevens; pianist/composer/arranger with Rob McConnell's 'Boss Brass' winning Grammy and Juno Awards; accompanist and/or writer for Peggy Lee, Nancy Wilson and many others.
Selective Filmography: *THE EXECUTION OF RAYMOND GRAHAM,* TV, 85, CDN, Comp/Cond; *TIMING,* Th, 85, CDN, Co-Comp/Cond; *MARKHAM,* In, 85, CDN, Comp; *ACTRA AWARDS,* TV, 85, CDN, Comp/Cond; *GENIE AWARDS,* TV, 85, CDN, Comp/Cond; *NHL AWARDS,* TV, 85, CDN, Comp/Cond; *BEST OF BOTH WORLDS,* Th, 84, USA, Comp; *'BIZARRE'* (167 eps), TV, 84-78, CDN/USA, Comp; *'SONNY AND CHER'* (100 eps), TV, 75-71, USA, Comp/Cond; *WACKY WORLD,* TV, 74, USA, Comp; *'ANDY WILLIAMS'* (50 eps), TV, 71-69, USA, Comp/Cond.

DAVIES, Victor

AFM, CAPAC, DGC, GCFC. Lily Pad Productions, 102 Lyall Ave., Toronto, Ont, CAN, M4E 1W5. (416)698-5995.
Types of Production & Categories: Th Film-Comp; TV Film-Comp.
Genres: Drama-Th&TV; Musical-Th&TV; Children's-Th&TV.
Biography: Born 1939, Winnipeg, Manitoba. Has studied piano from age 5; B. Mus. in composition, Indiana University, 64. Freelance composer, pianist, conductor, musical director; has composed scores for TV, radio, theatre. President, Canadian League of Composers, 79-82.
Selective Filmography: *'LET'S GO'* (200 eps), TV, 85-77, CDN, Comp; *THE JOURNAL OF LAN TRAN,* TV, 84, CDN, Comp; *POSSESSION,* Th, 83, CDN, Comp; *AND WHEN THEY SHALL ASK,* Th, 83, CDN, Comp; *'AMERICAN CAESAR',* TV, 83, CDN, Comp; *THE PEDDLER,* TV, 82, CDN, Comp; *THE CATCH,* TV, 81, CDN, Comp; *LATITUDE 55,* Th, 80, CDN, Comp; *THE CURSE OF PONSONBY HALL,* TV, 79, CDN, Comp; *'MAN AND NATURE'* (13 eps), TV, 78, CDN, Comp; *WILDERNESS TRAILS,* Th, 75, CDN, Comp; *THE PIT,* Th, 71, CDN, Comp; *THE BEGINNING AND END OF THE WORLD,* Th, 71, CDN, Comp; *REGINALD THE ROBOT,* TV, 71, CDN, Comp; *THE MAGIC TRUMPET,* TV, 69, CDN, Comp.

DOLGAY, Marvin

AFM, AMPAC. 146 Hampton Ave., Toronto, Ont, CAN, M4K 2Z1. (416)466-0537. Tambre Prod.Inc., 55 Berkeley St., Toronto, Ont, CAN, M5A 2W5. (416) 367-9797.
Types of Production & Categories: Th Film-Comp; TV Film-Comp; TV Video-Comp.
Genres: Drama-Th&TV; Comedy-Th&TV; Variety-TV; Commercials-TV.
Biography: Born 1955, Toronto, Ontario. Music Director, President, Tambre Productions Inc. Music and audio production for many TV and radio commercials which have won Art Directors and Chicago Commercial Festival Awards. Apprenticed under Paul Hoffert for 1 1/2 years. Former member of pop/rock groups: Stampeders, Charity Brown, James Leroy.
Selective Filmography: *MAGIC GLASSES,* Th, 86, CDN, Comp/Snd Des/P Audio; *YOPLAIT FISHBOWL/SUNLIGHT DETERGENT,* Cm, 86, CDN, Comp/Snd Des/P Audio; *CROWN X/YAMAHA MUSIC,* In, 86/85, CDN, Comp/Snd Des/P Audio; *THE BLUE MAN,* Th, 85, CDN, Comp; *'4 ON THE FLOOR'* (13 eps), TV, 85, CDN, Mus Dir/Theme Comp; *TRUE GIFT OF CHRISTMAS,* TV, 85, CDN, Snd Des; *ALWAYS KNOCK FIRST,* Th, 85, CDN, Mus Dir; *SICK KIDS TELETHON,* TV, 85, CDN, Comp; *HEART FUND,* Cm, 85, CDN, Comp;

(cont/suite)

PERFECT TIMING, Th, 84, CDN, Comp; *PARADISE,* Th, 84, CDN/IL, Mus Ed; *YAMAHA OUTBOARDS/TAVIST STUNTMAN/ENCORE COFFEE/ PANADOL HEADS,* Cm, CDN, Comp/Snd Des/P Audio.

DOMPIERRE, François

UDA. 786-B Champagneur, Outremont, Qué, CAN, H2V 3P8. (514)271-5138.
Types de production et Catégories: l métrage-Comp; c métrage-Comp; TV film-Comp.
Types d'oeuvres: Drame-C&TV; Comédie-C&TV; Variété-C&TV; Action-C&TV.
Curriculum vitae: Né en 1943, Ottawa, Ontario. Cours de musique (piano-orgue) au Conservatoire de Montréal. Arrangeur, chef d'orchestre et réalisateur d'une dizaine de microsillons. Récipiendaire de plusieurs Prix Félix (Gala de l'Adisk) pour ses propres disques.
Filmographie sélective: *LE MATOU* (THE ALLEY CAT), C, 85, CDN/F, Comp (GENIE); *TOBY McTEAGUE,* C, 85, CDN, Comp; *LE DECLIN DE L'EMPIRE AMERICAIN* (THE DECLINE OF THE AMERICAN EMPIRE), C, 85, CDN, Comp; *LE SANG DES AUTRES* (THE BLOOD OF OTHERS), C, 84, CDN/F, Comp; *MARIO,* C, 84, CDN, Comp (GENIE); *VIVRE EN CE PAYS,* C, 83, CDN, Comp; *BONHEUR D'OCCASION* (THE TIN FLUTE), (aussi 5 ém-TV), C, 82, CDN, Comp; *PARTIS POUR LA GLOIRE,* C, 75, CDN, Comp; *OK LALIBERTE,* C, 73, CDN, Comp; *IXE 13,* C, 71, CDN, Comp; *YUL 871,* C, 66, CDN, Comp.

DUGUAY, Raôul

UDA. 1707 chemin Beaulac, St-Armand, Qué, CAN, J0J 1T0. (514)248-3536.
Types de production et Catégories: l métrage-Comp.
Types d'oeuvres: Drame-C; Science-fiction-C; Expérimental-C.
Curriculum vitae: Né en 1939, Val d'Or, Abitibi, Québec. Docteur en philosophie (esthétique phonétique); chercheur en holisme (physique, chimie, biologie); spécialiste des harmoniques (sons diphoniques); aussi réalisateur et acteur.
Filmographie sélective: *LES FLEURS SAUVAGES,* C, 80, CDN, Comp; *O OU L'INVISIBLE ENFANT,* C, 73, CDN, Réal/Sc/Com.

ERBE, Micky

ACTRA, GCFC. 17 St.Andrews Gardens, Toronto, Ont, CAN, M4W 2C9. (416) 961-1017. Mickymar Productions Ltd., 663 Yonge St., Suite 203, Toronto, Ont, CAN, M4Y 2A4. (416)960-2281.
Types of Production & Categories: Th Film-Comp; Th Short-Comp; TV Film-Comp; TV Video-Comp.
Genres: Drama-Th&TV; Comedy-Th&TV; Musical-Th&TV; Documentary-Th&TV.
Biography: Born 1948, Paterson, New Jersey; landed immigrant status in Canada. Studied at Manhattan Academy; studied composition/arranging with Torrie Zito and Charlie Callello; trumpet with John Ware. Produces, arranges records and commercials; Clio and Craft Award winner, 4 time Juno Award nominee for 'The Spitfire Band'; 2 time Genie nominee. Has written for Canadian Brass, Maureen Forrester, The Nylons; a specially commissioned viola concerto for Rivka Golani-Erdesz.
Selective Filmography: *THE DREAM IS ALIVE,* Th, 85, CDN/USA, Co-Comp; *FREEDOM TO MOVE,* Th, 85, CDN, Co-Comp; *'FRONTRUNNERS'* (3 eps), TV, 85, CDN, Co-Comp; *PRIME TIME,* Th, 85, CDN, Co-Comp; *JOINT CUSTODY* (MOMMY'S HOUSE, DADDY'S HOUSE), TV, 85, CDN, Co-Comp; *CINEMA ET CINEMA,* TV, 84, CDN, Co-Comp; *'GREAT MOMENTS'* (3 eps), TV, 84, CDN, Co-Comp; *ABORTION: STORIES FROM NORTH TO SOUTH,* Th, 84, CDN, Co-Comp; *NUNS: BEHIND THE VEIL,* Th, 84, CDN, Co-Comp; *HAIL COLUMBIA,* Th, 82, CDN, Co-Comp; *UTILITIES,* Th, 82, CDN, Co-Comp; *THRESHOLD,* Th, 80, CDN, Co-Comp; *TICKET TO HEAVEN,* Th, 80, CDN, Co-Comp; *KELLY,* Th, 81, CDN, Theme Co-Comp/Co-Comp; *HARRY*
(cont/suite)

TRACY, Th, 80, CDN, Co-Comp; *HARD FEELINGS*, Th, 80, CDN, Comp; *IMPROPER CHANNELS*, Th, 79, CDN, Co-Comp/Theme Co-Comp; *NOMADS OF THE DEEP*, Th, 77, CDN, Co-Comp; *GRANDPA AND FRANK*, TV, 77, USA, Co-Comp; *'SESAME STREET'* (sev seg), TV, 77, USA, Co-Comp; *ONTARIO/SUMMERTIDE*, Th, 76, CDN, Co-Comp/Theme Co-Comp; *OCEAN: TIME MACHINE*, Th, 75, CDN, Co-Comp; *TELL ME MY NAME*, TV, 75, USA, Co-Comp; *1000 MOONS*, TV, 74, CDN, Co-Comp; *NORTH OF SUPERIOR*, Th, 70, CDN, Co-Comp.

FOREMAN, Howard

AFM. 6270A Westbury, Montreal, Que, CAN, H3Y 2X3. (514)739-0919. Montage Creative, 5154 blvd. St. Laurent, Montreal, Que, CAN. (514)271-7422.
Types of Production & Categories: Th Film-Comp; Th Short-Comp; TV Film-Comp.
Genres: Drama-Th; Musical-TV; Educational-TV; Children's-Th.
Biography: Born 1957, Montreal, Quebec; Canadian-US citizenship. Educated through university in Canada; session guitarist, Muscle Schoals Sound Studio, Alabama; many national commercials in Canada and US; solo albums in Canada and Europe; music videos; produces radio spots, jingles, records and film soundtracks; adapter of lyrics for film. Tour guitarist for international acts.
Selective Filmography: *N.G.T.* (QUEBEC GOV.), In, 86/85, CDN, Comp; *THE PEANUT BUTTER SOLUTION* (OPERATION BEURRE DE PINOTTES), Th, 85, CDN, Comp/Lyrics; *HERE'S THE LAST TIME*, MV, 85, CDN, Act; *THE PRODIGAL*, TV, 84, CDN, Comp; *RUNNING SCARED*, TV, 84, CDN, Comp; *MUSIC ETV*, TV, 84, USA, Act; *RAFFINEE*, TV, 84, F, Comp.

FREEDMAN, Harry

CLC. 35 St.Andrew's Gardens, Toronto, Ont, CAN, M4W 2C9. (416)921-5530.
Types of Production & Categories: Th Film-Comp; Th Short-Comp; TV Film-Comp; TV Video-Comp.
Genres: Drama-Th&TV; Musical-Th&TV; Documentary-TV; Children's-TV.
Biography: Born 1922, Poland; came to Canada, 25; naturalized Canadian citizen, 31. Languages: English, French. Senior matriculation (Honours), High School of Art, Royal Conservatory of Music; Tanglewood Scholarship, R.C.M. Scholarship. Has written music in all forms including 3 symphonies, 9 ballets, a one-act opera, chamber music, choral music and scores for film, TV and theatre. Founding member of Canadian League of Composers; Guild of Canadian Film Composers. Part-time film animator and painter (Japanese sumi-e).*ALL THAT GLISTENS* won a Gold Award, N.Y. Int'l Film & TV Fest.; *AGAINST OBLIVION* won a Bronze Chris Plaque, Columbus. He was named Canadian Music Council Composer of the Year, 79; Officer, Order of Canada, 84.
Selective Filmography: *CONNECTIONS*, TV, 85, CDN, Comp; *AGAINST OBLIVION/ALL THAT GLISTENS*, 'HAND AND EYE', TV, 83, CDN, Comp; *SOMETHING HIDDEN: A PORTRAIT OF WILDER PENFIELD*, TV, 81, CDN, Comp; *PYRAMID OF ROSES*, Th, 80, CDN, Comp; *KAVIK THE WOLF DOG*, TV, 78, CDN, Comp; *1847*, 'THE NEWCOMERS', TV, 77, CDN, Comp; *THE BELLS OF HELL*, TV, 73, CDN, Comp; *THE PYX*, Th, 73, CDN, Comp; *TILT*, Th, 72, CDN, Comp; *NOVEMBER*, Th, 70, CDN, Comp; *ACT OF THE HEART*, Th, 70, CDN, Comp **(CFA)**; *ISABEL*, Th, 68, CDN, Comp; *THE MILLS OF THE GODS*, TV, 66, CDN, Comp; *THE ROOTS OF MADNESS*, TV, 66, USA, Comp; *LET ME COUNT THE WAYS*, TV, 65, CDN, Comp; *700 MILLION*, TV, 65, CDN, Comp; *ROMEO AND JEANETTE*, TV, 65, CDN, Comp; *SPRING SONG*, TV, 64, CDN, Comp; *JOURNEY TO THE CENTRE*, TV, 64, CDN, Comp; *THE DARK DID NOT CONQUER*, TV, 63, CDN, Comp; *PALE HORSE, PALE RIDER*, TV, 63, CDN, Comp; *'THIS HOUR HAS SEVEN DAYS'*, TV, 62, CDN, Comp; *20 MILLION SHOES*, TV, 62, CDN, Comp; *MICHELINE*, TV, 61, CDN, Comp; *INDIA*, TV, 59, CDN, Comp; *WHERE WILL THEY GO?*, TV, 59, CDN,

(cont/suite)

COMPOSERS/COMPOSITEURS

Comp; *THE DOUKHABORS*, TV, 58, CDN, Comp; *THE BLOODY BROOD*, Th, 57, CDN, Comp; *SHADOW OF THE CITY*, TV, 56, CDN, Comp.

FREWER, Terry

ACTRA, AFM. 1444 Argyle Ave., West Vancouver, BC, CAN, V7T 1C2. (604) 926-6288.
Types of Production & Categories: Th Short-Comp; TV Film-Comp; TV Video-Comp.
Genres: Musical-Th&TV; Documentary-TV; Commercials-TV; Industrial-Th&TV.
Biography: Born 1946; Canadian. Bachelor of Music, University of British Columbia, 69. Vocalist, musician, composer, producer; has had orchestral works performed by major Canadian symphony orchestras; featured vocalist in performance with Vancouver Symphony Orchestra, 72. Musical director for Ann Mortifee, Carroll Baker, Terry Jacks; wrote 'Old Rock & Roller' recorded by Tom Jones and Carroll Baker. Extensive work on shows for various Expo 86 pavilions.
Selective Filmography: *'LOTTO WEST'*, TV, 86/85, CDN, Comp; *BATHYSPHERE*, TV, 86, CDN, Comp; *MAZDA*, Cm, 86, CDN/USA, Comp; *HARVEY'S/CHEVY/PONTIAC*, Cm, 85-84, CDN, Comp; *'ZIGZAG'*, TV, 83, CDN, Theme Comp; *'SPORTS WEEKEND'* (CBC), TV, 78, CDN, Theme Comp; *CHALLENGE OF ALASKA/HAPPINESS IS/SKI B.C.*, In, 72/70, CDN, Comp; *PATAGONIA*, TV, 71, CDN, Comp; *VERTICAL DESERT*, TV, 71, CDN, Comp; *'STORY THEATRE'* (40 eps), TV, 70, CDN/USA, Comp; *LIFE AND TIMES OF CHESTER ANGUS RAMSGOOD*, Th, 70, CDN, Comp; *A FACE IN THE CROWD*, TV, 70, CDN, Comp; *THE PLASTIC MILE*, Th, 69, CDN, Comp; *SUMMER CENTER*, Th, 69, CDN, Comp; *DESERT RANCH/THE DRAGGERS*, 'THIS LAND OF OURS', TV, 68/67, CDN, Comp; *SERAPHINE*, TV, 68, CDN, Comp.

FRITZ, Sherilyn

2161 Prairie Ave., Port Coquitlam, BC, CAN, V3B 1V6. (604)941-4413.
Types of Production & Categories: Th Short-Comp.
Genres: Musical-Th.
Biography: Born 1957, Princeton, British Columbia. Bachelor of Music, University of B.C.; Masters in Music Composition, U. of Alberta. Has won many awards including the William Rea Award. Has been involved with studio and stage productions, Vancouver; taught at U.B.C., Vancouver Community College, U. of Alberta.
Selective Filmography: *AUDITION*, Th, 80, CDN, Comp/Mus Dir; *ELEVENTH HOUR*, Th, 79, CDN, Comp/Mus Dir; *OBSERVANCES*, Th, 79, CDN, Comp/ Lyrics/Mus Dir.

FUREY, Lewis

Ralph Zimmerman, Great North Artists Mgmt., 345 Adelaide St.W., #500, Toronto, Ont, CAN, M5V 1R5. (416)593-2587.
Types of Production & Categories: Th Film-Comp.
Genres: Drama-Th; Musical-Th; Children's-Th.
Biography: Born 1949, Montreal, Quebec. Educated at McGill University and Juilliard, NY. Began career at age 11 as violin soloist with Montreal Symphony Orchestra. Began making albums, 75; recorded 10. Director/actor/composer of various TV variety specials and musical stage shows; feature film director, 85. *NIGHT MAGIC* was the official Canadian selection, Cannes, 85.
Selective Filmography: *SAUVE TOI LOLA*, Th, 86, F, Comp; *NIGHT MAGIC*, Th, 85, CDN/F, Dir/Co-Scr/Comp (**GENIE**); *THE PEANUT BUTTER SOLUTION* (OPERATION BEURRE DE PINOTTES), Th, 85, CDN, Comp; *AMERICAN DREAMER*, Th, 84, USA, Comp; *MARIA CHAPDELAINE*, Th, 83, CDN/F, Comp (**GENIE**); *FANTASTICA*, Th, 80, CDN, Comp/Act; *SEE YOU MONDAY* (AUREVOIR...A LUNDI), Th, 79, CDN/F, Comp; *RUBBER GUN*, Th, 77, CDN,

(cont/suite)

COMPOSITEURS/COMPOSERS

Comp; *L'ANGE ET LA FEMME*, Th, 77, CDN, Comp/Act; *LA TETE DE NORMANDE ST-ONGE*, Th, 75, CDN, Comp (CFA); *JACOB TWO-TWO MEETS THE HOODED FANG*, Th, 75, CDN, Comp.

GAGNON, André
a/s Guy Latraverse, 3962 ave. Laval, Montréal, Qué, CAN, H2W 2J2. (514)288-2743.
Types de production et Catégories: l métrage-Comp; TV film-Comp.
Types d'oeuvres: Drame-C&TV; Documentaire-C.
Curriculum vitae: Formation en musique classique. Jusqu'en 1967, fut le pianiste accompagnateur et l'arrangeur pour plusieurs artistes dont Claude Léveillé, Monique Leyrac, et Renée Claude. Depuis, il a présenté des spectacles à la Place des Arts et dans des salles à travers le monde; a représenté le Québec à l'Exposition Universelle d'Osaka, 70. A enregistré 13 microsillons dont 'Les Turluteries', 'Neiges', 'Mouvements' et 'Virage à gauche' (tous des disques d'Or). Compositeur de la musique du ballet 'Mad Shadows' (Ballet National du Canada); a joué plusieurs fois avec l'Orchestre Symphonique de Montréal.
Filmographie sélective: *'DES DAMES DE COEUR'* (26 eps), TV, 86, CDN, Comp/Arr; *CYRANO*, TV, 85, CDN, Comp/Arr; *LE FIL D'ARIANE*, C, 85, CDN, Comp/Arr; *LA CELESTE BICYCLETTE*, TV, 83, CDN, Comp/Arr; *TELL ME THAT YOU LOVE ME*, C, 82, CDN/IL, Comp/Arr; *HOT TOUCH* (FRENCH KISS), C, 81, CDN, Comp/Arr; *PHOBIA*, C, 80, CDN, Comp/Arr; *RUNNING*, C, 79, CDN, Comp/Arr; *LES JEUX DE LA XXIe OLYMPIADE*, C, 76, CDN, Comp/Arr; *'LES FORGES DU ST-MAURICE'*, TV, 73-70, CDN, Comp/Arr; *KAMOURASKA*, C, 72, CDN, Comp/Arr.

GELINAS, Marc
CAPAC, SARDEC, UDA. 495 de la Colline, C.P.1757, Ste-Adèle, Qué, CAN, V0R 1L0. (514)229-6707.
Types de production et Catégories: l métrage-Comp; TV vidéo-Comp/Sc.
Types d'oeuvres: Comédie-C&TV; Variété-C&TV; Enfants-TV.
Curriculum vitae: Né en 1937, Montréal, Québec; bilingue. Trente ans de carrière comme auteur compositeur, chanteur, comédien. Plus gros vendeur de disque canadien français, 69. Auteur compositeur pour plusieurs annonces publicitaires.
Filmographie sélective: *'TRABOULIDON'* (5 eps), TV, 85/84, CDN, Co aut; *'BRAVO'* (65 eps), TV, 81, CDN, Co conc/Co aut/Comp thème; *'ROSA'* (52 eps), TV, 75, CDN, Comp; *UN SHOW QUI ME TENTE AVEC DU MONDE QUE J'AIME*, TV, 74, CDN, Aut comp; *BYE BYE* (3 ém), TV, 73-71, CDN, Aut comp/Sc; *TIENS-TOI BIEN APRES LES OREILLES A PAPA*, C, 71, CDN, Comp thème/Aut comp; *RED*, C, 70, CDN, Aut comp/Comp thème; *'TOUR A TOUR'* (39 eps), TV, 69, CDN, Aut; *FOODLE DUDDLE*, TV, 69, CDN, Aut comp; *'DU FEU S'IL VOUS PLAIT'*, TV, 68, CDN, Comp thème.

GODFREY, Patrick
AFM, GCFC. 37 Spruce St., Toronto, Ont, CAN, M5A 2H8. (416)920-3998.
Types of Production & Categories: Th Short-Comp; TV Film-Comp; TV Video-Comp.
Genres: Drama-TV; Variety-TV; Documentary-Th&TV; Animation-Th.
Biography: Born 1948, Toronto, Ontario. Performer, composer; piano and harpsichord are main instruments. Three Solo records released: 'Ancient Ships' (80), 'Bells of Earth' (82), 'Small Circus' (85).
Selective Filmography: *FRAGILE HARVEST*, 'THE NATURE OF THINGS', TV, 86, CDN, Comp; *THE BIG SNIT*, Th, 85, CDN, Comp; *'FRONTRUNNERS'* (4 eps), TV, 85, CDN, Comp; *'ENERGY - SEARCH FOR AN ANSWER'* (8 eps), TV, 84, CDN, Comp; *ALL OF OUR LIVES*, Th, 84, CDN, Comp; *PICK ME UP AT PEGGY'S COVE*, 'SONS AND DAUGHTERS', TV, 82, CDN, Comp; *DREAM CITIES*, 'VISTA', TV, 82, CDN, Comp; *UPPER REACHES*, TV, 80, CDN, Comp; *BELONGING*, TV, 79, CDN, Comp.

COMPOSERS/COMPOSITEURS

GRAY, John H. - see WRITERS

HABIB, Don

ACTRA, AFM, GCFC, UDA. 64 Salaberry North, Chateauguay, Que, CAN, J6J 4K2. (514)691-6470. Con Alma Enterprises, C.P.57, Chateauguay, Que, CAN, J6J 4Z4. (514)691-6470.
Types of Production & Categories: TV Film-Comp.
Genres: Drama-Th; Musical-TV; Documentary-TV; Children's-TV.
Biography: Born 1935, Montreal, Quebec; speaks French, English and Arabic. Enrolled at McGill University in Master's programme in Music Composition, 86; 8 years, assistant professor, Concordia U.. Has worked with Penderecki, Mancini, Michel Legrand, Skitch Henderson; underscored in collaboration with director/composer François Cousineau.
Selective Filmography: *CRIES OF THE DEEP* (PIEGES DE LA MER), TV, 82, CDN, Arr; *SUZANNE*, Th, 80, CDN, Arr; *L'ANGE GARDIEN*, Th, 79/78, CDN, Mus Dir/Arr; *CLOWNS OF CHRISTMAS*, TV, 76, CDN, Arr; *AS EAGLES FLY*, TV, 75, CDN, Comp; *'FANTASTICA'*, TV, 74, CDN, Comp; *THE ART OF COOKING*, TV, 74, CDN, Comp.

HARDY, Hagood

ACTRA, AFM. Hagood Hardy Productions Ltd., 133 Lowther Ave., Toronto, Ont, CAN, M5R 1E4. (416)967-6373.
Types of Production & Categories: Th Film-Comp; TV Film-Comp.
Genres: Drama-Th&TV; Documentary-TV; Animation-TV.
Biography: Born 1937; Canadian-US citizenship. Married, 4 children. Has recorded 10 albums: 3 Gold, 1 Platinum, 1 Double Platinum. Composer/arranger, over 50 features and TV films; commercial jingles. Selected Billboard Magazine's recipient for the award of American Instrumentalist of the Year; received the William Harold Moon Award; 3 time Juno Award winner.
Selective Filmography: *'FRONTIER'* (6 eps), TV, 86, CDN/GB/F/D, Comp; *ANNE OF GREEN GABLES - THE SEQUEL* (mini-series), TV, 86, CDN/USA, Comp; *THIS CHILD IS MINE*, TV, 85, USA, Comp; *ANNE OF GREEN GABLES* (mini-series), TV, 85, CDN, Comp; *'DURRELL IN RUSSIA'*, TV, 85, CDN, Comp; *WILD PONY*, TV, 83, CDN, Comp; *'THE AMATEUR NATURALIST'*, TV, 83, CDN, Comp; *THE CARE BEARS* (special), TV, 83, CDN, Comp; *'MAZES AND MONSTERS'*, TV, 82, USA, Comp; *FORBIDDEN LOVE*, TV, 82, USA, Comp; *THE CHRISTMAS EXPRESS*, TV, 81, CDN, Comp; *PORTRAIT OF AN ESCORT*, TV, 81, USA, Comp; *IMAGES OF IRELAND*, TV, 80, CDN, Comp; *MY ISLAND*, TV, 80, CDN, Comp; *DIRTY TRICKS*, Th, 80, CDN, Comp; *ANATOMY OF A SEDUCTION*, TV, 79, USA, Comp; *'THE SECRET RAILROAD'*, TV, 79, CDN, Comp; *KLONDIKE FEVER*, Th, 79, CDN, Comp; *AN AMERICAN CHRISTMAS CAROL*, TV, 79, USA, Comp; *TUKIKI*, TV, 79, CDN, Comp; *I, MAUREEN*, Th, 78, CDN, Comp; *JUST JESSIE*, Th, 78, CDN, Comp; *HOME TO STAY*, TV, 77, USA, Comp; *BETHUNE*, TV, 77, CDN, Comp; *TELL ME MY NAME*, TV, 77, USA, Comp; *HAILEY'S GIFT*, TV, 77, CDN, Comp; *TOM AND JOANNE*, TV, 77, USA, Comp; *RITUALS*, Th, 76, CDN, Comp; *SECOND WIND*, Th, 76, CDN, Comp; *'THE NEWCOMERS'*, TV, 76, CDN, Comp; *DOSTOEVSKY*, TV, 75, CDN, Comp.

HARRISON, Ron

GCFC. Harrison Music Ltd., 1532 King St.W., Toronto, Ont, CAN, M6K 1J6. (416)535-4984.
Types of Production & Categories: Th Film-Comp; TV Film-Comp; TV Video-Comp.
Genres: Drama-Th&TV; Comedy-TV; Action-TV; Documentary-Th&TV.
Biography: Born 1932, Hamilton, Ontario. Music education: Royal Conservatory of Music; 7 years private tutelage (Gord Delamont); 1 year, Oscar Peterson School

(cont/suite)

(scholarship); 1 year, Eastman School of Music; 1 year, UCLA, Film Scoring. Composed music for more than 450 TV and feature films.
Selective Filmography: *'PROFILES IN NATURE'* (65 eps), TV, 86-84, CDN, Comp; *'LAWYERS'* (7 eps), TV, 85, CDN, Comp; *GALAPAGOS,* TV, 83, CDN, Comp; *'THE CHINESE'* (6 eps), TV, 81, CDN, Comp; *'WILD CANADA'* (13 eps), TV, 80, CDN, Comp; *'THE CANADIAN ESTABLISHMENT'* (7 eps), TV, 80, CDN, Comp; *'THE WATSON REPORT'* (104 eps), TV, 80-78, CDN, Comp; *'MATT AND JENNY'* (26 eps), TV, 79, CDN/GB/D, Comp; *WINGS IN THE WILDERNESS,* Th, 77, CDN, Comp; *'FLIGHT: THE PASSIONATE AFFAIR'* (4 eps), TV, 76, CDN, Comp; *'TO THE WILD COUNTRY'* (13 eps), TV, 74/73, CDN, Comp; *'ADVENTURES IN RAINBOW COUNTRY'* (26 eps), TV, 69, CDN/GB/AUS, Comp; *'FABULOUS WORLD OF SKIING'* (26 eps), TV, 68, CDN, Comp; *'AUDUBON WILDLIFE THEATRE'* (78 eps), TV, 67, CDN, Comp.

HOFFERT, Brenda

ACTRA, AFM. Hoffert Music Corporation, 73 Brookview Dr., Toronto, Ont, CAN, M6A 2K5. (416)781-4191.
Types of Production & Categories: Th Film-Comp/Lyr; TV Film-Comp/Lyr.
Genres: Drama-Th&TV; Comedy-Th&TV; Musical-Th&TV; Documentary-Th&TV.
Biography: Born 1944, Toronto, Ontario. Studied 8 years, Toronto School of Drama; regular in continuing series of 'Children's Theatre of the Air'; grade XIII piano; studied voice, Royal Conservatory and with Aura Rully; co-leader of 'The Lizard People' (children's performing ensemble), 79-81; writer/director/ producer of numerous commercials; creative director of Morgan Earl Sounds, 79-83. Received numerous Clios and other advertising awards.
Selective Filmography: *SPECIAL DELIVERY,* TV, 85, CDN, Lyrics; *WILDCAT,* TV, 85, CDN, Lyrics; *THE EXILE,* TV, 85, CDN, Lyrics; *PERFECT TIMING,* Th, 84, CDN, Lyrics; *ONE NIGHT ONLY,* Th, 84, CDN, Lyrics; *SLIM OBSESSION/PASSENGERS,* 'FOR THE RECORD', TV, 83/81, CDN, Lyrics; *ONE FINE WEEKEND,* TV, 82, CDN, Wr/Co-Prod; *CIRCLE OF TWO,* Th, 80, CDN, Lyrics; *THE ELEPHANT WHO COULDN'T FORGET,* ED, 80, CDN/ USA, Mus Prod; *WILD HORSE HANK,* Th, 78, CDN, Lyrics; *THE THIRD WALKER,* Th, 78, CDN, Lyrics; *OUTRAGEOUS!,* Th, 77, CDN, Co-Comp; *IT SEEMED LIKE A GOOD IDEA AT THE TIME,* Th, 74, CDN, Lyrics; *SUNDAY IN THE COUNTRY,* Th, 73, CDN, Lyrics; *LIGHTHOUSE,* TV, 73, CDN, Cont.

HOFFERT, Paul

AFM, GCFC. Hoffert Music Corporation, 73 Brookview Dr., Toronto, Ont, CAN, M6A 2K5. (416)787-7728.
Types of Production & Categories: Th Film-Comp; TV Film-Comp.
Genres: Drama-Th&TV; Musical-Th&TV; Action-Th&TV; Science Fiction-Th&TV.
Biography: Born 1943, Brooklyn, New York; Canadian citizenship, 71. B.Sc., University of Toronto. Adjunct professor of film music, York U., 86. Extensive experience in scoring feature films (26) and TV specials. Awards include San Francisco Film Festival, P.R.O. Film Composer of the Year, 80; 4 Juno Awards, Clio. Author of text 'Synchronizing Music in Film & Television'. Reputation in 3 fields: symphonic, orchestral and contemporary; 4 gold records, 1 platinum for 'Lighthouse'.
Selective Filmography: *UNIVERSE,* Th, 85, CDN, Comp; *'THE HITCHIKER'* (6 eps), TV, 85/84, CDN/USA, Comp/Theme Comp; *HEAVENLY BODIES,* Th, 84, CDN, Mus Dir; *FANNY HILL,* Th, 83, GB, Comp; *MAGIC PLANET,* TV, 83, CDN/USA, Comp; *TORONTO TRILOGY* (3 shows), TV, 83, CDN, Comp; *STRAWBERRY ICE,* TV, 82, CDN, Comp (**2 ANIK**); *PARADISE,* Th, 81, CDN/ IL, Comp; *FIREBIRD 2015,* Th, 80, CDN, Co-Comp; *CIRCLE OF TWO,* Th, 80, CDN, Comp; *DOUBLE NEGATIVE,* Th, 79, CDN, Comp; *MR. PATMAN,* Th,

(cont/suite)

79, CDN, Comp; *WILD HORSE HANK,* Th, 78, CDN, Comp; *SHAPE OF THINGS TO COME,* Th, 78, CDN, Comp; *THE THIRD WALKER,* Th, 78, CDN, Comp; *HIGH-BALLIN',* Th, 77, CDN, Comp; *OUTRAGEOUS!,* Th, 77, CDN, Co-Comp **(CFA)**; *IT SEEMED LIKE A GOOD IDEA AT THE TIME,* Th, 74, CDN, Co-Comp; *SUNDAY IN THE COUNTRY,* Th, 73, CDN, Co-Comp; *GROUNDSTAR CONSPIRACY,* Th, 72, CDN/USA, Comp; *FLICK* (FRANKENSTEIN ON CAMPUS), Th, 70, CDN, Comp; *THE OFFERING,* Th, 66, CDN, Comp; *WINTER KEPT US WARM,* Th, 65, CDN, Comp.

JONES, Cliff - see WRITERS

KARDONNE, Rick

1050 Yonge St., #33A, Toronto, Ont, CAN, M4W 2L1. (416)921-9607.
Types of Production & Categories: Th Film-Comp.
Genres: Comedy-Th; Documentary-Th.
Biography: Born 1947. Composer, lyricist, author of 6 stage musicals including 'Sweet Reason', 75; 'Salon', 82; 'House of Pride', 83; composer, lyricist of lead song on Salome Bey's 'Pickwick' album: 'Hit the Nail Right on the Head'. Music director for countless stage, variety productions.
Selective Filmography: *RIP-OFF,* Th, 71, CDN, Co-Comp; *CATTLE DRIVE* (HOW THINGS HAVE CHANGED), Th, 70, CDN, Comp/Lyrics/Arr.

KOBYLANSKY, Karl

2725 Lyndene Rd., North Vancouver, BC, CAN, V7R 1E2. (604)980-0053. Capilano College, 2055 Purcell Way, North Vancouver, BC, CAN, V7J 3H5. (604) 986-1911.
Types of Production & Categories: Th Film-Comp; TV Video-Comp.
Genres: Drama-Th&TV.
Biography: Born 1932, Winnipeg, Manitoba. Languages: English, Russian, Ukrainian. Conductor, Vancouver Pro Musica Art Ensemble; Capilano Symphony Orchestra; recording sessions for NFB films. Teaches music composition, counterpoint, harmony, Capilano College, 86; has scored many college and community TV productions.
Selective Filmography: *DEAD WRONG,* Th, 83, CDN, Comp.

LAING, Alan R.

GCFC. P.O. Box 1772, St.Mary's, Ont, CAN, N0M 2V0. (519)284-1942. Ron Leach, Characters, 150 Carlton St., Toronto, Ont, CAN. (416)964-8522.
Types of Production & Categories: TV Film-Comp; TV Video-Comp.
Genres: Drama-Th&TV.
Biography: Born 1937; working knowledge of French. Has composed scores for dramatic productions (theatre, TV) in Canada, USA. Former actor, director, conductor, concert recitalist. Plays 10 instruments professionally; has had a long association with the Stratford Festival.
Selective Filmography: *CAT'S PLAY,* TV, 77, CDN, Comp; *A GIFT TO LAST,* TV, 76, CDN, Comp.

LANGLOIS, Jérôme

CAPAC. 5316 rue Fabre, Montréal, Qué, CAN, H2J 3W5. (514)527-6905. Les Prod. Molignar inc., 1599 A rue Panet, Montréal, Qué, CAN, H2L 2Z4. (514)522-2339.
Types de production et Catégories: l métrage-Comp; c métrage-Comp; TV film-Comp; TV vidéo-Comp.
Types d'oeuvres: Drame-C&TV; Comédie musicale-C&TV; Documentaire-C&TV; Animation-TV.
Curriculum vitae: Né en 1952, Providence, Rhode Island; citoyen canadien; bilingue. Etudes: cours classique; Conservatoire de musique, Montréal et cours privés de

(cont/suite)

COMPOSITEURS/COMPOSERS

composition avec André Prévost; contrepoint, harmonie avec Jacques Faubert. Fondateur, compositeur principal du groupe 'Lasting Weep' (68-72) et de 'Maneige' (72-76); a enregistré 2 microsillons. Depuis 76, a joué ses compositions en concert à plusieurs reprises; écrit pour la danse, le théâtre et la chanson.
Filmographie sélective: *'THE ADVENTURES OF ALBERT & SIDNEY'* (150 eps), TV, 86, CDN/USA, Comp; *VISAGE PALE* (PALE FACE), C, 85, CDN, Comp; *LE FILM D'ARIANE* (PETITES HISTOIRES DE FEMMES), C, 85, CDN, Comp; *MOTHER'S DAY*, ED, 85, CDN, Comp; *LES PETITES CRUAUTES/LA TERAPENE*, 'PETITS CONTES CRUELS', TV, 84, CDN, Comp; *'LES ARTS: CLARENCE GAGNON'* (3 eps), TV, 84, CDN, Comp; *LES ENFANTS DES NORMES POST-SCRIPTUM*, TV, 83, CDN, Comp.

LAUBER, Anne

LCC. 372 A Fairmont ouest, #2, Montréal, Qué, CAN, H2V 2G4. (514)279-7992.
Types de production et Catégories: 1 métrage-Comp; c métrage-Comp; TV film-Comp.
Types d'oeuvres: Drame-C&TV; Documentaire-C&TV.
Curriculum vitae: Née en 1943, Suisse. Compositeur et chef d'orchestre; nombreuses musiques de concert, oeuvres de tous genres: musique de chambre, musique vocale, symphonique, oratorio pour soliste et orchestre. Nombreux concerts et enregistrements radiophoniques; 2 disques. Enseigne à l'Université de Montréal et du Québec; titulaire de l'Orchestre des Jeunes de Ville d'Anjou, 83-84. Doctorat en Musique, 86.
Filmographie sélective: *LOUKY BERSIANICK,* TV, 86, CDN, Comp; *NICOLE BRASSARD,* TV, 86, CDN, Comp; *JOVETTE MARCHESSAULT,* TV, 86, CDN, Comp; *MARIE UGUAY,* TV, 81, CDN, Comp; *L'AFFAIRE COFFIN* (THE COFFIN AFFAIR), C, 79, CDN, Comp/Chef d'orch.

LAZEBNIK, Betty

AFM, CAPAC. 16 Fairview Blvd., Toronto, Ont, CAN, M4K 1L9. (416)466-5354.
Types of Production & Categories: Th Film-Comp; Th Short-Comp; TV Film-Comp; TV Video-Comp.
Genres: Drama-Th&TV; Comedy-Th&TV; Documentary-Th&TV; Animation-TV.
Biography: Born 1954, Toronto, Ontario. B.F.A., Music, York University, '76; Eastman School of Music, summer 80. Has also composed, arranged and produced music for commercials, TV and radio. Has received 2 Genie award nominations.
Selective Filmography: *RENO AND THE DOC*, Th, 83, CDN, Comp; *GUILTY PLEASURES,* Th, 82, CDN, Comp; *PASSING THROUGH*, TV, 81, CDN, Comp; *SKIPPY PEANUT BUTTER/GIRL GUIDES/KINNEY SHOES*, Cm, 81/80, CDN, Comp; *LAUGHLINES*, Th, 79, CDN, Comp.

LEGRADY, Thomas

AFM, CAPAC, GCFC. 58 Van Horne Ave., Willowdale, Ont, CAN, M2J 2S9. (416)494-9306.
Types of Production & Categories: TV Film-Comp; TV Video-Comp.
Genres: Comedy-TV; Variety-TV; Musical-Th&TV; Documentary-Th&TV.
Biography: Born 1920, Budapest, Hungary; Canadian citizen; speaks English, French, German, Hungarian. Ph.D., Political Science; Masters in Music Composition and Orchestra Direction. First Prize in Canadian Composition Competition, 64; OMTA Award as Music Director, 85. Four band compositions published in Canada by Gordon Thompson; two in the Netherlands by Molinara.
Selective Filmography: *'FRONTRUNNERS'* (1 eps), TV, 85, CDN, Comp/Cond; *CHARLIE GRANT'S WAR,* TV, 84, CDN, Comp/Cond; *'A LA ROMANCE'* (39 eps), TV, 59-56, CDN, Arr; *'COURONNE D'OR'* (39 eps), TV, 59-56, CDN, Arr; *'GENERAL MOTORS VOUS INVITE'* (78 eps), TV, 59-57, CDN, Arr; *'CHANSONS CANADIENNES'* (117 eps), TV, 59-56, CDN, Arr; *SUNSHINE AND ECLIPSE*, Th, 56, CDN, Comp; *THEY SAW LONDON,* ED, 56, H, Comp;
(cont/suite)

AGGTELEK, ED, 55, H, Comp; *THE BLOOD,* ED, 54, H, Comp; *AGROLSZAKADT URILANY,* Th, 46, H, Arr.

MacDONALD, Brad

AFM, AMPAC. 25 Janellan Ter., Scarborough, Ont, CAN, M1E 3M8. (416)282-0170. MacDonald-Daller Prod., 48 Yorkville Ave., Toronto, Ont, CAN, M4W 1L4. (416)964-1885. Jerry Lomberg, Bookings, 304 Richmond St.W., Toronto, Ont, CAN, M5V 1X2. (416)599-5816.
Types of Production & Categories: TV Film-Comp; TV Video-Comp.
Genres: Documentary-TV; Children's-TV; Animation-TV; Commercials-TV.
Biography: Born 1950. Professional composer, musician with classical and pop experience; writes commercials for nat'l broadcast; recognized by Clios, N.Y. Art Directors. World class Fairlight operator.
Selective Filmography: *'PETER USTINOV'S RUSSIA'* (6 eps), TV, 86, CDN, Comp/Arr; *'SUNDAY REPORT',* TV, 86, CDN, Comp/Arr; *'WONDERSTRUCK'* (13 eps), TV, 86, CDN, Comp/Arr; *'WHAT'S NEW'* (26 eps), TV, 86/85, CDN, Comp/Arr; *'BUCKSTOPPERS'* (13 eps), TV, 86, CDN, Comp/Arr; *ONTARIO HYDRO/PANASONIC/MR CLEAN/PETRO CANADA/KELLOGS,* Cm, 85, CDN, Comp/Arr; *FIRST CHOICE/BIC/I.G.A./MENNEN,* Cm, 85/84, CDN, Comp/Arr; *HOCKEY NIGHT IN CANADA,* TV, 84, CDN, Comp/Arr.

McCAULEY, William

AFM, CLC, GCFC. 44 Goodyear Crescent, Willowdale, Ont, CAN. (416)469-4612.
Types of Production & Categories: Th Film-Comp; TV Film-Comp.
Genres: Drama-Th&TV; Documentary-Th&TV.
Biography: Born Tofield, Alberta. B. Mus., University of Toronto; Associate of Toronto Conservatory of Music; M.A. and Doctorate of Musical Arts, Eastman School of Music. Worked for Crawley Films, 49-60; composer of 175 TV documentaries, theatrical shorts and industrials; composer of 'Miniature Overture' recorded by The Canadian Brass; arranger, conductor, 6 albums. Music Director at the O'Keefe Centre since 60; conductor of North York Symphony since 72.
Selective Filmography: *CITY ON FIRE,* Th, 79, CDN, Co-Comp/Cond; *RIEL,* TV, 78, CDN, Comp/Cond; *IT SEEMED LIKE A GOOD IDEA AT THE TIME,* Th, 74, CDN, Co-Comp/Cond; *SUNDAY IN THE COUNTRY,* Th, 73, CDN, Co-Comp/Cond; *'THE WHITE OAKS OF JALNA'* (12 eps), TV, 71, CDN, Comp/Cond; *FESTIVAL,* Th, 69, CDN, Comp/Cond.

MILLS-COCKELL, John

AFM, GCFC. 154 Indian Rd.Cres., Toronto, Ont, CAN, M6P 2G3. (416)762-1360. Great North Artists Mgmt., 345 Adelaide St.W., Ste. 500, Toronto, Ont, CAN, M5V 1R5. (416)593-2587.
Types of Production & Categories: Th Film-Comp; Th Short-Comp; TV Film-Comp; TV Video-Comp.
Genres: Drama-Th&TV; Action-Th; Horror-Th&TV.
Biography: Born 1943, Toronto, Ontario. Education: University of Toronto: Royal Conservatory, Faculty of Music; won the BMI student composer Award. Fifty percent of his work has been in conventional media, yet he is a specialist in electronic music with an interest in science fiction; has recorded often in Europe, USA.
Selective Filmography: *'THE LITTLE VAMPIRE'* (13 eps), TV, 85, CDN/GB/D, Comp/Cond; *HALF A LIFETIME,* TV, 85, CDN, Comp; *STRIKER'S MOUNTAIN,* TV, 85, CDN, Comp/Cond; *LABOUR OF LOVE,* TV, 84, CDN, Comp/Cond; *MAGGIE AND PIERRE,* TV, 84, CDN, Comp; *MOVING TARGETS,* 'FOR THE RECORD', TV, 83, CDN, Comp; *SNOW,* Th, 83, CDN, Comp; *GONGGA SHAN: WHITE PEAK BEYOND THE CLOUDS,* TV, 82, CDN, Comp; *CHALLENGE: THE CANADIAN ROCKIES,* TV, 82, CDN, Comp/

(cont/suite)

Cond; *'ARK ON THE MOVE'* (13 eps), TV, 81, CDN/GB, Comp/Cond; *HUMONGOUS,* Th, 81, CDN, Comp; *THE ITALIANS,* 'THE NEWCOMERS', TV, 81, CDN, Comp **(CFTA)**; *TERROR TRAIN,* Th, 80, CDN, Comp/Cond; *'CITIES'* (4 eps), TV, 80, CDN, Comp/Cond; *DEADLY HARVEST,* Th, 78, CDN, Comp; *THE CLOWN MURDERS,* Th, 77, CDN, Comp; *'THE STATIONARY ARK'* (L'ARCHE IMMOBILE), (13 eps), TV, 75, CDN, Comp; *'A THIRD TESTAMENT'* (6 eps), TV, 75, CDN/GB, Comp/Cond.

MOLLIN, Fred

ACTRA, AFM. 311 Adelaide St.E., Toronto, Ont, CAN, M5A 1N2. (416)863-9316.
Types of Production & Categories: Th Film-Comp; Th Short-Comp; TV Film-Comp; TV Video-Comp.
Genres: Drama-Th&TV; Comedy-Th&TV; Musical-Th&TV; Children's-Th&TV.
Biography: Born 1953, New York; has resided in Canada for over 15 years. Three time Juno Award-winning record producer.
Selective Filmography: *HIGH SCHOOL NARC,* TV, 85, USA, Comp; *MAKING IT YOUNG,* TV, 85, CDN, Comp; *LOOSE SCREWS,* Th, 85, CDN, Comp; *TUCKER AND THE HORSE THIEF/WORKING FOR PEANUTS/MY FATHER,MY RIVAL,* 'FAMILY PLAYHOUSE', TV, 84, CDN, Comp; *HOCKEY NIGHT,* TV, 84, CDN, Comp; *GREAT MOMENTS IN CANADIAN SPORTS,* TV, 84, CDN, Comp; *'IN MOTION'* (26 eps), TV, 84, CDN, Comp; *YOUTH STRESS,* TV, 83, CDN, Comp; *SPRING FEVER* (SNEAKERS), Th, 82, CDN, Comp; *'HEART OF GOLD'* (3 eps), TV, 82, CDN, Comp; *MISDEAL* (BEST REVENGE), Th, 80, CDN, Comp; *THE DREAM NEVER DIES,* Th, 80, CDN, Comp; *FAST COMPANY,* Th, 78, CDN, Comp.

MORLEY, Glenn

AFM, GCFC. 47 Huntley St., Toronto, Ont, CAN, M4Y 2L2. (416)929-9324.
Types of Production & Categories: Th Film-Comp; TV Film-Comp; TV Video-Comp.
Genres: Drama-Th&TV; Comedy-Th&TV; Documentary-TV; Educational-TV.
Biography: Born Toronto, Ontario. Languages: English, French, Spanish. B.F.A., York University. Partner: Morley/Shragge Multi Media Music; extensive theatrical work as composer, musical director; approximately 85 productions in Canada and abroad. Musical and technical director for York U. Graduate Program in Theatre, 75-76; lecturer in musical theatre, George Brown College, 79-81; numerous concert works performed by the Toronto Symphony, National Arts Centre Orchestra etc.. Composer, orchestrator, arranger, numerous jingles and record projects; music director on live extravaganzas: Bicentennial Showcase, Mitchener Gala, industrial showcases.
Selective Filmography: *'PARENTS AND READING'* (6 eps), TV, 86, CDN, Co-Comp; *'NATURE OF THINGS',* TV, 86-80, CDN, Theme Comp; *'MAN ALIVE',* TV, 86-84, CDN, Theme Comp; *'THE CAMPBELLS'* (22 eps), TV, 85, CDN/USA/GB, Co-Comp; *THE EXILE,* TV, 85, CDN, Co-Comp; *'SPIRIT BAY'* (7 eps), TV, 85/84, CDN, Co-Comp; *CLASS OF PROMISE,* TV, 85, CDN, Co-Comp; *ONE MAGIC CHRISTMAS,* Th, 85, CDN/USA, Cond/Orch; *OVERNIGHT,* Th, 85, CDN, Co-Comp; *SPECIAL DELIVERY,* TV, 85, CDN, Co-Comp; *SLIM OBSESSION,* 'FOR THE RECORD', TV, 84, CDN, Co-Comp; *'COUNTRY CANADA',* TV, 84-80, CDN, Theme Comp; *'HOME FIRES'* (31 eps), TV, 83-80, CDN, Co-Comp; *A CASE OF LIBEL,* TV, 83, USA, Co-Comp; *TIES THAT BIND,* 'HAND & EYE', TV, 83, CDN, Comp; *BEST OF BOTH WORLDS,* TV, 82, CDN, Co-Comp; *PASSENGERS,* TV, 82, CDN, Co-Comp; *THE KGB CONNECTIONS,* TV, 81, CDN, Co-Comp; *COMING OUT ALIVE,* TV, 81, CDN, Co-Comp; *POPULATION OF ONE,* TV, 81, CDN, Co-Comp; *'THE WINNERS'* (8 eps), TV, 81, CDN, Co-Comp; *MUST FREEDOM FAIL?,* TV, 80, CDN, Comp; *'MEETING PLACE',* TV, 80, CDN, Theme Comp; *THE MASSEYS* (2 parts), TV, 78, CDN, Co-Comp.

COMPOSERS/COMPOSITEURS

NAYLOR, Steven J.

GCFC. P.O. Box 3731, Halifax South, NS, CAN, B3J 3K6. (902)422-7760.
Types of Production & Categories: TV Film-Comp; TV Video-Comp.
Genres: Drama-TV; Documentary-TV; Children's-TV.
Biography: Born 1949, Woodstock, Ontario. B.A., Waterloo University College (English), 69; Bachelor of Independent Studies, U. of Waterloo (Music), 73; additional studies in composition, film composition, electronic music techniques; various scholarships, grants. Experience in music for theatre (children's); background in pop music and folklore.
Selective Filmography: *'SESAME STREET'* (sev seg), TV, 85, USA, Comp; *THE LAST LOG DRIVE,* TV, 85, CDN, Comp; *KOUCHIBOUGUAC,* ED, 85, CDN, Comp/Mus Prod; *THE JOB,* TV, 85, CDN, Comp/Mus Prod; *GETTING TO WORK* (pilot), TV, 85, CDN, Mus Prod; *DON CONNOLY'S HALIFAX,* 'CITYSCAPES', TV, 84, CDN, Comp; *'LE TERRAIN D'ACADIE'* (3 eps), ED, 84, CDN, Comp/Mus Prod; *JUST SO STORIES,* TV, 84, CDN, Comp; *VALSE TRISTE,* TV, 84, CDN, Comp; *THE REGIMENT,* TV, 84, CDN, Comp; *'SAFE AT HOME'* (3 eps), ED, 81, CDN, Comp/Mus Prod; *JENNY KOOKOO,* TV, 81, CDN, Comp/Mus Prod; *SARAH JACKSON,* TV, 80, CDN, Comp/Mus Prod; *SPINNER BOY/CLOCKWORKS,* 'EXCEPTIONAL CHILDREN', TV, 80, CDN, Comp/Mus Prod; *THE KING OF HEARTS,* TV, 76, CDN, Comp; *ASHLEY'S CHRISTMAS PRESENT,* TV, 74, CDN, Comp.

NIMMONS, Phil

CLC, GCFC. Nimmons 'N' Music Ltd., 114 Babcombe Dr., Thornhill, Ont, CAN, L3T 1N1. (416)889-9980.
Types of Production & Categories: Th Film-Comp; Th Short-Comp; TV Film-Comp.
Genres: Drama-Th&TV; Variety-TV; Musical-Th&TV; Documentary-Th&TV.
Biography: Born 1923, Kamloops, British Columbia. B.A., University of British Columbia; Juilliard School of Music, NY ; composition, Royal Conservatory of Music, U. of Toronto. Co-founder, teacher, Advanced School of Contemporary Music, Toronto, 60-63. Composer: contemporary classical works for piano, strings, instrumental; over 400 original jazz compositions; radio and stage plays; has recorded 10 albums; band leader, Nimmons 'N' Nine; composer for numerous TV series and specials, 60-70. Has won many awards including: BMI (68), Juno (76) and P.R.O. Canada (80); recipient of a Toronto Arts Award, 86.
Selective Filmography: *THE TROJAN WOMEN,* Th, 78, CDN, Comp/Arr; *POWER BY PROXY,* TV, 60, CDN, Comp/Arr; *THE YOUNG AND THE BEAT,* Th, 57, CDN, Comp/Arr; *A DANGEROUS AGE,* Th, 56, CDN, Comp/Arr.

POLGAR, Tibor

GCFC. 21 Vaughan Rd., #1903, Toronto, Ont, CAN, M6G 2N2. (416)654-7835.
Types of Production & Categories: Th Film-Comp; Th Short-Comp; TV Film-Comp; TV Video-Comp.
Genres: Drama-Th&TV; Musical-Th&TV; Documentary-Th&TV; Educational-Th&TV.
Biography: Born Budapest, Hungary; Canadian citizen. Languages: English, German, Hungarian. Attended Humanistic Gymnasium; University-Faculty of Philosophy. Head of the Music Dept. and conductor of the Hungarian Radio Symphony Orchestra for 25 years. As a composer, has written music for stage and scores for 200 Hungarian films (features, documentaries, cartoons). In Canada, has worked for CBC Radio and TV; has also written music for films and commercials. Awarded Senior Arts Fellowships by the Canada Council, 66 and 67.
Selective Filmography: *IN PRAISE OF OLDER WOMEN,* Th, 78, CDN, Comp; *THE HOUSE ON FRONT STREET,* Th, 77, CDN, Comp; *ENERGY,* ED, 76, CDN, Comp; *THE CUTTY STOOL,* TV, 76, CDN, Comp; *THE GLOVE,* TV, 75, CDN, Comp; *DRACULA,* TV, 75, CDN, Comp.

RAINE-REUSCH, Randy

AFM. Box 1119, Stn. A, Vancouver, BC, CAN, V6C 2T1. (604)255-2506.
Types of Production & Categories: Th Short-Comp.
Genres: Documentary-Th; Educational-Th; Experimental-Th.
Biography: Born 1952, Halifax, Nova Scotia. Composes and performs on over 130 instruments; specialist in ethnic and world music. *SOLUS* won an Award at the New York Dance and Film Festival; Best Film in it's class, Chicago Film Festival.
Selective Filmography: *KANGAROOS UNDER FIRE,* Th, 85, CDN, Comp; *SOLUS,* Th, 84, CDN, Co-Comp; *RIVER OF ICE,* Th, 82, CDN, Co-Comp; *THE LONG FIST,* Th, 81, CDN, Comp.

RATHBURN, Eldon

641 Bathgate Dr., Ottawa, Ont, CAN, K1K 3Y3. (613)745-9340.
Types of Production & Categories: Th Film-Comp; Th Short-Comp; TV Film-Comp.
Genres: Drama-Th&TV; Documentary-Th&TV; Animation-Th&TV.
Biography: Born 1916, Queenstown, New Brunswick. Staff composer, NFB, 47-76. Studied with Healey Willan at the Royal Conservatory. Recordings: 'Labyrinthe' (Expo 67), 'The Metamorphic Ten - Canadian Brass Rag'; composed 'Rise and Fall of the Steam Railroad - Turbo-Junction'. Won the Los Angeles Young Artist Award, 44.
Selective Filmography: *FINAL CHAPTER,* 'THE CHAMPIONS', TV, 86, CDN, Comp; *TRANSITIONS,* Th, 86/85, CDN, Comp; *CANADA'S SWEETHEART: THE SAGA OF HAL C. BANKS,* TV, 85, CDN, Comp; *J.W. MORRICE,* Th, 85, CDN, Comp; *SKYWARD,* Th, 84, CDN, Comp; *I LIKE TO SEE THE WHEELS TURN,* TV, 81, CDN, Comp; *WHO HAS SEEN THE WIND,* Th, 76, CDN, Comp; *FOR GENTLEMEN ONLY,* TV, 76, CDN, Comp; *THE HECKLERS,* TV, 76, CDN, Comp; *THE ROAD TO GREEN GABLES,* TV, 75, CDN, Comp; *CIRCUS WORLD,* Th, 74, CDN, Comp; *DEATH OF A LEGEND,* Th, 71, CDN, Comp; *FIELDS OF SPACE,* Th, 70, CDN, Comp **(CFA)**; *FIELDS OF SACRIFICE,* Th, 64, CDN, Comp; *CITY OF GOLD,* Th, 57, CDN, Comp.

ROBERTSON, Doug

AFM. Robertson Music, 42 Rumsey Rd., Toronto, Ont, CAN, M4G 1N8. (416) 467-1515.
Types of Production & Categories: TV Film-Comp; TV Video-Comp.
Genres: Drama-TV; Commercials-TV; Industrial-TV.
Biography: Born 1952, Toronto, Ontario. B. Music, University of Toronto, 76. Composer/arranger/lyricist for 400 radio commercials; composer/producer for 'Pizza-Pizza' radio commercials, 83-86.
Selective Filmography: *SUMMER CITY,* In, 86, CDN, Comp; *ONCE UPON A TIME IN TRICKLE FALLS,* TV, 85, CDN, Comp; *HAMILTON BUSINESS,* In, 84, CDN, Comp; *NION IN THE KABARET DE LA VITA,* TV, 84, CDN, Comp; *DAVID ROCHE TALKS TO YOU ABOUT LOVE,* TV, 84, CDN, Comp.

ROBERTSON, Eric

AFM. 34 Westmount Park Rd., Weston, Ont, CAN, M9P 1R6. (416)245-3151.
Types of Production & Categories: Th Film-Comp; TV Film-Comp; TV Video-Comp.
Genres: Drama-Th&TV; Science Fiction-Th; Horror-Th; Documentary-Th&TV.
Biography: Born 1948, Edinburgh, Scotland. Educated at Daniel Stewart's College; studied organ piano and composition with Eric Reid, Dr.E.F. Thomas, W.O. Minay; emigrated to Canada, 63; scholarship student, Royal Conservatory of Music with Dr. Charles Peaker, Dr. Sam Dolin; A.R.C.T. and Fellowship degree, Royal Canadian College of Organists. Has composed/arranged hundreds of advertising
(cont/suite)

jingles; musical director, TV and radio variety; record producer, awarded numerous platinum and gold awards.
Selective Filmography: *ISLAND LOVE SONG,* TV, 86, CDN, Comp; *'STREET LEGAL'* (6 eps), TV, 86, CDN, Comp; *IN THIS CORNER,* TV, 85, CDN, Comp; *THAT'S MY BABY,* Th, 85, CDN, Comp; *MICHAEL AND KITTY,* TV, 85, CDN, Comp; *THE CUCKOO BIRD,* TV, 84, CDN, Comp; *LOVE AND LARCENY,* TV, 84, CDN, Comp; *THE OTHER KINGDOM* (mini-series), TV, 84, CDN, Comp; *GENTLE SINNERS,* TV, 83, CDN, Comp; *SPECIAL PEOPLE,* TV, 83, CDN/USA, Comp; *SHOCKTRAUMA,* TV, 83, CDN, Comp; *HIDE AND SEEK/SNOWBIRDS/BY REASON OF INSANITY,* 'FOR THE RECORD', TV, 83-81, CDN, Comp; *IF YOU COULD SEE WHAT I HEAR,* Th, 82, CDN, Comp; *SCORN OF WOMEN,* TV, 82, CDN, Comp; *DEATH BITE* (SPASMS), Th, 81, CDN, Comp; *THE UNEXPECTED,* TV, 81, CDN, Comp; *WINNIE,* TV, 81, CDN, Comp; *KILLER INSTINCT,* Th, 81, CDN, Comp; *THE HIGH COUNTRY* (THE FIRST HELLO), Th, 80, CDN, Comp; *THUNDER,* TV, 79, CDN, Comp; *PLAGUE* (MUTATIONS), Th, 78, CDN, Comp; *THE TAR SANDS/KATHY KARUKS IS A GRIZZLY BEAR,* 'FOR THE RECORD', TV, 77, CDN, Comp; *INSURANCE MAN FROM INGERSOLL,* TV, 76, CDN, Comp; *A QUIET DAY IN BELFAST,* Th, 74/73, CDN/GB, Co-Comp; *ALONG THESE LINES,* Th, 74, CDN, Comp.

SEREDA, John

1763 E. Pender, Ste. 202, Vancouver, BC, CAN, V5L 1W5. (604)253-3998.
Types of Production & Categories: Th Film-Comp; TV Film-Comp; TV Video-Comp.
Genres: Drama-Th&TV; Educational-TV; Commercials-TV; Industrial-TV.
Biography: Born 1953, Alberta. Involved in performance/writing/production of concerts, recordings, theatre, TV, jingles. Juno Award for Album recorded with Tommy Banks Orchestra at the Montreux Jazz Festival; wrote lyrics for Jesse Award-winning 'Sex Tips for Modern Girls'.
Selective Filmography: *WAITING FOR SERGIO,* Th, 86, CDN, Comp; *IT WORKS BOTH WAYS,* ED, 85, CDN, Comp; *TOO MUCH TOO SOON,* TV, 85, CDN, Comp; *CONVEYOR MADNESS,* In, 85, CDN, Comp; *MONSTER MACHINE,* Cm, 84, USA, Comp.

SHORE, Howard

AFM. 1619 Broadway, #94, New York, NY, USA, 10019. (212)265-7621.
Types of Production & Categories: Th Film-Comp; TV Film-Comp.
Genres: Drama-Th; Comedy-Th&TV; Horror-Th.
Biography: Born 1946, Toronto, Ontario. Attended Berklee School of Music, Boston. Music producer: Randy Newman's 'Live from the Odeon'.
Selective Filmography: *THE FLY,* Th, 86, USA, Comp; *HEAVEN,* Th, 86, USA, Comp; *FIRE WITH FIRE,* Th, 86, USA, Comp; *BELIZAIRE, THE CAJUN,* Th, 86, USA, Mus Prod; *AFTER HOURS,* Th, 85, USA, Comp; *PLACES IN THE HEART,* Th, 85, USA, Comp; *NOTHING LASTS FOREVER,* Th, 84, USA, Comp; *VIDEODROME,* Th, 82, CDN, Comp; *SCANNERS,* Th, 80, CDN, Comp; *'SATURDAY NIGHT LIVE'* (121 eps), TV, 80-75, USA, Comp; *THE BROOD,* Th, 79, CDN, Comp.

SHRAGGE, Lawrence

67 Sullivan St., Toronto, Ont, CAN, M5T 1C2. (416)977-4532.
Types of Production & Categories: Th Film-Comp; Th Short-Comp; TV Film-Comp; TV Video-Comp.
Genres: Drama-Th&TV; Musical-Th&TV; Action-Th&TV; Documentary-Th&TV.
Biography: Born 1954, Montreal, Quebec. Education: Berklee College of Music, Eastman School of Music.

(cont/suite)

Selective Filmography: *'THE CAMPBELLS'* (52 eps), TV, 86/85, CDN/USA/GB, Comp; *SPECIAL DELIVERY*, TV, 86, CDN, Co-Comp; *'SPIRIT BAY'* (13 eps), TV, 86/85, CDN, Comp; *'HOOKED ON READING'* (6 eps), TV, 86/85, CDN, Comp; *THE SILENT PARTNER*, TV, 86, CDN, Comp; *WHERE'S PETE*, Th, 86, CDN, Comp; *THE EXILE*, TV, 85, CDN, Co-Comp; *ONE NIGHT ONLY*, Th, 85, CDN, Comp; *'EDUCATING THE SPECIAL CHILD'* (6 eps), TV, 85, CDN, Comp; *CLASS OF PROMISE*, TV, 85, CDN, Co-Comp; *WILDCAT*, TV, 85, CDN, Comp; *THANKS FOR THE RIDE*, Th, 84, CDN, Comp; *SLIM OBSESSION*, 'FOR THE RECORD', TV, 84, CDN, Co-Comp; *A CASE OF LIBEL*, TV, 84, USA, Co-Comp; *'HOME FIRES'* (31 eps), TV, 83-80, CDN, Co-Comp; *PARADISE*, Th, 83, CDN/IL, Orch; *THE BEST OF BOTH WORLDS*, TV, 82, CDN, Co-Comp; *'TALES OF THE HAUNTED'* (5 eps), TV, 82, CDN/ USA, Comp; *THE ELEPHANT WHO WOULDN'T FORGET*, TV, 82, CDN, Comp; *THE WAY OF THE WILLOW*, Th, 82, CDN, Comp; *PASSENGERS*, TV, 82, CDN, Co-Comp; *THE KGB CONNECTIONS*, TV, 81, CDN, Co-Comp; *'THE WINNERS'* (8 eps), TV, 81, CDN, Co-Comp; *FIREBIRD 2015*, Th, 80, CDN, Co-Comp; *POPULATION OF ONE*, TV, 80, CDN, Comp; *COMING OUT ALIVE*, TV, 80, CDN, Co-Comp; *'LOVE AT THE CROSSROADS'* (5 eps), TV, 80, CDN, Comp.

SKOLNIK, Bill

AFM-145, AFM-149. 6362 Ash St., Vancouver, BC, CAN, V5Z 3G9. (604)324-1248.
Types of Production & Categories: Th Film-Comp; Th Short-Comp; TV Film-Comp; TV Video-Comp.
Genres: Drama-Th&TV; Documentary-Th&TV; Educational-TV; Animation-TV.
Biography: Born 1950, Montreal, Quebec; bilingual. Degree in Political Science, University of Toronto. Has worked for CBC, CTV, TVO, Global and PBS.
Selective Filmography: *IT CAN'T BE DONE*, Th, 86, CDN, Comp/Arr; *TALES OF THE MOUSE HOCKEY LEAGUE*, TV, 86, CDN, Comp/Arr; *INDUSTRY IN B. C./THE SALMON FISHERY*, ED, 86, CDN, Comp/Arr; *MY AMERICAN COUSIN*, Th, 85, CDN, Arr; *'SESAME STREET'* (lyrics-26 seg), (56 seg), TV, 85-83, USA, Comp/Arr; *'CHALK TALK'* (15 eps), TV, 84, CDN, Comp/Arr; *TO ANNEDALE AND BACK*, Th, 84, CDN, Comp/Arr; *COWBOYS DON'T CRY*, Th, 84, CDN, Comp/Arr; *SEASONS OF THE MIND*, Th, 82, CDN, Comp/Arr; *PETROCAN*, In, 82, CDN, Comp/Arr; *EYEOPENER MAN*, TV, 81, CDN, Comp/Arr; *THEY LED THE WAY*, Th, 81, CDN, Comp/Arr; *'THE SCIENCE ALLIANCE'* (26 eps), TV, 81, CDN, Comp/Arr; *'THE BODY WORKS'* (40 eps), TV, 80, CDN, Lyrics/Comp/Arr; *'KIDSWORLD'* (26 eps), TV, 78, CDN, Comp/ Arr; *'THE FRENCH SHOW'* (13 eps), TV, 77, CDN, Comp/Arr; *'LES BOUCANIERS D'EAU DOUCE'* (13 eps), TV, 77, CDN, Arr; *25 MINUTES TO POST-TIME*, Th, 76, CDN, Arr; *BUFFALO BILL AND THE INDIANS*, Th, 75, USA, Arr.

SOLOMON, Maribeth

ACTRA. 17 St.Andrews Gardens, Toronto, Ont, CAN, M4W 2C9. (416)961-1017. Mickymar Productions Ltd., 663 Yonge St., Suite 203, Toronto, Ont, CAN, M4Y 2A4. (416)960-2281.
Types of Production & Categories: Th Film-Comp; Th Short-Comp; TV Film-Comp; TV Video-Comp.
Genres: Drama-Th&TV; Comedy-Th&TV; Musical-Th&TV; Documentary-Th&TV.
Biography: Born 1951, Toronto, Ontario. Education: York University, Royal Conservatory of Music for piano theory harmony; studied flute with Robert Aitken; harmony and composition with Gordon Delamont. Toured US and Canada extensively; wrote songs recorded by Anne Murray and others; has won Clios, Radio & TV Awards for commercials; 2 Genie nominations; produced Juno Award-winning recording artists; plays piano, synthesizers and flute.

(cont/suite)

Selective Filmography: *THE DREAM IS ALIVE,* Th, 85, CDN/USA, Co-Comp; *FREEDOM TO MOVE,* Th, 85, CDN, Co-Comp; *'FRONTRUNNERS'* (3 eps), TV, 85, CDN, Co-Comp; *PRIME TIME,* Th, 85, CDN, Co-Comp; *JOINT CUSTODY* (MOMMY'S HOUSE, DADDY'S HOUSE), TV, 85, CDN, Co-Comp; *CINEMA ET CINEMA,* TV, 84, CDN, Co-Comp; *'GREAT MOMENTS'* (3 eps), TV, 84, CDN, Co-Comp; *ABORTION: STORIES FROM NORTH TO SOUTH,* Th, 84, CDN, Co-Comp; *NUNS: BEHIND THE VEIL,* Th, 84, CDN, Co-Comp; *HAIL COLUMBIA,* Th, 82, CDN, Co-Comp; *UTILITIES,* Th, 82, CDN, Co-Comp; *TICKET TO HEAVEN,* Th, 80, CDN, Co-Comp; *KELLY,* Th, 81, CDN, Co-Comp/Theme Co-Comp; *THRESHOLD,* Th, 80, CDN, Co-Comp; *HARRY TRACY,* Th, 80, CDN, Co-Comp; *IMPROPER CHANNELS,* Th, 79, CDN, Co-Comp/Theme Co-Comp; *NOMADS OF THE DEEP,* Th, 77, CDN, Co-Comp; *ONTARIO/SUMMERTIDE,* Th, 76, CDN, Co-Comp/Theme Co-Comp; *OCEAN: TIME MACHINE,* Th, 75, CDN, Co-Comp; *NORTH OF SUPERIOR,* Th, 70, CDN, Co-Comp.

TATE, Brian

AFM, CAPAC, CLC. 4079 W.15th Ave., Vancouver, BC, CAN, V6R 3A2. (604) 228-1696.
Types of Production & Categories: TV Film-Comp/Prod; TV Video-Comp/Prod.
Genres: Variety-TV; Educational-TV; Industrial-TV.
Biography: Born 1954, Vancouver, British Columbia. Studied composition with Elliot Weisgarber, University of B.C., B.Music, 76; with Sir Lennox Berkeley, London, 77. Assistant conductor, Hammersmith Symphony, Ariann Chamber Orchestra, Toronto, 79-81. Received several commissions for new works including Toronto Symphony Brass Ensemble; conductor with Royal Conservatory's Training Program, Vancouver, 81-. Music director, composer: musical theatre, film, radio drama, a/v, concert stage.
Selective Filmography: *THE LEGEND OF SINTER KLAAS,* TV, 86, CDN, Comp/Mus Prod; *'TAKE PART'* (65 eps), TV, 86, CDN, Comp/Mus Prod; *THE GREAT DIVIDE,* 'LANSCAPE AS HISTORY', ED, 85, CDN, Comp/Mus Prod; *EXPLORATIONS IN MASS COMMUNICATIONS / CONTROL TECHNOLOGIES,* In, 85, CDN, Comp/Mus Prod; *'MIXED COMPANY'* (daily), TV, 85, CDN, Comp/Mus Prod; *GROWING UP WITH LOGO/ORDER FROM CHAOS/OUT OF HARM'S WAY,* ED, 85, CDN, Comp/Mus Prod; *HOLLYWOOD SHOWCASE* (pilot), TV, 84, USA, Comp/Mus Prod; *'VENTURE CAPITAL'* (13 eps), TV, 84, CDN, Comp/Mus Prod; *GEROL* (pilot), TV, 84, CDN, Comp/Mus Prod; *PLAY, GYPSIES,* TV, 83, CDN, Assist Mus Dir/Arr.

TEDMAN, Keith

CLC, GCFC. 5245 Provence St., Pierrefonds, Que, CAN, H8Z 2M3. (514)620-6167.
Types of Production & Categories: Th Short-Comp; TV Film-Comp; TV Video-Comp.
Genres: Science Fiction-Th; Documentary-Th&TV; Children's-Th&TV; Animation-Th&TV.
Biography: Born 1947, London, England; Canadian citizen; bilingual. Ph.D. in Music, University of Sussex, 83; M.M.A., B.Mus. in music composition, McGill University, 72, 75. Has written concert works for various ensembles and orchestras, performed and broadcast in Canada and U.K., Publication by Waterloo Music Co.. Awards in composition from Canada Council, Quebec Cultural Affairs Ministry. Chris Plaque and Learning Magazine Award for *MAGIC FLUTE.*
Selective Filmography: *SUMMER LEGEND,* Th, 85, CDN, Comp; *STARLIFE,* Th, 83, CDN, Comp; *'SESAME STREET'* (sev seg), TV, 83, CDN, Comp; *THE TOWN MOUSE AND COUNTRY MOUSE,* Th, 80, CDN, Comp; *TALE OF TWO TURKEYS,* ED, 80, CDN, Comp; *HALLOWEEN JUST ISN'T THE SAME,* ED, 80, CDN, Comp; *IMAGE MAKERS,* TV, 79, CDN, Comp; *THE UNBROKEN*
(cont/suite)

LINE, Th, 79, CDN, Comp; *THE MAGIC FLUTE,* Th, 77, CDN, Comp; *WATERWAYS TO EXPLORE,* TV, 75, CDN, Comp.

WALKER, Russ

AFM. The Media Centre, 397 Donlands Ave., Toronto, Ont, CAN, M4J 3S2. (416) 422-4636.
Types of Production & Categories: TV Film-Comp; TV Video-Comp.
Genres: Drama-TV; Documentary-TV; Commercials-TV; Industrial-TV.
Biography: Born 1954, Toronto, Ontario. Educated extensively in both classical and electronic music; travelled all over the world studying local music in different countries. Has released 3 records with WEA and RCA Records; worked for 9 years as a recording engineer/producer; began composing for film, 79.
Selective Filmography: *THE BIRTH OF LANGUAGE,* TV, 86, CDN, Comp; *KEYS TO THE OFFICE,* TV, 86, CDN, Comp; *THE JOY OF STRESS/TIEM/ THE FUTURE'S PAST/WE ARE MOTION/IDEA CORP.,* In, 86/85, CDN, Comp; *THE OTHER FACE OF LEPROSY,* 'NATURE OF THINGS', TV, 86, CDN, Comp; *SPEAKING OUT,* TV, 85, CDN, Arr; *SUTTON PLACE,* Cm, 85, CDN, Arr; *THE NO NAME SHOW,* TV, 84, CDN, Comp; *FROM GRAPE TO GLASS,* TV, 82, CDN, Comp; *CIDA/MOTOROLA/ALGOMA STEEL/INTER METCO,* In, 82-79, CDN, Comp; *CHILDREN'S THEATRE SPECIAL,* TV, 82, CDN, Comp; *JOSHUA'S CARVING/LENA IN THE KINGDOM OF GLASS,* 'SPREAD YOUR WINGS', TV, 81/80, CDN, Comp; *RICHARD'S TOTEM POLE,* 'SPREAD YOUR WINGS', TV, 81, CDN, Comp; *MADELAINE,* TV, 81, CDN, Comp; *BOUNCE FABRIC SOFTENER/NORTHSTAR SHOES/ EVINRUDE MOTORS,* Cm, 81-79, CDN, Comp; *DIRTY SKY, DYING WATER,* TV, 80, CDN, Comp; *FAST FORWARD,* TV, 80, CDN, Comp; *SENTINEL OF THE SEA,* TV, 79, CDN, Comp.

ZAZA, Paul

ACTRA. Zaza Sound Productions Ltd., 322 Dufferin St., Toronto, Ont, CAN, M6K 1Z6. (416)534-4211.
Types of Production & Categories: Th Film-Comp; TV Film-Comp; TV Video-Comp.
Genres: Drama-Th&TV; Horror-Th&TV.
Biography: Born 1952. President, owner of Zaza Sound; has composed scores for over 30 feature films and has numerous credits in the recording and television industries.
Selective Filmography: *BULLIES,* Th, 85, CDN, Comp; *BIRDS OF PREY,* Th, 85, CDN, Comp; *'KIDS OF DEGRASSI STREET',* TV, 85/84, CDN, Orch; *PINK CHIQUITAS,* Th, 85, CDN, Comp; *HIGH STAKES,* Th, 85, CDN, Comp; *'MANIA'* (4 eps), TV, 85, CDN, Comp; *TURK 182,* Th, 85, USA, Comp; *'JUST JAZZ'* (52 eps), TV, 85/84, CDN, Mus Dir; *BREAKING ALL THE RULES,* Th, 84, CDN, Comp; *LOVERBOY* (MEATBALLS III), Th, 84, CDN, Comp; *THE VINDICATOR* (FRANKENSTEIN FACTOR), Th, 84, CDN, Comp; *ISAAC LITTLEFEATHERS,* Th, 84, CDN, Comp; *SIZE SMALL,* TV, 84/83, CDN, Comp; *MODESTY BLAISE* (pilot), TV, 83, USA, Comp; *A CHRISTMAS STORY,* Th, 83, CDN/USA, Comp; *'SOUNDS GOOD',* TV, 82/81, CDN, Mus Dir/Host; *PORKY'S II - THE NEXT DAY* (CHEZ PORKY - LE LENDEMAIN), Th, 82, CDN, Comp/Orch; *MELANIE,* Th, 82, CDN, Comp; *MR WIZARD'S WORLD,* TV, 82, USA, Comp; *'TALES OF THE KLONDIKE'* (3 eps), TV, 82, CDN, Comp; *CURTAINS,* Th, 81, CDN, Comp; *'FIFTIES CONNECTION',* TV, 81/80, CDN, Mus Dir/Host; *PORKY'S* (CHEZ PORKY), Th, 81, CDN, Comp; *GAS,* Th, 81, CDN, Comp; *BEING DIFFERENT,* TV, 81, CDN, Comp; *OCEAN'S ALIVE,* TV, 81, CDN, Comp; *KIDNAPPING OF THE PRESIDENT,* Th, 80, CDN, Comp; *TITLE SHOT,* Th, 80, CDN, Comp; *PROM NIGHT* (LE BAL DE L'HORREUR), Th, 79, CDN, Comp; *MURDER BY DECREE,* Th, 79, CDN, Comp (**GENIE**).

Bold Numbers Represent Pages Where Complete Listings Appear.

Bold Numbers Represent Pages Where Complete Listings Appear.

Bold Numbers Represent Pages Where Complete Listings Appear.

Bold Numbers Represent Pages Where Complete Listings Appear.

Bold Numbers Represent Pages Where Complete Listings Appear.

Bold Numbers Represent Pages Where Complete Listings Appear.

Bold Numbers Represent Pages Where Complete Listings Appear.

INDEX

M

Bold Numbers Represent Pages Where Complete Listings Appear.

Bold Numbers Represent Pages Where Complete Listings Appear.

INDEX

Bold Numbers Represent Pages Where Complete Listings Appear.

Bold Numbers Represent Pages Where Complete Listings Appear.

Bold Numbers Represent Pages Where Complete Listings Appear.

INDEX

Bold Numbers Represent Pages Where Complete Listings Appear.

INDEX

Advertisers / Commanditaires

Advertising Director — Marcia Hackborn